Short Story Criticism

Guide to Gale Literary Criticism Series

When you need to review criticism of literary works, these are the Gale series to use:

If the author's death date is:	You should turn to:
After Dec. 31, 1959 (or author is still living)	**Contemporary Literary Criticism** for example: Jorge Luis Borges, Anthony Burgess, William Faulkner, Mary Gordon, Ernest Hemingway, Iris Murdoch
1900 through 1959	**Twentieth-Century Literary Criticism** for example: Willa Cather, F. Scott Fitzgerald, Henry James, Mark Twain, Virginia Woolf
1800 through 1899	**Nineteenth-Century Literature Criticism** for example: Fedor Dostoevski, Nathaniel Hawthorne, George Sand, William Wordsworth
1400 through 1799	**Literature Criticism From 1400 to 1800** (excluding Shakespeare) for example: Anne Bradstreet, Daniel Defoe, Alexander Pope, Francois Rabelais, Jonathan Swift, Phillis Wheatley **Shakespearean Criticism** Shakespeare's plays and poetry
Antiquity through 1399	**Classical and Medieval Literature Criticism** for example: Dante, Homer, Plato, Sophocles, Vergil, the Beowulf Poet

Gale also publishes related criticism series:

Children's Literature Review

This series covers authors of all eras who have written for the preschool through high school audience.

Short Story Criticism

This series covers the major short fiction writers of all nationalities and periods of literary history.

ISSN 0895-9439

Volume 4

Short Story Criticism

Excerpts from Criticism of the Works of Short Fiction Writers

8178

Thomas Votteler
Editor

Gale Research Inc.

DETROIT · NEW YORK · FORT LAUDERDALE · LONDON

STAFF

Thomas Votteler, *Editor*

Sean R. Pollock, David Segal, Robyn V. Young,
Shannon J. Young, *Associate Editors*

Cathy Falk, Rogene M. Fisher, Mary K. Gillis, Susanne Skubik, Bridget Travers,
Debra A. Wells, *Assistant Editors*

Jeanne A. Gough, *Permissions & Production Manager*
Linda M. Pugliese, *Production Supervisor*
Jennifer Gale, Suzanne Powers, Maureen Puhl, *Editorial Associates*
Donna Craft, David G. Oblender, Linda Ross, *Editorial Assistants*

Victoria B. Cariappa, *Research Supervisor*
Karen D. Kaus, Eric Priehs, Maureen Richards, Mary D. Wise, *Editorial Associates*
H. Nelson Fields, Judy L. Gale, Jill M. Ohorodnik, Filomena Sgambati, *Editorial Assistants*

Sandra C. Davis, *Permissions Supervisor (Text)*
H. Diane Cooper, Kathy Grell, Josephine M. Keene, Kimberly F. Smilay, *Permissions Associates*
Maria L. Franklin, Lisa M. Lantz, Camille P. Robinson,
Shalice Shah, Denise M. Singleton, *Permissions Assistants*

Patricia A. Seefelt, *Permissions Supervisor (Pictures)*
Margaret A. Chamberlain, *Permissions Associate*
Pamela A. Hayes, Lillian Quickley, *Permissions Assistants*

Mary Beth Trimper, *Production Manager*
Evi Seoud, *Assistant Production Manager*

Arthur Chartow, *Art Director*
C. J. Jonik, *Keyliner*

Laura Bryant, *Production Supervisor*
Louise Gagné, *Internal Production Associate*
Kelly Krust, Sharana Wier, *Internal Production Assistants*

Contents

Preface

Short Story Criticism (SSC) presents significant passages from criticism of the world's greatest short story writers and provides supplementary materials—biographical and bibliographical—to guide the interested reader to a greater understanding of the authors of short fiction. This series was developed in response to suggestions from librarians serving high school, college, and public library patrons who had noted an increasing number of requests for critical material on short story writers. Although major short story writers are covered in such Gale literary criticism series as *Contemporary Literary Criticism (CLC), Twentieth-Century Literary Criticism (TCLC), Nineteenth-Century Literature Criticism (NCLC),* and *Literature Criticism from 1400 to 1800 (LC),* librarians perceived the need for a series devoted solely to writers of the short story genre.

The Scope of the Work

SSC is designed to serve as an introduction to major short story writers of all eras and nationalities. For example, the present volume includes commentary on Jorge Luis Borges, a central figure in modern Latin American literature, and Robert Penn Warren, the Pulitzer Prize-winning first Poet Laureate of the United States who also published distinguished short fiction; D. H. Lawrence, one of the most original English writers of the twentieth century, and Nikolai Gogol, a seminal nineteenth-century Russian writer and a forefather of the modern short story. Since these authors have inspired a great deal of relevant critical material, *SSC* is necessarily selective, and the editors have chosen the most important published criticism to aid readers and students in their research.

Twelve to fifteen authors will be included in each volume, and each author entry presents a historical survey of the critical response to that author's work: some early criticism is included to indicate initial reaction, later criticism is selected to represent any rise or decline in the author's reputation, and current analyses provide a modern view. The length of an entry is intended to reflect the amount of critical attention the author has received from critics writing in English and from foreign critics in translation. Critical articles and books that have not been translated into English are excluded. Every attempt has been made to identify and include excerpts from the most significant essays on each author's work. In order to provide these important critical pieces, the editors will sometimes reprint essays that have appeared in previous volumes of Gale's literary criticism series. Such duplication, however, never exceeds twenty-five percent of the author entry.

The Organization of the Book

The author entry consists of the following elements: author heading, biographical and critical introduction, a list of principal works, excerpts of criticism (each preceded by an explanatory note and followed by a bibliographical citation), and references for further reading.

- The **author heading** consists of the author's full name, followed by birth and death dates. The unbracketed portion of the name denotes the form under which the author most commonly wrote. If the author wrote consistently under a pseudonym, the pseudonym will be listed in the author heading and the real name given in parentheses on the first line of the biographical and critical introduction.

- The **biographical and critical introduction** contains background information designed to introduce a reader to the author and to the critical debates surrounding his or her work. Parenthetical material following the introductions provides references to biographical and critical reference series published by Gale, including *CLC, TCLC, NCLC,* and *LC, Children's Literature Review, Contemporary Authors, Dictionary of Literary Biography,* and *Something about the Author.*

- *SSC* entries include **portraits of the author.** Many entries also contain illustrations of materials pertinent to an author's career, including holographs of manuscript pages, title pages, dust jackets, letters, or representations of important people, places, and events in the author's life.

- The list of **principal works** is chronological by date of first publication and lists the most important works by the author. The first section comprises the short story collections, novellas, and novella collections. The second section gives information on other major works by the author. For foreign authors, the editors have provided original foreign language publication information and have selected what are considered the best and most complete English-language editions of their works.

- **Criticism** is arranged chronologically in each author entry to provide a useful perspective on changes in critical evaluation over the years. All short story, novella, and collection titles by the author featured in the entry are printed in boldface type to enable a reader to ascertain without difficulty the works discussed. Also for purposes of easier identification, the critic's name and the publication date of the essay are given at the beginning of each piece of criticism. Unsigned criticism is preceded by the title of the journal in which it appeared. When an anonymous essay is later attributed to a critic, the critic's name appears in brackets at the beginning of the excerpt and in the bibliographical citation.

- Critical essays are prefaced with **explanatory notes** as an additional aid to students and readers using *SSC.* The explanatory notes provide several types of useful information, including: the reputation of a critic, the importance of a work of criticism, and the specific type of criticism (biographical, psychoanalytic, structuralist, etc.).

- A complete **bibliographical citation,** designed to help the interested reader locate the original essay or book, follows each piece of criticism.

- The **further reading list** appearing at the end of each author entry suggests additional materials on the author. In some cases it includes essays for which the editors could not obtain reprint rights.

Cumulative Indexes

Each volume of *SSC* includes a cumulative **author index** listing all the authors who have appeared in *SSC, CLC, TCLC, NCLC, LC,* and *Classical and Medieval Literature Criticism (CMLC),* as well as cross-references to the Gale series *Children's Literature Review, Authors in the News, Contemporary Authors, Contemporary Authors Autobiography Series, Dictionary of Literary Biography, Something about the Author, Something about the Author Autobiography Series,* and *Yesterday's Authors of Books for Children.* Users will welcome this cumulated author index as a useful tool for locating an author within the literary criticism series.

Each volume of *SSC* also includes a cumulative **title index.** This index lists in alphabetical order all short story, novella, and collection titles contained in the *SSC* series. Titles of short story collections, novellas, and novella collections are printed in italics, while all individual short stories are printed in roman type with quotation marks. Each title is followed by the author's name and the corresponding volume and page numbers where commentary on the work may be located. English-language translations of original foreign language titles are cross-referenced to the foreign titles so that all references to discussion of a work are listed in one place.

Suggestions Are Welcome

Readers who wish to suggest authors to appear in future volumes, or who have other suggestions, are cordially invited to contact the editors, either by letter or by calling Gale's toll-free number: 1-800-347-GALE.

Acknowledgments

The editors wish to thank the copyright holders of the excerpted criticism included in this volume, the permissions managers of many book and magazine publishing companies for assisting us in securing reprint rights, and Anthony Bogucki for assistance with copyright research. We are also grateful to the staffs of the Detroit Public Library, the Library of Congress, the University of Detroit Library, the University of Michigan Library, and the Wayne State University Library for making their resources available to us. Following is a list of the copyright holders who have granted us permission to reprint material in this volume of *SSC*. Every effort has been made to trace copyright, but if omissions have been made, please let us know.

COPYRIGHTED EXCERPTS IN *SSC*, VOLUME 4, WERE REPRINTED FROM THE FOLLOWING PERIODICALS:

America, v. 139, September 30, 1978 for "The Changing Church and J. F. Powers" by Michael True. © 1978. All rights reserved. Reprinted by permission of the author.—*American Book Collector,* v. XVII, November, 1966. Copyright 1966 by The American Book Collector, Inc.—*American Literature,* v. 26, 1954-55. Copyright © 1954 Duke University Press, Durham, NC. Reprinted with permission of the publisher.—*American Quarterly,* v. X, Spring, 1958 for "Jack London's Heart of Darkness" by Sam S. Baskett. Copyright 1958, renewed 1986 American Studies Association. Reprinted by permission of the publisher and the author.—*The American Scholar,* v. 45, Winter, 1975-76. Copyright © 1975 by the United Chapters of Phi Beta Kappa. Reprinted by permission of the publishers.—*Américas,* v. 25, November-December, 1973. Reprinted by permission of the publisher.—*Arizona Quarterly,* v. 22, Winter, 1966 for a review of "Death in Midsummer and Other Stories" by Robert J. Smith. Copyright © 1966 by *Arizona Quarterly.* Reprinted by permission of the publisher and the author.—*Books Abroad,* v. 45, Summer, 1971. Copyright 1971 by the University of Oklahoma Press. Reprinted by permission of the publisher.—*Book Week—New York Herald Tribune,* August 23, 1964. © 1964, *The Washington Post.* Reprinted by permission of the publisher.—*Caliban,* v. XII, 1975. Reprinted by permission of Université de Toulouse-Le Mirail.—*Carolina Quarterly,* v. XXXV, Spring, 1983. © copyright 1983 *Carolina Quarterly.* Reprinted by permission of the publisher.—*CLA Journal,* v. VII, March, 1964. Copyright, 1964 by The College Language Association. Used by permission of The College Language Association.—*Commonweal,* v. CIII, March 12, 1976. Copyright © 1976 Commonweal Publishing Co., Inc. Reprinted by permission of Commonweal Foundation.—*Critical Inquiry,* v. 12, Autumn, 1985 for "Thresholds of Difference: Structures of Address in Zora Neale Hurston" by Barbara Johnson. Copyright © 1985 by The University of Chicago. Reprinted by permission of the publisher and the author.—*Critique: Studies in Modern Fiction,* v. XI, 1969; v. XXIV, Fall, 1982. Copyright © 1969, 1982 Helen Dwight Reid Educational Foundation. Both reprinted with permission of the Helen Dwight Reid Educational Foundation, published by Heldref Publications, 4000 Albemarle Street, N. W., Washington, DC 20016.—*The D. H. Lawrence Review,* v. 16, Fall, 1983. © James C. Cowan. Reprinted with the permission of *The D. H. Lawrence Review.*—*Eire-Ireland,* v. III, Spring, 1968; v. VII, 1972. Copyright © 1968, 1972 Irish American Cultural Institute. Both reprinted by permission of the publisher.—*Four Quarters,* v. XXI, May, 1972. Reprinted by permission of the publisher.—*Genre,* v. 7, March, 1974 for "The Fit of Gogol's 'Overcoat': An Ontological View of Narrative Form" by Charles Sherry. Copyright 1973 by Donald E. Billiar, Edward F. Heuston, and Robert L. Vales. Reprinted by permission of the University of Oklahoma and the author.—*The Georgia Review,* v. XXII, Winter, 1968. Copyright, 1968, by the University of Georgia. Reprinted by permission of the publisher.—*Hispanic Review,* v. XXXVI, April, 1968. Reprinted by permission of the publisher.—*The Hudson Review,* v. XI, Summer, 1958. Copyright © 1958, renewed 1986 by The Hudson Review, Inc. Reprinted by permission of the publisher.—*Irish University Review,* v. 7, Autumn, 1977 for "The Fiction of Mary Lavin: Universal Sensibility in a Particular Milieu" by Janet Egleson Dunleavy. © *Irish University Review.* Reprinted by permission of the author.—*Jack London Newsletter,* v. 2, May-August, 1969.—*Journal of the Short Story in English,* n. 8, Spring, 1987 for "Mary Lavin's 'The Becker Wives' Narrative Strategy and Reader Response" by Susan Asbee. © Université d'Angers, 1987. Reprinted by permission of the author.—*The Kilkenny Magazine: An All-Ireland Literary Review,* n. 12 & 13, Spring, 1965.—*Latin American Literary Review,* v. III, Fall-Winter, 1974. Reprinted by permission of the publisher.—*Los Angeles Times Book Review,* March 19, 1989. Copyright, 1989, *Los Angeles Times.* Reprinted by permission of the publisher.—*The Markham Review,* v. 2, May, 1970. Reprinted by permission of the publisher./ v. 5, Winter, 1976. © Wagner College 1976. Reprinted by permission of the publisher.—*Midcontinent American Studies Journal,* v. 7, Fall, 1966 for "Of Time and the River: 'Ancestral Nonsense' vs. Inherited Guilt in Cable's 'Belles Demoiselles Plantation' " by Howard W. Fulweiler. Copyright © Mid-America American Studies Association, 1966. Reprinted by permission of *American Studies,* formerly *Midcontinent American Studies Journal,* and the author.—*The Mississippi Quarterly,* v. XXX, Fall, 1977. Copyright 1977 Mississippi State University. Reprinted by permission of the publisher.—*Modern Fiction Studies,* v. IX, Winter, 1963-64; v. 18, Summer, 1972. Copyright © 1964, 1972 by Purdue Research Foundation, West Lafayette, IN 47907. All rights reserved. Both reprinted with permission.—*New Pages,* n. 10, Winter-Spring, 1986.—*The New Republic,* v. 153,

Authors to Be Featured in *SSC* , Volumes 5 and 6

Hans Christian Andersen, 1805-1875. (Danish fairy tale writer, poet, short story writer, novelist, travel writer, autobiographer, and dramatist)—One of the most distinguished and best-loved writers of fairy tales, Andersen created an enduring legacy of lively and inventive literature that includes such tales as "Thumbelina," "The Princess and the Pea," and "The Ugly Duckling."

Kay Boyle, b. 1902. (American novelist, short story writer, poet, essayist, and translator)—An eminent author of the American expatriate movement of the 1920s, Boyle is noted for her intriguing and innovative prose style. Her stories often reflect an ardent commitment to social activism and convey an impassioned concern with the individual's search for love and understanding.

Pearl S. Buck, 1892-1973. (American novelist, short story writer, dramatist, essayist, editor, biographer, autobiog-rapher, translator, and author of children's books)—Best known for her Pulitzer Prize-winning novel, *The Good Earth,* Buck is distinguished as the first American woman to have received the Nobel Prize in Literature. Critics applaud Buck's astute descriptions of setting and character in both her novels and her short stories.

F(rancis) Scott (Key) Fitzgerald, 1896-1940. (American novelist, short story writer, essayist, scriptwriter, and dramatist)—Renowned for his classic novel *The Great Gatsby,* Fitzgerald is considered one of the most influential novelists and short story writers of the twentieth century. In such stories as "May Day," "Babylon Revisited," and "The Diamond as Big as the Ritz," Fitzgerald depitcs the prosperity, excess, and subsequent disillusionment that characterized America's Jazz Age.

O. Henry, 1862-1910. (American short story writer and novelist)—A major figure in the history of the short story, Henry is renowned for his poignant caricatures of life in early twentieth-century New York City. Considered a master of the "suprise ending," Henry is perhaps most readily recognized for such widely anthologized stories as "The Gift of the Magi" and "The Last Leaf."

Franz Kafka, 1883-1924. (Czechoslovakian-born German short story writer and novelist)—Frequently identified as a genius who gave literary form to the disorder of the modern world, Kafka's prophetic and profoundly enigmatic stories often describe modern human degradation and cruelty. His well-known and widely studied short story "The Metamorphosis" is regarded as a masterpiece of the genre.

Doris Lessing, 1919- . (Persian-born English novelist, short story writer, essayist, dramatist, poet, nonfiction writer, journalist, and travel writer)—Considered among the most powerful contemporary novelists, Lessing has explored many of the central ideas, ideologies, and social issues of the twentieth century. Three of her most acclaimed volumes of short fiction, *Five: Short Novels, The Habit of Loving,* and *African Stories,* focus primarily on racial concerns and the emancipation of modern women.

Frank O'Connor, 1903-1966. (Irish short story writer, novelist, essayist, and critic)—O'Connor is one of Ireland's major literary figures. His stories are widely read and cherished for their realistic and humorously sensitive portrayals of Irish life.

Liam O'Flaherty, 1896-1984. (Irish novelist, short story writer, autobiographer, and travel writer)—O'Flaherty is considered an important figure in the Irish Renaissance, a literary movement that sought inspiration in Celtic cultural tradition. Best known for novels that chronicle the Irish struggle for independence from England, O'Flaherty is also respected for short stories that vividly portray the arduous peasant life of his native Aran Islands.

Mark Twain, 1835-1910. (American novelist, short story writer, journalist, essayist, autobiographer, and dramatist)—Regarded as the father of modern American literature, Twain is credited with freeing American fiction from the staid literary conventions of the nineteenth century. Although best known for his novel *Adventures of Huckleberry Finn,* Twain also wrote such acclaimed stories as "The Man That Corrupted Hadleyburg," and "The Celebrated Jumping Frog of Calaveras County," which caustically-satirize hypocrisy and social injustice.

Additional Authors to Appear in Future Volumes

Agnon, Shmuel Yosef
  1888-1970
Aiken, Conrad 1889-1973
Aldiss, Brian 1925-
Aleichem, Sholom 1859-1916
Asimov, Isaac 1920-
Atherton, Gertrude 1857-1948
Babel, Isaac 1894-1941?
Baldwin, James 1924-1987
Balzac, Honoré de 1799-1850
Barth, John 1930-
Beattie, Ann 1947-
Beerbohm, Max 1872-1956
Bellow, Saul 1915-
Benét, Stephen Vincent
  1898-1943
Bierce, Ambrose 1842-1914?
Boccaccio, Giovanni 1313?-1375
Böll, Heinrich 1917-1985
Brentano, Clemens 1778-1842
Bunin, Ivan 1870-1953
Caldwell, Erskine 1903-
Calisher, Hortense 1911-
Camus, Albert 1913-1960
Carter, Angela 1940-
Carver, Raymond 1938-1988
Cassill, R. V. 1919-
Cervantes 1547-1616
Chandler, Raymond 1888-1959
Chaucer, Geoffrey 1345-1400
Chopin, Kate 1851-1904
Conrad, Joseph 1857-1924
Coover, Robert 1932-
Cortázar, Julio 1914-1984
Crane, Stephen 1871-1900
Dahl, Roald 1916-
Dante Alighieri 1265-1321
Davenport, Guy 1927-
de la Mare, Walter 1873-1956
Dick, Philip K. 1928-1982
Dinesen, Isak (ps. of Karen
  Blixen) 1885-1962
Disch, Thomas M. 1940-
Doyle, Arthur Conan 1859-1930
Elkin, Stanley 1930-
Ellison, Harlan 1934-

Fast, Howard 1914-
Flaubert, Gustave 1821-1880
Forster, E. M. 1879-1970
France, Anatole (ps. of Anatole-
  François Thibault) 1844-1924
Friedman, Bruce J. 1930-
Gaines, Ernest J. 1933-
Gallant, Mavis 1922-
Galsworthy, John 1867-1933
García-Márquez, Gabriel 1928-
Gardner, John 1933-1982
Garland, Hamlin 1860-1940
Gass, William H. 1924-
Gide, André 1869-1951
Gilchrist, Ellen 1935-
Golding, William 1911-
Gordimer, Nadine 1923-
Gordon, Caroline 1895-1981
Grau, Shirley Ann 1929-
Greene, Graham 1904-
Grimm, Jakob Ludwig
  1785-1863
Grimm, Wilhelm Karl
  1786-1859
Hammett, Dashiell 1894-1961
Harris, Joel Chandler
  1848-1908
Harte, Bret 1836-1902
Heinlein, Robert A. 1907-
Hesse, Herman 1877-1962
Hoffmann, E. T. A. 1776-1822
Hughes, Langston 1902-1967
Jackson, Shirley 1919-1965
James, Henry 1843-1916
James, M. R. 1862-1936
Jewett, Sarah Orne 1844-1909
Jhabvala, Ruth Prawer 1927-
King, Stephen 1947-
Kipling, Rudyard 1865-1936
Knowles, John 1926-1979
Lardner, Ring 1885-1933
Laurence, Margaret 1926-1987
LeFanu, Joseph Sheridan
  1814-1873
LeGuin, Ursula K. 1929-
Machado de Assis, Joaquim
  Maria 1839-1908

Malamud, Bernard 1914-1986
Mann, Thomas 1875-1955
Mansfield, Katherine 1888-1923
Masters, Edgar Lee 1869?-1950
McCullers, Carson 1917-1967
Maugham, W. Somerset
  1874-1965
Mérimée, Prosper 1803-1870
Oates, Joyce Carol 1938-
O'Brien, Edna 1936-
O'Faolain, Sean 1900-
Olsen, Tillie 1913-
Ozick, Cynthia 1928-
Paley, Grace 1922-
Pasternak, Boris 1890-1960
Pavese, Cesare 1908-1950
Perelman, S. J. 1904-1976
Pritchett, V. S. 1900-
Robbe-Grillet, Alain 1922-
Roth, Philip 1933-
Saki (ps. of H. H. Munro)
  1870-1916
Saroyan, William 1908-1981
Schwartz, Delmore 1913-1966
Scott, Sir Walter 1771-1832
Solzhenitsyn, Alexander 1918-
Spark, Muriel 1918-
Stafford, Jean 1915-1979
Stead, Christina 1902-1983
Stein, Gertrude 1874-1946
Steinbeck, John 1902-1983
Stevenson, Robert Louis
  1850-1894
Sturgeon, Theodore 1918-1985
Tagore, Rabindranath
  1861-1941
Taylor, Peter 1917-
Thackeray, William Makepeace
  1811-1863
Tolstoy, Leo 1828-1910
Turgenev, Ivan 1818-1883
Updike, John 1932-
Vonnegut, Kurt, Jr. 1922-
Wells, H. G. 1866-1946
West, Nathanael 1904-1940
White, E. B. 1899-1986
Zola, Émile 1840-1902

Jorge Luis Borges

1899-1986

(Also wrote in collaboration with Adolfo Bioy Casares under the joint pseudonyms Honorio Bustos Domecq, B. Lynch Davis, and B. Suarez Lynch) Argentinian short story writer, essayist, poet, translator, critic, biographer, travel writer, novelist, and scriptwriter.

Regarded as among the foremost figures in modern Latin American literature, Borges is acclaimed for his esoteric and intricate short stories in which he combines fantasy and realism to address complex philosophical questions. His works often defy classification, synthesizing elements of both fiction and the essay, while generally eschewing the use of complex characters and realistic settings. In his writings, Borges employs paradox and oxymoron to examine such metaphysical issues as the existence of a supreme being, the malleability of personal identity, and the impotency of human intelligence. Ana María Barrenechea observed: "Borges is convinced that nothing in Man's destiny has any meaning. This incredulity incites him, nonetheless, to create a literature out of literature and philosophy in which the metaphysical discussion or the artistic problem constitutes the plot of the story. His literary creativity vitalizes what, *a priori,* would otherwise seem abstract, and he is capable of infusing drama and the throbbings of adventure into thoughts which in themselves lack narrative substance."

Borges was born in Buenos Aires, where he lived for most of his childhood. His father was Jorge Guillermo Borges, a respected lawyer, author, and educator, and Borges once commented: "If I were asked to name the chief event in my life, I should say my father's library." From an early age, Borges absorbed a wide range of world literature. He learned to read English before Spanish due to the influence of his English grandmother, and when he was seven years old, he translated Oscar Wilde's parable "The Happy Prince." Borges's first original story, "El rey de la selva," was published when he was thirteen. While his family was stranded in Switzerland following the outbreak of World War I, Borges enrolled at the Collége de Genéve, where he studied French and German and familiarized himself with such European philosophers as Arthur Schopenhauer and George Berkeley. Upon graduating in 1918, Borges traveled to Spain. There, he published reviews, essays, and poetry and associated with the Ultraístas, an avant-garde literary group whose fiction combined elements of Dadaism, Imagism, and German Expressionism. Striving in their poetry to transcend boundaries of time and space, the Ultraístas championed metaphor as the ultimate form of expression, and their influence permeates much of Borges's early work, particularly *Fervor de Buenos Aires,* his first poetry collection.

Borges returned to Buenos Aires in 1921. During this time he helped develop several small Argentinian publications, including the literary magazine *Prisma* and the journal *Proa.* He also became reacquainted with Macedonio Fernandez, a writer and colleague of his father whose friendship and guidance greatly influenced Borges. Encouraged by Fernandez to develop his interest in metaphysics and the complexities of language, Borges began publishing essays on these topics,

many of which were later collected in such volumes as *Inquisiciónes* and *El tamaño de mi esperanza.* In 1938, Borges developed septicemia, a form of blood poisoning, from a head wound he suffered in a fall down a staircase. Concerned that the condition had impaired his writing ability, Borges published a short story as his first work after the accident, intending to attribute its possible failure to inexperience in the genre rather than a loss of literary skill. The tale, "Pierre Menard, autor del Quijote" ("Pierre Menard, Author of Don Quixote"), unexpectedly garnered positive reactions, and Borges's ensuing short fiction earned increasingly widespread critical recognition in Argentina.

Borges's early tales, which closely resemble his essays in style and subject matter, are often interpreted as parables that illustrate the limitations and possibilities of art. In his early story, "Pierre Menard, Author of Don Quixote," for example, Borges focuses upon a modern writer who sets out to create his own version of Miguel de Cervante's *Don Quixote* yet composes a text that corresponds precisely to portions of the original work. In the prose piece "El acercamiento a Almotásim," which appears in *Historia de la eternidad,* Borges questions conventional perceptions of reality in the form of a bogus review of a nonexistent Indian detective novel. Borges's collection *Historia universal de la infamia (A Universal*

History of Infamy) purports to be a criminal's encyclopedia of knife fighters, rogues, and felons that includes fabricated sketches of such historical figures as Billy the Kid, mafia boss Monk Eastman, and nineteenth-century slave trader Lazarus Morell. Also included in the translated edition of this work is "The South," a tale in which a fastidious librarian, desiring the chivalric lifestyle of an Argentinean gaucho, enters into a fatal knife fight that may exist only in his imagination.

In 1943, after signing a manifesto denouncing Argentinian military dictator Juan Perón, Borges was demoted from his government post as an assistant librarian to poultry inspector, a position he refused, however, in favor of becoming an itinerant lecturer and teacher. Following the ousting of Perón in 1955, Borges was named director of the prestigious National Library of Argentina and later awarded the Premio Nacional de Literatura, the country's highest literary honor. Yet, Borges remained largely unknown outside Latin America. In 1961, Borges and Irish dramatist Samuel Beckett shared the Prix Formentor, an international prize established in 1960 by six avant-garde publishers to recognize authors whose work they deemed would "have a lasting influence on the development of modern literature." This achievement closely coincided with the publication of his short fiction collection *Ficciones* and helped establish his reputation throughout the world.

Ficciones, which includes material originally published in Argentina under the title *El jardín de senderos que se bifurcan,* is generally regarded as Borges's most significant work. Primarily concerned in these stories with conflicts between reality and imagination, Borges utilizes what he considered to be the four fundamental aspects of fantasy, which James E. Irby recounted in his introduction to *Labyrinths:* "the work within the work, the contamination of reality by dream, the voyage in time, and the double." In "Tlön, Uqbar, Orbis Tertius," one of his most frequently analyzed stories, Borges combines fiction with such elements of the essay as footnotes and a postscript to describe the attempts of a secret philosophical society to create an invented world free of linear space and time. As their ideas cohere, objects from their imagined realm surface in reality. Frances Wyers Weber commented: "The story develops the contrasts not only between the cohesiveness of Tlön and the incomprehensible, unstable realities of the experienced world, but also the inevitable mutilation that order imposes. The utopian world of unlimited capricious speculation becomes a carefully wrought complex that eliminates all alternatives and bewitches humanity with its utter intelligibility."

Among other stories collected in *Ficciones* is "La lotería en Babilonia" ("The Babylon Lottery"), the tale of an unidentified company whose lottery system controls the most intimate aspects of Babylonian society. Meting out punishments as well as prizes, the lottery promotes a "controlled chaos" that ultimately replaces chance as the dominant factor in the lives of Babylon's citizens. In the piece "La muerte y la brújula" ("Death and the Compass"), Borges draws upon the detective fictions of Edgar Allan Poe and G. K. Chesterton. The protagonist, Lönnrot, is a coolly analytical investigator who pursues the murderer of three rabbis, certain that the killings hold religious significance despite evidence that implicates Red Scharlach, the detective's antithetical double and former adversary. Following a lengthy chase through a labyrinthine manor, Scharlach traps Lönnrot and reveals that the murders were in fact part of his plot to kill the sleuth, whose overconfi-

dence in his superior intellect ultimately betrayed him. D. P. Gallagher observed: "Such is the nature of Borges's amused critique of pure reason, and of his playful dramatization of the impossibility and vanity of definitive knowledge. For like Lönnrot we can only piece together infinitesimal fragments which in turn we can only interpret through a spectrum of limiting assumptions."

In his next collection, *El Aleph* (*The Aleph*), Borges continued to dismantle what he viewed as the false absolutes of space, time, and identity. The simultaneity of the universal and the particular that characterizes much of Borges's fiction is evident in the "Aleph" of the title story, a stone that encompasses all visual images of the universe and contains all points of space, signifying humanity's limitless, if misguided, possibilities. The Aleph's opposite, described in the story "El Zahir," is a coin that symbolizes the religious doctrines and scientific theories used to systematize the universe. In addition to these highly metaphysical pieces, *El Aleph* contains several stories in which abstract experience blends with realistic characterization and settings. In "La espera" ("The Wait"), for instance, a mobster dreams that he successfully eludes a gang of assassins. When he wakes he is emboldened by his dream, and he calmly confronts the gunmen, who shoot him rather than vanish as they had in his imagination. In "Emma Zunz," one of Borges's most realistic stories, the title character, a young factory worker, plots to murder her employer, Loewenthal, whose false accusations prompted her father's suicide. As part of her scheme, Emma deliberately loses her virginity to a stranger, planning to claim that Loewenthal raped her and that she killed him in self-defense. Yet Emma is so disgusted by her encounter with the stranger that she murders Loewenthal for reasons arising from her feelings of violation rather than revenge. Gene H. Bell-Villada asserted: " 'Emma Zunz' is one of the few great Borges stories in which the decisive factor is not an abstraction, not a bookish or mental pattern, but the forces of sheer passion, albeit passion slightly twisted. This is a story that, to an astounding degree, peers into the depths of a simple human heart."

Borges continued his straightforward approach to character and plot in *El informe de Brodie* (*Doctor Brodie's Report*), a collection consisting of such pieces as "La señora mayor" ("The Elder Lady"), the story of a centenarian who ignores her central role in a patriotic celebration, and "Historia de Rosendo Juárez" ("Rosendo's Tale"), the sequel to Borges's earlier "Hombre de la esquina rosa" ("The Streetcorner Man"), in which he chronicles violence in the Argentinian underworld. Ronald Christ remarked that in *Doctor Brodie's Report,* "Borges confronts the provincial, the petty and the stupidly cruel—exactly that world he avoids in his great fiction—at the same moment that he attempts to understand the nature of his own experience not from the heights of his former metaphysic but from an unintellectually contemplative, reluctantly lyrical point of view." Borges's collection, *El libro de arena* (*The Book of Sand*), although similar to *Doctor Brodie's Report* in its traditional treatment of character and plot, returns to the fantastical themes of his earlier fiction. This volume includes the long tale "El congreso" ("The Congress"), in which a world parliament attempts to incorporate all of humanity's diverse ideologies and thoughts in a collection of books housed in one remote library. The congress eventually realizes the arbitrary nature of their task and agrees that all historical knowledge restricts the intellect. They abandon their project and destroy the books, concluding that "every few centuries, the library of Alexandria must be burned down."

In the late 1950s, Borges's eyesight declined due to a hereditary disease, and he limited his literary output to essays and easily recalled, metrically structured poems, which he later collected in such anthologies as *El hacedor* (*Dreamtigers*), *Elogio de la sombra* (*In Praise of Darkness*), and *The Gold of the Tigers: Selected Later Poems*. During this period, Borges's mother increased her role as his secretary, a position she had occupied throughout his career, taking dictation of his work and reading to him in Spanish, English, and French. In 1985 Borges was diagnosed with liver cancer, and he left Buenos Aires for Geneva, Switzerland, where he married his companion and former student, María Kodama. Three weeks later, at age eighty-seven, Borges died.

Among the first contemporary Latin American authors to achieve international recognition, Borges is lauded for his stylistic and philosophical innovations, which have redefined the boundaries of fiction and the essay. Citing his imaginative infusion of fantasy into South America's essentially realistic literary tradition, critics often attribute Borges's influence to the works of such ensuing Latin American authors as Julio Cortázar, Gabriel García Márquez, and G. Cabrera Infante. While several commentators have faulted Borges for his refusal to address social or political issues, most agree with Octavio Paz's contention that "he was brave when faced with the circumstances of his country and of the world. But above all he was a writer, and the literary tradition seemed to him no less alive and present than current events." Jaime Alazraki observed: "Borges' stories, which trite criticism insists on seeing as an evasion of reality, bring us in fact much closer to reality . . . an essential reality which reduces us to a fortuitous number in a gigantic lottery and at the same time links us with everything that was and is to be, to a reality which transforms us into a cycle which already has occurred and yet teaches us that a minute can be the receptacle of eternity, to a reality which effaces our identity and yet converts us into depositories of a supreme Identity—in short, an improbable, contradictory, ambiguous, and even absurd reality."

(For further information on Borges's life and career, see *Contemporary Literary Criticism*, Vols. 1, 2, 3, 4, 6, 8, 9, 10, 13, 19, 44, 48; *Contemporary Authors*, Vols. 21-24 rev. ed.; *Contemporary Authors New Revision Series*, Vol. 19; and *Dictionary of Literary Biography Yearbook: 1986*.)

PRINCIPAL WORKS

SHORT FICTION

Historia universal de la infamia   1935
   [*A Universal History of Infamy*, 1972]
El jardín de senderos que se bifurcan   1942
   [*The Garden of Forking Paths* published in *Ficciones*, 1962]
Seis problemas para don Isidro Parodi [with Adolfo Bioy Casares under the pseudonym Honorio Bustos Domecq] 1942
   [*Six Problems for Don Isidro Parodi*, 1981]
Ficciones, 1935-1944   1944
   [*Ficciones*, 1962; published in England as *Fictions*, 1965]
El Aleph   1949; enlarged edition, 1962
   [*The Aleph, and Other Stories, 1933-1969* (enlarged edition), 1970]

Obras completas. 10 vols.   (short stories, essays, and poetry) 1953-1967; published as one volume, 1974
Manual de zoología fantástica [with Margarita Guerrero] 1957; also published as *El libro de los seres imaginarios*, 1967
   [*The Imaginary Zoo*, 1969; also published as *The Book of Imaginary Beings* (revised and enlarged edition), 1969]
Labyrinths: Selected Stories and Other Writings (short stories and essays) 1962
Crónicas de Bustos Domecq [with Adolfo Bioy Casares under the pseudonym Honorio Bustos Domecq] 1967
   [*Chronicles of Bustos Domecq*, 1976]
El informe de Brodie   1970; published in *Obras completas*
   [*Doctor Brodie's Report*, 1972]
El libro de arena   1975
   [*The Book of Sand*, 1977]

OTHER MAJOR WORKS

Fervor de Buenos Aires   (poetry) 1923
Inquisiciónes   (essays) 1925
Luna de enfrente   (poetry) 1925
El tamaño de mi esperanza   (essays) 1926
El idioma de los Argentinos   (essays and lectures) 1928
Evaristo Carriego   (essay) 1930
Discusión   (essays and criticism) 1932
Historia de la eternidad   (essays) 1936
Poemas, 1922-1943   (poetry) 1943
Otras inquisiciónes, 1937-1952   (essays and lectures) 1952
   [*Other Inquisitions, 1937-1952*, 1964]
Antología personal   (poetry and prose) 1961
   [*A Personal Anthology*, 1967]
El hacedor   (prose and poetry) 1960; published as Volume IX of *Obras completas*
   [*Dreamtigers*, 1964]
Obra poética, 1923-1967   (poetry) 1967
   [*Selected Poems, 1923-1967*, 1972]
Nueva antología personal   (poetry and prose) 1968
Elogio de la sombra   (poetry and prose) 1969
   [*In Praise of Darkness*, 1974]
El oro de los tigres   (poetry) 1972
Borges on Writing   (interviews) 1973
La rosa profunda   (poetry) 1975
The Gold of the Tigers: Selected Later Poems   (poetry) 1977; includes English translations from *El oro de los tigres* and *La rosa profunda*
Historia de la noche   (poetry) 1977
Prosa completas. 2 vols.   (prose) 1980
Siete noches   (lectures) 1980
   [*Seven Nights*, 1984]
Antología poética, 1923-1977   (poetry) 1981
Atlas [with María Kodama]   (prose) 1984
   [*Atlas*, 1985]

ANA MARÍA BARRENECHEA   (essay date 1965)

[*In the following excerpt, Barrenechea focuses upon Borges's symbolic treatment of the universe as a chaotic labyrinth.*]

Jorge Luis Borges was born in the very heart of Buenos Aires on August 24, 1899. He was:

   the son, grandson, great-grandson, and great-great-grandson of native-born Argentinians . . .

who contributed their Spanish, English, and Portuguese blood to his veins. He often mentions his ancestors in his works, and the meaning of their presence therein must be understood. . . . (p. 1)

As a writer who feels temporality so deeply:

> I who am Time and blood and anguish.

Borges is enabled, through the union with the males in his lineage, to experience the incarnation of Time in the prolongation of some of their anxieties and hopes. This union already evolves under the guise of the temporal labyrinth and the cyclical returning which confront the same destinies (Nietzsche), or under that of an immortality which is not personal but is achieved through the succession of generations (Schopenhauer), or else under that of the simple occurrence which leads to death.

Such throwbacks are also justified by the intense symbolism which characterizes his work. Borges discovers key moments in men's lives, moments which explain their destinies. At the same time, he emphasizes that writers and other artists create symbols of the universe, of human destiny, and of themselves through contained oscillations which attempt to convey at once that Man wanders through life blindly and that each man is all men and therefore no one. (pp. 1-2)

His childhood was spent in the house in the Palermo district, in the hotel, and later in the house in Adrogué where the family resided during the summer months. The town of Adrogué appears from time to time in his poems, essays, or stories with a magic which restores the lost days of scenting honeysuckle or eucalyptus, or is useful in contaminating with unreality some of the stories which are populated with statues, useless fountains, rhombic glass doors in yellow, red, and green; it is the unreality of childhood remembrances which memory sifts and fantasy elaborates.

In his earlier works Borges revived memories of the Palermo district with its exploits of brawlers because he was motivated by the nostalgia for adventure and the interest in recreating unpublished aspects of his land in the thematic manner used by Carriego. But afterward, the house in Palermo represents that symbolic closed perimeter wherein the child reads interminable stories by Kipling and Stevenson, as well as those in *The Arabian Nights*. (pp. 3-4)

[From the beginning, Borges] was attracted to many diverse aesthetic and philosophical questions. In his literary essays appear Argentinian authors alongside chosen foreign ones: Spaniards, Englishmen, Germans, Americans. His impassioned meditations on language are focused on the conflict between the Spanish and vernacular forms, as well as on the problematical nature of all language. Next to an exalted remembrance of Buenos Aires is found a speculation on Berkeley's idealism or on the negation of the "I." (p. 9)

Borges applies his capacity for synthesizing human destinies and emphasizing their symbolic character to life itself, converting it into a parabola of his work. He sees himself imprisoned in a house (which becomes a prison-labyrinth without exit) and condemned endlessly to construct literary labyrinths. This is and will remain his task: poems, essays, and stories are definitively oriented toward the universal forms of the fantastic-metaphysical plane. But this does not mean that he separates himself from his country to become an uprooted artist. He has always been an Argentinian; as he himself has

noted, one either belongs or does not belong to an area, and this happens naturally, not by design. He does, however, disown local color, those aspects of language consciously set off, and a programming of the Argentinian theme.

He chooses to allow the theme to appear whenever it becomes "necessary," whenever universal suffering present in national human values or national suffering projected in universal terms demand it. . . . Besides, since he abandoned his "studiously native" attitude, the fusion of the two themes is achieved without hardship and often by obscure routes. A disreputable tenement in Buenos Aires becomes the Hindu house where the eternal Final Judgment of **"The Man on the Threshold"** is held; a vision of its desolate neighborhoods persists in the nameless city of **"Death and the Compass"**; gauchos and *compadritos* try to appeal to, supplant, or elude the Divinity, or themselves become the Divinity in **"Funes the Memorious"** and **"The Dead Man."** The resonance of the local may accentuate what is dramatic or satirical in a story. (p. 11)

[The Argentinian] reaction with respect to Borges is a very special affair. From the beginning there was controversy over his work and a resultant split among contenders into impassioned supporters and pitiless detractors . . . when he had yet to write the stories which have made him universally known. Everyone recognized the mastery of his style, a style which was not only copied—along with his world of fantastic stories—by his followers, but penetrated surreptitiously into that of some of his detractors. His enemies charge him with "foreignism," nihilism, evasion of reality, dehumanization, unfounded use of the imagination, while extremists accuse him of being a writer for the select few who has forgotten the people. If they concede that he has concerned himself with Argentinian life, they then limit the concession by saying that he has done so only in a slight or partial manner; if they emphasize his foreignness, his metaphysical preoccupation, and his strange literary preferences, they also find him superficial and a mere copy of European writers superior to him. (pp. 13-14)

In 1930, Nestor Ibarra could analyze his work and deny him any standing as a narrator. It was not until 1933 and 1934, in a series of works published in *Crítica* and later collected in *A Universal History of Infamy* (1935), that he began to evolve as a storyteller through the reworking of known tales and the direct translation of others. In spite of the maturity they revealed, Borges himself severely considers them as the provisional exercises of a writer who was delving into a new field. . . . (p. 14)

To 1935 corresponds **"The Approach Towards Al-Mu'tásim"** . . . where the characteristics which have made his stories renowned are fully defined. However, Borges did not yet possess a clear awareness of his stature as a narrator. In 1938, he wrote **"Pierre Menard, Author of the *Quijote*"**; afraid that he would lose his writer's faculties during a painful period when a type of septicemia clouded his mind, Borges created that story with a purpose: if he failed with it the consolation would be that he was working in a genre in which he would never distinguish himself. But its success was evident in the rapid succession of stories thereafter; these he collected in *The Garden of Forking Paths* (1941). By that time Borges' fiction had achieved the stature it holds today.

Borges has reached a high literary level through strange and lucid narratives. He constructs poetic and hallucinatory fantasies—of ancient India, of the cruel México of the Conquest, of his own Buenos Aires—which revive the fantastic literature of the Spanish language in order to express the human condition: Man is lost in a chaotic universe and anguished by the passage of time. Borges' wonderment at the mystery of life has been emphasized, but more fundamental yet is his astonishment at the theories of those who attempt to interpret a world and a destiny which are unmistakably impenetrable. The idea of God, of the Trinity, of Heaven and Hell, of Platonic archetypes, of pantheism, and so many other religious or philosophical contrivances which their creators consider the exact explanation of reality or which the believer accepts like a revelation, these are of great interest to Borges because of their strange magic. Therefore he looks for those which offer him the greatest aesthetic possibilities and a supernatural suggestion in order to place his own fables in a phantasmal world where the boundaries between life and fiction have been erased.

Within those confines exist beings who oscillate from one pole to another. Some act on the level of reality, labor in their human undertaking, and only in the end discover that they are shadows or automatons. (In **"The Dead Man,"** the protagonist thought himself master of his own destiny and found he was only the toy of a God who had condemned him from eternity; in **"The Circular Ruins,"** the principal character thought of himself as a real man only to discover in humiliation that he was the dream of another man; in **"The Theologians,"** their personal pride is shown to be worthless when the protagonists reach Paradise.) Others proceed through an inverted route from a nebulous world to a confrontation with irrevocable events, (In **"The Garden of Forking Paths,"** the man who dreams of multiple twisting roads finds only the single exitless alley of crime and punishment; in **"A New Refutation of Time,"** Borges attempts his own concoction of eternity, knowing it is useless; in **"The Wait,"** all temporal magic fails and death arrives assuredly.) In many of his works unreality reigns almost supreme; in very few . . . is there solely the expression of destiny without a means of escape.

Borges has spoken of the surprising effect produced by the map-within-a-map in Josiah Royce's *The World and the Individual,* by the play-within-a-play in *Hamlet,* by the novel-within-a-novel in *Don Quixote,* and by the twin inclusions in *The Arabian Nights* and *The Ramayana.* To readers and spectators who consider themselves real beings, these works suggest their possible existence as imaginary entities. In that context lies the key to Borges' work. Relentlessly pursued by a world that is too real and at the same time lacking meaning, he tries to free himself from its obsession by creating a world of such coherent phantasmagorias that the reader doubts the very reality on which he leans.

To undermine the reader's belief in the concreteness of life, Borges attacks those fundamental concepts on which the security of living itself is founded: the universe, personality, and time. The universe is converted into a meaningless chaos abandoned to chance or ruled by inhuman gods, or perhaps into a ciphered cosmos whose secret key cannot be found. Personality is dissolved within pantheism. Motion disintegrates time or deceitfully promises eternity. Along with this, the reader senses the constant presence of infinity which demolishes and overwhelms him, or sees matter disappear in reflections, dreams, and images along those lines of idealistic philosophy or religious and legendary ideas which nullify it. (pp. 14-16)

Perhaps the most important of Borges' concerns is the conviction that the world is a chaos impossible to reduce to any human law. At the same time that he so vividly experiences the madness of the universe, he realizes that as a man he cannot avoid searching for some meaning in it. . . . It might be said that rather than look for a solution which he knows beforehand is doomed to failure, he comments on or elaborates the literary and philosophic propositions of greatest imaginative range in order to communicate the drama or magic of human destiny.

He sometimes emphasizes the absurdity of the human condition through the exposition of Man's simple, elemental terror in the face of physical pain, for which no intellectual justification can be found. . . . Living, therefore, is a chaotic and arbitrary mass in which the predominant characteristics are the marks of disorder and chance—the nightmare, irrationality and madness, Man's solitude and helplessness. Nonetheless, contrary to what might be expected, Borges' style is not shapeless and disorganized. . . . He always insists that rigor should govern the organization of fiction in contrast to the disordered and confused reality. . . . According to this ideal, Borges presents the concept of a chaotic and illusory world by means of a few lucid details and a narrative structure that is well planned and coherent. Disorder, on the other hand, takes root in the occurrences to which he refers, in certain coined symbols, and in a sector of his vocabulary.

Several of his stories develop a central theme which becomes the symbol of the absurd universe in which Man must live. Who can forget the "lottery" that dictates the destinies of the Babylonians, or the monstrous "library" of Babel, or the "palace" where the lonely Asterion meditates? **"The Babylonian Lottery"** is, for example, the fable of a world engrossed in the caprices of chance. It relates the history of an organization with mysterious origins in which are mixed legend, magic, familiar memories, and even a version of contemporary reality satirically transcribed as ancient Babylonian tradition of doubtful authenticity:

> My father related that in the past—a matter of centuries, of years?—the Babylonian lottery was a plebeian pastime. He related (I do not know whether truthfully) that in exchange for copper coins barbers gave out rectangles made of bone or parchment decorated with symbols. In broad daylight, a lottery was held; those favored received, without further corroboration of chance, minted silver coins. As you can see, the process was elementary.

The description of chaos is not present as something static and established. That it might include greater drama and scope, it is developed through a progressive narration of varied vicissitudes, conquests, and setbacks in which the will of the masses imposes its right to partake in the universal disorder. Allusions to divinities and magic symbols (Baal, Beth, Ghimel, Aleph), to bloody rites, to the occult power of the Company (a veiled reference to the Jesuits?), contrast with a description of the lottery's procedure which often expresses horror in bureaucratic terms, or accepts it with the indifference toward the commonplace, or studies it with apparently historical objectivity. The bureaucratization of horror is not the most frequent expression in Borges and it is that fact that separates him from Kafka. The most important point of divergence, however, is in their attitudes toward reality: Kafka's anguish derives from being excluded from participation in an order in which he exists; Borges is indifferent because he does not believe in that order. Besides, Borges is completely divorced from the idea of guilt and from the biblically-related religious sense which are always present in Kafka.

The picaresque touch of masking a known reality (the barbers who sell lottery tickets in Argentina) in a story that disfigures and leaves it in an intermediate zone of mixed historical implication and legend, is an innocent game of tricks on the reader like others in which Borges indulges. . . . [It] is the counterpart of that other vision of what seems to be fantasy but possesses aspects of reality. Both function, like the mixture of real and fictitious books and authors, under the disfiguring and confusing roles of boundaries.

[**"The Babylon Lottery"**] begins with a biographical affirmation which employs the adjective *vertiginous* to submerge the reader in the madness of a world where nothing is certain—one could be executing a divine command, or falsifying it, or merely acting as a plaything of chance. . . . It concludes with a series of the author's favorite interpretations of the universe which, through its negative aspect, culminates in the completion of the initial vertigo. . . . (pp. 50-3)

Next to the concept of a monstrously misshapen world and beings lost on capricious paths, Borges usually places the concept of a cosmos governed by the Divinity. This permits him to accentuate the irrationality of the universe through means other than chance, that is, by deepening the unbreachable separation between God and Man; thus Man will never be able to penetrate the designs of the divine mind.

In the congregation of experts which creates Tlön, [in **"Tlön, Uqbar, Orbis Tertius"**], he emphasizes the coherent legislation which contrasts with the chaos of earth, and the hierarchies that lucid human minds can plan: . . .

> How would it be possible not to submit to Tlön, to the minute and vast evidence of an ordered planet? It is useless to reply that reality also is ordered. Perhaps it is, but in accordance with divine laws—I translate: inhuman laws—which we can never perceive. Tlön may be a labyrinth, but it is a labyrinth contrived by men, a labyrinth destined to be deciphered by men.

Inhuman, upon alluding to its double meaning (the etymological one of nonhuman and the common one of implacable cruelty), heightens the separation of the two incompatible worlds and the impenetrability of the universe's meaning. In a later passage, he designates the human organization of this artificial world as the rigor of chess players rather than of angels, because the science of mathematics attempts to simplify and bring order to an infinitely complex world which can only be known in all its variety by God and the angels. Nonetheless, geometry and numbers, the most human of creations along with language, serve Borges on other occasions as metaphors which express that nonhumanity of the divine. For their simplicity alludes to an aseptic perfection devoid of passion and doubt. The geometric architecture of **"The Library of Babel,"** the precision of letters, and the deployment of numbers have been thought up to transmit the impression of a self-sufficient world which excludes any participation by Man, a world which, in itself, is that blind divinity without beginning or end.

Perhaps the most powerful symbol which Borges has created to show the contrast God-Man and the irrationality of the world is the palace of the Immortals. He has constructed it by removing the reason-for-being from architectonic elements, like an absurd inversion of functional theories. . . . The horror of the city is heightened by the labyrinthine route that leads to it, and by the already disclosed contrast of desert-universe; its symbolic value is heightened by its presentation as a city consciously elaborated by men toward that end:

> As for the city whose renown had extended to the Ganges, nine centuries had elapsed since the Immortals had razed it. With the relics of its ruins they erected, in the same place, the incongruous city I had traversed—parodic or reversible destiny and, likewise, temple of the irrational gods who control the world about whom we know nothing, except that they do not resemble Man. The building was the last symbol to which the Immortals condescended.

The existence of a God whose nature and intentions Man ignores gives diverse intonations to the expression of an incomprehensible world. The Gnostic theogonies and cosmogonies assist in its configuration because their conception of the universe as a mirror of the heavens (whether inverted or not) and their descending hierarchies of circles reflected one within the other accentuate the inanity. What is more, they add the touch of the chaotic and decadent with their ideas of creation as the handiwork of minor deities, who have been driven mad or are dead. Borges also relates to these those Christian and Hebraic beliefs which somehow insinuate the magic or symbolic aspect of the universe. (pp. 53-5)

Disturbing the mixture, Gnostic theogonies flow into Borges' tales—the mad or malevolent gods, the demiurges or inept angels who created the world, a melancholy god who no longer remembers having done so, an inferior god who uses it to communicate with a devil. And above all these lurks the idea that the Creator has died. . . . This idea intensifies Man's helplessness and absurdity, condemned as he is to repeating fixed gestures infinitely by a divinity who has disappeared, or to acting disjointedly outside the divinity's control (the opposite of that world without men presided over by an implacable and solitary Lord augured in **"The Library of Babel"**). . . .

But even more common is the other sector of ideas bred in Gnostic speculations—that which holds that earth is an inverted copy of the celestial order. Such convictions likewise engender a dual lineage—they accentuate Man's phantasmagoric quality because of his condition as a simple reflection, and they complicate the enigmas of a universe which, being an image of the superior order, ought to contain a meaning and a message.

In his eagerness to discover the key to the world, Borges adds other themes which preoccupy him: God's foreknowledge and predestination, magical and cabalistic sciences, the cipher or the all-powerful Name, the Book dictated by the Divinity and the ancient Hebrew-Christian *topos* of "The Book of Nature."

Articles, poems, and stories express the anguish over the secret meaning of the cosmos under various guises. In one of these, everything repeats the superior hierarchy, inverting it, and even the most horrendous thing on earth finds its justification above. . . . Borges' phantasmagoria endows the multiform heresies described in **"The Theologians"** with terror and splendor; it is an erudite narrative with quotations which combine real and fictitious names, and constructed in imitation of theological discourses in which distorted biblical segments and allusions to heinous crimes and the extravagant or curious statement alternated. (pp. 55-7)

It often occurs in Borges' work that an idea is reflected in the literary structure, that is, it manifests itself in the architecture of his own stories or in that of the imaginary books whose précis he includes therein. (p. 57)

Setting out to verify the supernatural power of a divine sentence hidden in the world that surrounds Man (cabala, Gnosticism, simple belief in magic), Borges chooses the image of the tiger [in **"The God's Script"**]. To Blake he owes the splendid suggestion of the metaphor:

> which brings together the decorative and the piti-
> less;

to Schopenhauer, the concept of an eternity in which the message is confided to the species, not to the individual, and which is magnified to the point of incredulity by the vastness of a time traceable to the beginning of creation and of a space which encompasses empires and heavenly bodies as well as the numerosity of generations of cereals and men. The importance of the symbol is such that the whole economy of the story seems to be subordinated to its existence. . . . (pp. 57-8)

[In **"The God's Script,"** the] priest of Qaholom discovers the key to the universe . . . but the success is an exception in Borges. Man lives in helplessness, and the suspicion that perhaps the chaos has a meaning makes him even more pathetic when it promises him a divine power he can never achieve. Thus hope and frustration instill drama into **"The Library of Babel"** through their contrast; thus in **"The Babylonian Lottery"** no one knows whether Man's role is that of impostor or secret agent of the Company; thus in Babylonia, Tlön, and Babel, it is impossible to know what is fundamental and what is merely accessory to the divine mind. In later works, peace may be found through the acceptance of an Order in the universe. Perhaps Borges "disbelieves" in it, but it must satisfy him aesthetically as essential and eternal shapes satisfy him. In that secret justification Man at last finds his reason for being and his place in the universe; in that way, the sorrow of Dante and that of the leopard have a meaning in the divine economy. . . .

Since the earliest essays, Borges showed an interest in the Hebrew veneration for books and in the belief in a work dictated by God, therefore, one which is perfect and sacred in itself, an oracle of the Lord destined for Man. . . . (p. 58)

Borges' alert awareness of the marvel of certain human imaginings—fantastic tales in themselves—should be noted. . . . But he has yet to allude to nature as being a divine book, thus fusing both ideas. This appears later in "The Mirror of Enigmas" and, especially, in "On the Cult of Books," where Borges traces the evolution of the metaphor "Book of Nature." In **"Tlön, Uqbar, Orbis Tertius"** the topic is reduced, through the Gnostic influence, to the world interpreted as the writing which an inferior god invents to communicate with a devil, while the anguish of not being able to comprehend the celestial message formulates the extravagant proposition:

> that the universe is comparable to those cryptographies in which all symbols are invalid, and that only those things are true which occur every three hundred nights.

The vision is complicated by the discussions on predestination (whether the Lord ordains even the minutest details of the planet or only its general patterns); when turned inside out, the last hypothesis ironically presents a Divinity occupied only with the unimportant things, as in **"The Babylonian Lottery."** (p. 59)

In a lecture on Poe, Borges analyzed some of the procedures used by the artist to create a mood of unreality and horror; among these he emphasized the labyrinthine architecture of the school where the protagonist of "William Wilson" was educated. Borges, too, makes profuse use of labyrinths in his work and often stirs an inevitable uneasiness merely by making a simple reference to corridors, stairways, or interminable streets, to doors, salons, or patios that are repeated, or simply to the doubt of returning to the same place. . . .

The thought of monstrosity stands always as a dramatic overtone, be it in the minds of those who created the labyrinth (that reproach which is almost remorse and that intellectual horror of Homer-Rufus in **"The Immortals"**), be it in the construction realized, or in the relationship of the architecture to the being enclosed in it, [as in **"The House of Asterion"**]:

> What is important is the profound correspondence
> of the monstrous house to its monstrous inhabitant.
> The Minotaur amply justifies the existence of the
> labyrinth.

Borges enhances the phantasmagoric impression by relating the labyrinths to nightmares. On the one hand, he describes nightmares in which the protagonists believe themselves to be enclosed within labyrinths, and, on the other, he describes labyrinthine constructions with metaphoric terms from the realm of fantasy. . . . (p. 60)

The exitless labyrinth where Man wanders erringly finally becomes the double symbol of the Infinite and chaos. The dream of Rufus the Tribune in **"The Immortal"** traces, with anguishing precision, the path toward a perceivable but untenable goal; the library of Babel is a monstrous labyrinth which likewise alludes to the Infinite. Through its corridors and stacks men will travel, vainly searching for their justification.

But the library is also the universe, and it is that labyrinth-universe metaphor which gives the concept of chaos its grandeur and horror. In **"The House of Asterion,"** narrated by the protagonist from his own viewpoint, it constitutes the core of the story through slight observations that only have meaning for the alert reader and through a final sentence which reveals to the common reader the personality of the Minotaur. Borges says that he wrote it under the inspiration of a painting by Watts in which a pensive Minotaur looks out toward the horizon while leaning on the parapet of his labyrinth, as if meditating on the world beyond the walls. Thus, Asterion meditates melancholically on the nature of the palace and sees it as exceeding its limits and multiplying itself throughout the earth. In the same way, the gangster interned in the villa-labyrinth at Triste-le-Roy senses that the world is another web of anguish; the sinuous imaginings of Ts'ui Pên exceed the garden, the novel he invented, the small English village where the drama evolves, and expand throughout the entire world; and Rufus the Tribune enters and leaves the City of the Immortals through a labyrinth, retiring with the growing fear that the symbolic palace might be prolonged endlessly in the universe.

Borges frequently accumulates his procedures, repeating them with variations. In **"The Immortal"** he assembles multiple labyrinths—the infinite desert, the premonitory dream of the unreachable water jar, the labyrinthine path of wells and corridors, the irrational palace; in **"The Garden of Forking Paths"** he also includes a quadruple labyrinthine construction in which poetry, vagueness, and mystery are mixed—the ancestor's labyrinth imagined first in the form of vast boundaries, the cyclically interpreted novel, the same novel later relived in a plurality of destinies, and the suggestiveness of the path which leads him to the crime, from the station to the house.

The concrete labyrinths he describes—houses, palaces, cities—give occasion to comparisons with philosophic, mathematic, or literary themes such as the concepts of Nicholas of Cusa or Pascal, postponements, Eleatic professions, cyclical or deviatory time; through a shuttlelike movement that inverts the scheme, metaphysical or literary metaphors are given the name of labyrinths. (pp. 61-2)

Dreams of labyrinths also appear in the anguish of a nightmare or in hallucinations, and at the same time, the intricate and chaotic forms of the fantasy, even without the labyrinths as mainstays, are given the key name:

> From the unending labyrinth of dreams, I returned
> to my unbearable prison as I would to my house.

Not only do houses and palaces become labyrinths—with their corridors, galleries, patios, circular chambers, wells, basements, winding staircases—but also streets, plazas, cities (Banaras, Buenos Aires, London), as well as the infinite desert, waterways, and vast geographic areas wherein marshes and swamps tend to accentuate the chaotic with infernal connotations inspired by Dante. . . .

Borges insistently employs the labyrinth in a mental outline which resembles that of the "secret drawing." All translate the idea of the divine presence (which embraces past, present, and future), combining an old Christian topic with the legend of the magician who hears his enemy's footsteps or sees the figure outlined by them. Some of these expressions symbolize Man's aimless wandering through the world without understanding the meaning of his life; others symbolize the possible key to his actions which the Divinity knows and rarely chooses to reveal. . . . (pp. 62-3)

With *labyrinth* and *drawing* Borges employs a rich variety of images that express the hidden key of Man's life and are characteristic of his style: *name, countenance, letter, cipher, symbol, emblem, metaphor, adjective, attribute, image, form, shape, map, mirror, dream, simulation.* Sometimes he accumulates them, as in this excerpt wherein he conjures up a cortege of dreams, symbols, images, and imaginary worlds, showing their falseness disguised as reality, their appearance which promises and defrauds, and their vagueness:

> Dreams, symbols, and images pierce the day; a disorder of imaginary worlds flows incessantly into this world; our own childhood is as undecipherable as Persepolis or Uxmal.

Religious and magical ideas are predominant in *name, letter,* and *cipher:*

> they omit his real name—if we even dare to think that there is such a thing in this world; that night when he finally heard his name; perhaps without being aware that they were the symbols and letters of his destiny; I think I perceive in them a cipher of Chesterton's history, a symbol or mirror of Chesterton.

The "real name" was perhaps suggested by Bloy's text which he quotes in "On the Cult of Books," although there were sufficient biblical passages available on the Last Judgment and "The Book of Life." All this terminology alludes to divine foreknowledge, to the belief that all things are the creation of the Word, to the power of the secret name of God, or to the more general idea that words, letters, and numbers possess powers of enchantment and that they are identifiable with the named. *Cipher,* in its turn, combines the significance of synthesis, or compendium, and number, a cabalistic element like letters. The magical connotations are, undoubtedly, the most efficient in such a genus of expressions. (pp. 65-6)

Another group of words—*drawing, form, map*—translates God's foresight and his capacity to intuit a life simultaneously into a visible scheme. *Form,* at least in ["Conjectural Poem"], points to the Platonic archetypes, to universal shapes liberated from time and divinity. An "invisible drawing" and a "secret shape" are united to express the occult meaning of life or the work . . . and to insinuate pantheistic repetitions suggested by Schopenhauer's philosophy. In certain cases, *form* takes us to another series of metaphors which accentuate the sensation of unreality—*shadow, dream, reflection, copy, simulation, image.* . . . They, too, are related to Platonism on the one hand (because they translate a world which is merely a reflection of eternal ideas) and to Berkeley's idealism on the other.

Mirror is one of the most interesting in this group. Sometimes the phantasmal and blurry properties are predominant in it, but it also contains deforming ones. . . . (pp. 67-8)

Image has the dual meaning of a figure which reproduces a model and of *metaphor,* another of the key words, with its literary significance. He says that the Chinese Wall is an enormous metaphor, that is, a symbolic achievement. The circle is closed with *symbol* and *emblem* which insist on the secret message, in the sign that must be deciphered. What's more, *symbol, image, metaphor, attribute, adjective, predicate,* and *epithet* relate the interpretation of life to the literary task, through a characteristic penetration of one world into the other. . . . (p. 68)

Like all writers, Borges knows that the artist selects and emphasizes certain significant elements which he considers fundamental to the expression of his message. An attitude, an object, an incident from the life of a character, reveal his makeup better than any long explanation [In **"The Dead Man"**], Borges inverts planes and presents a reality wherein literary procedures are valid:

> Thereafter, into Benjamin Otalora's destiny came a ruddy horse with black mane and tail, which Acevedo Bandeira brought from the south, bearing inlaid appointments and saddle cloths with tigerskin borders. That liberal horse was a symbol of the master's authority and thus the boy covets it, just as he craves spitefully the woman with the resplendent hair. Woman, appointments, and horse are attributes or adjectives of a man he aspires to destroy.

It is typical that the explanation of reality and the allusion to the literary exercise coexist easily in his fiction. They mix with an extraordinary narrative flair that heightens both aspects through the reflection of one in the other. Besides, setting out to analyze the work of the novelist or poet, he does not consider the greater or lesser veracity of the events (he is that sure of the impossibility of reliving them as they were), but focuses on the representative value given them. This explains or clarifies the manner of narrating the story **"The Dead Man."** When the protagonist reaches the summit of his career, his success is affirmed by the possession of the previously indicated symbols:

> A bullet pierced his shoulder, but that afternoon Otalora returned on the master's ruddy horse to die, and that afternoon a few drops of his blood stained the tigerskin, and that night he slept with the woman of the shining hair. Other versions change the order of these events and deny that they occurred in one day.

The original accumulation, with its poetic truth, and the posterior clarification, with its possible reflection of historical truth, refer indirectly to the narrator's task and heighten the symbolic stature of the three objects as well as the freedom to group them artistically. (p. 69)

Along with the previously indicated terms which express the meaning of the universe, Borges uses adjectives that underline the hidden and almost untenable aspects of symbols—*arcane, occult, recondite, invisible, dark, obscure, secret.* . . . It has been shown that the *drawing* could be *invisible,* but so, too, could the *labyrinths.* Anything mysterious is *obscure* or *dark,* as is anything subconscious, unknown, and chaotic. . . . *Secret* is the adjective he uses constantly when referring to the subterranean cipher imbedded in events. . . . *Suspect, guess,* and *conjecture* describe the task of the man who tries to decipher the symbols preferred by the planet. *Secret, obscure,* and *dark,* besides *central, blind, elemental, fundamental, irresistible,* and *profound* suggest an intimate message, an undeniable destiny, an essential aspect that is impossible to elude. . . . (p. 70)

Borges insists on the theory that Man does not recognize his real self; but he also desires to show Man at that instant of his life when he is confronted with the revelation. Thus, he investigates decisive moments in the lives of historical personages and writes a narrative structure around these through which he translates that point of view. . . . [The plot of **"Biography of Tadeo Isidoro Cruz"**], acquires tension and drama when it is given as a schematic narrative of informative rapidity which has gaps Borges does not care to fill so as to arrive quickly at that episode which forms the cipher of a human destiny:

> (A fundamentally lucid night awaited him, secreted in the future: the night when he finally saw his own face, the night when he finally heard his name. Well understood, that night exhausts his history; better yet, an instant of that night, an act of that night, because acts are our symbols. Any destiny, no matter how long and complex it may be, is aware of reality *at only one moment:* that moment in which Man knows eternally who he is.

An action performed by Cruz becomes the emblem and key of his life, but in his turn, that fictional creature becomes a symbol of Argentinians and all Hispanic men with their radical individualism, in the sense that Borges is and would like all men to be such a symbol. Having selected Cruz's fight in defense of Martín Fierro as his topic, Borges gives the tale the prestige of the classic in which all Argentinians recognize

The first photograph of Borges, taken when he was ten months old.

themselves, as well as the rustic and elemental sense of courage of the face-to-face duel of men and knives. (pp. 70-1)

The importance of Borges' utilization and interpretation of events in his work, as well as its reflection in his vocabulary and in the construction of stories and essays, is most obvious. Nonetheless, it would be worthwhile to examine further the literary value he assigns his symbols. . . . [He] quotes Chesterton in the defense of it as one more language which Man has attempted to use in his inability to comprehend the universe. Yet, he observes that interpretation does not exhaust these symbols because many are superior to the dry reality they substitute and because, as in dreams, there are double and triple levels in them. Persons, things, and acts may be symbols. The fact that the Chinese Wall is a symbol of Emperor Shih Huang Ti projects over the individual all that is remote, grandiose, and strange in it.

What Borges does not indicate, though he is undoubtedly aware of it, is the contrary interplay of influences. If the symbol reflects its light on the object symbolized and enriches it, reality in turn influences the symbol, increasing its prestige (already enhanced by its very status as a symbol) through the qualities which the object symbolized confers on it. In **"Deutsches Requiem,"** the Jewish writer David Jerusalem is

a symbol of a detested zone

in the protagonist's soul—Christian charity and compassion—which makes his personality more complex; and the Nazi officer himself, when he becomes aware of his symbolic role, increases his stature monstrously, encompassing Germany, the universe, and the future in a life prolonged after death:

Tomorrow I shall die, but I am a symbol of future
generations. . . .

Perhaps there is too much subtlety in uniting a type of story
that particularly appeals to Borges with the idea of the secret
key to the universe, but there are tales which narrate certain
events and hint at other possible interpretations which may
be uncovered in time by astute readers, yet these are only
fully revealed at the end.

His first story, **"The Pink Corner Man,"** already demonstrates this peculiarity in its definitive text. **"Tlön, Uqbar,
Orbis Tertius"** contains a conversation with Bioy Casares on
a first-person story with traces

that would permit some few readers—a very few
readers—to divine an atrocious or banal reality.

Borges applies this scheme under several variations to **"The
House of Asterion," "The Immortal,"** and **"The Shape of the
Sword,"** while in **"The Zahir"** he injects the plan for a similar
story based on the theme of the treasure of the Nibelungen.
But he achieves something even more complex. In **"The
Theme of the Traitor and the Hero"** he incorporates the readers' task to the plot because he narrates the hardships of one
who investigated the truth of hidden or at best half-disclosed
deeds in the public life of Kilpatrick:

In Nolan's work, the least dramatic passages are
those in which he imitates Shakespeare; Ryan suspects that the author interpolated them in the hope
that someone in the future would arrive at the
truth.

It could be said that Borges is guided solely by aesthetic interests, enjoying the designing of a story with a final surprise
well calculated through the measurement of evidence, like
the expert writer of detective fiction who sufficiently veils his
clues that the criminal might not be recognized. Is he not the
author of **"Death and the Compass"** and **"The Garden of
Forking Paths"**? Doesn't he enjoy the interplay of fictitious
authors, apocryphal texts, and altered quotations (the epigraph of **"The House of Asterion"** has been altered, for example)?

But there is another motivation which is more profound. On
telling the story of a valiant Irish rebel as if he were one, the
cowardly Vincent Moon becomes the courageous conspirator
and is fused with him in a somewhat symbolic way. This
forms the basis of **"The Theme of the Traitor and the Hero."**
Likewise, the ending of the tale of the Nibelungen suggests
the impossibility of knowing the true meaning of life. . . .
(pp. 73-5)

Perhaps it would be fitting to see in the manner of presenting
such narratives, along with the literary reasons, a further
manifestation of human insecurity with regard to the key of
the universe, and a vague, pantheistic allusion to the fusion
of the most opposed destinies. And perhaps Tlön's characteristic phrase—that a deed could be atrocious or banal—may
be helpful in the reinforcement of the dual interpretation.
Commenting on a story projected by Hawthorne, Borges sets
out to select the horrible or trivial deed from the point of view
of artistic efficiency. But he also cites Kierkegaard and his
story of expeditions to the Pole, where the factor is not
whether the act is important or prolix, but rather its symbolic
role. Borges' own narratives often point to the uselessness of
Man's attempt to decipher a divine message in which he can-

not distinguish the fundamental from the accessory. (pp.
75-6)

Borges is an admirable writer pledged to destroy reality and
convert Man into a shadow. . . . (p. 144)

This entire phantasmal world is expressed in highly original
stories and essays which Borges decorates with those themes
and situations which universal philosophy, theology, and literature make available. And all three should be placed on the
same level because all interest him for the imaginative possibilities they offer and their capacity for stirring the deepest
feelings. His work does not contain the coherent evolution of
metaphysical thought nor a doctrine which he adopts as the
single and real key to the universe because Borges is convinced that nothing in Man's destiny has any meaning. This
incredulity incites him, nonetheless, to create a literature out
of literature and philosophy in which the metaphysical discussion or the artistic problem constitutes the plot of the
story. His literary creativity vitalizes what, *a priori*, would
otherwise seem abstract, and he is capable of infusing drama
and the throbbings of adventure into thoughts which in themselves lack narrative substance.

Besides this, he oscillates between the lucidity of an intelligence which knows Man's limitations and indulges in the fullest usage of irony or skepticism, and the passion of one who
is deeply stirred by his destiny as a man lost in the universe.
His satire may sometimes create farcical situations but it
never loses its fundamental sobriety; his maneuvers with
time, the individual, and the cosmos enfold a desolate anguish. Borges himself explains the motive for such an irritating sentiment. The answer to the logic of his art may be found
in the final words of *Other Inquisitions* where he unites his
preferred metaphors:

Denying the temporal succession, denying the "I,"
and denying the astronomic universe are ways of
apparent despair and secret consolation. Our destiny (differing from Swedenborg's Hell and the Hell
of Tibetan mythology) is not frightful because of its
unreality; it is frightful because it is irreversible and
composed of iron. Time is the substance of which
I am made. Time is a river which drags me away,
but I am the river; it is a tiger which destroys me,
but I am the tiger; it is a fire which consumes me,
but I am the fire. Unfortunately, the world is real;
I, unfortunately, am Borges.

Nonetheless, a purely negative and false idea of Borges' work
should not result. Only one aspect of the writer's work—the
expression of irreality—has been treated; but Borges' creativity is characterized by the richness and complexity of his art.
Even within the limited scope here, some of the observations
made above would be sufficient to destroy that nihilistic impression. One of these would be the constant allusion to the
practice of literature; this is so wisely intertwined with the
narrative that, without dampening or disturbing it, it conveys
the depth of aesthetic problems. Another is his fervent poetry
in the midst of the basic solitude of Man (like that of Averroes, the Martín Fierro of **"The End,"** the Chinese spy of
"The Garden of Forking Paths," the dreamer of **"The Circular Ruins,"** the Homer of **"The Immortals,"** the Borges himself of "Cyclical Poem"). Another, that manly courage in accepting implacable destiny (as with those heroes who meet
their test in humiliation and defeat, the lucid analysis of the
ignorance and limitations of reason, the death of Cruz, Martín Fierro, and Láprida). Another, perhaps the most power-

ful, is the creative joy of the author who sees in the imaginings of others as well as in his own the true force capable of overcoming the limitations of the human condition. (pp. 144-45)

Ana María Barrenechea, in her Borges: The Labyrinth Maker, *edited and translated by Robert Lima, New York University Press, 1965, 175 p.*

FRANCES WYERS WEBER (essay date 1968)

[*In the following excerpt, Weber utilizes Borges's stories in* Ficciones *to explore the author's approach to fiction.*]

The essays and stories of Jorge Luis Borges must be placed in an intermediate zone between the critical and the imaginative, the intellectual and the poetic, the real and the invented. But in discussing the stories alone one might feel obliged to follow Borges's own lead and regard them as purely fictitious, as dream, as artistic structures devoid of any ideological intentions: "When I write a story I do not think too much about the metaphysical meaning it may possess, because if I did, perhaps, it would not let me dream the plot. . . . The ideal reader of my work would be a person who greatly resembles me, one who would not look for too many intentions in what I have written but would abandon himself to the reading." "Metaphysical meaning" is always subordinate to the playfulness of art. Borges has observed in himself a tendency to evaluate philosophical systems according to aesthetic criteria. The conscientious critic would then respect the autonomy of the stories and refrain from wondering if Borges's elegant fictions have other than literary relevance. (p. 124)

If Borges shows that the distinctions between the world of fiction and our own "real" world are doubtful, precarious or non-existent, it would seem quite proper to assert that the stories not only create an imaginary realm but also comment on possible ways of knowing and picturing the world we live in. . . . Instead of establishing an entirely independent realm of game and conjecture, Borges's fiction-making irradiates its ambiguity and playfulness to all the activities of the mind.

The advantage of fiction as a means of representing experience is precisely its acknowledged deceptiveness. And Borges's fantasies make their illusory nature thoroughly apparent . . . The most direct demonstration of the story's fictitiousness is a pattern of ideas and motifs that refute themselves. It is not only in the literature of Borges's imaginary world of Tlön that all books have their counter-books and no philosophical thesis is complete without its antithesis. The theory or postulation that negates itself is one of the author's favorite topics and it determines the structure of several stories. His themes generally involve an initial polar contrast of images or ideas; that duality is then destroyed or collapsed in the course of the story. Yet the final identification can be understood only by going through the story, by following the steps from primary opposition to eventual coalescence. In this essay I shall examine the contradictory thematic development of four of these self-reversing tales, **"Tlön, Uqbar, Orbis Tertius," "La lotería en Babilonia," "El inmortal,"** and **"El jardín de senderos que se bifurcan."** I hope to show that the progression of the plot is itself a working out of the ideal of fiction—complete provisionality and ambiguity—and that this ideal can be extended to other forms of thought. All representations of the world, whether given as "fact" or fiction, should display an equal awareness of their tentative nature.

The essay-like quality of **"Tlön Uqbar, Orbis Tertius,"** the numerous references to non-existent works by real scholars, critics, and writers (Bioy Casares, Martínez Estrada, Alfonso Reyes) from the beginning make its genre dubious—essay or fiction. The story is a peculiar blending of the conceptual and the aesthetic, similar to that of fiction. The mixture of forms is a reflection of the plot itself which traces the gradual insertion of an ideal scheme into concrete reality. In Part I the narrator describes his discovery of Uqbar, whose legends and myths refer to two imaginary regions, Mlejnas and Tlön. . . . The narrative's disclosure of information about Tlön is piecemeal: first we read an apparently marginal description of it in relation to Uqbar's literary epics; then we find out, to our surprise, that not only Borges, but other well-known writers have been puzzling about it for some time (why did he conceal this fact at the beginning of his accounts?); finally we are faced with the prospect of succumbing to its total rule. The gradual penetration of Tlön into the reader's awareness reproduces the action of the story—Tlön's invasion of the experienced world.

Yet the passage of Tlön into reality contaminates the pure ideal universe with disorder and chance and inevitably entails a restriction of the immense scope and flexibility of its ideas. We notice that as Tlön proceeds to take over our world, certain contradictions necessarily arise within its system.

The mythical planet represents, at least in its origins, an inversion of common sense. At the very beginning of the story the threatening and monstrous mirror in the hallway of the villa in Ramos Mejía announces not only the theme of an illusory physical reality (mirrors and copulation are abominable because they multiply the number of men) but also the possibility of a reversal of ordinary perceptions and beliefs. Tlön is a world of pure idealism. . . . The heresy of materialism is so fantastic that language can scarcely formulate it; to the people of Tlön it is as strange and unbelievable as Berkeley's idealism to the common sense realist. Paradoxically enough, in this world of independent mental acts, we can observe a certain evolution—the "history" of Tlön is one of increasing idealism. At first it is pure temporal sequence. Many of its schools of thought undermine the bases of succession and one of them goes so far as to deny time. Yet a few pages after the mention of this theory we learn about the mental fabrication of secondary objects, the *hrönir,* which has been going on for some one hundred years (the *hrönir* as concretizations of thoughts or desires, anticipate the "realization" of Tlön in our world). Their methodical production has permitted the modification of the past. They radically alter the sequential, temporal nature of ideality; they destroy time. The question that arises is how one can speak of this process as having gone on for any specific number of years. And what kind of validity can be attributed to the discovery of Tlön's origins and history outlined in the postscript? . . . Indeed, what happens to the history of Tlön's emergence into our world? . . . The history of Tlön is the destruction of the very possibility of history. The narrator refers to Bertrand Russell's postulation of a planet created a few minutes ago, inhabited by people who "remember" an illusory past; the story can be seen as the creation of such an imaginary or fictitious remembrance.

The contradictions involved in Tlön's refutation of time are equally evident in the story's treatment of causality. The mental world of Tlön is thoroughly comprehensible and orderly. Yet in infiltrating our disorderly reality Tlön makes use of what Borges considers one of our world's distinguishing features—chance. . . . [In the story, it appears that] chance is not chance but the working out of a complete though as yet unperceived scheme. And beyond that scheme we may discover an even more inclusive contingency. This leads to the general problem of order as opposed to chaos or, more specifically, the relation between order and sheer arbitrariness.

Men are enchanted by Tlön because of its perfect rigor . . . Reality yearns to give in to total coherence. Yet this final coherence, the story shows, is also a contraversion of its own principles. In the idealism of Tlön, speculative sciences exist in almost "innumerable number." Since philosophies are dialectical games, they multiply indefinitely. The inhabitants of the strange planet recognize that any system means the subordination of all aspects of the universe to a single one of them. They provide a corrective to this unavoidable narrowness in the unchecked proliferation of metaphysical theories, each one of which is balanced and countered by its contrary. . . .

Yet this corrective must be abandoned if Tlön is to introject itself into our world. Tlön can be utopian only in the realm of pure thought. As soon as it tries to invade reality it must subject its own diversity to exact organization. A meaningful pattern is necessarily based on the arbitrary selection of a single configurative principle. Order is an attempt to overcome contingency, yet it is inevitably tied to it. And Tlön's order is more all-encompassing than any previously devised: it integrates all realms of mental effort, offering a thoroughly congruent cosmology, geography, literature, falsified history, etc. In its over-all articulation it is more "totalitarian" and threatening than dialectical materialism, anti-semitism and nazism, which are only poor fragmentary symmetries "con apariencia de orden." When the world is Tlön, even expressive variety will disappear; our languages will be forgotten. . . . Tlön will be the perfect dictatorship. The story develops the contrasts not only between the cohesiveness of Tlön and the incomprehensible, unstable realities of the experienced world, but also the inevitable mutilation that order imposes. The utopian world of unlimited capricious speculation becomes a carefully wrought complex that eliminates all alternatives and bewitches humanity with its utter intelligibility.

The theme turns in upon itself and in so doing illustrates the very function of fiction. While Tlön slowly establishes itself as the only truth, the plotting of the story shows that truth to be limitation and distortion. "Truth" remains intact only by making no claims on reality—only by holding itself aloof. In a sense it can exist only in that fiction which makes obvious its fictitiousness, in the story as tentative, ironic formulation.

Tlön is a labyrinth contrived by men, destined to be deciphered by men. Reality, the narrator tells us, is organized according to divine laws, that is, inhuman laws. **"La lotería en Babilonia"** is a description of how those laws might operate. As in **"Tlön,"** the institution of the lottery is presented historically, and as in **"Tlön,"** the principles of the lottery destroy all possibility of history. The lottery grew from an ordinary one that gave out a limited number of prizes to a complicated distribution of rewards and punishments. The company early assumed complete public control and decreed that its operations should be free of charge and apply to all the inhabitants of Babylonia. . . . The Babylonians believe that the lottery is an intensification of the random nature of events, a "periodic infusion of chaos into the cosmos." They reason that chance should therefore determine all the steps of a draw-

ing—not only a given reward or punishment but the way it is carried out as well. These scruples at last brought about certain reforms. Because of the lottery's totalitarian extension, it becomes impossible to tell the difference between mere chance, "accidental" or "mistaken" drawings, and official chance; errors would only corroborate the arbitrariness of the entire program. The system is finally so intricate that every action requires an infinitive number of drawings. Some seem to cause only minimal alterations in the physical world but they have, at times, terrible consequences.

The adverbs I have used in this summary, "at last," "early," "finally," "at times" would seem to make a separation between events which occur as part of an expected sequence and those which lie outside that series. Yet by the end of the story, it is apparent that no such separation can be made. No pattern of causality (no "history") can be perceived in a world entirely ruled by chance. As the narrator proceeds with his tale, the reader realizes that it is a mythical or pseudo-historical explanation of the experience of total contingency. . . . The speaker slyly tells us that he has perhaps covered up "alguna misteriosa monotonía," the monotony of reality itself, of all-too-well known disorder and insecurity. Strangely enough, history is cultivated in Babylonia; the historians have invented a method to correct chances. . . . Just as men have sought to find in the incomprehensible workings of the world evidence of a divine plan, the Babylonians theorize on the "divine" significance of the lottery. The company's silent functioning is "comparable al de dios" and gives rise to the same kind of conjectures that a despairing consciousness might make about God in the face of the world's complete meaninglessness. . . . [Borges suggests] that it doesn't matter if we affirm or deny the shadowy corporation because Babylonia is nothing else than an infinite game of chance. This . . . supposition would, of course, negate the entire projected history of the lottery. The narrator's account of its development is nothing but an illusory memory, the invention of an impossible sequence. The detailed description of the rules of chance demonstrates the capriciousness of the rules. The "divine" laws of the company are indistinguishable from pure chaos.

Both **"Tlön"** and **"La lotería"** are historical accounts of what cannot possibly have historicity. **"El inmortal"** develops a paralled contradiction. It is the autobiography of a man who is all men—or no man—and who cannot possibly have a biography. A manuscript is found in the last volume of Pope's *Iliad;* written in the first person, it tells the story of Marco Flaminio Rufo, tribune of a Roman legion at the time of Diocleatin. Rufo sets out to find the City of the Immortals and the river whose waters are said to abolish death. He unwittingly discovers the river, a miserable dirty stream, and the city, an incomprehensible confusion of architectural forms. Among the speechless troglodytes who live near the river's edge is one who eventually reveals himself to be Homer. Rufo later realizes, through a reconsideration of certain slips and peculiarities in his own narrative, that he too is Homer and that he has been all men. He tries to rid himself of the intolerable burden of immortality.

The theme of mortality/immortality is tied to that of order/disorder; in a sense the two might be seen as the temporal and spatial elaborations of the same basic polarity—the limited, the particular, the ordered as opposed to the incommensurable, the undifferentiated, the totally disordered. The double-layered labyrinth Rufo traverses after drinking from the magic river prefigures the rest of the story's plot, which moves from a limited but coherent human world to the utter meaninglessness of the immortal world. The substructure of the resplendent City of the Immortals is a blind chaos of sordid galleries. It is, nevertheless, a true labyrinth, a house built to confuse men but a house whose secret internal plan can conceivably be grasped. One might make one's way through a maze by following the single hidden pathway that leads to the entrance of the city above. But the City of Immortals has no purpose and no secret plan; it is utterly confounding. . . . As is often the case with Borges's labyrinth images, the idea of a manageable (though sometimes sordid, cruel, or tyrannical) human order is opposed to a far more inclusive arrangement that can only be described as complete disorder or thoroughly bewildering multiplicity. This upper construction is not that city of perfect and classical beauty whose fame had spread as far as the Ganges and which Rufo traveled to find. The Immortals had destroyed their first city and built on its ruins a parody or reversal, a temple to the irrational gods who rule the world. This architectural confusion is the last symbol to which the Immortals condescended. Again, human order is superseded by divine disorder, cosmos by chaos.

The narrator too passes from the human world to the inhuman, immortal one and loses thereby all sense of meaningful design and of human dignity and uniqueness. Given infinite time, all things occur to all men. Given infinite time, infinite circumstances and changes, it is impossible not to write, at least once, the *Odyssey.* Rufo is Homer and he is all men, which is to say he is no one or he is not. . . . To such a being every act and thought becomes a mere echo of all past acts or a faithful foreshadowing of future ones. Nothing can happen only once. . . . Therefore all acts are justified and all are indifferent. Just as the terrible senselessness of the City of the Immortals contaminated the past and the future, eliminating the possibility of value or happiness, so too immortality destroys the prized individuality of men. . . . The narrator and all the other impossibly pluralized Immortals seek the magic river whose waters restore mortality (they reason that if the universe is a system of precise compensations—a corollary of the theory that in infinite time all things occur to all men—the river that confers immortality must be encountered by one that abolishes it). After accidentally discovering this river, Rufo-Homer looks forward to death. Yet mortality, which supposedly gives pathos and value to men, turns out to be strangely similar to immortality. It is only another version of the identification of one man with all men or with no one. The immortal has been all men, therefore he has not been; the mortal will be all men when he is *nadie,* when he dies, when he ceases to be. . . . The progress of the story's argument is as follows: the escape from mortality, from the limitations of human reality and the ultimate annihilation of death proves to be the entrance into a still more dreadful realm of ceaseless repetition, of perfect and perpetual annihilation. But after developing the disastrous consequences of immortality against the apparent "benefits" of mortality, the narrator collapses the latter into the former. Borges spreads out the play of two apparent antitheses and then reduces them both to the same formula: "ser todos: ser nadie."

"El jardín de senderos que se bifurcan" is a spy story with a pseudo-historical setting. A revelation by one of the characters undercuts the historicity and suggests that the account we are reading, for all its references to real people and real events, may actually be part of a vast fiction. And then the fiction itself becomes a dream or nightmare in the mind of one

of the characters so that finally the entire story hovers enigmatically between truth and fiction, between history and invention. The protagonist Yu Tsun is a spy for Germany in the First World War. To communicate a secret (the whereabouts of an allied military installation) to the German chiefs of staff, he must kill Stephen Albert, a man he does not know and who turns out to be the discoverer of a secret far more important than his own. Albert's discovery is intimately related to Yu Tsun: it solves the mystery of the labyrinth and the strange, chaotic novel left by the latter's ancestor Ts'ui Pen. Albert had found out that the two legacies were really the same thing: a bewildering novel that develops multiple contradictory plots, every one of which has several denouements that, in turn, serve as the starting points of still more bifurcating narrative lines. This fictional world has infinite temporal levels, innumerable pasts, presents, and futures; in other words, it has no time, no sequential progression, no single continuity in which all episodes are linked in lineal order. If there is no time, causality does not operate. In any given plot within the novel, the resolution is inevitable but the chain of occurrences within it is variable. . . . The antecedent of an event has no necessary connection to it; it does not cause it nor in any way affect it. There is nothing in any moment that determines those following it. Each present is discontinuous and autonomous, and the future, since it is not tied to a causal chain, is no more subject to willful modification than the past. No character can determine his fate. Every future in this many-layered novel is irrevocable, though entirely different sequences may lead up to the same conclusion. The novel is not infinite but it implies infinity (Ts'ui Pen had set out to construct an infinite labyrinth); if it were sufficiently extended, all things would eventually occur to all the characters.

It is obvious that Ts'ui Pen's work is more than mere fiction; it is, Albert says, "an incomplete, though not false, image of the universe." The universe portrayed consists of innumerable temporal series; it is a growing and vertiginous network of diverging, converging, and parallel times. As Albert describes it, the image seems to become confused with the universe itself; the novel ceases to be a mere symbol and extends to the "real" world of the story's characters. Albert speaks of himself and of Yu Tsun as if they were figures in Ts'ui Pen's novel or as if the implications of the novel applied to their real lives. He tells Yu Tsun that in most time spheres they do not exist; in others only one of them does; when they coincide their destinies vary; at one time Albert is dead when Yu Tsun finds him, at another he appears as a ghost. The summary of these potential encounters may simply be a personal example of how the novel works or it may indicate that the two men have been absorbed into that fictional world. (pp. 125-36)

["El jardín de senderos que se bifurcan"] starts out as an apparently veridical report of an episode in the First World War (presented as a first-person narration in a "found" manuscript). Then the development of the plot indicates first that the whole "reality" of the report has been swallowed up into the fictitiousness of Ts'ui Pen's novel, next that such fictitiousness is a vain and evasive dream in the protagonist's mind, a dream destroyed by the undeniable reality of his pursuit, capture, and execution, and finally, in the closing lines, that the entire action is just one of the many opposing plots in a vast web of infinite times. The story seems to reverse itself twice so that we can never be sure whether it is real or imaginary, whether Yu Tsun and Albert are "real" persons in a historical, autobiographical account, or shadowy, infinitely fictitious beings repeated in numberless novelistic situations.

The themes of Borges's stories—a utopian world of pure mental content, the sacred order of the universe, immortality, the assimilation of temporal sequence into an eternal and total labyrinth—would seem to point to an atemporal realm of complete and enduring stability. Yet the implications of those themes are always carried to the point of reversal and final dissolution. The mechanism is similar to that of the surprise ending. . . . We might describe three steps in the story's effect on the reader: 1) we read from beginning to end and are forced to reconsider the entire course of the action; 2) we re-read and experience the story not only as narrative, as a sequence of episodes, but as a suspended complex of interrelated images and themes; 3) we then realize that the very progress of the narrative prevents any permanent or simultaneous order (although at the same time the indications of simultaneity destroy any meaning the progression might have). Tlön negates the past and the possibility of history and thereby negates the history of its own gradual intrusion into the real world that is recorded in the narrative. **"La lotería en Babilonia"** historically develops the denial of history. **"El inmortal"** fuses the contrary poles of mortality and immortality into a single annihilation that precludes any stable or unchanging form. It is not clear if Yu Tsun's political mission constitutes a unique and irrevocable destiny or merely one of infinite fictional possibilities. In other words, the forced temporality of the story has, in its contrary effects, a kind of "message," and that message involves the complete undermining of the subsistent order suggested by the story's themes and by the illusion of simultaneity.

Such a pattern subverts not only the apparent reality of the story's events, but its opposite as well; it dissolves both the common sense world organized by time and causality and the "ideal" world of order, eternity, infinity. The contradictions established within the fictions set the disorder of the material world against the abstract order of an ideal one, but they also set that ideal realm against itself. Order either simplifies its own principles and becomes totalitarian or it is so wonderfully complex, intricate, and all-inclusive that it is indistinguishable from complete chaos. The stories act out an ironic and total destruction of all realities and all abstractions.

This persistent dissolution is certainly nihilistic. Some critics want to defend Borges against the charge of inhuman nihilism or "negative" thinking. But negative thinking, Borges shows, is the least deceptive, the most intelligent, and the most fruitful. Since the world forever escapes the mind's attempts to grasp it, thought should be continually self-critical. In one of his essays, he observes that there is no classification of the universe which is not arbitrary and conjectural. The impossibility of penetrating the divine scheme does not dissuade us from proposing human schemes, although we know they are provisional. The important point is to keep their provisionality always in mind. Indeed, we should make an effort to dramatize and heighten it. . . . The stories' self-refuting, self-digesting form acts out the realization of the fragility of all mental constructions. Because they are transparent inventions that at every turn give evidence of their imaginative origins, the fictions organize experience without distorting it. Each fiction is, like Ts'ui Pen's novel "an incomplete, but not false, image of the universe." If divine order is the delusive tag for total chaos, the artist's order is, in the

awareness of its incomplete and hypothetical nature, vastly superior.

At this point, it is no longer necessary to separate fiction and philosophy. The attitudes useful in artistic creation may also be useful in speculative thought. Certainly their products are frequently indistinguishable. Borges confessed to the serious omission in his anthology of fantastic literature of the genre's unsuspected and greatest masters—Parmenides, Plato, Duns Scotus, Spinoza, Leibniz, Kant, Frances Bradley. In his stories Borges does not set everyday reality against a more convincing "reality" of thought; in fact, he scrupulously blurs the differences between these two levels. But in the pattern of all of them is the implicit opposition between bewitchment or blind faith and ironic comprehension. In an essay he quotes Novalis's description of man's self-deception: the greatest wizard is the one who enchants himself to the point of taking his own fantasmagoria for autonomous appearances. Borges argues that such is our case. We have dreamed the world but we have left certain tenuous interstices of unreason in order to know that it is false. By calling attention to these nebulous zones, we make ourselves aware of the conjectural character of all knowledge and all representation. . . . And Borges's fictions, in playing out a drama of postulation and dissolution, illustrate what should be the ironic and playful ideal of all mental activities. The aesthetic is the final attitude towards the tentative formulations of the mind. Fiction-making turns out to be the proper exercise of intelligence. (pp. 137-41)

Frances Wyers Weber, "Borges's Stories: Fiction and Philosophy," in Hispanic Review, *Vol. XXXVI, No. 2, April, 1968, pp. 124-41.*

DONALD A. YATES   (essay date 1971)

[*In the following excerpt, Yates examines Borges's short fiction, particularly the prose work "Pedro Salvadores," and illustrates the author's characteristic concern with philosophy, language, drama, and his Argentinian heritage.*]

In these brief remarks on the narrative prose of Jorge Luis Borges, I propose to attempt something at once seemingly impossible and totally obvious. Viewing the immense richness and complexity of Borges' narrative resources, one quickly perceives the apparent impossibility of describing that author's artistic orientation in a short essay. Yet like the fiction of no other contemporary writer (to judge from the growing amount of critical comment accorded to his work), Borges' prose writings invite, inspire, perhaps even demand analysis and interpretation. . . .

To ascribe to Borges' artistic world four key aspects, four cardinal points, is, to be sure, arbitrary. Still, this approach need not produce necessarily invalid judgments. Schematic yes, but with any luck, in some way telling.

The narrative prose encompassed by these observations extends from **"Hombres de las orillas,"** published in September of 1933, to **"Pedro Salvadores,"** which appeared in the English translation . . . in the *New York Review of Books* in mid-August 1969. (p. 404)

"Pedro Salvadores" is, in Borges' words, a "straightforward story" of a new type he has begun to write. The first narrative of this new style was **"La intrusa,"** published in 1966. The general observations of this paper, I feel, apply as fully to this later narrative mood as to the above-mentioned first story by Borges (which in its subsequent appearances carries the title **"Hombre de la esquina rosada"**). And for those familiar with the author's more celebrated in-between stories—those of *Ficciones* and *El Aleph*—the appropriateness of these cardinal points will, I hope, be apparent.

Borges believes in the superiority of his recent narratives—**"La intrusa"** especially, which he now refers to as his best story, and **"Pedro Salvadores,"** which pleases him for its simplicity. He has excused his earliest story as (again his own words) "psychologically false" and as so much "fancy work." Urged to consider that it was his first story and showed signs of having been carefully worked over and polished, he has replied, "Yes, but I think I may have overdone it."

Let us examine, then, these points of reference as they relate to Borges' fiction. They seem conveniently to characterize the stories he fashioned from his own materials—the stories of the late thirties and of the forties. But to put the theory to the test, we shall see how they apply to his latest fiction, specifically to **"Pedro Salvadores,"** the two-page account that Borges prefers to call an anecdote, something *not* his but only recounted to him. I hope to show in some detail how, in the retelling, this episode of the Rosas terror becomes his.

The cardinal points of Jorge Luis Borges are four and may be considered as corresponding to the points of the compass. Borges' south is, of course, his deeply sensed nationality as an Argentine. It is reflected not only in his literary use of Argentine settings and events, but also in the manner in which he absorbs and synthesizes borrowings from the most disparate sources. (pp. 404-05)

The circumstances of the author's life have combined to produce a man who, owing to chronic nearsightedness which led gradually to virtual blindness, has withdrawn from aggressive participation in the present, and has seen fit to draw drama and excitement vicariously from many sources, none perhaps more noteworthy than the participation of his ancestors in the turbulent events of his country's history. . . .

If Borges has any identity whatever, it is as an Argentine, and, as an American poet has expressed it, "that has made all the difference." Those who would call him "Europeanized" and criticize his indifference to Argentine reality surely understand very little about the writer. . . .

If the direction north has special significance as the principal point of orientation, then I would be inclined to say that Borges' north is most evidently language—this being extended to include its chief mode of aesthetic expression, literature, as well as the preoccupation with the techniques of that expression, literary style. Borges has stated on numerous occasions that the most significant feature of his childhood (and I have heard him extend "childhood" into "lifetime") was his father's library of English books. There is perhaps no more eloquent testimony to the truth of this statement than Borges' admission that the most vivid images that remain with him of his early years in Palermo are not of people or places or events, but of books, their feel, their smell, and the illustrations they carried. A curious statement, but one that illuminates the paths along which his life subsequently led him. His destiny, he understood at an early age, was to be a writer. (p. 405)

Borges' literature is made up of other literatures, and he is quick to acknowledge influences in his work. . . . When his sight failed some fifteen years ago, he made a decision not to content himself with the wealth of familiarity with literature he had already acquired. . . . He took down from the upper shelves of his library a collection of books on Old English that he could no longer see, and with his students embarked on a journey back into the beginnings of that tongue which, more than any other, has enriched his life. Thus, language, in a broad, fundamental sense, continues in his later years to be a point to which he is oriented, a north by which he still guides himself.

The east of Borges' compass may be said to constitute the most distinctive feature of his writings. It could be described as a fascination with philosophical and metaphysical questions that manifests itself, in part, in the incorporation of these problems as elements of his prose fiction. His interest in these matters goes back to the philosophical works he read as a boy and discussed with his father, a teacher of psychology. . . .

Following a seven-year period of education and literary apprenticeship in Switzerland and Spain, Borges returned to Buenos Aires where, waiting at the pier to welcome the family home, was his father's friend Macedonio Fernández, the man who was to influence Borges' attitude and style of thought more than any other person. With Macedonio, Borges subsequently developed an intellectual skepticism toward most commonly held beliefs of a spiritual or practical nature as well as a fondness for a personal brand of philosophic idealism that Macedonio had evolved. Together they read and discussed many books and writers in a genial tone; among them Schopenhauer, Hume, and Francis Bradley. (p. 406)

Borges acquired many things with Macedonio Fernández, and when Borges began to write his first stories, in the late 1930s, the essentially philosophical concepts and metaphysical questions (especially those touching on time, infinity, and identity) that had been so firmly and—thanks to Macedonio—so casually assimilated as part of Borges' literary environment, were quite naturally incorporated as fictional or narrative elements of his prose. After the first two stories signed with his own name had been published—**"Pierre Menard, autor del *Quijote*"** and **"Tlön, Uqbar, Orbis Tertius"**—the narrative formula was set, and thereafter his very peculiar, very original prose style would be instantly recognizable. Borges himself, perhaps more clearly than anyone else, has described this feature of his writings, saying: "I am quite simply a man who uses perplexities for literary purposes."

The remaining point, the west of Borges' compass, is the least studied aspect of his narrative mood. . . . [Critics] have talked vaguely and occasionally of the uncommon abundance of knives, swords, murders, *guapos, compadritos,* conspiracies, intrigues, violence, vengeance, ambushes, plots, and executions. But only recently . . . is serious attention given to what I consider the fourth and final cardinal point: the strong, ever-present narrative ingredient of drama. This element may take the form of vivid color, melodrama, mystery, or very tight clockwork plotting, but it is characteristically present in his fictions and occupies the place that, in the stories of others, would be occupied by psychological probing or exposition—features notably absent in Borges' tales.

Borges' inordinate fondness for western films, gangster movies, fantastic literature, and detective fiction (perhaps explained by the concept of psychological transference or compensation), has accounted for much of the enjoyment he has derived from everyday life. All of these interests have exerted a great influence on his writing. To begin with, he has produced in collaboration with his close friend Adolfo Bioy Casares: the don Isidro Parodi detective stories, an extravagant detective tale entitled *Un modelo para la muerte,* two Argentine gangster film scripts, two fantastic tales included in a book called **Dos fantasías memorables,** two anthologies of detective short stories, as well as a successful detective novel series (*El Séptimo Círculo*). . . . These interests no doubt have accounted for the tone of certain of his own stories—the remarkable **"La muerte y la brújula," "El jardín de senderos que se bifurcan," "Emma Zunz," "El acercamiento a Almotásim," "La espera,"** and others. But most significantly, his passion for fantasy and detective fiction, for gangster films, tales of *guapos, mavelos,* and *compadritos* has influenced the narrative structure of virtually all his prose fiction. Drama, usually in obvious and explicit form, is a feature of his style (we recognize him by it); moreover, it has come to represent for him a fundamental quality of the aesthetic effect he ideally hopes to achieve. It is in *Ficciones* that we find the following statement, perhaps one of the most significant formulations in all his work: "El hecho estético no puede prescindir de algún elemento de asombro," [or, "the aesthetic work cannot do without some element of astonishment."]

That "asombro" [or "astonishment"] is translated, in Borges' fiction, into the various forms of drama, melodrama, or sudden revelation that hold his stories firmly together. We need only recall those tales we have read to understand that the aesthetic effects Borges attains—the impression or impact they leave with the reader—are derived from the "asombro," that is, the culmination not of a single reflection or insight, but rather the discharge of narrative tension accumulated by an intricately plotted and controlled dramatic situation.

Now, to test the applicability of these four features, let us turn to an example of Borges' new, "straightforward" fiction—the succinct narrative, **"Pedro Salvadores,"** found in his latest work in Spanish, *Elogio de la sombra.* If this proposed scheme is at all valid, it should lead to a reasonably full appreciation of Borges' art as manifest in this tale. (pp. 406-08)

"Pedro Salvadores" is Borges' account of a true story, a story he had heard many years before he wrote it down. In the first paragraph he states, in his own voice, two things:

> I want to leave a written record (perhaps the first to be attempted) of one of the strangest and grimmest happenings in Argentine history. To meddle as little as possible in the telling, to abstain from picturesque details or personal conjectures is, it seems to me, the only way to do this.

Here we have two quite different aspects. There is starkness and honesty in the author's intention to leave "a written record" of this incident (such, of course, is the function of prose), and the professed determination to accomplish this without descending to "fancy writing" is both disarming and subtly deceptive. But we are drawn closer by a promise of drama—the relating of "one of the strangest and grimmest happenings in Argentine history." In one paragraph, two sentences, three of the four aspects discussed above are evoked. The fourth, the author's concern with philosophical ideas, quickly comes into play in the next expository paragraph. Here we are given once more a forthright look into the narrator's art; like the magician before his trick, Borges shows us his hand, seeming to fulfill the promise he has just made: "A

man, a woman, and the overpowering shadow of a dictator are the three characters. The man's name was Pedro Salvadores; my grandfather Acevedo saw him days or weeks after the dictator's downfall in the battle of Caseros." In these lines Borges proceeds directly to the telling of the story he has announced; and a key element in the structure of the inner narrative has been inserted (as we shall see) in the reference to the meeting between Borges' grandfather and Pedro Salvadores.

Next appears the first feature of a philosophical nature—a brief allusion to the concept of destiny, and the casual evocation of the question of identity, which the author will develop more fully near the story's end: "Pedro Salvadores may have been no different from anyone else, but the years and his fate set him apart." The paragraph continues, providing, in terms as succinct as those in which the cast of characters was presented, the setting of the story. The scene of the events is suggested as being as typically anonymous as Salvadores is himself. . . . Now the stage is set and the announced drama begins. In the next paragraph the only violent incidents of the story occur. The sparse and unembellished account of the rapid series of happenings both fulfills the author's promise "to abstain from picturesque details" and reflects a cinematographic narrative technique that Borges has used successfully before (e.g., in **Hombre de la esquina rosada**").

> One night, around 1842, Salvadores and his wife heard the growing, muffled sound of horses' hooves out on the unpaved street and the riders shouting their drunken *vivas* and their threats. This time Rosas' henchmen did not ride on. After the shouts came repeated knocks at the door; while the men began forcing it, Salvadores was able to pull the dining-room table aside, lift the rug, and hide himself down in the cellar. His wife dragged the table back in place. The *mazorca* broke into the house; they had come to take Salvadores. The woman said her husband had run away to Montevideo. The men did not believe her; they flogged her, they smashed all the blue chinaware (blue was the Unitarian color), they searched the whole house, but they never thought of lifting the rug. At midnight they rode away, swearing that they would soon be back.

There now occurs a curious paragraph. While it contains necessary information, it is the least effective of the entire story. For this, I think, there is a reason. Something must be said about Salvadores here (the next paragraph will deal with his wife). Yet after the period of his confinement is specified there is little Borges tells about Salvadores' underground existence—that is, until he is ready to consider, from a philosophical viewpoint, what the meaning of Salvadores' adventure might be. And this will not occur until two paragraphs later. The conclusion we may draw from this is that the details of Salvadores' confinement interest Borges much less than the conjectures he might draw from it or the interpretation he might suggest for it. This, of course, coincides with the scheme of narrative values we have discussed. (pp. 408-09)

But now comes a masterful paragraph. In half a dozen lines Borges relates the nine-year tribulation of Salvadores' wife. He has compressed into these few lines, still abstaining from "picturesque details or personal conjecture," the image of an extraordinary woman, all the facts we need to know about her life during the nine years, and an arresting and almost gratuitous dramatic surprise:

His wife let go all the servants, who could possibly have informed against them, and told her family that Salvadores was in Uruguay. Meanwhile, she earned a living for them both sewing uniforms for the army. In the course of time, she gave birth to two children; her family turned from her, thinking she had a lover. After the tyrant's fall, they got down on their knees and begged to be forgiven.

The last sentence breaks the time sequence because the balance of the story is about Salvadores, and his wife's situation needs to be resolved here before we return to his experience.

The next paragraph is the justification, in Borges' eyes, for the narrative. In it he searches, characteristically, for the possible significance behind the facts. The questions that begin the paragraph, even after Borges gives them extended consideration, remain unanswered at the end. And it is out of this final perplexity that Borges, a few lines later, draws the story's concluding reflection. In this "justifying" paragraph we observe the limpid, precise language and the poised, perceptive, but fundamentally interrogative attitude that, in turn, justify Borges to his reader:

> What was Pedro Salvadores? Who was he? Was it his fear, his love, the unseen presence of Buenos Aires, or—in the long run—habit that held him prisoner? In order to keep him with her, his wife would make up news to tell him about whispered plots and rumored victories. Maybe he was a coward and she loyally hid it from him that she knew. I picture him in his cellar perhaps without a candle, without a book. Darkness probably sank him into sleep. His dreams, at the outset, were probably of that sudden night when the blade sought his throat, of the streets he knew so well, of the open plains. As the years went on, he would have been unable to escape even in his sleep; whatever he dreamed would have taken place in the cellar. At first, he may have been a man hunted down, a man in danger of his life; later (we will never know for certain), an animal at peace in its burrow or a sort of dim god.

The final sentence of the story is properly a part of the paragraph just cited. But Borges withholds it, with considerable effect, while he occupies himself with resolving the external structure of the narrative. Now we have a reference to the encounter between Borges' grandfather and Salvadores that was prefigured at the story's beginning. The balance of the brief paragraph generates a calculated falling, anticlimactic tone, which provides the necessary contrast with the story's last sentence:

> All this went on until that summer day of 1852 when Rosas fled the country. It was only then that the secret man came out into the light of day; my grandfather spoke with him. Flabby, overweight, Salvadores was the color of wax and could not speak above a low voice. He never got back his confiscated lands; I think he died in poverty.

Now the final element of the tale: "As with so many things, the fate of Pedro Salvadores strikes us as a symbol of something we are about to understand, but never quite do." Close readers of Borges will perceive a familiar ring in this final line. It is a lucidly expressed insight. . . . (pp. 409-10)

I hope it is clear that in **"Pedro Salvadores"** Borges blends the four aspects we have discussed into a prose narrative in which we cannot fail to sense the presence of his hand. The

consciousness of his Argentine nationality, his acute awareness of language and the theory and practice of literary art, his persistent artistic concern with the perplexities of philosophical and metaphysical speculation, and his highly developed appreciation of the essence of drama are surely all present and apparent in this story. It may even be said that they constitute the principal ingredients of the prose style of Jorge Luis Borges. (p. 411)

> *Donald A. Yates, "The Four Cardinal Points of Borges," in* Books Abroad, *Vol. 45, No. 3, Summer, 1971, pp. 404-11.*

THOMAS O. BENTE (essay date 1973)

[*In the following favorable review of* Doctor Brodie's Report, *Bente compares Borges's treatment of complex themes to that of his earlier volumes* Ficciones *and* El Aleph.]

Perhaps it is because readers have grown so accustomed to the Borges of forking paths, libraries of infinite volumes, and suspended time sequences, that Borges' latest collection of stories in English, **Doctor Brodie's Report,** has caused such interest in—indeed, controversy over—the apparent departure from the Borges who was known and appreciated before. Some reviews of the latest anthology have characterized the change in quasi-psychiatric terms, approaching the volume, in light of the differences it shows from earlier works, as a doctor might approach a patient whose erratic behavior gives every evidence of pronounced schizophrenia—disrupted patterns of behavior in comparison with previous "normality." . . . Comments on **Doctor Brodie's Report** have become, then, a balance between a discussion of how the stories are different or new and an attempt, in some cases, to justify them. The point of departure has been more "How could Borges do this to us?," rather than "What has Borges done and how has he accomplished it?"

The essence of this article will, alas, probably not be much different in tone from other reviews of **Doctor Brodie's Report** . . .

Yet there is something more that must be included . . . , especially insofar as **Doctor Brodie's Report** is concerned— simply an evaluation and appreciation of the anthology in view of Borges' total work; an attempt to view the latest short stories not so much from an approach that emphasizes their differences from the earlier fiction but rather from a perspective that shows that although the subject matter and thrust of many of the stories are modified, their essence is still very much within the Borges vein, and the reader should not be alarmed with the new configurations the stories take. Borges has not disappointed us by completely abandoning his illusions and literary preferences of the 30's and 40's; he has shown, in spite of his age and the laurels earned from earlier creativity, that he is immensely capable of retaining essential vestiges of earlier periods and remolding them in a modified type of fiction that we as readers may not have expected. In this sense, Borges reveals himself again as the innovator we have always known.

As far as Borges himself is concerned, there is little doubt that he views the literary production as a short story writer, the creative effort first seen in **Historia Universal de la Infamia,** the sketches that appeared in the *Crítica* of Buenos Aires in 1933 and 1934, as the most significant work bue has done. (p. 36)

Borges and his sister Norah (left rear) in Geneva, Switzerland, 1916, two years after they became stranded with their family in Europe during World War I.

The early 40's, however, mark a definite turning point in Borges' literary career. Published in Victoria Ocampo's *Sur* . . . several short stories appeared that were later included in *El Jardín de Senderos que se Bifurcan,* 1941, later altered and retitled *Ficciones* and published in 1944. It is, without doubt, in *Ficciones* that Borges' imagination takes flight, carrying the reader on a cosmic journey to regions unexplored in Hispano-American literature until its appearance. Such well known stories as "Tlön, Uqbar, Orbis Tertius," "Las Ruinas Circulares," "La Biblioteca de Babel," and "El Jardín de Senderos que se Bifurcan" are included. With *Ficciones* the reader also begins to determine the basic preoccupations that have fascinated Borges in his short stories: time and space, the labyrinth, differing personal realities, thought, memory, and individual versus multiple personality. *Ficciones* is indeed a key work for appreciating the Borges who has become so famous.

Late in the 40's, the second volume of stories for which Borges is well known appeared: *El Aleph,* 1949. Even within the decade of the 40's, an important shift—if not in technique at least in emphasis—may be noted. *El Aleph* includes such masterful selections as "El Inmortal," "Emma Zunz," and "Deutsches Requiem." The period of the mystery or detective story has begun. If *Ficciones* plays with the reader's fantasy and intellect in that order of importance, *El Aleph* reverses the order; each element is important in both of these major works, yet the change is apparent from one to the other.

The reason for indicating such a shift in emphasis is not simply to point out what may, indeed, be regarded as literary history; rather it is to suggest that Borges' literary career has never been static. It is as unreasonable to assume that Borges as a poet in the 20's is to be equated with the Borges of *Ficciones* and *El Aleph* as it is to expect that the Borges of the 40's is the Borges of the 60's. *Doctor Brodie's Report* is a case in point. . . .

[*Doctor Brodie's Report*] is a collection of eleven stories first published individually in other sources. . . . [The] stories represent, individually, the latest in Borges' short story creativity. . . . (p. 37)

Apart from the intrinsic literary value of the volume, *Doctor Brodie's Report* offers a collection of stories that are, collectively, another turning point in the writer's career. The change is not, however, nearly as dramatic or shocking as some of the critics have led us to believe. Unifying the work and distinguishing it from earlier collections of Borges' stories is the undercurrent of realism, as opposed to fantasy or illusion, that marks the narratives. Individually, the stories share much in common with the earlier Borges.

Perhaps the most convenient approach to reading the stories of *Doctor Brodie's Report* is to identify certain characteristics of Borges' writing which have been explored *vis-à-vis* the earlier fiction in an effort to see how they are molded into the latest fiction. We might, therefore, focus on the reality Borges creates in his stories and the types of characters the author presents, with some mention of the questions of time, destiny, and chance.

One of the constant traits of Borges' earlier fiction is the creation of a story plot and development that is highly complex, a technique that often gives his stories all the outward appearances of fact as opposed to literary fiction. The reader immediately recalls "El Inmortal" or "Deutsches Requiem" as examples of this particular stylistic characteristic—stories in which an accumulation of details, some based on fact, some on fantasy, contribute to create an appearance of reality, an illusion of verisimilitude. Even the most perfunctory reading of *Doctor Brodie's Report* reveals that Borges has not abandoned this stylistic technique. In the first paragraph of "The Unworthy Friend," the second story in the collection, for example, both the story teller as a personage in the narration as well as Santiago Fischbein, a Jewish bookseller fond of esoteric intellectual pursuits, are introduced. The introduction—a type of quasi-prologue that establishes the relationship of the narrator to the deceased Fischbein—serves only to lead the reader into the body of the story, which becomes Fischbein's first-person account, told earlier to the narrator, of an incident from his childhood in which he resisted the temptation of evil but betrayed a friend as a result. The curious characteristic of the story—not unlike many of Borges' others—is that a relatively simple narration is rendered significantly more complex through the addition of preliminary detail. This, of course, is also a frequent structural characteristic of Borges' fiction—introductory paragraphs which contribute little to the actual development of the story, but which create an aura of authenticity for the fiction.

"Rosendo's Tale," the fifth story, based on an earlier story entitled "Streetcorner Man," employs the same technique. The story begins with an introductory paragraph and

> It was about eleven o'clock at night; I had just entered the old grocery store-bar (which today is just

a plain bar) at the corner of Bolívar and Venezuela. From off on one side, a man signaled me with a 'psst.' . . . This is what the man told me. . . .

The narrator then changes voices (no longer the storyteller but rather Rosendo, the man from the bar) and proceeds to relate an episode of his life in which he killed another man, took flight, and later refused to fight again, preferring to be branded a coward rather than accept the risk of killing a second time. The lineal development of the story is essentially quite simple, at least insofar as the chain of events in Rosendo's life is concerned, yet the mention of countless characters, the round-about way in which the reader finally comprehends Rosendo's tale, although the story is no more than eight pages in length, give it a baroque quality—an immensely simple and understated narrative adorned with a surface, structural façade that is highly complex.

"Juan Muraña," the eighth story in the collection, reveals much the same technique. Borges enters his prologue, again set off from the story, by naming himself as a character on board a train who encounters an old school acquaintance, Emilio Trápani. The latter becomes the narrator as the body of the story unfolds and we, the readers, together with Borges in the story, hear Trápani's account of his uncle, Juan Muraña. Curiously, however, both the title and the prologue, which lead us to suppose the central figure of the story is the uncle, are misleading; the circumstances described happened ten years after Muraña's death. In a circuitous way the story focuses, really, on an episode concerning an eccentric aunt—Muraña's wife—who killed the family's landlord out of frustration and irritation over an eviction notice. Perhaps Muraña is, in a way, the axis of the story, however; the aunt states—and believes—that her husband's knife, obeying the impulse of Muraña, committed the murder. Borges again converts an ostensibly simple plot into an amazing complexity of the unexpected, compounding the story into an intricacy of chance encounters, multiple personages, and the metaphysical suggestion of a transmigration of identity or soul from human to object. Clearly, many of the stories in *Doctor Brodie's Report,* although apparently more simple than Borges' earlier fiction, reveal a similar sophistication in the cleverness with which the story unfolds. Borges adroitly molds the surface structure of his narrative to appear simple, while at the same time he probes another tale which is, in many cases, peripheral to the apparent simplicity of the story but which actually becomes the point of focus.

One of the limits of the short story as a genre . . . is the extent of characterization that may be accomplished within the necessarily imposed restrictions of length. This is why a short story is so frequently limited to the denouement of only one episode, and why the characters are so frequently "flat," to use E. M. Forster's word. We as readers have little time to determine whether the characters are convincing. We share, generally, only one major experience with the personages and know them only in the context of one major situation. What, therefore, marked Borges' characters of his earlier stories as particularly identifiable or recognizable, and in what way are the characters in the stories of *Doctor Brodie's Report* similar to or different from those created earlier?

One recalls Borges' characters from his most famous stories as being, frequently, creations of fantasy with greater than life proportions ("El Inmortal," "Las Ruinas Circulares"), occasionally people of such intellectual acumen that what might otherwise be their strongest trait proves to contribute to their

downfall ("Funes, el Memorioso," "La Muerte y la Brújula"), and at times protagonists of such astute cleverness that they are reduced in significance when compared with their inventiveness ("El Jardín de Senderos que se Bifurcan," "Emma Zunz"). One of the most striking features of *Doctor Brodie's Report,* and doubtless one of the factors that has led some critics to consider the collection as such a departure from the earlier Borges, is the absence of characters whose literary existence reveals the above personality dimensions. The personages of the stories in the latest collection are simply not so extra-humanly complex, and in their lack of complexity or design they gain a human quality that may not have been a general characteristic of Borges' personages earlier. Richard Burgin in his book *Conversations With Jorge Luis Borges* asked Borges about the change in direction his stories are taking. Borges' responded,

> . . . I feel that the kind of stories you get in *El Aleph* and *Ficciones* are becoming rather mechanical, and that people expect that kind of thing from me. So that I feel as if I were a kind of high fidelity, a kind of gadget, no? A kind of factory producing stories about mistaken identity, about mazes, about tigers, about mirrors, about people being somebody else, or about all men being the same man or one man being his own mortal foe. And another reason, that may be a rather malicious one, is that there are quite a few people all over the world who are writing that kind of story and there's no reason why I should go on doing it. Especially as some of them do it far better than I do, no?

Perhaps the most notable example of an unpretentious and entirely realistic character is found in "The Elder Lady," the ninth story in the collection. The story is, without doubt, a *tour de force* of magnificent proportions in the brief but poignant presentation of an old woman, María Justina Rubio de Jáuregui, " . . . the last surviving daughter of any of the soldiers who had fought in the South American War of Independence. . . . " Because of this distinction, a party in her honor is given. The lady is so old and (we believe) senile, however, that the celebration is incomprehensible or—at best—without great significance to the guest of honor. The story is basic and uncomplicated; it does not provide a source for mental gymnastics over hidden meanings or philosophical meanderings, but it is a masterful example of its genre.

Yet if the creation of characters whose literary existence may be appreciated on a human, flesh and blood level and not solely on a cerebral level marks the collection, Borges has not completely abandoned the types of individuals who occupied his earlier interest, nor has he failed to give his newer characters certain traits reminiscent of earlier personages. Characters distinguished by their esoteric, intellectual pursuits abound. . . . (pp. 37-9)

One of the most widely discussed characteristics of Borges' fiction from the days of *Ficciones* and *El Aleph* has been the common unity of man; the concept that although an individual exists as an entity unto himself, his existence—the experiences of his life and indeed his very personality—is a shared existence with other men, either past or contemporary. Although the concept is complex and related to Borges' view of time and events, reduced to its simplest explanation it is as though one man stands before a single mirror bordered by double mirrors on either side. Soon another man approaches and stands side by side with the first. The image in the front mirror is of two individuals, yet there is a fusion in the multiple reflections cast from the side mirrors.

In **"The Duel,"** the third story, two women share an understanding between them—consciously or unconsciously—yet vie for honors as painters. Although they are very different women and in spite of the fact that each attempts to outdo the other (the duel), the reciprocity of sentiment and sharing of personality is so great that the death of one not only inhibits but actually incapacitates the artistic creativity of the other.

In **"Guayaquil,"** one of the most fascinating stories in the collection, the question of whether the narrator or Dr. Zimmerman will examine newly discovered letters of Simón Bolívar is pursued. Among the letters is Bolívar's account of what took place during his celebrated meeting with San Martín in Guayaquil in 1822. As the story develops, and during the encounter between the narrator and Dr. Zimmerman, both qualified historians, it becomes clear that both they—and we as readers—are witnessing a reenactment of what may well have taken place between the two generals decades before. . . . In another story, **"Rosendo's Tale,"** mentioned earlier, one of the characters says, " . . . and finally he came out and asked me to fight. Then something happened that nobody ever understood. In that big loudmouth I saw myself, the same as in a mirror, and it made me feel ashamed."

"The Meeting," the seventh story, presents an interesting suggestion of animism in the transference of personality and identity, also seen in **"Juan Muraña."** An evening dinner party leads to a knife fight between two guests during which one is killed. The fight, which is presented as so matter-of-fact that it causes neither surprise nor shock from the reader, is essentially little more than a situation devoid of human consequences. It serves only for the narrator, who witnessed the tragedy, to suggest that the two knives, which years before belonged to two Gauchos who used them to fight each other, may actually have been the adversaries in the latest scrap, and not the two men. . . . Of course the suggestion of personification of the two knives is not identical to the "one man is all men" concept, yet it does reveal a striking parallel to the fluid, encompassing nature of individual identity for which Borges has been known. These examples suggest that while Borges may not dwell on the common threads of shared experiences and personality with the same emphasis as he did earlier, they are certainly still present, albeit in a more subtle fashion.

There are other examples of the Borges of earlier years in *Doctor Brodie's Report.* The question of probability and chance is apparent in **"The Gospel According to Mark,"** the first story of the collection which also relies on a recognizable characteristic of Borges' fiction—the surprise ending—for much of its power. The interest in geometric design or arrangement . . . is seen in **"The Meeting,"** and the common Borges belief that time is not fixed or universal but rather individual permeates several of the stories.

Borges' latest collection is, nevertheless, unusual in its diversity of stories. Two are specifically concerned with Gaucho life: **"The End of the Duel,"** and **"The Intruder,"** the tale of two Gaucho brothers whose sibling friendship is so powerful as to cause the murder of a young woman whose presence threatened to come between them. The story, written in 1966, has already become well known and marks, by Borges' own

admission, " . . . the first of my new ventures into straightforward storytelling."

[*Doctor Brodie's Report*] is somewhat of an unusual tale for Borges because of the subject; the diary of a missionary and his experiences among a tribe of primitive men called the Yahoos. Nonetheless, the introduction or preface to the story is certainly very much Borges; the narrator tells the reader that the manuscript, from which the story is taken, was discovered among the pages of a volume of the *Arabian Night's Entertainments* that belonged to David Brodie, D.D., a Scottish missionary. Borges has again couched his story in circumstances that lend the illusion of reality, and while the report of life among the Yahoos may be far removed from the setting of most of Borges' stories, its imagination, inventiveness, and unusualness are certainly noteworthy.

Doctor Brodie's Report should not, in last analysis, surprise the reader as such a departure from the familiar Borges of earlier years. Much less should it provoke mildly condescending remarks of how the Argentine storyteller, who has become so dear to many, has somehow failed to maintain his knack in his older years. To say that the present Borges is any less valid than the earlier Borges is to impose a critically pedantic limit on the artistic creativity of an author whose literary career has been marked by trends and evolution in expression. The latest collection retains many of the characteristics of the fiction of earlier years and at the same time adds new dimensions which Borges had not explored previously. Time and international acclaim have proven the enduring success of *Ficciones* and *El Aleph;* let the reader now prepare to read an easily identifiable Borges who is not really so different after all, and who is showing us that the literary progression he has made is but one more example of the creative genius that has long been recognized in his work. (pp. 39-40)

Thomas O. Bente, "Borges Revisited," in Américas, Vol. 25, Nos. 11-12, November-December, 1973, pp. 36-40.

D. P. GALLAGHER (essay date 1973)

[*Gallagher is a faculty member at Oxford University specializing in Spanish-language authors. In the following excerpt from his critical survey* Modern Latin American Literature, *Gallagher examines the metaphysical dimensions of Borges's short stories, which, he asserts, refute the systematization of unknowable reality while affirming the existence of infinite possibilities.*]

In Latin America, and especially in Argentina, Borges is usually either revered or detested. For the apostles of committed literature he is an irrelevant, reactionary aesthete. For others, he is the stylistic genius who has taught a whole generation of Latin American novelists to write Spanish, and he is above all the man who has restored the imagination to its proper place in Latin American literature, by liberating fiction from the duty to document 'reality'. Yet whether revered or detested, Borges is someone no Latin American writer can easily escape. He is a monumental point of reference for every Latin American novelist, even for those who write in reaction to him, and he fulfils therefore a role in prose fiction similar to that of Vallejo and Neruda in poetry.

How can one account for this formidable position? There is perhaps no writer more difficult to write about than Borges. He has been an amateur philosopher all his life and his work is full of *ideas*. Yet to abstract those ideas from his work is to reduce it to a string of perhaps not very startling propositions about the human condition. All too often when reading books on Borges one begins to wonder what all the fuss is about, and to feel that Borges might have done better to leave, say, time and identity to the experts. Yet if one then returns to his actual writing, the spell is reborn. (p. 94)

The most recurring concern of Borges's work is to reveal the gap that separates our intellectual aspirations from our intellectual limitations. In most of his stories, he presents us with the spectacle of men who set out to 'decipher the universe', only to discover that they cannot even decipher an infinitesimal fragment of it, not even that which constitutes their own person. Sometimes, maybe they think they have found the answer. If they do, they are ultimately all the more comically pathetic. The metaphysical systems they doggedly conceive are in the end arbitrary. An irreducible universe intimidatingly reasserts itself.

Borges's work abounds in emotive descriptions of that moment of reassertion and its consequent defeat of the intellectual quest. Thus, the Arab scholar Averroes: 'The fear of the crassly infinite, of mere space, of mere matter touched Averroes for an instant. He looked at the symmetrical garden; he felt aged, useless unreal.' Paradoxically, the role of metaphysics turns out to be the opposite of what it set out to be. Rather than explain the universe, metaphysics shows it up to be inexplicable, serves in the end rather to shake our initial complacent belief in a possible solution. The more we speculate, the more perplexed we become, and we can only conclude with 'that lucid perplexity which is metaphysics' only claim to fame, its remuneration and its source'; for metaphysics is the 'art of being puzzled'.

A healthy, lively scepticism has always pervaded Borges's work. It is a scepticism that was probably originally inherited from his father, whom Borges has described as a 'philosophical anarchist': 'Once he told me that I should take a good look at soldiers, uniforms, barracks, flags, churches, priests, and butcher shops, since all these things were about to disappear, and I could tell my children I had actually seen them. The prophecy has not yet come true, unfortunately.' There has always been a sceptical, almost Voltairean streak in Borges with regard, for instance, to Christianity. Take this lapidary assault on the Trinity, from an early essay, "Historia de la eternidad" (1936):

> Imagined at a stroke, its conception of a father, a son, and a phantasm, articulated in one single organism, seems like a case of intellectual teratology, a deformation which only a horrific nightmare could have yielded. Hell is mere physical violence, but the three inextricable persons are a horror of the intellect, an infinity as stifled and specious as that of mutually reflecting mirrors.

He is no less devastating on Platonic archetypes. 'Of those conveniences of the intellect I can no longer offer an opinion: I suspect that no man will be able to intuit them without the assistance of death, fever, or madness.' Ultimately, no hypothesis about the afterlife can be tested without a visit to it. Yet it is paradoxically our very limitations which are the principle source of our yearning to surpass them, while remaining the obstacle that prevents us from doing so. (pp. 95-6)

How do these propositions manifest themselves in the stories?

One of Borges's favourite expedients to symbolize or re-enact the problem of the limitations of knowledge is to present us with a detective with a limited command over the limited evidence at his disposal. The best example is the story called **"La muerte y la brújula"** (**"Death and the compass"**). A close look at that story will, I hope, reveal many of Borges's concerns and techniques.

The bare outline of the plot is as follows. Two detectives, Lönnrot and Treviranus, are called to investigate the murder or Dr. Marcelo Yarmolinsky, the delegate from Podolsk to a Third Talmudic Congress that is to be held in the unnamed city in which the story is set. They find, in the hotel room where Yarmolinsky has been killed, the following inconclusive sentence written on a sheet of paper on his typewriter: 'The first letter of the name has been uttered.' Treviranus suggests that the murderer has mistaken Yarmolinsky's room for that of the Tetrarch of Galilee across the corridor: the Tetrarch owns the most famous sapphires in the world. Lönnrot insists there is a less mundane, more 'rabbinical' explanation, and he gathers up the books on Yarmolinsky's bookshelves, most of them on Jewish mysticism, in order to look for clues.

A further two crimes occur which seem to bear out Lönnrot's conclusion that the murders are connected with a search for the secret name of God, the Tetragrammaton, for again the criminal has left messages to the effect that in turn 'the second' and then 'the last' letter of the name have been uttered. The three crimes have been committed moreover at points equidistant from each other which when joined form a perfect equilateral triangle, and they have been committed on the third of each of three successive months. Everything suggests both a mystical motive and that the series has been completed in the form of a 'mystical' triangle that is equilateral both in time and in space.

Yet Lönnrot encounters an underlined passage in a book (Leusden's *Philologus Hebraecograecus,* 1739) found on the scene of the third crime, to the effect that *'the Jewish day begins at sundown and ends the following sundown.'* According to the Jewish calendar the crimes have therefore been perpetrated on the *fourth* of each month. A compass helps him find the point where he surmises that the *fourth* and last crime will take place. The sacred figure drawn by the assassin must be a rhombus, not a triangle. The ineffable Tetragrammaton is, after all, a *four*-letter word. Lönnrot visits the scene of the fourth crime the day before it is to be committed, in order to savour his imminent victory over the simple-minded Treviranus, in order to gloat on the assassin's impending apprehension. The assassin, alas, is there waiting for him: Lönnrot himself is the intended fourth victim. The assassin, Red Scharlach, a notorious bandit from the Southside who has never been able to forgive Lönnrot the imprisonment of his brother, has invented the whole series in order to trap him. The first crime was indeed a mistake as Treviranus had maintained. Scharlach got the idea for the rest of the series when he read that Lönnrot was seeking a 'rabbinical' explanation. In the second crime he killed two birds with one stone: he further stimulated Lönnrot's erudite intellect while usefully disposing of the subordinate who failed to acquire the Tetrarch's jewels. The third crime was a put-up job—the 'corpse' the assassins rushed out from the tavern where the 'crime' took place was alive and well: Red Scharlach himself, in fact. The simple-minded Treviranus, by the way, had guessed this too, much to Lönnrot's indignation at the time.

From this bare outline it can be seen that **"Death and the** compass" can be read as a cautionary tale about the vanity of the intellect. The simple-minded detective, Treviranus, was always much nearer a solution because he was free of intellectual pretensions. It took a *clever* man, Lönnrot, to perceive the clue about the Jewish day, and to think therefore in terms of the rhombus figure. A 'clever' reader might have picked up other clues suggesting a rhombus. On the scene of the second crime, the message about the secret name of God is scrawled 'on the wall, on the shop's conventional red and yellow *diamond* shapes'; in their third foray, the 'assassins' are dressed as harlequins with 'costumes of red, green, and yellow *lozenges*'. Red Scharlach plants recondite clues in order to trap Lönnrot. Yet it is only because Lönnrot is *clever* that he perceives them. That is his undoing.

Many of Borges's stories seek to demonstrate the extent to which the quality of an argument rests on the quality of its premise. A flawless argument may be elaborated in blissful innocence of the fact that the premise that initiated it was faulty. Lönnrot's argument is flawless, but his original premiss, that the first crime was 'rabbinical' in nature, was a mistaken one.

Another problem encountered by Borges's investigators is the problem of the nature and quality of the evidence investigated. A detective, for instance, in order to solve a crime, must work on the evidence that *happens to come his way*. He may deduce a solution from that evidence, but how can he know that the evidence is complete? How can he be sure that a clue as yet unperceived by him will not come to throw fresh light on the case, and force him to a radical reappraisal of his solution? How, moreover, can he be sure that the clues really signify what they *appear* to signify? How can he be certain that his interpretation of them is correct?

In a story called **"Funes el memorioso" ("Funes the memorious")** Borges describes [Funes], an Uruguayan farm-hand who is incapable of forgetting anything, and who is able to perceive every conceivable detail of his environment:

> We, at one glance, can perceive three glasses on a table; Funes, all the leaves and tendrils and fruit that make up a grape vine. He knew by heart the forms of the southern clouds at dawn on 30 April 1822, and could compare them in his memory with the mottled streaks on a book in Spanish binding he had only seen once and with the outlines of the foam raised by an oar in the Rio Negro the night before the Quebracho uprising. . . . Two or three times he reconstructed a whole day; he never hesitated but each reconstruction had required a whole day.

In order really to think empirically, in order to make sure that *none* of the evidence on which an argument is based is missing, one must be a Funes. Yet for Funes every detail perceived was so unique that 'Not only was it difficult for him to comprehend that the generic symbol *dog* embraced so many unlike individuals of diverse size and form; it bothered him that the dog at 3.14 (seen from the side) should have the same name as the dog at 3.15 (seen from the front)'. Funes, in short, was not able to think at all. 'To think is to forget differences, generalize, make abstractions. In the teeming world of Funes, there were only details, almost immediate in their presence.'

We are left with an unsurmountable paradox, central to Borges's work and to Lönnrot's dilemma. In order to think properly, it is necessary to marshal *all* the evidence, for only then

will it be certain that a clue is not missing which will throw light on or even contradict the rest. Yet to marshal all the evidence is to become imprisoned by it, to end up by seeing nothing *but* clues. And *what* clues? The tens of thousands of impressions stored in Funes's brain each day are merely the percepts that happen to be available to a man who is confined to an Uruguayan shack, for Funes is, significantly, paralysed and therefore chair-ridden (and very limitingly provincial). His world of innumerable fragments is therefore itself but an infinitesimal fragment of the universe. And even if Lönnrot were a Funes, he would be no better off. For as in the case of any investigator, it is not sufficient that he should merely perceive with competence what is given. There is always something (an invisible criminal for instance) beyond his field of vision, beyond his immediate grasp. The problem is therefore not only one of how much he can afford to 'forget' of what is before him but also one of how much relevant evidence is wholly unsuspected by him and outside his field of vision.

Lönnrot's field of vision is not only limited topographically, but also mentally, because he brings to bear notorious *a priori* assumptions on the evidence. 'Here's a dead rabbi', he declares. 'I'd much prefer a purely rabbinical explanation, not the imagined mistakes of an imagined jewel thief.' Of course, we don't all limit our fields of reference so brutally. We don't all look at evidence through a spectrum of rabbinical assumptions, although no doubt we all have assumptions of our own, albeit less recondite ones. Lönnrot's very spectacular assumptions are merely hyperboles of the fact that it is impossible to look at any evidence without some assumption or other.

Lönnrot's solution of the crime then is based on limited evidence, and on an interpretation of that limited evidence that is limited too in view of the interpreter's limited assumptions. The 'pure reasoning' Lönnrot is said to exercise therefore turns out to be a limited and vain enterprise. Worse still, it is not as pure (what reasoning is?) as he imagines it to be, for although 'Lönnrot thought of himself as a pure logician, a kind of Auguste Dupin . . . there was aslso a streak of the adventurer and even of the gambler in him.' The limited game fails not only because it is limited but also because it can never be played to perfection. But finally Lönnrot's hypothesis collapses as a consequence of its negligence of specific detail, as a consequence of its abstracted formality and resultant innocence of reality. (pp. 96-101)

Such is the nature of Borges's amused critique of pure reason, and of his playful dramatization of the impossibility and vanity of definitive knowledge. For like Lönnrot we can only piece together infinitesimal fragments which in turn we can only interpret through a spectrum of limiting assumptions. Indeed the joke is not only on Lönnrot, it is on all intellectual enterprises, and not least on the reader's attempt to decipher the story. Some readers, unlike Lönnrot, may spot those diamonds and lozenges before Scharlach explains them at the end, and they might imagine themselves at their peril to be cleverer even than Lönnrot. The story is in fact full of traps for the reader in the form of clues that point to the significance of the figure three and the figure four alternately. (p. 101)

There is no end to the game of recondite exegesis that Borges invites the reader to play. Like Red Scharlach with Lönnrot, Borges delights in allowing the reader the illusory gratification of his intellectual vanity. Let us then fall headlong into the trap, and investigate two possibilities, one that Red

Scharlach is God, and the other that Red Scharlach and Lönnrot are the same person.

The first clue to the possibility that Red Scharlach is intended to stand for God is presented, characteristically, in the form of a joke. The editor of the *Judische Zeitung* comes to interview Lönnrot about the first crime. Yet instead of talking about the crime, Lönnrot, obsessed with the Tetragrammaton, talks to him about the various names of God. 'The following day, in three columns, the journalist stated that Chief Detective Erik Lönnrot had taken up the study of the names of God in order to find out the name of the murderer.' This devastating irony of the journalist at Lönnrot's expense is also an irony of Borges's, for the game that equates Scharlach to God is played throughout the story. (p. 102)

In Borges's work, God steps in where the intellect breaks down. Where explanations no longer hold water, where man's intellectual quest for them collapses, there is God. Yet 'God' in Borges's stories is often something more active than a mere symbol of intellectual confusion. Let us turn momentarily to Borges's favourite image, the labyrinth. In nearly every story, there are allusions to labyrinths, and many of the stories describe specific labyrinths. Yet the labyrinth need not be a specifically concrete one—for Borges the universe itself is a labyrinth, as is any intellectual puzzle (such as an enigmatic crime) that a man may attempt to solve. Now Borges has said that he uses the labyrinth rather than any other image to express the bewilderment of man because labyrinths are places that have been constructed artificially and *deliberately* to confuse. The confusion of those that enter it is the labyrinth's sole purpose. Now a good criminal is like a labyrinth-maker. If he plants false clues for the detective it is so as to lead him down false trails—the planting of false clues is a skill that all Borges's criminals possess. Suppose the criminal is God, and there emerges the image of a God who deliberately plants false clues, who deliberately goads man's intellectual vanity into the belief that he is arriving at a solution only to laugh in his face in the end by killing him. For the death that God provides for all men is, like the death that Red Scharlach provides for Lönnrot, the ultimate mockery of all those vain attempts at rational explanation they may have indulged in.

We have seen how fundamentally sceptical Borges is, how grimly he endeavours to demonstrate that nothing is knowable. Yet if nothing is knowable, nothing can be affirmed to be impossible. Borges reveals in the description of weird exotic sects, ridiculously limited theologies, arbitrary rituals all in conflict with each other. But he does this not only to show how absurd it is to incite the suspicion that anything is possible. Borges is as superstitious as he is sceptical, and not inconsistently. For if you cannot *know* even that the world exists, or who Borges is, neither can you *know* that, say, the markings on a jaguar's hide are not a secret message from God [as in [**"La escritura del Dios"**], or that four simpletons do not unconsciously control the universe in each generation [as they appear to in **"El hombre en el umbral"**].

A labyrinth-maker constructs his artifice deliberately in order to confuse, yet *he* knows its secret order. Red Scharlach plants his clues deliberately in order to confuse Lönnrot, but *he* knows what he is doing. Similarly, the ultimate labyrinth, the universe, may have been constructed with an aim to confuse its inhabitants by Someone cognizant of its arcane design.

Among the books found by Lönnrot in Yarmolinsky's room there is one *Vindication of the Cabbala*. It is a typically mischievous joke of Borges's that this is the title of an essay by Borges himself. Yet Borges's interest in cabbalism is not a joke. For if the universe has an arcane design, and if everything is possible because nothing is knowable, it may well be that all things, let alone the Bible, mean something very different from what they appear to mean. Borges can sympathize with Leon Bloy's belief that 'Every man is on earth in order to symbolize something he is ignorant of and to realize a particle of a mountain of the invisible materials that will serve to build the city of God.' He can sympathize, like Bloy, with the words of St. Paul (1 Corinthians 13:12): 'Videmus nunc per speculum in aenigmate: tunc autem facie ad faciem.' The visible ingredients of the world are signs pointing to something else, and what they will ultimately signify may be very different from what they appear to signify now. Who knows? Maybe 'the steps a man takes from the day of his birth until that of his death trace in time an inconceivable figure. The Divine Mind intuitively grasps that form immediately, as men do a triangle. This figure (perhaps) has its given function in the economy of the universe.' If everything in the world perhaps signifies something arcanely different from what it appears to signify, then the evidence from which we infer our explanations of the universe might well signify something very different from what we have imagined it to signify. We return therefore to the point that such explanations are impossible not only because the evidence they draw upon is by definition fragmentary but also because the evidence may be of deceptive appearance; thus the deceptive nature of the evidence Red Scharlach plants. There are several other stories by Borges (such as **"Emma Zunz"**, **"El muerto"**, or **"Tema del traidor y del heroe"**) which explore situations where elaborately contrived evidence has been erected from which plausible conclusions can be inferred that turn out however to be wildly off the mark simply because the evidence was deliberately designed to deceive.

It is possible to read **"Death and the compass"** therefore as a fable about a man (Lönnrot) who attempts to explain God's (Red Scharlach's) deeds not suspecting that his apparent success is an illusory gratification God (Red Scharlach) has condescended to allow him before invalidating it by killing him, not suspecting that the evidence he has worked from is the make-believe of an elusive conjuror.

Now let us start again and explore another possibility, that Lönnrot and Red Scharlach are the same person. To quote a typically devious commentary by Borges on the story:

> The killer and the slain, whose minds work in the same way, *may* be the same man. Lönnrot is not an unbelievable fool walking into his own death trap but, in a symbolic way, a man committing suicide. This is hinted at by the similarity of their names. The end syllable [*rot*] means red in German, and Red Scharlach is also translatable, in German, as Red Scarlet.
>
> (pp. 102-05)

Now the victim and the killer are the same person in the first place because for Borges all men are somehow the same person. For Borges the history of the world is potentially contained in one day in the life of any one man. A man who hates is all men who have hated; a man who loves is all men who have loved; a man who kills or dies is all men who have killed or died. Nowhere is this sense that nothing fundamental changes, that everything repeats itself, better expressed than in a short prose-poem "La trama" ("The Plot"), collected in Borge's book *El hacedor (The maker)* and his *Personal Anthology*:

> To make his horror complete, Caesar, pursued to the base of a statue by the relentless daggers of his friends, discovers among the faces and blades the face of Marcus Junius Brutus, his favourite, his son perhaps, and he ceases to defend himself to exclaim, *"You too, my son!"* Shakespeare and Quevedo echo the pathetic cry.

> Fate takes pleasure in repetitions, variants, symmetries. Nineteen centuries later, in the south of Buenos Aires province, a gaucho is assaulted by other gauchos, and, as he falls, recognizes a godson and with gentle reproach and gradual surprise exclaims (these words must be heard, not read): 'But *che!*' He is killed and never knows he dies so that a scene may be re-anacted.

Although Borges does not deny that every infinitesimal instant is unique, and that every incident, however archetypal in its essence, is different—the overtones for instance of the remark 'Pero *che!*' are inexorably if subtly different from those of the remark 'Et tu, Brute!'—the sense that *fundamentally* everything repeats itself has always pervaded his work. (pp. 105-06)

That we live only to re-enact the fundamental emotions and perceptions of those that have lived before is both true and horrifying. For one, our freedom of choice is annulled, or narrowed down to a choice of mere trivial detail. Each man's life is moreover a vain repetition of others' lives. For Borges copulation is abominable as mirrors are abominable: both multiply the species and therefore vainly repeat what was already there. Now if one feeling emerges from Lönnrot's final journey to the villa in which he is to be murdered it is that he is doomed, that he is being driven by an irrepressible destiny. This is of course particularly true if we consider the sequence retrospectively (i.e. after we know what was in store for him), but then it is always in the present that our sense of free will exists, whereas events seen in the past generally look altogether more inevitable. He is doomed because he is a man, because the intellectual enterprise of man is doomed and because man is doomed to death. He is all the men who have conducted an intellectual enterprise before, and he is all the men who have failed. Red Scharlach is doomed too, for Lönnrot's death merely prefigures his own. That I think is partly why for Borges murder is somehow suicide, and the killer is his victim. It is Red Scharlach as much as Lönnrot (in so far as they are not the same person and one can distinguish between them) who is committing suicide, for by killing a man he is killing Man, he is killing himself, his mirror image. Lönnrot, incurably intellectual to the end, suggests to Scharlach that in *another incarnation* he employ a simpler labyrinth to hunt him down, that ancient maze of Zeno, the straight line, for 'in your maze there are three lines too many.' The point is not only that Lönnrot is doomed to be incurably intellectual down to the most desperately unpropitious moment but also that Scharlach (man) will be hunting Lönnrot (man) down to the end of time (it is noteworthy that he speaks to Lönnrot with a 'hatred the size of the universe') and that to the end of time Lönnrot's irrepressible intellectual quest will wither down the same labyrinthine path. (pp. 106-07)

Now if there is a temporal reason why Scharlach and Lönnrot may be read as the same man, namely that all men through the ages are because all men through the ages re-enact the same intellectual failure, there is another possible reason. Given that Scharlach may also be read as God, it can be argued that this 'God', this arch-deceiver, this planter of false trails, this frustrater of the intellect, is merely a sector of the deceived and frustrated intellect itself. Man is his own labyrinth-maker, man is his own labyrinth. The obstacle that impedes the intellect's progress is nothing other than the very intellect itself. And that evidence that Scharlach plants in order that Lönnrot's hypothesis may be substantiated is simply the evidence any thinking mind might plant for itself, in order to substantiate its own *a priori* assumptions. Borges's stories continually attempt to demonstrate the fact that it is possible to marshal evidence to prove or justify anything—thus in **"Deutsches Requiem"** he shows how easy it is to justify Nazism, or in the memorable **"Three versions of Judas"** how it is possible to substantiate the hypothesis that Judas, not Jesus, was the Saviour. Unwittingly, all men tend to justify their assumptions by finding means to substantiate them, whether they be philosophers, detectives, or ordinary men making everyday decisions. The intellect, in the end, is the intellect's principal deceiver. The God that entices man's vanity into believing he has achieved a solution is merely man's own instinct to wish-fulfilment. The labyrinth in the end is to a large extent the labyrinth of its victim's own mind, a fact that gives further richness to Borges's propensity to describe *mirror*-mazes which dramatize the extent to which man is ultimately incapacitated largely by *himself.* (pp. 107-08)

"Death and the compass" has many supplementary richnesses that have not yet been explored. Not to forget the obvious it is of course a good detective story, but it is also a parody of the genre and a meditation on its implications. Many of the clichés of the genre are deliberately included: a mysterious telephone call cut off at the most interesting moment, the lone detective entering through a creaking gate into a large house which may or may not be deserted, the genius detective in conflict with a simple-minded colleague, the revelatory denouement, and so on. Yet one notes that ultimately the clichés are stood on their head. The 'genius' detective is wrong, the simple-minded policeman is right: it is as though Sherlock Holmes or Father Brown, not Scotland Yard, had made spectacular blunders. I mention Father Brown because Borges has always been an avid reader of Chesterton, and it is in particular the Father Brown pattern that is being meditated upon in this story. In the Father Brown stories, as Borges has pointed out in his essay "On Chesterton", an apparently supernatural crime is always solved by the sober commonsense of the eponymous hero. What appeared to be a fantastic event turns out to have been a very ordinary one. The same, of course, occurs in **"Death and the compass"** but with a very significant difference, for it is the criminal alone, not the detective, who is aware of the commonplace truth. In the Father Brown stories, moreover, the world is presented as an apparent fantasy which however becomes easily explainable when subjected to the scrutiny of reason. In **"Death and the compass"** it is the reasoning mind that turns a perfectly commonplace event into a recondite fantasy. By presenting the Father Brown pattern in inverted form, Borges is therefore implying a criticism of Chesterton's faith in reason, although one should say that there is another fundamental difference between Father Brown and Lönnrot. Father Brown brings to bear an eclectic commonsense on the fantasy, whereas Lönnrot does not question the fantasy as a premiss from which to argue in a logical vacuum which excludes all other possible premisses.

"Death and the compass" is one of Borges's earlier short stories (it was first published in 1942), yet it is as good an example as any of Borges's methods and ideas. Certainly, there are many others which could have been discussed at similar length for the same purposes of showing how Borges's stories work and what they aim to demonstrate. Borges's ideas do not indeed differ greatly from story to story. The stories differ rather in emphasis, with the result that they fertilize each other. Memories of one story often help to elucidate the more recondite points of another. (pp. 109-10)

Some stories emphasize the *moral* implications of arguing from questionable premisses. Take the Histriones, for instance, a sect described in **"The theologians"**. Their main premiss is St. Paul's dictum 'for now we see through a glass darkly', from which they conclude that 'everything we see is false.' The line from Matthew 11:12 'the kingdom of heaven suffereth violence' leads them to believe, moreover, that 'the earth influences heaven', and from the *Zohar* they learn that 'the higher world is a reflection of the lower.' Thence:

> Perhaps contaminated by the Monotones, they imagined that all men are two men and that the real one is the other, the one in heaven. They also imagined that our acts project an inverted reflection, in such a way that if we are awake, the other sleeps, if we fornicate, the other is chaste, if we steal, the other is generous. When we die, we shall join the other, and be him. . . . Other Histriones reasoned that the world would end when the number of its possibilities was exhausted; since there can be no repetitions, the righteous should eliminate (commit) the most infamous acts, so that these will not soil the future and will hasten the coming of the kingdom of Jesus.

Of course not all thinkers argue from premisses as questionable as these and not all are driven to crime as a result of their consequently faulty reasoning. Yet it is not only the Histriones who have committed crimes in the name of some more or less spurious reasoning. Not so long ago priests found it easy to rationalize the burning of their fellow men. In **"Tlön, Uqbar, Orbis Tertius"** Borges describes how the existence of an imaginary planet with a rigidly ordered metaphysical system came to be believed in by everyone on earth. Is this surprising, he asks? 'Ten years ago any symmetry with a semblance of order—dialectical materialism, anti-Semitism, Nazism—was sufficient to entrance the minds of men.' So Borges's distrust of the intellect plainly has a moral dimension. One can discern it in many other stories, but nowhere more than in **"Deutsches Requiem"**, a story which some critics have absurdly thought to show Borges in unwitting sympathy with Nazism. On the contrary, its aim is to demonstrate the case with which one can justify the most repugnant actions on the most rational grounds. One should be sceptical about the intellect's powers not only because it is vain but also because it is morally dangerous not to be.

Other stories emphasize the extent to which our knowledge and our values—in general, our interpretation of the evidence, as it were—depend on the assumptions of our cultural environment. Here Borges's most frequent technique is to present a first-person narrator (such as the Cretan Minotaur, or a citizen of a 'Babylon' where everyone's life is governed by an arcane lottery system) who makes statements that are alien to us but which the narrator takes for granted. Thus the narrator who turns out to be the Cretan Minotaur in **"La casa de Asterión"** makes odd statements like 'Even my detractors admit there is not *one single piece of furniture* in the house.' His assumptions about furniture are clearly different from ours. But the effect is to make us question our own assumptions too, and to make them seem just a little bit more gratuitous and relative. (pp. 110-12)

Borges is not lacking in sense of humour. Indeed, his stories are usually very funny indeed. Sometimes they are funny on the surface. Stories like **"The Aleph"** and **"The Zahir"**, while being concerned with vaster issues, find time to furnish often hilarious satires of society ladies, second-rate poets, academicians, critics, nationalists, and so on. With Bioy Casares, Borges has indeed produced several books whose principal aim it has been to satirize the more pompous aspects of Argentinian life. The most notable is their *Seis problemas para don Isidro Parodi* (1942), a book in which social satires are woven into the plots of six Chestertonian detective stories. Yet there is a much more fundamental humour in Borges's own stories which underlies its incidental manifestations. For Borges's stories are comedies of the intellect, of an intellect doomed to trip over a banana skin. As comedies they are particularly effective because, as we have seen, the joke falls heavily on the reader too. But the generally light-hearted tone of the stories at the incidental level makes the reader's reaction to his own tripping up one not of anguish but rather of grateful self-mockery. We can laugh at ourselves reading Borges moreover because Borges laughs so readily at his own self. And we can feel gratitude because the stories continually help to jolt our complacent belief in the order and sense of our environment. Such dispersal of complacency leads not only to confusion, but also to a joy in the fact that the world is a more fabulously mysterious place than we had perceived it to be. Moreover the more metaphysical stories may well attempt to spell the vanity of metaphysics, but in that very vanity there is a kind of splendour. For Borges there is something splendid in the spectacle of men striding out to explain the universe. That they do so is a measure of their spirit, indomitable against overwhelming odds. There may be a contradiction here, in view of what has been said about the moral danger that underlies man's attempt to explain the world. But Borges would not want to deny himself the right to self-contradiction. For, after all, part of the mystery of the world for Borges is that it is sustained on paradox. And the perception of paradox has its own cerebral rewards, its own beauty. Borges's stories entertain one, absorb one as puzzles do, thrill and amaze one, and, one hopes, make one wiser; but they do not make one despair.

Just as metaphysics for Borges is ultimately an absorbing game, a willed suspension of time and place which has little relation to anything but itself, so is literature ultimately a game too, self-regulating and autarchic. Every story by Borges has built into it more or less recondite a reminder of its fictive status. With great subtlety we are reminded that what we are reading is a mere story, a fiction. (pp. 112-13)

One of Borges's favourite ways of undermining the status of his stories is by discrediting the competence of his narrator as a witness to the events he is describing. On one occasion it is hinted that the narrator was drunk when the story he is telling occurred (**"La forma de la espada"**, **"The shape of the sword"**). Usually the narrator's problem is one of faulty

A portrait of Borges as a young man.

Quixote is something of a different book according to whether or not we approach it after reading, say, Nietzsche. Similarly, the books we read after *Don Quixote* will affect our memory of it. The same is true of memory in general: the shape and import of any event in the past changes constantly in the light of subsequent experience. And it is as a result of this fundamental creativeness of memory that every remembered fact is a fiction. Since, moreover, a writer draws on memory in order to compose a story, a story must, by definition, be fictive, a *creation,* not an expression of what really happened.

Let us take some typical comments the narrators of *El informe de Brodie* make on their own memory:

> I do not know whether there were two or three emptied bottles on the floor or whether an excess of movies suggests this false memory to me.

> The intervening years of course have exaggerated or blurred what I saw.

> Anyway, here is the story, with the inevitable variations brought about by time and good writing.

> I see in advance I shall give in to the writer's temptation of emphasizing or adding certain details.

> [The old lady] related historical events, but always with the same words and in the same order, as though they were the Lord's prayer, and I suspected that the words no longer corresponded to images.

The last example is the most important, for it stresses the gap that separates words from the images in the past they purport to describe. An old lady who has told the same anecdote over several decades is left only with the almost memorized words of the anecdote, not with the real images that prompted them. Similarly a man who has written something many years earlier and who one day reads it over, will find there nothing but words, as though they had been written by another—'Words, displaced and mutilated words, words of others'. So the past exists only in our creative memory of it, or in the fictive words we wrote when we were living it.

In a story called **"La busca de Averroes" ("Averroes's search"),** Borges evokes one Averroes, a Moorish scholar in medieval Spain. At the end of the story we learn that Averroes disappers 'as if fulminated by an invisible fire', and with him his entire surroundings disappear, including 'the houses and the unseen fountain and the books and the manuscript . . . and perhaps even the Guadalquivir'. For the Averroes of this story is merely a creature of words, alive only so long as the words are there to describe him. There may have been a real Averroes, but like any real person, even the most famous historical personage, he is doomed to become a fiction the moment he dies, for he can only survive after death either in the words that were written about him, and all words are simplificatory fictions, or in the creative memories of others. In the end, the 'realistic' stories of *El informe de Brodie* read as though they had been written in order to demonstrate that realistic stories are as fictive as fantastic ones, because language and memory, the stuff of which they are made, are fictive by definition.

Another devious game that Borges plays in order to question the status of his stories is to inject fragments of his personal life into some of their most unlikely characters. Thus Otto Dietrich zur Linde, the unrepentant Nazi of **"Deutsches Requiem"** shares with Borges a cavalry-charging ancestor, an

memory. It is for instance a characteristic irony of Borges's that the narrator who evokes the impeccably memorious Funes uses the words 'I remember' almost obsessively throughout the story. Thus on the first page alone of the story we have 'I remember him (I have no right to utter that sacred verb)', 'I remember (I think) his angular, leather braiding hands', 'I clearly remember his voice', and so on.

A large proportion of Borges's stories are tales of fantasy; they describe such things as imaginary plants, imaginary books, a city inhabited by immortals, situations in general in which it is not clear where the line can be drawn between fantasy and reality. Yet Borges has always written realistic stories too, and the realistic mode is predominant in his most recent book, *El informe de Brodie* (1970), in the preface of which he asserts that the stories 'observe . . . all the conventions of a genre [realism] which is no less conventional than any other'. Now it is significant that it is in this very 'realistic' book that his discrediting of the narrator's memory is most insistently exercised. Often the narrators of these stories were *children* when the events they are describing occurred. In the intervening years, how many other experiences have got tangled in with what they witnessed at the time? Or to what extent has their perspective of what happened so long ago significantly changed? In **"Pierre Menard, autor del Quijote" ("Pierre Menard, author of Don Quixote"),** Borges demonstrated how our reading of a given book is affected by what books we have read before, or conversely how our memory of a book is affected by what we then read afterwards. *Don* interest in Schopenhauer, a love of Brahms (the only classical composer Borges enjoys), a preoccupation with tigers, an opinion about Whitman, and a notion about the destiny of the precursors of great literature. All this despite the well-known fact that Borges has always detested Nazism. In **"El duelo"** (**"The duel"**) an absurd society lady shares Borges's much publicized opinions about the Spanish language, and in **"Guayaquil"**, the two leading characters, though they loathe each other, both share with Borges a great many traits. In the first place one of them, the narrator, shares with Borges a notoriously bookish disposition, and also an ancestor called Suárez who led a cavalry charge at the battle of Junín. And yet he is, unlike Borges, a professor of history and blatantly anti-Semitic (Borges, who wrote a euphoric poem about the Six Day War, is devoted to the Jewish cause). The narrator's rival, Zimerman, though unlike Borges a Jew, shares with Borges the view that Government should be as invisible as possible (cf. Borges's remark in the preface of *El informe de Brodie,* the book in which the story appears: 'I believe that in good time we will deserve to have no governments') and an almost insulting modesty, which Borges characteristically mocks. Both characters share with Borges an interest in Schopenhauer and, more reconditely, an interest in Gustav Meyrink's *Der Golem.*

"Guayaquil" is therefore an exercise in self-mockery, in that for instance a character who sounds so much like Borges is made to utter lapidary remarks against the Jews whereas the Borgesian modesty of the other character turns out to be an aggressive sham. The story is moreover self-mocking in another, more subtle manner. It depicts the rivalry of two historians. Which of the two will be chosen to investigate some newly discovered letters of Simón Bolívar? These letters are said to throw light on the *rivalry* between Bolívar and San Martín at their famous meeting in Guayaquil in 1822. The story therefore is a characteristically Borgesian meditation on the eternal return of archetypal situations. The archetypal situation that repeats itself in this case is a Schopenhaurean one: the triumph of one will over another. For Zimerman talks the narrator by sheer force of will into not pressing his claim just as Bolívar is supposed to have talked San Martín into resigning his command. Yet it is the mischievous spirit of the story that Schopenhauer and eternal return turn out to be mere fantasy consolations for the narrator in that they endow his sheer feeblemindedness with a grandly archetypal dimension and better, with a *distinguished* precedent. Characteristically, Borges has erected a grandly metaphysical design in this story only self-mockingly to demolish it. At the very point that the narrator and Zimerman appear to have magically 'become' San Martín and Bolívar respectively, we realize that they have become so only in the narrator's self-consoling fantasy.

The autobiographical ingredients of **"Guayaquil"** and other stories constitute a final, deliberately ironical comment on the nature of writing. Whatever you set out to describe, 'realistically' or otherwise, you are i the end writing, however obliquely, about yourself as much as about what you set out to describe. And writing is therefore fictive not only because the limitations of language and memory make it so, but also because it is subjective. Inexorably the subject transforms (creates) the object it perceives, and converts it into a projection of itself. (pp. 114-18)

Borges's work is indeed an image of himself. If one man is all men, it is an image of man too, but there are certain char-

acteristics in it which are peculiar to Borges's personality. His very style is perhaps his most revealing image. Borges writes, on the *surface* at any rate, an English-sounding Spanish, full of understatements, of affirmations by negation, of phrases like 'not without a certain ostentation', 'not without a tremble', 'the memory of which the years have not erased'. There is an elegant delicacy about Borges's writing that signifies a very particular kind of man, a rather Edwardian gentleman, perhaps. Yet behind his elegant stylistic mask, assuming that it is a mask, there is a similar tension in Borges to the one he intuited in Chesterton, of whom Borges once wrote that the Catholic faith was a disguise for the Poe or Kafka buried within him: 'Something in the mire of his self tended to nightmare, something secret, blind, and central.' Borges's own work, despite its apparent cerebral coolness, is furnished with oblique images of the intimate dreams and nightmares that reside in 'the mire of his self'. To take an example, his stories are full of brave rough men expert at handling a knife—these would seem to be inverted images of what he has often described as his own fear of physical violence, or images of his longing to overcome it, or of his longing to have been a man of action, not a librarian and a writer. Of course he may well be not all that unhappy that he is a librarian. For action is seen in his stories as ultimately both gratuitous and destructive. His men of action always die, and they die compulsively, as though they could not stop themselves. Yet Borges cannot stop himself from admiring them, as he admires the fierce tigers that pace his fiction, emblems of the real tigers in the jungle who hunt down their own quarry and live in the open, and which no writer can pin down in a poem. In contrast, the mirror, Borges's most pressing image, reveals the 'detested face' from which he cannot escape. It will never be the face of a knife-fighter or of a tiger. It is the fated face of Borges, the sign of his destiny. Mirrors for Borges are horrifying because they remind him of all that is inescapable but also because they help to confirm his suspicion that though he cannot escape them, neither Borges nor the world may exist at all, that Borges too for instance may been an insubstantial reflection of something else, just as his mirror-image is an insubstantial reflection of him. Mirrors intolerably underline a central paradox of Borges's work: that not only is the world inescapable; it may also be unreal. (pp. 119-20)

Borges's stories, in the end, are not only cooly lucid cerebral games but often highly affective, poetic expressions of the fragility of the world and of man. Again, that fragility is not a desperate one. It has a certain splendour. It is a measure of the odds against man and a measure therefore of his spirit. (p. 121)

> *D. P. Gallagher, "Jorge Luis Borges (Argentina, 1899-)," in his* Modern Latin American Literature, *Oxford University Press, 1973, pp. 94-121.*

TED LYON AND PJERS HANGROW   (essay date 1974)

[*In the following excerpt, Lyon and Hangrow discuss Borges's subversion of conventional religious and philosophical belief through heretical imagery and language.*]

As early as 1930, heresy and its resultant frustrations occupy prominent position in the prose of Jorge Luis Borges. By 1936, in the essay "Circular Time," Borges is talking of heresy, heresiology, heresiarchs, and the human consequences of such doctrines and beliefs. From his most brilliant decade, the 1940's, to his most recent fiction, **"El congreso"** [**"The**

Assembly"], 1971, heresy is a constant motif, a basic recurring element which grants thematic unity to his extensive collection of short stories.

As here defined, heresy is defiling, challenging or opposing that which is considered sacred or divine. In the limited context of Christianity such heresies as salvation through knowledge alone (Gnosticism) or the affirmation that Christ was merely an inspired man and not a God (Christology) are already well known. Yet Borges goes much beyond Christianity in discovering heresies and explores its many facets in a universal setting. Not only does he base his prose on creeds and countercreeds of world religions, he also delves into sacred personal beliefs and venerable national myths. He does not avail himself of heresy to denounce or criticize religion but rather as a literary device to expand his created world, to reveal basic themes of life and existence.

No specific religion, sect or dogma comes under direct fire in the author's prose; he is a universalist, not confined to one historical time or place. Judaism, and especially the mystery-delving Kabbalists, most often provides ideological bases (**"Death and the Compass," "The Aleph," "The Theologians"** and the poem **"The Golem"**). Islam, Hinduism and certain Eastern religions rank second in the canon of organized religions serving as inspiration for writings on heresy (**"The Circular Ruins," "The Two Kings and the Two Labyrinths," "The Garden of Forking Paths,"** etc.). Christianity and its multiple doctrines follow—**"The Gospel According to Mark," "Three Versions of Judas," "El congreso,"** etc. In **"The God's Script"** Borges even uses the backdrop of ancient Mayan belief although the ideas are based on the Kabbalah and the resultant mixture comes out a heretical hybrid of philosophy and religion. The creeds of these religions offer the metaphysical elements which may assist in explaining the complex universe, a constant yearning among Borgesian characters.

Borges frequently refers to "God" and to the "divine," but seldom makes qualitative remarks regarding what god, or which divinity. His works present a god that simply "is"; Borges rarely evokes traditional religious notions of god but instead makes reference to an infinite, unconditional, and indefinable deity, a god whose presence pervades the universe, one who created all, Tillich's god, the "ground of being." Certainly Borges is not alluding to an anthropomorphic deity, nor to any type of god that can be limited or conditioned. . . . Without trying to form a complete analysis of Borges' complex theology, it is here sufficient to recognize that his prose assumes a "divine presence"; most of his works exude such a being. What exactly he conceives that presence to be he does not prescribe, considering it an impossible task to approach god through words or rituals. For Borges to describe the god(s) hovering above nearly every story would be tantamount to personal heresy.

It is likewise heretical to think that the universe can be explained in terms of a philosophy or a theology. Definitions, words and theories are insufficient expressions of the true nature and meaning of the intricate universe. . . . Philosophy is at best only a meager representation of the way the universe seems to be, and with time, each particular philosophy inevitably loses its meaning and importance, becoming "a mere chapter, if not just a paragraph or a name, in the history of philosophy."

In numerous stories Borges represents the universe as an intricate maze, and even suggests that "God" created the world in that confusing manner for a specific purpose. However, it is not necessary for man to understand that purpose, and further it is an act of heresy to try to approach the mind of god, which man does when he attempts to discover purposes. In presenting the universe as a labyrinth, Borges suggests that the world is an enormous, complex drama. In this drama each event is a key part of the total, each individual action is integral to the universal act, and each man is "performing a secret drama determined and premeditated by God." Thus, "the history of the universe—and our lives and the most trifling detail of our lives—has an unconjecturable, symbolic meaning." Each act is universal; man must comply with the requisites of the complete universal production. Since those requisites have been framed by god, it is not for man to discover them but rather to act out the total scheme. The universe, therefore, appears as a labyrinth to the human mind; man will never fully understand its processes nor its meanings.

Despite this position in the scheme, man, by his very nature, is destined to try to order his world and thus the concept of heresy is built into Borges' labyrinthal universe. Many of his characters are active personages who are not content to sit back and perform their part of an existence which seems meaningless. Even at the risk of committing heresy, they struggle with the meaning of the world around them and their place in history, despite the futility of ever perceiving the order for which they search. Indeed, the very act of heresy is essential for Borges' characters to achieve their full humanity; if they remain passive and avoid the struggle for meaning they will certainly not fall into heresy but neither will they ever reach full stature. Searching for order and perspective in life and death, Borgesian characters formulate philosophies and theologies that attempt to explain the unseen and the seen. Thus, philosophy becomes heresy, for as man attempts to order the universe and reason out his existence, he meddles with the divine.

In this struggle man frequently winds up inventing realities that are more logical and easier to accept than the actual world. (pp. 23-5)

In **"The God's Script"** Borges suggests what might happen were man to somehow stumble upon the secret meaning of the universe. Tzinacán posits that from the beginning, god saw the end and wrote a coded message, one that would give its user unlimited power. As the last priest in his known world, Tzinacán expects this privilege and commences his search for the secret and sacred symbol that will unlock divine knowledge and power. After considering and eliminating thousands of possibilities, he postulates that the coded message is inscribed on the skin of the jaguar. Deciphering the meaning and formulating it into words occupies uncounted years but like a successful Kabbalist, Tzinacán envisions a giant wheel, a type of "Aleph," that unites all time and space, the entire universe. However he wisely realizes that he could never reveal this personal secret, to do so would amount to betrayal and heresy, giving him power over god's creations. Such power would alter his existence, making him a god rather than the prisoner he really is. . . . Tzinacán realizes that it is impossible for finite man to decipher and control the universe, for in the hypothetical instant in which he might, he would lose his identity and become infinite. And in Borges, even the thought of approaching the infinite is traumatic, as seen in **"Averroes' Search."** . . . Clearly, the infinite, the divine realm, is not intended for man, yet still he searches for its key. It is thus that he turns to philosophy, and it is thus that in "the history of philosophy are doctrines, probably false, that exercise an obscure charm on human imagination."

Borges' characters invariably strive for the meaning of their existence through diverse methods; one is no more valid than another; all lead to some type of frustration. Borges has added a distinct flavor to the existentialist tradition of the Twentieth Century, although he by no means could be classified solely an existentialist. . . . Rejecting philosophical idealism, Borgesian fiction emphasizes the failure of philosophical theories to adequately represent the realities of the world and universe. Indeed, as these philosophies boldly attempt to interpret reality, they not only fail as theories but also enter the realm of heresy. (pp. 26-7)

As already stated, the Borgesian universe is labyrinthal, a maze fashioned by the unfathomable mind of divinity, destined to remain eternally indecipherable to man. Scharlach states (**"Death and the Compass"**): "I felt that the world was a labyrinth, from which it was impossible to flee." As already seen, Borges' view of existence necessitates a belief in the divine, although he does not attempt to define or delimit this deity, for to do so would be a form of heresy. Rather, Borges attempts to accede to divine power, so perfectly demonstrated in **"The Library of Babel"**: "Man, the imperfect librarian, may be the product of chance or malevolent demiurgi; the universe, with its elegant endowment of shelves, of enigmatical volumes, of inexhaustible stairways . . . , can only be the work of a god."

This god, or gods, whom man cannot question or comprehend, has created an ordered chaos of the cosmos wherein man must wander constantly yet unsuccessfully, endeavoring to decipher the supreme puzzle. This universe does not preclude use of man's inherent intelligence, though to attempt to unravel the labyrinth of the universe is not within his jurisdiction and constitutes usurpation of the powers of deity. . . . (pp. 27-8)

The heresy of imitating god's attributes, a challenge to that which is considered divine, is an integral part of the heresy in Borges' framework of the world. His protagonists, regardless of time and circumstance, again and again outstep their mortal limits, seeking either to disentangle their personal enigmas or to structure their own labyrinths, all courses of action which bear serious consequences. Life, Borges suggests, is a riddle, an intricate puzzle with ever-changing rules that man must accept with flexibility or break himself trying to solve. And yet, with all its confusion, life for Borges is still more preferable than the immortal state of deity. An analysis of several short stories demonstrates the pervasiveness of this theme of divine imitation, surfacing in much of fiction.

The contrast between **"Death and the Compass"** and **"Story of the Warrior and the Captive"** offers insight into the Borgesian concept of heresy. Lönnrot, in the first story, fancies himself "a pure reasoner," and uses his intelligence to unravel a maze of mystery and murder. He has supreme confidence in his rational ability to decipher the name of God and to thus discover the assassin. But reason is a tool of man, and Lönnrot, the smug heretic, discovers all too readily the fallacy of reasoning which leads him to the solution of the maze and to his simultaneous destruction. Droctulft, the barbarian, and the Englishwoman-savage of **"Story of the Warrior and the Captive"** provide the direct antithesis to Lönnrot. The war-

rior willingly abandons his own army during a siege against an intricate and advanced city to fight and die for a complex labyrinth of civilization he will never be able to understand. . . . The blond captive woman, conversely, chooses the life of barbarism, and contentedly drinks animal blood to indicate her isolation from that same civilization for which Droctulft gives his life. Although directly opposite in action, the warrior and the captive are similar in method, never attempting to decipher the complexities and confusion of their lives but instead yielding to "a secret impulse, *an impulse more profound than reason,* and both heeded this impulse, which they would not have known how to justify." Both accept the insoluble labyrinth of life, leaving inviolate the powers of deity, and finding happiness therein.

One of the most sacrosanct attributes of divine intelligence is the power of creation. In **"The Circular Ruins"** and **"Tlön, Uqbar, Orbis Tertius"** this power is usurped by man, as the stranger in the first story shaped from his dreams a living son, the most arduous and heretical task that man can conceive. Nevertheless, the dreamed creation could not be interpolated into reality until the multiple gods of the temple granted the magical gift of life. The creation of an entire planet is the purpose of a secret society in **"Tlön, Uqbar, Orbis Tertius,"** on the condition that the association, under the direction of an eccentric American millionaire, Ezra Buckley, make no pact or covenant with Jesus Christ. This heresy, the rejection of divine assistance in a project requiring the usurpation of divine powers, evokes a delightful Borgesian comment. "Buckley did not believe in God, but he wanted to demonstrate to this nonexistent God that mortal man was capable of conceiving a world. Buckley was poisoned in Baton Rouge in 1828." . . . In this rapid juxtaposition of time and space (suggesting perhaps cause-and-effect), the heretic is rewarded.

To decipher a god's identity and his writings is likewise heresy, for man does not have that power; to do so he must intrude on divine right. In **"The God's Script"** Tzinacán struggles to find the secret writings in order to take upon himself the powers of God. A similar heresy is performed in **"Three Versions of Judas"** wherein Runeberg postulates that Judas is the actual embodiment of God; to complete Christ's glorious purpose, there was a need for betrayal, and so God fulfilled the plan and selected the vilest destiny of all, to be the betrayer Judas. As the mortal Savior/traitor, he voluntarily selected hell because happiness is also a divine attribute denied to man. And for the heretic Runeburg, who blasphemously divulges the terrible secret of identity, the future holds only suffering and death.

A variation on man's usurpation of the divine is found in **"The Secret Miracle."** A Jew sentenced to death by the Third Reich is apparently able to suspend chronological time, a power which man does not actually possess, after asking for god's intervention. The assistance is given only after he discovers god by chance, randomly and not rationally, . . . after which his request for an additional year to finish his literary labors is granted. In Hladík's mind, a year does transpire between the final command for execution and moment of his death, although in actuality he dies at the set hour. The condemned finishes his work within the maze of his mind and thus justifies his entire existence. The heresy inherent in such an attempt to control time is mitigated by Hladík's supplications to the divine mind, and his reliance on impulse and chance to guide his plea.

An actual physical labyrinth is created by the King of Babylon in **"The Two Kings and Their Two Labyrinths."** This imitation of the divine design of the universe is scandalous "for confusion and marvels belong to God alone and not to man." In **"Theme of the Traitor and the Hero,"** Ryan solves the maze of history, an integral part of the divine power to order time, only to lose all desire to make known the solution, similar to the aforementioned Tzinacán.

The Nazi zur Linde, condemned to death in **"Deutsches Requiem,"** perceives in his final moments the circular labyrinth of life that time and divinity have shaped for men and nations. In the defeat of Hitler and Germany, zur Linde finds happiness, not because he seeks punishment nor because he realizes that to deplore a part of the scheme of the universe is to blaspheme god, rather, he glimpses the totality of the maze, the "secret continuity" of the world, and perceives in the fall of the Third Reich the perfected destiny of Germany. In the divine plan it matters neither who the victims nor the victorious are, as long as the circle is complete and the necessary results prevail. Zur Linde avoids heresy because he recognizes and accepts man's inability to order the labyrinth of the universe, and consequently, finds peace in this knowledge.

In **"The Gospel According to Mark,"** man takes upon himself a divine role, and later he must of necessity bear the immediate consequences of playing Christ. This heresiarch, Espinosa, attempts to solve the enigma of the Gutres by placing himself as the supreme intelligence, the source of all knowledge; later he receives the same fate as Christ. Emma Zunz takes upon herself the role of avenger in the death of her father, a role normally reserved for divine justice only. And even though she sees the fulfillment of her vengeance, she finds no satisfaction in that fulfillment. A novel twist to the concept of heresy is man's attempt to limit and order the paths of the labyrinth of life leading to the supreme essence. For in man's attempt to reach the divine, to define the orthodox and heretical through the establishment of religious dogma, the usurpation of sacred rights occurs, so postulated in **"The Theologians"** where two rivals, Aureliano and Juan de Panonia, expend their lives in the refutation of various heresies, attempting always to beat the other in the rational treatises they present. Irony, a common Borgesian tool, succinctly appears in the use of Juan's successful refutation of the heresy of circular time as the decisive factor in his conviction for heretical opinions. That two directly opposed philosophies could both be branded as heresy points to the absurdity of man's endeavor to define religion and orthodoxy. (pp. 28-31)

[Borges'] preference for man's confused wanderings in the universal labyrinth of immortal existence is shown in **"Funes the Memorious."** Through a chance accident Ireneo receives a perfect memory, another divine attribute usually denied man. . . . But a perfect memory becomes a form of hell because each recollection of the past is an exact duplicate, requiring the same amount of time as the original experience. Sleep is an extreme difficulty and "forgetting differences, generalizing, abstracting," an impossibility. Such an existence expanded infinitely into immortality bothers Borges, as witnessed in the lucid story **"The Immortals."** Here a tribune of a Roman legion seeks for immortality, only to find its manifestation in the irrational gods who have created the labyrinth that man calls life. These divine intelligences are described as naked, barbaric troglodytes who must exist with the terrible knowledge of their own immortality. Indifferent, because all things happen to those who live forever, unpitying, the immortals live in a total world of thought, never speaking, mov-

ing, nor in reality living. Nothing holds any value because nothing is unique and will not happen over and over again. An existence equatable to hell, the ultimate search of the immortals becomes one for the river that can again grant mortality and death.

Thus, Borgesian man exists in a labyrinth he can neither understand nor control. Neither can he define nor duplicate the supreme powers that fashioned it. Life is neither orderer nor rational, and man cannot make it so. To strive for such an impossibility, to seek to unravel the eternal enigma, is to defile and challenge the sacred, to commit heresy. This recurring motif throughout Borges' works, in all its infinite variations, stems from the same basic root, the usurpation of divine power by man. Whether the heretic tries to unveil the name of god or assumes the actual power of creation, he violates the maze of mortality by attempting to imitate the attributes of a deity who reigns in seeming confusion and chaos. In such a maze, man must wander and be content to accept the whims and caprices of the labyrinth's creators, recognizing that life's only peace lies in the knowledge of self limitation. . . .

The concept of heresy hardly seems the place to find humor. . . . Yet through Borges' skeptical intellect and ability to see the world with new light, the possibility of subdued laughter *does* exist. Humor in heresy rarely produces bellysplitting guffaws; neither is it explicit in the story. As an element of audience involvement, the reader must mentally carry the story to conclusion, wherein he may discover elements of wit and humor. In this fashion the reader is placed in a position superior to the story and enjoys the advantage of chuckling at human foible; such humor usually arises from the final disposition of major characters. Lönrott's extermination [in **"Death and the Compass"**] is more comic than tragic; by delving into mysteries he weaves his own death web. Pierre Menard's heretical attempts to be Cervantes and re-write his works [in **"Pierre Menard, Author of Don Quixote"**] evoke an ironical humor unparalleled in Latin American literature. Funes achieves near omniscience through perfect memory but in so doing destroys himself. The dreamer (**"The Secret Miracle"**) creates man in his own image but is mockingly denied the crowning achievement of death and is hopelessly condemned to immortality. The most obvious element of humor confronting the reader is satire, wherein Borges turns from his philosophical concepts of the universe to reconcile himself with the mundane and somewhat artificial complexities of the life that surrounds. Overtly conscious of the frailty of man-made institutions, Borges seeks through laughter not so much to tear them down as to inspire their reexamination or renovation.

"Ibn Hakkan al-Bokhari, Dead in His Labyrinth" evokes such revision. The heresy in this work (building an unsolvable labyrinth), is also an element of humor, for in recounting the story, it becomes obvious that while attempting to clarify the circumstances surrounding King Zaid, the two intellectuals wind up hopelessly muddling the whole affair. Borges' dramatic blending of satire with overstatement, is comparable to a small child possessed of an over-grown imagination. Upon further interrogation the child supplies necessary facts (Borges even supplies false historical data) which are very clear and distinguishable to him but which leave the listener completely perplexed. Borges employs this technique of parody and humor in heresy to further develop his well-known theme of the ambiguity of reality and the false importance man has placed on "information." (pp. 31-3)

By contrast, **"The Immortals"** employs a humor based on understatement. . . . Heresy here pokes fun at the commercial sale of immortality, an immortality so estranged from its usual context that it becomes revolting and undesirable. The element of horror, the desired effect in the story, is emphasized by the use of a heretical theme combined with humorous understatement. The highlight of humor is the used-car-salesman jargon directed at the successful marketing of a grotesque "immortality."

Borges himself, the unashamed creator of new, deity-challenging literary worlds, may also be considered a heresiarch; he would take delight in such a classification. Humor in his works serves to extend and expand the results of heresy; laughter and smiles in this very serious world compound the effects of defiling the sacred. By telling a story with diverse possibilities Borges calls attention to the vain importance that man has placed on certain artificial "truths." As previously noted, humor may arise through reader afterthought, rather than the intrinsic situation of the story. One of Borges' greatest concerns is to cause man to recognize the folly of his present existence, of times through humorous exposition of life and the human condition. . . .

Challenging the structure of the universe, competing with God by fashioning artificial labyrinths, attempting to control time, or even creating a golem-being, Borges' heretics end in frustration and death. No one is allowed to enjoy the fullness of realization; for to do so would place him above the "divine" that seems to gently hover over the author's prose. Yet no one is censured by moralistic divinity nor burned in the fires of the Inquisition; the heretic himself works out his own punishment, usually through the realization of his inability to control forces already in progress. For some it is immediate death. . . . Others drag themselves through the drawn-out process of impending death, unable to alter the future any longer. . . . The creator of a dreamed off-spring seeks the crown and freedom of death only to realize, an echo of old Gnostic belief, that he too is only dreamed and hence frustratingly condemned to immortality. . . . The realization of helplessness and the inability to modify existence are the most characteristic frustrations. . . . (pp. 33-4)

Intellectual heresy, as practised by Borges' creation, is a lonely occupation. Shutting himself off from others the heretic is left alone to ply his trade: Abenjacán hides in a crimson labyrinth of his own making; Dahlmann (**"The South"**), seeking to control the manner in which he dies, ends his life in a dingy hospital room (or on a lonely plain). . . . Yet despite their forced isolation, the reader perceives that these characters are the real "heroes" of Borges' created worlds. They have chosen to *not* accept the divine scheme, rather to delve into exciting mysteries, to attempt to exert control over the future, to order an apparent chaos. They are the Doers, the Makers, Borges, "el hacedor," not content with the world of darkness that settles around them. Yet their discontent leads only to frustration and death and as the narrator of **"The Two Kings and Their Two Labyrinths"** tersely concludes, "Glory to Him who lives forever."

Heresy in Borges does more than merely provide an innovative literary base; its functions are broader than simply creating humor. For Borges heresy serves to elucidate the essence of being. Man has a dualistic, oxymoronic nature; his inner contradictions may at one time deny all that he has previously held sacred and complete. Man is both hero and traitor, creator and dreamed creation, Christ and Judas, savage and civilized, friend and assassin; prisoner and priest. Heretical belief and practice demonstrate the non-static nature of man's existence, his inherent contradictions. Borges uses heresy to challenge rigid belief. Heresy implies an a priori system of ideas and concepts that are true inscrutable realities; Borges defies anything so precise and closed. The past, life, a library, a book, man's mind, time, and the universe have all been symbolically represented by the author as a labyrinth. Anyone who pits his own wit or wisdom against the labyrinth ends in frustration. Yet these labyrinth-challengers are the author's true and tragic heroes, fighting against an uncontrollable destiny larger than themselves. (pp. 34-5)

Ted Lyon and Pjers Hangrow, "Heresy as Motif in the Short Stories of Borges," in Latin American Literary Review, *Vol. III, No. 5, Fall-Winter, 1974, pp. 23-35.*

MARY McBRIDE (essay date 1977)

[*In the following excerpt, McBride analyzes Borges's short story "The Aleph" as an existentialist work.*]

"The Aleph" is a concept story, projecting a main concern of human analysis—the relativity of human perception, the inadequacy of man's reason to explain the enigma of the universe. In this story Borges illustrates the existentialistic assumption that existence has no meaning for a human being except the meaning created by that individual's experience. Basically, the author gives form to four important ideas which are a part of or close to existentialism: (1) it is impossible to know truth; (2) the personality is determined by one's experience and therefore changes constantly; (3) language is expressed and interpreted according to experience and thus is unreliable as a means of communication; (4) men build up masks to conceal reality, and thus render real communication impossible.

The impossibility of knowing truth, first among these four tenets, is the burden of the story, overshadowing and often including the other three. Personality, which constantly changes with new experience; language, which never has exactly the same meaning for the speaker and the hearer; and masks, which are used to hide reality—these factors obscure truth, or, further, may make its existence impossible. Carlos, in the story, thought that he had found truth in the Aleph. A bright spot in his cellar, this phenomenon contained all other points, and in it he saw "all other points in the universe." It was the *multum in parvo*, the embodiment of all that exists. (p. 401)

The reader soon notices that the world seen by the narrator was the world of his own experience; it was not *the* universe but a universe of his own. It was a product of his own mind, the only reality perceivable to man—relative and never absolute. Thus the Aleph of Carlos and the narrator, this alleged spot of absolute truth, was judged false. A seeming crystal reflecting the whole world, it was merely a figurative mirror reflecting Carlos, the narrator, or whoever looked.

Moreover, the reflection changed, and the more times the viewer looked at the Aleph, the more new things he must have seen. "Our minds are porous and forgetfulness seeps in," the narrator concludes; "I myself am distorting and losing, under the wearing away of the years, the face of Beatriz." Beatriz was dead and was herself unchanging; yet she continued to change as his view of her changed. His image of her, though ostensibly solidified by death, continued to vary as his experiences continued to alter his concept. Thus her personality was solidified only when she was no longer remembered.

If she continued to change in his concept after death, her personality was even less fixed during her life. Photographs described at the beginning of the story reveal her as she changed with new experience, . . . various poses indicating various changes in her personality. It is with skilled irony that the narrator preceded these descriptions with a statement of his own false feeling of constancy in a changing world: "The universe may change but not me, I thought with a certain sad vanity"—an illusion which disappeared by the end of the story where he observed that his own forgetfulness was seeping in and that he was "distorting and losing, under the wearing away of the years." Thus personality, or the concept of it, is the sum of one's experience and therefore changes with every new experience.

A third idea projected in the story illustrates still another existentialistic view—the idea that the meaning of language also depends on experience. The speaker or writer uses words to which he ascribes meanings determined by his experiences, and the hearer or reader interprets the same words in terms of his own different set of experiences. Thus words may be an inadequate, unreliable medium of communication. (pp. 401-02)

A fourth idea in the story concerns man's masks—a further hindrance to real communication. Borges makes frequent and effective use of the mask concept in his story, revealing lesser masks like that removed by Carlos's cognac and like the narrator's mask of silent endurance to conceal his strong aversion to Carlos's poetry. The most significant mask, though, involves the Aleph. It was for Carlos a microcosm of universal infinity—but it was this only because Carlos made it so. Its meaning to Carlos was the mirror of his own life. The problem of Carlos was that he was mistaking his own limited world for an absolute universe, a sum of all mankind. Thus it is that man can view reality only in the limited sphere of his own experience, yet he may allow this limited view to masquerade as absolute and thus may render it false.

In the story, Carlos reacted with woe when his ancestral

Borges in 1971, kneeling on the shore of the Dead Sea in Israel, where he had traveled to receive the fifth biennial Jerusalem Prize for his contributions in literature to the world's understanding of the freedom of the individual in society.

home with his Aleph in the cellar was to be razed. But this Aleph was false; it was his own Aleph masked as absolute. Years later, after the house was destroyed, Carlos became a nationally celebrated poet, and the narrator comments with cogent force that this productive Carlos was "no longer cluttered" by the Aleph. He was free from the shackle of masquerade.

Clearly, then, the thrust of Borges's story involves the subjectivity of interpreting reality, the existential concept that man and things in general exist, but that these things have no meaning except that which man creates for them from his own experience. Thus it is impossible to know absolute truth, even if it exists. Such truth is obscured, perhaps prevented, by deterrent factors emphasized in Borges's story and in the existentialistic view—impediments created by constant change in personality, individual and varied interpretation of language, and ubiquitous masks behind which man hides actuality. These concepts are predominant in **"The Aleph."** (pp. 402-03)

> *Mary McBride, "Jorge Luis Borges, Existentialist: 'The Aleph' and the Relativity of Human Perception," in* Studies in Short Fiction, *Vol. 14, No. 4, Fall, 1977, pp. 401-03.*

DAVID I. GROSSVOGEL   (essay date 1979)

[*In the following excerpt, Grossvogel evaluates Borges's use of the detective story to convey the enigmatic nature of God and the universe, particularly in "Death and the Compass."*]

Jorge Luis Borges has noted how nearly akin is his writing to his "other" self, that private world of anxiety, desire, and perplexity. It is not simply, as he has written in "The Reaches of My Hope," that, in the end, all writing is autobiographical; the act of writing is more like the splitting of self into sentience and commentary that he describes in "Borges and I," ending, "I do not know which one of us has written this page"—a conclusion that stresses the problematic nature of the act. Borges's inner anxiety, which intends to escape from the containment of his fiction, derives from a sense of the absolute nature of the unknown that may be analyzed as the mystery of time, . . . of the infinite, . . . or of the refusal of the unknown to be reduced to either coherence or permanency. . . . (pp. 128-29)

The possibility of a *reality* emerging from the printed page through more than the symbolism of its words (as well as the special place that books occupy in Borges's cosmogony) derives in part from the fact that Borges is himself a bookish creation. He describes his existence, in which "life and death have been lacking," as "infested with literature". The first part of the statement is subject to caution: there is indeed a coldness and a distance in the Borges pages that talk about blood and death that gives those pages a metallic and artificial quality. But the anxiety that suffuses so many of the stories is evidence of the many ways in which a sense of life and death has affected Borges. And his references to metaphysics and philosophy are ironic reminders that before their specialized analyses became academic, metaphysics and philosophy belonged to religion, and their purpose was to help cope with the ambient darkness of a human life. (p. 129)

A book is an ordering; . . . its very being denies, and will convey less than adequately, the structureless and unpronounceable chaos, the infinity of space and formlessness that extends beyond man's ability to measure and to shape. Nevertheless, Borges is concerned with that sense of chaos in much of his writing and so he faces the technical problem (which may also be a metaphysical problem) of articulating that sense through his fiction, without that fiction becoming, for him or for his reader, a surrogate ordering.

The temptation the book represents as the Absolute Book, as perfect order, or as "The God's Script" is one of the pervasive influences on the thought and fiction of Borges: if such an absolute ordering were possible within a book, then the unknown, the "god," would be manifest within it. But the perverse nature of books, like the nature of the unknown, is that their ordering is never more than partial and that their most forceful disclosure about mystery is that it cannot be disclosed. **"Tlön, Uqbar, Orbis Tertius"** describes "a labyrinth devised by men, a labyrinth destined to be deciphered by men." Tlön begins as only the thought of men, and its only tangibility, at first, is the spurious tangibility of texts. . . . Founded by Berkeley and other members of a "benevolent society," it is intended as a realm of human control. . . . Eventually, the language of Tlön that resists formulation ("Every mental state is irreducible: the mere fact of naming it—i.e., of classifying it—implies a falsification") invades the earth as tangible evidence: the letters around the edge of a compass. And the book devised by benevolent humanists who intended it as a replacement for the unfathomable labyrinth of god becomes just one more divine Script, wholly impenetrable, and about which men can only speculate: "One of the schools of Tlön [theorizes] that the history of the universe—and in it our lives and the most tenuous detail of our lives—is the scripture produced by a subordinate god in order to communicate with a demon." The book, in its exacerbated desire to become the sum and the ordering that will eclipse all mystery, may go as far as to create the objects of a new world, but it will do so only in order to renew, once again, the frustration of attempting to achieve that sum and that ordering.

"I owe the discovery of Uqbar to the conjunction of a mirror and an encyclopedia"; the mirror, the perfect Berkleyan instrument that contains nothing but shows everything that is *seen in it,* also inverts reality (or the illusion of reality): the encyclopedia, in which men had hoped to establish an ordering of all things reduced to their symbols (the symbol, like the mirror, is a container only by virtue of our willingness to grant it a thing contained), ends, in **"Tlön, Uqbar, Orbis Tertius,"** by returning to our world nonsymbolic and mysterious objects. . . . After the failure of reflecting symbols, the hermetic object returns and is deified as the latest avatar of the unknowable.

The mirror also multiplies: "For one of those gnostics, the visible universe was an illusion or (more precisely) a sophism. Mirrors and fatherhood are abominable because they multiply and disseminate that universe"; the mirror image is the equivalent of a world that is illusory or it is an adequate image for a world whose quintessence cannot be apprehended. The mirror's image, which is not spatial, renders accurately of a spatial world only what is not in that world: it is thus an emblem for the unavailing mind that cannot ever fully grasp its object, while at the same time it is the ironic counterpart of that object—a negation of the original negation. In Tlön, one of the metaphysical hypotheses . . . proposes "that while we sleep here, we are awake elsewhere and that in this way every man is two men." The fantastic literature of Borges, which is sometimes a kind of metaphysics, oc-

casionally prescribes such a trajectory for his character: it represents yet another avatar of the mirror when, as in Tlön, the reflection becomes flesh. At such times, Borges suggests a lunge at the unknown that is of such desperate power as to carry the lunger to the other side of the metaphysical barrier without having been able to penetrate it: . . . the insubstantial reflection of the mirror becomes the image (even as it begins to devise fictional structures of its own) of this failure.

Dreams and time are similarly attempted and with as little success. The character in **"The Circular Ruins"** dreams a creature into being . . . only to understand at the end "that he too was a mere appearance, dreamt by another." The dream dreams the dreamer dreaming and, as in Tlön, which was the climactic effort of (philosophical) idealists to construct a controllable universe, the discouraged mind ultimately suspects that all being, all creation, is *someone else's* communication—the reference to a "subordinate god" suggesting that the process is infinitely recessive, like that of the mirror, and thus contrives simply one more image or sense of the infinite.

This vision of cyclical time and a cyclical return, associated by a number of critics with the Nietzschean concept, appears to be still another instance in which the fictional event attempts to pattern itself on the metaphysical concept in order to show the ineffectuality of concepts. Nietzsche emphasized the *Ubermensch's* exhilaration in the knowledge of an identical rebirth because of the possibility of escape from a Judeo-Christian morality of enslavement confined to the present cycle, stressing the extent of the condemnation imposed by an awareness of such recurrences on the slavish mind. Borges, on the other hand, telescopes time and duplicates personality without exultation, as coldly as the mirror whose interreflections occur within a wholly closed space, however deep their illusory space might be. Borges believes that while metaphysics develop freely within the self-containment of the mind, they founder in their actualization within the *seeming* they intended to dissipate: the metaphysical speculation is an act with no extension, and the actual act that extends from it becomes a dream with no more substance than the thought that was its impetus.

An act attempted is likely to be dissipated in the ineffectuality of the dream since Borges suggests on more than one occasion that the percipient of the idea is likely to be created by the idea. In **"The End of the Duel,"** Borges contrives without a shudder a story of murder and abomination. His explanation leaves us somewhat dissatisfied: "You're given the impression, I hope, of a rather grim country where the kind of story I'm going to tell is thought of as a joke." The authorial voice cannot separate itself as clearly as the commentator from participation in this kind of "joke." In order not to be contaminated, in order not to sound as harsh and inhuman, the authorial voice must be subsumed within a vaster joke—a metaphysical joke, in fact—where no blood actually flows because the substance of the joke concerns the problematic substance of personality and the problematic nature of its description. The faceless creatures of Borges bleed less for being the figures of an equation written on the lunar surface of his landscapes. The extent to which those surfaces are reinvested with human depth as they "create" the reader (or author) who creates them remains to be analyzed, as do the ways in which that reverse creation is attempted.

Borges is both the victim and the perpetrator of his joke. His fiction, so consistently woven out of speculative essays, confirms the judgment of **"The Immortal;"** that "there is no pleasure more complex than that of thought"; but the uneasiness Borges feels at being adrift in a chaotic and timeless universe becomes dismay (serious or ironic) when he considers the efforts of those who attempt to encapsulate the unknowable within their theories. Not infrequently, Borges makes his ironic point by projecting a character into the realized world of such theory and watching that character founder within substitute shadows that grow into a surreal intensification of the darkness that the rational construct was meant to reduce. . . . As in Tlön, men have only words, and they become as unsatisfactory as mirrors: a world that cannot be *penetrated* is only *reflected* by symbols that are no more than another part of the illusion. Still, the words spill over: in the same way that the fiction enlarges and echoes for Borges a private uneasiness, his fictional comment is extended into an existential multiplicity of interviews, discussions, [and] postfaces about his stories. . . . [Words] and ideas create palliative activity within a world that denies the possibility of deeds.

Up to this point, Borges loses the game, even though his ironic *Weltanschauung* may benefit from the loss: fictional commentary (intended to be more than an instance of the metaphysical failure), that evidences such exuberant health as it spills out of the book, requires a metafictional comment in order to remain within the author's control and the limits of his original intent. It is evident that Borges has been a ready contributor to this metafictional commentary. But he has also tried to make his fiction oscillate between the text's containment and the reader's parafictional world in ways that are more complex.

Tlön is a planet perplexed by language, evidencing a genetic peculiarity that links it, beyond fiction, to the book (Borges's) that creates it as a literary fiction about a literary fiction. Since the limits of language are an instance of human limitation, the writer in search of his formulation provides an instance as well as an emblem for man in quest of a structuring answer. In the story about the revelatory power of a mystical object, **"The Aleph,"** Borges encounters the difficulty of presenting its magical simultaneity (that is to say, total and unequivocal revelation) through language, man's inadequate instrument, which is perforce sequential and partitive. . . . In the end, the fictional voice of **"The Aleph"** will doubt both possibilities—the possibility of the magical realization within the fiction as well as the possibility of the actual transcription to suggest a fictional realization: "Does this Aleph exist in the heart of a stone? Did I see it there in the cellar when I saw all things, and have I now forgotten it? Our minds are porous and forgetfulness creeps in." But this discouragement, because it is so pervasive and because it is the state of mind of the author Borges attempting this story, this sense of failure begins the process of linking two worlds that are utterly different in kind—the world of the fiction and the world of the reader in which the fiction may attain an entirely new dimension.

Before this discouragement, a postscript to the "ineffable core" of the story provides what the fiction claims as parafictional evidence—documentation that would establish the fact of a nonfictional Aleph and thereby cast doubt on the reality of the fictional one. Through a clever and ironic play of fictional mirrors, . . . Borges offers the evidence of the parafictional world to stress the fraudulence of his fiction. The rejection of the fiction as truth rehabilitates that fiction at another

level, since the "real" world cannot comment on the devising of a fiction (that is, something that does not exist in "reality") without being itself fictionalized: the evidence of a real Aleph outside the referential fiction of Borges invalidates his Aleph (it is only a fiction) but requires that fiction for its own claim to reality, without which it cannot invalidate its fictional mirror. The interplay of these fictional (and parafictional) reflections begins to give **"The Aleph"** the dimension of an Aleph—the story becomes a special kind of revelatory mirror.

A part of the interreflections of these mirrors leaves the printed page. Still, Borges wants their very substance to be caught in the same oscillation between the spurious world of the story and the actual world of the reader. In the same way as did Sartre two years earlier (in *Nausea,* 1938), Borges attempts the leap from fictional to phenomenal object through the tangible hybrid the reader holds in his hands. In **"The End of the Duel,"** Borges begins with an autobiographical note that commits the subsequent story: "It's a good many years ago now that Carlos Reyles, the son of the Uruguayan novelist, told me the story one summer evening out in Adrogué": at this point, the story might well be simply an expansion of the biographical fact. Later, in a Columbia University seminar (now in print), Borges absorbs both the prefatory note and the story itself within the web of his explication:

> Well, this is a mere statement of what actually happened. I got the story from somebody else as well, but since it would have been awkward to mention two names and have two characters, I left out my other friend. Adrogué means a great deal to me because it stands for my boyhood and for my youth. It was the last place my father went before he died, and I have very pleasant memories of it. Adrogué was once quite a fine little town, to the south of Buenos Aires, but now it has been spoiled by flats, garages and television. But in its time it was full of *quintas,* with large gardens, and was a fine place to be lost in. Adrogué was a kind of maze, and there were no parallel streets. Reyles was the son of a famous Uruguayan novelist.

This is a way, not uncommon for Borges, to either stress the autobiographical part of his fiction, or turn the fiction into a form of autobiography (see the collection called, in its English translation, *The Aleph and Other Stories,* where each story is given a postscript—a "commentary"—that makes it an *event* in the life of the author). Borges knew that he had at least one illustrious predecessor in these attempts— Cervantes. When the author of the first *Quixote* became aware of the pirating of his work, he hastened the completion of a second *Quixote.* But he also gave an added reality to his original work . . . by making it the object of a commentary in the second work: those comments were no longer simply "fiction" since they referred to an actual object, and both books thus acquired a parafictional dimension that the author enlarged by having the minor characters of the second book encounter principals that now existed in two worlds. This was the hybrid literary object that Borges chose to weave into his **"Pierre Menard, Author of Don Quixote,"** a commentary meant to be read as fiction. The story, which Borges calls "a halfway house between the essay and the true tale," is essentially a reading of three lines of *Don Quixote* in book 1, chapter 9. Since the fiction tells about a Pierre Menard who has been able, by dint of effort, to write a *Don Quixote* identical to that of Cervantes, the difference between the two texts will be determined by the way in which Borges's reader reads them. In order to determine those differences, the reader must first become a fictional character—the one who reads Cervantes (alongside Menard) through a genuine historical distance so as to inform the lines with their seventeenth-century modernity. It is only then that he will be able to note in the identical lines of the modern Menard an archaism of tone and idea (especially as it pertains to the nature of history). Inserting the phenomenological object that is the Cervantes text within his fiction, Borges coerces from his reader the performance that the fiction requires of that reader—understanding the archaic text as a modern one and then understanding the selfsame text, when the fiction claims it to be modern, as if it were archaic.

This fiction that oscillates between the worlds of parafictional commentary and those of its making, because of the insertion of a text that had already been placed within such an oscillation by Cervantes, emerges as commentary alongside the other commentaries that Borges has made on the curiously hybrid nature of the *Quixote*. In the essay called "Partial Magic in the *Quixote*," Borges is reminded that in the now parafictional object, a parafictional wedge in the form of a fictional object had already been introduced by Cervantes, whose own *Galatea* is found in the Don's library and upon which the "barber, a dream or the form of a dream of Cervantes, passes judgment." And in the "Parable of Cervantes and the *Quixote*," Borges notes how time has changed the nature of the original fiction in a way that is identical to the intent of his own fictional tricks and those of Cervantes, though Borges, through sheer perversity, confirms the equation by inverting it. Recalling the reality of the Spanish region of La Mancha, Borges remarks that the original story juxtaposed and contrasted "the unreal world of the seventeenth century." But by now, that "ordinary" world has ceased being part of *our* "everyday" and has receded for us as far as the unreal world contrived by books of chivalry. One "unreal" is now as "unreal" as the other and, in the fullness of time, the once-real La Mancha has become as mythical as the mythical Montiel. What Borges does not tell us here, but what his belief in the dream dreaming the dreamer allows us to infer, is that the real La Mancha, now buried within the depth of centuries, reacquires phenomenological presence as the myth that focuses our comment.

The specular interreflection is thus an image that turns into a process relating a reader and a text—a reading that obtrudes an *object* into the world of the reader even as it absorbs that reader into its own. The "object" created by the specular mechanism of "Pierre Menard" is the reader made for the purpose of reading "Pierre Menard," in a devising that subverts the expectation of control that such a reader would otherwise bring to his text. Within the infinite recession of the dream dreaming the dreamer dreaming, . . . the reader is thrust through the fiction into a confrontation with the unknowable that creates the existential sense that the fiction is investigating. In "Tlön, Uqbar, Orbis Tertius," the author despairs of knowing a reality that his fiction is also in the process of subverting: "It is useless to answer that reality is also orderly. Perhaps it is, but in accordance with divine laws—I translate: inhuman laws—which we never quite grasp. Tlön is surely a labyrinth."

A labyrinth created so as to be decipherable would lack the defining essence of god's labyrinth—its nondecipherable nature. In order for the design of "Tlön" to be like god's, it loses those who venture into it. Several labyrinth stories of Borges

instance and discuss how the text becomes an accurate labyrinth. In "The Two Kings and Their Two Labyrinths" (which purports to be a trope for another story, "Ibn Hakkan al-Bokhari, Dead in His Labyrinth"), the chronicler quoted by the fictional voice records that "in former times there was a king of the isles of Babylon who called together his architects and his wizards and set them to build him a labyrinth so intricate that no wise man would dare enter inside, and so subtle that those who did would lose their way. This undertaking was a blasphemy, for confusion and marvels belong to God alone and not to man." . . . A lesson of Babel is that the word that cannot penetrate the unknown can at least lose its user in such a way as to give him a sense of the unknown. The author thus becomes an ultimately futile intercessor but one who is nevertheless lustered with some of the mystery that he attempts; and Borges, faithful to his way of populating his fiction with aspects of his own quandaries, is likely to turn his victims into such unavailing intermediaries dwelling at the outer limits of the unknown and on whom some of the mystery rubs off. These ambiguous figures, like that in "The Circular Ruins," are mere appearances, as distant from the unknowable as those for whom they mediate the unknowable, but who, like their author, distill some of its flavor through proximity or concern.

The labyrinth of "Tlön" is a device of language; its failure to reach the unknown is a failure of language. For the author, that failure is both confirmation of his participation in the human condition and an unacceptable evidence that his writing attempts to cancel. But, as we have seen, it is the specular and speculating part of the fiction that contaminates speculation, entrapping not only the commenting Borges but his own commentators as well. Monegal, who appears as an episodic character in "The Other Death" (a part of the maze through which the narrator tries to get to the story he is attempting to tell), notes how "Pierre Menard" devises even a critic of its own making. . . . [Parafictional] and concentric expansions of the fiction provide Borges with an enlargement of the maze, extending it like the interrelations of the mirror over two worlds through which Borges moves, now as the writer entrapped within his fiction, and again as the "I" who escapes from it, and forcing the reader who follows him to go through similar avatars. At one level, the reader confronts, instead of his fictional object, another existent—Borges, engaged in the process of writing. But if the reader attempts that passage out of the maze, Borges fictionalizes himself, reentering, from the opposite end as it were, his specular construct.

The philistine mind will conclude that these speculations and specula, these alternations of the reader and his reading, the modification of the author and his object in their respective functions, are only mental postures—and Borges would most likely not disagree: however doggedly the human mind attempts the unknowable, it is always thrown back upon itself, it contrives only another posture. If metaphysics is ultimately, as in Tlön, only another form of fiction, a branch of fantastic literature, then Borges will gentle the exacerbation of the metaphysical quest through the irony and the games of his fiction. In time he will reduce the whole metaphysical quandary to a detective (short) story—though even this ultimate reduction will be approached cautiously. . . . (pp. 129-40)

About "Death and the Compass," Borges has said that it is a "nightmare version of the city [Buenos Aires]," a work that "should stand or fall by its general atmosphere, not by its plot"—as ever, in Borges, the statement merits some reflection. Even if one excludes the H. Bustos Domecq stories that Borges began writing in the early forties in collaboration with Adolfo Bioy Casares, much of Borges's writing could be thought of as detective story-writing: one need only allow an unallowable departure from the strict definition of the genre—the fact that the riddle proposed by Borges is seldom resolved in his resolution. A labyrinth successfully traversed is a labyrinth no more, and the Borgesian labyrinth must remain a labyrinth at the end of even a detective story. That persistent labyrinth accounts for both the detective nature and the "atmosphere" of Borges's stories.

One way of reducing the detective story to its simplest definition is to say that it concerns a detective who is looking for a name—the identity of the culprit (identity that is, in a genre not overly concerned with identity, little more than a name). So defined, the quest reminds Borges that the mystery for which god is a substitute concept also becomes, as any enduring mystery must, the object of an exacerbated quest: "I learned that the holy fear of uttering God's Name had given rise to the idea that that Name is secret and all-powerful. I learned that some of the Hasidim, in search of that secret Name, had gone as far as to commit human sacrifices."

The Tetragrammaton hides the four mystical consonants of God's Name. . . . The Tetragrammaton is an object, not an idea. God creates his world out of the alphabet's letters, and those who decipher his world do so by reading the evidence of God's text in the very symbols that create his text. I have had occasion already to point out how the peculiar economy of Borges requires him to create a text about (and ultimately as undecipherable as) the "Book of God" (for example, in **"The Circular Ruins"**). **"Death and the Compass"** is perhaps the most explicit of such Borgesian exercises, even though, as the trajectory that contrives a detective story, it appears to be considerably less than that.

Again in the simplest terms, **"Death and the Compass"** is about a criminal's vengeance on a detective: Lönnrot has arrested and "put away" the hood Scharlach's brother. Seriously wounded, "Red" Scharlach mulls an exemplary revenge during the nine days of his delirium. His opportunity comes when, one day, through treachery and a mistake, one of his men kills the Talmudic scholar Marcel Yarmolinsky. Since Talmudic scholars and detectives are decipherers of tangible signs, the Borgesian Scharlach sees in this conjuncture the possible form of a retribution to be exacted from Lönnrot, and one his delirium had suggested to him before ever the opportunity arose: what could be more devilish than to entrap a detective within the web of a maze of his own making? Or, from the point of view of a devilish story-writer, what could be more devilish than to entrap a reader within the expectation of a resolvable mystery? (Both detectives and their readers live within a similar expectation.) Accordingly, Borges devises a "Jewish" story, in which the four-parted Tetragrammaton and the four-pointed compass conceal a mystery whose *events* will have a resolution to the extent that this is a detective story—even though the mystery itself will not be dissipated: the Tetragrammaton does not yield the mystery associated with it.

The first murder, Rabbi Yarmolinsky's, allows Borges to place his story within the world of the book: once again, the text of the story is about a text and its elucidation is about the elucidation of a text. Yarmolinsky brings with him to the Talmudic congress "His many books and his few suits of clothes." Among these, two are of special interest. One, the

Vindication of the Kabbalah, is in fact an essay by Borges himself, who thus lends his reality to his fiction (while stating, at the same time, his own parafictional interest) with an expectation of the consequences that we have previously described in this kind of Cervantine ploy. The other book is the *Sefer Yetzirah. . . .* [The] *Sephirot,* or ten primordial numbers, and the twenty-two letters of the alphabet out of which God "produced everything that is and everything that will be": these are among the revelations of the books in which Lönnrot will steep himself as he gradually becomes a part of the case he is investigating. But in becoming a Kabbalist (for the Kabbalistic texts, which Lönnrot also reads, derive from the *Sepher Yetzirah*), Lönnrot falls not only into a Borgesian posture, but into that of the Borges who falls into the posture of God for whom the world is a text: "For the Kabbalists, the letters of the Torah are the mystical body of God, and from this it follows that the Creation is just a reflection or emanation of the Holy text." (pp. 140–43)

[As] Borges points out, the Tetragrammaton is a recent awareness of Lönnrot's: he reads with the haste of a neophyte, or perhaps with the haste of someone hurried, and hurrying on, to his destiny. In a text about the phenomenological evidence of text and world, and of world through text, Lönnrot makes the mistake (which is perhaps part of an ultimate plan) of reading with his mind objects that are more arcane than their symbolism. The logical process of his deductions speeds him to the southern part of the city and the villa Triste-le-Roy. In his recent Kabbalistic learning, Lönnrot has discovered that "Tradition [the meaning of the Hebrew word *Kabbalah*] lists ninety-nine names of God; Hebrew scholars explain that imperfect cipher by a mystic fear of numbers; the Hasidim argue that the missing term stands for a hundredth name—the Absolute Name." As Lönnrot now hurries to Triste-le-Roy, Borges notes that the "mystery seemed almost crystal clear. He felt ashamed for having spent close to a hundred days on it": but the absolute name that is to be revealed within a perfect cipher is meant to elude him.

Lönnrot has already become a piece of the puzzle he is fitting together. . . . At Triste-le-Roy, where the "two-faced Hermes [that casts] a monstrous shadow" is but a symbol of the doublings that, like images caught within facing mirrors, turn the villa into an issueless labyrinth, Scharlach is waiting to kill Lönnrot. And the red thread that has been running through the blood splattering previous corpses, coloring "the garish sunset" that helps number correctly the appointed days, through the crimson of the prophetic lozenges, that thread suddenly draws together, in their respective names, Lönnrot (whose last syllable means *red* in German) and "Red" Scharlach (whose name in German means *scarlet*). Remembering the interreflecting mirrors of Triste-le-Roy and the straight-line maze of Zeno the Eleatic, Lönnrot tells Scharlach: "When in another incarnation you hunt me down, stage (or commit) a murder at A, then a second murder at B, eight miles from A, then a third murder at C, four miles from A and B, halfway between the two. Lay in wait for me then at D, two miles from A and C, again halfway between them. Kill me at D, the way you are going to kill me here at Triste-le-Roy." And Scharlach, who all along has been well aware of circularities, answers, "I promise you such a maze, which is made up of a single straight line and which is invisible and unending."

The awareness of another incarnation, of a reversal of this particular hunt (though it is hard to say with certainty who is the hunter and who the hunted), the similarity of the thought that has enabled Scharlach to think Lönnrot thinking his way to the center of the maze at Triste-le-Roy, these make of Lönnrot and Scharlach the same man at point D of a straight line maze that has already been drawn as inescapably as the infinite line of images caught in the facing mirrors of the villa.

This much Borges himself is willing to confirm. But there is a third man as well at point D, the one who entered the story earlier as the author of the *Vindication of the Kabbalah*—Borges himself. For Triste-le-Roy is a part of the author's private maze. It is the "beautiful name invented by Amanda Molina Vedia [to whom the story is inscribed]." Furthermore, it "stands for the now demolished Hotel Las Delicias in Adrogué. (Amanda had painted a map of an imaginary island on the wall of her bedroom; on her map I discovered the name Triste-le-Roy)." We know of Adrogué already, which Borges confirms in "An Autobiographical Essay" to be indeed "some ten or fifteen miles to the south of Buenos Aires". Adrogué is the place of Borges's childhood summers, to which he returned for many years thereafter, the stuff of "so many memories" of his and about which he wrote "a longish elegy" by the same name. What dies at the point of the circle called Triste-le-Roy is not only the possibility for Lönnrot-Scharlach to decipher the criminal's name, but, deep within the intimate memory of Borges, the possibility for him to inscribe within his fiction the Absolute Name out of which, as out of God's Torah, the world is made.

"For the Kabbalists, the letters of the Torah are the mystical body of God, and from this it follows that the Creation is just a reflection or emanation of the Holy text." At the melancholy point named Triste-le-Roy where the author and his characters merge within a Kabbalistic story that preserves, as in a maze, the mystery that is the mirror of a deeper Mystery, the tale of this particular Tetragrammaton ends: [although Lönnrot discovers its first three letters, which are planted as clues to the murders by Scharlach], its fourth letter remains unknown, and with that missing letter, the unutterable remains unuttered. Like other unsanctified intercessors, Borges has stolen from the mystical sign only an amulet, and his power—like theirs—is only the distillation of a Kabbalistic flavor, a sense of the unknown and the unknowable, within the text of a story concerned with the mystery, the power, and the limits of texts. And the modern reader, reading with his head because the head can best control the metaphysical shudder, confronts an object that is wholly closed and refractory, a *thing* of the author's making, which, like the four mystical consonants of the Tetragrammaton, becomes a physical epitome of all mystery. And so, the reader's head notwithstanding, the shudder returns. (pp. 144-46)

> *David I. Grossvogel, "Borges: The Dream Dreaming the Dreamer," in his* Mystery and Its Fictions: From Oedipus to Agatha Christie, *The Johns Hopkins University Press, 1979, pp. 127-46.*

GENE H. BELL-VILLADA (essay date 1981)

[*In the following excerpt from his comprehensive study* Borges and His Fiction, *Bell-Villada examines Borges's thematic approach to violence and death in stories from his short fiction collection* El Aleph.]

El Aleph contains a number of tales dealing with various types of physical violence—underworld executions, rustic

machismo, political killings, even pathological revenge. Borges's famed erudition and fantasy tend to be absent from these stories, which are generally in the lean, unadorned, hard-boiled tradition. The only overt signs of "Borgesian" fancifulness in them are an occasional secondary conceit such as the blurred identities in **"The Waiting"** and **"Emma Zunz"** or the final play of contradiction in **"The Dead Man."** The one exception to this is **"The Other Death,"** with its erudite and oneiric machinery every bit as elaborate as that in **"Averroës's Search"** or **"The Secret Miracle"**; in this story, however, the narrative legerdemain is set, not in far exotic lands, but in twentieth-century Argentina and Uruguay. By contrast, **"The Intruder"** and **"Deutsches Requiem"** conspicuously avoid all fantasy and, surely not accidentally, these two stories are among the weakest in the volume.

On the other hand, Borges has given us one of his most powerful little tales in **"The Waiting,"** a story about big-city gang executions, the kind of mobster bloodlettings one still reads about in American newspapers. Early one morning a man arrives by cab at a guest house in northeastern Buenos Aires. Clearly worried, he absent-mindedly pays the driver with a Uruguayan coin, regretting it immoderately. When the landlady asks his name, he replies "Villari" because nothing else comes to his mind. A simple man, who is unaware of the artifice involved in having assumed his enemy's name, he lives from day to day. . . . He treasures little things like tobacco and *maté* and tries to live purely in the present without thoughts of past or future. In a recurring dream he confronts Villari and actually shoots him down. One dark July (that is, winter) morning, two silent men—the real Alejandro Villari and a henchman—appear in his room and wake him. In a haunting gesture, the man asks them to wait and turns to the wall, hoping perhaps that they might be a dream. Then the two toughs blast him.

The protagonist of this story has chosen to wait or, as the title indicates, lives a life of "waiting." But unlike Samuel Beckett's tramps, who wait for a Godot that obviously will never come, Borges's gangster sits around waiting for the inevitable. Particularly striking is the banal and ordinary nature of "Villari" and his wait. Here we have what could be any middle-aged retired man living somewhere in seclusion . . . with the disquieting knowledge, cutting through all this everyday banality, that the end will be a violent one. In keeping with his ordinary quality, "Villari" lives in a remote niche of the sprawling Argentine metropolis, lost in urban anonymity in a quarter where there are no fellow Italians to remind him (or us) of his roots. Except for his Italian ancestry and his obvious gangster background, we know nothing of "Villari"—his looks, his temperament—other than the general remarks about his being neither more nor less courageous than anyone else. On top of this, Borges purposely blurs the identity of victim with that of victimizer. . . . (pp. 175-76)

Despite its surface realism, ruffled only by scattered hints of fantasy, **"The Waiting"** eludes all elementary analysis of actions or motives. It is true that "Villari" could have left town, hidden himself in disguise anywhere around Buenos Aires, or sought protection from cohorts of his own. He could have adopted any of a series of survival measures, ranging from flight to fighting back, for he obviously is neither a dunce nor a coward; indeed, he is rather quick to defend himself when someone jostles him on the street. Similarly, as regards the executioner, there are no reasons given for Villari's desire to eliminate the unnamed stranger, no explanations suggested as to how the boss man succeeds in tracking down a quasi-hermit who lives virtually sequestered in a remote guest house. In this special world of mysterious violence, where the usual real-life motives and explanations carry no weight and are without analytical value, both victim and victimizer ritually act out their predetermined roles. Villari-the-victim, who simply knows that someday he will be hunted down and shot, dedicates his remaining days to waiting for that moment; Villari-the-executioner simply finds his man one day—and that is all we are allowed to know. What is noteworthy about Borges's yarn, then, is what he leaves out; the entire drama is boiled down to the elemental experiences of pursuit, hiding, waiting, fear, and death. Even a precise sense of time is absent; while Borges vividly conveys the feeling of day-to-day monotony, there is no indication in the story as to just how many months or years actually have gone by in that rooming house.

On the other hand, one cannot but feel struck at the slight role played by the fantastic in so enigmatic, so dreamlike a narrative. Aside from the cautious use of the Double (in which the protagonist casually assumes the name of his victimizer-to-be), the only overt use of fantasy in **"The Waiting"** is to be found in the few scattered references to dreams. When the man in the rooming house considers the off-chance that Alejandro Villari might already have died, he also infers from this the possibility that his own life might be a dream, a notion he quickly discards. More significantly, every night at the crack of dawn, the man has dreams (based, as usually is the case, on recent incidents and images) in which he successfully shoots it out with Villari and his henchmen; these dreams could be seen as a vivid imaginary fulfillment of the man's wishes. In a striking coincidence—striking not for reasons of meaning but because of its sheer eeriness—the two killers arrive at the identical hour during which the protagonist usually has his dreams. The stranger then turns to the wall, with the touching speculation ventured by Borges that "Villari" may have hoped to transform the killers into the accustomed dream of that hour of the morning.

But these dreams have no larger narrative aims, no effects other than atmospheric; if anything, **"The Waiting"** subtly highlights the powerlessness of the imagination, its lack of relationship and relevance to the prosaic, brutal world of daily survival in the city. Despite the protagonist's often active dreaming, his life slouches quietly but inexorably on to the dread moment of cold, businesslike execution. Its haunted air notwithstanding, in this story the imagination and its uses are expressly played down. . . . Art and artifice are, for any number of reasons, of little consequence to "Villari" and his precarious life situation.

Although **"The Waiting"** is in the gangster-story tradition, its atmosphere and meaning set it apart from that tradition. In this regard, one might compare Borges's piece with Hemingway's celebrated story "The Killers." . . . Hemingway's concretely realistic piece—with its considerations of motive, its precise narrative point of view, and its portrayals of ordinary men who do exclusively ordinary kinds of things—contains none of the oblique hints, the brooding suggestiveness, the "Kafkian" overtones of Borges's story, where the surface events seem to stand dimly for something else. Borges's very title points to the ongoing situation rather than to any of the participants in the events. Indeed, despite its realistic trappings, **"The Waiting"** impresses one as being vaguely allegorical, a symbolic parable of the inevitability of dying.

Borges (right) with his collaborator and close friend Adolfo Bioy Casares.

The elusiveness and banality of its setting and actors and the stereotyped quality of the two killers give an impression that one is observing more than a gangster yarn. One seems to witness an eternal drama in which Everyman awaits the onset of death. Despite its impression of brittle hardness, **"The Waiting"** is one of Borges's most provocative and pathetic little stories.

On the face of it, **"The Dead Man"** is a much simpler story, a fast-moving yarn of nineteenth-century frontier violence, capped with a surprise ending in which the discrepancy between Borges's stark title and Benjamín Otálora's feverish life is explained. Nevertheless, Borges's puzzles are subtly at work here and, as we shall see, there are even allegorical hints of the kind we saw in **"The Waiting."**

A nineteen-year-old Buenos Aires hoodlum named Otálora stabs a man and flees to Uruguay to meet with Azevedo Bandeira, an underworld boss. In Montevideo, during a drunken brawl, he saves an old man from attack by a knife artist and finds out that the near-victim is Azevedo himself. Otálora, now in the good graces of the boss man, is engaged as an apprentice gaucho. . . . One afternoon at Azevedo's city house, the boss summons Otálora to bring him his *matè*. As he looks at the legendary chieftain, who is sick in bed and fondling his redheaded mistress, Otálora is angered that this old geezer, whom he could kill at a blow, somehow enjoys such prestige. Later, at a desolate ranch called *El Suspiro* ("The Sigh"), Otálora launches a plot. He conspires with Azevedo's bodyguard Suárez, regularly disobeys Azevedo's orders, mounts Azevedo's horse, takes over the command (but retains Azevedo as figurehead), and beds down with Azevedo's redhead. Then the reversal: at a New Year's Eve celebration, just when a drunken Otálora is vaunting his power publicly, Azevedo and Suárez seize the redhead and hurl her at Otálora. In a sudden insight, Otálora realizes that his gains came about precisely because he had been sentenced to death. . . . Suárez disdainfully shoots the upstart boy.

"The Dead Man" tells a story, among other things, of inordinate political ambition and personal pride bringing about a man's own downfall. . . . Otálora, of course, is quite ambitious and, more important, extremely brave—but he lacks all prudence. As Borges's Spanish version observes, he possesses "no virtue other than an infatuation with courage." . . . Otálora's courage is a raw, immature, and self-serving kind, a blind force that rushes on with no awareness of the importance of personal loyalties and group needs; thus, Otálora can simply tear up his letter of introduction or murder a fellow-smuggler, acts of self-reliance at its very starkest. This obliviousness to forces outside himself is another way of saying that Otálora has absolutely no political savvy and no aptitude for the cool calculation necessary for the most violent power struggles; only for the briefest spell can this brash and impetuous young man cover up, by means of simple audacity and force, those leadership qualities he lacks. (pp. 176-80)

In the end, Otálora—like a figure out of tragedy—receives the consolation prize of enlightenment, the realization that he was doomed from the start. Until then, Otálora never appears to take note of certain clues suggesting a set-up. For much of Otálora's story suggests that Azevedo's plot to do the boy in had existed from the very first encounter, that even the drunken brawl and the narrowly averted murder may have been a ruse. One is struck by the sudden return to normalcy immediately following the brawl and the rapid acceptance of Otálora within the next few hours. Moreover, the very same gaucho who had nearly knifed Azevedo sits afterwards at the boss's right-hand side, joins in the men's reveling with no hint of disgrace, and the next day is sent to fetch Otálora—curious goings-on which a shrewder person would certainly have questioned. . . . Only at the last minute does Otálora discover that he had consistently misread all the signals in his own favor and that everything pointed to a trap. Azevedo's men had led *him* on, baited him, deluded him, filled his head with exaggerated notions of his own power, and crowned him king of fools, only to dispose of him thereafter. Hence Otálora is bold but obtuse, intrepid but not wise; he simply likes to fight and lord it over, with no sense of the unwritten rules of authority and force. His deficiencies are not purely moral—though amoral he certainly is—but intellectual as well; he has an incapacity for understanding the relationship of others to him, plots included.

All of this unfolds within a formal framework whose surface simplicity is as deceptive as the events encouraging Otálora's rise. Actually, throughout this fast-moving tale of the underworld, one finds present the hand of Borges the master. The entire story is told in the present tense, imparting a vivid immediacy to the reckless youth's headlong rush to power; by using the rather common device known as *presente histórico* (the customary Hispanic way of writing history and biography), Borges places the **"The Dead Man"** within a familiar literary tradition. Borges's approach to Otálora's adventures also recalls the procedure he employed in **"Theme of the Traitor and the Hero"**: the story we are to read, the author initially informs us, is not in its final definitive form, and other versions may exist. Hence, when we read of Otálora's success in taking Azevedo's horse and mistress the very same day, Borges goes on to mitigate the unlikely nature of these easy victories by invoking alleged accounts that claim greater time lapses between the two deeds. Borges thus gets the most out of fast action, but also soothes the incredulous reader by suggesting more believable alternatives. Above all, Borges never lets us lose sight of the fact that we are reading a story, a written object whose shape is contingent on the facts he chooses to tell and on the way he actually tells them. Much as in the above-mentioned Irish tale, where the narrative is presented as a general "theme" not bound to any single time or place, Borges sets forth the story of Otálora in mere outline, the details of which he will purportedly expand in future.

In spite of Borges's modest apologies for the shortcomings of

"The Dead Man," this piece is artfully structured for formal coherence and clarity. Otálora's first meeting with Azevedo and his gang is at a drunken free-for-all; he dies at the greatest brawl of them all, a New Year's Eve party in which the mobsters almost ritualistically eat freshly slaughtered meat. The death of Otálora, which takes place exactly at midnight, neatly rounds off a cycle and coincides with the end of the calendar year as well. Similarly, when Otálora first sees the redhead in Azevedo's room, she is "barefoot and half-dressed"; this illicit carnal appeal is accentuated in the dramatic closing scene when, as prelude to Otálora's execution, she is dragged out by force, once again "barefoot and half-dressed." The story is further built around a series of cultural oppositions such as city versus country . . . Argentina versus Uruguay . . . , and Hispanic countries versus Brazil. . . . (pp. 180-82)

A marvelous little thriller, **"The Dead Man"** resembles **"The Waiting"** in its suggestion of forces standing beyond man's grasp and control. This is particularly brought out by the story's final little twist, the notion that Otálora has been considered a dead man all along (an idea that some readers may find hard to accept). After all, within the actual body of the narrative, Otálora is never dead; indeed, he only dies *after* the last line of the story. To Azevedo's men, however, Otálora is "dead" because from the very first encounter they have conspired to seduce him into dreams of grandeur and then shoot him. In a more metaphysical way, one could think of Otálora as dead because his brazen character and his paths of glory have led him inevitably to the grave. A marked man, condemned from the outset, Otálora's great success serves (in a kind of inverted Calvinism) as a harbinger of doom. Even his resonant name "Otálora" carries dark hints of predestination because it echoes the words *a tal hora* ("at such an hour"). His abandoning of home turf and urban roots to die in a more primitive land (the back country of Uruguay) brings to mind the way in which "Villari" readies himself to die in a remote corner of Buenos Aires; "Villari," however, dies in a resigned, accepting spirit in contrast to Otálora's intoxicated self-deception. **"The Dead Man"** is a thriller with parable overtones; it has the ring of those old moral fables in which the harshly sealed fate of one overly presumptuous individual seems to stand as a cautionary tale to us all. (p. 182)

Of all the stories in *El Aleph* that deal with criminal violence, **"Emma Zunz"** is the most highly achieved, the most vivid and powerful, and by far the most moving. One summer evening, eighteen-year-old Emma arrives home from her factory job and finds a letter informing her of her father's suicide in Brazil. Caught in the complex web of shock, nostalgia, guilt, and fear, Emma recalls how the happier days of six years ago were shattered when Aaron Loewenthal (then manager of the factory and now owner) framed her father for embezzlement and forced him to flee the country. Reflecting upon this secret bond between herself and the deceased, Emma hatches a plan that same sleepless night. The next day she routinely goes to work, takes in strike rumors, chats with girl friends, and feels embarrassed when they talk of boys, for—an emotional idiosyncrasy that will color subsequent events—the opposite sex arouses in Emma "an almost pathological fear." Saturday morning Emma makes preparations for her plan: after verifying ship sailing dates, she telephones Loewenthal, poses as an informer, and sets an appointment for the evening. That afternoon she heads for the red-light district, picks up a coarse-looking Scandinavian seaman, follows him through a maze-like house of assignation, and—in a ritual that repels Emma, who feels horrified that her father could have so possessed her mother—goes to bed with the sailor.

Remaining alone, Emma tears up the money, gets dressed, leaves unnoticed, and takes a trolley through the dark streets. She heads for the factory, above which Loewenthal, a pious miser and widower, lives alone. . . . Before her arrival, she had rehearsed at length the moment in which, after seizing his pistol, she would confront him, accuse him, extract a confession, and shoot him. But her fury over the physical outrage to which she has just been subjected virtually overwhelms her; as a result, Emma shoots the miser from behind at the first opportunity, too hastily for her speech to make any sense, and she thus never vindicates her father before a dying Loewenthal. Emma then makes a plausible mess of the room, picks up the telephone, and says what she was to say on countless future occasions—that Loewenthal had abused her and she killed him in self-defense. Her strange tale eventually convinces everyone because "substantially it was true. True was Emma Zunz's tone, true was her shame, true her hate. True also was the outrage she had suffered: only the circumstances were false, the time, and one or two proper names."

In that resounding final cadence (probably one of Borges's most perfect and beautiful single passages) there is a conceit by itself fascinating: that Emma's rage—against the sailor, against her father for having abused her mother, and even against men in general—could effectively and justly override circumstantial falsehoods of time, persons, and place. Emma's deposition contains details that are fictional, but, in a more significant way, her claims are true to a larger reality, true to the strength of her conviction, and above all true to the passionate and righteous anger brought on by those who had, however unknowingly, wronged her.

Emma's explanation of the murder arises out of a situation fraught with ironies. Emma does achieve her purpose of liquidating Loewenthal, but, when she actually shoots him, her act of violence takes on a meaning totally different from that which she had had in mind. What was first conceived as a vendetta for her father turns quite unexpectedly into a vindication of herself, her revenge against the sailor, and more. Hence, although Emma does avenge her father on the face of it, at the moment of execution the issue of filial vengeance has dwindled in importance. Similarly, Emma plots her crime in such a way as not to be found out and succeeds to a degree beyond reckoning. . . . Emma escapes censure and prison because of an unforeseen emotion—her fury at having been used and victimized by a man (albeit not the same one); this feeling gives her added energy and heightened powers of persuasion. . . . (pp. 183-84)

This remarkable little narrative stands out because of its special differences from the rest of Borges's oeuvre. **"Emma Zunz"** is the only major Borges story in which the chief character is a factory employee and, more important, a woman. Owing perhaps to this central circumstance, the piece conveys a sense of everyday life too often missing in Borges. . . .

In addition, **"Emma Zunz"** is one of the few great Borges stories in which the decisive factor is not an abstraction, not a bookish or mental pattern, but the forces of sheer passion, albeit passion slightly twisted. This is a story that, to an astounding degree, peers into the depths of a simple human heart. On one hand, we are witness to Emma's fear of the male sex, a condition attributable to anything from psychological damage or frigidity to immaturity or mere shyness.

Borges, however, is concerned not with etiology but with the manifestations and consequences of this young woman's disorder. . . . (p. 185)

In spite of Borges's own confessed dislike for psychological art and science, **"Emma Zunz"** focusses with a rare intensity, a rich sympathy and authenticity, upon the psychologies of loss, unformed sexuality, and resentment—all in the space of some eight pages.

Two things in particular help make **"Emma Zunz"** a uniquely powerful story: its density of urban images, feelings, and atmosphere, and its varying shades of darkness. Emma's childhood remembrances excepted, the narrative is filled with people, places, objects, and activities that are typically urban. . . . More important than this cityscape, however, is its relationship to the orphaned protagonist, a late adolescent who is alienated in some degree from her surroundings. (p. 186)

Throughout **"Emma Zunz"** there prevails a sombre feeling of night, a look of blacks and greys. The story covers three calendar days, with the overwhelming bulk of the action occurring at or after sundown. (p. 187)

Paradoxically, despite the gloom and darkness pervading **"Emma Zunz,"** it is considerably more optimistic a piece than are most of Borges's writings. Unlike other Borges thrillers, the protagonist here is less an unwitting pawn of circumstances than a thinking being who creates her own circumstances, painful and sordid though these may be. If Emma in the end is driven by emotion, it is at least her own emotion and not that of others. Moreover, she succeeds in her enterprise, even though (as often occurs in real life) its realization works out rather differently from what was first planned. As if this were not enough, Emma persuades others of the rightness of her act by the sheer force of her personal conviction. . . . (pp. 187-88)

Borges's characters are usually depicted as tossed about and deceived by outside forces. In **"Emma Zunz,"** by contrast, a person can choose a course of action, and the difficulties that present themselves may even fuel one's will to take action. It might be additionally noted here that **"Emma Zunz,"** besides being a superb instance of the psychological thriller, has the makings as well of a classic women's story. Despite Borges's own problems with the opposite sex, he manages to write with great empathy, without a hint of condescension, about the inner plight of a shy and sexually troubled young woman and about her ingenious vendetta as well. **"Emma Zunz"** is a story in which a woman triumphs, as does the justice that its female protagonist creates.

On the other hand, the remaining three stories that deal with criminal violence (**"The Intruder," "The Man on the Threshold," "Deutsches Requiem"**) are the least satisfactory of all the pieces gathered in *El Aleph.* It seems almost inconceivable that the same man who created **"Emma Zunz"** could also have written **"The Intruder,"** a disturbing yarn of jealousy and frontier violence that implicitly celebrates a male companionship strengthened by misogyny. There it is, however, with its roustabout protagonists, two Nielsen brothers who are always together as teamsters, gamblers, rustlers, cop-killers, brothel-frequenters, and drunkards. Their intimate bond is threatened when Cristián, the elder of the two, brings home an attractive woman named Juliana Burgos. (p. 188)

"The Intruder" contains no mental fancies, no magic, and no significant formal novelties; its direct and simple prose exhibits no apparent ironies, ambiguities, or artfully placed rhetoric. This is perhaps Borges's only foray into the psychology of adult interpersonal relationships and their attendant emotions. Love and jealousy, family, and the precarious ties of friendship are themes notably absent from Borges's tales. In this story, however, he touches upon such matters as suppressed love changing to anger or third-party jealousy and the subjective struggle against it—glimpses of a realm not customarily found in Borges. The tie stressed here, of course, is of a rather archaic sort, the macho bonds between men in the wilderness. . . . Alas, Borges's sketchy presentation of his materials does not allow for an adequate development of the subject. The two brothers are virtually indistinguishable except by obvious tags such as names and relative age and by the admittedly ingenious device of having only the elder of the two ever speak.

Worse still, Juliana Burgos comes across as little more than a vague shadow. Her presence is created only by Borges's brief first introduction and later by the indirect medium of the Nielsens's behavior. Otherwise she remains an invisible abstraction throughout, without emotions, reactions, changes, or traits of her own. Because of this serious lacuna, one finds no psychological enlightenment as to why the Nielsens should have taken any real interest in this particular woman, let alone fall in love with her. On Juliana's own side, we find not the slightest hint of why she accepts such brutal treatment. As a result, she never comes to life, be it as repressed rebel, beguiled lover, willing slave, or some combination of these. . . . One is forced to conclude that **"The Intruder,"** in spite of its careful understatement, suspenseful buildup, and polished prose, is a rather shallow story.

It goes without saying that the story's gratuitous violence against a female can only strike negative chords at this moment in history. . . . Oddly enough, Borges consistently singles out **"The Intruder"** as one of his two or three best pieces. One wonders why; but Borges's critical judgments of his own writing and that of others are notoriously questionable.

Still less convincing is **"The Man on the Threshold,"** a "Kiplingesque" tale of exotic violence. Set in colonial India, the plot centers around the mysterious kidnapping of a hated British judge named Glencairn. Charged with the task of finding Glencairn, the narrator (one Dewey) combs the unnamed city in vain, asks countless natives about Glencairn, and, to his anger and dismay, gets nothing but false answers. . . . [Following a large crowd into a particular house, Dewey] finds a naked man holding a bloody sword, and sees Glencairn's bloody corpse in the back.

"The Man on the Threshold" is a more clever story than **"The Intruder."** Some passages have a lively immediacy, in particular Dewey's feverish account of his innumerable interrogations and false leads. At the same time, the idea of the colonial government assigning as investigator an unaccompanied Englishman (instead of a group of native informers) rings a trifle inauthentic. . . . A key problem here is one we saw in connection with **"The Intruder,"** that of insufficiently profiled characters. Dewey is colorless and unmemorable. . . . A closely related difficulty is that, of all the stories found in *Ficciones* and *El Aleph,* only **"The Man on the Threshold"** attempts to draw a specific and recent Oriental locality instead of inventing a fictional Eastern realm. Not surprisingly, the exotic mise-en-scène never comes to life because, in contrast to the situation in **"Averroës's Search,"** the

local color in **"The Man on the Threshold"** is set up unquestioningly, with no hint of irony. . . . **"The Man on the Threshold"** would undoubtedly have come off somewhat better had Borges set the action in a Buenos Aires slum.

"Deutsches Requiem" is a great deal more complex and ambitious, but these traits only succeed, as we shall see, in making the story that much more flawed. The resonantly named narrator, Otto Dietrich zur Linde, first introduces himself by listing his distinguished military ancestors. Pleading guilty in an unspecified war crimes trial to charges of torture and murder, zur Linde feels no remorse and seeks no pardon; rather, he hopes his own statement will help to elucidate the nightmarish history of Germany. . . . [In] 1941, Otto zur Linde was assigned to head a concentration camp at Tarnowitz, Poland. From that vantage point of power, he made every effort to avoid committing the capital "crime of mercy." He almost succumbed to this unthinkable sin when one David Jerusalem was added to his roster of prisoners. Jerusalem was a purportedly renowned poet whose Whitmanesque verses celebrated human existence so much that Otto zur Linde was nearly moved by him. Eventually, due to zur Linde's exertions, the poet went mad and killed himself. The accused now explains this sordid incident; it was motivated not out of racism but out of a personal need to destroy his own sense of compassion, "a detested area of my soul." Formerly jubilant at the victories of the Nazi Reich, the defeat of his homeland arouses in zur Linde a like exultation. Beyond the hell-fire of the war just finished, he perceives a hidden continuity; for, as long as there is violence (even Allied violence against Germany), as long as everyone rejects "servile Christian timidity," there is satisfaction in Otto zur Linde's heart.

"Deutsches Requiem" is Borges's only extended attempt at "political fiction." Strictly speaking, however, the narrative deals not with Nazi politics as such but with a species of intellect and personality, a cultural type. This limited focus is of a piece with Borges's own political strengths and weaknesses, for though he consistently opposed nazism and its local Argentine offshoots, he never demonstrated the slightest historical understanding of how a collective phenomenon such as the Third Reich can arise. . . . **"Deutsches Requiem"** suffers from a . . . lopsided quality

The protagonist of **"Deutsches Requiem"** suggests that his life and testimony could shed light on German history. Borges's avowed aim with zur Linde, then, resembles that of Thomas Mann with his composer Adrian Leverkühn in *Doktor Faustus;* in both works one man embodies those aspects of German culture and character which may have led to nazism. (pp. 188-92)

Otto zur Linde's own mental portrait is sketched out via his artistic and literary preferences. In his early youth he liked Brahms, Shakespeare, and Shopenhauer but later he fell under the spell of Nietzsche and Spengler. These tastes are in keeping with a well-known paradox: that, in addition to the military realm, German culture has distinguished itself above all in two of the most otherworldly activities—metaphysics and music. . . . Though Schopenhauer belongs to that long tradition of German idealist philosophers, he stands out because he has a completely pessimistic outlook about the worth of any social reform, an attitude with underlying fascist implications. More important, Schopenhauer's antirational and antidemocratic ideas were to exert a prime influence on Nietzsche, a thinker notorious for his consistent idealization of aristocratic warrior races, his contempt toward ordinary human beings, and of course his status as semiofficial philosopher for the Nazi regime. Nietzsche was the most eloquent modern spokesman for warlike values and ruthlessness. . . . (pp. 192-93)

These twin materials, the German militarist past and the prowar, antidemocratic, apocalyptic strain in German philosophy, are presented as key elements in the making of nazism. Unfortunately, as an accounting for the rise of Nazi power, such tags as "German militarism" and "Nietzsche" are rather conventional explanations, ready-made formulas one encounters in casual streetcorner talk about the whys and wherefores of German fascism. Static clichés, they convey no specific sense of the historical development of German society. As such, they leave vast areas of experience unresolved—for example, why England and France, with militarist and reactionary traditions of their own, did not succumb to native fascisms. Similarly, to link so directly the ascendancy of nazism with the writings of Nietzsche and Spengler is to attribute to books a disproportionate role in bringing about political events. Despite its artful literary trappings, **"Deutsches Requiem"** treads a much-beaten path.

The one notable strong point of **"Deutsches Requiem"** is its highlighting of certain notorious Nazi traits: namely, the rejection of mercy (even mercy that is politically useful), the unquestioning submission to higher authority, and a dizzy taste for apocalypse and hyperbole. . . . [Zur Linde] expresses "faith in the sword" and hopes that what is to reign will be "violence, not servile Christian timidity." The thinking here closely parallels that "spiritualizing and intensifying of *cruelty*" extolled by Nietzsche as the necessary alternative to Christian meekness and nonviolence. Otto zur Linde, neither a killer by nature nor insane, is actually the dutiful follower of a principle, "an ethic of infamy," as Borges called it in an interview. Neither cynical nor corrupt, zur Linde is presented as a very special sort of individual, "a saint who is unpleasant and stupid." He is the devout believer of a quasi-religious creed that hails cruelty as its prime virtue.

None of this intellectual scaffolding appears ample or adequate enough for the vast and recent subject taken on by Borges. The stark historical reality looms far too large behind Borges's cerebrations. To present Nazi cruelty by way of mental conceits and Nietzschean phraseology is simply to put us at too great a distance from the physical, moral horror of the real-life events. Nazism is dealt with on the same plane as a metaphysical problem, which it obviously is not. In the same way, Borges resorts to his familiar apparatus of scholarly footnotes; he mixes authentic and invented literary allusions and mingles historical references with phony ones. Although this technique is a reliable and fruitful resource for his fantastical fables, in this story it seems woefully inappropriate to the sheer enormity of the topic. The net result is an ostensibly political narrative that is bookish and abstract, even precious; it is almost a scholar's remote appreciation of nazism but without the factual utility of ordinary scholarship. The Nietzschean snippets in particular seem a formal contrivance, a mental construction deliberately brought in to give shape to Otto's ravings. (pp. 193-95)

Throughout **"Deutsches Requiem,"** therefore, Borges applies ready-made outside schemes that cannot cope with the inordinate monstrosity under examination. One of these outside schemes happens to be nothing less than the author's own temperament and background. . . . The narrative result is a troublesome confusion of voices. One virtually *hears* Borges

reciting his life and loves to an interviewer, autobiographical tidbits that sadly interfere with his portrait of a Nazi and rob it of autonomy and objectivity. Some of these personal congruences are disquietingly intimate: an ancestor of zur Linde's led a decisive cavalry charge, as did a great-grandfather of Borges's; Brahms is included among Otto's favorites for no apparent reason other than the fact that Brahms is about the only classical composer Borges actually knows. Otto zur Linde therefore comes across not only as an intellectual mouthpiece for Nietzschean slogans but also as a very close replica of Borges's personality and preferences. He is a dim shadow of his literary progenitor. These procedures (the grafting of the author's own traits and interests onto an unsympathetic character and the excess philosophical baggage brought to bear upon an experience that is fundamentally sociopolitical in nature) make **"Deutsches Requiem"** one of Borges's least satisfying narrative creations. Although trick stories like **"The Shape of the Sword"** can be read as animated if flawed trifles, the weightiness and solemnity of **"Deutsches Requiem"** render the piece not only off-target intellectually but artistically static and opaque as well.

The most complex and ingenious of all of Borges's tales of violence is also one of the best stories in the book—**"The Other Death,"** a magic thriller set in Argentina and Uruguay in 1946. Its narrator (named "Borges") reads in a letter from his friend Patricio Gannon that Don Pedro Damián, after having relived in a final delirium the bloody battle of Masoller, has just died. A volunteer in the gaucho army during the 1904 Uruguayan uprising, Damián returned afterwards to his sheepshearing job in northern Argentina and lived a quiet forty years; that brief war was his one special moment. "Borges," who met Damián briefly in 1942 and found him taciturn and dull, now seeks data on Masoller and obtains from Emir Rodríguez Monegal a letter of introduction to Dionisio Tabares, a colonel in that battle. The Colonel feverishly narrates the bloody events but, to "Borges's" surprise, remembers Damián as a braggart who lost his nerve at the high point of combat. . . . Some months later, "Borges" returns to Montevideo for additional details from the Colonel, in whose company he finds a Dr. Amaro, another Masoller veteran. When "Borges" bitterly recalls Damián as the half-breed who cowered before the bullets, both men stare at him in perplexity: the Colonel is unable to remember Damián, and the Doctor asserts that the boy actually died a heroic death, heading a battle charge. . . . Later, when "Borges" heads north to make on-the-spot inquiries, Damián's ranch has vanished, none of the villagers recognizes the name, and one Abaroa, who witnessed Damián's death, just recently breathed his last. As if this did not suffice, a photograph of the man "Borges" thought was Damián turns out to be that of an Italian tenor.

A bewildered "Borges" now plays with three conjectures: (1) that there are two Pedro Damiáns (a hypothesis that still fails to explain the colonel's triply varied responses), (2) a speculation, ventured by one of "Borges's" female friends, that Damián may have returned as a ghost, and (3) "Borges's" own grand leap that starts from the assumption of Damián's original cowardice and survival. This last fact was so shameful to the young man, however, that he thereafter set out to strengthen his resolve in preparation for the moment when he could once again prove his courage. And the time did come (in the form of a last-minute hallucination in Damián's head) during which the battle of Masoller repeated itself in all its destructive glory and Don Pedro Damián went back in history to die a hero's death. (pp. 195-96)

This remarkable piece depicts the classically "Borgesian" type of action—the irruption of fantastic, miraculous, or otherwise unreal elements into the ordinary, everyday world of reality. The fantastical source here is not an encyclopedia but a dream, a wishful delirium that imposes itself upon the world and, in the process, modifies the sense of the past hitherto held by all concerned. The story takes as its intellectual point of departure a theological question as to whether God's powers include the capacity to undo and remake past events. Ever since the time of Thomas Aquinas, it has been the standard church line to negate this possibility. . . . But a celebrated eleventh-century churchman named Pietro Damiani (St. Peter Damian in English), known mostly for his monastic reforms, did toy with this notion in his minor treatise *De omnipotentia.* Borges's **"The Other Death,"** however, shows the feat being performed not by God (at least not seemingly so) but by agency of the powerful imagination of a determined, courageous individual. Moreover, the material *events* of forty years ago are not erased or altered, much less the entire ensuing historical fabric, but the *memory* of these slight events and the *idea* of Damián entertained by other people are obliterated, as well as a few vestigial items (a picture, a ranch, a friend) associated with him, these last two being virtually exorcised out of existence. In short, what changes is the private and public identity of Damián, who evolves from a surviving onetime coward to a hero dying young; who, in the eleventh-hour act of the will, wipes clean his cowardly past; who, in so doing, transforms what little remaining historical record there is of that past.

The turn-of-the-century world within which Pedro Damián's dream operates, one might emphasize, is a concretely real if distant one. The political context of his personal adventures happens to have been one of the major crises in Uruguayan history. When the renowned reformist José Batllé y Ordóñez was elected to the presidency in 1903, a gaucho nationalist uprising broke out, led by the flamboyant military-political caudillo of the Blanco party, Aparicio Saravia. Most of the year 1904 was taken up by a bloody civil war, with fierce battles at Illescas, Tupambaé, and Masoller. . . . [Masoller] is a major event, as awesome to Uruguayans and Argentinians as the battle of Gettysburg was to North Americans. Even more important, the revolution of 1904 was the last time the rural gauchos, with their traditional values of manly courage and *machismo,* acted as a major political force in the River Plate region. The defeat at Masoller is thus a milestone, a moment of special historical significance to antigaucho liberals like Borges; it signals the end of one era and the beginning of a very different one. (pp. 197-98)

The history in **"The Other Death,"** then, is a very real if remote entity; to mid-twentieth-century inhabitants of the Plate region it is a vivid remembrance of other worlds past. The geographic setting here is comparably real but of a special sort, an alternative kind. The action takes place chiefly in Uruguay (to Argentinians, I should reiterate, a more primitive country). Much of it occurs not in Montevideo but far off in the rural backlands, almost at the border of Brazil. . . . Similarly, in a procedure familiar from **"Tlön, Uqbar, Orbis Tertius,"** Borges peoples his fantastical text with real-life individuals. Patricio Gannon, who first informs "Borges" of Pedro Damián, is an occasional writer, scion of a rich Anglo-Argentine ranching family in Entre Ríos. At the time of Bor-

ges's writing **"The Other Death,"** Emir Rodríguez Monegal was a promising young man of Uruguayan letters; today he is a leading critic of Latin American literature, a Yale University professor, and author of the official biography of Borges. The aristocratic-sounding "Ülrike von Kühlmann" is a fanciful pseudonym coined by the author for an unidentified upper-class Argentine lady quite close to him, one of Borges's numerous platonic friendships with the female sex. The narrative also mentions a photograph of Enrico Tamberlik (1820-89), a famed Italian tenor who spent much of his life in Madrid and was particularly renowned for his high notes.

The plot of **"The Other Death"** develops around an intellectual contradiction and moves from a well-established axiom to its unsettling logical opposite. It starts with Emerson's poem "The Past," which emphatically asserts time's irreversible nature, and ends with Pier Damiani's stray notion that God can undo what has passed. . . . The concept of the inviolate past is commonsense wisdom, orthodox philosophy, even basic science. The poem, immediately associated with Gannon's first report of Damián's recent death, thus stands there as something that is about to be refuted, neutralized, canceled out, challenged by events. As is therefore appropriate, when Gannon unknowingly feels the effects of the other death . . . and forgets about the old soldier, his former interest in Emerson's unshakable past equally eludes him. As the narrative proceeds to demonstrate the possible truth in Pier Damiani's speculation, the ironclad, absolute statements of Emerson's poem recede from Gannon's as well as from the reader's memory. Even as triumph in battle belongs to Pedro Damián, so does the triumph of an idea redound to Pier Damiani.

"The Other Death," permeated by a factual reality that it later partly negates, works precisely by a dialectical interplay between two opposition forces: real, objectively known history versus Damián's elusively subjective history; real-life palpable individuals versus the slippery identity of one man; frozen past versus changeable past (or the memory thereof); Emerson versus Damian. In addition to all this, Borges himself intrudes in the penultimate paragraph and compounds the confusion by casting doubt on the dependability of what we have just read. As he confronts the curious fact that only he and "Ülrike von Kühlmann" seem aware of the mysterious upsets going on in the world about them, he inevitably wonders if his own imagination might have invented some of it, if the old gaucho really was called Pedro Damián, if the name was perhaps unconsciously prompted by his reading of Pier Damiani, or for that matter if Pedro Damián ever existed at all. . . . The result of such juggling and mental mystification (dazzling artistry and delicious humor aside) is that it softens the effect of the actions depicted and counteracts the sheer farfetchedness of the ideas set forth. Obviously, a dying man's delirium could never erase public memories of his past nor cause relevant physical objects to disappear, though the possibility of such extraordinary powers is interesting to contemplate. Borges, however, preempts readers' resistance and incredulity by stating that, actually, some or much or even all of **"The Other Death"** may be false.

In addition to these lighthearted mystifications played in public, Borges's narrative contains a subtle but significant revision of historical reality in the photograph of Tamberlik, who is portrayed "in the part of Otello"; this photograph is an impossibility, inasmuch as Tamberlik had retired from the stage in 1878, while the world premiere of Verdi's *Otello* took place in 1887, a scant two years before Tamberlik's own death. This concealed contradiction, however minor, reproduces in miniature the ambiguities of Damián's own career; a portrait of Tamberlik in a concocted situation furnishes yet another instance of possibilities not fully actualized, of "what-might-have-been" in history. (pp. 198-200)

[One] of the themes implicitly dealt with in **"The Other Death"** is the thorny problem of what elements can constitute a man's final and definitive biography. In 1904, Pedro Damián acted like a coward; in the forty-odd years that followed, however, he lived poised for his moment of heroism. Had Damián been granted a second opportunity for combat, he would have fought bravely and perhaps died a hero's death. The fact that the occasion presented itself only in dreams does not vitiate Damián's potential for courage, though there does remain the dilemma of the "real" past versus his merely possible present. One might venture to say that Borges's story reverses the well-known "Sartrean" idea by suggesting that an individual's life can be judged as the sum total of his *potential* acts, which could even cancel out what he had previously and palpably done. In dreams begin our personal identities.

"The Other Death" is many things at once. On one level, it is a playful parable on the nature of the past or on how individuals look upon the past. For although it is true that events of the past remain unmovable, nonetheless the knowledge and interpretation thereof can vary widely according to individual, group, and epoch; indeed, events can be altered or suppressed if someone possesses such power and has a stake in doing so. . . . [The story] shows how forces such as subjective desires, dreams, and inner strengths might erase the memory of one's own cowardice. Finally, it must be noted that, philosophical dalliances aside, **"The Other Death"** is a most amusing story because of the pranks it plays on the objective world and above all those it plays on Borges's fictional self. Especially entertaining are the two successive scenes in which Colonel Tabares topples the narrator's preconceptions about Pedro Damián's moral fiber. There is a vivid immediacy to these dialogues, a colloquial, conversational, almost auditory quality to the language employed. All these elements—the philosophical-parable overtones, the identity theme, the use of fantasy, the evasive formal trickery, and the humor—combine to form a story that stands unmistakably among Borges's five or six richest. (p. 201)

Gene H. Bell-Villada, in his Borges and His Fiction: A Guide to His Mind and Art, *University of North Carolina Press, 1981, 292 p.*

FURTHER READING

Alazraki, Jaime. *Jorge Luis Borges.* New York: Columbia University Press, 1971, 48 p.
    Contends that Borges's fiction is based upon a confrontation between opposites that challenges the reader to transcend conventional notions of reality.

Ayora, Jorge. "Gnosticism and Time in 'El inmortal.'" *Hispania* 56, No. 3 (September 1973): 593-96.
    Discusses Borges's affinity with the early Christian cult of Gnosticism, centering upon his short story "The Immortal."

Bagby, Albert I., II. "The Concept of Time of Jorge Luis Borges." *Romance Notes* VI, No. 2 (Spring 1965): 99-105.
    Asserts that Borges posits time as an intellectual projection of our subconscious that allows only for the eternal present.

Barili, Amelia. "Borges on Life and Death." *New York Times Book Review* (13 July 1986): 1, 27-9.
    Interview with Borges conducted just prior to his death in which he discusses the philosophical aspects of his fiction.

Botsford, Kenneth. "The Writings of Jorge Luis Borges." *The Atlantic Monthly* 219, No. 1 (January 1967): 99-104.
    Critical overview of biographical and philosophical aspects of Borges's work.

Carter, E. D., Jr. "Women in the Short Stories of Jorge Luis Borges." *Pacific Coast Philology* XIV (October 1969): 13-19.
    Relates the minor role of women in Borges's short stories to the author's changing attitude toward sexuality.

di Giovanni, Norman Thomas. "'Streetcorner Man' Revisited." *Western Humanities Review* XXVI, No. 3 (Summer 1972): 213-18.
    Borges's translator and collaborator recounts the process by which he and Borges translated the author's short story "Hombre de la esquina rosa" into English.

Dyson, A. E. "'You, fictional reader . . .': Jorge Luis Borges." *Critical Quarterly* 21, No. 4 (Winter 1979): 5-27.
    Contends that Borges's fiction demonstrates the superiority of provocative images over abstract philosophical concepts without raising moral or psychological issues.

Enguidamos, Miguel. "Imagination and Escape in the Short Stories of Jorge Luis Borges." Translated by Mildred Boyer. *The Texas Quarterly* IV, No. 4 (Winter 1961): 118-27.
    Examines Borges's skepticism toward such concepts as individuality and the existence of God.

Gass, William H. "Imaginary Borges and His Books." In his *Fiction and the Figures of Life,* pp. 120-33. New York: Alfred A. Knopf, 1970.
    Analyzes Borges's relationship to such literary figures as Dante, G. K. Chesterton, and Oscar Wilde.

Gillespie, Robert. "Detection: Borges and Father Brown." *Novel* 7, No. 3 (Spring 1974): 220-30.
    Compares Borges's examination of evil and the supernatural to that of G. K. Chesterton.

Isaacs, Neil D. "The Labyrinth of Art in Four 'Ficciones' of Jorge Luis Borges." *Studies in Short Fiction* VI, No. 4 (Summer 1969): 383-94.
    Reviews Borges's symbolic use of the labyrinth in such stories as "The Babylonian Lottery," "The Library of Babel," "Tlön, Uqbar, Orbis Tertius," and "The Garden of the Forking Paths."

Johnston, Martin. "Games with Infinity." In *Cunning Exiles: Studies in Modern Prose Writers,* edited by Don Anderson and Stephen Knight, pp. 36-61. Sydney: Angus and Robertson, 1974.
    Discussion of Borges's philosophical perceptions and his use of such symbols as the labyrinth, library, book, and knife.

Lorich, Bruce. "Borges's Puzzle of Paradoxes." *Southwest Review* LVIII, No. 1 (Winter 1973): 53-65.
    Uses Borges's short story "The South" and other pieces to demonstrate his subversion of conventional reality.

Maurois, André. Introduction to *Labyrinths,* by Jorge Luis Borges, pp. ix-xiv. New York: New Directions, 1962.
    Traces Borges's European literary heritage.

Modern Fiction Studies 19, No. 3 (Autumn 1973).
    Special issue devoted to Borges with essays by David William Foster, Emir Rodríguez Monegal, Robert Lima, and others.

Murillo, L. A. "The Labyrinths of Jorge Luis Borges: An Introductory to the Stories of *The Aleph*." *Modern Language Quarterly* 20, No. 3 (September 1959): 259-66.
Contends that the labyrinths in Borges's short fiction collection *The Aleph* symbolize humanity's fears and frustrations when confronted with a chaotic universe.

Natella, Arthur A. "Symbolic Color in the Stories of Jorge Luis Borges." *Journal of Spanish Studies: Twentieth Century* 2, No. 1 (Spring 1974): 39-48.
Studies Borges's symbolic use of the colors gray, red, and yellow in his conception of the universe.

O'Mara, Richard. "Literature's Mozart." *The Virginia Quarterly Review* 54, No. 3 (Summer 1978): 552-59.
Laudatory review of Borges's short fiction collection *The Book of Sand*.

Ortega, Julio. "Borges and the Latin-American Text." In his *Poetics of Change: The New Spanish American Text,* translated by Galen D. Greaser and Julio Ortega, pp. 20-32. Austin: University of Texas Press, 1984.
Critical discussion refuting the assumption that Borges's work does not evoke the cultural realities of Latin America.

Paz, Octavio. "In Time's Labyrinth." Translated by Charles Lane. *The New Republic* 195, No. 18 (3 November 1986): 30-4.
Combines personal reminiscences and an analysis of Borges's literary aesthetic.

Pritchett, V. S. "Medallions." In his *The Mythmakers: Literary Essays,* pp. 174-84. New York: Random House, 1979.
Uses the stories in Borges's short fiction collection *The Aleph* to examine the author's mythical constructs.

———. "Borges." *The New Yorker* LVII, No. 14 (25 May 1981): 137-40.
Favorable review of Borges's detective stories written in collaboration with Bioy Casares under the pseudonym of H. Bustos Domecq and collected in *Six Problems for Don Isidro Parodi*.

Rodríguez Monegal, Emir. *Jorge Luis Borges: A Literary Biography.* New York: E. P. Dutton, 1978, 502 p.
Detailed biography.

Stabb, Martin S. *Jorge Luis Borges.* New York: Twayne Publishers, 1970, 171 p.
Biographical and critical survey of Borges's career.

Stark, John O. *The Literature of Exhaustion: Borges, Nabokov, and Barth. Durham: Duke University Press, 1974, 196 p.*
Considers Borges's work to be representative of the principles expounded in his essay "The Literature of Exhaustion," which asserts that all literary possibilities have been already explored and utilized.

Sturrock, John. *Paper Tigers: The Ideal Fictions of Jorge Luis Borges.* Oxford: Clarendon Press, 1977, 227 p.
Favorable analysis of Borges's short stories.

Tri-Quarterly 25 (Fall 1972).
Special issue devoted to Borges with essays by Adolfo Bioy Casares, Jaime Alazraki, Carter Wheelock, and others. In addition, this collection features an anthology of Borges's work and an interview with Norah Borges, the author's sister.

Wheelock, Carter. *The Mythmaker.* Austin: University of Texas Press, 1969, 190 p.
Discusses Borges's use of myth, through which he attempts to transcend the gulf between human perception and reality.

———. "The Subversive Borges." *The Texas Quarterly* XVIII, No. 1 (Spring 1975): 117-25.
Asserts that Borges's subversion of reality in his fiction demands a personal courage that transcends religious or philosophical dogmas.

Whiston, T. "An 'Irish' Story of Jorge Luis Borges: 'Tema del triador y del héroe.' " *Hermathena,* No. 114-CXIV (Winter 1972): 23-8.
Explication of Borges's story "The Theme of the Traitor and the Hero," centering upon the fallibility of history and the redeeming nature of art.

George Washington Cable

1844-1925

(Also wrote under the pseudonyms Drop Shot and Felix Lazarus) American short story writer, novelist, essayist, journalist, and historian.

An important writer of his generation, Cable is regarded as a major catalyst in the development of modern Southern fiction through his accurate portrayal of post-Civil War Southern society and honest treatment of complex racial issues. In his novels and short fiction, Cable eschewed the style and themes of traditional antebellum literature, focusing instead on the social and moral milieu of the Creole people, descendants of the French and Spanish colonists of Louisiana who settled predominately in and around New Orleans. While critics contend that Cable's works often suffer from sentimental plots and melodramatic endings, his authentic renditions of Creole dialect earned him distinction. Carl Halliday asserted: "[Cable] opened an absolutely new field in the world's literature. The novelty alone would have given him some notoriety. But only the hand of a real artist could have compelled an abiding interest in these remote and up to his time little-heard-of people. To him belongs largely the honor of having preserved the history, traditions, and customs of a fast-vanishing form of civilization."

Cable was born in New Orleans to wealthy and influential parents. His father was a major supplier of goods for settlements along the Mississippi River, and his mother was an austere Calvinist who instilled her religious beliefs in her children. In 1859 Cable's father died, following a series of financial misfortunes that decimated his business empire, and Cable went to work as an apprentice bookkeeper to help support his family. In 1863 Cable enlisted in the Confederate Army as a cavalry soldier, and after the war he returned to his job as a bookkeeper and began contributing articles and sketches under the pseudonym Drop Shot for the *New Orleans Picayune*. He was released from the paper in 1871, however, when he refused to write theatre reviews because attending the theatre offended his religious convictions. Cable was later rehired by the *Picayune* when the paper came under new ownership, and in 1873 he received an opportunity to publish his fiction in a national magazine through Edmund King, an editor at *Scribner's Monthly* who was touring the South in search of new literary talent. Impressed with the local-color pieces Cable wrote for the *Picayune*, King arranged for Cable's story " 'Sieur George" to be published in the October, 1873, issue of *Scribner's*. Considered one of Cable's best short works, particularly for his subtle and evocative use of setting, atmosphere, and tone, this piece revolves around a destitute gambler who agrees to raise the daughter of his best friend as his niece, only to involve the girl in his degenerate obsession with the lottery. Philip Butcher described " 'Sieur George" as a "masterpiece of local color," and many critics have stated that this story contains elements that became distinguishing characteristics in much of Cable's subsequent fiction.

Cable's first collection of stories, *Old Creole Days,* was published in 1879. Incorporating " 'Sieur George" and six other pieces previously published in *Scribner's Monthly,* this vol-

ume demonstrates Cable's mastery of local color and dialect. While these tales offer quaint depictions of romance, honor, and chivalry among the Creole population of antebellum New Orleans, they also contain subtle condemnations of slavery, the disfranchisement of freed blacks, and the plight of the quadroon and octoroon castes. "Belles Demoiselles Plantation" focuses upon Colonel DeCharleu, a Creole aristocrat, and his unscrupulous attempts to trade his ancestral land and mansion, which are threatened by erosion, for a townhouse owned by his half-breed cousin Injin Charlie. DeCharleu successfully negotiates the transaction but is overcome by guilt and confesses his true intentions just as the mansion crashes into the Mississippi River, killing DeCharleu's seven daughters. *Madame Delphine,* a novella published separately in 1879 and incorporated in later editions of *Old Creole Days,* explores the dichotomous existence of the quadroon and octoroon castes. Legally considered neither black nor white yet subjected to similar restrictions as blacks, these individuals are portrayed by Cable as victims of sexual exploitation and symbolic reminders of ancestral sin.

Cable earned substantial critical praise for *Old Creole Days,* especially in the North, where exotic and romantic tales set in the antebellum South were extremely popular. His depictions of Creole society, however, caused much resentment among southern critics and established Creole families who felt that Cable had misrepresented them, and his examination of miscegenation provoked hostility among the Creole elite. Many also took issue with Cable's handling of dialogue between his Creole characters; the mixture of standard English, African-American patois, and French-American dialect in his stories was considered deprecating. Perhaps Cable's most serious trangression, however, was his sympathetic portrayals of octoroons, quadroons, and blacks. Edmund Wilson observed: "George Cable was the first Southern writer to try to deal in a serious work of fiction with the peculiar relationships created by the mixture of white and Negro blood; and it was not to be till fifty years later, when William Faulkner wrote *Go Down, Moses, Absalom, Absalom!* and *Intruder in the Dust,* that a Southerner who had lived with these situations would have the courage to treat them in fiction again."

Cable attempted to appease the Creoles by publishing *The Creoles of Louisiana* in 1884, a historical overview highlighting their influence on Louisiana culture and politics. This concilatory gesture proved to be unsuccessful, and, fearing for his family's safety, Cable moved to Northampton, Massachusetts, the following year. Yet he continued to write about the South in his fiction. *Bonaventure: A Prose Pastoral of Acàdian Louisiana* is a trilogy of stories centering on the tribulations of a Creole teacher who was raised among the Acadians, descendants of French Catholic settlers who were expelled from Nova Scotia by the British in the mid-1700s. Cable's subsequent collection of short fiction, *Strange True Stories of Louisiana,* which originally appeared as a continuing series of individual episodes in *Century Magazine,* is essentially the fictionalization of actual incidents in Louisiana history. Cable explained in the book's introduction that he had translated and edited old manuscripts, archives, and journalistic accounts of colonial settlements which, over time, became local legends in New Orleans. "Salome Müller, the White Slave," for example, is based on an 1844 Louisiana Supreme Court decision that decreed Müller, the daughter of German immigrants who was erroneously classified as a mulatto and sold into slavery, was white. Another tale, "The 'Haunted House' in Royal Street," derives from a 1834 scandal in which Madame Lalaurie, a prominent Creole matron, was suspected of torturing her slaves. When her sadistic proclivities were exposed, Madame Lalaurie fled to France and her home was turned into an integrated school for girls. Years later, during Reconstruction, an angry mob stormed the school and expelled all pupils who were of mixed racial ancestry.

After resettling in the North, Cable's literary career began to deteriorate. During this period, he published several pamphlets and book-length nonfiction works that espoused civil rights for disenfranchised blacks, particularly their right to equal education, and argued against the use of convicts as forced laborers, a practice then popular in the South. While Cable earned acclaim in the North for his position on such issues, his views caused further resentment among his fellow Southerners. Some commentators have suggested that the quality of Cable's later fiction suffered immensely because of his political convictions, and the pieces in his last two short story collections, *Strong Hearts* and *The Flower of the Chapdelaines,* are generally perceived as didactic and inferior to his local-color writings of earlier years. Louis D. Rubin, Jr. observed: "[Cable] did not recognize the contradictions within his own personality—the desire for social approval in New Orleans as contrasted with the desire to protest the injustice being done to the Negro; the desire for approval by the Gen-

teel Tradition in literature as contrasted with the desire to deal with the often raw and unpleasant realities of the life around him. . . . The polarity, the ambivalence, are abundantly present in his best fiction; but to judge from his letters and his other writings, apparently it was only *as fiction,* in the concrete particularity of characters and situations, that he was ever to express them."

(For further information on Cable's life and career, see *Twentieth-Century Literary Criticism,* Vol. 4; *Contemporary Authors,* Vol. 104; and *Dictionary of Literary Biography,* Vols. 12, 74.)

PRINCIPAL WORKS

SHORT FICTION

Old Creole Days 1879
Madame Delphine 1881; also published as *Madame Delphine: A Novelette and Other Tales* 1881
Bonaventure: A Prose Pastoral of Acadian Louisiana 1888
Strange True Stories of Louisiana 1889
Strong Hearts 1899
"Posson Jone' " and Père Raphaël, with a New Word Setting Forth How and Why the Two Tales Are One 1909
The Flower of the Chapdelaines 1918
Creoles and Cajuns: Stories of Old Louisiana 1959

OTHER MAJOR WORKS

The Grandissimes: A Story of Creole Life (novel) 1880
The Creoles of Louisiana (essays) 1884
Dr. Sevier (novel) 1885
The Silent South, Together with the Freedman's Case in Equity and the Convict Lease System (essays) 1885
The Negro Question (nonfiction) 1888
The Southern Struggle for Pure Government (nonfiction) 1890
The Busy Man's Bible and How to Study and Teach It (nonfiction) 1891
A Memory of Roswell Smith, Born March 30, 1829, Died April 19, 1892 (nonfiction) 1892
John March, Southerner (novel) 1894
The Cavalier (novel) 1901
Bylow Hill (novel) 1902
Kincaid's Battery (novel) 1908
The Amateur Garden (nonfiction) 1914
Gideon's Band: A Tale of the Mississippi (novel) 1914
Lovers of Louisiana (To-Day) (nonfiction) 1918

[EDMUND GOSSE] (essay date 1881)

[*Gosse was a British critic, poet, and lecturer who was one of the most important English translators and critics of Scandinavian literature. Among his other works are studies of John Donne, Thomas Gray, Sir Thomas Browne, and important early articles on nineteenth century French literature. In the following excerpt, Gosse praises Cable's depiction of antebellum New Orleans in* Madame Delphine *and considers him to be a writer of great promise.*]

As the author of a collection called ***Old Creole Days,*** and of an interesting novel entitled *The Grandissimes,* Mr. Cable has already shown himself to be master of a new field in fiction—namely, the curious Creole and Quadroon population of the city and environs of New Orleans. In **"Madame Delphine"** he takes a series of idyllic scenes from the same unexhausted source, and delights us with pictures of a strange, old-world, timid civilization of which it is safe to say that English readers know nothing. Those who have read the *Grandissimes* must not expect to find in **"Madame Delphine"** any situation so tragically pathetic as the death of the old, indomitable African king; in his latest story Mr. Cable has given himself up to the warmth and perfume of the tropical city, to the romance rather than to the tragedy of its population, and to the pathos of its divided races. At the same time, a certain dimness of style that gave a hazy effect to some of the pages of the earlier novel gives place in **"Madame Delphine"** to a more incisive and exact manner of writing. It should be said at once that Mr. Cable writes exceedingly well, with a rich and musical prose that suits his subject; his fault as a stylist is that he introduces too incessantly a profusion of ingenious detail, and is not content to let enough simplicity divide his "purple patches" from one another. But this severity is "what Nature never gives the young," and its absence is not to be very sternly reprimanded in the present dearth of novelists who take any thought whatever about their style. . . .

In those days there existed in New Orleans a class which had sprung up between the Creoles and the negroes, and which belonged to neither. This was the free quadroon caste, a race illustrious for the extreme beauty and grace of the women, often almost absolutely white, with massive regular features, lustrous eyes and hair, and manners of the most bewitching grace and refinement. Yet, by the whim of that cruel law which forbade marriage with a white man until the ninth departure from the negro had been reached, these lovely quadroons and still lovelier octoroons were unable to form any legitimate attachments with men scarcely their equals in social standing. Out of this evil state of legislation there arose a condition of things which encouraged a universal laxity of manners, and which entailed, at the best, shame and embarrassment on the next generation. Mme. Delphine was euphemistically called the widow of an American with whom she had long lived happily in this house of perfumes and shadows; but he had been dead nearly twenty years, and she was still living on the property which, in defiance of the law, he had left her. Their one child had been brought up in the North by his mother and sisters; but, after being separated for sixteen years, the mother's heart had yearned for her daughter, and Olive was now on her way back to New Orleans to live with Mme. Delphine. (p. 237)

It would not be fair to Mr. Cable to tell the plot any further. How the hero contrives to become acquainted with Mme. Delphiné, how the unsurmountable barrier between him and Olive is honourably removed, how roughly the course of their true love runs, and what a sublime sacrifice is made at the last by poor old Mme. Delphine, for all this we must recommend the reader to the pages of the novel itself. He is not likely to put the book down until he has finished it.

We think that a novelist's quality is often best shown in his conduct of a short story. **"Madame Delphine"** is followed by three tales, which really form part of the same study of old Creole life. The first of these, **"Belles Demoiselles Plantation,"** would be more striking if the reader were not irresistibly reminded by its conclusion of Edgar Poe's "The Fall of the House of Usher." It might very well have been written

by a man who had never read the earlier story, but for readers of Poe the similarity destroys the necessary shudder of surprise. **"Madame Délicieuse,"** on the other hand, is one of Mr. Cable's perfectly original pictures of the glittering, lazy, graceful life of the Creole population in its old palmy days. But we recommend any one who is still unconvinced that in Mr. Cable we have gained a novelist with new powers and of brilliant promise to read the last story, **"Posson Jone' "**; we have every confidence in the result. For, unless we are greatly mistaken, he will recognize in the treatment of this short tale a skill in depicting riotous Southern masses of people, in full sunlight, moved by sudden passion to the exercise of whimsical and cruel revenge, combined with a sense of the gentleness and placability which make these races a paradox to Northerners, such as no writer of modern times, except Flaubert, has displayed. The destruction of the circus, and the horrible game played with the tiger and the buffalo, in this story of **"Posson Jone',"** may be recommended as certain to give the jaded reader that *frisson nouveau* of which he is so much in need. We must add a word on the dialect which Mr. Cable uses. It is new, and must be learned; but it is simple, and easy to learn. It is merely an alternation of French corrupted by English, and English directly translated from French; a soft and languid speech, invented by the easy Creole for his needs. (p. 238)

[Edmund Gosse], in a review of "Madame Delphine," in The Saturday Review, *London, Vol. 52, No. 1347, August 20, 1881, pp. 237-38.*

THE NATION, NEW YORK   (essay date 1888)

[In the following excerpt, the critic offers a positive review of Bonaventure.]

The noble simplicity of a life like Bonaventure's would be welcome from any hand. From Mr. Cable's [***Bonaventure: A Prose Pastoral of Acadian Louisiana***] it is doubly so; for, with the example of a worthy life full of sincerity, of elevation, and of sacrifice, made only the more lovely because of the unconsciousness with which it is given, one at the same time enjoys the pleasure of surrendering one's imagination to Mr. Cable's, and following the threads of his simple story, benefiting by his exquisite workmanship, his minute observation, and his artistic feeling, without a thought behind. It is a pleasure which is afforded one only too seldom in the fiction of the day. The number of writers now making novels whose work it is safe or at all possible to read with one's critical judgment left to one side, may be numbered on one hand. Even Mr. Cable has faults: refined and subtle as his humor is, to some he may seem a little over-fond of it. Though he imagines comprehensively, and observes with closeness and fidelity, it may justly be complained, nevertheless, that his imagination now and then strains a point, while at other times his faculty of observation has everything its own way. Yet, for all that, one cannot seriously find fault with the story of Bonaventure, or, rather, the cluster of stories growing out of his, and beautifully showing the breadth and power of influence which a simple, sincere, and high-minded man may wield. They are so unpretentious, so devoid of the claptrap and sensationalism which the public demands—and generally gets, one must sorrowfully admit—that a sympathetic reader is not only pleased by reading them, but also elevated and made better. This not alone because the stories are unaffected in their simplicity, and free from the taint of melodrama, of course, but because at the same time they are pervaded with a spirit of faith, a faith in the nobility of truth, however, homely, in the beauty of unselfishness, however simple.

Mr. Cable's power of seizing on the points of a character, otherwise commonplace, and conveying along with the sense of its highest attributes the homely aspects of its environment, the every-day life of an untutored, unambitious people, and never once lapsing into sentimentality or bathos, is an invaluable one, especially when it is joined with the deep respect for his art which Mr. Cable shows in every turn. It is due to two things: the belief which the writer has in the things he places highest, and in his sense of humor. The one enables him to write sincerely, the other prevents him from writing foolishly. For the rest, his charm, his interest, his freshness—they come from his materials and his workmanship, rather than from his native power and talent. But, with these qualities all combined, he gives us stories for which we can freely feel thankful.

> *A review of "Bonaventure: A Prose Pastoral of Acadian Louisiana," in* The Nation, *New York, Vol. XLVI, No. 1200, June 28, 1888, p. 529.*

THE CRITIC, NEW YORK (essay date 1890)

[*The following is excerpted from a review of* Strange True Stories of Louisiana.]

[In many cases, Mr. Cable's **Strange True Stories of Louisiana** are] not 'stories' at all, but genuine historical documents full of interest and dramatic power. Several of them are translated from the queer misspelt MSS. of old French ladies in whose hand the papers came through 'many a winding bout'; one is compiled from the judicial records of Louisiana; and another is the painful diary of a Union woman in New Orleans and Vicksburg during the war. All reveal the singular wealth of the region in materials for exciting fiction set in a pictorial background and compounded of many tints. The mixed nationalities, the romantic history, the poetical traditions, the varied and dramatic incident which weave a many-colored tapestry out of the story of Louisiana, are reproduced in these narratives with telling power. The 'Land of Evangeline' has not been described by Longfellow himself in more graphic touches than those used by the charming Creole grandmother who contributes **"The Adventures of Francoise and Suzanne"**—not so graphic, for Longfellow was drawing on his imagination while the Creole lady is a part of the scene she describes. **"The Young Aunt with the White Hair"** is too terrible for publication,—a cry from the wilderness of ancient Louisiana when the Indians were cannibals and the 'Young Aunt' herself contributed a slice of her living flesh to their feast.

In **"Salome Müller"** another horror looms up—a *cause célèbre* familiar to many people now living,—a brand plucked from the burning of slave Louisiana when white people could be sold into bondage under a system called the 'redemptioner' system. No 'Confederate' or 'Federal' can read the Union woman's diary without pitying her predicament and admiring her courage. The writer of this review was in New Orleans and near Vicksburg at the time, and can testify to the wonderful accuracy of the outline, no less than to the hardships, terror and tribulation endured by the young bride with muzzled lips and masked face. Mr. Cable graphically recounts—in rather foreign English which uses *plead* as a participle—how these MSS. came into his hands and introduces fac-similes of

them in the text. Many of them he bought, and translated, and his translations are usually idiomatic and vicacious. It was a good thought to publish them, and one can only hope that the originals, uncorrected in their virginal French, with all their vagaries of spelling and phonetics, will some day be printed for their philological value.

> *A review of "Strange True Stories of Louisiana," in* The Critic, *New York, Vol. XIII, January 18, 1890, p. 26.*

CORNELIA ATWOOD PRATT (essay date 1899)

[*Pratt was an American novelist and journalist. In the following excerpt, she comments on the longevity of* Old Creole Days *and contends that Cable's short fiction is superior to his novels.*]

The attempt to explain why charm is charming is always a thankless task. There are other literary qualities which may be reduced to their constituents, and these last weighed and ticketed, but the charm of a tale, like that of a personality, is always irreducible, defying the critic and delighting the world at large, apparently elusive and yet, so far as fiction is concerned, the one indestructible element. A little charm carries far and lasts forever.

It is the possession of this element of charm that gave Mr. Cable's early work its immediate success and insured its lasting popularity. The long-famous collection of stories published under the title of **Old Creole Days** has, it is true, many more tangible excellences. The tales dealt with wholly fresh material, and opened, to Northern readers, a new world in a land which they had always vaguely apprehended to be the region of romance. This material was deftly handled. The stories were told in a manner sufficiently direct and vigorous to give the effect of intensity, and yet sufficiently deliberate and measured to convey the alluring golden atmosphere of a land where it is always afternoon. They were unencumbered with any lengthy, tiresome explanations of the social conditions which made the very essence of their dramatic intensity, and yet managed to make those conditions perfectly clear. They were full of the picture-conveying phrases which throw such strong illumination upon the background of a situation. For one instance out of a hundred, recall Père Gerome's dingy and carpetless parlor where "one could smell distinctly the vow of poverty," or the latter-day aspect of Madame Delphine's house, whose batten shutters are closed "with a grip that makes one's knuckles and nails feel lacerated." They appealed exquisitely to the finer feelings . . . and their handling of things emotional is always that delicate, sane, sweet touch which puts the emotions safe upon the high levels we would have them always keep. Even when they were painful stories, their pain was always on the side of righteousness or moral beauty. But chiefly they were playful, tender, human. Over their pages dripped softly the luxurious Creole-English which affects the eye and ear as honey does the palate. Whether charm subsists in the sum of all these qualities or is a product arising from their chemical combination, or is something behind and beyond them all, does not greatly matter if only the world is so cordially agreed concerning its presence as has been the case in **Old Creole Days**. It is almost twenty years since these stories became a part of our literature, but the fact is one difficult to realize, since the book has the gift of the perennial youth and freshness always seeming to belong, if not exactly to the current hour, at least to a near and beloved yesterday.

Of a lovableness almost equal to **Old Creole Days** are Mr. Cable's stories of Acadian Louisiana, **Bonaventure** and the rest. It is only in facing the author's longer novels that the critic escapes from the tyranny of charm, and becomes able to use again the implements of his trade which the magnetic qualities of the other work we have been considering render useless for the time.

Perhaps the best test of the absolute finality of a man's call to labor in any field of art is found in his persistent devotion to the ends of art through middle age and after, and in the power his work shows of resisting the encroachment of the other mental interests which are naturally and righteously far more absorbing to the normal man than are the ends of art. The question is not only, to paraphrase Mr. James, "Can he keep his talent fresh when other elements turn stale?" but even more is it, "Can he keep his talent disentangled from his religion, his sense of affairs, his political perceptions, his historical sense, and all the invading horde of lively and legitimate interests which go to make up the intellectual life of a man beyond thirty?" The implication of the question is not, of course, that all these things cannot serve art, but rather that art must not serve them.

If one were to arraign any of Mr. Cable's work for any cause—and in its mildest form the labor is not a gracious one—it would be his novels, on the ground that they are over-weighted with other than the human interest which is the compulsory one in fiction. Other things are good only so long as they make or explain personality; they begin to be bad when personality is made subservient to them. (pp. 250-52)

[Mr. Cable's novels are] essentially manly, intellectually vigorous, and natural, but it is not the attitude of one who is fundamentally an artist. Also, his attitude, while it does not make the books any less good to read in a large way, does distinctly lessen their legitimacy and excellence as fiction. They have interest as history and ethics rather than as life and art. They hold us by chapters and pages rather than as wholes, because in them the writer's creative ability has been sacrificed to his power of reflection.

It seems safe to assume that this sacrifice must have occurred by conscious or unconscious choice, since Mr. Cable's novelettes and short stories give abundant evidence of his ability to tell a story that is a story, existing for its own sake and moving directly, if with the grace of leisure, to its appointed end. This being the case, we can only regret that the choice has been so made, for reflective work in literature is as plentiful as creative work is rare, and to spend upon the one a talent capable of the other seems an unpardonable rudeness to the gods who give of their best sparingly. (pp. 252-53)

Cornelia Atwood Pratt, "The Stories of George W. Cable," in The Critic, *New York, Vol. XXXIV, No. 861, March, 1899, pp. 250-53.*

THE CRITIC, NEW YORK (essay date 1899)

[*In the following excerpt, the critic comments upon the spiritual qualities that underscore the stories in* Strong Hearts.]

There are three stories in Mr. Cable's new volume [**Strong Hearts**], and as he tells us frankly, "Behind the sub-titles and changes of time, scene, and characters, this tale of strong hearts is one. . . . In each of its aspects it sets forth, in heroic measures and poetic fates, a principle which seems to me so universal that I think Joseph would say of it also, as he said to the sovereign of Egypt, 'The thing is established of God.' " In its briefest expression this principle is that "religion without poetry is as dead a thing as poetry without religion,"— that is to say, to the love of God, even as to the love of man or woman, we must of necessity bring imagination, tenderness, grace. We must keep the commandments with spiritual intelligence, and bring the finer resources of our nature to bear upon the performance of duty. All the spiritual stimulus of the world—that which sets our motor activities going in the right direction—is one, and whether we say we are moved by religion or poetry, it is one; for on the highest plane the two are identical. Incidentally it follows from this that "being good" is an art, though an unconscious one, and counts among its rewards the subtle joy of the artist mingled with the more tangible exultation of the saint. But it is not with the reward of goodness, but rather with what one may call its chemistry, that these stories concern themselves.

Let not this preamble frighten the reader away from **Strong Hearts**, lest he fall into a Sunday-school book unaware. Mr. Cable has three definite and interesting stories to tell. **"The Solitary"** is the story of a man who found the way to outwit a world which was too big and hard and full of temptations for his strength. **"The Taxidermist"** is the story of Pastropbon Manouvrier, who stuffed birds in an obscure little shop and passed serenely unmoved through the experience of acquiring unearned wealth, without knowing that he was undergoing the crucial test of character. **"The Entomologist"** is the story of two women, one of whom was wise and one of whom was foolish. They are all tales of New Orleans, and their skeleton of ethical import is covered with the rose-flesh of that soft Southern life which the writer knows so well how to depict. This covering is perhaps a little insufficient in **"The Entomologist,"** for Mr. Cable lacks the moral patience to make his erring heroine acceptable to us. She is so very foolish in her dilettante assumption of an illicit passion that she alienates interest as well as sympathy. To our thinking, **"The Taxidermist"** is the richest and sweetest of the tales, perhaps because the hero rarely explains himself save by action, and the author refrains from comment on his obvious nobility. The story equals in charm and strength the best of Mr. Cable's notable work in the same field, and creates a lively appetite for more of its happy kind. (pp. 564-65)

A review of "Strong Hearts," in The Critic, *New York, Vol. XXXIV, No. 864, June, 1899, pp. 564-65.*

FRED LEWIS PATTEE (essay date 1923)

[*An American literary historian, critic, poet, and novelist, Pattee was a pioneer in the study of American literature. In such works as* A History of American Literature, with a View to the Fundamental Principles Underlying its Development *(1896) and* The First Century of American Literature *(1935), Pattee called for the recognition of American literature as distinct from English literature and contended that literature is the popular expression of a people, rather than the work of an elite. In the following excerpt, Pattee discusses romantic elements in Cable's short fiction.*]

George Washington Cable must be ranked first of all as a pioneer: he was the first literary voice of the New South.

It was by no means a precocious phenomenon that had been discovered, not at all a genius unexplained and dominating: he was twenty-nine when his first story, " 'Sieur George," appeared in *Scribner's;* he was thirty-six when *The Grandissimes,* his second book, brought him wide recognition. His apprenticeship had been as long and exacting as even Hawthorne's. And yet, like Harte, he seemed to have come full fledged. To read him to-day one begins with no callow material: there is no *Fanshawe* in his list. One finds in his first volume, *Old Creole Days,* what is really his best work, and it is because he mastered his art in obscurity and did not—could not—publish until he had reached his highest form. He was not a Creole as at first was reported—there was in him no French or Spanish strain; he was not even an unmixed Southerner—his mother was of New England stock: it accounts for a Puritan quality within him; it accounts for his later forced exile from the South. And yet he was by no means a Northerner. He had been born and reared in *ante bellum* New Orleans; the mark of the old city was broad upon him: an exotic strangeness, a Gallic predilection to artistry, a tropic efflorescence in style and diction, an unhurried lingering over the amenities of life, a patrician fastidiousness that avoided as by instinct the unlovely and the coarse. (pp. 256-57)

He delved in [the city archives of the old Spanish-French-American metropolis] with all the zest of an antiquarian, and found them excitingly rich in strange history and romantic tradition—how rich, indeed, one has but to open *The Grandissimes* or the *Strange True Stories of Louisiana* to realize. And he brooded over them as Hawthorne had brooded over the Puritan traditions, and he wrote them at length into romance. "Money, fame, didactic or controversial impulse I scarcely felt a throb of. I just wanted to do it because it seemed a pity for the stuff to go so to waste."

Material it was that it was hardly possible to treat realistically. It covered not one *ancien régime,* but three: the era of Spanish beginnings, the era of French domination with its pirates in the gulf, its indigo planters, its Creoles and its Acadians, and the era of American domination after 1804, ended dramatically by the storm of the war which made even the days of Cable's youth seem like romance. There is no sharpness of line in the stories that make up *Old Creole Days:* all is mellowed and softly tinted and idealized. In his own words, descriptive of a tale by one of his characters, "There shone a light of romance upon it that filled it with color and peopled it with phantoms." So with his own work. The exquisite dialect effects, the impressionistic backgrounds, the dainty etchings of Creole femininity, the humorous Dutchmen and chivalrous Gulf pirates seemed to the North the very essence of realism, but old New Orleans did not at all accept them as photographs. A little later Grace King turned to fiction for no other purpose than to correct Cable's picture and to show to the North what Creoles really are.

Cable was a romancer with a manner all his own. He had learned his art in solitude in a corner of the world, and it was unconventional in the extreme. Nowhere else in American literature, save in Lafcadio Hearn, may one find a tang so individual. It is like mangoes or alligator pears: one must acquire the taste. Everywhere a suggestion of French influence—in the artistry, in the lightness of line, in the style: often paragraphic, elided of verbs, subtly suggestive. The technique shows faintly the influence of Poe. The early short stories have uniformity of tone, atmosphere, culminating effect; they are strong in characterization; they bring out a certain unique or single effect. They lack, perhaps, what Poe called momentum—the fault with which he had charged De

Béranger: they are beautiful, sparkling, brilliant, but they move slowly, they have a Southern disregard for rush and immediacy. The backgrounds are etched in without regard to proportion, the character descriptions go to extremes; in "**Madame Delphine**" a chapter of analysis and description is given to each character.

It was caviar to Northerners when it first came, and they acquired the taste slowly. After five years only seven of his stories had found place in the magazines, and when in 1879 they were published as *Old Creole Days* there was no excitement anywhere, no real enthusiasm, though to-day we realize that the book was a classic. . . . It was *The Grandissimes* that gave Cable his entrance to the Valhalla of American fiction. In 1880 the novel was still the supreme literary form: the short story was still an amusing trifle.

Undoubtedly it was his materials rather than his art that gave Cable his first vogue. His own confession that he was led to write simply because of his materials and his reaction after his success with *The Grandissimes* are both significant. After his first two or three volumes, which are the real Cable untouched by outside opinion, we find him turning more and more to merely picturesque presentation. . . . His short-story fountain dried up almost in a moment. His total product is less than a dozen if we count only his real achievements: it includes the seven in *Old Creole Days,* later swelled to eight by the inclusion of "**Madame Delphine**" "**Père Raphael**," and perhaps the three parts of *Bonaventure,* which undoubtedly are of short-story texture. Little that he wrote in later days really matters. When he left the South in 1879 he became like a tropic tree transplanted into Northern soil: he lost somehow that indescribable tang that had made his early work so distinctive.

His influence upon the American short story, however, has been a marked one. He helped to swell the stream of dialect and local peculiarity that was slowly gathering now, to break shortly in a veritable flood; he called attention anew to style as an essential of short-story art, and by the great success of his work he inspired new writers everywhere to search for the unique and to put the emphasis upon material and characterization. In quantity he did little for the form, but the little he did do is distinctive. He is one of the rare few of whom, even while he is living it may be said, he added a permanent volume to the none too large library of American masterpieces. (pp. 257-59)

Fred Lewis Pattee, "The Era of Localized Romance," in his The Development of the American Short Story: An Historical Survey, *Harper & Brothers Publishers, 1923, pp. 245-67.*

EDWARD LAROCQUE TINKER   (essay date 1934)

[*Tinker was an American novelist, biographer, critic, and historian who was an authority on the French period in Louisiana. In the following excerpt, Tinker examines the animosity between New Orleans Creole society and Cable after the publication of* Old Creole Days.]

The two people most heartily hated by the Creoles of Louisiana were "bloody" O'Reilly, who, when governor, executed five of their compatriots for conspiring against Spanish rule, and George Washington Cable, who had the temerity to write of their race. Although these offenses would appear to differ materially in degree of moral turpitude, they seem to have

Cable's birthplace on Annunciation Square, New Orleans, Louisiana.

differed not at all in the amount of vindictive rancor they engendered in the Creoles—an animosity that persists today as fierce and malevolent as ever.

While various causes abetted its birth, the real root reason for this deep-seated spleen against Cable was that his every hope, habit, thought, and even his religion, were in direct conflict with the Creoles. He was as much of a misfit in French New Orleans as a turtle hatched in a peacock's nest; as alien to his birthplace as an Eskimo might have been. The city then was as unbridled a port as any on the continent. Bull-baiting, cock-fighting, and gambling in every form were rampant. Slavery was considered sanctioned by Holy Writ, and pretty cream-colored quadroons, tricked out in ribbons, were exposed for sale as "fancy girls" in the windows of slave marts. Sailors from every country, "Kaintucks," rawboned and fur-capped, who had floated their produce down the Mississippi in flatboats, and boatmen, "half-horse, half alligator," held nightly revels in the "swamp," and there was scarcely a dawn that the watch did not stumble over the body of a man, knifed or shot in a brawl. Gentlemen prosecuted their quarrels in more formal fashion and misunderstandings were settled by the duel. The Creoles, enriched by slave labor and nourished by French culture, had developed a life of great luxury, their houses filled with tapestries and fine French furniture. Pride of possession added to pride of race had made of them a haughty, high-strung tribe. (p. 313)

Cable began to put on paper the Creoles he met and the tales he heard about them [while on the staff of the *Picayune*]. It was not strange that this race should seduce his pen, because for this slow, plodding, rather prudish writer they must have had all the charm of the dissimilar, and while he felt it his duty to disapprove of some of their characteristics, many of their very faults endeared them to him. The irksome monotony of his toil-filled existence must have made him secretly envy the gay impulsiveness of the Creoles, their graceful insouciance, their debonair courage, their spontaneous bursts of extravagance, their lily-of-the-field philosophy, and their instinctive clutch at immediate pleasure with no counting of future costs. Perhaps the describing of their volatile emotions may have assuaged his own inhibitions, and writing of their

warm, exotic, impetuous love affairs, and of the quadroon balls, may have given him a certain psychological release.

He approached the task of telling his tales with a mind that was a *tabula rasa* so far as the influence of other fiction writers was concerned, for he considered the reading of novels sinful—an opinion he did not change until, in middle age, he chanced to read George Macdonald's *Annals of a Quiet Neighborhood,* and was persuaded that some fiction might be innocuous. After that he read some of Victor Hugo, Thackeray, Tourgenieff, and Hawthorne. Although this partial insulation from literature deprived him of the joy and profit of many masterpieces, it had the advantage of keeping him from the influence of poor books and allowing him to form his own style and to treat the characters of the new fictional field he had discovered, in a far more original way than he would otherwise have done. Especially did it keep him free of the outworn *clichés* and grandiose ideology of the Southern literature of his day. This was a real boon, for the early books of the South were written for haughty, aristocratic land-owners whose pride had been further fostered by the ownership of a servile race. (pp. 315-16)

Saved from this baleful influence, it was not surprising that Cable's stories should have a new flavor. . . . **"Sieur George"** appeared in [*Scribner's Monthly*] in 1873, and during the next few years all the stories were published which were later collected in Cable's first book, **Old Creole Days.** They had an immediate success in the North, and the "Yankees" were enthusiastic about these fresh tales of an exotic, foreign life so full of color and quaintness, the existence of which they had never before imagined. **"'Tite Poulette,"** one of the stories, received a reception as warm as Boucicault's *Octoroon.* It recounted the pathetic struggle of an octoroon mother to preserve her daughter's virtue in defiance of a social order that doomed these near-white women to an almost inevitable life of immorality. . . . [It] was quite natural for the former abolitionists to welcome enthusiastically this new attack upon one of slavery's consequences—the tragedies born of miscegenation. Deep hatreds die hard, and perhaps no book since *Uncle Tom's Cabin* stirred up so much enthusiasm as did **Old Creole Days.** These stories were so vivid, interesting, and full of sentiment that they could stand upon their own merits; and even in England, where no such bias existed, they were immediately hailed as masterpieces. Indeed one Englishman, after reading **"'Tite Poulette"** and a later story, **"Madame Delphine,"** said that if the octoroon mothers were half as noble and self-sacrificing, and their daughters half as alluring and virtuous as Cable depicted them, he, for one, regretted the abolition of a slavery that had produced such splendid characters.

The very reasons which made Cable famous in the North made him infamous in the South. Not one of her authors had ever before dared to write of the Negro except as a loyal, humble family retainer, or as a black-face buffoon. The Negro as a flesh-and-blood human being, as a living problem in adjustment, was so sore a subject that by tacit agreement Southern society ignored the existence of this aspect and, on pain of ostracism, permitted no one to discuss it. This was easy to understand, for the Louisianians had been deeply humiliated by the Negro rule which the Carpetbaggers had forced upon them during Reconstruction and, having but recently engaged in a bloody fight to bring back white supremacy, they could not forgive Cable, a Southerner born, for sympathizing in print with the quadroon cause. They felt that this was most subversive because they believed the Negro must be ruthlessly crushed. The Creoles considered Cable more loathsome than a Carpetbagger; called him a renegade scalawag; and when they mentioned his name they spat. "Besides," they asked, "were there no Southern ladies and gentlemen to write about, that he had to parade quadroon women across his pages as heroines and dish up the very dregs of society?"

They felt that they had special reason to be incensed; for Cable, not content with describing the quadroon balls of the *rue d'Orleans* and with advertising the fact that they were frequented by Creole gentlemen, went even further. In **"Belles Demoiselles Plantation"** he made a well-born Creole chaffer, and none too honestly, for a piece of ancestral real estate owned by an illegitimate relative with a mixed strain of Negro and Indian blood. It only made matters worse that he added:

> One thing I never knew a Creole to do. He will not utterly go back on the ties of blood, no matter what sort of knots those ties may be. For one reason he is *never ashamed of his or his father's sins;* and for another,—he will tell you he is 'all heart!'

It was more than they could stand, for they inherited from Old World ancestors an arrogant pride so sensitive that they never forgave a mention in print, and they feared that people in other parts of the country who read his stories would get the impression that their race was not of unsullied white descent. Their sense of personal dignity was further offended because Cable made his Creole characters speak a quaint lacerated dialect. Whether or not his notation of their peculiarities of pronunciation was philologically correct is open to discussion; but that many of the Creoles of his day spoke English with a decided foreign accent and used strange literal translations of French idioms, cannot be denied. When his characters were speaking French, Cable was fair enough to put correct English in their mouths; but even this could not persuade the Creoles that he was not holding them up to ridicule and advertising them to the world as an ignorant, unlettered people. The whole *Vieux Carré* boiled with rage, but nothing prevented Cable from writing every minute he could. . . . (pp. 317-19)

In *Old Creole Days* Cable had been completely the creative artist fascinated with his material and entirely absorbed in his narrative. Some of these tales, however, were centered upon the injustices meted out to the colored people, and much mulling over the subject had aroused his crusading fervor. . . . The Creoles would not believe that his missionary fervor and sympathy for the colored race were perfectly honest. Instead, they insisted that he championed the Negro merely for the purpose of selling his books to the Yankees, even though the plausible explanation of his fanatical evangelism was that it came as a direct legacy from his witch-burning ancestors and that he really thought he had a divine call to right the wrongs of the oppressed and to spread the word of God. (pp. 320-21)

The present generation of Creoles, with few exceptions, although they have never read his books, have inherited a garbled version of the reasons for their indignation, and one of them was heard to explain that Mme. Lalaurie refused to receive Cable because he had colored blood, and that in order to get even with her, he wrote **"The 'Haunted House' in Royal Street,"** in which he described how a mob, learning of her brutal treatment of her slaves, sacked her house just after she had fled. There are only two minor inaccuracies in this statement: the first being that Cable had no Negro blood; and

the second, that he never saw Mme. Lalaurie, because she escaped to France in 1834, ten years before he was born. . . .

Announcing that he wished to be closer to his publisher, he left New Orleans in 1886. (p. 324)

Cable the artist had always been at war with Cable the Sunday school teacher, but in this new congenial atmosphere his evangelistic predisposition conquered. He indulged in a very orgy of proselyting. Every Saturday afternoon he taught a huge Bible class of two thousand members, at Tremont Temple in Boston, and another class on Sundays at Northampton; he founded the People's Institute, Culture and Garden Clubs for working families, and even became a member of the Simplified Spelling Board. He reinforced all his preaching by publishing two small books on the twin objects of his zealous propaganda, *The Busy Man's Bible* and *The Negro Question.* All these preoccupations so filled his mind with extraneous problems that his literary output was seriously affected.

Without implying any criticism of his manifold activities aimed at reforming society, the truth must be told: his pedagogic excesses murdered his creative ability. . . . Cable became a dull writer, his novels, prosy, platitudinous and choked with copybook morality. Of the books published after his hegira only two have any merit. **Bonaventure** is good because its three stories were written before he left his native state; and **Strange True Stories of Louisiana,** because he merely edited other people's manuscripts. The remaining books he produced are negligible, commonplace, run-of-the-mill romances.

A second factor also contributed to Cable's literary degeneration. Like Lafcadio Hearn, he did not have the creative type of mind. His inspiration had to be fed by continuous surface impressions of the life around him—new turns of phrase, new incidents. These he could fashion into books with all the ingenuity and meticulous care of a Swiss watch-maker. But after he left the South he still continued to write about it, although he was cut off from all the impressions he had been accustomed to receive from daily contacts with his models, from all new accretions of picturesque incident. His mind was not sufficiently fertile nor his memory vivid enough to supply this lack; and this was a contributing reason why his later books lacked authenticity and vital interest; why they became pale shadows of his early successes. In spite of this Cable will always be remembered for two books, **Old Creole Days** and *The Grandissimes,* and also because he is the legitimate father of the literary movement which is producing such splendid fruit in the South today. Cable first, among Southern writers, treated objectively and realistically the life he saw around him, and was first to break the taboo against writing about the Negro. His courage freed the authors who followed him of the necessity of fulsome praise for all things sectional; taught them their right and duty to analyze and portray truthfully, even, if necessary to criticize, the social conditions under which they and those around them live. All this Cable accomplished at the cost of practical ostracism among his own people; so he may well be called the first martyr to the cause of literary freedom in the South. (pp. 325-26)

Edward Larocque Tinker, "Cable and the Creoles," in American Literature, Vol. 5, No. 4, January, 1934, pp. 313-26.

KJELL EKSTRÖM (essay date 1950)

[*In the following excerpt, Ekström investigates the accuracy of Cable's portrait of Creole society, manners, and dialect.*]

Did Cable give an accurate picture of the Creoles? Was his rendering of their dialect correct? Was his presentation of them intended as an attack on them? Those are questions that present themselves to the student of his early Creole stories. To give a definite answer to them is, however, very difficult.

The spokesmen of the Creoles maintained . . . that Cable's description of them was in every—or almost every—way false. There were, however . . . , some Creoles who held a different opinion, but they seem to have been in the minority. Since, according to his own word, Cable had contemporary Creoles for his models, one way to judge of the realism of his Creole characters would be after the picture we can make of those Creoles. His Creole critics seem to have taken it for granted that he described contemporary Creoles—"We are not like that," they said. The problem is, however, made more complicated by the fact that in many cases Cable may have changed his models to make them fit better into the historic milieu; or he may have created wholly imaginary figures or drawn characters after people he had read about during his studies of history. Now it seems impossible to say which characters belong to each of these categories, and it would be as wrong to judge all of them as Creoles of the time in which the stories are laid as it would be to consider them all to be Creoles of the 1870's or 1880's.

Since I do not presume to solve this problem, I shall content myself with presenting some further evidence on this question. (pp. 172-73)

In the Boston *Literary World* of January 24, 1885, there appeared an article by W. S. Kennedy, entitled "The New Orleans of George W. Cable". Kennedy, who, after reading Cable's stories, had gone to New Orleans to study Creole life, writes:

> the essential facts of the representations are true and sharply accentuated. I have heard from different Creoles bits of speech which were familiar from my having met with them in *The Grandissimes* or *Old Creole Days.* You soon discover that the class feeling, the ancient national antipathy of French and Saxon, makes of Canal street—separating the French from the American quarter—a line of demarcation as distinct as that which divides the water of the Mississippi from those of the Gulf. The Creoles are proud and poor; hold themselves aloof—have their own paper—L'Abeille de la Nouvelle Orleans—and will read no other; and have formed a society for the preservation of the French language. They rate English, rarely speaking it with willingness, or without a shrug of the shoulders.

Here we have an unprejudiced critic from the North, who, having made a special study of the subject, came to the conclusion that in essentials Cable's picture of the Creoles is true. (p. 174)

A Creole correspondent to the New Orleans *Times-Democrat* wrote:

> I acknowledge the truthfulness of the Creole characters as far as he (Cable) depicts them. I concede that they are vivid, living; that I seem to recognize the individuals; but I protest at such being raised above their proper level, and made to appear as representative types of any other than the class the author has chosen to use for purposes of fiction.

This is interesting as being—as far as I know—the only *public* admission by a Creole of that time that there existed such Creoles as Cable depicted.

In a letter to Cable from a member of the Soniat family there is a description of an old Creole lady who seems to beat the most eccentric Creole ever portrayed by Cable. Here is an extract from that letter:

> I wish you knew some of the old creoles I do, there is one old lady in our family who knows *everything* concerning *everybody* who lives, or has lived below Canal Street within this century, she could furnish you material for your brain to embroider on forever. Within the same square resides another "antique" who came up town six years ago to call on me, it was the first time she had "crossed the Rubicon" (Canal Street) in fifteen years, and I am sure she has not seen "le haut de la ville" since, it is an unknown region to her. . . .
>
> Those old folks are fossils of a past age and are as different in opinions and ways from the creole society lady of the present as can be; but if I wanted anecdotes of the past, good gumbo or hard common sense advice these are the ones I would apply to. The Creoles are a peculiar, a *very* peculiar people, they are made up of opposites.

(pp. 174-75)

In view of the evidence presented it seems incredible that Cable's picture of the Creoles is as false as some of his Creole critics would have us believe. This does not preclude the possibility that, for artistic or other reasons, Cable may have exaggerated certain traits in them. Neither must it be forgotten that Cable did not write about those few Creoles who went to Paris for their education or about the drawing-room life of the uppermost Creole society. His choice of characters from all other walks of life, being a break against the literary tradition of the Creoles, or indeed of the whole South, was, of course, shocking to the leading Creoles.

Was Cable's rendering of the English spoken by the Creoles accurate? (p. 176)

It is very difficult to judge now in this matter, no linguistic work, as far as I have been able to find out, having been made to elucidate it. It is, however, evident that Cable made no attempt to reconstruct the English of the Creoles of the early nineteenth century but took the artistic liberty of putting into their mouths the English of contemporary Creoles. Now it is hard to imagine that his rendering of their language was wholly false. He had a very fine ear for music, and it is known that he was able to write down from memory melodies he had heard. It seems probable that his ear for languages was equally acute. In his notebook we find many instances of his having written down dialectal peculiarities overheard by him.

I have also found some evidence that Cable's rendering of the English of the Creoles was not so incorrect as Gayarré maintained.

In a review of *Old Creole Days* in the New Orleans *Picayune* we read the following: "The careful rendering of the dialect reveals patient study of living models; and to any reader whose ear is accustomed to the broken English, as heard in the parts of our city every day, its truth to nature is striking."

This reviewer, being a New Orleans journalist, must be supposed to be a competent judge in this question. Another New Orleans journalist, Charles W. Young, wrote this to Cable: " 'The Grandissimes' is immense. And the dialect. I could almost fancy I was once more among my old friends in the Second District (right about that am I not?) I used to have a great many Creole friends down on Esplanade Street and thereabouts." Here, again, is evidence in favour of the accuracy of Cable's rendering of Creole speech given by a man, who, having had many Creole friends, may be considered a competent critic.

G. H. Clements, who was well acquainted with the New Orleans Creoles, also praised Cable's rendering of their English. " 'Tis amazing how you catch their idioms," he wrote to Cable in 1881. He went on to tell him about an old aunt of his who thought that Cable greatly exaggerated the peculiarities of the Creoles' speech; "we'd read a bit of dialogue to her, she'd fume: 'tees not so, he naver hyar peeple talk so.' " Ten years later he gave evidence that some Creoles had not yet learned to master the English language. Then he wrote to Cable:

> Now that they are learning English they fairly gloat over the less-favored ones. Mina's sister said to me at dinner last night, "you are sober"—of course what do you expect?—"well I notice you were sober last night, too, you took no ham". She explained that she meant I was temperate in eating. "Not for Meester Cable make de creole to talk so—is's think we is niggers!"
>
> (pp. 177-78)

There is also evidence that Sidney Lanier held a very high opinion of Cable's ability to render dialect in his fiction. In 1880 Allen Redwood wrote to Cable: "But you must admit Sidney Lanier to evidence upon a point concerning which he is peculiarly fitted to testify—the phonetical accuracy of your dialect study. Well, he says, you are the *only* man who has mastered the *sounds* of dialect."

This evidence cannot be said to have *proved* the accuracy of Cable's rendering of the Creoles' English; but in view of the evidence presented, it seems hard to believe that it was a fabrication of Cable's as Creole critics maintained. However, only after extensive linguistic research can we hope to give definite judgement in this question.

Was Cable's presentation of the Creoles in his early fiction intended as an attack on them? Gayarré, Fortier, and other spokesmen of the Creoles were obviously convinced that such was the case. But many critics in the North wondered at the furious Creole reaction to Cable's Creole stories, as they thought that Cable had given a most charming picture of Creole life. Many of the thrusts at the Creoles, in *Old Creole Days* particularly, are, it is true, woven into the fabric of the stories in such an artistic way that they may easily escape a less careful reader. But the reader who looks below the surface of romantic plots in a colourful milieu will notice them. (p. 180)

The predominating problem in New Orleans at the time when the *Old Creole Days* stories were written and *The Grandissimes* conceived was the Negro question. It was on this question that Cable wished to throw some light by putting it in its historical context; he wished to regard it "in the light of that past history—those beginnings—which had so differentiated the Louisiana civilization from the American scheme

of public society". And he meant to make *The Grandissimes* "as truly a political work as it has ever been called". It is obvious that he intended to show the bad effects of slavery as well on the individual as on the whole society.

It seems also as if Cable regarded the Creoles as particularly unprogressive, although there is no evidence that he hated them, as some Creole spokesmen maintained. It is more probable that in his reformatory zeal he wanted to teach them "some fundamental lessons of society and government", as Boyesen put it. The innate differences in temperament and attitude towards life between the pleasure-loving, easy-going Latin Creoles and Cable, the Presbyterian Anglo-Saxon, must not be overlooked in this connection. On the whole, however, it seems as if the Latin peculiarities of the Creoles struck Cable as amusing and appealed to his artistic sense. He certainly did not wish to do away with the colourful traits in Creole life. But he objected to Creole unprogressiveness and Creole pride, in ancestry particularly; and it was mainly towards them that he directed his thrusts. (pp. 181-82)

> *Kjell Ekström, in his* George Washington Cable: A Study of His Early Life and Work, Vol. X, *Cambridge, Mass.: Harvard University Press, 1950, 197 p.*

JAY B. HUBBELL (essay date 1954)

[*An American critic and educator, Hubbell was considered an authority on Southern literature. In the following excerpt, he explores Cable's reputation as a "Southern Yankee" and asserts that his artistic decline began after the 1881 publication of* Madame Delphine.]

When the Creoles of New Orleans found themselves portrayed for Northern readers in a manner repugnant to their sensitive natures, they denounced George Washington Cable . . . as a "Southern Yankee," an Abolitionist at heart, who had wilfully misrepresented their speech, their manners, and their morals so that he could sell more of his books to Northern readers. In other parts of the South many persons read with pleasure his *Old Creole Days* and *The Grandissimes*; but when in the middle eighties Cable began airing in Northern magazines his heretical views on the Negro question, he provoked widespread condemnation. From all over the South came the cry: "He is none of us."

The notion that Cable was a "Southern Yankee" now seems absurd. He had been born, brought up, and educated in Louisiana, which is more remote from New England than any other Southern state except Texas. On his father's side he could trace his ancestry back to the Old Dominion. He had fought in the Confederate army. He had written his best books while living in New Orleans; and if *Old Creole Days* and *Madame Delphine* are not Southern literature, what is? Cable did not remove to New England until he was a famous writer forty years old. Surely he was right when in 1893 he said at an Authors Club dinner in New York: "Southerners' utterances to the contrary, I am—after being first of all an American citizen—a Southerner. . . ." (p. 804)

Cable's chief offense against the South was that he had deliberately violated what Southerners understood to be the meaning of the Compromise of 1877. They had accepted the end of slavery and of secession with the understanding that the Negro was the Southerners' problem and the North would not again interfere. When Cable began writing in Northern magazines about "civil equality," they thought he was deliberately stirring up trouble. It seemed to them that he was advocating "social equality," perhaps even miscegenation. On the race question the New South was intolerant and uncompromising. The now Solid South did not care to be reminded that there had always been natives of that region who on one issue or another had refused to conform to prevailing opinion. There are—in part because of Cable's courageous stand—many more of them today. (p. 805)

Cable has often been represented as bursting upon the American literary scene like a meteor, but the acclaim he won with **Old Creole Days** and *The Grandissimes* came only after more than a decade of writing, and it was preceded by repeated failures to interest the house which eventually published these books. (pp. 809-10)

Cable had found the Northern magazine editors difficult to please. [*Scribner's Monthly* editors Josiah Gilbert Holland and Richard Watson Gilder] were enthusiastic about the stories which they accepted, but most of these seem to have been considerably revised before publication. *Scribner's Monthly* rejected "Dr. Goldenbow," "Hortensia," and "Ba'm o' Gilly," which was apparently never published anywhere. They declined "Bibi" as too horrible, and so did [William Dean] Howells when Cable submitted it to the *Atlantic Monthly*. It finally became the Bras-Coupe episode in *The Grandissimes.* Holland and Gilder also rejected **"Posson Jone','"** certainly one of Cable's finest stories, presumably because they feared the effect upon their subscribers of an intoxicated Protestant preacher. Eventually Edward King succeeded in placing it in *Appletons' Journal.* (p. 811)

[After] reading the manuscript of **"Madame Délicieuse,"** in which he had found "a lot of little awkwardnesses," Gilder wrote to Cable: "You bother me. Your conception of character is strong—artistic—your style is bright and witty—your plots are generally good—your field is all your own—and I consider your stories a great acquisition to the monthly—but you lack in the capacity to edit yourself. This is the only thing that makes me fear for your literary future." It was not until later that Gilder discovered that in Cable the artist was being threatened by the propagandist. (p. 812)

The deterioration of the artist in Cable had already progressed very far indeed. He was to write nothing during the remaining forty-odd years of his life as good as **"Madame Delphine"** (1881).

Meanwhile Cable had discovered that lecturing, singing Creole songs, and reading his stories from the platform were more profitable and less laborious than writing and rewriting stories which must pass the gauntlet of editor and publisher. He gave his first public address at the University of Mississippi in June, 1882. "Literature in the Southern States" was a vigorous plea for a national point of view. "We have been," he said, "already too long a unique people. Let us search provincialism out of the land. . . ." He did not object to the author's choosing Southern subjects. "Only," he insisted, "let them be written to and for the whole nation. . . ." Joel Chandler Harris had expressed much the same view in the Atlanta *Constitution* a year earlier, and Lanier had before 1875 come to regard himself as a national rather than as a sectional poet. (pp. 813-14)

In March of the next year, while lecturing at the Johns Hopkins University in Baltimore, Cable discovered how effective his own stories were when he read them aloud to a sympathetic audience. In 1884 on an invitation from Mark Twain he joined forces with the great humorist in what in a letter to his wife Cable once facetiously referred to as "the old highway-robbery business." It has been generally supposed that Cable was by much the less popular member of the team; but Fred W. Lorch, who in 1952 retold the story of the 1884-1885 tour from the abundant newspaper accounts, reached a different conclusion. By 1884 Cable had become an accomplished platform performer, and he was as well known to his audiences as Mark Twain. He was also a controversial figure whom audiences were eager to see and hear. In *Dr. Sevier,* published in September, 1884, he had boldly stated that in the Civil War the cause of the North was a "just" one. "The Freedman's Case in Equity," which appeared in the *Century* in January, 1885, provoked a storm of protest from the South. . . . In Southern eyes, however, what Cable had done was to violate the Compromise of 1877, by which Southerners understood that the North would not again interfere with the treatment of Negroes in the South. Northern indifference to the Negro question irritated Cable also, and so he spoke out boldly. The South interpreted his demand for "civil equality" as a demand for "social equality," perhaps even for erasing the color line completely, and labeled him an "Abolitionist" and a "Southern Yankee." (pp. 814-15)

Even Southern liberals like Henry W. Grady found altogether unacceptable the views of the Negro question which Cable was freely expressing in Northern and not Southern periodicals. Conservatives like Hayne and Gayarré regarded him as a traitor to the South. Cable . . . owed much to Gayarré's historical studies of Louisiana; and it was a debt which he never adequately acknowledged anywhere in print. In Northern eyes it was now the author of *The Creoles of Louisiana* and not Gayarré who was the historian of Louisiana. (p. 815)

On April 25, 1885, Gayarré delivered at Tulane University a lecture, *The Creoles of History and the Creoles of Romance,* in which he attacked Cable's various insinuations that the Creoles had African blood in their veins. Of Cable's fiction Gayarré seems to have read only, and not very carefully, *The Grandissimes.* . . . In his lecture Gayarré attacked Cable's assertion that " . . . the pilgrim fathers of the Mississippi Delta were taking wives and moot wives from the ill specimens of three races." In his indignation Gayarré had forgotten that he himself had written of "the promiscuous herd of thieves, prostitutes, vagabonds, and all sorts of wretches of bad fame who had been swept together, to be transported to Louisiana."

The Creoles looked to Paris and not to London or New York. Their culture was French. American literature as it came to them from the Northern states seemed prudish; it lacked color and warmth. For all of Cable's reading in French literature, his fundamental aims were very un-French. The sex morals of the Creoles had a continental freedom repugnant to Cable, and they resented his pictures of quadroon balls, which were in fact far from being the romantic affairs that Cable made of them. In the eyes of the proud and sensitive Creoles the *"Américains,"* especially those of the merchant class to which Cable belonged, were vulgar outsiders, pushing and ill-bred. The Creoles understood better the aristocratic Southern planter.

To be portrayed unsympathetically by an outsider, by a "Southern Yankee," was intolerable. As Cable himself said, "A Creole never forgives a public mention." The Creoles' resentment mounted with the publication of each new book by

Cable, for, as they rightly saw, he portrayed them less and less favorably in each new story. **"Madame Delphine"** was peculiarly offensive. In that story a Negro woman of the quadroon caste manages to get her daughter, who is seven-eighths white, across the color line. When in 1883 this [novella] was included in a new edition of **Old Creole Days,** the Louisianians were certain that in the eyes of Cable and his Yankee readers the proud Creoles had Negro blood in their veins. This insinuation was even harder to bear than Cable's representing men who prided themselves on their excellent French as speaking broken English. It is eighty-one years since Cable's first story appeared in *Scribner's Monthly,* but there are still Creoles who have not forgiven Cable.

Louisiana readers saw in *The Grandissimes* satiric thrusts which were likely to escape the Northern reader. In that book, for example, Cable ridicules the Creoles' "ancestral, perennial rebellion against common sense" and again: "Those Creoles have such a shocking way of filing their family relics and records in ratholes." The Creole men, as Cable paints them, are proud, vain, ignorant, boastful, quarrelsome, fond of gambling and of quadroon mistresses. His Creole women, on the other hand, are beautiful, fascinating, amiable, and vivacious. When James Barrie was in New Orleans in 1896, several Creole ladies warned him against accepting Cable's account of the Creoles as accurate. Barrie's reply was that he "supposed it must be so, no ladies in the flesh could be quite so delicious as the Creole ladies of Mr. Cable's imagination." There was in the author of **Old Creole Days** a certain susceptibility to the voluptuous such as one feels in the sage and serious Spenser's description of the Bower of Bliss in *The Faerie Queene.*

In July, 1884, the Cables left New Orleans for a long stay in Simsbury, Connecticut. The next year they settled permanently in Northampton, Massachusetts. The reasons that Cable gave for leaving Louisiana were his wife's poor health, the need to be closer to editors, publishers, and the audiences to whom he lectured and read his stories. He desired also, he says, to study American life in other sections. He never admitted that Southern hostility, which had become acute in 1884, had anything to do with his change of residence, but one wonders. On January 24, 1880, he had written to Robert Underwood Johnson: "I see no good reason why I should leave Louisiana; why should I? What advantage is supposeable?" In his later years Cable was only at long intervals to revisit New Orleans.

In New England Cable gave much of his time to the promotion of Home-Culture Clubs and to teaching Sunday School classes. In 1891 he published *The Busy Man's Bible.* In later life he modified his stern religious creed much as Lanier had done some years earlier. He also modified his theory of the function of the novel. In April, 1900, he wrote to Waitman Barbe: "A novel's most obvious aim—the aim which should never for a moment be evidently directed by any other purpose—should be to entertain, not to inform." It cannot be said, however, that the adoption of his new theory resulted in the writing of better novels.

Cable's new theory of the function of fiction seems to have come during the writing of *John March, Southerner* (1894). When in August, 1890, Gilder read the manuscript of that novel, he is said to have wrung his hands in despair. He had found it "a tract, not a story." He had been hoping that Cable could work off his preoccupation with reform in addresses and essays and keep his novels free from propaganda. Even

after Cable had worked hard to meet Gilder's criticisms, the editor found in it "less charm" than in any of Cable's earlier stories. *John March* did not seem to him "to have its origin in a deep sense of art." (pp. 816-18)

Cable's deterioration as an artist, which so greatly disturbed the editors of the *Century,* has troubled every critic who has discussed his work. It has been suggested that his loss of creative power was due to his removal from the region which he knew best, but Cable's best books had all been written three years before he removed to New England. They had all been written in fact by the time he was free to devote himself entirely to literature. Cable's decline in power disturbed William Malone Baskervill, who in his *Southern Writers* (1897) placed Cable in "the class of thoroughgoing men, actuated by thoroughgoing logic, lovers of abstract truth and perfect ideals, and it was his lot to be born among a people who by the necessities of their situation were controlled by expedience. They were compelled to adopt an illogical but practical compromise between two extremes which were logical but not practical." This cast of mind explained to Baskervill why Cable gave "a prejudiced, incorrect, unjust picture of Southern life, character, and situation. This domination of one idea," Baskervill concluded, "has vitiated the most exquisite literary and artistic gifts that any American writer of fiction, with possibly one exception, has been endowed [with] since Hawthorne. . . ." Baskervill, who would probably have approved of Cable's later theory of the function of fiction, did not live to read the later novels.

Howells, writing in *Harper's Magazine* in October, 1888, took another view: "It is the conscience of Mr. Cable that gives final value to all he does." The Southern condemnation of Cable, he thought, was "narrow-minded, the censure of a people who would rather be flattered than appreciated." A somewhat similar view has been expressed much more recently by Cable's Swedish biographer, Kjell Ekström, who maintains that Cable's deterioration as a novelist was due to the fact that "being no longer fired with a reformatory zeal, he was unable to create really moving literature" [see excerpt dated 1950]. The difficulty with Ekström's theory and those of other critics is that it does not explain the decline in the quality of Cable's work in the years 1882-1894, when he was still deeply concerned with reforms. A similar decline in artistic power is seen in nearly all of Cable's local-color contemporaries. In nearly every instance the writer's first book is his best, and it is a book of short stories rather than a novel. Few of them indeed wrote novels of any distinction. Was Van Wyck Brooks right when in "The Literary Life in America" (1922) he maintained that there is something in the American environment which prevents the writer from developing his full potentialities?

Whatever be the explanation of Cable's decline, it seems clear that the delicate balance between the love of beauty and the desire to make over the world which one finds in **Old Creole Days** is less in evidence in *The Grandissimes* and has practically disappeared in *John March, Southerner.* Cable's best work was done before his attitude toward the Southern problem had hardened into a fixed creed. His best work was done while he was young, ambitious, and enthusiastic and while he was willing to be guided by the editors of *Scribner's Monthly,* whose sense of literary form was keener than his. His first two books angered the Creoles, but other Southerners were enthusiastic about them. After he had published "The Freedman's Case in Equity" in January, 1885, the South practically disowned him. I believe that Southern condemnation had a profounder effect upon Cable than he was ever willing to admit. He was no longer one of his own people, and the life of the slaveholding South had little attraction for him. By the time he had lost his deep concern with the Southern problem and had altered his theory of fiction, the literary fashion had shifted away from romantic local-color stories of the Old South. He was by training a romancer and not a realist, and he was unable to write successful realistic studies of contemporary American life in the manner of Howells. The time for new stories like those in **Old Creole Days** was long past. I do not wish, however, to be understood as regarding Cable's later novels . . . as uninteresting or altogether unimportant. (pp. 819-20)

Before Cable's death in 1925 Ellen Glasgow, Mary Johnston, and James Branch Cabell had begun to follow his example and were attacking Southern traditions in literature and in life with a freedom which among the writers of the New South only Cable had dared to claim. They were to be quickly followed by T. S. Stribling, Paul Green, Julia Peterkin, Erskine Caldwell, William Faulkner, and others who would seem to conservative Southerners to belong to the tradition of Cable and Mrs. Stowe rather than that of Thomas Nelson Page and Grace King. Cable was an important literary pioneer. His attack upon Southern conservatism hastened the time when Southern writers would be able to describe the life of their region with the freedom which had prevailed in the days of George Tucker, Jefferson, and Madison. (pp. 821-22)

> *Jay B. Hubbell, "The New South, 1865-1900: George W. Cable," in his* The South in American Literature: 1607-1900, *Duke University Press, 1954, pp. 804-22.*

RAYBURN S. MOORE   (essay date 1954-55)

[The following is a review of "Don Joaquin."]

With the exception of **"Posson Jone',"** which appeared in *Appletons' Journal,* April 1, 1876, most students of Cable have assumed that the teller of Creole tales published in *Scribner's* all the short stories he succeeded in getting printed in the great monthly magazines in the 1870's. During this decade, however, Cable presented to the periodical-reading public another story to which he apparently never later referred. This tale, **"Don Joaquin,"** written probably as the result of the author's visit to Havana, Cuba, in July, 1875, appeared in *Harper's New Monthly Magazine* in January, 1876. (p. 418)

Presumably Cable did not wish **"Don Joaquin"** to be retained in the canon of his fiction. In spite of certain similarities to **"Café des Exilés,"** a contemporaneous story, in technique and in the use of the Cuban-English dialect, he probably thought that the former did not fit into the pattern of his work in that particular period. . . . **"Don Joaquin,"** though not without merit and finish as a story, was based on a Cuban background that was somewhat alien to the writer's previous local-color material.

In **"Don Joaquin"** most of the action takes place in Havana, and the plot is centered on the love affair of Don Joaquin Justiniani, a wealthy Cuban, and the beautiful Señorita Luisa, a proud young Cuban Creole. Pride on the part of both lovers had prevented a marriage in Marianao six years before the story begins, and in his sorrow over the apparent loss of his beloved, who had left Cuba, Justiniani turns for consolation

to the gruff but kind Simpson, an English merchant. The Englishman urges the Cuban to forget his troubles and concentrate his energies in the building of a beautiful home. Under the direction of Monasterio, a Cuban architect, the construction of the Don's house proceeds according to plan until the Señorita Luisa arrives in Havana. Monasterio and Simpson begin immediately to pay court to the beautiful señorita, but Justiniani does not realize at first that the new arrival is his former sweetheart. The two soon meet, however, in true Spanish style (the Don observes the señorita through the iron grating of her drawing-room window), and the old flame of love is rekindled. Justiniani concludes that Simpson by devoting his attention to the Señorita Luisa has been false, and he plans to kill his English friend. Through a misunderstanding over the señorita's surname, Simpson had not realized that he was courting his Cuban friend's beloved. All ends well, though, when the Englishman explains his error to Justiniani and the Señorita Luisa capitulates to the long-suffering Don through the subtle device of a personally designed doorknocker for his (their) new home.

Cable, however, was not primarily concerned with Cuba in his fiction. From 1875 to 1879 . . ., he was interested in collecting his stories about the Creoles of Louisiana and publishing them together in a volume. With this object in mind he suggested in a letter to the publishing firm of Scribner, Armstrong and Company, when the publication of **Old Creole Days** was being arranged, that **"Posson Jone',"** which had originally appeared in *Appletons' Journal,* be included in the selection of stories. For obvious reasons Cable did not mention **"Don Joaquin."** His reasons for neglecting the story thereafter cannot be determined with authority at this date. (pp. 419-21)

> *Rayburn S. Moore, " 'Don Joaquin,' A Forgotten Story by George W. Cable," in* American Literature, *Vol. 26, 1954-55, pp. 418-21.*

ARLIN TURNER   (essay date 1956)

[Turner was an American critic and educator who specialized in Southern literature. In the following excerpt taken from his seminal study George Washington Cable: A Biography, *Turner provides an overview of* Bonaventure *and* Strange True Stories of Louisiana.*]*

As with his Creole stories, a primary aim of Cable's was to represent the Acadians truthfully. On his trips among them, he sought out what was commonplace in their communities and yet peculiar to them. In 1887 while he was writing **"Au Large,"** he visited the southwestern parishes again and at Franklin went over the manuscripts with Mme de la Houssaye, who had long been his friend and his authority on the Acadians of the past and the present. [**Bonaventure**] has a simplicity in its action not found in either of Cable's earlier novels, a simplicity the reader feels is appropriate to the directness and outward naivete of the Acadians which conceal the intensity and the depth of their characters. The author's purpose is to hold close to the line dividing reality from absurdity; if he avoids falling into absurdity, as in the spelling bee on which hangs the future of Bonaventure and also the school he teaches at Grande Pointe, he is saved because his characters are of such directness and simplicity that the action of melodrama is natural to them. The three stories all bear out one theme—selfless devotion to others as the key to happiness. In **"Carancro"** Bonaventure finds himself through a search which obviously represents self-abnegation and self-discipline reached through the standing off of temptation. At Grande Pointe in the second story he wins out in his venture and wins personal happiness because he has held to the faith reached through the testing of the earlier story. In **"Au Large"** it is one of Bonaventure's pupils, Claude St. Pierre, who proves again that one's happiness is always in "some other one's hands" and that concern for others before self is requisite to true nobility.

Bonaventure has the charm of the Acadian villages. Elemental in their natures and devoid of intricacy or subtlety, the characters live a story similarly direct and uncomplex. The book has no characters and no scenes to stick in the reader's mind as do those of Cable's earlier books, but the total picture is impressive, the picture of a gentle people, delightful in their simplicity and heroic in their minor way. (pp. 236-37)

To some reviewers *Bonaventure* was a welcome fusion of realism and idealism; it proved the methods of realism could produce something besides unleavened photography of life. It displayed a richness of life, the Boston *Literary World* said, even in the most stringent poverty. . . . Some credited Cable with success where he had failed in his earlier books: in the character of Bonaventure he had made the force of goodness strong and active and utterly believable. They found his usual charm and humor and the faithfulness they had come to expect of him in his laying with delightful exactness the background of terrain, customs, and speech.

In November, 1888, Cable began a series of pieces in the *Century* which ran for twelve months and then formed the volume *Strange True Stories of Louisiana.* The opportunity to retell true stories was welcome to him. He could include the factual documentation he was tempted to crowd into his fiction and yet could give it an imaginative interpretation unsuited to historical writing. The occasion invited him to demonstrate his belief that true stories, but slightly dressed up, often have the interest of fiction. (pp. 237-38)

He first began collecting the true stories in 1883, and by the end of that year had in his desk the chief manuscripts and other documents relating to five of the seven he published later. Three of the stories came from Mme Sidonie de la Houssaye, a widow bringing up her children at Franklin, a village in St. Mary, one of the Acadian parishes. With literary inclinations and a wealth of information on the history and traditions of French Louisiana, much of it coming to her from ancestors among the early settlers, she published several books, in French, and wrote others that did not find a publisher. She had also trunks full of manuscripts, some of them aged through the greater part of a century. (p. 238)

Before acquiring the first manuscript from Mme de la Houssaye, Cable had been put on the track of another true story by his friend Dr. Francis Bacon in New Haven, the story of Salome Müller, who the Louisiana Supreme Court decided in 1844-45 was white, a German immigrant of 1818, who had somehow passed into slavery as a child. Explored in the newspapers and the court records, this story became **"Salome Müller, the White Slave."** The story **"Attalie Brouillard"** came orally from a judge of the author's acquaintance. It tells how a shrewd free man of color drew a will, in the role of a man just dead, for the benefit of a quadroon woman who had been something more to the deceased white man, apparently, than a landlady. Convinced after inquiry that this "tale was true so many more times than was necessary," Cable told it

with the lightness and humor appropriate to relieve the grimness some of the other stories have.

"The 'Haunted House' in Royal Street" is the grimmest of the seven tales. . . . Its history has been told over and over in print since Cable's time. His narrative contains two episodes, the second of which tells how in December, 1874, when the house was used for an unsegregated girls' high school, a mob expelled the pupils not of white blood. It was to protest against this act and the supporting editorials and mass meetings that Cable wrote two letters to the editor of the *Bulletin*. Later he read an account of the incident written by Dora Richards Miller, who had been a teacher in the school at the time. She had laid it aside because she would lose her place teaching in New Orleans if she published it.

The earlier and stranger episode, the one that gave the house its haunts, dated back to 1834, when Mme Lalaurie had entertained Creole society at sparkling dinner parties in part of the house while at the same time torturing nine of her slaves in other parts with a cruelty reminiscent of the Dark Ages. Cable began with Harriet Martineau's account as she learned it in New Orleans two years after the event and reported it in her *Retrospect of Western Travel.* James B. Guthrie and Mrs. Miller searched newspapers and documents for him and interviewed people whose memories dated back to 1834. The materials Cable had in his hands when he wrote the narrative of the Haunted House are fascinating in themselves and testify as to the care with which he used his sources. Where the reports did not agree in details, he sifted them for the points of agreement and qualified his account where there was not agreement. It is true that the subject involved two touchy subjects, slavery and the Creoles, but he no doubt was following his customary method of historical research.

The last of the *Strange True Stories of Louisiana* came from a manuscript of Dora Richards Miller's. While he was first assembling the tales in 1883, she brought him a diary she had kept during the war. The Vicksburg portion Cable published in the *Century* war series, the remainder along with the other true stories, and the complete diary in the volume. A Union sympathizer during the war, Mrs. Miller had returned to teaching in New Orleans afterward and had to conceal her authorship. She was in constant fear, as it was, lest the school board learn of it; though the names were changed in the published diary, several families in New Orleans recognized it as hers. A widow with children to support, she was glad to sell the manuscript to Cable and to earn wages doing research for him. (pp. 239-40)

In 1884 Cable had suggested that she write up her experiences during the insurrection on the island of Santa Cruz in 1848. After she had written the account and had tried for a year to find a publisher, he bought it in 1887 and laid it aside. He published it in *Scribner's Magazine* (December, 1892) as **"A West Indian Slave Insurrection."** In introducing it in the magazine, he said it was taken exactly from the manuscript of a friend, the Dora of the narrative, and reiterated that it was hers, not his. Actually he overstated, as he had done in publishing the war diary, his closeness in following the manuscript. Mrs. Miller was disappointed, however, at having herself identified only as Dora. After the *Times-Democrat* of December 4, 1892, had cited a paragraph from the "Slave Insurrection" for commendation, she wrote a letter for the December 11 issue of the paper stating that she was the Dora of the story and citing Cable's printed denial that he had done more than minor revising. She had no doubt, she said, that Cable

English author James M. Barrie and Cable.

would want her to make this statement. An anonymous letter in the same issue, no doubt drawing information from her, converted the matter into a charge that Cable had engaged in sharp dealings. The same charge was expanded in other publications and in at least one anonymous letter to Cable's publishers. At the request of the editor of the *Critic* Cable wrote an explanation for the issue of February 4, 1893. Dictated in haste on the train, he said, it was a reply only to Mrs. Miller's letter in the *Times-Democrat,* but he was obviously thinking more of the abusive charges others in New Orleans had written. Consequently he refuted more firmly the implications of her letter than he would have done otherwise, indicating how extensive his revision had been in reality, and added that the implications that he had concealed her literary ability should take account of her failure to publish her writings independently. Still he insisted that she was the writer of the story and he only the editor. (p. 241)

After the *True Stories* had been completed in the *Century,* Cable printed two supplementary letters. One of them, published in September, 1889, was written in embarrassment to explain two anachronisms in the story, **"Alix de Morainville"** which had escaped his attention and seemed to compromise the genuineness of the manuscript he had used. The other letter answered objections that had been raised to the implications in the account of the Haunted House that the White League was organized against the black race. During Reconstruction the White League, a semimilitary, semisecret organization, had been the spearhead of the efforts of white Democrats to wrest the government from the carpetbaggers. Cable replied in the issue of April, 1890, that "there are harms deeper and far more lasting than bodily injuries," and that every man in the state, black or white, had suffered from the extralegal action of the White League. He was still deeply involved in the Southern controversy, as he had been while collecting and publishing the true stories. Four of the seven dealt with phases of the great sore question, and he would not have gainsaid that the tales reflected his own coloring. He might have argued that the strongest stories of Louisiana always touched on the question somehow.

In the ten years after the publication of *Dr. Sevier,* Cable's only important addition to his literary work was *Bonaventure.* The *Strange True Stories of Louisiana* and some of the

lesser pieces, such as the articles on Creole songs and dance, had been well received; but they were primarily historical and antiquarian. The fact is that Cable in those years was a literary man only with his left hand, and a fiction writer hardly at all. That fact he regretted, and he winced when it was said that he had let his reform work draw off his energy from literature. Yet in so far as that was true, to his mind it was putting first things first. He hoped his creative work would not suffer, and he was reluctant to admit that it did, but if such was the case, it simply had to be. (p. 242)

> *Arlin Turner, in his* George W. Cable: A Biography, *Duke University Press, 1956, 391 p.*

EDMUND WILSON (essay date 1962)

[*Considered America's foremost man of letters in the twentieth century, Wilson wrote widely on cultural, historical, and literary concerns. He is often credited with bringing an international perspective to American letters through his discussions of European literature. Wilson examined the social and historical implications of a literary work, particularly literature's significance as "an attempt to give meaning to our experience" and its value "for the improvement of humanity." In the following excerpt taken from* Patriotic Gore *(1962), Wilson assesses Cable's career as a precursor of modern Southern literature.*]

[George Cable's] work during the seventies and eighties—influenced though it partly was by the more banal conventions of Victorian fiction—is astonishing, in a stuffy period and coming from the demoralized South, for its intelligence, its boldness and its brilliance. George Cable emerges in New Orleans as a phenomenon which could not have been predicted and of which, as a matter of fact, neither Northerners nor Southerners knew what to make. Not merely did the author of *Old Creole Days* possess a remarkable literary gift; he had a kind of all-around intellectual competence that was very unusual at that period in men of letters in the United States. The ups and downs of his early life, the drop from prosperity to poverty and the subsequent neccessity of regaining his place, had brought the young Cable into contact with all sorts of conditions and races. He had been through the yellow-fever and the cholera epidemics, and in the former had lost a son (these epidemics figure in several of his stories); he had witnessed the capture of New Orleans (which he describes in two of his novels) and he had fought in the Civil War (also described in two); he had acquired, through his father's interests, some firsthand knowledge of steamboating (the subject of another novel called *Gideon's Band*); and since he had spent ten years of his life—1871-81—first as manager of finances and head of the accounting department of a prominent cotton broker and then as secretary of the Finance Committee of the New Orleans Cotton Exchange, he had a practical grasp of business (the complications of which in his novels occasionally become a bore). From his days as a reporter for the *Picayune,* he had come to know who lived and traded and more or less what was going on in every street in New Orleans, as, from his researches in the city archives, he had mastered its early history. As secretary of a grand jury, he had been led to look into conditions in the prisons and asylums of the state (there is an episode about this in *Dr. Sevier*), and he had organized a movement to reform these institutions. It has been said of George Cable that he possessed at that time a more detailed and comprehensive knowledge of the state of Louisiana than anybody else alive. He was, in any case, appointed by the federal government to make the report on his state for the tenth United States census, and in connection with this census he carried out a special study of what must have been the only element of the population of Louisiana that he did not already know well—the French-speaking Acadians, known as "Cajuns," of the southwestern part of the state, descendants of those French Nova Scotians who had been expelled from Canada in the seventeen-fifties for refusing to take the oath of allegiance to the English and whom Longfellow had idyllized in *Evangeline.* He was also much interested in folklore, studied African voodoo and witchcraft, and made a collection of songs in the Creole language. (pp. 557-58)

What is unique in the work of this Southerner is the exercise of a Protestant conscience in a meridional and partly Catholic community, in which it is, however, completely at home. The violence and the scandal he writes about are the conditions of the world he lives in, but presented from a point of view that is quite distinct from the point of view of those who commit them or suffer them. It is also undoubtedly true that Cable had derived certain benefits from growing up in this mixed milieu. The lucidity and accuracy of French had, both in style and in thought, served him well, and New Orleans had a regional culture such as no other Southern city possessed. The New Orleanians loved theater and opera, and there was a certain amount of literary activity (which had begun with early writings in French and was to continue in English through our twenties). Cable had for his associates in his early days—they later became his enemies—the Franco-Spanish Creole historian Charles Gayarré, of an older generation, and his near-contemporary Lafcadio Hearn. The *Picayune,* for which he wrote, maintained a literary standard that was unusually high for the South. And the piquant variety in New Orleans of races, religions and nationalities had given Cable a kind of international experience which he could hardly, in the pre-war period, have got anywhere else in the United States. (pp. 562-63)

George Cable was the first Southern writer to try to deal in a serious work of fiction with the peculiar relationships created by the mixture of white and Negro blood; and it was not to be till fifty years later, when William Faulkner wrote *Go Down, Moses, Absalom, Absalom!* and *Intruder in the Dust,* that a Southerner who had lived with these situations would have the courage to treat them in fiction again. I do not imagine that Faulkner has been influenced by Cable; but it is interesting to note that their methods are in certain respects rather similar and seem inevitably to have been forced upon them by the nature of the material itself. In Cable and Faulkner both, the truth about family imbroglios in which a mixture of blood is involved is likely at first to be concealed from the reader, then presently in an unobtrusive way implied—allowed to leak out in some confidence of a character or made suddenly to emerge like the cat from the bag. It is treated, in other words, in the way that the Southerners treat it, and in Faulkner and Cable the suspense for the reader is likely to be created by the presence of a secret, and the climax will be a surprise.

There is in Cable's case a certain machinery of the conventional Victorian plot, but the effectiveness of his early fiction depends on the startling relationships, the unexpected courses of action that result from the queer situation of two races living side by side, entangled with one another but habitually ignoring this fact, proceeding more or less at cross-purposes but recurrently brought up short by love, sympathy

or consanguinity. Hence the violence, the scandal, the constant frustration—to which is added that other frustration of intervention by an alien power: in the early days the "Americans," in the years after the war the Yankees. The pretense that the past has not happened, that ancient history is not still with us here, makes the terror of this Southern world, the tragic irony of Cable's fiction. That episode unanimously rejected by the editors of the Northern magazine—now given a new title by the author: "The Story of Bras-Coupé"—is embodied in *The Grandissimes,* and reverberates all through the novel. The first version of the story was evidently written—by 1873—before Cable had read Turgenev, but we know that he did read the Russian in 1874, and he must have reworked it before it was published, in 1880, as a part of the novel. At any rate, it reminds one of such stories of serfdom of Turgenev's as "Mumu" and "The Wayside Inn," and it hangs over the novel of *The Grandissimes*—being part of the background of the Grandissime family—as a horror, a hideous crime, from the consequences of which they can never escape, a little as Turgenev's memories of the atrocities committed by his mother are felt as a motif of fear that runs through the whole of his work. *The Grandissimes* is Cable's best book, and the other strong things in his work are likely to repeat this theme. So in **"The 'Haunted House' in Royal Street,"** one of the *Strange True Stories of Louisiana,* the terrible Madame Lalaurie, who lived with the utmost elegance in a house full of chained and tormented slaves—we are reminded again of Turgenev's mother—and had to flee for her life from a mob when a fire revealed these infamies, is the real ghost whose presence is felt in the accursed house in Royal Street. This house has been converted by the Reconstruction government into a non-segregated high school for girls, but when the federal ascendancy has weakened, it is invaded by a local white mob, who cross-examine the students and drive away all the girls who cannot prove that they do not have black blood. (pp. 564-65)

Old Creole Days and *The Grandissimes* were not especially well received by the Creole population of New Orleans. They thought Cable had made them ridiculous by representing them as speaking bad English and even dropping into Negro patois, and they believed that he had led the public to suppose that all Creoles had Negro blood. He attempted to counteract this by doing justice to their Latin virtues in the course of recounting their history in *The Creoles of Louisiana,* published in 1884. But when he persisted—through public statements as well as through his subsequent fiction—in his searching inquiry into Southern affairs, he eventually roused up against him virtually the whole white South. In the eighties, he was publishing as articles or delivering in the form of addresses a whole series of studies of conditions in the states of the late Confederacy, which he later—in 1885 and 1890—collected in two small books, *The Silent South* and *The Negro Question.* These are among his most valuable writings, and they ought to have been recognized as classics in their field, but they appeared at a time when it happened . . . that neither the North nor the South desired to be harassed further by these problems for which the proposed solutions could never be made to come out right. They were for years almost never read by anyone save the few special students of Cable. (pp. 566-67)

The slow strangulation of Cable as an artist and a serious writer is surely one of the most gruesome episodes in American literary history. We have seen that **"The Story of Bras-Coupé"** was rejected in its original form, and that the harmless and amusing **"Posson Jone' "** was refused by four editors before it was accepted by *Appleton's Journal.* It was complained that there was no love interest in **"Posson Jone',"** and the editor of *Harper's* objected that "the disagreeable aspects of human nature are made prominent, and the story leaves an unpleasant impression on the mind of the reader." Richard Watson Gilder of *Scribner's* censored a figure of speech in another story, **" 'Tite Poulette,"** and urged Cable to "omit a touch or two of horror in **'Café des Exilés.' "** "Write something intensely interesting," he added, "but without the terrible suggestion you so often make use of." Three stories at this time were refused on account of their political implications, and were never afterwards published. "It is tempting," [Cable's biographer Arlin Turner] says, "to speculate on the kind of fiction Cable would have produced if from the time he first submitted "Bibi" onward his work had been judged by an editor less fearful of the unpleasant and the touches of horror." Mr. Turner has found two versions of the manuscript of *The Grandissimes,* which came out serially in *Scribner's,* and they show the constant carping and nagging to which the author had to submit. When he suggested doing a sequel to *The Grandissimes,* the editors would not have it at any price, for—even though complaints from the South were not yet making themselves heard—they did not want to publish in their "family magazine" any more uncomfortable stories about people of mixed blood. They really wanted nothing from Cable but little love stories of queer old New Orleans—the romance and charm of the French Quarter, those Creoles with their droll way of talking—and they did not care in the least that Cable had no natural bent for the conventional kind of romance, that his interests and his capabilities all lay in the direction of imaginative history and realistic social observation. (pp. 579-80)

One of the features of his early fiction had been his scrupulously accurate rendering of the dialects, accents and lingoes of the mixed population of the South, from Negro French and illiterate West Floridian to the English and French of the upper-class Creoles. His skill at this kind of mimicry was one of the things that made his readings successful, and he seems to have set out in [*Dr. Sevier*] to provide a certain number of scenes which would keep his mainly well-schooled audiences in gales of good-natured laughter. You have in *Dr. Sevier* not merely Negro and Creole, but also the imperfect English of Irish, German and Italian Americans, all set down with phonetic precision and stuck full of so many apostrophes that their dialogue becomes an obstacle. This conscientious book suffers, too, from a kind of miscalculation that sometimes occurs with novelists when a curious or striking true story, transposed into a work of fictions turns out to give an impression of implausibility and, in the case of *Dr. Sevier,* to seem rather pointless as well, and hence uncharacteristic of Cable. **Bonaventure,** which followed in 1888, when Cable had been warned off the subjects that aroused his unwelcome emotions, turned out, in spite of careful descriptions of the "Cajuns" and their rather wild country—the author calls the book a "prose pastoral" and is trying for the poignant-idyllic—to have been rendered completely non-memorable by a kind of wholesome insipidity and a sentimentality that fails to function. (pp. 581-82)

The real canon of Cable's books, the five of them that ought to be read by every student of American literature—*Old Creole Days, The Grandissimes,* **Strange True Stories of Louisiana,** *The Silent South* and *The Negro Question*—were all written by 1890. Though somewhat hampered in the novels that

immediately follow by the demands of the popular taste, the author of *The Grandissimes* is still trying to maintain his standing on the higher level of literature; but these books show Cable at a serious loss—witness *Bylow Hill*—as to what to do with his talents. And in the interval between **Strong Hearts** and *Bylow Hill,* he had, for the first time in his life, deliberately mustered his powers for a full-scale exploitation of the popular taste. (pp. 584-85)

> *Edmund Wilson, "Novelists of the Post-War South: Albion W. Tourgee, George W. Cable, Kate Chopin, Thomas Nelson Page," in his* Patriotic Gore: Studies in the Literature of the American Civil War, *Oxford University Press, 1962, pp. 529-616.*

HOWARD W. FULWEILER   (essay date 1966)

[*Fulweiler discusses Cable's juxtaposition of romance and realism in "Belles Demoiselles Plantation."*]

In his New Orleans tale, **"Belles Demoiselles Plantation,"** George Washington Cable describes the psychological compulsions that bind the aristocratic Colonel de Charleu and his half-caste kinsman, Injin Charlie, to their respective family homes as "ancestral nonsense." We are not entirely surprised at reading such a comment from the platform companion of that mytho-clastic realist, Mark Twain. Ironic commentary on the romantic idealism of the south comes as naturally to the local colorist Cable as it does to Mark Twain in the local color portions of *Life on the Mississippi.* The pragmatic and provisional quality of later nineteenth-century American thought, as it appears in the realistic modes of Twain, James, Howells or genre writers like Mary E. Wilkins Freeman and Sarah Orne Jewett, is often shared by Cable. Recent reevaluation of Cable's fiction has been especially fruitful in demonstrating just this aspect of his work. Two perceptive essays by Louis Rubin and Edmund Wilson ably connect Cable to his own milieu and even suggest his relationship to serious contemporary southern regionalists, especially Faulkner. Both Rubin and Wilson have particularly emphasized Cable's realism and the astonishing astuteness and courage of his social criticism of the post-Civil War South. This approach, however, has caused them to neglect the more commonly read local color stories of **Old Creole Days.** It has also caused them to overlook, I believe, some of the literary qualities in Cable's work which give it added dimension beyond social criticism on the one hand or the bizarre romanticism of so much local color on the other. (pp. 53-4)

Since Lafcadio Hearn remarked in 1883 that **"Belles Demoiselles Plantation"** was the "most singular tale" in Cable's **Old Creole Days,** criticism has been uniformly respectful of the story's charm, but has offered little explanation of its artistic success. This story, however, is more than charming. Its continued popularity is not the result of Cable's "love of mystification," or his treatment of "quaint" regional eccentricities. Instead, a mature control of plot, character and symbolism give it a powerful unity of theme, which raises it above the typical slickness of so much local color fiction.

The theme of **"Belles Demoiselles Plantation"** is composed of two parts which are closely and intricately related. The first and more apparent aspect of the theme is mutability, the precariousness of human institutions and distinctions—social, racial or economic. The second, and perhaps more important aspect for Cable, the Presbyterian Sunday School teacher, is the Biblical drama of judgment, the inevitable justice of Providence, whose agents are mutability and nature: time and the river. Added to this seemingly romantic theme is the subtly ironic tone of the narrator, the pragmatic and provisional commentator whose "common sense" realism deftly highlights the "ancestral nonsense" in the rigid attitudes of the protagonist and antagonist of the story. The tale achieves its peculiar quality of richness and depth by its craftsmanlike tension between a romantic theme of ancestral guilt and mutability and a sensitive, if ironic and pragmatic, point of view—a point of view almost Jamesian in its sense of the ongoing, unfolding quality of experience.

Judgment in **"Belles Demoiselles Plantation,"** as in so much American literature, early and late, is exacted not only for the sins of the present generation, but also for the sins of past generations. Early in the story Cable tells us with a characteristic deadpan irony that the first Count de Charleu had left his Choctaw wife behind when he was recalled to France "to explain the lucky accident of his commissariat having burned down with his account-books inside." The Count's excuses were accepted for this almost Faulknerian accident, and he was rewarded by a grant of land. Cable then introduces the ancestral guilt of the De Charleu family ironically: "A man cannot remember every thing! In a fit of forgetfulness he married a French gentlewoman, rich and beautiful and 'brought her out.' " The artistry of the narration is apparent in its evenly balanced tension. Although Cable treats the concept of ancestral guilt ironically, he nevertheless takes the fact of guilt quite seriously. His irony shifts to a mordant indictment of the Count's indifference in the next sentence: "However, 'All's well that ends well;' a famine had been in the colony, and the Choctaw Comptesse had starved, leaving nought but a half-caste orphan family lurking on the edge of the settlement." From this first crime, which resulted in the founding of the De Charleu dynasty, Cable carefully unfolds the consequences, the pragmatic results of the crime. He shows how the inevitable working of judgment, operating in time, destroys the external values—money, prestige, family, property—that the first Count and his descendants so cherished.

Since the first Count sacrificed his integrity for prestige, for the continuance of his "name" in all its feudal inconsequence, Cable comments indirectly on the results of this act by a subtly modulated ironic symbolism. The fragility of the legitimate branch of the family increases, as we see it rise, "generation after generation, tall, branchless, slender, palm-like." This symbolic attenuation of the masculine strength of the house finally flowers "with all the rare beauty of a century-plant"—which blooms only once before death—in the present Colonel's daughters. The "name," therefore, of which the Colonel is so proud cannot, despite his day-dreams, be passed on. As time destroys the male vitality of the legitimate branch of the family, so also the other branch, with the sole exception of the childless Charlie, "diminished to a mere strand by injudicious alliances, and deaths in the gutters . . . was extinct." Similarly, the De Charleu inheritance is slowly worn away by constant attrition from the Mississippi River. (pp. 54-5)

Until his final recognition of the truth, Colonel De Charleu avoids confrontation with the realities of time and judgment. Although his own plantation is heavily mortgaged, the old man confidently plans to buy and rebuild the decayed property of De Carlos, the last descendant of the Count and his Indian wife. Cable skillfully develops the contrast between external appearance and inner reality. As the river quietly erodes the foundation upon which De Charleu's outer facade

of wealth and position is displayed, so inner corruptions gnaw secretly underneath the seemingly unchanged appearance of the man. "He had had his vices—all his life; but had borne them, as his race do, with a serenity of conscience and a cleanness of mouth that left no outward blemish on the surface of the gentleman." Moral emptiness underlies the Colonel's aristocratic shell as sterility and death lurk behind the final bloom of the century plant. Even De Charleu's Creole virtue, that he "will not utterly go back on the ties of blood," is ironically related to his moral insensitivity and the ancestral guilt of his family. "He is never ashamed," Cable tells us of the Creole, "of his or his father's sins." Under the courtly exterior, there is only pride and self-love. Cable's incisive realism removes the mask of southern gentility. "With all his courtesy and bounty, and a hospitality which seemed to be entertaining angels, he was bitter-proud and penurious, and deep down in his hard-finished heart loved nothing but himself, his name, and his motherless children." One remembers, as no doubt the Bible scholar Cable remembered, that it was Lot, the inhabitant of Sodom, who entertained angels before judgment was executed on his home, and his daughters were rendered motherless.

The intricate dialectic between romantic theme and realistic point of view is further intensified as Cable continues to unfold his narrative. His realistic, though comic, treatment of the aristocratic Colonel's ludicrous and pathetic attempt to bolster his decaying external identity by acquiring Injin Charlie's house in town balances with delicate irony the transcendent theme of the story against the humorous *facts* of the situation. Although the attempts of the two old men—one of them deaf—to speak English are comic, mutability and judgment are always present, modifying and transforming the quality of the humor. (pp. 56-7)

In the careful unraveling of the drama, the Colonel has been offered a choice: he has been given the opportunity to acknowledge the common humanity he shares with his kinsman, a brotherhood symbolized by the two inherited houses. This is the common humanity the first Count De Charleu denied in order to have a "name." The Colonel, like his ancestor, refuses to acknowledge his human brotherhood with De Carlos and in so doing refuses self-recognition as well.

The beginning of De Charleu's self-recognition comes some months after he has refused Charlie's final offer to trade his city block for the plantation house. Sitting on the levee, he muses on the emptiness of his past life, paralyzed and made useless by "pride," "gaming," and "voluptuous ease." Nevertheless, "his house still stood, his sweet-smelling fields were still fruitful, his name was fame enough; and yonder and yonder, among the trees and flowers, like angels walking in Eden, were the seven goddesses of his only worship." As the Colonel begins to perceive the attrition of time and vice on his personality, he turns complacently to the external possessions that have hitherto been his substitute for character—house, name, property, daughters. At this moment he hears a slight sound which brings him to his feet. "There came a single plashing sound, like some great beast slipping into the river, and little waves in a wide semi-circle came out from under the bank and spread over the water." The bank upon which his house stands, the material foundation of his life, which had seemed so solid, has begun to cave in. Like Henry James's John Marcher, the Colonel has always avoided contact with the real substance of life until, with feral stealth, it slips into his life "like some great beast." Yet this first revelation does not cause a moral awakening in De Charleu; he only sees with brutal clarity the reality of time and decay.

At the threat of losing his property, in which he has always based his sense of identity, De Charleu's moral collapse becomes complete, and he hurries frantically back to town to trade his house for Old Charlie's block. It is not until the two men return to look at the property, that he finally has a true vision of himself; he recognizes that he is about "to betray his own blood," that he does share a common humanity with Charlie which he is ready to violate. Although he warns Charlie, time and the river are inexorable. The thoughtless superficiality and the self-seeking pride of the De Charleus, with their dependence upon externals, are judged. "Belles Demoiselles, the realm of maiden beauty, the home of merriment, the house of dancing, all in the tremor and glow of pleasure suddenly sunk, with one short, wild wail of terror—sunk, sunk, down, down, down, into the merciless, unfathomable flood of the Mississippi." If Cable has suggested God's punishment of Sodom and Gomorrah early in the story, he suggests finally His judgment of the contemporaries of Noah.

By this final symbolic action of the river Cable fuses his two themes into one. The river, as type and metaphor of time and mutability, the ever-flowing substance that has joined together the generations of the De Charleus and now washes them away, emerges as the agent of divine justice.

What conclusions are we to draw then from our close reading of this local color sketch? . . . Our reading shows clearly, it seems to me, that Cable is making use of the universal themes of mutability, sin, guilt and judgment presented in romantic, idealistic and sometimes gothic modes in the earlier fiction of Poe, Hawthorne or Melville. Does this mean that Cable's story is simply a continuation of the romantic symbolism of the earlier nineteenth century? Not exactly. Our reading seems to show differences and modifications as striking as the likenesses. Cable's delicate control of narrative point of view, his ironic balancing of pragmatic and unsentimental comment with romantic theme, and his sense of the ongoing, unfolding quality of experience relate him to the tradition of critical realism.

What general conclusions may we arrive at, then? Perhaps the work of Cable's friend and colleague, that sometime local colorist and frontier humorist, Mark Twain, may be instructive. It is a continual source of paradox that the elemental themes of a book like *Huckleberry Finn* have made inevitable mythic and romantic interpretations of Twain, a conscious, even self-conscious realist. In **"Belles Demoiselles Plantation"** we have a similar fusion of realistic technique with romantic theme. Does not our close reading, perhaps, make it possible to see Cable as more than an intelligent and socially aware critic of his own time or as a quaint romancer of superficial eccentricities? Do we not see another link in the chain of American literary history? I would like to suggest that in the realistically handled unravelling of the fate of the last of the De Charleus we may perhaps see even more clearly a stage in development from the openly romantic treatment of mutability, guilt and retribution in, say, "The Fall of the House of Usher" or *The House of the Seven Gables* toward the realistic myth of Yoknapatawpha County in the twentieth century. And is it not just this sort of concrete example of change, this fusion of traditions, that both illuminates and validates *our* concept of what Parrington might have termed a "main current" of American thought. (pp. 57-9)

Howard W. Fulweiler, "Of Time and the River: 'Ancestral Nonsense' vs. Inherited Guilt in Cable's 'Belles Demoiselles Plantation'," in Midcontinent American Studies Journal, Vol. 7, No. 2, Fall, 1966, pp. 53-9.

LOUIS D. RUBIN, JR. (essay date 1969)

[*Rubin is an American critic and educator who has written and edited numerous scholarly studies of Southern literature. In the following excerpt, he analyzes Cable's use of local color and treatment of Creole morality in relation to the "Genteel Tradition" of American literature.*]

The typical local color story, as written by Thomas Nelson Page, Joel Chandler Harris, Mary Noailles Murfree, and, in his less original moments, Cable himself, was a hybrid literary form. It provided close detail of setting and, within limits, a realistic descriptive texture, but these were grafted onto an essentially romantic plot structure, commonly a love story. The characters, though given the particularities of regional life, tended to be types, with little depth or complexity to them, designed to exhibit the quaint eccentricities of provincial life. The typical local color story was a form of pastoral romance, with an emphasis on setting; if in their quaintness and simplicity the characters constituted something of a rebuke to the complexities and urgencies of post-Civil War urban America, the rebuke was gently administered, and comforting to the nation's widespread wish to believe that the simple American virtues of prewar days still existed. In any event, the appetite of the American magazine reading public for picturesque provincial tales seemed unquenchable, and the mass magazines competed for circulation with story after story of local color fiction.

Because it was shaped for a mass market and designed for family consumption, magazine fiction accepted the ideals and the inhibitions of the dominant Genteel Tradition. Sex was to be treated obliquely, and depiction of physical passion was taboo. Ideality was the pervading mode; religion was sacrosanct. Overt unpleasantness of setting or characterization was frowned upon; the rigors of life on the farm in a time of failing farm prices and widespread rural poverty, the exigencies of a meager existence in the defeated cities of the South, were not permitted to infringe upon the romantic plot structure and quaint descriptions of an idealized provincial life. Controversial topics and attitudes were to be avoided; when Southern writers such as Page ventured to exhibit traces of lingering Confederate prejudices, such passages were carefully excised. The world was essentially good, and magazine fiction must perforce reflect the goodness.

Thus, if in the history of American literature the local color movement represents a stage in the development of a realistic fiction, it is primarily because its technique, involving the detailed description of provincial life, served to introduce a more diversified subject matter and to place a premium upon accurate, if very much selected, observation. When, as sometimes happened in Cable's fiction, the attempt to render the details of regional experience drew the artist's eye toward the inclusion of unpleasant and even ugly elements, the magazine editors who guarded the sensibilities of their readers were quick to protest.

The story entitled **"Posson Jone',"** perhaps the best of Cable's early stories—all of which appeared in magazines before being published in book form under the title *Old Creole*

Days in 1879—is an example of the problems that a writer like Cable faced in his dealings with the magazine editors of the Genteel Tradition. This story, which involves a drunken preacher who is willing to gamble away his church's money, was rejected by *Scribner's Monthly,* and then in succession by the New York *Times,* the *Galaxy,* and *Harper's.* When Henry Mills Alden, editor of *Harper's,* returned it, he commented that "the disagreeable aspects of human nature are made prominent, and the story leaves an unpleasant impression on the mind of the reader," adding later that the stories in *Harper's* "must be of a pleasant character and, as a rule, must be love tales." Ironically, **"Posson Jone' "** when published proved to be the most widely commended of all of Cable's stories, and was praised by Charles Dudley Warner for showing that actual life, even low life, could be heightened to gain an idealistic effect. (pp. 44-6)

The public taste for local color provided, therefore, both a signal opportunity and a potentially severe liability for George W. Cable in his drive to become a successful writer. There can be no question of Cable's good fortune in having been born and raised in New Orleans; the lavish color, the romantic history, the exotic mixture of races and civilizations, provided him with a setting that was ideally suited to the growing American interest in provincial life, and his own descriptive talents were precisely those best calculated to take advantage of the situation. Highly conscious of racial differences, strongly interested in society and the relationships between people, alert to the sensuous possibilities of life in a richly complex Southern city with a strong Latin heritage, he was admirably equipped to answer the demand for fiction that emphasized a rich textural surface. The sound, shape, feel, and smell of everyday life was his metier; he was a master of the composition of place, writing at precisely the time when that quality was in great demand. As for Cable's other qualities—a strongly developed social conscience, a talent for probing boldly into the moral and social subterfuges of the life around him, an unwillingness to accept half-truths and convenient rationalizations—these were less well adapted to the demands of his editors and the public. But at first, as he wrote the stories that would make up *Old Creole Days,* these liabilities did not seem crucial. (p. 46)

The story, " 'Sieur George," contains in miniature almost everything out of which Cable was to make his art, and it is dominated by a particular tone and his major theme, the Creoles of New Orleans. The tale of an *Américain* gentleman who spends the better part of his life and all of his fortune gambling unsuccessfully with tickets on the Cuban lottery, **" 'Sieur George"** has about it an air of pervading languor, the futility and decadence, with a hint of the voluptuous, of a Latin race living in slothful ease in a Southern city under warm skies. The protagonist, known first as "Monsieur" and later, as his fortunes decline, merely as " 'Sieur George," dwells for fifty years in two rented rooms in a brick house in the French Quarter. His origins are unknown. Like the Creole landlord Kookoo whose attempts to find out the secret in his tenant's hair trunk constitute the framework of the story, we view 'Sieur George from without, a somewhat imposing but not quite heroic figure, who makes his living in obscure ways, drinks a great deal, and tells nobody about himself or his past. From the very first there is the sense of ruin, embodied in the description of the building, which itself stands for what we shall finally perceive is the moral ruin of 'Sieur George:

> With its gray stucco peeling off in broad patches, it has a solemn look of gentility in rags, and stands, or, as it were, hangs, about the corner of two ancient streets, like a faded fop who pretends to be looking for employment.
>
> (pp. 46-7)

When 'Sieur George first moved in, he brought a small hair trunk; and when Kookoo took hold of this trunk to help in arranging the apartment, 'Sieur George had threatened to hit him, thus arousing the landlord's deepest curiosity as to its contents. After 'Sieur George had gone off to fight in the Mexican War—for he surprised them all one day by stepping out of the old house in full regimentals—Kookoo had hoped at last to find out what was in the trunk, but 'Sieur George's apartment was at once occupied by a Creole lady and servant who in their aloofness offered him no opportunity to look within. After the war, 'Sieur George fails to return for some time. When eventually he does so, it is with a scar from a saber wound on his forehead, and a friend in tow, a "tall, lank, iron-gray man." For a while it seems to everyone that 'Sieur George is preparing to marry the woman inhabiting his apartment, but apparently it was the tall friend who won the lady's hand. After the wedding, 'Sieur George returns to dwell in the apartment again. Turned momentarily garrulous, he tells Kookoo and others how the tall man, a "drunkard" for whom he had little regard, had attached himself to him during the war, and he makes it clear that he disapproves of the marriage. Then his forebodings are justified; the wife dies, 'Sieur George brings home her infant child, and soon afterward the father is found drowned. 'Sieur George raises the child by himself; he has reformed, no longer comes home drunk. Eventually the child turns sixteen, reaches womanhood. One evening there ensues a final dramatic scene, which the eavesdropping Kookoo witnesses. 'Sieur George tells the girl that she can no longer live with him. . . . (pp. 47-8)

The girl weeps pathetically, sobbing that she cannot bear to leave the old man. Whereupon—and here Cable's instinctive artistry thoroughly redeems the story from the sentimental romance it has seemed to be turning into—'Sieur George "was encouraged by the orphan's pitiful tones to contemplate the most senseless act he ever attempted to commit." He tells the girl that she is not really blood kin to him, and that there is one way whereby she can with propriety continue to live with him:

> She looked up at the old man with a glance of painful inquiry.
>
> "If you could be—my wife, dearie?"
>
> She uttered a low, distressful cry, and, gliding swiftly into her room, for the first time in her young life turned the key between them.
>
> And the old man sat and wept.

This startling dénouement, with its sense of degradation, its suggestion of near depravity, its furtive understatement, destroys whatever admiration has been building for 'Sieur George in the reader's mind. His moral degradation is clear. When the girl departs to take up life in a convent, and 'Sieur George slumbers away in a drunken stupor, we learn the secret of his troubles; Kookoo steals into the apartment, manages to look into the mysterious trunk, and finds it filled with a mass of worthless tickets on the Havana lottery. We last glimpse 'Sieur George sleeping out in the high grass along the edge of the prairie, and still seeking in vain to talk to the girl in order to borrow ten dollars for yet another try at the lottery.

" 'Sieur George," we are told, so puzzled Richard Watson Gilder and his fellow editors at *Scribner's Monthly* that before it was accepted for publication Cable was asked to insert several clarifying sentences and to write a final paragraph. One can understand why; what is told is stated indirectly, and a great deal of the appeal and strength of the story comes from its delicate gliding over matters that if presented directly would doubtless never have won Gilder's approval. The sense of decadence, of moral ruin, is so artfully embodied in the physical dilapidation and decay that it is difficult to point to any actual, direct statement of the story's chief appeal, its depiction of sensual indulgence and moral squalor. The statement that Kookoo is "of doubtful purity of blood," the remark that the young Creoles of the neighborhood think that the mulatto maid, "a tall, straight woman," is "confound' good lookin'," and above all the eloquent understatement of the passage in which 'Sieur George's niece recoils at his proposal . . . are almost the only specific sexual references in a story with nonetheless profoundly sensual overtones. The extent of Gilder's comprehension of the story's true nature may be gauged from his statement to Cable that he must "work as religiously as if you already had Bret Harte's reputation—and perhaps you may have one as lasting."

Bret Harte, with his sentimental prostitutes, tender-hearted gold miners, and the like, was hardly of the same rank as Cable; the unsentimental, almost savage depiction of human degradation in " 'Sieur George," with its acceptance of decadence, strikes a note that Harte never attained. The statement of Gilder's assistant, Robert Underwood Johnson, that "it was a fresh and gentle southwest wind that blew into the office in 1873" when the story arrived at *Scribner's Monthly* seems almost comically inappropriate. (pp. 48-50)

In any event, " 'Sieur George" is a remarkable psychological study, and in its time and place seems all the more startling; critics who complain of its absence of plot and its insipidity as social criticism miss the point. Its plot is completely appropriate to what the story has to say, and the story moves beyond mere social criticism to offer a compelling picture of human degradation. The artistry is a great deal more like that of James Joyce in *Dubliners* than that of even the best of Cable's contemporaries. If only, one laments, Cable had enjoyed editorial tutelage equipped to recognize what he had to offer, and critics able to perceive the nature of his artistic gift. But this was never to be.

Though Cable made his degenerating protagonist in " 'Sieur George" one of the *Américains,* his depiction of the Creoles, primarily through the landlord Kookoo, was hardly flattering. His remark that "your second-rate Creole is a great seeker for little offices," his description of Kookoo as "an ancient Creole of doubtful purity of blood," his insistence upon the pretensions of the little landlord, as in his statement that Kookoo "felt a Creole's anger, too, that a tenant should be the holder of wealth while his landlord suffered poverty," above all his depiction of the Creole as venial, acquisitive, and "intensely a coward," were not calculated to endear the author to Creole New Orleans.

"Belles Demoiselles Plantation," the second story to appear, fastens upon miscegenation. Like all the tales of *Old Creole Days,* the story takes place in the early years of the nineteenth century. Cable begins by describing two lines of the distin-

Cable in the study at Tarryawhile, his estate in Northampton, Massachusetts.

guished Creole family of De Charleu: the legitimate branch which "rose straight up, up, up, generation after generation, tall, branchless, slender, palm-like"; and the sinister branch, product of a union of the original De Charleu and a Choctaw wife, its name corrupted by Spanish contact to De Carlos, now "diminished to a mere strand by injudicious alliances, and deaths in the gutters of old New Orleans," of which the single surviving representative is one Injin Charlie. The latter, "sunk in the bliss of deep ignorance, shrewd, deaf, and, by repute at least, unmerciful," owns a block of dilapidated buildings left to the Indian side of the family by his great grandfather, while the legitimate De Charleus, consisting of Old Colonel Jean Albert Henri Joseph De Charleu-Marot and his seven beautiful daughters, inhabit lovely Belles Demoiselles Plantation at a point below New Orleans on the Mississippi. (pp. 50-1)

The story revolves about the Colonel's attempt to persuade his half-breed relative to sell him his town property—for the Colonel's seven beautiful daughters have been badgering him to move from Belles Demoiselles into New Orleans and its gay social life. Injin Charlie steadfastly refuses; what would people say? he demands: "dey will say, 'Old Charlie he been all doze time tell a blame *lie!* He ain't no kin to his old grace-gran-muzzer, not a blame bit! He don't got nary drop of De Charleu blood to save his blame low-down old Injin soul! . . . ' " He proposes to trade his property for Belles Demoiselles, but the Colonel will have none of this— until he realizes one day that the Point on which the plantation house is located is eroding so rapidly that the house must soon be washed away. He then determines to make the trade, and Injin Charlie assents. But at the last minute the ties of blood are too strong to permit the Colonel to defraud his half-breed cousin; he takes him out to inspect Belles Demoiselles, then declares: "My God!—old man, I tell you—you better not make the trade!" "Because of what?" Injin Charlie asks "in plain anger," whereupon, as the two of them watch, "Belles Demoiselles, the realm of maiden beauty, the home of merriment, the house of dancing, all in the tremor and glow of pleasure, suddenly sunk, with one short, wild wail of terror—sunk, sunk, down, down, into the merciless, unfathomable flood of the Mississippi." The stricken Colonel, his seven beautiful daughters drowned in the river, lives on for a year longer, nursed by old Injin Charlie, until at last he dies, dreaming of his daughters in the garden. . . . (pp. 51-2)

Despite the sensational melodrama of the conclusion, **"Belles Demoiselles Plantation"** is an effective tale, not least for its depiction of Injin Charlie. This dissolute, half-deaf old man, living in semi-squalor and idleness with an aged and crippled Negress, is a much more convincing figure than the proud Colonel; in his lazy corruption and sybaritism, he represents very much the same image of decay and unregenerate hedonism that characterizes the milieu of **" 'Sieur George."** For all his squalor, there is something at once exotic and attractive in his disdain for the hard work of moneymaking, his preference for sitting placidly in the sun on his bench in the garden, under a China tree. And despite the fact that throughout his fiction Cable's conscious sympathies are usually with the energetic, bustling *Américains* rather than with the indolent, pleasure-loving Creoles whether of higher or lower caste, one senses here, as often in Cable's fiction, a kind of admiration for and even envy of the lazy, sensual way in which the Creoles accommodate themselves to their circumstance. It is not that Cable portrays the Creoles as nonmaterialistic, but simply that their natural indolence keeps them from working too hard for anything. The portraits of both Injin Charlie and the Colonel, however, and particularly the emphasis on the mixed blood lines, were hardly flattering to the Creoles.

Lax Creole morality plays an even more striking part in the story entitled **" 'Tite Poulette,"** this time in direct contrast to Nordic, or more precisely, Dutch attitudes. This story, the first, save for the rejected "Bibi," in which Cable dealt directly with the Negro situation, involves an octoroon woman, Zalli, called Madame John, and her lovely daughter, "white like a waterlily! White—like a magnolia!" who live across the street from Kristian Koppig, a rosy-faced, beardless young Dutchman. Zalli had been the mistress of a Creole, Monsieur John, who had loved her and had left her not only a daughter known as 'Tite Poulette, but also ample funds when he died. The money has long since been lost in a bank failure, however, and to earn her living Zalli, her identity masked, dances at one of the famed quadroon balls, which at this stage in New Orleans history have become quite degenerate. The Creole manager of the ball, having once spied 'Tite Poulette in company with her mother, seeks to force his attentions on the beautiful young woman. When he refuses to go away from their door, Kristian Koppig slaps him across the face.

Later, upon learning that Madame John must dance at the ball out of financial necessity, however much she loathes the task, Koppig goes to urge her not to do so, but discovers he is too late. So he goes to the ball himself to ask her to leave, and there is set upon and stabbed repeatedly by the manager and his friends. Madame John has him taken to her apartment, where she and 'Tite Poulette nurse him to health. The young Dutchman declares his love for 'Tite Poulette and proposes marriage, but the distraught maiden cannot accept— "it is against the law" for one of part-Negro blood to marry a white man. Whereupon Madame John reveals that 'Tite Poulette is not her child and Monsieur John's, but the child of a Spanish couple that Monsieur John had befriended— both of them having died of the fever: "I have robbed God long enough! Here are the sworn papers—here! Take her; she is as white as snow—so! Take her, kiss her; Mary be praised! I never had a child—she is the Spaniard's daughter!"

The happy ending, though Cable attempted to prepare for it

by earlier hints, is very much a *deus ex machina* contrivance and, as Cable knew well, did not constitute a realistic solution to what he felt was the injustice of racial discrimination; in a later [novella], **"Madame Delphine,"** he would confront the matter more directly. Still, in presenting so forcefully the plight of the quadroons, Cable was criticizing racial discrimination both as it had existed back in antebellum days and, by inference, in the New Orleans of his own times, which still legally forbade persons of mixed blood to marry whites. And in presenting the Creoles as the perpetrators of the quadroon system, he was again placing them in an unfavorable light. (pp. 52-3)

The famed **"Posson Jone',"** which appeared first in *Appletons'* because the editors of *Scribner's Monthly* and several other magazines found it too coarse, also contrasts Creole and Anglo-Saxon morality, this time for purposes of comedy. One Jules St.-Ange, an indolent young Creole down on his luck, leaps at the opportunity to bilk a tall American preacher from West Florida of his roll of banknotes belonging to Smyrny Church. He succeeds in getting the *Américain* drunk, but when the huge West Floridian preaches to a jeering multitude come to see a battle between a tiger and a buffalo, then lifts up the tiger and single-handedly places him upon the back of the buffalo in order to demonstrate that "the tiger and the buffler *shell* lay down together!", the little Creole is so overcome by admiration that he extricates the preacher from jail. Posson Jone' is filled with remorse, for he has lost the money entrusted to him by his parishioners. Jules, who has won a large sum of money playing cards, seeks to give the money to the parson to make up the loss; Posson Jone' refuses, but when he boards the schooner to go home, it turns out that his Negro slave has safeguarded his money all along. So moved is Jules St.-Ange by the whole thing that he resolves to pay his debts and become an honest man.

Here Cable, in spite of his satire of the naïve country American preacher, presents the Anglo-Saxon as morally superior to the Creole. In several fine dialogues, their attitude toward religion is humorously contrasted; Jules's religion is a mere form, in no way binding upon his conduct, while Parson Jones is theologically narrow and naïve, but, as Jules says, "the so fighting an' moz rilligious man as I never saw!" If Jules can separate an *Américain* from his money, he "might find cause to say some 'Hail Marys!' " . . . Both the Creole and the Protestant preacher are equally convinced of the complete inferiority of Negroes, and the portrait of neither could be said to be flattering, but it is the parson who inspires the Creole to act in untypical Creole fashion and pay his debts. (p. 54)

In retrospect it seems especially unfortunate that of all the stories of his early years, it was **"Posson Jone' "** that Cable had the greatest difficulty in placing for publication, for the discouragement surely had the effect of helping to convince him that this kind of broad, detached humor, which took no sides and made sport of the naïveté of Southern Protestantism, was an unprofitable literary business. The much greater acceptability of his more romantic, idealistic tales must have indicated to him that this, and not broad comedy, was the direction in which he should move in his future writings.

In the story entitled **"Madame Déliceuse,"** there is no direct confrontation of Creole and Anglo-Saxon. Very much a romance all the way, it centers on the efforts of a young Creole woman, Madame Déliceuse, to reconcile her friend General Hercule Mossy de Villivicencio, a pompous and martial old veteran of the War of 1812-15, with his son, Dr. Mossy, physician and (unknown to his Creole neighbors) distinguished scientist, whom she loves. The General resents the fact that his son shows no interest in military matters and heroic attitudes, and for some years they have not spoken, but Madame Déliceuse cleverly arranges their reconciliation, and all ends happily with the espousal of Mossy and Madame Déliceuse. The story, however, contains considerable humor about the Creoles' vanity and showiness. There are digs at the Creoles' lack of awareness of what goes on in the world beyond New Orleans; they have no idea that Dr. Mossy is a distinguished man of science, and consider him only a mild little physician. Furthermore, the doctor at first refuses to fight a duel to defend his father's honor, and Cable makes it clear that his attitude toward dueling not only makes him morally superior to the Creoles but, even though he is himself a Creole, very much untypical of the race. As for Madame Déliceuse, though she is an admirable woman, she is so in Creole fashion, with "her principles, however, not constructed in the austere Anglo-Saxon style, exactly (what need, with the lattice of the Confessional not a stone's-throw off?)" She is virtuous and generous, but very much acquainted with the ways of the world, and by no means averse to using deceit if the ultimate goal be good. The story is slight, touches on no important themes, and makes its appeal entirely through the quaint characters and the exotic atmosphere of early nineteenth-century New Orleans. (pp. 55-6)

"Jean-ah Poquelin," by contrast, is perhaps the most somber of all the stories of *Old Creole Days.* Old Jean-ah Poquelin, an indigo planter once, later a smuggler and slave trader, is a recluse. He lives in an old plantation house on a canal early in the nineteenth century, not long after American rule over Louisiana has been established. Once he had been popular and highly respected, but after returning from a slaving trip, he went into seclusion. There had been a brother whom he had revered, but who had disappeared from sight after the final trip. There are rumors of a ghost out on the Poquelin place, and some suspicion that the brother is being kept there. Meanwhile, New Orleans is expanding beyond the old city, and streets are laid out past the Poquelin place; old Jean-ah has sought to get the American authorities to forbid the draining and filling in of the swamp near his house, but in vain. A development company wishes to purchase the house, but the old Creole will not negotiate. . . . Finally a horde of Creoles, at the instigation of the Americans, goes out to the Poquelin place one night to shivaree its owner. . . . Not until then does the secret of the Poquelin place reveal itself; from the half-ruined old mansion come a deaf-mute servant with the coffin of Jean-ah Poquelin, followed by a figure as white as snow—Jacques Poquelin, the long-hidden brother, now a leper. The crowd watches as the Negro mute and the brother go off with the coffin into the swamp, toward the leper colony there.

In this story the old Creole's nobility and loyalty to his brother stand out in sharp contrast both to the Americans who are bent on developing new areas of the city, and to the unfeeling, exuberant Creole townsfolk who go out to shivaree the old man. Only Little White, the secretary of the development firm, is able to appreciate the dignity and courage of the old Creole. With its stark outlines, its sense of tragedy, its playing off of the commercialism of the Americans and the callousness of the Creole mob against the lonely dignity of Jean-ah Poquelin, faithful to his terrible burden, the story is one of Cable's best. Cable gives a tragic dignity to the Creole past

manfully confronting its sins (it was in Africa, on a slaving expedition, that Jacques Poquelin had contracted his dread disease), in doomed resistance to the irresistible forces of progress and commercial development. Yet the story could hardly be read with pride by Cable's Creole neighbors; the fact that old Jean-ah Poquelin had been a smuggler and slave trader, and the depiction of the brother as a leper, scarcely constituted a complimentary portrayal of Creole society.

The remaining story in *Old Creole Days,* **"Café des Exilés,"** deals not with the old French-Spanish Creoles of pre-American Louisiana, but with a group of Spanish exiles from Cuba during the 1840's, who meet at the Café des Exilés to plot an expedition to Cuba and to plan ways of smuggling weapons out of New Orleans. Philip Butcher cites the story as an example of Cable's racism; the hero, he notes, is an Irish adventurer: "Always the male partner belongs to a race commonly regarded by Americans at the time as superior to the race of the woman. A beautiful Creole girl may win the love of an Anglo-Saxon, or an octoroon may capture a male Creole, but the coin is never reversed." This is not strictly accurate: the tall man who wins the hand of the sister of 'Sieur George is apparently a Creole, while 'Sieur George and presumably his sisters are Americans; and in Cable's second novel, *Dr. Sevier,* Irish Kate Riley marries Italian Rafael Ristofalo. It is true, however, that Cable, himself a Protestant of German and New England stock, tends to make his villains dark-complexioned and his heroes light-hued, and he often seems to equate darkness, especially of the Creole sort, with lax morals—though not always, as witness Mossy and 'Sieur George. (pp. 56-8)

Creole beauty fascinated Cable; his Creole heroines, whether of mixed or entirely white blood, are among his most alluring creatures. He admires the utter femininity and helplessness of Zalli and 'Tite Poulette; he finds the element of mixed blood allied with pure whiteness of complexion quite enthralling. What appeals to him as artist, and so distinguishes his New Orleans stories, is the physical texture of Creole life. For all his religious belief, as a writer he is secular in a way that almost no other American novelist of his century is.

The stories of *Old Creole Days* present a densely packed social panorama of class and caste. Cable's art is very much of the everyday, the ordinary; it is not the sometimes highly romanticized plots—Belles Demoiselles Plantation being swept away by the river, the beautiful Creole maiden nursing Kristian Koppig back to health, and so forth—that constitute the chief appeal. Rather it is the social scene, the rich variety of social life, with the coming and going of people, the confrontation of Creole and Anglo-American attitudes and customs, the impact of racial admixture. The art of the stories in *Old Creole Days* is founded upon realistic social observation. (pp. 58-9)

What is largely missing from these stories, however, is any important attempt at social *criticism.* Except for the implied relevance of the plight of the quadroons in **" 'Tite Poulette"** to the plight of the Negro in post-Civil War New Orleans, there is relatively little evidence of the author's desire to protest social inequities. The attack on racism that is so prominent even in his next book, *The Grandissimes,* is hardly evident here at all. Only in occasional remarks—Jules St.-Ange and Posson Jone' on the subject of Negroes and heaven, the abrupt sale of 'Sieur George's sister's slave after her marriage—does Cable touch on racism, except in **" 'Tite Poulette."** To be sure, there is considerable *implied* criticism. The fact that 'Sieur George's ruin comes because of his mania for the lottery is not without its relevance to the existence of the infamous Louisiana State Lottery of Cable's own day. **"Jean-ah Poquelin"** comments obliquely but meaningfully on commercialism at the expense of human compassion. **"Madame Déliceuse"** has things to say both about dueling and about intellectual insularity. And certainly Cable goes to considerable lengths to criticize the democratic failings of the Creoles of Louisiana. But the point is precisely that most of this is suggested obliquely; it grows out of the fiction, and is in most instances a part of the characterization and the story line. The stories generally succeed on their own merit as fiction. (pp. 59-60)

"You bother me," Richard Watson Gilder had written to Cable after reading **"Madame Déliceuse"**: "Your conception of character is strong—artistic—your style is bright and witty—your plots are generally good—your field is all your own—and I consider your stories a great acquisition to the monthly—but you lack in the capacity to edit yourself. This is the only thing that makes me fear for your literary future." Gilder was by no means an infallible critic; his role in Cable's eventual development is open to considerable question, and it is doubtful that the kind of self-editing he wanted Cable to be capable of was what should have been done. All the same, he may well have sensed, however indistinctly and vaguely, what might prove to be a severe limitation indeed to Cable's artistry: not an inability to edit his material as such, but literally an inability to edit *himself*—to recognize what it was that he was really trying to do, and to shape his material to that end. (p. 61)

> Louis D. Rubin, Jr., in his George W. Cable: The Life and Times of a Southern Heretic, *Pegasus, 1969, 304 p.*

JOSEPH J. EGAN (essay date 1970)

[*In the following excerpt, Egan examines Cable's use of myth and symbolism to comment upon the demise of the old Creole order in* "Jean-ah Poquelin."]

Throughout **"Jean-Ah Poquelin"** picturesque description, apropos to the local color tradition, takes on subtle symbolic overtones. The Poquelins' "old colonial plantation-house half in ruin" externalizes the decay and approaching death of the Creole order of early nineteenth-century Louisiana in the wake of "the newly established American Government": "It stood aloof from civilization, the tracts that had once been its indigo fields given over to their first noxious wildness, and grown up into one of the horridest marshes within a circuit of fifty miles." This change-regression motif is paralleled in the life of the plantation's owner, Jean Marie Poquelin, "once an opulent indigo planter, standing high in the esteem of his small, proud circle of exclusively male acquaintances in the old city; now a hermit, alike shunned by and shunning all who had ever known him." Significantly, old Jean Marie is " 'the last of his line' "—the archetypal Creole, unable to resist the advance of an immigrant culture.

Jacques Poquelin vivifies both the antithesis and complement of his elder half-brother's qualities; indeed, their finely balanced personalities and mutual love and respect create a noble life of psychological wholeness: "They had seemed to live so happily in each other's love. No father, mother, wife to either, no kindred upon earth. The elder a bold, frank, impetuous, chivalric adventurer; the younger a gentle, studious,

book-loving recluse; they lived upon the ancestral estate like mated birds, one always on the wing, the other always in the nest." Although these representatives of the Creole heritage attain a spiritual vitality, despite Jean's involvement in the slave-trade, which, in characteristic simplicity, he regards as "a vital public necessity," their own impracticality causes a pecuniary decline. . . . Even the venture in the slave-trade proves ultimately disastrous, and in having Jacques return from the Guinea Coast "a leper, as white as snow," and Jean begin a life of mysterious retirement to protect the family's hideous secret, Cable implies the Poquelins' total lack of status in contemporary New Orleans.

The thematic conflict dramatized in **"Jean-Ah Poquelin,"** then, concerns the opposing spiritual and material orders, the Creole brothers being, as we have seen, unable to integrate the two; but the extent of their success or failure can be estimated only by comparing their achievement with that of "the Anglo-American flood that was presently to burst in a crevasse of immigration upon the delta." In bringing physical improvement and economic growth to Louisiana, the newcomers obviously succeed where the Creole has failed. . . . This material prosperity, however, brings with it a disintegration of human relationships noticeably at odds with the complete "brotherhood" attained by the Poquelins. To appreciate the difference in values between the two societies, the American and the French Creole, we have only to note the "sharp" business practices and perverse rationalizations of the newly formed Building and Improvement Company: " 'Mr. President, this market-house project, as I take it, is not altogether a selfish one; the community is to be benefited by it. We may feel that we are working in the public interest (the Board smiled knowingly), if we employ all possible means to oust this old nuisance from among us." A further indictment of the new "civilization" is suggested when Cable parallels this animosity for profit with the antagonism the lower-class Creoles show Jean Marie, an antagonism that, under the influence of American customs, hardens naive superstition into malicious intolerance:

> How easily even the most ultra Louisianians put on the imported virtues of the North when they could be brought to bear against the hermit. "There he goes, with the boys after him! Ah! ha! ha! Jean-ah Poquelin! . . . The old villain!" How merrily the swarming Américains echo the spirit of persecution! "The old fraud," they say—"pretends to live in a haunted house, does he? We'll tar and feather him some day. Guess we can fix him."

This image of the human being, rejected and ostracized by the loveless majority, draws the various strains of Cable's story into an impressive pattern of symbolism. The tragedy of Jacques Poquelin, the leper, enfolds the fate of the other characters who cannot assimilate the arbitrary, harsh conventions of the Northern settlers and their Creole minions: the dissenters are met with mistrust and "shunned like lepers." Just as the voice of persecution denounces Jean Marie's desire for privacy, so also does it cry down the example of Christian charity supplied by Mr. White, the "mild, kind-hearted little" Secretary of the Board and eventual defender of Poquelin. . . . As his name is perhaps meant to imply, White represents the potential for redemption in the soul of the "white" American. When his plea for compassion goes unheard during the cruel *charivari* of Poquelin, whose "bronze . . . face" and "black" eye manifest a dark, Latin descent, the "white" Anglo-American community is that much the closer to self-destruction, its spiritually diseased and deteriorated condition being wryly, pathetically reflected in the "ghostly white" color of the "leper" it abhors. This ironic reversal of the moral connotations associated with *fair* and *dark, healthy* and *sick* gives additional emphasis to the ambiguities that pervade the tale. Significantly, the African mute, who is the "mute" witness of the Poquelins' past ascendancy and, in his own way, an outcast from white society, elects at the end to accompany the corpse of Jean Marie, "killed" by ignorance and prejudice, and "the living remains" of the leper, Jacques, into exile in a forbidding place, no more forbidding, however, than the prosperous city they leave behind. . . . (pp. 6-7)

The insistence on the idea of Jacques Poquelin as "the walking death" calls attention not only to the eclipse of the proud Creole culture but also to the death of the spirit implicit in the greed and pitilessness of the present inhabitants of New Orleans. Though Jean Marie's marsh "grew as wild as Africa," we are made to feel that the new men, who "civilized" the marsh and put it to profit, are, ironically, more primitive in soul than he. Throughout Cable advances the generic truth that material progress need not make a society more humane by intimating this paradoxical relationship between the gradual taming of the land and the growing savagery of the people: " 'Gentlemen,' said little White, 'here come the last remains of Jean Marie Poquelin, a better man, I'm afraid, with all his sins,—yes a better—a kinder man to his blood—a man of more self-forgetful goodness—than all of you put together will ever dare to be'." The mythic meaning of **"Jean-Ah Poquelin"** and all of the story's artistic design thus persistently carry us back to the proposition that the measure of a civilization depends upon the value it assigns to the feelings of the heart. (p. 7)

> *Joseph J. Egan, " 'Jean-Ah Poquelin': George Washington Cable as Social Critic and Mythic Artist," in* The Markham Review, *Vol. 2, No. 3, May, 1970, pp. 6-7.*

ETIENNE DE PLANCHARD   (essay date 1975)

[*Planchard is a French critic and educator. In the following excerpt, she analyzes Cable's political observations in the romance "Madame Délicieuse."*]

[**"Madame Délicieuse"**] deals with Louisiana a few years after it had entered the Union, and draws its name from the heroine, an intelligent beautiful young Creole lady, known all over New Orleans for "her kind offices and benevolent schemes." A compulsive peace maker, she has determined to reconcile two friends of hers, a father and his son, who have become so estranged as to go under different names. The father, General Hercule Mossy de Villivicencio, a veteran of the 1812-15 war against England, is a typical Creole "gentilhomme," a handsome martial-looking giant who has remained faithful to the old mode of thinking borrowed from the French and Spanish courts and holds the opinion that the only occupation worthy of an aristocrat is being an officer. In an effort to preserve the traditional civilization of the Creoles he is running for the governorship of Louisiana. His son, by contrast, is a small sedate man who opposed his father's wish of seeing him join the French army and became a doctor and a scholar. He styles himself Dr. Mossy.

Madame Délicieuse, playing the game of "fausses confidences" and using her influence over the general who is in love with her, succeeds in having the father visit his son. The latter proposes the help of his pen for the general's campaign, an offer which is somewhat sarcastically accepted. The very next morning, a vicious attack against the Villivicencio ticket is published in the "Américain" newspaper. There ensues a scene reminiscent of Corneille's *Le Cid* in which the general asks his son to vindicate his honor. After refusing to fight a duel which he considers would be plain murder, Dr. Mossy promises to settle the quarrel and leaves. While his father is waiting in the doctor's office, Madame Délicieuse comes in and, taking advantage of the general's growing anxiety, forces him to acknowledge his love for his son and then confesses that she wrote the libel in order to create a crisis that would bring father and son together again. She discloses the deeper motive of her conciliatory efforts: she has been in love with the doctor for ten years, but the latter could not marry her on account of his having been disinherited. The story ends with the general accepting the marriage and withdrawing his candidacy.

This short story meets all the prerequisites of local color fiction. It harmoniously blends romance and sentiment with a picturesque and accurate description of the setting. The characters are eccentric enough to be entertaining, but none is unpleasant. The heroine is worshipped as is the rule in typical Southern fiction, and her character appears as a happy mixture of mild realism (she is a Latin woman, taking some liberty with truth but for worthy causes only) and exotic charm that will appeal to every reader, male or female. The satirical comments upon the Creole way of life are delivered in a gentle ironical tone and are counterbalanced by the obvious admiration of the author for Madame Délicieuse. The barbs of the attack on the Villivicencio ticket are blunted by the fact that it came from a Creole in order to arouse the general's anger. And the highly sentimental ending resulting from the intricate and improbable plot misdirects the judgment of the reader who is left with the feeling that politics are subsidiary and instrumental to the story.

A closer study shows us the true purpose of the author which he unobtrusively reveals at the end of his narrative, thus investing it with a deeper meaning. Cable links the sentimental plot and the political subplot, with General de Villivicencio renouncing simultaneously the love of Madame Délicieuse and the governorship of Louisiana.

> My daughter! said the stately general; this—is my son's ransom; and, with this—I withdraw the Villivicencio ticket.

The relationship between courting the Creole lady as a lover, and Louisiana (a female character) as a candidate, could not be more clearly established. The story appears in a new light because with our attention focused on the subplot, we notice its parallelism with the plot. The structure of both follows the same triangular pattern. Madame Délicieuse is disputed by two men—an older and a younger one—, and two communities—the Creole, the older and the American, the younger—, compete for Louisiana in the election.

The parallel can be extended to the contestants, both in the plot and in the subplot. General de Villivicencio represents Creole aristocratic society, not only because he is its flagbearer, but also because he embodies its qualities and defects. They are summed up in the aptest possible way by Dr. Mossy's comment upon his father's chances of being elected:

> They could not elect one more faithful.

This sentence is typical of Cable's genius for subtle statements which hit upon the truth without being offensive. Indeed what characterizes General de Villivicencio and his staff is faithfulness. Faithfulness to traditions, "time-honored customs," to "good old Bourbon morals and manners," in short to the old European monarchic order. We shall see later that this very faithfulness is the cause of their failure, but is there a greater compliment to pay them while respecting the truth?

Dr. Mossy, if he is not an American by birth, is nevertheless very much Americanized. First, he has broken with his European past and adopted a democratic English-sounding name. Beside, he writes in English, a barbaric language for the Creoles, has become a devotee of the Yankee gospel of work, and believes in public opinion that must be dealt with the pen and not with the sword as is his father's wish.

The parallelism between plot and subplot is now demonstrated, and as a consequence the criticism of the Creoles, which previously appeared as mere banter becomes pregnant with a deeper meaning. The light comedy turns into a lesson in politics. For faithfulness, though an endearing quality, and most revered by the Creoles, can prove disastrous. General de Villivicencio and his staff resolved "to make one more stand for the traditions of their fathers." But this stand was made in a democratic system imposed by the Americans. The candidacy of the ticket was presented according to "time-honored customs" which were not adapted to the conditions of the contest. For the Creole conception of democracy is typical of an aristocratic society. A few self-styled leading citizens, "a band, heroically unconscious of their feebleness," placed the general's name in front of public opinion without any attempt to ingratiate the candidate with his voters. The "leading citizens" were consistent with themselves since, in a monarchic system, people are not expected to vote for a program, but to be faithful to a man. Unfortunately for them, the system was no longer monarchic but democratic. By refusing to follow the rules of the game while taking part in it, they made sure they would lose it. . . . And in a democratic system, the majority wins. (pp. 121-25)

"Madame Délicieuse" teaches us that, just as a young woman has rather marry a young than an old man to enjoy long happiness, a country must be wed to the present, rather than to the past, in order to have a future. Greybeards are no more successful in love than old timers in politics. These are facts of life. General de Villivicencio reverted to wisdom, the distinctive quality of old age, and bowed to his son in order to restore peace in his family. The Creoles, the representatives of the past, are asked to yield before the Yankees, the champions of progress, to ensure a harmonious development of the American family.

But, at the time when Cable wrote this short story, the lesson was of little use to them, since they had long been integrated in the national community. Yet there was another family strife still going on. . . . Both North and South had long been estranged, like the general and his son. Both the Creoles and the South had been compelled to yield to the Yankees. Both had tried to recapture the power that had eluded them so as to reestablish the former political order. Both preferred clannish loyalty to justice and progress. Why should not the teaching of the fable benefit the Southerners? They could breech the family quarrel by abjuring their unprogressive ideas and surrendering to the ideal of democracy which is so essential to the American people.

"Madame Délicieuse" is very interesting because it throws some light on the true nature of Cable's genius, as well as on his shortcomings. As he was highly successful in recapturing the romantic atmosphere of New Orleans and its people, he achieved fame as one of the best local colorists of the time. But his very success in that field eventually proved to be as lethal to his talent as Nessus's shirt. When he wanted to tackle problems that mattered to him, he met first with the disappointment, then the hostility, of his editors who wanted more exotic love stories about old Louisiana, and none of the unpleasantness that resulted from dealing with actual situations. (pp. 125-26)

Cable's understanding of social and political problems, his ability to rise above a purely sectional point of view and cast a lucid look over the Reconstruction period in particular, and American history in general, not only makes him the ablest advocate of the reconciliation between North and South among the many writers who chose to exploit that popular theme, but also the first great political novelist in American literature. Unfortunately, he is betrayed by an artistic technique which remains conventional. He relies exclusively upon love story plots which the taboos and demands of his time, and probably his own sensibility too, caused to be treated with stilted mawkishness. To convey his everlasting concern for unity, he repeatedly uses the symbol of marriage, the best to express the fusion of two in one. But the device has been too often used, and I should say misused for the above mentioned reasons, and it has lost some of its magic.

But when he does not get entangled in his sentimental plots, Cable displays a fine talent. He excels in rendering the atmosphere of a town, unravelling the intricate skein of society life, and discerning the hidden motivations of people. His acute perception of the contradictions of the American experience, his generous efforts to reconcile them and contribute to the unity of the nation by laying bare the causes of disunion, give him a special place in the literature of the United States. (p. 126)

> *Etienne de Planchard, "'Madame Délicieuse': A Political Fable," in* Caliban, *n.s. Vol. XI, No. 1, 1975, pp. 119-26.*

JOHN CLEMAN (essay date 1976)

[*In the following excerpt, Cleman asserts that the concept of nature in Cable's fiction is a central yet often ignored feature of his works. Cleman examines Cable's garden and wilderness imagery in such stories as "Gregory's Island," "The Solitary," "Jean-ah Poquelin," and "Belles Demoiselles Plantation."*]

The importance of nature in the American experience generally and to America's major 19th Century writers especially seems obvious. That such a judgment should apply to the work of George W. Cable, however, has not been so obvious, and the main lines of discussion about him have dealt with the degree of realism in his treatment of Southern life and with his championing of Negro rights. However, throughout his career, the natural environment was a central part of his writing and other activities. . . . If we examine this writing we find that Cable's attitudes toward nature frequently reflect the transitional aspect of the late 19th period, a time when older Transcendental and still lingering Puritan attitudes toward nature were being modified by Darwinism and by the actualities of an emerging industrial, urban society. Cable's attitudes toward nature, like his views of the South generally, are indeed ambivalent, but a reasonably consistent pattern of his sensibilities can be described, and more important, this pattern, or at least his view of nature, appears as a central part of his major literary concerns. (pp. 24-5)

In a sense Cable brings to nature two different although not exclusive sensibilities: one allows him to recognize and depict the starker realities of brute nature while he finds in it a fascinating appeal that does not require him to bring it to heel first; the other tends to generalize nature into a set of principles or values, to render it a thoroughly domesticated set of social, moral, and political ideals even in its wilder aspects. Central to both perspectives is the insistence that what ultimately matters is man. Cable's ability to find appeal in the raw wilderness was sometimes strong, producing some of his most powerful natural descriptions, but it was never his final position. Running through all his garden writing is the notion that the garden and the practice of gardening—that is the enhancement of nature through art—is useful. Principally, it provides spiritual and moral enrichment for man, and the potential for this is in nature itself, but art or at least the presence of man is required for this potential to be realized.

With these attitudes and responses toward nature in mind, we can turn to the four stories. Originally published as **"Gregory's Island"** (1896), **"The Solitary"** [1899] presents the theme of man's conflict with nature more purely than in any other single work. Gregory apparently has a drinking problem, but mostly he lacks the "spiritual breadth and stature" to deal with life. A coward, Gregory seeks isolation in nature not only to separate himself from specific temptation, but also, hopefully, to reduce existence into simple enough terms for him to handle. (pp. 25-6)

Gregory's Gulf Coast Island, therefore, is more than just a self-assumed prison. While there he learns from nature, first the pleasures of solitude, quiet, and a sense of renewal: "Each dawn he rose from dreamless sleep and leaped into the surf as into the embrace of a new existence." Then he discovers a more immediate sense of God: "Skyward ponderings by night, canny discoveries under foot by day, quickened his mind and sight to vast and to minute significances, until they declared an author known to him hitherto only by tradition." Quite obviously there is a Thoreauvian cast to these experiences which is reinforced as he eventually learns "a way of reading by which sea, sky, book, island, and absent humanity, all seemed parts of one whole, and all to speak together in one harmony, while they toiled together for one harmony some day to be perfected."

However, Cable does not see the education into nature to have only transcendental value, to result in Gregory's remodelling his life according to nature's universal plan. In fact, nature's lessons, as such, are clearly not enough to save Gregory. . . . The "old usurer," of course, is Demon Rum, Gregory's insatiable thirst, which never leaves him entirely free and which would surely have destroyed him had not the hurricane intervened and removed any possibility of his leaving early.

What brings Gregory peace, then, is not benign natural beauty, a sense of a peaceful or an ameliorative center to the natural order, or even a recognition of God's hand in creation, but a sense gained during the violent storm and in the calm days afterward of the immense power of the natural world and at the same time of his capacity to be in harmony with that world. He is humbled by the storm's power—but he does not

resign himself either to share in its violence and destructiveness or to be overwhelmed into some kind of sheepish submissiveness. In a way that significantly characterizes most of Cable's treatments of this theme, Gregory's inner struggle with his thirst is paralleled by an outward struggle with or within nature. . . . Cable suggests quite explicitly that Gregory's personal problem is to find some measure of control over a tempestuous weakness within himself, to find sources of strength within his weaknesses, to harbor in his own nature for some good. Just as alcoholism is never completely cured, storms are never contained, but limited accommodations to both are possible.

In these terms the "moral" of **"The Solitary"**—and it is clearly more a parable than a bit of realism—reflects precisely the attitudes of the garden writing and his garden sensibility. Nature is to be controlled, but not brought under heel. Not only must Gregory deal with his weakness all his life, but he must accommodate his natural experiences to the "human world," to civilization. Specifically, he goes into business raising cattle on his island, putting the natural environment, even the otherwise sterile conditions of his island, to use. This point needs to be kept in mind, for the "alliance" he pledges to his "wild prison" as he looks down on "the majestic after-heavings" of the storm is a rather sentimental celebration of the silver lining to every dark cloud, and the promise he finds there is translated into an ideal of progress which is realized ultimately in the civilized and not the natural world. The wildness depicted in the marsh region, despite its beauty and power, is less appealing in itself than in the quasi-transcendental idealism that is derived from it.

Subjugation of nature, of course, is a major part of the Idea of Progress current in the nineteenth century. Cable's emphasis is less directly on technology than on individual, moral improvement, but the index of progress for him is still control of nature. **"Jean-ah Poquelin"** [1875], because it deals with the problems of civilization more directly, illustrates this point better than **"The Solitary."** . . . Old Jean Poquelin typifies the early New Orleans aristocrat whose old world ways clash with the values and enterprise of the burgeoning American civilization. "Once an opulent indigo planter," highly esteemed, with the indigo market's decline Jean turns to "larger, and, at that time, equally respectable profits, first in smuggling, and later in the African slave trade." One trip to the slave coast ends mysteriously, and Jean, apparently without his beloved scholar brother, Jacques, returns home to live the life of a recluse, a feared, mysterious figure bedeviled by small children but shunned by almost everybody else. For most of the story his personal tragedy (some suspect it is a dark crime) remains in the background, and the central issue is whether his backward, reclusive life style, so vividly identified with the natural environment in which he lives, will be able to withstand the onrush of the *Americain*.

Cable takes some care in describing where Jean lives, suggesting the primary conditions of his life in relationship to the changing community nearby. The house itself is like a bulwark not only against "the Anglo-American flood" but also against prior, more harrowing dangers, or more appropriately it is like "a gigantic ammunition wagon stuck in the mud and abandoned by some retreating army." The battle imagery of this passage is appropriate not only to Jean's imminent struggles with the government, but also to a struggle he has already lost with nature. Cable makes it clear that the house stands "aloof from civilization"; that the land around it, which had once been cultivated for indigo, has since "grown up into one of the horridest marshes within a circuit of fifty miles." . . . Cable develops much of the Gothic atmosphere of the story through descriptions of the swamp and Jean's house, and the swampland is much like what appears in *The Grandissimes, Bonaventure* (1888), *Gideon's Band* (1914), and *The Creoles of Louisiana* in the attention to detail and the dark overtones, but unlike those other treatments of the wilderness, the descriptions of the swamp surrounding Jean's house are unrelieved by any exotic beauty. They present images of ugly, coarse, chaotic growth with implications of decay and death, almost totally forbidding, but beyond mere frightfulness, these descriptions suggest how much Jean has consigned his life away from the lives of other men. Moreover, by describing the marsh to be a "jungle" or "wild as Africa," Cable may imply that it was in Jean's choice of the African slave trade that he sealed his own fate and became locked in a past which the wild marsh in part symbolizes.

If the marsh is Jean's bastion against change and exposure, then the draining of it is a sign of progress, of approaching civilization, just as it is in *The Creoles of Louisiana,* and this is precisely how Cable develops his theme in **"Jean-ah Poquelin."** As the "alien races" begin to expand beyond the bounds of old French New Orleans, signs of civilization, particularly roads, houses, and cultivation, appear and eventually surveyors' marks reach into the seemingly inviolate, "haunted ground" of Jean's swamp. The changes wrought not only endanger Jean's secret, but also bring beauty and fruitfulness to the land. (pp. 26-7)

In these terms the argument is all in favor of progress and civilization, but as critics have repeatedly recognized, Jean, particularly in his loyalty and pride, comes off better than members of the new order who try to push him out. However, too much can be made of Jean's virtues as contributing to a critique of the new order, for Cable is here ambivalent about both sides of the issue. The Poquelin brothers' tragedy is partially that they have been victimized by fate and by an inevitable clash of values, but it also grows out of their weaknesses, their inability rather than refusal to progress in the right direction. Thus, while "certain enterprising men" were shifting from indigo to sugar, Jacques was "too apathetic to take so active a course," and Jean, like so many others, committed his fortunes directly to a slave economy, which Cable deplores for the morally enervating indolence it produces in the masters, as well as for the cruelty and degradation it visits on the slave. In addition, Jean is a gambler and a high liver before his fateful visit to Africa, and these failings, echoing the weaknesses of Gregory, indicate a giving-in to the sensuous life, a letting-go whose meaning is made clear as the brothers' formerly cultivated land slips back to its natural state, good for nothing but seclusion. While we are certainly to feel sympathy for Jean, it is clear that the old order he represents is not to be long lamented. The revelation at the end is not that we should modify our view of progress, but that Jean is a better man than we have supposed and that the supernatural horror turns out to be the real and natural horror of leprosy, contracted on the last slaving mission. In the end Jean's fate seems both inevitably and ironically tied to the natural realm, for his casket is borne off by his ex-slave "with the strength of an ape" and by Jacques "into the jungle" toward "the ridge in the depth of the swamp known as the Leper's land."

Cable's argument about controlling nature, however, is even clearer in the figure of Little White, who is the best represen-

tative of the new, Anglo-American order, showing compassion and good sense where the others do not. The key point about him is that unlike many of the Creoles and Anglos, he lacks fear, or at least he is able to control his fear, and this enables him to make the crucial discovery about Jean that changes his thinking and leads, in turn, to his heroic actions at the end. Part of Gregory's achievement, it will be recalled, is mastering his general fear of life to the point where he can serve some useful purpose, and the link between fear and nature in **"Jean-ah Poquelin"** is pointed to in Cable's using the natural descriptions as the primary vehicle for creating the sense of terror in the story.

"Jean-ah Poquelin," therefore, should be understood as much in terms of these issues of nature and progress as the more superficial conflict between Creole and Anglo-American cultures. . . . **"Jean-ah Poquelin"** also reveals more of the wilderness sensibility than was found in **"The Solitary"**, insofar as there is no tendency to idealize or find transcendental value in Jean's marshes. While rejected, the image of the wilderness is present without much qualification, except as some of the ambivalence about Jean may transfer to the environment with which he is associated. In **"Jean-ah Poquelin,"** however, little if any of this ambivalence is carried in the natural descriptions themselves, but if we look at *Bonaventure, The Grandissimes,* or *Gideon's Band* the wilderness is more complexly represented. (p. 27)

As in most of Cable's fiction **"Belles Demoiselles Plantation"** involves an ancestral conflict, in this case between the birthrights of Colonel De Charleu and Injin Charlie, but more than in most of Cable's fiction the natural environment of **"Belles Demoiselles Plantation"** figures directly in the action. Consequently, the most significant image of the river, the main feature of that environment, is developed at the outset in a passage suggesting a primal, elemental force, a brute or beast. . . . Perhaps reflecting his wilderness and garden perspectives, Cable presents this vignette of the *pointe* as a transformation in two stages, first the majestic giant, the river, literally taking its course and then man altering what is left through cultivation. The seething, and again fascinating dynamism of the river gives way to the more placid bend, the rustling cane, and the assumption of permanence in the natural conditions that underlie them.

Stability and a classically benign facade—everything in its place—are inserted in the more general description of the plantation that follows the river passage:

> The house stood unusually near the river, facing eastward, and standing four square, with an immense veranda about its sides, and a flight of steps in front spreading broadly downward, as we open arms to a child. From the veranda nine miles of river were seen; and in their compass, near at hand, the shady garden full of rare and beautiful flowers; farther away broad fields of cane and rice, and the distant quarters of the slaves, and on the horizon everywhere a dark belt of cypress forest.

Thus, in setting the scene Cable develops something like a gradation we find in his garden writing: the angular "four square" fixity of the house, the artificially beautiful garden, the useful fields, and the dark line of the wilderness, somewhere distant and somewhat vague for those at the house but vivid and more sinister for the reader who remembers the image of the same level of nature, the flowing, turbulent, violent river presented at the outset.

The impressions of solidarity appear not only in descriptions of the plantation and the levee, but also more tellingly in the Colonel's dreams of his city home. "The house should be of stones fitly set," he explains, and there is to be a "big stone gate." Allied with these impressions, however, is the even more predominant image of the garden and the refinement of nature, the dominance and control of nature, that the garden implies. In fact, the garden represents the most refined assumptions of solidarity, the most visible and the most blinding assurances that the Colonel holds to as a levee against all that is violent, turbulent, unpleasant, and uncontrolled around him. Cable uses the garden, or, more accurately, the image of the family in the garden, as the primary symbol of the Colonel's happiness. . . . [The] idyll continues for two more paragraphs, and the essence of it is the sense of pleasure, beauty, harmony, and happiness identified with that existence. The daughters, in fact, come to seem little more than part of all that beauty. They are neither individualized nor particularly personalized—seven animate flowers, whose only apparent human trait is the collective wish to move to town for more elegant surroundings. They are almost inevitably pictured in the garden, and the importance of this connection is most fully realized when the Colonel sits on the levee "on a summer afternoon of uncommon mildness" shortly after he and other New Orleanians have temporarily defeated the river by buttressing their levee. He begins musing over his past woes: "yet his house still stood, his sweet-smelling fields were still fruitful, his name was fame enough; and yonder and yonder, among the trees and flowers, like angels walking in Eden, were the seven goddesses of his only worship." The main irony of this image of natural benignity is obvious. No sooner does the Colonel envision his plantation as Eden than he hears the first crack of his inevitable doom. Even as he approaches Belles Demoiselles for the last time with Injin Charlie, nature seems to mock him. . . . It seems "like a gem, shining through the dark grove, . . . like a great glow worm in the dense foliage."

The point of this irony, the opposed images of river and garden, is not only that nature is unpredictable and uncontrollable or that man is a fool to think otherwise. The image of happiness that the Colonel finds in his plantation and daughters buffers areas in his own life that seem out of his domination. The pride in his fateful musings on the levee top, the joy he finds in helping to keep the river from destroying the levee, are compensations for his inability to control Charlie. But more than a victim of Charlie's pride, he is a victim of his own, and ironically so, Cable makes clear, because there is in his past of "mad frolic" and "elegant rioting" no more justification for his pride than there is for his Indian relative's. There are, in short, two spheres to the Colonel's life; "he had had his vices—all his life; but had borne them, as his race do, with a serenity of conscience and a cleanness of mouth that left no outward blemish on the surface of the gentleman." Glossing over the reality of licentiousness and poverty is his love of "nothing but himself, his name, and his motherless children." To these he erects the facade of happiness and idyllic beauty, and for them "had they even required him to defraud old De Carlos—," Cable "can hardly say," but we can see him willing to do so almost to the point when the river makes the question academic.

Thus, at the moment of the cave-in there are two parallel struggles taking place—the river with the land and the Colonel with his base impulses. At the eleventh hour, the Colonel seems to choose honesty. . . . Altogether it appears he is fi-

nally gaining control of his basest inclinations, but he has played his game too long, and the river's victory robs him for a time of an assurance of his own moral conquest. The issue of the folly of ancestral pride is reflected in the larger contest of forces between man and nature, and it is this meaning of the tale that is embodied in the central images of the setting.

The proof of this argument is in the concluding passages. If we left the tale at this point we would seem to be arguing some naturalistic interpretation, suggesting that inexorable nature defeats moral intent. But Cable in his fiction as in almost all his activities is highly moral. The river as a symbol of nature in **"Belles Demoiselles Plantation"** is not malignant nor entirely indifferent. When it takes the house, the river is a naturalistic, "merciless, unfathomable flood," but as the Colonel recuperates, "by the window came in a sweet-scented evergreen vine, transplanted from the caving bank of Belles Demoiselles." In this way, which echoes the after-storm scenes of **"The Solitary,"** Cable seems to affirm that nature is capable of blessing as well as destruction. It is made up of unfathomable forces that include not only devastating rivers but evergreen plants growing out of caving banks. Significantly Charlie has brought the plant there, and he "wants to see the vine recognized," precisely, it would seem, to encourage the Colonel back to a faith in some beneficent moral purpose overriding all tragedy and signaled in the plant's beauty. . . . At the very least, a key sign of his renewed moral health, concurrent with his physical decline, is that he can look on that plant "with beaming eyes." He can see beauty in the world, and the implication of his changing condition is that he is literally being spiritualized as he moves closer to his death.

At the end there is no bitterness, no black denunciation of God's hand in worldly affairs. "Mes belles demoiselles!" he whispers, "In paradise; in the garden; I shall be with them at sunrise." Thus, in a fashion entirely consistent with his "garden sensibility" and with his orthodox Christian upbringing, Cable presents the Colonel's reward for virtuously refusing to cheat his distant relative, seemingly denied in nature, to be affirmed after all in the vine and in the promise of heaven. In essence, by virtuously giving up the worldly paradise he so ardently sought, he eventually gains a more lasting happiness.

Recognizing the role of nature in **"Belles Demoiselles Plantation,"** the reader may still find the closing scenes of the story sentimental, the message trite, but Cable's power rarely rests in his conventional moral dogma. **"Belles Demoiselles Plantation's"** strength is, of course, in its main characterizations, and even more, I would argue, in the particular ironies worked out with respect to the natural image and the resulting tensions with the opposed garden image. The tendency of Cable's garden sensibility was to smoothing of lines, shaping the coarser realities of nature to suit certain proprieties of art and morals and to reflect rather generalized and conventional spiritual values. The garden ideals of tranquility and control, in short, tended to result in a rather placid social vision and was not conducive to his best art. In a sense I am arguing a view of literature held by Melville in his review of Hawthorne's "Mosses from an Old Manse" which has, in fact, become one staple of modern criticism, that American literature in particular derives much of its interest and strength from a dark vision, a "power of blackness." In Cable this power, when it exists, is less overtly psychological than in Poe, Hawthorne, Melville and others, but the ambivalence he feels toward the wilderness nevertheless draws on some of the same basic fears of death, isolation, the not-man, and even sex, when we recognize the naturalness, which is both terrifying and attracting, but decidedly sexual, in Palmyre Philosophe of *The Grandissimes.*

My point, however, is not to argue that deep down Cable is a dark romantic, but that this is one element along with a number of others both dark and light that comprise a central feature of his art. The pervasiveness of his concern with the theme of self control as linked to a larger issue of controlling nature and progress should not be overlooked if we are to recognize the fullest implications of the cultural conflicts in his novels. Thus, self control in some form is an issue for, among others, Sieur George, whose weakness is gambling; for Posson Jone', whose behavior when drunk has been described by one critic as atavism; for Vignevielle, who in **"Madame Delphine"** (1881) gives up pirating when, like Gregory, he reads the lessons of nature; for Agricola Fusilier, who Charlie Keene at one point says is reverting to the pure physical naturalness of his Indian ancestors; for Honoré Grandissime, who must place the interests of society above his own love interest; for John March, who must similarly work for the general good and learn to control his temper; for Bonaventure, whose whole life becomes a model of renunciation, of struggle with his selfish passions; for the entomologist, in **Strong Hearts,** whose consuming and destroying passion is not only science, but hunger; and for Arthur Winslow in *Bylow Hill* (1902), who is obsessed and destroyed by jealousy. The atavism of Posson Jone', Bras-Coupé, Agricola, Jeff-Jack Ravenel, and the black insurrectionists in **"A West Indian Slave Insurrection"** suggests that the attitudes toward nature I have described were further touched by the interest in evolution of the period, but there are other instances where the natural setting is simply an appropriate backdrop for love scenes. Cable's attitudes toward nature, indeed, were a combination of various beliefs and esthetic values, but the wilderness-garden parameters seem to me to describe the vital center of those attitudes.

It would be going too far to say, finally, that all of Cable's social, political, and esthetic theory grows out of a central set of attitudes toward nature, but these attitudes play a more vital role in his thought and in his fiction than has been previously recognized. Rather than the sole source of other beliefs, nature seems to be an index of a rather wide range of conflict and ambivalence in Cable's work. Furthermore, when the specific image of the wilderness is only dimly realized or when the garden sensibility predominates, frequently something is lost to his art. . . . However, in a number of the **Old Creole Days** stories, in *The Grandissimes,* in **Bonaventure,** and in *Gideon's Band,* the vital issues of plot and characterization are centrally linked to a complex treatment of landscape, of the natural wilderness, which deepens and intensifies those issues and gives the works further meaning and power. Nature may not be the whole key to Cable's art, but to ignore its role, I think, misses a great deal and risks turning his fiction into sociological tracts. (pp. 28-31)

> John Cleman, "College Girl Wildness: Nature in the Work of George W. Cable," in The Markham Review, Vol. 5, Winter, 1976, pp. 24-31.

WILLIAM BEDFORD CLARK (essay date 1977)

[*An American educator and critic, Clark has published numer-*

Samuel Clemens (Mark Twain) and Cable, posing for a photograph promoting their 1884 lecture tour.

ous essays on Southern and Western literature. In the following excerpt, Clark examines the theme of miscegenation in Old Creole Days *and* The Grandissimes, *contending that Cable's treatment of sexual transgression is symptomatic of the South's greater sin of racial oppression.*]

In 1889, George Washington Cable responded to the all-but-universal denunciation his ideas had met with in the South by writing a lengthy autobiographical essay entitled "My Politics." That essay not only recounts the young Cable's inner struggle to reconcile the South's defeat in the Civil War with what he had earlier accepted as the unquestionable righteousness of secession and slavery, but it also reveals the intimate role his writing played in the working out of his final position. In undertaking a work like *The Grandissimes,* Cable tells us, he was involved in slowly and patiently guessing out the meaning of "the riddle of our Southern question"; and the success of much of his best writing stems from the determination with which Cable wrestled with the past and present of his region in his search for a viable answer to that riddle.

In this connection, **"The Haunted House on Royal Street,"** one of Cable's **Strange True Stories of Louisiana,** is worth looking at in some detail, for it not only contains some excellent local color and serves as a powerful statement of many of the author's deepest feelings about his region, but it also stands as a remarkable example of the way in which the Southern past yielded its secrets to Cable's inquiring imagination. **"The Haunted House"** begins with the author conducting his reader on a kind of literary guided tour of the Vieux Carré. In a symbolic sense, the walk from the newer sections of New Orleans into the old Quarter constitutes a trip back into the city's past. After spending several pages in establishing a firm sense of place in the reader's imagination, Cable turns his attention to the history of the haunted house itself, formerly occupied by a certain notorious Madame Lalaurie. Although now in something of a state of disrepair, the house was once a favorite showplace of Creole society. Just as Madame Lalaurie, its former owner, was ostensibly a kind and gentle lady, her luxurious house gives no overt indication of the horrors once perpetrated behind its walls. Nevertheless, in the old days rumors of Madame's sadistic abuse of her slaves were persistent among the people of New Orleans. . . . (pp. 597-98)

Despite the frequency of such rumors, relatively little is done to intervene in what is clearly the private affair of a high-born Creole lady until fire breaks out. In the course of evacuating the building, the rescuers discover Madame Lalaurie's slaves, whose bodies bear the irrefutable evidence of her systematic cruelty. Shocked and outraged, a mob storms the house and the mistress is lucky to escape before the assault.

For Cable, "the gloomy pile, even when restored and renovated," stands as a "ghost-ridden" symbol of the evils which the institution of slavery made possible. While he is careful to point out that Madame Lalaurie was in no way a typical slaveholder, Cable nevertheless insists that "any public practice" is "answerable to whatever can happen easier with it than without it." That such inhumanities as those of Madame Lalaurie were nurtured by the practice of slavery is evidence enough to convict the institution as a whole.

Ironically, after the Civil War, Madame Lalaurie's house is converted into an integrated girls' school. Daughters of the white citizenry and of the city's old "free-colored" caste are taught under the same roof and by the same teachers until members of the White League enter the school forcibly and set about expelling those students they believe to be of black ancestry. Cable handles the subsequent inquisition scene with particularly devastating irony. As each of the hysterical girls is interrogated by the representatives of the League, a banner on one wall solemnly proclaims, "The eye of God is on us"; and there is further irony in the farcical unreliability of the mob's attempt to separate the sheep from the goats. Some of the "colored" students are so white as to escape detection altogether, and one girl of obviously Negroid background avoids eviction when she claims Spanish blood and threatens that her brother will challenge her accusers to an affair of honor. (pp. 598-99)

In relating the story of Madame Lalaurie's maltreated slaves, Cable brings in a blanket indictment of the "peculiar institution" itself by revealing the propensity for evil inherent within it, and, in relating the arbitrary expulsion of the "colored" pupils (who are for all practical purposes white) from a public girls' school, he is able to demonstrate both the pathos and the absurdity of caste distinctions in general, specifically as they were to be reinforced as a result of the South's alleged maltreatment during Reconstruction. When **"The Haunted House"** is viewed in this light, it seems particularly fitting that Cable should have built the climax of his narrative around the theme of mixed blood, because the problem of miscegenation, particularly with respect to the New Orleans quadroon caste, was a theme that exerted a very evocative influence over his creative imagination. Cable's interest in this

question no doubt reflects his personal awareness of the sexually dehumanizing aspects of racial relations in the South both before and after the Civil War, and it is in his handling of this and related themes that he comes closest to solving that "riddle" of Southern life noted previously.

One of the most familiar of Cable's stories centered around the issue of mixed blood is **" 'Tite Poulette."** Written in the early 1870's and incorporated into *Old Creole Days,* the story is clearly an outgrowth of the "tragic mulatto" tradition, and Cable's major concern in writing it was a professed attempt at capitalizing on the romantic potential of a situation in which love surmounts the color-line. Consequently, the pronounced social criticism found elsewhere in Cable's works is only implicitly a part of " 'Tite Poulette." Still, the narrative has considerable interest of its own and is important because of its relationship to a later work, the remarkable little masterpiece **"Madame Delphine."**

On the surface, " **'Tite Poulette"** concerns itself with the ancient theme of love tested and found true. The male protagonist, a rather bungling young Dutchman by the telling name of Kristian Koppig, is a newcomer to New Orleans whose Protestant conscience is shocked by many of the customs of that predominantly Latin city. Directly across from his window stands the house of Madame John, a quadroon, who lives with her daughter 'Tite Poulette, a girl possessed of a complexion so white as to excite expressions of admiration from the youthful Creoles she meets on the street. Slowly, almost imperceptively, Kristian develops an interest in the lovely daughter, but the fact of her mixed racial ancestry troubles him. . . . Koppig's ambivalent emotions continue to plague him, but the pathos inherent in 'Tite Poulette's situation is best understood by the two women themselves. At one point, Madame John sums up the alienation of the quadroon caste when she exclaims, " 'There is no place in this world for us poor women. I wish that we were either white or black'."

The plot thickens when economic pressures induce Madame John to accept employment as a dancer at the "ball," and her new employer takes a predatory interest in her daughter. Kristian's sense of honor, spurred to recklessness by his growing interest in 'Tite Poulette, brings him into a violent confrontation with the lascivious Creole, and in a subsequent encounter he is stabbed. The two women, sensing their role in the young man's misfortune, nurse him through his crisis, during which Kristian unknowingly reveals the extent of his feelings for 'Tite Poulette, as well as his residual aversion to black blood: " 'Take her away,' [he says,] waving his hand, 'take your beauty away. She is jet white. Who could take a jet white wife?' " Nevertheless, when he recovers consciousness, Kristian declares his love for the girl and expresses his wish to marry her; thus, he passes the test secretly insisted upon by Madame John, who rewards the selflessness of his love by revealing that her "daughter" is indeed white—the child of two Spanish immigrants who died of yellow fever.

With this single melodramatic stroke, Cable removes all the complications separating his lovers and brings his narrative to a happy end. This resolution, a severe disappointment to many readers, has all the facile artifice of a fairy tale. While he raises several vital issues in " **'Tite Poulette,"** notably the irony of a law that forbids legitimate intimacies between the races but does nothing to prevent them on an illicit basis, Cable skirts such problems whenever they appear. In his first novel, *The Grandissimes,* he was less disposed to do so. (pp. 599-601)

["Madame Delphine"] stands in this writer's estimation as Cable's most successful utilization of the theme of mixed blood as an index to the complexity of the Southern riddle. Written at the request of a quadroon woman who, after reading the compromised " 'Tite Poulette," petitioned the author to tell the whole truth about the tragedy of her caste, "Madame Delphine" is a more honest retelling of the earlier story, an artful fable of miscegenation and collective Southern sin.

On the surface, Cable's tale centers around the love between a beautiful octoroon, Olive, the daughter of the title character, and a reformed pirate and smuggler. While the bulk of the plot is devoted to bringing these two lovers together and reconciling the difficulties of law and custom that separate them, the unifying concept behind it is the Old Testament notion of collective societal guilt, a favorite theme of the devoutly Presbyterian Cable. . . . This concept surfaces throughout the story and is repeatedly sounded by saintly Père Jerome, a Catholic priest of recognizably Protestant sensibilities. Père Jerome puts it this way early in the narrative:

> We all participate in one another's sins. There is a community of responsibility attaching to every misdeed. No human since Adam—nay, nor Adam himself—ever sinned entirely to himself. And so I never . . . contemplate a crime or a criminal but I feel my conscience pointing at me as one of the accessories.

In a special sermon he is called upon to deliver at the St. Louis Cathedral, Père Jerome reiterates this idea, and specifically connects it with the institutionalized sin responsible for the very existence of the city's quadroon caste:

> "My friends, there are thousands of people in this city of New Orleans to whom society gives the ten commandments of God with all the *nots* rubbed out! . . . . if God sends the poor weakling to purgatory for leaving the right path, where ought some of you go who strew it with thorns and briars!"

There is a sociological as well as a theological soundness to Père Jerome's assessment of this question when he attempts to recreate what he feels is God's attitude toward the quadroon concubine in the abstract: " ' . . . all the rights of her womanhood trampled in the mire, sin made easy to her— almost compulsory—charge it to account of whom it may concern!' "

But the sexual sin involved in the creation and perpetuation of the quadroon caste is only symptomatic of a greater and more widespread evil, racial oppression itself, as Cable makes clear through Madame Delphine's attack upon the *Code Noir* that stands in the way of her daughter's marriage:

> . . .from which race do they want to keep my daughter separate? She is seven parts white! The law did not stop her from being that; and now, when she wants to be a white man's good and honest wife, shall that law stop her? . . . what a law!

In order to subvert so hypocritical a law, Madame Delphine swears that her daughter is white and paves the way for the marriage of Olive to her suitor. In thus bearing false witness, she jeopardizes her own soul and, out of an ironic sense of guilt, goes to Père Jerome for absolution. Her subsequent fatal swoon in the confessional, sentimental as it is, neverthe-

less provides Cable with the chance to effectively reinforce the thematic focus of his story. Père Jerome's intercessional prayer, "Lord, lay not this sin to her charge!" is damning in its implications as to where the blame is ultimately to rest. "Madame Delphine" is, in a way, *The Grandissimes* writ small. That the story stops short of portraying the eventual consequences of the white South's racial transgressions is hardly a fault in its overall design. Those consequences would have been only too apparent to an audience in the post-Reconstruction era.

William Faulkner is only the most distinguished of a long line of Southern novelists to till the literary ground broken by Cable in works like *The Grandissimes* and "Madame Delphine" and the vision of Southern history put forward in *Absalom, Absalom!* and *Go Down, Moses* remarkably parallels the solution to the Southern riddle arrived at by the earlier writer. Faulkner's Isaac McCaslin meditates on his family's and his region's histories and the role miscegenation plays therein only to seek to repudiate his share in the past. Faulkner always insisted, however, that a man must do more than repudiate. . . . [Cable's] self-imposed exile in the North was in no way an effort at escaping the burden of history; it was a consequence of his determination to right past wrongs through present action. (pp. 607-09)

> *William Bedford Clark, "Cable and the Theme of Miscegenation in 'Old Creole Days' and 'The Grandissimes',' in* The Mississippi Quarterly, *Vol. XXX, No. 4, Fall, 1977, pp. 597-609.*

PATRICK SAMWAY, S. J. (essay date 1982)

[*Samway is an American critic and scholar whose best-known work is a study of William Faulkner. In the following excerpt, he offers a thematic comparison of the stories "Posson Jone' " (1876) and "Père Raphaël" (1901).*]

George Washington Cable's New Orleans, with its fashionable society leisurely strolling down Chartres Street, its haunting quadroons hidden behind imposing walls, and its exotic mingling of Creole, mulatto, and *américain,* provided not only a locus, but also a focus for his creative imagination. In her essay, "Place in Fiction," Eudora Welty has stressed the significance of place in fiction:

> I think the sense of place is as essential to good and honest writing as a logical mind; surely they are somehow related. It is by knowing where you stand that you are able to judge where you are. Place absorbs our earliest notice and attention, it bestows on us our original awareness; and our critical powers spring up from the study of it and the growth of experience inside it. It perseveres in bringing us back to earth when we fly too high. It never really stops informing us, for it is forever astir, alive, changing, reflecting, like the mind of man itself.

Cable's two stories, **"Posson Jone',"** and **"Père Raphaël,"** one about a Protestant minister and the other about a supposed Catholic priest, both happen to be located in the same place: the French Quarter. Cable considered the first, **"Posson Jone',"** originally published in *Appleton's Journal* in 1876. . . , as a companion story to **"Père Raphaël,"** originally published in 1901; eventually they were brought out by Scribner's in 1909 in a single volume. . . . Yet, as Miss Welty suggests, by choosing the French Quarter, Cable has provided an environment in which his characters not only can express themselves freely, but they can also make judgments about the society they live in.

"Posson Jone' " rates as one of Cable's more famous stories; it is included in *Old Creole Days* and was a favorite when Cable read it while on tour with Mark Twain. Like "Père Raphaël" it blends realism with idealism, the flamboyant with the introspective, refined society with low life, and colorful Creole dialect with delightfully muted prose descriptions. Unlike Miss Welty's stories in *The Golden Apples,* for example, Cable has not linked these two stories together in a sequential manner, nor has he juxtaposed them in counterpuntal variations as Faulkner did in *The Wild Palms.* "Posson Jone' " and "Père Raphaël" are distinctive stories capable of being read separately, yet they do penetrate one another. Their juxtaposition is rather unique in American literature since both stories relate events and situations that happen simultaneously, not unlike the cyclical patterns in *The Sound and the Fury,* but without the intricate time periods so important to Faulkner's novel. The events and characters in "Posson Jone' " are seen again in different ways in "Père Raphaël"; "Père Raphaël," in turn, dramatizes a fuller, more nuanced version of "Posson Jone'." . . . Reading these two stories one after another is like watching two movies at the same time, movies which reveal the same plots but from a variety of angles. (pp. 61-2)

Cable discovered in these two stories three related thematic situations, the first two in "Posson Jone' " and the third, inchoatively developed in "Posson Jone'," as Cable suggested, but more explicitly developed in "Père Raphaël":

1. Providence, not law, ultimately governs human affairs.
2. Friendship cannot be calculated in monetary terms.
3. Romantic love overcomes all obstacles including parental opposition and authority.

Initially when Posson Jones, the West Floridian preacher, attracts the interest of Jules St-Ange because of the money Jones possesses, Jules tricks him into gambling, even though this goes against Jones' moral sensibility. One Sunday afternoon, the two attend a circus, in the Roman sense, where buffaloes and tigers are slaughtered; eventually these two men, so opposite, become good friends, such that Jules is willing to bail Jones out when he has been thrown into jail and, in addition, to give him some money. Characteristically, Jones refuses Jules' offer. Subsequently Jones' Negro servant, Colossus, returns the five hundred dollars he had secretly taken from Jones for safe-keeping. In all of this, Providence has brought these two men together. Money is not the basis of their friendship. Eventually Jules sees how to use his money; that is, he will pay his debts, a maneuver which will put him in the good graces of his family and friends.

In developing these thematic relationships, Cable sensed he needed two stories to reveal the dimensions of romantic love that were not explicitly portrayed in "Posson Jone'." . . . In this story, romantic love seems to have its origin in divine Providence. As Florestine, Jules' girlfriend, says in the last sentence of "Père Raphaël": "Me, the same like Jules, I am discourage' to be wicked any mo', those Providence get al'ong so well without." Here, Cable's religious sensibility concerning Providence seems more social than theological, yet there is, as in many of his novels and stories, most notably in "Madame Delphine" in *Old Creole Days,* a pervading religious tone congruent with, and conducive of, romantic love.

In these two stories, Providence governs the destinies of these characters, as they frequently admit. Even the law, whether established by a parent or by the state, ultimately does not thwart the designs of Providence. While no one really undergoes a radical *metanoia,* perhaps because Père Raphaël is an imposter, lifestyles and attitudes are gradually modified throughout the course of the two stories. Jules, initially described as an "elegant little heathen" taught by the Capuchins that this world "is a cheese to be eaten through," seems to have nibbled considerably into this cheese-world and still lacks friends and money. Gambling satisfies Jules' needs; friends are to be acquired for the sake of winning money. . . . Jones, a man of giant stature, with a slight stoop in his shoulders and with a face marked as Cable says, "more by weather than by age," just happens to converge on the same street as Jules and at the same time. Providence, or circumstance to see it in its secular guise, has brought them together. Thus, place, religious background, and money or the lack of it (Jones has money in his hat belonging to the Smyrna Church) are the decisive elements in their first meeting. Jones says, "It seems like a special provi*dence.*—Jools, do you believe in a special provi*dence*?" When Jules thinks of the bank notes in Jones' possession, he agrees and admits the existence of such a Providence.

Cable has juxtaposed Providence, which supposes an intelligent being behind it and which can shape men's lives, with gambling, pure chance, that is seemingly unpredictable and without any intentionality. What we do not realize is that it is not by sheer chance that "a short, square, old Negro, very black and grotesque" named Colossus, Jones' body-servant, takes Jones' money. Cable stresses this notion of Providence in unexpected ways; Jones believes, for example, "there would always be 'a special provi*dence* again' cotton untell folks quits a-pressin' of it and haulin' of it on Sundays.' " Likewise, Jules' malapropism about Providence shows his easy compliance and lack of understanding: "I thing you is juz right. I believe, me, strong-strong in the improvidence, yes." Jones even disapproves of Jules mixing religion and mercantilism, particularly when Jules tells the story of assisting his father in blessing sugar with holy water to form a *quitte.* To this Jones finally comments, "I reckon you must be a plumb Catholic." But Jules knows how to respond to Jones and still keep in his good graces: "I am a *Catholique, mais* . . . not a good one." No false humility here! Just a come-back that reflects a worldly man who adjusts to the situation very quickly—and keeps his sense of humor while doing it.

As Cable develops this notion of Providence, he intertwines it with the notion of friendship, to show that friendship cannot be assessed in monetary terms. Life cannot be reduced to a single preoccupation. In portraying Jules before his first encounter with Jones, the narrator shows that the French Quarter seems to have a sympathetic relationship with Jules, in such a way that the nature reflects the human spirit. . . . Yet Colossus, in spite of the pleasant surroundings, is wary of Jules and tries to prevent this budding friendship from continuing. But it is too late; the magnetic forces have started working and the human attitudes and emotions are lining up in a discernible pattern. After both Jules' and Jones' servants are sent off, religion and money are further linked when Jones says, with an irony he is unaware of, concerning Colossus, "He's a powerful smart fool. Why, that boy's got money, Jools; more money than religion, I reckon." The narrator warns the reader, however, that the fascination we might have towards Colossus because of his eloquence would be misplaced; Colossus' castigation of drinking liquor and violating the Sabbath by playing the fiddle must not mislead anyone. Above all "this is a story of a true Christian; to wit, Parson Jones."

Providence guides these two friends, not by prophetic voices nor by religious decrees, but by allowing them to listen to their consciences and to follow some inner moral and religious imperatives. This matter of conscience first reaches a crisis when Jules wants to buy some "noble" coffee in the French market rather than drink the restaurant coffee. Jones objects since purchasing coffee in the French market would, in his mind, violate the Sabbath. . . . Though the parson makes his own rules, such as never visiting on Sunday, except with Church members, he likewise makes his own exceptions. Thus, he finds himself with Jules not, as he might have hoped, in some Church member's home, but in a theatre, sub-let to gamblers. Once inside the gambling-den Jones is adamant; he will listen to the voice of Providence and not lend Jules money: it's "a matter of conscience with me, Jools." To which Jules responds, *Mais, oui! 'tis a matt' of conscien' wid me, the same.*" And yet, it is not the same because Jules does grow in his awareness of his moral obligations; his conscience becomes more sensitive and exacting. Eventually both Jules and Jones put aside their verbal quarreling and become more expansive, reflected in the festive mood Cable depicts when the two protagonists visit Cayetano's Circus in the Congo Plains; buffalo and tiger fights, singing, boisterous preaching, the companionship of Baptiste and Colossus all contribute to the joyous relationship of these two men. In his exuberance, Jones misquotes Isaias' prophecy when he says that the buffalo and the tiger shall lie down together; he compounds his mistake by referring to Daniel's apocalyptic vision of going into the "buffaler's den." Unfortunately, this mood does not last; the tiger and the buffalo are slaughtered and Jones is taken to jail.

When Jules wins six hundred dollars by a specious providence he attempts to effect the release of a most reluctant Jones, a man now aware even more of his own faults and shortcomings. Yet, surprisingly, they pray together and Jones accepts his freedom. Jules attempts to give his money away, earned "in a mysterious way," to Jones, but is rebuffed. Finally when Colossus arrives at the boat, the *Isabella,* which will transport Jones and Colossus to their homeland, he hands over the money he had previously taken and Jules, in turn, resolves to pay all his debts with the money he had won. Thus, both Jules and Jones, rich in money and friendship, have listened to their consciences; love has guided them to a happy resolution of their situation. As Cable writes at the conclusion of **"Posson Jone',"** the "ways of Providence are indeed strange." Strange, too, is the fact that Jones never knew he was a spiritual force in Jules' life: "In all Parson Jones's after life, amid the many painful reminiscences of his visit to the City of the Plain, the sweet knowledge was withheld from him that by the light of the Christian virtue that shone from him even in his great fall, Jules St.-Ange arose, and went to his father an honest man." This reference to Jules' father links the two stories together because in the first sentence of **"Père Raphaël"** the judge who released Jones from jail was, in fact, Jules' father, René De Blanc St.-Ange. Thus up to this point, the direction of the story has indicated that Providence, whether specious or special, is not at the mercy of the law since Jones is released from jail through the friendship of Jules. Although at the end of **"Posson Jone',"**

the West Floridian preacher and the son of a wealthy Creole are richer than either one had thought possible, at least during their time together, one element is missing, the one Cable himself refers to in his introduction, and the one Miss Welty likewise stresses in her essay on analyzing the short story: romantic love. (pp. 63-8)

By initially linking **"Père Raphaël"** with **"Posson Jone',"** in mentioning the identity of Jules' father, Cable places us at the beginning of the second story half-way back into the first; yet, we do not feel dislocated because of the sense of place, particularly the corner of Rue Royale and Conti Street. In fact, the gambling-den adjoins the judge's house and he himself plays cards every night, further linking these two stories by games of chance. Though Jules is a bitter disappointment to his father because of his apparently reckless way of living, his father is not above gambling on Sunday, provided, of course, that the game is fair. Thus the card game, representative of one dimension of Providence, is pitted against human ingenuity in resolving the father-son dilemma. In addition, in **"Père Raphaël,"** Cable has introduced a situation which had not been adumbrated in **"Posson Jone'"**; Abigail Meriwether, whose mother is a friend of the judge, is in love with Dimitry Davezac, whom she cannot marry until he produces someone who can vouch for his character. Though the judge is familiar with Père Pierre, as Jules is friendly with Parson Jones, it is Dimitry who suggests another religious person, **"Père Raphaël,"** to be his character witness. This suggestion occurs at the same time we hear the noise and shouting from Cayetano's Circus in the Place Congo; place continues to link these two stories, even when the characters from the first story are not really active in the second.

Since Caroline has overheard Père Pierre tell the judge not to prevent the marriage of Jules and Florestine, Florestine decides to masquerade as Père Raphaël; she will not be discovered if she wears a cowl down low since the judge has to shield constantly his sore eye. As in *Twelfth Night* and *Much Ado About Nothing,* Cable uses the device of eavesdropping to bring the romantic lovers together since this is the one device whereby some can learn what others think without verbally disclosing their own point of view; the audience sees the total picture, a picture that no one else is quite aware of since mutual communication is prohibited to the eavesdroppers. Abigail, however, "still in a tremor of hope, longing, and self-blame" sees Caroline instruct Baptiste about informing Jules of the judge's willingness to repay his son in a two-fold manner. Florestine, in turn, sees Abigail peering after Dimitry, while outside Jules encounters Dimitry, presumably for the first time: the "spying maidens, from Florestine's high chamber, could see Dimitry, though not Jules." At this point, Jones enters the story and ties together the plots and themes of both stories. And thus, "the maidens took courage when they heard the parson set forth his theory of special Providence and Jules profess a like conviction." In a clever way, Cable has helped to assure Providence's success: Jules and Jones go gambling, the St.-Anges go to Mass, and the others go to the pawn shop.

During the meeting between Père Raphaël "with unlifted cowl" and the judge, Florestine knows the judge's penchant for cards and ingratiates herself by saying that she enjoys cards too; also, in passing, she acknowledges Dimitry as a worthy candidate for Abigail's hand. Thus, Dimitry who has pawned all of the judge's bric-à-brac has commenced to prove himself. Jules, however, must do more than commence; he must finish. The roar of the circus seems to confirm and remind the reader of Jules' habits; Dimitry is winning but Jules seems to be losing. After Jones is put in jail, Jules returns home and with Père Raphaël, Dimitry, and his father, plays cards. Jules wins. The money he wins from Dimitry and Raphaël is actually the money they had received from the pawn shop. Thus, Jules is unaware of the real providential source and cunning behind this card game, one deliberately set up so that he would be reconciled with his father and thus be placed in a position to marry Florestine. Yet Jules will not pay his debts because he owes a greater debt to Jones who had lost his money. As Jules repeats " 'tis a matt of conscien'," the final scene in the suburb of St. Jean on the Bayou Road, a repetition of the final scene in **"Posson Jone'**," is seen in an entirely new light, uniting as it does Providence, friendship, and romantic love. As in a Shakespearean play, the main characters reappear slowly to face the final resolution of their particular problem; one is particularly reminded of Sir Thopus in *Twelfth Night* and Friar Lawrence in *Romeo and Juliet,* a pseudo and a real priest who serve as literary catalysts. After Père Raphaël's disguise is removed, the judge finally realizes "to commance, 'tis enough!" The judge sees clearly now, as we all do, and Jules agrees to pay his debts. Before all, the father and son exchange mutual absolution. With this note of reconciliation, Cable has not only brought these two stories to a conclusion, but he has suggested that characters will continue to interact with one another.

Thus Cable has revealed in these stories that the New Orleans of his imagination does, in fact, have a conscience, one that can make decisions and seek to resolve problems. Unfortunately, Cable does not probe the depth of the relationships he creates, whether they be male-male in the case of Jules and Parson Jones, or female-male in the case of Florestine and Jules. The strength of these stories lies partly in the manner in which they are related and partly in the descriptive passages concerning New Orleans and environs. Cable remains within the genteel tradition; his characters enter and retreat from the polite society they live in and are themselves judged in terms of its customary, and often superficial standards. Though the circle appears quite wide and seems to include individuals who might be considered marginal, all remain within limits that are quite acceptable. Cable's sense of harmony, normally seen as a positive characteristic of his technique, can to a certain extent work against him; one would almost think that had he left some element unbalanced (Catholic/Protestant, profane/spiritual, Providence/human creativity), he might have ventured into new territory rather than remaining comfortable within the confines of the Vieux Carré. Yet, for all this, these stories lack neither vibrancy nor subtlety and, especially when seen as companion pieces, one builds on and reinforces the literary strengths of the other. (pp. 69-72)

Patrick Samway, S. J., "Cable's 'Posson Jone'' and 'Pere Raphael': 'Tis a Matt of Conscien'," in Revue de Louisiane, *Vol. 11, No. 1, Summer, 1982, pp. 61-72.*

FURTHER READING

Bilke, Lucy Leffingwell Cable. *George W. Cable: His Life and Letters.* New York: Charles Scribner's Sons, 1928, 306 p.
   A compilation of Cable's diaries and letters by his daughter.

Brooks, Van Wyck. "The South: Miss Murfree and Cable." In his *The Times of Melville and Whitman,* pp. 378-94. New York: E. P. Dutton & Co., 1947.
   Provides a brief social history of New Orleans and examines Cable's use of local color.

Christophersen, Bill. " 'Jean-ah Poquelin': Cable's Place in Southern Gothic." *South Dakota Review* 20, No. 2 (Summer 1982): 55-66.
   Demonstrates that "Jean-ah Poquelin" parallels William Faulkner's "A Rose for Emily" in thematic development and compares similarities and differences in treatment by the two authors.

Downs, Robert B. "Romantic New Orleans: George W. Cable's *Old Creole Days.*" In his *Books That Changed the South,* pp. 148-55. Chapel Hill: University of North Carolina Press, 1977.
   Views *Old Creole Days* as both a historical and sociological document of antebellum New Orleans.

Hicks, Granville. "A Banjo on My Knee." In his *The Great Tradition: An Interpretation of American Literature since the Civil War,* pp. 32-67. New York: Biblo and Tannen, 1967.
   Places Cable in the regionalist tradition as represented by such authors as Bret Harte and Mark Twain.

Perret, J. John. "Strange True Stories of Louisiana: History or Hoax?" *Southern Studies* XVI, No. 1 (Spring 1977): 41-53.
   Asserts that some of the pieces in this collection are fabrications.

Pugh, Griffin T. "George W. Cable's Theory and Use of Folk Speech." *Southern Folklore Quarterly* XXIV, No. 4 (December 1960): 287-93.
   Discusses Cable's use of dialect in his short fiction and novels.

Ringe, Donald A. "The Moral World of Cable's 'Belles Demoiselles Plantation.' " *Mississippi Quarterly* XXIX, No. 1 (Winter 1975-76): 83-90.
   Refutes Howard W. Fulweiler's interpretation of this story as a parable of divine justice [see excerpt dated 1966].

Trotman, C. Jones. "George W. Cable and Tradition." *The Texas Quarterly* XIX, No. 3 (Autumn 1976): 51-8.
   Brief reassessment of Cable's fiction.

Turner, Arlin. "George Washington Cable's Literary Apprenticeship." *Louisiana Historical Quarterly* 24, No. 1 (January 1941): 168-86.
   Examines Cable's years as a journalist on the *New Orleans Picayune* and its influence on his fiction.

———. Introduction to *Creoles and Cajuns: Stories of Old Louisiana,* by George W. Cable, edited by Arlin Turner, pp. 1-19. Garden City: Doubleday, 1959.
   Surveys Cable's portrait of urban Creole society and the rural Acadian communities.

———. *Critical Essays on George W. Cable.* Boston: G. K. Hall & Co., 1980, 251 p.
   A collection of critical essays on Cable's writings. Commentators include Lafcadio Hearn, James M. Barrie, and W. D. Howells.

Warner, Charles Dudley. "On Mr. Cable's Readings." *The Century Magazine* XXVI, No. 2 (June 1883): 311-12.
   Account of one of Cable's public readings of *Old Creole Days.*

Nikolai (Vasilyevich) Gogol

1809-1852

(Born Nikolai Gogol-Yanovsky; also transliterated as Nikolay; also Vasilevich, Vasil'yevich, Vasilievich, and Vasilyevitch; also Gogol and Gógol; also wrote under the pseudonyms V. Alov and Rudy Panko) Russian novelist, dramatist, short story writer, essayist, critic, and poet.

Gogol is regarded as one of Russia's greatest prose stylists and a seminal influence on his country's literature. While he is perhaps best known for his novel *Mërtvye dushi* (*Dead Souls*) and his drama *Révizor* (*The Inspector-General*), Gogol, along with American writers Nathaniel Hawthorne and Edgar Allan Poe, is acknowledged as a progenitor of the modern short story. His fiction, written in an idiosyncratic style that combines elements of realism, fantasy, comedy, and the grotesque, typically features complex psychological studies of individuals tormented by feelings of impotence, alienation, and frustration. In addition, several of Gogol's stories humorously expose negative aspects of Russian society. Often cited as a major inspiration to such authors as Fedor Dostoevski and Franz Kafka, Gogol's work, while ultimately considered unclassifiable, has elicited a variety of critical interpretations.

Gogol was born into a family of Ukrainian landowners. As a young boy, he attended boarding school, where he developed an interest in literature and drama. After failing both to find employment as an actor and to sell his writing, Gogol used his own money to publish his epic poem *Hanz Küchelgarten*. When this work received only negative reviews, Gogol collected and burned all remaining copies of the book. Soon after, he obtained a civil service position in St. Petersburg and began writing *Vechera ná khutore bliz Dikanki* (*Evenings on a Farm near Dikanka*), a volume of mostly comic folktales set in his native Ukraine. In these stories, Gogol depicted the world of the Cossack peasantry through an engaging mixture of naturalism and fantasy. Immediately acclaimed as the work of a brilliant young writer, *Evenings on a Farm near Dikanka* brought Gogol to the attention of celebrated poet Alexander Pushkin and noted critic Vissarion Belinsky, who was an early champion of Pushkin and now recognized similar promise in Gogol. Pushkin proved to be Gogol's strongest literary inspiration, and their association from 1831 to 1836 fostered Gogol's most productive period.

Mirgorod, Gogol's next cycle of stories, comprises four tales that encompass a variety of moods and styles. "Starosvetskie pomeshchiki" ("Old-World Landowners") is a light satire of peasant life, while "Taras Bulba," often referred to as the "Cossack *Iliad,*" is a serious historical novella that portrays the Cossack-Polish wars of the sixteenth and seventeenth centuries. "Viy," described by Gogol as "a colossal product of folk-imagination," is a tale of supernatural terror reminiscent of Poe, and "Kak possorilsya Ivan Ivanovich s Ivanom Nikiforovichem" ("The Tale of How Ivan Ivanovich Quarrelled with Ivan Nikiforovich"), considered one of the most humorous stories in Russian letters, details the end of a long friendship due to a trifling argument that culminates in an absurd series of lawsuits.

The three stories in *Arabeski* (*Arabesques*) rank among Gogol's finest works. Demonstrating a shift from Ukrainian settings to the more cosmopolitan milieu of St. Petersburg, capital of the Russian empire, these pieces form part of what was termed Gogol's Petersburg Tales in the two-volume collection *Sochinenya* (*The Works of Nikolay Gogol*). Each of these three stories reveals the city as nonsensical, depersonalized, and dreamlike. "Nevski Prospekt" ("Nevski Prospect") illustrates the illusory nature of the principal thoroughfare in St. Petersburg through the experiences of two men in pursuit of women whom they believe represent ideal beauty. Their expectations are shattered, however, as one man kills himself when he discovers that his perfect woman is a prostitute and the other receives a beating from the husband of his inamorata. In "Portret" ("Portrait"), Gogol examines conflicts between artistic integrity and financial security, and in "Zapriski sumasshedshago" ("Diary of a Madman"), Gogol's only first-person narrative, he recounts in diary form events that lead to a minor civil servant's delusion that he is the king of Spain. This story has been interpreted as an indictment of the dehumanizing effects of Russian bureaucracy and a comment on the futility of ambition.

Gogol's final two Petersburg Tales, "Nos" ("The Nose") and "Shinel" ("The Overcoat"), are considered among the greatest short stories in world literature. Both pieces exhibit Gogol's subtle intertwining of humor and pathos and, like "Diary of a Madman," focus on the bizarre fate of petty government officials. "The Nose" centers on a vain, ambitious bureaucrat whose nose, apparently severed by his barber, assumes a life of its own and is later encountered while dressed in the uniform of a high-ranking Russian officer in the streets of St. Petersburg. Several unsuccessful attempts to regain his nose induce the protagonist's humiliation and loss of self-esteem, until one day he notices it has grown back as mysteriously as it disappeared. While recognized as a satire on Russian bureaucracy and human vanity, some Freudian critics have analyzed "The Nose" as an example of Gogol's castration anxiety. "The Overcoat," deemed by some critics as the greatest short story in the Russian language, has generated much criticism and myriad interpretations. The story revolves around an impoverished clerk, Akaky Akakyvitch, who undergoes extreme deprivation in order to save money for a new overcoat, which he views as essential to his happiness. After Akaky finally acquires the garment, it is stolen. His calls for help go unheeded, and he subsequently catches cold and dies. After his death, however, a ghost resembling Akaky appears and roams the city stealing overcoats. While most readers of Gogol's day construed "The Overcoat" as an example of social realism, believing that the author displayed deep sympathy for his beleaguered hero, later scholars have viewed the story from a psychological perspective, asserting that the overcoat symbolizes a mask that enables Akaky to disguise his spiritual destitution. Others have taken a metaphysical viewpoint, interpreting the ironic loss of the coat and Akaky's futile pleas for help as indicative of humanity's spiritual desolation in an indifferent cosmos. Despite such diverse views, critics have consistently noted the resonant irony and lyrical power with which Gogol invested this story.

Toward the end of his life, Gogol became increasingly convinced that his works should spiritually enrich his readers. *Vybrannye mesta iz perepiski s druzyami* (*Selected Passages from Correspondence with My Friends*), a collection of didactic essays and letters, which many of Gogol's previous admirers condemned as reactionary, reflects this growing religious and moral fanaticism. Following the critical failure of *Selected Passages from Correspondence with My Friends*, Gogol recommenced composition on a second section of his novel *Dead Souls*, a project he had previously abandoned due to a nervous breakdown. By this time, however, Gogol had fallen under the influence of Matthew Konstantinovsky, a maniacal priest who insisted that he burn his manuscript and enter a monastery. Gogol agonized over the decision but finally complied, convinced that this act would save him from damnation. At Konstantinovsky's insistence, Gogol undertook an ascetic regimen in order to cleanse his soul. He began a fast that weakened his already precarious health and died shortly thereafter.

Gogol's influence on Russian literature continued into the twentieth century and is perhaps most evident in the poetry of the Russian Symbolists. Such poets as Andrey Bely and Aleksandr Blok cite Gogol's rich prose and visionary language as embodiments of supreme fantasy. Nevertheless, many critics maintain that Gogol's mixture of realism and satire has proved to be his most influential achievement. Perhaps internationally renowned writer Fedor Dostoevski best summarized the extent of Gogol's influence when he acknowledged Russian literature's vast debt to Gogol by stating, "We all came from Gogol's 'Overcoat.'"

(For further information on Gogol's life and career, see *Nineteenth-Century Literature Criticism,* Vols. 5, 15.)

PRINCIPAL WORKS

SHORT FICTION

Vechera ná khutore bliz Dikanki [as Rudy Panko] 1831
  [*Evenings in Little Russia*, 1903; also published as *Evenings on a Farm near Dikanka*, 1906]
*Arabeski (short stories and essays) 1835
  [*Arabesques*, 1981]
Mirgorod 1835
  [*Mirgorod*, 1842]
Sochinenya. 2 vols. (short stories, dramas, and novel) 1842
  [*The Works of Nikolay Gogol*. 6 vols., 1922-1928]

---

*This work includes the short story "Taras Bulba"; also published as "Taras Bulba" [revised edition], 1842.

OTHER MAJOR WORKS

Révizor (drama) 1836
  [*The Inspector-General*, 1892; also published as *The Government Inspector* in *The Government Inspector, and Other Plays*, 1927]
Mërtvye dushi (novel) 1842
  [*Tchitchikoff's Journeys; or, Dead Souls*, 1886; also published as *Dead Souls*, 1915]
Zhenit'ba; Sovershenno neveroyatnoye sobitye (drama) 1842
  [*The Marriage: An Utterly Incredible Occurrence* published in *The Modern Theatre*, Vol. IV, 1955-1960]
Igroki (drama) 1843
  [*The Gamblers* published in *The Modern Theatre*, Vol. III, 1955-1960]
Vybrannye mesta iz perepiski s druzyami (essays and letters) 1847
  [*Selected Passages from Correspondence with My Friends*, 1969]
Letters of Nikolai Gogol (letters) 1967

IVAN YERMAKOV (essay date 1923)

[*A psychoanalyst, Yermakov was strongly influenced by Sigmund Freud. Using Freud's concept of the creative process as the basis of his analysis in the following excerpt, Yermakov draws general conclusions about Gogol's psyche. He maintains that Gogol, like Freud, understood the significance of dreams and thus revealed his characters primarily through their own dreams. The essay from which this excerpt is taken was originally published in Russian in 1923 in Yermakov's book* Ocherki po analizu tvorchestva N.V. Gogolya.]

Gogol's fantastic tale **"The Nose"** occupies a special position among those works of his which are linked, if not exactly by the same theme, then by the tormenting questions he put to himself and endeavored to resolve. Included in this group are a number of his best stories, such as **"Viy," "The Tale of How Ivan Ivanovich Quarrelled with Ivan Nikiforovich," "The Nose," "The Overcoat,"** and **"Diary of a Madman."** To be sure, it is to some extent arbitrary and artificial to lift just a few stories out of the corpus of Gogol's works, all of which are organically interconnected; for . . . the theme of **"The Nose"** had long been in the making, in stories where the nose itself had not yet been assigned the role of protagonist. This fact makes it clear that Gogol did not borrow his theme from elsewhere, as literary historians suppose; he was not simply echoing certain literary fashions of the beginning of the nineteenth century; rather, he responded to them, interpreted them, and gave them a particular form, out of an inner need and compulsion to do so. (p. 158)

In his letters and his works of fiction, Gogol betrays an irrepressible need to observe, describe, and castigate the shortcomings of others and of himself as well. In neither case is he free, for he is obeying the command of his unconscious. Gogol torments himself in order to have the right to torment others.

All of a writer's works are nothing more than a confession and self-revelation. Gogol—and he speaks of this specifically in **"An Author's Confession"**—saw his works as a kind of mirror in which he scrutinized and studied himself. This, it seems to me, explains his narrative method, his use of colloquial language and *skaz,* [a form of narration in which the speaker's style is as significant as the story], and his habit of putting himself into everything he wrote. The clash of two opposing tendencies in the confession—one revealing, the other concealing—produced a compromise solution to the task that Gogol set himself, and forced him to resort to jests, puns, and unfinished utterances. The attempt to say what cannot be directly expressed in civilized society leads to ambiguity and to witticism. Gogol regarded his works as a confession, an exhibition, for all to see, of something important and significant. (pp. 159-60)

In the complex and interesting course of Gogol's search for his unique, Gogolian self, there is a natural demarcation of two phases, although they are very intimately interconnected. The first is one of open self-ridicule; the second finds him directing his gaze more deeply into the hidden recesses of his own experiences and seeking out "nastiness" there. **"The Nose"** is one of Gogol's confessions that belongs to this second phase, along with **"Viy," "The Overcoat," "Nevsky Prospect,"** and others.

Two sides of Gogol's personality are revealed in the first phase of the development of his work as a satirist: his attempt to depict both comic and terrible things. Here his tendency to try to discredit other people does not go beneath the surface, and his humor is sometimes not of a very high order. He does hit on some very apt names and situations for his characters; but we also constantly find many awkward and rough-cast attempts, such as Dovgochkhun, Pupopuz, Krutoryshchenko, and others.

The second phase is marked by greater care in the selection of such names; the dark and terrible side of life, which was localized in the countryside in the *Dikanka* stories, is now transformed into universal evil, of which every man is the vehicle.

In the first stage, the writer participates in the stories himself, he consistently does the narrating, as if he were retelling old tales and adapting himself to the people he is talking about, putting himself, as it were, on their level. But in the second stage the situation changes. To be sure, Gogol hews to the same narrative method as before. But fundamentally new is his focus on himself, his desire to reveal and identify in him-

self the same traits he sees in others. In other words, there comes a time in the development of Gogol's work when, preoccupied with self-purification and self-analysis, he gradually shifts to the confessional form until finally, and with complete consistency, he entitles one of his last works **"An Author's Confession."** As this inner development proceeds, Gogol begins to take a different view of his early works, which had made him famous overnight. He does not find in them what is now most important to him: the *spiritual* element, which attracts him and fills his life above anything else. (pp. 160-61)

[Two] opposing and endlessly conflicting tendencies underlay Gogol's art: self-depreciation and self-exaltation. The conflict was explicitly reflected not only in what Gogol wrote, but also in the way he wrote, in the style and the imagery he used. . . .

In his early works Gogol liked to introduce and even elaborate on heroic themes, together with themes drawn from ordinary life. For example, *Taras Bulba,* **"Al-Mamun," "Rome,"** and others contain epic descriptions and characterizations that might well have been taken from Homer. These two styles—the one intense and epic, the other commonplace—intertwine throughout all his writings, for instance in **"Diary of a Madman,"** in *Dead Souls,* and, as we shall see, in **"The Nose"** as well, even though they are concealed there.

There is something very significant about the ease with which noble and ignoble themes interweave and unfold in tandem. (Gogol's follower, Dostoevsky, brought this tendency to full flower.) Very often such themes develop in unexpected ways; but they grip us, they seem to dull our critical faculties, and we do not notice how outwardly unmotivated and unexpected they are. Among such instances we should include the so-called lyrical digression at the beginning of **"The Overcoat"** and those in *Dead Souls,*—the passage in chapter eleven, for example, where the courier gallops by, shouting imprecations and shattering the reverie into which the writer has fallen. (p. 162)

In his art [Gogol] constantly moves between two abysses, falling now into one, now into the other. This is what some critics see as his tendency toward the extreme, the ultimate. These two natures are the masculine and the feminine, the active and the passive, the holy and the sinful, the pregenital and the genital. Laughter and tears, pleasure and pain are expressed simultaneously in Gogol's works; and the coexistence of these two opposing tendencies is intimately linked with his sexual experiences and is marked both by auto-erotism and by fear or bitter repentance for such self-gratification. Active behavior is repressed and directed against the self. (pp. 162-63)

In moving toward the extreme, or the ultimate, Gogol, like many fantasts, consistently starts from reality, from some story he has been told, from anecdotes or incidents current in society. He fixes an inquisitive eye on the world around him as he studies man—his words, his gestures, his expressions, and, above all, his nose, to which he attaches a special and very vital significance. One could compile a whole little anthology from the passages in Gogol's works that mention the nose, so tirelessly does he describe the taking of snuff, nose-blowing, and so on. (p. 163)

We must . . . study **"The Nose"** from the viewpoint of that most unusual work of Gogol's, **"An Author's Confession."** A confession is a serious act. . . . [Gogol] is faced with the equally important task of neither revealing nor concealing anything completely. These two opposing drives give rise to conflicting needs. They very often cross and produce so-called compromise solutions, which end up as puns and double entendres. . . . (p. 191)

Feeling absolutely unrestricted, and burning with a desire to repent, Gogol sought an opportunity to bare everything that lay in the depths of his soul, and to make a confession as a great sinner. The most blasphemous scenes, the most unforgivable similes, the most cynical images and possibilities pass before his mind's eye; it is his tremendous capacity for self-analysis which allows him to accept them and to regard their exposure as a heroic deed. To discern these conflicting drives within himself, to bring them out for himself and even for all to see, to invite laughter and ridicule and to know that he is "laughing at himself"—this is what makes it possible for Gogol to confess and reveal himself to the ultimate. It is at this ultimate—this realm of our basic, archaic self, this primitive fabric on which the patterns of our life are later embroidered, this dark, unknown, nether-world of the mind into which man is usually so ready to cast everything he finds cumbersome in his conscious life—it is here that the most contradictory drives come into collision and prove to be identical. Here the same word, the same symbol takes on two completely different meanings at the same time. Here religious fervor is blasphemy, things of the greatest value are valueless, good deeds are evil and sinful. Only after he has reached this ultimate, only after he has brought forth the essence of this basic self can a writer free himself from everything accidental and temporary, touch and understand the innermost secrets of the soul, and then forge a truthful and genuine image of man, and thereby a work of art.

But perhaps there is something dubious about this approach. Perhaps "The Nose" is simply a joke, a trifle, with none of the serious purposes that we have indicated here. (pp. 191-92)

[The] problem posed in "The Nose" is a sexual one. It throws light on the question of the autonomy of man's sexual activity as symbolized by the separate existence of the nose. (The same thing can be seen in the quarrel between the two Ivans.) Sexual activity asserts its rights, which run counter to the urgings of the ego and the norms of society. The thing that cannot be displayed or talked about without shame and embarrassment—"the nose"—itself evokes a feeling of shame and embarrassment if it is not in its proper place, between the two cheeks. The result is an insoluble problem: it is uncomfortable to have a nose but just as uncomfortable not to have one: the two situations are equally discrediting and disgraceful. (p. 192)

In trying as best we can to decipher "The Nose," we must say that two things underlie the story: the fear of castration, which goes along with the repressed wish to possess an enormous sex-organ; and the desire for unlimited erotic pleasures. These desires lead to aggressive acts directed against social life and cultural values, and must be repressed. However, a frivolous individual like Kovalyov is not guided by anything except his own egotistic interests. His activities run counter to the demands of civilized life. They create a feeling of guilt in him which he does not wish to recognize, but which reveals itself to him in the form of an extremely oppressive dream (the dream of castration). But it has been only a dream; on awakening, Kovalyov tries to ignore his painful experiences, and he resumes his interrupted activities. We find him making fun of a military man whose nose is the size of a waistcoat

button; he is even buying the ribbon of some order, but it is not known why, since he has not been so honored. In other words, life has once again fallen into its old rut. The mysterious disappearance of the "nose" remains as mysterious as ever to Kovalyov. (p. 194)

Something that could have brought about catharsis, awareness, purification, further growth and development, a turning point in life (an "annunciation"), has been lost beyond recall. The laughter in the story is suffused with tears, the bitter tears of the author: no, man will not become aware of all his vileness, he will not understand what he is really like. Even in the case of a "learned" collegiate assessor such as Kovalyov, the unconscious attempt to reveal his essential inner self in the form of images and actions has passed without leaving a trace.

In keeping with the structural requirements of the humorous story, Gogol is obliged to bring off a happy ending. But somehow, we feel like saying, as he himself does at the end of **"The Two Ivans"**: "It's a dreary world, my dear sirs!"

All these surprisingly perceptive discoveries are the result of the same process we observe at work in psychoanalysis: one must be honest and courageous when faced with oneself. Gogol possessed a sufficiency of honesty and therefore succeeded in bringing out a great many things in his own mind and the minds of others, things which need much more extensive elucidation and analysis.

For the present, however, we can draw two conclusions from our analysis of **"The Nose."** First of all, what strikes the reader as being mere chance, "nonsense," a dream yet not quite a dream; what makes Ivan Yakovlevich and Kovalyov constantly test themselves to see whether they are asleep or losing their minds—all this has its own logic and has been skilfully prepared by the author. From here it is only a step to the assertion that sleeping and dreaming are not such nonsense after all. The statement that the nose was found by a near-sighted police officer with a mother-in-law who could not see anything either is fraught with significance. Does it not say that the real meaning of the loss of the nose can be discovered and revealed only when a person is near-sighted, when he can see nothing but his own nose, or, in other words, nothing but a dream?

[Second], Gogol's characters frequently carry on meaningless conversations that would hardly be conceivable for normal people. Evidently they do not understand what they are saying or why. But it is just such utterances which best characterize individuals; in psychoanalysis they are called free associations, and they reveal that area of the mind that contains drives which man cannot understand but which nonetheless determine his actions. (pp. 195-96)

["The Nose"] makes it clear that Gogol grasped the significance of the dream as a phenomenon that threatens us and compels us to give serious thought to ourselves. He discerned the possibility of crisis in Kovalyov's petty and intimidated soul—in his useless running around and in his cynical attitude toward women. He created a tragedy, a tragicomedy, and thereby posed the question: what is more important, the sexual or Kovalyov? Is the sexual subordinate to Kovalyov, or Kovalyov to the sexual? The nose comes off by itself and declares its independence of Kovalyov; so far as it is concerned, Kovalyov is nothing more than a carriage for it to ride in. Kovalyov laughs at himself for being foolish enough to take a dream for reality. He does not notice that it is precisely his predicament in the dream which perhaps does more than anything else to expose the emptiness of his life and the humiliation of being utterly dependent on his own nose. Whenever it seems as if the meaning of these events is about to be revealed, everything is shrouded in fog. Kovalyov is not allowed to see; he does not want to see the person who is to blame for everything: himself.

Gogol says that although such cases are rare, they do happen: this is a subtly ironic commentary on people who do not understand the significance of dreams, and who consider outer reality truer than inner. But Gogol understands. He takes the fashionable "nosological" theme which intrigued so many writers before him, and does something more with it than simply reshuffle its familiar components. And he is able to make us understand what every person is tormented by, and what must be resolved and grasped so that man can free himself from the power of the dark forces of primitive instinct. He seems to be refusing to give a solution; he leaves the reader baffled; but any attentive eye can see that Gogol knows something about why such dreams occur; and he prods us into "action," into making an effort to see our own dreams in Kovalyov's dream and hearken to the voices that challenge us to evaluate the life and activity of such an individual. (pp. 197-98)

> *Ivan Yermakov, "The Nose," in* Gogol from the Twentieth Century: Eleven Essays, *edited and translated by Robert A. Maguire, Princeton University Press, 1974, pp. 156-98.*

THE TIMES LITERARY SUPPLEMENT   (essay date 1926)

[*The following excerpt from a review of* Evenings on a Farm near Dikanka *praises Gogol for his charming and knowledgeable use of Ukrainian folklore and Cossack traditions.*]

There are eight stories in [*Evenings on a Farm Near Dikanka*] all of which originally appeared in various magazines when [Gogol] was twenty-one or twenty-two. Published shortly afterwards in book form, they purported to be tales told by a village sacristan and written down by Rudy Panko, a bee-keeper. The bee-keeper introduced something quite new into Russian literature (this was in 1831) and Gogol won instantaneous recognition.

A native of the Ukraine, he was born in the very village which he celebrated in the first of the stories, **"The Fair at Sorotchintsy."** Into his stories he poured his knowledge of Ukrainian folk-lore and Cossack traditions, describing the customs and legends, the festivals and costume of previous generations with a mixture of realism and humour that is wholly captivating. His attitude towards native superstitions about the Devil, witches and "the unclean powers" in general was precisely the attitude of the Russian peasant; he set great store by them and made them the subject of farcical episodes. In spite of the verbal luxuriance of the descriptive passages (some of the more glowing pictures of the Ukraine are classic models) Gogol's method is essentially naturalistic, almost homely. With one exception only, the stories are conceived in the outwardly humorous manner of *Dead Souls,* rather than in the romantic manner of Gogol's most famous Cossack tale, **"Taras Bulba."** What is grotesque in them, however, is not discordant with the general truth and liveliness of the picture; there is as yet no personal animosity in the writer. . . .

Gogol's letters to his mother at the time the *Evenings* were written abound in requests for information concerning old-time custom. His itch for self-expression made good use of the material she supplied, but, having tasted success, he was no longer content to be merry and picturesque, or to detach himself from the life he portrayed. Thenceforth his tormenting egotism shows itself in the malice of his portraiture. The stories in this volume are by no means Gogol's best work. But the reader who knows only the stupid, shiftless, vicious, cunning creatures of his more mature art will welcome their spontaneous charm.

> *"Gogol's Early Stories," in* The Times Literary Supplement, *No. 1269, May 27, 1926, p. 349.*

HENRY JAMES FORMAN (essay date 1926)

[*Forman is an American critic, editor, and short story writer whose books include* In the Footprints of Heine *(1910) and* The Story of Prophecy *(1936). In the excerpted review below of* Evenings on a Farm near Dikanka, *Forman acknowledges Gogol's skill as a humorist and notes the potential for genius that would surface in his later works.*]

Evenings on a Farm Near Dikanka was written by Gogol when he was barely 20, just after he came to St. Petersburg from his ancestral estate in the Ukraine. In the great world of the capital he laughed—how he laughed!—at the superstitions and robust humors of his native land, but there was a touching homesickness in his picture:

> Do you know the Ukrainian night? Oh, you do not know the Ukrainian night! Look at it: the moon looks out from the centre of the sky; the immense dome of heaven stretches further, more inconceivably immense than ever; it glows and breathes. . . . All the countryside is sleeping. But overhead all is breathing; all is marvelous, triumphal. All the soul is full of the immensity and the marvel; and silvery visions rise up in harmonious multitudes from its depths.
>
> Divine night! Enchanting night! And suddenly it all springs into life—the woods, the ponds and the stones. The glorious clamor of the Ukrainian nightingale bursts upon the night, and one fancies the moon itself is listening in mid-heaven. * * * The hamlet on the upland sleeps as though spell-bound.

This passage is not easy to render in all its ecstasy, but it is famous in Russian literature. And what, you may ask, happens against this background? Well, young people make love and make merry and circumvent older people, who always, it seems, have to be circumvented. And one of the chiefest of sports is circumventing the devil.

A young man sees his father, the head of the village, making love to his (the boy's) sweetheart. From that moment he becomes a devil himself, almost, in devising tricks and practical jokes to make his pompous father look ridiculous. Robust humor, as we conceded, and doubtless in the original it appears more natural. But a hundred years ago this region was in the fourteenth century, and in many respects it is there still.

To outwit the devil, however, is even greater sport than to outwit stubborn old men.

In almost every story the devil figures as a character. In **"The Revenge"** a Cossack chieftain guarding the marches of Poland finds that his own father-in-law is at once wizard, devil and spy—just about as confused as those incult intellects that lived by war. A Cossack carries a letter to the Empress Catherine; sure enough he has an adventure with witches and devils on the way—after hearty potations the previous evening.

The devil is all but omnipotent, as the story demands, yet he is always a fool. Any able-bodied Cossack or peasant ultimately and invariably gets the better of him. . . .

"Christmas Eve" is one of the longest and most characteristic of the tales. It is a variant of the ethnically peculiar legend of the Blacksmith and the Devil. The man who works with blackened face and hands at a lurid forge must have some contact with the Devil. In this tale, together with much realistic Christmas Eve merriment, carol singing and lovemaking, is set forth the adventure of a young blacksmith in procuring a pair of the Empress Catherine's slippers for his haughty sweetheart, who had laughingly promised to marry him if he accomplished the feat. Here the devil plays the part of the djinn in Arabian tales. He carries the compelling blacksmith to St. Petersburg and brings him back in a night—with the prized slippers of the stout, sensual little German woman who was the Empress Catherine in his pocket. The blacksmith appearing as a courtier with the devil in his pocket is in itself rich humor. And Gogol does not fail here or elsewhere to give the opulent, incisive, realistic picture of Catherine's court.

It must be admitted that other volumes of Gogol will probably prove of more general interest than the present one. The play *Revizor* (*The Inspector General*), *Dead Souls* and "Taras Bulba" are doubtless of a more universal appeal. But these first tales of Russia's great humorist in a manner indicate the pedigree and origin of the genius that later produced the greater works. It is richly worth reading for those interested in Russian literature.

> Henry James Forman, "Gogol's Gay Tales of the Russian Ukraine," in The New York Times Book Review, *August 15, 1926, p. 5.*

THE TIMES LITERARY SUPPLEMENT (essay date 1928)

[*The following excerpt offers detailed descriptions of several stories in* Mirgorod.]

[The stories in **Mirgorod**] continue the strangely jeering humour and the opulent fancy of *Evenings on a Farm near Dikanka;* there is the same caricaturist's sense of humanity (except, of course, in the famous "Taras Bulba"), and there are the same ornate, highly coloured descriptive passages, positively glowing with poetic imagery and full of the most musical rhythms and cadences. But there is something else in addition: the fusion of naturalistic detail and fantastic temper in a way that foreshadows Gogol's later and greatest work. This is quite obvious at the start. "Old-World Landowners," the first story in the book, provides what seems to be a faithful and affectionate picture of the Ukraine of his childhood. Here are two old people withdrawn from the world, living their infinitely harmless lives in eating and sleeping. Even their gluttony has an undeniable "old-world" charm, so idyllic is the scene Gogol conjures up for us. But, if the picture is true, why the lingering fondness and the elegiac note on which the narrative is sustained? Why this idealization of reality? It is because Gogol's driving force is his inability to live in the present, not his strict sense of the past.

With what completeness he escaped from the present and his peculiar mental chaos (to which he succumbed towards the end of his life) is shown in "Taras Bulba," which has been called—rather too often—the "Cossack Iliad." It is at once the most romantic and the most objective of Gogol's works, capturing in all its poetic vigour the spirit of the old Cossack warriors. It is conceived entirely in the heroic vein; and, unless we except the somewhat pallid figure of the Polish maiden for whose sake Andrey, the old man's younger son, deserts the besieging Cossack force, there is nothing to mar its heroic splendour from beginning to end. The battle scenes have an epic grandeur; the Cossacks themselves, although only a few of them are sharply individualized, are all of recognizable human stature; and the dominating figure of old Bulba, an authentic creation on the epic scale of the Greek, towers wonderfully above the historical tradition.

As for the Polish maiden, it is with her that we come back to the personal world of Gogol's art. She is merely a woman of dazzling beauty; we know no more of her than that. Gogol describes her charms in great detail and with positive awe, but even her loveliness is inhuman. That is one of the strangest things about Gogol's work; himself, he seems to have had no experience of love, and the result is, first, that his few love scenes are pure fantasy; secondly, that the woman almost invariably appears as an instrument of evil. "Viy," the story which follows "Taras Bulba," reminds us of Poe, not merely because of its supernatural terrors but because of the morbid sexlessness suggested by its idea of feminine beauty. True, Gogol himself described the story as "a colossal product of folk-imagination" and professed to have written it down precisely as he heard it. The fact remains that this tale of a philosopher who was destroyed by a witch of surpassing beauty was one which would touch him closely, tormented as he was by fears associated with an abnormal eroticism. And the gruesome humour he lavished upon the theme was again a device which would enable him to express, in a grotesque form, the relief he sought to his own hallucinations.

His humour takes a purer turn in the last story, "How Ivan Ivanovitch Quarrelled with Ivan Nikiforovitch." The subject could not very well be slighter; as with all Gogol's excursions into realistic comedy, the idea is simple in the extreme. The two Ivans, amiable, stupid worthies, have been bosom friends for many years. A mere trifle serves to end their friendship, and they become the most implacable of enemies. To the consternation of the whole town, each brings a lawsuit against the other, reinforcing it with wild charges of high treason and atheism. The litigation goes on and on, until the chief of police tries to effect a reconciliation; everything is carefully planned, and there is every chance of success. Up to this point the farce is delicious; Gogol puts no check upon the hilarity and the riotous nonsense he extracts from the situation. Nowhere else, save perhaps in his play *Marriage,* is his fun so spontaneous. But the entire mood of the story changes when the attempt at reconciliation breaks down. The two silly men, vowing eternal enmity, become grey-haired and ruined in the course of their litigation. The town of Mirgorod is no longer the same when the narrator visits each of them in turn and listens to their prophesyings of vengeance; the fields are black, the rain beats down, drenching crows and jackdaws, and there is not a gleam of light in the sky. The symbolism is unmistakable. "It is gloomy in this world, gentlemen!" is the celebrated conclusion.

Of the causes of Gogol's depression we know a great deal.

Even without the testimony of his letters and of his contemporaries, however, we can find sufficient illumination in his work itself, and more particularly in the solemn pretensions of the work of his last years, "Selected Passages from the Correspondence with My Friends." That extraordinary farrago of religiosity and egotism, although it is scarcely literature, is of peculiar interest to the student of Gogol. Nothing illustrates more clearly the moral struggle from which springs the whole of Gogol's art. Intensely conscious of his own shortcomings of character, he proceeded, in his own words, "to depict in my heroes my own nastiness." An inordinately self-centred creature, almost pathologically introspective, he magnified his own faults, it might be said, until they were large enough to embrace the whole of Russian society.

> *"Nikolay Gogol," in* The Times Literary Supplement, *No. 1400, November 29, 1928, p. 930.*

DMITRY CHIZHEVSKY (essay date 1938)

[*In the following excerpt, Chizhevsky emphasizes the craftsmanship and technical significance of "The Overcoat." He also details the study of "skaz," a form of narration used in this story and commonly employed in Russian literature of the period, in which the speaker's style is as significant as the story. The essay from which this excerpt is taken was originally published in Russian in 1938 in the journal* Sovremennye Zapiski.]

In ["The Overcoat"], the same virtually meaningless word is repeated with extraordinary frequency: *"even."* Within the thirty-two to forty pages that **"The Overcoat"** takes up in the usual editions of Gogol, this little word crops up no fewer than seventy-three times. Moreover, in some places, it is especially frequent: we run across it three, four, and even five times on a single page. Is this just accidental? (pp. 296-97)

First of all, repetition of exactly the same word is characteristic—in Gogol and in other writers—of conversational speech or *skaz*, as the literary historians now call it. In **"The Overcoat"**—and we must mark this well—the story is, to all appearances, told not by Gogol himself but by a narrator whom Gogol very deliberately keeps at a certain distance or remove from himself. Here Gogol follows the narrative technique of **Evenings on a Farm Near Dikanka** and **Mirgorod.** He uses various devices to emphasize that the story is being told by some narrator (who is not himself further characterized). For example, he uses parenthetical expressions such as "nothing is known of that"; "I don't remember from what town"; "Akaky Akakievich was born—if my memory doesn't betray me—sometime on the night of March 22"; "it's hard to say on precisely what day." . . .

Gogol employs digressions for the same purpose. For example, at the very beginning of the story—"In the department of . . ."—the narrator breaks off: "But it's better not to specify in just which department"—and twenty lines of digression follow, after which the story begins all over again: "And so, in a certain department there worked a certain clerk. . . ." (p. 299)

But the narrator is made to resemble Akaky Akakievich in a certain way. This is done by the repetition of certain unnecessary words. For example, in place of words which modify substantives in an expressive and meaningful way, we find qualifiers which have no meaning whatsoever; "a certain" ("a certain police inspector," "a certain director," etc.); "some . . . or other" ("some attitude or other," "some town

or other," etc.); "something or other"; "somehow or other"; etc. Gogol himself draws attention to his hero's way of speaking: "It must be noted that Akaky Akakievich expressed himself for the most part in prepositions, adverbs, and last but not least, in particles of a kind that have absolutely no meaning. And if the matter was very complicated, he even had the habit of not finishing a sentence at all." . . . (pp. 299-300)

The impoverishment of the narrator's diction is therefore no accident. Obviously Gogol was unable to bring it all the way down to the level of the speech of Akaky Akakievich. . . . [The] result would have been no story at all. However, Gogol does to some degree make his narrator's diction resemble that of his heroes. This is the purpose of the peculiar impoverishment of the language of **"The Overcoat."** Such impoverishment would seem to contravene the fundamental, intrinsic law of every work of art, which necessarily strives to achieve the greatest possible richness, fullness, and plenitude. But in this case, the possibilities for a richness and fullness of diction are obviously limited by the inarticulateness that is so characteristic of the narrator and the heroes. (p. 300)

The later development of the naturalistic style in Russian literature provides examples of such language which go far beyond the modest first steps that Gogol made. Examples from Dostoevsky are the speech patterns of Makar Devushkin, in *Poor Folk,* and of the anonymous narrator of *The Double.* On certain pages a reader who has not grasped the author's intention sometimes feels some irritation: why make narrators out of stammerers like these? (pp. 300-01)

The comic element in Gogol consists of a distinctive play of oppositions, or antitheses, between something meaningful and something meaningless. These antitheses alternate, so that one particular thing—a phrase, a word, an idea—which has seemed to make sense suddenly proves to be nonsense; or, vice versa, what has seemed like nonsense proves to make good sense. Among such instances of word-play is the way in which "even" is used. "Even" introduces an intensification, a heightening: it marks a tension, an anticipation; and if no heightening follows, if the thing that is anticipated does not come off, we feel thwarted and surprised, and Gogol has achieved a comic effect. Instead of intensification, Gogol sometimes introduces a "zero meaning" after "even" (meaningless phrases are very common in Gogol); and sometimes we are surprised by a slackening instead of an intensification. Thus there is an alternation of the serious and the humorous; and if a rise in the level of diction is given special emphasis by highly emotional and rhetorical intonation, then even ordinary diction looks like nonsense: having soared too high into the realm of intense emotion, the diction suddenly breaks off and everything ends in nothing, in trivialities—exactly the opposite of what the reader was anticipating. (pp. 302-03)

In **"The Overcoat,"** the word "even" very often . . . introduces phrases and ideas which lack the anticipated logical connection or perhaps in fact any connection at all with what precedes. Thus, "even" robs what is meaningful of its meaning. And what seems meaningful is not always so: such is Gogol's artistic plan here. Some examples: "The clerk's surname was Bashmachkin. From the name alone it is already clear that it was derived from the word for shoe [*bashmak*]; but when, at what time, and in what manner it derived from 'shoe'—of this nothing is known. His father, his grandfather, and *even* his brother-in-law, and absolutely all the Bashmachkins wore boots, merely having them resoled about three times a year." After the first break in logic—the transition to the brother-in-law, who, after all, is not a blood relative of Akaky Akakievich—there follows still another break—the transition to the soles [*podmyotki*], a word that bears absolutely no resemblance to the name Bashmachkin.

Similar breaks in the logical train of thought, all introduced by "even," go along with the narrator's distinctive ideas about the relation of the weather and fate to the higher levels of the Russian "table of ranks." The St. Petersburg cold makes "the forehead ache and tears come to the eyes . . . *even* in those who occupy higher positions"; or: "Various misfortunes are strewn on the path of life not only of titular, but *even* privy, actual, court and all other councilors, *even* those who give no counsel to anyone, nor themselves take it from anyone." . . . (pp. 303-04)

[Through this device, Gogol] reveals the insignificance of the realm or segment of life that he is depicting. What comes after "even" proves to be trivial and insignificant. This means that in this particular realm of life, insignificance, emptiness, "nothingness" are represented as being significant and essential. (pp. 305-06)

A story gains in psychological intensity when the author moves close to his hero. It is precisely in the interest of getting closer that Gogol introduces a narrator, who takes everything seriously. The same effect is achieved in **"Diary of a Madman"** through the diary form, which affords the reader a glimpse into Poprishchin's soul. Dostoevsky brings it off in *Poor Folk,* by having his hero write letters. In his Ukrainian stories Gogol gets close to his heroes with amazing ease, and even merges with them through his narrators (Foma Grigorievich, in **"St. John's Eve"**) and through his use of two levels of language: literary Russian saturated with Ukrainianisms. (pp. 308-09)

The task of establishing a close identity with the hero and his inner world is far more difficult in **"The Overcoat."** . . . [It] is much harder to depict emptiness, insignificance, and nothingness than great and elevated things. It would have been utterly impossible to have Akaky Akakievich himself tell about his own adventures and experiences. It is really not so easy to create a type of narrator who is close to Akaky Akakievich.

Nonetheless Gogol does try to transport us into the inner world of his hero wherever he can, and to show us how Akaky Akakievich looks at life. To a large extent, Gogol shows us the angle from which Akaky Akakievich views the world by means of those everlasting "evens." "Even" indicates how many things and people there are in the world that the poor clerk looks up at from below. After all, "even," logically, points to things or objects which are higher, elevated, significant, unattainable. And as it happens, there is a great deal that lies in this higher realm as far as Akaky Akakievich and the narrator of his story are concerned: overcoats with beaver collars and velvet lapels; state councilors, court councilors and other councilors who are not subject to the operations of those laws of nature and fate that a poor clerk is. This is also the world of the other characters in the story: a new overcoat is an unusual event not only for Akaky Akakievich but for his tailor as well.

The small world or microcosm of a poor clerk is a big world for him precisely because it is filled with objects that he looks up at from below. It is just this sort of existence that Gogol wished us to understand; hence the innumerable "evens" that mark out the configuration of the hero's inner world, his spir-

itual posture. The small world—the big world: it is on this antithesis that the movement of the entire story depends. **"The Overcoat"** is built on the oscillating rhythm of contrasting experiences. Gogol transports us into Akaky Akakievich's little world; we cannot remain there, because we do not find it easy to reincarnate ourselves as Akaky Akakievich. Over and over again our own awareness that his world is a microcosm shatters any illusion that we are in a big world and are experiencing a profound tragedy which decides the matter of the hero's life and death. (pp. 309-10)

"The Overcoat" represents one stage in the development of a theme which is so characteristic of Russian literature—that of the poor clerk. Next to **"The Overcoat,"** the best-known stories in this genre are those of Dostoevsky . . . :*Poor Folk, The Double,* "A Faint Heart," and "Mr. Prokharchin."

Of all the versions of this story (which have been numbered at around two hundred by literary historians), Gogol's is the most successful and effective. . . . However, if social protest really were at the center of the story, would Gogol not have achieved a much greater effect by drawing a portrait of an individual of depth and complexity working in a low-level job? Let us not forget that in his youth Gogol himself had to snatch time for his literary labors from sterile and inane office work. Of course, a reading of Gogol's story as a moral, ethical protest ("I am your brother") is more in line with his own moralizing tendencies; but is Akaky Akakievich a literary type who can successfully illustrate the idea of "I am your brother" to the reader? One does not, after all, have to be particularly snobbish to refuse to see a brother in Akaky Akakievich, whose life is a pitiable and ridiculous tragedy. Should not Gogol have understood that the plot of the story and the mind of Akaky Akakievich being what they are, many, very many readers have to acknowledge Akaky Akakievich not as a brother but, at most, as some very distant relative? (pp. 310-11)

The idea that every human being is our brother was axiomatic in Gogol's Christian view of life and he deemed it necessary to remind us of that at the beginning of the story. But actually, if we read even this passage carefully, without any preconceived ideas, the person who comes out as a human being, as a counterweight to the inhumanity of Akaky Akakievich's fellow clerks, is not Akaky Akakievich himself, but that same young man for whom "everything seemed to change." The theme of **"The Overcoat"** is much more closely associated with a problem that is central to Gogol's view of life: that of "one's own place." (p. 311)

[Gogol speaks of Akaky Akakievich's overcoat] in a language of passion and love, in an erotic language; and there is no doubt that he does so intentionally:

> He had even grown quite accustomed to going hungry in the evenings; but he did partake of spiritual nourishment, for his thoughts were constantly on the eternal idea of the future overcoat. From that time on, his very existence seemed to become somehow fuller, as if he had gotten married, as if some other person were present with him, as if he were no longer alone but were accompanied by some agreeable helpmeet who had consented to walk the road of life with him. This helpmeet was none other than the new overcoat, with its warm padding and its sturdy lining, something that would never wear out. . . . Nevertheless, just before the end of his life he was visited by a radiant guest in the guise of

an overcoat, which for a brief moment enlivened his drab existence.

The reader is apt to interpret such lines more as a mockery of the poor clerk than as an expression of real sympathy or as evidence of a feeling of brotherhood for him. But it is only in this "erotic" context that certain small details in Gogol's story become intelligible. For example, the thief does not merely strip Akaky Akakievich of his coat but, for some reason or other, says: "But this coat belongs to me!" Is not this nocturnal robber a variant of the powerful-rival type in love stories? Love for the overcoat is the only thing that is capable of arousing any erotic feelings in Akaky Akakievich. He runs after a charming lady, and studies an erotic picture in a shop window. And is not the appearance of a ghost searching for an overcoat a kind of parody of the romantic "dead lover" who rises from the grave in quest of his bride? (pp. 312-13)

The theme of **"The Overcoat"** is the kindling of the human soul, its rebirth under the influence of love (albeit of a very special kind). It becomes evident that this can happen through contact with any object—not only with one that is grand, exalted, or important (a heroic deed, one's native land, a living human being such as a friend, a beloved woman, etc.), but also with one that is common and ordinary too. . . . And it is not only love for what is grand and important that can destroy a man or pull him down into a bottomless pit; so too can love for an insignificant object, once it has become the object of passion, of love. (p. 315)

[In] **"The Overcoat"** the hero's fervor is of a lower order than anywhere else in Gogol. Yet Akaky Akakievich does have a fervor; he displays the object of this fervor—the overcoat—to his fellow workers and rejoices that he can show himself in it "even in the evening." The intensity of his enthusiasm for the object of his fervor somehow places him in the ranks of Gogol's other heroes, both serious and humorous. He has something in common with Gogol's fops, accumulators, and unhappy lovers. (pp. 316-17)

Gogol not only wished to present Akaky Akakievich as our "brother"; the main purpose of **"The Overcoat"** was to point to the danger that lurks even in trivia, even in the daily round: the danger, the destructiveness of passion, of passionate enthusiasms quite apart from the object they attach to, even if that object is only an overcoat. For Gogol, the word "even" serves as the means for emphasizing this basic idea. "Even" carries our thoughts to the heights, like an arrow, like an irrepressible thrust of passion, only to let them fall, all the more impotent, and plunge into the common ruck. Akaky Akakievich's impotent aspiration is directed at an unworthy object and is toppled from an illusory height ("even") by the Devil, who is the one responsible for providing such a prosaic yet fantastic goal for this aspiration.

And Akaky Akakievich's aspiration, his earthly love, does conquer death itself; this means, for Gogol, the utter loss of self, a loss that extends even to the life beyond the grave. By returning from the other world to the cold streets of St. Petersburg, Akaky Akakievich shows that he has not found peace beyond the grave, that he is still bound, heart and soul, to his earthly love. The illusory victory of earthly love over death is therefore really the victory of the "eternal murderer," the evil spirit, over man's soul. Gogol's story of the poor clerk is not humorous, but terrible. (pp. 320-21)

Dmitry Chizhevsky, "About Gogol's 'Overcoat,' " in Gogol from the Twentieth Century: Eleven Essays, *edited and translated by Robert A. Maguire, Princeton University Press, 1974, pp. 295-322.*

VLADIMIR NABOKOV   (essay date 1944)

[*A Russian-born American man of letters perhaps best known for the novels* Lolita *(1955) and* Pale Fire *(1962), Nabokov was a prolific contributor to many literary fields. He was fascinated with all aspects of the creative life: in his works, he explored the origins of creativity, the relationships of artists to their work, and the nature of invented reality. In the following excerpt from his biography* Nikolai Gogol *(1944), Nabokov considers Gogol to be a strongly visual writer who excels primarily as a stylist. He concludes that Gogol's work "is a phenomenon of language and not one of ideas."*]

Gogol was a strange creature, but genius is always strange; it is only your healthy second-rater who seems to the grateful reader to be a wise old friend, nicely developing the reader's own notions of life. Great literature skirts the irrational. *Hamlet* is the wild dream of a neurotic scholar. Gogol's **"The Overcoat"** is a grotesque and grim nightmare making black holes in the dim pattern of life. The superficial reader of that story will merely see in it the heavy frolics of an extravagant buffoon; the solemn reader will take for granted that Gogol's prime intention was to denounce the horrors of Russian bureaucracy. But neither the person who wants a good laugh, nor the person who craves for books "that make one think" will understand what **"The Overcoat"** is really about. Give me the creative reader; this is a tale for him.

Steady Pushkin, matter-of-fact Tolstoy, restrained Chekhov have all had their moments of irrational insight which simultaneously blurred the sentence and disclosed a secret meaning worth the sudden focal shift. But with Gogol this shifting is the very basis of his art, so that whenever he tried to write in the round hand of literary tradition and to treat rational ideas in a logical way, he lost all trace of talent. When, as in his immortal **"The Overcoat,"** he really let himself go and pottered happily on the brink of his private abyss, he became the greatest artist that Russia has yet produced.

The sudden slanting of the rational plane of life may be accomplished of course in many ways, and every great writer has his own method. With Gogol it was a combination of two movements: a jerk and a glide. Imagine a trap-door that opens under your feet with absurd suddenness, and a lyrical gust that sweeps you up and then lets you fall with a bump into the next traphole. The absurd was Gogol's favorite muse—but when I say "the absurd," I do not mean the quaint or the comic. The absurd has as many shades and degrees as the tragic has, and moreover, in Gogol's case, it borders upon the latter. It would be wrong to assert that Gogol placed his characters in absurd situations. You cannot place a man in an absurd situation if the whole world he lives in is absurd; you cannot do this if you mean by "absurd" something provoking a chuckle or a shrug. But if you mean the pathetic, the human condition, if you mean all such things that in less weird worlds are linked up with the loftiest aspirations, the deepest sufferings, the strongest passions—then of course the necessary breach is there, and a pathetic human, lost in the midst of Gogol's nightmarish, irresponsible world would be "absurd," by a kind of secondary contrast.

On the lid of the tailor's snuff-box there was "the portrait of a General; I do not know what general because the tailor's thumb had made a hole in the general's face and a square of paper had been gummed over the hole." Thus with the absurdity of Akaky Akakyevich Bashmachkin. We did not expect that, amid the whirling masks, one mask would turn out to be a real face, or at least the place where that face ought to be. The essence of mankind is irrationally derived from the chaos of fakes which form Gogol's world. Akaky Akakyevich, the hero of **"The Overcoat,"** is absurd *because* he is pathetic, *because* he is human and *because* he has been engendered by those very forces which seem to be in such contrast to him.

He is not merely human and pathetic. He is something more, just as the background is not mere burlesque. Somewhere behind the obvious contrast there is a subtle genetic link. His being discloses the same quiver and shimmer as does the dream world to which he belongs. The allusions to something else behind the crudely painted screens, are so artistically combined with the superficial texture of the narration that civic-minded Russians have missed them completely. But a creative reading of Gogol's story reveals that here and there in the most innocent descriptive passage, this or that word, sometimes a mere adverb or a preposition, for instance the word "even" or "almost," is inserted in such a way as to make the harmless sentence explode in a wild display of nightmare fireworks; or else the passage that had started in a rambling colloquial manner all of a sudden leaves the tracks and swerves into the irrational where it really belongs; or again, quite as suddenly, a door bursts open and a mighty wave of foaming poetry rushes in only to dissolve in bathos, or to turn into its own parody, or to be checked by the sentence breaking and reverting to a conjuror's patter, that patter which is such a feature of Gogol's style. It gives one the sensation of something ludicrous and at the same time stellar, lurking constantly around the corner—and one likes to recall that the difference between the comic side of things, and their cosmic side, depends upon one sibilant.

So what is that queer world, glimpses of which we keep catching through the gaps of the harmless looking sentences? It is in a way the *real* one but it looks wildly absurd to us, accustomed as we are to the stage setting that screens it. It is from these glimpses that the main character of **"The Overcoat,"** the meek little clerk, is formed, so that he embodies the spirit of that secret but real world which breaks through Gogol's style. He is, that meek little clerk, a ghost, a visitor from some tragic depths who by chance happened to assume the disguise of a petty official. Russian progressive critics sensed in him the image of the underdog and the whole story impressed them as a social protest. But it is something much more than that. The gaps and black holes in the texture of Gogol's style imply flaws in the texture of life itself. Something is very wrong and all men are mild lunatics engaged in pursuits that seem to them very important while an absurdly logical force keeps them at their futile jobs—this is the real "message" of the story. In this world of utter futility, of futile humility and futile domination, the highest degree that passion, desire, creative urge can attain is a new cloak which both tailors and customers adore on their knees. I am not speaking of the moral point or the moral lesson. There can be no moral lesson in such a world because there are no pupils and no teachers: this world *is* and it excludes everything that might destroy it, so that any improvement, any struggle, any moral purpose or endeavor, are as utterly impossible as changing the course of a star. It is Gogol's world and as such wholly different from Tolstoy's world, or Pushkin's, or Chekhov's or my own. But after reading Gogol one's eyes may become gogolized and

one is apt to see bits of his world in the most unexpected places. I have visited many countries, and something like Akaky Akakyevich's overcoat has been the passionate dream of this or that chance acquaintance who never had heard about Gogol.

The plot of **"The Overcoat"** is very simple. A poor little clerk makes a great decision and orders a new overcoat. The coat while in the making becomes the dream of his life. On the very first night that he wears it he is robbed of it on a dark street. He dies of grief and his ghost haunts the city. This is all in the way of plot, but of course the *real* plot (as always with Gogol) lies in the style, in the inner structure of this transcendental anecdote. In order to appreciate it at its true worth one must perform a kind of mental somersault so as to get rid of conventional values in literature and follow the author along the dream road of his superhuman imagination. Gogol's world is somewhat related to such conceptions of modern physics as the "Concertina Universe" or the "Explosion Universe"; it is far removed from the comfortably revolving clockwork worlds of the last century. There is a curvature in literary style as there is curvature in space,—but few are the Russian readers who do care to plunge into Gogol's magic chaos head first, with no restraint or regret. The Russian who thinks Turgenev was a great writer, and bases his notion of Pushkin upon Chaïkovsky's vile libretti, will merely paddle into the gentlest wavelets of Gogol's mysterious sea and limit his reaction to an enjoyment of what he takes to be whimsical humor and colorful quips. But the diver, the seeker for black pearls, the man who prefers the monsters of the deep to the sunshades on the beach, will find in **"The Overcoat"** shadows linking our state of existence to those other states and modes which we dimly apprehend in our rare moments of irrational perception. The prose of Pushkin is three-dimensional; that of Gogol is four-dimensional, at least. He may be compared to his contemporary, the mathematician Lobachevsky, who blasted Euclid and discovered a century ago many of the theories which Einstein later developed. If parallel lines do not meet it is not because meet they cannot, but because they have other things to do. Gogol's art as disclosed in **"The Overcoat"** suggests that parallel lines not only may meet, but that they can wriggle and get most extravagantly entangled, just as two pillars reflected in water indulge in the most wobbly contortions if the necessary ripple is there. Gogol's genius is exactly that ripple—two and two make five, if not the square root of five, and it all happens quite naturally in Gogol's world, where neither rational mathematics nor indeed any of our pseudo-physical agreements with ourselves can be seriously said to exist.

The clothing process indulged in by Akaky Akakyevich, the making and the putting on of the cloak, is really his *disrobing* and his gradual reversion to the stark nakedness of his own ghost. From the very beginning of the story he is in training for his supernaturally high jump—and such harmless looking details as his tiptoeing in the streets to spare his shoes or his not quite knowing whether he is in the middle of the street or in the middle of the sentence, these details gradually dissolve the clerk Akaky Akakyevich so that towards the end of the story his ghost seems to be the most tangible, the most real part of his being. The account of his ghost haunting the streets of St. Petersburg in search of the cloak of which he had been robbed and finally appropriating that of a high official who had refused to help him in his misfortune—this account, which to the unsophisticated may look like an ordinary ghost story, is transformed towards the end into something for which I can find no precise epithet. It is both an apotheosis and a *dégringolade*. Here it is:

> The Important Person almost died of fright. In his office and generally in the presence of subordinates he was a man of strong character, and whoever glanced at his manly appearance and shape used to imagine his kind of temper with something of a shudder; at the present moment however he (as happens in the case of many people of prodigiously powerful appearance) experienced such terror that, not without reason, he *even* expected to have a fit of some sort. He *even* threw off his cloak of his own accord and then exhorted the coachman in a wild voice to take him home and drive like mad. Upon hearing tones which were generally used at critical moments and were *even* [notice the recurrent use of this word] accompanied by something far more effective, the coachman thought it wiser to draw his head in; he lashed at the horses, and the carriage sped like an arrow. Six minutes later, or a little more, [according to Gogol's special timepiece] the Important Person was already at the porch of his house. Pale, frightened and cloakless, instead of arriving at Caroline Ivanovna's [a woman he kept] he had thus come home; he staggered to his bedroom and spent an exceedingly troubled night, so that next morning, at breakfast, his daughter said to him straightaway: 'You are quite pale today, papa.' But papa kept silent and [now comes the parody of a Bible parable!] he told none of what had befallen him, nor where he had been, nor whither he had wished to go. The whole occurrence made a very strong impression on him [here begins the downhill slide, that spectacular bathos which Gogol uses for his particular needs]. Much more seldom *even* did he address to his subordinates the words 'How dare you?—Do you know to whom you are speaking?'—or at least if he did talk that way it was not till he had first listened to what they had to tell. But still more remarkable was the fact that from that time on the ghostly clerk quite ceased to appear: evidently the Important Person's overcoat fitted him well; at least no more did one hear of overcoats being snatched from people's shoulders. However, many active and vigilant persons refused to be appeased and kept asserting that in remote parts of the city the ghostly clerk still showed himself. And indeed a suburban policeman saw with his own eyes [the downward slide from the moralistic note to the grotesque is now a tumble] a ghost appear from behind a house. But being by nature somewhat of a weakling (so that once, an ordinary full-grown young pig which had rushed out of some private house knocked him off his feet to the great merriment of a group of cab drivers from whom he demanded, and obtained, as a penalty for this derision, ten coppers from each to buy himself snuff), he did not venture to stop the ghost but just kept on walking behind it in the darkness, until the ghost suddenly turned, stopped and inquired: 'What d'you want, you?'—and showed a fist of a size rarely met with *even* among the living. 'Nothing,' answered the sentinel and proceeded to go back at once. That ghost, however, was a much taller one and had a huge moustache. It was heading apparently towards Obukhov Bridge and presently disappeared completely in the darkness of the night.

The torrent of "irrelevant" details (such as the bland assumption that "full-grown young pigs" commonly occur in private

houses) produces such a hypnotic effect that one almost fails to realize one simple thing (and that is the beauty of the final stroke). A piece of most important information, the main structural idea of the story is here deliberately masked by Gogol (because all reality is a mask). The man taken for Akaky Akakyevich's cloakless ghost is actually the man who stole his cloak. But Akaky Akakyevich's ghost existed solely on the strength of his lacking a cloak, whereas now the policeman, lapsing into the queerest paradox of the story, mistakes for this ghost just the very person who was its antithesis, the man who had stolen the cloak. Thus the story describes a full circle: a vicious circle as all circles are, despite their posing as apples, or planets, or human faces.

So to sum up: the story goes this way: mumble, mumble, lyrical wave, mumble, lyrical wave, mumble, lyrical wave, mumble, fantastic climax, mumble, mumble, and back into the chaos from which they all had derived. At this superhigh level of art, literature is of course not concerned with pitying the underdog or cursing the upperdog. It appeals to that secret depth of the human soul where the shadows of other worlds pass like the shadows of nameless and soundless ships. (pp. 140-49)

Vladimir Nabokov, in his Nikolai Gogol, *New Directions Books, 1944, 172 p.*

HERBERT E. BOWMAN   (essay date 1952-53)

[*In the following essay, Bowman characterizes "The Nose" as a satire on Russian bureaucracy and human vanity.*]

If, in an effort to understand Gogol''s fantasy, ["The Nose"] one turns from the intricacies of plastic surgery, Slawkenbergian caprice, and even Gogolian psychology—to say nothing of the labyrinth of castration fears—if one stands aside from all this and fixes one's full attention on the nose itself, one can make several easy discoveries.

The discovery which may provide the key to Gogol''s story is the simplest one of all, namely, that the nose (taken as a physical structure independent of the sense of smell) is perhaps the least important organ of the human body—yet it is at the same time the most conspicuous. And it is conspicuous not only by reason of its protuberant location in the head but by being extremely and proverbially individual in its shape and size.

A second striking fact about the nose is that, with all its conspicuousness, it is seen only by others and hardly at all by its owner, unless, like Major Kovalyov, he keeps a mirror handy. Perhaps only the madman Poprishchin has attempted to explain this physiological circumstance: **"The Diary of a Madman"**, it may be recalled, explains, in one of Poprishchin's last entries, that we cannot see our noses, because they all live on the moon.

As a third important feature of the nose we might take the somewhat odd, but nevertheless evident fact that there is something ridiculous about the nose. It is likely to appear in expressions that carry a note of ridicule or disparagement. A nose that is too conspicuous makes its owner something of a clown—either a sad clown, like Cyrano de Bergerac, or a happy one, like Jimmy Durante.

These are at least several of the distinctive traits of the nose. They suffice to make of the nose a perfectly appropriate vehicle for Gogol'. A ridiculous appurtenance, performing no real function, yet occupying the most advanced position in the human form, in the very middle of the face itself; a lazy, empty, foolish member; a thing of no value to its owner except for purposes of public show—what better object than the nose could have provided Gogol′ with a humorous representation of his characteristic world of hollow and ludicrous 'appearance'?

That Major Kovalyov, who loses his nose, is the epitome of empty appearance, is emphatically clear. His first act on awaking is to call for his mirror. He is the world's slave and the world's darling. His objectives in life are chiefly two—to win promotion and to marry 'well'. His very title 'major' is a reminder of his self-regard: ' . . . in order to give himself still more weight and distinction he never called himself simply a collegiate assessor, but always a major'. As a promising young official and a dashing young Don Juan, he dresses smartly, scrutinises the least pimple on his nose, wears ornate side-whiskers, and strolls along the Nevsky Prospect every day. 'Therefore the reader may judge for himself what the major's position was when he saw, instead of a . . . nose, a ridiculously flat smooth place.'

The loss of his nose troubles the major for only one reason: it ruins his appearance. All his thought is of how he will look—to his friends, sweethearts, colleagues. 'Where in the world can I let myself be seen, looking like such a buffoon? I have respectable acquaintances.' It is, indeed, his sense of personal importance that makes the loss of his nose so particularly painful: 'It is possible for some huckster-woman selling peeled oranges on the Voskresensky Bridge to sit there without a nose, but I have prospects . . .'

Of all the parts of his body which the major might have lost, it is his considered opinion—and one which we can share—that the most grievous to lose is precisely the insignificant and idiotic nose. (pp. 206-08)

Gogol's use of the nose as a gauge of personal esteem perhaps finds its most incisive dramatic statement in the major's encounter with his nose in the streets of St Petersburg. For it turns out that the nose is the major's superior by several grades: the nose appears, in fact, in the accoutrements of a state councillor, so that when Kovalyov addresses his nose, he stands as a major addressing a general. In this farcical scene, we are given a sharp perception both of the major's deference to rank and of Gogol′'s mockery of rank. Even to his own nose, once it gets into the uniform of a superior, the major is ready to bow and scrape, with frequent 'dear sir's'. By this same scene Gogol′ reveals that the major's nose is the best part of him—indeed, the major's nose is the major's superior, for the nose is now clearly all that the major has lost, in brief, his standing in the world. When and if the major succeeds in becoming a general, it will be through the good offices of his 'nose'. Thus Gogol′ takes a bitter pleasure in showing us how the major, perfect creature of worldly ambition, is led around by the nose.

Gogol′'s indulgence in grotesque fantasy—achieving, through fantasy, spiritual vision—is characteristically supported here by a refreshing and diverting concreteness. If it is true that the nose can appear as an officer, because it is the very sign of external appearance; it is also true that the nose makes a passable officer, because any general, muffled up in the habiliments of office, appears to any passer-by as hardly more than a disembodied nose.

Gogol′ thus makes the two-sided suggestion that a nose is an officer and an officer is a nose. Not content with cutting off the major's nose to spite his face, Gogol′ proceeds to tweak the nose of all generals.

If **"The Nose"** is taken as a grotesque laugh at the absurd importance of appearance in a world of appearance, then it becomes easy to interpret the central figure of the major and the strange accident which befalls him.

Around this focus Gogol′ proceeded to fill out the canvas of his story, primarily by the episodes built out of various responses to the major's predicament. Thus we are given a scene at the newspaper office where Kovalyov tries in vain to insert an advertisement for his nose. There follows a scene at the office of the police inspector, who finally outrages the major by his reaction of stupid complacency when he announces that 'no decent man would get into such a predicament'. The doctor whom Kovalyov summons, after the police have brought the nose back, turns out to be similarly useless, although full of medical advice. Kovalyov's next step, a desperate accusation of a staff-officer's wife as the cause of his nose-trouble, leads only to an exchange of letters hopelessly entangled in double-meanings. Meanwhile, the general public demonstrates its morbid curiosity about the major's nose, which is rumoured to be walking about in various parts of the city.

Gogol′ has thus availed himself of the occasion for satirising a variety of stock attitudes, stock figures, stock responses within the official and public life of St Petersburg. The loss of his nose reduces the major to playing the part of a sad and anxious Khlestakov, calling out in the society around him its own absurd reactions to his absurd personal situation.

This series of encounters, which occupies so much space in the story, is, however, essentially additional and complementary to the principal theme of **"The Nose"**. To argue that Gogol′ took the major's nose away merely in order to create out of the nose-chase a picaresque adventure among the institutions of St Petersburg is, in other words, to miss the first point of the story.

In this connection, the documentary evidence is revealing: the history of the original manuscripts of the story shows that part of the detailed account of the reaction of St Petersburg to Major Kovalyov's strange case was a later development in Gogol′'s composition.

Not only this question of where the main emphasis of the story lies, but other minor structural features also are thrown into perspective once we are clear about Gogol′'s original 'inspiration'.

Psychologically, if not historically, this thought stands at the source of **"The Nose"**: Here am I, Major Kovalyov, a young man with a promising future, influential acquaintances, fascinating lady-friends—clearly a man on the make. What if I were to wake up one morning with some absurd disfigurement! What would be the most demoralising accident that could happen to me? To lose a hand, perhaps. Or a foot. Both ears? My *nose*! . . . Imagine the figure I should cut if my *nose* suddenly disappeared!

It is surely some such reflection in Gogol′'s imagination that found its way into Major Kovalyov's nightmare. However Gogol′ was to tell the major's story, it was certain that the main idea would retain its character of playful hypothesis: 'What would happen if . . .'

As it turned out, Gogol' first considered telling his story as a dream *(Son)*. To cast the imaginative hypothesis into the form of a dream is obviously the most straightforward procedure. But the major's dream is more real than reality itself. However fantastic, the major's story is not *mere* fantasy. Perhaps to strengthen that realisation in the mind of the reader, Gogol' abandoned the dream-mechanism and made his story 'real'—thus making it, of course, all the more fantastic.

In order to provide a setting of 'reality' for the fantasy, Ivan Yakovlevich, the barber of Part I, serves a primary purpose: by his confusing and complicating presence in the story, he prevents the major's tale from reverting to its original simplicity as a nightmare or a daydream. We may not have believed the major's denial that his nose-trouble was a dream or a pink elephant, but we are forced to take his story seriously when a second person, the barber, clearly not the creature of Kovalyov's imaginings, gets mixed up in the incident.

To be sure, the barber's tale (Part I) and the major's tale (Part II) never mesh. Perhaps this is a defect in Gogol''s creation. On the other hand, this very incongruity increases the power of the narrative to engage and mystify.

Another structural detail which has been frequently criticised may likewise be made understandable by the foregoing interpretation. The story seems to suffer from a structural incoherence, a fragmentariness which seems to become extreme at the end of both Part I and Part II, which fade away in an all-enveloping 'mist', as well as in the character of Part III, obviously tacked on for the purpose of making an unceremonious restitution of his nose to its proper position on Major Kovalyov's face.

We may be less inclined to consider this narrative off-handedness a defect if we refer again to the 'origin' of the story. The major's accident and all that follows from it (Part II) are the literary illustration of an hypothesis, an imaginary situation, to which the barber's adventures (Part I) are attached. If Gogol' had kept his story in the form of a dream, the dream would have simply ended in an abrupt awakening—as is actually the case in the earlier version. In its final form the story ceases to be a dream and becomes a fantasy of real life. But it does not thereby lose its original character as a mental mustering of imagined consequences attendant on a man's loss of his nose. Once those consequences are envisaged, once the imagination has had its sport with the idea, it simply lets the train of thought evaporate into 'mist' and hands the major back his nose.

And it is not as if a real major had had a real nose taken from him. Gogol' never seems to try to make his protagonist into a real person. All the major's characteristics conduce to turning him into an epitome—the typical man of ambition, with all the hackneyed attitudes that belong to the world of appearance, whose creature he is. Although required to move through the thin air of purest fantasy, he is the very embodiment of a moral type. He is a major not only without a nose, but without any face at all. (pp. 208-11)

Herbert E. Bowman, " 'The Nose,' " *in* The Slavonic and East European Review, *Vol. 31, 1952-53, pp. 204-11.*

MILDRED A. MARTIN (essay date 1956)

[*In the following excerpt, Martin analyzes "The Overcoat" from a Christian perspective.*]

"The Cloak," by Gogol, invites the reader first of all to consider the relation between self-respect and pride and then raises further questions. Akaky, a simple-minded letter-copying clerk in a Moscow office, is the butt of the jokes of his office mates. They declare that his landlady, a woman of seventy, beats him; pretend that he is to marry her, and strew bits of paper over his head calling them snow. He bears all their gibes meekly, until their joking becomes unbearable. When they jog his hand and make him miss a letter in his copying, he exclaims, "Leave me alone! Why do you insult me?" Akaky's cry does not spring from pride, from a sense that anything is due him as Akaky, but from self-respect. Christian self-respect arises from the knowledge that one is a child of God and is loved by Him. As a child of God, Akaky is the brother of his tormentors and does not deserve insult. Gogol makes the point explicitly: "In these moving words, other words resounded—I am thy brother." Akaky respects himself also because he is so good a copyist, but this fact does not elevate him in his own eyes or make him proud. He loves his copying, during most of his life has no desires beyond doing his little task well, and is without anxiety as to what others may think of him.

Just as "The Thief" [by Fedor Dostoevski] may be read as an example of humility of behavior and as a powerful reminder that the outcast and ne'er do-well may be a Christian, so **"The Cloak"** may be read as a reminder that the simple are also human beings, and our brothers. We are prone to the pride of intellect which not only ridicules those less quick than we are, but may even lead us to feel them to be morally inferior to us. It is easy to ridicule Akaky. He cannot do anything but copy without the least alteration what is stuck under his nose and this mechanical task he loves passionately. "Aside from his copying, it appeared that nothing existed for him." Thinking only of his work, he is unaware of where he is, does not notice scraps of melon rind flung from an upper window onto his hat, and cannot bring out a coherent sentence. He is, in short, a laughable figure, but with Akaky's words resounding in our ears, laughter dies suddenly on our lips.

Akaky's vagueness is such that he is not much aware of other people, and in that respect he is unlike Emelian. However, he does not fall into the sin of self-regard. As he walks through the Moscow streets, he is thinking, or rather dreaming, of his work. He does not notice and pity the misfortunes of others; neither does he engage in malicious observation. . . . His simplicty of heart keeps him from thinking of himself or thinking unkindly of others.

The greatest event in Akaky's life is his purchase of a new cloak, and his death is indirectly caused by the theft of the cloak. While it is obvious that Akaky cannot be called a proud man, one may ask whether his interest in his cloak and his grief over its loss means that he has a taint of pride. The cloak certainly means a great deal to him. When he begins to save, that he may accumulate the necessary sum for buying the material and having it made, by going without tea in the evening, by walking lightly, almost on tiptoe over the cobblestones in order not to wear out his shoes, by burning no candles and by doing without a fire, he finds that his existence becomes "fuller," and his character now grows firmer, "like that of a man who had made up his mind, and set himself a goal." The daring thought of having marten fur on his collar flitted through his mind. When the tailor had finished the cloak, and Akaky wore it to the office, "several times he laughed with internal satisfaction." Finally, when the cloak was stolen, and he was scolded by the prominent official to whom he had gone for help in recovering it, he fell ill of a fever and died. How does Gogol treat this material, which in another context might be an indication of pride?

In the first place, the cloak is needed for warmth. Akaky's old cape is worn out beyond repair, and Moscow winters are cold. The new cloak is not a possession which will enhance his prestige in his own eyes or in those of others, but is compared to a person, "a friend who had consented to travel along life's path with him." The thought of the marten fur made him absent-minded, and he "nearly made a mistake, so that he exclaimed almost aloud, 'Ugh!' " The "nearly" and "almost," and Akaky's perturbation at his near mistake place the thought of the marten fur in a humorous light and throw into relief the simplicity of a man whose vanity can be expressed so innocently. Besides, in the end, he has cat fur which "might, indeed, be taken for marten at a distance," but which is cheaper. At the office, when his colleagues gathered around to congratulate him on his new cloak, he was "ashamed," and when they said they must have a party to christen the cloak, "He stood blushing all over for several minutes, trying to assure them that it was not a new cloak, that it was in fact the old cape." These are not the actions of a proud man. However, it is true that if he had not tried to recover the cloak after it was stolen, he would not have been scolded so severely that he fainted; nor would he have fallen ill of a fever and died because of grief and exposure. In comparison with Emelian he is less Christian, since he is attached to something material, and Emelian, whose cloak is full of holes, never thought of having a new one. Emelian's besetting weakness was drink, which has no connection with pride. Akaky's love for his cloak has to be handled skillfully, and this Gogol does, to prevent its being a symbol of pride.

But there is a real symbol of pride here, even arrogance, that of the "prominent personage" whose severity caused Akaky to faint; and this throws Akaky's meekness and simplicity into bold relief. The prominent personage is not only important in contrast with Akaky, but is a fairly complete study in pride, and the only proud character in the three stories. The rank of this personage had only recently been attained, and his position was not considered prominent "in comparison with others still more so." His behavior is typical of that of the proud person who has not yet established himself; he uses every device to try to increase his importance, such as managing to have inferior officials meet him on a lower stair of the staircase, sending all visitors to his secretary first, and adopting three phrases to use with inferiors: "How dare you?" "Do you know whom you are speaking to?" and "Do you realize who is standing before you?" The prominent personage, chatting idly with a friend, keeps Akaky waiting a long time in order to show him "how long officials had to wait in his anteroom." On seeing Akaky's "worn uniform and modest mien" he speaks curtly to him, and finally scolds him so severely for not having presented his case through proper channels that Akaky faints, whereat the important personage is gratified. Gogol comments that the official's heart "was accessible to many good impulses," but that "his rank often prevented him from showing his true self." His uneasiness in his new rank, and his real knowledge of his lack of worth, which he tries

to hide from himself and from others, cause him through pride to commit an injustice toward Akaky. When he learned of Akaky's death, "he hearkened to the reproaches of his conscience, and was out of sorts for a whole day." The phrase "a whole day" shows the superficiality of his repentance, but after his own cloak is snatched from his shoulders by Akaky's ghost, he seriously begins to mend his ways, is careful before he says "How dare you?" to learn the facts of the case.

Since in the western world we are more likely to encounter the apparently ridiculous person, like Akaky, than the ne'er-do-well, like Emelian, this story may be more effective in arousing our pity than the more powerful story by Dostoevski. We are forced to identify ourselves with the newcomer in Akaky's office, who has joined the rest in making fun of this pathetic figure, but who realizes his inhumanity when he hears Akaky's cry, "Why do you insult me?" Gogol says:

> And the young man covered his face with his hands; and many a time afterwards, in the course of his life, shuddered at seeing how much inhumanity there is in man, how much savage coarseness is concealed beneath refined, cultured, worldly refinement, and even, O God! in that man whom the world acknowledges as honorable and upright.

When we read such a story as this, to use Jean-Paul Sartre's phrase, "Our innocence is destroyed" and we are no longer able to be blind to our own conduct. We are now forced, with shame, to see ourselves more clearly. (pp. 16-20)

Mildred A. Martin, "The Last Shall Be First: A Study of Three Russian Short Stories," in Bucknell Review, Vol. VI, No. 1, March, 1956, pp. 13-23.

PETER C. SPYCHER   (essay date 1963)

[In the essay excerpted below, Spycher refutes Russian critic V. Setchkarev's position that "The Nose" is merely a joke, maintaining instead that it is a dramatization of Gogol's own sexual anxieties under the pretext of a farce as well as a satire on social climbers.]

One of the more recent Gogol' biographers, V. Setchkarev, has advanced the following, at first rather alluring and certainly very convenient opinion. Interpreting Puškin's artistic creed as art for art's sake, Setchkarev argues that, in creating **"The Nose,"** Gogol' deliberately applied this artistic principle, and simply played with the various devices of storytelling, and thus fooled the reader who always looks for a "deeper meaning" if not for a downright clear-cut moral. **"The Nose,"** in Setchkarev's view, is nothing but a nonsensical jest, brilliantly told in such a fashion as to produce an illusion of some kind of reality. (p. 361)

The characterization of **"The Nose"** as a nonsensical jest would of course dispense with a lot of thinking on the part of the reader. Yet I hope to be able to demonstrate in some detail that this story is by no means a nonsensical jest. It is relatively easy to perceive that Gogol' must have intended it as a satire on social climbers, a subject very dear to his heart throughout his life. But it will become clear that the story has also a more hidden level of meaning, on which, under the guise of a grotesque farce, a drama of sexual failure is enacted.

The setting of **"The Nose"** is St. Petersburg. The story is divided into three parts: the first dealing with the extravagant experiences of Ivan Jakovlevič, the barber; the second, with those of Kovalev, the collegiate assessor; the third bringing the two protagonists briefly together, and closing with the comment of the narrator upon the "author's" strange story which the narrator has re-told.

It is interesting to note that Gogol' originally planned to present **"The Nose"** explicitly in the form of a dream. In its final shape it still retains dream-like features, not so much because of its "improbable" plot as because of other circumstances, such as the fact that the action begins on 25 March and ends on 7 April—the former the day of the Annunciation according to the Julian, the latter according to the Gregorian calendar, suggesting virtually no time elapse between the beginning and the ending of the story. It is also significant that both protagonists, Ivan Jakovlevič and Kovalev, discover certain startling changes in their lives—the finding and the loss, respectively, of Kovalev's nose—upon awakening, which sometimes denotes the opposite: the start of a dream; that the sequels to these startling changes are both finally shrouded in a fog; and that, upon awakening again, Kovalev, "looking quite accidentally into the mirror," sees his nose, miraculously, in the place where it ordinarily belongs, while shortly afterwards Ivan Jakovlevič, having come to shave his regular customer, mutters: "Well, I never!" as he glances at Kovalev's nose. Several additional elements of this kind could be cited, but at this point I want to mention just one more. There is an exchange of rather sharply worded letters between Kovalev and Mme. Podtočin, whom Kovalev accuses of having deprived him of his nose by witchcraft. Now, when Kovalev, with his nose again firmly planted in his face, meets Mme. Podtočin and her daughter in the street, they, oddly enough, greet him "with joyful exclamations," which might indicate that the exchange of letters has taken place only in Kovalev's dream.

Let us first concern ourselves with Kovalev. Assuming that he does have a dream, what are its most salient events? They are the loss of his nose, the frantic search for it, and its eventual recovery. What, furthermore, is the meaning of the nose, its loss, and its recovery? In trying to find an answer to this question, I should like, for the time being, to move on a certain level (that of the satire on social climbers) and then to shift to another level (that of the comically enacted drama of sexual failure).

In the story **"Nevskij Avenue,"** Lieutenant Pirogov and all those "gentlemen with side-whiskers" are small people with petty wants who give themselves airs; they do not cultivate their souls and minds but attach great value to external, deceptive symbols of their pretended importance. Of all of them we can say what the narrator of **"Nevskij Avenue"** says of "that gentleman who is strolling about in the immaculate coat": "You think he is very rich, don't you? Not a bit of it: he carries all his wealth on his back." Essentially this is true of Kovalev, too: he wears all his wealth on his face, and his wealth is his fairly handsome nose. Indeed, he has no center of being, he is all periphery. Thus "he could never forgive an insult to his rank or his calling." He is not really a human being but a conceited puppet of a certain rank—preferring the then non-existent military equivalent of "major" to his rank of "collegiate assessor" (he obtained this rank while serving in the Caucasus, which means that it is less valuable than that of a regular collegiate assessor)—and he aspires to the post of a "vice-governor" or, failing that, of "an administrative clerk in some important department." He takes excessive care of his clothes, sports excellent whiskers, likes to flirt

with girls and women, is "not averse to matrimony, either, but only if he [can] find a girl with a fortune of two hundred thousand," meanwhile playfully and fraudulently holding—or trying to hold—the attention of "ladies of good position," such as Mme. Cextarev, the widow of a state councillor, and Mme. Podtočin, the widow of a first lieutenant, and her marriageable daughter, and of many others as well: in fact, the whole story literally swarms with ladies to whom he feels indiscriminately attracted.

For all these reasons he needs his handsome nose, "such a conspicuous part of [himself]," a nose which should, if possible, not even be disgraced by as little as a small pimple. (pp. 361-63)

Under the circumstances, what should be so surprising about the fact that the run-away nose becomes a roguish impostor who pretends to be a state councillor with a gold-embroidered uniform, a large stand-up collar, chamois-leather breeches, a sword, and a plumed hat, who rides around in a carriage, pays a visit to the Kazan Cathedral, where he poses as a pious man, secures himself a passport to travel west (the "cultured" West) as far as Riga (which was however, still in the Russian Empire), so as to be fully able to assert: "I am *myself*"? And why should not the nose, at least temporarily, intimidate Kovalev since the state councillor nose can see "from the buttons of [Kovalev's] uniform that [he is] serving in a different"—and lower—"department"? After all, the drives and aspirations of a man who has no center but is all periphery must be centrifugal; and it is easy for the most important part of his periphery (which is practically everything while the center is nothing—Kovalev himself states that his nose is himself) to tear itself off, to become independent, a being in its own right, a being, moreover, that poses as the very ideal—a specious ideal—of that which its original owner has yearned to become. But of course, the nose only pretends to be this ideal; in reality it is nothing but a white, solid object which can be wrapped in a rag or a piece of paper—in a way something about as worthless as Kovalev the whole man is.

And why should we be surprised that Kovalev, upon discovering the loss of his nose, makes a fuss, rushes off to see the commissioner of police (only to find that he has just left), the authorities at the City Police Headquarters . . . , and later on the police inspector of his district . . . , and, anticipating the possibility of the nose's decision to leave St. Petersburg and thus perhaps to seal Kovalev's sorry fate, tries to place a lost-ad in one of the city's newspapers, craving for his dear nose much as that countess craves for her inferior bitch? Yet everywhere he meets with fake martiality, stupidity, incredulity, suspicion, empty prattling, and lazy inefficiency. And the frustration of his search is increased by his own untimely infatuation with all sorts of women.

In his rage, he ascribes his humiliating disfigurement—quite wrongly, as he eventually realizes—to witchcraft employed by the exasperated Mme. Podtočin, who wanted him to marry her daughter but could not pin him down, or to the devil himself. (But here, the devil is surely not Gogol''s true devil, the representative of the universe's evil power; the devil here is only a creature of Kovalev's furious false fancy in which he wishes to put the burden of responsibility for the loss of the nose on somebody—anybody—else's shoulders.) However, just as Kovalev's spirits are at their lowest ebb, a police officer—the one from the Isaakievskij Bridge, to whom we shall return in another connection—brings his nose back.

There are some mocking aspects to this scene: the retriever of the nose is a member of the very authority which has hitherto been unavailable or has been unwilling to co-operate, and he is—in contrast to Kovalev in his present state—"of a handsome appearance, with whiskers that [are] neither too dark nor too light and with fairly full cheeks." It is as if he were secretly saying to Kovalev: "Why have you made all that fuss? Everything is all right, and you will be a true man again, just like me." But alas, this is not the case! Kovalev, to be sure, is at first overjoyed. He even ignores the police officer's claim that the chief accomplice in the whole affair was that scoundrel of a barber, Ivan Jakovlevič, that thief and drunkard who regularly shaves Kovalev. Incidentally, why should Kovalev discount the barber so persistently? Why should he rather accuse Mrs. Podtočin without any foundation in fact? We shall leave this question open for the moment. At any rate, Kovalev is overjoyed. But soon enough he is forced to recognize that it is one thing to hold his detached nose in his "cupped hands," and quite another to place it back "between his two cheeks."

What follows, viz., Kovalev's vain attempts to fasten the nose to his face; the appearance of the doctor, who, after making several almost crudely futile efforts, suggests that Kovalev "better leave it to nature"; Kovalev's exchange of letters with Mme. Podtočin; the foolish rumors spreading through St. Petersburg about the independent nose's manifold adventures (whereupon "a thick fog descends on the whole incident, and what happened afterwards is completely unknown"); finally, Kovalev's incorrigible, unrepentant, increasingly strutting conduct after he has discovered that his nose is where it belongs: all these scenes may be understood as various facets of a satire on ignorant, gullible, self-righteous, conceited people.

Upon closer examination, however, one is struck by the fact that these same scenes, as well as most of the others, are bathed in a solution of eroticism and sex. It might, therefore, be well for us now to shift our attention to this aspect of our story. As a matter of fact, Gogol' makes it perfectly clear that for Kovalev his nose is a symbol *both* of his social status and his success with the ladies. There is certainly no contradiction between these two meanings of the symbol; but while the social-status meaning should not be underplayed, we may suspect that it is the erotic and sexual meaning which constitutes Kovalev's chief—though probably unconscious—concern. Gogol' himself may be alluding to the two meanings and their respective significance when he has the commenting "re-narrator" of the story muse: "Quite apart from the really strange fact of the supernatural displacement of the nose and its appearance in various parts of the town in the guise of a State Councillor [social-status meaning], how did Kovalyov fail to realize that he could not advertise about his nose in a newspaper? . . . It's improper, awkward, not nice [erotic and sexual meaning]!"

Thus we are inclined to maintain that what Kovalev anxiously longs for is externally respectable status, not only expressed by professional rank but also, even more urgently so, by erotic and sexual success, or at least the semblance of it. And if this is true, then the hypothesis that Kovalev's nose symbolizes his sexuality and, more specifically speaking, his sexual organ, will be regarded as neither too daring nor too shocking. (pp. 363-65)

Kovalev's dream about the loss of his nose is actually a dream about the loss of his sexual organ, or of his sexual power: an impotence or castration dream. He himself does not know why, how, and through whom or what his member got lost; he claims to be ignorant and innocent of the loss. He is terrified at his nightmare, to be sure, but when he discovers that his accustomed appearance has been restored, he demonstrates clearly that he has neither understood nor learned anything and that he will remain unreformed forever. We readers, however, realize that Kovalev's dream has revealed his guilt, for he is unwilling and unable either to surrender to the total experience of true spiritual and physical heterosexual love or to renounce it resolutely and perhaps humbly; he only plays with love, he only tries to appear to be a lover, and only a status-seeking lover at that.

[Ivan] Ermakov believes that the separation of the nose from its owner and the adventures it embarks upon signify the insubordination of sexuality (the "Id") to man's conscious morality (the "Ego") (the terms "Id" and "Ego" to be conceived in the Freudian sense) [see excerpt by Yermakov dated 1923]. It is Kovalev's dilemma, according to Ermakov, to be embarrassed *both* at possessing sexual drives and at imagining himself as being deprived of them. Ermakov declares: "At the basis [of the story] lies fear [of sex], corresponding to the repressed desire of having an enormous [sexual] organ, and of the possibility of unlimited erotic satisfaction." I do not know whether I see Kovalev's problem exactly in the same light. Fear of sex there is in Kovalev, to be sure; but it is certainly not the fear of the savage force of his own sexuality, nor is it the fear of a clash between society's moral code and the immorality or amorality of sexuality; it is rather the fear of the female sex, the fear of being unable to prove himself as a male in front of a woman. And if the adventures of the nose as a state councillor should be meant to symbolize the insubordination of chaotic sexuality to man's conscious morality, why is it, then, that those adventures of the nose are so tame and timid, almost as tame and timid as Kovalev himself has always been? Indeed, Kovalev's sexuality is weak, underdeveloped, immature. We shall see later on that the regrettable state of Kovalev's sexuality is feared to have been decisively conditioned by one particular factor.

We have barely said a word yet about Ivan Jakovlevič, the barber. What is the matter with him? And what, we should like to know, is his relationship with Kovalev?

Significantly, Ivan Jakovlevič's surname is lost (even on his signboard); He does not count as a member of society. He is a wretched, filthy drunkard and thief, and a "cynic," wearing a stained frock coat at all times, in a pathetic attempt to cover his abominable other pieces of clothing. He is mercilessly bossed by his wife, "a highly respectable lady." As a barber, he likes to lather his customers abundantly and to pull violently at their noses with his dirty and stinking hands while he does the shaving.

This fellow, too, may be said to have a dream (simultaneously with Kovalev's). He dreams that one morning, at breakfast, he finds a nose in a loaf of bread baked by his wife, a nose which he at once identifies as that of his customer Kovalev, the collegiate assessor. It is Ivan's wife who indignantly accuses him of having cut it off, but even though he cannot explain to himself how on earth he could have done it, he does feel eminently guilty and is frightened at the idea of the police detecting the nose at his home and charging him with having cut it off. Therefore, he wraps the nose in a rag and goes out to dispose of it in all secrecy. As he stops on the Isakievskij Bridge to throw the parcel into the Neva, he is summoned by a police officer who has been watching him (it is the same police officer that returns the nose to Kovalev) and is questioned by him about his odd doings. "But here the incident is completely shrouded in a fog and absolutely nothing is known of what happened next" (except that the police officer tells Kovalev that he has locked up Ivan in a cell at the police station—and except that Kovalev's own dream describes in detail "what happened next").

From what we learn about Ivan Jakovlevič we can easily infer that he is not a status-seeker by any means but a miserable wretch without any ambitions or pretensions. And his dream is certainly not the nightmare of a social climber who is afraid to be deprived of status; instead it is—as is, in the last analysis, Kovalev's dream—the drama of a sexual problem.

Ivan's irrepressible urge to pull with his dirty and stinking hands at the noses of his customers and to lather their faces "wherever he [fancies]," together with the fact that his "highly respectable" wife holds him in contempt and bosses him, might suggest that he is sexually deficient, perhaps somewhat abnormal, perhaps a masturbator. His dream seems to express his guilt feelings in this regard. Significantly enough, it is his wife who finds a nose, who guesses without hesitation that it is the nose of one of Ivan's customers and that Ivan must have cut it off, and who revengefully puts it in a loaf of bread baked by herself so that it will be a reproachful surprise for her husband. And after he has found the nose, she gives him a terrible dressing-down, screaming in her indignation: "Blackguard! Drunkard! I shall inform the police against you myself," and: "All you know is to strop your razor. Soon you won't be fit to carry out your duties at all, you whoremonger, you scoundrel, you!" And Ivan stands there, "utterly crushed." This scene signifies an exposure of Ivan's "sinful" secret sexual behavior and at the same time a punishment for a behavior which is bound to end in total sexual impotence. Ivan's subsequent efforts to get rid of the nose, which are hampered by his encounters with respectable citizens and above all with the police officer at the Isaakievskij Bridge who watches him throwing the nose into the Neva, in their turn, signify his feelings of guilt towards what he recognizes to be the official moral standards in sexual matters; and so does his imprisonment. Yet it must be said that he is enough of a degenerate to feel relieved at being rid of the nose, at being rid of his sexual obligations toward his wife.

This interpretation of Ivan's dream would, I believe, be quite satisfactory were it not for one circumstance: the fact that Ivan has cut off not his own nose but that of Kovalev. We should, however, be able to remove this difficulty, too. Let us now take the next and decisive step: let us examine the relationship between Ivan and Kovalev.

Is it not a remarkable coincidence that both Kovalev's and Ivan's dream should deal with two perfectly complementary parts of one and the same subject? The circumstance that Kovalev is one of Ivan's regular customers would surely not help to explain such a coincidence.

One is very much tempted to conclude that the two dreams are not really separate dreams dreamt by two separate individuals, but that a third person dreams what comprises the entire story **"The Nose"**! And this is indeed the conclusion I propose to draw. This third person is the "author," about whom the commenting "renarrator" remarks that it is difficult to see how he could have chosen such a subject for a story.

Incidentally, the use of the term "dream" as a designation of

what happens to Kovalev and to Ivan, and now to the "author," is a little problematic. On the one hand, the dream-like character of Kovalev's and Ivan's experiences and of the story as a whole cannot be overlooked, as we have pointed out earlier; on the other hand, the story is presented as a "true" one; the narrator says: "The world is full of all sorts of absurdities. Sometimes there is not even a semblance of truth." Or: "Say what you like, but such things do happen—not often, but they do happen." At any rate, our use of the term "dream" does not imply, of course, that **"The Nose"** is an actual dream recorded by Gogol'; the story is to be characterized as a fantasy; a term which, in contrast to that of "dream," presupposes the exercise of active, purposeful, controlled artistic imagination on the part of the creator.

And now everything will fall into one coherent and meaningful pattern provided we agree that Ivan Jakovlevič and Kovalev are but two manifestations of one self: Kovalev being that part of the self which would like to attain "respectable" social and, above all, sexual status, a spurious status if it cannot be a real one (and it can hardly be a real one); and Ivan Jakovlevič being that miserable other part of the self—strenuously ignored by Kovalev—which unwittingly threatens to spoil success by "sinning." Ivan Jakovlevič is in fact the true Kovalev stripped of his pretensions.

Now we understand why Ivan cuts off, not his own but Kovalev's nose, and why Kovalev, in his turn, refuses to believe that Ivan has cut off his nose and instead prefers to charge the innocent Mme. Podtočin with the deed. And we also understand why the barber has only a first name and a patronymic, whereas the collegiate assessor has virtually only a surname (his first name, Platon, figures once in the signature of his letter to Mme. Podtočin; his first name and his patronymic appear once in Mme. Podtočin's reply): the two parts put together form a full name. And perhaps the circumstance that the whole action takes place on the day of the Annunciation is not without significance either: the idea of virgin birth, a sacred miracle for the faithful Christian, a contradiction in terms from a purely human point of view, an impossible combination, yet one that appeals to the "author" of the story, shines as an ironic sun over the grotesque and sad landscape of **"The Nose."**

In the final analysis, the "author's" nightmare is Gogol''s own. We know that he was never successful with women. And there is probably even a bond between his twisted and negative relationship with the world of "reality" in general and his inability to establish erotic and sexual contact with a woman. Thus it seems that in **"The Nose"** Gogol' has artfully expressed the tragedy of his own personal sexual failure. No wonder he has cloaked it in such an outwardly funny story. (pp. 367-71)

> *Peter C. Spycher, "N. V. Gogol's 'The Nose': A Satirical Comic Fantasy Born of an Impotence Complex," in* Slavic and East European Journal, *n.s. Vol. VII, No. 4, 1963, pp. 361-74.*

ISAAC BASHEVIS SINGER (essay date 1964)

[*A Polish-born American novelist, short story writer, translator, and author of children's books, Singer is widely regarded as the foremost contemporary writer of Yiddish literature. Awarding Singer the 1978 Nobel Prize in Literature, the Swedish Academy cited him for "his impassioned narrative art which, with roots in a Polish-Jewish cultural tradition, brings universal human conditions to life." In the following review of* The Collected Tales and Plays of Nikolai Gogol, *Singer discusses style, themes, and characterization in Gogol's short fiction.*]

Gogol's literary method is Homeric; his tales are a stark presentation of facts and images without commentary or psychological explanation. Like his Cossacks, Gogol was never afraid of sudden veerings. In his stories he shifts tone and point of view without warning. He is the antithesis of the psychological school which tries to explain and justify all actions, constantly skeptical of its power to convince the reader.

As have many great writers, Gogol turns again and again to a milieu he knew so well that there was no chance for error. (pp. 1, 15)

Gogol had one great weakness: he was incapable of describing love and carnal passion. In writing about either of these, he became completely banal and used expressions that were cliches even in his time. . . . His men in love have but one desire: to sacrifice their lives for their beloved.

Such banality stemmed in some part from the very life of the people Gogol described. Until very late the Cossacks kept faith with a chivalry that was an anachronism even in Cervantes' time. War and pillage were men's chief occupations. Their wives and mothers worked the fields and were the real providers of the families. Like medieval knights, they lived very little with their women. . . .

The Cossack was a collectivist; love and sex as they are understood in modern times were almost unknown to him. Some Cossack men nursed hidden homosexual inclinations. It was easier for Gogol to convey devotion from man to man than for him to describe love between the sexes. The result is that Gogol's characters find their real individuality in comedy, in odd or incongruous situations in which love plays no part. His great power is in involving ordinary people in extraordinary situations and in portraying characters ludicrous or tragic in their pettiness. Many of Gogol's characters are types who are credible not because of their uniqueness but because they belong unmistakably to a certain group or class, as do most of the characters in, for example, *Evenings on a Farm Near Dikanka.*

But even in cases where the situation is grossly exaggerated or fabricated, the story is redeemed by Gogol's adherence to characteristic rhythms of speech and forms of conduct. Being a master of idiom, Gogol loses more in translation than Tolstoy, Dostoyevsky or Turgenev. That his power is felt even in translation shows how rich in expressiveness this master was, how much he could lose without seeming impoverished.

Like Chekhov, Gogol was always on the brink of melancholy. He saw in man a blind and helpless creature, a plaything for powers which he could never fathom. Gogol often shows his characters asleep—fatigued Cossacks stretched out in the bewitched Ukrainian night, with the innocence of animals ignorant of the meaning of evil and of the misfortunes that befall them. But while Chekhov's pessimism was the beginning and the end of his philosophy, Gogol not only hints but says openly that the solution to the riddle of being can exist beyond this world. Gogol's despair may have been greater than Chekhov's, but so was his faith that the Creator was not thoroughly malicious. Gogol's devils are as vulnerable as man. His imps can easily be thrown into a sack or driven away by incantations. If he becomes God's Cossack, man can fight Satan and conquer him. . . .

Reading Gogol not only gives great enjoyment and an important lesson in the methods of literary creation, but also serves as a commentary on and explanation of the great Russian literature that came soon after him. Like Tolstoy, like Dostoyevsky and Chekhov, Gogol lived all his life in an atmosphere of impending catastrophe and in fear of man's malice and God's indifference. (p. 15)

Isaac Bashevis Singer, "Bewitched, Bothered and Benighted," in Book Week—New York Herald Tribune, *August 23, 1964, pp. 1, 15.*

RICHARD F. GUSTAFSON (essay date 1965)

[*In the following excerpt, Gustafson views "The Diary of a Madman" as an atypical Gogol story for being psychological, rather than social or moral, in focus.*]

The **"Diary of a Madman"** is not simply the story of a poor insignificant clerk who is driven insane by the frustrations and humiliations received from the ranking figures in a powerful bureaucratic machine. Popriščin is not a passive Akakij Akakievič who can vent his anger only by a fantastic return from the dead. His evenings are spent not in copying documents for his own pleasure, but in writing a diary to justify himself and wreak his vengeance upon the world. Popriščin dominates the story as no other Gogolian hero does. The whole meaning of the diary is intimately connected with the personality of its author. The **"Diary of a Madman"** is psychological, rather than social or moral, in focus, almost unique in Gogol"s work. It is the only first-person narrative the creator of *Dead Souls* wrote. We are asked to enter into the workings of a deranged mind, and we must do this through the words produced by that mind. The story falls into two parts, before and after the madman's ascent to the throne. There is little change, however, in the patterns of the insane clerk's personality. Let us now look at the author of the diary, the creator of this mad world, Aksentij Ivanovič Popriščin.

Popriščin is angry. The world, he thinks, has done him wrong. All are against him, existing only to insult and injure him. He sees himself as a victim, suffering from the torments of an inhuman world. The chief of his section at the office does nothing but harass him; the cashier will not give him an advance on his salary out of sheer stinginess; even the lackeys treat him with disdain. The madman sees a menace in everyone, of high or low rank. And to all he responds with anger. This anger usually takes the form of an aggressive attack. The section chief is reduced to something less than a human being; he has a face like a druggist's bottle and is called a "damned heron." The cashier is attacked by rumor; the madman reports that at home his cook beats him. "Everybody knows it." To the lackeys' failure to recognize him as a man of "noble birth," he responds with an indignant and dramatic departure from their presence. The clerk's only enjoyment in life comes from the theater, where he laughs at "amusing plays" in which the authors make jibes at lawyers, collegiate registrars, merchants, and journalists. Even his sense of humor is aggressive.

Of course, the madman is caught in the vicious circle of paranoia. He blames his feelings of frustration on others and sees threats even where there are none. The aggression he feels toward all becomes projected onto others. Underneath the aggression, however, lies envy. He covets a position of authority or at least the feeling of superiority he senses in the lackeys.

Typically he projects his envy onto others. The section chief, he believes, envies his alleged favored position as head pencil-sharpener for the director. Even the dog Medži is jealous of him.

Popriščin's need for dignity and authority is accompanied by a compensatory fantasy of dignity and authority. He insists upon his own nobility and associates himself with glorified figures of authority. His initial reaction to the director is awe: "And just look into his face! Aie! what importance in his eyes!" The clerk imagines that he has a position of special importance to the director, acquiring dignity, as it were, by associating with it. Most important of all, however, is the fantasy "newspaper world" in which he lives. His own life, even in the first half of the story, is intimately associated with the great rulers and governments of Europe: France, England, Austria, Spain. He reads the news of the world in *The Northern Bee* and projects his own life into the historical events of the day. The Emperor of Austria, Polignac, and the Dey of Algiers are his fantasy associates. The transformation into the King of Spain takes place after the clerk has read of the vacant Spanish throne in the newspapers. In solving this political problem, he solves for a moment his own personal one.

Associated with the fantasy of power is the imagined love quest. Popriščin is a knight errant in search of his beloved. Sofi is wondrously idealized: She is a dazzling beauty, dressed sumptuously in white, as are most Gogolian women. She carries a handkerchief which exudes the aroma of nobility. Her lips are sugary sweet, her eyes flash like the sun. She is a swan, a canary. She lives in elegance; her rooms are filled with mirrors and china and bottles of perfume scenting the air with the fine fragrance of femininity. In her boudoir, as Popriščin imagines, "there must be marvels . . . a paradise, such as is not to be found in the heavens." To this paradise the madman has no entrance. Sofi is unattainable, as courtly ladies should be. All Popriščin can do is gaze upon her (the Gogolian theme of voyeurism), lie on his bed dreaming of her (the repeated entry, "for the most part I lay on my bed," with its suggestion of masturbation), and remain silent (the repeated entry, "aie! aie! never mind, never mind . . . silence"). Sofi is literally beyond words.

The political and erotic fantasies are both compensatory. They arise from Popriščin's need to bolster his ego, to prove himself. Humiliated by the drab realities of his everyday existence, the clerk attempts to correct them by associating himself with a dignified world and, when that fails, by proving himself sexually, if only in fantasy. Throughout the story the madman tends to alternate between these two fantasy worlds. Reality is assiduously avoided.

However hermetically sealed the first-person world of the madman is, reality has a way of creeping in. In his naiveté Popriščin has a penchant for quoting the derogatory statements of others. For example, he reports in his diary the following unflattering words of his section chief:

> Come, think what you are about! Why, you are over forty. It's time you had a little sense. What do you imagine yourself to be? Do you suppose I don't know all the tricks you are up to? Why, you are philandering after the director's daughter! Come, look at yourself, just think what you are! Why, you are a zero and nothing else! Why, you haven't a penny to bless yourself with. And just look at yourself in the mirror—how could you think of such a thing!

Popriščin takes this assessment as an aggressive attack and responds with his own assault ending with "I spit on him." The difference between the director and the section chief lies in the fact that the director remains silent and the section chief speaks out. The director is awesome in his distance, the section chief menacing in his penetration into Popriščin's world.

The most striking exposure of reality comes in the dog's letters which the madman copies into his diary. Here the clerk learns that his great idol, the director, is no different from the rest of God's grovelling creatures; he too is ambitious. Once exposed, the idealized figure of authority becomes menacing and is attacked: he is a Mason, a cork. Of course, for Popriščin ambition is the greatest sin; this one fault taints the image of his idol, because it makes him resemble the madman. It is the clerk who is truly ambitious and who, in the second half of the story, projects his own ambition upon the whole world. Sofi, too, is exposed. She, we learn, is in love with a court chamberlain and finds Popriščin ridiculous. To the madman, this news is unbearable, and in revenge he tears up the letters.

The destruction of the dog's letters is a highly symbolic act. Popriščin associates dogs with a certain form of knowledge or intelligence unavailable to men. . . . This special knowledge of the dogs is always associated with the political theme: "Dogs are clever creatures, they understand all diplomatic (*političeskie*) relations." Popriščin hopes to discover himself in the midst of the political world the dogs know so well. Ironically, he does, but it is not the world he wants or needs. Rather Medži, in telling of her own amorous life, speaks in terms which seem to be a grotesque of the madman's fantasy affair with Sofi: "I must confide to you that I have a number of suitors. . . . One is a very clumsy mongrel, fearfully stupid, stupidity is painted on his face; he walks about the street with an air of importance and imagines that he is a distinguished person and thinks everybody is looking at him." The clumsy mongrel resembles the clerk, just as his title (*dvornjaga* 'mongrel') resembles Popriščin's own (*dvorjanin* 'nobleman'). In the reality of the dog world the madman is a mongrel. Popriščin's response to this letter is ironically revealing: "How can anyone fill a letter with such foolishness! Give me a man! I want to see a man. I want spiritual sustenance—in which my soul might find food and enjoyment." He refuses to accept the truth and attempts to destroy it by tearing up the letters of the "stupid dogs."

In reality, we must assume, the letters never existed. They are a figment of the madman's mind, part of him, just as they are part of his diary. But they proceed from that area of his mind which has still retained some touch with reality. After all, in part one the mad clerk still functions in the real world: he works at the office, attends the theater, and keeps track of the days. When Popriščin destroys the letters, he destroys his one last bit of sanity.

The destruction of the truth-revealing letters is followed immediately by Popriščin's so-called rebellion.

> It's always a court chamberlain or a general. Everything that's best in the world falls to the court chamberlains or the generals. If you find some poor treasure and think it is almost within your grasp, a court chamberlain or a general will snatch it from you. God damn it! I'd like to become a general myself, not in order to receive her hand and all the rest of it; no, I should like to be a general only to see

how they would wriggle and display all their court manners and *équivoques* and then to say to them: I spit on you both. Oh, damn it!

But is this a rebellion against the system? Is this Popriščin's attempt to assert his humanity in the face of bureaucratic oppression? First of all, Popriščin merely wants to find a better station within the system; there is no Dostoevskian rebellion against the whole order of things. Secondly, the madman ostensibly rebels because he has lost Sofi's hand to the court chamberlain. Surely, however, Popriščin, as a human being, had little to offer a young lady of society; his protest is one of sour grapes. Finally, in his anger the clerk forgets himself. He wants to become a general "not in order to receive her hand." He wants revenge. Popriščin wants to wield his power over those who he imagines are oppressing him. The victim wants to be the victimizer. The madman's interest in Sofi was never really amorous. His erotic desires were aroused by his feelings of humiliation and his need to assert himself. Sofi was his one last chance to prove himself a man.

Once the erotic fantasy fails, Popriščin turns back to his newspaper world. He begins to wonder whether his dreams of power and glory might not have some foundation in reality:

> Why am I a titular councilor and on what grounds am I a titular councilor? Perhaps I am not a titular councilor at all? Perhaps I am a count or a general, and only somehow appear to be a titular councilor. Perhaps I don't know myself who I am. How many instances there have been in history: some simple, humble tradesman or peasant, not even a nobleman, is suddenly discovered to be some sort of powerful personage *(vel'moža)* and sometimes even a ruler *(gosudar')*. If a peasant can sometimes turn into something like that, what may not a nobleman turn into?

The dividing line between reality and fantasy begins to fade: the madman no longer knows who he is. The stage is set for the metamorphosis. Popriščin has only to turn to the newspapers and discover that the Spanish throne is vacant. Interestingly enough, the insane alternation of the political and erotic fantasies comes to the fore in Popriščin's pondering of the Spanish problem: "It seems to me extremely peculiar. How can the throne be vacant? They say that some Donna is supposed to ascend the throne. A Donna cannot ascend the throne, she cannot possibly. There ought to be a king on the throne." The clerk spends the next few days *lying on his bed* and thinking about the Spanish question: the sexual motif is replaced by the political one. Only in part two of the story will the two fantasies merge.

Popriščin is concerned for his social image and his self-image. He feels alienated both from the world and from his own being. His fantasy quests for power and love represent his search for a public and private identity. His inability to achieve these, he believes, arises from his social status. He remembers that he is a titular councilor (ninth rank); his section chief is a court councilor (seventh rank). Popriščin is lower down on the scale of being. Like most Gogolian heroes, the insulted and injured clerk sees the assigned ranks in the service as symbols of real value, a way of defining a person. They are an absurd categorizing of humanity into good and bad, a menacing judgment of men. That the madman thinks this way is clear from his treatment of the male figures: none is named, but everyone is given a title, a state in life above or

below Aksentij Ivanovič Popriščin, titular councilor, nobleman. He dreams of being a collegiate councilor (sixth rank, higher than his section chief), a general (second to fourth rank), or "even something higher." He wants to raise himself on the ladder of being. But in doing so his anger comes forth: he seeks revenge. Unlike the Underground Man, Popriščin does not see that in attempting to gain revenge he is asserting the very values of the system which he believes is so oppressive. He cannot rebel against the system because he knows no other. He is caught in his own self-centered, solipsistic world of diaries, masturbation fantasies, and dreams of glory. The steady drum beat of the first-person pronoun, often accompanied by the obsessive phrase "I am a nobleman," becomes his death knell. (pp. 268-73)

The clerk's first task as King of Spain is to complete the miracle of metamorphosis by a suitable disguise. In the beginning he is obliged to go around incognito, because he does not yet have the appropriate royal attire. Popriščin, like many Gogolian heroes, believes that clothes literally make the man. In part one he asserted, addressing himself in his mind to the section chief: "Give me a fashionably cut coat and let me put on a necktie like yours—and then you wouldn't hold a candle to me." Once king, therefore, the madman sets out to get himself a proper mantle. The tailors, it turns out, however, are asses involved in all sorts of shady deals, so Popriščin, unlike his counterpart Akakij Akakievič, sits behind locked doors and sews his own overcoat: he secretly fashions his own image. Once attained, the new mantle disguises the real Popriščin: "the style has to be completely different." He is the King of Spain because he dresses like him. The theme of the disguise, the mask over reality, I need not mention, is common in Gogol', and usually is associated, as here, with illusions or delusions of grandeur. (p. 274)

Like Kant, Gogol' saw the comic in desire frustrated. This theme runs through many works by Gogol'. However, in the **"Diary of a Madman,"** where the above old rule is repeated almost verbally in the "rebellion" speech, the rule supplies the organizational principle of the story. In part two, Gogol' leads Popriščin through a series of discoveries; some form of the word "discovery" *(otkrytie)* is repeated each time. Part two, one should note, opens in a "new light": "it burst upon me like a flash of lightning."

The first discovery is Popriščin's new identity. Once the simple clerk becomes the King of Spain, a whole new world is opened up to him; he believes that formerly he was living in a fog, but that "now everything has been revealed *(otkryto)* to me." Of course, only Popriščin knows of his new identity; the humor in the second half arises from the madman's knowledge of this miracle and ignorance of the truth coupled with the world's apparent incredulity or simple ignorance of the metamorphosis. But from Popriščin's point of view all is well, as he has succeeded in remaking his public image.

Having gained his dignified status, Popriščin seems to dismiss his erotic interests by his second discovery. After making a quick visit to Sofi's rooms and telling her of the great happiness that awaits her, the King of Spain observes:

> Oh, woman is a treacherous creature! I have discovered now what women are. So far no one has found out with whom Woman is in love: I have been the first to discover it. Woman is in love with the devil. Yes, joking apart. Scientific men write nonsense saying that she is this or that—she cares for nothing but the devil. You will see her from a box in the first

tier fixing her *lorgnette.* You imagine she is looking at the fat man with the medals. No, she is looking at the devil who is standing behind his back. There he is, hidden in his medals. There he is, beckoning to her! And she will marry him, she will marry him.

As in the first half of the story Sofi is not blamed for her failure to love the clerk. She is lured away from him, the victim of the devil's devices. Sofi's "paradise" has a serpent lurking in it. It is important to notice that Popriščin's hidden guilt about sex comes to the surface: he associates sexual attraction with evil, with the devil himself. He self-righteously dismisses his "canary." Significantly enough also, the apparent dismissal of amorous interests comes at the beginning of Popriščin's reign as King of Spain. At the point when the frustration of his ambitions has been temporarily alleviated by his fantasy of political power, he can reassess his erotic needs. As the new fantasy advances, however, the erotic impulse will reappear, but as befits the second part of the story, in a "new light."

The fantastic anxiety vision—the devil lurking in the medals—is followed by many more such visions as Popriščin becomes more and more deranged. The diary entries now demand interpretation. The third great discovery, which is again an anxiety vision, is that China and Spain are really the same place: if you just write Spain on a piece of paper, you will see that it turns out to be China. Popriščin's newspaper world gets the best of him; this discovery marks his complete estrangement from reality. The entry headings with their distorted dates underline the loss of touch with time. This new discovery emphatically stresses his loss of touch with space. Insane asylum equals Spain, Spain equals China. Of course, we are never told that the madman is in an asylum; we might interpret his move to Spain as a figment of his imagination, a fantasy of travel. But we do know that what Popriščin describes as his life at the royal court takes place in a madhouse. Perhaps the hero's own ironically naive words, which appear right at the moment he discovers his new identity, suggest this to us: "It's a good thing no one thought of putting me in a madhouse." . . . Like Kafka, Gogol' knows how to sustain the one point of view, to see everything from his hero's eyes.

The new discovery is closely associated with Popriščin's next anxiety vision: "Tomorrow at seven o'clock a strange phenomenon will occur: the earth will sit on the moon." Popriščin replaces the common-sense view of spatial relations with his own. His reaction to this sad event is significant: "I must confess that I experience a tremor at my heart when I reflect on the extreme softness (*nežnost'*) and fragility of the moon." The moon is traditionally associated with many things, one of which is love (here intimated by the tender, poetic, even amorous associations of the word *nežnost'*) and another is insanity (as the English words lunacy and lunatic suggest or as the Russian word *lunatizm* shows). The sensitive and fragile moon at the moment of eclipse is a symbol for Popriščin himself, the insane lover eclipsed by court chamberlains and generals. But what does the earth stand for? Is it the menacing world in which the madman believes he lives or that reality he fears but refuses to accept? As the language becomes more symbolic, the two images of the hero become more entwined.

The anxiety vision continues:

> You see the moon is made in Hamburg, and very badly made too. I am surprised that England hasn't taken notice of it. It was made by a lame barrel

maker, and it is evident that the fool had no idea what a moon should be. He put in tarred cord and one part of lamp oil; and that is why there is such a fearful stench all over the world that one has to stop up one's nose. And that's how it is that the moon is such a soft globe that man cannot live on it and that nothing lives there but noses. And it is for that very reason that we can't see our noses, because they are all in the moon. And when I reflected that the earth is a heavy body and when it falls may grind our noses to powder, I was overcome by such uneasiness that, putting on my shoes and stockings, I hastened to the hall of the Imperial Council to give orders to the police not to allow the earth to sit on the moon.

The moon is the abode of noses. The nose, of course, is a common image in Gogol'. In the **"Diary of a Madman,"** however, the image recurs throughout the work in a particular complex of associations. In a December entry, as the clerk reacts to the imminent marriage of Sofi to the court chamberlain, he remarks: "You don't get a third eye in your head because you are a court chamberlain. Why, his nose is not made of gold but is just like mine and everyone else's; he sniffs (*njuxaet*) with it and doesn't eat with it, he sneezes (*čixaet*) with it and doesn't cough with it. I have often tried to discover what all these differences come from." The nose is something essential to a human being; it defines him as such. It is, if you wish, a least common denominator of all men. When it comes to such a basic thing as a nose, all men are equal, or at least they should be. But in the above quotation, because of the context, the nose is associated with Popriščin's erotic interests. His nose is as good as the court chamberlain's, and yet Sofi wants to marry the court chamberlain, not him. The nose is often associated with sexuality in Gogol', as many scholars have shown. But here (and elsewhere, I believe) the erotic themes and images are themselves symbolic: Popriščin's fear that the noses will be crushed, the obvious symbolic castration fear, suggests the fear for his own identity. The one thing that makes him a man may be destroyed.

The above quotation about the court chamberlain's nose appears in part one where the dominant theme is Popriščin's erotic fantasy quest for Sofi. An excellent example of the obsessive madness of the diary can be seen in the repetition of this passage in part two. In the second half the dominant theme turns from the erotic to the political fantasy. Consequently this reworking of the above passage: "An Englishman is very politic (*politik*). He pokes his nose into everything. All the world knows that when England takes a pinch (*njuxaet*) of snuff, France sneezes (*čixaet*)." The total effect is the gradual merger of the two fantasies.

In the vision of noses crushed into powder, Popriščin reveals his greatest fear: the search to prove himself may end in failure. But something else also comes through his words. Earlier the madman associated the erotic impulse with evil: woman is in love with the devil. Here Popriščin ostensibly protests this order of things. Why, he asks, has the lame cooper failed to make the moon correctly? Why is there such a horrible stench that the nose is offended and must be stopped up? The moon now seems to stand for the female sexual organ. Again Popriščin finds something wrong with women. In part one, where the erotic fantasy plays the major role, women are idealized: they are associated with cleanliness and aromatic scents. In the first entry Mavra brings Popriščin cleaned boots and later Sofi exudes exotic perfumes. In part two, however, this imagery is reversed. In the first entry

Mavra is said to clean boots poorly and the symbolic moon stinks. In his protest Popriščin reveals a disgust with sex, a sign of his fear of women, his fear that the one last chance to prove he is a man may end in failure. He would rather condemn women and sexual relations as evil and dirty than face the test. It is significant that the erotic theme, seen in a new light, reappears in the very entry where Popriščin records his arrival in Spain, that is, in the insane asylum. As the political fantasy begins to fail, as the humiliations of the royal state become clear, the erotic impulse recurs.

To some it may seem too far-fetched or too Freudian to say that Gogol′ uses the nose and the moon as sexual symbols or that he underlines this suggestion with the erotic overtones in the phrase "the earth will sit on the moon." However, the erotic impulse, as we have seen, runs through the whole story. Furthermore, Popriščin himself will not let us rest with an easy dismissal of the question. Shortly after this anxiety vision, the madman makes one final discovery: "However, I was rewarded for all this by the discovery I made today. I found out that every cock has a Spain, that it is under his wings" [not far from his tail]. The realm of torment (insane asylum, Spain, China, moon) is here clearly associated with the sexual organs. This last discovery, couched in the symbolic statement of the insane man, is Popriščin's undoing. Since the nose—or the phallus—stands in the madman's mind for the basic value or worth of the individual, his discovery is that the tortures (Spain) are located in the real self. He, and no one else, is the cause of his own failure. Public and private image cannot be separated. The final irony, perhaps, is the most telling, for the rooster, the bird which appears in Popriščin's insane babblings, has almost no phallus at all. The poor clerk learns the horrible and pathetic truth: he has nothing to give. The political and erotic fantasies collide and collapse. Popriščin is a zero.

It is significant that this entry, the next to the last, begins with the clerk's refusal to respond to the Grand Inquisitor's call: "At first he shouted 'Popriščin!' I didn't say a word. Then: 'Aksentij Ivanov! Titular councilor! Nobleman!' I still remained silent. 'Ferdinand VIII, King of Spain!' " And still Popriščin remained silent. He answers to none of his titles; his true identity, he has discovered, lies elsewhere. This last discovery, however, destroys the delusion. The hero is unmasked. Of this Spain he is no king.

The final discovery, that the source of torment rests not in the world but in the self, leads directly to the last entry in the diary, the lyrical outburst of anguish. The completely insane clerk is crushed by the failure of his delusion. The desired object, now the glorious public image of king rather than the enticing Sofi, is again removed to a great distance. The last entry will once more present the situation in a new light. The "old rule" functions twice in the story. (pp. 274-78)

There are two Popriščins, the suffering clerk frustrated and humiliated by man's inhumanity to man, symbolized for him by the system of ranks, and the pretender who usurps a fantasy throne to make his dreams of power and glory come true. Both Popriščins take their origin in traditional literary types: the insulted and injured clerk (činovnik), the farcical braggart (xvastun), and the pretender (samozvanec). But from these types the author creates a character which is truly his own. Popriščin is a typical Gogolian hero, a dehumanized, depersonalized pathetic being who exists and is content with life until bitten by the bug of desire to be someone. The habit (privyčka) of life is broken by the passion (strast′) to prove

oneself. Popriščin wants to find his place in the world, to establish his ontological identity. However, he knows only the false rational ordering of humanity symbolized by the ranks. He thinks in terms of this system. His attitudes and reactions are inappropriate to the real situation. He is caught in his own self-centered view of the universe and seeks his identity where it does not exist. Unlike Dostoevskij, Gogol′ does not portray characters who rebel against the false values of the rationalistic ethic itself. Popriščin's attempt to establish his identity is doomed from the outset. Alienated from the world and from himself, he remains ignorant of any set of values which would recognize, in Dostoevskij's phrase, "the human being in the person" (čelovek v čeloveke). The first effect of the madman's failure is guilt, expressed in this story in sexual terms. The diary ends with the loss of the concrete existence of the hero: Popriščin is wafted off in a troika into the void, where there is nothing, nothing. Gogol′'s works often close with a sense of nothingness or death: a frozen tableau, a jump through a window, a paroxysm of death at the sight of a monster's eyes, the jingle of bells on a troika going nowhere. The work may end where it began, so that life is presented as a vicious circle, ever turning but staying in the same place. Gogol′'s hope for a reordered existence does not enter his fiction. Beyond the false world of ranks and rationalistic ethics there is only the void. In this shock of nothingness lies the terror of Gogol′'s vision. Man's search, however sympathetic, is ridiculed because it is in vain: everything is inappropriate because no true values exist. (pp. 279-80)

> *Richard F. Gustafson, "The Suffering Usurper: Gogol's 'Diary of a Madman,' " in* Slavic and East European Journal, *n.s. Vol. IX, No. 3, September, 1965, pp. 268-80.*

LEON STILMAN (essay date 1967)

[*In the essay excerpted below, which was originally published in Russian in 1967 in the journal* Vozdushnye puti, *Stilman discusses visual themes in Gogol's writing.*]

Themes connected with vision, with seeing, occupy an important place in Gogol's writings. They appear in many variants. Let us note two of them. One is that of the magic, lethal power of a glance, or the fear of being seen. The other is that of vision which encompasses very large, "boundless" spaces and resembles the vision of an all-seeing divinity; this expanded vision sometimes takes the form of viewing things from a height, a tower, or a very tall building. (p. 376)

The first of the two motifs mentioned above—that of the lethal glance, of terror at being seen—plays an especially prominent part in the account of the death of the heroes of two of Gogol's stories—the seminary student ("Philosopher") Khoma Brut, in **"Viy,"** and the artist Chartkov, in **"The Portrait."**

In **"Viy,"** Khoma is in the church, reading prayers over the coffin of the "young lass" (actually the witch); and he wards off "diabolical powers" by uttering incantations and by tracing a magic circle around himself. The third and fateful night arrives: demons and monsters fill the church, but neither they nor the witch, who rises from her coffin, can step across the "mysterious circle" drawn by Khoma. Then, at the witch's behest, Viy is brought in: he is the "chief of the gnomes," with "long eyelids that reach right down to the ground." He is led up to Khoma, and then the following occurs:

"Raise my eyelids. I cannot see!" said Viy, in a voice that seemed to come from the depths of the earth—and the whole swarm of creatures rushed to raise his eyelids. "Don't look!" an inner voice whispered to the Philosopher. But he could not resist, and he looked.

"There he is!" shouted Viy, and pointed an iron finger at him. And all, the whole swarm of creatures, hurled themselves on the Philosopher. He fell lifeless to the ground, and his soul fled from his body in terror.

Thus, Khoma dies from fear the moment Viy sees him. And Viy sees him when Khoma himself looks, unable to resist and heedless of the inner voice. Khoma is betrayed by his own glance, so that "not to look" here means "to be invisible": you must not look at something horrible; the temptation is great, but you must not yield to it; if you do look, then you yourself will be seen, and there is no salvation for you.

In a note to the title of the story, Gogol explains that "Viy is a colossal creation of the folk imagination. This is the name that the Little Russians use to refer to the chief of the gnomes, whose eyelids reach right down to the ground. . . ." However, Viy is unknown in Ukrainian folklore; so, in fact, are gnomes, who in all likelihood migrated into Gogol's story from Grimms' fairy tales. Viy therefore is a creation not of the imagination of "the folk" but rather of Gogol himself. And the word "Viy" was most likely derived by Gogol from the Ukrainian *viya,* meaning "eyelash." In any event, the long eyelids of the "chief of the (Grimm brothers'!) gnomes, and his name, which serves as the title of the story, are both associated with a glance, with eyes, with vision.

In **"The Portrait"** the artist Chartkov has committed a crime against art by buying up and destroying the work of other artists. The evil that takes possession of him issues from the dreadful eyes that glare from the portrait of the mysterious money-lender. And at the end of the first part there is the following description of Chartkov's delirious visions, as he lies dying:

> He began to be haunted by the long-forgotten, living eyes of the strange portrait, and then his frenzy was terrible. All the people standing around his bed looked to him like horrible portraits. The portrait doubled and quadrupled before his eyes; all the walls seemed to be hung with portraits that fastened their motionless, living eyes on him. Terrible portraits looked down from the ceiling and up from the floor, the room opened up and expanded endlessly to provide more space for these staring eyes.

"The Portrait" is very close in structure to the somewhat earlier story **"A Terrible Vengeance."** In **"The Portrait,"** after the death of the hero, the narrator is introduced in part two. He is the son of the artist-turned-monk who painted the mysterious portrait. Similarly, in **"A Terrible Vengeance,"** after the death of the sorcerer, an "old bandore-player" is introduced in the final chapter, and he sings a song "about a happening of old." Both the son of the artist and the bandore-player, in their narrative epilogues, present a *Vorgeschichte* of the events described in the text, and provide a clue to the mysterious happenings which tell the story of a curse. In **"The Portrait,"** this curse is embodied in the portrait of the money-lender, a variant of The Wandering Jew; in **"A Terrible Vengeance,"** it is in the sorcerer, the last in the line of the Cossack Petro who murdered his sworn brother Ivan (the

Cain motif). As a result of this curse, the sorcerer—a "sinner without parallel"—himself perpetrates many monstrous crimes.

Ivan, who has been "murdered" by his brother in the days of King Stefan (i.e., Stefan Batory), carries on a kind of semi-earthly existence, wandering through the Carpathian Mountains as a gigantic knight in shining armor. His soul will find peace only when vengeance is visited upon the last in the line of his murderer.

Chapter fourteen of **"A Terrible Vengeance"** begins with a description of the following event:

> An extraordinary miracle occurred outside Kiev. All the nobles and hetmans came together to marvel at this miracle: suddenly one could see far away, to the very ends of the earth. Far off the blue glimmer of the Dnieper estuary was visible; beyond it spread the Black Sea. Men who had travelled recognized the Crimea too, rising like a mountain out of the sea, and the marshy Sivash. To the left the Galician land could be seen.
>
> "And what's that there?" the assembled people inquired of the elders, pointing at gray and white crests that shimmered far off in the sky and looked more like clouds than anything else.
>
> "Those are the Carpathian Mountains!" said the old men. "There are some among them that the snow never leaves; and the clouds cling to them and spend the night there."
>
> Then a new marvel appeared; the clouds slipped off the very highest peak, and atop it, in full knightly regalia, appeared a man on horseback with his eyes closed; and he could be seen just as distinctly as if he had been standing nearby.

The sorcerer, who is standing in the crowd, recognizes the knight as the one destined to punish him for his sin and tries to hide. He gallops on his horse through that immense space, which is now being watched by hundreds of eyes and which offers no hiding-place. He loses his sense of direction, and, after a mad gallop, his horse carries him to the Carpathians and to Krivan, the highest peak—and there awaiting him is the "motionless horseman," the knight in armor, the Cossack Ivan, who was long ago murdered by an ancestor of the sorcerer. He sees that the horseman "stirred and suddenly opened his eyes; he caught sight of the sorcerer galloping toward him and began to laugh. His wild laughter echoed through the mountains like a thunder-clap." The horseman seizes the sorcerer with his mighty hand; the "terrible vengeance" is carried out.

In all three works, then, to be seen means to be doomed. In all three works the death of the hero comes in retribution for an act that has been committed; the instrument of this retribution is a person who is "dead" but who carries on a sort of supernatural existence somewhere between life and death.

In **"Viy"** and **"The Portrait,"** the death of the hero represents a victory for demonic or satanic powers; in **"A Terrible Vengeance"** it is a sinner—a murderer and incestuous father—who perishes, and the vengeance is taken with God's consent—although the consent is given somewhat reluctantly, according to the old bandore-player's account. The motif of the doom-dealing glance is common to all three works we have examined; but in **"A Terrible Vengeance"** still another motif appears: that of expanded vision. An immense stretch becomes visible to all; people can see the whole earth from the Black Sea to the Carpathians. Vengeance is to be exacted in accordance with God's will; and vision—which resembles the all-seeing eye of God—becomes a miraculous gift that is given to all for a certain period of time.

Expanded vision—the miracle that is described at the beginning of chapter fourteen of **"A Terrible Vengeance"**—is a free motif in this particular story, in the sense that it is not tied to the development of the narrative-line, and is not organic to the structure of the work. It seems to emerge from a store of images and ideas lodged within the author himself.

The idea of expanded vision as a special gift that he possesses or needs is found repeatedly in Gogol, particularly in his statements about *Dead Souls,* as well as in the text of the novel itself. Gogol conceives of it as looking from a height (a tower), i.e., downward, or else—and this is a peculiar equivalent of height—as taking in vast expanses from a great distance, "from the beautiful far-away."

Characteristically, the images of the tower or the tall structure are used for the most part as a means of parodying Gogol's own ideas of what we have chosen to call the "all-seeing eye." (pp. 376-80)

In the last chapter of Part 1 of *Dead Souls,* after Chichikov's hasty departure from the provincial town of X, there is a lyrical digression which contains something reminiscent of the miracle in **"A Terrible Vengeance"**: things can be "seen" over an enormous distance. But here, this miraculous power of sight is granted only to the author: "Russia! Russia! I behold thee, from my wonderful and beautiful far-away do I behold thee. . . ." And at the very end of the book, this power of sight becomes a vision, and Russia, in a somewhat unexpected metaphor, is transformed into a troika which "cannot be overtaken," and before which other peoples "stand aside."

But earlier, one finds a somewhat different image of Russia, as seen "from the beautiful far-away": "Exposed and empty and flat is everything in thee, thy low-lying towns like dots, like specks, are barely perceptible amidst the plains. . . ." These words create the impression that one is looking not so much from a distance as from a great height. On the other hand, in the strange dialectic of "An Author's Confession," distance seems to replace height. Gogol starts out by saying: "I began to think of a way I could . . . place myself at some point from which I could see the whole mass . . . ," and this naturally suggests the idea of elevation, albeit metaphorically; but then height is somehow replaced by distance, and it turns out that the solution to the problem lies in going abroad.

The motif of surveying great expanses from a height, from a tower or a tall building, appears several times in Gogol. The first mention of a tower seems to occur in the article entitled "On the Architecture of the Present Day," which was written at the end of 1833 or the beginning of 1834, and was included in *Arabesques:*

> Huge, colossal towers are essential in a city, quite apart from the importance of their function for Christian churches. Besides adding a vista and ornament to the city, they are necessary to give the city distinctive features, to serve as a beacon which points the way to every traveler, not letting him lose his way. The need for them is even greater in capital cities, for observing the environs. In our country they are usually limited to a height from

> which just the city itself can be seen. But in a capital city it is essential to see at least 150 versts [about 100 miles] in all directions; and for this you need perhaps only one or two extra stories and everything changes. As you ascend, the horizon opens out in extraordinary proportion. The capital gains a substantial advantage by being able to survey the provinces and foresee everything in advance; a building takes on grandeur by virtue of having become somewhat higher than the ordinary; the artist gains, being more disposed to inspiration by the colossal size of a building, and feeling a stronger creative tension within himself.

What is curious in this passage is the attempt to convince, to persuade; curious too is the combination of fantasy and hyperbole with the pseudo-efficiency, the pseudo-practicality which are generally characteristic of Gogol's writings when he gives advice—whether to his mother, in letters from "the beautiful far-away" to his home village of Vasilievka, or to his compatriots as a whole, in *Selected Passages from Correspondence with Friends*—advice which can rarely be followed, but which is detailed, concrete, and insistent to the point of being rather importunate. Of the towers which are "essential" in cities, Gogol writes that they can serve as an ornament, as landmarks, as a source of inspiration for the artist, and as a means of surveying the surrounding areas. And the capital must see "at least 150 versts in all directions"—a minimum of 150 versts. Characteristic here is the concern for the interests of the state: by "capital" Gogol obviously means the authority of the state, the imperial government which is situated in the capital. And it is essential for the government to have a colossal watch-tower in order to keep an eye on the environs and thereby to "foresee everything in advance" which, by the way, is an odd idea, where removal in space somehow merges with removal to future time. (pp. 382-83)

The tower, it seems to us, signifies two things. First, and metaphorically, it signifies the ability to survey vast expanses, the sort of vision that resembles the all-seeing eye of the Divinity—in essence, that is to say, knowledge which comes close to divine, or, more precisely, to prophetic knowledge or omniscience. . . . In the second place, the tower—for the observer atop it—signifies an elevated and dominating position, one that rises above the mass of ordinary mankind, the crowd of "existers." Both these meanings—all-seeing or all-knowing, and the predominance over the mob that is associated with distance from it (symbolically it is expressed vertically, as an upward distancing, but in actuality, it was a horizontal distancing, as expressed in Gogol's going abroad)—were undoubtedly present in Gogol's conscious mind and ran throughout his life. (p. 386)

Leon Stilman, "The 'All-Seeing Eye' in Gogol," in Gogol from the Twentieth Century: Eleven Essays, *edited and translated by Robert A. Maguire, Princeton University Press, 1974, pp. 376-89.*

PETER ROSSBACHER (essay date 1969)

[*In the following excerpt, Rossbacher compares the function of insanity in the heroes of Čexov's "The Black Monk" and Gogol's "Notes of a Madman," observing that Gogol is more uncomfortable with his protagonist's mental disorder than is Čexov and that his aim is to rectify this condition through his work.*]

Both Kovrin in Čexov's "The Black Monk" and Popriščin in

Gogol''s **"Notes of a Madman"** not only are exceptions to their authors' literary type, they embody its very opposite, its anti-type. Moreover, both protagonists are megalomaniacs, which raises the question: What is the function of insanity in Čexov's "The Black Monk" and Gogol''s **"Notes of a Madman"** against the background of the authors' literary type, the specific variety of character found in their works?

This question is based on the assumption that Čexov and Gogol' have a definable literary type. In the case of both writers it is possible to speak of such a type, since their responsiveness to artistically relevant stimuli is highly selective. Both writers experience reality by a few categories which constantly come to the foreground of their artistic attention, create a basic disturbance, and set the creative process in motion which gives birth to a certain literary type. (p. 191)

As early as 1832, we find Gogol''s literary type in **"Ivan Fedorovič Špon'ka and His Aunt."** Gogol' has Stepan Ivanovič Kuročka narrate about Špon'ka: "So it happened that when his fellow officers went to visit our small landowners, he stayed at home and occupied himself with matters proper only for a meek and kind soul: he would clean buttons, read a fortunetelling book, place mouse-traps in the corners of his room, or, finally, after taking off his uniform he would lie on his bed." After Špon'ka's resignation from the army, at age thirty-eight, we see him at a rendezvous: "The light-haired young lady stayed and sat down on the divan. . . . The silence continued for about a quarter of an hour. The young lady was still sitting in the same place. Finally, Ivan Fedorovič found enough courage. 'In summer, there are many flies, my lady,' he said in a half-trembling voice. 'Very many,' said the young lady, 'My brother purposefully made a fly-swatter from one of mama's old shoes; but still, there are many flies.' Here the talk again stopped. In no way could Ivan Fedorovič regain the gift of speech." The theme underlying these lines occupied a dominant position in Gogol''s works, clearly revealing that his sensitivity got stuck in man as a stupid, freakish being, living unaware of his high destiny, approaching life with a wrong perspective. Out of the encounter between Gogol''s artistic sensitivity and this aspect of man's life grows a literary type which can be defined in Čiževskij's words: "In this 'mundane' world there prevails a mundane point of view, a mundane attitude toward everyday and lowly things. They are seen 'from below.' Thus in the eyes of people engrossed in the life of this world what is ordinary and trivial is transformed into something grandiose and magnificent."

As in the case of Čexov, the nature of Gogol''s artistic sensitivity is also manifested in remarks on various phenomena that attracted his attention. At the age of seventeen, Gogol' wrote to his schoolmate Vysockij that all the animal-like beings who inhabited Nežin had strangled man's high destiny with the crust of their earthiness and miserable smugness. Already in these words we see what attracts Gogol''s attention: the discrepancy between what is—man an animal-like being—and what should be: man aware of his high destiny. Fifteen years later, in a digression in *Dead Souls,* Gogol' defined himself as a writer whose fate it was to show what indifferent eyes did not see, the terrifying, shocking morass of trivial things in which man's life was entangled. It is this aspect of reality to which Gogol''s artistic sensitivity cannot remain indifferent. On the contrary, it terrifies and shocks him. The religious nature of this shock becomes obvious if we read Gogol''s words against these lines written by Pascal almost

200 years earlier: "And the same man who spends so many days and nights in rage and despair for the loss of office or for some imaginary insult to his honor [cf. **"About How Ivan Ivanovič Quarreled with Ivan Nikiforovič"**] is the very same who knows without anxiety and without emotion that he will lose all by death. It is a monstrous thing to see in the same heart and at the same time this sensibility to trifles and this strange insensibility to the greatest objects." (pp. 194-95)

As with Čexov, Gogol' was aware that he had not consciously chosen his literary type. In a digression in *Dead Souls* he sees himself as a writer destined by a miraculous power to create strange heroes. Like Čexov, he was, however, aware of the nature of his type and had a definite attitude toward it. . . . Gogol''s attitude toward his literary type is one of rejection through hateful ridiculing.

There is another equally significant difference in attitude. Unlike Čexov, Gogol' is deeply disturbed by the nature of his typical character. This disturbance has its root in Gogol''s understanding of art, which, in Berdjaev's words, places him at the beginning of the didactic movement in Russian literature. Gogol' saw in art an instrument to clean Russian heads of ideals stuffed into them by French novels, and to create images which would become irresistible guidelines for man's life. The difference between Čexov's and Gogol''s understanding of the function of art can be reduced to a basic difference in their world outlook. . . . If the agnostic Čexov has no message for the artist Čexov, the believer Gogol' has a message for the artist Gogol'. Gogol' shows one aspect of the human predicament and considers it his task to overcome this aspect in his work. The inability of the artist to embody the message of the believer is at the basis of Gogol''s profound disturbance by his literary type. After the publication of the first part of *Dead Souls,* this disturbance became so intense that Gogol' refused to recognize his literary type as the content of his vision. The idea of his task as a mission imposed on him by God further intensified the conflict between Gogol''s artistic vision and his world outlook. For four years Gogol' tried to create a new literary type. This type was to be given life in the second part of *Dead Souls,* about which Gogol' wrote that in it the Russian man would no longer appear from his trivial side, but in all the depth of his nature, in all the majesty of his character. Whatever Gogol''s efforts (a pilgrimage to Palestine, close communications with his father confessor Matvej Konstantinovskij), his artistic vision remained closed to a new literary type. Whenever Gogol' worked on the second part of *Dead Souls,* his freakish literary type appeared instead of a positive hero. Terrified by the result of four years of work, he burned the manuscript. Trying to understand the nature of his creative paralysis, he wrote to father Konstantinovskij that the devil had often misled him into thinking that he had power over a theme to which he so far only aspired, a theme which he found only in his head, but not in his heart. This insight is the repetition of a thought he had expressed thirteen years earlier in a letter to his mother: "Literature is not at all an outcome of reason, but an outcome of feelings, in the same way as music and painting."

Against the background of the preceding considerations, we can now look at Popriščin, the megalomaniac protagonist in **"Notes of a Madman."** As in the case of Kovrin, Popriščin's insanity develops gradually, which allows us to compare the insane Popriščin with the sane Popriščin.

The sane Popriščin is a typical Gogolian type. A civil servant of ugly appearance spends his life sharpening pens for His Excellency. He takes pride in the nobility of his service which he sees in the cleanness of his office and mahogany tables. He is in love with Sofi, his director's daughter. Whenever he sees her, he is thrown into a feeling of being doomed, absolutely lost. Aware of his unworthiness, he asks her to execute him. When he sees her put on a stocking in her boudoir, he is robbed of the gift of speech and coherent thought. Later he is struck by the realization that there in this boudoir is the answer to his life. There he suspects miracles, a paradise that cannot even be found in heaven. When Sofi prefers a gentleman of the Emperor's bedchamber to him, Popriščin is crushed. In the same vein, his director inspires in Popriščin feelings of awe. He seems to belong to a different order of being. Reflecting on his misfortunes, the sane Popriščin reduces all his sufferings to the fact that he is only a titular counselor. The riddle of his existence remains inexplicable to him.

The insane Popriščin looks at his world with a different perspective. He can say: "I demand that food which would nourish and delight my soul, but instead I get such trifles . . . ." Sofi's world is seen as a world where people talk about a certain Bobov who in his jabot looks very much like a stork. Her suitor is simply a dog. This metaphor leads Popriščin to a generalizing statement which places the man-woman relationship in a different dimension. From its physiological basis, this relationship is raised to a plane where women are seen as beings who are in love with the devil. The insane Popriščin sees in his director a stupid creature, living for a ribbon. Moreover, the whole world of officialdom is a group of Judases, ready to sell mother, father, and God for money. Popriščin now experiences his world not only as a source of nonsensicality and evil, but as a source of unbearable pain. The new perspective leads to a total rejection of this world and the desire to leave it. "Sit down, my coachman, ring, my bell; rear horses, and carry me away from this world. . . . Mother, save your poor son . . . he has no place in the world." These are Popriščin's last words. Gogol''s yearning for a man with the right perspective has been fulfilled in an insane character.

Perhaps the function of insanity in Čexov's "The Black Monk" and Gogol''s **"Notes of a Madman"** can be understood by reference to Šestov's comment about megalomania (in *Penultimate Words*): that serious seeking brings a man to lonely paths which end in a great wall that sets a fatal bound to his seeking. A megalomaniac is understood as a man who, facing the questions of how to go beyond this wall, feels strong enough to shatter it. Applying Šestov's thought to the problem posed by the megalomaniac protagonist, it can be argued that the latter is capable of doing what the corresponding literary type cannot do, to shatter the wall before which the literary type got stuck, be it the wall of suffering or of a wrong perspective. Shattering this wall, the megalomaniac protagonist points to another aspect of his author's artistic vision. About this aspect of a writer's artistic vision Čexov wrote: "The writers whom we call eternal or simply good writers . . . have one common and very important trait: they go somewhere and call you there too, and you feel not with your mind but with all of your being that they have some goal. . . . The best writers are realists and write about life as it is. Since . . . you feel, in addition to life as it is, life as it should be, and that captivates you."

Čexov's and Gogol's artistic vision is based on an assump-

tion that is implicit in this vision and can be made explicit. . . . In Gogol''s artistic vision man is experienced as a being with a wrong perspective. However, the assumption determining this type of vision is: Man should be aware of his high destiny. Gogol''s literary type is "saturated with the awareness of this goal" in the sense that his very existence is the result of the negation of this assumption by reality as it is experienced in Gogol''s vision. The insane Popriščin, as the literary anti-type, embodies this assumption.

An answer to the question of the function of insanity in Čexov's "The Black Monk" and Gogol's **"Notes of a Madman"** can now be given. The insane protagonist can go beyond the point where the literary type got stuck, for he reveals the basic assumption implicit in the author's artistic vision and, as the anti-type, makes it explicit. (pp. 196-99)

Peter Rossbacher, "The Function of Insanity in Čexov's 'The Black Monk' and Gogol's 'Notes of a Madman,' " in Slavic and East European Journal, Vol. XIII, No. 2, 1969, pp. 191-99.

CHARLES SHERRY (essay date 1974)

[*In the following excerpt, Sherry assesses from a structural perspective the comic and grotesque aspects of "The Overcoat."*]

In **"The Overcoat"** man appears as a functionary, and regards other men, while becoming visible to them in turn, solely in terms of the use one man may be to another. Gogol's obsession with the deceptive and often evilly ambiguous nature of the functionary's presence in most of the work written during the great period of his maturity (1833-1842) makes that work particularly valuable and available for an exercise in a criticism which begins with the ambiguous presence of things disclosed in narrative space. (pp. 5-6)

Almost everyone of importance to the narrative of **"The Overcoat"** is a civil servant belonging in one capacity or another to the government. Akaky Akakyvitch is the son of a civil servant who was himself presumably the son of a civil servant. The Very Important Person is likewise the son of a civil servant, and his son is already in service. Everyone of real importance of Gogol's story belongs to a bureaucratic hierarchy; this hierarchy is the source of what really matters and the fountainhead of what is looked upon as real.

What a man really is is determined by his place in the hierarchy of the governmental bureaucracy. A man exists, with an exact calibration, to the degree determined by his place in that hierarchy. Those who are higher up in it are entitled, because they are higher up, to an existence of greater amplitude than those lower down; they possess, as it were, a more elaborate and glittering apparatus of happiness. Whether in fact they are happier, or whether or not they really do somehow exist to a greater degree upon some absolute existential scale is irrelevant; what is important for them is that they appear to others both lower down and higher up in the hierarchy—and thus to themselves—to be what their position allows them to be by filling precisely the space allotted to them, as did the official who divided his already quite small office in order to create an audience or presence chamber, complete with two men in ornate jackets to open the doors and admit petitioners, while leaving barely enough room for his own desk: "The story is even told of some titular councillor who, on being made chief of some small office, immediately partitioned off a special room for himself, calling it 'the presence chamber,' and placed two commissionaires in coats with red collars and galloons at the door with instructions to take hold of the door handle and open the door to any person who came to see him, though there was hardly room in 'the presence chamber' for an ordinary writing-desk."

Two words are of special importance here: *appearance* and *function*. In the world of **"The Overcoat"** man is a functionary, an operator whose sole purpose is to appear to fill the space allotted to him on the scale of existence established by the St. Petersburg hierarchy. That space is filled by making it impinge upon those lower down in order to make them feel the weight of the position of the one higher up and by bearing up under the pressure of those above—without pushing upward too hard. The functionary operating with maximum efficiency is simultaneously light and heavy. This disjunction in his actions—something Socrates would call unintelligible and illusory—is symptomatic of a deeper, more schizophrenic split in his very existence, a division of human from inhuman attributes which constitutes the aesthetic and moral focus of **"The Overcoat"** and is the source of what is at once morally and aesthetically grotesque in it. A man's life is lived at the very edges of his position in the bureaucratic hierarchy; the center of that life is hollow; all energy and intelligence flow outward toward the creation of a presence that exists solely for the sake of the onlooking gaze of others. Things too serve only to fill up, but not to overfill, the place one occupies, and act as well as signals to those around one of the positions one holds; but beyond that they have no real existence—only as a function does anything exist. (pp. 6-7)

For Gogol this bureaucratically dominated world is permeated by an irreality of its own manufacture, which has disconnected it from a world more real, which one could characterize as more permanent and stable, where appearance and reality are more or less the same, in that things remain what they appear to be. In the artificial world of the Russian official, things are not what they seem to be, they only seem to be, and beyond that seeming there is no human reality. Bureaucratic relationships have taken the place of those more human relations which enable one man to see another man as his brother. The irreality of this bureaucratic world comes to be through a single essential act, repeated an infinite number of times in innumerable variations, whose most elemental quality is the will to transform all things, including oneself, into functioning components of a system set in motion to order and control life. This world is alien, even hostile, to the warmth, depth and complexity of the human personality, and it confers "real" existence and value only upon that part of man, his rational will, which serves its ordering and containing purposes:

> Suffice it to say that the Very Important Person had become a Very Important Person only quite recently, and that until then he was quite an unimportant person. Moreover, his office was not even now considered of much importance as compared with others of greater importance. But there will always be people who regard as important what in the eyes of other people is rather unimportant. However, the Very Important Person did his best to increase his importance in all sorts of ways, to wit, he introduced a rule that his subordinates should meet him on the stairs when he arrived at his office; that no one should be admitted to his office unless he first petitioned for an interview, and that everything should be done according to the strictest order: the collegiate registrar was first to report to the provin-

cial secretary, the provincial secretary to the titular councillor or whomsoever it was he had to report to, and that only by such a procedure should any particular business reach him. In Holy Russia, we are sorry to say, every one seems to be anxious to ape every one else and each man copies and imitates his superior.

The craze for imitation which seems to dominate life in Holy Russia defines also the moral atmosphere in which Akaky Akakyvitch's destiny is worked out. This ordered, smoothly functioning world of endless imitation is what is most real and important in the lives of all it touches; yet it fabricates the artifices of its own irreality, a mode of fabrication whose action constitutes one of the chief themes of Gogol's work. (pp. 8-9)

The supposition that the uniform a man wears . . . makes him in some qualitative manner a larger, more valuable, and more existentially gifted person in the eyes of others becomes in Gogol's work an essential illusion of civilized life. Such a uniform is a mask concealing, even from the one who wears it, authentic human potentialities and relationships. For those caught up in the vortex of this illusion, the emblems one manipulates to signal to others the quality of one's existence become confused with that existence itself and are mistaken for it. A uniform is not an emblem signifying the achievements of a talent. The reverse is true: one becomes talented by putting on a uniform, and in doing this one assumes through the regard of the others in one's world, the only gaze there is, the power and quality of that uniform in one's self. But when the thing itself is confused with its emblematic representation, the reality with the manifestation of that reality, then everything becomes free-floating appearance. One's identity would cease to exist if it were withdrawn from the sphere of appearance which has become its reality: one functions according to the way it appears that he should function, and becomes thereby a function of that appearance, becomes in effect mere appearance, and falls victim to the whimsicality which constitutes the essence of appearance.

Gogol's vision of the "wondrous whimsicality" of the structure of Russian society constitutes the basis for both the comic and the grotesque aspects of his art. The sheer arbitrariness of the way man has arranged his relations with other men constantly amazes, amuses, and, upon occasion, terrifies Gogol. Such an arrangement is not made by society according to the talents and capacities people actually possess; but, in that there is so often such a discrepancy between the place a person occupies in society and his actual ability to perform well in it, society seems capriciously to assign positions within a hierarchy which fail to correspond to the qualities of the person assigned. There is, as the mad clerk in **"A Madman's Diary"** says, no good reason for anyone to occupy the place he does. . . .

For Gogol, the world man has made for himself is capricious and arbitrary in its arrangement. Things happen to be established as they are, but there is no reason why they could not very well be some other way. Yet it is only under the most extraordinary circumstances that man is able seriously to question the totality of his existence, to throw into question everything he has regarded as real, with the full expectation that it might not be. It is precisely those situations to which man reacts by questioning the very basis of the world as he knows it, or which could lead to such an inquiry (given greater awareness in the character), that constitute the moral and aesthetic center of so many of Gogol's stories. Often the shift of mood or the accidence of perspective is all that is necessary to throw a character out of his habitual relationship to society and thrust him into an uncanny situation where he questions the very existence of the world to which he no longer belongs and whose illusions he no longer can sustain as reality. (pp. 11-13)

The real disagreement of the formalists with the ethical interpretations of **"The Overcoat"** is over the meaning of two structurally quite similar moments in the narrative. They are central, and any interpretation of the narrative must account for them. The first is that moment early in the story when Akaky Akakyvitch, tormented beyond endurance by the young clerks in his office, pleads to be left alone in such an effective manner as to pierce through the callous sensibility of one of them. . . . The second of these moments occurs in the effect upon the Very Important Person of Akaky Akakyvitch's ghost, who returns to snatch the coat off his back as he is riding to visit his mistress:

> Pale, frightened out of his wits, and without his overcoat, he arrived home instead of going to Karolina Ivanovna's, and somehow or other managed to stagger to his room. He spent a very restless night, so that next morning at breakfast his daughter told him outright, "You look very pale today, Papa!" But Papa made no reply. Not a word did he say to any one about what had happened to him, where he had been and where he had intended to go.

> This incident made a deep impression upon the Very Important Person. It was not so frequently now that his subordinates heard him say, "How dare you, sir? Do you realize who you're talking to, sir?" And if he did say it, it was only after he had heard what it was all about.

According to the ethical interpretation of these moments, their meaning is constituted by the disclosure they make of man's inhumanity to man. In making this revelation the narrative takes up a critical, "realist," attitude towards its social environment. Carried to its extreme, the ethical point of view can find in **"The Overcoat"** little more than a sustained polemic against the injustice of social conditions in Russia.

For [Boris] Ejchenbaum, whose essay was the first and is still the finest formalist interpretation of **"The Overcoat,"** these moments become models of the stylistic grotesque. The grotesque, as he defines it, has its origin in the detachment of the events in the narrative from their links with reality. This is not done with the intent to satirize or to create an allegory, but in order to open up as wide a field as possible to a "play with reality," a play which renders conventional relationships amongst things unworkable. Ejchenbaum's interpretation of the grotesque in **"The Overcoat"** transforms the didactic social criticism of the ethical point of view into the free play of the stylistically oriented grotesque, which, in isolating the events of a narrative from any connection with the real world, transposes the elements of that work into a purely stylistic order. These two perspectives, the ethical and the formalist, tend to cancel one another out. Yet from an ontological perspective this cancellation may prove to be premature, or even unnecessary.

As we have seen, the world disclosed in the narrative space of Gogol's work is essentially whimsical in nature. The existence of what comes to a presence in the narrative space of

"The Overcoat" possesses a reality only in terms of its relation to the bureaucratic structure of Russian society, a structure whose reality is its appearance. It is the pressure of the presence of those entities whose being is appearance that determines the contours of narrative space in **"The Overcoat."** The contours of that space become visible in Gogol's work only when a character is thrust out of his normal relationship to the world and it becomes possible to see that world as it is in itself, at the point where it ceases to function for that person.

The two moments in **"The Overcoat"** which I have indicated constitute just such a break in the continuity of a character's relationship to a stable external world. Akaky Akakyvitch is the instrument of those moments. I would like to attempt to show how this is so and to bring out, in the process, the ontological significance of those moments.

Even at the outset of his life, Akaky Akakyvitch did not fit very well into the world of the St. Petersburg bureaucracy. He cried at his christening, as though, the narrator tells us, he knew already that he would become a clerk. Both his appearance and his attitude toward his work set him off from those around him. He is a function, not a functionary; a simple extension of his pen in a shabby old uniform. Because of this he is vulnerable in ways other men are not; he is the butt of office jokes and the man the hall porters do not even notice. His appearance is the cause of many of his difficulties and the source of the ridicule he has to endure. His uniform is old and faded, and the collar has shrunk, which makes his neck seem extraordinarily long. His work has a meaning for himself alone. He is in love with his calligraphy—a mild and harmless form of narcissism. But his attitude toward his copying serves also to separate him from the others with whom he works; they work in order to become like those over them, while Akaky Akakyvitch does his work for its own sake. It is only when they keep him from his copying that he is moved to complain. For the rest, he is almost oblivious to what happens about him, not knowing whether he is in the middle of the street or in the middle of a sentence. Others' lives are infinitely remote from him, yet he is unaware of the distance separating him from them. His shabby uniform betrays his lack of regard for the way in which others look upon him; and his narcissistic love of his own handwriting, his total absorption in his work, announces to others his absolute lack of ambition, an attitude they cannot comprehend, for every man in a bureaucracy wishes to be like his superiors, to emulate them, and to rise to their position.

Akaky Akakyvitch buys a new overcoat because he must. It is not something he wishes to buy in order to play the swell on Nevsky Avenue or to create a favorable impression upon his fellow workers, but something he wants for its two advantages: warmth and goodness. His coat will be warm and good, in that order: good because it is warm, and not because it is a signal to others of his station in life, and good, too, because he has given so much of himself to it. Even before he realizes that he must buy a new overcoat, Akaky Akakyvitch is described as a simple function in the department where he works; yet, in order to buy the overcoat he needs, he turns himself into a function in the machinery of his own life. To save money for it, Akaky Akakyvitch establishes a systematic savings plan: eating less, burning fewer candles—his landlady's when he can, walking less in his shoes, and wearing his underwear only when he must. After months of such behavior, he is able, with the help of a lucky bonus, to put together the money he needs for the overcoat—but at what price?

Other critics have commented upon the erotic nature of Akaky's relationship to his overcoat-to-be. My own feeling is that the tenderness he feels for his "Companion" is the same affection he has for certain letters of the alphabet which he forms with much pleasure and animation as he copies them down. He even used to bring his work home to occupy the evening hours. Apart from his work, his life had no content. But with the savings project for the coat, his existence assumes a greater amplitude. His life feels somehow fuller with it; but is it the overcoat itself that creates this effect, or is it the systematic organization which his life undergoes as he disciplines himself for his purpose? I think it is the latter, that capacity to transform one's life into a tiny finite series of repeated operations moving toward a clearly marked goal. There is a real difference between repeatedly performing an act an infinite number of times to no real final conclusion and performing the same act a finite number of times for a stated purpose. Doing the latter invests each act with a significance it could not have if it were only one in an infinite series of acts. The decision to purchase the overcoat from the tailor Petrovitch enhances the quality of Akaky's life through the enactment of his frugality, and it enlarges the meaning of his everyday acts: now even the way he walks, to preserve as best he can the leather of the soles of his shoes, becomes important. . . . Akaky's gestures, the way he walks or sits or moves about, all reflect a single meaning, which is contained in the warmth and goodness of the overcoat for which he is saving. I find it difficult to see anything really very erotic in the transformation of a man into a systematic savings machine. Akaky, in saving for his coat, has transferred the systematic procedures of his office to the last vestiges of his private life, and has made himself into his own function. In this way he is able to pay the price of his overcoat.

Akaky Akakyvitch is both scapegoat and threat to those with whom he lives. His vulnerability, his being a function in a world of functionaries, invites the ridicule of others; but his response to their cruelty, interpreted to mean "I am your brother," reveals the inhumanity of their lives. In both moments, for the young clerk and for the Very Important Person, the injustice and outrage committed against Akaky Akakyvitch discloses the harsh cruelty of life, which civilization seems to conceal. It is a cruelty that is not immediately obvious to those who live daily with it. It is only when the effects of their civilized cruelty are seen in their injustice toward Akaky Akakyvitch that they realize, if only in a partial manner, the brutality of official relationships. Akaky Akakyvitch's plea to be left alone fissures the world of the young clerk. He is touched by what Akaky says, and in being moved by it he is able for a moment to perceive the deceptive structure of the civilized world. The returning ghost of the outraged Akaky Akakyvitch affects the conscience of the Very Important Person in a similar fashion.

Just as the water from the Neva Delta oozes up through the cracks in the stone streets of St. Petersburg, so what is suppressed by its bureaucracies leaks through the breaks which occur in the well-ordered edifice of official existence. Life, or, if we can trust the narrator's interpretation of Akaky Akakyvitch's plea to be left alone, the brotherhood of man, is glimpsed at certain moments when the inhumanity of human relations which have become official relations is revealed through the actions of a simple clerk; but it is a brotherhood

seen as something quite remote and alien from the life one leads in government offices and departments. And once this has been seen, one can only turn back into the bureaucratic life with a shrug of the shoulders.

Yet why is it through Akaky Akakyvitch that this disclosure becomes possible? We must return, I think, to the quality of his vulnerability for an answer. He is vulnerable because he is a function and not a functionary. He is attacked by the young clerks in his office for this; but, in the rush of that attack, one young clerk runs right into what is after all a human being. He discovers in Akaky's plea the great distance that separates the pathetic old clerk from other men, and at once glimpses the civilized brutality of the world that creates such distances. What he had treated as an object—not only of his ridicule—becomes, when it speaks, a human being like himself; and the gap which opens up between the way in which he had regarded Akaky and the human quality of his speech frightens the young clerk into silence. To the Very Important Person Akaky Akakyvitch is likewise simply an object representing to him a means of demonstrating to his friend, as well as to himself, the power of his position, and nothing more: he even calls him a young man, when it is evident that Akaky is older than he is. But in Akaky Akakyvitch he discovers the man who will yield to his authority all the way, fainting in silence before it. Such absolute submission troubles the Very Important Person slightly, but it is only when his own overcoat has been snatched off his back by Akaky's outraged ghost that the enormous distance which separates him from his subordinates is revealed to him. Only then does he soften in his behavior toward them. But for neither the young clerk nor the Very Important Person is the experience of that discovery of any significant value, nor does it lead to any important change in them. It is as though one had looked into Pascal's abyss and then turned away with a shrug of the shoulders. (pp. 20-5)

In the mastery of the terror which seizes man at the moment when his world collapses lies the essence of the tragic moment. But in Gogol there is no such attempt at mastery; there is only a retreat back into the realm of appearances. In Gogol's world there is nowhere else to turn, no weapon to confront disillusion with but illusion—or a retreat into madness. From this situation tragedy cannot arise, only the grotesque.

In his *The Grotesque in Art and Literature* [see excerpt above] Wolfgang Kayser offers an extremely interesting interpretation of Christoph Wieland's definition of the grotesque:

> But Wieland found the very essence of the grotesque to lie in its complete detachment from reality. In his opinion, grotesques are not imitations but products of a "wild imagination." Like Gottsched, Wieland defined the grotesque in exactly the way in which the Renaissance Italians had defined it, namely, as *sogni dei pittori.* According to him, the grotesque is "supernatural" and "absurd," that is, it contradicts the very laws which rule our familiar world . . . . The basic feeling, however—if I understand Wieland correctly—is one of surprise and horror, an agonizing fear in the presence of a world which breaks apart and remains inaccessible.
>
> I am fully aware of the fact that, by interpreting Wieland's argument in this manner, I read something into it which it does not literally state. But it seems safe to assume that this is what he really wanted to say. By viewing our surprise as an ago-

nizing fear of the dissolution of our world, we secretly relate the grotesque to our reality . . .

For Wieland the essence of the grotesque lies in its detachment from reality. It is this freedom from the rules governing reality which elicit one's surprise and horror when confronted with the grotesque. However, to be able to include **"The Overcoat"** in Wieland's definition of the grotesque, we will have to alter that definition somewhat. For in Gogol's work the grotesque has an ontological origin. It is in the perception of the real as unreal, of the true as false, that the grotesque originates for Gogol. Entities emptied of their meaning become grotesque, and in the realization that one's world has been drained of its meaning the collapse of the relationship of the individual consciousness to a stable external world occurs. It is the revelation that beings themselves have no real existence save as appearance that makes the grotesque as style possible.

Unlike the tragic situation, which elicits the attempt at mastery over the terror of existence, the grotesque, in revealing a world ruled by whimsicality, elicits only surprise and horror, but no attempt at mastery of these emotions. In the grotesque there is no hidden meaning to be revealed: reality is simply an arbitrary, but ordered, series of appearances. Behind them is nothing. Having been surprised and frightened, there is nothing left to do but to go back to work or go mad. The grotesque elicits a shrug of the shoulders and motivates at best a retreat back inside the civilized cocoon man has spun for himself. The irruption of the extraordinary into the continuity of one's existence is either quickly forgotten, as with the Very Important Person, or else one goes mad and dies, the way Akaky Akakyvitch dies, never having recovered from the shock of his encounter with the Very Important Person.

Since the being of things as it is disclosed in the world of **"The Overcoat"** is utterly whimsical, the boundaries between the real and the unreal, the natural and the supernatural, collapse, and one penetrates the other. Thus it would not be unusual to see a ghost, nor would it be impossible to put one in jail. Those moments in the narrative when these boundaries dissolve constitute the ontological basis of the grotesque in the narrative. When they occur, the contours of the space man inhabits become visible. They are derivable from the presence of those entities whose being is disclosed as completely arbitrary. This is an ontological situation from which the formal and ethical dimensions of the narrative can be derived. Their structures would be repetitions of the arbitrary and grotesque nature of their ontological base.

The formalist interpretation of the stylistic grotesque as *skaz*, as a structure composed of many diverse and whimsically combined elements, is complemented by an analysis of the ontological structure of the narrative space of **"The Overcoat."** To show exactly how this is true would require another paper, however.

The ethical interpretation is, on the other hand, made more difficult by the ontological, for it is not easy to see how a polemic against the existing social conditions in Russia can be made from a view of existence which treats it as essentially unreal and whimsical. True, it is through injustice that the inessentiality of things is disclosed; but that revelation itself, as grotesque, precludes action of, say, a Sartrean kind upon a world revealed in literature as one's task. I do not wish to exclude the possibility of an ethical interpretation of **"The Overcoat,"** since I feel that the possibility of one remains la-

tent in the nature of the acts of injustice and outrage in it; but how such an ethical interpretation would keep itself free of metaphysics is very difficult to see. That is, if the world is revealed as arbitrary in its very being, then what would be the nature of an ethical criticism of it which would not be at the same time an attack upon the cosmos? Gogol's stories are narratives of place. Individuals figure in them of course, but ultimately it is always one place or another which acts as the real hero in them.

Akaky Akakyvitch's great error was to purchase an overcoat which fit him in a world where men are made to fit the overcoats they wear. Living at the edges of the image they have fabricated for themselves leaves the inner life of these men strangely distorted and empty. It is this distortion in their lives which produces the grotesque and aberrant space disclosed in the narrative of **"The Overcoat."** I hope that I have shown the ontological origin of that distortion. (pp. 25-7)

Charles Sherry, "The Fit of Gogol's 'Overcoat': An Ontological View of Narrative Form," in Genre, *Vol. 7, No. 1, March, 1974, pp. 1-29.*

CHARLES C. BERNHEIMER (essay date 1975)

[In the excerpt below, Bernheimer contends that the reflexive structure of "The Overcoat" serves as a defense mechanism for Gogol's fear of being annihilated by "the other."]

"The Overcoat" is one of the most elusive as well as one of the greatest of literary creations. Though subjected to innumerable interpretations, this enigmatic text has obstinately refused to "make sense." Boris Eichenbaum ascribes the peculiarities of the story to the character of its narrator, a playful juggler with reality and fantasy whose skillful puns, expressive sound effects, and tangential verbosity are part of a carefully contrived grotesque comedy. Eichenbaum's stricture that "in a work of art, not a single sentence can be in itself a simple 'reflection' of the personal feelings of the author, but is always a construction and a performance" provides a salutary antidote to reductive biographical and moralizing criticism. But his formalist method, illuminating as it is, fails to account for the function of the text as a performance put on not only for an audience but also for the writer himself. Both through its dramatic plot and in its narrative technique, the literary construction may express its creator's attitude toward the very act of writing. As I propose to demonstrate in this essay, Gogol's text has a reflexive structure by which it insists on its purely literary status, an insistence that simultaneously operates as a defense mechanism for Gogol himself. **"The Overcoat"** dramatizes Gogol's schizoid fear of being obliterated by the other even as its self-consuming structure provides him with a hiding place from the demands and definitions of life. (p. 53)

For Gogol to write "The Book" would be equivalent to a fixing of his personality, to an act of definition that would subject his secret soul to understanding, to penetration and violation by the other. . . . The solution Gogol devised, the inauthenticity of which was a source of unending anguish during his last years, was to coerce his "secret" self to fuse with an entirely suprapersonal, crudely dogmatic set of moral and religious doctrines (see *Selected Passages from Correspondence with Friends*). In articulating this preexistent code, Gogol could feel that he was being spoken through, that he was simply the mouthpiece for a totally impersonal truth, a mouthpiece that must constantly purify itself of individual identity in order to be worthy of its "divine" message. The paradox is that it is just this masochistic expurgation of identity that Gogol repeatedly describes in his correspondence as a soul-searching process of self-discovery. Once more Gogol masks his true self even as he claims to be engaged in a morally uplifting project of self-revelation. He protects his fragile ego by immuring it within the confines of a world governed by the superego. But the arrogant assertiveness of this persona is accompanied by an increasingly acute fear of inner emptiness: "All I can tell you now is—have faith in my words! I do not dare myself not to believe in my words!"

When writing **"The Overcoat"** (1839-41), Gogol did "dare" to doubt the truth of his words, but this ironic disbelief actually performed the same function of self-concealment as his later "faith." The narrative technique in the story is designed to dissolve all traces of an original authorial voice into a field of ventriloquistic freeplay. The narrative is constantly shifting from one rhetorical convention to the next, from the ironic detachment of the realist to the lyrical immediacy of the romantic, from chatty digression to elevated moralism, from commonplace detail to fantastic absurdity. No one of these alternatives can be said to define the narrator's true commitment, the ventriloquist's own voice. The narrative has no fixed origin; rather, it is structured through a play of substitutions around an absent center.

"The Overcoat" opens with a digression. On the one hand, this excursus about the dangers of naming official authorities introduces us to the rambling, forgetful style of the casual narrator who, unable to erase an unwanted beginning, seems to be chatting with us rather than composing a written text. On the other hand, since the self-canceling beginning is fixed before us on the printed page, subject to repeated rereadings, it makes us aware that the oral style of the narrator is, after all, a deliberate fabrication of the writer. The approach-avoidance gambit then appears to be a strategy by which the author manages somehow not to authorize his tale. It is as if he felt guilty about arbitrarily breaking in upon the silence that prevailed prior to his speech and apprehensive about the consequences of naming, a department or anything else. Thus the narrator's apparently eccentric digression conveys something more than his creator's fear of censorship. It expresses, satirically, Gogol's acute awareness that to use speech meaningfully is to establish an identity and to be actively involved in the world and that such involvement entails submission to the temporal powers ("departments, regiments, government offices, and indeed any kind of official body") that are the public guardians of authorized language.

No sooner, however, has the narrator expressed this sense of vulnerability than Gogol's text acts to protect him by dissolving any identity he may already have acquired. The description of Akaky Akakyevich, which follows in the second paragraph, is, as Eichenbaum says, "not so much a *description* of appearance as a *reproduction* of it in an imitative verbal gesture." This highly sophisticated use of words, which emphasizes sound impressions over signified content, hardly seems to be within the capacity of the gossipy, irresponsible narrator. And what is one to make of the account of Akaky's naming, presented to us by the narrator so that we should realize "that it could not have happened otherwise, and that to give him any other name was quite out of the question"? But it is perfectly clear to us that the account proves no such thing. Rather, like the digressive opening of the story itself, it draws our attention to the arbitrariness of any act of fictional origi-

nation. By ironically proving that Akaky could not have been named otherwise, Gogol brilliantly demonstrates that the void from which all fictional characters emerge harbors no notion of inevitability. The narrator, who asserts the opposite, seems to have lost all sense of reality and logic. Yet, a little later, he makes an impassioned plea for brotherhood in highly colored rhetorical prose. And this is soon followed by a self-conscious reference to the literary conventions that it behooves him to follow—though he manages somehow to avoid doing so.

Is it possible to find a recognizable continuity behind all these shifting masks? The pervasive use of the adverb *dazhe* ("even"), ingeniously analyzed by Dmitri Cizevsky, seems at first to point to the presence of a single narrative voice and, in fact, Cizevsky designates this usage as a means of characterizing the bumbling narrator's verbally impoverished oral style. However, it seems evident that a narrative that includes as many elaborate puns, sound effects, and plays on words as this one does can hardly be suffering from what Cizevsky calls "the lexical impoverishment of the narrator's speech" [see excerpt dated 1938]. Moreover, the word *dazhe,* as Cizevsky suggests, functions to empty the world of meaning, to show its inner void, and this revelation of nothingness holds not only for Akaky's life but also for the lives of Akaky's colleagues, of the VIP, and of all the other characters who appear in the story. "Human nothingness appears in everything," writes Cizevsky. But if the narrator really has such a nihilistic view of the world, then how is it that he so strongly advocates the brotherhood of man? Here Cizevsky's argument, which does not account for the full range of Gogol's irony, runs into trouble once more and he finds himself rather embarrassed to explain what the famous "humane" passages are all about.

The recurrent *dazhe* can, I think, be more accurately seen as a subtle reminder of the nothingness out of which *all* linguistic utterance quite arbitrarily asserts its tenuous existence. Instead of the awaited intensification, the emphatic "even" is followed by deflation ("his father, grandfather, and, why, even his brother-in-law as well as all the rest of the Bashmachkins, always walked about in boots"); instead of a logical continuity, "even" introduces a logical absurdity (the frost causes tears to come to the eyes even of those officials who occupy the highest posts). The point is that in the world freed through the activity of narrative play, logical discourse is only one among many equally valid alternatives. While *dazhe* may occasionally be used to characterize the quirky speech of a particular narrative persona, its more important function is to stress literature's independence from the restrictive system of priorities current in life. By refusing to range the important and the trivial, the large and the small, in a coherently intelligible spectrum, Gogol's narrative asserts its freedom from any centered structure of meanings. (pp. 54-5)

Eichenbaum terms "grotesque" this technique by which "Gogol can unite the incompatible, exaggerate the small and minimize the great" thereby "giving scope for *a playing with reality,* for breaking up and freely displacing its elements, so that the usual correlations and connections (psychological and logical) turn out, in this newly constructed world, to be unreal." But this disjunctive "unreality" perfectly defines the freedom specific to literature, a freedom that Gogol flaunts on numerous occasions by having a narrator openly admit his ignorance, indifference, or sheer incapacity. I say "a" narrator because the troubled voice which asks, "How indeed is one to delve into a man's mind and find out what he is thinking about?" seems to have little in common with the all-knowing individual who, in the following paragraphs, provides a detailed account of Akaky's response to the party given in his honor. These masks of omniscience or skepticism are points of arbitrary arrest in a potentially infinite free play of epistemological perspectives. Thus Gogol celebrates the capacity of literature to be discontinuous, disruptive, decentered, a capacity that he illustrates in the peculiarly absent, displaced quality of his protagonist's existence.

Akaky is described as a compendium of rhyming approximations ("neskolko riabovat, neskolko ryzhevat, neskolko dazhe na vid podslepovat"—somewhat pockmarked, somewhat red-haired, he even looked somewhat weak-sighted). He is an individual who is not quite one, a barely definable by-product of certain syntactic rhythms and repetitions. In fact, Akaky does not so much originate as he repeats. His fellow clerks come to believe that "he must have been born into the world entirely fitted out for his job, in his Civil Servant's uniform and a bald patch on his head." His name, which he has as much difficulty in acquiring as Gogol has in getting his story started, is simply the repetition of his father's. And his work in life consists in transcribing the language of others. The one time he is asked to alter the words of a particular document he breaks into a sweat and declares, "No, I can't do it. You'd better give me something to copy."

For Akaky, happiness consists in a total immersion in the words of others, not as meaningful discourse but as an absence of meaning. He finds in the tracing of individual letters "a multifarious and pleasant world of his own" ("a safe separate world" according to the penultimate version of the story quoted by Driessen). So entirely does he dissolve into his world that "you could, it seemed, read on his face every letter his pen was forming with such care." Thus, in a sense, Akaky actually becomes a text, a text, however, that can be deciphered not as a series of significant signs but only as a succession of discrete letters.

Living in this manner inside the alphabet is not alienating for Akaky because he hardly ever uses words to convey the needs and desires of a distinct self. When he does find it necessary to express himself, he feels embarrassed, cannot find any continuity in his articulation, stutters, mumbles, forgets to finish sentences, speaks "in prepositions, adverbs, and lastly, such parts of speech as have no meaning whatsoever." Akaky's language is an approximation because his self is only approximate. His experience is not constituted out of a confrontation between self and other; rather, it occurs almost entirely within the field of meaningless language out of which he has never quite emerged as a fully defined fictional character. Thus when Akaky walks in the street his urban environment appears to him as a text copied out in his own neat handwriting. His senses are largely inoperative. He does not care about the taste of his meals nor is he concerned about the bits of garbage he carries around on his hat. He never gives a thought to his clothes. He is, in effect, almost totally disembodied. "Outside . . . copying," we are told, "nothing seemed to exist for him."

The seamless web of verbal transcription that Akaky creates is torn only on a few rare occasions. In the office, the teasing by his fellow workers sometimes results in his arm being jogged and his work interrupted, prompting his famous "pathetic" outburst: "Leave me alone, why do you have to tor-

ment me?" (my revision of Magarshack's trans.). Or occasionally, when he is walking through the city, a horse blows on his cheek, suddenly making Akaky "aware of the fact that he was not in the middle of a line but rather in the middle of the street."

But these rips in the linguistic fabric of Akaky's world are few indeed. For the most part he seems to exist somehow outside of time, prior to any particularizing articulation, in a mode of repetition close to that described by Kierkegaard. "Repetition," writes Kierkegaard, "signifies freedom itself, . . . a transcendency, a religious movement by virtue of the absurd, which comes to pass when it has reached the borders of the marvelous." From the perspective of everyday life, however, Akaky's quasi-religious absurdity appears only as pathetically comic inadequacy. In true Bergsonian manner, we laugh at the unresponsive, mechanically repetitive quality of Akaky's existence, at his self-absorbed blindness and mute hesitancy, exulting thereby in our own flexibility and freedom. But the joke is really on us. We feel superior to Akaky in our adaptability to this world, but he has found a mode of being that eschews all such degrading compromises. Akaky is as undefined as an individual as the letters he traces are devoid of meaning. He has no family ties, no coherent language, no private desires. His dreams of the future are limited to "wondering what the good Lord would send him to copy." His happiness, and it must be stressed that he *is* happy, derives from the almost perfectly self-enclosed autonomy of his universe. Here the alphabet doubles back on itself, acts as its own mirror, encloses itself in the infinite space of its own reduplication. Akaky is implicated neither in the evil materiality of the world of difference nor in the limiting intentionality of the world of meaning. Having barely entered the narrative stream of temporal duration, he has remained close to his fictional origin, to pure repetition, to meaninglessness.

"A great enemy" shatters this transcendence. This enemy, identified by the narrator as "our northern frost," is in a larger sense the sheer force of physical, temporal reality. When the need to protect himself from the cold becomes manifest to Akaky, he discovers his self as different from the external world. No longer can he absorb that world into a homogeneous text copied out in his own handwriting. Since external reality threatens to destroy him, he must assert his identity against its annihilating power. The purchase of the overcoat constitutes such an assertion, but, simultaneously, it causes Akaky's fall into the world of otherness, of difference, of desire, into the traditional world of narrative action.

Here we have the central paradox of the story: even as it makes Akaky more of a goal-oriented subject by doing away with "all the indeterminate and shilly-shallying traits of his character," the acquisition of the overcoat causes him to lose the autonomy of his private universe of literal repetition and to become an object in the manipulative power plays of the everyday world. This awareness that by becoming a visible, well-defined subject one simultaneously becomes subject to the overwhelming hostile forces of reality was, as we have seen, Gogol's controlling obsession. In the letter to Pletnev quoted above, he describes himself as "a secretive person in whom everything is inside, whose character hasn't even taken shape," a phrase that applies perfectly to Akaky before he acquires his new coat. Significantly, Gogol's earlier description of the poet's role is also applicable to prelapsarian Akaky: "like a silent monk he lives in the world without belonging to it, and his pure unspoiled soul can converse only with God."

I do not want to suggest by this that Gogol "is" Akaky. I am arguing, rather, that Akaky's story dramatizes Gogol's attitude toward writing, that the story as a sequence illustrates its author's ambivalent feelings about the role of literary creation in relation to the external world and to his own identity. At the outset of his story Akaky's tenuous being seems to be almost entirely textual in nature. He is practically without centeredness-in-self, his universe being composed of a potentially endless series of literal substitutions. This originless universe is analogous in structure to the ventriloquistic narrative itself. And such a structure, according to the sweeping generalizations of contemporary French criticism, constitutes the very essence of literature. . . . The space of writing (*écriture*), as the structuralists define it, is a polysemic field, without center or "author," which can be traversed but not penetrated. It is, says Michel Foucault, "the opening of a space into which the writing subject never ceases to disappear." This disappearance is exactly what Gogol sought in his narrative technique and what he shows as Akaky's accomplishment through copying. Thus Akaky's movement out of his alphabetic universe into a world of meaningful self-definition is weighted with Gogol's own fears about acquiring a "finished shape" to his secretive personality, a shape that would subject him to the judgments of "an awesome and truthful posterity." As we have observed, later in his life Gogol did attempt to give himself a definite center through an identification with dogmatic religious teachings. But the annunciation of moralistic clichés coined by others defined his self in much the same inauthentic way that the overcoat made by the devilish Petrovich defines Akaky. In fact, one might say that Gogol made doctrinaire Christianity his personal overcoat.

When Akaky puts on his luxurious new coat he is making himself visible to others, he is giving himself an external appearance recognizable in their eyes. In a sense which Gogol loads with irony, he is losing his original celibacy and entering the community of married men: "His whole existence indeed seemed now somehow to have become fuller, as though he had got married, as though there was someone at his side, as though he was never alone". Edward Said has recently shown that in nineteenth-century narratives marriage is represented with increasing frequency as the end of originality and the absorption into the banality of life's normal generative processes. But whereas most nineteenth-century celibate heroes and heroines assert their originality by willfully pursuing the fulfillment of their private visions, adulterous ambitions, or illicit dreams, Akaky's originality is more self-reflecting, paradoxically more a matter of repetition than of origination. His freedom from the world is achieved by remaining close to his linguistic origins rather than by attempting, like Julien Sorel for instance, to authorize his existence in the temporal world. He maintains his near absence in a purely verbal space where letters repeat themselves, mirror themselves, duplicate their own images, and thereby indefinitely postpone their and his deaths.

The moment Akaky is forced to step out of his universe of linguistic doubling he is caught in an existential double bind: he will die from cold if he does not purchase a new coat; he will be destroyed by the hostile forces of reality if he acquires a self-defining cloak. Gogol's irony is particularly sharp when he speaks of the "spiritual nourishment" Akaky gains from "the great idea of his future overcoat" or when, later, he calls the overcoat a "Bright Visitant" which "brought a ray of sunshine into [Akaky's] drab, poverty-stricken life." For it is just the acquisition of the overcoat that destroys the fabric of Akaky's autonomous "safe" universe and implicates him fully in the material world. His loss of originality, ironically symbolized by his "marriage" to the overcoat, is his very entry into the flow of temporal duration, into the diachronic world of self and other. Here it is no longer language that is reflexive but consciousness. Akaky becomes aware of himself by using the other as a mirror in which his own existence is confirmed. Whereas earlier he had not cared at all about his appearance, now his self-consciousness is so acute that "not for a fraction of a second did he forget that he had a new overcoat on his back." His senses awaken. He observes activity in the street "as though he had never seen anything like it in his life," enjoys his food immensely, and even experiences, somewhat to his own bewilderment, the long-dormant urges of eros.

However, as soon as Akaky's newly found identity becomes visible to the world its vulnerability is recognized and the predictable attacks follow (predictable, that is, given Gogol's peculiar paranoia). In claiming the overcoat as his own, one of the thieves does no more than reclaim for the material world what is clearly its devil-inspired product. Next, the VIP shatters Akaky's still fragile sense of identity by imperiously questioning the clerk's right to even minimal self-assertion. . . . The VIP has trained himself, "in the solitude of his room in front of a looking glass," to reproduce in his own speech the hostile tones and rhythms of purely impersonal power. Hurling words at Akaky as if they were weapons, he seems to claim for himself, that is, for his official rank, all rights to language and ego. The very device of verbal repetition, which had been the source of Akaky's happiness as a copying clerk, now is used to demolish his fragile identity. Letters whose physical, material properties had given Akaky transcendent joy now are prostituted to form linguistic projectiles directed against him. This confrontation with the embodiment of annihilating otherness reduces Akaky to a nearly unconscious state, and the freezing Petersburg weather, Akaky's original enemy, finishes him off. Molestation and death are the price to be paid for attempting to authorize one's existence in the temporal world.

But literature need not be subject to that world if it chooses not to be. The "fantastic ending" of **"The Overcoat"** triumphantly asserts literature's independence from the repressive forces of reality and gleefully demonstrates its freedom to play with the realms of matter and spirit, life and death, to which it refers but by which it is not bound. The final section of Gogol's tale plunges the reader into a space that defies his habitual category distinctions. Akaky, who has "given up the ghost" (*dukh,* literally, "spirit"), returns, not in the bodiless form of a ghost, as Magarshack and most of the other translators have it, but as a corpse (*mertvets*). The police are told to catch this *chinovnik-mertvets* ("civilservant-corpse"; the hyphenated phrase furthers the ambiguity) "dead or alive and to punish him most severely as an example to others" (my revision of Magarshack's trans.). The fact that the reader begins to ask himself how the police might punish a live corpse is an indication of how mixed up things are becoming.

The confusion reaches a climax in the last paragraph. After Akaky's corpse has finally been laid to rest, a "real" ghost (*prividenie,* "apparition" as distinguished from *mertvets*) is sighted by a frail-bodied policeman who, we are informed, was once knocked over by an "ordinary, full-grown suckling pig rushing out of some private house" (my revision of Magarshack's trans.). Apart from the fact that "suckling" and "full-grown" are normally successive stages in the maturation process, the reader wonders what *any* live pig is doing in *any* private house. Then, climactically, he finds out that the ghost has an immense fist and huge mustachios and suddenly realizes that it is none other than Akaky's original assailant. This realization sparks off a whole series of inconclusive speculations: Was Akaky's "corpse" then "really" Akaky's aggressor? If so, how is it that both a departmental clerk and the VIP recognized Akaky? Does the VIP see Akaky's traits in those of his assailant only because of his personal sense of guilt? But the pervasive rumor throughout Petersburg is that it is a civil servant's corpse that is committing the thefts. Even if one grants that the ghost seen by the frail policeman was "really" the original thief of Akaky's overcoat, that ghost is not necessarily the same as the earlier "corpse" which, after all, we have been explicitly told has ceased to appear. Thus Leon Stilman's claim that "in 'actual fact' [the VIP] is robbed by the same man who robbed Akaky cannot be proved. The nonconclusion of the story denies any notion of factuality and leaves the reader afloat in a fluid world of shifting metamorphoses. The narrator at this point has dropped all pretense to authority, whether reliable or unreliable, and fused with the world he is describing. He is no longer ignorant or forgetful of it: the world is itself forgetful, mad, fantastic, discontinuous.

Thus the "fantastic direction" taken by the story in no way prevents it from being as "perfectly true" as Gogol claims it to be. For it is true to the essential nature of its medium. . . . As it doubles back upon itself, Gogol's narrative recovers its unique autogenerative powers and incorporates that law of reflection which, according to Andrey Biely, determines the musical orchestration of Gogolian prose.

Reabsorbed into literary freeplay after his foolhardy excursion into the material world, Akaky Akakyevich becomes the agent of what is aptly called "poetic justice." Thereby he fulfills Gogol's most deeply cherished fantasy: that he may revenge himself on reality while remaining inside literature; that he may exercise power while never becoming a definable, and hence vulnerable, presence in the world. Akaky as corpse is the presence of an absence. He operates within reality while remaining immune to its hostile force. And, once revenged, he disappears entirely within the polysemic shifts of the linguistic medium out of which he had, to begin with, only reluctantly and hesitantly emerged.

The reader, emerging with comparable reluctance from under the spell of **"The Overcoat,"** finds himself in a peculiar state of disequilibrium. He feels exhilarated by the sheer inventiveness of the verbal play he has witnessed but he also feels uneasy that the field of this play seems so remote from the real world, which once more surrounds him, and seems so irresponsible in its terms. In effect, from an existential standpoint this field is the playground of ontological insecurity. The effacement of an "original" self through the adoption of numerous masks and the creation of an autonomous world uncommitted to objective reality are, according to R. D. Laing, two of the characteristic strategies of the insecure, schizoid individual.

Akaky's story traces the loss and recovery of just such a self-enclosed world while displaying a discontinuous narrative style that repeatedly asserts its own autonomy. Gogol dramatizes his fantasy of becoming transcendent and omnipotent even as the constant slipping of the narrative persona from mask to mask ensures him this very unconditioned invulnerability. Thus, both as dramatic story and as narrative structure, **"The Overcoat"** functions for Gogol in much the same way as what Laing calls a "false-self system" functions for someone in a schizoid condition. The "false-self system," writes Laing, "exists as the complement of an 'inner' self which is occupied in maintaining its identity and freedom by being transcendent, unembodied, and thus never to be grasped, pinpointed, trapped, possessed. Its aim is to be a pure subject, without any objective existence." In literary terms, this purity corresponds most closely to the silent, unarticulated space prior to any beginning, to that space which, as Laing says of the overprotected inner self, "is endless possibility, capacity, intention." This is the inviolable subjective space inhabited, according to Gogol, by the "pure unspoiled soul" of the poet and within which he claimed to be building a palace and to be hiding the key to the secret subject of *Dead Souls.* As we have seen, the structure of literary free play served him to evoke this absence by making it the activating principle in a game of constant semantic displacements.

In psychological terms, however, such a pure, autonomous freedom is achieved at great expense, for, as Laing explains, "this shut-up self, being isolated, is unable to be enriched by outer experience, and so the whole inner world comes to be more and more impoverished, until the individual may come to feel he is merely a vacuum." This feeling arises above all when the owner of a false self is suddenly forced into confrontation with a hostile force that threatens to remove his artificial covering (or overcoat): "In so far as he feels empty, the full, substantial, living reality of others is an impingement which is always liable to get out of hand and become implosive, threatening to overwhelm and obliterate his self completely." In Akaky's case this threat is carried out. But then Gogol, having expressed through the account of the clerk's death his own worst fears of implosive destruction by the other, returns the story to a disembodied realm of fantasy where such fears dissolve into free play. "Without reference to the objective element," comments Laing, "[the self] can be all things to itself—it has unconditioned freedom, power, creativity."

Here perhaps we are getting to the real source of the reader's ambivalent response to the story's ending. He participates in the narrative's exuberant recapture of its freedom and omnipotence while simultaneously realizing that, to the extent he feels himself committed to "the objective element," that omnipotence must be viewed as impotence, as self-duplicity, as an irresponsible schizoid game. What is ontological insecurity from the point of view of being-in-this-world is liberating free play from the point of view of linguistic structure. Whereas Shakespeare ends his comedies by returning us to a world whose stability has been reaffirmed through the seemingly chaotic play of magical forces—think of a *A Midsummer Night's Dream*—Gogol ends his comic story by plunging his reader into the thick of metamorphic forces whose chaos remains unresolved. We feel ourselves to be inside a labyrinth of mirrors, some concave, some flat, some convex, unable to test the accuracy of the reflected images against any original reality. Despite the dynamic interplay of reflections, a silence surrounds us. Hence the fear, the bewilderment, and the anxiety. (pp. 56-60)

Charles C. Bernheimer, "Cloaking the Self: The Literary Space of Gogol's 'Overcoat,'" in PMLA, *Vol. 90, No. 1, January, 1975, pp. 53-61.*

ANTHONY HIPPISLEY (essay date 1976)

[*In the excerpt below, Hippisley discusses the spiritual significance of "The Overcoat" and its relationship to Gogol's personal life.*]

In his article about **"The Overcoat"** in this journal John Schillinger draws a parallel between Gogol''s story and *The Life of Saint Acacius of Sinai.* Schillinger concentrates chiefly on externals; he points out techniques of the hagiographical style that are evident in travestied form in **"The Overcoat"** and observes similarities in the lifestyles of the two central characters. Some interesting questions flow naturally from Schillinger's article: Did Gogol' mean to imitate the hagiography of Acacius, and if so, why? Does the pseudo-hagiographical form point to a content that has hitherto not been noticed? Although Schillinger discusses Akakij Akakievič in some detail, he hardly mentions the title-subject, the overcoat itself. It is the purpose of this article to suggest that **"The Overcoat"** has a spiritual meaning bearing closely on the author's own personal experience, that it symbolizes the sinner's pursuit of salvation represented by the coat itself. (p. 121)

The obvious streak of anxiety running through even the funniest works of Gogol' has been interpreted in various ways. [F. C.] Driessen sees it not so much in existentialist terms as something purely psychological (an unconscious Oedipus complex), just as Gogol's stomach ailments were psychosomatic (Driessen). But the most persuasive explanation of Gogol''s anxiety seems, especially in the case of **"The Overcoat,"** to be the religious one. **"The Overcoat"** was composed in the summer of 1840 in Vienna, during the sudden creative outburst between Gogol''s first stay in Rome (1836-39) and what Močul'skij refers to as the crisis of 1840, when Gogol' fell ill and was so convinced he was going to die that he took his recovery to be a miraculous sign that God had called him to a special mission. The first period in Rome, following the apparent failure of *The Inspector General* in 1836, was the happiest spell in Gogol''s life, though there has been disagreement as to whether this happiness should be classed as spiritual or worldly. Merežkovskij expounded the idea of a dualistic conflict raging in the heart and mind of Gogol' between the Christian principle and the pagan and argued that this first period in Rome represented the zenith of Gogol''s paganism, Roman Catholicism and carnal ancient Rome being polar to Eastern Orthodoxy and the spiritual life (Merežkovskij). V. Zeńkovskij, who also stressed the religious aspect of Gogol''s world outlook, pointed out that his religious beliefs were inextricably bound up with his concept of aesthetics, leading him to conclude that during that same first stay in Rome Gogol' attained his greatest *spiritual* tranquility. This tranquility was achieved largely through Gogol''s involvement with Roman Catholicism. He was deeply impressed by the quiet and reverent atmosphere inside the churches in Rome, by the beauty of the architecture and services, and he would frequently go there to pray and meditate. At this same time he made the acquaintance of Princess Zinaida Volkonskaja, a Russian convert to Catholicism, who with her circle of Polish Jesuit monks tried hard to convert him also. Although Gogol' seems to have acted disingenuously in falsely raising the princess's hopes, he was certainly at-

tracted by Catholicism, though not as an alternative to Orthodoxy, for, as he told his mother in a letter of December 1837, Orthodoxy and Catholicism are one and the same thing. This tranquility was shattered in 1839 by the lingering death of the young Count V'el'gorskij, the last close attachment Gogol' ever made. Watching his friend's life ebb away, Gogol' was brought face to face with the ineluctability of death and the horror of what lay beyond. When he himself lay ill the following year, what he experienced was "that same anguish, that horrible uneasiness that I had seen in poor V'el'gorskij during the last moments of his life" (Močul'skij). However perfect his spiritual equilibrium had been in Rome, it was quickly upset by this confrontation. Such a spiritual crisis must indeed have been traumatic, and consequently one might reasonably expect it to leave a trace upon **"The Overcoat,"** which was written just at that time. While not dismissing the idea that Gogol' might have been expressing in **"The Overcoat"** an existential predicament or a psychological *Angst* (not to mention a social protest), I suggest that a spiritual crisis is the real substance of the tale and that to express it the author drew upon the symbology of clothing with which he was familiar both through the Bible and through the Orthodox Liturgy.

Clothing is frequently used in the Bible to symbolize righteousness, beginning with the fig leaves of self-righteousness in which Adam and Eve presumed to stand before God in the garden of Eden, and ending with the saints in the book of Revelation who had "washed their robes, and made them white in the blood of the Lamb" (Rev. 7:14). More specifically, the Bible speaks of man's sinful state as dirty or worn-out clothing: "All our righteousnesses are as filthy rags" (Isa. 64:6); and of his need of restoration in terms of the need of a change of clothing: "I will greatly rejoice in the Lord, my soul shall be joyful in my God; for he hath clothed me with the garments of salvation, he hath covered me with the robe of righteousness" (Isa. 61:10). This verse from Isaiah is recited by the priest and deacon of the Eastern Orthodox Church as they put on their vestments in preparation for the Divine Liturgy. The vestments are worn in order to distinguish them not only from other men, but also from their own sinful selves. In his *Meditations on the Divine Liturgy* Gogol' displays sensitivity towards the symbolic meaning of these garments:

> The priest completes his vesting by putting on the chasuble (phelonion), the uppermost vestment, covering all the others and symbolizing the all-embracing justice of God, and says: "Let Thy priests be clothed with righteousness; and let Thy saints shout for joy, always, now and ever, and to the ages of ages. Amen" (Psalms 132:9). Thus invested with the divine instruments, the priest is now another man.

The parallel in **"The Overcoat"** is obvious, for Akakij Akakievič exchanges his filthy rags for a beautiful new coat and becomes a new man.

There are two important moments of truth in Akakij Akakievič's life: the realization of his need of greater protection against the cold and his decision in the tailor's shop to order a new coat. The first moment of truth comes on a day when the frost is particularly severe. The frost, "the mighty enemy of all people earning about four hundred rubles a month," symbolizes Satan, the enemy of mankind, who first brought about man's sinful condition. Gogol' says that the rich are scarcely affected by the frost because they are warmly clad. One might also say that the cloak of self-righteousness is thick enough to insulate the rich against an awareness of their sinful state. The titular councillors, however, are extremely vulnerable (note Gogol''s use of soteriological terminology): "The only salvation consists in running the five or six blocks as fast as possible in a threadbare little overcoat." But this is not true salvation, and Akakij Akakievič becomes painfully aware that his overcoat is not protecting him against the attacks of the enemy. "It occurred to him finally that there might be some defects [*grexi 'sins'*] in his overcoat," and on examining it he discovers it has become threadbare on the back and shoulders. One might wonder how it was he never before thought to look over his coat, until one recalls the symbolism: man is usually blind to his spiritual condition, only at certain moments of truth in his life does he catch a glimpse of himself as a sinner before God. Akakij Akakievič has reached this moment of truth and decides to take his coat to the tailor to have it mended.

This tailor has an unmistakable air of authority as he sits, "cross-legged like a Turkish pasha." His position relative to Akakij Akakievič recalls that of a priest, possibly even a pope, his name Petrovič suggesting the apostolic succession from St. Peter. In his papal capacity Petrovič makes devastating pronouncements *ex cathedra,* the *cathedra* upon which he sits being a "broad unpainted wooden table." The judgment pronounced by Petrovič on the coat—"No, it cannot be mended!"—strikes the same terror in the heart of Akakij Akakievič as does rejection by God in the soul of the sinner. Akakij Akakievič pleads with Petrovič to find some new pieces of cloth and sew them onto the coat where it is most worn, but Petrovič replies: "Well of course I can find pieces, pieces can always be found . . . but it is impossible to sew them on: the cloth is quite rotten. You would just have to touch it with a needle and it would fall apart." This is precisely the analogy that Jesus Christ used in order to explain the state of the sinner relative to God: "No man also seweth a piece of new cloth on an old garment: else the new piece that filled it up taketh away from the old, and the rent is made worse" (Mark 2:21). God will not mingle his righteousness with man's unrighteousness; indeed, contact between the consuming fire of God's righteousness and the unrighteousness of sinful man can only result in the destruction of the latter. To be acceptable before God, man must be adorned in the righteousness of Christ. This is the point Akakij Akakievič now reaches; it may be called his second moment of truth. The decision which confronts him is whether to keep his old coat and continue to try to survive, or whether to order a new coat and make whatever sacrifices might be required of him in order to obtain it. His decision to order a new coat may be compared to the sinner's decision to return to God and beg for forgiveness and salvation. When the Prodigal Son reached this moment of truth he said to himself: "I will arise and go to my father, and will say to him, Father, I have sinned," with the result that the father welcomed him with open arms and then gave this significant command to his servants: "Bring forth the best robe, and put it on him" (Luke 15:18,22). Schillinger points out that after this decision is made Akakij Akakievič's life undergoes a radical change, and that the overcoat "becomes for [him] an object of veneration worthy of great personal sacrifices" (Schillinger). This is not to be wondered at when one considers that the new overcoat symbolizes Christ himself.

The price quoted by Petrovič for the overcoat so dumbfounds Akakij Akakievič that he nearly faints. It makes the attainment of his goal almost impossibly remote. This has its parallel in both Roman Catholic and Eastern Orthodox (though not Protestant) theology, which sees salvation as a prize received not merely by faith, but also after much penance and many good works. It is this period of the protagonist's life, and not his downtrodden existence heretofore, as Schillinger says, that may be compared to the life of St. Acacius, for it is only after his decision to save up for a new coat that Akakij Akakievič becomes a "candidate" for salvation and begins his life of penance, becomes a monk, as it were. It is during this period that, although physically hungry, "he was nourished spiritually, constantly carrying about in his thoughts the idea of the future overcoat."

After unheard-of privations and sacrifices Akakij Akakievič has enough money and goes to fetch the coat on a day described by Gogol' as "the most solemn day in [his] life." It is solemn because it is the day of his salvation; he is about to put on the robe of righteousness, Jesus Christ. (pp. 122-25)

Several scholars have argued that the overcoat is one of those petty passions (*zador*) which bring ruin to Gogol''s characters, such as the gun in the story of the two Ivans. It is what Victor Erlich calls the homunculus's "overinvestment in trivia." This idea, expounded by Gippius, developed by Čiževskij, who sees such *zadory* as Satanic agents ("Zur Komposition von Gogol''s *Mantel* "), and reproduced by Vsevolod Setchkarev, fits some of Gogol''s works adequately, e.g., **"The Portrait"** and *Dead Souls.* The case of **"The Overcoat,"** however, is not so clear-cut. Čiževskij suggests that the devil employs Petrovič to ensnare Akakij Akakievič in the toils of materialism, represented by the new coat, and thus destroy him. But, as Driessen points out (*Gogol as a Short Story Writer*), it is not the coat or its purchase that brings about the protagonist's downfall, but rather its loss (quite the reverse of the acquisition of money by Čertkov and Čičikov's greed for dead souls). This does not mean that Čiževskij's interpretation is to be rejected, but that a modification might be suggested in the light of the clothing analogy. It is possible that Satan, the father of lies and master of counterfeit, has perpetrated a grand deception upon Akakij Akakievič, and that the overcoat is not what it appears to be. But the bait which Satan has thrown across his path (if, indeed, the whole thing is a diabolical trick) is not the temptation of materialism, i.e., an expensive coat, but the temptation of an illusory salvation. In other words, something that is still on the spiritual plane. Such a reading of the tale, with Scripture being quoted by the demon Petrovič in order to lead Akakij Akakievič into a hopeless pilgrimage towards a Christ who turns out to be a Satanic illusion, is consistent, for the clothing analogy still points to Christ and salvation. Čiževskij's interpretation (according to which the overcoat represents materialism), on the other hand, is not consistent. One does not, for example, become an ascetic in order to acquire material wealth. The question of whether the coat represents a true or an illusory salvation is neither easy to resolve nor in the long run very important, for either way Akakij Akakievič ends up unsaved and is forced to meet a wrathful God in the person of the general.

The relationship between this Important Personage and Petrovič was pointed out recently by R. A. Peace, who, pursuing the theory that Akakij Akakievič's inability to communicate verbally is related to the fact that he is at the mercy of other people's words (rather than their actions), drew a parallel between the way Petrovič delights in observing the effect of his own words on Akakij Akakievič and the similar way in which the general notes with pleasure that "his word was even able to render a person unconscious." We have already noted that Petrovič is invested with sacerdotal authority. It is interesting that as the tailor passes judgment on the coat Akakij Akakievič begins to lose consciousness and his eye becomes fixed on Petrovič's snuffbox, with its picture of a general. This general anticipates the Important Personage. The face of God is so "important" that no mortal eye may look upon it and live, which explains both why the face is missing on Petrovič's sacred image and why it is Akakij Akakievič's face-to-face encounter with the Important Personage, and not the mugging he had suffered earlier, which is the real cause of his death. While Petrovič's words dumbfounded Akakij Akakievič, the general's words literally annihilate him. He has lost his salvation, and the only possible consequence is to be destroyed by the consuming fire of God's righteous anger.

The sinner's ultimate encounter with an angry God, which Gogol' had dreaded since childhood, is played out here by Akakij Akakievič. The only thing that could have protected him was the robe of righteousness, and whether it was a genuine salvation or a Satanic delusion, it is gone. (pp. 126-27)

In the final section of **"The Overcoat"** Akakij Akakievič's ghost returns to wreak vengeance on his tormentors. Although there is no scriptural foundation for the belief that departed souls come back and haunt the living, Gogol' was particularly vulnerable to such ideas, as his earlier works testify. . . . Bearing in mind that the final section of the tale is part of its *Urstoff*—Gogol' originally conceived a story with the title "The Tale of the Civil Servant Who Stole the Overcoat"—we can see how in the final redaction it has been invested with a poignant spiritual meaning: the soul of Akakij Akakievič comes back to seek a salvation of which he has been robbed, or which perhaps he never possessed.

It should by now be clear both why Schillinger's analogy between Akakij Akakievič and Acacius is helpful, and also why it is misleading. It is helpful because it forces us to look at **"The Overcoat"** for its spiritual meaning, which is very rarely done nowadays. It is misleading, because it invites one to view Akakij Akakievič as a holy martyr who is persecuted during his earthly pilgrimage, but who receives his crown in the hereafter, an analogy that fails to take into account the meaning of the overcoat. An equally plausible parallel is at hand in Bunyan's Christian, who in chapter 3 of *The Pilgrim's Progress* reaches the cross and meets three Shining Ones, the first of whom tells him that his sins are forgiven, while the second "stripped him of his rags, and clothed him with a change of raiment." Gogol''s pilgrim gets little beyond this point, for a catastrophe of blasphemous enormity befalls him and his robe of righteousness is snatched away from him. No martyr's crown awaits the Gogolian Acacius; he is awaited by a horror of outer darkness. (pp. 127-28)

> *Anthony Hippisley, "Gogol's 'The Overcoat': A Further Interpretation," in* Slavic and East European Journal, *Vol. 20, No. 2, Summer, 1976, pp. 121-29.*

GARY COX (essay date 1980)

[*An American critic, Cox is the author of* Tyrant and Victim in Dostoevsky (1984). *In the following excerpt, he examines the conflict between urban and rural mores in the collection* Evenings on a Farm near Dikanka.]

One of the central themes of Gogol''s first collection of short stories, *Evenings on a Farm near Dikanka* (*Večera na xutore bliz Dikan'ki,* 1831-32), is the tension between urban and rural values. Country life is elaborately extolled by the homespun narrators, and implicitly ridiculed as the reader becomes aware of their stupidity. Citified narrators, who have left their rural roots behind, present opposing values, but fare little better in the reader's esteem. But the opposition is much deeper and more complex than the mere competition between the countrified raconteur Foma Grigorevič and the city writer Makar Nazarovič. An examination of the interconnecting systems of sociological, sexual, and stylistic contrast in the stories reveals that the opposition between urban and rural values is reflected on several levels. An opposition between immobility and dynamic motion is central to all of these systems of bipolar contrast.

The tension between static countryside and dynamic city is dramatized by the patterns of family structure and generation conflict. Rural life is represented by a closed family structure with strong, at times even indecently strong parent-child bonds. The dramatic conflict of many of these stories involves the young person's revolt against that family structure, against the tyrannical or even incestuous parent. This youthful rebellion is associated with several of the characteristics of city life and urban values as they are presented in these stories. The patterns of family conflict here reproduce in microcosm the tension between urban and rural value systems.

These contrasts have a parallel in the patterns of sexual imagery used in nature descriptions. Both narrators connect natural beauty with sexuality and death, but in very different ways. The urban narrator does so through explicit sexual imagery and a view of nature as motionless and dead. The rural narrators avoid explicit sexual images, but they display a fear of expanded vision, which may be seen as an expression of repressed sexuality, and they connect this panoramic vision with a primal infanticide which gives rise to family disorders such as incest. The dichotomy is reinforced by a stylistic contrast. The rural narrator is preoccupied with all types of sensuous imagery except the visual, and he conveys through this imagery a sense of repose. The urban narrator, on the other hand, relies heavily on visual imagery and uses it to convey a sense of dynamic, but fragmented and disruptive, motion.

These themes are resolved in the stories **"The Lost Letter"** (**"Propavšaja gramota"**) and **"The Bewitched Spot"** (**"Zakoldovannoe mesto"**), where the folk narrative tradition is discredited, and in **"Ivan Fedorovič Špon'ka and his Auntie"** (**"Ivan Fedorovič Špon'ka i ego tetuška"**), where the flight from the countryside, from the parent, and from sexuality is shown to be finally impossible.

Hugh McLean has given us a cogent and interesting interpretation of Gogol''s second collection of short stories, *Mirgorod.* This reading of the stories is based on psychoanalytic sexual theory, and McLean notes an interesting aspect of Gogol''s work: the more mature and satisfying the literary product, the less mature the forms of libidinal outreach depicted there. The early stories present youths struggling against parental oppression to achieve adult expression of the libido, culminating with *Taras Bul'ba* where these forms of expression are decisively punished. In the later works, generally of far greater literary value, the treatment of these themes suggests a less mature stage of development.

McLean does not find the earlier collection of stories, the

Dikan'ka cycle, particularly interesting, except as preludes to the Oedipal drama of **Taras Bul'ba.** He calls them "conventional . . . operetta love stories in which picturesque Ukrainian lads woo their pretty black-eyed lassies beneath a bright Ukrainian sky." "These local-color romances," says McLean, "seem too obviously derivative, too lacking in 'felt' experience to be regarded as revealing any basic psychological tendency on the author's part. They form a series of variations on the familiar fairy-tale pattern. . . ." McLean's attitude has much justification; derivative these stories certainly are. But even the derivative author must choose his model and arrange the details, and in doing so Gogol' reveals interesting psychological patterns, particularly with regard to family structure and generation conflict.

Leaving aside for the moment the narrative frame (including the prefaces and final stories in each volume), we have in the Dikan'ka cycle six stories with a remarkably similar cast of characters. In each story there is a pair of young lovers and one of two parent figures. The male parent is typically the heroine's father, and the female parent, if there is one, her stepmother, although there are significant variations on this pattern. The stepmothers are always domineering types who either are or resemble witches. This atmosphere of feminine domination culminates in the figure of Špon'ka's aunt.

The warmest relationships in these stories are between parents and children of the opposite sex. This close parental bond parallels the closed and circumscribed life of the rural village with its strong ancestral ties. Relationships between parents and children of the same sex, on the other hand, are always hostile in these stories. In **"Christmas Eve" ("Noč' pered roždestvom")** the bond between the young hero and his mother is paralleled by that of the heroine and her father. Here generation conflict is at a minimum for there are no filial bonds between parents and children of the same sex. The parents oppose the young lovers only because marriage between their children would make their own marriage plans (and the financial gains which would result) illegal. There are some *pro forma* fights between the blacksmith and his future stepfather/father-in-law, but all conflicts are resolved happily. The four-sided structure is composed of two filial pairs and overlapping them two romantic pairs. The possibilities of incest multiply, for the young bride and groom will become siblings if their parents marry, while the older bride and groom will become inlaws if their children do so. It is finally the young lovers who marry, but this four-sided incestuous structure suggests a sexual basis for family ties in the rural village.

The incestuous undercurrent in these stories comes dramatically to the surface in **"A Terrible Vengeance" ("Strašnaja mest'")**, but it is suggested humorously as early as **"The Fair at Sorocincy" ("Soročinskaja jarmarka")**. After the young hero has humiliated his future father-in-law, Čerevik, as a means of forcing approval of his marriage to his beloved daughter, we find the following exchange:

> Čerevik peeked in at the door at that moment and stopped, seeing his daughter dancing before the mirror. He watched for a long time. . . . But when he heard the familiar sounds of a song, his pulse stirred within him and . . . he began to dance, forgetting all his troubles. The matchmaker's loud laugh startled both of them: "Here's a fine thing, the father and daughter themselves have been getting up a wedding right here. Step lively, the bridegroom's here."

By itself the incestuous suggestion of this passage would be minimal, but in conjunction with the prevalence of the incest theme throughout these stories it is significant.

"A May Night, or The Drowned Maiden" ("Majskaja noč', ili Vtoplennica") presents interesting variations on these themes, exceptions which serve to prove the rule in certain ways. This is the only story in the entire collection in which the father figure is the hero's biological father rather than his future father-in-law. This is also the only story in which the close bond between father figure and young heroine is an actual flirtation.

The older man is also the town mayor, and in this capacity he exercises something like a *droit de seigneur* with the young girls of the town. . . . His dominion over the young men is sexual as well as political, and as a result, sexual competition and envy play an important role in their rebellion against him. One of them cries out as they begin their revels: "Aren't we from the same clan (*takogo rodu*) as he is?" and elsewhere the narrator remarks, "Which of the lads would not have liked to be the mayor?" The social rebellion of the lads is also an Oedipal rebellion against a sexually tyrannical father figure. The incestuous parent symbolizes the close ancestral ties of the rural community, but this is also the source of youthful rebellion, since it sets off an Oedipal hostility between same-sex parent figure and child. The dynamism of youthful rebellion is an attack on the static nature of village life, but it is also an attack on the incestuous bond, which is viewed as the core of rural equilibrium.

The Oedipal situation is echoed in the parallel story of the drowned maiden. Here an almost indecently warm father-daughter relationship is threatened by the father's impending remarriage:

> "Will you care for me as of old, papa, when you take another wife?"—"I will, my daughter, still more closely than before will I press you to my heart. I will, my daughter, still brighter will be the earrings and necklaces which I will give to you!"

The stepmother turns out to be a witch who drives the daughter from home and into a watery grave. It is the spirit of this drowned maiden that helps Levko, the hero, to overthrow his father, in return for his assistance in catching her witch-stepmother in her watery underworld. The drowned maiden is clearly a double for Ganna, the heroine, whose hostile mother is mentioned in the same paragraph in which the drowned maiden's wicked stepmother is described. This story contains two parallel incidents of the overthrow of parents by children, and in each case the cause of enmity is competition between same-sex parent and child, a classic Oedipal (or Electra) situation.

The interest in father-daughter incest becomes fully explicit in **"A Terrible Vengeance,"** where the rivalry between the young Cossack hero and his incestuous father-in-law, the old sorcerer, results in the hero's death fairly early in the story. The theme takes on certain cosmic or primeval overtones in this story, for the ancestral crime revealed in the closing pages is presented as the source of the magician's evil desire for his daughter. The murder of Ivan and his infant son by Petro (the sorcerer's ancestor) functions as an original sin which perverts family relationships in future ages. We would expect it to be the murder of a family member, then, of a father, perhaps, as in Dostoevskij's *The Brothers Karamazov* or Freud's *Totem and Taboo*. Instead, it is the murder of a sworn brother, not even a blood brother. That is, the murder of a close friend, almost of an alter ego, is at issue here. But although it does not involve the killing of one's own father, it does destroy a father-son pair, in fact, the only loving father-son pair in this collection of stories. Ivan and his infant son, riding along asleep before Petro throws them off the cliff, almost seem to represent the paternal counterpart to a madonna and child. It is as though the father-son relationship itself is attacked in this murder, through the icon representing it. Both members of the pair are killed; father and son are treated as a single unit, suggesting the identity of father and self in this attack, all the more since the father attacked is a sworn brother or alter ego. The primal crime in Gogol''s system of family relationships is an attack on fatherhood, friendship, and one's very self, and it results in sexual desire, known only in the perverted form of father-daughter incest. In the ensuing conflict between the young man and his bride's father, the parent is the temporal victor, but all are ultimately destroyed. As in *Taras Bul'ba,* the parent punishes the child for making the transition from adolescence to adulthood. And this punishment is one which is transmitted from generation to generation.

This closing scene of **"A Terrible Vengeance,"** giving the reason for the "vengeance," finds a parallel in the other child murder in the cycle, in the story **"St. John's Eve" ("Večer nakanune Ivana Kupala").** In this story the hero is prevented from marrying his sweetheart by her father, who does not think he is wealthy enough. The demon Basavrjuk offers the hero sufficient funds, with the condition that he murder his bride's little brother. Thus it is a potential brother-in-law that is killed, and the murder is a stepping-stone to marriage with the child's sister. As in **"A Terrible Vengeance,"** the murderer is named Petro, and perhaps equally revealing, he is called Petro the kinless. So a family disorder is both cause and result of this fraternal infanticide, as in **"A Terrible Vengeance."**

As suggested earlier, the tensions of family life parallel the tensions between rural and urban life in these stories. The close family bond between parent and child is echoed in the self-contained rural community with its strong ancestral allegiances. At times there is even a confusion of identity in this ancestral bond. . . . The homespun narrators reserve their strongest contempt for youthful rebellion against these ancestral ties in favor of urban learning, as in Rudyj Pan'ko's anecdote about the latinate noun endings of the returning schoolboy in Foma Grigorevič's tirade at the beginning of **"St. John's Eve."**

Youthful rebellion is allied in these stories with certain features of urban life, particularly with a carnival atmosphere, not unlike that described by Mixail Baxtin in his book on Dostoevskij and Menippean satire, in which the ordinary rules of human interaction are temporarily abrogated. The town of Soročincy is not much of an urban center, except by contrast with the even smaller Dikan'ka; certainly it is dwarfed by the metropolis of Mirgorod. But because of the fair there, it seems to hum with urban excitement. The trip to that fair is associated with the restless yearning of youth to escape the constraints of family and rural community life. . . . The carnival atmosphere of Soročincy provides a backdrop for the youthful rebellion which culminates in the union of the young lovers. A similar carnival atmosphere characterizes the youthful revels in both **"A May Night"** and **"Christmas Eve,"** where even the laws of physics seem to be temporarily abrogated. Just as the intimate family bond is allied with static rural life in these stories, so is the Oedipal rebellion of youth associated with the dynamism of urban life.

The contrast between urban and rural life is underscored by the narrative structure of the collection. It is set up as a storytelling contest between a sophisticated urban writer who has left the rural community, and a homespun local raconteur. Both have absolute contempt for each other, and this hostility is dramatized in Rudyj Pan'ko's prefaces and in the introductions to the stories of Foma Grigorevič, the homespun narrator. The contrast between them is one of literary style: Foma Grigorevič's style is conversational and colloquial, while that of Makar Nazarovič, the city slicker, is more formally literary.

But the contrast is also expressed in their different ways of viewing the world, and particularly in the different sorts of imagery they use in nature descriptions. Both depict the same type of motionless panorama, punctuated by terrifying sound, and for both it is an occasion for terror. But for the sophisticated narrator it is explicitly linked with sex and death, while the folk narrators connect it with the danger of expanded vision and use it as the background for the primal crime which gives rise to family disorder. Each narrator fears what the other represents; the urban narrator fears the stagnation and sexuality he sees in the countryside, while the rural narrator fears the broadened scope which threatens the ancestral, rural way of life.

Many critics have commented upon the use of sexual imagery in certain nature descriptions in the Dikan'ka stories, yet it is particularly interesting in this context that this is characteristic only of the stories of Makar Nazarovič, the city narrator. The view of the countryside as sexual and dead reflects an urban mentality for Gogol'. . . . Not only is nature seen in sexual terms, but it is pictured as sleeping or even dead. The occasional sounds which interrupt the stillness only punctuate and highlight the sense of repose. This combination of sexual imagery and stillness is characteristic of nature descriptions throughout Makar Nazarovič's two stories; he views nature as static and sexual. The urban narrator's view of nature as static and sexual coincides with the picture of rural life which has been abstracted from the kinship structures in these stories.

Another interesting feature of static nature for urban narrators in Gogol''s works is that they are capable of inspiring terror. There is an element of awe in the descriptions of deathlike nature in Makar Nazarovič's stories, but in the later story **"Old World Landowners" ("Starosvetskie Pomeščiki"),** where the narrator is again an urban writer returning to his rural haunts, this awe turns to terror. Here the sexual imagery is absent, but the scene is the same: deathlike and beautiful stillness, punctuated by occasional sounds, which here are terrifying. . . . Lack of motion implies death for Gogol''s urban narrator, and the combination of sexuality and immobility he sees in a country setting terrifies him.

The folk narrators handle such natural scenes quite differently. The narrator of **"A Terrible Vengeance"** does not share the conversational style of the village narrators, but he is linked with them by his glorification of Cossack life. Here is the beginning of his famous description of the Dniepr:

> Marvelous is the Dniepr in quiet weather, when its massive waters move freely and smoothly through forests and mountains. It makes no ripple, no sound. You look and cannot tell whether its majes-

tic expanse is moving or not. And it seems
(*čuditsja*) to be made of molten glass, as though a
blue road made of mirror, measureless in width,
endless in length, were winding and twisting
through the green world.

Again nature is depicted as sleeping and motionless. Explicit
sexual imagery is absent; the closest thing to it is the narcissistic forest's admiration of its reflected image in the glassy
water, a far cry from the voluptuous embraces of earth and
sky described by Makar Nazarovič. But a new element is
added, the danger of seeing too much. . . . The view of the
Dniepr is panoramic, but this expanded vision is frightening
to the narrator. This detail may be viewed from a Freudian
vantage point as an indication of repressed sexuality. The sexual aspect of the natural scene, so vividly described by the
urban narrator, is repressed by the rural one, and the phobic
attitude toward expanded vision is the product of this repression.

But the rural narrator also fears expanded vision since it
threatens to undermine the family ties so basic to the self-
enclosed rural community. When he describes, almost as an
afterthought, a storm on the Dniepr, the scene reminds him
of the separation of mother and son: "The watery hillocks
rumble, striking against the mountains, and run back again,
flickering and moaning, and they weep and pour into the distance. Thus might lament an old mother of a Cossack when
she sees her son off into the army." The image seems ill-
chosen at first, but actually it fits in perfectly with the system
of imagery found in these stories. A terrifying scene in nature
reminds the rural narrator of something equally terrifying, the
dissolution of the family ties which form the basis of rural
life, and particularly the breakup of the bond between parent
and child of the opposite sex.

A few pages later this narrator's terror of expanded vision is
realized as the story reaches its conclusion:

> Outside of Kiev an unheard-of wonder ap-
> peared . . . suddenly the distant ends of the earth
> became visible in all directions. The Dniepr estuary
> shone blue in the distance and beyond it flowed the
> Black Sea. Experienced travellers recognized the
> Crimea as well, jutting like a mountain out of the
> sea, and the swampy Sivaš. On the left the land of
> Galicia was visible.

Once again the panorama is linked with the dissolution of
family ties, for this panorama is the backdrop for the punishment of the sorcerer, the incestuous father of the heroine. The
terrifying stillness of the mountains is punctuated by the
more terrifying sound of the avenging horseman's laugh. The
work closes with the story of the infanticide which gave rise
to all of these family disorders. It is narrated by the blind
troubador, the apotheosis of the folk narrator. Here again the
act takes place high in the mountains, giving a sense of expanded, panoramic vision.

The other scene of child murder in these stories is also told
by a folk narrator—Foma Grigorevič in **"St. John's Eve"**—
and the same kind of sensuous imagery pervades the scene.
Panoramic vision and stillness are punctuated by intermittent, terrifying sounds: "But suddenly lightning flashed in the
sky, and a whole bank of flowers appeared before him. . . .
All became silent. Basavrjuk appeared, sitting on a tree
stump, blue as a corpse. Not a rustle all around. Ukh,
terrible. . . . But suddenly a whistle was heard, which made
Petro's blood run cold. . . ." The stillness of the natural

panorama, interrupted by occasional sounds, inspires terror
in both urban and rural narrators, but its meaning is different
for each. The citified writer connects the natural scene with
the sexuality and stagnation which alienate him from village
life, while the country storyteller fears panoramic vision since
it exposes the primal murder which underlies ancestral and
familial bonds, and thus threatens those bonds.

These patterns are further reinforced by the contrasting use
of sensuous imagery by these opposing narrators. The rural
narrators, fearing expanded vision, avoid visual imagery.
Makar Nazarovič, by contrast, relies on visual imagery to
represent the dynamism of the urban environment. Rudyj
Pan'ko, the country bumpkin who narrates the prefaces, uses
images relating to all of the senses except vision in his description of rural gatherings: " . . . the spindles hum, the songs
pour forth, and none of the women turns her eyes from her
work. But as soon as the fellows burst into the hut with a fiddle, the merry shouts are raised. . . . " He is particularly
glowing in his description of gustatory pleasures. It should
be remembered that the pleasures of eating are again connected with the quiet country life in **"Old World Landowners."**
Foma Grigorevič, on the other hand, is particularly fond of
auditory imagery, and especially the sounds of storytelling:
"The spindle hummed and we children gathered into a little
group and listened to grandfather who hadn't crawled off his
stove for more than five years because of his old age". Note
the connection between grandfather's customary repose and
his embodiment of rural literary values. . . . The folk narrators seem to connect all kinds of sensuous imagery with the
sedentary comforts of rural life. But they avoid visual imagery and particularly dread expanded vision, as though any
kind of broader vision posed a threat to the closed and circumscribed life of the village.

Makar Nazarovič, by contrast, uses both auditory and visual
imagery to convey the hustle and bustle of the city-like
fair. . . . The impression is one of fragmentation and confusion, quite unlike the comfortable wholeness of village life in
the narrations of Foma Grigorevič or Rudyj Pan'ko. The dynamism of urban life threatens to dissolve social cohesion,
just as the static nature of rural life can be suffocating.

Not only does Makar Nazarovič use visual imagery; it is important for him as a narrative device. His stories do not seem
to be orally presented as do those of Foma Grigorevič,
but seem to be passing visually before our eyes. Witness
the remarks " . . . one needed only to lift one's eyes a
bit higher to see the reason for this obsequiousness. . . ."
and "The Psel river began to be visible to the eyes of our travellers . . .". The visual metaphor is as important for the
urban narrator as it is frightening for the rural ones. This
presages the direction Gogol''s prose was to take later in his
urban stories. It results in an impression of social life as dynamic but fragmentary, and of nature as voluptuously static.

These geographical, sociological, and sexual tensions are thematically resolved in the two brief tales about Foma
Grigorevič's grandfather, where the rural tradition is exposed
to ridicule, and in the story of Špon'ka and his aunt, where
the idea of escape from parental bonds is depicted as futile.
The two stories about Foma's grandfather close the two volumes of the collection, and by this time, Foma has succeeded
in establishing a tone of warm respect for this ancestor as the
founder of the narrative tradition he himself represents, even
though the reader may have some doubts about Foma
Grigorevič's credibility. In fact, that ancestral narrative tra-

dition is part of the generational continuity which characterizes the rural community, and which is the object of the rebellion of the younger characters.

These two stories, **"The Lost Letter"** and **"The Bewitched Spot"** irrevocably puncture our admiration for Foma's grandfather, and as such they end the collection of stories with a sense of a break in the continuity of generations. The first of these stories only hints at this. Up to this point, storytelling has been linked with the cozy warmth of the village and with extreme sensuous pleasure. In **"The Lost Letter"** we meet a Zaporozhian Cossack who tells stories frenetically, even desperately, and his narrative art is distinctly connected with the possibility of demon possession:

> A frightful gift of gab seized our Zaporozhian. Grandfather wondered whether perhaps a demon had possessed him. Where did he get it all? He told anecdotes and stories of such wild goings on that several times my grandfather held his sides and nearly split from laughing. But the further they went into the field, the darker it became, and at the same time the chatter of the young gallant became more disconnected. At last our narrator fell silent and shuddered at the slightest rustle.

This is not the first suggestion of a connection between folk narrative art and the demonic world. At the beginning of **"St. John's Eve,"** the narrator attributes quasi-magical powers to his grandfather's stories.

Grandfather's assault on the underworld in this story is only partly victorious, and one of its long term results is an annually recurring spell in which his wife dances uncontrollably: "No matter what she set out to do, her legs had a mind of their own and something would force her to dance." The theme of involuntary dancing is encountered again in the last story about Foma's grandfather, **"The Bewitched Spot."** That story begins with Foma's complaint about the constant demand for his stories: "My Lord, I've had my fill of storytelling by now. So what do you think? Honestly, it gets boring—you tell stories and more stories and then there's no getting out of it!" When the master storyteller tires of his craft, it is clear that something has gone amiss in the ancestral narrative tradition. This is followed by a scene in which grandfather alternately dances against his will and is unable to dance when he wishes to: "I noticed that his legs wouldn't stay still in one place; it was as though something were tugging at them. . . . As soon as he got to the middle of the dance and wanted to do some fancy steps . . . his feet just wouldn't move and that was all there was to it." As an artistic activity the dancing is parallel to his storytelling, and his inability to control his art signifies the downfall of the ancestral artistic tradition. It is significant that his problem involves an inability to move or to control his motion. It is as though the static nature of life in the rural village finally paralyzes even the folk artist who was its best representative.

Convinced that demonic powers are to blame, grandfather decides that the spot on which he was trying to dance is bewitched, and that a treasure is buried beneath it. He digs for the treasure (an activity which was associated with demon possession in Foma Grigorevič's earlier story **"St. John's Eve"**) and finds instead a bucket of garbage. We last see him, covered with garbage, and looking utterly ridiculous. The tradition of folk narrative art has been discredited and paralyzed.

Makar Nazarovič also uses the theme of involuntary, robot-like dancing at the end of **"The Fair at Soročincy,"** and here also the image has ominous overtones. The fair is ending and the people are going home when a musician brings them a moment of unity, but it is a unity achieved only through dehumanization. . . . The urban dynamism of the carnival appeared as a disruptive force in Makar Nazarovič's story, producing images of a fragmented society. Here a moment of harmony is achieved, but the characters lose their individuality and will. Collective nouns and neuter pronouns and verbs are used repeatedly to describe the group as a whole. There are no individuals here. And the actions of the group are involuntary, puppet-like, dehumanized.

In these passages, then, both poles of the dichotomy between rural and urban values are rejected, even by the narrators who represent them. It is Foma Grigorevič's own picture of his grandfather, in **"The Lost Letter"** and **"The Bewitched Spot,"** that finally discredits the folk narrative tradition. And Makar Nazarovič's pictures of urban dehumanization make city life an unappealing alternative.

But the most vivid images of the futile attempt to break out of the stagnation produced by rural life and parental bonds are presented in the story **"Ivan Fedorovic Špon'ka and his Auntie."** The narrator of this story, Stepan Kuročka, is not closely allied with either the rural or the urban narrators. He hails from the neighboring hamlet of Gadjač, but his more or less formal literary style links him with the urban group. His name, which suggests "chicken," dehumanizes him, as does Rudyj Pan'ko's simile comparing him to a windmill.

As the story opens the hero, Špon'ka, has no trouble breaking parental ties and establishing himself in the outside world, although his arena of activity is absurdly circumscribed there, and his rank in that arena quite low. But then a stronger parent figure comes on the scene, Špon'ka's unisexual auntie, and the ties of home and family life prove to be stronger than ever. Here there are no incestuous overtones to the parent-child relationship, hence no conflict between parent and prospective spouse. But the parental stranglehold becomes all the stronger as a result. The spouse is selected by the parent and the marriage is presented as an obligation to the parent. Thus the spouse becomes a proxy of the domineering parent and the marriage an extension of her dominion.

This supposition is reinforced by a glance at Špon'ka's nightmare with an eye toward the distinction between motion and immobility, so crucial to the tension between village and city in these stories. At first Špon'ka is surrounded by noise and motion, and he himself is in motion. . . . But then he is caught by his wife and imagines (*predstavljalos' emu*) that he is already married. Even the verbal root here (*stav*) suggests immobility. In the section which follows, most of the verbs referring to the wife are present tense verbs of stationary position (*sidit* 'she sits,' *stoit* 'she stands') or elided verbs of being. The phrases referring to Špon'ka all suggest frustrated motion ("he turns to the side," "he rushed to run into the garden," "he hopped on one leg"). Finally all of the participants of the dream are dehumanized, turning into bell towers, bells, geese and quantities of cloth. The quagmire of sexuality produced by rural life and parental control is finally seen as being just as dehumanizing as the fragmentation produced by the urban dynamism in these stories.

Both poles of the dichotomy are implicitly rejected, even by the narrators who represent them. The tradition of folk narration with its perversely strong family ties, its emphasis on cozy sensuous pleasures, and its fears of expanded vision which might lead beyond the closed rural community, is finally made to appear ridiculous. On the other hand, the youthful rebellion against rural family ties and social bonds leads to a view of nature as static and sexual and a view of urban life as fragmented and dehumanizing. Finally, in the Špon'ka story, the attempt to escape the parental stranglehold is depicted as futile. Marriage appears as a trap designed by the parent figure to preserve her domination. (pp. 219-31)

> *Gary Cox, "Geographic, Sociological, and Sexual Tension in Gogol's Dikan'ka Stories," in* Slavic and East European Journal, *Vol. 24, No. 3, Fall, 1980, pp. 219-32.*

RICHARD PEACE (essay date 1981)

[*In the following excerpt, Peace provides in-depth analyses of "The Diary of a Madman," "The Nose," and "The Overcoat."*]

In the figures of Piskarev and Chartkov in **"Nevsky Prospekt"** and **"The Portrait"** madness is presented as the outcome for an artist unable to realise his true ideal. Gogol's title for his story devoted to insanity itself had originally been 'Notes of a mad musician', but for this 'artistic' figure, he ultimately substituted a madman whose life depended on writing: a minor civil servant.

"The Diary of a Madman" is Gogol's one work of sustained first-person narration: its hero is the only character whom the author 'gets inside'. In **"The Portrait"** Gogol warns of the boundaries the artist crosses at his peril, but in portraying Poprishchin he himself has crossed the line separating imagination from inner reality; has stirred up the 'black sediment'. He himself has taken the 'anatomist's knife' and, for the first and only time, has opened up the inner man to reveal *otvratitel' nyy chelovek:* 'man in all his horror'.

This self-revelation of increasing madness is skilfully and convincingly handled, yet, for all the tragic seriousness of the theme, it bears the recognisable Gogolian stamp of 'laughter through tears'. Laughter, which treats madness as comic, is not that of a modern sensibility, but its cruelty is redeemed by pathos which is implicit throughout, and which rises to a poignant climax in the justly famous ending. Here the Gogolian formula is seen at its most striking. The sudden descent from the high note of genuine pathos to the grotesque inconsequentiality of: 'And do you know that the King of France has a lump right under his nose?' is not 'laughter' which mocks the preceding 'tears', it is rather a sudden tension projected on to the mood of pathos, which heightens and sharpens its impact.

The story is usually translated as the "diary" of a madman, but more accurately it should be 'notes' (*zapiski*). The fact that it purports to be a written self-revelation is important, since the concept of writing is central to the whole work. Poprishchin's madness is a crisis of identity, which reaches its climax in the delusion that he is the King of Spain, but the origin of his malaise lies in his sense of insecurity within the civil service hierarchy. He is a titular counsellor, a rank of ambiguous distinction, since it conferred the all important status of 'noble' (*blagorodnyy*) on the holder but not on his descendants (this could only be achieved through promotion to the next rank of collegiate assessor). In real terms Poprish-

chin's status depends on his ability to write: he is 'noble' by virtue of his job as a copy clerk. More than once he himself points to the connection. Thus, in a moment of apparent lucidity at the opening, he writes: 'Yes, I admit, if it were not for the nobility of the service, I would long ago have left the department'. And later in his reaction to the hallucination of reading the letters of a dog: 'May I never receive a salary: I have never in all my life heard that dogs could write. Only a nobleman can write correctly'.

Nevertheless, it is precisely his own ability to write correctly which is called in question; at the very outset he quotes the criticism to which he is subjected by the head of his section: 'Why, my lad, is there always such a jumble in your head? Sometimes you run around like a madcap and at times you so muddle up your work that Satan himself would not be able to make it out. You put a small letter in a title, and you don't put down either a date or a reference number'. It seems likely that it is because of these shortcomings that he is often assigned to the more humble task of sharpening pens for the director.

Poprishchin seeks to counter his feelings of insecurity at work (so intimately connected with status) by one of Gogol's favourite devices–inversion: his menial task in the director's office is a mark of special favour; the criticisms of the head of section are occasioned not by dissatisfaction but by envy; civil servants, as noble and dashing fellows, are not a whit the inferior of any officer. His negative fears have all been turned into positive attributes and as his madness progresses inversion achieves its most glaring form: consciousness of himself as a complete nonentity becomes the conviction that he is the King of Spain.

Poprishchin's feelings of insecurity are clearly discernible in his opening entry. Not only is the criticism of his incompetence on his mind, it seems borne out in fact: he is late for the office and claims that he would not be going there at all were it not that he wanted an advance on his salary (later he admits that he knows these hopes to be vain). His confusion seems to be mirrored in his description of a 'brother' civil servant who precedes him along the street (the only other man of 'noble' status there). Poprishchin first describes him as 'trudging along', but immediately reinterprets his progress as 'hurrying', yet not to the office (like himself) but rather on some amorous pursuit. His speculation on the dashing way that civil servants, like himself, have with women is suddenly interrupted by an unexpected encounter with Sophie, the director's daughter, with whom he is secretly in love. In alarm he shrinks into the background, and his behaviour thus gives the lie to the brave words which have gone before.

Sophie sweeps into a shop without noticing him, and her lapdog, Madgie, is also left unnoticed on the pavement. Therefore another and different parallel for Poprishchin's behaviour may also be drawn, and it is at this point that the reader first becomes aware that all is not well. Poprishchin claims that Madgie is addressed by another dog, significantly called Fidèle, who reproaches her for a breakdown in their relationship. This, though patently absurd, is nevertheless explicable in psychological terms; for just as Poprishchin had earlier projected his own desire for self-assertion on to the civil servant in the street, he now projects a re-awakened sense of his own inferiority on to the dogs: the 'faithful' dog reproaches the dog of his mistress with Poprishchin's own failure: that of communication. Such a substitution is not only a re-interpretation of a real situation, it also serves as a shield against it. When Poprishchin a second time resorts to its protection, this communication between dogs, significantly, takes the form of writing.

Working at close quarters with the director and seeing his daughter, Poprishchin is in the tantalising situation of being with them, but not of them. So deprived of any real entrée into their lives and thoughts, he finds it through the hallucination of discovering letters from Sophie's lap-dog to the dog Fidèle. From the condescending tone it is obvious that these missives are addressed to a social inferior, thus the gulf between Poprishchin and his masters, though bridged, is still maintained. The correspondence also puts the critic of his own writing skills in his place: 'The letter is written very correctly. The punctuation and even the letter *yat'* is everywhere in its proper place. Yes, even our head of section simply cannot write like this, even though he makes out that he has studied somewhere or other at a university'. The dog's letters are an hallucinatory device, the underlying purpose of which is to cope with the unpalatable truth of his own situation in the household, and the rumours of Sophie's impending marriage. They are a means of filtering reality, slowly and indirectly, into a consciousness, which is far too vulnerable.

The letters begin well, but every time they touch on the all important subject of Sophie, Poprishchin, as a reader, imposes his own veto: 'silence!' It is scarcely surprising that he finds them less and less satisfactory. Yet, significantly, a failure at the level of content he interprets as deficiency of form: 'An exceedingly uneven style. It is immediately obvious that they were not written by a man. It begins as it should, but ends in a doggy-fashion'. The next letter he criticises for one of his own clerical shortcomings: it does not bear a date. It is this letter which broaches the central problem of Sophie's intended marriage and the reality of his own position, but it does so in terms of the dogs who are Madgie's suitors. One is an exceedingly coarse mongrel; the other is the greatly admired Trésor, whose name is a phonetic echo of Teplov–the suitor of Sophie herself. Having moved one step nearer the truth, Poprishchin is pained, yet at the same time frustrated: 'Pah! Devil take it, what rubbish! How can one fill letters with such stupidities? Give me a human being! I want to see a human being. I demand food, such as will nourish and content my soul. But instead of that, what trifles!' Poprishchin's plea for human, rather than canine, protagonists is granted in the next letter, but their intrusion is hardly food 'to nourish and content the soul'.

This next letter tells him what he must have known all along: Sophie is to marry Teplov, a gentleman of the royal bedchamber: Poprishchin, she regards merely as a clumsy, comic figure, who performs the function of a servant in her father's study. These two views of himself Poprishchin had already unwittingly recorded in his entry of 4 October, where he comments that Sophie had almost smirked as he picked up her handkerchief, and where he reveals his annoyance that the servants treat him in a familiar way, as though they are on equal terms with a 'nobleman'. Nor could the attentions of a highly-placed suitor have escaped the notice of one who watched Sophie's movements so assiduously. The letters have failed in helping him come to terms indirectly with the facts. Writing, originally seen as putting the head of section in his place, is now seen, after all, as having been inspired by him: 'As though I don't know whose tricks these are. These are the tricks of the head of the section. After all the man has sworn

implacable hatred, and here he is causing harm, causing harm, at every step causing harm'.

The next stage in the development of Poprishchin's madness marks his ultimate retreat from reality. The inescapable fact of Sophie's impending marriage to the gentleman of the bedchamber causes him to question the very nature of rank and what it means to be a titular counsellor. On the other hand the very 'nobility', which the rank of titular counsellor obviously confers, must somehow be a pledge of something greater:

> Perhaps I am some count or other, or a general, and only just seem to be a titular counsellor. Perhaps I myself do not know who I am. After all, how many examples are there, according to history: some simple fellow, nothing like a nobleman, but simply some petty tradesman or other, or even a peasant–and suddenly it is revealed that he is some kind of bigwig, and sometimes even a sovereign. If such a thing can sometimes become of a peasant, what then can become of a nobleman?

Poprishchin's crisis of identity is here at its most acute, and its solution is no less extreme: he claims a rank which enables him to look down on all those whom he considers to have injured him, Sophie included: he is none other than the missing King of Spain. Yet his megalomania is merely a refurbishing of his status as copy-clerk-titular-counsellor ('if such a thing can sometimes become of a peasant, what then can become of a nobleman') so he cuts up a new uniform to make his regal robes, and his shortcomings as a scribe are now boldly blazoned forth at the head of each new entry in the 'diary', in the form of fantastically jumbled dates. His belief that he is king of Spain, for example, starts on a day in the doubly chiliastic year 2000. The month, suffering from similar pretensions to grandeur, is recorded as 'April 43rd'. The confusion of dates grows ever more absurd until with the final entry it reaches its apogee of inversion and distortion. His muddling is no longer evidence of mere incompetence, it is the mark of ever-increasing insanity.

In the office, when he is given a document to sign, Poprishchin now puts the signature 'Ferdinand VIII' in the place reserved for the director, and the kingdom of Spain itself may be interpreted as the realm of scribal madness: 'I advise everybody purposely to write down Spain on paper, and China will come out'. Jumbling the letters of *Ispaniya* (Spain) does not produce *Kitay* (China) but it could result in *pisaniya*–the act of writing itself, that very activity on which his true status is based: a nobility which his own muddling had seemed to place in jeopardy. By a simple inversion of letters, scribal faults have turned 'writing' into 'Spain' and a 'nobleman writer' into its 'king'. A related discovery is that every cockerel has its Spain and that this is situated under its pens.

Both the form and the progress of Poprishchin's madness clearly indicate its origin as a crisis of identity and of status. His very name suggests 'career' (i.e. *poprishche* = 'career', 'arena of activity') but although he claims that he can gain promotion through service, and that he is capable of becoming a colonel, his incompetence as a copy clerk suggests quite the reverse. The gulf between his name and his actual position is borne in on him through the dog's letters: 'His surname is exceedingly strange. He always sits and sharpens pens. . . . Papa always sends him on errands instead of the servants'.

On the other hand, many commentators see the root of Poprishchin's problems to be sexual. The erotic is undoubtedly an element in the story, nevertheless sexual anxiety is mixed with the more dominant concern about his social status. Thus Poprishchin is almost equally fascinated by the father as by Sophie herself; he is attracted by the power and prestige which she represents as the daughter of a general. Thus the embarrassment he feels, when alone with her in the same room, is not only sexual, it is excruciatingly social: ' "Your excellency", I almost wanted to say, "will you not order my execution, and if you want to execute me, then execute me with your little general's hand" '. When, shortly afterwards, she drops her handkerchief, he rushes to pick it up, but the fragrance it exudes is not sexual allurement, it is the attraction of status: 'Fragrance, absolute fragrance. It so smelled of general'.

There are moments which are more openly erotic. Thus he thinks of her in her boudoir, having just risen from bed and putting on white stockings. Nevertheless, later, in his madness, when he does gain access to this forbidden boudoir, his designs are not explicitly erotic, he merely seeks to confront her with his new regal status.

The curious thing about Gogol's one attempt to go beyond the boundaries and penetrate the 'inner man' is that the world he discovers is just as absurd as the fantastic reality of appearance and surface which he describes in **"Nevsky Prospekt"**: madness, it seems, is the outer world's lack of harmony transferred to the inner realm. The anatomist's knife in revealing 'man in all his horror', strangely enough, has shown the reader nothing new; for the phenomena of Poprishchin's inner world are reminiscent of that bizarre kaleidoscope of objects which Gogol elsewhere seeks to present as outward reality. Poprishchin's inner self is compounded of random external phenomena–a civil servant in the street; encounters with dogs and their letters; events in Spain. In Gogol the external world is always to some degree 'psychological'. This is obviously true *a fortiori* when that outer world has become the inner one, and on the one occasion when it clearly has done so, the condition is identified as madness. In the next story **"The Nose"** such madness will be placed back again in the external world itself.

> Major Kovalev had the habit of strolling every day along the Nevsky Prospekt. The collar of his shirt front was always extremely clean and starched. His side whiskers were of the sort that one can see even now on provincial and Ukrainian regional land surveyors, architects and regimental doctors, as well as those performing various police duties, and in general on all those men, who have full ruddy cheeks, and play boston whist very well. These whiskers go along the very middle of the cheek and stretch right up to the nose.

Thus major Kovalev [in **"The Nose"**] appears to be one of the 'thousand unfathomable characters' of the Nevsky Prospekt. His chief attributes are a shirt front and masculine appendages which not only mark his social status (in the pseudo-sociological manner, reminiscent of **"Nevsky Prospekt"** itself) but ominously 'stretch right up to the nose', an organ which is, in fact, the focus of Kovalev's anxiety about status; for in the course of the story it will leave his face and assume the guise of a civil servant of higher rank than he is himself. This fact alone is sufficient to suggest that the fantastic occurrences which befall Kovalev are similar in origin to those which afflict the hero of the **"Diary of a Madman"**. Indeed the opening of each story is almost identical, but in **"The Nose"**, Gogol has taken his treatment of psychology in terms of the fantastic a stage further; for although the fantastic happenings which Poprishchin records in his 'diary' can all be explained by the hero's madness, there is no attempt in **'The Nose'** to provide any logical handle by which the reader might grasp the story's absurdity.

Nevertheless, Kovalev's search for an explanation of his plight recalls Poprishchin; initially both wonder whether they are drunk, though, significantly, Kovalev links his drunkenness to shaving: 'Perhaps somehow or other by mistake, instead of water, I drank the vodka, with which I rub my beard after shaving'. Kovalev's other 'explanation' is to think that he is dreaming. This too is dismissed, but in the original manuscript version everything had been explained as a dream. Gogol removed this logical resolution when he sent the story to Pushkin's *Contemporary* (possibly because Bulgarin had criticised Pushkin's own story, 'The Undertaker', for a similar dénouement). The effect in the original version is certainly weak: 'but everything that is described here was seen by the major in a dream'. Moreover it is unconvincing, since even in this version the 'dream' is recounted by a narrator who knows about the reality of Kovalev's life: his earlier career; his daily walks along the Nevsky Prospekt; his future hopes. Nevertheless, as Janko Lavrin has pointed out, the very title *Nos* (Nose) is merely the Russian word for 'dream' written backwards, and this observation suggests the story as a literary joke, though at the same time it recalls the inversion of words associated with Poprishchin's madness. Whatever may have been Gogol's reason for eliminating overt explanation as a dream, the story certainly gains from being uncompromising in its absurdity.

The author himself is puzzled by his own story. He seems to be in a position similar to that of the postmaster in *Dead Souls* when he has narrated the incredible story of Captain Kopeykin. It is only after the story has been told, that he appears to realise just how absurd it really is: 'Now, after taking the whole of it into consideration, do we see that it contains much that is improbable'. Then, pretending to discuss the various absurdities in his tale, Gogol mockingly points to the strangest thing of all:

> But what is the strangest, what is the most incomprehensible of all is how it is that authors can take such things as subjects. I admit it is completely incomprehensible, it is just . . . no, no, I don't understand it at all. In the first place there is absolutely no advantage to the fatherland, and in the second place . . . but in the second place there is again absolutely no advantage. I simply don't know what it . . .

Thus the absurdity of the story is thrown back at the reader as something which defeats even the author himself, and he, disclaiming his story in this fashion, is in effect perpetrating a joke against the reader. **"The Nose"** is the Gogolian equivalent of the 'shaggy dog story': the joke is not for the reader but against him. To this extent the term *shutka* (joke), used by Pushkin to describe **"The Nose"**, seems valid–at least on one level.

Absurdity is everywhere in this story. It inheres not merely in the subject itself, but also in the manner of narration. Thus, in effect, there is not one story of the disappearance and reappearance of a nose: there are at least two.

First of all the barber Ivan Yakovlevich finds a nose baked

in a loaf of his wife's bread, and realises that it belongs to Major Kovalev, whom he shaves every Wednesday and Sunday. He disposes of his 'guilt' by throwing it from a bridge into the river Neva.

The second account concerns Major Kovalev himself, who wakes up one morning to find his nose has vanished from his face. However, he sees it in the street in the guise of a civil servant and pursues it into the Kazan Cathedral, where he accosts it, but his attention is distracted and the nose disappears.

Both these accounts open with their chief protagonists brought from sleep into the waking world by their noses: Ivan Yakovlevich by the smell of his wife's bread; Kovalev by his desire to see in the mirror whether a pimple has disappeared from the side of his nose. What they both wake to is a detached nose; in the first case an unwanted presence; in the second a mysterious absence. Yet these two stories are essentially different. In the barber's tale the nose is something thrice dead. It is first cut from a living face (he suspects, by himself), then baked in an oven by his wife, and finally drowned by the barber in the river. In Kovalev's story the nose is very much alive. It rides about in a carriage, talks, wears a uniform, makes visits, and prays in church.

Because of the accusations of his wife, and his own inability to remember the events of the previous day, Ivan Yakovlevich suspects himself of the deed. Kovalev, for his part, has no such suspicions:

> The barber Ivan Yakovlevich had shaved him on the Wednesday, and throughout the whole of Wednesday, and even the entire Thursday, his nose was intact. This he remembered, and knew very well. Moreover he would have felt pain and undoubtedly the wound could not have healed up so quickly and be smooth like a pancake.

The incongruity is therefore complete. The two stories touch at only one point: both protagonists recognise the nose as belonging to Kovalev.

It is as though Gogol is taking the structural device of the diptych, which he had used for the purposes of commentary in **"Nevsky Prospekt"** and **"The Portrait"**, and now in this 'joke' is mocking his own procedures. Yet the central theme introduced by **"Nevsky Prospekt"**, and carried on in all the St. Petersburg tales, is incongruity, and in the diptych of **"The Nose"** incongruity has developed into a narrational perception of reality which is almost schizophrenic. Moreover the dichotomy reflects another obsessional theme: 'dead and alive', which points to the problem underlying Gogol's very methods of characterisation.

There is, however, yet a third narrative strand which attempts some form of reconciliation between the disparate plots. After disposing of the nose in the Neva, Ivan Yakovlevich is apprehended on the bridge by an officer of the law. It is this same officer who later returns the nose to Kovalev, but the nose he has seized was the living one, with the passport of a civil servant, sitting in a stage coach and on his way to Riga. Yet the nose he returns is wrapped up in a piece of paper, and is carried in his pocket: it is the 'dead' nose. When Kovalev attempts to put it back in place, he not only notices that it feels wooden, but it falls on the table with a strange sound like a cork. All his attempts to affix it fail, and it is only thirteen days after its appearance in the freshly baked bread of Ivan Yakovlevich that it unexpectedly returns to its right-

ful place on the face of Kovalev. Although all this appears to have little to do with the activities of the barber, it is nevertheless he, whom the policeman blames, though he manages to suggest that it is somehow more a case of drunkenness and theft. These jumbled narrative lines are further complicated by fresh rumours of the nose taking a regular stroll along the Nevsky Prospekt at three o'clock (the hour for civil servants according to the narrator of **"Nevsky Prospekt"**), or being seen in a fashionable shop there, or even in the Taurida Gardens.

In this narrative cause and effect are completely disconnected. The whole story seems merely a series of logical dislocations, even in its minor details. Thus, on first discovering the loss of his nose, Kovalev's first response is to go to the police rather than to seek medical advice, and despite the fact that the police officer, who brings the nose back, roundly accuses the barber for its loss, Kovalev still prefers to think it was really the work of a female acquaintance Podtochina, whose name is connected with *podtochit'* –'to undermine' (e.g. of a person's health or powers). He writes her an absurd letter of accusation, which from the threat of legal action passes directly to:

> But with complete respect for you, I have the honour to be
> Your humble servant,
> Platon Kovalev

At the end of the story when the nose is miraculously restored to Kovalev's face, its reappearance is followed almost immediately by the usual professional visit of Ivan Yakovlevich. Yet Kovalev allows himself to be shaved by the very barber accused of its loss without a word of reproach. His only fears are not about the clumsiness of the barber's hands, but about their cleanliness. Such psychological dislocations are everywhere apparent: the discovery of a nose in his wife's bread is not a cause for Ivan Yakovlevich to scold her, but rather for her to scold him; and when Kovalev returns home to find his servant spitting at the ceiling he reproves him not because the habit is disgusting, but because it is foolish.

The closing words constitute a 'tongue in cheek' justification of the story's absurdities: 'and well then, where are there no absurdities? All the same, if you think a bit about it, it is true there is in all this something or other. Whatever anybody says similar occurrences do happen on this earth, seldom, but they do happen'. The incongruities in the story can be justified by reference to the absurdities of the real world; they are not the faithful reflection of such incongruities, but rather their imaginative projection in art. Thus synecdoche in art parallels synecdochal values in Russian society where, as in the story itself, one 'member' can represent the entire 'body': 'But Russia is such a land of miracles, that if you say anything about one collegiate assessor, then all the collegiate assessors, from Riga to Kamchatka, will invariably take it as referring to themselves. And the same goes for all titles and ranks'. Kovalev himself exemplifies these values; for him the titular 'part' is greater than the human 'whole': 'He could forgive everything that might be said about himself, but just could not forgive anything which referred to his rank and title'. It is in such a world that a nose can be of higher rank than its owner.

Alogism and dislocation are often used to make a social point, to mirror a discrepancy between private interest and public duty. Thus when the policeman who brings back the nose suddenly breaks off his official business to discuss his private life, the dislocation is intended as a 'jolt' to remind Kovalev that money is called for.

The efficiency of this policeman may be further judged by his 'short-sightedness', which is such as to prevent his seeing the very two features which the 'culprit' has removed from the face of the 'victim': 'If you were to stand in front of me, I can see only that you have a face, but neither your nose nor your beard. I don't notice anything at all'. The bribe-taking of yet another policeman is presented as an eccentric passion for sugar: 'In his home the whole of the entrance hall, as well as the dining room were heaped round with blocks of sugar, which merchants had brought to him out of friendship'.

The fact that Kovalev regards the loss of a nose as a police rather than a medical matter is an absurdity with its own social implications. A doctor actually lives in the same house, but he is the last person Kovalev turns to for help; for although the doctor takes good care of his own health, he is unable, even unwilling, to help Kovalev. He claims it would be worse for his patient if he were to fix the nose back in its place, and seems more interested in acquiring it as an object to exhibit for money. . . . Through the doctor's interest in acquiring the nose for exhibition Gogol seems to suggest a certain connection between the medical profession of his day and the role of mountebank.

The central incident with the nose is the most absurd of all the logical disconnections in the story. It may be taken on one level, as a joke against the reader, but there also lies behind it a more serious significance. A key word throughout the whole story is *mesto*–(place, position, job). Thus *mesto* is Kovalev's sole reason for being in St Petersburg: 'Major Kovalev had come to St Petersburg on necessary business, to be precise to look for a position fitting to his title' (i.e. *iskat' prilichnogo svoyemu zvaniyu mesta*). Kovalev is very conscious of his title, the civil service rank of collegiate assessor: 'He had only had this title two years, and therefore could not forget it for one moment. Yet his way of 'not forgetting it for one moment' exhibits a striking dislocation of logic: 'But in order to give himself a bit more nobility and weight, he never called himself collegiate assessor, but always major'. Kovalev is a civil servant masquerading as a military man, and he is not even sure of his status as a collegiate assessor, as the text slyly hints:

> But meanwhile it is necessary to say something about Kovalev, so that the reader can see what sort of collegiate assessor he was. One cannot in any way compare collegiate assessors who receive this title with the help of diplomas of learning, with those collegiate assessors who are made in the Caucasus. They are two types completely on their own.

Thus there are 'educated' (*uchennyy*) collegiate assessors and 'Caucasian' collegiate assessors. Kovalev belongs to the latter. It is implied that he has gained this title by virtue of having served in a distant outpost of the empire, but that he lacks the educational qualifications to achieve the rank in the capital. Yet it is precisely to St Petersburg that he has now come in search of a position, and is trying to cover up his true title by calling himself major.

The phrase 'a position fitting to his title', therefore, has an ironic ambiguity, and this is reflected in the two posts he has in mind: either that of a vice-governor (ridiculously ambitious), or the job of *ekzekutor* (more fitting to his rank). Instead of either of these 'places', however, Kovalev wakes up one morning to find 'a very stupid, even and smooth place' (*preglupoye, rovnoye i gladkoye mesto*): the place, in fact, that was once occupied by his nose. When Kovalev pursues his nose into the Kazan Cathedral, 'place' again is uppermost in his mind: 'It seems strange to me, dear sir, I think you ought to know your place'. The use of the word *mesto* here is ambiguous: the nose should know its 'place' to be on Kovalev's face, and not in the Kazan Cathedral praying; but the nose should also know its social 'place'. It is, after all, dressed up as a state counsellor, a rank three 'places' above Kovalev himself, and one more fitting for his own ambition to be a vice-governor. Kovalev seems to feel that without a nose he cannot further his career but he breaks off without mentioning the 'place' he hopes to receive, asserting instead that he mixes in company of equal rank to the nose (i.e. a state counsellor's wife–Chekhtyreva). The nose in reply claims independence, and in words which not only have physical but social and psychological ambiguity: 'there can be no close relationships between us'. He appears to mean that they each work in different departments, yet the statement that he himself serves in education is phrased in terms of an 'educated part' (*ya zhe po uchenoy chasti*, which could also be interpreted: 'whereas I–according to an educated part'). The 'Caucasian' nature of the collegiate assessor is thus mocked by the superiority of his 'educated' part, and the irony is further strengthened by the connotations of foolishness associated with 'nose' in Russian.

Apart from differences of rank and education the superiority of the 'part' to the 'whole' is emphasised throughout. Thus Kovalev has to walk because he cannot get a cab: the nose is riding around in its own carriage. In the cathedral the nose is absorbed in prayer: the less spiritual Kovalev is distracted by thoughts of an amorous adventure. So that there is obvious irony in the subsequent statement: 'One could already see from the nose's own replies, that for this man there was nothing holy'. The nose seems to represent all Kovalev's own pretensions, all his efforts to reach beyond himself. It is his most prominent external feature, but it seems to assume significance for his inner world: the baseless psychological projection of his own character becomes identified, through fantasy, with a detachable physical protuberance. Thus the loss of the nose he equates directly with the loss of career prospects and the inability to make an advantageous marriage, whereas its sudden appearance as a civil servant in its own right mocks him in the form of a 'double' which is in every sense his better, and yet can have no connections with him.

For Kovalev, as for Poprishchin in **"The Diary of a Madman"**, status seems to be linked with amorous aims. The statement about his ambition to become a vice-governor or an *ekzekutor* is followed immediately by another possibility: 'Major Kovalev was not against getting married even, but only on condition that his bride should have two hundred thousand in capital behind her'. As we have seen he does not finish his sentence to the nose about his hopes for preferment, but goes on to mention his acquaintance with Chekhtyreva and other ladies. When visiting the newspaper office his eye lights on the name of a pretty actress in a theatre announcement, and once more a sexual response seems intimately connected with the question of status; 'staff officers in the opinion of Kovalev ought to sit in the orchestra stalls'.

On the other hand women seem, somehow, to be connected with the loss of his nose. In spite of everything Kovalev is convinced that its disappearance is the work of Podtochina, and when, in the Kazan Cathedral, he allows himself to be distracted by a pretty girl his nose 'disappears' a second time.

The fact that the loss of the nose both springs from, and further inhibits, Kovalev's relations with women seems to suggest that the protuberance might be equated with a more obviously masculine organ. Such an identification has good literary antecedents, and the story is a happy hunting ground for critics of a Freudian bent. (pp. 124-38)

The story ends happily for Kovalev. With the restoration of his nose we witness the restoration of Kovalev himself. He is shaved as usual by Ivan Yakovlevich, as though nothing had happened, and his actions on its return seem to recreate in a positive sense his behaviour on first discovering its loss. He now orders a cab (there was none available on the first occasion); goes into a pastrycook's and is served (previously he was not); he looks into the mirror and reassures himself about the nose's presence (it was not there when he looked in the pastrycook's mirror before). Moreover, the nose seems now to establish his 'military' superiority: 'He turned round quite happy and with a satirical expression, slightly closing one eye, he looked at two military men, one of whom had a nose not a whit larger than a waistcoat button'. At the end both his overweening ambition and his amorous proclivities seem to have been reinstated in full vigour: 'After this Major Kovalev was to be seen always in a good mood, smiling, determinedly pursuing all pretty ladies and even once stopping in front of a stall in the *Gostinyy dvor* and buying a ribbon for some decoration or other, why is unknown because he himself was not a knight of any order at all'.

Word-play is important for the story. Gogol exploits the idea of 'nose', not only conceptually as a kind of metaphor, but also verbally, much as he does that other key concept 'place'. Thus Podtochina, in her reply to Kovalev's strange letter, thinks that his references to the nose are allusions to the Russian idiom *ostat' sya s nosom*—'to be duped' (literally: 'to remain with a nose') a verbal ambiguity already anticipated in Kovalev's complaint to the doctor; 'How can I remain without a nose?' (*Kak zhe mne ostavat' sya bez nosa*?) There is also the frequent identification of noses with buttons.

Such elements help to reinforce the view of the story as a joke, yet, at the same time, they may be taken as devices of ambiguity pointing to a serious psychological undertone. The story may be interpreted as a joke, or, in spite of Gogol's suppression of the original ending, it may be seen as the fantasy of dream. There are other tentative straws of explanation at which the reader might also clutch. Thus it could be related to silly rumours, garbled in the salons of St Petersburg: 'And all these events were extremely gratefully received by all those society gentlemen, the indispensable visitors at evening gatherings, who loved to make the ladies laugh, and whose store at that time had been completely exhausted'. Again it might all be a form of hypnotic illusion: 'It was precisely at that time that everybody's mind had been turned to exceptional things. It was not long before that experiments on the effects of magnetism had been the talk of the town'. Indeed the doctor, who refuses to put back Kovalev's nose, has this quality of magnetism in his voice.

There is the possibility, again, of taking the story as an allegory. The clerk in the newspaper office refuses to print Kovalev's advertisement for his nose, from fear that it might have a hidden meaning. He quotes the case of an advertisement about a runaway, black-haired poodle, which turned out to be an attack on the treasurer of some institution. Kovalev's reaction to this is, in itself, revealing: 'But, after all, I am not making an announcement to you about a poodle, but about my very own nose: therefore it is almost the same thing as about myself'.

"The Nose" is indeed a sort of allegory 'almost about Kovalev himself', which at the same time has overtones of authorial self-confession. On the surface it can be read as a joke: a bizarre story which proceeds by verbal associations and logical dislocations rather than by the cause and effect of the everyday world. To this extent it looks forward to the next story about St Petersburg, **"The Overcoat"** in which another civil servant makes vain efforts to retrieve a lost synecdoche–a coat (with overtones of a human being) which will only be restored to him, as in the case of Kovalev, by supernatural means. (pp. 139-40)

"The Overcoat" has long been held up as a key work in the Russian realist tradition, but in the twentieth century the view that the story is 'realistic' has been strongly challenged. The opening paragraph, in itself, should act as an *avis au lecteur*. It is little more than a verbal arabesque which at its end returns the reader to the very point of its opening: 'a certain department'. The intervening verbiage has mocked the reader for his social susceptibilities in literature and established an authorial tone of playful mystification. Moreover, since the whole impetus behind the arabesque has been provided by the one word 'department', the reader should be warned that here is a story in which words have a wayward dynamism all their own: they are more capable of retarding or advancing the plot than mere actions.

This opening prepares us, not for realism, but for the sort of incongruous world already encountered in a story like **"The Nose"**. The absurdity is carried on in the depiction of the central character, where for realistic description Gogol substitutes the verbal formula: Akakiy Akakiyevich is 'a little bit pockmarked, a little bit red-haired, a little bit blind in appearance'. Two other verbal formulae take the place of real biographical detail; for at birth the hero pulls a face which suggests he senses himself as a future titular counsellor: later when people see him in the office they think that he must have been born 'ready made' complete with uniform and bald patch. . . . The nature of this service has entirely swamped his private and inner world. As he walks along the street, he sees only his own handwriting on everything, and if he is suddenly brought to his senses by bumping into a horse: 'Only then would he notice that he was not in the middle of a line, but rather in the middle of the street'.

Such verbal play detracts from any serious, realistic presentation of the hero and through visual effects he is reduced to the grotesque. Thus his neck is compared to that of a wagging plaster kitten; things permanently adhere to his clothing because of an unfortunate gift of always managing to be under a window whenever rubbish is thrown out; he eats his food without noticing either the taste or the dead flies, and only realises that he has had enough when he sees that his stomach has swelled.

The realist approach to the story stresses the social theme of humble destitution, but it is difficult for the reader to understand Akakiy Akakiyevich's poverty. He has no dependants, no extravagances, not even any amusements; he has a very careful system of saving money, is not at the very bottom of the civil service hierarchy and has been in his position for longer than anyone can tell, yet he appears to be unable to afford such a basic necessity as a winter overcoat to keep out the St Petersburg frost. The description of his meagre possessions and of the methods he employs to save wear and tear to his clothing and boots is comic. The poverty of Akakiy Akakiyevich, in real terms, is absurd: it is presented hyperbolically.

The coat, too, is presented with hyperbole, not merely as regards its material quality, but also in respect of the effect it has on its wearer. Under its influence he becomes a new man; he experiences something akin to an awakening of the senses. The coat replaces his obsession with copying and in its turn dominates his existence, whilst at the same time offering a pledge for a new and fuller life. At this point it is as though Gogol has taken up one of the 'myriad characters' on the Nevsky Prospekt, a man who consists entirely of his clothing, and devoted a whole study to him. Yet his analysis is not pursued by going inside the character, as in **"The Diary of a Madman"**, the psychological world of Akakiy Akakiyevich, such as it is, is projected through externals: the whole tale is a finely spun cocoon which houses a 'dead soul'.

Almost everything in the tale can be seen as 'psychological'. The poverty of Akakiy Akakiyevich is presented in the same grotesque way as is the central character himself. The narrator's verbal onslaught, in the enormous sentence which contrasts the life of other minor civil servants with that of his hero, suggests (in spite of certain verbal flourishes) that he is deprived of all amusements through the dearth of inner resources rather than a lack of financial ones. He is a man with one obsession–copying; his work, humdrum though it may be, has become his private pleasure, and he is happy with his inner world of stereotyped creativity, unable to communicate with others and little interested in them.

The outward poverty of Akakiy Akakiyevich is a metaphor of his spiritual indigence. The coat, too, is lined with metaphor: his outward wrapping is identified as a 'lifelong lady friend', and on acquiring it, it is 'as though he has got married'. Having put it on he assumes a new personality, or, at the very least, a new frame of mind. The coat seems to open up a whole new possible life of conviviality, drinking, even amorous adventure. He goes to the apartment of the assistant chief clerk and is forced to drink champagne; on his way there he had chuckled at an erotic picture in a shop window; on his way back he almost chases after a woman in the street.

These outward and return journeys must in themselves be taken as metaphors of inner movement. The outward journey is from the darkness and meanness of his own quarter of the city towards the growing light and bustle of his convivial destination: the way home is the same spiritual journey in reverse. Thus the streets of St Petersburg, which in **"Nevsky Prospekt"** were both a sociological metaphor and a catalyst for human folly, here assume a psychological function. Setting forth he had increasingly been opening his eyes and seeing–for the first time; returning to his old life, he closes his eyes, and is robbed of his coat. The thieves are men with large moustaches (a recurring symbol of male sexuality in Gogol) and the phrase of expropriation is significant: 'but the coat is mine'.

Akakiy Akakiyevich is deprived of something that was never really fully his. The awakening of his senses, which he experienced under the influence of the coat, was merely a wraith-like potential, which was never fully convincing. After his embryonic erotic experiences on the streets of St Petersburg,

Akakiy Akakiyevich is now thrown back on his seventy-year-old landlady, about whom his fellow clerks used to tease him, pouring paper 'snow' on his head, and asking when he was going to marry her. Now when he returns covered in real snow, his reception by his landlady seems to recreate in ironic terms the essential features of the erotic picture, which had first stirred something unknown within his breast: a man in a doorway looking at a woman with only one shoe on her foot (the erotic irony is underlined by the fact that the landlady has just jumped out of bed and is holding her nightshirt to her chest 'out of modesty').

The ostensible plot of the story is, of course, the acquisition and loss of an object–the overcoat, but in some strange way this gets mixed up with psychological awakening and eroticism: a confusion which may be observed even in the reaction of the policeman to whom Akakiy Akakiyevich first turns for help: 'The district superintendent received the story of the theft of the coat in an exceedingly strange way. Instead of turning his attention to the main point of the matter, he began to question Akakiy Akakiyevich on why it was that he was returning home so late, and hadn't he called off and been in some disorderly house or other?'

The police prove entirely unhelpful. The policeman (*budoch-nik*) who witnesses the theft is not prepared to act, and Akakiy Akakiyevich is told by his landlady that it will be useless to go to the local police officer (*kvartal' nyy*). She advises him to apply directly to the district superintendent, who, as we have seen, has his own oblique view of the matter. As the normal channels seem so perverse, the pursuit of the coat takes its own obliquity: Akakiy Akakiyevich seeks to recover it through the intercession of a person of significance. His exact office is unknown, it is sufficient that he is a 'significant person'; but just as the coat had been seized by aggressive men with moustaches, so now the insignificance of Akakiy Akakiyevich quails before the 'significance' of this man, and he is robbed of his life by a verbal bully.

The story assumes its final obliquity in the account of Akakiy Akakiyevich's vengeance. He returns to the streets of St Petersburg as a ghost, and poetic justice is done, when he takes the overcoat of the significant person in circumstances which seem to reflect the symbolic potential of Akakiy Akakiyevich's own coat. The significant person has just been to a party; he too has drunk two glasses of champagne, and instead of returning home is entertaining thoughts of an erotic encounter. At this point his coat is seized from his back with the words: 'Your coat is the one I want.' With its loss the 'significant person' becomes a different man, and the ghost itself disappears. The only sighting reported later is of an 'apparition', which turns out to be a figure strikingly like the original coat thief.

The plot of this story is scarcely less oblique than that of **"The Nose"**: 'titular' poverty forces a titular counsellor to make sacrifices to acquire a coat, which is somehow more than mere clothing. It is stolen by robbers and when he tries to retrieve it through civil-service channels he is put so firmly in his place that he dies. He returns as a ghost, but exacts retribution for his stolen coat not from the thieves but from the 'significant person'. The obliquity is reinforced on a verbal level. The hero is a clerk who cannot use words, but yet is obsessed by their calligraphic reproduction. He is at the mercy of the verbal effects of the tailor Petrovich, and, more devastatingly, those of the 'significant person'. An automaton, to whom a coat has brought the pledge of feelings, is devastated by one who is: 'absolutely delighted by the thought that a word from him could even deprive a man of his feelings. Akakiy's awakening had been the development of feelings'. Formerly copying had engulfed his life in entirety: 'It is not enough to say that he worked with zeal. No, he worked with love'. This 'love' was transferred to the coat and from this, in turn, there stems a dimly awakened interest in such erotic objects as the picture of the woman with the shoe, and the woman in the street whose body is full of movement.

Gogol presents his theme through verbal play and literary joke, gently mocking in turn his hero's surname, Christian name and rank. The narrator himself calls attention to the verbal undercurrents of the story when he claims that the hero's name has been derived from a shoe (an object, which, as an erotic symbol, is a motif both for his outward journey and for his return). The disingenuous narrator finds it strange that the name could be derived from a shoe, since all his relations wore boots. (pp. 141-45)

Akakiy Akakiyevich has the rank of titular counsellor, and the narrator pretends to disapprove of writers who poke fun at those who bear it (Gogol's own story **"The Diary of a Madman"** might be a case in point). Nevertheless, his own treatment of his hero is scarcely less mocking than that of Akakiy Akakiyevich's colleagues in the office. The ambiguous distinction of the rank of titular counsellor has already been noted, but it seemed anomalous in yet another way. All the senior grades in the hierarchy (rank one excepted) were various degrees of 'counsellor' (ranks two to seven inclusive); the titular counsellor, however, was separated from these 'real' counsellors by the career threshold of rank eight, the collegiate assessor. He was thus a 'counsellor' only in name. At the very end of the section introducing his hero, the narrator plays with the words 'counsellor' and 'counsel'. He talks of the misfortunes which bestrew the path not only of titular counsellors, but of privy, actual, court and all counsellors 'even those who give no one counsel, nor take it from anyone else'. As a 'counsellor' Akakiy Akakiyevich is obviously in the latter category: he is incapable of performing any duty other than routine copying.

The official responsible for the death of Akakiy Akakiyevich must be a true counsellor (probably actual state counsellor) as he has recently attained the rank of general, nevertheless he is always referred to as the 'significant person', *znachitel' noye litso* (literally–'significant face'). It is through this formula that further word-play is possible, suggesting the essential link between this verbal tyrant and his victim. (p. 146)

By contrast 'significance' is a quality which, in both its senses, Akakiy Akakiyevich completely lacks. He is so insignificant, the narrator tells us, on his death, that he would not have attracted even the attention of an entomologist. Significance, in yet another respect, is foreign to him: he copies words without understanding them, and his own speech is incoherent and lacks meaning: 'It must be explained that Akakiy Akakiyevich expressed himself, for the most part, in prepositions, adverbs and ultimately in particles which had absolutely no meaning [i.e. *znacheniye*] whatsoever'. His favourite all-purpose phrase is *togo*–'and that . . . ' and when confronted by the general, he is so overwhelmed by his 'significance' that he uses more of this semantic debris than normal. Ironically, he is annihilated by formulae of significance which are little more than the practised copying of stereotyped phrases: the exercise to which Akakiy Akakiyevich has devoted his own life.

The final section of the story contains the ultimate identification of the hero as a 'dead man/civil servant' (*chinovnik-mertvets*). Akakiy Akakiyevich returns as a ghost (*mertvets*=literally 'corpse') and the whole of this ludicrous sequence is permeated by punning on the concept 'dead and alive'. Such verbal play goes to the root of Akakiy Akakiyevich's character; for, paradoxically, when he was alive he seemed one of the walking dead, whereas after death he shows more 'life' in his behaviour as a ghost.

Verbal play, as we have seen, runs all through the story. Although it adds to the humour, its chief contribution lies elsewhere: it is intimately connected with definitions, with names, titles, states of being. Its function is to suggest another meaning below the level of the blandly smiling surface of a joke, and as such it may be compared to the device of a 'coat', which is not a coat, and 'poverty', which is not poverty, or even the naive narrator, who is really the sophisticated author himself.

The tale may be related to the genre of the *skaz*. The story is filtered through the unsophisticated consciousness of an inept narrator, who places unusual emphases on unimportant areas of his narrative, whilst neglecting others altogether. A desire to be accurate about dates and street names obsesses him when it is least called for, and deserts him on other occasions. His naive incomprehension of the psychological motivation of his characters is almost as great as the innocence of Akakiy Akakiyevich himself. The focus is one of distortion: Petrovich's big toe and his snuff box loom larger than the man himself; Akakiy Akakiyevich's baptism is described with mock seriousness. The relative positions of mother, godfather and godmother are recorded with fastidious accuracy, yet the conventional hierarchy of virtues is inverted (the mother is described merely as 'a very good woman', while the godfather is 'a most excellent man', and the godmother is a 'woman of rare virtues').

Behind his simpleton-narrator lurks the wily author himself, who laughs at his narrator, at his heroes, but above all at his readers. Mockery of the reader is present, as we have seen, in the very opening of the tale, and one of the ironies of the genre is that a tale told by an 'inept' narrator posits the need for a sophisticated reader.

The fact that the author also laughs at his hero, would seem to undermine the traditional view, that in **'The Overcoat'** Gogol is the champion of the underdog: the little man persecuted by authority. It was this view that Eykhenbaum and others attacked, interpreting the 'humanitarian' passage of the awakening of a conscience in a fellow clerk as a mere artistic device. It cannot, however, be denied that there is both 'laughter' and 'tears' in the presentation of Gogol's 'little man', but unlike Karamzin he does not seek to redeem the sufferings of his central character through the sympathetic tears of his readers; there is only a nod in the direction of Sentimentalism. On the other hand the 'medieval' morality demands strict recompense: a justice which is both supernatural and of this earth. It is this that Gogol has given us in the ghost who steal overcoats.

The ghost sequence is no less absurd than the fantastic world of **"The Nose"**, or the hallucinations of Poprishchin. Indeed **"The Overcoat"** has much in common with **"The Diary of a Madman"**. Both heroes are titular counsellors, for whom the copying out of documents is intimately connected with their self-regard. One, whose writing is perfect, lacks imagination and any inner life other than that provided by his passion for copying; the other, whose writing is full of aberrations, falls prey to imagination and an inner aberration which swamps his sense of reality. Poprishchin, to achieve a new identity cuts up his uniform, and becomes the King of Spain; clothing brings the promise of a new personality to Akakiy Akakiyevich. For Poprishchin status is mixed with eroticism, and the 'new self' of Akakiy Akakiyevich, as we have seen, also has its erotic overtones.

Yet in one thing the stories are radically different: Poprishchin, through his diary, is seen from the inside; the narrator of **"The Overcoat"** refuses categorically to get inside his characters. He states this at two crucial points in the psychological development of his hero: once, when Akakiy Akakiyevich, on his way to the party, is confronted by the titillating picture, and a second time when the situation is reversed, and he returns to his landlady without the coat. Just as the narrator refuses to speculate about the arousal of his hero: 'For it is impossible to get into the soul of a man and learn all that he is thinking', by the same token he leaves the psychology of defeat to the empathy of his readers: 'and how he spent the night there, can be left to the judgement of him, who can to any extent imagine the situation of another'.

"The Overcoat" is probably the most famous story in the Russian language. Its germinal significance for later writers seems to be enshrined in the apocryphal remark attributed to Dostoevsky: 'We have all come out of Gogol's **"Overcoat."** ' For Dostoevsky himself this is largely true. He began his career by rewriting Gogol and earned overnight acclaim with *Poor Folk,* which is a conscious attempt to humanise and psychologise Gogol's story of a poor clerk. It is interesting that for this purpose Dostoevsky goes back to the earlier, and sentimental, form of the novel in letters, in order to do what Gogol refuses to do: 'get into the soul of a man'. Dostoevsky's novel is more openly sentimental, and he presents psychology directly and analytically, rather than in the devious and oblique method of Gogol. The promise of a saving relationship in Dostoevsky's work is not with a coat, but with a girl; correspondingly the hero's name, Devushkin, is not 'derived from a shoe' but from the word for a girl *devushka*. Devushkin is not a clerk obsessed by mere copying, writing has real significance in his life. He communicates through letters and even tries his hand at *belles lettres*. His interest in literature leads him to read **"The Overcoat"**, which he severely censures, finding Akakiy Akakiyevich unconvincing.

It is Dostoevsky, not Gogol, who brings realism to the depiction of poverty and the theme of the downtrodden clerk. Yet one of the chief differences between them lies in their treatment of psychology. Gogol, as we have seen, uses external poverty as a psychological metaphor. Dostoevsky's method is the very reverse of this: outward poverty is not used to hint at an inner state of mind, it is rather psychology which is used to explore poverty as a physical state. In polemicising with Gogol, Dostoevsky shows a great perspicuity and subtlety. He understands Gogol fully but disagrees with his methods. (pp. 147-50)

> *Richard Peace, in his* The Enigma of Gogol: An Examination of the Writings of N. V. Gogol and Their Place in the Russian Literary Tradition, *Cambridge University Press, 1981, 344 p.*

FURTHER READING

Bonnett, Gail. "Deity to Demon: Gogol's Female Characters." *Proceedings, Pacific Northwest Conference on Foreign Languages* XXIII (1972): 253-67.
> Investigates Gogol's treatment of his female characters and their function as literary devices.

Driessen, F. C. *Gogol as a Short Story Writer: A Study of His Technique of Composition.* Translated by Ian F. Finlay. The Hague: Mouton & Co., 1965, 243 p.
> A critical guide to all of Gogol's stories, including detailed plot summaries and listings of major themes.

Eichenbaum, Boris. "How Gogol's 'Overcoat' Is Made." In *Gogol from the Twentieth Century: Eleven Essays,* edited and translated by Robert A. Maguire, pp. 267-92. Princeton: Princeton University Press, 1974.
> A structural analysis of "The Overcoat."

Erlich, Victor. *Gogol.* New Haven and London: Yale University Press, 1969, 230 p.
> General study of Gogol's life and works designed to provide a complete survey for the English-speaking reader.

Garrard, John G. "Some Thoughts on Gogol's 'Kolyaska.' " *PMLA* 90, No. 5 (October 1975): 848-60.
> Exploration of why "Kolyaska" has been critically neglected and a defense of its status as a paradigm of Gogolian fiction.

Gregg, Richard. "The Curse of Sameness and the Gogolian Esthetic: 'The Tale of the Two Ivans' as Parable." *The Slavic and East European Journal* 31, No. 1 (Spring 1987): 1-9.
> Explores the theme of monotony and spiritual impoverishment in "How Ivan Ivanovič Quarrelled with Ivan Nikiforovič " commenting on its relation to Gogol's view of art.

Holquist, James M. "The Devil in Mufti: The *Märchenwelt* in Gogol's Short Stories." *PMLA* LXXXII, No. 5 (October 1967): 352-62.
> Argues that Gogol's short stories extended the parameters of the German literary fairy tale by imbuing the form with profound moral significance.

Hughes, Olga Raevsky. "The Apparent and the Real in Gogol's 'Nevskij Prospekt.' " *California Slavic Studies* VIII (1975): 77-91.
> Analyzes the discrepancy between surfaces and essences in "Nevsky Prospect."

Lavrin, Janko. *Gogol.* London and New York: George Routledge & Sons, 1925, 263 p.
> Biographical and critical appreciation of Gogol's life and works. Lavrin states that his objective is "to introduce to English readers a great and complex foreign author in as simple terms as possible."

Massey, Irving. "Metamorphosis in Gogol: 'The Nose.' " In his *The Gaping Pig: Literature and Metamorphosis,* pp. 59-75. Berkeley: University of California Press, 1976.
> Comprehensive analysis of the nature of metamorphosis in "The Nose."

McLean, Hugh. "Gogol's Retreat from Love: Toward an Interpretation of *Mirgorod.*" In *American Contributors to the Fourth International Congress of Slavicists,* pp. 225-44. The Hague: Mouton & Co., 1958.
> Explores the role of love in the stories in *Mirgorod.*

Oulianoff, Nicholas I. "Arabesque or Apocalypse? On the Fundamental Idea of Gogol's Story 'The Nose.' " *Canadian Slavic Studies* I, No. 2 (Summer 1967): 158-71.
> Refutes common critical opinion that "The Nose" is a frivolous joke and maintains that it contains monstrous elements similar to those depicted in the paintings of Hieronymus Bosch.

Proffitt, Edward. "Gogol's 'Perfectly True' Tale: 'The Overcoat' and Its Mode of Closure." *Studies in Short Fiction* 14, No. 1 (Winter 1977): 35-40.

> Detailed analysis of the controversial ending of "The Overcoat."

Rowe, William Woodin. *Through Gogol's Looking Glass: Reverse Vision, False Focus, and Precarious Logic.* New York: New York University Press, 1976, 201 p.

> Examines Gogol's creative process. Rowe emphasizes the world of vision and perception in Gogol's writings.

Stilman, Leon. "Gogol's 'Overcoat'—Thematic Patterns and Origins." *The American Slavic and East European Review* XI, No. 2 (1952): 138-48.

> Exegesis of the story "The Overcoat."

Trahan, Elizabeth, ed., *Gogol's "Overcoat": An Anthology of Critical Essays,* edited by Elizabeth Trahan. Ann Arbor: Ardis, 1982, 105 p.

> Detailed analyses by five critics of "The Overcoat," including Boris Eichenbaum's influential essay "How Gogol's 'Overcoat' Is Made."

Tschizewskij, Dmitrij. "The Composition of Gogol's 'Overcoat.' " *Russian Literature Triquarterly,* Nos. 14-16 (1977): 378-401.

> An analysis of narrative style in "The Overcoat" focusing upon the use of repetition.

Waszink, Paul M. "Mythical Traits in Gogol's 'The Overcoat.' " *The Slavic and East European Journal* 22, No. 3 (Fall 1978): 287-300.

> Examines mythical elements in "The Overcoat."

Woodward, James B. "The Threadbare Fabric of Gogol's *'Overcoat.'* " *Canadian Slavic Studies* I (1967): 95-104.

> Study of the stylistic technique of "The Overcoat."

——. *The Symbolic Art of Gogol: Essays on His Short Fiction.* Columbus, Ohio: Slavica, 1982, 131 p.

> Interpretative essays on five of Gogol's most celebrated and complex stories, including "The Nose," "The Overcoat," and "Old-World Landowners."

Zora Neale Hurston

1891-1960

American novelist, folklorist, short story writer, autobiographer, essayist, dramatist, librettist, and anthropologist.

Hurston is considered among the foremost writers of the Harlem Renaissance, an era of unprecedented excellence in African-American art and literature during the 1920s and 1930s. Although her fiction, which depicts the common black folk of her native Southern Florida, was largely unconcerned with racial injustices of the time, Hurston's works have undergone substantial critical reevaluation since the advent of the black protest novel and the rise to prominence during the 1950s of Richard Wright, Ralph Ellison, and James Baldwin. In addition to having published four novels, three nonfiction works, and numerous short stories and essays, Hurston is acknowledged as the first modern black American to collect and publish folklore. Lillie P. Howard stated: "[Hurston's] works are important because they affirm blackness (while not denying whiteness) in a black-denying society. They present characters who are not all lovable but who are undeniably and realistically human. They record the history, the life, of a place and time which are remarkably like other places and times, though perhaps a bit more honest in the rendering."

Hurston was born in Eatonville, Florida, the first incorporated black township in the United States and the setting for most of her fiction. At age fourteen, Hurston left her hometown to work as a maid with a traveling Gilbert and Sullivan theatrical troupe. In 1923, she entered Howard University, a predominantly black college in Washington, D.C., where she published short stories in *Stylus,* the university literary magazine, and attracted the attention of noted sociologist Charles S. Johnson. With Johnson's encouragement, Hurston moved to New York City in 1925 and subsequently secured a scholarship to Barnard College with the assistance of Annie Nathan Meyer, a white philanthropist and well-known supporter of Harlem Renaissance artists. While at Barnard, Hurston studied anthropology under Franz Boas, one of the most renowned anthropologists of the era, and after her graduation in 1928, she continued her work with Boas as a graduate student at Columbia University. During this period, Hurston began publishing short stories and establishing friendships with many important black writers. In 1927, together with Langston Hughes and other artists, Hurston founded *Fire!,* a literary magazine devoted to African-American culture that ceased publication after its premiere issue as a result of financial difficulties and a fire that destroyed the editorial offices.

With the aid of fellowships and a private grant from a New York socialite interested in "primitive Negro art," Hurston returned to the South to collect folklore. Between the years 1927 and 1931, she traveled to Alabama, Louisiana, and Florida, living among sharecroppers and workers lodged in labor camps whose primary form of entertainment consisted of telling tall tales, or "lies." In one of these camps, Hurston was cautiously scrutinized by the workers because of her expensive apparel and automobile and was not accepted until she "confessed" that she was a bootlegger fleeing from justice. In 1935, Hurston published *Mules and Men,* a collection

of African-American folktales that expanded upon her academic studies and anthropological field work. In addition to tales and descriptions of voodoo practices and beliefs, *Mules and Men* included work songs, legends, rhymes, and "lies," all of which contained hidden social and philosophical messages considered essential to survival in a racist society. Hurston categorized her findings in *Mules and Men* under such themes and motifs as biblical events, moral lessons, variations of plantation stories as delineated in the works of Joel Chandler Harris, and explanations of natural phenomena. The story "Why the Waves Have Whitecaps," an example of a tale about natural occurrences, relates the tragic consequences of a rivalry between the anthropomorphic figures Mrs. Wind and Mrs. Water. In the tale, Mrs. Water, jealous of her adversary's children, drowns them in the sea, so that whenever Mrs. Wind grieves for her offspring, her sorrowful voice forms white caps on the ocean's waves.

Mules and Men became a popular success. Although many critics praised the book's readability and entertaining qualities, some cited an absence of scholarly analysis and comparative notations and an abundance of authorial intrusions. Others accused Hurston of ignoring racial oppression and exploitation in the South—accusations that recurred throughout her literary career. Recent commentators, however, have refuted these charges. Theresa R. Love asserted: "[Hurston's goal] was not merely to collect folklore but to show the beauty and wealth of genuine Negro material. In doing so, she placed herself on the side of those who saw nothing self-defeating in writing about the black masses, who, she felt, are more imaginative than their middle-class counterparts."

Hurston's short stories and novels also dramatize the lives of the black masses. She was especially praised for her recreation of Eatonville's landscape, social customs, and colorful dialect. Hurston published nearly all of her stories in *Opportunity,* a black American magazine produced by the National Urban League, prior to the publication of her first novel, *Jonah's Gourd Vine,* in 1934. "Drenched in Light," Hurston's earliest story, is an initiation piece centering on a high-spirited girl whose sense of adventure and independence is constantly undermined by her puritanical grandmother. "Sweat" is a tale of hatred and revenge involving a long-suffering washwoman and her brutal, adulterous husband. "Muttsy," one of Hurston's few stories set in the North, revolves around a young Southern woman who moves to Harlem and falls in love with a professional gambler. Hurston returns to the rural South in "John Redding Goes to Sea." Basically an extension of the story "Drenched in Light," this later work focuses upon John Redding, a restless young man torn between leaving Eatonville for new adventures and settling down to appease his family. After marriage fails to suppress his dreams of flight, John is liberated from his directionless life when he drowns during a hurricane while saving another person's life. Hurston's last story, "The Gilded Six-Bits," was published in *Story* magazine in 1933 and is considered her best work of short fiction. Described by Robert Bone as "a drama of sin and redemption, a symbolic reenactment of the Fall," this piece concerns Joe and Missie May, a newlywed couple whose idyllic marriage is nearly destroyed by Slemmons, a smooth-talking Northerner who operates an ice cream parlor in Eatonville. Impressed with Slemmons's affluence and sophisticated demeanor, Missie May takes him as a lover but quickly discovers that his lifestyle is as fallacious as the "gold" coins and jewelry he used to seduce her. These and other tales were collected in 1985 in *Spunk: The Selected Stories of Zora Neale Hurston,* which received substantial praise from critics. Grace Ingoldby commented: "Hurston has the vitality of Dickens and the South Americans; to read her is to realise how cautious much contemporary writing has become."

Many critical studies of Hurston have focused extensively on her private life. Early in her literary career she depended heavily on white patronage for financial assistance. Langston Hughes wrote in his autobiography, *The Big Sea,* that Hurston was "simply paid just to sit around and represent the Negro race." Other writers who knew Hurston during the 1920s and 1930s contend that she deliberately played the role of an exotic curiosity in order to advance her career. While some have questioned Hurston's integrity, her work is significant for its insights into the human condition. In a dedication to *I Love Myself When I Am Laughing . . . and Then Again When I Am Looking Mean and Impressive: A Zora Neale Hurston Reader,* Alice Walker summarized Hurston's achievements: "We love Zora Neale Hurston for her work, first, and then again (as she and all Eatonville would say), we love her for herself. For the humor and courage with which she encountered a life she infrequently designed, for her absolute disinterest in becoming either white or bourgeois, and for

her *devoted* appreciation of her own culture, which is an inspiration to us all."

(For further information on Hurston's life and career, see *Contemporary Literary Criticism,* Vols. 7, 30; *Contemporary Authors,* Vols. 85-88; and *Dictionary of Literary Biography,* Vol. 51.)

PRINCIPAL WORKS

SHORT FICTION

Mules and Men   1935
Spunk: The Selected Stories of Zora Neale Hurston   1985

OTHER MAJOR WORKS

Color Struck   (drama)   1926
The Great Day   (musical revue)   1932
Jonah's Gourd Vine   (novel)   1934
Their Eyes Were Watching God   (novel)   1937
Tell My Horse   (nonfiction)   1938; also published as *Voodoo Gods: An Inquiry into Native Myths and Magic in Jamaica and Haiti,* 1939
Moses, Man of the Mountain   (novel)   1939; also published as *The Man of the Mountain,* 1941
Dust Tracks on a Road   (autobiography)   1942
Polk County: A Comedy of Negro Life on a Sawmill Camp, with Dorothy Waring   (drama)   1944
Seraph on the Suwanee   (novel)   1948
I Love Myself When I Am Laughing . . . and Then Again When I Am Looking Mean and Impressive: A Zora Neale Hurston Reader   (fiction and nonfiction)   1979
The Sanctified Church   (essays)   1981

ZORA NEALE HURSTON   (letter date 1934)

[*The following excerpt is from a letter that Hurston wrote to Franz Boas, famed anthropologist and her former instructor at Columbia University. Here Hurston requests that Boas write the introduction to her folklore collection* Mules and Men *(which he did; see excerpt dated 1935) and outlines her publisher's concern that the book have popular appeal in addition to scholarly value.*]

I am full of tremors, lest you decide that you do not want to write the introduction to my **Mules and Men.** I want you to do it so very much. Also I want Dr. [Ruth] Benedict to read the ms. and offer suggestions. Sort of edit it you know.

Mr. Lippincott likes the book very much and he will push it. His firm, as you know probably publishes more text-books than any other in America and he is conservative. He wants a very readable book that the average reader can understand, at the same time one that will have value as a reference book. I have inserted the between-story conversation and business because when I offered it without it, every publisher said it was too monotonous. Now three houses want to publish it. So I hope that the unscientific matter that must be there for the sake of the average reader will not keep you from writing the introduction. It so happens that the conversations and incidents are true. But of course I never would have set them down for scientists to read. I know that the learned societies are interested in the story in many ways that would never interest the average mind. He needs no stimulation. But the man in the street is different.

So *please* consider all this and do not refuse Mr. Lippincott's request to write the introduction to **Mules and Men.** And then in addition, I feel that the persons who have the most information on a subject should teach the public. Who knows more about folk-lore than you and Dr. Benedict? Therefore the stuff published in America should pass under your eye. *You* see some of the preposterous stuff put out by various persons on various folk-subjects. This is not said merely to get you to write the introduction to my book. No. But an enormous amount of loose writing is being done. (pp. 163-64)

> *Zora Neale Hurston, in a letter to Franz Boas on August 20, 1934, in* Zora Neale Hurston: A Literary Biography *by Robert E. Hemenway, University of Illinois Press, 1977, pp. 163-64.*

FRANZ BOAS   (essay date 1935)

[*Boas, the most distinguished anthropologist of his era, was Hurston's professor at Columbia University in the late 1920s. At her request (see excerpt dated 1934), he wrote the following appreciative introduction to the original edition of her folklore collection* Mules and Men.]

Ever since the time of Uncle Remus, Negro folk-lore has exerted a strong attraction upon the imagination of the American public. Negro tales, songs and sayings without end, as well as descriptions of Negro magic and voodoo, have appeared; but in all of them the intimate setting in the social life of the Negro has been given very inadequately.

It is the great merit of Miss Hurston's work [**Mules and Men**] that she entered into the homely life of the southern Negro as one of them and was fully accepted as such by the companions of her childhood. Thus she has been able to penetrate through that affected demeanor by which the Negro excludes the White observer effectively from participating in his true inner life. Miss Hurston has been equally successful in gaining the confidence of the voodoo doctors and she gives us much that throws a new light upon the much discussed voodoo beliefs and practices. Added to all this is the charm of a loveable personality and of a revealing style which makes Miss Hurston's work an unusual contribution to our knowledge of the true inner life of the Negro.

To the student of cultural history the material presented is valuable not only by giving the Negro's reaction to every day events, to his emotional life, his humor and passions, but it throws into relief also the peculiar amalgamation of African and European tradition which is so important for understanding historically the character of American Negro life, with its strong African background in the West Indies, the importance of which diminishes with increasing distance from the south. (p. 5)

> *Franz Boas, "Preface to 'Mules and Men,'" in* Zora Neale Hurston, *edited by Harold Bloom, Chelsea House Publishers, 1986, pp. 5-6.*

JONATHAN DANIELS   (essay date 1935)

[*The following is excerpted from a favorable review of* Mules and Men.]

When Zora Hurston set out with an education in anthropolo-

gy and a Chevrolet to collect the folk-lore of dark laughter and dark magic she counted much on her own Negro blood to make it possible for her "to penetrate through that affected demeanor by which the Negro excludes the white observer from participating in his true inner life." But no advantage of skin or blood could have produced the book [**Mules and Men**] which Miss Hurston brought back from the gay "woofing" of Florida's lumber camps and the tawdry rituals off the little sinister streets in New Orleans's Vieux Carré. Only an ability to write, a rare conjunction of the sense of the ridiculous and the sense of the dramatic, could have produced this remarkable collection of Negro folk tales and folk customs.

Perhaps not all that Miss Hurston has collected is true folk lore unless the minstrel show, the vaudeville act, and the joke book before her were unacademic collectors of the folk humor of the Negroes. Perhaps some readers will halt in skepticism as Miss Hurston advances in solemnity into the mysterious rites of Hoodoo. But her book is rich enough to stand both skepticism and familiarity. Strung together on the story of her quest for them are tales like those of Joel Chandler Harris's Brer Rabbit and of Roark Bradford's Scriptures in black face. There is material for a whole lusty and amusing book in the hilarious adventures of Old Massa and John (not John Henry, who Miss Hurston says is as modern as Casey Jones). And steadily through the book's pages there is plenty of the humor of grand black exaggeration:

> "My ole man wouldn't farm no po' land like dat," said Joe Wiley. "Now, one year we was a kinda late puttin' in our crops. Everybody else had corn a foot high when papa said, 'Well, chillun, Ah reckon we better plant some corn.' So Ah was droppin' and my brother was hillin' up behind me. We had done planted 'bout a dozen rows when Ah looked back and seen de corn comin' up. Ah didn't want it to grow too fast 'cause it would make all fodder and no roastin' ears so Ah hollered to my brother to sit down on some of it to stunt de growth. So he did, and de next day he dropped me back a note—says: 'passed thru Heben yesterday at twelve o'clock sellin' roastin' ears to de angels!'"

> "Yeah," says Larwins White, "dat was some pretty rich ground, but whut is de poorest ground you ever seen?"

> Arthur Hopkins spoke right up and said:

> "Ah seen some land so poor dat it took nine patridges to holler 'Bob White.'"

Altogether **Mules and Men** is a satisfying book. In a foreword, Dr. Franz Boas of Columbia University points out its value to "cultural history." It is also valuable to current entertainment.

> *Jonathan Daniels, "Black Magic and Dark Laughter," in* The Saturday Review of Literature, *Vol. XII, No. 25, October 19, 1935, p. 12.*

THOMAS CALDECOT CHUBB   (essay date 1936)

[*In the review of* Mules and Men *excerpted below, Chubb praises the book's characterization, language, and humor.*]

[**Mules and Men**] purports to be sociological, and in the strictest sense it is, but not even that ponderous classification can spoil it. For if *Jonah's Gourd Vine* is a story with a background of sociology, **Mules and Men** is a social study with gusto of a story. Indeed, it is hard to think of anybody interested in the negro whom this new book will not delight. The southern raconteur who justly prides himself upon his large store of stories about the colored man will here find himself beaten on his own ground, but having gained a new supply of tales to tell. The student of folk-lore will find a well-filled source-book. And he who loves the negro, or is amused by him, or burns for his wrongs, or thinks he ought to know his place, will find, each of them, as good a portrayal of the negro's character as he is ever likely to see.

Not, either, a one-sided portrayal. The gaiety, the poetry, the resourcefulness and the wit are set down, but so also are the impulsiveness, the shiftlessness, the living in the moment only. Short of associating with the negro daily, there is no way you can learn more about him. Indeed, from Miss Hurston you will find out many things that, even if you live surrounded by negroes for a long time, you might never know. For as she says, "the negro, in spite of his open-faced laughter, his seeming acquiescence, is particularly evasive." He tells the white man what he thinks the white man wants to know, or what he feels he ought to know.

The book is divided into two parts. The first part deals with "Folk Tales" and the second with "Hoodoo." I find the second part interesting, but dare not judge it. I am aware that hoodoo plays a great part in the lives of certain negroes, but I have the teasing conviction that it has always been, and always will be over-emphasized because of those who like its appeal to the romantically macabre. The first part, however, is magnificent. It is a collection of negro anecdotes, negro brags, and negro folk tales. They are all rich and full. In the accuracy of their language, they are superior to "Uncle Remus"; and as stories they average very nearly as high.

Quite expectedly, most of these stories are humorous, and a large part of what remain are fantastic; but there are a few grim, a few ghostly and a few sardonic. Of the humorous stories, the greater part deal with slaves who outwit "de ole marster," or with animals, representing the negro, who outwit animals representing the white man. For I am sure everybody must now realize that Brer Rabbit is "the brother in black," as is also Brer Gopher when he outwits rather than outruns Brer Deer. Such ugliness as there is, is mainly in the background. There you see the negro lusting, fighting, drinking coon dick and living in such an atmosphere of squalor as would crush—as it has crushed on various occasions—any less resilient race.

And laughing as the escape therefrom. For laughing is the negro's *catharsis*. It is what lets him keep his resilience. . . . (pp. 181-82)

Thomas Caldecot Chubb, in a review of "Mules and Men," in The North American Review, *Vol. 241, No. 1, March, 1936, pp. 181-83.*

DARWIN T. TURNER (essay date 1971)

[*A noted literary historian and critic, Turner has written and edited numerous studies of African-American literature, including* Images of the Negro in America *(1965) and* In a Minor Chord: Three Afro-American Writers and Their Search for Identity, *from which the following is excerpted. In this study, which examines Jean Toomer and Countee Cullen in addition to Hurston, Turner characterizes* Mules and Men *as lacking both scholarliness and artistry and asserts that the*

book is overpowered by Hurston's own personality and perceptions.]

Ironic, psychologically perceptive stories first brought [Zora Neale Hurston] to the attention of Charles S. Johnson and various other editors. **"Spunk"** and **"The Gilded Six-Bits"** typify this early work.

"Spunk" reveals the fickleness of the mob. The townspeople praise Spunk Banks when he fearlessly steals Joe Kanty's wife. Then they redirect their praise to Joe when, infuriated by insinuations that he is a coward, he attacks Spunk, who is armed. After Spunk kills Joe, the people play upon his superstitions until he accidentally kills himself. Having murdered two men and destroyed a woman's happiness, the gossips turn to a new subject.

"The Gilded Six-Bits" is equally ironic and poignant. When Joe Banks learns that his wife has been seduced by the gilded six-bit coin of Otis D. Slocum, an arrogant Northern visitor, he begins to treat her as though she is a prostitute. He changes his attitude only after the appearance of their newborn child convinces Joe that he, not Slocum, is actually the father. The story ends ironically. Ignorant of the dissension, a white confectioner who sells Joe a reconciliation gift voices his envy: "Wisht I could be like these darkies. Laughin' all the time. Nothin' worries 'em."

Miss Hurston revealed the same talents in her novels. The simply narrated tales, the credible, likable characters, and the colorful dialogue evoke tenderness and amusement. (pp. 99-100)

[*Mules and Men* and *Tell My Horse*] clearly evidence Zora Neale Hurston's talents as a reporter and her weaknesses as a scholar. Both books resulted from research grants which were awarded to enable Miss Hurston to gather folklore of Africans in the United States and the Caribbean. Although William Wells Brown had published folktales in *My Southern Home* (1880) and a few Afro-American writers had used folklore, no Afro-American before Zora Neale Hurston had compiled and published a significant, substantial collection of folklore.

The more valuable of her two collections, *Mules and Men,* includes folklore of Afro-Americans in Florida and in Louisiana. . . .

The usual hero is John, whom Miss Hurston carefully distinguished from John Henry, a creation—so Miss Hurston reported—of white storytellers. The black folk hero John is superhumanly strong and fast, and he is extremely cunning. Although somewhat awed by God, he glories in his ability to outwit a white man or the devil. The rabbit, the animal self-image of the Afro-American in much of his folklore, appears in surprisingly few tales. Miss Hurston has explained that native Floridians tell their stories about the gopher, the Florida equivalent of the rabbit. (p. 116)

Although *Mules and Men* is interesting, it is disappointingly superficial for the reader who desires more than entertainment. Miss Hurston repeatedly identified herself as an anthropologist, but there is no evidence of the scholarly procedures which would be expected from a formally trained anthropologist or researcher in folklore. Instead of classifying or analyzing tales, she merely reported them in the chronological order and the manner in which they had been told to her. Furthermore, she failed to ask or to answer essential questions. For instance, her internship as a witch doctor required her to prescribe charms and cures. Although a reader eagerly wishes to learn some results of her treatments, Miss Hurston dropped the matter after reciting the details of the prescriptions.

It cannot be said in her defense that Miss Hurston regarded the folklore with the eye of a novelist rather than a scholar. Although interested in the personalities of the storytellers, the idiom spoken by Afro-Americans, and the banter and the flirtation which accompany and encompass the storytelling sessions, she did not attempt to transform the folktale into art, as Joel Chandler Harris did with the Uncle Remus materials or as Charles Waddell Chesnutt did in "The Goophered Grapevine." Perhaps Miss Hurston neglected these matters because she was overly concerned with her major topic— Zora Neale Hurston, who travels, who learns to collect material, who is initiated into strange rituals, and who enjoys her visits. Nevertheless, despite the superficiality which limits its scholarly importance, *Mules and Men* is an enjoyable work of competent journalism, which offers valuable insight into a class of people and a way of life. (p. 117)

> Darwin T. Turner, "Zora Neale Hurston: The Wandering Minstrel," in his In a Minor Chord: Three Afro-American Writers and Their Search for Identity, *Southern Illinois University Press, 1971, pp. 89-120.*

ROBERT BONE   (essay date 1975)

[*A noted American critic, Bone is the author of the critical histories* The Negro Novel in America *(1958) and* Down Home: Origins of the Afro-American Short Story. *In the following excerpt from* Down Home, *which was originally published in 1975, Bone surveys Hurston's short stories, stressing the tension that they develop between urban and pastoral values. Bone asserts that Hurston's story "The Gilded Six-Bits" best expresses this concern and stands as her principal achievement in the short story genre.*]

The thirst for experience was always strong in Zora Hurston's soul. In her autobiography, *Dust Tracks on a Road,* she writes of herself as a child:

> But no matter whether my probings made me happier or sadder, I kept on probing to know. For instance, I had a stifled longing. I used to climb to the top of one of the huge chinaberry trees which guarded our front gate, and look out over the world. The most interesting thing that I saw was the horizon. Every way I turned, it was there, and the same distance away. Our house, then, was in the center of the world. It grew upon me that I ought to walk out to the horizon and see what the end of the world was like.

Far horizon never ceased to beckon, and the urge to explore it formed the basis of her picaresque adventures. That urge was momentarily suppressed, however, by the stifling atmosphere of a provincial, racist, and male chauvinist society. Everywhere she turned she encountered restrictive boundaries which designated certain areas as "off limits" to a Southern black girl. These limits were enforced no less by the black than the white South; hence the abrasive conflict between this imaginative youngster and the black community. Again and again she was reminded by her elders that, being black, she must settle for a good deal less than far horizon. And she rebelled with every fiber of her being.

To escape from the cramped quarters of her childhood was the central thrust of Hurston's adolescence. This thrust toward freedom, whose literary mode is the picaresque, is dramatized in three early stories, **"Drenched in Light," "John Redding Goes to Sea,"** and **"Magnolia Flower."** At the same time, a conflicting impulse is apparent in Hurston's early fiction: namely, the urge to celebrate the singularity of Eatonville, the all-black town in Florida where she was born and raised. This local-color strain, which manifests itself in stories such as **"Spunk"** and **"Sweat"** flowers ultimately into pastoral. (pp. 141-42)

Eatonville is the roosting place of Hurston's imagination; it is what she counterposes to the modern world. Founded during Reconstruction by Northern abolitionists, this independent township was the breeding ground of the frontier virtues celebrated in her fiction. Six of Hurston's stories and two of her novels are set in Eatonville, and when she abandons this familiar setting she does so at her peril. Hers is an imagination bound to a specific landscape: its people, its folkways, and its pungent idiom. This deep attachment to the Florida lake country accounts for both the strengths and limitations of her art, since what she gains in density of texture she sometimes dissipates in the depiction of a purely surface world. (p. 144)

In approaching Hurston's short fiction it is well to bear in mind that this was her apprentice work. Six of her eight stories were published from 1924 to 1926, while she was still an undergraduate. Only **"The Gilded Six-Bits,"** which appeared in *Story Magazine* of August 1933, is representative of her mature achievement. Of the apprentice pieces of the 1920's, **"Magnolia Flower"** and **"Muttsy"** are hopelessly incompetent. **"John Redding Goes to Sea,"** and **"Sweat"** hover on the borderline of art and fantasy, while **"Drenched in Light"** and **"Spunk"** display something of the power that is generated by her best fiction.

"Drenched in Light" (*Opportunity,* December 1924) is a remarkable first story, whose impetus derives from the author's childhood. Here is the relevant passage from Hurston's autobiography:

> I used to take a seat on top of the gate-post and watch the world go by. One way to Orlando ran past my house, so the carriages and cars would pass before me. The movement made me glad to see it. Often the white travelers would hail me, but more often I hailed them, and asked, "Don't you want me to go a piece of the way with you?" They always did.

The story that derives from these materials is a portrait of the artist as a young girl. The plot depicts a high-spirited child, full of mischief and invention, in conflict with a Calvinist, repressive, and experience-prohibiting society. The white-shell road that beckons to the child's imagination is a symbol of experience. Her picaresque adventures, undertaken in defiance of adult authority, are emblematic of the budding artist's unavoidable collision with the narrow outlook of the folk community. Grandma Potts, who functions like the Widow Douglas in *Huckleberry Finn,* embodies this restrictive outlook, while the child-heroine, whose name is Isis, symbolizes joy, laughter, and the pagan attitude toward life.

One day, on the occasion of a village barbecue, Isis makes off with Grandma's new red tablecloth and wears it as a Spanish shawl. Thus adorned, she performs a gypsy dance to the delight of her immediate observers. Among them are two white men and a lady who befriend the vagrant child, take her "a piece of the way" in their car, and interpose themselves and their authority between the malefactor and her grandma's wrath. In the woman's confession that she is in need of brightness, while the child is "drenched in light," adumbrations of the myth of primitivism may be seen.

It is highly significant that the white upper class, in the person of Lady Bountiful, should support the child in her imaginative exploits, and her conflict with the folk community. This woman is the fictional projection of a series of white patrons who encouraged Zora Hurston's art. At a deeper level, the episode suggests that in Hurston's unconscious mind, having access to experience was tantamount to being white. Hurston makes much of the fantasies that she indulged in as a child, devoting an entire chapter to the subject in her autobiography. It is clear from **"Drenched in Light"** that one of her most potent fantasies—imaged as a princess, wearing stately robes and riding on a white horse to the far horizon—was that of being white.

"John Redding Goes to Sea" (*Opportunity,* January 1926) is essentially a sequel, taking up where **"Drenched in Light"** leaves off. The imaginative child—this time a boy—longs to go to sea and experience something of the world, but his desire is stubbornly opposed by his mother. Mrs. Redding, like Grandma Potts, embodies the narrow and provincial outlook of the folk community, which cannot cope with the artistic temperament. Images of stasis and stagnation dominate the tale, expressive of the fate awaiting John if he lacks the courage to be free. Grown to manhood, but still intimidated by his mother, he is offered a chance to be a hero, when a bridge is threatened by a hurricane. In an ironic dénouement he drowns, escaping mediocrity only through a kind of crucifixion.

In his young manhood, John Redding is caught in an agonizing dilemma. To remain in Eatonville is to be trapped forever in superstitious ignorance, symbolized by his mother. But to depart is to be disloyal to the folk community where he was born and bred. This is the central dilemma of Hurston's life, and a common predicament among black artists. It is resolved, in Hurston's case, by her assumption of the bardic role. Guilty for having left the folk community in order to pursue her personal ambitions, Hurston seeks atonement through her art. She is determined to avoid stagnation by transcending her milieu, but equally determined to give voice to that milieu, to become its spokesman. The result is her bardic fiction, written in the local-color vein.

Two of these local-color stories, **"Spunk"** and **"Sweat,"** are closely related to the Brer Rabbit tales. In their central polarities between the cruel and powerful and the weak and oppressed, echoes of the master-slave relationship are unmistakable. Like the animal fables from which they are descended, these tales are exercises in the art of masking. The secret theme of **"Spunk"** is the violation of black womanhood; of **"Sweat,"** the deadly hatred nurtured in the hearts of the oppressed. The racial implications are effectively disguised by an all-black cast of characters, but the emotional marrow of these tales is a sublimated racial anger.

"Spunk" (*Opportunity,* June 1925) is concerned with two varieties of courage or definitions of manhood. Spunk Banks is a giant of a man who carries off his neighbor's wife and defies him to redress the injury. Joe Kanty, the aggrieved husband,

Hurston in her mid-twenties.

hesitates to challenge his tormentor, but taunted by the village men, he attacks him from behind, only to be shot to death. The men function as a chorus, observing and commenting on the action. At the outset Spunk wins their admiration through his fearlessness, while Joe is despised for his apparent cowardice. In the end, however, a villager proclaims that "Joe was a braver man than Spunk." Amid the derisive shouts of his audience he explains that it requires a greater courage for the weaker to attack the stronger man.

Behind the two antagonists loom the archetypal figures of Brer Rabbit and Brer Bear. Joe Kanty, as his name suggests, would be helpless in an open test of strength; his only hope lies in a surprise attack. The story thus endorses the survival values of subterfuge and treachery, up to and including an assault from behind. Two conflicting codes, one "honorable" or Anglo-Saxon, the other "cowardly" or Negro, are juxtaposed. The story repudiates conventional morality and affirms the outlaw code imposed upon the black man by his social subjugation. Hurston thus invokes the ancient wisdom of the folktale to reconcile the frontier virtues of courage and manliness with the brutal facts of caste.

"Sweat" (*Fire,* November 1926) is a less successful tale. The heroine is Delia Jones, a long-suffering laundress whose life is made unbearable by a brutal, tyrannous, and flagrantly philandering husband. Sykes attempts to kill his wife by concealing a rattlesnake in her laundry basket, but in an ironic reversal, he is destroyed by his own villainy. Throughout the story, man and wife are locked in a mutual hatred so intense that it acquires the force of myth. Behind their murderous domestic quarrel we discern the ancient animosities of Brer Rabbit and Brer Wolf. Like the cruellest and most sadistic of the animal fables, this story serves to vent illicit feelings of hatred and revenge.

The story has an ending that can only be described as self-indulgent. In the episode depicting Sykes' ordeal, Hurston loses her composure and rejoices in the torture of her villain. **"Sweat"** is thus reduced to a revenge fantasy. While such fantasies are a common feature of the animal fables, a more sophisticated medium demands a commensurate advance in emotional control. Nor does the story succeed as a horror tale, for naming the emotion that a reader is supposed to feel is not the same as compelling him to feel it. Hurston is an amateur in horror, and compared to Eric Walrond's "The White Snake," this story is a visit with the children to the Bronx Zoo.

From stories in the local-color vein, Hurston's imagination flowered into pastoral. But not until her disillusionment with urban life was complete. **"Muttsy"** (*Opportunity,* August 1926) is her story of recoil from the black metropolis, similar in tone and psychological significance to Claude McKay's Harlem tales. **"Drenched in Light"** and **"John Redding Goes to Sea"** portray the self setting forth from its place of origin in quest of wider horizons. **"Muttsy"** Hurston's sole attempt to deal with the urban scene, depicts the self in jeopardy from false, urban values. **"The Gilded Six-Bits"** brings the theme full circle as the self, reconciled to its provincial origins, returns to its spiritual home in Eatonville.

"The Gilded Six-Bits" (*Story,* August 1933) is Hurston's principal achievement in the short-story form. The tale inaugurates the second and most creative phase of her career, which followed her return to Eatonville in 1932. She now was a mature woman: her ambivalent feelings toward the folk community had been resolved; her adolescent impulse to escape it, mastered. Her curiosity to witness something of the larger world had been appeased, and she was ready to accept her destiny. That destiny, she now perceived, was to embrace her folk experience and give it form. The fruit of self-acceptance was a burst of creativity, beginning with the present story and extending through three novels.

The story is concerned with a crisis in the lives of Joe and Missie May. They have been happily married for a year when Slemmons, an urbanized Negro from Chicago, opens an ice-cream parlor in Eatonville. Dazzled by his fancy clothes and city ways, Missie May forgets herself and takes him as a lover. Joe discovers the deception and drives Slemmons off, but it is many months before he can forgive his thoroughly remorseful wife. Structurally speaking, the woman functions as a pivot between two value systems: the one urban and "sophisticated," the other rural and elemental. At first she chooses falsely, but in the end the deep and abiding values of the countryside prevail.

"The Gilded Six-Bits" is essentially a drama of sin and redemption, a symbolic reenactment of the Fall. As the story opens, Joe and Missie May frolic in prelapsarian innocence. Their pastoral surroundings and simple way of life constitute a Paradise where "all, everything was right." Into this happy Eden comes the Tempter, Slemmons, who proffers not an apple but a ten-dollar gold piece suspended from his watch

chain. That the gold should prove to be illusory is Hurston's bitter comment on the Great Migration. Through Slemmons the city is exposed as a repository of false values.

The shallowness of urban culture is conveyed through Slemmons' attitude toward time. In the modern world of progress and improvement, of which the ice-cream parlor is an emblem, time is a commodity. The capitalist ethos, with its obligation to convert time into money, is symbolized by Slemmons' golden watch charm. But the peasant world of Joe and Missie May responds to natural rather than artificial rhythms: "Finally the sun's tide crept upon the shore of night and drowned its hours." In this world, time has a moral and theological rather than economic significance. It is primarily a healing force, repairing the breach that guilt has opened in the human soul.

"The Gilded Six-Bits" thus reveals the central core of Hurston's values. In this story, written in the depths of the Depression, she attacks the acquisitive society from a standpoint not unlike that of the Southern Agrarians. For the first time her social conservatism, inherited from Booker Washington by way of Eatonville, finds in pastoral an appropriate dramatic form. At the same time that her values coalesce, her narrative voice assumes a new authority. A mature style emerges whose metaphors, drawn from folk speech, function as a celebration of agrarian ideals. Having discovered her subject and mastered her idiom, she turns to those longer works of fiction where, for the most part, her achievement as a writer lies. (pp. 144-50)

> *Robert Bone, "Three Versions of Pastoral," in his* Down Home: Origins of the Afro-American Short Story, *Columbia University Press, 1988, pp. 139-70.*

THERESA R. LOVE (essay date 1976)

[*Love discusses the subject matter and language of the folktales collected in* Mules and Men, *noting particularly Hurston's use of slang and dialect.*]

Warning that there is an inherent danger in seeing oneself through the eyes of others, DuBois urged Afro-American writers to remember that "in art and literature, we should try to loose the tremendous emotional wealth of the Negro and the dramatic strength of his problem through writing, the stage, pageant, and other forms of art. We should resurrect forgotten ancient Negro art and history, and we should set the black man before the world as both a creative artist and a strong subject for artistic treatment." This belief of Dr. Du-Bois's is reflected in Langston Hughes's statement that one of the aims of *Fire* [a literary magazine founded by several writers of the Harlem Renaissance] was "to burn up a lot of the old dead conventional Negro white ideas of the past, 'épater le bourgeois.' "

Miss Hurston took such pronouncements seriously. Her goal was not merely to collect folklore but to show the beauty and wealth of genuine Negro material. In doing so, she placed herself on the side of those who saw nothing self-defeating in writing about the black masses, who, she felt, are more imaginative than their middle-class counterparts. Consequently, few of the latter are included in her works. Often, her characters work and live in sawmill camps. Some are sharecroppers. Some work on railroads. Most are uneducated and provincial. A statement from her short story, **"John Redding Goes to Sea,"** sums up their way of life: "No one of their community had ever been farther than Jacksonville. Few, indeed had ever been there. Their own gardens, general store, and occasional trips to the county seat—seven miles away—sufficed for all their needs. Life was simple indeed with these folk." To the anthropologist, their economic and cultural isolation made them the proper source for folk materials in their purest form.

While most of Miss Hurston's subjects are Floridians, many are West Indians, for her interest in folklore led her to the Caribbean Islands, where she again concentrated on the legends, superstitions, music, and dances of the folk. She was especially intrigued by the blacks in the Bahamas, whom she regarded as more prolific and better composers of music than their American counterparts. And then there is Jelly, of **"Story in Harlem Slang,"** the New York "pimp" who has his own variety of "racial prejudice," which he describes to a friend in these words: "Man, I don't deal in no coal. Know what I tell 'em? If they's white, they's right! If they's yellow, they's mellow! If they's brown, they can stick around. But if they come black, they better get way back!"

This passage suggests another important aspect of Zora Hurston's work. Her decision to write about the ways of the folk necessitated her use of their dialect as a means of achieving verisimilitude. Of course, the careful student of a writer must always remember that the writer's rendition of a dialect may or may not be authentic. Many writers are merely following a literary tradition—that of attributing certain speech patterns to a given social or ethnic group for artistic reasons. Inasmuch as most of Miss Hurston's characters are represented as being speakers of Black Dialect, and inasmuch as she herself abandons her use of the General Dialect when she pictures herself as a researcher among those who speak the variant dialect, it would appear to be relevant to determine whether or not she is merely using a literary convention or is being scientific in her work as an anthropologist.

The following excerpt from *Mules and Men* reveals her use of the speech patterns of many blacks:

> God was sittin' down by de sea makin' sea fishes. He made de whale and throwed dat in and it swum off. He made a shark and throwed it in and then he made mullets and cats and trouts and all swum on off.
>
> De Devil was standin' behind him lookin' over his shoulder.
>
> Way after while, God made a turtle and throwed it in de water and it swum on off. Devil says, "Ah, kin made one of those things."
>
> God said: "Devil, Ah know you can't make none, but if you think kin make one go 'head and make it and Ah'll blow de breath of life into it for you."
>
> You see, God was sittin' down by de sea, makin' de fish outa sea mud. But de Devil went on up de hill so God couldn't watch his workin', and made his outa high land dirt. God waited nearly all day befo' de Devil come back wid his turtle.
>
> As soon as God seen it, He said, "Devil, dat ain't no turtle you done made."
>
> Devil flew hot right off. "Dat ain't no turtle? Who say dat ain't no turtle? Sho it's a turtle."
>
> God shook his head, says, "Dat sho ain't no turtle,

> but Ah'll blow de breath of life into it like Ah promised." . . .
>
> So God blowed de breath of life into what de Devil had done made, and throwed him into de water. He swum out. God throwed him in again. He come out. . . .
>
> God says: "See, Ah told you dat wasn't no turtle."
>
> "Yes, suh, *dat* is a turtle."
>
> "Devil, don't you know dat all turtles loves de water? Don't you see whut you done made won't stay in there?"
>
> Devil said, "Ah don't keer, dat's a turtle. Ah keep a 'telling you."
>
> God disputed him down dat it wasn't no turtle. Devil looked it over and scratched he head. Then he says, "Well, anyhow it will go for one." And that's why we have gophers!

Even a cursory glance at this myth will show that the anthropologist and writer has been quite faithful in recording the speech patterns of her subjects. There are phonological deviations from those of the General Dialect: the substitution of the *d* sound for the *th* sound and that of *k* for *c* (kin); morphological features: the double negative ("Ah know you *can't* make *none*"); the inflection of strong verbs as if they were weak ("throwed"); overinflection ("All turtles loves *water*"); and the variant use of pronouns ("and scratched *he* head"). Yet there are other patterns which linguists have attributed to Black Dialect and which do not appear in this passage at all: the omission of the *s* signal as an indication of the third person singular present tense ("he eat") and the use of the pronominal appositive ("the gopher he couldn't stop"). These omissions are interesting because they represent two of the most frequently recurring features of the variant dialect. As a result, it would seem that Miss Hurston's use of Black Dialect forms substantiates the theory that she is willing to sacrifice her interest in anthropology—which discipline would emphasize the need for photographic descriptive passages—for the sake of artistic expediency. Otherwise her works might now be facing the same fate as those of Joel Chandler Harris, whose Uncle Remus tales are seldom read because of the difficulty which the modern reader has with the heavy, nineteenth-century Black Dialect in which they are written.

A careful student of Zora Neale Hurston must also distinguish between her use of slang and her use of dialect. In the short story in which Jelly appears, **"Story in Harlem Slang,"** there is Black Dialect, but there is also "black slang." For example, there are these terms: "trying to jump salty," "gum beatin'," "ziggaboo," "coal scuttle blond," "conk buster," and "gut bucket." Interestingly enough, these terms almost never appear in her novels, in which she is discussing the inhabitants of Florida, or in her books of folklore, but they do appear in this story about two Harlem pimps, who would like to think that they are irresistible to women, especially since they depend on women for a livelihood. They would also like to think that they have become more urbane since they have come north. They are not the simple, naïve men who watch girls from the porch of Joe Clark's store, which is the setting of most of Miss Hurston's works. They are, in the common vernacular, "hip." The writer thus gives them an appropriate vocabulary and thereby shows how skillfully she can combine her learning and her artistic abilities. (pp. 425-28)

Mules and Men, the tales which Joe Wiley, Jim Allen, Larkins White, and their friends tell the anthropologist, deals with a variety of . . . subjects. Many of the tales are based on Biblical situations. An example is a tale about a woodpecker, whose natural instinct to peck wood is stronger than Noah's warning that if he does not abstain from doing so, he will drill a hole in the ark and cause it to sink. As a result, Noah, angered by the bird's disobedience, bloodies his head with a sledge hammer, and "dat's why a peckerwood got a red head today." The possum also incurs an unfortunate incident with Ham, Noah's son, who loves to play the banjo and the guitar. During the great flood, Ham runs out of strings for his instruments, and so he goes down into the hold of the ship, finds the possum, and shaves the hairs off its tail, and that is why the possum's tail is without hairs today. In another tale, God is sympathetic to the snake, whom he suffers to crawl on the ground to ornament it. When men start treading on the defenseless creature, however, God gives him poison to protect himself. He also gives him rings to rattle, as a warning that man is near. This is done so that man may avoid stepping on him. Only when man does not heed the warning, may the snake strike. This last tale is designed to emphasize the mercy and justice of God. Many of the tales are moral lessons. Among them are those that show that selfishness and greed are punished, while virtue is rewarded. An example is a tale of a cat who eats nine fish, which are all of the food that a starving family and its dog possess. Eventually all die of starvation, except the cat who dies because he has eaten too much. When they reach heaven, God is so angry with the cat's selfishness and greed that he has his angels throw him out. The cat falls for nine days, "and there ain't been no cats in Heben since." The cat still has those nine lives in his belly and that is why "you got to kill him nine times before he'll stay dead." (pp. 429-30)

Not all of the tales which Miss Hurston recounts in *Mules and Men* are based on Biblical situations, nor do all teach moral lessons. Some attempt to explain elemental matters; **"Why the Waves Have Whitecaps"** is one of the most moving and touching of these. This myth moreover, is important, for it reveals that a sympathetic bond exists between the huge bodies of water which carve Florida into a peninsula and the people who inhabit it. In the Hurston version Mrs. Wind and Mrs. Water try to outdo each other in bragging about their children. Each claims that hers are the more gifted. Eventually, Mrs. Water tires of Mrs. Wind's bragging and begins to hate Mrs. Wind's children so much that one day, when they come over to her house for a drink of water, she grabs them and drowns them all. The grief-stricken mother goes over the ocean calling them, and every time she does so, the white fringes of their caps rise, and that is why the sea waves have white caps, and so, "When you see a storm on de water, it's de wind and de water fightin' over dem children." (p. 430)

The frequent religious and moral flavor of the myths and legends of black people might be taken as an indication that religion plays a strong part in their lives, and, certainly, the works of Zora Neale Hurston would seem to suggest that she thought so herself. Any discussion of her attitude toward the religious practices of blacks must, however, take into account the fact that she makes a distinction between those who practice true Christianity and those who are hypocrites.

The distinction is made clear when one studies the behavior of the men and women who throng the "jooks" on Saturday night, as contrasted to those whom she pictures as frequenting the churches on Sundays. The former drink, swear, and carry switch blades, which they use at the drop of an epithet; yet they are the epitome of kindness and love. For example, Big Sweet in *Mules and Men* is pictured as preferring jooks to churches, but there is no one who is more loyal and true than she. In fact, it is she who helps Zora Neale escape the knife of the jealous Lucy, for when Big Sweet gave her word that "I aims to look out for you . . . do your fighting for you," she meant it, and nobody bothers Big Sweet, not even the Quarters Boss, for she is so tough that if God gives her a pistol, she will send him a man.

In Miss Hurston's fiction, few examples of such devout love can be found among those characters who profess to be Christians, for she depicts many of them as being full of greed and malice. The incident in *Mules and Men* dealing with the traveling preacher and his two women companions—one on his left side and one on his right—may serve as an illustration. One evening, when the sun had set behind the living quarters of the sawmill workers and when their children had finished playing "Shoo-round," and "Chick-mah-chick," the "stump beater," as the novelist calls him, and his two females come walking into the area. After the woman on his left has sung "Death Comes a Creepin'," he announces his text, "Behold de Rib!" His message is that since God made the first woman from a man's rib, He means for men and women to work side by side—not one before, nor one behind, just side by side. When he has delivered this profound message, the preacher takes up a collection and leaves. Miss Hurston's satirical tone suggests that he was called to preach by hard work in the sun, as one of the quarters-women puts it, rather than by God. (pp. 433-34)

Theresa R. Love, "Zora Neale Hurston's America," in Papers on Language & Literature, *Vol. 12, No. 4, Fall, 1976, pp. 422-37.*

ALICE WALKER   (essay date 1976)

[*An American novelist, short story writer, poet, and critic, Walker is noted for works that powerfully express her concern with racial, sexual, and political issues, particularly the black woman's struggle for spiritual and political survival. She is best known for her novel* The Color Purple *(1982), which was awarded both the American Book Award and the Pulitzer Prize. Walker played a major role in the rediscovery of Hurston in the 1970s. She wrote an article recounting her journey to Hurston's hometown, during which she placed a headstone over Hurston's unmarked grave (see Additional Bibliography), and edited* I Love Myself When I Am Laughing . . . and Then Again When I Am Looking Mean and Impressive: A Zora Neale Hurston Reader *(1979), an important gathering of selections from Hurston's work. In the following excerpt from her foreword to Robert E. Hemenway's biography of Hurston, Walker testifies to the significance of* Mules and Men *as a work of literary art and an invaluable document of African-American folk culture.*]

I became aware of my need of Zora Neale Hurston's work some time before I knew her work existed. In late 1970 I was writing a story that required accurate material on voodoo practices among rural southern blacks of the thirties; there seemed none available I could trust. A number of white, racist anthropologists and folklorists of the period had, not surprisingly, disappointed and insulted me. They thought blacks inferior, peculiar, and comic, and for me this undermined—

no, *destroyed*—the relevance of their books. Fortunately, it was then that I discovered *Mules and Men,* Zora's book on folklore, collecting, herself, and her small, all-black community of Eatonville, Florida. Because she immersed herself in her own culture even as she recorded its "big old lies," i.e., folktales, it was possible to see how she and it (even after she had attended Barnard College and become a respected writer and apprentice anthropologist) fit together. The authenticity of her material was verified by her familiarity with its context, and I was soothed by her assurance that she was exposing not simply an adequate culture, but a superior one. That black people can be on occasion peculiar and comic was knowledge she enjoyed. That they could be racially or culturally inferior to whites never seems to have crossed her mind. (p. xi)

When I read *Mules and Men* I was delighted. Here was this perfect book! The "perfection" of it I immediately tested on my relatives, who are such typical black Americans they are useful for every sort of political, cultural, or economic survey. Very regular people from the South, rapidly forgetting their southern cultural inheritance in the suburbs and ghettos of Boston and New York, they sat around reading the book themselves, listening to me read the book, listening to each other read the book, and a kind of paradise was regained. For Zora's book gave them back all the stories they had forgotten or of which they had grown ashamed (told to us years ago by our parents and grandparents—not one of whom could *not* tell a story to make us weep, or laugh) and showed how marvelous, and, indeed, priceless, they are. *This is not exaggerated.* No matter how they read the stories Zora had collected, no matter how much distance they tried to maintain between themselves, as new sophisticates, and the lives their parents and grandparents lived, no matter how they tried to remain cool toward all Zora revealed, in the end they could not hold back the smiles, the laughter, the *joy* over who she was showing them to be: descendants of an inventive, joyous, courageous, and outrageous people: loving drama, appreciating wit, and, most of all, relishing the pleasure of each other's loquacious and *bodacious* company.

This was my first indication of the quality I feel is most characteristic of Zora's work: racial health—a sense of black people as complete, complex, *undiminished* human beings, a sense that is lacking in so much black writing and literature. (In my opinion, only Du Bois showed an equally consistent delight in the beauty and spirit of black people, which is interesting when one considers that the angle of his vision was completely the opposite of Zora's.) Zora's pride in black people was so pronounced in the ersatz black twenties that it made other blacks suspicious and perhaps uncomfortable; after all, *they* were still infatuated with things European—*everything* European. Zora was interested in Africa, Haiti, Jamaica—and, for a little racial diversity (Indians), Honduras. She also had a confidence in herself as an individual that few people (anyone?), black or white, understood. This was because Zora grew up in a community of black people who had enormous respect for themselves and for their ability to *govern* themselves. Her own father had written the Eatonville town laws. This community affirmed her right to exist, and loved her as an extension of itself. For how many other black Americans is this true? It certainly isn't true for any that I know. In her easy self-acceptance, Zora was more like an uncolonized African than she was like her contemporary American blacks, most of whom believed, at least during their formative years, that their blackness was something wrong with them.

On the contrary, Zora's early work shows she grew up *pitying* whites because the ones she saw lacked "light" and soul. It is impossible to imagine Zora envying anyone (except tongue-in-cheek), and, least of all, a white person for being white. Which is, after all, if one is black, a clear and present calamity of the mind.

Condemned to a deserted island for life, with an allotment of ten books to see me through, I would choose, unhesitatingly, two of Zora's: *Mules and Men,* because I would need to be able to pass on to younger generations the life of American blacks as legend and myth, and *Their Eyes Were Watching God,* because I would want to enjoy myself while identifying with the black heroine, Janie Crawford, as she acted out many roles in a variety of settings, and functioned (with spectacular results!) in romantic and sensual love. *There is no book more important to me than this one.* (pp. xii-xiii)

> *Alice Walker, "Zora Neale Hurston—A Cautionary Tale and a Partisan View," in* Zora Neale Hurston: A Literary Biography *by Robert E. Hemenway, University of Illinois Press, 1977, pp. xi-xviii.*

ROBERT E. HEMENWAY (essay date 1977)

[*Hemenway is the author of Hurston's critical biography, excerpted below. Here he discusses several issues surrounding* Mules and Men, *including narrative stance, literary technique, and issues of scholariness.*]

The intimacy of *Mules and Men* is an obtained effect, an example of Hurston's narrative skill. She represented oral art functioning to affect behavior in the black community; to display this art in its natural setting she created a narrator who would not intrude on the folklore event. A semifictional Zora Neale Hurston is our guide to southern black folklore, a curiously retiring figure who is more art than life. The exuberant Zora Hurston who entertained the Harlem Renaissance is seldom in evidence in *Mules and Men.* In her place is a self-effacing reporter created by Hurston the folklorist to dramatize the process of collecting and make the reader feel part of the scene.

Mules and Men begins in Eatonville as the young collector returns to her native village to listen to "all them old-time tales about Brer Rabbit and Brer Bear" and "set them down before it's too late." Her next stop is Polk County, "where they really lies up a mess and . . . where dey makes up all de songs." By the time she leaves central Florida, her seventy tale texts have been recorded and two-thirds of the book written. She then heads for New Orleans to collect hoodoo. This last section describes the rituals of five different power doctors she studied with, supplemented by an appendix listing conjure paraphernalia and root doctors' prescriptions.

It is easy to overlook Hurston's craft as she mediates between self and material in this presentation; yet she shaped *Mules and Men* in somewhat the same manner in which Henry David Thoreau created a unified experience in *Walden.* His two years of residence at Walden Pond were condensed into a book structured around one year's seasonal cycle. Hurston condenses a two-and-a-half-year expedition into one year and nine months, with a one-year segment (Florida) and a nine-month segment (New Orleans). Her two return trips to Eatonville in 1927 and 1928 are telescoped into a single dramatic homecoming. At the end of the Florida section she claims to have "spent a year in gathering and culling over folk tales."

Actually, she spent only six months in Florida before heading for New Orleans; but a year makes possible an orderly transition to the new section: "Winter passed and caterpillars began to cross the road again. . . . So I slept a night, and the next morning I headed my toe-nails toward Louisiana."

Hurston had to provide a frame for the adventures and insights of a complicated experience; she had to select from a multitude of situations and personalities. One way to unify could have been, like Thoreau, to stress the personal significance of the various encounters. Yet *Mules and Men* is ultimately a book very different from *Walden* precisely because Hurston did not choose the personal option. Her adventures go purposely without analysis. While Henry David Thoreau embarks on a voyage of spiritual discovery, Zora Neale Hurston always remains close to the shore, her description directed away from the inner self toward the words of her informants.

The scholarly folklorist of the thirties was expected to subordinate self to material in the interests of objectivity. The intent was to leave the emphasis on the folklore texts that were being added to the "body of knowledge." After describing the corpse, the folklorist could perform an autopsy in order to learn how the living organism functions. The cold text, isolated on the page for scientific study, implied the living folk, but the folk themselves were secondary to the artifact collected. Hurston knew such training, and she had written two articles for the *Journal of American Folklore* in a proper scholarly manner, dispassionately reporting her texts and offering theories about the relationships between Afro-American and Afro-Caribbean folklore. As she acknowledged in the letter to Boas [see excerpt dated 1934], she was well aware of how *Mules and Men* departed from this accepted mode, and she worked hard to make sure that her personal saga did not become the book's focus. Much of *Mules and Men* is a simple reporting of texts, an approach similar to that of another prominent black folklorist of the era, J. Mason Brewer. Yet Hurston also breathed life into her narrative by presenting herself as a master of ceremonies, a transitional voice. Instead of observing a pathologist perform an autopsy, the reader keeps in sight a midwife participating in the birth of the body folklore. The effect is subtle and often overlooked. *Mules and Men* does not become an exercise in romantic egoism; it celebrates the art of the community. Where the reader of *Walden* comes away with visions of separating from society in order to gain spiritual renewal, the reader of *Mules and Men* learns a profound respect for men and women perpetuating an esthetic mode of communication; the impulse is not to isolate oneself, but to lose the self in the art and wisdom of the group.

From the very first pages Hurston creates a self-effacing persona inviting the reader to participate in collective rituals. She arrives in Eatonville knowing that even if she had given birth to a "Kaiser baby" (that is, had had a child by the Kaiser), she would still be John and Lucy's daughter; college degrees mean nothing to the loafers on the store porch, for they will define their community in their own terms, identify people according to kin. They are like African *griots* who preserve the genealogy of a tribe which has not developed a written language. Hurston portrays herself as a town prodigal returned to collect "them big old lies we tell when we're jus' sittin' around here on the porch doin' nothin'." She is an educated innocent whose memory of the village folklore has been diminished by her urban experience and academic study; she must renew community ties.

Portrait of a young Hurston.

Yet Arna Bontemps testified that many of the *Mules and Men* tales were a vivid part of Hurston's storytelling repertoire when she arrived in New York, well before she ever studied or collected folklore. A short story like **"Black Death"** confirms the accuracy of that memory. The Zora Neale Hurston of *Mules and Men,* then, is deliberately underplaying her knowledge of Eatonville so that the reader will not feel alienated. Because she saw from a dual perspective, both from within the community and from without, Hurston the writer could select those experiences which would attract the reader and let the folk speak for themselves. Hurston the narrator admits only to a desire to hold a microphone up to nature.

This technique, which falls somewhere between scientific reporting and personal journalism, produces a repeated pattern of experience. Zora becomes a member of each community she encounters, accepted by virtue of race and her sympathy with communal ways. As she is accepted, so is the reader. Each experience in the book begins with her admission into a group. She starts in Eatonville not only because she can collect there without harm or danger, but also because she is by definition of birth a part of that village. When she travels to Polk County she must establish a right to be in the lumber camp before she can retire and listen. She is accepted only after a fugitive status is created, an extensive repertoire of folksongs is demonstrated, and her "$12.74 dress from

Macy's" is put away. The dress is an obvious example of Hurston's narrative posing for the benefit of her readers. Given her collecting experience, it seems extremely unlikely that Zora Neale would actually be wearing such a dress in a lumber camp. Yet by suggesting a certain distance between herself and her informants—symbolized by her clothes—the narrator manages to ease the reader into the alien environment.

There is an ambivalence here that has sometimes been criticized. Is **Mules and Men** about Zora Hurston or about black folklore? If the former, the self-effacement makes the reader want to know more about what was going on in her mind, more about her reaction to the communities that embraced her. If the latter, there is a need for folklore analysis. Are hoodoo candles a form of fire worship comparable to the use of fire in Christian ritual? What is the cross-cultural structure of the folktale? These deficiencies are the price Hurston paid for her two-fold purpose. On the one hand, she was trying to represent the artistic content of black folklore; on the other, she was trying to suggest the behavioral significance of folkloric events. Her efforts were intended to show rather than tell, the assumption being that both behavior and art will become self-evident as the tale texts and hoodoo rituals accrete during the reading.

Hurston presents the artistic content in the communication by stressing how "facile" is the "Negro imagination." The participants in a tale-telling session are all capable of verbal adornment: "A'nt Hagar's son, like Joseph, put on his many-colored coat and paraded before his brethren and every man there was a Joseph." A storyteller is someone who can "plough up some literary and lay-by some alphabets." The scholar never steps in to stress the ingenuity of a particular metaphor or the startling effectiveness of an image. She wants to reveal, in her words, "that which the soul lives by" in a rural black community; although there was a need for a transitional voice, only by stepping to the background could she allow unhampered expression. She did not want her readers reminded too often that a folklorist was there to take it all down, a fact that is reflected in her collecting technique. When Alan Lomax asked her, in 1935, "How do you learn most of your songs?" he got a precise reply: "I just get in the crowd with the people and if they sing it I listen as best I can and then I start to joinin' in with a phrase or two and then finally I get so I can sing a verse. And then I keep on until I learn all the verses and then I sing 'em back to the people until they tell me I can sing 'em just like them. And then I take part and I try it out on different people who already know the song until they are quite satisfied that I know it. Then I carry it in my memory. . . . I learn the song myself and then I can take it with me wherever I go." Hurston's technique, in other words, was to become one of the folk, a position which did not allow for the detachment of the analytical observer.

This deliberate lack of analysis places a special responsibility on the reader. The tales of **Mules and Men** are *not* quaint fictions created by a primitive people. They are profound expressions of a group's behavior. Readers have frequently overlooked the fact that Hurston represented this in a tale-telling context; because context is often essential to understanding an orally rendered story, they have also failed to perceive the behavioral significance of the particular tale. The following story illustrates the point:

You know Ole Massa took a nigger deer huntin'

and posted him in his place and told him, says: "Now you wait right here and keep yo' gun reformed and ready. Ah'm goin' 'round de hill and skeer up de deer and head him dis way. When he come past, you shoot."

De nigger says: "Yessuh, Ah sho' will, Massa."

He set there and waited wid de gun all cocked and after a while de deer come tearin' past him. He didn't make a move to shoot de deer so he went on 'bout his business. After while de white man come on 'round de hill and ast de nigger: "Did you kill de deer?"

De nigger says: "Ah ain't seen no deer pass here yet."

Massa says: "Yes, you did. You couldn't help but see him. He come right dis way."

Nigger says: "Well Ah sho' ain't seen none. All Ah seen was a white man come along here wid a pack of chairs on his head and Ah tipped my hat to him and waited for de deer."

The tale is best understood as that of a slave outwitting his master, thwarting his plans, then escaping punishment by retreating behind the mask of stupidity. The mask is effective because the white man's racism disables him; to believe that the black man is intelligent enough to trick him would destroy his presumption of superiority. It is the time-honored technique of "puttin' on ole massa." The key to this interpretation of the tale is the context Hurston established for it. It is told on a day when the men in the logging camp discover that they will not have to work because the train to transport them to the woods has been sent away. This occasion produces a series of tales about how white men have imposed labor on blacks, and how black men and women, since slavery, have both suffered from the imposition and cunningly escaped it. Directly preceding the antlers—pack-of-chairs story are an account of a field hand saying "More rain, more rest," then changing his line to "more rain, more grass" when asked to repeat by the overseer; speculation that there "must be something terrible wrong" at the lumber camp "when white folks get slow about putting us to work"; a story about a straw boss "so mean dat when the boiler burst and blowed some of the men up in the air, he docked 'em for de time they was off de job"; a tale about John's tricking Ole Massa into holding a bear by the tail; and a story about how the white man obtained pen and ink from God and "so ever since then de nigger been out in de hot sun, usin' his tools and de white man been sittin' up figgerin', ought's a ought, figger's a figger, all for de white man, none for de nigger." Hurston's context emphasizes white unfairness and black ingenuity. Applied to the story, this context suggests that when the slave refuses to shoot, he is escaping from labor, just as the field hand did when it rained; his action protests the presumption that a white skin endows one with the right to give orders or demand a Jim Crow acknowledgment—the tip of the hat—of white authority. The slave's explanation enables him to gain ascendency in a situation where those orders have not been carried out. The ludicrous picture of a white man with a rack of chairs on his head undermines the image of white dominion. The denouement places the master in a situation where his wishes have been thwarted, his appearance has been mocked, and his own labor has been made as unrewarding as that of his slaves.

One characteristic of folktales is that they lose their original context. Like ancient religious rituals, the form is kept while the function changes; the meaning gets lost. Hurston knew that this was a characteristic of all folklore, and her immediate report of this revolutionary tale, no doubt taken from her field notes, reveals how the function of the tale may have been distorted. Providing an interpretation of the tale that sharply contrasts with Hurston's context, the teller concludes, "Some colored folks ain't got no sense, and when ah see 'em like dat, ah say, 'My race but not my taste.' "

It may be that this was simply the closing formula for the tale, passed from generation to generation, insuring that its ironic content would not be detected. If so, the closing lines mean exactly the opposite of what they say. But as one commentator has argued about the phrase "if you're black get back," expressions like "some colored folks ain't got no sense" may feed racial self-hate and encourage a group inferiority complex. There is a fine line between seeing the tale as cunning and seeing it as ignorance.

One must challenge any interpretation of ignorance because there are so many overt protest tales in *Mules and Men* of the same form and structure as the antlers—pack-of-chairs story. The pattern is basically that a dutiful slave performs a task and the situation results in a thwarting of the master's wishes. The tales from the John-Marster cycle are almost all of this general structure; the emphasis is upon John's ingenuity in turning a situation to his advantage. As one storyteller puts it, "John sho was a smart nigger now. He useter git de best of Ole Massa all de time." Hurston observed that this quality makes John "the wish fulfillment hero of the race." (pp. 164-71)

Mules and Men is not all folktales and hoodoo. It also contains many sayings, fragments of songs, rhymes, and legends. There is little explanation, however, of how all this folklore assumes any significance beyond the immediate entertainment. When a story ends "Stepped on a pin, de pin bent / And dat's de way de story went," it is up to the reader to speculate about the traditional closing formulas of the folktale. In actuality, the rhyme functions like "and they lived happily ever after." When one man tells another, "Don't you like it, don't you take it; here's mah collar, come and shake it," there is no explanation of how verbal formulas direct aggression into socially acceptable forms. Rhyme as a creative response to a prosaic world goes unanalyzed. Brer Rabbit is not discussed as an allegorical figure symbolizing black cunning. Hoodoo as an alternative science with a worldview as valid as any other goes unexplored. The universality of trickster figures like John goes unanalyzed. There is deliberately no cross-cultural reference, although many of the tales also appear in other cultures. There is no reference at all to the scholarship in the field.

These remarks are not necessarily criticisms, for Hurston makes *Mules and Men* a very readable folklore book. But the subordination of Hurston the scholar to Hurston the narrator can cause the reader to miss her attempts to provide the data for scholarly study. There is a consistent and subtle attempt, for example, to demonstrate how traditional tales are perpetuated. A small boy is encouraged to speak, then praised for the "over average lie" he contributes to the lying session. Presumably he will grow up a storyteller. When Joe Wiley asks if anyone has heard the story about "Big Talk," the reply is, "Yeah, we done heard it, Joe, but Ah kin hear it some 'gin." When a man says he will tell a tale for his wife, his listener

responds, "Aw, g'wan tell de lie, Larkins if you want to. You know you ain't tellin no lie for yo' wife. No mo' than de rest of us. You lyin' cause you like it." There is psychic satisfaction in the repetition of narratives.

Similarly, Hurston summarized the difference between an active and a passive tradition-bearer:

> "Didja ever hear de White man's prayer?"
>
> "Who in Polk County ain't heard dat?" Cut in Officer Richardson.
>
> "Well, if you know it so good, lemme hear *you* say it," Eugene snapped back.
>
> "Oh, Ah don't know it well enough to say it. Ah just know it well enough to know it."

The active tradition-bearer produces the text; the passive tradition-bearer is a self-correcting force insuring that the text will not be altered in any significant way.

The tale-telling context is often humorous, a kind of game-playing; but tales can also be used to deflect a potentially violent encounter. Hurston chose such an event to give one of her infrequent, indirect explanations of folkloric process: how proverbs serve as religious texts for a secular moment, and how specially gifted storytellers function as secular priests. The following exchange demonstrates Hurston's contextualism; the explanation occurs in the form of an argument between the storytellers:

> Jim Allen commented: "Well, you know what they say—a man can cackerlate his life till he git mixed up wid a woman or git straddle of a cow."
>
> Big Sweet turned viciously upon the old man. "Who you callin' a cow, fool? Ah know you ain't namin' *my* mama's daughter no cow."
>
> "Now all y'all heard what Ah said. Ah ain't called nobody no cow," Jim defended himself. "Dat's just an old time by-word 'bout no man kin tell what's gointer happen when he gits mixed up wid a woman or set straddle of a cow." "I done heard my gran'paw say dem very words many and many a time," chimed in Larkins. "There's a whole heap of them kinda by-words. Like for instance:
>
> " 'Ole coon for cunnin', young coon for runnin',' and 'Ah can't dance, but Ah know good moves.' They all got a hidden meanin', jus' like de Bible. Everybody can't understand what they mean. Most people is thin-brained. They's born wid they feet under de moon. Some folks is born wid they feet on de sun and they kin seek out de inside meanin' of words."
>
> "Fack is, it's a story 'bout a man sittin' straddle of a cow," Jim Allen went on.

The narrative which follows concerns a man who sends his son to college and upon his return asks him to help milk a troublesome cow. The boy "scientifically" concludes that to kick the milking bucket the cow has to hump her body; thus, the way to stop the hump is to tie his father astraddle her back. The cow breaks loose and goes down the road with her rider, to the great amusement of the "uneducated."

While logically this story has little to do with the argument preceding it, imagistically it is appropriate. The lying session provides for exactly this kind of free association. By the time the tale is finished, the argument, which was playful to begin with, has been forgotten. The listeners are ready for another story. One of the effects here is to emphasize folklore as a dramatic vehicle for community expression. There is a drama involved in all tale-telling contests, and the potential violence of these actors is disarmed by the verbal ceremonies they participate in. They are performing before an audience in a ritualized way, just as the tale-teller becomes the main actor and the story spun is a form of one-act "play"—the verbal noun being particularly appropriate. The dispute becomes both a serious matter and a game. Hurston's attempt to recreate this dramatic context in *Mules and Men* was informed by considerable thinking about the relationship between folklore and drama. (pp. 172-74)

> Robert E. Hemenway, in his Zora Neale Hurston:
> A Literary Biography, *University of Illinois Press,*
> *1977, 371 p.*

HENRY LOUIS GATES, JR.   (essay date 1978)

[*Gates, a noted American critic specializing in African-American literature, is the author of such books as* The Signifying Monkey: Towards a Theory of Afro-American Literary Criticism *(1988) and* Figures in Black: Words, Signs, and the Racial Self *(1987). He has also edited numerous distinguished volumes, including* The Classic Slave Narratives *(1987) and the thirty-volume* Schomburg Library of Nineteenth-Century Black Women Writers *(1988). In the following excerpt from a review of Hemenway's biography of Hurston (see excerpt dated 1977), Gates briefly discusses Hurston's spiritual and artistic legacy among contemporary black writers.*]

The deeply satisfying aspect of the rediscovery of Zora Neale Hurston is that black women generated it largely, and generated it primarily for literary reasons. Alice Walker's moving foreword [to Robert Hemenway's biography; see excerpt dated 1976] recounts her attempts to find Miss Hurston in the Garden of the Heavenly Rest, a segregated cemetery at Fort Pierce, Fla. Miss Hurston has become the metaphor for the black woman writer, if not of all black writers. Of Alice Walker, Toni Morrison, Gayl Jones and Toni Cade Bambara, none shares Miss Hurston's political inclinations. But, in markedly formal ways, each approaches her craft through Miss Hurston, especially Miss Walker and Miss Morrison. Their attention to Miss Hurston signifies a new sophistication in black literature: They read Miss Hurston not only for the spiritual kinship inherent in such relations, but also because she used language in subtle and various ways and, in her novels—particularly in her masterpiece, *Their Eyes Were Watching God*—used the coming to consciousness so absent in other black fiction as the fundamental framework for her work. (pp. 13, 30)

Re-reading Miss Hurston, I was struck by the density of experience she cloaked in a verdancy of words. It is this concern for words, for what a character in *Mules and Men* calls "a hidden meaning, jus' like de Bible . . . de inside meanin' of words," that unites Miss Hurston's anthropological studies with her fiction. For the folklore Miss Hurston collected so meticulously as Boas's student became metaphors in her novels—the traditional, recurring metaphors of black culture. Much more a novelist than a social scientist, even Miss Hurston's academic collections center on the quality of imagination, "the image-making faculty," that makes these lives whole and splendid. . . . This concern for language and for the "natural" poets who "bring barbaric splendor of word

and song into the very camp of the mockers" not only connects her two disciplines but as well makes of "the suspended linguistic moment" a thing to behold indeed. Always Miss Hurston's writing depends for its strength on the text, not the context. . . .

Miss Hurston's theory of language and behavior, as exemplified in *Mules and Men,* is that the capacity to forge myths in commanding images is an unadulterated sign of psychic health. Using "the spy-glass of Anthropology," her works celebrate rather than moralize; they show rather than tell, so that "both behavior and art become self-evident as the tale texts and hoodoo rituals accrete during the reading." She, as author, functions as a "midwife participating in the birth of a body of folklore," the "first wondering contacts with natural law." The myths she describes so accurately are in fact "alternative modes for perceiving reality," and never just condescending depictions of the quaint. "The Dozens," for example, that age-old ritual of graceful insult, Miss Hurston sees as, among other things, a verbal defense of the sanctity of the family, conjured through ingenious plays on words. Though attacked by Wright and virtually ignored by his literary heirs, Miss Hurston's theory of language and her conception of craft became the warp and the weft of Ralph Ellison's *Invisible Man,* which remains the classic black novel. Indeed Ellison's art, even more than Miss Morrison's and Miss Walker's, is heir to Miss Hurston's theory of the novel. (pp. 30-1)

> Henry Louis Gates, Jr., *"Soul of a Black Woman,"*
> in The New York Times Book Review, *February*
> *19, 1978, pp. 13, 30-1.*

ROBERT E. HEMENWAY   (essay date 1978)

[*In the following introduction to the 1978 edition of* Mules and Men, *Hemenway discusses the book's weaknesses as well as its strengths and includes some details about Hurston's later life in Florida.*]

In the spring of 1951 Zora Neale Hurston arrived in the coastal village of Eau Gallie, Florida, carrying a few clothes and a portable typewriter. She moved into a long-vacant, one-room house that rented for five dollars a week. Weather-beaten and isolated, on a large lot, the frame shack was covered by vines and surrounded by weeds. Five huge oaks loomed over it, cabbage palms dotted the yard. She began transforming the place, making it livable; she reported to a friend: "I have to do some pioneering, but I find that I like it. I am the happiest I have been in the last ten years. . . . I am up every morning at five o'clock chopping down weeds and planting flowers and things. . . . It looked like a jungle three weeks ago, and it took a strong heart and an eye on the future for me to move in when I arrived. The place had run down so badly." She brought in electricity, cleaned and painted, and began landscaping the grounds. Clearing out an artesian well, she then constructed a fountain and arranged butterfly ginger around it. She planted bright red and yellow poppies, scattering the seeds throughout the grass.

It was not the first time Zora Hurston had lived in Eau Gallie, nor the first time she had come to stay in this isolated, one-room shack. She labored hard—"I still must remove tons of junk, old tin cans, and bottles from the premises"—because she hoped to restore the property to its original image in her memory. It was here, twenty-two years earlier, that she had first begun to write *Mules and Men.* When she first stayed in the house, in the spring of 1929, it served as a way station for a very energetic folklore collector who needed to organize her field notes; she had been transcribing materials for eighteen months while criss-crossing the rural South, and she needed to assess the significance of what she had found. Surrounded by 95,000 words of folk-tale material, dozens of children's games, hundreds of folk songs, and a confusing compilation of hoodoo rituals, the youthful scholar quickly saw that her collections could alter the popular conception of the Southern black folk. Although she stayed for only three months and *Mules and Men* was not published until 1935, Eau Gallie was where the book really began. That single room and the grounds surrounding it held some of the best of an author's memories, and when she returned in 1951, Hurston looked beyond tin cans and weeds, willing herself a vision of another "pioneer," a vibrant young folklorist at the height of her powers. At the age of fifty, Zora Neale Hurston was searching for her past, seeking to reclaim the creative magic that had made her famous. (pp. xi-xii)

[The publication of *Mules and Men*] was historically important, the first book of Afro-American folklore collected by a black American to be presented by a major publisher for a general reading audience. In the nineteenth century, black novelists William Wells Brown and Charles Chesnutt had reported on the folklore of slaves and ex-slaves. The establishment of an American Folklore Society chapter at Hampton Institute in 1893 led to the reporting of folklore in the Institute's journal, the *Southern Workman,* but it had only a limited circulation. Many popular periodicals had reported on black folklore during and after the Civil War, but the collectors were always white and often looked upon the material as quaint or exotic. The second issue of the *Journal of American Folklore* in 1888 called for the study of the "lore of Negroes in the Southern states of the Union," and the *Journal* printed many Afro-American materials, but the plantation context so prominent in the popular accounts was frequently present in these scholarly reports as well, and, again, the collectors were usually white. The twentieth century saw increasing interest in black folkways, but generally speaking, Afro-American folklore between 1850 and 1930 was almost always collected by whites and usually preselected to conform to either the collector's romantic notion of black people (humble, God-fearing, simple folk) or racist stereotype (inferior beings lost in a complex society).

For a variety of reasons black folklorists were few. When *Mules and Men* appeared, only two other black scholars, J. Mason Brewer and Arthur Huff Fauset, had professional training similar to Hurston's. *Mules and Men* is a pioneering book, and Hurston thought of it as part of a mission; she wrote that she was "weighed down by the thought that practically nothing had been done in Negro folklore when the greatest cultural wealth of the continent was disappearing without the world ever realizing that it had ever been."

If there is a theme to the folk tales and hoodoo of *Mules and Men,* it is that the folklore of the black South is an expressive system of great social complexity and profound esthetic significance. *Mules and Men* was published at a time when racism and racist stereotypes were very evident. Minstrel shows were a popular form of American entertainment; the United States Senate could not agree that lynching was a crime; many newspapers still refused to capitalize the word Negro. At a time when the men on Joe Clarke's store porch were considered by whites to be lazy and ignorant, Hurston pre-

sented these storytellers as the tradition-bearers for an Afro-American world view. At a time when spirituals were accepted because they had become so harmonized that they were barely distinguishable from Bach chorales, when Paul Robeson and Roland Hayes were being praised for concert interpretations of the "sorrow songs," Hurston claimed, "Robeson sings Negro songs better than most, because, thank God, he lacks musical education. But we have a cathead man in Florida who can sing so that if you heard him you wouldn't want to hear Hayes or Robeson. He hasn't the voice of either one. It's the effect." At a time when hoodoo was considered a bizarre superstition, she compared it to Christianity:

> I am convinced that Christianity as practised is an attenuated form of nature worship. Let me explain. The essentials are a belief in the Trinity, baptism, sacrament. Baptism is nothing more than water worship as has been done in one form or the other down thru the ages. . . . I find fire worship in Christianity too. What was the original purpose of the altar in all churches? For sacred fire and sacrifices BY FIRE. . . . Symbols my opponents are going to say. But they cannot deny that both water and fire are purely material things and that they symbolize man's tendency to worship those things which benefit him to a great extent. . . . You know of course that the sacrament is a relic of cannibalism when men ate men not so much for food as to gain certain qualities the eaten man had. Sympathetic magic pure and simple. *They have a nerve to laugh at conjure.*

Mules and Men refutes the pathological view of uneducated rural black people. Hurston's method is presentational, and she does not impose folklore theory on the reader. She operates from the premise, however, that what she presents is "the greatest cultural wealth of the continent," and as a trained anthropologist she understood the world "culture." *Mules and Men* does not exactly ignore the brutal oppression of black people in the South, but it subordinates the economic and social deprivation to achieve a cultural perspective. Even in the face of an historically brutal experience, black people affirmed their humanity by creating an expressive communication system that fostered self-pride and taught techniques of transformation, adaptation, and survival. The tales of *Mules and Men* prove that human beings are not able to live without some sense of cultural cohesion and individual self-worth—no matter how hard their circumstances, no matter how much effort is directed toward denying them a sense of personal value. Why is the slave John, as Hurston claims, "the wish fulfillment hero of the race"? Sack Daddy, a sawmill worker from Polk County, answers: "John sho was a smart nigger now. He useter git de best of Ole Massa all de time."

Aware of the historical importance of her effort, Hurston paid considerable care to the choice of approach for *Mules and Men,* the communication context she would offer the reader. Her decision was to report from a black communal perspective. As the black poet June Jordan has stated, "white America lies outside the Hurston universe . . . you do not run up on the man / the enemy"; in Hurston's work black people put aside the "warrior postures" that enable them to deal with that enemy and adopt the "person postures" that enable them to relax and freely express themselves. Hurston reports on what happens on Clarke's store porch after the day's labors. The tale-tellers at Clarke's store understood the ancient black folk song:

Got one mind for white folks to see,
Nother for what I know is me;
He don't know, he don't know my mind.

The verse affirms identity; the singer knows that there is a *me*, that this person is someone quite different from the stereotypical figure seen from the outside. Even though white possessiveness may seem to consume all, it cannot take possession of the private self.

Black identity receives expression in Afro-American folklore because folklore permits the presentation of emotions so deeply felt that they often cannot be openly articulated. Hurston understood this process in a way Joel Chandler Harris did not. The Uncle Remus tales are always told from within the plantation tradition; the context is always a serene, kindly old darky relating animal tales to pre-adolescents—the mask is never dropped. In *Mules and Men* the folklorist works in a different setting, encounters tale-tellers in a different frame of mind:

> They are most reluctant at times to reveal that which the soul lives by. And the Negro, in spite of his open-faced laughter, his seeming acquiescence, is particularly evasive. . . . The Negro offers a feather-bed resistance. . . . The theory behind our tactics: "The white man is always trying to know into somebody else's business. All right, I'll set something outside the door of my mind for him to play with and handle. He can read my writing but he sho' can't read my mind. I'll put this play toy in his hand, and he will seize it and go away. Then I'll say my say and sing my song.

The sayings and songs of *Mules and Men* document a culture. The tales here are *not* the quaint, childish entertainments of a primitive tribe. They are the complex cultural communications permitted an oppressed people, their school lessons, their heroic biographies, their psychic savings banks, their children's legacies. Black folk tales illustrate how an entire people adapted and survived in the new world experience, how they transformed what they found into a distinctive way of life; they describe the human behavior the group approves, indicate when the behavior is appropriate, and suggest strategies necessary for the preservation of the group in a hostile environment.

Consider, for example, the John-Massa tale told in Chapter Five. Newly transported to America as a slave, John is taught a language: the white man's house is called a "kingdom"; his fireplace is a "flame vaperator"; his bed is "his flowery bed of ease." When forced to communicate in this new vocabulary, John does so only up to a point, then breaks through the pretense of the artificial nomenclature and speaks directly.

Such a tale resonates with historical, cultural, and psychological significance. Although the tale is known in many cultures, it was adapted to the Afro-American experience. It recreates the unsuccessful attempt at cultural genocide the slaves overcame. There was an attempt to strip the African of his language, penalizing him, as Alex Haley has so recently shown, for the desire to preserve the linguistic fragments of Africa. The tale reminds us that whoever attempts to control language, the naming process, attempts to control our understanding of who we are, our definition of reality. What kind of person would call a fireplace a "flame vaperator"? A person given to pretentious labels, one who wished to measure self-worth by material objects, one unwilling to look upon reality (bricks and mortar) and call it by its correct name. A

person, in other words, characteristic of the master-oppressor class, looking upon slavery and calling it beneficent. Such whites, thanks to the labor of slaves, sleep on a "flowery bed of ease," and psychic satisfaction arises from the opportunity to label it truthfully. The twist at the end of the tale, John's dropping of the pretense that he has accepted the artificial nomenclature, is the final triumphant irony of the tale. It objectifies the secret knowledge that John had held from the first. He had always known what the truth was, and his master had known that John knew. They were participating in an elaborate ritual of self-delusion. Black listeners did not have to look far to apply the tale's truths. White people might say "separate but equal," and black people might temporarily have to accept the label, but both knew that they were participating in a verbal hoax. Sooner or later the institution had to collapse from the weight of illusion language had been asked to serve.

Mules and Men is a storehouse of such revelations, a repository of coded cultural messages preserved and passed by word of mouth from generation to generation. When it was published, Carl Sandburg called it "a bold and beautiful book, many a page priceless and unforgettable." Alan Lomax calls *Mules and Men* "the most engaging, genuine, and skillfully written book in the field of folklore."

Any book purporting to present an interior view of black Americans is bound to create controversy, since no single book can capture the rich diversity of Afro-American culture. *Mules and Men,* although generally well received at the time of its publication, also has had its critics. There have been understandable complaints about its lack of cross-cultural analysis, comparative notes, and scholarly apparatus. There have been objections to the absence of social consciousness in Hurston's storytellers, the charge made that their lack of bitterness creates a false image of romantic pastoralism for the black South. It is worth mentioning, however, that the expectations of scholarly form were relatively unsophisticated in 1935, and that in any case Hurston knew very well she was not presenting her collections in the normal, scholarly fashion. . . . In a letter to Boas [see excerpt dated 1934], she admitted that "I have inserted the between-story conversation and business because when I offered it without it, every publisher said it was too monotonous. Now three houses want to publish it. So I hope the nonscientific matter that must be there for the sake of the average reader will not keep you from writing the introduction." Boas refused to go ahead until he had checked the entire manuscript for authenticity, then stressed in his preface the value of these conversations [see excerpt dated 1935].

The between-story "business" is only unscientific in the sense that Hurston is apparently calling upon her collecting memories to provide continuity between tales. She told Boas, "It so happens that the conversations and incidents are true"; although she may be creatively rearranging them, they have seemed to modern scholars to simulate tale-telling situations, at least in a selectively edited form. That is, Hurston's invention seems to have been limited to condensation and arrangement; she did not invent any folklore for the book. Her informants may not have told quite so many tales while walking to the lake to fish, but the words are their own, not Zora Neale Hurston's.

Finally, ethnographic observations occur in these "between-story conversations." When challenged to tell a story, one man says, "Ah don't know it well enough to say it. Ah jus'

Portrait of Hurston probably taken in New York City.

know it well enough to know it." He clearly understands his role as a passive tradition-bearer, a self-correcting force who will insure that the active bearer—the tale-teller—will not violate too extensively the community's expectation of a given performance. While most folklore collections include objective discussions of the field techniques used to collect the data, Hurston shows rather than tells the same information. Folklorist Sandra Stahl has remarked on Hurston's temporary role-playing to gain the trust of her informants. This field methodology, which would be discussed operationally in conventional ethnography, is dramatized in *Mules and Men.*

The charge of romantic pastoralism is more complicated, and may best be summarized by Sterling Brown, poet, scholar, folklorist, one of the distinguished Afro-American artists of the twentieth century. Brown reviewed *Mules and Men* in 1936 and praised it for its simplicity, raciness, earthiness, and plausibility. However, he objected to the lack of political awareness among Hurston's storytellers. Brown had collected folklore in the South and saw people living "in a land shadowed by squalor, poverty, disease, violence, enforced ignorance, and exploitation." He concluded: "From the reviewer's own experiences he knows that harsher folk tales await the collector. These people brood upon their hardships, talk about them 'down by the big gate,' and some times even at

the big house. They are not blind, and they are not being fooled; some have lost their politeness, and speak right out. *Mules and Men* should be more bitter; it would be nearer the total truth."

Such criticism is still relevant. The Eatonville of the 1930s, with such a high unemployment rate that Hurston felt compelled to solicit funds to help the town, is seldom in evidence. Yet Zora Neale Hurston was not blind to racial prejudice, or the economic hardship that her people bore. From the age of ten until twenty she knew the smell of poverty, with its "dead dreams dropping off the heart like leaves in a dry season and rotting around the feet."

Hurston's personal experience of poverty and her commitment to an integrated society were subordinated in *Mules and Men* so that she could address the negative image of the black folk publicly held by most Whites and by some Blacks. (Some of Hurston's strongest opposition came from middle-class black people who thought of the folk heritage as something which should be forgotten, a legacy of ignorance which could be used to justify racism.) The problem was that too many people confused material and ideological poverty. Because the men at Joe Clarke's were sometimes unemployed, often uneducated, occasionally hungry, it was assumed that no significant *ideas,* expressive *forms,* or cultural *creations* could emanate from the store porch. The black folk were placed in a kind of ideological strait jacket that interpreted their responses to the environment as either the product of social pathology, cultural deprivation, or an understandable, but simplistic desire to "protest."

Mules and Men creates a black communal perspective in order to emphasize the *independent* cultural creation of black people. Because Hurston was not a theorist, and *Mules and Men* was meant for the "average reader," her method was presentational. The folklore was expected to speak for itself. It said many things, but one of the most important was that Afro-American culture was not simply a *reactive* phenomenon. Black people's behaviors could not always be interpreted in the light of white oppression. What much of *Mules and Men* demonstrates, to paraphrase Ralph Ellison, is that black Americans are not the creation of the white man. As Ellison puts it, "Negro folklore, evolving within a larger culture which regarded it as inferior, was an especially courageous expression. It announced the Negro's willingness to trust his own experiences, his own sensibilities as to the definition of reality, rather than allow his masters to define these crucial matters for him."

Hurston once told Langston Hughes that he should make a Southern tour and read his poetry in sawmill camps and turpentine stills, on docks and levees: "There never has been a poet who has been acceptable to his Majesty, the man in the gutter before, and laugh if you will, but that man in the gutter is the god-maker, the creator of everything that lasts." Hurston identified with that figure, whom she called the "Negro farthest down"; *Mules and Men* was meant to affirm his place in the artistic universe. She was less interested in the economic system that made him poor than in the sensibility that enabled him to create a God. The book was written so that the folk's artistic works—anonymous in their authorship, dramatized in performance, transmitted orally—would not be forgotten. Hurston told a Chicago reporter, "It would be a tremendous loss to the Negro race and to America if we should lose the folklore and folk music, for the unlettered Negro has given the Negro's best contribution to America's culture."

In a sawmill camp, the jook was the dance hall and bar in which men and women danced, drank, and gambled. A "jook woman" was not noted for her spotless reputation, a "jook man" was prone to violence, good times, and rough talk. Zora Neale, with her Barnard degree, learned to be at home in such surroundings, because she knew the significance of what went on there. In 1934 she reported: "Musically speaking, the jook is the most important place in America. For in its smelly, shoddy confines has been born the secular music known as blues, and on blues has been founded jazz. The singing and playing in the true Negro style is called 'jooking.'"

Mules and Men was an attempt to present a "true Negro style," one which had been ignored and maligned by a racist society. It is not the whole story of Blacks in the South, or even a comprehensive anthology of all forms of Afro-American folklore. It remains today, however, as it was at the time of its publication, one of the most important collections of Afro-American folklore ever to be published.

It is a long way from a jook's noisy excitement to a quiet Barnard classroom, but it is not so far from a sawmill jook in Polk County, Florida, to a one-room house in Eau Gallie. The middle-aged woman in the tropical sunshine struggling to reclaim past glories has largely shared her fate with the artists who perform in **Mules and Men.** American society has tended to forget about them both, tale-teller and collector, while the tales live on. That fact is both an affirmation of the communicative art in Afro-American folklore and a commentary on the way black artists have been received in this country.

As for Zora Neale Hurston, she understood the whole process but did not spend a moment in regret. As she said, "I have been in sorrow's kitchen and licked all the pots." (pp. xviii-xxviii)

> *Robert E. Hemenway, in an introduction to* Mules and Men *by Zora Neale Hurston, Indiana University Press, 1978, pp. xi-xxviii.*

LILLIE P. HOWARD (essay date 1980)

[*In her critical study of Hurston excerpted below, Howard surveys Hurston's short stories, noting that many of them share the common theme of a free human spirit trapped by oppressive individuals or institutions.*]

"John Redding Goes to Sea" was Hurston's first fictional work. A groping melodramatic story of dreams deferred, of ambition, determination, and expectations mocked to death by time, its main character, John Redding, like Janie Crawford of *Their Eyes Were Watching God,* anticipates the horizon, but unlike her, never achieves it while alive. Whereas Janie's grandmother limits her horizon to a speck, John Redding is limited by his mother and his wife.

From his early childhood, John had known the pain of being limited and hindered. One of his first experiences was with twigs, which John called ships and placed on a stream to sail away. More often than not, however, the ships would be swept in among the weeds and held there, a foreshadowing of the fate John himself would soon suffer. When he grew up and wanted to explore the horizon, he was hindered by his mother who believed that he should marry, settle down, and forget about wandering. To Matty Redding, marriage was the solution to everything. Perhaps to please his mother, John did marry, but he soon began to "saunter out to the gate to gaze wistfully down the white dusty road; or to wander again to the river as he had done in childhood. To be sure he did not send forth twig-ships any longer, but his thoughts would in spite of himself, stray down river to Jacksonville, the sea, the wide world—and poor home-tied John Redding wanted to follow them." John quickly discovered that marriage did not make happiness; it could not pacify that urge to wander, that quest for experience; sometimes it only brought pain and chains.

As John explained to his wife, marriage was a mistake because he could not "stifle that longing for the open road, rolling seas, for peoples and countries I have never seen." Because neither his wife nor his mother understood or encouraged him, he was a stifled free spirit, trapped in the cage of an unhappy marriage. He begged his mother to "let me learn to strive and think—in short, be a man." Ironically, though appropriately, Redding is killed in a storm and his body floats out to sea where he is free to search, explore, and realize his dreams. John Redding is a dreamer in a world which does not treat dreamers kindly. In his weakness he allows himself to be manuevered by his mother and his wife. By the time he has gathered enough fortitude to assert himself, it is too late.

"John Redding Goes to Sea," like the stories that follow it, treats many subjects that Hurston later embodies in her works. Like Isis of **"Drenched in Light,"** Janie of *Their Eyes Were Watching God,* and Hurston as she presents herself in *Dust Tracks,* John Redding has a vivid imagination and always pictures himself on the open road. Sometimes he was "a prince, riding away in a gorgeous carriage, . . . a knight bestride a fiery charger, . . . a steamboat captain piloting his craft down the St. John River. . . . He always ended by riding away to the horizon." Like most of Hurston's male characters, John aspires to be a man, to improve himself, to be somebody. As with all dreamers, however, there are obstacles to be overcome. John only overcomes his by paying the ultimate price—his life. Sometimes, however, suggests Hurston in *Their Eyes Were Watching God,* that is the way it must be: "Ships at a distance have every man's wish on board. For some they come in with the tide. For others they sail forever on the horizon, never out of sight, never landing until the Watcher turns his eyes away in resignation, his dreams mocked to death by Time. That is the life of men."

"Drenched in Light," Hurston's first contribution to the black literary and cultural awakening called the Harlem Renaissance, is "a portrait of the artist as a young girl." The subject is Isis Potts, a free-spirited eleven-year-old black girl, filled with imagination, energy, love, and vitality. Secure in self, Isis bustles with pride, talent, and self-confidence as she searches for self-actualization. Unfortunately, she is stifled and limited by the restrictions imposed by her provincial grandmother.

The story is set in Florida, and focuses upon a day in the life of Isis. From sunup to sundown, the impish Isis romps with the dogs, turns somersaults, dances, perches upon the gatepost in front of her home, races up and down the road to Orlando "hailing gleefully all travelers," begging rides in cars and winning her way into the hearts of "everybody in the country." Typically, she gets into all kinds of mischief, even attempting at one point to shave her grandmother's beard ("No ladies don't weah no whiskers if they kin help it. But Gran'ma gittin' ole an' she doan know how to shave like me.") while the old lady sleeps. When the outside world fails to amuse, Isis turns inward to her vivid imagination for entertainment. She wears "trailing robes, golden slippers with blue bottoms," rides "white horses with flaring pink nostrils to the horizon," pictures herself "gazing over the edge of the world into the abyss." She is busy making the most out of life, much to the chagrin of her grandmother.

The only conflict in the story is caused by Grandma Potts, an old, traditional parent who sanctions corporal punishment for anything which goes against her seasoned principles. She thus mets out punishment for such crimes as sitting with the knees separated ("settin' brazen" she called it), whistling, playing with boys, or crossing legs. Obviously there is no peace for Isis when Grandma is around.

Grandma Potts seems to be the natural product of the slavery tradition. When Helen, for instance, a white stranger who has been captivated by a gypsy dance Isis performed at a local barbeque, her grandma's new red tablecloth draped about her shoulder as a Spanish shawl, requests that Isis be allowed to accompany her to her hotel to dance for her, grandma, bowing and dissembling, happily turns her granddaughter over to the woman. Because the grandmother does not really know Helen, the reader at first assumes that she allows Isis to accompany her only because the woman is white, a member of that ruling class whom grandma has grown accustomed to obliging without question. When we are told that the grandmother is secretly bursting with pride, however, we begin to suspect that she understands and appreciates Isis's worth and only keeps up a stern front to keep the girl in line, to perhaps break her spirit (as Zora's father tried to do hers) so that she will not fall victim to a world which had little tolerance for spirited blacks. On the other hand, perhaps the grandmother was pleased because the "missus" was pleased. Isis, though ignorant of even the name of her patron, only knows that someone finally appreciates her talents, and she is happy to be rescued from a grandmother who stifles her.

Helen is sincere in her feelings for Isis; she longs for Isis's vitality. Since life has gone out of her own existence, she is determined—like the whites who hungrily flocked to Harlem during the 1920s to be liberated by the "exotic primitive"—to snatch excitement from other sources. She determines to absorb Isis's light, to live delightfully, vicariously, through Isis. When one of her male companions sarcastically suggests that Isis has adopted her as a surrogate mother, Helen is quick to reply: "Oh, I hope so, Harry . . . I want a little of her sunshine to soak into my soul. I need it."

The story is partly autobiographical and anticipates what is to come in the later works. Potts was Hurston's mother's maiden name; Isis's village seems to be Hurston's own Eatonville, and some of the events of the story are also found in autobiographical pieces written by Hurston. (pp. 58-61)

"Drenched in Light" is undeniably Isis Potts's story. She is the heroine and subject of most of the action. Though children appear in other Hurston works, this is the only work in which a child figures significantly in the plot. The work is filled with a child's laughter, imagination, and energy. It possesses a child's charm, though it discusses more adult themes—the lasting effects of slavery and the boredom and emptiness of white adult life—in passing.

"Spunk," Hurston's next work, takes its title from its protagonist, Spunk Banks. The title, however, does double duty, for it not only refers to the name of the story's main character

but also to his audacious attributes. The plot is a classic one of *hubris* punished, for it develops the story of a man who uses his spunk to intimidate and manipulate others, only to eventually lose his nerve and his life.

Set in a village which, though unnamed, is apparently Eatonville, the story is told by a narrator and by the townfolks who function as catalyst and chorus, precipitating the serious action of the story, filling in details of what happens off stage, and judging the main characters. When the story opens, Spunk has already established a reputation in the village as a hero. He is a man to be feared, "a giant of a brown skinned man," a man who "ain't skeered of nothin' on God's green footstool—nothin!" More importantly, like the white massa, he intimidates and takes what he wants—"He rides that log down at the saw-mill jus' like he struts 'round wid another man's wife—jus' don't give a kitty." In this case, Spunk wants Lena Kanty, the wife of the town's coward, Joe Kanty. The story is based upon Spunk's desire for Lena, his realization of that desire, and the fatal consequences that arise therefrom.

When the story begins, Spunk and Lena have been together long enough for the townspeople to know of the relationship, and for Joe Kanty, the cuckolded, nervous, and cowardly husband, to nerve himself (i.e., gather spunk) and demand the return of his wife. Spurred and shamed by town gossip, Kanty is prompted to try a sneak attack; he confronts Banks's Army 45 with a pocket razor and dies. It is a clear case of self-defense, and no man dares dispute it. After a brief trial, Spunk is free and ready to marry Lena. Before he can do so, however, he is bothered by a big, *black* bob-cat that he cannot shoot (he believes the cat is Joe's ghost "done sneaked back from Hell!") and he claims that the saw at the mill (which he used to ride just for fun) is loose and that someone is pushing him into its blade. None of these things is happening, of course; and yet, in Poe-like fashion, they are all happening. Either Spunk's conscience and imagination are successfully working against his sanity, or a supernatural force is intervening to right the wrongs of the world. The next evening Spunk is mysteriously caught in the saw—pushed by Joe, he swears—and killed. The man of whom everyone else was afraid has brought about his own death (a natural explanation) or Joe's spirit has caused Spunk's death (a supernatural explanation). The reader must decide which. The townspeople clearly do not question the validity of the supernatural explanation. To do so is to question a very real part of the rituals upon which their society is built. In Eatonville and in many other black communities, superstitions, the supernatural, and voodoo were as common as cape jasmine bushes and sweet potatoes. At any rate, Joe seems more powerful, more *present* after his death. Perhaps, as one of the townsmen believes, Joe has been the braver man after all.

By Hurston standards, however, Kanty is not a MAN; he's one of those puny characters who are more of a nuisance than anything else. Although Banks is a MAN, on the other hand, he is a wrongheaded one, the tragic hero with too much pride who, by imposing his will upon others without proper regard for their feelings, brings about his own downfall. Too, after Spunk kills Kanty, he loses his spunk and thus becomes as cowardly and despicable as Kanty.

Ironically, Spunk Banks, who had been such a powerful man while he lived, is quickly forgotten once he is gone. Three sixteen-inch boards on saw-horses served as his "cooling board" while a dingy sheet served as his shroud. Instead of mourning his death, the townswomen "ate heartily. . . . and wondered who would be Lena's next," while the townsmen "whispered coarse conjectures between guzzles of whiskey." Life continues to flow. (pp. 62-4)

["Muttsy"] documents the experiences of an innocent little Red Riding Hood, Pinkie Jones, as she enters the bewildering forest of Harlem. When the story opens, Pinkie, who has journeyed North in search of refuge, has already fallen prey to the wolfish atmosphere of "Ma Turner's back parlor," a "house" run by Forty-dollars-Kate. There Pinkie feels "shut in, imprisoned, walled in with women who talked of nothing but men and the numbers and drink and men who talked of nothing but the numbers and drink and women." A gambler named Muttsy is immediately taken with Pinkie and wants to marry her. In order to win her, he gives up a lucrative gambling career for a job on the docks because Pinkie likes a man "that works for a living." A month after the marriage, however, Muttsy is on his knees with a friend shooting a perfect seven. After he has won the friend's money, he tells him to "send de others roun' heah one by one. What man can't keep one li'l wife an' two li'l bones? Hurry em up, Blue!" Pinkie has obviously, and credibly, been unable to change her husband's ways. That Muttsy has returned to his gambling does not particularly bode ill. Pinkie will probably have to modify her "likes," but a happy marriage between Muttsy and Pinkie still seems possible.

"Sweat" is a story of marriage gone sour, of hard work and sweat, of adultery, hatred, and death. Set in Florida (most of the action of the piece takes place on the outskirts of the town rather than in it), the story explores the relationship between a married couple, Delia and Sykes Jones, and the hatred that emanates from their marriage after love has disappeared.

Although the couple appear to be in love when they marry, Sykes soon tires of his wife—"Two months after the wedding, he had given her the first brutal beating"—and seeks companionship with various women of the town, finally settling with Bertha, a big, fat woman described by one of the townsmen as a "greasy Mogul . . . who couldn't kiss a sardine can Ah done thowed out de back do' 'way las' yeah." Delia stays home and does the laundry of white folks to earn a living for herself since her husband spends his money elsewhere. She is really the head of the household and has worked for fifteen years to pay for the house Sykes wants to give to Bertha.

When he has become so enamored of Bertha that he wishes to marry her, Sykes begins to prey upon his wife's obsessive fear of snakes. Not only does he throw his snakelike bull whip into the room to scare her, but he also pens a rattlesnake near the back door. When that is not enough to run Delia away, he moves the snake to her clothes hamper knowing that, it being Sunday, Delia will soon begin to sort the clothes for the weekly Monday washing. He hopes that the snake will kill her, thereby removing her from his sight forever. Delia escapes, however; Sykes himself is bitten—"hoist with his own petards," as it were—and dies. Delia could have warned him, saved him, but she understandably does not. She has been hardened by his constant abuse and has built up a "spiritual earthworks" against him. Poetic justice has been rendered. He had made Delia's life miserable; he had beaten her, cheated on her, and refused to provide for her. He had taken advantage of her by taking things for which she had worked and paid to Bertha's and by flaunting Bertha daringly around the community and around Delia. He had even paid Bertha's rent at Della Lewis's—"the only house in town that would

have taken her in"—and promised her his wife's house. Sykes had done everything, in short, which would turn Delia, observers in the community, and the reader against him.

The story itself, however, is not as simple as the plot summary suggests. One of the reasons that Sykes cannot bear the sight of his wife, for instance, is because her work makes him feel like less than a man. He resents her working for the white folks, washing their dirty laundry, but he does not resent it enough to remove the need for her to do so. Or perhaps his wife's work has removed the need for him to be a man. Clearly Delia is an independent woman, by necessity, it seems, having worked for fifteen years to support herself and her husband, and having even paid for the house they live in. Whether she needs Sykes at all is questionable, and perhaps he senses this and looks elsewhere for someone who does need him.

Though Sykes's vulnerability and uncertainty about his own masculinity are understandable, he is still contemptible. He has not loved, trusted, understood, and appreciated Delia—a man must do these things if he is to survive in the Hurston fictional world—but has instead hated, tricked, and beaten her. As one of the townsmen noted, Sykes had "beat huh 'nough tuh kill three women let 'lone change they looks." He is one of those men "dat takes a wif lak dey do a joint uh sugar-cane. It's round, juicy an' sweet when dey gits it. But dey squeeze an' grind, squeeze an' grind an' wring tell dey wring every drop uh pleasure dat's in 'em out. When dey's satisfied dat dey is wrung dry, dey treats 'em jes lak dey do a cane-chew. Dey throws 'em away. Dey knows whut dey is doin' while dey is at it, an' hates theirselves fuh it but they keeps on hangin' after huh tell she's empty. Den dey hates huh fuh bein' a cane-chew an' in de way." Like Spunk Banks, Sykes obviously deserves and brings about his fate. (pp. 65-8)

"The Gilded Six-Bits" was Hurston's last published short story before she tried her skills with the novel. It foreshadows much of what was to come in her later works and presents the self "reconciled to its provincial origins." It has more depth than the other stories, its characters are more developed, and its dialect has much of the texture we are to see in her novels. "The Gilded Six-Bits" is the most often anthologized of Hurston's works.

Set in Eatonville, "The Gilded Six-Bits" is the story of a beautiful marriage beset by difficulties, of trials and successes, of appearances and reality. Having as its theme the old adage that all that glitters is not gold, the story centers around the married life of two people, Missie May and Joe Banks, the force which tests and threatens their relationship, and their subsequent attempts to allay this force. The narrative falls logically into three parts, each of which centers around the welfare of the marriage. We see the marriage in a state of health, and in a state of ill health followed by a long, but successful, convalescence.

At first the marriage between Missie and Joe is a happy one. They show their love in small but significantly generous ways. Missie keeps a spotless home for Joe and cooks his favorite food while Joe buys her little tokens to show his love. They are so happy that there is even "something happy about the place" where they live. Their life together seems perfect, the Garden of Eden. When the serpent arrives in the form of Otis D. Slemmons, however, the Banks begin their fall.

Otis D. Slemmons is a city slicker-womanizer who sports gold teeth, a five-dollar gold piece for a stick pin and a ten-

Portrait of Hurston taken November 9, 1934.

dollar gold piece for a watch charm. He and his gold impress Missie so much that she wants some of the same for her husband and takes Slemmons into her bed as a means of getting it. Although her intentions are naively good—Joe has admired Slemmons and expressed his desire to be like him—they precipitate the deterioration of the marriage.

When Joe returns home earlier than usual from work one night and catches Slemmons awkwardly trying to get into his pants, he attacks him, accidentally grabbing the gold watch charm as Slemmons makes a timely escape. In spite of his discovery, however, Joe remains with Missie. She becomes hopeful when Joe makes love to her after three months of abstinence, but when she finds Slemmons's piece of money under her pillow the next morning, she is confused. A close examination reveals that the money isn't gold at all, but is a gilded half-dollar. What disturbs Missie most, however, is that Joe has left the money under her pillow as though he were paying for her services—"fifty cents for her love." Misery.

When Missie becomes pregnant and bears a fine boy who resembles Joe, shadows lift and happiness once again seems possible. Determined to let bygones be gone, Joe goes shopping for the first time since the Slemmons incident and buys fifty cents worth of candy kisses with the gilded money. The marriage has come full circle, but it will never be the same.

The carefree innocence which characterized the early marriage has been replaced by painfully gained maturity and knowledge. The lesson has been costly but because the foundation upon which the marriage was built has been strong, the marriage has survived. Missie and Joe genuinely love each other and both have enough courage, determination, and trust in each other to weather the storm. Thanks to their joint efforts, their marriage is well on its way to recovery.

"The Gilded Six-Bits" clearly shows that the promises of the city—to which blacks were flocking by the thousands during the Great Migration of the early part of the century, and indeed throughout the Harlem Renaissance—were often gilded. The city, be it New York, Pittsburgh, Chicago (from which Slemmons hailed), etc., promised hope and opportunity. Promises were deferred, however; the land of opportunity became a vicious jungle, and blacks were thrown back upon themselves. They were able to compare the pastoral, the rural, natural folk experience with the urban experience, and they found the urban experience lacking. Wiser and stronger, they thus became content with their quaint folkways, found value and truth and strength in themselves.

Significantly, four of the five stories Hurston published between 1924 and 1933 deal with marriage and marital problems, a major theme in Hurston's works. Instead of portraying marriage romantically, however, Hurston presents it frankly, replete with infidelity, jealousy, violence, and hatred. There were certain characteristics she considered essential to a successful marriage—courage, honesty, love, trust, respect, understanding, and a willingness to negotiate differences, to prop each other up on every side. As her stories and some of her novels show, those who did not subscribe wholeheartedly to her successful marriage formula could suffer disasters.

Curiously, in the unsuccessful marriages, the male is always eliminated, i.e., killed—an unusual and hard fate—and the woman is left intact, available, as it were, for another, hopefully happier marriage. A flawed man is obviously less forgiveable in the Hurston world than a flawed woman. When the woman is at fault, however, as in **"Spunk," "The Gilded Six-Bits,"** and *Seraph on the Suwanee,* she is made to suffer, though her punishment is mild when compared to that of the men. Lena Kanty loses both of the men in her life within a few days; Missie is taunted and tortured by her conscience and her husband for almost a year; and Arvay Henson of *Seraph on the Suwanee* torments herself throughout most of the novel, most of her life.

Though Hurston herself did not find marriage palatable—she married twice, divorced twice, after spending only a few months, maybe less, with each husband—she did advocate it highly for her characters. She recognized that for some, finding a suitable mate who will love, cherish, respect, trust, understand, and encourage is the "be-all" of life, just as she realized that for others, like herself and John Redding, marriage wasn't meant to be. In her works, she presents marriage as varied and realistically beset by hardships. To her, it was an important institution capable of various possibilities which she explores sometimes beautifully, sometimes unmercifully, but always realistically.

As Bone has noted [see excerpt dated 1975], Hurston's story plots often pit the weak against the strong—John Redding against his mother, Isis Potts against her grandmother, Joe Kanty against Spunk Banks, Delia Jones against her husband Sykes, Missie and Joe against Slemmons. Though the strong may often win, however, their victory is shortlived: John's mother loses him entirely; Banks and Sykes Jones eliminate themselves; Missie and Joe's marriage weathers the storm. Hurston, as creator, will, more often than not, remove the source of the oppression and free the stifled or threatened spirit. Even **"John Redding Goes to Sea"** is not a sad story because John, though dead, is at last free. (pp. 69-72)

> Lillie P. Howard, in her Zora Neale Hurston, Twayne Publishers, 1980, 192 p.

BARBARA JOHNSON   (essay date 1985)

[*In the essay excerpted below, which was originally published in* Critical Inquiry, *Autumn, 1985, Johnson offers a deconstructionist analysis of the problems of identity and address in* Mules and Men.]

In preparing to write this chapter, I found myself repeatedly stopped by conflicting conceptions of the structure of address into which I was inserting myself. It was not clear to me what I, a white deconstructor, was doing talking about Zora Neale Hurston, a black novelist and anthropologist, or to *whom* I was talking. Was I trying to convince white establishment scholars who long for a return to Renaissance ideals that the study of the Harlem Renaissance is not a trivialization of their humanistic pursuits? Was I trying to contribute to the attempt to adapt the textual strategies of literary theory to the analysis of Afro-American literature? Was I trying to rethink my own previous work and to re-referentialize the notion of difference so as to move the conceptual operations of deconstruction out of the realm of abstract linguistic universality? Was I talking to white critics, black critics, or myself?

Well, all of the above. What finally struck me was the fact that what I was analyzing in Hurston's writings was precisely, again and again, her strategies and structures of problematic address. It was as though I were asking Zora Neale Hurston for answers to questions I did not even know I was unable to formulate. I had a lot to learn, then, from Hurston's way of dealing with multiple agendas and heterogeneous implied readers. . . .

One of the presuppositions with which I began was that Hurston's work was situated "outside" the mainstream literary canon and that I, by implication, was an institutional "insider." I soon came to see, however, not only that the insider becomes an outsider the minute she steps out of the inside, but also that Hurston's work itself was constantly dramatizing and undercutting just such inside/outside oppositions, transforming the plane geometry of physical space into the complex transactions of discursive exchange. In other words, Hurston could be read not just as an example of the "noncanonical" writer, but as a commentator on the dynamics of any encounter between an inside and an outside, any attempt to make a statement about difference.

One of Hurston's most memorable figurations of the inside/outside structure is her depiction of herself as a threshold figure mediating between the all-black town of Eatonville, Florida, and the big road traveled by passing whites:

> The front porch might seem a daring place for the rest of the town, but it was a gallery seat for me. My favorite place was atop the gate-post. Proscenium box for a born first-nighter. Not only did I enjoy the show, but I didn't mind the actors knowing that I liked it. I usually spoke to them in passing. . . .

> They liked to hear me "speak pieces" and sing and wanted to see me dance the parse-me-la, and gave me generously of their small silver for doing these things. . . . The colored people gave no dimes. They deplored any joyful tendencies in me, but I was their Zora nevertheless.

The inside/outside opposition here opens up a reversible theatrical space in which proscenium box becomes center stage and small silver passes to the boxholder-turned-actor.

Hurston's joyful and sometimes lucrative gatepost stance between black and white cultures was very much a part of her Harlem Renaissance persona, and was indeed often deplored by fellow black artists. Langston Hughes, who for a time shared with Hurston the problematic patronage of the wealthy Charlotte Mason, wrote of Hurston:

> Of the "niggerati," Zora Neale Hurston was certainly the most amusing. Only to reach a wider audience, need she ever write books—because she was the perfect book of entertainment in herself. In her youth she was always getting scholarships and things from wealthy white people, some of whom simply paid her just to sit around and represent the Negro race for them, she did it in such a racy fashion. . . . To many of her white friends, no doubt, she was a perfect "darkie."

"Representing the Negro race for whites" was nevertheless in many ways the program of the Harlem Renaissance. While Hurston has often been read and judged on the basis of personality alone, her "racy" adoption of the "happy darkie" stance, which was a successful strategy for survival, does not by any means exhaust the representational strategies of her *writing.* (pp. 172-74)

In the opening lines of her introduction to [*Mules and Men*] Hurston writes:

> I was glad when somebody told me, "You may go and collect Negro folk-lore." In a way it would not be a new experience for me. When I pitched head-foremost into the world I landed in a crib of negroism. . . . But it was fitting me like a tight chemise. I couldn't see it for wearing it. It was only when I was off in college, away from my native surroundings, that I could see myself like somebody else and stand off and look at my garment. Then I had to have the spy-glass of Anthropology to look through at that.

The journey away to school does not confer color and fixed identity . . . but rather sight and self-division. "Seeing" and "wearing" (significantly, not seeing and being) cannot coincide, and we cannot always be sure which side of the spyglass our narrator is standing on. The ambiguity of the inside/outside opposition involved in "see[ing] myself like somebody else" is dramatized in many ways in Hurston's collection of folk tales, songs, and hoodoo practices, resulting in a complex interaction between the authority of her spyglass and the rhetorical nature of her material.

Mules and Men is a book with multiple frames: it begins with a preface by Franz Boas, Hurston's teacher [see excerpt dated 1935], and ends with a glossary and appendix. As we have seen, Hurston's own introduction begins with a paraphrase of the 122d Psalm which replaces the biblical "they" with an unnamed "somebody," and it ends by placing itself geographically just outside the town line of Eatonville: "So I rounded Park Lane and came speeding down the straight stretch into

Eatonville. . . . Before I enter the township, I wish to make acknowledgments to Mrs. R. Osgood Mason of New York City. She backed my falling in a hearty way, in a spiritual way, and in addition, financed the whole expedition in the manner of the Great Soul that she is." And Part One begins: "As I crossed the Maitland-Eatonville township line. . . ." That line is the line between the two ends of the spyglass, but it is also supposed to stand as the line between the theoretical introduction and the tales. Yet Hurston has already told the first tale, a folk tale she remembers as she drives, a tale of creation and of the unequal distribution of "Soul." Hence, not only does the first tale subvert the opposition between theory and material, but the tale itself comments doubly upon the acknowledgment to Mrs. Mason: what Mrs. Mason backed is called a "falling"—both a postcreational Fall and a losing hand in the "Georgia Skin Game" often referred to in the text. And since the story is about God's promise to redistribute "soul" more equally in the future, it sheds an ironic light on the designation of Hurston's wealthy patron as a "Great Soul."

Hurston does, however, offer some theoretical remarks in her introduction:

> Folk-lore is not as easy to collect as it sounds. The best source is where there are the least outside influences and these people, being usually underprivileged, are the shyest. They are most reluctant at times to reveal that which the soul lives by. And the Negro, in spite of his open-faced laughter, his seeming acquiescence, is particularly evasive. You see we are a polite people and we do not say to our questioner, "Get out of here!" We smile and tell him or her something that satisfies the white person because, knowing so little about us, he doesn't know what he is missing. The Indian resists curiosity by a stony silence. The Negro offers a feather-bed resistance. That is, we let the probe enter, but it never comes out. It gets smothered under a lot of laughter and pleasantries.
>
> The theory behind our tactics: "The white man is always trying to know into somebody else's business. All right, I'll set something outside the door of my mind for him to play with and handle. He can read my writing but he sho' can't read my mind. I'll put this play toy in his hand, and he will seize it and go away. Then I'll say my say and sing my song."

The shifts and reversals in this passage are multiple. Hurston begins as an outsider, a scientific narrative voice that refers to "these people" in the third person, as a group whose inner lives are difficult to penetrate. Then, suddenly, she leaps into the picture she has just painted, including herself in a "we" that addresses a "you"—the white reader, the new implied outsider. The structure of address changes from description to direct address. From that point on it is impossible to tell whether Hurston the narrator is *describing* a strategy or *employing* one. Is her book something set "outside the door" for the white man to "play with and handle," or is the difficulty of penetrating the featherbed resistance being described in order to play up her own privileged skill and access to its inner secrets? In any event, theory is here on the side of the withholder.

The text itself is a frame narrative recounting Hurston's quest for folk tales along with the folk tales themselves. It is a tale of the gathering of tales, or "lies," as they are called by the tellers. Hurston puts herself in a position to hear the tales

only to the extent that she herself "lies." When she tells the townspeople that she has come to collect their "lies," one of them exclaims, "Shucks, Zora, don't you come here and tell de biggest lie first thing. Who you reckon want to read all them old-time tales about Brer Rabbit and Brer Bear?" Later, when Hurston leaves Eatonville to gather more tales elsewhere, she is snubbed as an outsider because of her car and expensive dress until she lies and says that she is a bootlegger fleeing from justice. With her loss of difference comes a flood of tales. The strategy to obtain the material becomes indistinguishable from the material obtained.

This is not to say that the anthropological frame is entirely adequate to its task of accurate representation. The following tale can be read as a questioning of the framing activity:

> Ah know another man wid a daughter.
>
> The man sent his daughter off to school for seben years, den she come home all finished up. So he said to her, "Daughter, git yo' things and write me a letter to my brother!" So she did.
>
> He says, "Head it up," and she done so.
>
> "Now tell 'im, 'Dear Brother, our chile is done come home from school and all finished up and we is very proud of her.' "
>
> Then he ast de girl "Is you got dat?"
>
> She tole 'im "yeah."
>
> "Now tell him some mo'. 'Our mule is dead but Ah got another mule and when Ah say (clucking sound of tongue and teeth) he moved from de word.' "
>
> "Is you got dat?" he ast de girl.
>
> "Naw suh," she tole 'im.
>
> He waited a while and ast her again, "You got that down yet?"
>
> "Naw suh, Ah ain't got it yet."
>
> "Now come you ain't got it?"
>
> "Cause Ah can't spell (clucking sound)."
>
> "You mean to tell me you been off to school seben years and can't spell (clucking sound)? Why Ah could spell dat myself and Ah ain't been to school a day in mah life. Well jes' say (clucking sound) he'll know what yo' mean and go on wid de letter."

The daughter in the tale is in a situation analogous to that of Hurston: the educated student returns home to transcribe what her forebears utter orally. She has learned a notation system that considers itself complete, but that turns out to lack a sign for (clucking sound). The "inside" is here commenting on the "outside," the tale commenting on the book as a whole. It is not by chance that this should be a tale precisely about mules and men. The non-coextensiveness of oral signs and written signs is a problem very much at the heart of Hurston's enterprise. But lest one fall into a simple opposition between the tale's orality and the transcriber's literacy, it is well to note that the orality/literacy relation is the very *subject* of the tale, which cannot be appreciated by those who, like the father *in* the tale, cannot write. Its irony is directed both ways.

Despite Boas's prefatory claim that Hurston has made "an

unusual contribution to our knowledge of the true inner life of the Negro," the nature of such "knowledge" cannot be taken for granted. Who does Boas mean by "we"? . . . [Her] collection of folk tales forces us to ask not whether an "inside" has been accurately represented but what is the nature of the dialogic situation into which the representation has been called. Since this is always specific, always a play of specific desires and expectations, it is impossible to conceive of a pure inside. There is no universalized other for the self to reveal itself *to*. Inside the chemise is the other side of the chemise: the side on which the observer can read the nature of his or her own desire to see.

Mules and Men ends, unexpectedly, with one final tale. Hurston has just spent 150 pages talking not about folk tales but about hoodoo practices. Suddenly, after a break but without preamble, comes the following tale:

> Once Sis Cat got hongry and caught herself a rat and set herself down to eat 'im. Rat tried and tried to git loose but Sis Cat was too fast and strong. So jus' as de cat started to eat 'im he says "Hol' on dere, Sis Cat! Ain't you got no manners atall? You going set up to de table and eat 'thout washing yo' face and hands?"
>
> Sis Cat was mighty hongry but she hate for de rat to think she ain't got no manners, so she went to de water and washed her face and hands and when she got back de rat was gone.
>
> So de cat caught herself a rat again and set down to eat. So de Rat said, "Where's yo' manners at, Sis Cat? You going to eat 'thout washing yo' face and hands?"
>
> "Oh, Ah, got plenty manners," de cat told 'im. "But Ah eats mah dinner and washes mah face and uses mah manners afterwards." So she et right on 'im and washed her face and hands. And cat's been washin' after eatin' ever since.
>
> I'm sitting here like Sis Cat, washing my face and usin' my manners.

So ends the book. But what manners is she using? Upon reading this strange, uncommented-upon final story, one cannot help wondering who, in the final analysis, has swallowed what. The reader? Mrs. Mason? Franz Boas? Hurston herself? As Nathan Huggins writes, after an attempt to determine the sincerity of Hurston's poses and self-representations, "It is impossible to tell from reading Miss Hurston's autobiography who was being fooled" [see Further Reading]. If, as Hurston often implies, the essence of telling "lies" is the art of conforming a narrative to existing structures of address while gaining the upper hand, then Hurston's very ability to fool us—or to fool us into *thinking* we have been fooled—is itself the only effective way of conveying the rhetoric of the "lie." To turn one's own life into a trickster tale of which even the teller herself might be the dupe certainly goes far in deconstructing the possibility of representing the truth of identity.

If I initially approached Hurston out of a desire to re-referentialize difference, what Hurston gives me back seems to be difference as a suspension of reference. Yet the terms *black* and *white, inside* and *outside,* continue to matter. Hurston suspends the certainty of reference not by erasing these differences but by foregrounding the complex dynamism of their interaction. (pp. 179-83)

Barbara Johnson, "Thresholds of Difference: Structures of Address in Zora Neale Hurston," in her A World of Difference, *The Johns Hopkins University Press, 1987, pp. 172-83.*

RUTHANN ROBSON   (essay date 1986)

[*The following appreciative assessment of Hurston's short fiction is excerpted from a review of* Spunk.]

Although [Hurston] is better known as a novelist than as a short story writer, her stories deserve a place in the anthologies *at least* on an equal basis with Faulkner and Flannery O'Connor. Her dialects are faultless and accessibly rendered, her plots smooth and flawless and her tensions maintained. She writes of men and women with equal scrutiny, knowledge and sympathy.

The most witty selection in ***Spunk*** is the never before published **"Book of Harlem."** Structured in numbered verses like the Bible, this story is full of sardonic playfulness and absolute seriousness. It is clever and wonderful and has not lost its timeliness although it is set "in those days when King Volstead sat upon the throne in Hokum, then came a mighty drought upon the land" and "then did the throat parch and the tongue was thrust into the cheeks of many voters," in other words, during Prohibition.

Both Harlem and the Bible appear in other selections in this collection, but the majority are early stories apparently written from her life in the Black community of Eatonville, Florida. Central Florida was unerringly rural then, though when one reads one of the characters referring to the road to Orlando, it is difficult not to think of Mickey Mouse ears and the giant Disney complex responsible for the phenomenal "development" of Orlando. Yet Hurston's stories are not quaint remembrances of a by-gone era, for they involve complex human emotions and actions and relationships.

Hurston is a first rate fiction writer. . . .

Ruthann Robson, in a review of "Spunk," in New Pages, *No. 10, Winter-Spring, 1986, p. 19.*

GRACE INGOLDBY   (essay date 1987)

[*Ingoldby provides a very appreciative review of* Spunk.]

[The best short stories] reveal the virtuosity that exists within the form: in some it is the unmistakable sound of a particular voice that keeps one reading; with others, like those of the late Zora Neale Hurston, it is the range of voices and their vitality that dazzles.

Hurston, hailed as the inspiration behind modern black American writing, left quite a legacy when she died in 1960. In any culture hers would be a tricky act to follow, for her stories are no more about black American women than Picasso's drawings are about bulls, three-faced women and guitars. The stories in ***Spunk*** transcend the particular without any sense that Hurston knows how far she's leaping: unselfconscious, exuberant, tragi-comic, they are, to wipe the grime of overuse from a good word, brilliant.

In **"Sweat"** Delia the washwoman, once a 'right pretty li'l trick' has been hollowed out by husband Sykes who has a charming way with women. 'Tain't no law on earth dat kin make a man be decent if it ain't in 'im'; Sykes treats his old lady like a chew of sugar cane. He grinds her up, he wrings her, he concentrates on getting all that's in her out—a process observed by the porch philosophers who comment that such men, 'when deys satisfied dat dey is wrung dry, dey throws 'em away'. This story has a fairy-tale ending; Sykes gets killed. Joy bursts out of simple tales, sadness seeps. Hurston has the vitality of Dickens and the South Americans; to read her is to realise how cautious much contemporary writing has become. (p. 29)

Grace Ingoldby, "Multiple Echo," in *New States-man*, *Vol. 114, No. 2936, July 3, 1987, pp. 29-30.*

SUSAN WILLIS (essay date 1987)

[*In the following excerpt from her book-length study of Afri-can-American women's writing, Willis discusses the "subver-sion of domination" inherent in Hurston's choice of language. The critic also explores the social and economic contexts of the folktales collected in* Mules and Men.]

When, as a teenager, Zora Neale Hurston took a job as a lady's maid to a young starlet in a traveling Gilbert and Sulli-van troupe, she became an instant success, a new "play-pretty" for the entire company. To explain the fascination the actors and musicians felt for her, Hurston discounts the fact that she was the only black in the group and attributes her popularity, instead, to her Southernness, particularly her use of language:

> I was a Southerner, and had the map of Dixie on my tongue. They were all Northerners except the orchestra leader, who came from Pensacola. It was not that my grammar was bad, it was the idioms. They did not know of the way an average Southern child, white or black, is raised on simile and invec-tive. They know how to call names. It is an every-day affair to hear somebody called a mullet-headed, mule-eared, wall-eyed, hog-nosed, 'gator-faced, shad-mouthed, screw-necked, goat-bellied, puzzle-gutted, camel-backed, butt-sprung, battle-hammed, knock-kneed, razor-legged, box-ankled, shovel-footed, unmated so-and-so! Eyes looking like skint-ginny nuts, and mouth looking like a dishpan full of broke-up crockery! They can tell you in simile exactly how you walk and smell. They can furnish a picture gallery of your ancestors, and a notion of what your children will be like. What ought to happen to you is full of images and flavor. Since that stratum of the Southern population is not given to book-reading, they take their compari-sons right out of the barnyard and the woods. When they get through with you, you and your whole family look like an acre of totem-poles.

Aside from the rich array of barnyard epithets, this passage includes another, more subtle feature, all the more suggestive of Hurston's relationship to language and writing. Contrary to the author's own good opinion of her grammar, the para-graph is based on a number of awkward and misleading shifts in the pronouns. This ungrammatical use of pronouns occurs throughout Hurston's autobiography, *Dust Tracks on a Road,* where it articulates the contradictory nature of Hur-ston's project as a black woman writer and intellectual at-tempting to mediate two deeply polarized worlds, whose terms include: South/North, black/white, rural/urban, folk tradition/intellectual scholarship. Hurston begins this pas-sage with the first person and positions herself as a Souther-er in opposition to the body of Northerners represented by the third-person pronoun "they." "*I*" was a Southerner." "*They* were all Northerners." *They* did not know how a Southern child uses language. However, at this point, the third-person pronoun abruptly takes on a new referent. "*They* know how to call names." Here the pronoun repre-sents Zora's own Southern neighbors, from whom Hurston now differentiates herself. She might have maintained her identification with the group of Southern speakers had she continued with the first person, using the pronoun "we" in-stead of shifting to the third person, "they."

The shift in pronouns is significant in relation to the introduc-tion of the pronoun "you" later in the paragraph. "They can tell *you* in simile exactly how *you* look and smell" and so on. Who can this "you" be but the Northern audience, the white patron who financed much of Hurston's research and writing and the basically white, intellectual readership, who, in 1942, might have been expected to buy this book. The pronoun shifts have two functions. They suggest Hurston's inevitable turmoil and ambivalence over being in the middle and being mediator. And they suggest a certain smugness on the part of the author, "a poor black Southern girl" whose ungram-matical use of English is a deft ploy for turning the tables on the superior Northern establishment. One has the image of Hurston, standing back and chuckling over the "acre of totem-poles" she has just thrown in her reader's face, while she remains blameless because the shift in pronouns has sepa-rated the authorial "I" from the Southern "they."

Hurston's writing is full of tricks of this sort. As she explains in her introduction to *Mules and Men:*

> You see we are a polite people and we do not say to our questioner, "Get out of here!" We smile and tell him or her something that satisfies the white person because, knowing so little about us, he doesn't know what he is missing. The Indian resists curiosity by a stony silence. The Negro offers a feather-bed resistance. That is, we let the probe enter, but it never comes out. It gets smothered under a lot of laughter and pleasantries.

Again the pronoun shifts enable Hurston to be both Southern and not-Southern, black and not-black, inferior and not-inferior. This is not to say that she assumes a Northern, white identity; rather, she lifts herself, as a writer, out of any possi-ble inscription in the stigmatized view of Southern blackness. Bear in mind that this is the Jim Crow South. The passage is a remarkable example of how grammatical tricks make "feather-bed resistance" a form of subversion, whose deep hostility is masked by the displacement of aggression into "laughter and pleasantries." The entering "probe," and un-mistakable image of invasion and male domination, is neatly smothered by a feminine, castrating image, the "feather-bed," notwithstanding all the polite double-talk.

Nowhere is Hurston's subversive intent and smug demeanor more evident than in the conclusion to *Mules and Men.* Here, she tells the story of Sis Cat, who, having let one rat get away while washing her face and hands, decides to eat a second rat straight off. When the rat objects, "Where's yo' manners at, Sis Cat? You gong to eat 'thout washing yo' face and hands?" Sis Cat responds:

> "oh, Ah got plenty manners, . . . But ah eats mah dinner and washes mah face and uses mah manners afterwards." So she et right on 'im and washed her face and hands.

Hurston's concluding one-liner is: "I'm sitting here like Sis Cat, washing my face and usin' my manners." Having just served up the body of black Southern folktales to the Northern white readership, Hurston, gloating like the cat who's just devoured a rat, asks her reader, Now, who's swallowed who? In identifying herself with the aggressor, Hurston takes the subversive intent of her writing one step further than she was able to with her use of pronoun shifts. Rather than the displaced "I," lifted above the terrain of struggle between North and South, white and black, she is here the wily predator, using her "manners"—her writing—with confidence and satisfaction.

I'd like to return to the litany of barnyard names that began this essay and so astounded Hurston's traveling companions. From "puzzle-gutted" to "knock-kneed" and "unmated" this is the raw idiom, which Hurston inherits as a Southerner, particularly one born soon after the turn of the century and raised in a rural environment, and which she, as a writer, will have to transform. Full of assertive expressivity, this is basically still an oral idiom; and as such, it is limited both as a means of communication and as the basis for narrative. Notwithstanding their aggressive intent and vivid imagery, these words do not constitute a language for the audience to whom the book is intended. It is, instead a delightful object, a "play-pretty," like Zora Neale herself, who at this point is a fifteen-year-old pretending to be twenty, a flirtatious and talkative lady's maid, who doesn't yet see herself as a writer nor her discourse as the production of narrative.

One of the tasks Hurston will face as a writer is to develop a literary mode of discourse out of a folk tradition whose basic component is name-calling. The task is complicated by the fact that the tradition includes some qualities that an assertive and resourceful writer like Hurston would want to preserve in the course of developing a more properly literary style. When, in her autobiography, Hurston recalls her introduction to Big Sweet, we sense the dramatic strength that name-calling entails. And we get a glimpse of a woman who accomplishes in her outspoken use of the vernacular what Hurston will eventually achieve in writing:

> I heard somebody, a woman's voice "specifying" up this line of houses from where I lived and asked who it was.
>
> "Dat's Big Sweet" my landlady told me. "She got her foot up on somebody. Ain't she specifying?" . . . She was giving her opponent lurid data and bringing him up to date on his ancestry, his looks, smell, gait, clothes, and his route through Hell in the hereafter. . . . his pa was a double-humpted camel and his ma was a grass-gut cow, but even so, he tore her wide open in the act of getting born, and so on and so forth. He was a bitch's baby out of a buzzard egg.

Although "specifying" may "signify" within the group of "four or five hundred people on the 'job' [who] are listening to Big Sweet's 'reading'," it would not "signify" for an audience outside the rural South as anything more than stereotypically provincial. Big Sweet cannot directly speak her life to the reader, but her image as Hurston describes her, foot up on her opponent's porch, invective in her mouth, can embody something of her experience and gutsy spirit. "Specifying" may be the most self-affirming form of discourse, but it is bound up by its inscription within a specific group of language users. And it is circumscribed, held in check, by the

Hurston on a fishing trip during the late 1930s or early 1940s.

larger system of domination that defines the South and women like Big Sweet as marginal and inferior. As another of Hurston's informants makes clear in his rendition of a folktale, "specifying" is something you do to a neighbor or a fellow camp worker. It's not something you pull on a straw boss or "Ole Massa." As his story goes:

> During slavery time two ole niggers wuz talkin' an' one said tuh de other one, "Ole Massa made me so mad yestiddy till Ah give 'im uh good cussin' out. Man, Ah called 'im everything wid uh handle on it."

When the second man is later upbraided by the master he, too, decides to cuss Ole Massa out. But contrary to his friend's experience, "Ole Massa had 'im took down and whipped nearly tuh death." When the poor man asks his companion why he wasn't punished for the cussing he gave the master, the friend responds:

> "Man, you didn't go cuss 'im tuh his face, didja?"
>
> "Sho Ah did. Ain't dat whut you tole me you done?"
>
> "Naw, Ah didn't say Ah cussed 'im tuh his face. You sho is crazy. Ah thought you had mo' sense than dat. When Ah cussed Ole Massa he wuz settin' on de front porch an' Ah wuz down at de big gate."

If we remember the wily cat who swallowed the rat, then we might say that Hurston's project is analogous to cussing out the master. But because her medium is the narrative, rather than oral language, she can't take refuge down at the gate and do her cussing out in private. Instead, she must do her "specifying" in the form of a book Ole Massa can hold in his hands and read on his very own porch.

Whether or not we decide Hurston's writing achieves the subversion of domination inherent in its bold intent depends largely on how the act of "specifying" is transformed in the process of creating a literary language. As the distance between opponents is foreshortened and finally condensed into the narrative space between writer and reader, barnyard simile becomes metaphor and a lot of the invective is redirected. . . . I want to emphasize that the development of metaphor as a literary language is what differentiates Hurston's writing from that of her more realist contemporaries like Ann Petry and makes her the precursor of today's great modernist writers like Toni Morrison and Paule Marshall. However, because Hurston's work defines the incipient stages of black modernism (which also includes Jean Toomer's unique book, *Cane*), not all of her metaphors are the highly condensed, multireferential figures we have come to associate with Morrison's writing. In fact, many of Hurston's images occupy a midway point between "specifying" and metaphor. These, although drawn from colloquial expression, represent a more complex form of describing than the simple "calling out" and naming. One such example occurs as Hurston continues her account of Big Sweet. Recognizing the importance of befriending Big Sweet, Hurston remarks on her own feeling of insecurity and estrangement in the Polk County mill camp. As she puts it, "I felt as timid as an egg without a shell." And no wonder—with men and women carrying knives and apt to do more than "specify" at each other, Hurston was definitely in a precarious position. Describing herself as a "bootlegger," she showed an inordinate interest in the camp's male population—their songs, stories, and general practice of "woofing" on each other. Big Sweet would prove herself an important ally and lifesaver. In her own advice to Hurston, "You just keep on writing down them lies. I'll take care of all the fighting. Dat'll make it more better, since we done made friends."

When Hurston describes herself as feeling "as timid as an egg without a shell," she evokes absolute vulnerability and she does so in a language that is only one step removed from the barnyard, but on its way to a frame of reference that will no longer be purely animal. "Specifying" equates the opponent with a brute, and, by the very nature of animal existence, cannot give symbolic expression to feelings. In contrast, the colloquial image, even though it is still rooted in a rural system of specification, gives ample space for the expression of emotion. This is possible not only because of the explicit comparison "as timid as," but because the shell-less egg is no longer strictly a part of nature in the same way as a "puzzle-gutted" and "knock-kneed" animal is.

The "egg without a shell" is also a particularly female image. This is true because the egg is the most basic female cell and because eggs—especially shell-less ones, in pans and ready to be fried—summon up the range of women's domestic labor. Hurston often draws from this same register in the creation of images based on colloquial expressions. (pp. 26-33)

What enables Hurston to transcend colloquialisms . . . and write more complex and condensed metaphors is the same element of distance that allows her to look back on and study the folklore she was born into. As she puts it:

> From the earliest rocking of my cradle, I had known about the capers Brer Rabbit is apt to cut and what the Squinch Owl says from the house top. But it was fitting me like a tight chemise. I couldn't see it for wearing it. It was only when I was off in college, away from my native surroundings, that I

could see myself like somebody else and stand off and look at my garment.

When Hurston remarks that her culture once fit "like a tight chemise," she describes a situation most women will recognize as their own. Women wear their daily lives like a snug and intimate article of clothing, so familiar it's apt to be taken for granted. Very often only a significant transformation in situation or consciousness will bring women to scrutinize their daily surroundings and relationships. (p. 34)

Distance and alienation, then, give rise to some of the most beautiful images set forth in the history of black women's writing. Looking back on her childhood, but seeing it from her perspective as an adult, Hurston describes a memorable dream image:

> for weeks I saw myself sitting astride of a fine horse. My shoes had sky-blue bottoms to them, and I was riding off to look at the bellyband of the world.

This delightful image is Hurston's response to a friend's refusal to join her in a quest for the horizon. Always a wanderer, she recounts many instances of stifled wanderlust in her autobiography. Throughout her childhood, the desire for mobility would very often work its way out in images such as these until the day when, as a teenager, she would make her own "dust tracks on a road" headed North. The image of shoes with "sky-blue bottoms" captures the clarity and mind-stretching creativity of the best surrealist art. It elides a child's vocabulary and boundless desire with a sophisticated notion of the world turned topsy-turvy. With the sky brought down to earth and made accessible, one might easily capture the world's "belly-band." (p. 35)

As I see it, Hurston defined and worked in two very different forms, both of which express a social form as well as an aesthetic model. The first is exemplified by the collection *Mules and Men,* whose narrative topography includes the self-contained islands of the tales themselves, which are then interconnected and defined on a broader grid by the path of Hurston's journey and her conversations with the tale-tellers. The oral tales are the original text, which Hurston contextualizes through her own discourse and work as an anthropologist, finally producing yet another, properly literary, text: the book *Mules and Men.* The most basic formal feature to arise out of these layers of textualization is containment. This is a codifying and concretizing form that allows no room for narrative transformation. It is a text whose form mimetically reproduces the economy and social structures of the rural South. The tales, like the work camps, include great creative and human energies, but both are contained: the tale, by the closure of its form; the camps, by their isolation one from another and by their inscription within a larger economic system of domination. Although the camps were in many ways privileged zones, where men and women could hide from the long arm of white, Southern justice, these zones were included in a larger system, which required cheap labor, and so defined a part of its work force as "criminals."

How, then, does the figure of Hurston relate to the form of narrative containment? Born and raised only miles away from the Polk County work camps, she has returned as an anthropologist trained by Franz Boas and funded by a wealthy patron. As a mediator, her task is to transform the raw material of culture into a form accessible to a Northern, intellectual clientele. As a figure in the narrative, Hurston establishes and articulates links between the closed units represented by the tales. Her discourse creates the web of narrative context while it separates the tales from the bed of social context. Hurston's mobility and the larger text she writes break down the sense of closure that defines each tale told in isolation, but she does not so transform the tales as to make of them some new narrative form.

Part of the reason why the folktales themselves resist transformation resides in their internal structure, which, like the whole of Hurston's text, reflects the economics of an oppressed area as it is contained within a larger capitalist economy. A close reading of a single tale will demonstrate how these narratives partake of economic structures.

The story, which tells of Jack and the Devil, is typical of all the Devil stories in **Mules and Men** even though it is longer than most tales and includes more detail and narrative transitions. It is important to note that the Devil, although he has power and represents authority, is in no way comparable to the Ole Massa. The Devil, a trickster like the Jack or John of the stories, is an alternative representation of the black man, who, because he is another worldly figure, is not completely inscribed within the economic and social restraints common to the black population.

The story opens with an inheritance distributed equally between two brothers. The first brother uses his share to buy "a big farm" and "a pair of mules," and to settle down. This is the last we hear of this brother. What follows is all about the second brother, Jack, who "took his money and went on down the road skinnin' and winnin'."

Why is the first brother even mentioned? His part is very small and he's of no interest. Nevertheless, his function in the story is absolutely crucial. For the first brother represents the larger economy, the system of stability based on property ownership within which Jack's "skinnin' and winnin' " is inscribed. Although the whole of the story will focus on Jack's inventive and alternative economics, everything Jack does is contained by the system of capital that is in no way influenced or affected by the forms of exchange employed by Jack.

The first of these modes of exchange is gambling and features Jack pitted against an unbeatable opponent, who, having won all of Jack's money, suggests they keep the game going by staking Jack's life against "all de money on de table." This is a good lesson in the forms of equivalence that evolved under capitalism, which equates a human being with currency. The attachment of exchange value to human beings is, of course, as old as slavery, capitalism's first mode of labor control in this hemisphere.

Jack agrees to the wager, loses, and suddenly finds himself facing a "twelve-foot tall" opponent. "De man looked down on 'im and tole 'im says, 'De Devil is mah name and Ah live across de deep blue sea'." Within the terms of the wager and certainly by reason of his greater power, the Devil could kill Jack on the spot. But that would make a dull story and an unprofitable economics. As the Devil will show, and in keeping with the economics of slavery, Jack is more valuable alive than dead. So the Devil perpetuates the game, but changes its form, and in so doing, lifts Jack out of the economics of slavery and reconstitutes his relationship to him in terms of a system defined by debt peonage, not unlike the sharecropping system of the post-Civil War South.

The transformation to this new economic mode occurs after a transitional interlude in the story during which Jack must journey across the ocean to the Devil's house "befo' the sun sets and rise again." Jack accomplishes the journey on the back of a bald eagle, whom he must feed in midflight "everytime she holler." He has brought along a yearling bull for the eagle's meals. The first time the eagle hollers, "Jack was so skeered dat instead of givin' de eagle uh quarter of de meat, he give her de whole bull." This puts Jack in a terrible fix when the eagle makes a subsequent demand for food. Jack's response is to tear off his own arm and then a leg, so that when he finally arrives at the Devil's house and knocks on the door, he identifies himself as, "One of de Devil's friends. One widout uh arm and widout uh leg." The Devil quickly remedies the situation because, as we shall see, he wants an able-bodied worker, not a cripple:

> Devil tole his wife, says: "Look behind de do' and
> hand dat man uh arm and leg." She give Jack de
> arm and leg and Jack put 'em on.

What's remarkable about this passage is not Jack's self-mutilation and acquisition of new limbs per se. Such things happen throughout the mythic stories of Africa, the roots of the Afro-American storytelling tradition, as in Amos Tutuola's *The Palm-Wine Drinkard,* which at one point describes a man who, journeying from the market to his own village, returns all the limbs and body parts he borrowed from other people on his way to town. When he finally arrives home he is only a head. The Afro-American folktale, as Hurston records it, regards the loss and acquisition of body parts with the same matter-of-fact attitude we find in Tutuola's mythic writing. These narratives shift the focus away from the notion of a body as it belongs to an individual who might experience pain and loss; they demand that we instead consider the process of transformation itself and what it implies. Broadly speaking, the incident articulates the fluctuations in fortune an individual might experience. Gambling, sharecropping, and all the conniving schemes anyone like Jack might invent hold out the promise of instantaneous reward and the probability of rapid downfall. One minute, you're on top of the world; the next, you're hobbling around barely able to survive; and then, you're miraculously restored. The story of the eagle is a mythic device for describing the worldview of people whose lives ultimately are in someone else's hands.

Once at the Devil's house, Jack quickly learns his new economic status. Now in the Devil's debt for his arms, legs, and life, Jack is required to perform a number of tasks. With his labor, given in exchange for a debt that can never be paid, Jack now symbolizes another era in the economic history of this hemisphere, an era that assigned the Indians of Latin America to the haciendas and the emancipated blacks of North America to the peonage of sharecropping. First, Jack must clear a hundred acres for the Devil; then he must retrieve a lost ring from the bottom of a well; and finally, he must pluck two geese in a raging gale without losing a single feather. Luckily, Jack, who could never have performed the tasks in the amount of time allotted by the Devil, is aided by the Devil's daughter, who magically completes each of the tasks. It should be noted the women figures in the tales are never portrayed as stereotypically subservient peasant women, but exercise free will, guile, and intelligence. They make their own decisions and form their own alliances, often contrary to the wishes of male figures in positions of authority. The conclusion of the story features a new set of economic relationships. Jack, having fulfilled his obligations to the

Devil, marries his daughter and sets up housekeeping. The situation suggests his liberation from bondage and access to a form of freeholding. Although the Devil might be forced to accept Jack's independence as the logical result of their contract, he, as a domineering master, fails to accept the situation emotionally. This is evident one night when the Devil comes looking to kill Jack. As a free man, Jack is now worth more dead than alive. This is the reverse of his economic definition under slavery. Hurriedly, Jack and his wife escape in a buckboard pulled by two of the Devil's horses with the Devil in pursuit on his jumping bull.

The outcome of this section of the story has to do, significantly, with the manipulation of language. It suggests the historical function of black language and writing from slavery to the present, which has often reversed systems of domination. The horses Jack has stolen are booby-trapped. Named "Hallowed-be-thy-name" and "Thy-Kingdom-Come," they've been trained to fall to their knees every time the Devil calls their names. Jack is able to outdistance the Devil only because his wife knows the charm to reverse the Devil's spell each time she calls out. However, the Devil finally catches up with Jack, who has hidden in a hollow log, where he invents his own language trick to turn the tables on the Devil. When the Devil picks up the log, Jack cries out, "O Lawd, have mercy." His speech act parallels the Devil's use of holy names and has the effect of causing the Devil such a fright that he drops the log and attempts to flee. But in his haste, he orders his bull to turn around with such ferocity that "De jumpin' bull turnt so fast till he fell and broke his own neck and throwed de Devil out on his head and kilt 'im." So the Devil is mastered by himself and by Jack in the use of language.

"Dat's why dey say Jack beat de Devil." The conclusion of the story is a statement of closure. It separates the tale from the workers' daily lives. Although the story's characters and their relationships have spoken for the real-life situations of black people in this country, these lessons do not carry over to the daily life and toil in the camps. The story is a unit whose function is not to transform anyone's thoughts about his or her working and living conditions. Rather, the story and its telling affirm the group as a cohesive unit, whose members' real-life possibilities are just as contained as the form of the stories they tell.

Group definition and affirmation are the positive features of these stories, whose form, like the society in which they occur, denies transformation. Affirmation is their strength, but it is a strength evolved in response to containment. A good example are the stories of one-upmanship. One man begins: "I know land so poor it won't grow rocks." Thereafter, each of the tellers must respond with another, more impoverished and humorous example. The formula is the same in the "I-know-a-man-blacker-than" stories and the "uglier-than" stories.

> "Ah seen a man so ugly till he could get behind a jimpson weed and hatch monkies.
>
> Everybody laughed and moved closer together. Then Officer Richardson said: "Ah seen a man so ugly till they had to spread a sheet over his head at night so sleep could slip up on him."
>
> They laughed some more, then Clifford Ulmer said:
>
> "Ah'm goin' to talk with my mouth wide open. Those men y'all been talkin' 'bout wasn't ugly at all. Those was pretty men. Ah knowed one so ugly

> till you could throw him in the Mississippi river and skim ugly for six months."

Who wins in a "lying" contest? Is it the best man and the best tale? Or is it the group, "Everybody laugh[ing] and mov[ing] closer together"? Telling stories like these affirms the group more than its individual members. It allows each participant to experience the force of cohesion. But it does so on the basis of derision, and this, too, is a feature of the oppressive system that contains the storytellers and their tales. The stories look at blackness like they look at ugliness. They affirm race, but they do not then transcend racial prejudice. This is, instead, the project for our time. The stories Hurston records begin in negativity; seize their negativity; and in so doing, position themselves on the brink of formulating an alternative vision. But they go no further. This is the significance of "lying," the rural black word for storytelling. From the point of view of the dominant white population, "Niggers lie and lie." Seizing the negativity, the black folk tradition affirms the right to "lie"—to tell tales—to give shape to the self and community. But "lying" can go no further because so long as racial domination exists, "lying" cannot transcend the boundary of otherness and inferiority defined from above. (pp. 38-45)

> *Susan Willis, "Wandering: Zora Neale Hurston's Search for Self and Method," in her* Specifying: Black Women Writing the American Experience, *The University of Wisconsin Press, 1987, pp. 26-52.*

FURTHER READING

Bethel, Lorraine. " 'This Infinity of Conscious Pain': Zora Neale Hurston and the Black Female Literary Tradition." In *All the Women Are White, All the Blacks Are Men, But Some of Us Are Brave: Black Women's Studies.* Edited by Gloria T. Hull, Patricia Bell Scott, and Barbara Smith, pp. 176-88. Old Westbury, N.Y.: The Feminist Press, 1982.

> A feminist appreciation and reevaluation of Hurston, focusing on her short stories and her novel *Their Eyes Were Watching God.*

Bloom, Harold, ed. *Zora Neale Hurston.* Modern Critical Views. New York: Chelsea House Publishers, 1986, 192 p.

> Contains nineteen biographical and critical essays on Hurston, including pieces by Langston Hughes, Fannie Hurst, Larry Neal, and Alice Walker.

Davis, Arthur P. "Zora Neale Hurston." In his *From the Dark Tower: Afro-American Writers, 1900 to 1960,* pp. 113-20. Washington, D.C.: Howard University Press, 1974.

> Overview of Hurston's work. While praising her as a fiction writer and folklorist, Davis portrays Hurston as disloyal to her own race and eager to gain the acceptance of whites.

Ford, Nick Aaron. Postscript to his *The Contemporary Negro Novel: A Study in Race Relations,* pp. 94-102. College Park, Md.: McGrath Publishing Co., 1968.

> Contends that Hurston's impersonal treatment of racism in her works accentuates negative racial stereotypes.

Gloster, Hugh M. "Zora Neale Hurston, Novelist and Folklorist." *Phylon* IV, No. 2 (Second Quarter 1943): 153-59.

> Survey of Hurston's life and career.

Helmick, Evelyn Thomas. "Zora Neale Hurston." *The Carrell* 11, Nos. 1 & 2 (June-December 1970): 1-19.
  Biographical and critical overview.

Huggins, Nathan Irvin. "Heart of Darkness." In his *Harlem Renaissance,* pp. 84-136. New York: Oxford University Press, 1971.
  Emphasizes Hurston's acceptance of the patronage of wealthy whites in what many critics consider a subjective and unflattering portrait of the author.

Kilson, Marion. "The Transformation of Eatonville's Ethnographer." *Phylon* XXXIII, No. 2 (Summer 1972): 112-19.
  Details Hurston's transition from a relativist anthropologist in her early writings to a critical ethnographer in the essays she wrote after 1942. Included is a discussion of the prominent themes of Hurston's fiction and an appendix listing Hurston's writings.

Lupton, Mary Jane. "Zora Neale Hurston and the Survival of the Female." *The Southern Literary Journal* XV, No. 1 (Fall 1982): 45-54.
  Discusses the tenacity of Hurston's female protagonists in her novel *Their Eyes Were Watching God* and her short story "Sweat."

Mikell, Gwendolyn. "The Anthropological Imagination of Zora Neale Hurston." *The Western Journal of Black Studies* 7, No. 1 (Spring 1983): 27-35.
  Examines the impact of Hurston's anthropological career on her creative writing.

Pinckney, Darryl. "In Sorrow's Kitchen." *The New York Review of Books* XXV, No. 20 (21 December 1978): 55-7.
  Review of *Mules and Men* and Robert Hemenway's literary biography of Hurston.

Pratt, Theodore. "Zora Neale Hurston: Florida's First Distinguished Author." *Negro Digest* XI, No. 4 (February 1962): 52-5.
  Memoir by a personal acquaintance of Hurston's.

Pryse, Marjorie. "Zora Neale Hurston, Alice Walker, and the 'Ancient Power' of Black Women." In *Conjuring: Black Women, Fiction, and Literary Tradition.* Edited by Marjorie Pryse and Hortense J. Spillers, pp. 1-24. Bloomington: Indiana University Press, 1985.
  Places Hurston with Alice Walker in a tradition of black female writers who use knowledge of their shared heritage to speak for all African-American women.

Southerland, Ellease. "The Influence of Voodoo on the Fiction of Zora Neale Hurston." In *Sturdy Black Bridges: Visions of Black Women in Literature.* Edited by Roseann P. Bell, Bettye J. Parker, and Beverly Guy-Sheftall, pp. 171-83. Garden City, N.Y.: Anchor Books, Doubleday, 1979.
  Traces elements of voodoo and numerology throughout Hurston's fiction and folklore.

Walker, Alice. "In Search of Zora Neale Hurston." *Ms.* III, No. 9 (March 1979): 74-9, 85-9.
  A reflection on Hurston's later life that also laments the lack of critical attention given to her after her death. Walker recounts a trip to Eatonville, Florida, Hurston's hometown and the inspiration for many of her writings, where she searched for Hurston's grave and talked to several people who had known the writer during her final years.

Wall, Cheryl A. "Zora Neale Hurston: Changing Her Own Words." In *American Novelists Revisited: Essays in Feminist Criticism.* Edited by Fritz Fleischman, pp. 371-93. Boston: G. K. Hall and Co., 1982.
  Critical overview of Hurston's fiction, including a brief discussion of the significance of *Mules and Men* as the first collection of black folklore compiled by an African-American.

Wallace, Michele. "Who Dat Say Who Dat When I Say Who Dat? Zora Neale Hurston Then and Now." *Voice Literary Supplement* No. 64 (April 1988): 18-21.
  An examination both of Hurston's reemergence in African-American literature after years of obscurity and of her artistic legacy among contemporary black writers. Includes an analysis of the diverse scholarly interpretations Hurston's works have elicited throughout the years.

Willis, Miriam DeCosta. "Folklore and the Creative Artist: Lydia Cabrera and Zora Neale Hurston." *CLA Journal* XXVII, No. 1 (September 1983): 81-90.
  Surveys the folklorist careers of Hurston and Cuban author Lydia Cabrera, exploring how both writers combined scientific methodologies and artistic intuition in their works.

Mary Lavin

1912-

American-born Irish short story writer and novelist.

Considered one of the foremost Irish short story writers of the twentieth century, Lavin instills her tales of the Irish middle class with insight into the dynamics of intimate relationships through her focus on the contrarieties of human emotions. The central figures of Lavin's stories tend to be sensitive individuals who have repressed or abandoned their dreams and are ultimately forced to confront regrets over the uneasy compromises of their lives. Sometimes faulted for lacking plot in her stories, Lavin frequently fixes her attention on seemingly trivial occurrences, investing them with hidden meanings and revealing their emotional significance. Though she has published works in several genres, Lavin's most significant literary contributions have been in the short story form. In the preface to her *Selected Stories* Lavin explains: "It is in the short story that a writer distills the essence of his thought. I believe this because in the short story shape as well as matter is determined by the author's own character. Both are one. Short-story writing—for me—is only looking closer than normal into the human heart."

Lavin was born in East Walpole, Massachusetts. When she was nine years old, she moved with her parents to Ireland and lived in Dublin, where she attended the Loreto convent school. In 1925, the family relocated to the Bective estate in County Meath, and Lavin subsequently attended University College, Dublin, receiving her M.A. in English in 1936. In 1938, Lavin wrote her first short story, "Miss Holland," on the back of a typed draft of her Ph.D. dissertation on Virginia Woolf. After several rejections, the story was accepted by editor Seumas O'Sullivan and published in the *Dublin Magazine* in 1939. O'Sullivan's agreement to seriously consider any other submissions that Lavin sent prompted her to abandon her dissertation and pursue a career as a writer. In 1940, the publication of Lavin's story "The Green Grave and the Black Grave" in the *Atlantic Monthly* introduced her fiction to an American audience and garnered high praise from such prominent Irish writers as Lord Dunsany and Frank O'Connor. In 1942, with the help of Dunsany, Lavin published *Tales from Bective Bridge,* her first collection of short fiction, and secured her status as a prominent literary figure.

Tales from Bective Bridge presents the essence of Lavin's artistic approach through stories in which she subordinates action to the underlying emotional dilemmas of her characters. "At Sallygap," one of the most critically acclaimed pieces in the collection, centers on Manny Ryan, whose unrealized dreams strain his relationship with his wife Annie. The story opens as Manny reflects on a forgone opportunity to play fiddle with the East Mary Street Band in Paris. His decision to stay in Ireland and marry Annie has left him with a mundane and unsatisfying life as a Dublin shopkeeper. Critics note that Manny Ryan is one of Lavin's more complex characters, and through his narration in "At Sallygap" readers witness his growing dissatisfaction with himself, his work, and his marriage. Because it focuses on a sensitive and artistic character caught in an emotionally stolid environment, this story is often compared in theme and style to James Joyce's work in

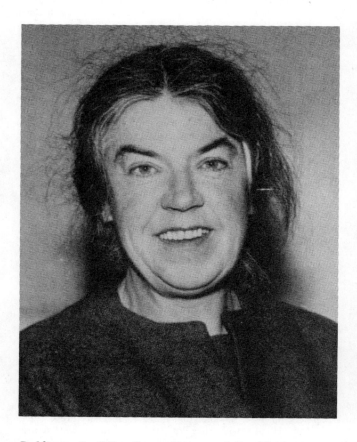

Dubliners. In "The Green Grave and the Black Grave," Lavin contrasts the falsity of emotions in the marriage of Manny and Annie Ryan, with the intensity of authentic love. Here, Lavin relies on the rhythmic qualities of Gaelic verse to convey what Richard F. Peterson has called "the myth-making character of the Irish people." Focusing on the profound devotion that prompts Bean Og Eamon to recover her husband's body from the "green grave" of the sea, Lavin creates a modern fable of humanity's vulnerability to the relentless indifference of nature.

Although *Tales from Bective Bridge* received high praise, many critics noted a lack of plot structure in these stories. Perhaps in response to such commentary, Lavin evinced a new emphasis on plot in her works collected in *A Single Lady, and Other Stories* and *Patriot Son, and Other Stories.* Lavin's fiction during this period garnered mixed reviews, and such stories as "Posy," "The Small Bequest," and "The Long Ago" have generally been faulted for intrusive narration and unrealistic characterizations. The tales collected in *In the Middle of the Fields, and Other Stories* and *Happiness, and Other Stories* reflect Lavin's interest in autobiographical fiction and mark a return to the impressionistic writing style that established her reputation. These collections include several pieces that center on the emotional challenges of widowhood through the character Vera Traske. Commentators agree that Lavin's "widow stories" are among her finest and note that Vera Traske is Lavin's most autobiographical character. The story "Happiness" is the last of the Vera Traske stories and has been referred to by critics as a representative capsule of Lavin's artistic and personal perspectives. In this story, Vera, like Lavin, endures the early death of her husband and is left to care for their three young children. Though Vera dies, this story reveals her enduring faith in the value of life. Told from the perspective of Vera's oldest daughter, "Happiness" exemplifies the emotional stamina and unyielding optimism that have sustained Vera through her personal tragedies.

Though she occasionally draws upon her childhood experiences in America as material for her stories, Lavin's predominant settings are rural Ireland, Dublin, and the Abbey Farm on the Bective estate, where she has spent most of her life. From her earliest attempts, Lavin has been successful in developing characters that reflect the essence of Irish culture as well as the boundless nature of human tragedies and triumphs. She has maintained a strong commitment to writing richly colored tales that test the emotional endurance of her characters, and though often pervasively despairing in their treatment of the tragic elements of human existence, Lavin's stories are considered poignant for their unwavering compassion and hopefulness.

(For further information on Lavin's life and career, see *Contemporary Literary Criticism,* Vols. 4, 18; *Contemporary Authors,* Vols. 9-12 rev. ed.; and *Dictionary of Literary Biography,* Vol. 15.)

PRINCIPAL WORKS

SHORT FICTION

Tales from Bective Bridge   1942;   revised, 1978
The Long Ago, and Other Stories   1944
The Becker Wives, and Other Stories   1946; also published
  as *At Sallygap, and Other Stories,* 1947
A Single Lady, and Other Stories   1951
The Patriot Son, and Other Stories   1956
Selected Stories   1959
The Great Wave, and Other Stories   1961
The Stories of Mary Lavin. 2 vols.   1964, 1974
In the Middle of the Fields, and Other Stories   1967
Happiness, and Other Stories   1969
Collected Stories   1971
A Memory, and Other Stories   1972
The Shrine, and Other Stories   1977
Mary Lavin: Selected Stories   1981
A Family Likeness   1985

OTHER MAJOR WORKS

The House in Clewe Street   (novel)   1945
Mary O'Grady   (novel)   1950

AUGUSTINE MARTIN   (essay date 1963)

[*Martin has written and edited several critical surveys of Irish*

literature. In the following excerpt, he offers an overview of the dominant themes in Lavin's works.]

Because of the curious position of Mary Lavin in the modern short story, this essay is in the nature of a rapid survey, a preface to criticism, rather than a formal critical essay. It attempts to examine briskly and consecutively (1) her technical and aesthetic approach to the form, (2) her fictional material and milieu, (3) the operation of her creative technique in a selected number of her stories, and (4) her dominant and recurring themes as exemplified in these and—more briefly—in other examples of her work. . . . Consequently the present purpose is to blaze some sort of trail rather than to set up critical monuments by the wayside.

Before setting out I find it necessary to make clear a few basic convictions about the stories of Mary Lavin. The first is that she belongs to the thin front line of Irish short-story writers—to the company of Liam O'Flaherty, Frank O'Connor and Sean O'Faolain. I have no idea how readily this rating of her work will be accepted because so far no body of criticism has grown up around her writings. The reason for this critical neglect, I feel, is almost wholly an extra-literary concern. An explanation of it would belong—to borrow a distinction from Dr Leavis—more to the history of publicity than the history of literature. Finally I feel that she occupies a unique position in the Irish short story. Mr O'Connor has written that the Irish short story is in the nature of a separate art-form. If this remark is true—and it is as true as such remarks can ever be—then Mary Lavin is outside the tradition.

The form of short story she has evolved owes less to Irish models—George Moore, James Stephens, Daniel Corkery, Seamus O'Kelly, O'Flaherty, O'Connor and O'Faolain—than to Turgenev, Tchehov, Katherine Mansfield and James Joyce, who was far more a European than a specifically Irish artist. (pp. 393-94)

Miss Lavin has provided us with only two comments that might be taken as guides to her creative method. The first, characteristically, is embodied in one of her short stories, a shrewdly self-critical piece entitled **"A Story with a Pattern"** and the other occurs in the preface to her ***Selected Stories,*** the only piece of formal literary criticism she has ever written. **"A Story with a Pattern"** tells how she 'finds' herself at a party, being taken to task by a rather forthright guest for failing to supply her stories with the sort of plot and pattern which, he claims, the normal reader demands. Ruthlessly telescoped, the argument goes like this:

> 'Now your stories,' he said, 'are very thin. They have hardly any plot at all.'
>
> 'But I don't think . . .'
>
> 'And the endings,' he said, 'your endings are very bad. They're not endings at all. Your stories just break off in the middle! Why is that, might I ask?'
>
> I'm afraid I smiled superciliously. 'Life itself has very little plot,' I said. 'Life itself has a habit of breaking off in the middle.'
>
> (p. 394)

This story is the closest the author ever gets to an artistic manifesto. . . . [But is] her aesthetic a simple negation of all pattern, her stories uncritical reflections of life's disorder? Her preface to the ***Selected Stories*** indicates a more positive stance:

I believe that it is in the short story that a writer distills the essence of his thought. I believe this because in the short story shape as well as matter is determined by the author's own character. Both are one. Short story writing—for me—is only looking closer than normal into the human heart. The vagaries and contrarieties there to be found have their own integral design.

Everything here is highly relevant. It seems that Miss Lavin's attitude does not entail any real repudiation of pattern in life or art. Life has its own pattern, a subtle pattern that inheres in 'vagaries and contrarieties' if one looks hard enough to find it. Hence she asserts that shape and matter are one. Form or pattern therefore must not be imposed from without. . . . That, as she tells the man at the party, would be—at least for her—'distorting the truth'. Instead she feels that it is her duty as a story teller to approach her living material with an intense and much more humble scrutiny; to find its intrinsic rhythms, choose its significant emphases and deploy them in a meaningful artistic sequence. If I have so far interpreted her position correctly the rest follows.

> And it is here that devices of concentration, poetic association and above all implication are sometimes needed. To interpret these devices the reader must be sensitive, alert and above all willing to come forward and take the story into his mind and heart.

This is very forthright, even challenging. The reader is being put on his mettle; his intelligence and sensitivity are made stand by; some of the onus is thrown on him if he is not to miss the story's point. The challenge might seem even righteously defensive if it were not for its peculiar truth and peculiar relevance to Miss Lavin's stories. But they do require in the reader this sensitivity and alertness. They do not deliver their impact in one flash of insight at the end, or through any internal progression of emphatic or cumulative incident; they seldom make use of dramatic tension or issue in dramatic resolution. They provide a minimum of kicks. But instead, if read attentively, they set up vibrations in the mind and the imagination which continue in the reader's mind long after the story has been put down. It is as if the author has so unerringly found the innate rhythms of her human material that the story goes on in the reader's mind and merges with his own experience. (pp. 395-96)

Let us test these general assertions against a selected number of her stories. To choose from the substantial body of her writing, stories that are at once typical and especially meritorious would be a most difficult task. My idea, therefore, is to start with a series of pieces dealing with the same family, which she has written over twelve years of her career and through three volumes. They concern the Grimes family and though they are not all typical of her best work they are typical of her milieu and serve to point up her characteristic techniques and some of her central themes. In this sense they are satisfactory as the purpose here is not to dispense accolades but to examine significant aspects of a writer's art and artistic material. For the main body of the author's work is set against the background and amid the milieu of Irish middle-class existence—the small town with its shop-keepers, priests and farmers from the surrounding country-side. On the surface it is a drab uneventful world where the chief occurrences are marriages, deaths and unspectacular scandals.

It is a world where outward, emphatic action scarcely exists, where human tensions are muted, where love, joy and desper-

ation are subsumed in to a common ethos of stoic respectability. But it is her especial genius to pierce beneath these colourless surfaces and wrest significance from the most outwardly commonplace situations. Hence it is altogether typical that the rather squalid saga of the Grimes family begins with an apparently insignificant visit to a disused graveyard where the mother of the family has been buried.

"A Visit to the Cemetery" appeared in her collection *A Single Lady* and it introduces Liddy and Alice Grimes, two daughters of the family who have come to visit their mother's grave. The cemetery has been closed for some time and it is a jungle of twisted grass and tottering headstones. Alice, the elder of the sisters, keeps expressing her disgust at the condition of the place and saying what a pity it is that her mother had not been buried in the bright new cemetery on the other side of the town. Having completed their devotions at the grave they are about to leave when Liddy, on seeing a dislodged bone, is suddenly struck by a horribly real sense of death. She gets a shuddering vision of her mother's body in the dank earth. Alice, the more pragmatical one, tries rather impatiently to console her.

> 'After all we must all die—we know that,' she said.

> But Liddy was incorrigible.

> 'That's what I mean,' she said quietly.

The desolate mood has completely taken hold of her:

> 'I cannot believe that I won't go on feeling: feeling the cold and the damp—you know, even after—'

The realization is borne in on Alice too; it seems almost as if death is reaching out at them from the dank earth. It is then that Alice makes the remark that magically transforms their mood and at the same time gives the story its shrewed ironical lift:

> 'Well thanks be to goodness we won't be buried here anyway!' she said, impulsively.

Liddy is shocked into curiosity. Alice rushes on to explain that their father will be the last to be buried there. As for themselves—

> 'there aren't any more plots to be got here now, thanks be to God, so our husbands will have to provide them—in the new cemetery—thanks be to God again.'

Our husbands—it was an intoxicating thought! Like a flash Liddy's depression lifts and a whole new vista is opened up to her imagination. The old cemetery with its dank emblems of decay loses its grip upon her as she rushes Alice out into the sunlight which has suddenly been switched on again. Now, by a natural, but quietly hilarious association the new cemetery becomes a symbol of life and marriage; a focus for all the romantic aspirations of young womanhood. The author, of course, makes no overt reference to this—but it is shrewdly planted in the dialogue. (pp. 397-98)

I feel that this story is a little masterpiece. If it were only for the accuracy with which the varying moods of the girls are caught in the descriptions and dialogue it would be masterly. But its genius is even more manifest in its rich suggestiveness, its specifically fabulous quality; and so its insights into life, love, human aspiration and human mortality take on the authority of a universal statement. And then there is the quality in Mary Lavin's stories to which I have referred already: their ability to set up vibrations in the mind, to capture the essential and characteristic rhythm of her chosen situation so that the reader's imagination can be carried forward in sympathetic resonance well beyond the limits of the story itself.

Thus at the end of **"A Visit to the Cemetery,"** not only can we see the girls walking around among the graves of the new cemetery—though it is not described—but we have a fair sense of what their future lives are to be like. Despite the strictures of the man at the party the story does not break off at the end; the whole point is that it goes on—at least for those who have picked up its imaginative frequency. This is surely the salient virtue of this type of story. (pp. 398-99)

Finally **"A Visit to the Cemetery"** has, as perhaps its most engaging quality, a complete absence of author comment; it is the most shameful case of literary eavesdropping. The transition of mood that changes a tombstone to a wedding cake is carried solely by dialogue and imagery. One could say quite accurately that it is all done with tombstones.

The next three stories in the Grimes saga occur in the author's next volume, **The Patriot Son.** . . . The first of the three **"An Old Boot"** is a rather slight piece, important only in that it introduces another one of the Grimes sisters, Bedelia the eldest, who is to play a pivotal role in the future fortunes of the family. The father of the family, Matthias Grimes, has by now turned odd with the death of his wife and Bedelia is preparing to get her claws on the family business. In **"An Old Boot"** we find her making crafty overtures to Daniel, the seedily eligible manager of the shop. In the midst of their furtive negotiations—no element of love seems to arise—they are rudely silenced by the clump of old mad Matthias Grimes's boot—'hot and smelly with the heat of a living foot'—on the ceiling above. But though their tepid intimacies are momentarily suspended, the reader has no doubt as to who shall be in control when the old man dies. Therefore at the beginning of the next story in the sequence, **"Frail Vessel,"** we find that the father has died and that Bedelia and Daniel—well in control of the business—are preparing for their marriage of convenience.

Apart from being a fine sample of the story-teller's art, **"Frail Vessel"** enacts a central theme in the author's consciousness, and its two chief actors, Bedelia and Liddy—the younger sister of **"A Visit to the Cemetery"**—represents two recurrent and crucial types in her stories. Bedelia cold, practical, inflexibly determined, is summed up in the author's phrase, 'a conniving woman'; Liddy is the opposite—warm, whimsical, romantic, outwardly frail. Liddy is the frail vessel of the title and against her is levelled all the very formidable artillery of Bedelia's ruthless connivance.

The first confrontation takes place when Liddy interrupts Bedelia's marriage preparations with a sudden request for permission to marry an unsuccessful solicitor, Alfonsus O'Brien, who has recently come to town. Bedelia, though deeply suspicious of O'Brien and secretly livid that Liddy should be so obviously in love, gives her consent for purely selfish reasons—the chief one is that she foresees certain embarrassments in having Liddy around the house when Daniel moves into her bedroom. But afterwards when both of them are married, she regrets her generosity, not because Liddy and her husband are wretchedly poor but because she realizes how useful Liddy would be to her, now that she is heavy with child. So by a series of calculated and unscrupulous financial

manoeuvres she breaks up the marriage, sends O'Brien packing and leaves Liddy no choice but to return to live with herself and Daniel. It is here that the muted irony of the story begins to accumulate. Too late Bedelia discovers that Liddy too is pregnant; instead of a dependent hand-maid she has an added encumbrance on her hands. Worse still she realizes that Liddy is still in love with her worthless husband; her secret store of happiness is still undamaged. Bedelia's carefully laid plans for power and patronage have blown up in her face. . . . (pp. 399-400)

This theme, the indestructibility of human love, given generously, is a constant energizing principle in Miss Lavin's stories. It occurs in **"The Will"** where the love of Sally, who married beneath her, survives all the pressures of her respectable and uncomprehending family; in **"A Happy Death"** where the dying man salvages from a lifetime of oppressive shrewishness an image of early love that irradiates his end; in **"A Tragedy"** where the act of surrender to conjugal love is proof against the corroding and malicious influence of a sister-serpent beneath the same roof. The converse position is equally dominant and articulate. Failure to give oneself generously in love carries its own punishment—that limbo of the affections inhabited, for instance, by Elgar in **"The Convert"** who neither marries Naida Paston whom he loves nor loves Mamie Sully whom he marries; or Rose Darker in **"A Gentle Soul"** who through sheer pusillanimity twice betrays the man she loves, once in life and once after his death; or Brede in **"Bridal Sheets"** who through some inscrutable meanness of spirit allows her hidden finery to stand between her and complete surrender to her husband's love, even after she has died.

(It seems to be a conviction of the author's that people, even when given a second chance, will behave exactly as they did before. Both Rose Darker and Brede reject their second chances to make amends: one by refusing to give the evidence that will vindicate her dead lover's character, the other by refusing the body of her dead husband the bridal sheets that she had never shown him in life.)

If **"Frail Vessel"** establishes the impregnability of romantic love, the next story in the sequence dramatizes the destructive and self-destroying power of connivance as it operates in the soul of Bedelia. In **"The Little Prince"** Bedelia sets about removing her younger brother Tom from the field of her activities. Tom is gentle but feckless and Bedelia has little difficulty in forcing him to emigrate. But Tom's very impracticality takes its revenge on her because he departs without claiming his share in the business and he never writes to let her know of his address. Her scrupulous husband Daniel lodges Tom's shares of the profits to his—Tom's—account in the bank every week, and as the years pass it grows into a substantial sum—an ever-present and maddening reminder to Bedelia of both her ruthlessness and lack of foresight. (In Mary Lavin's stories, as in life, extreme craftiness in some things is often accompanied by obtuseness in others.)

As time passes Bedelia becomes obsessed by anxiety—partly familial, mostly financial—about Tom's fate till eventually word reaches them from America that an old tramp called Tom Grimes is dying in a New York hospital. In desperation Bedelia and Daniel set out to identify him. During the voyage the author introduces a characteristic device, obliquely underlining the central theme. Bedelia takes up with a widow on the ship, a woman who is transporting the corpse of her husband for burial to America. The body in the hold becomes an almost obscene symbol of human chicanery. An Englishman remarks to Daniel as he watches the two women pacing the deck:

> 'I must say she looks a cold fish to me. I bet she has some shrewd motive in taking the poor stiff back to the States. Look at the face of her. I can't stand a conniving woman!'

It was with a shock that Daniel realized that the other had mistaken Bedelia for the owner of the corpse.

The voyage continues and so does Bedelia's equivocal remorse while the corpse in the hold is 'like a shuttle, rattled backwards and forwards with each uneasy movement of the water.' This macabre and inexorable motion brings Bedelia to New York and to the unresolved crises of her anxieties. Because there she fails to recognize Tom's corpse; she is brought up against the grey stonewall that she has been unconsciously raising between herself and her brother:

> She looked again into the dead man's face. But if it was her brother something had sundered them, something had severed the bonds of blood and she knew him not. And if it was I that was lying there, she thought, he would not know me. It signifies nothing that they might once have sprung from the same womb. Now, in this fateful moment they were strangers.

By her actions, by the whole crafty pressure of her life Bedelia has renounced the right to recognize her own flesh and blood; and so, fittingly, she is punished. And the mind of the reader acquiesces because the punishment is as much a part of the integral pattern of her life as were her grey ambiguous crimes. The biblical 'she knew him not' is justified. (I can find no such justification for the cliché 'this fateful moment' which arises from a stylistic carelessness of which the author is sometimes guilty.)

In Mary Lavin's scheme of things you cannot violate the ties of love, in any of its forms, without involving yourself in unhappiness. This has nothing to do with any doctrinaire invocation of poetic justice; it is the relentless working out of an organic human sequence.

I shall not dwell on the last story of the series "Loving Memory" chiefly because I find it especially problematical. It occurs in her volume *The Great Wave*. . . . I find it difficult to judge as an independent work in its genre because it *seems* to set out to explain why the Grimes family turned out as it did. It tells how the father Matthias Grimes first married their mother Alicia, a rather supernal young woman—a sort of reincarnation of Flora of "The Becker Wives"—and lived with her in an intense, exclusive, lifelong relationship with scarcely a thought for the children. It tells how Alicia died young and how Matthias, imprisoned even more rigorously within her memory, haunts her grave and slips slowly into madness. In it, one finds it difficult to be sure whether the author is committed to writing a fresh short story or to extending and rationalizing the Grimes saga. (pp. 400-02)

However, taken together with "A Visit to the Cemetery" and "The Little Prince" it raises a broader issue in the author's work as a whole—her virtual obsession with the theme of death. These three stories deal specifically with the power of the dead over the living and to them might be added at least three other stories involving this theme, "A Gentle Soul," "The Convert" and "Lemonade." Perhaps it is significant that the theme has had a strange attraction for many of the

great short story writers; one recalls at random Chekov's "Easter Eve," Joyce's "The Dead" and Katherine Mansfield's "The Stranger," all piercing and memorable tales. In Mary Lavin's stories it is difficult to generalize on its significance except to note that with one exception—"A Visit to the Cemetery"—the memory of the dead person acts so as to paralyse or impair the grip of the living upon living reality. Matthias Grimes, Bedelia, Rose Darker, Mad Mary and Elgar are all in different ways trapped within their memories. But the exception is so forceful as to reduce the validity of this generalization; Alice and Liddy are quite emphatically projected towards the future and the business of living by their epiphany in the graveyard.

This fixation of memory is only one of the many instances of the author's preoccupation with death; the theme looms large throughout the body of her work. Even a glance at the titles establishes its pervasive presence in the author's mind—"The Green Grave and The Black Grave," "The Cemetery in the Demesne" and "The Will" might be added to the titles already cited. An investigation of its provenance and causes would be unlikely to yield much of critical value—in fact it could be explained better in terms of sociology and Irish sociology in particular. But it ties up in a strange way with another stream of the author's sensibility which is likely to yield more specifically critical dividends.

In her work there is a whole range of characters who recoil from the more fullblooded implications of life and settle for a cool cloistered compromise; over against them stands an equal rank of figures who are characterized by their energetic committment to the hot realities of living. Several of her stories enact the conflict between these two basic life attitudes and it is especially significant that in one of her very earliest stories "Love is for Lovers" the tension is quite clearly epitomized. Here Matthew, a character of the first type, is almost tempted from his ordered, emotionally tepid existence by a stiflingly full-blooded widow, Mrs. Cooligan, but he retreats quite deliberately into the cool cloister of his bachelorhood. As it is an early story the author presents the issues less subtly than in her subsequent work and the contrast is quite aggressively deliberate:

> Life was hot and pulsing and it brought sweat to the forehead. He didn't know anything about marriage, but it must be close and pulsing too . . . Life was nauseating to him. Death was cool and fragrant. Of course, he had a long way to go before its green shade lengthened to reach him. But in the meantime he could keep away from the hot rays of life, as he had always done before he had got familiar with Rita.

Surely this is the death wish presented in a most assertive, not to say unnerving form. If it cropped up only in one early and rather clumsy story, one might dismiss it as a transitory if curious tangent of the author's creative imagination. But it reemerges inexorably though more subtly through her later work: in the contrast between Miss Holland and her fellow lodgers; in the contrast between the prim and pathetic spinster and her father in "A Single Lady"; in Daniel's rejection of the little servant girl in "Posy"—where even the heroine's nickname is redolent of the life principle; in the disparity between the vigorous and sweating Magenta and the two pallid old maids; and more subtly in the contrast between Mamie Sully and Naida Paston in the two stories in which they appear. This persistent dichotomy could be expanded and developed. There is little doubt that the author is on the side of life despite the fact that many of its protagonists in her work are little short of repellent—Mamie Sully, Annie Bowles, Rita Cooligan—and many of its deniers are sympathetically, almost tenderly evoked—Naida Paston, Miss Holland, Matthew and Daniel. Again it is difficult to be sure whether the author is—however unconsciously—presenting the death wish as something central in the human condition or merely posing the question of its peculiar relevance to Ireland. It is sufficient here to note that the psychological tensions which surround it are a constant principle of energy in her creative consciousness.

In centering this critique around the Grimes saga I have been forced to exclude, except for passing mention, several areas of the author's work which would have made incomparably more *exciting* material for criticism. There would have been much more colour and liveliness in stories like **"My Vocation"** or **"The Yellow Beret"** which are set against a Dublin background; again there are stories like **"The Haymaking,"** **"Brigid"** and that powerful and grievous story **"Asigh"** which exploit the ethos of agrarian society; finally it has been necessary to bypass that handful of stories set in Synge and O'Flaherty country, the western sea-board, stories like **"The Green Grave and The Black Grave"** and **"The Great Wave"** with its rich biblical implications. But for all their colour and excitement these stories are really on the periphery of her artistic vision. The centre of her focus is the 'vagaries and contrarieties' of the human heart as seen in its small-town habitat. This is her objective correlative and it is on this murky prism that she concentrates the strongest creative light; it is here that her human concern is most sustained and urgent. Out of this material she builds not only the Grimes cycle but her only other related sequence of stories—those featuring Naida Paston, Elgar and Mamie Sully—**"The Convert,"** **"Limbo"** and **"The Mouse,"** though in the last of these for some inscrutable reason she gives the character new names.

Outside of this small-town ethos Miss Lavin has written accomplished and powerful stories but it is within it, one feels, that she is most consistently close to the hard core of the human predicament. **"The Great Wave"** is more exotic and spectacular, more overwhelming in its symbolic overtones than say **"Frail Vessel,"** but it is also more remote from the authentic problems of living. With all its lyrical splendour it is really no more than an illuminated capital on the parchment of life. It is in the tedious and unadorned script of the Grimes history that life's meaning is to be read. It is the final proof of Miss Lavin's integrity as an artist that she has pursued this squalid chronicle with such relentless and minute concern and forced it to yield up its hidden and unexpected riches. Of course we must not be ungrateful that she has paused from time to time to give us such a finely worked capital as **"The Great Wave"** or such diverting and irresponsible marginalia as **"My Vocation"** or **"The Patriot Son"**—that irreverent footnote to Irish revolutionary literature.

Concluding, one gets the very strong impression that the really critical portion of Miss Lavin's career lies ahead. If she were to stop writing now she would, of course, have left an enduring corpus of work behind her but she would also have failed to exploit the full potentialities of which that work gives evidence. Frank O'Connor seems to have held such a view three years ago when he wrote of her [in *A Review of English Literature*, Vol. 1, No. 2, April 1960]:

> She fascinates me more than any other of the Irish writers of my generation, because more than any of

them, her work reveals that she has not said all that she has to say.

And while Mr O'Connor claims her for his generation it must be remembered that she is some ten years his junior. Consequently the years ahead ought to be artistically very rich if she determines to resist the temptation to write solely *New Yorker* type stories. This is not to suggest that her *New Yorker* stories are in any way inferior—it is the limitation of scope and amplitude that might prove most dangerous. I feel that Mr O'Connor is again absolutely right when he goes on to suggest that her best future work is likely to be in the *novella* where he foresees for her a story-form 'more expansive, more allusive, more calligraphic.'

This view is certainly warranted when we think of some of her longer stories like **"The Happy Death," "Asigh," "The Little Prince"** and above all her superb novella **"The Becker Wives"** which Mr O'Connor must have had in mind when he coined these three epithets. There is so far little evidence that Miss Lavin has exhausted her chosen material and milieu. She does not seem to share either Mr O'Connor's or Mr O'Faolain's impatience at the limitations imposed by the little island on which they live. . . . Miss Lavin has been content to carry on her tireless investigations of the Irish lower middle-class existence. She may be running a certain critical hazard here in a world that is apt to confuse geographical with artistic range. But then she can console herself with the thought that her country's most universal artist, James Joyce, was in this sense its most parochial.

If one can judge, however, from her most recent *New Yorker* stories her latest trend seems to be in the direction of more specifically personal material. This would indeed be a new development in a writer who has hitherto rigorously excluded the autobiographical element from her work. It would also be a most promising direction for one who has tempered her skill on the most unpromising material that her surroundings had to offer and built from it a body of the most authentic literature. (pp. 402-06)

> *Augustine Martin, "A Skeleton Key to the Stories of Mary Lavin," in* Studies, *Vol. LII, No. 208, Winter, 1963, pp. 393-406.*

ROBERT CASWELL (essay date 1965)

[*In the following excerpt, Caswell discusses the structural patterns in Lavin's fiction and comments on her use of timeshifts, irony, and humor in conveying the flux of her characters' emotions.*]

Among Irish short-story writers of the present, none occupies a higher position than Mary Lavin. At her best, her sense of nuance in human emotion is as fine as that of Joyce. Her sense of place, although she herself has stated that her stories could have happened anywhere, equals or surpasses any living Irish writer. Her craftsmanship in this difficult genre is continually impressive, while her profound understanding of "the vagaries and contrarieties" in the human heart is unequalled in contemporary Irish fiction. Her vein of humour, which she infrequently exercises, is rich and varied; it ranges from the broadly comic in **"My Vocation"** and **"Second Hand"** to the humorously ironic in **"A Small Bequest"** and **"My Molly"**; from the somewhat grimly humorous in **"Bridal Sheets,"** to the vision of the human comedy so warmly depicted in **"The Living."** As may be seen in such stories as **"Sarah," "A Story** with a Pattern," "A Gentle Soul," "Asigh," and "The Great Wave," Miss Lavin is also capable of a strong narrative line. A more familiar aspect of her work is those stories in which nothing much seems to happen and what does happen seems of little importance. The severest example of such a story is the brief **"A Visit to the Cemetery."**

Two qualities which are almost immediately apparent in Miss Lavin's work are intensity of observation and precision in presenting what she sees. She has written: "Short-story writing—for me—is only looking closer than normal into the human heart. The vagaries and contrarieties there to be found have their own integral design." The presence of the integral design obviously suggests that a pattern is not so much imposed as discerned by the writer, who must be certain of what is really present in the human heart. Although intensity of observation is not limited to the writer alone, the art of imaginative expression is. It is the distinction of Miss Lavin's art that the two qualities coalesce in her stories.

Her fictional world is variously peopled with shop-keepers, farmers, tradesmen, labourers and fishermen. . . . It is the world of the post-1916 rebellion whose diminished reality poses a problem for the Irish writer. (pp. 69-70)

Miss Lavin's solution to whatever problems arise for a writer working within the diminished reality of present-day Ireland (diminished in comparison with the Ireland of legend and saga or the Ireland of the years of rebellion), has been to concentrate upon the "contrarieties and vagaries" of the heart. These qualities she takes seriously, and through her art as a short-story writer she gives them a significance which is often delicate and always penetrating.

The conflicts frequently involve the violation of some class convention of the shopkeepers, farmers and tradesmen. It is a measure of her intensity of observation that she has built such a large body of fiction upon conventions which the ordinary observer would scarcely notice. (p. 70)

Although she uses the various distinctions made between or within these groups as a source of conflict in many of her stories, Miss Lavin does not merely record rural Irish manners, nor does she often satirize them. Instead, she focuses her attention upon the suffering which is the result of conflict with them. (p. 71)

What is more important, however, than the actual existence of the lower middle-class conventions Miss Lavin makes use of in her fiction is that she has not used these conventions as ends in themselves. If she had chosen to record carefully the manners of the class she so frequently writes about, her work would be dull. If she had concentrated on satirizing the manners of this class, the codes and customs could not possibly have sustained the importance which satire demands of its material. Whether through conscious choice or instinct—and it should be remembered that she was once a student of Jane Austen—Miss Lavin has maintained a balance between conventions and character. She has been provided with a social structure, the elements of which are not entirely local, through which she can present her characters in a coherent and meaningful conflict. The actual existence of the social structure she uses gives her greater freedom in "looking closer than normal into the human heart."

The structural pattern of a Lavin story is generally quite simple. The story begins with a statement or a question which arouses the reader's interest:

When Bedelia opened the green baize door that led from the lobby into the shop, she had only one purpose: she wanted to know where she stood. (**"An Old Boot"**)

At half-past three in the afternoon, while Elgar was up in the storeroom over the shop, he heard Miss Mongon calling upstairs to Maime, and he knew that everything was over. (**"The Convert"**)

'The child of a ghost—who'd marry me,' cried Alice. She was fifteen then, but years before that she knew she'd never marry, years before her mother died, she knew it. (**"Loving Memory"**)

Immediately, we want to know where Bedelia stands concerning what; what it is that Elgar realizes is all over, and why Alice considers herself the "child of a ghost." While our interest is arrested by the opening statement or question, Miss Lavin quickly moves from the present to the immediate or distant past. About one-third to one-half of a story concerns the reason or reasons for the opening remark, and the rest of the story concerns the present; but it is a present which has become meaningful because of our knowledge of past events.

In her finest stories, however, the structural pattern is more complex. The past events do not simply supply the reader with background information for action in the present; they work in conjunction with experience in the present to force the character to reinterpret assumptions upon which his life has been based for years. An example of this pattern is **"The Convert."**

When Elgar, the convert of the story, hears Miss Mongon calling to his wife, Maime, what he realizes is that Naida Paston is dead. The significance of this for Elgar is only gradually revealed to us through the memories which the death of Naida set in motion. The first memory concerns the failure of Elgar to visit Naida after he and Maime returned from their wedding trip to Dublin. He then reverts to his first arrival in the town as a young student on holidays looking for a quiet place to study. Because he was a Protestant, he lived in the home of the Pastons, who were also Protestant. Soon after Elgar's arrival, Naida's Catholic friend Maime Sully decided to win him for herself. Maime's sexual aggressiveness overcame whatever feeling Elgar may have had for Naida. Naida's attempt to prevent his becoming a Catholic was deliberately misinterpreted by his future wife. It is four years from the night of Naida's warning to the present time in the story, and the four years are traversed in Elgar's memory.

The use of Elgar's memory in recalling past events is more than just a convenient device to give the reader background material for what is to happen in the rest of the story. His memories, which begin as simple recollection, become a part of the story's action when the past forces him to reassess his previous actions. (pp. 71-3)

Naida, as we know, is dead; she has fallen to clay. However, four years prior to her death Elgar chose the bovine and sensual Maime Sully instead of the delicate and spiritual Naida. He also relinquished his spiritual heritage. On either count he was "maimed" and "sullied," and it is Elgar's increasing awareness of this fact as he recollects the past which is the centre of the story. When he is finished with memory, he stands naked before his own isolation and the worthlessness and ineffectualness of his life.

The full effect of the change in Elgar emerges in the remainder of the story, which takes place in the present. Looking out of the storeroom window, Elgar sees his small daughter. (p. 74)

A moment later, thinking of the child that Maime is carrying, he asks himself whom it will resemble. The image that comes to him is that of a little girl in a photograph in the Paston's house: ". . . but now he knew that the look upon its face was the look that he yearned for, but never would see, upon the face of a child of his own. For the child in the picture was Naida." This realization forces him to run from the storeroom in search of company, but in the shop he finds Miss Mongon, Maime and Owdie Hicks, an old boy friend of his wife, discussing the unborn child. Their vulgarity over such an intimate matter revolts him, and in a fury he tells them that he will not have such talk in his house "to-day of all days." Miss Mongon tries to avoid the implications of this remark by asking about how Protestants are dressed for burial. Since they are Catholics, they do not know; it is Maime who turns to her husband and asks:

> 'Elgar, you ought to know,' she said impatiently.
> 'What will she wear?'
> But when he looked at her so oddly, she stamped her foot at him.
> 'Naida, I mean,' she said impatiently. 'You ought to know.'

These final words of the story complete Elgar's isolation and also reveal that he has always been considered something of an outsider in this Catholic community. The convert was never really converted. What is more important is that Naida Paston was not the primary victim of Elgar's actions four years earlier; he himself was.

In addition to the use of a functional structure in her work, Miss Lavin manifests great imaginative precision in the way she traces the overtones of an emotion or a thought. The overtones may be oblique and tenuous, as they are in the conversation between the two children in **"A Visit to the Cemetery,"** or they may be direct and substantial, as they are in **"A Story with a Pattern."** In either instance, a sensitive response to shades of meaning and emotion is demanded of the reader. However, Miss Lavin frequently uses clusters of images which the context of the story gives symbolic overtones and which lead almost explicitly to the meaning of the story. An early example of this functional imagery may be seen in **"At Sallygap."** (pp. 74-5)

[Yet, a] more complex and significant use of clusters of images than that seen in **"At Sallygap"** may be found in **"The Pastor of Six Mile Bush."** The narrative consists of a visit which three young students make to a desolate parish in the west of Ireland. The three students are: Alexis, a seminarian, Giles and Marks, who are medical students. The purpose of the visit is to prove to Alexis that the pastor of Six Mile Bush, like most priests, does not live up to his early vows: in this instance, the pastor is accused of gluttony. The three make their way by moonlight to the priest's house only to discover that the food he is supposed to consume so wantonly is secretly given to starving children. After this discovery, the three young men return to the town.

The names of the three students have some significance. Alexis means "helper" or "defender,' and he functions in both capacities in the story; Giles means "kid", which can be taken as colloquial for a young person, and underscores his overly-simplified ideas about priests; Marks, ultimately de-

rived from Marcus, which may suggest Mars, the god of war, is the aggressively critical member of the group. The names used for the three characters re-enforce their roles in the narrative, but they are certainly not necessary to define roles which are readily available to us from the context of the story.

The journey of the three students takes place at night, and the intermittent moonlight illuminates the path to Six Mile Bush. The barrenness of the landscape suggests that the journey is through a land of both physical and spiritual death. . . . The landscape of death also contains a "garish white object, the bleached bones of a sheep's head, eerily intact with gaping eye sockets and a yawning jaw bone still sown with yellow teeth." Beside the presbytery is a grave yard with "a few flat tombstones and one or two granite crosses." Over the entire scene presides the aged, sallow-faced and shrunken priest, who suggests to Alexis the image of a moulting crow. In their journey to Six Mile Bush, the young men have reached what seems to be a spiritual nadir, which is concretely realized in the landscape depicted.

However, a closer look at some of the objects in the landscape prepares us for the spiritual resurgence at the end of the story. The tombstones and the granite crosses in the grave yard recall the "great slab-like formations" of rock, the "tortured tree," and the "first feeble blades of grass," respectively. The tombstones affirm that we are in a land of the dead, but they also have implications of eventual resurrection for the dead. The granite crosses are linked linearly and symbolically with the "tortured tree (the cross)" and also with the blades of grass, which are signs of physical life. Furthermore, the second part of the grass simile . . . (". . . like the first feeble blades that penetrate the surface lands locked under great floods of water."), suggests that the slab-like formations are the source of some kind of life. Since it is obvious that the kind of life is not physical, we must look for some form of spiritual or religious life.

While the three students watch through the window, the old priest carves himself a small portion from a huge joint of mutton and then hacks the joint to pieces. Hearing a noise outside the window, he brings the platter of mutton, minus the small portion for himself, to the window and hands it out to the unrecognized but bewildered Marks. The priest then returns to his meagre supper. Marks places the platter on a tombstone, and in a few moments a number of "ragged and miserable" children gather to eat the food.

> Not more brightly had the moonlight broken over the bogland than did the significance of the scene before them shine into their minds.
>
> And all at once Alexis felt Marks take his hand and press it.

The appearance of the moon is not a pathetic fallacy. Until now it has suggested sterility and death as it has shown intermittently over the barren landscape. However, with the "significance of the scene" with the "ragged and miserable" children there is a corresponding change in the significance of the landscape. Out of its barrenness has come an image of selfless love which has profoundly affected the three young men; in a land of death, they have discovered spiritual life.

In the final paragraphs of the narrative, Miss Lavin extends the implications of her story much further than those suggested in the previous paragraph. She begins building her final image with Giles discovering a path back to the main road through a small wheatfield. "Through the pale wheat a dark path ran like a river." Both the wheat and the river are images of life and are consistent with the change in Marks and the reaffirmation of his vocation in Alexis. Marks and Giles enter the path, but Alexis pauses to look back at the lighted window through which he sees the priest, about whom there is some "strange unhuman quality of those who are not only extremely old, but who are already withdrawn in spirit and desire from normal dealings with their human kind." This acme of detachment is Alexis' vision, his moment of insight and understanding of his vocation as a priest, who is a servant of Love. Reflecting earlier on the conditions under which the old priest has to live, Alexis had thought:

> It isn't right, Alexis's heart cried out—it isn't right. No man ought to be sent to live out a lifetime in a place like this. And yet! Where might not he himself be sent when his turn came?

His experience at Six Mile Bush has answered his doubts for him.

Alexis' moment of realization is reflected in his gladness that the path through the wheat field demands that the three must walk single file, "and the necessity to talk would be postponed for some time. He did not want to talk." . . . The earlier appearance of grass, with its suggestions of physical life and of all flesh being grass, which emphasized the landscape of the dead, is replaced by the patch of wheat. The wheat also suggests physical life, but, because of its traditional associations with Christ in a religious context, it also fulfills the religious theme of the story. The path which the three young men follow through the wheat field is also compared to a river, and, together with the wheat, obviously indicates the spiritual rebirth which has taken place in them through the baptism of experience. What we have witnessed in the second half of the story is a profound deepening of character through an experience which began as a little diversion for three bored students on their summer holidays.

Spiritual rebirth, or the achievement of a wholeness of vision in the characters, is less evident in the bulk of Miss Lavin's stories than the desolation which stems from an almost unaccountable failure of nerve or will at moments of crisis. Where a rebirth combines with the desolation, we have a tragic sense of life; in such stories she is without equal among contemporary Irish writers. This sense of life is most compellingly presented in the stories of love, not only the passion of love in premarital relations, but also love in marriage and in the family. In all three areas Miss Lavin has an uncanny ability to catch the nuance which almost defies expression, the nuance which begins as the slightest vibration of which the character is only dimly aware. The vibration is set in motion with the first sentence of the story, sounding a note which makes us immediately aware of the peculiar Lavin quality in her work, and continues to the end of the story until seemingly every variation has been sounded. (pp. 82-6)

The critics who take note of Miss Lavin's work have often commented upon her use of the past. Frank O'Connor has stated that

> She has the novelist's preoccupation with logic, the logic of Time past and Time future, not so much the real short story teller's obsession with Time present—the height from which past and present are presumed to be equally visible.

The suggestion is then made that perhaps the *novella* is her proper medium. However, the use of the past in her stories is not simply a structural device, nor is it simply a manifestation of a preoccupation with the logic of time past and future. It is essential to the way she sees life, a part of her vision of things. No doubt her elaborate use of the past creates problems for the short-story writer; but Miss Lavin has solved these problems in her best short stories, and we may expect that she will continue to do so. (pp. 88-9)

> Robert Caswell, "The Human Heart's Vagaries," in The Kilkenny Magazine: An All-Ireland Literary Review, Nos. 12 & 13, Spring, 1965, pp. 69-89.

ROBERT W. CASWELL (essay date 1968)

[*Here Caswell defends the apolitical orientation of Lavin's works and praises her focus on personal relationships, calling* Tales from Bective Bridge *one of the best Irish short story collections.*]

If some of the most memorable works in modern Irish literature are [as Frank O'Connor stated] "closely linked to the immediate reality of politics," this linkage is obviously due to the intense and widespread involvement of the people in the deeply troubled political events in Ireland during this period. Consequently, the "reality of politics" is the most common experience shared by the people and the writer. However, although it sometimes appears to be otherwise, rebellious politics are not the whole story of modern Irish life and play an ever diminishing part in the country's daily affairs. Furthermore, it would seem that the writers of the revival whose work is to a greater or lesser extent involved with the politics and the nationalism of that period will be increasingly of less use to young writers dealing with more normal events. (pp. 48-9)

The reason or reasons that enabled Mary Lavin to come through the political events of the thirties and forties unscathed could only be known if Miss Lavin were to write an autobiography, which she is most unlikely to do. However, from conversations with her it is obvious that she was acutely aware of the events; moreover, her father was involved to some extent in a few of them. As a matter of fact, if she chose to do so she could probably write a dozen or so stories on the period of an explicitly political nature. The fact that she has not, and most likely will not, should not be made an implicit adverse criticism of her work. Nor should the fact that she has but the one story on Irish nationalism ["**Patriot Son**"] be taken as an indication of some serious limitation. After all, as her work clearly reveals, Irish life is not entirely a thing of politics and nationalism.

The importance of Miss Lavin's first volume of stories, **Tales from Bective Bridge** (1943)—the year of the censorship debate over Eric Cross's *The Tailor and Anstey*—is due primarily to the way in which she retains certain ideas of Irish life with which we are familiar from the work of Moore, Joyce, and others, while at the same time she transforms these ideas into conceptions of a more than Irish value. In fact the transformation is so successful that, as she herself has said, her stories could take place anywhere. By not adhering to the "reality of politics," and by not exploiting nationalism in its widest sense, she risks losing the force of a specific Irish identity. So far she has not done so. Moreover, her approach enables her, even at the beginning of her work, to keep from coming enmeshed in certain images of Irish life that by now have become clichés.

To illustrate. The conflict in **"Lilacs,"** the first story in *Tales from Bective Bridge,* arises from the desire of the daughters of Phelim and Rose Molloy, Kate and Stacy, to get rid of the dung in which their father trades. To Phelim as a young man, the dung is a source of income which will enable him to marry Rose. Later, it is a source of income for giving a fine education, including music lessons for Stacy, to his daughters. Moreover, to Phelim there is at times a natural beauty in the dung. When the young Rose protests that it is dirty stuff, he replies:

> 'I don't know so much about that,' said Phelim. 'There's a lot in the way you think about things. Do you know, Rose, sometimes when I'm driving along the road I look down at the dung that's into the road and I think to myself you couldn't ask much prettier than it, the way it flashes by under the horse's feet in pale gold rings.' Poor Phelim! There weren't many men would think of things like that.

However, Rose "didn't like the smell of manure, then, anymore than after, but she liked Phelim." The remark helps to explain the title: the ideal, in this case love, and the real, in this case the wherewithal to support the love, are inextricably bound together; both, if life is to be something rich, must be accepted. Neither Kate nor Stacy ever realize this fact. After the death of the parents, Kate decides to expand the dung business so that she can make enough money to escape from the house she detests with a large dowry. Kate recognizes the necessity of coming to terms with the reality of the manure, of the necessity of using it to get the lilacs of freedom from the house and of marriage. However, she has no intention of coming to terms with the perennial fact of what is, to her, disgusting in life. It is something that she recognizes must be faced, made practical use of, and then put aside. This attitude is clear in the scene in which Stacy calls Kate's attention to the smell of Con O'Toole's pipe. To Stacy the smell is worse than that of the dung. Kate, who has not noticed the smell at first, later says that

> 'It *is* disgusting. I'll make him give up using it as soon as we take up residence in Rowe House. But don't say anything to him. He mightn't take it well. Of course I can say anything I like to him. He'll take anything from me. But it's better to wait till after we're married and not come on him with everything all at once.'

The calculation, the slight harshness of tone, are sufficient to indicate the distance between Kate and Con, on the one hand, and Rose and Phelim on the other. The tone, clearly enough, reveals the author's attitude towards this manipulation of the real and the ideal. Kate's thinking, however, is probably the best modern way of dealing with what is nasty in life, but clearly her thinking does not possess the wholeness and beauty that is natural to Phelim, and that Rose could respond to and accept without deluding herself in the matter.

If life for Phelim and Rose is an indissoluble union of lilacs and dung, and if life for Kate is a task of making use of the dung to get the lilacs, however impaired they may be as a result of her attitude, for Stacy life must be all lilacs. She is less bothered by the social stigma of the dunghill than Kate is, but the odor from the manure, especially on the days when fresh manure is delivered, causes severe headaches. Because of

them she can seclude herself in her room delivery days where at least she does not have to see the dung. It is Kate who notices Stacy's propensity for withdrawal from facing the unpleasant. . . . . Earlier, during one of her headache spells, Stacy has the following fantasy:

> . . . she lay in bed and thought of a big lilac tree sprouting up through the boards of the floor, bending the big bright nails, sending splinters of wood flying till they hit off the window-panes. The tree always had big pointed bunches of lilac blossom all over it; more blossoms than leaves. But the blossoms weighed down towards her where she lay shivering, and they touched her face.

There is a strangely erotic note in this passage, and the immensity of the somewhat phallic lilac tree here might suggest barrenness of physical love in her life. She is never paired with any male in the story. But however suggestive the fantasy may be along these lines the main thrust of the story renders such an interpretation peripheral. More to the point is the destructiveness of the lilac tree and the unnaturalness of the blossoms outnumbering the leaves. It is the dream or ideal unhinged from the reality of the manure. This point is made final in the closing scene of the story. After Kate marries and moves out of the house, Stacy informs Jasper Kane, the family solicitor, that she is at last going to get rid of the dunghill. "But what will you live on, Miss Stacy?" he said, and the story ends.

The implications in the line are various although they do not focus the entire story. Practical Jasper Kane literally points out a detail that the sensitive and impractical Stacy has simply never thought of, and the moment he does so the humor is delightful. The reader's answer to the question is, almost involuntarily, that she will live on lilacs, figuratively, of course, her day dreams—or perhaps her unused violin and piano? Impossible, and no doubt Jasper, as well as the reader, knows this even if Stacy does not. Clearly the course of Phelim, in making a living from the manure, which enabled him to marry Rose, and the course of Kate, in doubling the intake and sale of manure to insure a large dowry so that she could marry Con O'Toole, is preferable to Stacy's alternative. The sane thing for her to do is to deal in enough manure to make a living. The story, however, is more than a criticism or gentle mocking of the dreamer who gets unmoored from reality; the word "live" in the final sentence can carry more meaning than simply to make a living. Implicit in the word, although neither Jasper Kane nor Stacy seem aware of it, is the necessity for Stacy, if she is to have a life as meaningful as that of Phelim and Rose, with whom she is temperamentally akin, to find for herself the relationship, the abiding and necessary union, between the lilacs and the dung. Only in this way will her life, unlike that of Kate and Con, be a thing of beauty.

Had Miss Lavin fashioned the dung heap as an image of Ireland, and had she fashioned the lilacs as an ideal that was incompatible with life on the Irish dung heap, the story would be a variation on a familiar theme; presumably it would also be considered a work that adhered to the "reality of politics." What we have instead is a story that adheres to reality, Irish or otherwise.

Essentially the same adherence to reality is apparent in **"At Sallygap,"** Miss Lavin's only full-scale rendering to date of the familiar pattern of paralysis, decay, and spiritual death in Irish life with exile as the only ready solution. The central character in the story is Manny Ryan. As a young man he had almost gone to Paris as a fiddler in a band, but because of his pity for Annie, the girl whom he was courting at the time and whom he later marries, he decides not to go. For the rest of his life, as a Dublin shopkeeper in King Street, he regrets not having pursued his dream and regrets having been betrayed by pity. At the time of the story, he is at the Sallygap in the Dublin mountains in search of a farmer who will supply his shop with fresh eggs. In the course of the day, Manny thinks of going to Paris to look up the boys, or of taking a vacation in Liverpool instead. Then he realizes that it is Dublin and Dublin life only that he wishes to escape, if only briefly. . . . The importance of Manny's discovery, which breaks the familiar pattern already noted, is specifically commented upon by the author:

> He had found at last his real escape from the sordidness of the life he led, and perhaps in time the seed of sensitiveness that had lain sterile in his heart through his bleak and unnatural spring and summer might have had a rare and wonderful winter flowering.

However, the long years of spiritual poverty have drained Manny of the strength to capitalize upon his discovery. By the end of the story, he is already forgetting his happy hills. "He would never seek sanctuary among them again." Salvation for Manny resides in his discovery of nature, and although he is unable to act on his discovery, he at least makes it. (pp. 50-4)

With the exception of "At Sallygap," which, like "The Patriot Son," is unique in Miss Lavin's work, it is clear why Frank O'Connor is correct in saying that "she has stood a little apart from the rest of us. . . ." The separation is even clearer if *Tales from Bective Bridge* is thought of in conjunction with Moore's *The Untilled Field,* Joyce's *Dubliners,* Corkery's *A Munster Twilight,* O'Faolain's *A Midsummer Night's Madness,* O'Connor's *Guests of the Nation,* and O'Flaherty's *Spring Sowing.* From Moore to O'Flaherty we move in a fictional world that is dominated, to a greater or lesser extent, by the politics and nationalism of which O'Connor speaks. These two things dominated the life of the country, so naturally they dominated the life of the imagination. It need only be added that much of our image of Ireland is dominated by the work of these writers, and that much of our fascination with them is due to the singularness of the experiences depicted, or perhaps what to non-Irish readers is somewhat exotic. When that exotic note is missing, we are disappointed; we are not getting what we have come to expect from Irish writers. However, this note is present in *Tales from Bective Bridge* and in later works, but it is the *basso ostinato* of a much larger orchestration.

Tales from Bective Bridge is one of the truly significant volumes of short stories by an Irish writer, as important in its way as those which O'Connor singles out in *The Lonely Voice:* Moore's *The Untilled Field,* Joyce's *Dubliners,* and O'Flaherty's *Spring Sowing*—as important, but of course not as influential. Free of their domination, the stories indicated quite unconsciously a way out of the political and national trap that increasingly threatens an impasse for the Irish writer. One of the values of her way out is evident in the fact that her purely creative productivity is greater than that of her contemporaries or her near contemporaries. (pp. 58-9)

The best explanation of her especial orientation comes from an interview. Asked if she felt herself "part of a tradition of Irish writers," she replied:

> I do not feel aware of being a particularly Irish writer. Since I lived in Ireland for most of my life, the raw material was Irish. But I suppose that if I had not moved from Massachusetts at the age of ten, I would have written about Massachusetts and the people of Massachusetts. It is the people among whom we live that provide our objective correlative. They are our idiom. Anything I wanted to achieve was in the traditions of world literature. I did not read the Irish writers until I had already dedicated myself to the short story. Then I would have been a fool not to have studied them, masters as they were of the medium. I studied English and French in college and outside the curriculum I read widely among the Russians and the Americans. O'Connor, O'Faolain, and O'Flaherty were only a part of literature as I thought of it. I had read Tchekov and Tourgeniev, Flaubert and Joyce and the shorter works of D. H. Lawrence, Tolstoy and Henry James. As for influences, perhaps I owed most to Edith Wharton, the pastoral works of George Sand, and especially Sarah Orne Jewett.

Like Joyce, who also stood a little apart from the rest of them, she aimed for achievements "in the traditions of world literature."

The point, then, is that no matter how valid O'Connor's remark on the relationship of politics and Anglo-Irish literature may be, and no matter how much, as a result of achievements of the revival writers who adhered to "the immediate reality of politics," we have come to expect this relationship, we should not allow this orientation to affect our just appreciation of Irish writing that, as in the case of Mary Lavin and others, is playing a different tune. (p. 60)

> *Robert W. Caswell, "Irish Political Reality and Mary Lavin's 'Tales from Bective Bridge,' " in Eire-Ireland, Vol. III, No. 1, Spring, 1968, pp. 48-60.*

JOHN HAZARD WILDMAN (essay date 1970)

[*Wildman is a short story writer, novelist, poet, and critic. In the following exerpt from his review of Lavin's* In the Middle of the Fields, and Other Stories, *Wildman discusses Lavin's ability to create unity among the characters in her stories.*]

Affinity is the key word that, without announcing itself as a word, suffuses the mind of at least one reader when he lives within the stories of Mary Lavin. Maybe, it is more of a quality than a word: it is not nailed to a page in a dictionary; rather, it emanates from people in relationship with nature, with houses, with (rarely) the ways of cities, with, above all, each other—with all of these, in fluent conjunction. It also includes its opposite, for, through her tender irony, Mrs. Lavin causes loneliness itself to be a quality that does not categorize, but, rather, runs through, human kind. Contrast may often provide her dramatic effect; but unity is her theme.

No story in *In the Middle of the Fields* could illustrate this point with more beautiful firmness than "The Cuckoo-Spit." As in all of her narratives, the subject is simple, almost banal. She is not an author who has to prop up mediocre writing and lack of insight with off-the-trail excursions. Nor does she over-decorate simplicity. Even investigation is not her main interest. It is a hovering empathy that is her chief effect. She darts from character to character—centering, for emphasis, on one, but being all of them.

Here, she has taken the simple situation of a woman, beautiful through insinuation, who, having lost a husband she has passionately loved, meets a man much younger than she is. There is a strong mutual attraction and, eventually, the sad, open awareness of the impassable distance between the two of them. *Eventually* is probably the wrong word. Both seem to have known the situation all along, especially the woman. The story consists of how they openly tell this fact to each other—but, of even greater importance, openly tell it to themselves.

It is the woman on whom the story centers, for hers is the harder task. It is as if she must read aloud a clearly written sentence, whereas he has at least the temporary comfort of having to decipher, nearly aware of the message, but nevertheless retaining a blurred hope. And, of course, within the moody honesty of his youth, there also lies a quality the temporariness of whose nature he cannot know: resilience.

> " . . . I sometimes think love has nothing to do with people at all." Her voice was tired. "It's like the weather!" Suddenly she turned to face him. "But isn't it strange that a love that was unrealized should have—"
>
> "Given such joy?" he said quietly.
>
> "Yes, yes," she said gratefully. Then she closed the door behind them. "And such pain."
>
> "Goodbye," she said.
>
> Goodbye.

The last unquoted *Goodbye* brings the story to final impact. How similar in tenderness, how different in specific reception, the relationship has been to both of them. But the difference lies in the wideness of human experience, not in its lonely aloofness, part torn from part. Vera had had the greater suffering, the deeper perception. But *that,* one feels, is a difference of degree, not of kind: it comes from her age, and it lies before him just as surely as it remains within her at the time. *Goodbye* unites them. (pp. 515-16)

Surely, though, the big test for an author of Mrs. Lavin's stature is the taking of some of the drab constituents of life and, basing her story on one character yet moving from individual to individual, finding new insights into known human traits, new understandings. This is found in her story **"One Summer."** There is no apology for human weakness or attacks upon it. Again, there is empathy. But there is also a new look at the bared ironies of the human state, no comment made, but a suggestion of understandings. acceptance, as of a kind helpfulness before the dying, a thoughtful pause in hopeless movement, a stillness which is an action in itself, an acknowledgment of union.

The situation is that of a woman, motherless, with a father who has turned from a childhood guide and friend into a domineering force. The woman falls in love. She has almost the courage to leave her father; but the demands of her lover are that she must leave him completely—go away geographically, this action treated as the symbol of a total break. The father becomes extremely ill, dying. But the transition is made so inevitably as to be almost an intensification of a psychological state. Indeed, Mrs. Lavin's plotting is so simple that it can almost be predicted: it is essence for which she is

looking, with which she identifies herself; and it is the typical in which she finds it.

The woman's post-office-bold attempts to free herself, her cozy venture into danger, is, as the reader expects it to be, pathetically ineffectual. Circumstance surrounds her: strand by strand, it builds its fine, unbreakable web. Irony is not forced upon us; it is found in the seemingly inevitable turning of the dying father to the strong nurse, whose size and health and half-professional, half-natural joyfulness lift up his spirits, bring spurious life to encroaching death. The father is peevish with the daughter; and the fact to be noticed is that one cannot find a villain; for the daughter's forced fidelity is naturally tedious to him; the fat, largely impervious nurse *is* life and potential fertility. It is she, the professional cheer-spreader, who ties to firm point the sprawlingness of the gloomy house. She and the maid have men to whom they are engaged: immediately the two women take to each other. They have a bond. And when the daughter (also called Vera) receives letters from the man whom she has hoped to marry, the nurse and the maid come close to her, spontaneously. They do not know that the news is of the man's engagement to another woman.

Even the old woman who comes in as night nurse—somebody lost from Dickens but found and more than four-fifths transformed by Mrs. Lavin—joins in this pathetic human comedy. Somehow, one understands the grotesquerie of aged obtuseness as seen in the woman's breaking of the jug of water and then complaining, "Lily! You gave me a leaking jug." This is not Dickens, nor is it the result of bitter observation. Rather, it is a situation which is *there*. That is the point. It is small, but it is real; it is viewed in passing but with real understanding. The reader comes to see that he is on the side of both the old woman and of Lily, who giggles. In other words, this small incident stands as a microcosm of the art of completeness.

The country and nature and its characteristic parts play a large role in these stories; but they do not obtrude, take over, become a character or a rhetorical flourish on a banner or (much worse) all of these, as they tyrannically do in the case of some Southern writers of the United States. They are established in a phrase, in a delicately suggestive human relationship, as in **"The Lucky Pair"** in the description of a man seen beyond many dancers: "He was not sucked under even when in the final flourishes of a number the ends of dresses lashed together into a wild and briary foam." Very, very rarely is there overwriting, as in the description of diminishing sunlight on windows and their sills in the same story: "Evenly but diminishngly, they gave back the light, as a hand passing over the keys of a piano will give back notes divinely graded." The *divinely* hurts.

But this is to be picayune about a volume of stories whose delicacy of perception is matched only by firm control of situation and theme. Here is contemporary and honest storytelling, honorably unanxious about demand and successfully committed to greatness. (pp. 517-19)

John Hazard Wildman, "Affinity—and Related Issues," in The Southern Review, *Louisiana State University, n.s. Vol. VI, No. 2, April, 1970, pp. 515-19.*

V. S. PRITCHETT (essay date 1971)

[*Pritchett is a highly esteemed English novelist, short story writ-*

er, and critic. In his criticism, Pritchett writes in the conversational tone of the familiar essay, approaching literature from the viewpoint of an intelligent but not overly sensitive reader. He also stresses the value of his own experiences in interpreting literature rather than adhering strictly to a codified critical doctrine derived from a school of psychological or philosophical speculation. In the following excerpt from his introduction to Lavin's Collected Stories, *Pritchett comments on the colloquial color of Lavin's fiction and praises her insightful examinations of the psychological motivations of her characters.*]

[Mary Lavin] is writing most of the time about people who appear to be living, at first, in a state of inertia, in the lethargy of country life: then we notice that they are smoldering and what her stories contain is the smoldering of a hidden life. Her short stories are as dense as novels and we shall gradually apprehend the essence of complete life histories—as we do, for example in the first novel-like act of a play by Ibsen—and they make the novel form irrelevant. They give a real and not a fancied view of Irish domestic life and it combines the moving with the frightening. She excels in the full portraiture of power-loving women, downtrodden women, lonely women, bickering country girls, puzzled priests and seedy shopkeepers who might pass as country types first of all, but who soon reveal a human depth of endurance or emotional tumult in their secret lives. (p. x)

Many of these stories [in Lavin's **Collected Stories**] describe country deaths and widowhood, the jealousies of young girls, the disappointments of courtship, the terrible aspects of lonely lives, the sly consolation of elderly love; the picture of Ireland is a somber one, relieved only by the mean comedy of country calculations and watchfulness. Why is it that these stories are not merely depressing? Simply because Miss Lavin is a great artist; we are excited by her sympathy, her acute knowledge of the heart, her truthfulness and, above all, by the controlled revelation of untidy, powerful emotion. She has a full temperament. The tales are mutinies of an observant mind, a record of unrepentant tumult where one did not know it could exist. The truck driver who bores everyone at home because he won't stop opinionating, only does so because his life is lonely and, in fact, his capacity for finding someone anywhere to talk to lands him in a dreadful situation in which his talk is a blessing; and all the time, unknowingly, he is showing us an Ireland we would never have guessed. Miss Lavin goes into the deepest human instincts and is likely to find the epical and cleansing in what could easily be left as trivially sad. Her opening story, **"The Green Grave and the Black Grave,"** reads like a tale from the Gaelic; but it seems to me far more moving and richer in meaning than, say, Synge's *Riders to the Sea* and to have a subtler tragic force. The distinction it makes between the customs of love faced by death—for grief is a fundamental theme with her—is superbly managed. I cannot think of any Irish writer who has gone so profoundly without fear into the Irish heart. This fearlessness makes her remarkable.

Where else have we read stories of this kind? Not in English or American literature. The obvious suggestion is in the Russian of, say, Leskov, Aksakov or Shchedrin; not of Turgenev or Tolstoy. She has the same animal eye for everyday life, the same gift for immersing herself in people and not sacrificing the formlessness of their lives to the cleverness of a formal art. She feels too much to be adroit, anecdotal or "outside." Another aspect, I think, relates her to the Russians of the nineteenth century: women dominate her stories and they are likely to be women who are lonely; for just as in Russia the

women became lonely and powerful because the manhood of their men was destroyed by political tyranny, so, in Ireland, the departure of the men and the curious domestic belligerence, and even separation, of the sexes has put a special burden on women. Not that she is writing propaganda on their behalf. Far from it. Her stories are not the quick glances we get in other writers; they are long gazes into the hearts of her people. (pp. xii-xiii)

V. S. Pritchett, in an introduction to Collected Stories *by Mary Lavin, Houghton Mifflin Company, 1971, pp. ix-xiii.*

THOMAS J. MURRAY (essay date 1972)

[*In the following excerpt, Murray comments on the anecdotal nature of Lavin's writings in her* Collected Stories *and notes her use of an objective narrative voice to convey emotional conflicts among her characters.*]

Lavin's fiction cannot be placed alongside the best from other cultures, but it can be seen, at full maturity in a few stories, as a quietly respectable contribution to the mainstream narrative fiction of the Irish story. That fictional technique is not at all like the tendency in the great novels of Joyce, Beckett or O'Brien to lyricize itself through poetry into some grand design which creates out of its minutest parts cosmological and metaphysical schemes of reality. The great Irish novel of this century has always done well by lyrical narrative. The short story of narrative fiction has controlled its poetry by playing off certain felt tensions between feeling and form. And Miss Lavin's fiction shows more respect for the anecdotal rather than the poetic.

So little of the fiction in Lavin's present collection overtly reflects what Dennis Donoghue only this spring in the *Times Literary Supplement* issue on "Irish Writing Today" called "the story of fracture: the death of one language, so far as it is dead or dying or maintained as an antiquity, and the victory of another; the broken relation of one religion to another . . . the divergence of one Irishman from another." Two exceptions to this description are the stories titled **"The Green Grave and the Black Grave"** and **"The Great Wave,"** in both of which a remarkable ritualistic texture and sensitivity to poetic dialogue make strong symbols out of the sea and its simple followers. The men and women of these stories are like Synge's tragic folk; their knowledge of suffering and love is unequal to ordinary conversation, but it erupts in a strange incantatory power that makes the characters embodiments of some mythological force. " 'The sea is stronger than talk of love,' said Tadg Og, going out after him into the dark." Almost none of the other characters in other stories realize the truth of Tadg's remark, for their speech reveals not a knowledge either of love or death or the tragic but mere opinions of unfanciful social realities. The Bishop of **"The Great Wave"** recalls, on his confirmation visit to an off-shore island where he was born and raised, how he learned the darker realities of life that matter. Awakening from a harrowing storm that claimed the lives of all the island's menfolk who were after the mackerel run, he remembers turning to Seoineen, the only survivor and the island's only native to be ordained priest, and crying, "But it saved you your life."

"For what?" he asked. "For what?" And there was, in his voice, such despair that Jimeen knew it wasn't a question but an answer; so he said no more for a few minutes. Then he raised his voice again, timidly. "You saved my life too, Seoineen." Seoineen turned dully and looked at him.

"For what?"

But as he uttered them, those same words took on a change, and a change came over his face, too, and when he repeated them for the third time, the change was violent.

"For what?" he demanded. "For what?"

The youthful Jimeen of this story cannot hide in the folds of his episcopal regalia the desperate knowledge of a wrecked life that, in one question, helped him sort out the trivial from the real questions of life. "Who knows anything at all about how we're shaped, or where we're led, or how in the end we are ever brought to our rightful heaven?"

The Bishop's probity earned in suffering knowledge sets the standard against which Lavin measures the complacency and apparent indifference of many of her other middle class men and women. There is a sullen resignation or an ungenerous brooding in the air they breathe or the earth they fitfully walk, but in few of these mature stories is it the earth of people who have sunk roots in an ancestral past like the barbarous "good country people" the American reader sees in the short stories of Flannery O'Connor or Joyce Carol Oates. They are less curious, less interesting, and less concerned with the rites and myths of innocence and righteousness than are the gothic peacock strutters of O'Connor's red clay Georgia farms. Lavin's scenery is the territory staked out by shopkeepers, ordinary workers, serving girls, clerks and widows of some means but of uncommonly ugly tongues and silly pretentions. They almost unnerve a reader into worrying them into real fictional existence as he keeps asking, in story after story, what really aches their hearts. Many of them are Catholic, but that does not seem to matter as faith is not in crisis in the fictions. Many of them show no ambition for power or money or goods; many of them show no questioning of conscience or identity. They are very small neighborhood people of insular concerns, but curiously when they shut their doors after an evening walk, or a day's work, or Sunday Mass, or a minor business meeting, they remain the small crabbed people one associates with small dingy shops: cheapness and meanness. The Dublin jackeens, as the bewildered, mousy shopkeeper Manny calls his neighbors in the story **"At Sallygap,"** characterizes the lot—people who "couldn't tell you the difference between a bush and a tree" but who could "talk you out of your mind." . . . Although aware of the others' squalor, Manny's problem is precisely the same as theirs: a sterility that has killed long-repressed sensitiveness. In almost all of the relationships of these tradesmen types, a telling poison clots their blood and chokes their speech, turning an incipiently passionate hate into ineffectual passive resistance. Miss Lavin's finely ironic characterization makes both the Dublin and non-Dublin Mannies too tolerant of their own ordinariness. Likeable to themselves, to each other, and to the reader they are not unless the reader easily tolerates fools who accept their own moral sterility in the same way the fools accept dirty tea cups with caked, half-dissolved sugar and sloshy tea leaves.

It is these half-way people, belonging in neither city nor country but affecting the mean or boorish airs of both ways of living, who obviously fascinate Miss Lavin. She makes them work on a reader's rejection of them until he grudgingly accepts them in their own ordinariness as he might accept some

annoying and unnameable irritation. One cause of that irritation conditioning an attitude toward the characters is the woman's role as devourer of masculine fantasies. Lavin's women are not made into symbolic presences whose egos feed on monstrous greed or possessive jealousy; there is rarely the touch of the super-ego playing out its destructive forces in their lives. They are, however, more like the small, tidy, neat and efficient women or young girls who at best can only reluctantly let go of the man's heart strings when some improbable demand of his ego intervenes between their wills and his desires.

The theme of the killing of the male's fantasies is chillingly done in the story **"At Sallygap"** in which Annie, wife of the timid shopkeeper Manny, has so soured the husband that even a few hours outing outside Dublin, away for the first time in years from her and their fetid shop, makes him irritably nervous as he realizes the price he will have to pay for his stolen joy of watching the simple country people. His escape blends into fantasies of forgotten recklessness of childhood, and he is momentarily happy and free as he roams the country roads until he nervously remembers that Annie awaits him at the shop door, trembling in rage at this extravagant flightiness. Manny Ryan's aloneness in the country is not solitary or pleasant, for the clouds of confusion roll over him. And in that confusion he is made perfectly aware of Annie's fear; his unexpected bolt for the something different in life would be as nothing to her in comparison to the facing of existence alone she was made to experience in the few hours of his absence. "And tomorrow, if he were to try and persuade Annie to take a walk out in the country, she'd look at him as if he were daft." And his promise, uttered to no one but the air and the trees and the sky, that he would come back again, evaporates into the dark void of many other unfulfilled wishes Manny has never been able to realize.

If it were not his fear of Annie's scorn, why else would Lavin reduce the husband to an image of "a little boy who has lost the change, a little boy creeping in under fear of the whip"? In the instant of this recognition of his own helplessness, Manny's fleeting happiness dissolves into a "desolating joy." Although not a merciful or useful knowledge with which he can reorganize the marriage, Manny now knows clearly what before he had darkly understood. Annie's hate is the source of all that holds them hopelessly together. But the death of Manny's fantasies of escape into a healthier life is not the only death Miss Lavin masterfully dramatizes in this story. The shuttered and darkened shop which awaits Manny on his return to Dublin is a symbol of the closed heart Annie has nurtured ever since the day of her first victory over him when she persuaded him not to run off to Paris with his flighty musician friends in search of silly adventures. That dock-side scene of the few weeks before their marriage was played out in all the bed-side scenes of later years. As he steps into the darkened shop and dimly senses her presence in the room, Manny's mind darts to the past and summons up the ghost of the wife in his melancholy reminiscence. . . . Although Manny's complacency makes him a sexual impotent husband, it is finally his kindness and softness, too frail to contain the animal lustiness he had once hoped to find in marriage, which she insists on battling as weakness.

The Annie Ryans of Lavin country are legion. Their husbands' small and delicate strengths are never judged or used psychologically on their own terms for what they are. Their vicarious pleasures in other women's sexuality are joyless and illusory. How often the neighborhood women gossiping in Annie's shop tried to tell her how cruel their husbands' animality was. The ashes of indifference and resignation soon consume the woman's fantasies and the man's happiness. As the devourer of male frailty, the young woman of the story **"Sunday Brings Sunday"** plays her role as a vehicle of Lavin's parody interpretation of the church and family influences on an ignorant girl's fumbling sexual encounters. The dutiful and sweet girl Mona and the on-the-make Jimmy blindly stumble into sex once Mona, having left school and her family's protective custody, is apprenticed to a doctor. This story stunningly evokes the working-class girl's suppressed fears of sensuality and personal freedom. Mona's undoing, it seems, is her regimented conscience which the Church's fearful teachings about sin and guilt have turned into an overly refined instrument of shame and confusion. Her natural fantasies of power and love, so long dreamed of as coming alive at the moment when she can step outside the home and work independently as a serving girl for some local worthy whose respectability the awaiting boys would have to be impressed by, become a veritable nightmare. The weekly, priestly admonishment of "It is by prayer that we obtain the grace to avoid sin" sickens her delicate memory of hesitant sex with Jimmy until all of her girlhood memories of purity, obedience and simplicity churn into a stomach-heaving consciousness of shame. (pp. 123-28)

Sunday after Sunday, after the initial sexual experience with Jimmy whose apologetic shyness and dull-witted nature become a threat to the little joy she had expected from him, become wearisome rituals to conscience-stricken Mona. She finally sees her life as a projection of meaninglessness, the same nonsense uttered each Sunday by the old crone who repeats to the passers-by "Sunday brings Sunday." Mona could forgive Jimmy everything and herself even more, but the shame and ignorant confusion are too strong to dispell. . . . The humorlessness and heavy-heartedness of these adolescents, who are in truth more child-like than they would ever admit to, destroys the natural fantasies of power and release which they ought to feel rather than fear in innocent, companionable sex.

In another particularly well-made story of family estrangement Lavin comes as close to the heart of the problem as she does in any other story of isolating the effects of a woman's destruction of a male's vitality. Like so many of the husbands or single men who have lost or repressed the ability to turn the interesting experiences of daily life into a form of story telling, the carter in **"The Cemetery in the Demesne"** was, before the wife's tongue got hold of talkativeness, an ebullient story teller. Although no one ever listened very much, he had a great zest for his own idle and harmless chatter consisting mainly of anecdotes he picked up from people and incidents encountered along his delivery routes. Returning home one evening from a hauling job during the course of which he met up with a young mother whose fatally sick child is suspiciously simple-minded, the carter struggles to recall a similar incident from his past in which a sick child was cured by a priest's reading a gospel over him. In that dimly remembered incident the mother's luck turned black later on, and the carter is disturbed that he passed this folklore on to the mother. Of course, neither his wife nor nasty sister-in-law will indulge his fantasy about this bit of folklore the carter insists he heard from them. They use the incident as a joke against him. And his dreams of death, inspired by the encounter with the sick child, go no further than his unconscious. Although the wife

detects a strange despondency in the normally talkative husband, he is forced to cut her off from the rich stories and puzzling dreams of his imagination by retorting: "Don't ask foolish questions. . . . Women are always asking foolish questions. I never knew a woman yet that was happy with her mouth shut! It's talk, talk, talk, all the time. Why don't you shut up once in a while!" In settling for the banality of playing checkers each evening with the sister, the carter's wife is denied any glimpse into the strange and storied dreams of death and salvation struck by the chance music of the husband's loquacious chatter with a fretful mother and sick child.

The basis of this story's credibility seems to be contrived around the figure of the husband's sister-in-law until the reader sees that the wife herself is mainly guilty of damning up the springs of emotion begging for release on the husband's tongue. The reader sadly knows she will never bother to find out the cause of the husband's rejection of her because she is incapable of appreciating his desire to spin out tales which have little or no connection to her most immediate concerns. She, like many of the other women in different stories, seems not to realize that her immediate concerns provide no visible gratification to the other spouse, especially when those visible concerns are centered on the wife's perfunctory execution of a housewife's routines. One of the husbands, at least, is granted the clarity of perception which judges the failed and failing women of most of the stories for their true worth. Tom in **"A Tragedy"** stops short both his wife and guest-in-residence sister-in-law's aimless mouthing off about the tragedy of an air crash with the vehemently curt remark: "It is always the same in this country. . . . It's impossible to keep a conversation on the right level. There is no such thing as general conversation. Someone always butts in and drags it down to the particulars." Tom's sister-in-law, of course, knows a friend who knew someone who was almost killed in this almost tragedy in an almost unbelievable occurrence. Tom is sick of the loose language and the affectations of tragedy. Near-tragedy to Tom is closer to melodrama than to real suffering. And when his wife in bed begs him to listen to the sister-in-law's threat of suicide inspired by hearsay reports of the air crash, Tom retorts: "Well, I'll tell you what to do: ask her to tell it to the dead on Snowden, and see what they'll say to her." The wife instinctively recognizes the rightness of his words: " . . . not one of them, she knew, but would fling back, if he could, that mantle of snow and come back to it all: the misunderstandings, the worry, the tension, the cross purposes." Unlike the sister-in-law of this story Tom has always been able to discriminate finely between an experience and its contrastingly pale expression. He has taught his wife the cheapening effect of words. Moreover, despite the blood ties and common childhood experiences binding the two women of his household, he has given her a stringent lesson in not abiding fools gladly.

It is clear from these representative seminal stories that the anarchy which Frank O'Connor described as the energizing factor in any country's first-rate fiction is the anarchy of the heart. Not that the anarchy has any strong relationship in Miss Lavin's imagination with the intransigent vices of human nature, but the disturbed hearts of these people do suffer from a shattered composure. Their reluctances, fears, sourings, and spitefulness cause them to question joy, to withhold love, or to feel shame where none should exist. Their anarchy is much like the Irishman's regard for the weather; it sometimes, as the lovely but timid widow Vera states about love in **"The Cuckoo-Spit,"** "has nothing to do with people at all." Stormy or clear, it might just turn around and blow away the next moment if you don't pay it much worry.

Although the inhuman quality is gnawing at the heart of the characters, Miss Lavin's treatment of the malady is deceptive because her prose style is very straight and not in the least convoluted or involuted with verbal lyricisms which, if used, might reduce the tension of the narrative or inflate the banality of the dialogue into symbolically pregnant speech. Her admirable control of point of view works well to maintain an almost extremely cruel distance from the characters to the extent that at times it is impossible to say where her true sympathies are as judged from the distanced and neutral point of view. One value of this apparent objectivity is the absence from her fiction of stuck-on social issues as background scenery or of clichéd ideas of 'Irishness' as ingredients of characterization. Another is the humility she holds toward the characters as evidenced time and again throughout all the stories in the marvellously hearable and repeatable dialogue, strong enough to suggest that the story writer must also be a dramatist willing to forego the pleasurable sensation of hearing a detectable point of view through the speech of his characters. These assorted strengths are, perhaps, withheld only from the characterization of children who, unfortunately, are in many stories urged onto "the shores of adult knowledge—those bright shores of silt" with a precociousness their frail awareness of things does not warrant.

What matters, finally, is the readability of the fictional surfaces; there are few surprises in the narrative or imagistic detail to shock the reader with artistic self-consciousness as the scenes, situations, and possible larger metaphoric senses of design are controlled by a firm core of anecdote. In spite of the reader's uneasy dread which stems from his awareness of the short-circuited feelings of a husband and wife or a mother and her children, Miss Lavin's usual technique is a tell-tale sign of a shift in the rhythms of the characters' speech without making it a criss-cross of reflexive references stretching into poetry but keeping it on the safer side of spoken speech. The heavier technique would not do at all for people for whom "the habits of years were not to be broken so easily." Their questions are always: What could they say to each other? What would they say to each other? What should they say to each other? Questions? Perhaps not. Statements more likely because informed by a knowledge "that two people never are one, and that they were, as they always were, and always would be, two separate beings, ever at variance in their innermost core, ever liable to react upon each other with unpredictable results." (pp. 128-31)

Thomas J. Murray, "Mary Lavin's World: Lovers and Strangers," in Eire-Ireland, *Vol. VII, No. 2, 1972, pp. 122-31.*

JANET EGLESON DUNLEAVY (essay date 1977)

[*Dunleavy is an American scholar of Irish literature and the author of several children's books. In the following excerpt, he discusses Lavin's emphasis on physical detail in her stories, noting the relationship between her characters and their surroundings.*]

The surface of Mary Lavin's fiction faithfully records details of an exterior reality through which men, women, and children who resemble people she has known move from yesterday to today to tomorrow. Hidden in their words, gestures, and observations, however, is that which extends beyond the

limits of time, place, and individual character. What seems so solid and permanent in her stories is revealed, in afterthought, as fluid and temporal—the moment immobilized by the reader's willing suspension of disbelief in response to the artist's power to recreate milieu. What seems so fleeting and illusory is revealed as timeless—a fragment recognized, in afterthought, as essential human nature: The resulting interplay of universal sensibility and particular experience is what makes her work disarmingly simple on first reading, disturbingly complex on recollection, elusive, tantalizing, and seductive.

Each of Mary Lavin's stories appears linear in structure, supporting the first impression of simplicity. Between beginning and end, however, stretch particles of life, held by forces that both repel and attract, vibrating with unseen energy like the famous line that Marcel Duchamps perceived and tried to paint. Applied to the fiction of Mary Lavin, such metaphor and analogy are appropriate, because they introduce ideas that affect her work: as an artist conscious of and curious about the creative process, she is intrigued by all concepts and perceptions that challenge the human mind. Techniques and theories of other forms of art are, to her, applicable to literary art: she herself tries consciously to see with the eyes of a painter or sculptor, to hear with the ears of a composer or musician. But she is intensely interested also in those developments in the social and natural sciences that affect human understanding of the world in which she, we, and her characters live. The observations and speculations about the nature of the human species that these offer are refracted for her by the prism of human personality in response to questions that, attempting to understand these observations and speculations, she asks herself. . . . (pp. 222-23)

Such probing of personality, sometimes painful and relentless in its intensity, invites comparison with the work of Virginia Woolf. At the same time, the author's awareness of the self-protective limitations to human understanding seems similar to that of Henry James. And her evolution of a range of personality types, particularized in different roles and different situations, with different identities and different social and intellectual backgrounds, is not unlike Gertrude Stein's attempts to present "bottom nature". But this focus on character is never separate from consideration of milieu. Accidents of birth and environment are presented by Mary Lavin as forces that play on universal sensibility. Thus she exhibits also, for those seeking her literary antecedents, if not the English, something of the French naturalists.

Mary Lavin's characters are, on the one hand, farmers and fishermen in Irish villages; shopkeepers, blue-collar workers, clerks, domestics, and lodginghouse keepers in Irish towns and cities; and insulated, isolated, modestly comfortable to modestly affuent Irish, Italian, and American members of the middle class. Some are presented as materially or spiritually impoverished; some are emotionally impoverished as well. Often her children are vulnerable: most have not yet learned to distinguish between what adults do and mean to teach and what they say they do and pretend to teach. Her women are distinguished from those of other authors by her special sensitivity to conditions unique to the lives of women. But on the other hand, in the fiction of Mary Lavin, farmers, fishermen, shopkeepers, blue-collar workers, clerks, domestics, lodginghouse keepers, children, widows, and professional men and women all balance within them capacities for love, hate, greed, jealousy, fear, emotional blindness, and courage that establish among them affinities and analogies unrelated to—existing beyond—the social, economic, and cultural spheres by which they otherwise might be defined. This skillful building of the universal and the particular in her work is enhanced by her refusal to choose between the stasis of human nature and the kinesis of human environment as the single or consistently dominant force responsible for shaping human events. Like W. B. Yeats, Mary Lavin acknowledges that a stone may "trouble the living stream", but she knows also that "too long a sacrifice can make a stone of the heart". It is the relationship that she thus establishes between human events and time that is responsible for the double vision—the "extraordinary sense that what we call real life is a veil"—in such stories as **"The Sand Castle"**.

Although surely he is old enough to know that tides move in and sand castles fall, John, the eldest of the three children of **"The Sand Castle"**, throws himself seriously and wholeheartedly into creating a fated edifice. Emily, who just as surely shares his knowledge, works by his side with feverish energy and complete devotion to the task at hand. Alexander, too young to consider any moment beyond the now, asks only to be part of the human endeavour: he knows nothing of tides, and temporal existence; to be excluded is his only fear. He is given safe tasks that neither will interfere with John's conception of the finished castle nor will cause an interruption in the work in the form of intercession by Nurse.

Finished, the castle seems to all, even the two who persist in avoiding awareness of the approaching tide, a marvel beyond compare. "Gosh," exclaims Alexander, over and over, perhaps with more awe than the others because it is truly a creation beyond anything he alone could produce, yet he has had a part in it. Then he becomes the first to recognise impending disaster: "gosh, gosh," he hears the ocean repeat as it creeps closer and closer to the castle.

At first, like Cuchulain the children try to fight the invulnerable tide: subtly, the myth combines with their eternal childhood game to suggest a meaning out of place and time. Then, realising the futility of their efforts, Emily decides that if they cannot protect their castle, at least they can prevent its falling to the ocean by destroying it themselves. All jump and jump and jump, crumbling walls and battlements, forgetting the castle in their new game of seeing who can jump highest, jumping finally just for the joy of jumping. But, writes Mary Lavin, "as they rose up and down, in their hearts also there rose and broke, and rose again, and broke, the silent wave of a wild intuition that was carrying them forward, nearer and nearer to the shores of adult knowledge—those bright shores of silt." With those few words, the focus shifts, only slightly—but it is enough to carry the reader also to those same shores of adult knowledge, to the recognition that they are "bright shores of silt".

The outer world of **"The Sand Castle"** is a middle-class seaside resort to which children like John, Emily, and Alexander are brought by nursemaids; it presents, on the surface, middle-class life, comfortable but not ostentatious. Other Mary Lavin stories, nearly equal in number to those that depict the middle class, concern men and women for whom material comforts are few and simple, who must work hard and be thrifty to have any material comforts at all. A third and smaller group of stories concerns timeless people in a time outworn: fishermen and their families, farmers and their families, for whom life is not very different from that of their ancestors, despite the occasional introduction of a few of the advantages of a technological society. The invulnerable tide, always an undercurrent if not always perceived in the surface sequence of events, advances alike on tenement house and town house, cottage and estate. Meanwhile, other Johns and Emilys and Alexanders, grown to adulthood, plan, build, quarrel over, and destroy adult versions of sand castles, wage their own brand of warfare against the invulnerable tide, or seek transient joy, perhaps not in jumping, but in those other universal games that are played by men and women "on the shores of adult knowledge". (pp. 223-25)

The techniques used by Mary Lavin in [her story] **"At Sallygap"** seem, on the one hand, to be those of the naturalist. Accurate depiction of milieu is much more important than it was in **"The Sand Castle"**; indeed, the strength of the story depends in large part on the author's ability to present Manny Ryan and his wife as apparently overwhelmed by the twin forces of heredity and environment and to construct a detailed picture of working-class Dublin that surely would have satisfied Zola's concept of notebook observation of reality. On the other hand, the author uses narrative viewpoint in the manner of the symbolists: the factual data used to construct the outer worlds of Manny and Annie—ostensibly a single world that they both share—are selected from the myriad details available in plausible external reality to produce a double image consistent with the different psychological or inner words of each. It is a very different technique from that which, for example, Tennessee Williams used in *A Glass Menagerie* or Franz Kafka used in *The Trial:* the outer world is in no sense distorted by Annie's or Manny's perceptions. It is, on the contrary, historically accurate, although restricted to that which they, each creatures of universally shared emotions trapped in a particular world, each perceive; details are focused as either Manny or Annie, whose universally shared emotions respond to particular experience, would focus them. Manny Ryan's broken violin, for example, never becomes larger than life in Manny's memory, as does Luara's glass unicorn or her typewriter or the picture of his father for Tom Wingfield, nor does Manny consciously attach to it the symbolic significance it inevitably acquires for the reader: watching the mail boat sail for Holyhead, he simply remembers the early experience, as it occurred, and regrets, freeing a plausible train of memories and moods. . . . (p. 228)

In **"A Memory"**, a novella by Mary Lavin, city and country again provide contrasting setting, [as in **"At Sallygap"**], but the characters are intellectuals, not shopkeepers. Unmarried, James, a research professor, and Myra, a translator and editor, live half-lives on the fringes of society. Professionally successful, they are emotionally impoverished; each is in a sense self-exiled because each ignores the signposts and denies the goals that are regarded as "natural" and "right" in the social, intellectual, and economic circles to which they belong.

Alone in his Meath cottage, in the dark suit and white collar more appropriate to the city which he wears even in the country, tended only by Mrs Nully, who comes in for a few hours each day to give him a hot meal, James lives a celibate, cleric-like existence in which Myra seems to serve as a twentieth-century *virgo subintroducta*. For the most part, his academic work fills his days: he has no commitment to teaching. But on those rare occasions when he has to be at the University or, more frequently, when for some reason his work goes against him, he spends his evenings in Myra's mews house behind one of Dublin's Georgian squares.

Myra, who has "concocted a sort of cocoon of thought and

wrapped herself up in it", seems a perfect companion for James. In her free-lance work she regularly sets herself a goal of two thousand words a day which she meets without fail, persevering doggedly when she encounters difficulty, leaving a "residue of enthusiasm" for the next day when, "her mind . . . leaping forward like a flat stone skimming the surface of a lake", she reaches her daily quota with ease. Adept at cooking, sewing, and other housewifely accomplishments when young, she readily admits to having long since lost all domestic skills, "as if part of her had become palsied" by her single-minded commitment to the intellectual life.

For James, Myra's domestic failure makes her all the more attractive: "when they first met, it was her lack of domesticity that had been the essence of her appeal to him." When he thinks of her house, it is as a place with a "marvelously masculine air", although, to James, "Myra herself remained very feminine." He laughs with her when she tells of an incident in the National Library when, trying to repair a rip in her skirt, she accidently sewed back to front, turning it into trousers. He regards her lack of enthusiasm for cooking as a triumph of her intellect. At first, in their evenings together, they used to eat at a small cafe near her mews house. But they soon retreated to the privacy of Myra's sitting room where their minds (never their bodies) could achieve the union they desired. There they formed the habit of ordering two trays from the cafe—a solution to the problem of eating which eliminated not only cooking but also the domestic chore of washing up dishes. With the "menial jobs of living" thus taken care of, both considered themselves free to enjoy the intellectual companionship which both agreed to be the basis of perfect friendship. So, on the surface, which is all he regards, life seems very agreeable to James. He is aware of but does not speculate on the reasons for the "queer, unsettled mood" that sometimes comes over him, interfering with his work, driving him to "catch the bus for Dublin—and an evening with Myra." Nor does he connect it with the scent of her clothes, "at times quite disturbing, . . . the cause of giving her the victory" sometimes in their "really brilliant arguments".

A memory of himself at twenty-six reveals, however, that James has not maintained always that rigid denial of his own feelings, so evident to the reader throughout the story. The year he finished his PhD, he had been passionately, obsessively, in love with a girl named Emmy. She "stood out in his life because of the violence of his feeling for her. It was something he had never permitted himself before; and never would again." He is certain that his career would have been wrecked, his intellectual energies would have been sapped, had a travelling scholarship not taken him away until after Emmy had married someone else. For him, conventional marriage was "never really in the picture". His friendship with Myra is the more welcome for the "uniquely undemanding quality of her feeling for him". With her he had come to believe that a man and a woman can enter into "a marriage of minds".

Although **"A Memory"** draws on the same eye for accurate detail, the same ear for authentic sound, as **"At Sallygap"**, milieu does not serve the same artistic purpose in the novella. It contains no suggestion that James and Myra may be caught, even superficially, in the twin tides of heredity and environment; indeed, they pride themselves, according to James, on how little they are influenced by what other people do and are elevated, in his opinion, to "pure heights of integrity" by their independence and ability to resist social pres-

sures. Detailed descriptions of Dublin, the Meath countryside, James's cottage, and Myra's house in the mews provide less notebook observations of external reality, more an objective correlative of James's inner world. As the narrative follows his thoughts and observations, it presents a thorough study of his character and personality, including his ambivalent and repressed feelings, of which he is himself unaware, and the errors in his perceptions of others. The focus is on the world outside, but the double vision gives back a clear image of James himself. From time to time, in brief, tantalizing moments, James seems on the verge of looking inward, of seeing that image which is so clear to the reader. But always his eye turns outward again, and the opportunity is lost. When Myra loses the control he so admires and cries, "You have denatured me", predictably, James flees. Outside her mews house, as one impulse leads him to raise a hand, rap on the gate, and return to Myra, another stronger impulse overcomes him—"to make good his escape."

James does not escape, of course; he cannot, as the narrative makes clear, because he is trapped inside himself, inside the sand castle which he has spent a lifetime building, which for ten years Myra has helped him build. Indeed, as Emily of **"The Sand Castle"** has made John's fated edifice her own, Myra had joined in James's elaborate construction. Then suddenly an operation ("much messier than childbirth" and "worse for . . . a childless woman", according to James's sister, Kay) brought the incoming tide too near to be ignored. There on the shores of adult knowledge, the wave of wild intuition rising within her, Myra saw their castle begin to crumble, begged James to see it, too, sought to engage him in a relationship that might provide at least transient joy before the waves of time washed over them. But James remains unaware of what Myra has offered him—and despite his disturbing memory, he remains equally unaware of what Emmy also had offered, long ago.

The subtle development of **"A Memory"** depends on a slow, gradual release of glimpses into James's personality through a sequence of events that sustains interest in the "and then" story, even while the reader becomes aware that the chief characters are not what they believe themselves to be and their day will not end as they expect it to. The double vision presented in the descriptions of outer reality which serve also to depict inner reality contribute to suspense by diverting the reader, who may be caught up in the outer world of the story, even while aware that the main action is developing within James. The selective accuracy with which the outer world is perceived by James is also diverting, for it easily misleads the reader into contemporary acceptance as well of his perceptions of his inner world and his assessment of Myra's, despite growing evidence that warns against believing what James says about himself or Myra. In the end, the truth concerning James is clear, but with subtle artistry Mary Lavin leaves the reader's mind unsettled: Is James the sole author of his own tragedy? Does the intellectual androgyny of Myra and James offend natural law, causing the gradual disintegration of their physical beings and their artificially constructed lives? Or is Zola present in **"A Memory"** after all: are James and Myra unable to withstand the hereditary forces which determine male and female natures, do they succumb in the end to those environmental influences that pressure even those on the fringes of society to accept traditional male and female roles?

While Wicklow, Meath, and Dublin are the places in which Mary Lavin lives her daily life, where every day she hears and talks with real-life counterparts of her fictional working people, shopkeepers, intellectuals, and others for whom she creates addresses in or near Ireland's cosmopolitan capital city, her sensitivity to the interplay of universal emotion and particular experience is no less acute in stories set in the fishing and farm communities of the Gaeltacht, where Irish is still the vernacular for significant portions of the population and old traditions die slowly or survive in changing forms under the influence of tourism and television. In the island community of **"The Green Grave and the Black Grave"**, for example, news of a death in the hours before dawn must still be told by candlelight, there being no electric power to bring the comfort of instant day into a dark world, and the smudge of the oil lamps of **"Bridal Sheets"** brings the only sadness to the life of Brede, the new-made widow from the inlands, that she can talk about with the island women.

Tadg Mor and Tadg Og of **"The Green Grave and the Black Grave"** are the islander fishermen, father and son, who bring news of the death of Eamon Buidhe to the cottage of Seana Bhride and Brid Og. They had seen his black boat like a "wave blown up in the wind"; they have taken his body from the sea that his one-year-wife might give it proper burial in a black grave on the island. Death by drowning is a familiar end to life for these two almost indistinguishable figures. Like the litany of the mass or a passage from the ancient annals is their recitation of the names of those who went down in the lonely green grave of the ocean and those whose bodies were recovered for burial in the black grave of the land, where one day their sea widows might be buried with them. Lucky is the man, in their opinion, who is saved for the black grave; happy is the wife who knows that in eternity, at least, she and her husband will lie together. But Eamon Buidhe's one-year-wife from the inlands does not answer the door when they knock, and at the cottage of Seana Bhride they learn that the inland woman had decided to fight the sea, to go out in the black boat with her husband, to go down with him into the green grave, too, if the sea took him, where "her arms would be stronger than the weeds of the sea, to bind them together forever." At this news Tadg Mor and Tadg Og realise that they have done an unlucky thing in taking the corpse of Eamon Buidhe into their boat, for now she will lie lonely forever in the Black Grave of the land while his one-year-wife is "washed to and fro in the waves of the sea". But when they return to the shingle beach where they have left their boat filled with silver and opal fish and the body of Eamon Buidhe, they find the body gone and the boat floating free.

> "The sea is stronger than any man," said Tadg Mor.
>
> "The sea is stronger than any woman," said Tadg Og.
>
> "The sea is stronger than women from the inland fields," said Tadg Mor. . . .
>
> "The sea is stronger than talk of love," said Tadg Og.

But the inland woman who had tried to tame and best the sea had wrung from it at least a partial victory. The sea had provided a green wave where forever "Eamon Buidhe Murnane would be held fast in the white arms of his one-year-wife, who came from the inlands where women have no knowledge of the sea but only a knowledge of love."

Father and son of **"The Green Grave and the Black Grave"** share the same name, with *mor* (big) and *og* (young) added for purposes of distinction. They share, too, one vocabulary: sparse, economical, reinforced by repetition rather than elaboration. Black, green, yellow, brown, silver, opal, and white are all the colours of their world, of everything and everyone in it. Bright and dark, bad and good, life and death, provide the chief antinomies. The waves on which their own boat rises and falls, rises and falls, are sharply pointed, like those drawn by kindergarten children. Their distances are measured not in miles or acres but in sea fields.

The dialogue of Tadg Mor and Tadh Og is more chant than conversation. Its rhythm is picked up and varied, like a musical composition, in the narrative. Syntax is derived from Anglo-Irish, but no attempt is made to reproduce its phonemic characteristics; the effect strikes both the ear and the understanding, for it not only establishes an intonation pattern that evokes the island milieu but also deflects attention from the speakers to that which is spoken about, focusing on action or observation rather than on agent or observer. The result is that although the narrative follows Tadg Mor and Tadg Og throughout the entire story, reporting their dialogue almost exclusively, they are not central characters. The man and woman whom the story really is about are Eamon Buidhe and his one-year-wife.

The primitive quality of the word painting of **"The Green Grave and the Black Grave"**, the incantatory prose, the stylised, almost wooden figures of Tadg Og and Tadg Mor, and the ritualistic action of the story all combine to present an impression of an old tale with a new twist, a modern story with the appeal of folklore. Was it the power of the inland woman over the sea, a power unknown to Emily of **"The Sand Castle"**, that forced the waves to recover the body of Eamon Buidhe for her white arms to hold forever? Was it the challenge she threw to the sea, swearing that it needed "taming and besting", that led to the pyrrhic victory? Or are these but the explanations of a people still steeped in the folk tradition who live with childlike naïveté on the bright shores of adult knowledge, explanations that the modern, sceptical mind rejects?

"Bridal Sheets", by comparison, is a story of island life today. Except for the syntactical characteristics that communicate the flavour of Gaeltacht English and an expression or two perhaps peculiar to islanders, the colloquial speech of Peigin and Brede could be that of the "shawleys" who gossip with Annie Ryan. The narrative reflects the mind of Peigin, a familiar, likable woman who has drawn the unenviable task of sitting up all night with the new-made widow, Brede. In an adjoining room of Brede's cottage, the other women of the island perform a task which frequency has made commonplace: they are washing the corpse of Eamon Og, Brede's husband. Peigin wishes she were with the other women in the room beyond, for Brede is not only making an unseemly hullabaloo, in Peigin's opinion, but is maintaining, in the face of all attempts to comfort her, that no one knows what she is going through. Peigin finally blurts out:

> "Ah, wisha, will you quit saying we none of us know what you're going through. . . . Sure—isn't losing one's man a common class of sorrow altogether in this island, or any other island of the western wave? Doesn't the sea get them one and all in time!"

Then, half curious, half determined to perform her office as best she can, despite Brede, Peigin begin to question the other Woman: Is it the sound of the sea that ails her? Is there a child on the way? Is it the look of Eamon's corpse, which admittedly had been "a bit over-long in the sea"? Did she and Eamon quarrel just before he pushed his currach into the waves for the last time? With nothing but negative answers and continued moaning and sobbing in response to all her questions, Peigin's patience runs out: " 'If you want anyone to know what ails you, then why can't you tell it!' "

And so a truth is told: Eamon has gone to his death without seeing his four-month bride in her wedding costume, for they were married on "the wettest day ever came out of the sky". Nor had he ever seen the dainty shoes she had brought in her trunks, for they could not be used on the rocky paths of the island. Nor had she ever worn her new shifts for him, or put her linen bridal sheets on their bed, for fear they would be ruined by the sooty smoke from the island's oil lamps. For four months neither he nor anyone else on the island had seen her in anything but an old brown skirt and black jumper, her feet stuck into men's boots, and the yellow, patched sheets made of flour sacks that had been in the cottage when she arrived were all she ever had put on their bed.

Peigin, who at first accepts what Brede says as the truth of what "ails" her, is amazed, but soon she has a solution: they will lay out Eamon on the bridal sheets, and he will be a "proud man looking down from Heaven this night and seeing himself in such grandeur." To her surprise, Brede has reservations: linen is cold to the skin (Peigin points out the Eamon will not feel it); linen wrinkles easily (Peigin reminds her that "he'll have no carry-on that would put creases in sheets"). Reluctantly, Brede gives the fine sheets to the women, but after Eamon is laid out on them and Brede is left alone with him, Peigin finds her removing the fine linen and pushing the old, patched, yellowed sheets under him once again. " 'What in the name of God are you doing Brede?' " cries Peigin. "But" writes Mary Lavin, "she knew."

Like **"The Sand Castle"**, **"Bridal Sheets"** is not the simple story it appears to be on the surface. Unlike **"The Sand Castle"**, it does not withhold this fact until the last line but buries clues in scattered, parenthetical references to feelings of loneliness, homesickness, and disappointment that scarcely seem worth remembering on first reading. Not until Peigin's unanswered questions, "What in the name of God are you doing," is followed in the reader's mind by a silent but inevitable why, do all the scattered clues connect. The technique is subtle, for Brede's thoughts are not included in the narrative; the reader receives only what Peigin thinks, says, and does, only what Peigin sees Brede do and hears Brede say: Peigin has the telling of the story. But Peigin's perceptions are limited to those significant to her island milieu—she is time-bound and earthbound—while Brede, placed in a situation for which she is not prepared, expresses universal emotions that exceed the islanders' concept of proper widowhood. Yet Brede is not innately more sensitive than Peigin, nor has she any greater understanding of "Those bright shores of silt". In the face of frequent and unexpected death, the island women simply protect themselves with their rituals, while inland different rituals are learned. The island women's rituals cannot protect Brede, the inland woman, nor, far from home, her illusions of life having been washed away by the realities of island existence even before she had to face the inevitable, encroaching tide, can she protect herself. This, the unspoken truth, is what

Peigin finally "knew", as Brede's despair momentarily brushed aside the veil of real life. (pp. 229-36)

Janet Egleson Dunleavy, "The Fiction of Mary Lavin: Universal Sensibility in a Particular Milieu," in *Irish University Review, Vol. 7, No. 2, Autumn, 1977, pp. 222-36.*

SÉAMUS DEANE (essay date 1979)

[*Deane is an Irish critic, poet, and editor. In the essay excerpted below, he suggests that Lavin's attention to the nature of love is linked inextricably with the natural and social landscapes in her fiction.*]

Mary Lavin's work seems naturally to command the reader to respond, as most of her commentators have done, to a certain purity of execution, of phrasing, and, perhaps more peremptorily, of the kind of concentration which we properly associate with deep and patient study. The object of study in her case is, very simply, the nature of love. Sometimes its validity is tested, although this is rare. Sometimes its bitterness is revealed, and this is frequent. More often again, its endurance is made manifest in the form of an iron stoicism or in the shape of an ethereally intense conviction. At all times, there is a deep engagement with the social environment, although that environment is often more restricted for the central character than it is for the narrator, these two being very seldom identical. In fact, the restriction of people's lives in these stories is best confirmed for us by the number of celibates who inhabit them. The celibacy may be enforced by death—Mary Lavin writes with great force about the widowed—or chosen as a vocation by priests or by laymen or women who entertain a love the world cannot respond to satisfactorily. All the forms of celibacy are for her forms of fidelity to a lost love, whether it be lost in the past or lost in the sense that it was never attained. Despite this, sexuality is a strong and pervasive presence, breathing pantheistically through the Irish (particularly the County Meath) landscape. . . . (p. 237)

Morally, this is a severe world. Although Mary Lavin has, psychologically, an empathetic closeness with even the most brutal or selfish characters, she candidly denies them moral sympathy. Sympathy is for lovers. To earn it, they must overcome all barriers—of class, of family, of temperament. They must elope, take risks, "learn", as Clem says in **"The Gardener"**, "to distinguish". Out of love for his children and, generally, for the innocent, he killed his wife. It is that kind of distinction which the extraordinary sensibility of the lover must have the courage and lucidity to make. However, the feeling that someone has been judged is not coercive. It more usually comes as a kind of aftertaste. The stories are not morality tales; they adjudicate by implication, not by pronouncement. A great deal depends, therefore, on the tone of the narrative. I once referred to it as having a "nefarious sweetness" and see no reason to question that ascription (although it is less evident in the most recent volume *The Shrine and Other Stories* than it had previously been). Indeed the tone so beautifully blends the elements of sympathy and judgement that we can only wish that union (as does the field of meadow-grass in **"Asigh"**). Whether or not it be said that these erotic tensions are embodied in or transferred to the details of landscape, it is difficult to think of this action as a solely literary device. It bespeaks the attitude towards sexuality characteristic of the Ireland of the last half-century. It is not, in other words, just a technique of conscious or unconscious sublimation. Insofar as these stories are concerned with the oblique exposure of powerful feelings, we sense that their power is closely related to the social and psychological habits of social suppression and secrecy. There is no attempt, really, to criticise this typical aspect of Irish social life, although one can infer a certain amount of disagreement and bitterness towards its inevitable consequences. Mary Lavin very largely shares the mores of her society. The question for her is, given those mores, by what means do people who behave in accord with them, deal with the anxieties and longings for which no direct, outright expression is available? She is concerned with the preservation of dignity and worth in very unlikely and often demeaning circumstances. The subtlety of her scrutiny and the assurance with which she controls her narrative indicate the presence throughout all her work of a firm moral criterion by which worth can be judged and in accord with which people can come to embody such worth. That criterion is fidelity to the vocation of love. Mary Lavin had consistently found an appropriate narrative form in which to cast it. A writer who is so involved in the domestic, practical world is committed by that involvement to the demands of verisimilitude, even in the way in which the story is told. Occasionally, these demands are not met and the result is disquietingly artificial.

The awkwardness I refer to is most often found in those stories which are reported through an intermediary. In **"The Mouse"**, for instance, the story of Lelia, Mina and Arthur is told by a mother, who has recently renewed her friendship with Lelia, to her daughter, who is intrigued by the hidden tale of Lelia's lost lover, Arthur. The mother and Lelia are, as usual, attracted to one another by the enforced celibacy of their present state. The mother's husband is dead, Lelia's Arthur forsook her for another woman, Mina. Yet Lelia remains faithful to the love she had for him; and, more wonderfully, continues to believe in the love he had for her. At any rate, after many years of silence, Lelia finally tells how it all happened to her new-found friend. The mother, in turn, tells it to her daughter whose curiosity had provoked the whole confession. But the confession is reported verbatim. We are listening to Lelia's voice, disguised as the mother-narrator's voice. Although there is an effort to set the scene, to give a physical foreground, so to speak, to the telling of the story, we are conscious of a certain clumsiness and certain improbability in the whole matter. The mother may be cross, shivering with cold, she may fill the kettle for a cup of tea, but we know that these actions are merely efforts to disguise the fact that she is no part of the story's moral fabric, but is merely a fictional device. The same applies to the daughter. As a consequence, the story lacks that surety of tone and address which we meet with in such perfect stories as **"At Sallygap"**, **"An Akoulina of the Irish Midlands"**, **"Asigh"**, **"A Memory"**, **"Happiness"** and **"Senility"**. It is when Mary Lavin cannot find a satisfactorily probable way of getting the story told that she lapses into an excessive enumeration of small actions and physical details which have no direct bearing upon the story itself. The reader is diverted from the feeling in the story by the mock-cosiness of its address. It is possible that this kind of flaw is one endemic to short story writers. The fact of publishing story after story in magazines leads the author as much as it does editors or readers to expect of himself a certain kind of story. All the best short story writers— Tchekhov, Henry James, Babel, Kafka—produce works which are in some respects a stereotype, in some respects a caricature of their best stories. I think that Irish writers are

probably more prone to this failing than are most authors, for there is a certain expectation in their audiences (especially their American audiences) about what an Irish short story is like. The pressure of editors and audience is a very real one and Mary Lavin now and again succumbs to it, just as Frank O'Connor, far more often, also did. In Mary Lavin's case the house style of *The New Yorker* sometimes shows through. When it does, the effect is not good.

Even if this be so, **"The Mouse"** has moments which remind us of other, more enduring aspects of her work. Take, for instance, Lelia's description of her last moment with Arthur:

> I remember almost everything about that day as if it was a painting, and I was outside it, instead of in it. I remember a man with an ass and cart came down to the bank of the stream where we were sitting, with a big barrel to fill for the cattle grazing inside the ramparts. Well, I suppose anyone would remember a thing like that, but I remember every detail of it, and how when the barrel was filled, and he was leading the ass up from the stream, the wheels of the cart rocked, and little silver drops of water were tossed up in the air, and they seemed to hang in the air for a minute, like a spray of tremble-grass, before they fell back into the barrel. Fancy remembering that all those years! And I remember, just close to Arthur's face once, where he was lying back in the grass, a little black insect . . .

This is, to some extent, a set piece. It is description saturated by grief, but formally so. The grief arises both from the situation itself and from the innocence of Lelia, however willed we may feel that to be. The acuity of her perception renders the depth of her loss. If we compare that to another passage from a different story, we can see how subtly the description of landscape can operate with, in this case, a retrospective force. The story is called **"Asigh"**:

> Closed in by summer, the fields were deeper and lonelier than ever, and the laneway that led out to the road was narrowed by overhanging briars and the wild summer growth of bank and ditch.

This is a story of love frustrated by a father's brutality and by a lover's hard-nosed common sense. It is also a study of sexual pathology and its manifestation in social attitudes. Most memorable though, is the girl's longing to find an outlet for the love which has stirred to life inside her. If not through her suitor Tod Mallon, or even through the quiet vengeance of love for the father who destroyed her life, then at least, vicariously, through her brother and his girl-friend, Flossie Sauran. But that longing is disappointed too. We leave her as we found her, lost amid the stiflingly rich fields of Meath, emotionally starved in the midst of plenty. The world depicted here is a cowardly one, and its harsh male authority is shown to be the product of half-sensed but wholly submerged sexual longing. But it is the girl who is the primary victim. Her impulse is to give love, not merely to have it. On all sides, the gift is betrayed by people unworthy to receive it. Such stories reach the level of parable. They exemplify a great deal about Irish social life but so powerfully embody it in terms of natural description and narrated event that we feel the convergence of every detail towards a single, powerful impression. The landscape, as described above in the opening sentences of the story, incorporates in itself the claustrophobic loss of the young girl. In this case, we are aware of a venomous economy in the telling and a stiff resistance to any easing or sentimentalisation of the theme. Mary Lavin's women may be heroic; but their stature does not diminish their unhappiness; it is instead the consequence of that unhappiness.

It is, therefore, a mistake and an exaggeration to speak of Mary Lavin's stories as though they were, *au fond,* a version of Irish pastoral—a notion put abroad by many of her reviewers. Although love is their subject and the Irish landscape, lyrically evoked, is often their environment, there is a candid bitterness, an unforgiving spirit in many of them. The most notable fact about love is its wastage. . . . Those who waste it are terribly punished, like the vacuous academic James in **"A Memory"**; those who suffer from its loss are haunted like Bartley Crossen in **"In the Middle of the Fields"**, or Vera in **"One Summer"**, even Bedelia in **"The Little Prince"**. Widowhood, bachelorhood, spinsterdom, childhood, old age and death—these are the states in which Mary Lavin tests love's validity. Marriage too, but marriage in her stories is always anticipated, brought to a sudden end or is a form of living death. It is not a state in itself but one from which her people seek refuge or to which they aspire. Although it is a fixed institution, it is rarely inhabited in the present tense by a living soul. Physically too, the act of love is always, so to speak, postponed. It is indeed surprising how very seldom such intimate stories are involved with physical intimacy. A touch or a kiss may mark the physical horizon of a love affair. This may be taken to indicate a certain prudery, but I hardly think so. Instead it would seem to indicate a highly spiritualised conception of love which governs the selection of physical detail—whether of the body or of the surrounding world—in most of these stories. Sexuality is denied, not by the narrator, but by her characters. Because of this denial, its effects are oblique and savage. We have here an analysis of Irish puritanism, not a monument to it.

The true lover fights against the world. Widows fly from those who remember the dead husband; other people's versions of the beloved make him and the love he bore unreal. Vera Traske in **"The Cuckoo Spit"** and Mary in **"In a Café"** experience this. That which is given in love—perhaps no more than the memory of a face—is precisely what the world wishes to take away. Love is phantasmal, yet the only reality; the world is actual, yet not at all real. Innocence and simplicity are the emotional stigmata of the lover, but they only show up in the presence of loss. In these stories, the deepest passions are the most disappointed. As celibacy is the recurrent image of loss, fidelity is the recurrent virtue characteristic of that state. Marriages may be made in heaven, but when they are so they are rarely realised on this earth. Or at least, to make the point truer to the stories, their realisation is always in the past. Marriage is the past tense of love. It survives, though, as an order of values which contrasts with the meaner values of the loveless world, whether that be middle-class Dublin, the rural world of County Meath, the faded gentility of the Anglo-Irish or the shopkeeper world of the village. Conflict is inevitable and many of these stories demonstrate the various shapes which it can assume. The great virtue of the lover is to maintain the integrity of passion, the great vice, to violate or betray that integrity. It is worth emphasising that passion is not subdued or granted a merely desultory role. Passion is kept intact by celibacy, just so long as we understand the celibacy to be a form of fidelity and not as merely a repudiation of the physical.

The conflict I have spoken of can sometimes, as in a story like **"Brother Boniface"** take a very simple form. In that story, the world of the shop and that of the monastery are clearly

seen as opposites to one another, but they are not in any deep sense inimical. Brother Boniface's uselessness in worldly matters is merely proof of his contemplative saintliness in an other-worldly realm. More often, we find that these stories pit two different types against one another. One type is ethereally gentle, consumed by passion so completely that his or her physical presence is slight; the other type has a more dominant, even a grosser, physical presence and an accompanying set of worldly values. Women in particular often fulfil the roles of Martha and Mary, with painfully contrasting fates as their reward or punishment. One thinks of Mary and Sis in **"A Tragedy"**, Bedelia and Liddy in **"Frail Vessel"**, Mae and Essy in **"Second-Hand"**. But perhaps it is **"An Akoulina of the Irish Midlands"** which best exemplifies this contrast. This is one of Mary Lavin's finest stories, a small masterpiece which is not at all overshadowed by its reference to Turgenev.

Still, it would be false to think of this body of work as conducive to a simple kind of type-casting. We are almost always aware of the small, irreducible pressures of Irish social life being exerted in a variety of ways upon individuals who are in part formed by that pressure, who in part embody it themselves and who, less often, have a conception of themselves which is independent of the formative influences of their environment. In some easily identified ways we can follow the evolution of Irish society in the last forty years by noting some social indications in these stories. An aspect of Irish middle-class feeling, the so-called "Fairyhouse Tradition", towards the movement for national independence is nicely caught in **"The Patriot Son"**; **"Scylla and Charybdis"** gives us a small, reverberative instance of the social distance between the gentry and their employees; **"A Fable"** uses the relationship between the Big House and the village as a ground for a parable about Beauty and Belief; the increasing importance of the university world for the middle classes is evident in stories like **"The Lucky Pair"**, and the more recent **"The Shrine"**. We learn that Tod Mallon in **"Asigh"** "was one of the first in the countryside to own a motor-car". In **"The Mock Auction"** Mrs. Lomas's respectable Protestant world collapses in squalid ruin in the period of transition between travel by pony and trap and travel by motor-car. Then there are other stories—**"Trastevere"**, **"Villa Violetta"**, **"A Memory"**—which belong to a less enclosed, more obviously contemporary Ireland and Europe. . . . (pp. 238-44)

As we observe the mutations of social life in these stories and compare these to the near-intransigent preoccupation with love which gives them their moral stability, we gain an insight into Mary Lavin's role in modern Irish writing. She is not, in any technical sense, an innovator. Equally, the reader is not troubled by the traditional form of her fiction any more than he would be by the same phenomenon in O'Connor, O'Faolain or O'Flaherty. (p. 244)

Yet Mary Lavin wears her Irish rue with a difference. Only Elizabeth Bowen equals her in the exercise of a peculiar kind of authority—the authority of the artist as a woman. Neither is doctrinaire on account of her sex. But each is highly sceptical of the importance of the "male" worlds of politics and work. There is no such thing as a career in the lives of their people; careers become vocations, and the vocation is always understood as a devotion to the complexities of human feeling. I think that because of this we never find in the work of these two women the kind of aggressive, domineering relationship to the world which is so typical of the many artist heroes in modern Irish writing. The pronoun "I" loses its customary importance in their work. The singular individual's relationship with the mediocre world is not their concern. Instead, as we read, we become aware of a very closely meshed nexus of feelings in which their protagonists are bound. Men are not men of affairs but men who have had or are having affairs. With this, there is a less hectoring and less anxious search for brilliance, charms, the edgy phrase-making of the conventional Irish short-story writer. (One would have to make an exception in Mary Lavin's case for stories like **"The Green Grave and the Black Grave"** or even **"The Great Wave"**, which strike me as professional Irish stories). Narratives may focus on an individual but not to the degree that we become diverted from this centre by the eccentric individualism of the narration itself. It is for instance only rarely that Frank O'Connor found a subject other than his own personality. He did not so much write stories as search in his work for a way in which to write with a Cork accent.

But Mary Lavin could not be accused of having a style in that sense of the word. More precisely, she deploys a rhetoric, just so long as we retain for the latter word its traditional and honourable meaning. Style is what we speak of when an individual seeks to discover in words the unique flavour, the particular mode of performance of his own sensibility. In rhetoric, the object is not the display of self, but the deployment of language for the sake of illuminating a particular situation or problem. One is the romantic, the other the classical mode of writing. Mary Lavin is classical. Her ethic is communal; the writing bears witness to commonalty in its traditional address, syntax and tone. Love, after all, is the great classical, not romantic, subject. The great romantic subject is the self. Love demands relation. Relation requires the exercise of certain controls which can become values, like those of loyalty, truth-telling, self-restraint.

Of course the dishevelled Irish community of which Mary Lavin writes does not embody these virtues. However she perceives in that community a peculiar combination of traditionalism and of rootlessness. Social institutions like the Church are powerful, yet artificial. The loyalties of people are strangely disturbed by its presence. Like the villagers in **"Sarah"**, they experience a curious ambiguity:

> There was greater undestanding in their hearts for sins against God than there was for sins against the Church.

The public practice of traditional beliefs is not often possible in such a society. Its ambience is sympathetic, its final decisions are loveless. For Mary Lavin the basic values are practised by the minority of lovers, almost all of them abandoned, almost all of them faithful to that which has caused them so much pain. They are the constituency of the elect in whom the human value of society is embodied but against whom its inhuman impulses are directed. The celibates become martyrs in the end. Like Liddy in **"Frail Vessel"**, who in her abandonment has still the better, spiritually, of her grossly competent and respectable sister Bedelia, they can murmur, "Even so . . . Even so". Great stories concentrate on individual moments but they articulate communal values. Mary Lavin has given us an astonishing number of these. (pp. 245-46)

> *Séamus Deane, "Mary Lavin," in* The Irish Short Story, *edited by Patrick Rafroidi and Terence Brown, Humanities Press, Inc., 1979, pp. 237-48.*

PATRICIA K. MESZAROS   (essay date 1982)

[*In the following excerpt, Meszaros examines Lavin's treatment of the relationship between femininity and creativity, commenting on the biographical elements in her later stories.*]

Although Mary Lavin's portrayal of the Irish middle-class character has been compared with some justice to the portraits in *Dubliners,* only a few of her many fine short stories are quintessentially Irish in setting or plot, and little of her work is known except among specialists in Irish literature. She herself has said [in a 1967 interview], "I did not read the Irish writers until I had already dedicated myself to the short story," and she claims to have been influenced most by "Edith Wharton, the pastoral works of George Sand, and especially Sarah Orne Jewett." Before she thought of becoming a writer, she had prepared herself at University College Dublin for an academic career, completing a master's thesis on Jane Austen and beginning a doctoral dissertation on Virginia Woolf. A recent study of her work estimates that sixty percent of her stories have a female protagonist or narrator [see Kelly in Further Reading list], and a number of her later stories form a quasi-autobiographical cycle exploring widowhood and the attainment of self-sufficiency in a solitary, middle-aged woman writer. That Mary Lavin's work has continued to suffer neglect is surprising, while both the women writers she most admires and those (like Doris Lessing and Jean Rhys) who are her near-contemporaries are receiving a great deal of critical attention. (p. 39)

Part of the reason, perhaps, is hinted at in the title of the critical study by Angeline Kelly cited above: Lavin is not a feminist in the contemporary sense; she is a "quiet rebel" who prefers to take an ironic stance, like Jane Austen, directing her detached gaze upon the foibles of men and women alike. Her vision has little in common with that of Doris Lessing, or of Sylvia Plath, or even Virginia Woolf, whose work and life inspired her own first attempt at writing fiction. Yet the treatment of women in Lavin's stories, particularly her treatment of the woman as artist, is at least as central to an understanding of her work as her treatment of the Irish character. . . . If Lavin's treatment of the relationship between femininity and creativity differs in important ways from the treatment of similar themes in the work of more fashionable writers, that is all the more reason to enrich our understanding of "the female sensibility" by paying close attention to her work.

The biographical fact most often advanced as essential to an understanding of Lavin's later fiction is that she was widowed when she was forty-two, after twelve years of marriage, left with a farm to run and three young daughters to rear. Her experience of widowhood, indeed, informs most of her middle and later work, both indirectly, in her searching and compassionate portrayals of loneliness and sometimes willful isolation, and directly, in her stories about widows, including her writer figure, Vera Traske. Oddly, however, these stories reveal very little about the feminine creative sensibility; Vera is a woman, a widow, who just happens (like the author) to be a writer. One of Lavin's earliest published works, **"A Story with a Pattern,"** and one of her most recent, **"Eterna,"** allude to the tensions in the lives of creative women more explicitly, as does her richly resonant and complex but unsettling novella, **"The Becker Wives."** Even though Lavin's interest in the woman as artist spans her whole career as a writer, her treatment of the creative woman is always oblique and ambiguous. Creative women are never narrators or centers of consciousness in the stories in which they appear, and evidence of their talent is either unreliable or unavailable. The focus of these stories is instead upon the effects such women have upon those around them, and the pervasive irony makes the author's attitude toward her female artist-figures difficult to assess.

On the other hand, Lavin's attitude toward her own work is not ambiguous. Very early in her career she recognized that the short story was to be her *Métier,* and she has repeatedly spoken slightingly and apologetically of her two novels, *The House in Clewe Street* and *Mary O'Grady.* In her frequent comments about the craft of the short story, she has made fascinating suggestions of a direct relationship between her life as a *woman* writer and her esthetic as a writer of *short stories.* The experience, the temperament, and the talent that fashioned this esthetic, as I hope to show, also account for the author's ambivalence toward her female artist characters. Such ambivalence is most evident in **"The Becker Wives,"** the most extended treatment in Lavin's fiction of the woman-as-artist theme. The meaning of this novella (or long short story) itself can also be illuminated by placing it in the context of other stories making direct or indirect use of the theme and of the author's own statements on her work. **"The Becker Wives"** is thus the centerpiece, the primary exhibit, in my argument, but the purpose of the whole is to demonstrate that Mary Lavin's vision of the woman as artist is both highly individual and one that finds its perfect embodiment in the short story form.

The very early work, **"A Story with a Pattern,"** addresses explicitly the question of the nature of the short story and implicitly the situation of a young woman writer. The protagonist encounters at a party a middle-aged man who criticizes her published stories for their lack of plot and conclusive endings, saying that her work will never appeal to a wide audience because "a man wants something with a bit more substance to it." Pressed by the writer to give an example, the critic tells a "true" story with a neat, O. Henry-like twist at the end, but the writer offends the critic by objecting that life "isn't rounded off like that at the edges." The story's title obviously refers to the patterned tale told by the critic but may also refer to the larger pattern of the frame story, one that Lavin may already have begun to observe in her own development as a writer. Concerned to practice her craft in a way that would not falsify her experience and—like all young writers—to establish her identity, she had to confront traditional notions about the proper form and content of the short story. By placing the confrontation in **"A Story with a Pattern"** between a female author and a male critic in a social context, she demonstrates her awareness of the difficulties faced by the woman writer in the search for her own authentic voice in her fiction. At the time she wrote this story Lavin was receiving advice and encouragement from Lord Dunsany, one of her earliest admirers, who praised her in his preface to her *Tales from Bective Bridge* but who recommended to her in private correspondence that she place more emphasis on plot and that she take O. Henry as a model.

However, to claim that a specifically "feminist" consciousness is revealed in this story, or indeed in any of Lavin's other works, would be a distortion. The group of "widow stories" is a case in point. Some of them, like **"Happiness," "The Cuckoo-spit,"** and **"In the Middle of the Fields,"** focus on the widow's struggle to live independently in the present rather than in memories of the past, but they evoke at the same time

a strong sense of the emotional and sensual deprivation of the widow's life. Even more *á propos,* the stories which portray the widowed Vera Traske specifically as a writer—**"Villa Violetta"** and **"Trastevere"**—clearly make the point that both personal happiness and a secure environment conducive to work are to be found in male protection and companionship. These two stories, however, have less to tell us about the author's sense of the place of art and creativity in a woman's life than does another of the "widow stories" whose protagonist is *not* presented as a writer, even though Lavin has admitted that the "Mary" of **"In a Café"** is herself. This story, indeed, may represent a transition between the earlier stories that (despite the wariness of the protagonist of **"A Story with a Pattern"**) were sometimes marred by pat conclusions and the more searching, complex, and equivocal later work. As Lavin said in a recent interview, "For years I wrote for fun [see Koenig in Further Reading list]," but in the years immediately following her husband's death she became increasingly serious and self-critical.

"In a Café" links the motifs of a widow's new-found independence and the preservation of her husband's memory to esthetic vision in a significant way. Two women, one young and recently bereaved after a brief marriage, the other (the story's center of consciousness) older and two years widowed after a long and happy marriage, meet in a café frequented by students and artists. By chance they exchange a few pleasantries with a young man at the next table, a painter, some of whose work hangs for sale on the café's walls. Later, alone, the older woman seeks out the artist in his studio, telling herself that she will look at the rest of his paintings and perhaps purchase one of them. Receiving no answer to her knock at his door, she impulsively bends to peer through the slot of the letter-box, gaining only a partial view of the interior which is yet enough to tell her much about its inhabitant's poor and solitary existence: "an unfinished canvas up against the splattered white wainscot, a bicycle-pump flat on the floor, the leg of a table, black iron bed-legs and, to her amusement, dangling down by the leg of the table, dripping their moisture in a pool on the floor, a pair of elongated, grey, wool socks." The scene is at once comic and pathetic. A door from an inner room opens, and the young painter appears to her as two "large feet, shoved into unlaced shoes, and . . . bare to the white ankles. For, of course, she thought wildly, focusing her thoughts, his socks are washed!" She springs to her feet and runs away.

This grotesque experience both frees the widow from her past and enables her to reclaim it. Earlier in the story, we had been told of her inability, since his death, to recall her husband's face. Now as she walks back to her parked car, his image comes to her vividly. The story ends:

> Not till she had taken out the key of the car, and gone straight around to the driver's side, not stupidly, as so often, to the passenger seat—not till then did she realize what she had achieved. Yet she had no more than got back her rights. No more. It was not a subject for amazement. By what means exactly had she got them back though—in that little café? That was the wonder.

Clearly, the widow's regaining of "her rights" is closely connected in the story with esthetic experience. When she first sees the paintings in the café, we are told, "She knew what Richard would have said about them. But she and Richard were no longer one. So what would *she* say about them?"

When she peers through the hole in the letter-box into the painter's bare little flat, she has herself become a sort of artist, focusing, as does Lavin herself as the writer of short stories, on limited and selective but vivid and telling details, deriving from them a compassionate vision of human isolation. The articulation and acceptance of this vision enable the character to accept her own circumstances and thus to live her own life in the present while having her past restored to her as memory.

Some support of the view that this story expresses something of the author's faith in the restorative and even redemptive power of her craft comes from Lavin's only published piece of criticism, the "Preface" to her *Selected Stories,* in which she recounts a childhood experience, when she was taken by her father to see about having her "small gold watch" mended. With dismay the child notices that the watchmaker's hands are palsied, shaken by "some kind of ague," and that "all down the front of his waistcoat and jacket, stains and slops of food showed how badly he was disabled." But then the old man takes the watch in his hands, bracing his wrists against the side of the table, and the little girl marvels at "the fixity, the sureness of those fingers when once they had entered the intricate world of their craft." The moral Lavin attaches to this anecdote is that "like that old man, I . . . had applied myself so singly to the art of fiction that I had maimed, and all but lost, the power to express myself in any other form." The reader, however, may perceive a larger meaning. Obviously, the image of the watchmaker is appropriate, for like the writer of short stories he must have a delicate, precise touch. But the other parallel, not made explicit by the author herself, is with his apparent handicap. Later in the essay she speaks of the necessity of writing "in snatches of time filched from other duties, and particularly of late years when I have had to run the farm from which we get our livelihood." Even before her husband's death, soon after the publication of her first book, she had spoken in an interview of looking forward to "having the morning hours to herself in the autumn when the baby would be in her crib and the older girls in school." Lavin seems consciously to have developed her technique as a writer to accommodate her personal situation, and she even maintains that her work is the better for the demands placed on her time by her domestic responsibilities: "I believe that the things that took up my time, and even used up creative energy that might have gone into writing, have served me well. They imposed a selectivity that I might not otherwise have been strong enough to impose upon my often feverish, overfertile imagination. So if my life has set limits to my writing I am glad of it. I do not get a chance to write more stories than I ought; or put more into them than ought to be there." She seems to believe not just that her craft enables her to overcome what might be viewed as the handicap of her personal circumstances, but also that those circumstances in themselves have forced her to refine and develop her craft.

Clearly, Lavin's view of the particular conditions affecting the woman as artist, as presented both in her stories and in her remarks on her own work, is a highly personal and perhaps even unique one among twentieth-century women writers. Despite her early interest in and admiration for Woolf, she seems to have no inclination to yearn for a room of her own, and she seems almost entirely lacking in that sense of confinement within the social and esthetic conventions of a male-dominated world that feminist critics find to be so pervasive in writing by women. Although her later works, par-

ticularly the Vera Traske stories, must be seen at least partly as personal responses to a devastating personal loss, it is nevertheless significant that even in the early novella, **"The Becker Wives,"** where we find Lavin's most sustained treatment of the woman as artist, traditional concerns of women writers are handled in untraditional ways.

The novella explores the venerable theme of the disruptive influence of the artist on an ordered society. From Plato through Shakespeare to Goethe and Coleridge the motif has been sounded, but here it is modulated into a new key because the artist is a woman and therefore doubly mysterious, potentially more disruptive. An archetypal figure older than that of the artist with "flashing eye" and "floating hair" is the *fatal woman,* and Lavin has vested the power of both figures in the character of her woman-artist. Flora, the poet, the actress, is also *la belle dame sans merci.* At the same time, **"The Becker Wives"** resonates with questions that have filled the diaries, letters, and published works of talented women for at least two hundred years. Do the woman's traditional roles in society inevitably stifle her creativity? Is the creative impulse in women perhaps an unnatural deviance of the maternal instinct; or, to put it differently, is motherhood the natural end, the apotheosis indeed, of female creativity? Much of the richness and subtlety of this work derives from the way in which the author has brought to a single focus in her central character the romantic myth of the artist, the myth of the fatal woman who has been seen both as the artist's muse and as his nemesis, and the new myth of the destructive conflict between femininity and creativity endured by the woman-artist.

The mystery surrounding the woman-artist is enhanced in two ways by the narrative technique of **"The Becker Wives."** First, Flora is presented only from the outside, as the Beckers see and imagine her, so that we gain no direct insight into her consciousness. Second, the work is unique for Lavin in that it introduces into the solid, closely observed domestic world of middle-class Dublin not only a mythic dimension but also an element of almost gothic mystery, as if Ligeia had come to live among the Forsytes. Marianne Moore's definition of poetry describes the world of **"The Becker Wives"** almost exactly: an imaginary garden with real toads.

The toads are the Beckers themselves, a family of wealthy corn merchants—four brothers and a sister—who, like Galsworthy's Forsytes, are long on family solidarity and earnest materialism but short on grace, wit, and imagination. All the Becker children take spouses as like themselves as they in turn are like their parents; all, that is, except the youngest brother Theobald, who wants a wife with more to recommend her than "suitability for marriage and child-bearing." Theobald is actually no more enlightened than the rest of his family; he is merely more snobbish. Nevertheless, he manages to marry the beautiful, talented Flora, who paints, plays the piano, and writes poetry, but whose real talent seems to be for acting. From the beginning the Beckers are charmed by Flora's piquantly histrionic behavior: she brings "into all their homes, as into their lives, more air . . . more colour, more light," and with Theobald's brother Samuel as her ally, she improves their taste in furniture and art. Best of all, she entertains them with her pantomimes and impersonations, most frequently with one of the other Becker wives. As Flora's acting proves to be an obsession, Theobald's pride turns to irritation. Samuel, in contrast, begins to watch Flora almost compulsively, and as his pregnant wife Honoria takes to staying at home, he seeks Flora's company in the evenings.

The Becker wives are prolific; at any given time two or three of them are to be found in various stages of pregnancy. But Flora remains slim and ethereal, and though her sisters-in-law privately pity her, she seems unconcerned. Eventually, however, the other wives notice that the object of Flora's impersonations has become almost exclusively Honoria. Finally one day Flora sits in a corner sewing a small white garment, refusing to answer to her name. Begging the family not to tease her, she points toward Honoria, basking in the sun outside: "As for that one, . . . that wretched creature out there: if someone doesn't stop her from driving me mad, I won't answer for what will become of her." This is no impersonation; Flora has exchanged places in her own mind with Samuel's wife. To Samuel, Flora confides her secret, speaking in Honoria's voice:

> You're the only one I trust. You won't let her drive me mad, will you, like she's been driven mad herself? That's it, you see. No one knows but me and I didn't tell anyone before now. But I knew it all the time. She's mad. Mad! She was really always mad. Her family was mad—all of them. Her father died in a madhouse.

Just before Samuel closes the door on his appalled family, they see him put his arm around Flora's shoulders, saying tenderly, "Hush, Honoria. Hush, hush."

"The Becker Wives" can be most readily interpreted in terms of the most universal of the myths to which it alludes, as a fable about a fragile poetic sensibility which temporarily disturbs but is ultimately quelled by an uncongenial environment. One version of this classic story locates the seeds of destruction in the artistic sensibility itself; thus Peterson says that Lavin's novella "concludes with a troubling vision of the artist who goes too far," that it tells of "a young woman whose gift of insight becomes a maddening curse, preventing her from entering the comfortable, commonsense Becker world." At the same time, that world itself, the narrative makes clear, is not one in which the poetic temperament can thrive. At the end, Samuel reflects that Flora was "a flitting spirit never meant to mix with the likes of them."

Largely because of the presence of Samuel, the romantic myth of the artist proves to be inadequate to a full interpretation of the narrative, for while Flora is the story's central character, Samuel's expanding consciousness focuses our vision, his quickening imagination stirring our sympathy. To the extent that it is Samuel's story, "The Becker Wives" follows the classic pattern of a youth's encounter with seductive pleasures and his resulting loss of innocence. As the seductress, however, Flora represents not sensual gratification but the lure of a world of imagination from which the Beckers are insulated by their complacent materialism. When the two worlds are brought into conflict, the Beckers' dimension is rendered in specific physical detail, but Flora's dimension is rendered in archetypal images. Similarly, we can explore Samuel's responses and trace the development of his imaginative awareness because he clearly belongs, like the great majority of Lavin's characters, to a world in which the human psyche *can* be explored. Flora we can only know—because what she represents *can* only be known—in a series of avatars. The realm of myth is made to impinge upon the realm of literally represented reality in this narrative in a way that is directly related to its fullest meaning.

The first pages of the novella establish the Beckers as dull people, so lacking in interest even to themselves that, having dinner in a fashionable restaurant, they evince only a bovine placidity, sitting "stolid and silent, their mouths moving as they chewed their food, but their eyes immobile as they stared at someone or other who had caught their fancy at another table." In the following pages, however, the narrative expands in connotative richness as a shift in focus records for the first time Samuel's perceptions: "Like limelight the moon shone greenly down making the lighted windows of the houses appear artificial, as if they were squares of celluloid, illuminated only for the sake of illusion. He hoped Theobald wouldn't insist on dragging him back to reality." Samuel is evidently the one Becker susceptible to esthetic emotion, the only one who will be in any way prepared to understand Flora.

Before she herself appears, Flora is presented in images refracted from other imaginations, first in Theobald's casual remark to her sister Henrietta that "Flora doesn't eat as much as a bird," so that "Henrietta's imagination rose with a beat of wings, and before her mind's eye flew gaudy images of brightly plumed creatures of the air." Caught up in the image, Theobald then makes a quite uncharacteristic slip of the tongue when, speaking of his intention of surprising his sisters-in-law by introducing Flora at a family party, he says, "I'm not going to miss an opportunity like this for killing two stones with the one—I mean two *birds* with the one *stone.*"

The slip is not lost on Henrietta, and when that evening Theobald arrives with his bride-to-be as the family is finishing dinner, it occurs to her that "all the seated Beckers, and all their seated guests, seemed to have been turned into stone." Yet the woman who has produced this Medusa-like effect does not seem to Henrietta to be at all forbidding in appearance:

> Flora was small. She was exceedingly small. She was fine-boned as well, so that, as with a bird, you felt if you pressed her too hard she would be crushed. But in spite of her smallness, like a bird she was exquisitely proportioned, and her clothes, that were an assortment of light colours, seemed to cling to her like feathers, a part of her being. . . . She accepted her clothes as the birds their feathers: an inevitable raiment.

Henrietta's impressions seem to be highly subjective, however, for they are not corroborated by the other observers: Flora seems to have the power of exciting and confusing the imaginations of those who meet her for the first time. In James's mind she evokes "gaudy and tinsel images" of the dancers from the operettas of his youth, while to Samuel she appears as the goddess Flora, in "a vision . . . of a nymph in a misty white dress, with bare feet and cloudy yellow hair, who in a flowering meadow skipped about, gathering flower heads and entwining them in a garland," even though he notices that she is dressed not in the "assortment of light colours" that had seemed to Henrietta like feathers but in "a trim black suit."

More perceptive than the others, Samuel soon realizes that indeed the "real" Flora is protean, that she actually *becomes* what she imagines herself to be, even when she is alone, and fascinated, he becomes "more and more dependent" upon her friendship. Flora's influence on Samuel refines his sensibilities and heightens his awareness of character. He no longer attempts to impress Theobald or boasts that his wife is a heiress. His ability to recognize in Flora's secret transformations the "naive and childish" expression of his wife Honoria or the "cold and shallow" stare of Theobald implies a new clarity of judgment, and toward Flora he now exhibits exquisite tact. . . . The images in which Flora herself is described progress from the conventional and natural to the strange and hieratic. Initially seen by the Beckers as a bird-like creature, a dancer, a flower-goddess, Flora presents herself as a maker of images (a pretend photographer), as a flame "withering the life" out of people, as the keeper of an imagined "little green dragon" over which her fingers move "delicately, guardedly, as if her pet had some prohibitive quality, such as a scaly skin," and as a woman capable of "departing from her own body and entering that of someone else." So, although we see her through Samuel's eyes as a powerfully attractive woman, we know so little of her real nature that we can not feel her to be a sympathetic character.

The scene marking the highest point in the development of Samuel's awareness also most poignantly reveals Flora's essential mysteriousness. One evening Samuel calls to find Flora alone in an unlighted room, pressed against the side of a window, staring upward at "the thin spikes of the first stars." She seems "like the bowsprit of an ancient ship, . . . and as sightless." Samuel whispers, "Who is it? . . . Who are you now?" and although she answers in her normal voice, "Why Samuel! What a strange thing to ask! I'm Flora, of course, who else?" for Samuel the moment has been an epiphany:

> Yes, it was Flora: but if ever a person was caught in the act of self-impersonation, that person was Theobald's wife, for in that tense, motionless figure which a moment before had been unaware of his presence, he realized that Flora had concentrated her whole personality. And the essence of that personality was so salt-bitter that a salt-sadness came into his heart too.

He is prepared for the end, and when Flora retreats permanently into her fantasy world, Samuel knows "that the terrible terrible sadness that had settled on his heart would lie upon it forever." In the last scene, despair settles on him as he looks out the window at the fat, stodgy children of his other sisters-in-law, knowing that the child "his wife Honoria was carrying would be like them, as like as peas in a pea-pod."

Samuel is a victim of *la belle dame sans merci;* having lost his beloved "flitting spirit," he has been abandoned like Keat's knight, where "no birds sing." Flora is presented in such a way as to suggest many of the avatars of the *femme fatale.* Like Poe's Ligeia, her family origins and circumstances are obscure, and like her she attempts to usurp the identity—if not the body—of another woman. Like Lamia or Lilith, she might be regarded as the seducer of young men and the barren, envious stealer of other women's children. An allusion may even be made to the Celtic analogue of Lilith, Blodeuwedd or Blathnat, whose name means literally "flower-face," and who was turned into a bird—an owl, like Lilith—after she betrayed her husband. The Medusa is suggested in the way Flora seems to turn the Beckers to stone when they first meet her, and Samuel's apprehension of her agelessness and inscrutability ("like the bowsprit of an ancient ship, . . . and as sightless") is reminiscent of Pater's description of *La Gioconda:* "She is older than the rocks among which she sits; like the vampire, she has been dead many times, and learned the

secrets of the grave." The important difference between these versions of the *femme fatale* and Lavin's version is that Flora is not evil, certainly not sexually destructive. Her implied threatening of Samuel's wife and unborn child is pathetic rather than sinister, because she speaks as a passive and ineffectual "Honoria," directing her words toward a "Flora" who no longer exists.

If Lilith in her various incarnations expresses fear of the independent, dominant woman, seen as a sexually and socially destructive being, in this remaking of the myth by a female writer her emasculating, murderous aspect is suppressed while her exciting, disturbing aspect is retained and expanded by combination with the myth of the socially disruptive artist. Whatever danger this fatal woman represents is due not to her being a woman alone but to her also being an artist—she is something less and something more than the legendary *femme fatale.* Moreover, the "fatal" woman herself is ultimately destroyed; the woman-artist becomes her own victim. Here both the myth of the romantic artist at odds with society and the myth of the fatal woman merge with the myth of the conflict between femininity and creativity. In the light of this myth, we can see Flora as doomed not only by the frustratingly conventional environment into which she has married, but also by the role set for her as a woman in that society.

As *la belle dame* is traditionally sterile, so also the female artist is traditionally childless; at least in the popular imagination, there has been "an eternal opposition of biological and aesthetic creativity." It is probably no coincidence that Samuel's wife, the woman whose identity Flora tries to usurp, the woman who is almost indistinguishable from the other wives and whose child will be as like theirs "as peas in a pea-pod," bears the somewhat unusual name, "Honoria." **"The Becker Wives"** was first published in 1946. Given Lavin's interest in Woolf, she would likely have read the posthumous collection, *The Death of the Moth and Other Essays,* published in 1942. That collection contains the text of Woolf's talk on "Professions for Women," and the talk itself contains the now famous passage in which the author describes how, in order to find her own identity as a writer, she first had to kill the spectral "Angel in the House," that "ideal" woman who was sympathetic and self-sacrificing, who "excelled in the difficult arts of family life." The reference to the "Angel in the House" is of course an allusion to a popular Victorian poem by Coventry Patmore; the name of the heroine of that poem is "Honoria."

Flora may in this light be seen as a martyr to the untenable position imposed by her society upon the woman-artist. As Stewart describes the dilemma of the female writer, "To be a heroine, she must nurture, help, inspire; by defining her independence as an artist, she turns into a gorgon. . . . She must die as this mythic 'feminine' woman in order to give birth to herself as an artist." The fragile Flora, unable, under the pressures of Becker family life, to sustain her lonely artistic selfhood, succumbs to what for her can only be a spurious, borrowed identity. As one of the commentators on the work has said, "Her schizophrenia really represents for her an embrace of comfortable, sane, solid middle-class values: pregnancy and propriety." Ironically Flora, whose name is that of a classical fertility goddess, is "fertile" only in her imagination. She can give birth neither to a real child nor to herself as an independent artist.

That the work is rich and complex should be apparent, but the mythic patterns which delineate both its universality and originality, imposed on the narrative like templates, leave some ends and pieces uncovered. In the last analysis, Flora remains a highly ambiguous character, and although she is certainly pathetic, she is not tragic. The "salt-sadness" which appears to Samuel to be the essence of Flora's being may be interpreted by the romantic reader as the terrible isolation of the artist, but it may be only an early manifestation of the illness soon to overtake her. If we are to believe the final revelation spoken by Flora in Honoria's voice, we must relinquish the notion that the woman-artist has been "driven mad" by her impossible circumstances, for her madness in hereditary: "Her father died in a madhouse." Even what the Beckers take to be Flora's extraordinary acting ability may be a manifestation of schizophrenia rather than talent. Indeed, looking back over the narrative, we can find no clear evidence that Flora has attained more than a "ladylike" level of accomplishment in any of the arts, or that she is anything more than a lovely dilettante and follower of fashions.

The reader may have been taken in by the power of the myths invoked by the narrative, myths which express the fears of society about women and about artists—that the beautiful, independent woman is a dangerous seducer of innocent youth, that the artist is akin to the madman and just as dangerous to society, that the creative impulse in woman is a substitute for the maternal instinct and that the female artist is likely to be barren. **"The Becker Wives"** seems to explore the frightening possibility that all these myths may be true, but the narrative as a whole suggests that such myths at worst cause us to accept stereotypes as truths and at best obscure life's complexities and ambiguities.

In creating Flora, Lavin has admitted that the sources of creative energy are dark and potentially dangerous, and she has faced some of our worst fears (and perhaps her own) by portraying a dichotomous situation in which, on the one hand, the charismatic female artistic personality ends by destroying itself while, on the other, female domestic animals go on placidly reproducing their kind in a world devoid of beauty. At the same time, however, the ironic authorial voice seems to suggest that the dichotomy is false. Whether Flora is to be seen as a scapegoat or as a demon exorcised, her flaw is a too-vivid imagination that allows fantasy to over-balance reality and finally to obliterate it. That she remains a mystery is a clue to her significance for the author, who once deplored her own "feverish, over-fertile imagination" and proposed to control it within the limits of the short-story form, even while she felt constrained by her domestic responsibilities and yearned for more time to follow her creative bent.

That same ambivalence appears once more, in some of the same ways, in one of Lavin's most recent stories. In **"Eterna"** she again portrays a creative woman who apparently goes mad. Once again we see the woman only from the outside, through the eyes of a rather ordinary character. Once again we cannot know for sure whether the woman is genuinely talented, whether she is driven mad by her restrictive environment or has carried the seeds of madness within her from the beginning.

The story's center of consciousness is a mediocre provincial doctor, complacently married to a very ordinary woman. One day in the National Gallery of Dublin, where he has gone while waiting for his wife, he encounters a madwoman whom he recognizes as a figure from his past and is thus forced to remember an incident he would rather forget. Not long out of medical school, he had been called to a convent to treat a young nun, Sister Eterna, injured in a fall from a scaffold while she had been painting a mural. Several visits later, when she impulsively showed him her treasure, a battered catalog from the National Gallery, he had committed a breach of propriety and professional ethics by speaking too familiarly to her, saying he would love to show her the paintings there. Much later he had heard that she had left the convent. Upset at first to see the once haughty young nun in her present condition, he regains his equilibrium as his wife approaches: "People had to learn to clip their wings if they wanted to survive in this world. They had to keep their feet on the ground. That was what Annie had taught him to do—God bless her." Annie, with her bundles of children's clothing bought on sale, is one of the Honorias of the world, and the doctor, with his smug hypocrisy, is one of the Theobalds.

Consistently, unmistakably ironic toward the doctor and his wife, the narrative voice of **"Eterna"** is entirely silent about the nun, who does not appear as a character except in the reminiscences of the doctor. Eterna is even more of a mystery than Flora. Thus, still apparently fascinated by the relationship between female creativity and madness, still apparently moved by the restrictions and insults suffered by the artistic temperament, Lavin is yet unable or unwilling to present the woman as artist in other than an oblique and ambiguous way.

The world from which her mysterious women-artists retreat, on the other hand, is a real world, and its flawed actuality is reported with zest by a witty, ironic voice, the instrument of a shaping and controlling imagination. Like the widow of the story, **"In a Café,"** the artist as writer of short fiction organizes her experience by scrutinizing the world outside herself closely and compassionately but from an ironic distance. To conquer loneliness and isolation, she confronts them directly but keeps them contained within a small frame. The mysteries of creativity she refuses to look at directly, except through the veil of myth. Faced with conflicting demands upon her time and energy, the woman-artist steadies her wrists, as it were, like the old watchmaker, and concentrates all her craft upon the small but complex object before her. (pp. 39-52)

> *Patricia K. Meszaros, "Woman as Artist: The Fiction of Mary Lavin," in* Critique: Studies in Modern Fiction, *Vol. XXIV, No. 1, Fall, 1982, pp. 39-54.*

SUSAN ASBEE (essay date 1987)

[*In the essay excerpted below, Asbee comments on the narration of Lavin's "The Becker Wives," suggesting that Lavin purposely establishes a false correlation between real and imagined experience in an attempt to convey the instability of the lives of her characters.*]

Mary Lavin's long short story, **"The Becker Wives"**, depends, for its main effect, on the surprising denouement: we learn that the protagonist has not been inhabiting a world which is the fictional equivalent of our own, but one which is not only different, but a much more sinister version. In *A Structuralist Poetics* Jonathon Culler describes the relationship between the reader and a novel as a 'narrative contract'. 'The basic convention governing the novel' he writes, 'is the expectation that readers will, through their contact with the text, be able to recognise a world which it produces or to which it refers'. (p. 93)

"The Becker Wives" is written in violation of this; the narrative contract established between narrator and reader must necessarily be a tenuous one, although it feels firm initially, for it is established only in order to mislead. It is not simply a 'trick' at the readers' expense, however, because the protagonist too is not always aware of the exact significance of her actions, and her world is an unstable one.

In **"The Becker Wives"** Lavin exploits and ultimately exposes her reader's unquestioning acceptance of a correspondence between real and fictional worlds. The narrative conceals and hints at its own conclusion, but during the course of a first reading the author's use of traditional realism, including extensive use of seemingly concrete, palpable detail, lulls us into a false sense of security. A second reading, with all the benefits of advance retrospection, is a very different process and reveals points at which this realism breaks down. . . . [Undoubtedly] Lavin's story *invites* re-reading, and the second reading necessarily focuses our attention on her narrative art.

"The Becker Wives" is a social comedy in the manner of Jane Austen or E.M. Forster, but the ending of the story has terrifying implications which go beyond the comic seriousness of Forster. Isolation and lack of understanding and communication take on new proportions, and we the implied readers are left with the Beckers, bound forever in a middle-class world from which there is no escape.

The Beckers' staid notions of respectability and propriety are overthrown when they are introduced to, and subsequently captivated by, Flora. Samuel Becker, possessing more imagination than the rest of his family, provides a particularly sensitive and intelligent focus for the reader's perceptions of Flora. This seemingly innocuous narrative stance helps to mislead us, however. Samuel is obviously the character *most like us:* that is, while he remains within his family's milieu, he is capable of seeing beyond their limitations—the comedy of manners mode encourages this same perception in us. Theobald has pretensions—and of course we don't share those, though, like him, we too may be impatient with his family's aquisitiveness. Julia seems guided throughout by common sense, and alone resists Flora's charm: but we don't identify with her, as commonsense is not a seductive virtue when we are receptive and eager to embrace a new world—in this case a world of the text as well as of the imagination. Furthermore, we cannot imagine Julia, or any of the other wives, reading a book. But we can imagine Samuel reading; in a way he guides our response—he is the nearest we get to a reader in the text because of the narrative point of view. He marries for money and has an element of the social climber in his nature, yet very early on in the story Samuel shows a potentially sensitive side. . . . (pp. 93-5)

But it is this same slightly superior point of view which makes Samuel more susceptible to the entertaining world which Flora creates; like us, because of his imaginative streak, he is less well defended from it by the solid conventionality of his sisters-in-law and his brothers, but Samuel, like the reader, also falls short of understanding the full implications of Flora's charm. It is only at the end of the story that the Beckers and the readers realise that Flora's captivating unconventionality is the result of inborn or hereditary madness. (There is a hint given early on which, if we know Thomas Hardy and his *Tess of the D'Urbervilles*, we might pick up: Theobald explains that Flora 'comes from a very old family') However, at the end of the story we are told that:

> It was all over, the fun and the gaity. Their brief

journey into another world had been rudely cut short. They had merely glimpsed from afar a strange and exciting vista, but they had established no foothold in that far place. And the bright and enchanting creature that had opened that vista to them had been but a flitting spirit never meant to mix with the likes of them.

The first three sentences of that passage could be read as an analogy for all readers as they come to the end of all novels for by the very nature of fiction we cannot enter a fictional world. Lavin invites us to re-read the story, with the surprising ending still in mind. The second time we read, we realise that we have not been the victims of a shabby trick, but that all the evidence was placed before us—had we noticed, or read in a more perceptive way—the first time we read it. Equally, the 'Intended' first reading is undoubtedly the one where we are *not* aware of all the implications. The words are the same on each occasion, but our different perceptions mean that the second time we read, we read a different work in a different way. Like O'Brien in *The Third Policeman,* like Golding in *Pincher Martin,* and like Ambrose Bierce in his short story "An Occurence at Owl Creek Bridge", Lavin has created a masterly palimpsest. It is significant that each of these works is, in one way or another, a rather terrifying tribute to the power and creativity of human imagination.

Henrietta is a Becker by birth, but her brothers' wives are of the same ilk: 'Henrietta, Charlotte and Julia. There they sat, all three of them, all fat, heavy and furred, yet like Anna, their mother-in-law, all emanating, in spite of the money lavished upon them, such an air of ordinariness and mediocrity . . .'. Theobald, the unmarried, youngest son, is impatient of exactly these qualities, so when his brother Samuel, true to form, marries 'a great deal of money' Theobald remains unimpressed by her wealth, and contemptuous of her 'mediocrity' (Lavin carefully repeats the word). Theobald introduces his own intended wife, Flora, into the formal dinner party designed to welcome Samuel's bride-to-be. Theobald refuses to bring her as an invited guest, however: 'I thought I made it plain to you that Flora wouldn't understand sitting down to the big gorges that James and Charlotte provide . . . Flora doesn't eat as much as a bird'. The formal family mealtime sums up the concrete, physical, unimaginative world, and in contrast Lavin uses this image of Flora as a bird, developing it in such a way that unease is generated in the reader (if at all) very gradually. Theobald says, 'I'm not going to miss an opportunity like this [i.e. the dinner party] for killing two stones with one—I mean two *birds* with one *stone*" (Lavin's emphasis), but although the unhappy alliance which their marriage will become is emphasised and foreshadowed by Theobald's slip of the tongue (the text deliberately signals it: Henrietta, we are told, was particularly upset because 'her brother usually affected such a slow and deliberate manner of speech there was seldom any danger of verbal mishap such as he had just suffered'—verbal mishaps are dangerous!) but equally the Flora/bird image has not yet become established as a motif and so this incident does not carry the same weight of implication on a first reading as it does on successive ones. The narrative encourages us to see Flora as the Beckers see her: though clearly intrigued, they believe she is merely a 'born actress' and 'a wonderful mimic'. And at first we are misled by this audience within the text, even though Henrietta remembers Theobald's slip later:

> Suddenly she recalled Theobald's slip of the tongue
> about killing two stones with one bird, and whatev-

er about his fiancee, it seemed to her that when, at that moment the dining-room door was flung open by Theobald, all the seated Beckers, and all their seated guests, seemed to have been turned into *stone*.

The narrative reiterates the disturbing image, drawing attention to it.

Flora and Theobald arrive late at the dinner party, the others are already drinking coffee. But Becker akwardness and social embarassment at what they see as Theobald's social ineptitude is quickly dispelled by Flora who 'saved the situation':

> 'You simply mustn't move!' she cried. 'Such a charming group as you make . . . oh how I wish *I* was a photographer.' Then suddenly she did the funniest thing. 'Let's pretend that I *am* one,' . . . and bending down her head in the drollest way, just as if she had a tripod in front of her, and letting her yellow hair fall down over her face like a shutter curtain, she made a circle with her fingers and held them up to her eyes to act as a lense for her make-believe camera . . . When she had them all smiling, she reached down her hand and squeezed the imaginary rubber bulb that controlled the shutter, . . . It was exactly as if she was a real photographer. The Beckers had unconsciously stiffened into the unnatural and rigid postures of people being taken by the camera. Then, when the girl straightened up and pushed back her hair, the group came to life again. Realizing how ridiculous they must have looked . . . they all laughed . . . Above all Theobald laughed. He was delighted with himself. He looked proudly at his finance. She'd be able for any situation.

The irony in that last sentence is only apparent retrospectively for Flora repeats the phrase with reference to herself at the end of the story when it is clear to readers and Beckers alike that she is certainly not 'able for any situation'. Flora continues her pretence; as she is taken round the table and introduced to each person in turn, she takes individual 'portraits', and the staid and respectable Beckers respond to her and participate in the make-believe.

> 'I hope I didn't break the camera, my dear?' [James] said. Theobald's pride in Flora was infectious. It even infected stuffy old James. He was changed by her. Flora herself didn't smile. She was doing something to her camera. And her serious expression convulsed the group.

The narrative perspective is unreliable in the extreme. In the earlier passage I quoted, the idiom of the sentence 'Then suddenly she did the funniest thing', and the use of the word 'drollest', suggests that the speaker could be Charlotte, or Julia, or Henrietta, telling the story at a later date, the narrative perspective shifts almost imperceptibly. But 'Flora herself didn't smile. She was doing something to her camera' is first of all objective observation, and then from Flora's point of view. We know there is no real camera, but at the end of the story we also know that the camera was real for Flora, not an elaborate joke: so at that point the narrative has broken (to use Jonathon Culler's term) its contract with us.

Flora maintains the illusion, and does not acknowledge her performance to be a pretence even as she leaves the gathering:

> 'There's no doubt about it' Ernest said, 'Theobald is right. There is a touch of genius about her. Now that you mention it, I think I did notice that she

was carrying that thing a bit far at the end of the evening. I saw her pretend to pack her photographic equipment and when Theobald gave her his arm, she made as if she was changing it to her other hand. As a matter of fact Theobald didn't twig it at all: he's a bit slow sometimes in spite of his high opinion of himself. I saw the whole thing immediately. And I let her see I did. 'Why don't you let Theobald carry it for you?' I said, and went as if to assist her myself. 'That's alright,' she said, 'I can manage.' And she smiled. Good Lord, that smile!'

Her smile is reassuring—it disarms Ernest completely—but it reassures us in the wrong way. We understand it as Flora's acknowledgement that she is continuing her masquerade: not, as it would be from her point of view, that she is quite capable of carrying her camera for herself. The Beckers appreciate the joke, enter into the humour of the situation which Flora creates for them—and incidentally add to her madness by encouraging it? They are a little critical: Julia's remark, 'I thought once or twice that she carried it just a bit too far' should signal our own unease—earlier it was Julia who forcast a 'disastrous marriage' for Theobald; and Julia who cries that Theobald 'is the kind of person who makes the worst mistakes of all in the end'. But in that earlier conversation, significantly, 'Ernest wasn't listening', and neither, the first time that we read the story, do we, in spite of the fact that the authorial decision to include dialogue like this should act as a signal to alert us to the fact that disaster is being foreshadowed. In the passage which I quoted a moment ago, Ernest tentatively agrees with Julia—perhaps Flora did go a little too far, but on the whole the Beckers enter into the spirit of the comedy, and Julia's criticism merely underlines her own sense of decorum. They react with delight to the fantastic green dragon which Flora invents for her audience's and her own amusement. 'The affair of the photography . . . had been impromptu, but the green dragon was apparently part of a steady repertoire'. 'I don't *do* it, I *see* it' Flora protests when her new in-laws ask her to 'do' the green dragon. Theobald explains:

> 'Flora just stands up and looks in front of her and claims she sees it—sitting on the table or on a chair—anywhere in fact. That's all there is to it, but the way she stares at it, you'd swear it was there. Her way of looking at it is so convincing'.

At first Flora refuses to perform: 'I'm sorry I can't show it to you', she said. 'I don't see it anymore. It must have gone into the garden'. The narrator comments on her mastery of the situation. 'The green dragon's absence was almost as positive as his presence would have been. Theobald saw that his family could almost visualise the little creature.' As if the Becker's willingness to comply with Flora's vision is not enough to involve us, the narrative detail in 'little' creature helps make the absent dragon appear even more concrete. Eventually the dragon does 'appear', and Flora cuddles it in her arms as if it were a puppy or a kitten, except that her fingers 'moved delicately, guardedly, as if her pet has some prohibitive quality, such as scaly skin.'

> 'Genius. Sheer genius' Samuel said . . . Even James rose to the occasion with a rare flash of wit. 'Take him inside, my dear,' he'd said . . . 'Don't stand out here in the night air. *The little fellow might catch cold*' (Lavin's emphasis).

The narrator comments that this 'showed how he responded to his sister-in-law.' We respond in much the same way, eager to enter this delightful world of imagination, so different from the solid, stifling materialistic world of the Beckers.

Flora is not a brilliant actress and mimic, she genuinely sees the things which she evokes. Far from being refreshingly unconventional and a 'genius', the young woman is mad, daily inhabiting the world which her inlaws think she creates simply for enjoyment. The tone at the end forces us to re-appraise our estimate of both the Beckers and Flora, as the Beckers have to re-assess their previous feelings about her.

"The Becker Wives" has a basis in solid middle-class values; even if these are unfamiliar to the reader, he or she will understand them because the first third of the story firmly establishes the Beckers' way of life before Flora's disturbing name is even mentioned. The naming of so many objects, summed up best, perhaps, by the big brass bed in which the Becker father died, creates the illusion of a recognisable world. In contrast to this solidity Flora enters and gives an insight into a more imaginative, evanescent world. Both, of course, are equally fictional, and this is one of the artifices that the text weaves.

Flora is the protagonist, but the reader never has insight into her mind. At one point the narrator tells us that the diversions she creates—spontaneous visits to the theatre, outings in charabancs and so on—

> made no difference to Flora as long as she could escape from the tedium and boredom of the present, just as it didn't matter to her whether it was Henrietta or Honoria she was impersonating as long as she stepped out of her own personality and became another being.

This is almost a straightforward statement on the developing nature of her madness, but the emphasis is on the pleasure the Beckers derive from her spontaneity: Theobald asks himself 'Had the Beckers ever before laughed out loud like that in the street? A change had certainly come over them'. Possessions, symbols of reality, are treated with scant respect by Flora, who has the good taste to despise Julia's vase. Taking their cue from her, they throw out once prized possessions, symbols of their status and wealth, and 'into their houses, as into their lives' the narrator tells us, 'more air had come, more colour, more light'. At the moment when we might become uneasy about Flora's impersonations, the narrative re-assures us that change is for the better.

Flora has an effect before the Beckers meet her: her name conjures images of 'brightly plumed creatures' a lark, or maybe a chaffinch for Henrietta; an operetta for James, while Samuel recalls that 'the first instant he'd heard the name Flora, it had brought a vision to his mind of a nymph in a misty white dress . . .' and so on. It is as if the power of her imagination precedes her.

Flora is undoubtedly the protagonist of the story, though at first we might expect Theobald to be the focus of interest. Samuel seems to take over, because of his special relationship with Flora: we observe Flora's world and become accomplices in creating it, a dangerous occupation. Samuel himself could be said to be culpable in encouraging her, indeed, it is Samuel's wife that Flora eventually 'becomes'. We realise how delicate a tightrope Samuel walks, did he but know it, when we re-read the story, for Flora's increasing madness is seen through his eyes, and it is, the narrator tells us, 'his biggest pleasure'. He is her aide and abettor: 'Charlotte?' he

would whisper asking if he'd guessed correctly who she was being'. And she'd smile, not at his perception, but because at that moment she actually believed she *was* Charlotte. They meet, as we the readers meet the narrator, on different terms.

Flora, desperate to escape from her own identity and personality, finally tells her own story—but taking on Honoria's personality and speaking of herself in the third person, outraged at the wretched creature who impersonates her. If Virginia Woolf had written this story, it's likely that it would have been told from Flora's point of view throughout, the narrative would have disoriented and distorted our view of the world, the new perspectives would have been on display, the prose might well have been full of verbal fireworks. Undoubtedly the reader would have had a role to play in organising the world of the text; but Mary Lavin's subtle and deceptive method of narration is equally challenging: it is disguised as straightforward classic realism, but the reader is implicated in cocreating a work which subtly misleads. The art behind the narrative strategies conceals itself, it is complex, intricate and shifting, distracting our attention when we should be most alert. (pp. 95-101)

Susan Asbee, "Mary Lavin's 'The Becker Wives': Narrative Strategy and Reader Response," in Jour-nal of the Short Story in English, No. 8, Spring, 1987, pp. 93-101.

FURTHER READING

Burnham, Richard. "Mary Lavin's Short Stories in *The Dublin Magazine.*" *Cahiers du Centre d'Etudes Irlandaises,* No. 2 (1977): 103-10.
    Chronicles the early development of Lavin's fiction, tracing her correspondence and early story submissions to Seamus O'Sullivan, editor of *The Dublin Magazine.*

Caswell, Robert W. "Mary Lavin: Breaking A Pathway." *The Dub-lin Magazine* 6, No. 2 (Summer 1967): 32-44.
    Presents early criticism of Lavin's stories and comments on the development of both her fiction and her critical reputation.

Church, Margaret. "Social Consciousness in the Works of Elizabeth Bowen, Iris Murdoch, and Mary Lavin." *College Literature* 7, No. 2 (Spring 1980): 158-63.
    Commentary on Lavin's treatment of social issues in her fiction. Church suggests that Bowen, Murdoch, and Lavin have created a revival of Celtic themes in their fiction.

Dunleavy, Janet Egleson. "The Making of Mary Lavin's 'A Memo-ry.'" *Eire-Ireland: A Journal of Irish Studies* 12, No. 3 (Fall 1977): 90-9.
    Draws on personal conversations with Lavin to describe the author's process of creating her short stories. Dunleavy comments particularly on the imaginative genesis of "A Memory" and Lavin's detailed manuscript revisions of the work, noting similarities between characters in "A Memory" and "Love is for Lovers."

———. "The Subtle Satire of Elizabeth Bowen and Mary Lavin." *Tulsa Studies in Women's Literature* 2, No. 1 (Spring 1983): 69-82.
    Biographical approach to the works of Bowen and Lavin. Dunleavy examines the relationships between the cultural milieu of Ireland, the authors' personal lives, and their fiction.

————. "Mary Lavin, Elizabeth Bowen, and a New Generation: The Irish Short Story at Midcentury." In *The Irish Short Story: A Critical History,* edited by James F. Kilroy, pp. 145-68. Boston: G. K. Hall and Co., 1984.

Brief biographical and critical overview of Lavin's career. Dunleavy traces the development of Lavin's major themes and comments on her reputation among Ireland's most prominent short story writers.

Dunsany, Lord. Preface to *Tales from Bective Bridge,* by Mary Lavin, pp. vii-xiii. Boston: Little, Brown & Co., 1942.

Applauds the depth and perception of Lavin's character portraits. Dunsany predicts a warm critical reception for Lavin's collection and compares her style to that of the celebrated Russian short story writers.

Koenig, Marianne. "Mary Lavin: The Novels and the Stories." *Irish University Review* 9, No. 2 (Autumn 1979): 244-61.

Comments on Lavin's opinions of her own work. Koenig discusses the ironic and ambiguous tone in much of Lavin's writing and examines Lavin's relationship with the short story form.

Murphy, Catherine. "Mary Lavin: An Interview." *Irish University Review: A Journal of Irish Studies* 9, No. 2 (Autumn 1979): 207-24.

Group discussion in which Lavin responds to questions asked by students of Merrimack College. Lavin shares her personal views, comments on her changing opinions of her fiction, and discusses the significance of the short story form in an afterword to the interview.

O'Connor, Frank. "The Girl at the Gaol Gate." *A Review of English Literature* 1, No. 2 (April 1960): 25-33.

Places Lavin among the most prominent Irish short story writers and comments on her treatment of specific themes and her avoidance of political issues. O'Connor suggests that Lavin's style verges on the novelist's technique in its preoccupation with the past.

Peterson, Richard F. "The Circle of Truth: The Stories of Katherine Mansfield and Mary Lavin." *Modern Fiction Studies* 24, No. 3 (Autumn 1978): 383-94.

Comparative analysis of Mansfield's and Lavin's treatments of similar themes. Peterson discusses Lavin's opinions of Mansfield's work and points to similarities between specific stories of the two authors.

Scott, Bonnie Kime. "Mary Lavin and the Life of the Mind." *Irish University Review: A Journal of Irish Studies* 9, No. 2 (Autumn 1979): 262-78.

Details Lavin's interest in the psychology of her characters and discusses her presentations of female artists, noting an increasing biographical slant to her stories.

D(avid) H(erbert) Lawrence

1885-1930

(Also wrote under the pseudonym Lawrence H. Davison)
English novelist, short story writer, poet, essayist, critic,
translator, and dramatist.

One of the most original English writers of the twentieth century, Lawrence explored human nature through frank discussions of sex, psychology, and religion. In his lifetime he was a controversial figure, both for the explicit sexuality he portrayed in his fiction and for his unconventional personal life. Much of the criticism on Lawrence's work revolves around his highly individualistic moral system, which is based on absolute freedom of expression, particularly sexual expression. Human sexuality was for Lawrence a symbol of the "life force" and is frequently pitted in his works against a dehumanizing modern industrial society. Universally recognized for his achievements in such novels as *Sons and Lovers, The Rainbow, Women in Love,* and *Lady Chatterly's Lover,* Lawrence was also a highly esteemed short story writer whose tales were often based on experiences from his working-class youth in England's industrial midlands. Such stories as "The Prussian Officer," "Odour of Chrysanthemums," and "The Rocking-Horse Winner" are considered masterly and innovative examples of the genre and crucial to Lawrence's development as a novelist.

The fourth child of an illiterate coal miner and his wife, a former school teacher, Lawrence was raised in the colliery town of Eastwood, Nottinghamshire. From boyhood he shared a close relationship with his mother and grew to hate the debilitating mine work that he felt was responsible for his father's debased condition. Lawrence attended local grammar and high schools and later, from 1906 to 1908, studied at Nottingham University College, where he began writing short stories. In 1908, Lawrence moved to Croyden, just south of London, to teach school. While there he encountered Ford Madox Ford's *English Review,* where he published some of his early poetry and—more meaningful to the evolution of his fiction—discovered what he and others termed "the exciting new school of realism" in the works of such writers as Thomas Hardy, Henry James, Joseph Conrad, and Leo Tolstoy. In 1911, the onset of tuberculosis forced Lawrence to resign from teaching. That same year he published his first novel, *The White Peacock,* which was critically well received. When he was twenty-seven, Lawrence eloped to Germany with Frieda von Richthofen Weekly, the wife of one of his college professors, and the two were married in 1914.

In 1913, Lawrence published his first major work, the largely autobiographical novel *Sons and Lovers,* and also wrote "The Prussian Officer," one of his most celebrated stories. Both works are early examples of the psychological fiction that he later developed more fully. Lawrence returned with Frieda to England just before the outbreak of World War I and remained there until the war's conclusion. During the war, Lawrence and Frieda endured harassment by the English government because of his antipatriotic views and her German ancestry. Lawrence's next novel, *The Rainbow,* a complex narrative focusing on relationships between men and women, especially those of marriage, appeared in 1915. The

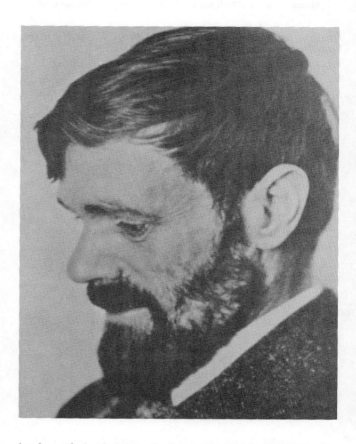

book was judged obscene for its explicit discussion of sexuality, and suppressed in England. These events intensified Lawrence's bitter struggle with social orthodoxy and the forces of modern civilization, which he increasingly came to believe were arrayed against him, and most certainly influenced his decision to leave England. His last major novel, *Lady Chatterly's Lover,* met with similar resistance and was available only in an expurgated version until 1959 in the United States and 1960 in England, when a landmark obscenity trial vindicated the book as a work of literature. After the war, the Lawrences lived briefly in Germany, Austria, Italy, Sicily, England, France, Australia, Mexico, and in the southwestern United States, where Lawrence hoped to someday establish a Utopian community. These varied locales provided settings for many of the novels and stories Lawrence wrote during the 1920s and also inspired four books of admired travel sketches. In 1930 Lawrence entered a sanatorium in Vence, France, in an attempt to cure the tuberculosis that afflicted him throughout his life. He died soon after.

Many critics consider Lawrence's short stories his most artistically accomplished writings and have attributed much of their success to the constraints of the form, which forced Lawrence to deny himself the elaborations, diversions, and repetitions that are integral but often burdensome elements of his full-length works. In comparison with his novels, Lawrence's short fiction is economical in style and structure. His early stories are written in the manner of Robert Louis Stevenson and Rudyard Kipling, whose anecdotes and tales of adventure epitomized the traditional nineteenth-century English short story. These first tales, which include "The White Stocking," "Legend," "The Vicar's Garden," and "A Prelude," largely emphasize plot, exhibiting clear narrative development and an obvious climax. Yet, in such a work as "The White Stocking," Lawrence's focus on erotic passion in the relations between the sexes prefigures much of his later endeavors. Most critics concur that "Odour of Chrysanthemums" marked the emergence of a second stage in the development of Lawrence's short fiction. Composed in 1911 and published in *The Prussian Officer, and Other Stories,* this piece incorporates the heightened realism of James, Conrad, and Tolstoy, and, like most of Lawrence's stories from the years 1909 to 1912, focuses on the familiar events and problems of twentieth-century industrial English society, while displaying concern for the lives of ordinary men and women. The title story from *The Prussian Officer, and Other Stories* is regarded by many as Lawrence's first completely visionary work. This piece signaled another change in the direction of Lawrence's writing, and to some critics, in the art of short fiction at large. Written in 1913, "The Prussian Officer" combines accurate social setting with penetrating psychological analysis, exhibiting Lawrence's eagerness to explore areas beneath the surface of human behavior. Characterized by compressed, intense observation, this and other works of the period before 1925 imply the depth and complexity of ordinary experience and retain Lawrence's sharp observation of character and place.

World War I was a major event in the evolution of Lawrence's aesthetic principles. Like many artists of the time, Lawrence viewed a cycle of apocalypse and rebirth as a necessary corrective to the apparent depravity of the modern world. In his post-war stories he presents intense personal engagements as essential in giving new life to people and societies on the verge of despair. Sensual love stands as an alternative to the mechanisms of modern warfare and technology, and the closed community that Lawrence valued and portrayed in his earlier writings becomes extended and reshaped to incorporate all of Western culture. To dramatize this concern for regeneration, Lawrence often utilized elements of religious ritual and myth. In "The Christening," for instance, he employs the rite of baptism to paradoxically evoke the disintegration of the old order. Critics have noted that Lawrence's use of such devices endeavors to invest the quotidian with significance. Lawrence's notion of rebirth subsequently came to be symbolized in his writings by the phoenix, the legendary bird that rose youthfully from the ashes of a pyre, and the emblem that eventually became associated with Lawrence himself. Other stories from this period include the title story from *England, My England, and Other Stories,* "Tickets, Please," and "The Horse-Dealer's Daughter." In "England, My England" Lawrence symbolizes the self-destructive yearning of the fading English gentility through the protagonist Egbert, an effete aristocrat who is killed at the front after enlisting in the army in an attempt to re-assert his masculinity. "Tickets, Please" is a sardonic tale of sexual role reversal revealed in a mock-heroic manner that climaxes in violent eroticism; and "The Horse-Dealer's Daughter" personifies the redemption of society through the erotic rejuvenation of a doctor and the girl he rescues from suicide.

Lawrence's longer short stories from this period, including "The Ladybird," "The Fox," "The Captain's Doll," and "St. Mawr," in some ways anticipate the techniques of his later works through their use of allegory, mythological structures, and imagery. "The Ladybird" employs the myth of Persephone to contrast sexless love with true passion, while "The Fox" makes explicit use of animal imagery to study the nature of human sexual relations. "The Captain's Doll" has been viewed as a comedic variation on Lawrence's abiding concern with male/female conflict. Some critics have accused Lawrence of displaying chauvinistic attitudes in several works of this period, notably "The Fox," "You Touched Me," and "The Border Line." The exotic story "The Woman Who Rode Away" culminates this trend in what some critics consider a misogynistic dramatization of female submission to male mastery in which a young white woman is captured and sacrificed to ancient gods by a group of aboriginal males. While many regard this tendency in Lawrence's work as transitory—by 1924 with "St. Mawr," he began to modify his views—throughout his career, Lawrence often demonstrated distrust and even fear of the power of women. The stories from this middle period of Lawrence's career are noted for their extensive range of themes, attitudes, settings, and characters, and critics have often commented on the steadiness and high quality of Lawrence's output during these years.

Lawrence's later short stories, from 1925 to 1930, display a dominant movement toward fabulation and satire. While in *Lady Chatterly's Lover,* his last novel, Lawrence returns to more representational forms, his short fiction emphasizes abstraction and argument. "The Rocking-Horse Winner" is a sardonic tale employing devices of the fairy tale and a mockingly detached tone to moralize on the value of love and the dangers of money. "The Man Who Loved Islands" is a parabolic story that ridicules idealism through the experiences of a man who flees the mechanistic modern world to three self-created island utopias, each of which fails due to the intrusion of his own human imperfection. In these and other late tales, Lawrence moves beyond the strictures of realism and encompasses a broad range of subjects and styles. Confronting such issues as materialism, idealism, conformism, women's movements, and traditional Christianity, these stories in some sense return to the legends and fables of his earliest works, yet manifest what many critics regard as keener insights, sturdier craft, and vaster experience.

Lawrence has come to be regarded as one of the twentieth century's most important short story writers. Through his innovative use of psychological themes and his distinctive application of a heightened realism to quotidian English society, he produced some of the earliest, and some critics believe finest, modernist prose. Lawrence demonstrated a wide imaginative range in his short fiction that was often lacking in his novels, and to many observers his fresh masterful approach extended the conventions of the short story genre. Although some critics fault several of Lawrence's stories for exhibiting failed symbolism, fanatical didacticism, and controversial views, he is nonetheless celebrated for his trenchant insights into the deepest impulses of life, his devotion to illuminating human passion, and his original perspective on the problems posed by human relationships.

(For further information on Lawrence's life and career, see *Twentieth-Century Literary Criticism,* Vols. 2, 9, 16; *Contemporary Authors,* Vol. 104, Vol. 121; and *Dictionary of Literary Biography,* Vols. 10, 19, 36.)

PRINCIPAL WORKS

SHORT FICTION

Prussian Officer, and Other Stories   1914
England, My England, and Other Stories   1922
"The Ladybird," "The Fox," and "The Captain's Doll"
    1923; also published as *The Captain's Doll: Three Novel-
    ettes,* 1923
"St. Mawr": Together with "The Princess"   1925
The Woman Who Rode Away, and Other Stories   1928
The Escaped Cock   1929; also published as *The Man Who
    Died,* 1931
Love among the Haystacks, and Other Pieces   1930
The Virgin and Gipsy   1930
The Lovely Lady, and Other Stories   1933
A Modern Lover   1934
The Tales of D. H. Lawrence   1934
The Complete Short Stories of D. H. Lawrence.   3 vols.
    1955

OTHER MAJOR WORKS

The White Peacock   (novel)   1911
The Trespasser   (novel)   1912
Love Poems and Others   (poetry)   1913
Sons and Lovers   (novel)   1913
The Rainbow   (novel)   1915
Amores   (poetry)   1916
Twilight in Italy   (essays)   1916
Look! We Have Come Through!   (poetry)   1917
New Poems   (poetry)   1918
The Lost Girl   (novel)   1920
Women in Love   (novel)   1920
Psychoanalysis and the Unconscious   (essay)   1921
Sea and Sardinia   (essays)   1921
Tortoises   (poetry)   1921
Aaron's Rod   (novel)   1922
Fantasia of the Unconscious   (essay)   1922
Movements in European History [as Lawrence H. Davison]
    (essays)   1922
Birds, Beasts and Flowers   (poetry)   1923
Kangaroo   (novel)   1923
Studies in Classic American Literature   (essays)   1923
Reflections on the Death of a Porcupine   (essays)   1925
The Plumed Serpent   (novel)   1926
Mornings in Mexico   (essays)   1927
The Collected Poems of D. H. Lawrence. 2 vols.   (poetry)
    1928
*Lady Chatterley's Lover   (novel)   1928
Pansies   (poetry)   1929
Nettles   (poetry)   1930
The Virgin and the Gipsy   (novel)   1930
Etruscan Places   (essays)   1932
Last Poems   (poetry)   1932
The Ship of Death   (poetry)   1933
The Spirit of the Place   (essays)   1935
Phoenix   (essays and criticism)   1936
Fire   (poetry)   1940
The First Lady Chatterley   (novel)   1944
The Collected Letters of D. H. Lawrence. 2 vols.   (letters)
    1962
The Complete Poems of D. H. Lawrence. 2 vols.   (poetry)
    1964
The Complete Plays of D. H. Lawrence   (drama)   1966
Phoenix II   (essays and criticism)   1968

John Thomas and Lady Jane   (novel)   1972

*This work is the third of three different versions. The other two
were posthumously published as *The First Lady Chatterley* and
John Thomas and Lady Jane.

―――――――――――

H. E. BATES   (essay date 1941)

*[Bates is considered a master of the twentieth-century English
short story. He is also the author of* The Modern Short Story,
*a highly regarded introduction to the history, development, and
pioneering writers of the genre. In the following excerpt from
that book, Bates suggests that Lawrence's short fiction is "a
more direct, more controlled, and more objective art" than his
novels and credits Lawrence with inspiring modern short story
writers to depict the immediate life about them in their works.]*

To consider Lawrence the short-story writer is a more
straightforward task than that of considering him as a novelist, and for various reasons. The novel will suffer almost any
kind of amplification of its theme, and Lawrence used it, to
its repeated detriment, as a means of disseminating a personal
gospel ("One has to be so terribly religious to be an artist")
that arose less from the head ("All scientists are liars!") than
from the solar plexus ("I don't feel it *here*!"). The statement
of this gospel, since Lawrence was no thinker and was nothing if not, [as Aldous Huxley stated in his introduction to the
Letters of D. H. Lawrence], "determined that all he produced
should spring direct from the mysterious, irrational source of
power within him," was often windy and diffuse, but the
novel contained it without bursting. Such a statement,
preached in passionate and often hysterical terms incapable
of modification ([Huxley declared]: "I have often heard him
say, indeed, that he was incapable of correcting"), would destroy any short story by the simple process of suffocation.
Lawrence, either intuitively or consciously, must have known
this, and in consequence his stories are always an expression
of a more direct, more controlled, and more objective art. In
them Lawrence has no time to preach, to lose his temper, to
go mystical, or to persuade the reader to listen to him by the
doubtful process of shouting at the top of his voice and finally
kicking him downstairs. Lawrence is for once bound to say
what he has to say within reasonable, and even strict, limits
of time and space. Ordinarily dictatorial, Lawrence is here
dictated to by the form he has chosen. The results have little
of that slobbering hysteria of the later novels; they are again
and again a superb expression of Lawrence's greatest natural
gifts, sensibility, vision, a supreme sense of the physical
(whether beautiful or ugly, human or otherwise), an uncanny
sense of place, and a flaming vitality. Unobscured by hysteria,
by the passion of theoretical gospels, these qualities shine
through three-quarters of the forty stories that Lawrence
wrote.

The publication of these stories began with *The Prussian Officer* in 1914. Lawrence, the son of a miner, had been brought
up in one of those dreary rows of working-class houses that
stand on the edge of the countryside they have robbed and
desecrated. And here, in these first dozen stories, Lawrence

aims to be nothing but the chronicler and interpreter of that life: a regional writer content to depict his own people. The vitality and authenticity of the pictures, strong with poetic realism, are striking. The eye recording them is clear, sharp, and vigorous, passionately observant, passionately responsive:

> The small locomotive engine, Number 4, came clanking, stumbling down from Selston with seven full wagons. It appeared round the corner with loud threats of speed, but the colt that it startled from among the gorse, which still flickered indistinctly in the raw afternoon, outdistanced it in a canter.

Ford Madox Hueffer seized on that passage as an indication of Lawrence's talent, and printed the story, **"Odour of Chrysanthemums,"** thus beginning Lawrence's career. He made no mistake; the man who could describe this:

> Like a stream the path opened into azure shallows at the levels, and there were pools of bluebells, with still the green thread winding through, like a thin current of ice-water through the blue lakes.

could also describe this:

> She served the dinner and sat opposite him. His small bullet head was quite black, save for the whites of his eyes and his scarlet lips. It gave her a queer sensation to see him open his red mouth and bare his white teeth as he ate. His arms and hands were mottled black; his bare, strong neck got a little fairer as it settled towards his shoulders, reassuring her. There was the faint indescribable odour of the pit in the room, an odour of damp, exhausted air.

There is no mistaking that. It is the voice of a man sensuously responsive to both beauty and ugliness; to whom all life will be, in increasingly involved and violent terms, a conflict arising from that contradictory power of vision. But it is also the voice of a man with narrative powers, with the gift of unfolding words, of exciting curiosity: the gift of the story-teller. In the short stories this gift can be seen more clearly and more consciously at work than in the novels; that spate of emotion, which Lawrence liked to call the expression of the daemon in himself, is regulated, held in check, directed. The novel, as a form, never imposed this duty on Lawrence so rigidly; in consequence the novels are often bad, shapeless, irritating in their insistent puerility and redundancy. (pp. 197-200)

Later generations will react to the novels of Lawrence much as we now react to the novels of Hardy. The philosophical rumblings will date; the wonderful pictures, the life directly projected, will remain. From such a test the short stories will emerge as the more durable achievement. In the earliest stories—**"Daughters of the Vicar," "The Shades of Spring,"** the beautiful **"Love Among the Haystacks,"** and so on—the daemon had not begun his dictation; in the later stories—among which **"The Man Who Loved Islands"** and **"The Fox"** are masterpieces—the daemon had either to be controlled or the story to lose its form as a story. In them Lawrence is still (and must be) obedient to one of his greatest gifts: that of narrative power, which in him is perhaps best described as the power of sustaining tension. Of that power, and its controlled use, **"The Fox"** and **"The Man Who Loved Islands"** are remarkable examples. In each such philosophy or moral as there is belongs to the bloodstream of the work, and is not a wild cloak flung on the body of it afterwards. And in each—and

here is an important distinction that must be drawn between the novels and the stories—the principal male figure is someone other than Lawrence himself. Lawrence is again and again the hero, the ego, of the novels (*The White Peacock, The Trespasser, Sons and Lovers,* and various others), but in the stories this is rarely true. Lawrence, for these short periods, proves capable of devoting his objective attention to someone else. True, these males are often despicable (the officer in **"The Prussian Officer"** or maliciously portrayed (the literary man in **"The Man Who Loved Islands"**), and have rarely that potent physical charm that characterizes Lawrence's own romanticized portraits of himself, but they are efforts, short but successful, in detached portraiture. That alone gives them a value which the novels often lack. They are impressed, but never oppressed, by the personality of their creator.

If Lawrence hated form and pretended to reject the idea of it in his own petulant way ("I won't"), it is nowhere obtruded, then, in the short stories. He proved amenable to whatever form the story imposed—long-short as in **"The Fox," "The Ladybird," "The Captain's Doll,"** and half a dozen others, or very short, as in **"Second Best," "Goose Fair," "The Christening,"** and others. Form here imposed on his genius the necessity for compression, and with fine results.

Clearly form was not Lawrence's primary contribution to the short story; nor, as with Katherine Mansfield, oblique narration; nor, as with Hemingway, a revaluation of style. Like Sherwood Anderson (with whom it is significant that he has often been compared) Lawrence turned his back on the conventionalized story in which most things hinged on artificially created problems or situations, and set to work to interpret his own people and the background of pit-heads, working-class houses, bluebell woods and hills, against which they lived. That, to Lawrence, must have seemed a very natural thing to do. Yet because Lawrence saw people as people his work was constantly stigmatized as shocking by the generation which had eagerly accepted the false and sadistic imperialism of Kipling and the scientific romancings of Wells. Yet Lawrence, being true to his own vision, will always be closer to life than either Kipling or Wells, and in that respect alone he set an example, as Anderson did in America, which a new decade of writers eagerly followed. Among the young short-story writers of 1940 you will find none, I think, who owe any important debt to Kipling or Wells; but you will find many who, as they depict the immediate life about them, have Lawrence to thank for the example. (pp. 201-03)

> *H. E. Bates, "Lawrence and the Writers of To-Day," in his* The Modern Short Story: A Critical Survey, *1941. Reprint by The Writer, Inc., 1949, pp. 194-213.*

GEORGE ORWELL   (essay date 1945)

[*An English novelist and essayist, Orwell is best known for his classic dystopian novel* Nineteen Eighty-Four *(1949). In the following excerpt from his review of* The Prussian Officer, and Other Stories, *Orwell asserts that Lawrence's talents are more suited to the short story than to the novel form.*]

[When, in 1924 or 1925, I got hold of *The Prussian Officer, and Other Stories,* both] **"The Prussian Officer"** and **"The Thorn in the Flesh"** impressed me deeply. What struck me was not so much Lawrence's horror and hatred of military discipline, as his understanding of its nature. Something told me that he had never been a soldier, and yet he could project himself into the atmosphere of an army, and the German army at that. He had built all this up, I reflected, from watching a few German soldiers walking about in some garrison town. From another story, **"The White Stocking"** (also in this collection, though I think I read it later), I deduced the moral that women behave better if they get a sock on the jaw occasionally.

Clearly there is more in Lawrence than this, but I think these first impacts left me with a broadly true picture of him. He was in essence a lyric poet, and an undisciplined enthusiasm for "Nature", i.e. the surface of the earth, was one of his principal qualities, though it has been much less noticed than his preoccupation with sex. And on top of this he had the power of understanding, or seeming to understand, people totally different from himself, such as farmers, gamekeepers, clergymen and soldiers—one might add coal miners, for though Lawrence himself had worked in the pit at the age of thirteen, clearly he was not a typical miner. His stories are a kind of lyric poem, produced by just looking at some alien, inscrutable human being and suddenly experiencing an intense imaginative vision of his inner life. How true these visions were is debatable. Like some Russian writers of the nineteenth century, Lawrence often seems to by-pass the novelist's problem by making all his characters equally sensitive. All the people in his stories, even those to whom he is hostile, seem to experience the same kind of emotions, everyone can make contact with everyone else, and class barriers, in the form in which we know them, are almost obliterated. Yet he does often seem to have an extraordinary power of knowing imaginatively something that he could not have known by observation. (pp. 31-2)

With few exceptions Lawrence's full-length novels are, it is generally admitted, difficult to get through. In the short stories his faults do not matter so much, because a short story can be purely lyrical, whereas a novel has to take account of probability and has to be cold-bloodedly constructed. In *The Prussian Officer* there is an extraordinarily good longish story called **"Daughters of the Vicar"**. An Anglican clergyman of the ordinary middle-class type is marooned in a mining village where he and his family are half-starved on a tiny stipend, and where he has no function, the mining folk having no need of him and no sympathy with him. It is the typical impoverished middle-class family in which the children grow up with a false consciousness of social superiority dragging upon them like a ball and fetter. The usual problem arises: how are the daughters to get married? The elder daughter gets the chance to marry a comparatively well-to-do clergyman. He happens to be a dwarf, suffering from some internal disease, and an utterly inhuman creature, more like a precocious and disagreeable child than a man. By the standards of most of the family she has done the right thing: she has married a gentleman. The younger daughter, whose vitality is not to be defeated by snobbishness, throws family prestige overboard and marries a healthy young coal miner.

It will be seen that this story has a close resemblance to *Lady Chatterley's Lover*. But in my opinion it is much better and more convincing than the novel, because the single imaginative impulse is strong enough to sustain it. Probably Lawrence had watched, somewhere or other, the underfed, downtrodden, organ-playing daughter of a clergyman wearing out her youth, and had a sudden vision of her escaping into the warmer world of the working class, where husbands are plen-

tiful. It is a fit subject for a short story, but when drawn out to novel length it raises difficulties to which Lawrence was unequal. In another story in this book, **"The Shades of Spring"**, there is a gamekeeper who is presented as a wild natural creature, the opposite of the over-conscious intellectual. Such figures appear again and again in Lawrence's books, and I think it is true to say that they are more convincing in the short stories, where we do not have to know too much about them, than in the novels (for example, *Lady Chatterley's Lover* or *The Woman Who Rode Away*), where, in order to be set into action, they have to be credited with complex thoughts which destroy their status as unspoiled animals. (pp. 32-3)

> George Orwell, "Review of 'The Prussian Officer and Other Stories' by D. H. Lawrence," in The Collected Essays, Journalism and Letters of George Orwell: In Front of Your Nose, 1945-1950, Vol. IV, edited by Sonia Orwell and Ian Angus, Harcourt Brace Jovanovich, Inc., 1968, pp. 30-3.

FRANK AMON (essay date 1953)

[*In the following excerpt from* The Achievement of D. H. Lawrence, *edited by Frederick J. Hoffman and Harry T. Moore, a collection of criticism that also includes essays by such noted figures as Aldous Huxley, James Thurber, Edmund Wilson, and Anthony West, Amons treats Lawrence's short stories, particularly "The Odour of Chrysanthemums," "The Prussian Officer," and "The Rocking-Horse Winner," as studies in the emotional and psychological states of his characters.*]

Lawrence, like Chekhov, stands for a distension in the form of the [short] story. Like Chekhov, he had the genius for portraying the intimate feeling of a place, a landscape, a conversation, or a character. Like Chekhov—but in a manner peculiar to his technique—he crystallized vacancy, frustration, inertia, and futile aspiration. We see that all of Lawrence's stories share one characteristic: all depend, as stories, upon subtle psychological changes of character.

With Lawrence's characters (as with Chekhov's) the subconscious seems to come to the surface and they communicate directly without the impediment of speech. Naturally the most interesting point for Lawrence is that at which the interplay of psychic forces is incomplete, where the adjustment is difficult, where the emphasis is on discord rather than on harmony. Consequently, Lawrence focused his attention, as Frederick Hoffman has said, "on the subtle complexity of an emotional state which a character assumes in a crisis."

The significance of this is that Lawrence has accomplished a transfiguration of experience. He lifts his characters from the surface experience of the concrete world onto new and immediate levels of psychic consciousness, and then returns them, sanctified and altered, to the concrete world in which they must continue. Inevitably this is the symbolic *rites de passage,* the ceremony or initiation or baptism, which ushers an individual into a new way of life; and in this, too, it is the spiritual death and rebirth motif of Lawrence's chosen symbol, the Phoenix.

If we take, for example, **"The Odour of Chrysanthemums,"** one of Lawrence's earliest stories, written in 1909, this *rites de passage* aspect comes out quite clearly.

The autobiographical setting of Lawrence's youth—the

lower-class colliery family—is of course common to many of his early stories and novels. But the theme, too, is central to Lawrence: the inviolable isolation of the individual psyche, the utter separateness of those with whom we share physical intimacy.

The revelation of the theme (of which for us the entire story is the qualifying and modifying symbol) comes to the wife through the death of her husband. Revelation through death then is the means of objectifying the theme. However, it is the *moment* of revelation with which we are concerned here and with the peculiar means of objectifying that moment.

Gradually, as the story unfolds, our interest in the chrysanthemums increases. At first, they hang dishevelled, "like pink cloths." A little later, Elizabeth's small son tears at the "ragged wisps of chrysanthemums" and drops the petals in handfuls along the path: " 'Don't do that—it does look nasty,' said his mother. He refrained, and she, suddenly pitiful, broke off a twig with three or four wan flowers and held them against her face." . . . [Later] Elizabeth's daughter wants to smell the flowers:

> "Don't they smell beautiful!"
>
> Her mother gave a short laugh.
>
> "No," she said, "not to me. It was chrysanthemums when I married him, and chrysanthemums when you were born, and the first time they ever brought him home drunk, he'd got brown chrysanthemums in his button-hole."

Here then is their significance: they are talismans of change, transition into a new way of life—a tragic way of life. They are markers of marriage, birth, and—inevitably—death. The chrysanthemums, we might say, are the omens, and it is through them that a great part of our interest is aroused and focalized; and it is through them (but not through them alone) that the father's death is foreshadowed. There is, however, a more subtle change than the physical death of the father. The dead man is brought in and laid out on the parlor floor. The wife and the husband's mother are present. The room is dimly lit by a single candle in a lustre-glass. Two vases of chrysanthemums exude a cold, deathly smell. Together the wife and mother strip the man naked and kneel on opposite sides to wash him of the pit grime. . . . Few readers will miss in this scene the obvious relation to a ceremonial preparation of the dead. For this ritual purification and consecration rite performed by the nearest kin has an archetypal significance. More specifically it resembles the ritual consecration of the archetypal parent, the father as the sacrificial King, the Fallen and Forsaken God.

It is significant, however, that Lawrence has chosen this symbolic enactment as the appropriate action to objectify the moment of inner revelation which comes across, it would seem, out of death; for as Elizabeth washes the dead body, she realizes the impregnable separateness of this man with whom she has been living as one flesh: "She had said he was something he was not; she had felt familiar with him. Whereas he was apart all the while, living as she never lived, feeling as she never felt." And she is "grateful to death, which restored the truth." It is the reversal of Donne's "No man is an island, entire of itself" to "*Each* man is an island, never fully known," a revelation through death of a mystery of life; and the living, as well as the dead, has undergone a transition: "She saw this

episode of her life closed." "Then with peace sunk heavy on her heart, she went about making tidy the kitchen."

Lawrence wrote this story when he was twenty-four; but he revised it five years later. We need not concern ourselves with the fact that Lawrence was reading Jane Harrison's *Ancient Art and Ritual* about the same time he was making his revision. What is important is that he could thoroughly incorporate into his art the most appropriate action—literal and symbolic—to objectify his theme.

We find incipient in this story such other patterns and motifs as the *Mater Dolorata,* possessive motherhood, lack of rapport between the sexes, and father-hatred-envy, which were to occupy Lawrence the rest of his life.

Lawrence developed rapidly as a writer, and his quickening command of form and subject matter is evident in his first six years of production. By the time he was twenty-five he had written one of the world's masterpieces of short fiction, **"The Prussian Officer."** Lawrence recognized its worth in a letter to Edward Garnett at the time: "I have written the best story I have ever done—about a German officer in the army and his orderly." It is this of course—and much more.

For the pattern of the Handsome Soldier and his tragic death has a mythic counterpart. It suggests that universal motif, the fable of the Fall of Man, the loss of Paradise. For the orderly is, on one level at least, Primal Man. Indeed, it is said of him that he seemed "never to have thought, only to have received life direct through his senses, and acted straight from instinct." (pp. 222-26)

If the orderly is the Adam of this Eden, the Captain is its Satan. Maleficent as he is, the Captain, like the arch-fiend in *Paradise Lost,* has a certain nobility of stature, an aura of the Fallen Prince about him ("He had ruined his prospects in the Army, and remained an infantry captain.") . . . In contrast to his orderly, he is a man completely "dominated by mind," a man of "passionate temper who had always kept himself suppressed." He had never married, for his position did not allow it, and "no woman had ever moved him to it." "Whereas the young soldier seemed to live out of his warm, full nature, to give it off in his very movements, which had a certain zest, such as wild animals have in free movement." And it is precisely this guileless nature that the Captain hates and tempts to action.

The Captain's predisposition to iniquity is innate in him, however, not the product of training or intellect but a trait hitherto repressed. It takes the form of an instinctive hatred for innocence and good, but a hatred so obsessive and even paranoid as to suggest the perversion of a still more deep-rooted love.

And if there are mythic overtones of the Biblical temptation and fall (the youth's limitations as a human being lead him to commit in fact a capital crime), there are also psychological undertones of homosexuality. For it is in effect the story of a courtship. From the first, the orderly feels that he is "connected" with the figure of the Captain—"and damned by it." While rubbing his Captain down, he admires the "amazing riding muscles of his loins." (pp. 226-27)

As for the Captain, he had "become aware of his servant's young, vigorous, unconscious presence about him." And it was like a "warm flame upon the older man's tense, rigid body." He is attracted to the youth's "strong young shoulders" and "the bend of his neck." We have the feeling throughout the story of a homosexual courtship: the older man, in spite of himself, wooing the younger; and the youth, sensing the advances, repudiating the Captain.

And with the soldier's denial, it becomes more difficult for the Captain to restrain himself: "As yet, the soldier had held himself off from the elder man. The Captain grew madly irritable. He could not rest when the soldier was away, and when he was present, he glared at him with tormented eyes. . . . he was infuriated by the free movement of the handsome limbs. . . . And he became harsh and cruelly bullying. . . ." And it would seem impossible to ignore this homosexual aspect in such a statement as "The officer tried hard not to admit the passion that had got hold of him. He would not know that his feeling for his orderly was anything but that of a man incensed by his stupid, perverse servant. So, keeping quite justified and conventional in his consciousness, he let the other thing run on."

Finally, the officer's passion culminates in an outburst of rage when the soldier in confusion ignores a question. As the orderly is crouching to set down a load of dishes before a stairway, the captain kicks him, sending the dishes tumbling; and as the soldier clings to the bannister pillar for support, the captain kicks him repeatedly. And afterwards, when the orderly confesses that he had been writing some poetry:

> "Poetry, what poetry?" asked the Captain, with a sickly smile.
>
> Again there was the working in the throat. The Captain's heart had suddenly gone down heavily, and he stood sick and tired.
>
> "For my girl, sir," he heard the dry, inhuman sound.
>
> "Oh!" he said, turning away. "Clear the table."

Here, on one level, is the Captain's realization that he can never succeed. The sinking of his heart and the curt dismissal of the orderly would seem to indicate his acknowledgment of a rival and the futility of the pursuit. In fact he erases the incident from his mind, denies it to himself—and is "successful in his denial."

With the soldier it is a different matter. He feels that he has been violated emotionally and physically, and he is filled with "one single, sleep-heavy intention: to save himself." The maneuvers are the following morning; and the combination of his bruises, the marching, the hot sun, and the violation of his inner self moves him—when he and the officer are alone—to attack the Captain and choke him to death. (pp. 227-29)

In one sense, this is a victory—a victory over and a release from the evil dominance of the Captain. But, in another sense, it is a capitulation, for this is what the orderly has been continuously fighting against. It is foreshadowed earlier in the story with the statement that "in spite of himself the hate grew, responsive to the officer's passion." And it is for this surrender to the Captain, as well as for the criminal act, that the orderly pays with his life.

I have postponed until now a consideration of the nature imagery in this story. For although it is intimately related to—and is in fact a part of—both the mythic and sexual patterns, it serves a wider and, if possible, more profound purpose. I refer specifically to the emotional significance of the valley-garden-mountain imagery which is wrought into the pattern of the story. . . . We perceive in terms of spatial contrasts the life of the body, down in the hot suffocating valley, challenged by the allurement of mountain heights. The contending opposites communicate a distinctive sense of the life of the earth in tension with the heaven of the spirit. The flux and heat of the soldier's sensuous experience—intoxicating and soporific—becomes at once a challenge and a bondage: a challenge because of the strange allurement of the mountain snows and a bondage or crucifixion because he cannot escape—or can escape only through death.

This theme—the conflict of the flesh and the spirit—is of course common to many of Lawrence's works, and the valley-mountain cluster with the same connotations can be found in such of his novels as *Women in Love* and *The Lost Girl*, in the poem "Meeting in the Mountains," and in the first pages of his travel essays (with a valuable commentary), *Twilight in Italy*.

In the story the theme becomes more and more explicit after the fateful beating. The orderly feels that the snowy peaks, radiant in the sky, and the "whity-green glacier river," in the valley below, seem almost supernatural, but at the same time he is going mad with fever and thirst. And near the end of the story, when he is in a delirium of fever, he sees "the mountains in a wonderlight, not far away and radiant. Behind the soft, grey ridge of the nearest range the further mountains stood golden and pale grey, the snow all radiant like pure, soft gold. . . . And like the golden, lustrous gleaming of the snow he felt his own thirst bright in him. And everything slid away." He remains in a state of delirium throughout the night, but in the morning, straight in front of him are the mountains: "He wanted them—he wanted them alone—he wanted to leave himself and be identified with them." And he does attain his realization—through death:

> There they ranked, all still and wonderful between earth and heaven. He stared till his eyes went black, and the mountains, as they stood in their beauty, so clean and cool, seemed to have it, that which was lost in him.

No one would suppose that the mythic, the psychological, and the image function separately, alternating perhaps from one level to the other like the negative and positive charges in a flow of electric current. One in fact *is* the other, and all operate more or less simultaneously while we follow the literal level. And we must never forget that the literal is there, for if it is not there, we have no story. It is important to note, however, that, regardless of levels of meaning, the distinctive characteristic is the flow and conflict of *opposites:* officer-soldier, aristocrat-peasant, evil-innocence, homosexual-heterosexual, mind-instinct, flesh-spirit, valley-mountain; and Freudians would see a father-son dichotomy. No one would suppose either that the complex of these three levels of meaning is *equivalent* to the story itself. In fact, I have ignored the social and political implications: the way in which the malady of the individual psyche can become the malady of modern civilization, the prostitution of the instincts by the perverted mechanized forces of the over-intellectualized world.

For the malady of the individual psyche reflecting the malady of modern civilization assumes various patterns in Lawrence's art. Paul, in *Sons and Lovers*, and Gerald, in *Women in Love*, depict different aspects of this theme. And in the story of Paul in **"The Rocking-Horse Winner"** Lawrence has adapted an age-old form to his subject matter.

"The Rocking-Horse Winner" is the story of Paul who secretly rides his rocking horse to pick winners in the horse races. Paul manages to win ten thousand pounds, five thousand of which he gives anonymously to his mother because she is "unlucky" and because the house whispers: *There must be more money!* His powers fail, however, and Paul becomes desperate and wild-eyed as the day for the big Derby draws near and he still does not know the winner. Finally, in the middle of the night, his mother finds him in a trance-like state furiously riding his rocking horse: "It's Malabar!" he screams. "It's Malabar!" and collapses in a brain fever. Paul is deliriously ill for three days, but on the third he learns that his horse has won, and he dies in the night, knowing that he *is* lucky. The tale ends with his uncle telling Paul's mother: "He's best gone out of a life where he rides his rocking-horse to find a winner!"

The allegorical implications of **"The Rocking-Horse Winner"** would seem evident in this last speech. More specifically, however, it has several characteristics common to the form of the fable or Märchen of folklore. Like the fable, it has two parts: the narrative which exemplifies a moral, and the statement of the moral appended in the form of a proverb. Moreover, the syntactical and rhetorical devices of the opening paragraph—"There was a woman who was beautiful, yet she had no luck. She married for love, and the love turned to dust."—exploit a formulaic beginning common to most Märchen, the characters not named, and some explanation concerning the cause of the difficulty which the story is to illustrate dramatically ("A King had a daughter who was beautiful beyond all measure, but so proud and haughty withal . . ."). And in fact the whispering house and the powers of divination ascribed to Paul (an ironic variation of the Rags-to-Riches motif through the supernatural powers of the first-born son) indicate to what extent Lawrence went to establish the tone and atmosphere of a modern moral fable.

The theme of the story is implied in the moral proverb that Lawrence invented: Don't ride your rocking horse to find a winner. The story illustrates the point. The mother realizes that she is unlucky, but she does not recognize the true reason as stated in the first paragraph: "At the center of her heart was a hard little place that could not feel love, no, not for anybody." She realizes that she is incapable of loving and that she is unlucky, but she does not equate the two in terms of cause and effect.

Instead she rationalizes the problem and tells Paul that they are the "poor members of the family" because his father has no luck. For she makes the common mistake of equating luck with money. Thus she tells Paul that luck is "what causes you to have money." Consequently, Paul is the victim, in a sense, of his mother's reasoning (a common pattern among Lawrence's heroes, with the subsidiary pattern of the father as scapegoat).

In reality, the family is not poor. They have a fine house and garden, servants and gardener; and the mother, as well as the father, has a small independent income. The fact is that each of them has expensive tastes and indulges them, for in spite of the shortage of money, "the style was always kept up."

The whole family is, in Lawrence's metaphor, riding its rocking horse to find a winner, riding furiously and fanatically and getting nowhere.

One also sees elements of the ritual dance in Paul's rocking-horse episodes. Lawrence of course knew the English morris and the Abbots Bromley Antler dance, both of which have hobby-horse riders. But more than likely he was remembering the famous hobby dance of Padstow, Cornwall or the New Mexican pueblos' saints' impersonations, called *maiyanyi*. But whatever Lawrence's source, his choice was a happy one. For the ritual riding of a hobbyhorse has a primordial depth and scope that extends into antiquity and throughout disparate cultures. In the Balinese *sanghang djanar,* for example, the rider—like Paul—rides in a trancelike state.

More fundamentally, the rocking horse (a "false" horse) is the perfect symbol to embody humanity's trancelike and mechanistic plunging onward to nowhere. Moreover, the choice of the rocking horse as the divining medium is psychologically sound. Divination is a form of sympathetic magic in which the *status* of the divining medium determines the future event. Both the indicator and the event are in a relation of logical harmony. And it is significant that the event divined, the horse race itself, is as appropriate a symbol as the rocking horse for mankind's materialistic and competitive race back to its point of departure. (pp. 229-33)

Lawrence has a special and unique contribution to offer in the art of the short story. I have not considered to any extent Lawrence's prose style, which serves its subject consummately. Rather I have dealt with his subject, the discovery under the social surface of more opulent realms of being.

For the effect of D. H. Lawrence's art, and it is also its value, is that it gives a new meaning to our experience. Lawrence's command of life, significant life, was such that we discover in his fiction a new content—an immediacy and relevance that was not previously perceived. An emotion with Lawrence is an apotheosis. Through its elemental and seminal processes of action it is a transition into another sphere of being, a *rite de passage*. And once having experienced this, a character is never quite the same. . . . Lawrence has captured this moment of transition, reinforced it with an emotionally charged symbol (chrysanthemums, valley-garden-mountain, rocking horse-horse race), and perpetuated it on the printed page.

Lawrence commanded his art so completely as to suggest less discipline than it had. There is in him an uninterrupted communication between his thought and his senses. This deceptive ease of style has contributed to a myth concerning his method of composition: that he preferred not—as most authors do when dissatisfied with what they have written—to file, clip, insert, and transpose . . . , but rather to rewrite entire new drafts straight off the pen in new bursts of spontaneity and intuition. (pp. 233-34)

This method attributed to Lawrence, however, has served several critics as a point of departure in attacking his "looseness" and "diffuseness." No doubt—like all great artists—Lawrence's first conception of an idea was involuntary, a "vital fortuity"; and perhaps his *first* drafts were written in bursts of spontaneity. But his revisions were certainly voluntary and meticulous.

My interpretations would argue that few artists could be more consciously and pertinently preoccupied with problems of method, technique, and form. (p. 234)

Frank Amon, "D. H. Lawrence and the Short Story," in The Achievement of D. H. Lawrence, *ed-*

ited by Frederick J. Hoffman and Harry T. Moore, University of Oklahoma Press, 1953, pp. 222-34.

F. R. LEAVIS (essay date 1956)

[*Leavis is an influential contemporary English critic whose methodology combines close textual analysis with predominantly moral and social concerns, emphasizing the development of "individual sensibility." The writer's role in Leavis's aesthetic vision is to eliminate "ego-centered distortion and all impure motives" from his or her work and to promote what Leavis calls "sincerity," or the realization of the individual's proper place in human society. Literature that accomplishes this he calls "mature," and the writer's judgment within such a work he describes as a "mature" moral judgment. Although Leavis's advocacy of a cultural elite, the vagueness of his moral assumptions, and his refusal to develop a systematic philosophy have alienated many scholars from his work, he remains an important, if controversial, force in literary criticism. In the following excerpt from his* D. H. Lawrence: Novelist, *a pioneering study of Lawrence's novels and short stories, Leavis presents a laudatory overview of the stories, commenting on several tales in terms of style, theme, tone, and subject matter and hailing the collective short fiction as "one of the major creative achievements of literature."*]

The range of [Lawrence's] tales, sure in touch and achievement as they are in all their various kinds—so convincingly right with so few exceptions—is immense. They constitute a body of creative work of such an order as would of itself put Lawrence among the great writers—not merely among the memorable, but among the great. (p. 307)

It is surprising how large a proportion of that first volume, published (to Lawrence's annoyance) as *The Prussian Officer,* is good. The title story and **"The Thorn in the Flesh"** are in an early Lawrence vein that he soon outgrew; sultrily overcharged, sensuously and emotionally, they seem to associate with *The Trespasser,* and, with all their unpleasant kind of power, they share essentially the same kind of immaturity as the negligible and more obviously immature **"A Fragment of Stained Glass."** But in that first volume too—the longest thing in it—is **"The Daughters of the Vicar."** The volume contains nothing else of the order of that masterpiece, but a great deal that goes very fittingly with it. **"A Sick Collier," "The Christening,"** and **"Odour of Chrysanthemums"** show Lawrence as the portrayer of the life he knew earliest, that of the miner's home. . . . [To render working-class life] in its distinctiveness (as he so incomparably does) is certainly Lawrence's preoccupation; but it is for him all the same just human life, and his attitude towards it differs in no way from his attitude towards human life anywhere, at any social level or in any conditions.

I have [elsewhere] . . . described that attitude as one of essential reverence, wholly unsentimental and unidealizing. The point of that description is enforced if we consider **"The White Stocking"** and think of Maupassant—consider it, say, along with two tales from *England, My England,* the next collection: **"Samson and Delilah"** and **"The Horse Dealer's Daughter."** The characters in **"The White Stocking"** are Elsie Whiston, a pretty, feather-brained incorrigible little work-girl flirt, her ordinary good-natured husband, and Sam Adams, his grossly bounderish employer, once hers too, who continues to send her presents which she accepts behind her husband's back because she can't resist them. It might seem that such matter was susceptible only of the lightest treatment, playing only for a lightly engaged response—the read-

er's interest to be one of superior, if not cynical, amusement. In Lawrence's actual treatment there is lightness right enough; but it is the lightness that registers a fulness of engagement in the writer. This for him is without qualification human life. It evokes, beyond any question, the free flow of his sympathetic consciousness; the lightness of the touch is the index, and is more remarkable than at first sight, perhaps, it is recognized to be. The success of the tale depends on our being made, as we are, to take the precisely right attitude towards the pretty, childish little coquette of a wife; one, that is, enabling us to sympathize with her husband's attitude towards her—to sympathize with it enough to see how a man we respect can be, and is, deeply attached to her. (And in our being made so positively to respect the steady, ordinary, good-natured Whiston we have a very significant power of Lawrence's art.) The play in Elsie Whiston of vanity, flirtatiousness, fear, defiance, and basic affection for her husband, on the one hand; and, on the other, the uneasiness of the even-tempered, wisely tolerant Whiston, rising to the ultimate eruption of anger, the blow on the mouth, and the decisive assertion of authority—there is no condescension in our interest in the drama. Whiston strikes his wife a blow on the mouth, but it is not a brutal view of life that we are given, but a positively and essentially humanizing one. (pp. 308-10)

What, to take the next instance, can any summary of **"Samson and Delilah"** suggest of the nature of that little tale? A summary here can tell nothing at all—it can only suggest falsely. A Cornish pub, a buxom middle-aged landlady, a party of billeted soldiers, a stranger who at closing-time says he is the landlady's husband and is going to stay, and whom, at the landlady's prompting, the soldiers, when he resists, tie up with her help and put outside, and who, a little later, comes in again through the unfastened door and is tacitly accepted as the husband, back after years of truancy—no elaboration can suggest what the tale actually is, and what interest it has for us. For its effect depends upon the working of vibrations, depths, and potencies—of psychic fields of force—that it takes a Lawrence to register. The actors have a deeper interest for Lawrence than, in such an affair, had we been the direct observers, they would have had for us, and the deeper interest is a richer human interest. This higher value, communicated to us, seems nevertheless to inhere implicitly and inevitably in the presented persons and facts, which, as we respond to them, we feel to belong to the ordinary life we know. The restored marital relations, part sensual attraction, part conflict, and part something else, between the returned tin-miner and the landlady of the village pub—we don't ask, at the end of the tale, why we should have been interested in them in this full, wholly uncondescending way. Nor, on the other hand, do we at all feel that the writer's art has brought off a *tour de force.*

When we come to **"The Horse Dealer's Daughter"** it is not so difficult to suggest, in description, the kind of thing it offers. And yet, the classical perfection of the tale in its simple human centrality is bound up with its remoteness from anything in the nature of cliché. There, at the opening of the tale, is the girl, isolated among her brutally egoistic brothers. . . . (pp. 310-11)

If we reflect how far from the spirit of Maupassant is this evocation of male brutality, we note too that there is no pathos of feminine charm or feminine helplessness about the girl. She is sullen, impassive, and, one would judge, well able to take care of herself. . . .

This absence of any obvious element of pathos conditions the intensity with which the fact of utter loneliness, the stark unendurable fact, is evoked. It *is* that fact which, with the extreme of economy, has been made present to us. . . . (p. 312)

It is remarkable how utterly without any touch of conventional pathos we are given her visit to the churchyard to tend her mother's grave. To the young doctor who by chance sees her there she "seemed so intent and remote, it was like looking into another world." The specific intentness and remoteness are conveyed with wonderful immediacy. The action in which they express their meaning, though it comes with a complete inevitability, comes still with its shock of surprise. The surprise is registered by the young doctor, when, again by chance, he sees her in the "thick, ugly falling dusk," across the sodden wintry field, enter the pond and walk slowly and deliberately, deeper and deeper, into the motionless water.

The doctor has his further surprise, one that makes us reflect how radically unlike (the unlikeness being his greatness) not only Maupassant but Eliot, Wyndham Lewis, Pound, and Joyce this writer is. The surprise is a complex one, and the complexity is conveyed with a compelling inevitability of truth that, in such a matter, one must recognize to be beyond the power of any but a very great writer. The unerring rightness of touch is, on reflection, hardly credible. There is the young woman lying, with newly recovered consciousness, in the ugly house to which the doctor has carried her back:

> Suddenly she sat up. Then she became aware of her own immediate condition. She felt the blankets about her, she knew her own limbs. For a moment it seemed as if her reason were going. She looked round, with wild eye, as if seeking something. He stood still with fear. She saw her clothing lying scattered.
>
> "Who undressed me?" she asked, her eyes resting full and inevitable on his face.
>
> "I did," he replied, "to bring you round." For some moments she sat and gazed at him awfully, her lips parted.
>
> "Do you love me, then?" she asked.
>
> He only stood and stared at her, fascinated. His soul seemed to melt.
>
> She shuffled forward on her knees, and put her arms round his legs, she stood there, pressing her breasts against his knees and thighs, clutching him with strange, convulsive certainty, pressing his thighs against her, drawing him to her face, her throat, as she looked up at him with flaring humble eyes of transfiguration, triumphant in first possession.
>
> "You love me," she murmured, in strange transport, yearning and triumphant and confident. "You love me. I know you love me. I know."

The horror of the young doctor—this, if it were all, would give us a situation that a number of writers might have imagined. But of course it is not all; **"The Horse Dealer's Daughter"** is a love-story—a story of the triumph of love and of life. For there is no irony (and, it must be added, no more sentimentality than irony): when the doctor finally answers "Yes" we have no doubt at all about his complete sincerity:

> "Yes." The word cost him a painful effort. Not because it wasn't true. But because it was too newly

true, the *saying* seemed to tear open again his newly-torn heart. And he hardly wanted it to be true, even now.

(pp. 312-14)

His unwilling response to her challenge is something profound and positive; it was prefigured in the impression made on him when he saw her at her mother's grave. The "portentous" eyes were intent on death, and death plays a major part in this story of the triumph of life. . . . (p. 314)

"The Horse Dealer's Daughter" is profoundly characteristic of Lawrence; it is at the centre of his treatment of the relations between men and women. For to speak of Lawrence as being preoccupied with "sex" is a wholly misleading emphasis. Maupassant deals in sex; T. S. Eliot in *The Waste Land* is preoccupied with sex; but Lawrence, for whom sex is a matter neither for disgust nor for cynical knowingness, and who hates "emancipation" (tough or sentimental) and reductive functionalism, is concerned always with the relations between individual human beings—the relations in all their delicate complexity. The actual variety of cases that he presents should surely be found very striking; he is an incomparable master of the field that has been supposed to be peculiarly the business of the novelist.

Against **"The Horse Dealer's Daughter"** may be set for contrast another tale in the same volume: **"You Touched Me."** One might be inclined to suggest the nature of the contrast by saying that the latter would hardly be called a love-story. Yet the question arises, getting its force when we think of the clear relation between this tale and **"The Fox":** if love is not the theme of **"You Touched Me,"** where does the boundary come between what *is* love and what is not? An attempted summary of the tale might suggest that Matilda Rockley was the victim of a callous league between the ruggedly perverse wilfulness of the Midlands "character," her father, and the calculating materialism of Hadrian, his adopted charity-boy son. But the way in which the actual tale differs essentially from anything that we could associate with Arnold Bennett is pointed to, of course, in the title. The touch of Matilda's hand in the dark, she having forgotten that her father no longer occupies *this* room, is what starts his interest in her. . . . (pp. 315-16)

We are made to feel at one and the same time the profound attraction (which is certainly not crudely and simply sexual) felt by him, and the incredibility to Matilda and her sister of any such thing in the small cocky charity-boy "mannie." It is the attraction that, felt by a man towards a woman, inspires him with the specific and deliberate conviction that he must marry her—that the fulfilment of his life depends upon his marrying her. . . .

When he proposes, Matilda and Emmie inevitably believe that what he wants is their father's money. (p. 316)

The surprise in the tale is the way in which Matilda does finally agree to marry him. It is true that the father, who is on his deathbed, tells her that if she doesn't, he will make a will leaving all his property to Hadrian. . . .

But, bad as is the shock produced by her father's threat, and unpleasant as is her situation, we are not allowed to suppose her simply forced into acceptance by material fears for herself or Emmie (Emmie vehemently urges defiance—"we can look after ourselves"). In however equivocal a way, there is something more subtle about the surrender. . . . (p. 317)

It is made plain that, in some way of which we cannot suppose her able to give a full account, Hadrian's argument and attitude—not his mere persistence, but the spirit and meaning of it—have told. The situation of the sisters, imprisoned in old-maidhood by class—"In a thorough industrial district, it is not easy for the girls who have expectations to find husbands"—has affinities with that of the girls in **"The Daughters of the Vicar."** In fact, Matilda and Emmie themselves, Matilda tall and graceful and "naturally refined and sensible," with the shorter and plumper Emmie looking up to her, have their clear recall of Mary and Louisa Lindley. But if Matilda's marrying Hadrian is most decidedly not the triumph of life figured in Louisa's resolute adhesion to her collier, neither is it the equivalent of Mary's marrying, for "safety," the little abortion. In the father's confident sense of things, Hadrian stands for life, and the marriage is the assurance of a living future; we know, without needing to be told in so many words, that essentially the dying man sees the dead end of old-maidhood in the Pottery House as a defeat of life. And we have been given too strong a sense of the symbolic value of the "square, ugly brick house girt in by the wall that enclosed the whole grounds of the pottery itself" to feel that old Rockley's interposition, his brutal assertion of will, is just the caprice of rugged masculine "character". . . . (pp. 318-19)

If the concluding "That's right! That's right!" is not, for the reader, the note of a happy ending, neither is it a pure irony. No simple judgment, no simple determination of the sympathies, is in place. Nor do we feel ourselves incited by the close to work out a sum of for or against by way of deciding whether Matilda chose on the whole rightly and her father did well, or whether the major truth is that she was cruelly compelled. What we do feel is the challenge to realize the full complexity presented, and the tale leaves us with a sharp sense of how much, to what rare effect, this is an art calculated to promote one's imaginative perception in the face of ordinary human life.

So, for that matter, does **"The Fox,"** which offers something different from that particular kind of complexity. It is a much longer tale, a good deal more than twice as long as **"You Touched Me,"** and goes in for other kinds of effect than those which depend on brevity of presentment and a wealth of undeveloped implication. Its strength lies—and it is one of the supreme things among the major tales—in the fulness, depth, and unambiguous clarity with which it presents its theme, the theme that bears so obvious a relation to that of **"You Touched Me."**

Instead of the two sisters marooned in the Pottery House, we have two land girls, March and Banford, committed, at nearly thirty, to making a life together on their isolated little farm. The nature of the miscalculation, the strain involved, and the impossibility (unrecognized by them) of success in any sense are fully conveyed to us before the supervention of the young man. Nothing goes right, and we see that nothing *can* go right: the misfortunes with heifers and fowls are only outward manifestations. In spite of March's protective devotion to Banford and Banford's affection for March, no vital flow goes into the joint enterprise; the farming cannot succeed, and no life they may make together can be really a life. (pp. 320-21)

Though March is the man of the two, she is nevertheless wholly a woman; "her eyes were big and wide and dark, when she looked up again, strange, startled, shy and sardonic at

once," and in the "something odd and unexplained about her" we recognize "unsatisfied tendencies" that no amount of time for hobbies or cycle rides can satisfy. The most striking thing about the tale is the way the fox is used to focus her characteristic "absent" state and reveal the significance of her oddities. (pp. 321-22)

The significance of [the fox's] possessing the "blank half of her musing" for weeks and months afterwards defines itself when Henry makes his appearance. Banford, when he has explained his arrival and been admitted, is "no more afraid of him than if he were her own younger brother," and gossips happily with him. But to March (who seized her gun when he made his entrance) he is the fox: "Whether it was the thrusting forward of his head, or the glisten of fine whitish hairs on the ruddy cheek-bones, or the bright keen eyes, that can never be said: but the boy was to her the fox, and she could not see him otherwise." (p. 322)

The strain involved in her life with Banford on the farm is symbolized for her by the search after the fox. It is also, without her distinguishing, at the same time the strain of keeping her mind sufficiently on the everyday business of the farm against the continual pull exercised by the fox in her profound "musing." The fox, of course, merely provided a focus for her "musing," and the significance of his doing so with such effect is not obscure. . . .

The whole fox motive in all its development is remarkable for its inevitability of truth and the economy and precision of its art. There are March's dreams. That which she has on the night of Henry's arrival (he is fair, we note, with whitish glistening down on his ruddy cheeks) comes before he has made any advances. . . . (p. 323)

The second dream, coming just after Henry has shot the fox, conveys with astonishing vividness and subtlety the emotional dilemma, the complication of her feelings, caused by her solicitude and fears for Banford, towards whom she has been the "man." The death of the fox has made a great impression, but in the dream the idea of death attaches, not to Henry, but to Banford; and, knowing "that it wasn't right, that this was not what she should have," it is in a fox-skin that she wraps her friend's dead body. . . . (p. 324)

It is such things that partly explain how the drama gets its emotional depth and dignity. These are very remarkable, seeing how unpromising the characters might seem to be. Banford, March, and Henry are all lower-middle-class and ordinary, with extremely limited powers of expression. Their speech hasn't the advantages of the vernacular that serves Lawrence so well in his working-class characters. That of the girls is just suburban—flat and uneducated in an elementary-school kind of way. It is perfectly got, and never transcended, for even March's "witless humour" that so puzzles Henry is merely silly and pointless. And yet there is nothing amused or ironical in the presentment of the characters. They are human beings—just human beings and fully human beings; and their emotional problems are seen as having a dignity and interest not lower than the highest we feel to inhere in our own. The tone of **"The Fox"** all the way through may be described as simply and overtly serious; there is in the tale no sardonic element and no irony. It illustrates Lawrence's range that not only **"The Ladybird,"** with its exalted incantatory mode, but also one of his best things, **"The Captain's Doll,"** the characters of which are upper-middle-class and aristocratic, and the tone of which has a flexibility corre-

A facsimile reproduction of the first page of the manuscript of Lawrence's story "The Fox" in its original version, apparently written late in 1919 at Middleton-by-Wirkswirth.

sponding to the range and resource of their speech, should have appeared in the same volume. (p. 325)

"Mother and Daughter" *is* sardonic comedy; but how much and how little that description says may be brought out by comparing the tale with *St. Mawr,* to which it bears so interesting a relation.

It is a very close relation—closer than that between **"You Touched Me"** and **"The Fox."** Mrs. Bodoin and Virginia *are* Mrs. Witt and her daughter, Lou Carrington. They are unmistakably the same persons, though Mrs. Bodoin (with more point) is Irish, a Fitzpatrick, instead of an American, and Virginia (who, like Lou, has a very slight and piquant cast in one of her brown eyes) earns her own living in the Civil Service as head of a department. The great difference between the two tales is the absence from **"Mother and Daughter"** of the stallion and what goes with him. It is a great difference of course. It means that **"Mother and Daughter"** is without the range, and without the marvellous flexibility of tone, for which *St. Mawr* is so notable. The sardonic comedy is there in *St. Mawr,* with so much else.

But the point can be made at once that, if in **"Mother and Daughter"** sardonic comedy hasn't those accompaniments, it is of a kind with which they have been demonstrated to be wholly reconcilable. And here we have one of the profits of comparing the two tales: it helps to explain the difference between Lawrence's ironic note everywhere and that of other writers who might seem to be practising the same kind of

thing. What is so remarkable about Lawrence's irony is that, astringent as it may be, it never has a touch of animus; never a touch of that egoistic superiority which makes the ostensibly comparable work of other writers seem cheap—so often cheap and nasty. The difference, one feels, is one of depth. What we notice is Lawrence's incomparable sensitiveness of touch and tone, and this, the juxtaposition of *St. Mawr* with **"Mother and Daughter"** suggests, is the index of the profound humanity that is implicitly present in the surface lightness. It brings home to us, this juxtaposition, how embracing and exquisitely sensitive is the organization engaged in the sardonic comedy of the latter.

The distinction of **"Mother and Daughter"** is that it exhibits its particular mode so perfectly: it keeps to its given limits and achieves perfection within them. Its range, of course, is less than that of *St. Mawr,* but not so much less as may appear at first sight, and the advantage it gains is the unquestionable, the immediately convincing, perfection. No doubt arises like that which puts itself when one has finished *St. Mawr:* would Lou Carrington really have maintained for long her heroic self-dedication to loneliness and the "wild spirit" of the region, "keeping to herself" on the "little wild ranch, hung right against the savage Rockies, above the desert"? The question throws no doubt on what goes before in the tale; it merely leads to reflections about the difficulty of bringing to a convincing close a work so boldly symphonic that, within so limited a compass, hazards so daring a scope. (pp. 346-47)

Lawrence has diagnosed a whole social setting, a representative mode of modern life. And that is always so, in his tales as in his novels: in Lawrence modern civilization has a student and analyst of incomparable range as well as insight. The personal problems and situations he presents are the problems and situations of persons with specific social contexts, and his presentations of individual lives have such force and reality because they are at the same time, and inseparably, studies of the society to which the individuals belong. (pp. 354-55)

[**"The Virgin and the Gipsy"**] is one of Lawrence's finest things and is itself enough to establish the author's genius as major. . . . The genius must be apparent to any reader in the ease and economy with which the rectory household is established; established in all its personal and physical actuality and its ethos. There it is for us, as it is for the two girls, returned from their finishing year at Lausanne. The rectory seems "almost sordid, with the dank air of that middle-class, degenerated comfort which has ceased to be comfortable and has turned stuffy, unclean." The family itself is life gone stagnant. As an ostensible social fact it is a decent, solid, self-respecting family, stronghold of soundness and moral stability, fronting the world with a natural and proper cohesion. What we see it to be in essential fact is a system of stagnation, maintained by fear of life, furtive self-love, and love of power. (pp. 362-63)

The tale is a tenderly reverent study of virginal young life. As such it seems to me unsurpassable, and it has certainly never been surpassed. The freshness, the inexperience, the painfully conscious ignorance, the confidence, and the need to believe in life are touchingly evoked. We have, beautifully done, the wisdom of the sisters' discussion of love and marriage; a wisdom that they have to assume in order to persuade themselves that they are not, as they are, wholly without bearings. There is no sentimentalizing of their very ordinary case; they are not represented as, in any obvious sense, anything but indulgently treated by their elders. . . . (pp. 366-67)

The most difficult achievement of the tale is yet to be mentioned. It is the most difficult to talk about. We have yet to consider Yvette's relation to the gipsy. The difficulty is not a matter of anything strange or abnormal about the relation: It is that the indispensable unambiguous precision is so hard to achieve: the terms to hand (a significant fact, bearing pregnantly on the essential difficulty of the achievement and its importance) are of so little use; the necessary definition required Lawrence's genius and the resources of his art. One can say that, for Yvette, the gipsy represents the antithesis of the rectory, with its base self-love, its fear of life, its stagnation, and its nullity. That, so far as it goes, is true. . . . (p. 367)

But the essential theme of the tale has nothing to do with Wraggle-taggle-gipsyism. It focusses in the look Yvette catches in the eyes of the gipsy, and the effect it has on her. The word one has to use is "desire." It is a necessary word, and Lawrence himself uses it, but it leaves, of course, a delicate work of definition to his art. The tale is concerned with defining and presenting desire as something pre-eminently real—"real," here, having its force in relation to the nullity of life at the rectory. (p. 368)

["The Virgin and the Gipsy"] is an achievement about which one can feel more unreservedly happy than about *Lady Chatterley's Lover*. The point of the comparison is perhaps plain enough. The latter is notorious, of course, for its hygienic undertaking in relation to the obscene vocabulary and the corresponding physical facts; but its essential aim commits it, for success, to the achievement of **"The Virgin and the Gipsy"**; that of disengaging unambiguously the fact, and the crucial significance, of desire—of indicating desire in the sense of compelling a clear and clean and reverent recognition. It may be that the offences against taste entailed in the hygienic enterprise can be justified on the plea of good achieved; but they remain—and must, I think, always remain—offences against taste. No such objection holds against **"The Virgin and the Gipsy."**

The thing is done there with a perfection of sensitiveness and tact. While there is not the faintest touch of sentimentality, a tender, reverent sense of the virginal quality of Yvette determines the tone. At the close there is the cool recognition that the affair (if it can be called an "affair") with the gipsy is no more than what it is—or, rather, has been (or *could* have been). . . . (pp. 369-70)

The thousand large pages of strong work [in the tales] not only contain their immense range of life and variety of art; the range and the variety give us a profound unity of creative purpose. Taken together, the tales represent one of the major creative achievements of literature. (p. 371)

F. R. Leavis, in his D. H. Lawrence: Novelist, *Alfred A. Knopf, 1956, 396 p.*

W. D. SNODGRASS (essay date 1958)

[*Snodgrass is a Pulitzer Prize-winning American poet whose collection* Heart's Needle (1959) *had a significant impact on the development of the "confessional" school of contemporary poetry. The essay excerpted below originally appeared in the* Hudson Review, *and was reprinted in* D. H. Lawrence: A Collection of Critical Essays, *which includes further criticism on*

Lawrence's short stories by Graham Hough, Mark Spilka, and Monroe Engel (see later excerpt dated 1958). Here Snodgrass illuminates the symbolic structure of "The Rocking-Horse Winner," discussing various levels of meaning and interpretation.]

"The Rocking-Horse Winner" seems the perfect story by the least meticulous of serious writers. It has been anthologized, analyzed by New Critics and force-fed to innumerable undergraduates. . . . Yet no one has seriously investigated the story's chief structural feature, the symbolic extensions of the rocking-horse itself, and I feel that in ignoring several meaning-areas of this story we ignore some of Lawrence's most stimulating thought.

Though the reach of the symbol is overwhelming, in some sense the story is "about" its literal, narrative level: the life of the family that chooses money instead of some more stable value, that takes money as its nexus of affection. The first fault apparently lay with the mother. The story opens:

> There was a woman who was beautiful, who started with all the advantages, yet she had no luck. She married for love, and the love turned to dust. She had bonny children, yet she felt they had been thrust upon her, and she could not love them . . . at the center of her heart was a hard little place that could not feel love, not for anybody.

We never learn much more about her problems, about *why* her love turned to dust. But the rhyming verb *thrust* is shrewdly chosen and placed; knowing Lawrence, we may well guess that Hester's dissatisfaction is, at least in large part, sexual. We needn't say that the sexual factor is the sole or even primary cause of her frigidity, but it is usually a major expression and index of it, and becomes causal. Lawrence wrote in an amazing letter to John Middleton Murry:

> A woman unsatisfied must have luxuries. But a woman who loves a man would sleep on a board. . . . You've tried to satisfy Katherine with what you could earn for her, give her: and she will only be satisfied with what you *are*.

There could scarcely be a more apt description of Hester's situation. As for her husband, we cannot even guess what he *is;* he gives too few clues. Failing to supply the luxuries that both he and his wife demand, he has withdrawn, ceased to exist. The one thing he could always give—himself, the person he is—seems part of a discarded currency. The mother, the father, finally the boy—each in turn has withdrawn his vital emotions and affections from commitment in and to the family. Withdrawing, they have denied their own needs, the one thing that could be "known" and "sure." They have, instead, committed their lives to an external, money, and so to "luck," since all externals are finally beyond control and cannot be really known. Thus, it is Paul's attempt to bring an external into his control by knowledge which destroys him. It is a failure of definition.

The father's withdrawal, of course, leaves a gap which encourages Paul in a natural Oedipal urge to replace him. And money becomes the medium of that replacement. So the money in the story must be taken literally, but is also a symbolic substitute for love and affection (since it has that meaning to the characters themselves), and ultimately for sperm. We know that money is not, to Paul, a good in itself—it is only a way to win his mother's affection, "compel her attention," show her that *he* is lucky though his father is not. That money has no real use for Hester either becomes only too clear in that crucial scene where Paul sends her the birthday present of five thousand pounds hoping to alleviate her problems, relax the household, and so release her affections. His present only makes her colder, harder, more luxurious. . . . The mother and father have driven themselves to provide the mother with what she, actually, needs least. And she has squandered it, one would guess, precisely to show her scorn for it and for the husband who provides it. Money as a symbolic substitute has only sharpened the craving it was meant to satisfy; the family has set up a vicious circle which will finally close upon Paul.

As several critics have noted, the story resembles many well-known fairy tales or magical stories in which the hero bargains with evil powers for personal advantages or forbidden knowledge. These bargains are always "rigged" so that the hero, after his apparent triumphs, will lose in the end—this being, in itself, the standard "moral." Caroline Gordon and Allen Tate sum up their interpretation [in *The House of Fiction* (see Further Reading list)]: "the boy, Paul, has invoked strange gods and pays the penalty with his death." Robert Gorham Davis goes on to point out that many witches supposedly rode hobby-horses of one sort or another (*e.g.,* the witch's broom) to rock themselves into a magical and prophetic trance. When he rides, Paul's eyes glare blue and strange, he will speak to no one, his sisters fear him. He stares into the horse's wooden face: "Its red mouth was slightly open, its big eye was wide and glassy-bright." More and more engrossed in his doom as the story progresses, he becomes "wild-eyed and strange . . . his big blue eyes blazing with a sort of madness." We hear again and again of the uncanny blaze of his eyes until finally, at his collapse, they are "like blue stones." Clearly enough, he is held in some self-induced prophetic frenzy, a line of meaning carefully developed by the story. When Paul first asserts to his mother that he is "lucky," he claims that God told him so. This seems pure invention, yet may well be a kind of *hubris,* considering the conversation that had just passed with his mother:

> "Nobody ever knows why one person is lucky and another unlucky." "Don't they? Nobody at all? Does nobody know?" "Perhaps God. But He never tells."

Whether Paul really believes that Gold told him so, he certainly does become lucky. And others come to believe that superhuman powers are involved. Bassett thinks of "Master Paul" as a seer and takes an explicitly worshipful tone towards him. He grows "serious as a church" and twice tells Uncle Oscar in a "secret, religious voice. . . . 'It's as if he had it from heaven.' " These hints of occultism culminate in Uncle Oscar's benediction:

> "My God, Hester, you're eighty-odd thousand to the good, and a poor devil of a son to the bad. But poor devil, poor devil, he's best gone out of a life where he rides his rocking-horse to find a winner."

So, in some sense, Paul *is* demonic, yet a poor devil; though he has compacted with evil, his intentions were good and he has destroyed only himself. At first metaphorically, in the end literally, he has committed suicide. But that may be, finally, the essence of evil.

It is clear, then, that the story is talking about some sort of religious perversion. But *what* sort? Who are the strange gods: how does Paul serve them and receive their information? We must return here, I think, to the problem of knowledge and intellection. Paul is destroyed, we have said, by his desire to "know." It is not only that he has chosen wrong ways of knowing or wrong things to know. The evil is that he *has* chosen to know, to live by intellection. Lawrence wrote, in a letter to Ernest Collings:

> My great religion is a belief in the blood, the flesh, as being wiser than the intellect. We can go wrong in our minds. But what our blood feels and believes and says, is always true. *The intellect is only a bit and bridle.* What do I care about knowledge. . . . I conceive a man's body as a kind of flame . . . and the intellect is just the light that is shed on to the things around. . . . A flame isn't a flame because it lights up two, or twenty objects on a table. It's a flame because it is itself. And we have forgotten ourselves. . . . The real way of living is to answer to one's wants. . . .

(I have italicized the bit and bridle metaphor to underscore an immediate relationship to the rocking-horse of the story.)

Not one member of this family really knows his wants. Like most idealists, they have ignored the most important part of the command *Know thyself;* and so cannot deal with their most important problem, their own needs. To know one's needs is really to know one's own limits, hence one's definition. Lawrence's notion of living by "feeling" or "blood" (as opposed to "knowledge," "mind" or "personality") may be most easily understood, perhaps, as living according to what you *are,* not what you think you should be made over into; knowing yourself, not external standards. Thus, what Lawrence calls "feeling" could well be glossed as "knowing one's wants." Paul's family, lacking true knowledge of themselves, have turned their light, their intellect, outward, hoping to control the external world. The mother, refusing to clarify what her emotions really *are,* hopes to control herself and her world by acting "gentle and anxious for her children." She tries to be or act what she thinks she should be, not taking adequate notice of what she is and needs. She acts from precepts about motherhood, not from recognition of her own will, self-respect for her own motherhood. Thus, the apparent contradiction between Hester's coldness, the "hard . . . center of her heart," and, on the other hand, "all her tormented motherhood flooding upon her" when Paul collapses near the end of the story. Some deep source of affection has apparently lain hidden (and so tormented) in her, all along; it was her business to find and release it sooner. Similarly, Paul has a need for affection which he does not, and perhaps cannot, understand or manage: Like his mother, he is trying to cover this lack of self-knowledge with knowledge about the external world, which he hopes will bring him a fortune, and so affection.

Paul is, so, a symbol of civilized man, whipping himself on in a nervous endless "mechanical gallop," an "arrested prance," in chase of something which will destroy him if he ever catches it, and which he never really wanted anyway. He is the scientist, teacher, theorist, who must always know about the outside world so that he can manipulate it to what he believes is his advantage. Paradoxically, such knowledge comes to him only in isolation, in withdrawal from the physical world, so that his intellect may operate upon it unimpeded. And such control of the world as he can gain is useless because he has lost the knowledge of what he wants, what he is.

This, then, is another aspect of the general problem treated by the story. A still more specific form of withdrawal and domination is suggested by the names of the horses on which Paul bets. Those names—like the names of the characters—are a terrible temptation to ingenuity. One should certainly be wary of them. Yet two of them seem related to each other and strongly suggest another area into which the story's basic pattern extends. Paul's first winner, Singhalese, and his last, Malabar, have names which refer to British colonial regions of India. (A third name, Mirza, suggests "Mirzapur"—still another colonial region. But that is surely stretching things.) India is obviously one of the focal points of the modern disease of colonial empire; for years Malabar and Singhalese were winners for British stockholders and for the British people in general. The British, like any colonial power or large government or corporation, have gambled upon and tried to control peoples and materials which they never see and with which they never have any vital physical contacts. (Lawrence's essay "Men must Work and Women as Well" is significant here.) They have lived by the work of others, one of the chief evils of which is that their own physical energies have no outlet and are turned into dissatisfactions and pseudo-needs which must be filled with more and more luxuries. And so long as they "knew," placed their bets right, they were rich, were able to afford more and more dissatisfactions. A similar process destroyed Spain: a similar process destroyed Paul.

Though these last several areas of discussion are only tenuously present, most readers would agree, I think, that the rocking-horse reaches symbolically toward such meanings: into family economy and relations, into the occult, into the modern intellectual spirit, into the financial and imperial manipulations of the modern State. But surely the sexual area is more basic to the story—is, indeed, the basic area in which begins the pattern of living which the rocking-horse symbolizes. It is precisely this area of the story and its interpretation which has been ignored, perhaps intentionally, by other commentators. Oddly enough, Lawrence himself has left an almost complete gloss of this aspect of the story in his amazing, infuriating, and brilliant article, "Pornography and Obscenity." There, Lawrence defines pornography not as art which stimulates sexual desire, but rather as art which contrives to make sex ugly (if only by excluding it) and so leads the observer away from sexual intercourse and toward masturbation. He continues:

> When the grey ones wail that the young man and young woman went and had sexual intercourse, they are bewailing the fact that the young man and the young woman didn't go separately and masturbate. Sex must go somewhere, especially in young people. So, in our glorious civilisation, it goes in masturbation. And the mass of our popular literature, the bulk of our popular amusements just exists to provoke masturbation. . . . The moral guardians who are prepared to censor all open and plain portrayal of sex must now be made to give their only justification: We prefer that the people shall masturbate.

Even a brief reading of the essay should convince one that Paul's mysterious ecstasy is not only religious, but sexual and onanistic. That is Paul's "secret of secrets." Just as the riding of a horse is an obvious symbol for the sex act, and "riding" was once the common sexual verb, so the rocking-horse stands for the child's imitation of the sex act, for the riding which goes nowhere.

We note in the passage quoted above that Lawrence thinks of masturbation chiefly as a substitute for some sort of intercourse. . . . This is one of several doctrinal points where the reader will likely disagree with Lawrence. Nonetheless, the idea was prevalent at the time of writing and is common enough today that most men probably still think of masturbation chiefly as a sex substitute. And like the money substitute mentioned before, it can only famish the craving it is thought to ease. So we find another area in which the characters of the story don't know what they need; another and narrower vicious circle.

The tightening of that circle, the destruction of Paul, is carefully defined; here, one feels both agreement with Lawrence's thought and a strong admiration for his delineation of the process:

> . . . He went off by himself, vaguely, in a childish way, seeking for the clue to "luck." Absorbed, taking no heed of other people, he went about with a sort of stealth, seeking inwardly for luck.

Stealth becomes more and more a part of Paul. We hear again and again of his secret, his "secret within a secret," we hear his talk with Uncle Oscar:

> "I shouldn't like mother to know I was lucky," said the boy.
>
> "Why not, son?"
>
> "She'd stop me."
>
> "I don't think she would."
>
> "Oh!"—and the boy writhed in an odd way—"I *don't* want her to know, uncle."

We may quote here a passage from "Pornography and Obscenity":

> Masturbation is the one thoroughly secret act of the human being, more secret even than excrementation.

Naturally, any act accompanied by such stealth is damaging to the personality and to its view of itself. It involves an explicit denial of the self, a refusal to affirm the self and its acts (an imaginative suicide) and consequently a partial divorce from reality. But this is only part of that same general process of isolation. In the essay, Lawrence says:

> Most of the responses are dead, most of the awareness is dead, nearly all the constructive activity is dead, and all that remains is a sort of a shell, a half empty creature fatally self-preoccupied and incapable of either giving or taking. . . . And this is masturbation's result. Enclosed within the vicious circle of the self, with no vital contacts outside, the self becomes emptier and emptier, till it is almost a nullus, a nothingness.

And this is the process dramatized by the story. Paul draws back from his family, bit by bit, until he becomes strange and fearful to his sisters and will speak to no one, has grown beyond the nurse and has no real contact with his parents. Even Uncle Oscar feels uncomfortable around him. Finally he has moved his rocking-horse away from the family and taken it with him "to his own bedroom at the top of the house."

Lawrence believes that man's isolation is an unavoidable part of his definition as a human being—yet he needs all the contact he can possibly find. In his essay on Poe [in *Studies in Classic American Literature*], Lawrence writes:

> Love is the mysterious vital attraction which draws things together, closer, closer together. For this reason sex is the actual crisis of love. For in sex the two blood-systems, in the male and female, concentrate and come into contact, the merest film intervening. Yet if the intervening film breaks down, it is death. . . .

> In sensual love, it is the two blood-systems, the man's and the woman's, which sweep up into pure contact, and almost *fuse*. Almost mingle. Never quite. There is always the finest imaginable wall between the two blood waves, through which pass unknown vibrations, forces, but through which the blood itself must never break, or it means bleeding.

Sex, then, is man's closest link to other human beings and to the "unknown," his surest link into humanity, and it is this that Paul and his family have foresworn in their wilful isolation. And this isolation is more than physical. Again in "Pornography and Obscenity," we find:

> The great danger of masturbation lies in its merely exhaustive nature. In sexual intercourse, there is a give and take. A new stimulus enters as the native stimulus departs. Something quite new is added as the old surcharge is removed. And this is so in all sexual intercourse where two creatures are concerned, even in the homosexual intercourse. But in masturbation there is nothing but loss. There is no reciprocity. There is merely the spending away of a certain force, and no return. The body remains, in a sense, a corpse, after the act of self-abuse.

To what extent Lawrence thinks this reciprocity, this give and take, to be physical, I am not sure; I *am* sure it could easily be exaggerated. Lawrence makes a sharp distinction between the physical and the material. At any rate, it seems to me that the most important aspect of this sexual give-and-take is certainly emotional and psychological and that the stimulus which enters in sexual intercourse lies in coming to terms with an actual sexual partner who is real and in no wise "ideal." Thus, such a partner will afford both unexpectable pleasures and very real difficulties which must be recognized and overcome. But in masturbation these problems can be avoided. Most psychologists would agree that the most damaging thing about masturbation is that it is almost always accompanied by fantasy about intercourse with some "ideal" partner. Thus, one is led away from reality with its difficulties and unpredictable joys, into the self and its repetitive fantasies. This may seem rather far from the story, but I suggest that this explains the namelessness of the rocking-horse. (It also, of course, suggests shame and is valuable in manipulating the plot.) The real partner has a name which is always the same and stands for a certain configuration of personality with its quirks and glories; the fantasy partner, having no personality, has no name of his or her own but is given the name of such "real" partners as one might wish from week to week.

These, then, are the gods which Paul has invoked. This sexual problem gives, also, a startling range of irony to the religious texture of the story. The "secret within a secret . . . that which had no name" comes to be not only the shame of Paul's masturbation, but also a vicious and astounding parody of the "word within a word"—that which cannot be named. It should be clear from the material already quoted, and even more so from a reading of "Pornography and Obscenity,"

that it is popular religion—Christian idealism—that Lawrence is attacking, for it supports the "purity lie" and leaves masturbation as the only sexual expression, even at times openly condoning it. The strange gods are the familiar ones; the occult heresy is popular Christian piety.

It is not clear, however, how Paul receives knowledge from his onanistic gods. Lawrence himself does not pretend to know *how* this comes about, he only knows that it does exist:

> The only positive effect of masturbation is that it seems to release a certain mental energy, in some people. But it is mental energy which manifests itself always in the same way, in a vicious circle of analysis and impotent criticism, or else a vicious circle of false and easy sympathy, sentimentalities. This sentimentalism and the niggling analysis, often self-analysis, of most of our modern literature, is a sign of self-abuse.

This momentary release of energy is, I take it, equivalent to finding the name of the "winner" in the story. Thus the two great meaning-streams of the story, intellection and masturbation, relate. Masturbation stands as the primary area: the withdrawal and stealth, the intellectual participation in the physical, the need to know and magically control the external, the driving of the self into a rigid, "mechanical gallop," the displacement of motive, the whole rejection of self, all begins here. And the pattern, once established, spreads, gradually infecting all the areas of life, familial, economic, political, religious. Here, again, the reader may feel a doctrinal disagreement, suspecting that masturbation is more symptomatic than causal. Such disagreement scarcely touches the story, however, whose business is not to diagnose or cure, but to create a vision of life, which it does with both scope and courage.

I want to quote finally, one more passage from the essay "Pornography and Obscenity" to round off the argument and tie up some loose ends, and also simply because of its value, its sincerity. It is a kind of summation of the story's meaning and opens with a sentence roughly equivalent to Uncle Oscar's judgment: "he's best gone out of a life where he rides a rocking-horse to find a winner":

> If my life is merely to go on in a vicious circle of self-enclosure, masturbating self-consciousness, it is worth nothing to me. If my individual life is to be enclosed within the huge corrupt lie of society today, purity and the dirty little secret, then it is worth not much to me. Freedom is a very great reality. But it means, above all things, freedom from lies. It is, first, freedom from myself; from the lie of my all-importance, even to myself; it is freedom from the self-conscious masturbating thing I am, self-enclosed. And second, freedom from the vast lie of the social world, the lie of purity and the dirty little secret. All the other monstrous lies lurk under the cloak of this one primary lie. The monstrous lie of money lurks under the cloak of purity. Kill the purity-lie and the money-lie will be defenseless.

> We have to be sufficiently conscious, and self-conscious, to know our own limits and to be aware of the greater urge within us and beyond us. Then we cease to be primarily interested in ourselves. Then we learn to leave ourselves alone, in all the affective centres: not to force our feelings in any way, and never to force our sex. Then we make the great onslaught on the outside lie, the inside lie being settled. And that is freedom and the fight for freedom.

There are few more courageous statements in our literature. (pp. 117-26)

> W. D. Snodgrass, "A Rocking-Horse: The Symbol, the Pattern, the Way to Live," in D. H. Lawrence: A Collection of Critical Essays, *edited by Mark Spilka, Prentice-Hall, Inc., 1963, pp. 117-26.*

MONROE ENGEL (essay date 1958)

[*The essay excerpted below originally appeared in the* Hudson Review *and was reprinted in* D. H. Lawrence: A Collection of Critical Essays, *which includes further criticism on Lawrence's short stories by Graham Hough, Mark Spilka, and W. D. Snodgrass (see earlier excerpt dated 1958). Here Engel assesses the recurring styles, themes, and devices of Lawrence's long stories, focusing on his use of analogy.*]

Lawrence's short novels are a special and sustained achievement belonging roughly to the last decade of his life. It is of course not clear at precisely what point the long story becomes the short novel, but with **"The Fox"** (1918-19; revised and lengthened in 1921), not only does Lawrence write a story that is appreciably longer than his earlier stories (about three times the length of **"The Prussian Officer,"** for example), but he establishes certain themes—and, more peculiarly, certain patterns and devices for vivifying these themes—that become generic for his longer stories.

"The Fox" is written in a markedly objective style verging on irony, or a kind of satire with only the mutest comedy. The elastic fluency of the style also allows direct seriousness, even earnestness. The opening pages describe a peculiar state of disorder suggested by the facts that the two girls in the story are known by their surnames; that March, who had "learned carpentry and joinery at the evening classes in Islington," was "the man about the place"; and that on the farm, nothing prospers: the heifer gets through the fences, and the girls sell the cow—not insignificantly—just before it is to calf, "afraid of the coming event." The fowls are drowsy in the morning, but stay up half the night; and the fox carries them off at will. All in all, the girls "were living on their losses, as Banford said," and they acquired a "low opinion of Nature altogether."

This detailing of disorder is perhaps overdone, labored, and some other elements in the story seem too insisted on also—a kind of heaviness from which the subsequent short novels do not suffer. For March—who is obviously from the first the more restive and savable of the two girls—the fox represents an escape from her present deadening life, an escape conceived in increasingly sexual terms. "Her heart beats to the fox," she is "possessed by him." Then, when the young man appears, he is at once seen in foxy terms. (p. 93)

The analogy is intentionally overt from the beginning. Lawrence says of the boy that "to March he was the fox"; and once March says to him: "I thought you were the fox." The effect then comes not from a hidden analogy suddenly bursting on the reader's consciousness with the force of discovery, but from the detailed accumulation of the analogy, supported by Lawrence's genius for the description of nature and animals. (p. 94)

The boy's fox-likeness matters—given Lawrence's beliefs—in ways other than simply his vital quickness, or his sexual splendor. There is also "always . . . the same ruddy, self-contained look on his face, as though he were keeping himself to himself." The essential concerns in this story are more nearly simply sexual than in the later ones, but even here this self-contained boy says: "If I marry, I want to feel it's for all my life." And part of his claim to March is that there can be more permanence for her in a relationship with him than in one with Banford. The permanent marriage of two self-contained people is close to Lawrence's ideal.

For of course here as elsewhere, Lawrence is trying to render imaginatively what the relationship between the sexes is and might be, and the contest—between the boy and Banford—for March, is a contest that appears repeatedly, though in various guises, in Lawrence's work: a contest in which the new kind of lover must win the still neutral beloved from the claims of the old kind of love. Banford and March are held together by the old kind of love. Whether that love is also abnormal is largely beside the point. It is not simply that March encases her soft flesh in manly dress for Banford, and shows it in female dress for the boy Henry—though this simple device has enormous and, once more, overt effect in the story. It is rather that March feels responsible for Banford's health and happiness and well-being, and feels safe and sane with her. Sanity and over-responsibility are the marks, in all the short novels, of the old love. It was from these self-destroying feelings that March "wanted the boy to save her."

With Henry—who kills Banford to free March for himself—she feels something else. The story is at its weakest in these final pages, expanded in Lawrence's 1921 revision, which attempt to get at what the nature of the new kind of relationship between man and woman will be. Lawrence, who wished to write social and prescriptive fiction, felt a responsibility to substantiate the better world he preached . . . Each of Lawrence's short novels has this kind of visionary finale, but they become increasingly successful.

"The Captain's Doll" (1921) is in a similarly objective style, with the author detached even from the proponents of his thesis. But there is less bent of irony this time than of wonder, for **"The Captain's Doll"** is peculiarly a story about beauty. Again, the meaningful working of the story depends on an overt analogy—between Captain Hepburn and the doll portrait that Hannele makes of him, but doesn't make him into. For this time the analogy is a kind of anti-analogy—the doll is what Captain Hepburn must not become: "any *woman,* today," the Captain says, "no matter *how* much she loves her man—she could start any minute and make a doll of him. And the doll would be her hero; and her hero would be no more than her doll."

All the short novels make heavy use of analogy. This is the only one, however, in which the analogy is to an inanimate object, and the inanimate fixedness of the doll limits its range of usefulness. The use it has, though, is exact and startling, and is at least inherent in the first unseemly appearance of the doll, flourishing head downwards.

Again, as in **"The Fox,"** the story starts with disordered relationships, and the action concerns the choice a neutral person, Hannele, must make between conventional love and a new kind of relationship. But the choice as posed here is more complicated and rich than in **"The Fox."** For one thing, conventional love is given formidable and deeply attractive proponents in Mitchka, the Regierungsrat, and Mrs. Hepburn, who has, in her husband's account of her at least, a quality of out-of-the-world or primitive magic that will recur in the subsequent short novels as a quality reserved for certain adherents of the new order only. Also, the new kind of relationship is suggested more exactly and coherently in **"The Captain's Doll"** than it was in **"The Fox,"** and is less simply sexual.

The dramatic acceptability of the doctrine in this story depends on its being given dramatic validity, rather than being merely sermonized as at the end of **"The Fox."** It comes too from the substantial impressiveness of Hepburn as a character, and from his and the author's nearly painful sense of the pull and attractions of the old ways, and particularly of the mortal painfulness of beauty (as in the bathing scene in Section xiii). And on the lake, at the very end of the story, we even get a flash of what the life of Hepburn and Hannele may be together, united in this new kind of marriage.

In **"The Ladybird"** (1921-22), Lawrence told Middleton Murry he had "the quick of a new thing." The "quick" lies chiefly in the character of the Bohemian Count Dionys, who is a resurrected man in a more intellectual, varied, and charming way than Hepburn. Dionys, of course, is purposefully named; but he is the magic Pan, not the vulgar Bacchus.

Again the objective style verges on irony, but this time it is a grave kind of irony, as seen in the opening description of Lady Beveridge. The style is subtle, the exact weight of meaning unfixed. Nothing but such complex fluency of style could make the scenes between Daphne and Count Dionys—and particularly the climactic scene in Count Dionys' bedroom—convincing, and free from any air of the ludicrous.

Again—as in the two previous stories—there is a contest for the neutral soul: the soul of Lady Daphne. But the forces in this contest are not in each case single figures. Lady Beveridge and Basil are a team—the fully civilized or naturally repressed characters, bound to the old civilized kind of selfless love. This is in contrast to Lord Beveridge and Lady Daphne, who are *un*naturally repressed—repressed, that is, in opposition to their own natures. With Lord Beveridge, the repression is nearly final, despite his choleric intransigence and personal integrity. But with Daphne it is not yet final. Even her body cannot accept it, is in disorder, as shown by the tendency to tuberculosis from which she suffers when under stress—a tendency, of course, that Lawrence also had, and which he seems often to have attributed to social causes, to his inability to find a healthy moral atmosphere in which to live. The character who has thrown off civilized repression, the other principal in the contest, is of course Count Dionys.

Perhaps the most remarkable scene in the active contest is the long debate on love between Count Dionys and Basil, the champion of conventional love, who has told Daphne that his love for her now is a sacrament, and that he considers himself an eager sacrifice to her, and could happily die on her altar. These champions of different attitudes toward love carry on their debate with Daphne sitting between them, finding it "curious that while her sympathy . . . was with the Count, it was her husband whose words she believed to be true." So the schism between her mind, educated to repression, and that other part of her which suffers under this repression, is made dramatically clear. It is an indication of the energy of the ideas and the fluency of the style, that this almost formal debate is always dramatic, never abstracted from the situation, and never tedious—even as is the nobly ludicrous debate between Hepburn and Hannele on the bus in **"The Captain's Doll."**

Again animal analogy is important in the story—principally the ladybird analogy from which it gets its title. The ladybird, on the crest of Count Dionys' family, is, he thinks, a descendant of the Egyptian scarab. This leads to a deceptively casual and not quite open exchange:

> "Do you know Fabre?" put in Lord Beveridge. "He suggests that the beetle rolling a little ball of dung before him, in a dry old field, must have suggested to the Egyptians the First Principle that set the globe rolling. And so the scarab became the creative principle—or something like that."
>
> "That the earth is a tiny ball of dry dung is good," said Basil.
>
> "Between the claws of a ladybird," added Daphne.
>
> "That is what it is, to go back to one's origin," said Lady Beveridge.
>
> "Perhaps they meant that it was the principle of decomposition which first set the ball rolling," said the Count.
>
> "The ball would have to be *there* first," said Basil.
>
> "Certainly. But it hadn't started to roll. Then the principle of decomposition started it." The Count smiled as if it were a joke.
>
> "I am no Egyptologist," said Lady Beveridge, "so I can't judge."

The analogy between Count Dionys and this usefully destructive ladybird is admirably clear. (pp. 94-7)

Again the resurrection to a new way is not easy, not a trick, but a painful, chastening separation of the self from the accustomed world and—most painfully, and for Daphne particularly—from its surface beauties. Yet at the end of **"The Ladybird,"** the reader is convinced that he has glimpsed in Daphne and Dionys some special capacity possessed neither by the other characters in the story, nor by himself.

In *St. Mawr* (1924) the objective style is at times a style of high comedy, and particularly when Mrs. Witt is on scene. Again, of course, the story depends on a central analogy—stressed by the title—between a human being and an animal. But the horse St. Mawr defines Rico not by similarity but by contrast. In this way, the analogy is something like that in **"The Captain's Doll."** Once more the analogy is entirely overt, and is suggested or anticipated well before the horse even appears, in a horsey description of Rico in the second paragraph. Rico is all fraudulent play, never the real thing (Mr. Leavis has pointed to the significance of his playing at being an artist). Even his sexuality is bogus. His marriage with Lou is "a marriage . . . without sex"; and so there is brutal irony in the circumstance that he wears a ring, sent him by a female admirer, bearing a "lovely intaglio of Priapus under an apple bough." What Lou requires—and Rico is not at all—is a Dionys, the Pan of the dinner table conversation with the painter Cartwright.

The only men in the story who are at all Pan-like are Phoenix and Lewis, the two grooms, and Phoenix doesn't quite make it either. Lewis, however, is the real thing. He and St. Mawr both avoid physical contact with women because—presumably, and as he says—modern women are incapable of the proper and necessary respect for their husbands. Again part of the real creative accomplishment of the story is that it can make ideas and notions that we might resist or find absurd out of context, convincing and moving in context. This is particularly true of the long conversation between Lewis and Mrs. Witt during the crosscountry ride they take together to save St. Mawr. The ride culminates with Lewis's refusal of Mrs. Witt's offer of marriage; but before this offer, which ends all exchanges between them, Lewis has shown himself another of the Lawrence characters endowed with otherworldly magic. Mrs. Witt, who in her relations with every other man she ever knew had "conquered his country," feels that Lewis looks "at her as if from out of another country, a country of which he was an inhabitant, and where she had never been." And this magic property is given simpler demonstration by Lewis's naive, stubborn, but only partially credulous talk about falling-stars and ash-tree seeds and the people of the moon. When he sees a falling-star, Lewis thinks to himself: *There's movement in the sky. The world is going to change again. They're throwing something to us from the distance, and we've got to have it, whether we want it or not.*

St. Mawr is an ambitious story. In the disaster in which St. Mawr is disgraced, he is the figure of unrepressed man ridden by repressed man, Rico. The accident occurs, not fortuitously, when the horse shies at a dead snake. And— supporting the same suggestions—this precipitates for Lou an overwhelming vision of evil.

The magic and visionary qualities emerging through all the preceding short novels, dominate the middle and end of *St. Mawr*. The very end—the description of the deserted mountain ranch in the American Southwest—is a vision of the potential and possibility that Lawrence in his more optimistic thoughts about America considered it to possess. Lou Witt is not saved here, but is to be brought—possibly—to the condition that precedes any radically new life, a kind of exalted waiting, without sexuality or, really, any connection with other human beings. Lewis and St. Mawr—who has finally found his mate in a long-legged Texas mare: a touch that surely fails to add to the seriousness of the story—drop out before the end, and Phoenix, too, is in effect disposed of. The final pages—marred only at times by Lawrence's preachy vein—give an affecting picture of the beauty and effort of man's attempt to bring order into chaos. And we have here again the Shelleyan attempt to envision with some concreteness the condition abstractly prescribed.

"The Man Who Died" (1927) is entirely visionary and miraculous. Here the objective style is more formal, to help convey the quality of myth, and again analogy is important. At first Lawrence had called the story "The Escaped Cock"—a title that accentuates the analogy, as do the titles of the other short novels. As usual, the overt import of the analogy requires no expounding.

The theme of the resurrected man (and the Pan-Christ) had occurred in several of the other short novels, in different degrees of importance. Dionys is a resurrected man, coming back to life after being near death, and after considering himself dead and wishing his death. So too is Captain Hepburn in "The Captain's Doll." In *St. Mawr*, Lou Witt—writing to her mother—says she wishes no more marriages, and understands "why Jesus said: *Noli me tangere*. Touch me not, I am not yet ascended unto the Father. . . . That is all my cry to all the world." And this, of course, is the repeated cry of the man who had died.

It is unnecessary, here, to outline Lawrence's sexual prescrip-

tions. But clearly of great moment in this story are the reverential and respecting wonder between the man and the priestess, and that they know and need to know so little about each other, thus retaining a kind of inviolate personal integrity. Nor is anything like mere sexuality being invoked—not, for example, the slavish sexuality of the slaves. And once more, the extraordinary beauty of the narrative, often gratuitous to its immediate intent, prevents import from becoming anything so meagre as doctrine.

These stories have a richness and intricacy—purposeful, and also nearly accidental virtues—that summary cannot suggest. What should be suggested is the achievement not only of form—which often appears to be lacking in the long novels of the same period—but of something very close to formula. There is a bold repetition—often with increasing evidence of intention—of certain elements, principally: the objective and fluent style; analogy—generally animal analogy; disordered relationships; the opposition of traditional love and a new kind of relationship between the sexes, dramatized by a contest between these forces for a neutral beloved; the use of magic; and the visionary ending, associated with the emergent theme of resurrection, and given final importance in "The Man Who Died." Altogether, these short novels constitute an extraordinary body of imaginatively realized thesis fiction. (pp. 97-100)

Monroe Engel, "The Continuity of Lawrence's Short Novels," in D. H. Lawrence: A Collection of Critical Essays, *edited by Mark Spilka, Prentice-Hall, Inc., 1963, pp. 93-100.*

FREDERICK R. KARL   (essay date 1959)

[*Karl is an American critic who has written extensively on Joseph Conrad. His* Joseph Conrad: The Three Lives *(1979) is generally considered the standard biography, and his monumental* American Fictions, 1940-1980: A Comprehensive History and Critical Evaluation *(1987) is noted for its treatment of such experimental writers as William Gaddis, Thomas Pynchon, and John Hawkes. The following is excerpted from an essay first published in* A D. H. Lawrence Miscellany, *an impressive gathering of material on Lawrence that includes criticism by John Middleton Murry, Kingsley Widmer, Katherine Mansfield, Richard Aldington, A. Alvarez, and Harold Bloom. In this piece, Karl assesses strengths and weaknesses in "The Man Who Loved Islands," a work he considers representative of Lawrence's fiction.*]

"The Man Who Loved Islands," while succinctly presenting important aspects of Lawrence's doctrines, also suggests criteria by which to judge his craftsmanship. It is apparent that Lawrence's most notable artistic successes often occurred in the short story or novella, and that his long novels, although significant and genuine, frequently overstate, repeat, or stress the obvious, excesses not nearly so prevalent in his work in shorter form. "The Prussian Officer," for example, with its control and pungency, is perhaps Lawrence's supreme artistic achievement. Though without making equal claim for "The Man Who Loved Islands," one can rank it artistically with "The Rocking-Horse Winner," "Daughters of the Vicar," "The Fox," and "England, My England," many of whose virtues and vices it also shares.

The most evident, and surely the most destructive, weakness in the story is caused by Cathcart himself. Too much a symbol and too little a person, Cathcart, like many of Lawrence's other villains the author evidently detests, lacks substance and dimension. Lawrence could not overcome the personal problem of the author who must make an essentially negative character come to life despite his obvious soullessness. Cathcart illustrates Lawrence's point too explicitly, and he only exists or stands for something in the author's mind. Lawrence, who could frequently bring objects and people brilliantly to life, cannot make Cathcart flesh and blood. In this connection, one should, to evaluate Lawrence's shortcomings, compare the islander with Conrad's Heyst (in *Victory*), another "islander" who also lacks will and the desire to "relate" himself in human contact, and yet a character fully human. If we carry the comparison one step further and measure Flora against Lena, we can see that Lawrence as well abstracted a woman, while Conrad, although not entirely successful, was able to create the semblance of a woman trapped by circumstances. In Lawrence, the small personal touches which occasionally bring Clifford Chatterley to life while also chastising him are here missing, and with them all possibility of artistic objectivity.

The prose itself, in places evocative and inevitable in its aptness, whips and lashes sarcastically about Cathcart; so even the style further diminishes the islander's stature and makes him like a captive rat running a maze devised by the author. This "trapped" quality is found in several passages:

> The Master pursed his own flexible mouth in a boyish versatility, as he cleverly sketched in his ideas to the other man, and the bailiff made eyes of admiration, but in his heart he was not attending, he was only watching the Master as he would have watched a queer, caged animal, quite without sympathy, not implicated.

Cathcart has no "extension" values; Lawrence is always catching and ridiculing him, playing with him, as if disallowing all foibles, all vanity: "The Master went for a short cruise in his yacht. It was not really a yacht, just a little bit of a thing." Moreover, not satisfied with destroying Cathcart's world, Lawrence toys repeatedly, puppet-master-like, with Cathcart's feelings. . . . (pp. 273-74)

Attacked and hedged in by Lawrence's sarcasm and invective, Cathcart cannot achieve normal stature, nor less tragic dimension. His flaws are too obvious, his decline too rapid, and his absurdity continually underscored by the author's relentless attack. These faults in Cathcart's presentation are characteristic of Lawrence's work in general—rarely indeed do his "tragic" stories contain tragic characters. The tragedy, rather, is in the conflict implicit in Lawrence's view of the world, *not* in his characters as they relate to the world. Lawrence, as suggested, lacked the objectivity that would provide freedom for his characters and without freedom, their problems often become more frustrating than tragic, and his fiction in this respect comes closer to doctrine than to art. When, for example, Lawrence has sketched in the *mystique* of the island's past as a place of "priests, with golden knives and mistletoe; then other priests with a crucifix; then pirates with murder on the sea," he turns to Cathcart: "Our islander was uneasy. He didn't believe, in the daytime, in any of this nonsense." Cathcart's prosaic nature must, under Lawrence's assault, reveal its antipathy for poetry, for anything, in fact, that extends beyond immediate self-gratification. All nature and all Lawrence are bracketed against Cathcart; it is no wonder that like Gerald Crich, Clifford Chatterley, and other similar emotional cripples, he cannot survive.

That **"The Man Who Loved Islands"** does succeed despite Cathcart's ineffectiveness and thinness is a tribute to Lawrence's powers of description in evoking a world of waste and decline. This story conveys a "logical" situation that remains under firm control from the opening evocation of the island as a place where in early spring "the little ways and glades were a snow of blackthorn, a vivid white among the Celtic stillness of close green and grey rock, blackbirds calling out in the whiteness their first long triumphant calls." Whenever pastoral elements are summoned, Lawrence asserts his genius for bringing even rock to life; conversely, whenever Cathcart appears, the style loses its grace and becomes sarcastic and charged with hatred. (pp. 274-75)

As soon, however, as Lawrence temporarily forgets Cathcart, he brightens perceptively, and, so too, the prose suggests the silence and majestic isolation of the island.

> Followed summer, and the cowslips gone, the wild roses faintly fragrant through the haze. There was a field of hay, the foxgloves stood looking down. In a little cove, the sun was on the pale granite where you bathed, and the shadow was in the rocks. Before the mist came stealing, you went home through the ripening oats, the glare of the sea fading from the high air as the fog-horn started to moo on the other island. And then the sea-fog went, it was autumn, the oatsheaves lying prone, the great moon, another island, rose golden out of the sea, and rising higher, the world of the sea was white.

As an artistic device, the white sea of course foreshadows the vast whiteness which sweeps in upon Cathcart on his third island. Whiteness, as Lawrence uses it, is both reality and illusion: real when it becomes Cathcart's destroyer, illusory when it is the pure whiteness of his "creamy-white serge" that physically distinguishes his figure from the workers. Whiteness enters again when Cathcart dreams of perfectibility—he has white hopes, which can never be realized by an imperfect person. Whiteness, finally, is the color of Cathcart's pure soul, which makes everything he does "automatic, an act of will, not of true desire." Therefore, that whiteness should destroy Cathcart is the paradox of the innocent being slaughtered as the result of their own purity, not despite it. For purity, to Lawrence, is self-denying, life-negating, unless it is purity tempered by the fires of living human contact. The snow, then, like the white sea and moon, is symbolic of Cathcart's own lifelessness; it nullifies his existence and buries him in a tomb of endless desirelessness. (p. 276)

Cathcart becomes Lawrence's classic statement of what has gone wrong with civilized man in the twentieth century. Cathcart, Lawrence claims, is really the *best* the century has to offer, like Egbert of **"England, My England"**; yet how incomplete and frail he is! Withal his intelligence, fairness, notions of democracy, even resiliency—the true Englishman in his virtues—he lacks Soul, the Female part that would complete him. It is not enough for Lawrence that Cathcart does not hurt anyone else; his type of passivity destroys the individual himself. Rather, Lawrence implies, that Cathcart were less fair and less "English" if he were able to realize himself by being a living person.

This side of Lawrence has been noted by several critics who have interpreted his ideas on individuality and found them non-democratic, dangerously aristocratic, socially unacceptable. But Lawrence was neither sociologist nor politician and certainly not a significant philosopher; fervent, sensitive, perhaps a little mad when he saw his ideas frustrated or circumvented, he tilted at windmills in his futile idealism. Therefore, Cathcart and his kind must be exposed, for they are the so-called "good" people of this world who are destroying it. Not fortuitously, Lawrence's villains are rarely bad people; their villainy destroys only themselves, rarely others. The "others," like Flora, escape because they are sufficient. Moreover, Lawrence's heroes are frequently unappetizing, for they are too busy saving themselves to be agreeable. Consequently, Lawrence does not seem pleasant or sympathetic even to the serious reader; his earnestness led to dissatisfaction, not to propitiousness. In these terms, the irony of Cathcart's demise is doubled, for he *is* pleasant, *is* amiable, *is* just. Yet because his money has given him a kind of power which he misuses, Lawrence must destroy him before his type becomes powerful.

In this story, all of Lawrence's fears and hopes come together; it is a true microcosm of his work, an epitaph on *The Rainbow, Women in Love, The Plumed Serpent,* and a forerunner of *Lady Chatterley's Lover,* whose ideas it almost entirely encompasses. Still, its artistic virtues are greater than these novels, although it retains in small the defects common to all of Lawrence's work. For this man who preached individuality and self-fulfillment could not, ironically, stop imposing his will on his own characters even if it meant crushing them and destroying their dramatic effectiveness in the process. (pp. 278-79)

> Frederick R. Karl, "Lawrence's 'The Man Who Loved Islands': The Crusoe Who Failed," in A D. H. Lawrence Miscellany, *edited by Harry T. Moore, Southern Illinois University Press, 1959, pp. 265-79.*

KINGSLEY WIDMER (essay date 1962)

[*In the following excerpt from his* The Art of Perversity: D. H. Lawrence's Shorter Fictions, *Widmer traces Lawrence's "negative ways to his affirmations" in "The Prussian Officer" and "The Man Who Loved Islands," focusing on Lawrence's notion of salvation through annihilation.*]

A legion of moralists tells us that the Western sensibility suffers from a crisis of values. For some time, our literature and thought have exposed, and often espoused, varieties of anguished nihilism. Depending on which school of despair one studies in, the history of that peculiar suffering starts with willful egotism's destruction of the medieval synthesis, or with science and skepticism's fragmentation of feeling and thought in the seventeenth century, or with revolutionary rationalism's undermining of myth and style during the Enlightenment, or with the industrial revolution's atomization of organic community and human relatedness, or with violent ideologies' deification of the arbitrary and the absurd in the postromantic present. We need not argue here which is the true and proper history for a world "gone to pot," but only note the tacit agreement as to the death of the "old idols" and the painful revelations of subconscious, subatomic, subhuman, and other subterranean powers and desires. Nihilism, at a number of levels, provides an essential focus—one at least to go through, if not remain in—if we wish to recognize our time, our place, and ourselves.

D. H. Lawrence, I hope to show, confronted much of that nihilism, and he attempted to make from it a dialectic simultaneously of destruction and of salvation. In his most intriguing

works, his sardonic tales, nihilism often seems to be the one preoccupation and informing spirit. Elsewhere, the spirit of destruction seems more oblique, with Lawrence displaying the very nihilism he is angrily denying. Put another way, the primary insights and arts of his work reveal themselves in images and gestures that insist on the annihilating, wayward, rebellious, demonic, and contumacious. A number of previous commentators on Lawrence have properly noted these peculiarities, although not, I think, in sufficient depth to give the perversity its full significance. In reading the immense criticism on Lawrence, one comes to feel that it proclaims a moral line, with those who condemn Lawrence and his perversity on one side, and on the other side those who praise him and deny his perversity. In contrast, I shall treat the perversity as matter for praise, as an authentic mode with excellent aesthetic possibilities and considerable human wisdom. (pp. 3-4)

Some of the shorter fictions will show more exactly than Lawrence's frequently suggestive but angry and obsessive arguments the insights premised on the longing for annihilation. Two stories centering on a death agony—one early and one late work—will suggest the paradigmatic knowledge of extremity. **"The Prussian Officer"** is a pre-World War I tale, written in Lawrence's early manner of sensuous elaboration of a melodramatic episode. In the simple plot, a young peasant orderly hates his superior officer, a sadistic Captain; he rebels, kills the officer, flees, and dies in his flight. The concluding scene of the officer and the orderly "together, side by side, in the mortuary" emphasizes the obvious irony of similarity in death for warped authority and desperate rebel.

The story is usually commented upon as a revelation of Prussian militarism and, with some niggling by genteel critics, as showing an exploratory concern with homosexual sadism. This seems true enough, although hardly sufficient. Covert homosexuality is a major element in Lawrence's fictions. (There appears to be very little acknowledgment of it in Lawrence's statements, other than a general recognition of the significance of sexual warpings and a repulsion to inverts.) The Captain is actually a full-drawn example: he dislikes women, is moved "like a warm flame" by the nearness of the youth's body, develops a "deep" and "undiscovered" physical interest in the youth, becomes obsessed with a scar on the youth's hand, tries to stop the youth from having anything to do with a girl, flies into jealous rages, tries to hide "the passion that had got hold of him," obtains "intense gratification of his passion" by brutally beating the youth's posterior, and so on. The very brutality of the aristocratic officer produces in the peasant orderly a personal emotion that is quite new, and "he felt at once a thrill of deep pleasure and shame." Despite his conscious wish to remain innocent of both fascination and hatred, the youth is trapped in the "chaos of sensations" that characterizes the Lawrencean lover and the extremity of alienating experience. His new emotions separate him from his fellows until he feels that there "were only two people in the world." This is the world of love and hate, which tests one's deepest nature.

There is something more than homosexuality here. The sexual sadism of the officer-servant relation rests on the covert sexual basis of all authority, but the narration emphasizes the subjective change in the youth as his innocence loses contact with home, fellows, sweetheart, obedience, and certainty. Forced to the extremity of feeling, the youth's rebellion becomes gratuitous murder. The "passion of relief" with which he chokes the Captain to death and his solicitude for the destroyed body have strong sexual elements, but the revenge is subordinate to his loss of purpose and inversion of reality. The image of authority is dead, but one-fourth of the literal narrative remains to explore the subjective abyss of simple innocence as well as the unresolvable fatality that always marks the confrontation of Innocence and Authority—the antitype of tragedy.

A sensitive reading must account for the style and metaphoric order of the work as well as for the psychology and archetypal pattern of action and character. (pp. 6-8)

From the beginning of the story, Lawrence's vivid sense of place and physical sensation shows a metaphoric heightening that will later be crucial. The repeated "on and on" toward the cool mountains—the "heaven" in the youth's mind—points the direction of escape from his burden of hatred; the violated innocent longs to get away from the passion and pain of the "dull hot diagram" of life and reach nothingness. (p. 8)

At almost all points Lawrence's style insists that we be aware of the relation of person and natural scene, and it is his aesthetic as well as his metaphysical principle that everything in life must be "one living *continuum* with all the universe." After the young soldier has been carried away from normal life into the extremes of love and hate, only the image of authority has any relation to him. When he kills that he loses his last relation to the living universe. He no longer desires "to save himself"; and "nothing . . . could give him back his living place in the hot, bright morning." Thus, all reality is lost: he is "disembowled, made empty, a shadow creeping under the sunshine." He was only his passion; with that dead he is in a "blackish dream." The very ripeness of the summer scene, maintained from the opening paragraph of the story, turns to dissolution: "The air was too scented, it gave no breath. All the lush green-stuff seemed to be issuing its sap, till the air was deathly, sickly with the smell of greenness." The human order dissolves with the natural order. A Dostoyevskean aloneness is his greatest pain: "He would not have minded anything, but he could not get away from the sense of being divided from the others." (p. 9)

To be the existentialist outsider, to be completely in the beyond of pure existence, is the most profound state of subjectivity and awareness, but it is also fatal. Wandering in the forest, the youth achieves a vision of wonder and magical knowledge: " . . . thick-golden light behind golden-green glitterings, and darkness further off, surrounding him, growing deeper. He was conscious of a sense of arrival. He was amid the reality, on the real, dark bottom." In the flight from the horror of injured innocence, the youth has found what the idealists call the "really real"—nothingness. There is one final image of light and longing, three times repeated—the snowy mountains with which the story opened. . . . The ecstasy of identification with the mountains continues the next morning:

> There, straight in front of him, blue and cool and tender, the mountains ranged across the pale edge of the morning sky. He wanted them—he wanted them alone—he wanted to leave himself and be identified with them. They were still and soft with white gentle markings of snow. Finally, in his death throes, he stared at the gleaming mountains. There they ranked, all still and wonderful between earth and heaven. He stared until his eyes went black,

and the mountains as they stood . . . so clean and cool, seemed to have it, that which was lost to him.

The guilty longing for the ultimate beauty, innocence, and purity beyond life becomes the annihilation of life. (p. 10)

Many years later, and after many other violent and amoral parables of the limits of experience, Lawrence is still using the same thematic crux and image, but the subjects are more sophisticated, the form more logical, and the style less sensuous and more sardonic. The fatal flaw becomes idealism, instead of innocence; and the dangerous force is escape, instead of authority. The flight into annihilation of **"The Man Who Loved Islands"** forms one of Lawrence's most precise fictions. It suggests syllogistic organization—three actions, three islands. On the first and largest island the hero is "the Master"; on the second and middling sized island he becomes the ordinary—and trapped—man; and on the third and smallest island his own logic and the elements master him. He who is a master of men is also a man, and therefore mastered.

The story opens with the detached tone of the fable: "There was a man who loved islands." Then comes a brief sketch of the "superior" Englishman, by birth and nature an islander in all the connotations of withdrawal into private means, Englishness, and rationalized sensitivity. He finds his native isle too complex and too crowded, and so he "wanted an island all his own . . . a world of his own." But the desire for a pure and private world has a hidden destructiveness, and on his very first island the hero begins to learn the metaphysical "danger of becoming an islander." Alone, one is liable to be cut off from the flux of tangible life and thrown back into the "dark mystery of time." The hero, with the usual idealist's naïveté about a man's inner company, learns that withdrawal into the simple self brings forth complex fears from the unconscious; and he is haunted by nightmarish images of violence and sacrifice.

The rationalist escapes from primitive solitude by way of an ideal community. The man who loved islands creates a willed utopia, mostly of employees, in which he wants everyone to be happy and "the little world to be perfect." "But," says the mocking narrator, "anyone who wants the world to be perfect must be careful not to have any real likes or dislikes. A general good will is all you can afford."

The mode of the Lawrencean fable is usually statement, followed by a brief action commenting upon the statement. General benevolence must confront the tangible desires that it obscures but does not eradicate. The crux, once again, is authority: the goodness of "the Master" merely breeds his own "egoism"; this in turn raises the defensive "malice" of the "servant." Authority masked as virtue, power that pretends to be benevolent, creates the personal deceit and the general destructiveness of rebellion that becomes "symbolic of the island." The atmosphere of the island utopia is to be found in its symbolic tone—the Lawrencean "spirit of place"—not on its rational surface. The Master's benevolent plans increasingly rely on economic prudence, but neither benevolence nor bookkeeping will stop the cow from falling over the cliff. Nor can rational goodness and authority produce the desires that create human community. The sensitive Master admits defeat when confronted with the breakthrough of the covert self, the subterranean and primitive past, which is always discounted in principles of benevolence and of rational social order. . . . The benevolent rationalist has been defeated by the covert malignity of place, principle, and self; and the utopian island—with typical Lawrencean sarcasm—is sold as a resort for honeymooners.

The second island, his next alternative, provides the sensitive and intelligent man a withdrawal into the purity of private life (Anglo-Saxon practical idealism). This small island has no past, no community, no economic purpose except simple comfort and quiet living. In his small house with a couple of servants, he is now "mister" instead of "master." Simplicity, solitude, study (a compendium of classical flower references), and an end to ambition, benevolence, and rational and social pretension make the hero safe. "The island was no longer a 'world.' It was a sort of refuge."

Purely private life creates a sort of harmony and he is "without desire, without *ennui*." But a lingering doubt of self-consciousness raises a question: "Is this happiness?" He answers himself: "I feel nothing, or I don't know what I feel." Lawrence thus shows that such harmony can hardly be distinguished from mental and emotional stupidity. But the actual world remains to belie tricks of consciousness. The needs of the body rather than the needs of the rational mind this time defeat the man who loved islands. Out of "a kind of pity," he becomes the lover of the girl who waits on him, and then realizes that his own abolition of will is not enough. He wills nothing, and so becomes the girl's lover because "*she* willed it." The assertion of willed order brought failure on the first, utopian, island; the negation of will brings failure on the second, escapist, island. Manipulation of the *will* as such simply won't do.

The man who loved islands is, however, a Lawrencean who explicitly believes that sex is "one of the great life mysteries." Like Lawrence, he also believes in the quiescence of sexual desire. Yet in the story the escape to a "stillness of desirelessness"—a typical Lawrencean tumor of phrasing that mars an otherwise lean prose—leads to the trap of sexual "automatism." Apparently willed benevolence and willed escape have sapped some essential quality of being, so that the Lawrencean belief is inadequate for Lawrence's hero. He wishes, later, to transform his relation to the girl, but somehow has not the strength to combat the usual female who wants dependence rather than desire, selfish submission rather than the integrity of passion. He dutifully marries the pregnant girl; and the independent man now has an island peopled by a wife, a daughter, a mother-in-law, and a nurse. In the comfort of matriarchy, in a "refuge" that has turned to the fatuousness of a "suburb," all selfhood and desire become burdensome, even "nauseous." Here we see Lawrence's diagnostic image of the pervasive morality of comfortable duty, ending in disgust.

This sardonic tale hovers on the edge of the absurd at many points, as is often true of Lawrence's mocking fictions, and the grotesque failures of the "good" sensitive man provide endless possibilities; but it is also characteristic of Lawrence that the third, final, and shortest episode of the fable becomes vehement psychological denouement. The hero still has enough of his "finer distinction" that he can bring himself to flee the destructiveness of ordinary life. Truly alone at last on a barren third island, except for a cat and some sheep, his quest for harmony and perfection has left the human realm. His obsessive consciousness is fictionally maintained by a systematic denuding of the scene. As in "**The Prussian Officer,**" the style depends upon turning psychological realism into a surreal magnification of the details to give the logic of the obsessive emotions. Thus, when "all interest had left him," each

fact of life becomes grotesque. He finds the bleating sheep of his pastoral escape "repulsive," "degrading"; he finds the "intrusion, the clumsy homeliness" of the fishermen who bring his supplies, sickening; and he even finds indirect reminders of his humanity and identity so upsetting that he "hated to read his own name on an envelope." The longing for the ideal has become self-hatred and self-destruction. "He felt ill, as if everything were dissolving. . . . Everything was twilight, outside, and in his mind and soul." Oneness has been reached.

The man who loved islands of the mind rather than the actual world ends by destroying all marks of the mind: he tore "the brass label from his paraffine stove . . . [and] he obliterated any bit of lettering in his cabin." His only pleasures are nihilism—the removal of the sheep, the disappearance of the cat, the cessation of supplies, the winter disappearance of the sun, and the final blanketing of the whole scene in snow. Nothing left but himself, the self becomes nothing: he achieves mystic dehumanization and ceases "to register his own feelings."

Negation is the final ecstasy. "Soon, he said to himself, it will all be gone, and in all these regions nothing will be alive. He felt a cruel satisfaction in the thought." His final assertion of negative individuality is that self-destruction must override the destructiveness of the universe; this is his heroic defiance, his Lawrencean gesture. He attempts to free his boat from the snow, not with any intention of escaping, but that he may be trapped by "his own choice, not by the mechanical power of the elements." But the nihilism of the cosmos is even greater than that of the ego, and the concluding image is another version of the snowy mountain of the beyond. On the bleak snow-covered rock in the wintry northern sea, there is only more and more "snow rolling over the sea" and "its breath on him." The cold cosmos, the very loss of the warmth of the human animal, provides Lawrence's concluding trope for frigid idealism. (pp. 11-15)

In "**The Man Who Loved Islands**" (and is it not also true of many other powerful modern fables?) there seems to be a deep disgust with the physically human—constant repulsion, sexual desire as "nausea"; a total disillusionment with society—it is treated as obvious that the hero flees civilization, and even the utopian society reverses to the malevolent; a degradation of culture—reading is a game, knowledge an esoteric hobby, sensitivity an illness. Nor can this nihilism be separated from D. H. Lawrence, the yea-sayer of life values. The hero is Lawrencean about the sexual mystery, the negation of modern society, the longing for a utopian community, and the doctrine of simplicity and solitude. The man who loved islands even has the old Lawrencean hobby of naming flowers. This story, too, is the "true" Lawrence, all the more so in that it contains implicit self-mockery. (p. 16)

The early story, "**The Prussian Officer,**" turns the exploration of its authority-innocence theme into heightened nature images of the good and simple youth's longing for destruction. The late story, "**The Man Who Loved Islands,**" explores the sensitive idealist's benevolence and follows his emotional logic through the covert longing for destruction. The form of the innocence theme is appropriately lavish in sensual and scenic detail; the form of the idealist theme is appropriately discursive and hyperlogical. But the cogency of these fictions goes beyond the apt fusion of theme and form. The yearning for the extremity of experience, and covertly for its destructive culmination, is the crux of much of Lawrence's art. . . . [We] might note now that it may be the negations that make

Lawrence so pertinently and appealingly "modern," rather than his formal carelessness, woozy passional prose, and sometimes irritable moralizing and prophecy. That Lawrence so vehemently insists on organic relations to person and place may be to counter not only the nihilism of the prevailing social-moral order, but a more ultimate nihilism within himself.

Lawrence is not the only perverse modern artist. The perversity, after all, reveals the effort to turn an awareness of the destructive into something meaningful, to turn pessimistic knowledge to an affirmation. Often Lawrence insists on the destructive aims . . . as a transvaluation: " . . . once we are driven on to nihilism we may find a way through." But **"The Prussian Officer"** and **"The Man Who Loved Islands"** dramatize, with some of Lawrence's best art, innocence and idealism ending in self-annihilation. (pp. 16-17)

Kingsley Widmer, in his The Art of Perversity: D. H. Lawrence's Shorter Fictions, *University of Washington Press, 1962, 258 p.*

GARY ADELMAN   (essay date 1963)

[*Adelman is an American novelist and poet. In the following excerpt, he interprets "The Prussian Officer" as an analogy of modern humanity's loss of self—and subsequent desire for death—through the corrupting influence of civilization.*]

"The Prussian Officer" is a dramatization of the consequences of twenty-five centuries of evasion and denial of life. Written in 1913 at a time when Lawrence was hotly involved in working out a system for evaluating and conceptualizing experience in an idealized direction (forming a philosophy and a style suitable for its expression), it is not surprising that his obsessive subject matter finds its way into the short story. Its title, originally "Honour and the Man," Edward Garnett retitled. The story is concerned with the lack of honor and manliness in captain and orderly, and, in a larger sense, in all modern men, for by *honor* Lawrence means faithful observance of the individual life in man which *by nature* gives to him his identity.

As the prototype German officer, the Captain represents (in Lawrence's poetic vision) an exaggerated picture of modern man. He is a consequence, along with our mechanistic society, of 2500 years of mechanical insistence on an ideal of impersonal service: "cold," "hostile," "cruel," "brutal"; "stiff," "tense," "rigid," "fixed"; never did he receive life "direct through his senses," never did he act "straight from instinct." He is one of the "unliving." The abrupt awakening of the man to desires he has with tragic insistence repressed and the consequence of these emotions which he can neither admit nor control are motivation for this masterpiece of Lawrence's short stories.

"Then the change gradually came." The Captain is suddenly aware of his young orderly's "vigorous, unconscious presence." He is aroused; "penetrated through [his] stiffened discipline"; "touched into life by his servant"; incapable, "in spite of himself," of regaining "his neutrality of feeling." His passion is intolerable, inadmissable. He is an officer, "a Prussian aristocrat, haughty and overbearing." His position dictates that he be impersonal; that he be "cold and just and indifferent" to an inconsequential servant. Schöner, the orderly, who has served him for more than a year, knew his duty, which "he took for granted, as he took the sun and the rain." He serves "the officer as if the latter were an abstract authori-

Lawrence in 1912.

ty and not a man." Agitated and irritable, the Captain struggles to "keep himself hard to the idea of the service," but the "affair" gets out of hand. "He could not get away from the sense of the youth's person." "He could not rest when the soldier was away, and when he was present he glared at him with tormented eyes."

As the Captain's passion grows "madly irritable," Schöner grows "more mute and expressionless." The young soldier refuses "to be forced into a personal interchange with his master." The Captain is enraged. He begins to bully him, "using contempt and satire," and to take up as much of his time as possible. He seems to be going "irritably insane" in an obsessive desire to destroy the young soldier's instinctive, unhampered nature. "He was infuriated by the free movement of the handsome limbs, which no military discipline could make stiff." Schöner, whose every instinct "was to avoid personal contact," in spite of himself, feels his hatred grow in response "to the officer's passion."

The Captain spurs his servant's hatred, exulting in an intimacy of fear and bewilderment, at the same time succumbing to an uncontrollable desire to touch him: a glove in the face, then the end of a belt, then repeated kickings, always in the thighs and loins, and always at these times, "deep inside him was the intense gratification of his passion . . . working powerfully." Horribly brutalized, Schöner puts everything out of existence but the Captain. The Captain becomes "inevitable." He feels that he "must move under the presence of [his] figure." He feels that there are only "two people in the world . . . himself and the Captain." Finally, in an anguish of uncontrollable emotions, Schöner kills him.

Lawrence creates an orderly who is, before the "affair," childlike in his innocence. He lives instinctively, whereas the rigidly disciplined older man has repressed his nature, succumbing to a sterile way of life in which a mechanical obedience to the "idea of the service" destroyed all that was free in him. As an officer, the Captain is a master among men. Not only does he control and domesticate them, but also he denies his own nature and enslaves it completely. Athletic, graceful, Greek: he is apparently a man.

The Captain's life has been one long denial. He reveals his mortal want not only in his passion for Schöner, but also in the pleasure he takes in his command, the gratification he finds in "the hot smell of men," and in his love for horses. With his "long, fine hands and cultivated movements," his "white and slender" body, he "never married"—"no woman ever moved him to it" and he never moved a woman to it—he is obviously effeminate, finding his identity in an arbitrary, unnatural convention. His passionate hatred and love for Schöner are a consequence of a terrifying self-realization: that he is only the simulacrum of a man.

Schöner awakens in him a conflict of desires. The officer wishes to be loved—mastered—by the pristine, wild and unhampered, male vitality of his servant. But the mechanisms of his life continue despite him. He must command the men. And yet Schöner is not any man. With terrible destructive impact on the mental cosmos in which the officer has lived, as in an impenetrable shell, he has become an unconscious necessity. Driven by compassions he cannot deny, the Captain loses his equipoise. In agony he lusts after personal contact with Schöner. He manages somehow to keep his life organized, while gradually, torn apart by the struggle of unconscious demands with his militant will, he sinks (as Lawrence dramatizes it) into a perverse compromise. He brutalizes his servant with love, beats him for the gratification of the contact while at the same time remaining obedient to the ideal of his position. But even in this compromise there is design, as if his mind were forced to answer the needs of his unconscious. The Captain is intent on driving Schöner to a passion which must conclude with the orderly's killing him. This is to be the officer's fulfillment.

The conflict tearing the Captain apart appears in the symbol of the horse. The horse is an archetypal symbol, a directing force from the unconscious which the officer has, until his affair with Schöner, repressed. He has the reputation as "one of the best horseman in the West"; the orderly admires "the amazing riding-muscles of [the] loins" of the officer who is always riding, always "wheeling on horseback." In controlling and domesticating the horse, the Captain represses his natural, spontaneous desires. In mastering the animal, he finds the masculine force he lacks: power, to move and to command his men. Off the horse he is not a man—"he came back in an agony of irritation, torment, and misery" from his stay with a woman, and "rode all the evening." The horse establishes his identity among men. It gives validity to his position as an officer—to his pose as a man.

Schöner becomes identified with the horse. He begins to feel that he is "connected with that figure moving so suddenly on horseback: he follow[s] it like a shadow, mute and inevitable and damned by it." "[He] must move under the presence of the figure of the horseman." When he sees "the light heel of the officer prick the belly of the horse . . . the tension grow[s] in his soul." The symbol suggests the grotesque picture of the Captain mounting his orderly—kicking him in the loins—intent on gripping between his knees the vitality of the young, "unhampered animal" and making it move and live for him. To the terrified servant, the figure of the horseman—"a dark shadow over his light, fierce eyes . . . mouth and chin . . . distinct in the sunshine"—is the figure of Death.

Unlike the Captain, who determines his life according to concepts and voluntary decisions of the ego, who perversely suppresses natural expression, substituting a ghastly mechanistic process for the natural interchange that should take place between the unconscious and consciousness, Schöner experiences the world naturally and spontaneously through the unconscious. Primitive, a "young, unhampered animal," this innocent child is singled out of the herd for his initiation into personal consciousness by a society which has produced the Captain and which finds spontaneity and natural expression incompatible with its ideals. Schöner is made to conform to the meaning of 2500 years of denial and evasion of life, and the gradual realization that he is not entirely forced, but in large part responds to the ugly, perverse, life-denying commitments of the new dispensation, finds them in fact gratifying, destroys him. Such is the horror and fascination of **"The Prussian Officer"**—Schöner is willfully involved.

During the beatings, the orderly's conduct is bewildering. He seems to provoke the madly irritated officer:

> "Why have you a piece of pencil in your ear?"
>
> The orderly hesitated, then continued on his way without answering. . . .
>
> The officer's eyes were dancing, he had a little, eager smile.
>
> "Why have you a piece of pencil in your ear?" he asked.
>
> The orderly took his hands full of dishes. His master was standing near the great green stove, a little smile on his face, his chin thrust forward. When the young soldier saw him, his heart suddenly ran hot. He felt blind. Instead of answering, he turned dazedly to the door. As he was crouching to set down the dishes, he was pitched forward by a kick from behind. The pots went in a stream down the stairs, he clung to the pillar of the banisters. As he was rising he was kicked heavily again and again, so that he clung sickly to the post for some moments. . . .
>
> The officer's heart was plunging. . . . Pale, as if intoxicated, he waited. . . .
>
> "Schöner!" he said.
>
> The soldier was a little slower in coming to attention.
>
> "Yes, sir! . . ."
>
> "I asked you a question."
>
> "Yes, sir."
>
> The officer's tone bit like acid.

"Why had you a pencil in your ear?"

> Again the servant's heart ran hot, and he could not breathe. With dark, strained eyes, he looked at the officer, as if fascinated. And he stood there sturdily planted, unconscious. The withering smile came into the Captain's eyes, and he lifted his foot.

Why doesn't he answer more quickly? Why doesn't he make up an answer? And if he is incapable of avoiding personal contact, why doesn't he turn to higher authority? Why doesn't he "want anybody to know" of his beatings ("No one should ever know. It was between him and the Captain")? That Schöner is a frightened "animal" and cannot find words or responses to answer an experience he cannot understand; that he is afraid to complain to higher authority; and that any involvement there is, is forced by the Captain, is in part true to the experience of the story. But there is something very suspicious about a man, or even a terrified animal, that insists on remaining cornered and beaten, that makes something personal out of his helplessness. Schöner's behavior raises at least one thought: that once involved, he begins to play an active role in the perverse love affair.

The imagery of the murder and of the delirium which follows it confirms this suggestion. . . . Why is the murder described as a sexual act—the "pressing," "blood exulting in his thrust," "heavy convulsions," "passion of relief"—if not to bring to consummation a love affair? And after the death, if the orderly were not heart and soul involved, why his feeling that "his own life also ended"? The narrative subsequently relates the rapid dissolution of the young man, his feeling of ugliness everywhere, the agony of his death, as if the substance of life in him has become rotten. His "horror of the little creeping birds" and his fear of squirrels; his unquenchable thirst; his revulsion for the "deathly, sickly" smell of grass and the "suffocating, hideous smell" of sheep; his "delirium of sickness and fever"; his loathing of life: these are not natural consequences of an act of self-preservation. The cause of Schöner's agony is a self-revelation too terrible to understand, too disgusting to accept. His death agony testifies to his full involvement. (pp. 8-14)

It is inevitable that Schöner play the role designated for him by the Captain and that in so doing he should be "disemboweled, made empty, like an empty shell," "empty like a shadow." It is inevitable that he be raped into "reality, on the real, dark bottom" which is our modern life, no longer bearing to live, horrified and revulsed by everything natural—birds, squirrels; the smell of grass, grain, and sheep; the satisfaction of water; "contact with anybody." It is inevitable that he be robbed of his manhood and feel himself "only a consciousness, a gap that could think and perceive." It is inevitable that he become like his master. Why this should be is the appalling answer to why Schöner finds gratification in his mutilation. And the answer to this question is the answer to the mystery of the Fall. For Lawrence, modern man insists on destroying simplicity and natural directness, and by so doing, commits himself to perversity and death. What is left of Schöner after the debauchery is, in Lawrence's vision of things, what is left of all men raped by the sexless monster of civilizing trends: slow, terrible corruption and an instinct for death. (pp. 14-15)

Gary Adelman, "Beyond the Pleasure Principle: An Analysis of D. H. Lawrence's 'The Prussian Officer,'" in Studies in Short Fiction, *Vol. I, No. 1, Fall, 1963, pp. 8-15.*

JULIAN MOYNAHAN   (essay date 1963)

[*In the following excerpt from his* The Deed of Life: The Novels and Tales of D. H. Lawrence, *Moynahan offers a thematic discussion of the tales, focusing on "The Odour of Chrysanthemums" and "The Man Who Loved Islands."*]

As one reads through the three volumes of short stories and the two volumes of short novels . . . it is rather easy to group many of the tales according to reasonably distinct categories; yet, as might be expected, it is the best work that finally eludes the simple category. One group can be put together from the several stories which read as suggestive footnotes to certain of the novels. The most weirdly interesting of these is the early **"The Shades of Spring,"** describing the return to his home valley of one John Syson, a young man who, like Paul Morel, had courted and then left a girl living on a farm. But this Miriam—her name is Hilda—has solaced herself in the arms of a local gamekeeper with whom she makes passionate love in a forest hut draped with the skins of wild animals. There are enough references to the past to show that Syson's former relation to this girl was cast in the same mold as the unhappy, inhibited affair of Paul and Miriam. Yet where Miriam remained passive and spiritual Hilda has become bold and sensual, with no interest in returning to Syson. He had considered her "all spirit," but she now considers herself "like a plant. I can only grow in my own soil." **"Shades of Spring"** is a kind of arch which ties together the erotic dilemma of *Sons and Lovers* and the final solution of the dilemma in *Lady Chatterley*. We may want to conclude that Lawrence, after all, had only one story to tell, which he went on reworking until the ending came right, but a more reasonable inference is that the Miriam figure was from the beginning much more a plastic imaginative construct than a mere travesty of Lawrence's childhood sweetheart Jessie Chambers.

A second category, consisting of a half dozen or so stories that make fun of or otherwise discomfit certain people in the Lawrence circle, may be passed by quickly. **"None of That"** travesties Mabel Dodge's lust for willed experience and imagines a more sordid outcome to her career than the actual tough-minded woman would ever have tolerated. No less than four stories—**"Smile," "The Border Line," "Jimmy and the Desperate Woman,"** and **"The Last Laugh"**—are aimed with some malice at J. Middleton Murry, the man to whom Lawrence most frequently assigned the role of Judas in the tragi-comedy of his relations with friends. **"Things"** distressed the American expatriate couple Earl and Achsah Brewster by exposing the materialism implicit in American upper-bohemian veneration of European antiquity, but these kind people still managed to remain on good terms with Lawrence to the very end of his life.

A third category consists of a few works of substantial length which remain ambitious failures, owing either to excessive schematism in the ideas underlying the story, or indifferent success in the attempt to represent fictionally states of being about which Lawrence was confused or perverse. **"The Ladybird"** (*pace* Dr. Leavis) is, stylistically, Lawrence's ugliest story; its concern with "mastery" suggests that it issued from the same unwholesome region of Lawrence's imagination in which the leadership novels had developed. The hero, Count Dionys Psanek, is a lineal descendant of Dracula, except that, like Mr. Bela Lugosi, he stultifies where he intends to thrill.

"The Woman Who Rode Away," although it contains some of Lawrence's most brilliant renderings of landscape, is, like *The Plumed Serpent*, a heartless tale *au fond*. Both the

Woman and Constance Chatterley "throw themselves away," the latter in the direction of renewed life, the former merely into an abyss of senseless blood sacrifice. The Woman's ritual disembowelment by Mexican Indians seeking to recover the power of command they have lost to gringos is neither excusable nor interesting; and the story contains one of the most depressing images in all Lawrence: a blonde woman crawling on hands and knees along a narrow mountain ledge, while her two Indian captors walk easily erect, one before, one behind, both indifferent to her discomfort and danger.

"The Man Who Died" is a near-success until the baroque conceit of "I am risen!" destroys the suspension of disbelief required for Lawrence's bold attempt to merge his own and the Christian myths of bodily resurrection. Analogous difficulties crop up in a spirit story like **"Glad Ghosts."** The lady ghost here remains too involved in problems of the life of the senses to persuade us that she is as other-worldly as the convention demands. She is apt to remind the reader of the last, unfinished canto of Byron's *Don Juan,* where Juan mistakes for a phantom a warm, nubile lady wearing a sheet.

One of the most clear-cut groups among Lawrence's short stories consists of **"Two Blue Birds," "The Lovely Lady," "Mother and Daughter," "Rawdon's Roof,"** and **"The Blue Moccasins."** These are united by their rather bitchy, facetious tone. The characters are middle- and upper-middle-class English people, and a recurring figure in several of these stories is the strong-minded, aging woman who has fastened herself parasitically onto someone younger and less clever than herself. Without abandoning his characteristic concern for vitality Lawrence successfully exploits here a talent for comedy of manners which he rarely employs in his novels. There is nothing to urge against these stories except that they are a bit too brittle and slight compared to his best work.

I could continue this categorizing—for example, the early stories of working-class life, the three thoroughly unsuccessful stories about sexual conflict set in or near London and obviously written during Lawrence's first years in London (**"The Old Adam," "The Witch A La Mode," "New Eve and Old Adam"**)—except that I am much less interested in my schemes as such than to suggest what a large body of first-rate work remains after the ground has been cleared of work that is merely interesting, flawed, or only good enough to have made the international reputation of a lesser writer. (pp. 176-79)

The opening paragraph of **"Odour of Chrysanthemums,"** first published in 1911, establishes a tension which is expressed everywhere in Lawrence's work but always most movingly in the setting of his own native Midlands. . . . (p. 181)

The principle of composition here is simple contrast, the whole suffused, like the last stanza of Keats's ode "To Autumn," in an atmosphere of diminishment and decline. . . . These arrayed contrasts between machinery and a natural setting, embodying a tension between the necessity of human survival which called the industrial system into existence and the instinct of all living things to maintain themselves freely in being, are disturbed by one anomalous feature. A woman stands motionless, trapped between track and hedge, neither free to take flight like the animals, nor bound into a steely pattern of mechanical movement like the locomotive. She disappears immediately from the story but the anomaly of this human entrapment remains and becomes the central, moving motive of the story.

The drab cottage of Elizabeth Bates, clutched by its bony vine and with its long garden containing a few apple trees and some failing chrysanthemums, presses up against the cinder roadbed of the line. The mother is tall, straight, handsome, and fruitful, and she is also tense, unhappy, and exhausted because of her collier husband's evening visits to the pub, with their inevitable consequence, a further reduction of the scanty housekeeping allowance. The family atmosphere, established by the scene of the supper and the talk between brother, sister, and mother, is warm and close, and includes the father, whose inexplicably prolonged absence on this particular evening is concretely felt by all three.

Yet this atmosphere is also suffused with a permanent tension. The mother's inevitable anger at her husband's fecklessness, like the miner's drinking bouts, continues from day to day, and the children react anxiously to both these disturbing features of the shared life of the family. Finally, the husband, although we never see him alive, is a figure of anomaly. On the one hand his life is bound in with the rhythms of the machine; for he descends into the mine and returns to the surface according to the rigid patterns of a work schedule; and perhaps the machine principle has even invaded his "free" time, since the drinking habits of workmen are at least partially determined by the overfatigue and boredom consequent on heavy industrial labor. On the other hand, his mother remembers the warm laugh, perfect health, and high animal spirits he had had as a boy. His wife has laid her "living flesh" against his and out of these conjunctions have come children and a child as yet unborn—new life that is unbound, unpredictable, alive with possibility.

In the central scene of the story—the account of the laying out and washing of the miner's dead body by Elizabeth and her mother-in-law—we seem to pass beyond these contradictions. . . . (pp. 182-83)

In this most moving of all the scenes in Lawrence's fiction Elizabeth, and the reader, seem to recover a Blakeian true vision of the fundamental, living reality of a man. But it is illusory. . . . He is dead. Yet the image of this inviolable reality lingers, and tortures Elizabeth in her grief as she reflects that she had never known him, or he known her. They had denied each other fundamentally. "And this had been her life and his life. She was grateful to death, which restored the truth."

The story's image of life in the industrial age is that of a sickly, autumnal flower growing beside a cinder track and appearing first in association with pregnancy—Elizabeth puts chrysanthemums in the band of her apron—finally in association with death. But we must be careful about this change. The flower is sickly, yet it has grown by itself until picked and will grow again. Bates's death restores the truth which the anomalous and alienating features of the industrial system have covered up. With perfect objectivity and compassion Lawrence describes a waste of life in order to affirm life and discriminates the point from which civilization must begin to reconstruct itself if we wish to recover a true, unanomalous vision of ourselves, one another, and the world. And this point is a recognition of the naive, inviolable, impregnable dignity of an ordinary workman laid out on the floor of a miner's cottage, his life wasted, the lives of his family blighted, his cooling body prepared for burial.

"**The Man Who Loved Islands,**" first published in 1928, is perhaps Lawrence's greatest story in what may be called the fable or parable form. In such narratives—"**The Man Who Died**" and "**The Rocking Horse Winner**" are other notable examples—Lawrence solved the problem of dealing effectively with special states of being and awareness by dispensing with much of the realistic machinery he customarily employed in his longer novels. The action of these stories is set at a carefully calculated distance from the world of contemporary civilization. Their characters are simplified figures who epitomize particular aspects of the human condition in relatively pure form. Their greatness lies in the fact that, while they embody familiar Laurentian assumptions usually represented as a mixture of realism and symbolism in most of the longer novels, these stories never emerge as flat allegories, and their characters manage to remain fully expressive and alive.

F. R. Leavis, [in his *D. H. Lawrence: Novelist*], in speaking of this kind of Lawrence narrative, uses the word "frame-effect" to designate what I have referred to as a fable or parable quality in the form. The frame-effect limits "the freedom of the reader's implicit reference from the world of the tale to the expectations and habits of ordinary everyday actuality." This explanation is valuable because it does not assume there is no connection between the story and ordinary life; it assumes only that the reader must not expect ready and obvious connections. In "**The Man Who Loved Islands**" the reader's stock expectations are inhibited from the opening sentence onward. This sentence—"There was a man who loved islands"—by itself evokes the formalized world of the fairy tale. A man with a peculiar passion is summoned into existence by an apparently naive narrator, and as the story unfolds, this passion is everything, and the only thing, the narrator tells us about. The passion is the story's premise, just as the continuously expanding lust of the fisherman's wife for power and riches is the premise of the well-known folk tale. Both stories concern themselves with effects; there is little direct inquiry into the causes of these consuming passions, although by the time one has finished "**The Man Who Loved Islands**" he is in a position to construct for himself the kind of previous experience which brought the hero to the point of indulging in his fatal ambition to possess fully an island. (pp. 184-86)

The action of "**The Man Who Loved Islands**" represents the disintegration of a self. This fate is brought on by the hero's steadily accelerating withdrawal from those relationships with the surrounding world which, on Lawrence's view, determine the health and integrity of any human being. The story's development may be described as the continual shrinking of a circle around another circle, until the inner circle of the self and the outer circle of the non-self nearly coincide at that moment just before death with which the story concludes. Alternatively, it may be described as the systematic, willed reduction of the varied colors of experience to the flat whiteness of death-in-life, that peculiar Laurentian simulacrum of being in which the isolated ego dissolves into pure abstractedness. In the final third of the story the hero becomes Faust in reverse, a rapt soul who attempts to diminish the universe to a dimensionless point, who tries to conquer otherness by thinking its modes of space and time out of existence. In his final cold agonies there is something magnificent about Cathcart. The grandeur of his presumption against life compels awe from the reader even as he recognizes the justness of his failure. (pp. 186-87)

Cathcart himself is the principal symbol of "**The Man Who Loved Islands,**" and the island settings are, on one level, images or mirror reflections of his thought. We apprehend his essence by studying descriptions of his surroundings. Conventional distinctions between inner and outer worlds dissolve as Cathcart purchases a series of miniature universes that he can "presume to fill . . . with [his] own personality." As this personality progressively deteriorates under its burden of disconnectedness, he moves deeper and deeper into abstraction. His ghastly metamorphoses of self are evidenced through differences in the appearance of successive islands. The first contains some miles of fertile, flowery, sea-encircled earth, the last some rods of bleak, snow-covered reef. A comparison of descriptions of landscape becomes a comparison of three conditions of a soul. . . . (pp. 190-91)

In the end Cathcart no doubt becomes a madman, but the story hardly permits the reader to dismiss the central figure as a harmless maniac. His disease is mind-derived, and he finishes by destroying only himself. Given other circumstances, the same ghastly habit of mind could ravage the entire civilized world. It was, of course, Lawrence's deep conviction that the ravages of the abstracted intelligence and will were evident throughout modern experience, corrupting the friendships, loves, and working associations of men and women everywhere. Cathcart is mad in that he does not take the world as it is into his reckoning. The mind, isolated from living truth, can create only deadness; and living truth for Lawrence involves the recognition that the only marvel is to be alive in the flesh, and to be linked up in a universe which is organically alive.

"**The Man Who Loved Islands**" dramatizes a modern habit of mind, the habitual assumption of the modern civilized man that the relations between the individual and his world are a matter of words and ideas, that organic ties do not exist. Lawrence is saying here, as he has said elsewhere, that man imposes his abstracted thought upon life at the cost of his own life, that we must live with rather than against the life teeming in and around us.

The art of "**The Man Who Loved Islands**" is well-nigh flawless. The fable of Cathcart and his islands sums up everything Lawrence has to say about the perniciousness of the abstract without rage, without faltering, without argument. The complete story is what Robert Frost calls a "constant symbol" of its meaning. Its descriptions evoke the beauty of the phenomenal world and the horrific emptiness of a world subdued to the irreverent mind of a man who aspires to a godlike condition but who cannot feel love for or connection with any created thing. This story, unlike so many of Lawrence's narratives, leaves no questions suspended at its close. Perhaps this suggests that Lawrence's prophetic vision of doom for modern man was more powerful than his vision of hope. Really, it does not matter. As the artist who could create a tale like "**The Man Who Loved Islands,**" he transcends the limitations of the prophet and works a permanent change in the thought and feeling of his reader. (pp. 195-96)

> *Julian Moynahan, in his* The Deed of Life: The Novels and Tales of D. H. Lawrence, *Princeton University Press, 1963, 229 p.*

LIONEL TRILLING   (essay date 1967)

[*A major figure in the development of modern literary criticism as well as a respected novelist and short story writer, Trilling has been described as a social critic who sought to present literature as an integral element of the society from which it emerges. His criticism is remarkable for its sense of historical perspective and for its lucid delineation of the conflict between the individual and society. Trilling believed in the power of art to sustain the self in this "adversary culture" and he contended that the authentic work of art "reveals reality" and "instructs us in our inauthenticity." His work encompasses a distinctive range of topics, including the relation of morality to politics and the aesthetic as well as political meaning of liberalism, and was profoundly influenced by the work and character of both Matthew Arnold and Sigmund Freud. Among his major works of criticism are* Matthew Arnold *(1939),* The Liberal Imagination: Essays on Literature and Society *(1950), and* Beyond Culture: Essays on Literature and Learning *(1965). The following excerpt originally appeared in the 1967 edition of* The Experience of Literature: A Reader with Commentaries, *which Trilling edited in collaboration with Charles Kaplan. Here Trilling interprets Lawrence's use of strikingly divergent prose styles in "Tickets, Please" as a dramatization of the change in American society's view of women after World War I.*]

From the tone of its opening paragraphs it would be impossible to predict the kind of story that **"Tickets, Please"** turns out to be. Lawrence is unblushing in the quaint whimsicality with which he personifies the little tramcar, telling us that it seems "to pause and purr with curious satisfaction," that it is "abashed by the great crimson and cream-coloured city cars, but still perky, jaunty, somewhat dare-devil. . . ." He refers to it with the coy, manipulating "we" that is deplorably used with children ("We don't spit at our little sister, do we?") or hospital patients ("We are going to have our injection now"). And with the same pronoun he contrives a companionable trio of tramcar, author, and reader, in which we are presumed to connive at the enthusiasm of his "Hurray!" and be reassured by his " . . . but what matter!" When he tells us, "Therefore, there is a certain wild romance aboard these cars—and in the sturdy bosom of Annie herself," it is as if he were cozily putting his arm around Annie's shoulder to introduce her as a really nice girl who is bound to prove a satisfactory heroine.

In short, the beginning of the story commits itself to a manner which is all too consciously "literary," all too aware of its airs and graces of style, and all too pleased with itself and its jolly intimacy with the reader. Prose of this kind, with its avowed intention of charming the reader and making him warm and comfortable, was common enough in the fiction of the Victorian period, but it has long since gone out of fashion. And it is at the furthest possible remove from the startling episode which makes the substance of the story and from the quick, spare language in which its violence is set forth: "He went forward, rather vaguely. She had taken off her belt, and swinging it, she fetched him a sharp blow over the head with the buckle end. He sprang and seized her. But immediately the other girls rushed upon him, pulling and tearing and beating him." Prose—not to say action—as direct as this puts all whimsy, coziness, and jollity to rout.

Whether or not Lawrence consciously intended a particular effect by his use of these two widely divergent styles we do not know. But once we become aware of the contrast between them, we can scarcely fail to look for meaning in it. And the meaning we are most likely to discover is social—the startling discrepancy between the way the story opens and the way it develops may be said to represent the difference between an old and a new conception of women. At the beginning of the

story Annie seems ready to be the satisfactory heroine of a Victorian novel; with her sturdiness go a modesty and reserve which would once have been praised as "womanly." She disappoints this first judgment in a sufficiently remarkable way. Her conduct exemplifies the drastic revision of the notion of womanliness that was made after the First World War.

All through the nineteenth century, in the United States and in certain countries of Europe, there had been an ever-growing awareness that the status of women could no longer remain what it had traditionally been. The First World War, if only because it required many women to come out of the home and do the work of men, effected a change in the relation of the sexes which had long been in preparation and which was perhaps the most radical that history can show. Its importance was not underestimated by the fiction and drama of the time. The relations between men and women came to be thought of as a "problem" which writers undertook to "solve" or at least to state as clearly and honestly as they could. And of all writers none responded to the new sexual situation quite so intensely as D. H. Lawrence, with so much sensitivity and awareness, and with so passionate a commitment of both feeling and intelligence.

Lawrence was certainly not the first modern writer to propose the idea that between men and women there exists an intense antagonism. Nor is that idea only a modern one. Chaucer celebrated the fidelity and docility of women but he also took full notice of their desire to resist male dominance and even to gain what he called "the mastery." And the imagination of the Greeks, as their drama and legends abundantly testify, was haunted by the thought of the hostility which women might bear toward men. But the idea of the antagonism of the sexes as propounded by modern authors—Ibsen, Nietzsche, Strindberg, and Shaw may be mentioned as Lawrence's predecessors in the treatment of the subject—came to the modern consciousness as a novelty and a shock. Especially for Lawrence, it was on the sexual battlefield that the fiercest conflicts of civilization announced themselves.

But Lawrence was no less engaged by the mutual dependence of the sexes. And it is his equal recognition of both the antagonism and the reciprocal need, and of the interplay between the two, that gives his writing about love its unique air of discovery and truth. **"Tickets, Please"** is one of Lawrence's early stories, but it constitutes a summary statement of the emotional situation with which Lawrence was to deal throughout his career as a writer.

In their dress, in their manner of life and in their deportment, these girl-conductors of the tramline strikingly describe this century's revolution in the life of women. They are spoken of as "fearless young hussies"—they have learned to live on terms of equality, or apparent equality, with men, and to accept the manners of a rough male society. They had never, it is true, pretended to the standards of behavior that prevailed for the women of the British upper classes, which had shaped the prevailing ideal of womanliness as it was celebrated in novels. These girl-conductors had not been brought up to be *ladies.* But most of them had certainly been brought up to be "respectable." They leave respectability a long way behind when they undertake to deal with Coddy Raynor.

The maenad-like behavior of these working-class girls did have, it is worth noting, a degree of upper-class sanction. It had been validated by the conduct of many women of the very gentlest breeding, for the suffragettes, as the women who agitated for the right to vote were called, came largely from the upper classes yet did not shrink from violent means to enforce their claim to political equality with men, pouring acid into letter-boxes, destroying the putting-greens of golf courses, beating cabinet ministers over the head with umbrellas, and fighting strenuously when the police took them into custody. But the suffragettes acted out of outraged pride at the implication that women were not worthy to vote. The girls who make up the fierce little vigilance party of **"Tickets, Please"** are no less moved by an outrage done to their pride, but what they resent is not the political and social superiority that men insist on but the male sexual advantage.

These women need Coddy more than he needs them, and all the more because the war has created a shortage of men. They are now independent economically, but they can fulfil themselves only in marriage, while for Coddy marriage represents nothing but a surrender of freedom, a submission to whatever woman he marries, a yielding of *his* pride. From the point of view of equity, the situation is infamous and not to be borne. And yet no sooner have the girls succeeded in redressing the balance against him, at least symbolically and for the moment, than they are appalled by what they have done. They undertook to destroy this arrogant male, to humiliate him and make him ridiculous; their success makes them feel lost and miserable. For it is exactly what they resent in Coddy Raynor—his masculine pride and arrogance, his lordly independence—that constitutes his attraction as a man and draws them to him. The rough justice that the girls deal out may have its rough rationality, but the situation they confront is not to be solved by rationality. Their desires and their needs transcend justice and reason.

And here Lawrence leaves the problem. He does not try to adjudicate between the sexes but only to set forth the actuality of the relationship—and to find pleasure in it. The pleasure is quite unmistakable. As between John Thomas Raynor and Annie Stone and her embattled comrades, Lawrence does not take sides. He delights in both parties to the sexual conflict. The actual physical embroilment is grim enough, and any reader—at least any male reader—is sure to share John Thomas's fear of the enraged women he has exploited and deceived. Yet Lawrence, without at all masking the grimness, treats it as only one element of a story that is curiously tender and predominantly humorous.

The essence of both the tenderness and the humor lies in the fact that the behavior of the girls, which is so extravagantly unwomanly, reveals them, especially Annie, in the full of their female nature—and reveals them so not only to us but to themselves. The conduct that "unsexes" them, as a Victorian moralist would have put it, makes plain the intensity of their female sexuality. (pp. 123-27)

> Lionel Trilling, " 'Tickets, Please,' " in his *Prefaces to The Experience of Literature*, *Harcourt Brace Jovanovich, 1979, pp. 123-27.*

LEO GURKO (essay date 1972)

[*Here Gurko cites "The Fox," "The Ladybird," and "The Captain's Doll" as works that serve as a microcosm of Lawrence's fiction and link his early writing style of personal relations with his later novels of ideas. He also discusses Lawrence's use of similar themes and techniques in these stories, particularly the emblem motif, the theme of equilibrium between the sexes, the fairy tale motif, and the theme of resurrection.*]

["The Fox," "The Ladybird," and "The Captain's Doll" constitute] probably Lawrence's most brilliant single assemblage of tales, and rank with Conrad's *Youth and Two Other Stories* and Joyce's *Dubliners* as the richest of their kind in modern English.

Their aesthetic quality is more evident than Lawrence's reasons for publishing them in the same volume. He did of course write them in the same period: he had begun **"The Fox"** in 1918 while still in England and had finished **"The Ladybird"** at the end of 1921 in Sicily. As stories, all three take place in Europe toward the end of the First World War and immediately afterward, the very time in which they were written. Yet the differences among them in tone, atmosphere, and even the social classes to which their characters belong are so striking as to overwhelm the surface unity supplied by dates of composition and historical locale.

In tone, they range from the rhapsodic, incantatory style of **"The Ladybird,"** to the impressionistic pathos of **"The Fox,"** to the worldly comedy of **"The Captain's Doll."** The atmosphere of **"The Ladybird"** is mystical, **"The Fox"** broodingly Freudian, **"The Captain's Doll"** playfully ironic and sophisticated. There is a spread in social status from the lower-middle-class farm girls of **"The Fox"** to the established aristocracy of **"The Ladybird,"** from the army private of **"The Fox"** to the Scottish captain of **"The Captain's Doll."** "It illustrates Lawrence's range," wrote F. R. Leavis, "that not only **"The Ladybird,"** with its exalted incantatory mode, but also one of his best things, **"The Captain's Doll,"** the characters of which are upper-middle-class and aristocratic, and the tone of which has a flexibility corresponding to the range and resource of their speech, should have appeared in the same volume."

Yet there they are, between the same covers. In so placing them, Lawrence invites us to do more than be impressed with their range. He challenges us to discover the tie that pulls them together, the shared principle that underlies their vivid differences. Harry T. Moore suggests that **"The Ladybird"** is based on the Sleeping Beauty motif of folklore. The motif is certainly present here, and in the two companion tales as well. Lady Daphne is emotionally "asleep" until "awakened" by Count Dionys. Her sleep is a disturbed one: she is vaguely conscious of unrealized feelings, of longings that find no outlet; she is oppressed by a sense of being cut off from some deeper self. Her freedom of movement is severely constricted. "She was nailed inside her own fretful self-consciousness," Lawrence says of her in one of the story's great phrases. Thus impaled, she can only wait for the stranger, with his special magic, to free her from the evil spell. The young soldier in **"The Fox"** does the same for March. Her heterosexual nature, slumbering beneath the lesbian surface, is released from its entombment by the insistent force of his desire for her. The sleeping beauty idea is less overtly present in **"The Captain's Doll,"** but even there the drugged way in which Captain Hepburn moves through the early stages of the story is in striking contrast to the alertness of his actions at the end; he too passes from sleep to wakefulness. The process has its obvious biographical prototype in Frieda Lawrence's well-known statement about the kind of life she was living as Frieda Weekley when Lawrence first appeared: she felt like a sleepwalker, sunk lethargically in a state of spiritual drowsiness, only half-alive. Lawrence, she claimed, released her from this emotional torpor for good and all.

Another theory has been advanced by George Ford [see Further Reading list]. Mr. Ford finds in **"The Ladybird"**—and in other works by Lawrence—a retelling of the Pluto-Persephone myth. In it the dark man (Pluto, Lawrence, Count Dionys) emerges from the nether world (Hades, the coal mine, Eastern Europe) and compels the blonde woman (Persephone, Frieda, Lady Daphne) to accompany him back to his domain. In the end, the call of the upper region is too strong and he is forced to share her with it. Lady Daphne remains part of the conventional world represented by her English husband and part of the underworld ruled over by the King of Darkness. The black-haired man, incarnating the dark gods that serve for Lawrence as a metaphor of psychic potency, was a standard figure in his fiction. He is plainly present in **"The Ladybird."** One notes that the German countess in **"The Captain's Doll"** is blonde and the Scottish captain dark; in the end, he carries her off from the light of Europe to the darkness of Africa. The pattern is not immediately applicable to **"The Fox"** where March, the Persephone figure, is dark-haired. But one might argue that she is sexually displaced, being presented as a man in the early stages of the story: "She would be a man about the place." "She looked almost like some graceful, loose-balanced young man." And that is the role she plays in her relationship with Banford. Her color is therefore reversed, for perhaps the same reason that Gerald Crich, in *Women in Love,* playing the dependent feminine role in his affair with Gudrun, is intensely blond.

There is no doubt that Lawrence is using these materials from fairy tale and mythology, but the stories have a larger scope and deeper resonance than are accounted for by them. The three principal characters in each set up a triangular relationship too complex to be adequately described by fixed patterns borrowed from the past. The ambience in which they move, unsettled, transitory, richly chaotic, is peculiar to Lawrence's art and not easily explained in schematic terms. **"The Captain's Doll,"** with its sense of deliberate comedy, is especially resistant to definition by traditional romance, whether folk or myth. We are encouraged to look more intently within the stories themselves for clues to their collective meaning.

The element first encountered is the titles, each containing a symbol for a figure within. The ladybird or scarab is the emblem for the Count, the fox for Henry, the doll for the captain. These emblem images are embodiments of some significant quality in the man, but because they represent only the one quality, they are caricatures. They are, in effect, to use one of Lawrence's favorite terms, *reductions* of the men. We see the men in them clearly enough, but in a shrunken way. The problem for each—the problem of the stories—is how to be freed from the emblem into themselves, how to escape from their imprisonment as caricatures and regain their living wholeness.

The liberation process is particularly marked in **"The Captain's Doll."** The Countess makes a doll of her Scottish lover as a sign of her exasperation with him. The doll is a perfect physical likeness, down to the tight-fitting tartan trews. Seeing it for the first time, the Captain says, "You've got me." But the point of course is that she hasn't got him. All that she has caught of him is his physical self, down to his straight, handsome legs mentioned several times during the course of the story. The visible part of him is all she can take hold of; the invisible side of him—vague, non-thinking, gazing at her with "that other, unseeing look"—eludes her. She is fascinated by it, but cannot pin it down, and in her frustration imprisons in the doll the part of him that she can pin down. The

doll expresses her relationship with the Captain when the story opens; it has been sexually satisfactory and emotionally baffling. As long as the doll stands between them, their relationship cannot progress.

The Captain is a doll not only to the Countess but also to his wife. With her "lardy-dardy middle-class English," her sense of ownership and her obsessively feminine determination to "protect our men," Mrs. Hepburn is triumphantly characterized. On their wedding night, she extracted from her husband a promise, delivered on his knees, to love and adore her. This suppliant position confirms his function as her doll, a possessed subservient object that feeds her emotionally. Even when he ceases to "love" and "adore" her, he continues, willingly and calmly, to make love to her—a fact that shocks the Countess. Paradoxically, she finds it hard to believe that the man of whom she has made a doll has been one for eighteen years to another woman.

With the wife's death, the Captain is freed from his bondage to her. He repudiates the love-adoration posture and sets off in pursuit of the Countess in search of another kind of relationship. But first he must get rid of the doll. He finds it staring at him uncannily in a Munich shop window, and later as part of a fashionable still-life canvas, surrounded by two sunflowers in a glass jar and a poached egg on toast. The doll disappears, but he buys the still-life, turns it over to the Countess when he finds her, and in the end, when a new and unexpected union between them is created, she burns the painting as a sign that the Captain's phase as a doll is over and his phase as a man has begun.

Something of the same process occurs in the other two novelettes. The fox raids the hen coops, and the women are helpless against his assaults. March is entranced by the fox, whom she encounters but is unable to shoot. He is a kind of demon that invades her unconscious:

> She lowered her eyes, and suddenly saw the fox. . . . And he knew her. She was spell-bound—she knew he knew her. So he looked into her eyes, and her soul failed her. . . . For he had lifted his eyes upon her, and his knowing look seemed to have entered her brain. She did not so much think of him: she was possessed by him. She saw his dark, shrewd, unabashed eye looking into her, knowing her. She felt him invisibly master her spirit.

The Biblical use of "know" here suggests the sexual elements in the encounter. The fox is young, male, arrogant, and triumphant. Henry, who appears presently, has all these qualities in human form. Inevitably, he slays the fox and replaces it in March's sexual and psychic life.

In **"The Ladybird"** there is also a movement from the emblem to the man. On a visit to England years before the story opens, the Count had given Lady Daphne a thimble as a present on her seventeenth birthday. The thimble has a beetle in green stone at the top: the beetle is the ladybird, the Count's family crest. Until she uses the thimble, the Count is only a remote, mysterious abstraction to Daphne, a vague emanation from Eastern Europe far from her ken. When she meets him again as a wounded war prisoner, he reminds her of the thimble and asks her to sew him a shirt with it. At this point, the process of his ceasing to be an abstraction and becoming a man gets under way. A shirt touches the skin, and we know that to Lawrence touch was the most sacred and personal of the senses. Daphne, inept at sewing and confused in her feelings, misplaces the thimble, and not until it is found again can her relationship with the Count proceed. As with the doll and the fox, the emblem must be found and disposed of before the man can begin.

The emblem motif underlines Lawrence's conviction that modern life tends to shrink human beings into objects and abstractions, and that it is the mission of art to reverse the process, to restore men to their original individuality and wholeness.

But while this motif powerfully affects the men in these stories, it does not take the women into account. Yet their fate depends on the equilibrium established with the men. This equilibrium had been set forth as a theory not long before by Birkin in *Women in Love,* and emerges as one of the binding elements in these tales at the beginning of the '20's. The Countess is too masculine and "free" at the start of the **"The Captain's Doll."** Her excessive independence, assertiveness, and desire to get hold of the Captain—his vagueness irritates and disorients her—are as much her response to the unsettled times as to the compulsions of her own nature. The Captain's elusiveness is due to his married subservience. He has yielded too much of himself to his wife. Not until she dies can his balance be regained and can he be free to create a new relationship with the Countess. The equilibrium they finally establish is achieved not through harmony, friendly negotiations, and prudent adjustments, but through argument, angry dialectic, and a period of prolonged tension. They are deeply attracted to one another, but the ground through which they must pass is a minefield of resentments, demands, ultimatums, and mutual rage. The quarrel over the words in the marriage ceremony is characteristic of these collisions. He wants her not to love but to honor and obey him. She is anxious to love him, but is not prepared to honor and obey. It is an outrage, she feels, for an emancipated woman thus to humble herself before a man. So they quarrel, argue, and drive at each other. She finally gives way, grudgingly, reluctantly, not at all in the state of passive radiance typical of the traditional heroine. The equilibrium they reach is an equilibrium of tension. Their opposing male and female selves do work out an understanding, but it is an uneasy truce that prevails, not a stabilized peace.

In his opposition to Christian love, Lawrence repudiated meekness and docility in his lovers. As with himself and Frieda, belligerence and anger led to the promised land much more surely than passivity and non-resistance. He became a great specialist on love that is prickly, tense, bellicose, and quarrelsome, the kind that has its profound satisfactions but never ends "happily." Anti-Christian and anti-chivalrous, it was a nervously modern conception of love, rooted of course in the equality of the sexes, where each lover has, in Joseph Conrad's words, "an amazing sensitiveness to the claims of his own personality." When March is torn away from Banford's orbit and drawn into Henry's, she resists him to the very end of **"The Fox."** He wants more of her than she is willing to give; she is fearful of losing herself in him entirely. As they prepare to leave England, the struggle between them is still going on full force, but it is a struggle of equilibrium, Lawrence's ultimate objective in his dramas of personal life. And in **"The Ladybird"** Daphne's distorted relationship with her adoring husband is pulled into balance by her newly forged, polyandrous connection with the Count.

The search for emotional equilibrium has its geographic analogues. The Captain, after marrying the Countess, will take her off to a farm in East Africa: the contact between sophisticated Europe and primitive Africa reveals Lawrence's instinct for bringing opposites together. Earlier, the Captain had disclosed a passion for astronomy, and he is observed gazing at the moon through a telescope: the crowded earth and the uninhabited moon are another pair of opposites being momentarily joined. In **"The Fox"** March and Henry are setting off for the New World: England, small and enclosed, is juxtaposed with Canada, vast and open. In **"The Ladybird"** Eastern and Western Europe meld briefly in the embraces of Daphne and the Count. The development of a new emotion in Lawrence seems to require a change of venue, or at any rate is always accompanied by one. Paul Morel, at the end of *Sons and Lovers,* leaves the countryside and moves toward the glowing town. Birkin and Ursula leave Europe altogether and flee southward. Aaron Sisson abandons England and gropes his way to Italy. So does Alvina Houghton in *The Lost Girl.* In the novels where everyone remains in the same place, like *The White Peacock* and *The Trespasser,* everything relapses in defeat.

The shifts in location, however, are not arranged haphazardly. It is not just a matter of picking oneself up and leaving, where any place will do. The two places in each instance are usually in the same stark contrast to one another as are the man and woman connecting them. Lawrence wishes to make them extraordinarily different from one another to emphasize the necessity of the man and the woman being as different from one another as possible, for only in preserving the purity and absoluteness of that difference can a new relationship between them be possible. Only then can they really come together. A successful fusion is therefore possible only to the degree that they remain distinct. This is the paradox that lies at the heart of Lawrence's psychic-sexual dramas. And it is a paradox reinforced at every point by the geographic arrangements that Lawrence, quite as much as Conrad before him, organizes in the service of his art.

Underneath all the ideas in these stories described so far, underneath the classical and fairy-tale motifs, the emblem-symbols, the equilibrium of opposites, there appears most powerfully and inclusively the theme that absorbed Lawrence during the last ten years of his life: the theme of resurrection. It had been impressed upon him in the non-conformist chapels he had attended as a boy, in the Methodist hymns he loved to sing, in the whole atmosphere of Evangelical Christianity in which he had been reared. The rebirth into Christ he later changed to rebirth into man, the resurrection in heaven he altered to resurrection on earth. This was the radical surgery he performed on orthodox Christianity. But the Christian conviction of death as a preface to rebirth he retained intact, and in each of the three novelettes death is not only the preliminary but the prerequisite to new life.

In **"The Captain's Doll"** it is the death of Mrs. Hepburn that releases the others to a fresh beginning. Though her fall from a hotel window is accidental, there is something deeply purposive about it. The Captain, reporting the event to the Countess, describes his wife as a caged bird trapped in the wrong environment, even speaking a language not native to her soul. Her death, while a physical shock, is a psychic relief. Lawrence wishes to free the event from the burden of contrivance, from being, too baldly, a device manufactured to make the main sequence of his story possible. He does so by endowing Mrs. Hepburn with a complex nature not wholly borne out by the facts. As we see her in action when alive, she is a possessive woman with a will to sexual ownership under-lined by her feverish attempt to secure the doll. After she dies, we are told by her husband of her imprisoned side, a side we must take on faith since it is not dramatized but only de-scribed. The description, however, is eloquent, and is deliv-ered in that tone of special wisdom, of Delphic emanation from the Captain's remote and hidden self that developed into Lawrence's special "art language." Mrs. Hepburn dies, but she dies from a compelled emotional position and not simply in an arranged moment of plot. Her death removes a relationship which by its devouring character sealed off the Captain's life energies.

The act of death is more deliberately willed in **"The Fox,"** and is no less decisive. Two living creatures stand in March's way; both are slain by Henry. One is the aggressive male fox that raids the coop, who exercises a spell over March so po-tent she is unable to lift her gun against him. In the contest between *his* natural maleness and her *assumed* maleness, his is plainly the more powerful. In slaying the fox, Henry ab-sorbs its power and draws March into his psychic field. The other obstacle is of course Banford, with whom March has a lesbian relationship. Henry kills her too, with the exercise of the same force of will that he exhibited over the fox. Warn-ing her to step aside from the path of the tree he is cutting down, Henry knows that the warning is precisely what will stiffen her resolve not to move. The tree falls, crushing the girl, and at the same time freeing March from a tie she is un-able to break of her own accord. Again the two deaths are more than episodes in the plot; they are also events in March's emotional life, embodying her deflected energies and clearing the way to her rebirth.

In **"The Ladybird"** death is not specific but generalized. "How many swords had Lady Beveridge in her pierced heart!" is the story's opening sentence. She had lost her sons and brother in the war, and "death seemed to be moving with wide swathes through her family." The war, devouring a whole generation, is the death agent that clears the ground, if horrifyingly, for emotional rebirth, just as the Count's war wounds, from which he is slowly recovering, lead to the puri-fication and intensification of his role as the agent of the heal-ing darkness. **"The Ladybird,"** and the other two stories as well, taking place as they do toward the end of and immedi-ately after the war, exploit the feeling always present at such times that the old ways are shattered as new ones maneuver to be born. Lawrence hated the war, but he exploited it to great advantage in his work.

The three types of death on display here—accidental, deliber-ate, and generalized—are repeated, with variations, in all of Lawrence's writings from this point on. The accidental kill-ing of Kangaroo is in line with Mrs. Hepburn's fatal fall. The ritualized murder of the young protagonist in **"The Woman Who Rode Away"** and of the three Mexicans at the hands of Don Cipriano in *The Plumed Serent* are akin to the slaying of Banford. The shattering effects of the war are taken up once more in *Lady Chatterley's Lover,* and the slowly healing wounds of Count Dionys reappear in the slowly healing wounds of the Christ figure in **"The Man Who Died."**

Each type of prefatory death presents Lawrence with an artis-tic problem. Accidental death carries with it the curse of con-trivance, the author arranging a haphazard event just to make his plot come out right. The deliberately willed death involves him in something far more serious: the inevitable arousing in the reader of feelings of nausea and horror that

run counter to and threaten to destroy the author's channels of sympathy. The murder of Banford, offered to us as a neces-sary and even humane act, creates a visible chill in the read-ing air. The story survives the shock of this ruthless event but it never entirely repairs the damage done to our deepest feel-ings, those very feelings that Lawrence is forever appealing to and proclaiming as the ultimate source of truth. (pp. 173-81)

In his assault on Christianity, Lawrence believed that hate, violence, and anger, sincerely felt, had as legitimate a right to expression as kindness and love. Whatever may be said for this in theory, it raises formidable problems in the actualities of conduct. Here Lawrence's attempt to reform our sensibili-ties was probably too radical as a life purpose, while it intro-duced into his art grave emotional complications that grew progressively more serious and became, at last, unmanage-able. Resurrection that depended on murder somehow de-stroyed itself.

"The Captain's Doll" and its two companion tales are the su-preme staging ground for Lawrence's ideas at a turning point in his life. A month after sending off the last of them to his publisher, he left Europe altogether for wanderings in other parts of the world. Like the Captain, like Henry, he abandons the old world and its old forms in search of new resurrections, and, with his belief in the spirit of place, such resurrections were most readily accessible elsewhere. In his fiction, the novel of personal relationships and personal conflicts was be-hind him for the time being, and the novel of ideas, of pro-grams, of social and political resurrection lay ahead. The sto-ries of this collection contain some of his best and most repre-sentative writing. Beyond that, they link the early Lawrence with the later, and thereby serve as a revealing microcosm of his career. (p. 182)

Leo Gurko, "D. H. Lawrence's Greatest Collection of Short Stories—What Holds It Together," in Modern Fiction Studies, *Vol. 18, No. 2, Summer, 1972, pp. 173-82.*

P. MICHEL-MICHOT (essay date 1975)

[*In the following excerpt, Michel-Michot analyzes the signifi-cance of setting in "Tickets, Please," focusing on the story's opening paragraphs.*]

"Tickets, Please" has not so far received much critical atten-tion, and when it has its introductory paragraphs have been altogether ignored or not considered in all their implications. Brooks and Warren [in their anthology *Understanding Fic-tion*] focus their comment on the Lawrentian theme of the " 'doubleness' of love, its strange mixture of aggressiveness and passivity, of cruelty and tenderness, of possessiveness and surrender". Lionel Trilling [see excerpt dated 1967], viewing the story as Lawrence's expression of the shift from the Victo-rian to the modern period, interprets its beginning as an illus-tration of "Victorian . . . whimsy, coziness and jollity"—also reflected in the language and style—which is later under-mined and exploded by the outburst of violence rendered in "quick spare language". Seymour Lainoff rightly draws at-tention to the wartime aspect of the setting but does not con-sider the full significance or the function of the setting as a whole. Indeed the opening paragraphs achieve more than just a placing in time (wartime) and place (Midlands) of the "singleline tramway system", they also present the perspec-tive in which Lawrence sets the main episode, a perspective which is supported by the structure of the story; and the first reference to wartime—"Since we are in wartime the drivers are men unfit for active service . . ."—does not so much define the period as account for the kind of drivers and conductors who run the tramcar. But, surely, this oblique wartime indication gets its full meaning at the end of the story when, after witnessing the development of the girls' wish for revenge and their attack on John Thomas, the reader extrapolates and realizes what a devastating light this story casts on war in general. I would therefore suggest that the tram-system-in-wartime is an extended metaphor used by Lawrence to express the wrongness of modern society's approach to and distortion of its dynamics: society is presented as mechanizing, regulating, misdirecting and eventually perverting its creative force, and favouring a similar reversal of values and attitudes latent in the man-woman relationship, a distortion which inevitably leads, on the individual as well as on the collective level, to violence, frustration and defeat.

The tramcar is at once presented by a third-person narrator as part of a "*single*-line tramway *system*" (italics mine), and the long, modulated, first sentence describing its route—from the county town through "the black, industrial countryside", "the long ugly villages of workmen's houses", past cinemas and shops, "boldly" "up hill and down dale" to its terminus on "the edge of the wild, gloomy country beyond"—gives a superficial and complacent picture of the physical, social, and economic aspects of the country and conveys the narrator's satisfaction about the system, and a sense of achievement he seems to share with the tramcar that has overcome all the difficulties on its route. The journey back to the county town is viewed as an adventure rich in thrills and sensations. . . . The point of view becomes almost that of the tramcar and finally, within the same sentence, shifts to that of a collective "we" making one with the tramcar, so that the shift in point of view suggests successively a complacent and documentary view—"There is in the Midlands a single-line tramway system"—then the thrills and sense of adventure experienced by the animal-like engine "purr(ing)with satisfaction", then a collective identity when "we" are back in town and the tramcar's "still perky jaunty somewhat dare-devil" attitude is compared to a "jaunty sprig of parsley out of a black colliery garden".

The sense of adventure and the excitement enjoyed by the passengers is clearly presented in the opening paragraph as a thrilling escape from the blackness of the industrial landscape, and the excitement gets its value by contrast with the ugly, dull surroundings as suggested by the parsley comparison. The animal-like and bold driving force which characterizes the tram is however confined within an organized and regulated system and stops short where the real adventure should begin, "on the edge of the wild gloomy country beyond". When we read further that the tram is driven by cripples and hunchbacks, i.e. by the physically deficient—and we know what this meant for Lawrence—who have "the spirit of the devil in them" and in whose hands the ride becomes a "steeplechase", we realize at the literal level the sense of exhilarating adventure, the sense of recklessness enjoyed by the people on the "civilian home front", their impulse to live dangerously too; but when we learn further on that the car, "packed with one solid mass of *living* people", often breaks down and comes "to a *dead* halt in the midst of the unbroken blackness" (italics mine), that the car is then "a haven of refuge" for the miners travelling "from village to village for a change of cinema, of girl, of pub", and that the passengers

are reluctant "to dismount" because "the nights are howlingly cold, black and windswept", we have enough Lawrentian landmarks to take us beyond the literal meaning of the tramway system and the sense of companionship shared by the passengers. Indeed the tramway system, its drivers and passengers, is a vast metaphor for society's rape of the natural countryside turning it into an unnaturally black, industrial area while prompting in the people a wish for escape and providing them with false, artificial, mechanised excitement that makes them cling to the tramcar as a refuge of *light* and refuse to enter the cold, natural blackness of the *night*, that darkness which, as so often in Lawrence's short stories, is associated with instinctive life and is the prelude to a regenerative death.

In his mock-heroic placing of the tram system Lawrence also presents it as a world of reversed values:

> This, the most dangerous tram-service in England, as the authorities themselves declare, with pride, is entirely conducted by girls, and driven by rash young men, a little crippled, or by delicate young men, who creep forward in terror.

The very structure and punctuation of this sentence, in combining the narrator's and the authorities' point of view (with the ironic relation between "dangerous", as applied to a public service, and "with pride"), conveys Lawrence's stance, which is further established when he has the "rash" yet "a little crippled" and the "delicate" and terrified young men drive the car, and when he defines the girl-conductors as "fearless young hussies" for whom the "step of the tramcar was (their) Thermopylae". The men are rash irresponsible weaklings, the girl-conductors have "all the *sang-froid* of an old non-commissioned officer." . . . The female is in charge, endowed with male aggressiveness, "ready to hit first". The double chiasm between "roaring hymns" and "antiphony of obscenities", the former happening downstairs, the latter upstairs, humorously underlines the abnormal quality of the tram world. (pp. 464-67)

The short dialogue that follows is a dramatic presentation of this upside-down world and, by a zoom effect, focuses the attention on Annie, addressed by the colliers as Miss Stone, while the next paragraph introduces the chief of the inspectors, not named in the social and work context of the tram-service, but who appears "when things are slack". So we gradually move from a work, public, social situation to a private, individual, man-woman relationship with its roots in the tram-service-in-wartime, but, significantly, developing outside working hours. As such it becomes a counterpart to the tram system and gives Lawrence his opportunity for a dramatic presentation of the sexual theme.

The sexual significance of the tram-service-in-wartime metaphor becomes obvious when the focus is narrowed on the love-hate relationship between Annie and John Thomas, and when the narrator bluntly says that "for some reason everybody employed in this tram-service is young: there are no grey heads. It would not do. Therefore the inspectors are of the right age, and one, the chief, is also good-looking". Surely, if the tram-service-in-wartime were to be taken at its literal level only, the tram staff would *necessarily* include grey heads.

Instead of the lighted tram driven by "cripples" and "fearless young hussies" taking "howling colliers" from village to village "for a change of cinema, of girl, of pub", we have John

Thomas Raynor "always called John Thomas except sometimes, in malice, Coddy" with a *"ruddy"* face and a "faint *impudent* smile" (italics mine) with a *"black* overcoat buttoned up to his chin" (italics mine) who becomes his true self at night when he *"walks* out" with a girl in the *dark night"* (italics mine), after work—"always providing she is sufficiently attractive, and that she will consent to walk". John Thomas's approach to sex and that of modern society, as imaged in the tram-service-in-wartime metaphor, are thus clearly contrasted.

Lawrence then presents the love-hate relationship between Annie and John Thomas, which illustrates in a dramatic, i.e. non-preaching form, the battle of the sexes; but here again the setting is important for the Statutes Fair world is an echo of the tram-service-in-wartime, and it is significant for our interpretation that the second time Lawrence alludes to war it is to present the Fair as a world of substitutes—just as the tram-service stands for modern society's substitute for the real thing, i.e. Lawrence's approach to sex: "In the coco-nut shies there were no coco-nuts, but artificial wartime substitutes". There, on a November "drizzling ugly night," John Thomas meets Annie and takes her on the *dragons* and the *horses.* As in the tram situation, the place is crowded and the people are offered substitutes that represent a cheapening of the real thing. Not only has modern society cut man from his natural roots, placing him in an ugly industrial setting, it has also provided him with mass technological entertainments which distort and corrupt the originally pagan tone and meaning of such festive occasions.

The scene of the lighted tram coming to a dead halt in the night and the passengers' refusing to go out into the dark is echoed but endowed with a different meaning when John Thomas is in charge and takes advantage of the dark, resulting from the breakdown of the projector in the cinema, to draw Annie towards him before he actually takes her out into the *natural* darkness of the night. In the fair episode Lawrence shows on the one hand how Annie, while responding to the stimuli provided by the fair world, tries to remain in the 'system' ("she was afraid her hat was on one side", later on "she put her hat straight"), and on the other how John Thomas cunningly uses these stimuli to make Annie more aware of himself and gradually, overcoming her social defences, takes her away from the fair for "a walk across the *dark, damp* fields" (italics mine) for a moment of Lawrentian love. Social taboos and misconceptions are seen to recede as Annie becomes subdued by John Thomas's warm presence and surrenders to his kisses, which are "soft and slow and searching". After Lawrence has thus revealed the purely instinctive attraction between John Thomas and Annie, her female passivity and surrender to the irresistible power of the male, he shows the other side of the coin: when Annie, as a true creature of the tram-service, takes an *intelligent* interest in him and wants an *intelligent* response, i.e. becomes a possessive female sure of her hold on him, John Thomas, who wants to remain "a mere nocturnal presence", leaves her and goes his own dark independent way, taking a more docile girl out. The love relationship is then reversed into a hate relationship: Annie's sense of frustration and wounded pride take command, her love turns to hate, and her original passivity and surrender turn to aggressiveness and cruelty. The girls' attack on John Thomas, a furious Amazonian revenge on the Don Juan of the tram-service, continues the mock-heroic vein sounded in the presentation of the tram system, and the struggle duly develops into an inverted love scene with the

girls in charge, active, aggressive, on top of John Thomas lying on his back.

It is significant for the present argument that the collective revenge takes us back to the tram-service world, to the girls' waiting-room, where they trap and corner John Thomas like an animal; and it is just before he enters the room that Lawrence, for the third and last time, alludes to war: "Outside was the darkness and lawlessness of wartime", which is soon shown to prevail inside as well. The waiting-room then becomes a microcosm for the world at war: in their furious collective revenge the girls, urged by their frustrated instincts, are further inflamed by each other's violence and overshoot their original aim, a mere prank "to take him down a peg or two" and become mere beasts madly scratching their victim all over. Here Lawrence at once echoes and comments on the "darkness and lawlessness of war", its possible motivation and inevitable, devastating results. An originally private and psychological war between John Thomas and Annie is related to society's violation of nature—in the landscape and the quality of life—and to its perversion or inversion of true instinctive life (as shown in the opening paragraphs), and is extended to a small community in which the silent majority led by Annie, a strong, frustrated will to power, are inevitably carried beyond themselves to extremes of violence and cruelty of which they are eventually only half aware. Indeed at the end they disclaim all responsibility and soon try to dismiss the 'incident' from their consciousness: "Tit for tat, old man (. . .) The girls were all anxious to be off. They were tidying themselves hurriedly, with mute stupefied faces." Annie, who has more insight than the others and is divided between desire and hate, yet was the most intent on humiliating the enemy, feels "something broken in her". By using force she has engineered her own defeat, for now she can only reject John Thomas's choice of her as his girl, a choice which he cunningly made knowing perfectly well that she could not accept it; and she turns away with bitter hopelessness, her face quivering "with a kind of agony". John Thomas, the 'enemy', is eventually hurt but not vanquished, and Annie is apparently victorious but actually defeated. This may be Lawrence's comment on war and violence, whether private or public, psychological or political.

This typically Lawrentian story is often anthologized because it gives what Widmer rightly calls "a condensed history of the rhythm of usual love—predatory male and possessive female moving from attraction to excitement to intimacy to possession to resentment". But an interpretation limited to this theme and dismissing the long and meaningful introduction is too reductive. Only a close analysis of the opening paragraphs and of the symbolic significance of the setting can make us aware of the full meaning of the story, whose title—**"Tickets, Please"**—is the epitome of Lawrence's covert criticism of modern society, this censure being expressed in the descriptions of the "single-line tramway system", the Statutes Fair and the girls' revenge in the waiting-room and presented in a humorous mock-heroic vein, which is a rare achievement in Lawrence. (pp. 467-70)

P. Michel-Michot, "D. H. Lawrence's 'Tickets, Please': The Structural Importance of the Setting," in Revue des langues vivantes, *Vol. XLI, No. 5, 1975, pp. 464-70.*

CHARLES KOBAN (essay date 1978)

[*In the following excerpt, Koban appraises "The Rocking-Horse Winner" from a religious and moral perspective.*]

W. D. Snodgrass' famous essay on Lawrence's **"The Rocking-Horse Winner"** [see excerpt dated 1958] is a very nearly exhaustive explication of the story's meaning, yet it is not I think totally exhaustive because Snodgrass—like critics in general—has overlooked one side of the story's meaning, namely the mystical side. It is very tempting to see the story as a kind of social commentary, as a "way to live" Snodgrass puts it in his title. Certainly, **"The Rocking-Horse Winner"** is a mordant commentary on the distorted and self-destructive values of the upper middle-class and of many of us living in a capitalist, money-dominated society. But it is worthwhile, as a corrective to socialistic approaches to Lawrence, to recall his famous pronouncement in a letter to Edward Garnett: "But primarily I am a passionately religious man, and my novels must be written from the depths of my religious experience." And it is interesting and I think valuable to take a "religious" view of **"The Rocking-Horse Winner"** not as a corrective but as a complement to Snodgrass' essay. A proper "religious" view of the story must of course consider the sublimation of human feeling in the form of money as a mystical force in family life, a topic that Snodgrass deals with from a moral point of view.

Lawrence did not consider money an evil in itself, or at least he considered it a necessary evil, as his letters to Frieda Lawrence reveal. To him marriage was first of all a mystical union, a coming together of two souls in understanding and love. One could go further—for Lawrence the only freedom a man could know was the freedom of losing himself in his love for a woman. Marriage has a special place in Lawrence's vision, for marriage institutionalizes the fusion of souls which ought ideally to exist between man and woman. And out of the ideal marriage comes the inner strength to cope unperturbed with the many problems of the modern world. . . . It is of course popular to interpret Lawrence's definition of love as primarily sexual, and sexual it unquestionably is. But even sex, or perhaps one should say especially sex, is interpreted mystically by Lawrence. One could cite numerous examples of his mystical interpretation of sex, but **"The Fox"** provides perhaps the clearest. March and Grenfel come together in the most purely mystical union before ever there is any sexual consummation of their—one hesitates to call it—love. At any rate, there is a flame-like fusion of two souls first—and marriage and sex follow inevitably.

But Lawrence knew that for the middle-class money was a *sine qua non* of marriage. . . . Lawrence hated money and the warping of modern man that scrambling for money caused. But he knew that no middle-class marriage could be successful without it. Money on the other hand must be kept in perspective and not romanticized into a substitute for love, as it is in **"The Rocking-Horse Winner."**

Hester in **"The Rocking-Horse Winner"** is a woman "who started with all the advantages, yet she had no luck. She married for love, and the love turned to dust." Lawrence does not describe the process of disillusionment that has occurred in Hester's marriage, but one can imagine it with the help of other of Lawrence's writings—the slow destruction of love between husband and wife in the Morel family, caused mainly by impecuniousness and the mother's middle-class ambitions; the disaffection that reduces love to mere passion then

hatred in **"England, My England,"** again caused by the husband's failure to be an adequate bread-winner and supporter of the family. The father in **"The Rocking-Horse Winner"** is clearly a failure as provider and family-head, so much so that we are scarcely conscious of his existence. He fades into the background. And his failure is aggravated by the high social position the family tries to maintain. "There was never enough money," we are told. "The mother had a small income, and the father had a small income, but not nearly enough for the social position which they had to keep up."

So when **"The Rocking-Horse Winner"** opens, the process of disaffection has already occurred, and the close love between husband and wife which would have generated the mystical energy necessary for the family's well-being has been transformed into an ugly passion, greed. In *Sons and Lovers,* Mrs. Morel finds an alternative to her husband's love in her closeness to her sons; and Winifred in **"England, My England"** finds in cold duty to her children the purpose in life which her husband fails to provide her. But Hester romanticizes the family greed into mystical love of money, as personified in the whispering house, which "came to be haunted by the unspoken phrase: *There must be more money! There must be more money!*" And her mystical abstraction communicates itself insidiously to the children, making them insecure and self-conscious just as the love between her and her husband if it still existed would have made them feel wanted and safe.

Still, Hester like Mrs. Morel and Winifred *is* closer to her children, especially Paul, than to her husband. Though she is incapable of love, she is out of a sense of duty at least solicitous for her children, for they are her link with life and vitality—with the mystical force of love that is nearly dead in her heart. What I would like to suggest is that the story can be read as the climax in the chronicle of the death of love in Hester, the death of her heart, and that as such it ought to be read primarily as an allegory of the death of the child in her, the death of innonce and love. Mystically and allegorically speaking, Paul's death is her death. At the beginning of the story we are told that "at the centre of her heart was a hard little place that could not feel love, no, not for anyone." The motif of Hester's hardness is repeated in the story though she clings to her anxiety over Paul, but by the end of the story when Paul has lapsed into a coma she is "heart-frozen." Just as Paul's eyes are like "blue stones," so his mother's heart is stonelike. "His mother sat feeling her heart had gone, turned actually into a stone." With Paul's death the death of spirit in Hester is complete, for he was her last contact with the mystical springs of love that well up in all of us only if we love some other human being, as Lawrence said, with complete "nakedness of body and spirit." The mystifying of greed is finally an empty mysticism which destroys the worshipper of money as it destroys Paul and as it destroys Hester.

The closeness between mother and son is carefully developed in the story. Their conversation and interaction make for the central human interest in the story, but the relationship is unfortunately blighted from the beginning by Hester's hardness of heart. She cares only for money and her terrible romanticism infects Paul in his solicitation for her. He is trapped in the web of mystified greed that she has woven and which she calls luck: ". . . he went about with a sort of stealth, seeking inwardly for luck. He wanted luck, he wanted it, he wanted it." Luck is money in the abstract, the mystical sense because luck will always bring money and, being divinely given, cannot (unlike money) be taken away. " 'It's what causes you to have money. If you're lucky you have money. That's why it's better to be born lucky than rich.' "

The spurious mystical net is cast by the mother and the son is caught in its cords. From this point on they are one in their self-destructive mystical union. At the point when the boy is in the depths of his agony over the upcoming Derby, the union grows particularly strong and weighty—the mother's "heart curiously heavy because of him." In an interview he advises her not to be anxious about him: "I wouldn't worry, mother, if I were you." " 'If you were me and I were you,' said his mother, 'I wonder what we *should* do.' " And it is so, as her response indicates: they are for the time one. The motif running throughout the story of the flaming, glaring, sometimes wild blue eyes of the boy reinforces the idea of their union. It is as if an alien spirit inhabited and drove him to seek for luck and the spirit is of course the spirit of his mother, the spirit of greed. She is inside of him, flashing out from behind "his big blue eyes blazing with a sort of madness." His madness is hers, and with his death she is left to a living death. (pp. 391-94)

It is wrong I think to analyze the boy from too strict a moral point of view, as Snodgrass does, as if the child consciously made the wrong moral choices and had somehow knowingly entered into a league with demons. He is innocent, naive, and even loving of his mother. It is his mystical openness to her that leaves him vulnerable to the terrible forces she unleashes in her own household. To take him too realistically is faulty criticism for he is very much a symbol of the childish innocence that his mother has sadly let die in her. He accepts her worship of luck unconsciously . . . and he pursues that nebulous entity under the almost religious guidance of Bassett, who "was serious as a church." In another context and under more admirable inspiration, the boy's death might even be seen as the supreme sacrifice, since he gives up his life to placate his mother's tormented spirit. Alas, she will not now have to worry about money: " 'My God, Hester, you're eighty-odd thousand to the good, and a poor devil of a son to the bad.' " Paul is finally pathetic rather than immoral, and pathetic too is the stony-hearted mother.

But Lawrence does not want us I think to see Paul as a kind of child-sacrifice; he scarcely wants us to see him in a moral light at all for the moral light is cast full upon Hester and by reflection upon the nearly invisible father and from them out upon our money-maddened, love-starved society. The story has to it an altogether unbelievable air, not that it lacks therefore conviction and meaning. The whispering house, the riding of a rocking-horse to find race winners, the motif of Paul's blazing, uncanny blue eyes—all give the story an eerie unreality that lifts it out of the moral realm into the sphere of mystical relationships where inexplicable forces shape our lives. Even Paul's death is finally mysterious and can only be explained as resulting from the destructive power of mystified greed in which his mother has enveloped him. Inasmuch as the boy's death marks the death of the last vestige of something vibrant, loving, and irrational in her life, it is also the death in Hester of mystical forces that sustain life while rendering it trying.

The style of much of Lawrence's fiction is abstruse, dense, and compact, but the style of **"The Rocking-Horse Winner"** is deceptively simple with the simplicity of a Biblical parable and with some of the same allegorical overtones. (pp. 394-95)

And Lawrence with little exception maintains the parabolic

style—the simple directness and economy and pointed matter-of-factness—throughout **"The Rocking-Horse Winner."** If style is an indication of meaning—and if New Criticism has taught us anything it has certainly taught us to be sensitive to *how* a literary work means—then the style of **"The Rocking-Horse Winner"** points definitely toward an allegorical meaning in the story. Taken together with the mystical dimensions of the story, the parabolic style makes us conscious of an abstract, indeed religious meaning of the work which changes Paul into something more than a morally flawed young man, which renders him a symbol of the child in his mother. Paul's death of course makes the story a tragic one; but just as tragic is the death of innocence and love, symbolized by Paul, in his unfortunate mother. (p. 396)

Charles Koban, "Allegory and the Death of the Heart in 'The Rocking-Horse Winner,' " in Studies in Short Fiction, Vol. 15, No. 4, Fall, 1978, pp. 391-96.

KEITH CUSHMAN (lecture date 1979)

[*Cushman is an American critic who has published several significant works of scholarship on Lawrence and his writing (see Further Reading list). The following excerpt is taken from a lecture that Cushman first delivered at the D. H. Lawrence Conference at Southern Illinois University, Carbondale, in April, 1979. Here Cushman asserts that the stories in* England, My England *mark a significant advance in artistry over the early tales in* Prussian Officer, *displaying Lawrence's growing literary confidence and maturity, particularly in terms of his detached tone and the consistently high quality of his writing.*]

The stories in the **Prussian Officer** collection and the early stories collected posthumously in *A Modern Lover* are rooted in autobiography or at least in the immediate world of Lawrence's childhood and young manhood. The early stories depend for their effect upon the sharply realized milieu of countryside, colliery town, and occasionally (as with **"The White Stocking"**) city. The emotional impact of the finest of the early stories is related to Lawrence's own identification with their materials. **"Odour of Chrysanthemums"** is the most obvious example.

Though the emotional richness of the early tales is impressive, nevertheless Lawrence has made a significant advance in *England, My England,* where he does not rely on personal experience in the same way. His new ability to break loose from his own experience, to imagine his fictions more freely, is a measure of growing artistic confidence and maturity. The pleasures of the **Prussian Officer** collection include intense authorial engagement. In contrast, many of the *England, My England* stories are marked by sardonic detachment.

Though a number of Lawrence's finest tales were written and collected later in his career, the stories collected in *The Woman Who Rode Away* and the posthumous *The Lovely Lady* are much more uneven in quality, much more likely to suffer from thinness. **"The Rocking-Horse Winner"** is matched by **"Glad Ghosts."** **"The Man Who Loved Islands"** must co-exist with the nervous satiric attacks on John Middleton Murry. Nothing in *England, My England* is as nasty as **"None of That"** or as feeble as **"The Last Laugh."** My case for *England, My England* is based in part on the book's high percentage of achieved success.

The *England, My England* stories are, appropriately enough, all about English characters in English settings. All are studies in the relations between men and women (though with an author like Lawrence that hardly says anything profound). I will proceed by exploring what I take to be the major unifying elements in the collection. First, the stories of *England, My England* grow out of the experience of World War I and out of a new sense that the England of Lawrence's best hopes has become a lost cause. Second, the stories reveal Lawrence using myth and fairy tale structurally and playing off established mythical meaning for his own purposes. . . . Third, the stories, unlike many of the later tales, are nondoctrinaire. Instead they are in the best sense ambiguous. Finally, for the most part the *England, My England* stories are written in a vein of Lawrentian comedy. (p. 28)

In a letter of 26 April 1913 Lawrence had said that he wrote because he wanted "folk—English folk—to alter, and have more sense." Such a sentiment can be powerfully felt behind such works as *The Rainbow,* but with the exception of Mabel Pervin and Jack Fergusson in "The Horse Dealer's Daughter," the English men and women of the *England, My England* stories are beyond the possibility of alteration. Lawrence has imaginatively detached himself from the situation of England, just as in his own life he was then pointing toward America. He seems almost to take delight in observing his characters as they march toward perdition.

In "The Ladybird" Lawrence says that "the years 1916 and 1917 were the years when the old spirit died for ever in England"; he of course refers to the period of the worst carnage on the Western Front. The title story of *England, My England* directly addresses the death of the old English spirit. In the other stories Lawrence seems content to accept the fact that the old England is no more. He has moved on beyond crisis.

At the same time this volume is nevertheless part of Lawrence's response to the war. The dislocation and breakdown found throughout the collection point to the war's impact. So perhaps does the fact that nearly all the love relationships in the book are battles. "Tickets, Please" illustrates this point especially well, for it concludes with the tram-girls physically assaulting their elusive male supervisor.

"England, My England" itself is the work that is Lawrence's most direct statement *about* the war. The "Nightmare" chapter of *Kangaroo* describes England during wartime more vividly and concretely, but in "England, My England" Lawrence makes a concerted attempt to analyze and understand why the war happened to England and why England lacked the spiritual resources to come through intact. Lawrence's story of the failure of the dilettante Egbert is really the story of the failure of his generation and indeed the failure of England. Significantly, the original version of the story was published as early as October 1915. Lawrence revised the story extensively in December 1921, transforming it into a fully considered statement about England and the war.

It is not generally noticed that most of the other *England, My England* stories are rooted in the English experience of World War I. In both "Tickets, Please" and "Monkey Nuts" the traditional sexual roles have been subverted because the men are off fighting. The battles between John Thomas Raynor and the tram-girls and between Miss Stokes and Albert for the affections of Joe are placed in the context of the dislocations of wartime and its immediate aftermath. Similarly, Samson comes back to reclaim his Delilah in the first year of the war, asserting his traditional rights at a time when the traditional order is visibly disintegrating.

In "The Blind Man" Maurice Pervin is able to live the life of "sheer immediacy of blood-contact with the substantial world" because he has been blinded in Flanders. For all the richness of this life, his blindness is the result of a wound. Maurice's experience in the trenches has made him less than a whole man. The war is obviously the occasion for the battle between the sexes in "Wintry Peacock," for the story revolves around a letter from a Belgian girl in which she claims that she has had a baby by the married Corporal Alfred Goyte. Hadrian in "You Touched me," like Henry Grenfel in "The Fox," comes home to win one of the unmarried women only after the war has ended and things can return to normal.

E. W. Tedlock [see Further Reading list] has commented that the *England, My England* stories "contain Lawrence's most direct treatment of the war's effect on life." Only in the title story does Lawrence show us a soldier fighting in the war and none too convincingly: the machine-gun Lawrence says Egbert is in charge of actually seems to be an artillery-piece. But the point is not the war itself. Instead Lawrence uses details from the war to support his perception of irrevocable change.

The *England, My England* stories have tight, strong structures. This is partly because Lawrence is making use of ready-made structures that he finds in myth and fairy tale. In turning away from the Midlands and his own experience, he discovers rich resources for his narrative. *England, My England* is a collection of Lawrentian myths and fairy tales.

Although he constructs the stories on a foundation of myth and fairy tale, he subverts the myths and fairy tales he makes use of. The Lawrentian meaning resonates against the traditional, received meaning it replaces. This effect—revisionary mythmaking—contributes to the great vitality of the stories.

"The Blind Man" is a notable case in point. Surely its invocation of the paradox of sight through blindness has both *Oedipus* and *Lear* behind it. Like the Duke of Gloucester, Oedipus sees truly only when he is blinded. The true perception in both plays is associated with the light of reason, and Lawrence is having none of that. Instead he finds genuine, enduring value in the darkness. Blindness is not merely the path back to light. At the same time Lawrence insists that neither darkness nor light is adequate in itself. It is wholeness of being that must be striven for.

"Tickets, Please" is Lawrence's version of the myth of Orpheus and the maenads. In the myth Orpheus returns to Thrace after his failure to rescue his beloved Eurydice from the underworld. He encounters some Ciconian women raging as maenads, and they tear him to pieces. The explanation for their violence varies, but one tradition has it that each of the women wants him for herself and battles to possess him.

Lawrence transforms the mythical artist and lover into the tram inspector John Thomas Raynor. The tram-girls are Lawrence's maenads, and, true to form, they are angered by John Thomas' male elusiveness. He goes walking with the girls at night, nonchalantly flirts, and refuses to become more than a mysterious "nocturnal presence." Annie organizes the girls, they corner John Thomas and demand that he choose. When he still refuses, they attack. . . . Lawrence's maenads are appropriately "maddened," and they "giggle wildly." But Lawrence's Orpheus is not destroyed. Forced to choose, he

The ruins of Beauvale Priory, northeast of Eastwood, Nottingham, containing "the window in question" in Lawrence's story "A Fragment of Stained Glass."

chooses Annie, and in so doing he conquers her: "Annie let go of him as if he had been a hot coal." Something is "broken in her," and the other girls seem similarly dazed.

Both myth and short story express a fear of female sexuality. The power of eros is so intense that it becomes destructive. The exalted love of Orpheus and Eurydice and the unbridled ferocity of the maenads are but two manifestations of the same phenomenon. Lawrence adds a social context to the myth by placing his story in wartime: the women are free to break away from traditional restraint and inhibition because the men are not there to control them. However, Lawrence significantly revises the myth. Though his Orpheus can be battered in body, the power of male sexuality prevents his destruction.

"Samson and Delilah" revises the Biblical story, seemingly in the interest of male ascendancy. Though Lawrence's Delilah has soldiers tie up the Samson who has come to reclaim her, she is unable to shear his locks. Indeed she does not wish to do so: after he frees himself from the loosely tied rope, he discovers to his astonishment that she has left the door unlocked. This Delilah cannot resist the power of Samson's "dark, bright, mindless Cornish eyes." At story's end he has reclaimed his rightful place in the relationship. She glowers at the fire and shudders while he insinuates his hand between her breasts and talks on. As we shall see, she has "the eyes of some non-human creature" herself, and the struggle between Samson and Delilah is far from over.

As George Ford has noted, [see Further Reading list], **"Fanny and Annie"** is a version of the myth of Persephone and Pluto. Fanny, a proud, beautiful lady's maid, returns reluctantly to her home town "to marry her first-love" after her "brilliant and ambitious cousin" has jilted her. Fanny's return is a descent into the underworld. . . . The cousin could have led Fanny out of the provinces into a larger world. Now she must settle for second best, and even worse, a "red-faced woman" stands up in chapel and denounces Fanny's old sweetheart, accusing him of being responsible for her daughter's pregnancy.

But Lawrence's Persephone *chooses* the darkness. If the flames of the industrial town conjure up Hades, there are flames to be found within Fanny herself as she responds to Harry's "physical winsomeness" and his "flesh" that seems "new and lovely to touch." Though at first she is "inflamed with a sort of fatal despair," soon enough the only fire is that of physical attraction: "Fanny felt the crisp flames go through her veins as she listened." With comic deftness Lawrence reveals that Fanny finds Harry more interesting and attractive *after* the denunciation. She will stick it out and go through with the marriage. This Persephone will be happy to live in the underworld with her working-class Pluto.

John Vickery has observed that **"England, My England"** makes use of the mythic pattern of the scapegoat. Egbert as scapegoat is expelled first from his family and then from England. Traditionally the community drives out the scapegoat in order to restore itself, but no such restoration is possible in **"England, My England."** Egbert perishes, and Lawrence seems to feel that England will perish in his wake. The horsemen Egbert sees shortly before his death are associated with the riders of apocalypse.

"The Horse-Dealer's Daughter" even sounds like the name of a fairy tale, and Mabel Pervin is a version of Cinderella. She is oppressed by her three brutish brothers, the prescribed number out of fairy tales. She does the dirty work in the household, cleaning up while they sit around and call her "the sulkiest bitch that ever trod." Mabel has no fairy godmother to transform her into a princess. Instead, she must find her own salvation; her new life must be earned. Paradoxically she can achieve this only after immersing herself in the dark waters of death and destruction. Mabel is rescued from her suicide attempt by no Prince Charming but instead by

Jack Fergusson, the country doctor, a man who is also suffering from the sickness unto death.

"The Horse-Dealer's Daughter" also makes use of "Sleeping Beauty." Like Sleeping Beauty, Mabel must go through the experience of death in order to be truly brought to life. Fergusson saves her from the dark pond and its "cold, rotten clay." New life comes not from a magical kiss from the handsome prince but from a ritual immersion in the waters of destruction, followed by a passionate commitment made by a man who does not understand what he is doing.

Lawrence also revises "Sleeping Beauty" in **"You Touched Me."** Matilda Rockley goes at midnight to her father's bedroom, not realizing that Hadrian is sleeping there instead. Her touch awakens Hadrian, and "the fragile exquisiteness of her caress startled him." Lawrence reverses the fairy tale, for here it is the prince who awakens. At that, Hadrian is rather a sorry substitute for Prince Charming. In **"You Touched Me"** the power of human contact is quickening and awakening for both man and woman; both are brought to life. It must be added that Hadrian and Matilda do not seem destined to live happily ever after.

Lawrence's use of myth and fairy tale is a topic that demands full-scale exploration. Persephone and Pluto span his career from the courtship of the Morels to **"Bavarian Gentians."** Sleeping Beauty can be found in Louisa in the early **"Daughters of the Vicar"**; she is also very much present in Connie Chatterley. Ultimately Lawrence would create his own original fairy tales in such stories as **"The Rocking-Horse Winner"** and **"The Man Who Loved Islands."**

In *England, My England* the inherited stories provide Lawrence with ready-made structures. More importantly, he subverts traditional values as he subverts the traditional stories he makes use of. The *England, My England* stories have so much vitality partly because of the way they reverberate against familiar myths and fairy tales. Lawrence takes considerable delight in his revisionary mythmaking, in telling the stories of Oedipus, of Orpheus and the maenads, of Cinderella, of Sleeping Beauty one more time—and telling them his way.

In contrast to many of the stories from Lawrence's later years, the stories of *England, My England* are undogmatic and nondoctrinaire. Though they of course explore some of Lawrence's central beliefs, they also seem to demonstrate that at this point he felt that such beliefs could not be maintained with anything like certitude. (pp. 29-33)

Many of the *England, My England* stories seem to dramatize Lawrentian truths, but these truths tend to disappear when scrutinized carefully. **"The Blind Man"** is an excellent case in point. The story is a brilliant evocation of the rich life of intense, direct contact with the physical world. Lawrence's artistry is so commanding that he makes us feel as if we have truly entered Maurice Pervin's sensuous world. (p. 33)

Actually the scene of ritual communion only serves to underscore Maurice's extreme isolation. The life of the senses is one-sided and incomplete. Though Maurice is generally happy enough in his new-found darkness, he is also subject to "devastating fits of depression which seemed to lay waste his whole being. It was worse than depression—a black misery."

The desperately lonely Maurice, cut off and painfully isolated by his blindness, yearns for a relationship with Bertie Reid, the brittle, superficial friend of his wife. " 'Touch my eyes, will you?—touch my scar,' " Maurice asks in the barn, and Bertie, under the blind man's hypnotic spell, must do as he is bid. Maurice is overjoyed and exults over the "new delicate fulfilment of mortal friendship." But while Maurice croons, " 'we shall know each other now,' " Bertie stands "as if in a swoon, unconscious, imprisoned," gazing "mute and terror-struck," "trying by any means to escape." Maurice feels triumphant only because he is blind and cannot see what has really happened. If the scene of ritual contact attempts to bring the physical and the mental together in living relationship, Lawrence's point seems to be that such a relationship is not easy to accomplish. Lawrence called the ambiguous end of the story "queer and ironical." The story is almost a parody of his lifelong imaginative effort to integrate the powers of darkness and light.

"The Horse-Dealer's Daughter" has no irony, and yet it too is open-ended. This story concludes with a moving declaration and commitment of love between Mabel Pervin and Jack Fergusson, her rescuer. The story seems to be a full-fledged embodiment of salvation through the dark mystery of sexuality. Yet there is nothing programmatic—or even fully resolved—about **"The Horse-Dealer's Daughter."** The reader would like Mabel and Fergusson to be redeemed by their passion, but it is also unmistakable that something dangerous and destructive has been unleashed. Forces have been set in motion which are not controllable. At the end of the story when Fergusson must go back to his office, Mabel worries that the spell of their passionate encounter will be broken. But her fear that he "can't want to love" her is unfounded. He can't *help* loving her—if "love" is the right word: " 'No, I want you, I want you,' was all he answered, blindly, with that terrible intonation which frightened her." Notice the association of the power of eros with blindness, which serves to link **"The Horse-Dealer's Daughter"** and **"The Blind Man."** Indeed Mabel and Maurice even have the same surname, Pervin, which is probably not accidental. Clyde de L. Ryals has described **"The Horse-Dealer's Daughter"** as a "vivid presentation of what Jung calls the rebirth archetype," and the story does fit that pattern. Yet there is something troubling about Mabel Pervin's rebirth: the story is more ambiguous than a Jungian reading allows.

The unleashing of passion has something of the same effect in **"Tickets, Please."** The tram-girls get more than they have bargained for, and so does John Thomas. Though victorious, he is battered and bruised. There is only qualified triumph in an exit taken with "his face closed, his head dropped." The girls, unsettled, upset, and embarrassed, are all "anxious to be off," and they tidy themselves "with mute, stupefied faces." Lawrence suggests that in the battle of the sexes, ultimately no one can be a winner. The conflict is too basic to be resolvable.

The husband in **"Samson and Delilah"** seems to regain supremacy over his wife just as John Thomas defeats the tram-girls. Samson has returned to reclaim what is rightfully his and to strip his wife of the power she has enjoyed in his absence. Indeed she is secretly eager for him to restore his dominant role.

Yet **"Samson and Delilah"** is anything but dogmatic. At the end when he touches "her between her full, warm breasts, quietly," "she started, and seemed to shudder" as she gazes into the fire, a response so ambiguous that it is almost indecipherable. And **"Samson and Delilah"** has such an open ending that the story breaks off in mid-sentence. . . . The concluding ellipsis tells us that though Samson seems to be fully in command, the war is not over. He has gained the upper hand over his Delilah, but she has survived and will fight again. She will also win her share of the battles. Instead of dramatizing man's inherent right to dominate woman, the story is only insisting that man and woman must struggle for domination. [In his *The Art of Perversity*], Kingsley Widmer simplifies when he argues that Delilah "submits finally to male purpose." Instead of offering sexist dogma, **"Samson and Delilah"** presents a dialectical process.

The conflict in **"Monkey Nuts"** leads to the defeat of Miss Stokes. But though the aggressive woman is humiliated, the net result is that the deathly relationship between the unformed, malleable Joe and the emotionally sterile Albert will continue. This is another story in which the battle leads to no victory. Though the soldiers rout Miss Stokes, "they had a weight on their minds, they were afraid."

In **"You Touched Me"** Lawrence once again seems to be dramatizing a belief in the primacy of the senses, and once again closer inspection reveals otherwise. The rat-like Hadrian pressures the spinster Matilda into marrying him because she touched him on the brow that fateful night, though by mistake. There is no denying "the fragile exquisiteness of her caress," which "revealed unknown things to him." Even so, Matilda and her sister's suspicion that he is after their inheritance is not entirely unfounded. For whatever reason, Hadrian will not be denied. The women's dying father sides with Hadrian seeming "to have a strange desire, quite unreasonable, for revenge upon the women who had surrounded him for so long." A story which seems to be presenting the power of physical attraction is actually once again illustrating the fundamental hostility between men and women. Matilda at last capitulates, and she and Hadrian are married. The story's conclusion parodies both conventional happy endings and Victorian deathbed scenes. This ending is as "queer and ironical" as the ending of **"The Blind Man"**:

> "Let's look at you, Matilda," [the dying father] said. Then his voice went strange and unrecognisable. "Kiss me," he said.
>
> She stooped and kissed him. She had never kissed him before, not since she was a tiny child. But she was quiet, very still.
>
> "Kiss him," the dying man said.
>
> Obediently, Matilda put forward her mouth and kissed the young husband.
>
> "That's right! That's right!" murmured the dying man.

And that is all there is. Such grotesqueness hardly speaks for any compelling belief in the positive power of touch.

Though the *England, My England* stories explore the key Lawrentian themes of this fruitful period, they do not seek to provide the themes with resolution. In the most sardonic stories in the collection—**"The Blind Man," "Tickets, Please," "Monkey Nuts," "You Touched Me,"** and **"Wintry Peacock"**—he seems almost to be playing games with his themes. If in *Women in Love* or *The Plumed Serpent* he seems to be searching for large answers, in *England, My England*

he is content to rest with ambiguity. Indeed he insists on ambiguity. (pp. 34-6)

Lawrence indeed seems to be having a good time in these stories. There is a kind of creative zest in the way he goes about doing over *Oedipus Rex,* the myth of Orpheus and the maenads, and the story of Sleeping Beauty after his heart's desire. The best of the stories display a marvelous ease and civilized poise—and a sardonic humor as well. The reversals I have been sketching in this essay are in part comic reversals.

"The Blind Man," "Tickets, Please," "The Primrose Path," "You Touched Me," "Wintry Peacock," "Samson and Delilah," "Monkey Nuts," and **"Fanny and Annie"** all contain elements of comedy, and with the exception of the warm-hearted **"Fannie and Annie,"** the comedy has an edge. This comedy has little in common with the broadly satiric comedy of **"The Christening"** or the flippant, jeering manner of **"The Captain's Doll"** or, most disastrously, *Mr. Noon.* Comedy in *England, My England* is much more delicate and deadpan, much more effective too. I am not arguing that the stories are purely comic but rather that comedy is an important, customarily unnoticed ingredient.

I have already touched on the comic dimensions of these stories in speaking about revisionary mythmaking and ambiguity. **"The Blind Man"** and **"You Touched Me"** end on utterly sardonic notes. John Thomas' victory in defeat, Joe's and Albert's defeat in victory, the unlocked door that follows forcible ejection in **"Samson and Delilah,"** and I should add the sensitive young narrator's confusion and discomfort as his uncle proceeds down the primrose path: these scenes are not simply comic, but comic they are. At this point in Lawrence's career the battle of the sexes is intrinsically a comic spectacle.

The little-known **"Wintry Peacock"** is decidedly in a comic vein, and the joke is at the expense of the incompatibility of men and women. The witch-like Mrs. Goyte asks the young narrator to translate a letter to her soldier-husband from a Belgian girl who claims he has fathered her illegitimate child. Though the narrator mistranslates the letter to protect the husband, he cannot allay the wife's suspicions. At the end of the story he comes across the returned Alfred Goyte and tells him about his encounter with Mrs. Goyte. Narrator and soldier instantly form a bond of maleness against the wife and against the female world.

Laughter resounds all through **"Wintry Peacock."** Mrs. Goyte bends "down, doubled with laughter" when the narrator reads an effusion in the letter about her husband's "beautiful English eyes." The husband breaks "into a short laugh," then laughs "aloud once more," and finally goes "into a loud burst of laughter that made the still, snow-deserted valley clap again" as the narrator explains his efforts at deception. The story ends with the narrator discovering that the Belgian girl is even more formidable than the wife and running "down the hill shouting with laughter."

Of course all this laughter has a hollow ring to it. The narrator shouts with laughter at the end because he has seen at firsthand how fully men and women are at odds. Mrs. Goyte is criticized throughout for her willfulness, but her husband is criticized for letting himself be dominated by women. Nor is the narrator immune from the laughter, for his behavior with Mrs. Goyte and her husband implicates him in the games of love and war. Though he is laughing at the married couple, the joke is that he is laughing at himself as well. All of which makes the comedy complex and sardonic. The "misogyny" Kingsley Widmer perceives is present, but Lawrence is critical of the men in the story as well.

Lawrence's use of comedy is a major topic that has never been adequately explored. Comedy is one of the keynotes of *England, My England.* In so many of these stories the attempt to bridge the gap between man and woman only produces a wider chasm. This failure of relationship is presented comically. And when all is said and done, stories entitled "Monkey Nuts," "Tickets, Please," "Fanny and Annie," "The Primrose Path," and "You Touched Me" *can't* be entirely serious.

It can also be argued that many of the *England, My England* stories reveal Lawrence's growing need to assert male domination over women. The volume after all belongs to the period between *Women in Love* and the leadership novels, a time when star polarity was en route to being transformed into male authority. The novellas that date from this period—"The Fox," "The Captain's Doll," and especially "The Lady-bird"—are all concerned with female submission to the male will. "Tickets, Please," "Monkey Nuts," "Samson and Delilah," "You Touched Me," and "Wintry Peacock" all dramatize the struggle for masculine supremacy and not always appealingly. In this context "The Horse-Dealer's Daughter" seems a throwback to Lawrence's earlier efforts to bring the sexes together in passionate harmony.

At least, however, in most of the *England, My England* stories—as in *Kangaroo* later on—Lawrence undercuts the notion of male authority at the same time he attempts to dramatize it. If it is an ideal he is striving for, it is an ideal he does not believe is attainable. As noted, John Thomas Raynor departs with his head bowed as well as bloodied, and Samson's victory is only provisional. The only thing certain is the struggle between man and woman, and in *England, My England* that struggle is presented with comic detachment.

Though the best stories in *England, My England* have received their share of critical attention, that attention has always been given to the stories in isolation. I have tried to suggest that the collection deserves to be taken seriously as a book, and I have tried to point out some of the reasons why. The *New York Times* reviewer said it all as early as November 1922: "By far the greater number of these stories have a subtlety, an evasive quality underlying yet penetrating the texture of the exterior plot. Even when they seem simple, they are in truth intensely complex, composed of innumerable tiny fibres of thought and feeling and instinct, passing into one another by imperceptible degrees." (pp. 36-8)

> *Keith Cushman, "The Achievement of 'England, My England and Other Stories,'" in D. H. Lawrence: The Man Who Lived, edited by Robert B. Partlow, Jr. and Harry T. Moore, Southern Illinois University Press, 1980, pp. 27-38.*

LYDIA BLANCHARD   (essay date 1983)

[*In the following excerpt, Blanchard examines the development of Lawrence's short fiction after World War I, focusing on* England, My England, and Other Stories.]

If D. H. Lawrence's personal reaction to World War I was one of unremitting anger and despair, Lawrence also knew that the war provided him a unique battleground. He saw this battleground as both destructive and creative, a stimulus offering him the opportunity to strengthen the thrust of his message and work out new directions for his art. . . . Seeing this creative challenge as a fighting line of its own, Lawrence had written Edward Garnett . . . , suggesting that his first collection of short fiction, *The Prussian Officer and Other Stories,* actually be called "The Fighting Line": "After all, this is the real fighting line, not where soldiers pull triggers" (*Letters,* II).

On that fighting line, Lawrence rethought the assumptions of his earlier work; and, for the most part, he was confident he had met the challenge. . . . The significant changes from *The Rainbow* to *Women in Love,* not only in Lawrence's ideas but also in his style, are dramatic evidence of his ability to respond to the war's challenge; Lawrence's increased preoccupation with perfecting his philosophy, with the writing of nonfiction in a variety of forms, is further evidence of his ability to grow. But while the war stimulated Lawrence to break new ground in the novel, to try nonfiction in a variety of new ways to spread his ideas, and to create poetry about which he was enthusiastic and proud, apparently the war provided no immediate stimulus for Lawrence's short fiction. The period from August 1914 to November 1918 is almost a void.

The publication of *The Prussian Officer* stories at the beginning of the war suggested otherwise—that Lawrence would instead continue his work in the short form. Although he was angry with Garnett for changing the title of "Honour and Arms" to "The Prussian Officer" and understandably disappointed with some of the critical responses to the collection, his letters after its publication contain numerous references not only to his pride in the work . . . but also to his interest both in new publishing arrangements for his short fiction and in the short fiction of others, particularly E. M. Forster. It was not until the next summer, however, that Lawrence returned to the short story form, to write "England, My England." . . . During the four years of the war, Lawrence produced only four short stories; a fifth ("The Mortal Coil") was rewritten from a 1913 manuscript. Of these five, he did not include two ("The Thimble" and "The Mortal Coil") in his next collection so that when *England, My England and Other Stories* appeared in 1922, it included only three stories written during the war ("England, My England," "Samson and Delilah," and "The Horse-Dealer's Daughter")—and two of these were extensively rewritten. Of the ten stories in the collection, six were written during a surprisingly short period from November 1918, the month of the Armistice, to June 1919. (pp. 235-36)

It was not until after the Armistice . . . that Lawrence wrote about . . . experimentation in the form of his short fiction and the connection between that experimentation and the war. In November of 1918, Lawrence told Katherine Mansfield, "If one is to do fiction now, one must cross the threshold of the human people." He had just finished "The Blind Man" and told Mansfield the end was "queer and ironical." And, in fact, just as a few years earlier Lawrence had been absorbed with working out new ways to create fictional character in *Women in Love,* now those energies were transferred to the short fiction. The end of the war also ended his dormancy in the shorter form; the six stories Lawrence wrote during the seven-month period from November 1918 to June 1919 are as different from the pre-war short fiction as *Women in Love* is from *Sons and Lovers* or even *The Rainbow.* On the other hand, the novels on which Lawrence worked during the period after he finished *Women in Love* and before the appearance of his second collection of short stories—that is, *The*

Lost Girl and *Aaron's Rod*—do not show the experimentation of *Women in Love*. His creative interests, now absorbed by the short fiction, did extend beyond the stories, however, though still to the shorter forms; Lawrence called **"The Fox"** and **"The Captain's Doll,"** novellas on which he was working at the same time as the *England, My England* collection, "so modern, so new: a new manner."

As a collection, *England, My England and Other Stories* is generally perceived, as Keith Cushman has argued, as "Lawrence's most outstanding accomplishment as a writer of short stories." Cushman (see excerpt dated 1979) and, in a very different way, D. Kenneth Mackenzie have argued the imaginative unity of the collection; not only are many of the stories frequently anthologized, considered among Lawrence's strongest achievements in the form, but they also work together thematically and stylistically in a way quite different from the earlier *Prussian Officer* collection. Cushman has shown how Lawrence revised the best stories in *The Prussian Officer* at the same time as he was developing his mature style: "It was in 1914, the time of *The Rainbow*, the time of the final *Prussian Officer* revisions, that Lawrence fully committed himself to the visionary art that he would make his own for the rest of his life." If the commitment came in 1914, however, much of the working out of that commitment took place in the writing of *Women in Love*, and a very different relationship exists between it and *England, My England:* the unity of the collection results from the fact that Lawrence had mastered most of the important artistic choices informing the stories by writing the novel first. While the *Prussian Officer* collection "allowed Lawrence to experiment with characters, events, and themes he was to use later in his novels," *Women in Love* allowed Lawrence to experiment with themes and, more important, with the style that would distinguish the *England, My England* stories.

In some ways, then, *Women in Love* can be considered an apprenticeship for the short fiction. As a work that breaks with the traditional narrative, *Women in Love* develops character primarily through associated imagery and repetition, repetition that Lawrence characterized as a "pulsing, frictional to-and-fro" (Foreword to *Women in Love*); because of its episodic nature, many of the novel's chapters can be read as if they were themselves short stories. Techniques of narrative disruption and repetition gain strength in the shorter fiction; for, in *Women in Love*, however great the novel, the repetition often becomes turgid; the discontinuity and emphasis on the inexplicable, frustrating. In the short fiction, the ideas of *Women in Love* are communicated with a kind of force different from that of the novel, with a greater clarity and a greater command over the techniques that Lawrence had worked out in the longer fiction. Often the strength of both ideas and style brings the stories into the realm of myth and poetry. . . . (pp. 238-39)

The significance of the transition that Lawrence made after the war in his short fiction, the changes from *The Prussian Officer* to *England, My England*, can be illustrated in part by looking at the differences between the one story in the *England, My England* collection written before the war, **"The Primrose Path,"** and the last written of the stories in the collection, **"You Touched Me."** Even in its revised version **"The Primrose Path"** is in several ways significantly different from the other stories of *England, My England*, with the possible exception of **"Samson and Delilah,"** a story that Lawrence disliked even when it was first published. Like the traditional narrative or written history of the nineteenth century and like the stories of the *Prussian Officer* collection, **"The Primrose Path"** makes motivation clear and provides sufficient background for emotions and actions. Character is fate.

"The Primrose Path" is the story of a man who returns from Australia to learn that the wife he had earlier deserted is now dying of consumption. Lawrence contrasts the visit to the wife with stories of how the husband had himself been rejected by one woman en route to Australia and had then been taken up by still another on his return to England, although the story's contrived ending makes clear that this last relationship will be no more successful than the earlier ones. **"The Primrose Path"** is rich in the realistic detail of the best of the *Prussian Officer* collection, with little authorial intrusion. Through dialogue and incident, the reader learns that Daniel Sutton is defensive, uneasy of conscience, fearful of his mortality, coarse, bullying, cowardly in the face of his wife's illness. Given what the story makes clear about Sutton's character, it is easy to accept the nephew's prediction that the next woman in Sutton's life will also leave him. Dialogue and incident both reveal Sutton's character and prepare the reader for the conclusion.

But in **"You Touched Me,"** the major event in the story, Matilda's decision to marry Hadrian, is precipitated accidentally. Matilda touches Hadrian's forehead when she mistakes him for her father, and that simple act leads to consequences far out of proportion to the touch's significance—at least as a similar touch would have figured in the world of **"The Primrose Path."** In the later story, the touch moves Hadrian to ask Matilda to marry him, an offer she rejects but her dying father demands she accept, altering his will to favor Hadrian and thus force her. Finally, Hadrian triumphs, and the marriage takes place, although not so much because of the practical considerations, the money, as because Matilda has been in some way touched herself, both she and Hadrian experiencing feelings they cannot understand.

Unlike in **"The Primrose Path,"** neither the plot nor the dialogue satisfactorily explains the final paragraphs of **"You Touched Me"**; the explanation comes at a level beyond the threshold of plot and character. As with the other stories written or revised after the war, motivation is not always clear, for either the reader or the characters; passions are often inexplicable; the conclusion of the story is open-ended. In **"The Horse-Dealer's Daughter"** and **"The Blind Man,"** as well as in **"You Touched Me,"** physical contact leads to a passionate declaration; and, as if to emphasize the importance of the touch rather than the reason for it, in different ways the physical contact comes in darkness. In **"The Horse-Dealer's Daughter,"** Mabel Pervin and Jack Fergusson realize their love when he pulls her from the mud and slime of a stagnant pond. In **"The Blind Man,"** Isabel and Maurice Pervin live in a "wonderful and unspeakable intimacy" because of his blindness; the power of that blindness and the sense of touch helps to break the "insane reserve" of a friend. Not surprisingly, the stories in the *England, My England* collection use the words "touch" or "touched" twice as often as the stories in the *Prussian Officer* collection; the word "dark" appears more frequently in the later collections as well, reinforcing the emphasis on the unspoken and unknown as part of the struggle Lawrence describes in his Foreword to *Women in Love:* "the struggle for verbal consciousness, . . . the passionate struggle into conscious being."

The difference between the way in which **"The Primrose Path"** and the later stories reveal that struggle is a reflection of Lawrence's increased confidence. He had mastered a new form. He did not need to show traditional motivation nor use traditional narrative structure to explain cause for the emotional and spiritual changes in his characters. At the end of *The Rainbow,* Ursula realizes the importance of breaking with her past, and the necessity for such a break becomes not only a theme of central importance to *Women in Love* and *England, My England* but also a theme reinforced by Lawrence's stylistic decisions. Discouraged with the England he knew during the war, Lawrence argued for the importance of destroying the past to allow for the future. . . . The increased complexity and richness of the ways Lawrence handled this theme are reflected in the differences between **"The Thimble,"** written in 1915, when Lawrence was between revision of *The Rainbow* and the start of *Women in Love,* and the longer **"Ladybird,"** written in 1921, probably as a revision of the earlier story (**"The Thimble"** being one of the two wartime stories that Lawrence did not include in *England, My England*).

Both **"The Thimble"** and **"The Ladybird"** grow out of the same occasion, the return of a wounded soldier from World War I and the transforming effect not only on him but also, more important, on his wife, in both stories a couple based on Lady Cynthia Asquith and her husband. In both stories, the wife has become dulled and dissatisfied, aware of some unhappiness, a void in her life, uncertain that she really knows her husband. Both stories use the occasion of the husband's return as a stimulus for change, for resurrection, a rebirth for both effected by a decisive break with the past. Both stories also develop several other themes of concern to Lawrence—the dissatisfaction, even the death that results from trusting to the intellect, to what can be seen and visualized, as a way of learning about the world and, conversely, the importance of responding to what cannot be seen or known, to what is sensed instinctually, in the dark; the importance of moving beyond a self-conscious love to one which respects the unknown otherness of the partner and a dependence on that otherness. All are realizations to which Ursula and Birkin also come in *Women in Love* and are realizations developed in the *England, My England* collection.

But the difference between **"The Thimble"** and **"The Ladybird"** in Lawrence's treatment of these themes is again a measure of the difference that writing *Women in Love* made on Lawrence's short fiction. Although Lady Cynthia Asquith expressed some puzzlement about the use of the thimble as a symbol in the earlier story, its associations are with the past; it is the probable gift of an Earl returning home from war in 1801. When the couple throw it away in the earlier story, they break with England's past as well as their own, a past lived in willed independence and self-consciousness. They have already achieved a resurrection of the body in their recoveries from a serious pneumonia and war wound; throwing away the thimble, they undergo a second and more important resurrection, a resurrection of the spirit which the reader—prepared by the earlier steps in their progress toward change—can accept.

In **"The Ladybird,"** however, the symbolism is far more complex, less easily identified. While the thimble in **"The Ladybird"** is clearly associated with the past, it also has a more complex association with the primitive past. The jewels encrusting the first thimble have been replaced by a gold snake and a ladybird, the crest of the Psaneks. But the ladybird, as Count Dionys points out, while connected with the past through its connection with the Egyptian scarab and the pharaohs, is also the symbol of creative as well as destructive principles. When the wife loses the thimble in the later story, it is a loss rather than a gain.

The narrative line is brought to a more clearly defined finish in **"The Thimble."** With the throwing away of the thimble in the final paragraph and its disappearance on the pavement opposite, the break with the past is effected. "Then a taxi-cab went by, and he could see it no more" is a true closure for the events of the story. But Lawrence does not end **"The Ladybird"** at what might have been a conclusive point, the resurrection of the wife; rather, he brings back the husband and Count Psanek in an indecisive conversation about brooding through eternity.

In **"The Thimble,"** Lawrence tells us explicitly a number of things left unsaid in **"The Ladybird"**: "They were naked and newborn in soul, and depended on each other," the narrator writes about the husband and wife in **"The Thimble"**; and, as if to emphasize the rebirth, the emergence of both into a new life, they speak the word "helpless" fourteen times in one page of the story, often coupled with the word "baby." The break with the past is also reported explicitly through dialogue, as is the connection with the dark. For example, when the wife asks, "What was I before—when I married you?" the husband replies, "I don't know what you were. I've had my head cracked and some dark let in, since then. So I don't know what you were, because it's all gone." To emphasize the wife's self-consciousness, Lawrence uses the metaphor of photography: "She sat obsessed, as if his disfigurement were photographed upon her mind, as if she were some sensitive medium to which the thing had been transferred."

Such techniques make clear a number of Lawrence's concerns during the period of the war, but the form does not reinforce these concerns. While the form of **"The Thimble"** clarifies the message (and certainly helps to clarify many of the ideas Lawrence was working toward in *Women in Love*), the clarity also works against the message, Lawrence saying what he wants to be unsaid, bringing to light what should be kept dark, giving a logical progression to what should be repetitive rather than sequential. In **"The Ladybird,"** however, as in *Women in Love,* the form itself reinforces the message. (pp. 239-44)

During the period of World War I, Lawrence saw a decay in England that he felt could not be remedied; positive change could come only with a decisive break with the past. But to argue for a break with the past, for a resurrection to new ways of thought, drawing out of the dark and the primitive past to apprehend the condition of modern life, also necessitated looking for new ways to write—both the traditional narrative structure and methods of character development could not reinforce the ideas that Lawrence believed were essential to address. The basic forms that Lawrence saw as necessary he perfected in *Women in Love* then adopted into the short fiction that came after the war.

Certainly the strength of the *England, My England* collection and of the post-war novella comes from Lawrence's having worked out structures in *Women in Love* that were particularly suited to the form of short fiction. Whether the decision to hold back on actually writing short fiction during the war was conscious we will probably never know, but the results of the decision are clear. Many of the techniques of *Women in Love* were more suited to short fiction than to the full-length form and thus were not used in *The Lost Girl, Aaron's Rod,* or indeed any of the longer fiction written after *Women in Love*. The rewards of the experimentation are instead in the short fiction. . . . The period immediately after the war was the height of Lawrence's work in short fiction; the short fiction that came after *England, My England* grew on the strengths of that collection. (pp. 245-46)

Lydia Blanchard, "Lawrence on the Fighting Line: Changes in Form of the Post-War Short Fiction," in The D. H. Lawrence Review, *Vol. 16, No. 3, Fall, 1983, pp. 235-46.*

JANICE HUBBARD HARRIS   (essay date 1984)

[*In the following excerpt from her* The Short Fiction of D. H. Lawrence, *Harris discusses the development of Lawrence's short fiction during the 1920s as it progressed from what she terms the "leadership tales" of earlier years, concentrating on the evolution of his female characters.*]

E. M. Forster once said that it takes a person of real character not to need religious faith as he moves into the middle years of his life. Though he would not have applied the sentence to Lawrence, by Forster's criterion Lawrence never had much character, and certainly lost what he had as he turned forty. In previous work, his religious impulse led him to see the world as alive with godhead. At any moment, the natural earth, other people, a situation could separate itself from the welter of normal living and stand revealed for a moment as the location of mana or theos. His earlier visionary tales capture these revelations of power, of crucial signs pointing toward life or death. In the period we are now looking at, something different occurs. (p. 189)

Through the leadership tales, [Lawrence's heroines] had been asked to worship male leaders. As Lawrence apparently saw, when the heroines acquiesced they robbed the leaders of all decent opposition, rendering them flat and affected in their aloof dignity. There was no way the heroes could deserve genuine worship. The reward for the woman was thus not the keen joy that comes of celebrating something truly larger than the self, but, when she would accept it, an ability to sleep and thereby avoid disillusionment and the desire to criticize. In Lawrence's late fiction, written after he had returned to Europe in 1925, he ridicules his leadership vision and generally avoids the issue of worship altogether. We do not think of *Lady Chatterley's Lover,* "**The Man Who Died,**" "**The Man Who Loved Island,**" "**The Rocking-Horse Winner,**" or "**The Lovely Lady**" as stories that focus on the need to worship. . . . [Four] of Lawrence's stories from 1924-1925—done during his last summer in America and in one case upon first arriving in Europe—provided him with the bridge that moved him out of his leadership vision toward the accomplishment of the late fiction.

In these four stories, Lawrence continues to try to find something to which a person can honestly submit. But he turns from a vision of secularized, human hierarchy to a more cosmic vision. Awe, the refusal to measure all things by oneself, the joy and terror implied in recognizing any vast power are no longer seen as the attitudes women must feel toward men, or inferior men toward superior men. These are the attitudes any person must have toward magnificence of any kind. In *St. Mawr,* for example, Lou Witt feels awe in response to a

stallion and a landscape, and her response saves her. It is the inability of the princess ever to recognize or touch a world greater than her own small imaginings that damns her.

But buried within the theme of right worship is a yearning that will become a central issue in the tales to come, the yearning to be alone. It is indeed wise to give over the desire to worship another human being, but to worship a landscape or the sun may be a covert withdrawal from all human intercourse. Only a few of these issues are raised in "**The Overtone.**" They become central in *St. Mawr, The Princess,* and "**Sun.**"

In each of these tales, the formerly disparaged figure of the searching woman returns justified to the center of the stage. She may not conduct a successful search (the princess is a signal failure) but her activity of seeking is seen once again as potentially honorable. Surprisingly, the secondary role Lawrence had urged upon his females in the leadership work falls here to the males. Having insisted for much of the last five years that their inherent superiority be recognized, they now seem exhausted or distracted by petty concerns. Romero, in *The Princess,* is an exception. In their stead Lawrence gives us women who crave something in this world worthy of belief and commitment, and thereby become leaders in their stories by example rather than rhetoric.

"**The Overtone,**" written in the spring of 1924, soon after "**The Last Laugh,**" "**Jimmy and the Desperate Woman,**" and "**The Borderline,**" reads like a quiet reconsideration of the issues that inform those bitter tales. The tale opens in the living room of an older, married couple, Edith and Will Renshaw. It is a soft, warm night; Mrs. Renshaw is talking to two women friends about state aid to mothers while Mr. Renshaw dozes on the sofa. One of the friends, a young woman named Elsa Laskell, eventually becomes our window on the tale. As Elsa sits vaguely attending to Mrs. Renshaw, to the sounds and smells of the night, she begins to assume the role of a judge presiding over the older couple's deep quarrel. First, she figuratively hears each partner's brief against the other, then she responds.

Through a silent reverie, Mr. Renshaw opens the hearing, presenting his view of the death of his marriage. Once, years before, he had asked his wife to make love with him high on a hill beneath the full moon. Lawrence's prose conveys the young husband's longing, his belief that he could rid himself of all embarrassment and shame if he could come naked to her, here, just this once. His desire is as clean and bright as the moon. But she will not, cannot, respond. At this point, we feel sympathy for the husband. But in a move distinctly different from the leadership tales, Lawrence then gives Mrs. Renshaw the floor. In a lyrical voice—also interior monologue—she presents her view of the death of their marriage. Because she had denied him once, six months after their wedding, he could never approach her again without fear or mistrust. With a mixture of cordial deference and cold disapproval, he has remained aloof through the years. Both have grown old in spirit, poor in hope and belief. Our sympathies have broadened.

After both speak their piece, Elsa Laskell takes over, adding, as Patricia Merivale comments [in her *Pan the Goat God*], her tone to the series of overtones. Mr. Renshaw has gone outside; Elsa joins him. He jokingly assures her not to be afraid of him, for " 'Pan is dead.' " He refers to himself, but she leads the conversation to cultural implications. Mrs. Renshaw comes out and enters the conversation. All begin with the assumption one hears in **"The Last Laugh,"** that Christ has killed Pan, that shame and law kill passion and freedom. The reader understands that the Renshaws are still sadly accusing each other, although Mr. Renshaw has begun to assume the greater portion of blame. But Elsa turns the conversation; in another significant departure from the tales of this time, she asserts that Pan is not dead and that only Christ and Pan together can create a complete world, a full self, a living relationship. Christ is day, ethical procedure, and marriage; Pan is night, amoral ecstasy, freedom. Not only does Elsa insist that both spirits are still alive, but she asserts that she partakes of both. She is no fragment or half-thing but a bright blend of light and dark, " 'a black bird with a white breast and underwings.' " With relief and gladness, she leaves the Renshaws. The implication, only touched on here, is that she has something to believe in, a Pan-Christ spirit that is alive in the world. The Renshaw's quarrel over who has hurt or betrayed whom need not detain her any longer.

After the Murry tales of a few months earlier [which are usually interpreted as attacks on John Middleton Murray and Lawrence's old circle of friends in London], with their adulation of the Pan spirits—Pan, Pinnegar, and Alan Anstruther—and disparagement of the martyred Christ figures—Marchbanks, Jimmy, and Philip—the balance Lawrence maintains in **"The Overtone"** marks a clear switch in his thinking. Here is no simple celebration of the whinnying Pan. On a related level, here is no sinful woman who has ignominiously criticized and betrayed her husband. And, here is no one-dimensional man, cool, reserved, superior. As if to comment on the previous tales, Lawrence calls our attention to the tones and overtones of the characters he has created, the issues he has raised. Even more surprising than the balances Lawrence builds into the tale, however, is his finally returning to the figure so compromised in his previous leadership tales, the figure of the searching woman. Brief as her role is, Elsa Laskell revives and reinvigorates the female seeker of earlier fictions, anticipating most directly Lou Witt, heroine of *St. Mawr,* discoverer of the god of two ways.

St. Mawr returns to issues raised in the leadership fiction, especially in **"The Woman Who Rode Away,"** but addresses them from a different stance. For example, in their human, political manifestations, the leadership characters fade. They default. But the need that stands behind them is carried forward. Further, the split . . . between the masculine gain in asserting self and the feminine gain in losing self disappears as Lou's search helps her recognize her *human* need to find *and* lose self. But most important, in *St. Mawr* Lawrence removes the dams he had constructed in the leadership tales. Lou Witt has a voice, a mind, and the freedom to use them. With her mother and the stallion, Lou Witt joins the woman who rode away in a journey out of her old culture and toward a new one. Like the woman, she finds something to worship, something to give herself to; but one of the tale's great strengths is that she continually questions herself and the objects she worships. The tale's key images, of St. Mawr and Las Chivas, reinforce Lou's healthy skepticism.

Presaging Kate Leslie of *The Plumed Serpent* and echoing Hannele of **"The Captain's Doll,"** Lou Witt and her mother are critical and intelligent characters. Like Kate, Lou struggles in passage after passage to know where she is going and where she has been. A world traveler, she finally decides to leave Rico and England, her husband and most recent home,

and try America. The impetus for leaving is the claustrophobia she feels in England and the danger St. Mawr is in. He is about to be shot or gelded. A richly ambivalent embodiment of alien life and consciousness, St. Mawr is one of Lawrence's laudable solutions to finding imagery to capture what "the Aeon of the little Logos," or the time before "the white man stole the sun," or the ladybug sought to convey. The stallion helps us visualize a concept of life and vitality as mysterious and amoral, beyond rational comprehension or ethics. . . . At the same time, there is a basic stupidity to St. Mawr; sometimes he is even equated with Rico. In himself he is not the miraculous presence Lou should worship. But the miraculous presence is in him; Lou succeeds in rescuing him. Once in Texas, St. Mawr saunters out of the tale, but Lou is left still questioning. (pp. 190-94)

Lawrence's description of Las Chivas, Lou's lonely, wild, New Mexican ranch, carries on the magnificence and ambivalence. In part it represents what characters like Dionys or the Indians or the ghostly Alan have presumably represented in previous tales, that is, a powerful alternative to safe, sterile, modern experience. Las Chivas is alive with color; the Michaelmas daisies are a purple mist upon the hillside, spangled with clumps of bright yellow flowers. There are dark pines and mariposa lilies. Few places could stand in more vivid contrast to Lou's claustrophobic English home. "It was the place Lou wanted. In an instant, her heart sprang to it. . . . *'This is the place,'* she said to herself." Yet Lawrence's marvelous description of the experience of the previous owner's periodic revulsion from her ranch also makes clear the difficulties, the horror, and the squalor of the uncivilized place. He speaks of the rat dirt, the bones of dead cattle and goats, the swarming of lower life. With its recognition of the beauty and the horror of Lou's ranch, Lawrence again gives the seeker something to worship that is vaster than any man, yet at the same time he insists that she recognize the duality of the god she has chosen. It is a god of creation and destruction, of Michaelmas daisies and of strewn bones and rats. (p. 194)

Through Lou's consciousness, *St. Mawr* also begins to face an issue that has been hovering in the background of Lawrence's fiction since *Women in Love,* the desire to be alone. Ursula laughs at one of Birkin's visions of the future, saying that all he really believes in or wants is grass: plain, lonely, unpopulated, and unengaging grass. Lilly continually yearns to be alone in *Aaron's Rod.* In many of the leadership tales of 1921-1923, the leaders covertly succeed. They like the human conquests they make, they believe in their new relationships, but they come, go, and, with a distant smile on their faces, remain essentially apart. By contrast, Lou admits and stands by her desire. As she explains to her mother: " 'I want to be alone. . . . I want to be by myself really.' " (pp. 194-95)

Lou's mother initially pretends not to understand or agree with Lou's desire, but eventually she capitulates. By the last pages, she respects Lou's marriage to a landscape, a spirit of place. In this tale, the issue is at least temporarily closed, as Lou is allowed to end up worshipful, but also where nearly all of Lawrence's male leaders have longed to be, alone, untouched. However, as one sees in *The Princess* and in Lawrence's last satires, once he imagines a character succeeding in this hermit's quest, he sees the sterility it invites.

In *The Princess,* Lawrence keeps his woman in search and yet undercuts the very movement toward consciousness and ambivalence that he had honored in *St. Mawr.* Reversing the argument, he exaggerates the critical aspects of Lou's character to an extreme. Lou's awareness of the horror of the vast, untamed, natural world is the princess's exclusive attitude. The princess feels none of Lou's simultaneous awe, as Lou's withdrawal from human touch becomes a hysterical purity in the princess. One more journey tale, *The Princess* follows Dollie Urquhart (one hears Irkheart) into the center of the Rockies. Once there, she destroys the character who is identified with those Rockies and goes mad. Through Romero's murder, Lawrence seems to be reminding his reader, himself perhaps as well, that if the return to more primitive religions and beliefs entails danger, the refusal to stand in awe of anything invites death and insanity. (p. 195)

Dollie Urquhart and her father are consummately delicate, conscious individuals. She can see only squalor in anything more corporeal than her fairylike father. The perfect lotus, she sees her frail, beautiful self as "the only reality." The princess and her father eventually come to the United States for part of each year. She grows older, twenty-five, then thirty. When she is thirty-eight, her father, who is slightly mad and occasionally violent, dies, leaving her with a companion, Miss Cummins. Dollie remains exactly as she has always been, a princess, a child, a delicate fairy. She and Miss Cummins decide to travel, ending up in New Mexico. There she meets Domingo Romero. And suddenly, appropriately, the tale's tone changes. Up until now, the narrator's tone has mimicked Dollie and her father. Now the narrator becomes essentially transparent as Romero takes over responsibility for communicating the tale's values.

Romero is the man with the demon between his eyes, the character we might have seen in earlier tales as a leadership figure. Like nearly all of them—Henry Grenfel, Count Dionys, Pan, Pinnegar, Alan Anstruther, the Chilchui Indians—he has been dispossessed of his rights in the present order. Like them, he is a stranger, exotic, quiet, somewhat sinister in the view of the tourists he serves, guides, and cooks for. Unlike them, however, he has little desire to dominate and no aversion to contact. For all the racial mystery and allure Lawrence gives him, he seems refreshingly open and human. Dollie wants him.

Obstinately, she urges him to take her on an overnight ride deep into the Rockies. Her desire has much the same tone as that of the woman who rode away; it is based on curiosity, the desire to be titillated by wilderness. She quite lacks Lou's capacity for awe. Once there, freezing in the cold autumn night, she invites Romero into her bed to make love to her. She is immediately repelled, however, and makes her disgust clear. Feeling used, Romero is humiliated, bitter, and understandably afraid that he will be charged with raping her. For three days, he keeps her trapped in the cabin. He is eventually shot in the back by a forest ranger. The rangers escort the princess down to the dude ranch and the narrator resumes his former, ironic tone. Mad, Dollie represses all knowledge of what occurred in the mountains.

As we might expect of the last American tale before Lawrence's return to *The Plumed Serpent,* the imagery here is powerful. Through natural imagery especially, Lawrence conveys his sense of a god of creation and destruction, his understanding of the beauty and horror, the elegance and cruelty, in any return to older faiths. Most vivid are the quaking aspen and cottonwoods posed shimmering and yellow against the cold, blue-black spruce of the Rocky Mountain forest. The princess of course continually seeks out and identifies herself with the idyllic, sunny places. Refusing to recognize the god of darkness and light, the princess wants only the delicate, fairy beauty of the virgin forest; the granite rocks, dark shadows, and "dense, black, bristling spruce" are anathema to her. She will not see that real virginity or newness of being can come only through accepting the same qualities of light and dark, of delicacy and oppressiveness, that mark the forest.

Also vivid is Lawrence's image of the princess's need. Freezing in the cabin on her first night in the mountains, she dreams that she is being covered by snow. It is a fine image of her consciousness. As no previous women have been in Lawrence's power-leadership fiction, the princess is entirely consistent in her hypersensitivity and overdeveloped individuality and intellectuality. In contrast to our response to the woman who rode away, we fully appreciate—both emotionally and mentally—the gain that would accrue to the princess could she give herself to someone, something. Further, for all their differences, Romero reminds us of Captain Hepburn in **"The Captain's Doll"** in that he is a hero who is complex and interesting. The difference between Romero's character and that of the Chilchui Indians may be seen in the way Lawrence has Romero respond to the princess's insult. Balked, hurt, and violent, he throws her clothes into the lake and forces her to have intercourse with him. But his acts are seen for what they are, vengeful and born of misery. Even she perceives that. There are no vivid, pornographic images associated with Romero's rape. Romero soon leaves her alone. Between the two all is dreary deadness. Finally, in the image of the princess's greying hair and blank, mad gaze at the end of the tale, Lawrence concisely and aptly measures her loss. There are no explanatory paragraphs, no switches of intention. What is now wrong with her has always been wrong, only more so. (pp. 195-97)

"Sun," written in late 1925 after Lawrence and Frieda had returned to Europe, is the last tale to study the issue of worship in the terms I have been employing here. As Mark Spilka first noted [in his *The Love Ethic of D. H. Lawrence*], this is not a tale about sunbathing nor is Lawrence tracing an action meant to symbolize the need for humans to regain awareness of their links with the natural world. Juliet literally turns to the sun as to a god. Infinitely grander than she or anything the modern world has to offer, the sun is awesome to her in the same way St. Mawr and Las Chivas were wonderful to Lou Witt. In this tale Lawrence drops his emphasis on the god of two ways and his interest in exploring ambivalence. A healthy critique of Juliet's devotionals is nevertheless a part of the story.

Although it explicitly rehearses ancient sun-worshiping rites, **"Sun"** is not a fable but a visionary tale, done in terms typical of Lawrence. There is an exemplum at the heart of the tale, but its terms are dramatized realistically. Lawrence uses a transparent, omniscient narrator, a specific and natural locale, clearly motivated characters, and complex, psychological conflicts. As he did in earlier visionary tales such as **"The Horse Dealer's Daughter,"** Lawrence starts with a ceremonial rite—here, sun worship—and makes it contemporary, believable. This is the opposite strategy from the fables and ghost stories to come, in which he begins with the contemporary and naturalistic and renders them timeless and mythic.

There are two versions of **"Sun,"** the first written by December 1925, the second in 1928. (pp. 197-98)

Frieda and D.H. Lawrence and some immigrant English friends on an excursion in New South Wales, Australia, in 1922.

Through the opening movements, both versions of **"Sun"** read much the same. Each begins with the heroine, Juliet, and her child sailing down the dark Hudson River, across the Atlantic, away from New York, her husband, and her own neuroses and despair. Settling in a beautiful villa along the Italian coast, during the early winter months she gradually learns to relax and give herself fully to the sun. Her little boy begins to accompany her, growing agile and rosy himself. For all its grand circularity, the sun is very much a cosmic phallus, rising each dawn, penetrating the woman's willing self, declining each night. At this point in the tale, the woman's experiences parallel Lou Witt's in *St. Mawr.* Yearning to give themselves, to relax within the power of something possessing genuine grandeur, both women turn away from the counts, farmers, even the ghosts that their earlier sisters have submitted to, and offer themselves instead to sun, mountains, cosmos. They are managing to fulfill their need to worship. But in both versions of **"Sun"** Lawrence goes beyond Lou Witt's love of her Las Chivas Ranch as he follows Juliet's progress out of her love affair with the sun. And it is in the next step, back into the world, that Lawrence indirectly critiques Juliet's sun worship; further, it is in that critique that the two versions of **"Sun"** importantly part ways.

In the first version, the journey back is relatively straightforward, its gains and losses balanced. In the second version, the return from solitude is hesitating, grudging. In comparing the two versions, Michael L. Ross judges the second to be superi-

or. He sees Lawrence improving the tale's language, symbolic suggestiveness, and narrative structure. In my view, Lawrence's revision intensifies the tale's solipsism to such an extent as to mar whatever gains he makes in enriching the tale's language. Also, I find the narrative structure in the second version awkward.

In both versions, Lawrence has Juliet's husband, Maurice, eventually visit her in Italy. Although Maurice is a different kind of failure, it is as though Lawrence had invited Rico to visit Lou Witt at Las Chivas. In the first text, his visit and her thoughts form a relatively brief conclusion to both the tale and her period of withdrawal. As they sip coffee on the hillside patio, Juliet looks down and sees an Italian peasant and his wife. It is the first we have heard of the peasant. In a single page, Lawrence explains that Juliet and the peasant have been aware of each other through the past months. We learn a bit about him, but mainly we follow Juliet's thinking as she faces her desire for the peasant and accepts Maurice's desire for herself.

Structured like Lawrence's other triangles, the last passages of the tale consist of a weighing of alternatives. With fine dramatic skill, Lawrence sets up the last scene to dramatize Juliet's situation and the paradoxes within it. She has repeatedly descended from her villa to lie open to the ascendant sun; if she so chooses she can now descend to the peasant and open herself to his ascendant power. The peasant is equated with the sun: "he would have been a procreative sun bath to her." But set against the momentary contact he offers—"Why not meet him for an hour, as long as the desire lasts, and no more?"—is the continuity represented by Maurice. There is a sureness to him that carries its own more mundane connotations with the sun. While it is clear that Maurice oppresses Juliet, making her feel trapped in circumstances, in this first version of the tale he is not an entirely undesirable mate. Juliet's wise servant woman sees him as "good"; Lawrence tells us that he is kind and shows us that he is generous. But, more explicitly, Lawrence explains that "There was a gleam in his eyes, a desperate kind of courage of his desire, and a glance at the alert lifting up of her breasts in her wrapper. In this way, he was a man too, he faced the world and was not entirely quenched in his male courage. He would dare to walk in the sun, even ridiculously." He watches Juliet with "growing admiration and lessening confusion." That Juliet decides she will remain with him and bear him another child is both a credible and relatively complex decision. In contrast to her alternative—that is, choosing the peasant—it is also the decision that ushers her back into the world of human relations. She will continue her sun rites but bear another child by Maurice.

In rewriting the tale, Lawrence alters the progress of Juliet's return from solitude. In the version of 1928, he develops two important lines of motivation that push Juliet out of her hermitage. The first relates to the state of Juliet's general sexual desire; the second, to her specific desire for the peasant.

Using an Eastern image, Lawrence says that Juliet's intercourse with the sun has opened her womb like a lotus flower; this in spite of herself, in spite of her wish simply to be peaceful. At times Lawrence's language is stilted and awkward, especially in phrases such as "the trouble of the open lotus blossom" or Juliet's desire for "man dew." But his metaphor for female arousal as a radiant series of outwardly moving waves, as "the purple spread of a daisy anemone, dark at the core" is good; compared to other contemporaneous attempts to describe female arousal it is very good. . . . Within this particular tale, the language Lawrence uses to describe Juliet's state of sexual excitement also complements and balances the phallicism of the sun. His potency is matched by hers, his ruddiness, streaming blue brilliance, and radiant, pulsing roundness are answered by her own. She may regret her renewed desire, but in her body's yearning she becomes as active a sexual being as he.

If this first added line of motivation and the language it employs are gains, however, the second line of motivation is a loss. Just before Maurice arrives, Lawrence gives us a long expository passage on the peasant. In much greater detail than before, we learn about him, his older, possessive wife, his awareness of Juliet. We learn that Juliet had sat on her patio one evening while he worked below in the fields. They had watched each other, aware of one another's desire.

As in the first text, Juliet must make a choice between husband and peasant. She ends up making the same decision, for the tale has committed itself to tracing this would-be hermit out of her hermitage, to making her worship of the sun lead to something beyond itself. But Lawrence alters the terms of her thinking, intensifying her bitterness toward Maurice. With a loss of economy and impact, Lawrence now has Juliet's contemplations extend through two somewhat repetitious sequences, the first occasioned by her initial watching of the peasant, the second by her having to decide what to do

about the arrival of Maurice. In both passages, Lawrence amplifies the idea that one of the pleasures of being with the peasant would be the lack of complicated engagement. Juliet's longing now seems based on the presumption that the peasant would never exist for her in any personal way. The real loveliness would lie in their never talking to each other. In these passages, Juliet sounds like the tired and touchy leaders we encountered earlier. She wants no real relationship, no conflict, no ties. "She was so tired of personal contacts, and having to talk to a man afterwards. With that healthy creature, one would just go satisfied away, afterwards." Neither the tale nor she admits it, but her longing for the peasant seems simply a fancy version of the old human longing for the perfect brief affair.

In the early text of **"Sun,"** Lawrence dramatized the understanding that he had implied in *St. Mawr* and *The Princess.* He indicated that prolonged solitude can lead to sterility and preciousness, that one-night stands are an unrealistic answer to human longings for relationship, that seeking out "wild ones" inevitably denies the "wild ones" their humanity. The peasant, like Romero, is a human being. In his later text, Lawrence seems to have temporarily lost these understandings. (pp. 198-201)

The journey out of the leadership fiction has been accomplished. No one is asking anyone else to choose a leader and kneel in awe. Awe and wonder remain human feelings crucial to the modern individual's ability to lose self in a way that will nourish and sustain self. But in choosing sun and earth as fitting objects for his newly awakened heroines to worship, Lawrence has imagined a reveille that carries within it the potential for solipsism. In the fictions to come, Lawrence continually recognizes that temptation, as he mocks preciousness and withdrawal in a wonderful variety of guises. (p. 202)

Janice Hubbard Harris, in her The Short Fiction of D. H. Lawrence, *Rutgers University Press, 1984, 333 p.*

JUDITH PUCHNER BREEN (essay date 1986)

[*In the following excerpt, Breen interprets "The Blind Man" and "Tickets Please" in terms of Lawrence's treatment of his female characters.*]

"The Blind Man" and **"Tickets, Please"** . . . dramatize [Lawrence's] ironic vision of World War I as an opportunity for the destruction of an exhausted culture and the rebirth of long-repressed erotic energies, energies embodied by the scarred and sightless Maurice Pervin in **"The Blind Man,"** and in **"Tickets, Please"** by the mysterious tramway inspector John Thomas. Both Maurice and John Thomas are figures with a double identity, in some respects less characters than masks that imperfectly conceal the dark gods of pagan fertility lurking behind them. For example, when Maurice lost his eyes in Flanders, he was at once wounded by a murderously corrupt society and blessed by the recovery of the sense of touch—to Lawrence the most sacred of the senses— thereby returning to a more primitive state of psychic organization "as if he rose out of the earth." In **"Tickets, Please"** the disruption of the home front, seen in the empowerment of the women who assume the jobs and the prerogatives of the departed soldiers, has summoned into its midst a similar god-man, the resurrected Dionysus, representative of phallic power and prophet of a revitalized culture.

The customary reading of both stories is that they dramatize conflict between this new phallic man and the surviving pre-war civilization. Thus in **"The Blind Man"** Maurice competes for possession of his wife, Isabel, with her dear friend and guest Bertie Reid, a successful but impotent intellectual dandy. In the end Maurice transcends this conflict in an effort to establish a bond of idealized, masculine friendship with Bertie and thus enlarge his life purpose. In **"Tickets, Please"** John Thomas (as type character the equivalent, in American slang, to "Peter" or "Dick") is overwhelmed by a Bacchante-like attack of enraged discarded girl friends and their leader, Annie, who seek to end his free and easy ways by forcing him to choose one sweetheart. However he snatches victory from defeat when he chooses Annie, making her sensible of the gift of rich love she has lost through her misguided possessiveness.

In this paper I am going to argue, however, that precisely the reverse takes place in each story. Beneath the manifest text lies a latent subtext, which reveals a quite different view of the battle between the sexes—a text less socially permissable, perhaps not fully acknowledged by Lawrence himself, but nevertheless expressive of his profoundest imaginings. In my reading of **"The Blind Man,"** Isabel, the apparently sympathetic wife and friend, immersed in the last weeks of pregnancy, represents in fact the omnipotent, indifferent nature goddess to whom, in Wolfgang Lederer's words, "all man's efforts and achievements are as the games of children" as she ruthlessly pursues her procreative instincts. Burdened by her husband at a time when she wishes to be able to devote herself to her infant, she sets up Maurice in a sham friendship with Bertie in order to get him off her hands. Far from being winners or losers, Bertie and Maurice are both victims of Isabel's self-interest.

If in **"The Blind Man"** the woman is the real winner, in **"Tickets, Please"** woman is forced to recognize in brutal physical terms the limits of her power. The attack of the angry women on the "cock of the walk" John Thomas has all the strange frenzy of sexual arousal; but while together they can vilify him, disrobe him, pummel him, they cannot impose the final humiliation and rape him. Only John Thomas has the power to penetrate, to choose. In the one story, then, woman at her most loving conceals her ruthless power; in the other, woman at her most aggressive conceals her fundamental impotence. As we shall see, the single source of both these apparently irreconcilabe faults is her failure to be a man.

"The Blind Man" opens on a subdued but intense note of crisis. At dusk on a rainy November at the Pervin's farm, near the end of the calendar year and the year of "wonderful and unspeakable intimacy" between Isabel and her husband since his blinding, Isabel listens for the sound of the trap she has sent to fetch Bertie. The impending arrival of Bertie alerts the reader to the mixed reception awaiting the other expected newcomer, the new baby. And both these anxieties provide a focus for the internal pressures that have increasingly troubled the wonderful intimacy of husband and wife during the past year. Isabel has been visited from time to time with feelings of *ennui,* of unexplained weariness, and Maurice by "devastating fits of depression," which have intermittently made their life unbearable.

In the past such painful episodes have served in some ways only to underscore the profound bond between husband and wife. As Maurice works around the powerful hind-quarters of the horses in his stable, feeling the earth with his feet as he goes, he appears to Isabel "a tower of darkness," some savage old earth spirit, as it were, who escaped suppression by the transcendent deities—or . . . , the demonic Pluto who rose out of darkness to claim Persephone for his bride. However, in other ways the primitive intensity of their bond explains the depressions disturbing the married couple. The unspeakable intimacy uniting Isabel and Maurice is to be taken literally, it is an intimacy that goes beyond the genital bond of husband and wife to recover the pre-genital, language-less tie between infant and mother. In this context the "unspeakable" element of the intimacy, referred to three times in the story, carries gothic hints of mother-son incest.

There is no space in the present study to discuss the many images in the story which identify Maurice as the infant-husband and focus on Isabel as the all-powerful mother whose magical maternal kisses, which once healed cuts and bruises, now heal the blind Maurice and give him his psychic and phallic strength; one example—"he did not even regret the loss of his sight in these times of dark, palpable joy. A certain exultance swelled his soul"—must do. It is clear, however, that such precognitive intimacy explains Maurice's depressions, as well as his palpable joys, for the son's developing ego, childishly dependent and fearful of destruction, may be threatened as well as empowered by the mother. The mirror-image of Isabel, caught in an unguarded moment, exposes this malign as well as benign side of the wife-mother: "her grey eyes looked amused and wicked, a little sardonic, out of her transfigured Madonna face."

Maurice's depression may be caused as well by the constraining domesticity of his wife. . . . However both these fears of engulfment and constraint are adumbrated in the overwhelming anxiety which dominates Maurice in the story, the fear of abandonment. It is as if through Isabel's pregnancy the blind man were wounded once more, damaged more profoundly by the war between the sexes than the war between the nations. For Lawrence presents Isabel in her maternity as sinking back into the deep sleep from which Maurice had awakened her: on the one hand she is a hostile Beauty who wishes to get rid of her Prince Charming and go back to bed ("Maurice was like an ominous thundercloud. She had to keep waking up to remember him"); on the other hand she is a fleeing Persephone who wishes to be "snatched away off the earth" that has enfolded her, to flee the dark cavern and return to the world of time and change, to the surface of life, in her role of mother, as it is conventionally lived. To formulate this dilemma in a slightly different way which underscores Lawrence's remarkable hostility to pregnancy in the story: Isabel has been defeated by Maurice's resistance to her desire to "possess her husband utterly"; now she longs to replace him with the infant she can completely possess. Bertie in the story functions in part as a surrogate for this other, more threatening visitor, who creates not an inclination but a compulsion within Isabel to reject the glory of what Lawrence calls "blood-consciousness" and fade into the light of common day.

This family romance is carefully delineated through the architectural details of the Pervin's house, particularly the twisting corridors, suggestive of the umbilical cord, which connect the front rooms, Isabel's domain, to the back rooms housing the resident farmer's family, and then to the narrow causeway leading to Maurice's territory, the dark, vibrant stable. Symbolic interchanges between stable and domestic quarters, as if the farmstead in between were a changing room, mark crucial stages in the story. Maurice travels twice from the barn to the front rooms, where the pungency of the living horses is replaced by the fragrance of *potpourri,* traditional talisman against the odors of the flesh. On the first visit Maurice sits like a sculptured monument during the uncomfortable dinner with Isabel and Bertie. In a gesture recalling the cowardly fop in Shakespeare's *1 Henry IV* who enraged Hotspur by raising a pouncet box between his nose and the stench of battle, Bertie, "without knowing what he did," raised a bowl of violets to his nose to deflect the terrible force of Maurice's wounds. On this occasion Maurice is soon defeated by Bertie's evasions and returns to the barn. However on his second trip to the house, as we shall see, Maurice feels that his influence triumphs.

Maurice's movements are bracketed by two corresponding visits from house to barn. The first is by Isabel, who anxiously goes to check on her husband in preparation for Bertie's arrival. Before crossing the cold causeway, half-relishing, half-fearing the stormy blasts to be met there, she dons a figure-masking shawl and a man's felt hat. With this gesture she manages the transition from the world of book reviews to the "strange swirl of violent life" she finds in the darkness, the almost mesmerizing power of the god she both creates and serves. But at the end of the story Isabel forgoes a second visit. Because she "did not want to make the physical effort," she sends Bertie to meet Maurice in her place.

What is the reader to make of this psychological traffic pattern? Unlike his Victorian predecessors, who divided women into angels or demons, Lawrence divides them into angels and demons, dubbing the frightening half of their sexuality "female," and the nurturing side which magnifies the male, "masculine." From this point of view Isabel's function in the story, when she wears the man's hat, is to mask Maurice's longing for a more perfect union—a union with a man. This explains Maurice's conduct when Isabel sends Bertie on the second trip to the barn. Now that Isabel's pregnancy has stilled her masculine passions, Maurice seizes the opportunity to replace her.

From Maurice's point of view, the attempt to substitute Isabel's friend for Isabel has clear advantages. His fingers rove sensitively over the face of Bertie just as they did in an earlier scene over the face of Isabel, performing a ritual reenactment of infant-mother bonding that allows him to maintain his heroic stature; at the end of the story he swells to a "colossus." When Maurice compels Bertie to explore his face in turn, he is living out a fantasy of male union in which he entirely circumvents the need for women so that he can become self-created, the author of his own powers.

But what of Bertie's enforced role in this fantasy? Ironically, Bertie has been sent to do a man's job when he is more deficient in this regard than Isabel; whereas she merely showed ambivalence in crossing the yard to the barn, Bertie "shrank from the wet and roaring night." Though he starts out to meet Maurice with his man's hat on, it is soon knocked off when the groping Maurice significantly misjudges his height. This weakness causes the ceremony of mutual bonding to short-circuit, and all unknowingly Maurice is left with a second sham marriage. Nevertheless Maurice's effort does look forward to a time when male brotherhood will pre-empt heterosexual marriage. If the damaged warrior does not arrive there, at least one barrier, Bertie's false intellect, has been crushed like the shell of a mollusk.

And what of Isabel? At the end of the story she knows Maurice can believe in his friendship with Bertie only because he is blind, and she knows Bertie suffers agonies from his encounter with Maurice. But she purrs contentedly to her husband, "You'll be happier now, dear," meaning instead that she'll be happier now Maurice is off her hands. In this final picture of Isabel, then, her false mask and the true image reflected in the mirror coalesce. Apparently all sympathy and kindness, she views with complacent indifference the consequences of the trap she set for Bertie, gladly sacrificing both husband and friend to the new life within her womb.

"Tickets, Please" shares with **"The Blind Man"** the same Lawrentian antinomies of the dark god and a sterile culture. But in this story, as if to emphasize his rejection of conventional love plots, Lawrence parodies the conventions of romantic love comedy, in which lovers typically meet in the world of an oppressive everyday; escape to a world of holiday where nature reigns, law relaxes, and the barriers to happiness are overcome; and return transformed to a purged and elevated everyday world. In **"Tickets, Please,"** though, there is no everyday, only a homefront disrupted by the departure for the trenches of all able-bodied men and the substitution of women, along with "cripples and hunchbacks," in their jobs as conductors on a tram line connecting villages and coal mines in the industrial countryside of central England. Moreover, as no everyday world remains, no clearly-contrasting holiday world exists either. When the action of the story shifts from the tram line to the Statutes Fair at nearby Bestwood, Annie finds her ride on the Dragons cozy, because of John Thomas's encircling arm, but less exciting than the plunging, tilting tram car. The circular rides the pair enjoy on the roundabout alert the reader to the equally futile motions of the trams shuttling back and forth to Terminus, past the industrial town which provides for the life-weary miners the meaningless stimulation of "a change of cinema, of girls, of pub."

There is finally no movement from everyday to holiday in Lawrence's story because there is no sense of place in it at all, as Jane Austen or George Eliot meant it, not even the stable stable which fosters Maurice's rooted strength; the only roots Annie is to know is her "rich, warm" place in John Thomas's arms. But if holiday is just a continuation of everyday, then of course nothing can be learned, and the palpable joy John Thomas offers loses its transforming power. The "intelligent interest" Annie begins to take in him, despite her full return of his passion, represents her inability to relinquish the possessive ways her culture has instilled. As the concluding battle between the sexes shows, for Lawrence the defeat of such an offspring of Rosamond Vincy is the only possible happy ending to love plots in the industrial age.

At the beginning of **"Tickets, Please,"** however, the dynamics of this mock love story are not absolutely fixed. When in the opening pages Lawrence describes his conductresses in their short-skirted uniforms and peaked caps as "fearless young hussies" who pounce on sneaky youths and tread on the toes of howling colliers, he seems to admire the new bread of masculinized women the way he admired the masculine energies of Isabel. If these new women remain linked to ominous hints of petticoat government, the reckless swoops of their trams are linked as well to infernal energies, their trail of sparks to the fire and brimstone in which Shaw as well as Lawrence saw the salvation of the modern world. But these new women lack fit suitors—the colliers on their run are indoor types who, like Bertie, shrink from the howlingly cold nights—until their very need seems magically to summon forth John Thomas, representing the rare presence of sensual power in modern culture.

As inspector of trams, this mythological John Thomas comes and goes by profession; as a type of fertility god he does so by inclination, and has his way with many of the working girls. His clothing—black overcoat buttoned up to the chin, tweed cap pulled down over the eyes—functions as a traditional stage disguise, wittily recalling the disguised royalty of Shakespeare's wartime king, Henry V, who also passed unrecognized as he revitalized his weary flock. The self-possessed Annie Stone, tired of the boy she has on the string, responds to the persuasive ways of this skillful lover, and John Thomas rightly prefers her above all others for "the soft, melting way in which she could flow into a fellow." The tactile images of interpenetration and suffusion in their love scenes recall the unspeakable intimacy of Maurice and Isabel.

However, Annie's kinship to Isabel suggests that her true mate really is her discarded boy-friend, as does the comedy of her rationalizations for yielding to John Thomas. For example, he is "discreet," and like a current fashion comes in the "right style"; "he paid each time so she could be but complaisant"; and on her ride on the merry-go-round with a "perfectly happy" John Thomas, she divides her attention between her lover and her crooked hat. This conflict between love and vanity in Annie, and the materialistic overtones of her language, explain her possessiveness and, in the end, her passion for revenge. When John Thomas falls short on what she considers their bargain, she makes her choice, and in an act of self-reification she "determine[s] to have her own back."

The trap Annie sets for John Thomas in the ladies waiting room at Terminus is the same trap Isabel set for her prey in the Grange; both use food, warmth and the charm of feminine culture to disguise their monstrous cunning. However John Thomas participates more in his own undoing than Maurice, who has been blinded by a corrupt war and a pregnant wife. John Thomas is self-blinding, and betrays his realm, the world of dark and lawless nature, for the flattering company of female admirers. But in Lawrence's comparison of John Thomas to some sort of swamp beast crawling out of the damp to sun himself, he shows that John Thomas's self-destructive urge to ravin down his bane is irresistible. Man is an amphibian in Lawrence's story, native to worlds of light and darkness. It is as natural to John Thomas to seek warmth—though a king, he suffers want like other men—as it is for the swamp beast, even though, with cloak doffed and hat recklessly pushed back in the warm waiting room, like the beast he exposes himself to peril.

The girls' revenge begins playfully but not randomly; after turning John Thomas's face to the wall, one after the other taps him on the back to see if he can tell one girl from another in the dark. But when Annie steps forward, taps turn to blows; she gives a smart box to John Thomas's head that sends his hat flying and stirs up the buried aggression of her followers, who are transformed into strange wild creatures hunting down a terrified animal. For the hatless man in this story is not, like Bertie, a sexless creature; the stripping away of his clothes (the "sight of his white, bare arm maddened the girls") stirs his attackers into a sexual frenzy. Like the Bacchantes, in their possession of the god they are "filled with supernatural strength."

This possession of the body of John Thomas has other implications as well, and Annie, as she kneels on his back in a reversal of the traditional missionary position, asserts the ascendency of her sex and assumes for herself the patriarchal right to force the seducer to marry: " 'You've got to choose,' she cried." In this assumption of male sexual perogatives, despite a secret misgiving because "she could not exact more," she appears to win the battle of the sexes.

Yet John Thomas "did not give in to them really—no, not if they tore him to bits"; he jerks his face loose from Annie's grasp and, in a voice "strange and full of malice," utters the words "I choose Annie." Instantly Annie collapses in "bitter hopelessness" and commands the girls to end their taunts. John Thomas's victory rests on her realization that while she can force him to the ground, only he can "exact more," and his choice of Annie vindictively reminds her of the realities of sexual politics. At the end of the story, then, Annie is not horrified because (as sentimental readers might feel) she has lost invaluable love through her possessive ways; rather "something" (her assumed masculine power, we can guess) "is broken in her," and she is tormented by her realization that she is too weak to wreak vengeance on her enemy. Male genital power, says Lawrence, is the final power.

If the title **"Tickets, Please"** suggests to many readers Lawrence's habitual misogyny—man pays a price to get in the gate—it also suggests a more fundamental, more disturbing point: no matter how strengthened by the freedoms brought by World War I, women can never be the equals of men. The source of their power remains in the underlining of the word *please*. Annie's essential failure in her own eyes—the most cruel element in her humiliation—as well as in those of John Thomas, is her failure to be a man. Beaten but undefeated, John Thomas reassembles the cloak and cap of his stage disguise. Annie herself produces the key to unlock the door of the escape, and he returns alone to his mist-filled darkness to await a better day.

What conclusions may be drawn from reading **"The Blind Man"** and **"Tickets, Please"** in conjunction? First of all, the brutal humiliation of Annie Stone, which is pushed beyond anything that buoyant heroine actually merits in the story (and helps earn for Lawrence his reputation with some readers as misogynist) can best be understood as a response to the remarkable inflation of Isabel's powers. Lawrence focuses so intently in his fiction on the short-comings of women because underneath that fantasy lies a far more terrifying fantasy, especially intolerable to the male artist, a fantasy which magnifies women's creative and life-giving strengths. One of Lawrence's primary gifts as a writer is his ability to discover and dramatize such hidden plots, which are in fiction so compelling, and in real life so destructive to women.

Second, Lawrence's glance back to Shakespeare's Henriad in **"The Blind Man"** and **"Tickets, Please"** reveals a nostalgia for the heroic possibilities of war, possibilities including Hotspur's celebration of his smarting wounds as the badge of manliness, and the sign of the willingness to take on directly the best and worst life has to offer. "The patriarchal world of Shakespeare's history plays is emphatically masculine," Coppélia Kahn has written. John Thomas, like Lawrence himself, expends his creative forces on the home front. But the proper setting for the majestic presence he conceals behind hat and overcoat was originally the military world of "simple, idealized male comradships" characteristic of *King Henry V,* and free of feminine influence.

Finally, this reading of **"A Blind Man"** and **"Tickets, Please"** suggests an important area of investigation for feminist critics. As Sandra M. Gilbert and Susan Gubar have argued in *The Madwoman in the Attic,* consciously or unconsciously women novelists frequently express unacceptable feelings such as anger or passion through the use of doubles and other encoding devices. So too in these stories Lawrence has encoded his secret plot of homosexual love within the parameters of more permissible plots. Whether or not his strategy can be generalized to the works of other male writers is beyond the scope of this study. (pp. 63-73)

> *Judith Puchner Breen, "D. H. Lawrence, World War I and the Battle between the Sexes: A Reading of 'The Blind Man' and 'Tickets, Please,'" in* Women's Studies, *Vol. 13, Nos. 1 & 2, 1986, pp. 63-74.*

FURTHER READING

Aldington, Richard. *D. H. Lawrence: Portrait of a Genius, But. . . .* New York: Duell, Sloan and Pearce, 1950, 432 p.
  Standard biography of Lawrence. Aldington frequently employs passages from Lawrence's works to illustrate a biographical point.

———— Introduction to *"St. Mawr" and "The Virgin and the Gipsy,"* by D. H. Lawrence, pp. 7-10. Middlesex, England: Penguin Books, 1950.
  Sketches events in Lawrence's life surrounding the composition and publication of these works.

Baim, Joseph. "Past and Present in D. H. Lawrence's 'A Fragment of Stained Glass.'" *Studies in Short Fiction* VIII, No. 2 (Spring 1971): 323-26.
  Contends that the tension Lawrence derives from an apposition of fifteenth-century and modern, industrialized England in this story is consistent with his recurring theme of humanity's need to experience regeneration through the resurgence of instinct and emotion.

Balbert, Peter, and Marcus, Phillip L., eds. *D. H. Lawrence: A Centenary Consideration.* Ithaca, N. Y.: Cornell University Press, 1985, 261 p.
  Compilation of criticism covering Lawrence's entire range of writing. Includes pieces by Mark Spilka, Robert Kiely, and Marjorie Perloff, and the essay "Potent Griselda: 'The Ladybird' and the Great Mother" by Sandra M. Gilbert.

Bloom, Harold, ed. *Modern Critical Views: D. H. Lawrence.* New York: Chelsea House Publishers, 1986, 329 p.
  Anthology of criticism on Lawrence. Includes two pieces specifically on the short fiction: "Aphrodite of the Foam and 'The Ladybird' Tales" by H. M. Daleski and "The Ontology of D. H. Lawrence's *St. Mawr*" by Margot Norris.

Brande, Dorthea. "Six Novels." *The Bookman* (New York) LXXVI, No. 3 (March 1933): 290-91.
  Review of *The Lovely Lady, and Other Stories.* Brande contends that Lawrence's fiction could be mistaken as "the work of a woman—a restless, unsatisfied, neurotic feminine genius."

Canby, Henry Seidel. "Too Soon—and Too Late." *The Saturday Review of Literature* IV, No. 45 (2 June 1928): 925-26.
  Review of *The Woman Who Rode Away, and Other Stories.* Canby describes this book as "a reptile house in a sophisticated

Zoological Garden" and expounds Lawrence's distinctive position in Western culture.

Cushman, Keith. *D. H. Lawrence at Work: The Emergence of the "Prussian Officer" Stories.* Charlottesville, N.C.: University Press of Virginia, 1978, 239 p.
  Detailed study of the creative process behind several of Lawrence's early stories.

Dawson, Eugene W. "Love Among the Mannikins: 'The Captain's Doll.'" *The D. H. Lawrence Review* 1, No. 2 (Summer 1968): 137-48.
  Asserts the influence of psychologist Trigant Burrow on Lawrence's later fiction and analyzes "The Captain's Doll" in this light.

Englander, Ann. "'The Prussian Officer': The Self Divided." *The Sewanee Review* LXXI, No. 4 (October-December 1963): 605-19.
  Purports that Lawrence confused the "story" and the "theory" of "The Prussian Officer," and as a result, the tale, "rather than illuminating, confuses our grasp of the characters and their interrelationships."

Ford, George H. *Double Measure: A Study of the Novels and Stories of D. H. Lawrence.* New York: W. W. Norton & Co., 1965, 224 p.
  Close study of a selection of Lawrence's fiction, interweaving relevant events from his life.

Gordon, Caroline, and Tate, Allen. "D. H. Lawrence: 'The Rocking-Horse Winner.'" In their *The House of Fiction: An Anthology of the Short Story with Commentary,* pp. 337-51. New York: Charles Scribner's Sons, 1950.
  Text-book style interpretation that moves quickly through a number of assertions and considers the story in the contexts of viewpoint, tone, technique, and theme.

Gregor, Ian. "'The Fox': A Caveat." *Essays In Criticism* IX, No. 1 (January 1959): 10-21.
  Questions the success of Lawrence's realization of his artistic intentions in this tale.

Greiff, Louis K. "Bittersweet Dreaming in Lawrence's 'The Fox': A Freudian Perspective." *Studies in Short Fiction* 20, No. 1 (Winter 1983): 7-16.
  Interprets this tale with regard to the theories of Sigmund Freud and Lawrence's own Freudian perspective, as put forth in his *Fantasia of the Unconscious.*

Hinz, Evelyn J., and Teunissen, John J. "Savior and Cock: Allusion and Icon in Lawrence's 'The Man Who Died.'" *Journal of Modern Literature* 5, No. 2 (April 1976): 279-96.
  Centers discussion on the interpretation of specific symbolic objects in this story.

Hudspeth, Robert N. "Lawrence's 'Odour of Chrysanthemums': Isolation and Paradox." *Studies in Short Fiction* 6 (Fall 1969): 630-36.
  Appreciative commentary focusing on "Lawrence's ability to fuse image, scene, and atmosphere."

Littell, Robert. Review of *"St. Mawr": Together with "The Princess,"* by D. H. Lawrence. *The New Republic* XLIII, No. 553 (8 July 1925): 184.
  Describes "St. Mawr" as "the result, not so much of a creative urge as of creative habits."

Moore, Harry T. *The Life and Works of D. H. Lawrence.* New York: Twayne Publishers, 1951, 400 p.
  Approaches Lawrence's life and career as a whole, providing, in Moore's terms, "information, interpretation, and evaluation."

———— *The Priest of Love: A Life of D. H. Lawrence.* Rev. ed. New York: Farrar, Straus and Giroux, 1974, 550 p.
  Well-documented biography making use of reminiscences by

acquaintances of Lawrence. This work is a revised and enlarged edition of a book originally published as *The Intelligent Heart* (1954).

Muir, Edwin. Review of *"St. Mawr": Together with "The Princess,"* by D. H. Lawrence. *The Nation and the Athenaeum* XXXVII, No. 9 (30 May 1925): 270-71.

Describes this book as "patchy," noting that Lawrence has never before been "so sure of himself and so unsure of his theme, so confident and at the same time so unconvincing."

Nehls, Edward, ed. *D. H. Lawrence: A Composite Biography.* 3 vols. Madison: The University of Wisconsin Press, 1957.

"Composite biography" primarily comprised of excerpts from letters, journals, diaries, and memoirs written by Lawrence, members of his family, and his friends.

Nuhn, Ferner. "Lawrence and the Short Story." *The Nation* CXXXVI, No. 3533 (22 March 1933): 324.

Review of *The Lovely Lady, and Other Stories.* Nuhn asserts that the short story form often served Lawrence "only for a gathering of chips left over from his novels," but that he also produced memorable pieces, notably "The Rocking-Horse Winner."

Pinion, F. B. "Shorter Stories." In his *A D. H. Lawrence Companion: Life, Thought, and Works,* pp. 218-48. New York: Harper & Row Publishers, 1979.

Overview of Lawrence's short fiction.

Ruderman, Judith. "The New Adam and Eve in Lawrence's 'The Fox' and Other Works." *Southern Humanities Review* XVII, No. 3 (Summer 1983): 225-36.

Documents Lawrence's many references in his writings to the biblical story of Adam and Eve and explores his use of this tale in his short fiction.

Stewart, Jack F. "Expressionism in 'The Prussian Officer.'" *The D. H. Lawrence Review* 18, No. 23 (Summer 1985-Fall 1986): 275-89.

Traces elements of expressionism in this tale, concentrating on Lawrence's use of imagery and atmosphere.

Tedlock, E. W., Jr. *D. H. Lawrence, Artist & Rebel: A Study of Lawrence's Fiction.* Albuquerque: The University of New Mexico Press, 1963, 242 p.

Comprehensive survey of Lawrence's fiction.

Thornton, Weldon. "'The Flower or the Fruit': A Reading of D. H. Lawrence's 'England, My England.'" *The D. H. Lawrence Review* 16, No. 3 (Fall 1983): 247-58.

Focusing on "England, My England," Thornton hails Lawrence as an innovative and demanding writer whose works display both psychological and artistic subtlety.

Toomer, Jean. "Notations on 'The Captain's Doll.'" *Broom* 5, No. 1 (August 1923): 47-9.

Detailed, formalist, and largely unfavorable review of *The Captain's Doll: Three Novelettes.* Toomer outlines five distinct components of Lawrence's style and technique in these stories and provides brief commentary.

Wasserman, Jerry. "'St. Mawr' and the Search for Community." *Mosaic* V, No. 2 (Winter 1971-1972): 113-23.

Marks "St. Mawr" as an important work in the development of Lawrence's fiction. Wasserman purports that this story encompasses the breakdown in society that Lawrence disclosed in his early works, while rejecting the advocacy of a sexual solution, which his later works firmly embrace.

Worthen, John. "Short Story and Autobiography: Kinds of Detachment in D. H. Lawrence's Early Fiction." *Renaissance and Modern Studies* XXIX (1985): 1-15.

Charts the composition of Lawrence's fiction against events in his life. This issue of *Renaissance and Modern Studies* is devoted entirely to criticism on Lawrence and his writing.

Jack London

1876-1916

(Born John Griffith London) American novelist, short story writer, essayist, journalist, and dramatist.

London was an important American literary figure whose immensely popular works combined high adventure and mysticism with elements from Charles Darwin's concept of determinism and the racial theories of Friedrich Nietzsche. Although some commentators have characterized London as an unabashed romantic for his often sentimental treatment of realistic themes, most agree that his simple yet innovative style, descriptive skill, and adherence to principles of literary Naturalism provided a foundation for the works of many subsequent writers, including Sherwood Anderson, Ring Lardner, and Ernest Hemingway. Of the fifty books he published during his relatively brief career, London's short novels *The Call of the Wild* and *White Fang* are the most famous and typify his concern with humanity's struggle between barbarism and civilization. Critics generally agree, however, that London's most consistent accomplishments were his short stories, and such tales as "Bâtard," "Love of Life," and "To Build a Fire" are widely regarded as popular classics of American literature.

Born in San Francisco, London was abandoned as an infant by his natural father and received the surname of his stepfather, John London. Due to his family's poverty, London was forced to leave school at age fourteen and gain regular employment. After several years of working for low wages in a cannery and as a longshoreman, among other occupations, London became known as the "Prince of the Oyster Pirates" for illegally scavenging seafood and selling it at a high profit to San Francisco's restaurant owners. These and other experiences from London's life were later recorded in his semi-autobiographical novel *Martin Eden.* While still in his teens, London tramped across the United States and observed the American underworld, which he later chronicled in essays collected in *The Road.* London educated himself by reading the works of such authors as Herbert Spencer, Karl Marx, and Rudyard Kipling. At age nineteen he enrolled in high school, completing his entire coursework in one year, and subsequently entered the University of California, where he joined the Socialist Workers Party. During this period, London began to espouse the seemingly contradictory world views that later surfaced in his works. The influence of Charles Darwin and Friedrich Nietzsche, for instance, is reflected in London's adventure novels through his inclusion of white supremacist ideas and portrayals of amoral *übermenschen,* or supermen, while his socialist convictions are set forth in essays collected in such volumes as *The People of the Abyss, War of the Classes,* and *Revolution, and Other Essays.*

London was among the first prospectors to travel to the Klondike river valley in Alaska's Yukon Territory during the gold rush of 1898. Although he returned to San Francisco penniless and in poor health a year later, his experiences provided material for his first collection of stories, *The Son of the Wolf: Tales of the Far North.* This volume received wide popular recognition for its violent yet colorful portrayals of men and animals fighting for survival amidst what London termed

the "white silence" of the Yukon wilderness. Although many critics applauded his youthful optimism, several initially accused London of imitating such authors as Rudyard Kipling in his concern with Anglo-Saxon dominance, Bret Harte in his romantic treatment of realistic themes, and Joseph Conrad in his depiction of rugged individuals whose adherence to a code of honor enables them to resist savagery when confronted with brutal situations. Later reviewers, however, have commended London for his originality, and several have favorably explored Conrad's influence on London's early adventure stories. Among London's works frequently compared to those of Conrad are "In a Far Country," a story from *The Son of the Wolf* in which two men confined to a cabin during the Alaskan winter kill one another because of escalating mistrust and declining rations, and *The Sea-Wolf,* a popular and controversial novel about the slow demise of a powerful sea captain as a result of his egotism.

Although London gained a wide readership with his second volume of short fiction, *The God of His Fathers, and Other Stories,* he was initially faulted for his schematic use of Nietzsche's racial theories to provide his stories with stimulus and action. Later critics, however, have considered London's view of race both ambivalent and contradictory, contending that he often portrayed his white protagonists as ruthless amoralists and American Indians as noble savages who inevitably, if tragically, yielded to a superior white race. In "The God of His Fathers," a chieftain of mixed white and Indian heritage is prepared to allow two white prospectors and their party to pass through his tribal lands providing they renounce Christianity. Upon learning that white priests had refused to legitimize the Indian's birth and to sanction his marriage to a white woman, the story's protagonist recognizes the injustice of the Indian's situation but maintains allegiance to his own race—the "god of his fathers"—and commits violence on behalf of the less noble prospectors. London stated that his next volume, *Children of the Frost,* was related "from the Indian's point of view, through the Indian's eyes, as it were." Racial extinction is again a prominent theme, and the stories in this and ensuing collections are generally regarded as increasingly dramatic, ironic, and tragic in their treatment of death and survival. In contrast to previous London heroes who exhibited a strong will to survive, the old Indian protagonist of the story "The Law of Life" who is left to die by his tribe in the Alaskan wilderness attains nobility only after accepting his imminent death.

In his short novel *The Call of the Wild,* London offers an alternative to the sentimental portrayals of animals found in his early stories. Buck, the dog who functions as the protagonist of this work, is unrestrained by the human emotions and morality that previously limited London's portrayal of nature's savagery, allowing readers to suspend guilt as they vicariously participate in his conquests. A similar technique is evident in "Diable—A Dog," a story later published as "Bâtard" and included in *The Faith of Men, and Other Stories.* In this tale, a ruthless man attempts to break the spirit of a wild dog through cruelty; ironically, however, the man is killed by the animal, who functions as an embodiment of nature's brutality. Nature is again the dramatic antagonist in *Love of Life, and Other Stories,* a collection of tales set in the Far North and California. In the title story, a prospector is left to die by his partner after twisting an ankle while traveling the Yukon trail. Abandoning icons of civilization—his gun and gold—after realizing their unimportance in the wilderness, the man survives while his partner is later found dead, clenching his worthless treasure. "To Build a Fire," one of London's most famous and frequently anthologized stories, concerns a young man who ignores the warnings of seasoned prospectors never to travel alone in the Alaskan wilderness during severe cold. Breaking through a patch of thin ice, the man fails in his attempts to build a fire and freezes to death. While some critics maintain that the man dies due to a lack of intuition or imagination, being unable to conceive of the possibility of his own death, others assert that he dies as a result of panic and the failure of his rational faculties.

While on a cruise in 1907, London became interested in Hawaii and the South Pacific region as locales for his fiction. Most critics, however, have regarded London's novels and short fiction set in the South Seas as inferior to his Alaskan stories, and later scholars have often analyzed these pieces as indicative of London's racial beliefs. In *South Sea Tales,* for example, London's white supremacist theories are reflected in his characterizations of Nordic or Anglo-Saxon heroes as conquerors of "inferior" island races. Several critics, however, have contended that London's prejudice was largely confined to races in which class, family lineage, and social status were absent or undefined. London could thus admire the chiefs and royal families of the Polynesian races yet, in "The Inevitable White Man," describe in sporting terms the

slaughter of a group of rebellious Africans by an Anglo-Saxon slavemaster. Many of the stories in London's next collection, *A Son of the Sun,* center on cannibalism, head-hunting, and barbarism among the Melanesian tribes of the Solomon Islands, while those in *The House of Pride, and Other Tales of Hawaii* are set in the Polynesian Islands. Several stories in the latter collection focus upon leprosy, particularly within the colony at Molokai, which London visited during his stay in the region. Although some natives accused London of misrepresenting conditions on the islands, several scholars have appraised his accounts as unsensational and accurate. *On the Makaloa Mat,* a volume of alternately gentle and satirical stories written just prior to London's death, focuses on such themes as marital infidelity and interracial dilemmas. During the final decade of his life, London occasionally purchased ideas from other writers, stating publicly that he wrote only for financial gain. Although similar to his early work in theme and subject, works in such later volumes as *The Night-Born, Smoke Bellew,* and *The Turtles of Tasman* have attained neither the popularity nor the critical acclaim of his early Alaskan stories.

Throughout his career, London wrote at least one thousand words per day. Many critics concur with H. L. Mencken's contention that London's "too deadly industry" resulted in a "steady emission of half-done books" that the author did not rework. Most agree, however, that despite occasional didacticism and stylistic lapses, London's best works retain moments of technical and emotional brilliance. In Earle Labor's estimation, London's stature as an artist derives from "his 'primordial vision'—the mythopoeic force which animates his finest creations and to which we respond without fully knowing why." Carl Sandburg identified the attraction London's works continue to hold when he stated: "The more civilized we become, the deeper is the fear that back in barbarism is something of the beauty and joy of life we have not brought with us." London's works offer a vicarious alternative, Robert Barltrop observed, because "their material does not reflect—indeed, it provides an escape from—life as the mass of people know it."

(For further information on London's life and career, see *Twentieth-Century Literary Criticism,* Vols. 9, 15; *Dictionary of Literary Biography,* Vols. 8, 12; *Concise Dictionary of American Literary Biography, 1865-1917;* and *Something about the Author,* Vol. 18.)

PRINCIPAL WORKS

SHORT FICTION

The Son of the Wolf: Tales of the Far North   1900; published in England as *An Odyssey of the North*
The God of His Fathers, and Other Stories   1901
Children of the Frost   1902
The Faith of Men, and Other Stories   1904
Moon-Face, and Other Stories   1906
Love of Life, and Other Stories   1907
Lost Face   1910
When God Laughs, and Other Stories   1911
South Sea Tales   1911
A Son of the Sun   1912
The House of Pride, and Other Tales of Hawaii   1912
Smoke Bellew   1912; published in England in two volumes entitled *Smoke Bellew* and *Smoke and Shorty*
The Night-Born   1913

The Strength of the Strong 1914
The Scarlet Plague 1915
The Turtles of Tasman 1916
The Red One 1918
On the Makaloa Mat 1919; published in England as *Island Tales*
Dutch Courage, and Other Stories 1922

OTHER MAJOR WORKS

A Daughter of the Snows (novel) 1902
The Call of the Wild (novel) 1903
The People of the Abyss (essay) 1903
The Sea-Wolf (novel) 1904
War of the Classes (essays) 1905
White Fang (novel) 1906
Before Adam (novel) 1907
The Road (essays) 1907
The Iron Heel (novel) 1908
Martin Eden (novel) 1909
Revolution, and Other Essays (essays) 1910
The Cruise of the "Snark" (essays) 1911
John Barleycorn (novel) 1913
The Valley of the Moon (novel) 1913
The Mutiny of the "Elsinore" (novel) 1914
The Little Lady of the Big House (novel) 1916
Letters from Jack London (letters) 1965

NINETTA EAMES (essay date 1900)

[*In the following excerpt from the* Overland Monthly, *a popular American journal in which London published his first story, "To the Man on Trail," Eames provides a biographical portrait of London and contends that his strong personality and varied interests indicate a promising career.*]

The Managing Editor, manuscript in hand, came briskly forth from the inner sanctum and faced his associate, a flush of interest in his eyes: "Have you read this story—**"To the Man on Trail,"** by some one who signs himself 'Jack London'?—*nom de plume,* of course!"

"No. Why, what's the matter with it?" The Associate Editor raised a reluctant glance from the proof he was correcting.

"Well, it's strong—something out of the common. I wish you would look it over and see if you can't crowd it into the next form—ought to have appeared in the Christmas issue."

The Associate Editor, grudging the time, began a hurried reading of the manuscript. Ten minutes later he was looking very much alive as he hastily refolded the sheets, scrawled a line on the back and called to the office boy who was lazily snapping beans at a fly. "Take this to the printer. No time to lose!"

Thus **"To the Man on Trail"** was duly given place in the January *Overland Monthly* of 1899, and there was no dissenting voice on the staff when the Managing Editor declared the story to be in the front rank of vivid and picturesque realism. Shortly after its publication he had a call from the author, a young man plainly dressed and of modest and even boyish appearance. He had with him a second story, **"The White Silence,"** one of the best of a series of eight Arctic tales classed

under the general title of **The Son of the Wolf,** and published thereafter in consecutive numbers of the *Overland.*

To this magazine, therefore, is due the introduction of Jack London to the reading public, and not long afterwards his stories, which dealt mainly with Alaskan fact and fiction, began to appear in various standard publications throughout the West and East. (pp. 417-18)

[As a child, London] turned instinctively and inevitably toward literature, his imagination and feeling drawing out the romance of surroundings which to others appeared mean and commonplace.

"All things interest me," he says; "the world is so very good." This innate and loving appreciation of universal nature and of man is, in fact, a marked characteristic of Jack London, and has stood him in good stead through years of sordid toil and hardship.

Up to his ninth year he spent a somewhat joyous childhood on California ranches, his chief pleasure the books that fell into his hands—Trowbridge's works for boys, Captain Cook's voyages, Paul du Chaillu's travels, Rip Van Winkle, and occasionally a "Seaside Library" novel borrowed from some farm hand. Then followed the moving of the family into Oakland, where the boy first had access to a free library—an inestimable privilege to one with his insatiate love of reading. (p. 418)

Between school hours and work Jack found time to pore over books of history, poetry, and fiction, and to nurse the secret wish to become a writer. He was graduated from the Oakland grammar school at fourteen and a few months later drifted into an adventurous life 'longshore. Here he shared the industries and pastimes of the marine population, huddled along the water-front, taking his chances at salmon-fishing, oyster pirating, schooner-sailing, and other bay-faring ventures, never holding himself aloof when comrades were awake, but when they slept turning to his book with the avidity of a mind athirst for knowledge.

About this period of his life his sympathies and emotions were deeply stirred by the wrongs inflicted upon the laboring classes, and with youthful fervor he took up their defense, haranguing the crowds nightly in the plaza and urging upon them the necessity of social and political reconstruction. He became known in Bay whereabouts as "the boy socialist," and more than one of his street-hearers looked upon him as a kind of secular evangelist.

When he was seventeen, young London shipped before the mast on a sealing schooner which cruised to Japan and up the north coast to the Russian side of the Bering Sea. (pp. 419-20)

[However], Jack did not take specially to a seafaring life, and not long after we find him again in Oakland, plunging with characteristic ardor into the study of sociology and economics. Not satisfied with a theoretical understanding of the problems involved in socialistic reforms, like Josiah Flint, he took to the road, living for months the life of a tramp, and learning by hard knocks the true import of the survival of the fittest under existing economic conditions.

Speaking of the outcome of this practical test, Mr. London says:

> The months I spent on the road bred in me a permanent interest in the institutions of man both

from an economic and an ethical standpoint. Among other things I learned that society is an organism, the inertia of the masses profound, and the evolution of institutions a slow and painful process. Like every normal man who has thought along these lines, I learned to temper my radicalism, and was helped in this by a deeper inquiry into the science of evolution as taught by a host of writers, Herbert Spencer in the lead. I am still a socialist, but an evolved product, possessing a faith in humanity equaled only by a conception of its frailties and faults.

(pp. 420-22)

[In 1897, impelled] by the promise of gold and adventure, Jack London was among the first to join the fall rush to the Klondike. He was among the few doughty Argonauts who at this season made it over the Chilcoot Pass, the great majority waiting for spring. As charges were forty-three cents per pound for carrying supplies a distance of thirty miles, from salt water to fresh, he packed his thousand-pound outfit, holding his own with the strongest and most experienced in the party.

And here in the still white world of the North, where nature makes the most of every vital throb that resists her cold, and man learns the awful significance and emphasis of Arctic life and action, young London came consciously into his heritage. He would write of these—the terrorizing simplicity of an Alaskan landscape, its great peaks bulging with century-piled snows, its woods rigid, tense, and voiced by the frost like strained catgut; the fierce howls of starving wolf-dogs; the tracks of the dog-teams marking the lonely trail; but more than all else, the human at the North Pole.

Thus it would seem that his actual development as a writer began on the trail, though at the time he set no word to paper, not even jottings by the way in a notebook. A tireless brooding on the wish to write shaped his impulse to definite purpose, but outwardly he continued to share the interests and labors of his companion prospectors.

After a year spent in that weirdly picturesque but hazardous life, he succumbed to scurvy, and, impatient of the delay of homebound steamers, he and two campmates decided to embark in an open boat for the Bering Sea. The three accordingly made the start midway in June, and the voyage turned out to be a memorably novel and perilous one—nineteen hundred miles of river travel in nineteen days! (p. 422)

When London reached California he learned of the death of his father, and thenceforth devolved upon him the care and support of his widowed mother and a six-year-old nephew. There were debts also to meet,—doctors' and undertakers' bills,—which the son resolutely faced, his mind bent determinedly upon earning a livelihood by his pen. His brain seethed with stories founded upon the wonderful life of the past year. Could he transcribe these simply and dramatically so as to appeal to the reader? If this were possible, then success was assured. He began at once, and the result excited his highest hopes; before the year was out Eastern publishers were making him flattering offers for stories and articles, and urging upon the young author the advisability of bringing out a book.

Few writers, in fact, have come into such unprefaced notice as Jack London. One year from the publication of **"To the Man on Trail,"** a leading Boston house had secured the right to publish in book-form the group of eight tales entitled *The*

Son of the Wolf, which volume, attractively bound, is now in the hands of reviewers. **"An Odyssey of the North"** . . . is one of this collection, and most critics will account it first in graphic conception and detail.

In *The Son of the Wolf* the author gives his testimony of Alaskan life through actual sojourn in the country he describes. This personal contact, as it were, with his subject gives the book a unique charm and value. The reader feels that he is following the footsteps of one familiar with the trail but in no wise servile to bald fact; for here and there interspersed are bits of delicious fantasy with more than a hint of frank and wholesome sentiment. There is, nevertheless, little of the ethereal idealist in Jack London's work. We find him always human—a humanness which the spiritual-minded can share with profit. At times he makes use of a quaint naiveté of expression,—the bold yet tender passion of a rudimental age. . . . (p. 423)

[In **"The Odyssey of the North"**], as in his other stories, Mr. London's adroit but graphic portrayal of character suggests scope and symmetry of thought rather than limitation and indefiniteness. His magnetic ardor and earnestness of thought move even the most stolid, notwithstanding an undercurrent of protest against certain inadvertencies—false syntax and the flagrant misuse of an occasional word—which are the result of inexperience or carelessness. In justice to the author, however, it must be admitted that these errors—most of which are not serious—are not of a nature to beget a distrust of his genius.

If this youthful California writer makes a study of literary style, it is not apparent, so simply and unaffectedly does he relate a story. There is, indeed, small showing of that painstaking polish so dear to the academic mind; this young man of twenty-four has something more virile to offer than finish. Crude as is his diction, he has learned the ways out of prescribed literature into a spontaneity and freedom that charm and invigorate. One sees no straining after effect, no circumlocution; he reaches the humanity of his readers by direct course.

In undertaking to depict the man-world in the Arctic and the austerity and sublime homogeneousness of a North Pole landscape, Jack London had set no light task for himself. His choice of subject was voluntary and made with a shrewd guess at its literary values. That he has in so short a period won enviable recognition from the critics, demonstrates the clearness of his judgment as to public taste and the availability of his genius.

There are those who think this writer no less strong in philosophy and economics than he proves himself to be in fiction, and that, when the time is ripe, he will give vital thoughts to the world along these more important lines. Certain it is that the "boy socialist" is not lost in the man, for to-day Jack London has the avowed belief in an ultimate democracy to be achieved by all peoples whose institutions, ideals, and traditions are ethnologically Anglo-Saxon.

"Not that God has given the earth to the Anglo-Saxon, but that the Anglo-Saxon is going to take the earth for himself," he declares convincingly.

His views herein have doubtless been somewhat colored by an extensive reading of Kipling, for whom he entertains an admiration amounting to devotion. A few short-sighted critics have even gone so far as to accuse him of being studiously

Kiplingesque—a charge wholly without foundation, unless one excepts the fact that Mr. London shares with the eminent English novelist an ingrained belief in Anglo-Saxon dominance, a belief that crops out everywhere in the writings of both. In truth, the most cursory reading of **"The Son of the Wolf"** leaves an impression of distinctive literary character which in itself is expressive of the author's personality—picturesque, vigorous, and suggestive of tremendous and varied activities. (p. 424)

It may be permitted to the writer of this sketch to express the belief that London's genius will long continue to present the world with literary products that must delight and edify a constantly growing circle of readers. His youth, his robust health, his assiduous application, his indomitable purpose, his rare discrimination in the choice of literary materials, and the facility and felicity of his style—these all give promise and prophecy of exceptional achievement. (p. 425)

> *Ninetta Eames, "Jack London," in* Overland Monthly, *Vol. XXXV, No. 209, May, 1900, pp. 417-25.*

LITERARY DIGEST (essay date 1906)

[*In the following excerpted review of* Moon-Face, and Other Stories, *the anonymous critic praises London's short fiction for its energy, diversity, and originality but cautions London against egotism.*]

The eight stories which comprise [**Moonface, and Other Stories**] exhibit in quite varied fields the dramatic quality and virile powers of expression for which Mr. London is noted. In general the stories maintain the level reached in *The Call of the Wild* and suggest that there may be truth in the claim put forth by some of his admirers that this writer is related to the breed of Kipling. There is a freshness and originality in these unconventional tales, a sort of primitive vigor and pulsing life, that lift them above the average of the short stories that now have such vogue. Here and there, it is true, his style is disfigured by a grotesque stroke, and not infrequently his horror of the commonplace leads him into exaggeration, but these faults are redeemed by the intensely human quality of his work.

Probably the most serious charge that can be brought against this lively and interesting writer—the evidence for it looms large in the present collection of stories—is an ultra-smartness probably related to his ethical and political principles, which are known to be of the most "modern" type. Too much cocksureness and self-reliance is a sad handicap even in great writers. Slang, no doubt, may be endured in its place, and when properly muzzled by quotation marks, but it is not pleasant to meet it ranging at large through the pages of a book.

As for the subjects treated of in **Moonface,** they could hardly be more varied or more characteristic, and they are well adapted to give a comprehensive idea of the style of this energetic young writer.

> *A review of "Moon-Face, and Other Stories," in* Literary Digest, *New York, Vol. XXXIII, No. 14, October 6, 1906, p. 474.*

FREDERIC TABER COOPER (essay date 1906)

[*An American biographer and editor, Cooper served for many years as a literary critic for the* Bookman, *a popular early twentieth-century literary magazine. In the following excerpted review of the story "Moon-Face," Cooper expresses disapproval with London's ignoble view of human nature but acknowledges his talent for creating grim physical and psychological conflicts.*]

There is a cold-bloodedness about Jack London which would make it impossible for him to write [a story of pathos or regret]. . . . In his men and women the physical life lords it insolently over the spiritual and moral life. It is well for a novelist to keep in mind that even in the most cultured men and women the primitive human animal is, after all, not so very far below the surface. But it is also worth while to remember that there are few so degraded who are not sometimes swayed by influences that have no kinship with the physical passions. Mr. London, when he errs, does so on the side of the flesh; there are moments, even in his most powerful work, when one is prompted to say, "That is a false note; human nature is nobler than that!" It is only when he is writing frankly of man, the human animal, the primitive Klondike Indian, the prize-fighter in the lust of battle, the dangerous victim of a fixed idea, that he is really at his best. **"Moon-Face,"** the tale that gives its name to his new volume [**Moon-Face, and Other Stories**], is an admirable example of the last-named class of subjects, a man swayed by an unreasoning hatred until murder, wanton, callous murder, becomes an obsession. John Claverhouse is the name of the hated man; he is described as a cheery, optimistic, moon-faced man, "whose great 'Ha! Ha!' and 'Ho! Ho!' rose up to the sky and challenged the sun." The other man hates him because he is happy, because he is moon-faced, because, in short, he is John Claverhouse, and not some one radically different. And so, under the working of this obsession the other man plans a means of killing him, so strange, so diabolically crafty, that no one can ever trace it to him, no one will even have suspicions—except the victim himself, and he only in the last agonising moments of his life. There are just two stories which inevitably come to mind in connection with **"Moon-Face"**, Poe's "Cask of Amontillado" is one, with which it suggests comparison for its general spirit of insane hatred; and the other is one of Maupassant's stories, the name of which does not for the moment come to mind, but which forms a close parallel in method—the story in which a feeble peasant woman trains a giant hound to perform for her the vengeance which her own hands are too frail to carry out. (p. 247)

> *Frederic Taber Cooper, "The Note of Untruth and Some Recent Books," in* The Bookman, *New York, Vol. XXIV, November, 1906, pp. 244-49.*

LITERARY DIGEST (essay date 1907)

[*In the following excerpted review of* Love of Life, and Other Stories, *the anonymous critic unfavorably compares London's short fiction to that of adventure writer Bret Harte.*]

After sundry divagations in other fields of fiction, as well as in Socialistic discussion, Mr. London returns to the land of his first love in [**Love of Life, and Other Stories,** a collection of pieces about] Alaskan life. They are quite equal to his previous accomplishments in this direction, and are not approached by the efforts of any other writers, save Elizabeth Robins's *The Magnetic North,* which remains the chief achievement in arctic romance. Mr. London, if anything, has intensified his method of presenting a scene in simple, forceful language that makes one forget the telling and realize the vision with inward sight; as when, in the title story ["**Love of Life**"], he describes the efforts of a starving man on the Northern coast to catch a ptarmigan:

> Once he crawled upon one that must have been asleep. He did not see it till it shot up in his face from its rocky nook. He made a clutch as startled as was the rise of the ptarmigan, and there remained in his hand three tail-feathers. As he watched its flight he hated it, as tho it had done him some terrible wrong. Then he returned and shouldered his pack. . . .

The grim humor of Mr. London's *The Sea Wolf* reappears in the story "**The White Man's Way**," in which Yamikan, an Indian, having killed a white man in self-defense, is taken to California for trial, and is kept in prison, well fed, for two years, returning to Alaska on his acquittal in fine condition. Whereupon, Bidarshik, another Indian, not understanding the legal reason for the acquittal, proceeds to kill a white man voluntarily, expecting a two-years' revel in luxury and idleness. His victim proves to be a naturalist in search of specimens. Bidarshik is hanged, and his old parents are much mystified at the "white man's way."

There are one or two stories with less sinister themes in the book, as "**The Story of Keesh**," wherein the little lad, Keesh, mystifies the hunters of his village by his wonderful feats in killing bears. Principally, however, the narratives deal with the baser passions of man, and, while interest is sharply held, yet the author does not make use of the art of combining tenderness with strength, which was Bret Harte's noteworthy quality, and which enabled the latter to maintain his vogue in a single field during a long succession of years.

> *A review of "Love of Life, and Other Stories," in Literary Digest, New York, Vol. XXXV, No. 18, November 2, 1907, p. 655.*

J. MARCHAND   (essay date 1907)

[*In the following excerpt, Marchand praises London's short fiction collection* Love of Life, and Other Stories *for its narrative strength and vivid imagery but faults its subject matter as predictable.*]

When a writer does what is apparently expected of him by the reading public, he makes the reviewer's task more difficult. We know now that we may expect virile, vivid stories of the North, stories of struggle with the elements, of struggle with savage men and savage beasts, when we take up a book signed by Jack London. Having said several times what there is to be said about them, it is not easy to find new phrases. Most of the stories in [*Love of Life, and Other Stories*] have appeared in the magazines, but they are pretty generally worth preserving in book form. They are stories of the Alaskan North and of California; stories of the horrors of the Trail; stories of dogs that are more than human in their loyalty and affection, and of humans worse than brutes in their cruelty. All just what we have learned to expect from Jack London. But when we weary even of the well-told tales of man's struggle with the primal forces of nature, when we long for the greater conflict of man's struggle with his own nature, and the primal emotions, the talented author has prepared a little surprise for us in the story entitled "**A Day's Lodging**."

Simply told, sketched in with a few pen-strokes, we have a tale of strong human interest, a happening remarkable in itself and yet sufficiently possible to hold our imagination. The closing scene of it, the man deliberately lowering himself in the eyes of the woman he once loved, that he might save himself from loving her again, is admirable as a bit of strong and simple writing, and still more admirable as a bit of soul-painting. It is bigger in some ways than anything else in the book. The little preface the author has given it leads us to expect something else, however, something less good. And might lead some cruder readers to expect something else also, and to be disappointed. But the story of itself is good, both in theme and construction, and excellent in the writing of it. ["**Love of Life**"] is a study of hunger, strongly written, and had its meed of praise when it appeared in a popular magazine. "**The White Man's Way**" is a good bit of irony, and "**The Unexpected**" a thoroughly characteristic Jack London tale. "**The Sun-Dog Trail**" is an acknowledged "stunt," the author telling you in the beginning of the story just what he intends to do. It would be better were it more condensed in form. Taken altogether, these stories have all the good points of their author's work—strength, aliveness, vividness of colouring. They give us no new side of his talent, but they give us what we have learned to expect of him.

> *J. Marchand, in a review of "Love of Life, and Other Stories," in The Bookman, New York, Vol. XXVI, December, 1907, p. 419.*

THE NEW YORK TIMES BOOK REVIEW   (essay date 1911)

[*In the following excerpted review of* When God Laughs, and Other Stories, *the anonymous critic affirms London's strengths as an author of short fiction rather than extended narrative forms.*]

A collection of short stories, which exhibits the peculiar literary gifts of Mr. Jack London, somewhere near their brutal best, is contained in the volume entitled ***When God Laughs, and Other Stories.*** Except in a very few instances—conspicuously in one where he has essayed the lighter touch with his usual failure to achieve lightness—Mr. London has undertaken to make each sketch a vivid dramatization of some raw, grim, primitive crisis. The crueller and the fuller of the "agony of bloody sweat" this crisis is the better.

The author has exercised a fertile invention in the matter of grisly situations, and it may be said that he has succeeded in his effects in almost exact proportion to the native horror of the raw material. This statement is in no wise intended to detract from the recognition due Mr. London's skill in staging that material. It means, rather, that he knows how to make every ugly detail tell, to work up every point which tends to make cold chills run along the spine and produce a hot, choking sensation in the gorge. These sensations are nature's tribute to the horrible in fact, and nature can hardly pay the imagined horror greater tribute than to behave toward it in the same way.

A curious fact may be noted about the titles of the sketches. Some of them are extremely poetical and allusive, like "**When God Laughs**" and "**Created He Them**"; some are deliberately selected in raw chunks of language, like "**Just Meat**" and "**A Piece of Steak.**" The story, by the way, which bears this last title, is doubtless the truest of the lot. It deals with an old prizefighter's final great battle with conquering youth. ["**When God Laughs**"], to gain its end of putting a razor-edge upon sensation, invades depths of life and heights of folly from which, as a rule, all but weird mystics and physicians shrink. It is the story of two lovers with the refrain "Who wins his love shall lose her," sardonically twisted to show that even if he does not win her, he shall not gain—or, as Mr. London has it, "cheat the gods." . . .

Altogether, in spite of the calculated exploitation of the brutal for the sake of the jaded reader's answering thrill—the method, at second-hand, of the bloody Roman circus with its gladiators and human victims torn by wild beasts—even his harshest critics must admit that there is a strength in Mr. London here that is utterly lacking when he undertakes to be a novelist. He should stick to his last.

A review of "When God Laughs, and Other Stories," in The New York Times Book Review, *February 19, 1911, p. 88.*

THE BOOKMAN   (essay date 1911)

[*In the following excerpted review of* When God Laughs, and Other Stories, *the anonymous critic provides an overview of two of the collection's prominent stories, "Just Meat" and "Chinago."*]

When God Laughs, by Jack London, is a volume that does not average as well as some of his earlier collections of short stories; but there are at least two tales in it that refuse to be forgotten. One of these two is **"Just Meat,"** a story of two burglars who have successfully carried out a diamond robbery on a gigantic scale. It happens that a member of a firm of wholesale jewelers has planned to defraud his partner and abscond with the bulk of the stock. To this purpose he has taken to his house secretly a fabulous quantity of gems of all kinds and sizes, intending during the night to escape with them on board a sailing vessel bound for South America. It happens that the burglars break into this house before he has started, capture the jewels and incidentally kill the man. Now the authorities assume that it is the man's partner who has committed the murder and taken the stones. The real burglars are for the time being safe. But as they sit in their room, gazing fascinated at this glittering cascade of wealth, sheer avarice drives them mad and simultaneously each conceives the idea of poisoning the other with strychnine. The story ends with remorseless grimness as the two men writhe in their death struggles in the midst of the useless wealth. The second story is another bit of sombre irony called **"Chinago."** It is just the story of a Chinaman, one of scores drudging the years away on a plantation on one of the big islands in the Indian Ocean. He does not mind the toil, because the strange mad foreigners who hire him pay wages for a day's work which it would take him a month to earn at home. He has a dream of amassing enough money to have some time a little garden spot of his own and a tranquil haven for his old age. But there happens to come a tragedy. There is a man murdered. . . . Our Chinaman has had no share in the matter, but it happens that his name is very like that of one of the other Chinamen and that a certain official had been drinking rather deeply at the time he made out the death warrant. And that is the way it happened that this particular Chinaman's dream of a little garden spot was never realised.

A review of "When God Laughs," in The Bookman, *New York, Vol. XXXIII, No. 2, April, 1911, p. 195.*

London in the Klondike river valley during the gold rush of 1898.

THE NEW YORK TIMES BOOK REVIEW   (essay date 1914)

[*In the following excerpted review of* The Strength of the Strong, *the anonymous critic proclaims London a noteworthy author of short fiction.*]

Mr. London excels as a short-story writer rather than as a novelist. He plunges into his subject and swims through it and clambers out on the other side and shakes himself vigorously, while the spectator applauds—it has been a fine sight. But sometimes, as in his recent **Valley of the Moon,** he just swims and swims.

[**The Strength of the Strong**] illustrates the first method, though the stories are by no means of equal merit. It is not necessary to consider them in detail, as most of them are already known to readers of the popular magazines. Two, however, **"The Sea-Farmer"** and **"Samuel,"** are in a class by themselves. They are tales of a little island off the north of Ireland coast, where "fathers and mothers are revered and obeyed as in few other places in this modern world." . . .

"The Sea-Farmer" reminds one of Kipling, though it is far enough from being an imitation—as **"South of the Slot,"** with its shrewd emphasis upon the bizarre streak in the most "inhibited" of natures, is the sort of theme that O. Henry delighted in. But **"Samuel"** is a story that is neither Kipling nor

O. Henry, nor—we had almost said—Jack London himself. It belongs to the small group of tales that bear no stamp of authorship, that "any one" might have written—only "any one" couldn't—that are simple, and human, and dreadful, all at once, as life is. It is the story of a woman who insisted on giving her child an ill-omened name, and, when it died, on giving it to the next-born, and so on until four had borne it and had died, most of them horribly. Her family and her friends forsook her; after the second fatality the minister refused to christen her babes, but she took one and then another to the mainland and had him given the name her soul loved. And to the end, though old, lonely, and abhorred as a murderer of innocents, her spirit never flinched. . . .

"Samuel" does not touch the high-water mark of the talent that we recognize as peculiarly Jack London's. But, in a less narrow sense, it is perhaps the finest and most moving story that he has ever written—a story of the mystery of liking, of the mystery of fate and of steadfastness in the face of fate, that any man might be glad to have written.

> *"Jack London's Stories," in* The New York Times Book Review, *June 14, 1914, p. 270.*

FREDERIC TABER COOPER (essay date 1914)

[*In the following excerpted review of* The Strength of the Strong, *Cooper acknowledges London's popular strengths but questions the author's white supremacist sympathies, as demonstrated in the story "The Unparalleled Invasion."*]

[The stories collected in *The Strength of the Strong*] are varied enough to suit the most diverse tastes, and in point of time they keep us skipping up and down the centuries, from primordial days to the dim vistas of futurity, as nimbly as though he were endowed with Mr. H. G. Wells's convenient *Time Machine.* The story [**"The Strength of the Strong"**] may be defined as a sort of sociological parable, told by a man of the stone age, a monkey man, bowed with years, who tells the eager circle of his great-grandchildren the history of the tribe's slow emergence from barbarism, their experiments in local government, their mistakes in private ownership of land, and their final victory through breaking up the monopoly of the few and uniting in a free and equal communism. All of which, while cleverly done, is rather tedious, blatantly unreal, and to the reader who does not happen to share Mr. London's economic convictions, quite unimportant. Of a very different class is the amazing and delicious piece of wholesale extravagance called **"The Unparalleled Invasion."** In it the author has taken one of his forward bounds, a century or two, and imagines that China has undergone a great awakening. Her population has multiplied beyond belief, and the yellow hordes have overrun the greater part of the continent of Asia. They conquer through sheer force of numbers. . . . All Europe and America are aghast. It is the old bugaboo of the Yellow Peril now come in grim earnest, the Yellow Peril magnified to the *n*th degree. But one day a certain quiet, unobtrusive little American calls at the White House, and what he has to suggest to the President results in a secret conference of the world's powers. Then follows the most astounding gathering of a gigantic host of the allied armies and navies of the civilised world, brought together, not for the purpose of invading China, but of drawing an immense cordon around her on land and sea, so that not one Chinaman can escape. And when arrangements are completed, a vast squadron of little aeroplanes are seen soaring over

the whole Chinese Empire, everywhere letting fall a rain of little glass tubes. And within a fortnight China is stricken, not with one plague, but with twenty: typhoid, leprosy, yellow fever, bubonic plague, the sleeping sickness, these and innumerable others, let loose in an unimaginable orgy of pestilence and corruption. It is a Dance Macabre on a gigantic scale; and the only reason why it in a measure defeats itself is that it is just a little too big, too ghastly, too wholesale in its horror for the human mind quite to visualise it. We end by feeling as little kinship for the expiring billions of tortured Chinese as for the same number of garden ants.

> *Frederic Taber Cooper, in a review of "The Strength of the Strong," in* The Bookman, *New York, Vol. XXXIX, August, 1914, p. 679.*

THE NEW YORK TIMES BOOK REVIEW (essay date 1916)

[*In the following excerpted review of* The Turtles of Tasman, *the anonymous critic asserts that London's diverse range ensures widespread popular appeal.*]

No matter what other fault may be found with [***The Turtles of Tasman***] by Jack London, it cannot be accused of a lack of variety. For, although two of the eight tales which make up the volume have their scenes laid amid the ice and snow of the Yukon, they differ greatly in other ways, while the rest range from fantasy to comedy and from comedy to the mixture of pity and repulsion excited by those in the "drooling ward" of a home for the feeble-minded. . . . [**"The Turtles of Tasman"**] is the tale of two brothers, unalike in almost everything save a certain physical resemblance. Of the two, one had been a wanderer, had journeyed all over the surface of the earth, seen strange people, had an abundance of adventures, enjoyed himself hugely, and presently, sick and penniless, came to his brother's home to rest, as he supposed; to die, as every one else, including his devoted daughter, knew very well: the other had remained at home, stifling his own desire for adventure, devoting himself to the care of his mother and of the great estate to develop which his father had given his life, improving an immense tract of country, bringing prosperity to many other people as well as himself. The reader's sympathies will go to one or the other of these two, according as to whether he shares with the author the popular affection for the self-indulgent prodigal, despising those who obey such a humdrum, colorless thing as duty and refrain from "dancing a hoedown on the Ten Commandments," or is so eccentric as to respect the man who curbed his own wish for travel and "the shining ways" in order to be "the dependable one" of the family and, incidentally, was able to save his mother from blindness.

Another story of two brothers is **"The Eternity of Forms,"** a cleverly done, modern sort of ghost story, and next comes **"Told in the Drooling Ward,"** a tale whose title gives sufficient indication of its somewhat unusual, if not very pleasant, character. It is one of the "feebs," a "high-grader," 28 years old, nearly all of whose life has been spent in the home, who tells of some of his experiences, of the time he was adopted out, of his fondness for "little Albert," one of the "droolers," and of his contempt for the high-grade "epilecs," who are "stuck up because they ain't just ordinary feebs." **"The Hobo and the Fairy"** is the kind of thing which, before the recent experiments in prison reform, was usually dismissed with a shrug as a mere piece of sentimentality. . . . Rosa Shanklin, tramp and ex-convict, who had "defied all keepers and survived all brutalities . . . had been triced up and lashed until he fainted, had been revived and lashed again," and come as a result to hate the world which from the time he was 17 had persistently misused him, would scarcely have seemed a promising object for a fairy's ministrations. But presently there came to him a child who was not afraid, and after that wonderful afternoon he swore "to make good." The situation is well handled, with deftness, restraint, and good taste, and without any touch of the banal or maudlin. **"The Prodigal Father,"** which follows next, is an amusing bit of comedy, the history of a New Englander who came to California with only a very few dollars, found prosperity, and returned to his old home, believing that now at last he could successfully combat one whom he had feared of old—and presently discovered his mistake. . . . [And soon] comes what is decidedly the best story in the book, as well as the one most characteristic of Mr. London—**"Finis."**

A grim tale of the Yukon, of a man driven to desperation and the committing of a great crime, this story grips the reader as does none of the others. Morganson's long vigil by the trail in the bitter cold, the obsession which grew upon him, the way of escape which opened out before him, then shut mercilessly, irrevocably—these compose a series of tense moments, vivid, dramatic, making the reader thrill and tingle. And then the climax; the crime, the frustration, the coming of that which he had so dreaded and fought against, only to find at the very last that it was not terrible at all, but something to welcome with "a tired sigh of comfort." It is a strong story, this **"Finis,"** horrible at times, but alive and intensely vigorous and real, worthy to stand beside those tales with which Mr. London won his reputation. **"The End of the Story"** is also a record of events which happened by the shores of the Yukon, but it lacks something of the grip and power and inevitability which make **"Finis"** notable. Nevertheless, the account of the coming of Tom Daw to the cabin by the Yukon and of the doctor's journey over the snow and the fast-thawing ice to the help of a man who would, it seemed only too probable, be beyond human aid long before he could cover the many and difficult miles stretching between them, makes a most effective narrative, graphic, swift-moving and colorful.

The very great difference in theme, type, and merit which renders it practically impossible to estimate or classify this collection as a whole makes it one which readers of widely varying tastes may take up, feeling quite sure that in it they will find at least one or two tales which will please them.

> *A review of "The Turtles of Tasman," in* The New York Times Book Review, *October 22, 1916, p. 439.*

THE NEW REPUBLIC (essay date 1916)

[*In the following excerpted review of* The Turtles of Tasman, *the anonymous critic contends that London achieves his most characteristic form when he writes directly from personal experience.*]

When Kipling chose an American setting for that imperishable boys' romance, *Captains Courageous,* he selected the gray waste of waters off the Newfoundland coast. It was a natural scene but of late years there has come to be a Pacific tradition of [American] saltwater fiction. And the prophet of that tradition is Jack London. He has written many a stirring novel, and he has made the phrase "red blood" as nationalistic as "four flusher." But he is too thoroughly an American

not to have the kind of imaginative temperament which finds readier and more brilliant technical expression in the short story than in the novel. Of all his short stories the most genuine are those of the sea. In [*The Turtles of Tasman*] only one, **"The Turtles of Tasman,"** is concerned directly with seafaring men. It is the pathos of an adventurer come home to die surrounded by the loving care of a brother who envies his wayward brother's daring and his reminiscent, picturesque friends. He has stayed at home and made money, but his brother has seen the world. Evidently Mr. London thought well of this story, for he put it first in the book and used it for a title. There are eight other stories: one, a preposterous bit of cave-man symbolism, **"The First Poet,"** another, a sharp picture of the feeble-minded in **"Told in the Drooling Ward,"** the inevitable technically clever monologue **"The Eternity of Forms,"** . . . and two really memorable stories of the North, **"Finis"** and **"The End of the Story."** When Mr. London thinks of DeMaupassant and the form-perfect French, he becomes just uninterestingly imitative. When he thinks of other American writers, he becomes clumsily humorous or sentimental. But when he writes of Alaska or the Klondike or the sea as he knows it and loves it, his stories have the qualities for which he is still famous. (pp. 55, 57)

> *A review of "The Turtles of Tasman," in* The New Republic, *Vol. IX, No. 106, November 11, 1916, pp. 55, 57.*

THE NEW YORK TIMES BOOK REVIEW (essay date 1919)

[*In the following excerpted review of* On the Makaloa Mat, *the anonymous critic offers a favorable analysis of London's short fiction set in Hawaii.*]

When Jack London died he left behind him a number of completed but as yet unpublished manuscripts. Most of these have now been printed, and according to the publisher's announcement this new volume of short stories and sketches, **On the Makaloa Mat,** is probably the last that will ever appear. Composed entirely of Hawaiian tales, sketches and episodes, the book as a whole gives a fascinating picture of life on those picturesque islands; and it is, moreover, a picture which differs very considerably from the majority of those with which we are familiar. For many of the numerous characters who move through these pages are of mixed blood, half or three-quarters or even seven-eighths white, men and women of wealth and dignity and fine personality, who on the native side trace their ancestry back through long lines of "aliis," or chiefs, being as they are descended from the intermarriage of chiefesses with the white adventurers who came to Honolulu. No less than they of mixed blood do many of those who are pure native embody to a greater or lesser degree the sharp contrast between the old and the new. This contrast is perhaps nowhere better illustrated than in the story called **"Shin Bones,"** perhaps the best of the seven tales in the book. Here ancient superstitions and weird rites of sorcery, modern manners, ideas and education, heredity, sociology, romance, philosophy, and some very vivid descriptions of scenery and of adventure are combined in the narrative related by Prince Akuli of Lakanaii, Oxford graduate, . . . while waiting for an automobile to come and rescue his broken limousine. Prince Akuli himself and his mother Hiwilani, who in her old age reverted to the ways and the gods of her forefathers, show in their own persons how sudden has been the transition from the old beliefs and customs to the new—a transition that has occurred within the space of a couple of generations. . . .

As the majority of writers on Hawaii have dealt almost exclusively with the common people, showing the chiefs only in their relation to these commoners and as they appeared to the commoners' eyes, so does Mr. London deal almost exclusively with the "aliis," showing us the commoners from the aliis' point of view. But by no means the least interesting among the many interesting people to whom the author introduces us are some two or three of these old men, loyal retainers of those whose fathers theirs had served. One of these elders, Ahuna, rich in ancient lore, was the only living being who knew where lay the secret burial place of the ancient aliis, where other and nameless things also lay, while another elder, Kumuhana, had himself narrowly escaped being the last "moepuu," or human sacrifice, what time the great Chief Kahekili died. It was in the olden days a serious matter for all commoners when a great chief died, and although the idols had been overthrown and the taboo broken, the priests and great chiefs still practiced certain of the ancient ways when Kumuhana was young. While the chiefs and chiefesses lived, however, there was much gayety in their lives and in those of their followers, and it is a most alluring description of youth and love and joy, of perfumed nights and laughter-filled days which Bella Castner, three-quarters white, gives while she tells the story of the two radiant weeks of her life, those weeks when, mounted on her splendid black horse Hilo, she rode with her gallant lover, Prince Lilolilo, in the royal progress of the Princess Lihue.

In Hawaii are to be found other races besides the white and the Polynesian, and one of the tales, **"The Tears of Ah Kim,"** shows how a Chinese coolie rose to affluence and dignity, and then fell in love with the twice widowed Li Faa, who was half Kanaka, and, from the Chinese point of view, a new woman and a feminist. [**"When Alice Told Her Soul"** introduces] Abel Ah Yo, the highly successful revivalist, a sort of Hawaiian Billy Sunday, who was one-fourth Portuguese, one-fourth Scotch, one-fourth Hawaiian, and one-fourth Chinese! From this mixture resulted a most remarkable power of language, which so affected Alice Akana, mistress of the hula house, and heretofore safe repository of all the secret scandals of Hawaiian society, that she presently "Told Her Soul" in public, to the extreme embarrassment of some persons, the intense delight of others, and the great benefit of old John Ward, drunkard and beachcomber, an "old-timer," who knew quite a few little things himself. The book certainly cannot be said to lack variety; this story of Alice Akana, the "penitent Phryne of Honolulu," is an amusing bit of social satire, applicable to almost any comparatively small community, while **"The Kanaka Surf"** is a tale of the eternal triangle, something by no means especially of Hawaii. But there are many old myths and legends and superstitions which enter into these stories that are essentially of Hawaii, and one brief hint of a past more ancient than that of even the oldest alii ancestry, a hint which would seem to indicate that it was Mr. London's opinion that the Polynesians had at some time a direct knowledge of and connection with Africa. For the priests whom Kumuhana heard talking a language entirely different from the ordinary tongue, "the old language, the priest language," sang, too, a Maori death chant over the body of the dead chief, and invoked the God of the Sun, whom the Hawaiians called La, by another name, and that the great name of him who was once all potent in hundred-gated Thebes—Ra.

Much of the contents of this book was written while the author was himself staying in Hawaii. It is full of light and color, with many vivid descriptions of sea and forest, of the frowning and terrible "Iron-Bound Coast," and the beauty and fragrance of the fertile land. Yet more interesting are the accounts of the people themselves, of the duties of the aliis, become more than a trifle difficult in these modern times, and of the effect upon them of their contact with Western civilization. Much of it is admirably written, and if not without moments of horror, it is quite unmarred by any tinge of brutality.

"Jack London's Tales of Hawaii," in The New York Times Book Review, *November 16, 1919, p. 649.*

KATHERINE MANSFIELD (essay date 1920)

[*Mansfield was an important pioneer in stream-of-consciousness literature and among the first English authors to write fiction dependent on incident rather than plot. This technique is considered to have significantly influenced the modern short story form and was often utilized by London in his own* works. *Originally published in the* Athenaeum, August 27, 1920, *Mansfield's review of* Island Tales *excerpted below faults London's later fiction set in Hawaii as predictable.*]

On the back cover of ***Island Tales*** there is a list of thirty-four of Jack London's books which are to be had in a cheap edition. To read the titles is to get a curiously vivid idea of their author, of not only the kind of thing he liked to write about, but even of the way in which he approached his subject. . . . [They] conjure up an impression of a simple-hearted teller of tales who has been up and down the world, who has a fondness for Nature in her extreme moods, and is by no means devoid of sentimentality. We feel as we glance down that long list that here was a genial, warm-blooded fellow, who liked a name to be a name, a snowstorm to be a snowstorm and a man to be a hero. He is one of those writers who win the affection of their readers—who are, in themselves the favourite book. But this very affection which he inspired is a something sentimental. That which prevented Jack London from ever being one of the real adventurers, the real explorers and rebels, was his heart; there was always the moment when his heart went to his head and he was carried away by passions which were immensely appropriate to the occasion, but which suffered from a histrionic tinge. Then his simplicity, smothered under a torrent of puffed-up words, obscured the firm outlines upon which his story relied, and we were left with the vaguely uncomfortable sensations of those to whom an 'appeal' has been made. (pp. 255-56)

When we turn to ***Island Tales*** we cannot help regretting that the gleaners have been so busy in the field where such a teeming crop has been reaped. For there is not a single story in it which is better than the average magazine supplies. True, his admirers would recognize them as having come from the Jack London shop; but they are machine-made, ready-to-read tales which depend for their novelty upon the originality of the Hawaiian ornament. It is a little sad to notice the effect of this ambrosial climate upon his style of writing. Words became hyphenated, bedecked, sentences were spun out until the whole reminded one of the wreaths—the 'Leis' or love-tokens—that the gentle savages love to hang about their necks. And then the Hawaiian greeting, 'Arms around,' as he describes it so often and with such delight, was no antidote to his sentimentality. It would not, however, be fair to judge him by this book. But it does confirm us in the opinion that his salvation lay in wolves, snow, hardship and toil. (p. 257)

Katherine Mansfield, "Hearts Are Trumps," in her Novels and Novelists, edited by J. Middleton Murry, Alfred A. Knopf, 1930, pp. 255-57.

FRED LEWIS PATTEE   (essay date 1922)

[*Pattee was a pioneering American literary historian, critic, poet, and novelist who regarded literature as a form of popular expression. In the following excerpt, Pattee asserts that London's fiction was highly romanticized, despite the claims of previous critics who had characterized his work as essentially realistic.*]

It was [London's] Alaska stories that gave him his first hearing. He had the good fortune to speak at the one moment when all would listen. In 1898 the imagination of the world had been stirred by the Klondike gold strike, and everywhere there was demand for material that was concrete, circumstantial, hot from first-hand observation. Of London's first six books all save one, a juvenile in *St. Nicholas,* were tales of the Alaska gold fields, vivid with pictures, breathing everywhere actuality; and it is upon these five—*The Son of the Wolf, The God of His Fathers, A Daughter of the Snows, Children of the Frost,* and *The Call of the Wild,* the last issued in 1903—that his ultimate fame must rest. All are of short story texture: even the novel *A Daughter of the Snows* is a series of episodes, and *The Call of the Wild* might have for its sub-title "Seven Episodes in the Life of the Dog Buck."

His method was the method of Kipling, as Kipling's had been that of Bret Harte. He would present a field new to literature by means of startling pictures; swift scenes flashed upon a screen with emphasis, even to exaggeration, upon the unique and unusual. Everywhere Bret Harte paradoxes: Hay Stockard is accused by the missionary of breaking all the commandments, and he is a blasphemer until "From the slipping of a snow-shoe thong to the forefront of sudden death his Indian wife would gauge the occasion by the pitch and volume of his blasphemy," and yet he dies rather than renounce the God of his Puritan fathers. In all this early fiction the rush of the narrative is compelling and the seeming fidelity to nature in the background convincing. (pp. 119-20)

We are won at the start by the positiveness of the author. We must take him on faith: few of us know how civilized men behave in the areas beyond the bounds of civilization, how men die of starvation, how dogs deport themselves in the Arctic night. He tells us in minute detail, with Defoe-like concreteness of touch upon touch. But are we certain it *is* the truth? We are not. He is no more a realist than was Harte. Like Harte he is writing from memory and imagination the story of a vanished period, a brief and picturesque day in a new environment, where youth is supreme and alone, and his fancy hovers over it fondly, and paints it and exaggerates it and idealizes it even to romance. (p. 121)

His characters are not actual men whom he has himself seen and known: they are demigods, the unsung heroes of a heroic age now put into epic setting. (p. 122)

Moreover, he adds to this the romance of a fading race. He dates **"The God of His Fathers"** at "the moment when the stone age was drawing to a close." His Indian women are a remarkable group: Ruth, wife of Mason, in **"The White Silence"**; Madeline in **"An Odyssey of the North"**; Unga in **"The Wife of a King"**; Passuk, wife of Sitka Charley;

Zarniska, wife of Scruff Mackensie; Sipsu, the Chief's daughter, in **"Where the Trail Forks"**; and Killisnoo, wife of Tomm, introduced with the remark: "Takes a woman to breed a man. Takes a she-cat not a cow to mother a tiger." By no means are they realistic studies. They are drawn from imagination rather than from notes made after observation; they are the type of primitive super-woman their author's imagination delighted in—Jees Uck for instance, with her "great blazing black eyes—the half-caste eye, round, full-orbed, and sensuous." . . . (pp. 122-23)

Romanticized and overdrawn as unquestionably they are, nevertheless these women are the most vital and convincing of all Jack London's characters. They are his only additions to the gallery of original characters in American fiction. Their doglike fidelity and honesty, their loyalty and self-sacrifice, their primitive resourcefulness in danger and privation, excite unconsciously our admiration and our pity.

It is not too sweeping to say that the primary purpose of all London's early fiction was pictorial. He would reproduce for us the White North. Everywhere pictures, flash-lights not only upon the surfaces of the scene but into the heart and meaning of it. (pp. 123-24)

His affinity is with Conrad; with him he might have said, "My task which I am trying to achieve is, by the power of the written word, to make you hear, to make you feel—it is, before all, to make you *see.*" (p. 125)

[The causes for London's eventual decline] lay in the author's temperament and in the nature of his literary field. In reality, after the first five books, he exhausted his Alaska claim; his lode petered out. Harte and even Kipling had discovered that to confine oneself to the recording of a primitive society is soon to run out of material. London had added nothing to Harte's outfit save a new set of drop scenery, a new fresh vigor of treatment, and a Gogol-like gruesomeness of detail, and these now had grown familiar. But the enormous vogue of *The Call of the Wild* gave him at once new latitude. He cleared his desk of early material—**"The Faith of Men,"** *The War of the Classes,* **"Moon Face,"** and the like—and then began to write as he pleased: his market allowed it. By nature and training he was an extreme idealist; a revolutionist, indeed. . . . From this time on he was constantly astride of hobbies, some of which he rode furiously. He had discovered in his tumultuous reading the evolutionary theory, the recapitulation theory, Gogol, Spencer, Karl Marx, Nietzsche. At the time of his death he was, to quote his wife's words, "enormously interested in psychoanalysis," and had he lived would have written a series of novels concerned with "research into the primitive, into the noumenon of things, in order to understand the becoming of what man is to-day," novels undoubtedly of the type of *The Star Rover.* (pp. 126-27)

Unquestionably [London] was not a novelist: he was too impatient, too headlong, to round out a large plan. He had not the patience to revise; he refused to read his earlier chapters day by day as he proceeded. As a result, the novels grew by accretions, and became, like *The Little Lady of the Big House,* masses of loosely-bound material for novels. Had patience been granted him, and restraint, he might, perhaps, have enlarged his vignettes into careful wholes; into novels even. (p. 129)

His range, however, is small. Of one whole rich area of human society he knew only the surface. The sordid misery of his childhood had warped his sense of values and narrowed the circle of human characters that he knew intimately enough to portray as a novelist should portray characters. His world, therefore, is lopsided and misleading. His socialism, unrelieved as it is by humor, is often ludicrous. His gospel, as one finds it in *The Sea Wolf,* for instance, and *Martin Eden,* is frankly and outspokenly materialistic, and materialism is the antipodes of all that we denominate art.

Moreover, within his own chosen field he is limited of range. After the voyage of the *Snark* he added the South Seas to his literary area and tried to do for them what he had done for Alaska, but it was only a changing of scenery. Instead of intense cold, intense heat; instead of the aurora, the glamour of the tropic night. The novel *Adventure* is *A Daughter of the Snows* transferred to the Solomon Islands, and Frona Wilse changes her name to Joan Lackland. Smoke Bellew becomes the David Grief of **"A Son of the Sun."** But there is a falling off in zest and vision. The South Sea tales do not leave so wholesome an impression as the earlier tales of the Arctic. He has chosen only the loathsome, the sensational, the unique; and one feels that he has chosen them simply to make salable copy. (pp. 130-31)

[London's] sea tales are contemporary with Conrad's and at many points there is parallelism. Both deal largely with outcasts; both exalt their leading characters into super-men—Captain MacWhir in *Typhoon,* Razumov with his "men like us leave no posterity"; both tell graphically of typhoon and violence; both are sonorous and gorgeous of diction. But Conrad is objective and London is prevailingly subjective; Conrad knows the sea better and he loves it with his whole soul. (pp. 132-33)

The final literary style of Jack London—and doubtless it is true of all men—was the product of his own temperament. He was too individualistic, too impatient long to follow the lead of other men. Directed as he was at first by Kipling and Gogol and O. Henry, he soon divested himself of their mannerisms and voiced only himself. He was writing now furiously for money and only for money. In an interview published with his sanction at the height of his career, he declared that he did not write because he loved writing. He hated it.

> Every story that I write is for the money that will come to me. I always write what the editors want, not what I'd like to write. I grind out what the Capitalist editors want, and the editors buy only what the business and editorial departments permit. The editors are not interested in the truth.

Everything in his life during the last decade of his work called aloud for money, and his only source of income was his pen. For a man of his temperament there could be but one result: one finds almost nothing in his writings that has been brooded over, that, like ripened wine, has body to it and bouquet. One thousand words a day, every day in the week, without vacation or rest, excited work unrevised and unreturned to, is journalism, the ephemerae of the Sunday supplement.

His temperament is everywhere visible. His sentences are short, often mere members of a sentence—the unit of measure of one excitable and headlong. There is no reserve, no restraint: everywhere exaggeration, superlatives; everything in extreme. In his later work he used the adjective "abysmal" until it became a mannerism that could even creep into one of his titles; *The Abysmal Brute.* . . . Even on literary topics he can render tongue-tied and silent Humphrey Van Weyden "the Dean of American Letters the Second," Van Weyden

"the cold-blooded fish, the emotionless monster, the analytical demon." Are we convinced? On the contrary we begin to doubt the accuracy even of his autobiographical confessions. *Can* this man tell the truth? Will his imagination and melodramatic impulses permit him, even if he tries? Can we believe, for example, that a healthy country boy—not a De Quincey under the influence of drugs—can have dreams as extreme and as circumstantial as those he describes in the autobiographical parts of *Before Adam?*

That London devoutly believed that he was a realist and that his extreme pictures came only from his thoroughness, there can be no doubt. In *Martin Eden* he has said: "Realism is imperative to my nature, and the bourgeois spirit hates realism. The bourgeois is cowardly. It is afraid of life." But realism is science, and scientist London was not. Surely his is not the realism of the French school that filled endless note-books with careful observations before it began to write. He has been on the spot, to be sure, and the reader is never allowed for a moment to lose sight of the fact, but he works not from scientifically collected data. He can weave a glorious web of impressions of an era over which time is throwing a mellowing haze, he can heighten its picturesque places and exaggerate its lights and shades, but this is not realism. Wherever he touches the things that we know, we are likely to find him even grotesquely unrealistic. His dialogue seldom rings true, never, indeed, in his later novels. (pp. 133-37)

In the field of action, however, especially action in the primitive areas of life, he stands with the masters. Few have surpassed him in power to present vivid moving-pictures: records of fights—dog-fights, prize-fights, bull-fights, the fight of a bull moose with a wolf pack, the battle of a Scruff Mackensie with a whole Indian tribe, the over-powering single-handed of a mutinous crew by a Wolf Larsen, the stand of a band of island lepers against the authorities. Scenes of battle and tempest arouse his imagination as nothing else: typhoons in the Solomon Islands, races with the Yukon mail, mutinies at sea, Arctic heroes conquering single-handed a whole firm of Wall Street sharpers. (p. 139)

At one time—about 1903 it was—O. Henry threw his influence over London's short stories, notably those in **The Faith of Men** and **Moon Face,** but between London and O. Henry there is this fundamental difference: London was passionately in earnest; he wrote without humorous intent; he wrote with a motif, and this he never forgot even in his most headlong moments of copy production. Behind his work was a principle that he fought for, a conviction that was Puritanic in its intensity. O. Henry, and also Bret Harte, lacked this element, and lacking it, they are in danger, despite their literary cleverness and their humor, of falling among the mere entertainers, useful people but not a class to be placed high in the major scale of values. (pp. 141-42)

> *Fred Lewis Pattee, "The Prophet of the Last Frontier," in his* Side-Lights on American Literature, *The Century Co., 1922, pp. 98-160.*

PATRICK BRAYBROOKE (essay date 1927)

[In the following excerpt, Braybrooke analyzes London's short story "The Unexpected."]

One day, not so very long ago, the morning papers announced with all their baldness, that Jack London had died. And, we who loved the grim realism and deep understanding of his books, realised that a writer of hurricane force had passed from the earth and the earth was the poorer for his passing. For Jack London was one of those writers who combined a very sound common sense with an extraordinary power of writing terrific melodrama. London understood life and he could write of its frantic struggles, its delicious romance and its startling, terrifying mystery and tragedy. London wrote with a pen that literally galloped and the galloping left the reader gasping for breath and yet eager to read on, even if the reading became almost a painful emotion.

In this Essay, I have taken one of Jack London's short stories and I have taken that remarkable tale which he called **"The Unexpected."** By an examination of this something can be seen of the philosophy of this melodramatic and brilliant man of literary thrills. For that is exactly what London was, a literary man who could thrill *par excellence.*

It is one of the most interesting things in the world to watch the effect of something that is unexpected on an individual. The unexpected may bring out the best qualities in an individual, it may quite equally bring out the worst. (pp. 113-14)

It is with the result of the unexpected on two people, that Mr. London deals in his story **"The Unexpected."** Mr. London is of the opinion that the application of the unexpected in life is a kind of test, the unexpected selects and it knows whom it will beat and by whom it will be beaten. This is the way in which Mr. London puts his proposition.

> When the unexpected does happen, however, and when it is of sufficiently grave import, the unfit perish. They do not see what is not obvious, are unable to do the unexpected, are incapable of adjusting their well-groomed lives to other and strange grooves. In short, when they come to the end of their own groove, they die.

I think that it may be wise, in so far as it goes, to accept what Mr. London postulates. But I am very firmly convinced that a very large number of people are perfectly able to adapt themselves to meet a progress of events that they had not thought about. . . . But it is perfectly true to say that those who cannot meet the unexpected die, for if they do not die physically, they die mentally and spiritually. Mr. London, in the story that I am writing about, deals with a woman who was able to meet the unexpected when it was thrust upon her in the most violent and dreadful way that it is possible to imagine. Any event which Jack London writes of, if it is at all dramatic, may be quite certain to be drama to the last degree.

And let us look at the chief character of this remarkable story, the type of woman that Mr. London thinks can withstand the onslaught of the unexpected. She is one; Edith Whittlesey and she is one of those women who will never be beaten because she is never smashed by the most terrific reversal of her fortunes. (pp. 114-16)

[When] Edith Whittlesey became Edith Nelson came the sudden rush of the unexpected, the sudden rush that swept away lives, the sudden rush that made madness draw near, the sudden rush that veiled the face of the sun, the sudden rush that made all dark and fearful and full of frightful eventualities and still more frightful possibilities.

But I am anticipating, I must not describe the coming of the actual unexpected to Edith Nelson for a little. I must describe their background so that we can *see* this wonderful woman

that Jack London has created, as well as read about her. Edith Nelson found herself one of a gold mining rush that tore away to the fastnesses of Alaska. And here in Alaska in a little wooden cabin dwelt Edith and her husband. And it was the duty of Edith to see to the cabin for you must know that no matter where your home be, in Park Lane or in the heart of Alaska, a woman must be there if you would have your home to be the blessed place that name implies. And it seemed as if life would move evenly, no untoward events, for if you are in a rough country you expect roughness, but the roughness is expected and so it does not hurt so much. (pp. 116-17)

Not a situation in which it might be expected that a dreadful tragedy only waited its evil opportunity to pounce. Perhaps evil is even more clever than we think, for it seems to wait until no one gives it even a passing thought, then suddenly like a vulture, it swoops, it cuts with a two edged sword and withdraws laughing at the bloody havoc it has created.

And now Mr. London swerves right into the drama. The curtain is raised, the eyes strain that they may see the fearful spectacle, the flesh creeps, the storm has broken and the lightning reveals a terrible scene. Tersely does Mr. London introduce us to the awful tragedy that is about to take place in that little cabin of happy and successful people.

> And then the unexpected happened. They had just sat down to the breakfast table.

A time when you would least expect tragedy, men well cheered by ample sleep, well filled by the delights of the table, with the prospect of a prosperous day's work in front. There is only the Irishman absent and such is the merriness of the party that they are laughing at the absence of Dennin. The dialogue is true of the careless chat of men with the combination of wanted food and anticipation of coming success to add to success already gained. (pp. 117-18)

And then in came the absent member:

> The sound had scarcely died away when the door opened and Dennin came in. All turned to look at him. He was carrying a shot-gun. Even as they looked, he lifted it to his shoulder and fired twice. At the first shot Dutchy sank upon the table overturning his mug of coffee, his yellow mop of hair dabblin in his plate of mush. His forehead, which pressed upon the near edge of the plate, tilted the plate up against his hair at an angle of forty-five degrees. Harkey was in the air in his spring to his feet, at the second shot, and he pitched face down upon the floor, his "My God!" gurgling and dying in his throat.

This frightful scene was, in the most dramatic sense, something to cause terror. Mr. London merely remarks:

> It was the unexpected.

The effect on Edith and Hans was one of paralysis. The most usual first effect of a very sudden experience of the unexpected, is a sense of paralysis, the brain cannot so suddenly leave an old path and enter on a new one. In Mr. London's story, the brain of Edith has to suddenly adapt itself to a situation of sudden death from the immediate forerunning laughter at a genial meal. At first the transition is too violent to be coped with. (pp. 118-19)

But the stunning effect of the murder does not last very long, the instinct for self preservation arouses the sense of adaptability in Edith. Thus Mr. London demonstrates a very well attested truth. Nothing rouses so much from any great shock as the appearance of danger to ourselves. Mankind is naturally selfish and naturally desirous to save itself from premature extinction. And Edith knew that Dennin meant to kill her and her husband, so she "recovers" from the unexpected. (pp. 119-20)

In the case then of Edith Nelson, the unexpected has the effect of making her equal very quickly to even the most horrible form of tragedy. Death in its hideous entirety is literally hurled at her in a moment of time. But, in another moment she is able to face and contend with the appalling situation. . . . Mr. London's psychology seems very sound.

In a sense Edith Nelson had the best opportunity possible of recovering from the effects of the unexpected. The instantaneous action demanded would restore her balance of mind at once. Mr. London says that certain people do not recover from the onslaught of the unexpected and die. I have already said that I believe this to be true. But quite likely the reason that these people do not recover, in many cases, is that there is really no instant need for them to do so. . . . There would be no pressing need to recover from the shock at once. But in the case of Edith Nelson, if she had not recovered immediately, a bullet would have been fired at her and then one for her husband. So she was *forced* to pull herself together. But I do not wish to say from this that I think Mr. London means us to infer that Edith only recovered from the unexpected because of dire necessity, I believe he means Edith to be a type who would be able to fall in line with life however startling its course might be. In the case of her husband, Mr. London makes him to be a little slower in regaining his mental balance. Perhaps a man always takes longer because it takes more to precipitate him into the realms of shock. (pp. 120-21)

And the effect again on the two is well brought out. The woman is cool but the man is near to madness. Blind rage has possessed him but calm determination has invaded the woman. Very skilfully does Mr. London bring out this essential difference in their temperaments. The rage of Hans is so frightful that Edith can hardly believe that it is her husband. (pp. 121-22)

Suddenly through such a small event they find that they are in a new world. A mere plate falling off the table. How well does Mr. London follow the extraordinary thing that we call life.

> The clang of the plate had aroused them to life in
> a new world. The cabin epitomized the new world
> in which they must henceforth live and move. The
> old cabin was gone for ever.

Dreadful words "for ever"; no matter that we shriek, it can never be the same again, no matter that we threaten, it can never be the same again, no matter that we say that we will kill God, it can never be the same again, then the God that we would have killed if we could, is the God that we thank, that if it can never be the same again, we can in time adapt ourselves to the new conditions. (p. 122)

Then Mr. London gives us a bit of real horror. It is so funny! let us howl with laughter, the breakfast isn't cleared away, the coffee hasn't been finished, the genial dear fellows round the table may want a second helping. And Hans is going outside. His wife asks him why he is going. "To dig some graves."

That is why we laugh; that still form on the bed, the half empty medicine bottles, the sunlight that comes creeping into the room. What is that noise? That noise of shovelling, someone is digging a grave, poor fools and we think the world and all its pomp matters one iota. For the man on the bed, the shovelling is going on. Mr. London has finished that breakfast, there is the persistent noise of shovelling graves, and a wasted cup of coffee!

The trend of the story of **"The Unexpected"** is that Dennin the murderer lives and is kept captive in the Nelsons' cabin. Mr. London uses a great deal of sound psychology in telling this great drama. It would be difficult to imagine a more curious situation than that depicted by Mr. London. There is the cabin, there is the frozen waste of Alaska, there is the murderer, there are the man and the woman, each having to guard the murderer by turns. The situation again demonstrates how different in every conceivable circumstance is the viewpoint of a man and the viewpoint of a woman. There is something that is almost an antagonism between Edith and her husband. Hans Nelson is obsessed by the idea that it is his duty to kill Dennin; Edith on the other hand "contended there was only one way to punish Dennin, and that was the legal way arranged by society."

It needs no imagination to conceive of the desperate horror of that hut, the trapped murderer, the husband full of the lust for blood and always just on the border line which separates madness from sanity. (pp. 123-24)

Mr. London shows how [Edith's] determination, her obstinacy, her doggedness prevented her from breaking down. But the sudden and terrific call of the unexpected, the shattering shots and the death cry of the man, made a naturally strong woman far more strong, the unexpected far from beating her had caused her to be the magnificent victor over herself. But the situation affected the man in a different manner. Mr. London brings it out with considerable skill. Hans was quite near to insanity, Edith was probably never more sane, that was the effect of a great shock on two different kinds of people, different in temperament and different in sex. (pp. 124-25)

[It] is the woman who all the time keeps her husband from killing Dennin from making himself a self-appointed judge, woman is the life giver and she is the life preserver, even a brutal murderer cannot let her lose her essential womanhood. . . . So she will not let her husband suddenly raise his gun and send the brains of Dennin splashing against the cabin wall. (pp. 125-26)

The situation in the cabin was obviously one that could not go on indefinitely, so Mr. London introduces a very skilful arrangement for getting rid of Dennin. His solution of the difficulty opens up the very interesting consideration of what really constitutes the law. Something tells Edith that Dennin must not be killed without some kind of trial. Who is to try Dennin? We are not in England but in the wastes of Alaska. . . . It is the time when it must be that "every man did that which was right in his own eyes." The law of the primitive, if you will, but a law of necessity. Dennin must be got rid of, he could not be allowed to escape, he would take the first opportunity of killing his captors. Mr. London decides that there shall be a tribunal. (p. 126)

So the cabin resolved itself into a court of law, the man and his wife were the jury and judge and sentence is passed that Dennin shall be hanged. A very logical and happy conclusion, justice in a rough cabin. Mr. London is able to be quite certain that no matter what are the conditions, justice is seldom entirely ignored. It is the working of the white man's law. (p. 127)

Whether the events in Mr. London's story **"The Unexpected"** are credible is a question with which I am not concerned. In this tale there is a profound study of psychology. The effect of a frightful shock is shown on two people. The two people are a man and a woman and in most ways the woman comes out best.

Mr. London shows by this story that certain people can grapple with and beat any situation, however terrifying, however strained. There seems to be practically no limit to human endurance. Edith and Hans Nelson undergo an ordeal that would have shaken the strongest nerve. Yet they win through. Mr. London loves to write of rough justice, he loves the atmosphere of the log cabin. With the greatest possible skill he introduces his dramatic event and as a sequel almost, he studies pretty minutely the effect of the unexpected on a married couple. If it is interesting to merely mention the *morality* of the story, there might be some controversy as to whether Edith and Hans were right in "trying" Dennin and executing him. In any case the background of the story has to be remembered. It is true that there should not be one law for the rich and one law for the poor, but it should not be forgotten that the law may have to be administered in a crude manner, when the environment is rude.

Perhaps in some ways the obvious thing to have done would have been to shoot Dennin at once and the defence that it was done in self defence would seem to be quite an adequate one. But the way in which the Nelsons behaved was a nobler one, it called forth infinite endurance and infinite restraint. For, if Jack London's story is a story of how the unexpected was contended with, it is also a story of a great restraint. It is further the story of a struggle, a struggle between the restraint of the woman and the impetuous violence of the man. And again the story is a great tribute to women, for the woman comes out best, she is restrained, in a frightful situation she keeps her sanity and she carries through her dreadful task to its logical and appointed finish. If that which is written by Jack London in this story is horror, what is not written, if we use any imagination, is made up of far greater horror. Imagine feeding a man who has killed your two best friends, imagine "nursing" a man who looks at you with eyes that blaze with a hatred that cannot be defined. Imagine the situation for a delicate woman. The horror of the unwritten is greater than the horror of the written. Mr. London is always a grim realist but he is also a philosopher. In the tale that Mr. London has written of the unexpected, he has given a combination of drama, deep psychology and grim horror.

"The Unexpected" is worth reading and it is worth thinking about and the thinking leads very far down into the complex thing that is human nature. (pp. 127-29)

> Patrick Braybrooke, "Jack London and the Unexpected," in his *Peeps at the Mighty, Henry J. Drane,* 1927, pp. 113-29.

GEORGE ORWELL (essay date 1946)

[*An English novelist and essayist, Orwell is considered significant in twentieth-century letters for his unwavering commitment to personal freedom and social justice. Throughout his career, Orwell attacked exploitation of the weak by the power-*

ful, whether in a modern democracy or a totalitarian state. His best-known novel, Nineteen-Eighty-Four *(1949), is considered among the most important works of twentieth-century literature. Orwell's prose style, especially that of his essays, is admired for its precision, clarity, and vividness. In the following excerpted introduction to London's short fiction collection* Love of Life, and Other Stories, *Orwell asserts that London's fascination with the cruelty of nature reflected his ambivalent Darwinist and Socialist beliefs and that his most successful stories concern contemporary industrial society.*]

[London] was a writer who excelled in describing cruelty, whose main theme, indeed, was the cruelty of Nature, or at any rate of contemporary life; he was also an extremely variable writer, much of whose work was produced hurriedly and at low pressure; and he had in him a [bourgeois] strain of feeling . . . which did not accord with his democratic and Socialist convictions.

During the last twenty years Jack London's short stories have been rather unaccountably forgotten—how thoroughly forgotten, one could gauge by the completeness with which they were out of print. So far as the big public went, he was remembered by various animal books, particularly *White Fang* and *The Call of the Wild*—books which appealed to the Anglo-Saxon sentimentality about animals—and after 1933 his reputation took an upward bound because of *The Iron Heel,* which had been written in 1907, and is in some sense a prophecy of Fascism. (pp. 23-4)

Jack London's great theme is the cruelty of Nature. Life is a savage struggle, and victory has nothing to do with justice. In the best of his short stories there is a startling lack of comment, a suspension of judgement, arising out of the fact that he both delights in the struggle and perceives its cruelty. Perhaps the best thing he ever wrote is **"Just Meat"**. Two burglars have got away with a big haul of jewellery: each is intent on swindling the other out of his share, and they poison one another simultaneously with strychnine, the story ending with the two men dead on the floor. There is almost no comment, and certainly no "moral". As Jack London sees it, it is simply a fragment of life, the kind of thing that happens in the present-day world: nevertheless it is doubtful whether such a plot would occur to any writer who was not fascinated by cruelty. Or take a story like **"The *Francis Spaight*"**. The starving crew of a waterlogged ship have decided to resort to cannibalism, and have just nerved themselves to begin when another ship heaves in sight. It is characteristic of Jack London that the second ship should appear after and not before the cabin boy's throat has been cut. A still more typical story is **"A Piece of Steak"**. London's love of boxing and admiration for sheer physical strength, his perception of the meanness and cruelty of a competitive society, and at the same time his instinctive tendency to accept *vae victis* as a law of Nature, are all expressed here. An old prize-fighter is fighting his last battle: his opponent is a beginner, young and full of vigour, but without experience. The old man nearly wins, but in the end his ring-craft is no match for the youthful resilience of the other. Even when he has him at his mercy he is unable to strike the blow that would finish him, because he has been underfed for weeks before the fight and his muscles cannot make the necessary effort. He is left bitterly reflecting that if only he had had a good piece of steak on the day of the fight he would have won.

The old man's thoughts all run upon the theme: "Youth will be served". First you are young and strong, and you knock out older men and make money which you squander: then your strength wanes and in turn you are knocked out by younger men, and then you sink into poverty. This does in fact tell the story of the average boxer's life, and it would be a gross exaggeration to say that Jack London *approves* of the way in which men are used up like gladiators by a society which cannot even bother to feed them. The detail of the piece of steak—not strictly necessary, since the main point of the story is that the younger man is bound to win by virtue of his youth—rubs in the economic implication. And yet there is something in London that takes a kind of pleasure in the whole cruel process. It is not so much an approval of the harshness of Nature, as a mystical belief that Nature *is* like that. Nature is "red in tooth and claw". Perhaps fierceness is bad, but fierceness is the price of survival. The young slay the old, the strong slay the weak, by an inexorable law. Man fights against the elements or against his fellow man, and there is nothing except his own toughness to help him through. London would have said that he was merely describing life as it is actually lived, and in his best stories he does so: still, the constant recurrence of the same theme—struggle, toughness, survival—shows which way his inclinations pointed.

London had been deeply influenced by the theory of the Survival of the Fittest. . . . In the late nineteenth century Darwinism was used as a justification for *laissez-faire* capitalism, for power politics and for the exploiting of subject peoples. Life was a free-for-all in which the fact of survival was proof of fitness to survive: this was a comforting thought for successful businessmen, and it also led naturally, though not very logically, to the notion of "superior" and "inferior" races. In our day we are less willing to apply biology to politics, partly because we have watched the Nazis do just that thing, with great thoroughness and with horrible results. But when London was writing, a crude version of Darwinism was widespread and must have been difficult to escape. He himself was even capable at times of succumbing to racial mysticism. He toyed for a while with a race theory similar to that of the Nazis, and throughout his work the cult of the "nordic" is fairly well marked. It ties up on the one hand with his admiration for prize-fighters, and on the other with his anthropomorphic view of animals: for there seems to be good reason for thinking that an exaggerated love of animals generally goes with a rather brutal attitude towards human beings. London was a Socialist with the instincts of a buccaneer and the education of a nineteenth-century materialist. In general the background of his stories is not industrial, nor even civilised. Most of them take place—and much of his own life was lived—on ranches or South Sea islands, in ships, in prison or in the wastes of the Arctic: places where a man is either alone and dependent on his own strength and cunning, or where life is naturally patriarchal.

Nevertheless, London did write from time to time about contemporary industrial society, and on the whole he was at his best when he did so. . . . Although the tug of his impulses was away from civilisation, London had read deeply in the literature of the Socialist movement, and his early life had taught him all he needed to know about urban poverty. He himself was working in a factory at the age of eleven, and without that experience behind him he could hardly have written such a story as **"The Apostate"**. In this story, as in all his best work, London does not comment, but he does unquestionably aim at rousing pity and indignation. It is generally when he writes of more primitive scenes that his moral attitude becomes equivocal. Take, for instance, a story like

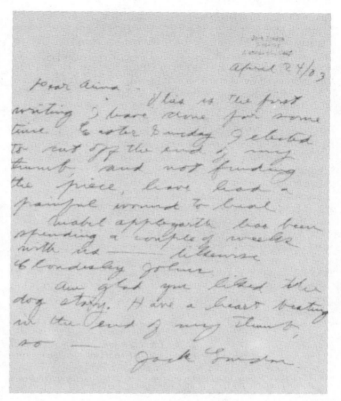

Handwritten letter fom London to his longtime friend Anna Strunsky.

"Make Westing". With whom do London's sympathies lie—with Captain Cullen or with George Dorety? One has the impression that if he were forced to make a choice he would side with the Captain, who commits two murders but does succeed in getting his ship round Cape Horn. On the other hand, in a story like **"The Chinago"**, although it is told in the usual pitiless style, the "moral" is plain enough for anyone who wants to find it. London's better angel is his Socialist convictions, which come into play when he deals with such subjects as coloured exploitation, child labour or the treatment of criminals, but are hardly involved when he is writing about explorers or animals. It is probably for this reason that a high proportion of his better writings deal with urban life. In stories like **"The Apostate"**, **"Just Meat"**, **"A Piece of Steak"** and **"Semper Idem"**, however cruel and sordid they may seem, something is keeping him on the rails and checking his natural urge towards the glorification of brutality. That "something" is his knowledge, theoretical as well as practical, of what industrial capitalism means in terms of human suffering.

Jack London is a very uneven writer. In his short and restless life he poured forth an immense quantity of work, setting himself to produce 1,000 words every day and generally achieving it. Even his best stories have the curious quality of being well told and yet not well written: they are told with admirable economy, with just the right incidents in just the right place, but the texture of the writing is poor, the phrases are worn and obvious, and the dialogue is erratic. His reputation has had its ups and downs, and for a long period he seems to have been much more admired in France and Germany than in the English-speaking countries. Even before the triumph of Hitler, which brought *The Iron Heel* out of its obscurity, he had a certain renown as a left-wing and "proletarian" writer—rather the same kind of renown as attaches to Robert Tressell, W. B. Traven or Upton Sinclair. He has also been attacked by Marxist writers for his "Fascist tendencies". These tendencies unquestionably existed in him, so much so that if one imagines him as living on into our own day, instead of dying in 1915, it is very hard to be sure where his political allegiance would have lain. One can imagine him in the Communist Party, one can imagine him falling a victim to Nazi racial theory, and one can imagine him the quixotic champion of some Trotskyist or Anarchist sect. But, as I have tried to make clear, if he had been a politically reliable person he would probably have left behind nothing of interest. Meanwhile his reputation rests mainly on *The Iron Heel*, and the excellence of his short stories has been almost forgotten. A dozen of the best of them are collected in [*Love of Life, and Other Stories*], and a few more are worth rescuing from the museum shelves and the second-hand boxes. . . . Much of Jack London's work is scamped and unconvincing, but he produced at least six volumes which deserve to stay in print, and that is not a bad achievement from a life of only forty-one years. (pp. 26-9)

> *George Orwell, "Introduction to 'Love of Life, and Other Stories' by Jack London," in* The Collected Essays, Journalism and Letters of George Orwell: In Front of Your Nose, 1945-1950, Vol. IV, *edited by Sonia Orwell and Ian Angus, Harcourt Brace Jovanovich, Inc., 1968, pp. 23-9.*

MAXWELL GEISMAR   (essay date 1953)

[*Geismar is considered one of the most prominent nonacademic historical and social critics in the United States. Although he admits that literature is more than mere historical documentation, Geismar's critical method suggests that social patterns and history, more than any other factors, affect the shape and content of art. In the following excerpt, Geismar provides a survey of London's short fiction and contends that London's contradictory allegiance to Socialist and Darwinian models of thought led to a moral myopia that adversely affected his art.*]

[Five years after London determined to become a writer], his Klondike tales established his fame. He was at once the author he had wanted to be—successful, rich, prominent—and a world-wide spokesman for revolutionary socialism in the United States. Moreover, the central paradox of London's career contained other ambiguous and contradictory elements in it. He had become a Marxian materialist, a disciple of evolutionary thought in its most literal aspects, and above all an advocate of a 'scientific' approach to life, society and art. "My life shall be free and broad and great," his literary spokesman declared, "and I will not be a slave to the sense delights that chained my ancient ancestry. I reject the heritage, I break the entail." Certainly not every man was capable of this action, London said. "But for some few of us, and I dare to include myself, the short cut is permissible." It was a key statement in London's early career, and one notices how often the variations of this central motif occurred in his early thinking. It was the short cut to satisfaction, he declared, that he wanted in his life. "This is my work. I would invent, overcome the roundabout, seek the short cut."

In this false dawn of the children of pure materialism, indeed, the secret of progress was "the elimination of waste"—and

the demon of efficiency had been added to the atavistic monsters, primordial brutes and bloodthirsty incubae of the Darwinian landscape at the turn of the century. We will see how Jack London converted both the structure of evolutionary thinking in Europe and the Marxian dialectic of history to a particularly native framework of pragmatism—to the methods of the laboratory, to the production lines of the factory. Under a program of denial his life, his writing, his modes of feeling, even, were to become a strictly mechanical or at best a well-regulated chemical process. There was also a Nietzschean influence in which the people became the masses and the masses the 'human herd' or worse during the course of his career; but it was surely an indigenous transvaluation of all values which led so directly to the fatal technics of literary engineering.

This was in brief the know-how of a native superman. For London's notion of human affection also led merely to the concept of convenience and efficiency in his own case. And "the fact, the irrefragable fact" to which he continually paid homage in his speech was also the fact of a false practicality and a relentless passage through life and through art that detoured primary human values. The success story of Jack London became a case history—very often ironical, morbid and illuminating—of thwarted ambition and moral corruption. (pp. 142-43)

London's first collection of Arctic tales, *The Son of the Wolf,* in 1900, was dedicated to the last of the frontiersmen "who sought their heritage and left their bones among the shadows of the circle." (p. 144)

Against the background of abstract splendor, there were the deeds of men's heroism, or cruelty, or the meticulous descriptions of moral and physical deterioration as in the scurvy, when muscles and joints began to swell, the flesh turned black, and gums and lips took on the color of rich cream. In **"In A Far Country"** two tenderfeet from the Southland lose their sanity in the silent space of an Arctic winter—are betrayed finally by nature's apparitions. "Their eyes were fixed upon the north. Unseen, behind their backs, behind the towering mountains to the south, the sun swept toward the zenith of another sky than theirs. Sole spectators of the mighty canvas, they watched the false dawn slowly grow." (pp. 144-45)

[London's second collection, *The God of His Fathers,* contained] writing that was completely fresh in its time, offering a contrast to the sweetness and goodness of popular fiction in the 1900's. The cadence of this prose only became completely familiar to us, indeed, in the work of the postwar generation of the 1920's. The frenzied epic of the gold rush was summarized in a vista of broken and dying animals (beside which the famous horses in Stephen Crane's work were almost untouched). In these tales of cupidity, of fear, of hunger, of the grim humor of murder and death, too, the will to survive—all that was left here of men's appetites and joys—was often viewed as another kind of phobia, ironical, insane. And in the lament of a northern gambler who was bankrupt and pursued by the shapes and forms of his crimes, merely waiting for death in the same unchanging position, London made his theme explicit. "Life's a skin-game. . . . I never had half a chance. . . . I was faked in my birth and flimflammed with my mother's milk. The dice were loaded when she tossed the box, and I was born to prove the loss."

But there were few instances in the short stories where London's sense of character was up to the level of the emotions he described, or where in fact the excellent material was not finally circumscribed by a shallow set of moral values. After the hero of **"The Great Interrogation,"** like many northern adventurers, had taken an Indian wife, he was urged by his former sweetheart, Mrs. Sayther, to renounce a debased form of marriage. . . . And this anthropological widow couching her love call in the clichés of popular Darwinism, expressed the central point of view in London's collection of Indian stories, *Children of the Frost,* in 1902. Although Sitka Charley, the half-breed, had been one of London's heroes in the earlier series of tales, even he, respecting, almost venerating the white man's power, had yet to divine its secret essence, so we are told—the honor of the trail, and of the 'law.'

Whose law, what law? The white man's law, of course, or at least the law in Kipling's romances of the white man's fate, as adapted to an imperial American audience of the 1900's. The geologist in the story called **"In the Forests of the North"** still remembered that he alone was "full blooded Saxon"; his blood pounds fiercely at the memory of Clive, Drake, Raleigh, even, somewhat remotely, of Hengist and Horsa. They were superior human specimens, apparently, when compared with the French-Canadian voyageurs in the tales or the strapping Crees from Manitoba-way. The white man in love with an Indian princess was also impelled by his race loyalty to "die at least with his kind." . . . (pp. 145-47)

The good stories, and London's authentic feeling for primitive culture and ritual, as in the sketch of the old man who was left by the tribe to die in the snow by the side of a dwindling fire, and submitted: "What did it matter after all?"— were subordinated to this vein of popular thought. And an early strain of sadism in London's work was linked with the sexuality of the inferior races or exploited in the guise of primitive virtues. . . . Yet a more accurate view of Indian culture dispersed before the white man's weapons of trade, liquor, disease, religion and superior fire power, was suggested at least in **"The League of Old Men,"** where an aboriginal chieftain recorded a desperate compact to kill off the whites before the tribal life had disappeared completely. (p. 147)

The history of increasing corruption in a genuine talent is both painful and fascinating. . . . Some of London's most brilliant passages of prose will describe the sensations of drawing steadily closer to a moral, if not now a social abyss. (pp. 178-79)

[London's protagonist in **"Planchette"** could be said to provide an] egocentric self-portrait. The story itself, technically poor, but interesting as personal history which was probably based on the break-up of his first marriage, was that of a fatal attraction between two lovers:

> She shivered at the sound of his voice—not from repulsion, but from struggle against the fascination of its caressing gentleness. She had come to know well the lure of the man—the wealth of easement and rest that was promised by every caressing intonation of his voice, by the mere touch of hand on hand or the faint impact of his breath on neck or cheek.

There, indeed, the symbol of masculine virility had been idolized to the point of possessing sexual traits usually identified with a feminine love-object.—You are universally lovable, the girl tells him again, every animal likes you, all people like you, "and the best of it is that you don't know it"—although, to be sure, the author of the story knew it. It was a myth of himself that London came to cherish, while the love affair

was based on a common taste for riding horses, grooms, the life of sport. It was the socialist smart set: a fatal romance of bohemians in the saddle. (p. 180)

The central mood in *Love of Life and Other Stories* (1906) and *Lost Face* (1910), two more collections of tales, was . . . one of inhuman, but almost mechanical misery. [**"Love of Life"**] concerned an Arctic prospector who won his desperate struggle to survive in the Northland only to fall victim to the delusions which had mastered him in the struggle. The atmosphere was that of pure nightmare, in which the prospector, starving and lost on the frozen, silent, northern waste, without ammunition but convinced he has one more cartridge left in his rifle, and repetitiously counting the matches which are his last bond with fire and life, sees food everywhere around him. . . . (pp. 187-88)

This was part Poe, of course, in a gray wilderness instead of dark gothic chambers. . . . [The prospector] eats the rushgrass on hands and knees, "crunching and munching like some bovine creature." He finds some ptarmigan chicks— "little specks of pulsating life no more than a mouthful"— thrusting them alive into his mouth. After his rescue he surrounds himself with stolen food as a refuge against another possible famine. Now **"Love of Life"** was typical of a series of London's stories in this vein: the solitary, obsessed individual; the self-enclosed world; the macabre struggle to survive; the ironic note of 'success' which obliterates everything the individual has survived for. It is probably the best of these stories, in the concentration of mood, the series of images and symbols of frustration and impotence, the coloring of fear, as London said, "that lies twisted about life's deepest roots."

The title story in *Lost Face* opened with a Cossack giant who has been captured by the Indians and lies prone in snow, moaning in pain. "The men had finished handling the giant and turned him over to the women. That they exceeded the fiendishness of the men, the man's cries attested." The sexual sadism was overt here; the theme of castration became explicit in [**"Lost Face"**]. Had the author, like his hero, the Russian explorer in the tale, already been condemned to perish "in this far land of night"? The last frontier of London's Alaska fiction had become, at any rate, a place of disease, torture, death, where the main effort of his heroes was to die decently and quickly. In the story called **"Trust"** the central image is a charnel pit of dying horses where the packers have tumbled their broken and useless animals. **"To Build a Fire"** is a famous story of a tenderfoot who is caught in the Alaska cold and loses his physical powers before he quite realizes it. . . . The central situation is that of the trap, again; and the gradual realization of impotence:

> The man looked down at his hands in order to locate them, and found them hanging on the ends of his arms. It struck him as curious that one should have to use his eyes to find out where his hands were. . . . He had an impression that they hung like weights at the ends of his arms, but when he tried to run the impression down, he could not find it.

But this was easily the best story in *Lost Face,* a brilliant little sketch whose prose rhythms, too, are still fresh. For the most part, however, the other stories were trite and careless, the writing was lifeless, even for London's commercial vein. (pp. 188-89)

When London had written two or three books a year during

the early part of his career, it was in part a display of sheer exuberance. During 1910 and 1911 he published four books each year. Only now he was beginning to work desperately (and carelessly) to re-establish his position on the commercial market—to make money. . . .

In the beginning, his realism, however circumspect in the final analysis, had revolutionized the tone of popular fiction in the 1900's. Now he capitulated cynically to the standards of the mass mind, and to the new vulgarity of a lower middle class audience that had been reached by the low-priced journals. . . . [The novel] *Adventure,* in 1911, the first of London's South Sea stories, was a popular romance in this vein. The contrast in London's work was not merely between the Arctic scene and the warm, lush tropics; but, as almost always, between what he could have done with this material, and what he did do. (p. 199)

South Sea Tales, in the same year, was a better collection of stories, however. **"The Whale Tooth"** was the ironical story of a missionary, consumed by religious fervor, who was murdered and eaten by the wily Solomon Islanders. There was the portrait of Bunster, the white trader who had fashioned a mitten out of sharkskin which, like sandpaper, could rub off a patch of black skin in one stroke—and the "big fella noise" that Bunster made when the savage Mauki skinned him alive with the mitten. That was the revenge of a secretive Negro slave. The true story of the white man's 'colonization' of the islands was suggested in these stories when the imperial schooners shelled the tribal villages and the natives were pursued in mass man hunts and wiped out by dynamite sticks, fire, or poisoned wells.

The portrait of Saxtorph in **"The Inevitable White Man"** . . . may have summarized the progress of the superior races. "He was certainly the most stupid man I ever saw, but he was as inevitable as death. There was only one thing that chap could do, and that was shoot." The story concerned a mutiny on a blackbirder during which the white man established himself on the slave ship's crosstrees and began to fire at the Negroes. . . . What was interesting here, of course, was the shifting of the focus to the [white man's] hot rifles rather than the dying human beings, and the stress on the spectator who observed the action with morbid fascination and described it in . . . glowing sporting terms. (The comparison with Hemingway's sketches of the First World War in *In Our Time* is obvious.) "Some of the long shots were magnificent. . . . It reminded me of trapshooting." But now indeed man had become quite literally the noblest game of all for his fellow men.

There are the wives of Old Koho in *A Son of the Sun,* another series of South Sea tales in 1912, and trivial except for the story called **"The Jokers of New Gibbon."** One of the women discovered in the story was the latest wife—

> She had been hung up by one arm in the sun for two days and nights. We cut her down but she died just the same. And staked out in the fresh running water, up to their necks, were three more women. All their bones were broken and their joints crushed. The process was supposed to make them tender for eating. They were still alive. Their vitality was remarkable.

The savage chieftain, "a head-hunting, man-eating Talleyrand" on the barbaric island of Malaita, was an interested spectator, too, at a scene of primitive dentistry. "His joy in

the torment of the patient was natural, for the world he lived in was a world of pain." . . . In their own pleasures and their state of imperial dominion, the Nordic conquerors in these stories are hardly superior, however, to the barbarians they have supplanted. One notices the drinking of the inevitable white men—or the inevitable drinking which, as in the case of the ruthless McAllister of **"Yah! Yah! Yah!"** (an obscene chant of the white man's contempt that runs through a saga of black misery) started punctually at six in the morning. As in the case of Saxtorph, who was quite helpless and incompetent except behind a rifle, the 'colonizers' are reduced to the extremes of savagery in order to compete with this primitive and savage existence. The abysmal hatred and malignancy of Koho were the dominant emotions in a world of pain, where pleasure consisted mainly in the suffering of others.

The Night-Born, in 1913, took its title from Thoreau's lines. "The Society Islanders had their day-born gods, but they were not supposed to be of equal antiquity with the night-born gods." Most surely London himself was an example of primitive and supernatural strains in the artist—of the darker and ancient side of life, of the buried instincts that in his case hardly rose to the human level. Yet these stories of pathology, insanity, or crime, were for the most part converted into popular tales, again with false or sentimental endings. (pp. 200-03)

[In **"The Kanaka Surf,"** a piece included] in *On the Makaloa Mat,* a collection of tales published posthumously in 1919, the theme was the break-up of a marital relationship through the wife's infidelity. . . . [The] husband makes an attempt to murder her, his brain drugged with opiates. The record of the rest of London's posthumous books is brief. (*The Turtles of Tasman,* 1916, contained [**"Told in the Drooling Ward"**], an almost Lardnerian tale of "a high-grade feeb" who emphasized his superiority to the low-grade droolers and epileptics in a state mental institution.) (p. 212)

[The heroine of **"On the Makaloa Mat"**], was a Hawaiian princess whose mixed blood, creating the "golden tawny brown of Polynesia," included "the splendid, sure, gracious, high-breasted, noble-headed port of which no outbreeding can ever rob the Hawaiian woman." She was descended from the chief stocks of Hawaii whose genealogies were chanted "a thousand years before written speech was acquired," and the story itself was set against a background of native royalty.

Many of the Hawaiian stories are in this vein, and one becomes aware that the vicious tone of London's theories of racial supremacy applied mainly, as it were, to *poor* Negroes— Negroes or the other 'inferior races' who were inferior precisely because they had not as yet acquired breeding, wealth or social tradition. (So his sympathies extended, in spite of himself, even to some of the barbaric 'nigger' chieftains of the Solomons, who were nevertheless of a true savage nobility.) But the equally barbaric race-thinking of the 1900's whose foremost literary exponent London himself became—and those distorted principles of social Darwinism which became, during this epoch, such a fundamental part of middle class thought in the United States—was from the very start the rationale of an economic struggle. It was the crude mythology of a rising social class that was seeking a hereditary line, as it were, on which to base a claim of superiority which was purely material and barely established. (pp. 213-14)

[A] desperate, monomaniacal and walled-in struggle to rise above the social pit was at the center of [London's] career. . . . Perhaps the sin (and main source of moral corruption) in this socialist and ex-socialist writer was not so much that he was drawn to such a specious philosophy, but that he, unlike the young Frank Norris who had accepted the same values almost unconsciously from the social milieu he belonged to—that he, Jack London, promulgated these ideas while he knew their falseness. (pp. 214-15)

[The] buried poet that always lay in the depths of London's temperament—but that had revealed itself only in the desolate howl of the huskies, the leap of the tiger, or the hee-hee councils of the half-men—emerged again, if only momentarily, before the final end. . . . But it was too late. The broken tone of the stories in London's final period, the uneven style of his later work as a whole, with bad and good jumbled together, showed the haste and recklessness with which he had poured out this virtuosity. (pp. 215-16)

> Maxwell Geismar, "Jack London: The Short Cut,"
> in his Rebels and Ancestors: The American Novel,
> 1890-1915, 1953. Reprint by Hill and Wang, 1963,
> pp. 139-216.

SAM S. BASKETT (essay date 1958)

[*In the following excerpt, Baskett compares London's short story "In a Far Country" to Joseph Conrad's "An Outpost of Progress."*]

Although there are certain obvious similarities in the fiction of Jack London and Joseph Conrad—both wrote tales of the sea as well as stories set in exotic lands, and frequently both peopled their fiction with rough characters engaged in violent action—Conrad's different emphasis, surer craftsmanship and more profound insight into the psychological motivations of his characters have made these similarities seem relatively inconsequential. London is often, even within the same book, an exponent of the cult of raw meat and red blood and a political expounder using fiction as a means of advancing the doctrines of socialism.

London's biographers and critics have given what seems to be the proper emphasis to the London-Conrad relation when they merely note in a sentence or so that London read the English author and that at one point or another their literary interests coincided extrinsically. Actually, however, it is as misleading to minimize their similarities as to exaggerate them; and to say that London exhibits *only* a superficial likeness to Conrad obscures a basic correspondence which is of some significance in an over-all consideration of London's fiction. (p. 66)

London's first story was published in January, 1899, and his 1915 letter to Conrad states that he began reading him about that time. Evidence of the impact of this reading on London is apparent in **"In a Far Country,"** London's fifth story, which was published in June, 1899; for this story seems to be a close parallel of Conrad's "An Outpost of Progress," first published in *Tales of Unrest* the preceding year. Walter F. Wright has commented on the similarity of theme in London's **"To Build a Fire"** and "An Outpost of Progress," noting that London in the physical realm as Conrad in the mental "has illuminated the mystery of existence," as he portrays a civilized man freezing to death in the arctic wastes. Actually, the earlier **"In a Far Country"** is much closer to Conrad's story in the description of characters, as well as in situation and incidents.

In "An Outpost of Progress," "Two perfectly insignificant and incapable individuals," Carlier and Kayerts, are left in charge of a trading post on the upper reaches of an African river. Since their existence had been "only rendered possible through the high organization of civilized crowds," the isolation of this outpost and "the contact with pure unmitigated savagery, with primitive nature and primitive man, brings sudden and profound trouble." They gradually deteriorate morally, emotionally and physically, eventually one kills the other and then commits suicide. In London's story, two "ordinary" men, the "Incapables" London repeatedly terms them, rather than undertake a hazardous thousand-mile journey with the remainder of their party, choose to spend the winter in an abandoned cabin on a tributary of the Yukon. Weatherbee and Cuthfert, "hardened to the ruts in which they were created," find the "pressure of the altered environment is unbearable, and they chafe in body and spirit" as they "face the savage youth, the primordial simplicity of the North. . . ." The story is a record of their quarrels, their concomitant disintegration. Finally each is successful in killing the other. (pp. 67-8)

Early in "An Outpost of Progress" Kayerts and Carlier are seen through the eyes of the director of the company who comments to another employee as they leave the two at their post: "Look at those two imbeciles. They must be mad at home to send me such specimens. . . . I bet nothing will be done! They won't know how to begin." The "old stager" replies with a quiet smile, "They will form themselves here." Sloper, in charge of the party in London's story, having previously marked the incompetence of Weatherbee and Cuthfert, comments to Jacques Baptiste, a native of the Northland, as they leave the two standing in the doorway of the cabin: "Now, these two men don't like work. They won't work. We know that. They'll be all alone in that cabin all winter,—a mighty long, dark winter. Kilkenny cats, well?" Baptiste responds with "an eloquent shrug, pregnant with prophecy."

Finally, the events illustrating the demoralization of the two pairs of men coincide in the following particulars: at first all goes well, but since they are unsupervised they do nothing except what is essential and even routine tasks are slackly performed. None of the men is fitted to grapple with this situation and as the slow days pass they degenerate mentally and physically. The memory of civilization recedes and they become ill from the lack of fresh food, their appearance altering to the extent that, in a scene in both stories, each comes on the other suddenly and fails to recognize him. In both stories the characters achieve a virulent, unreasoning hatred for each other and finally quarrel fatally over the same thing, the supply of sugar. In fact, there is only one important stage of "An Outpost of Progress" that does not have a counterpart in London's tale: the increasing moral obliquity of Carlier and Kayerts as dramatized through their passive acceptance of the selling of some friendly natives into slavery.

It is difficult to say, of course, whether London consciously borrowed from Conrad's story. It is apparent, however, that both the situation and the theme of the two stories are the same and that the theme of **"In a Far Country"** is much closer to Conrad than that of any of London's previous stories. London had handled each of his first four stories (**"To the Man on Trail," "The White Silence," "The Son of the Wolf,"** and **"The Men of Forty-Mile"**) as a tour de force. An unusual situation in each instance brings one of the central characters to confront violence and perhaps death. But once

London has delineated the situation, sketched the characters briefly and indicated the turn of action, the story is finished. **"In a Far Country"** also contains many of these elements. The theme, however, is not catastrophe (surmounted or not) but disintegration. **"In a Far Country,"** like "An Outpost of Progress," goes beyond the description of nature, and of man trying to exist on the "natural" physical level: Two unexceptional men, neither particularly good or bad, placed in isolation in an unfamiliar and unfriendly environment, reach a point of complete moral and emotional as well as physical breakdown. London himself was aware that this story differed from his first four, for in May, 1899, he wrote his friend Cloudesley Johns

> I wonder what you will think of **"In a Far Country,"** which comes out in the June Number (*Overland Monthly*) and which contains no reference to Malemute Kid or any other character which has previously appeared. As I recollect my own judgment of it, it is either bosh or good; either the worst or the best of the series I have turned out.

It seems possible and even likely that London's recent discovery and "mad appreciation" of Conrad may have been partly responsible for his somewhat different attempt in this story. (pp. 68-70)

> *Sam S. Baskett, "Jack London's Heart of Darkness," in* American Quarterly, *Vol. X, No. 1, Spring, 1958, pp. 66-77.*

A. GROVE DAY   (essay date 1964)

[*Day, whom James A. Michener has called "the world's foremost authority on Pacific literature," is a prolific editor and nonfiction writer who specializes in the history and biography of Hawaii and the Pacific region. In the following excerpted introduction to* Stories of Hawaii, *Day provides a critical and biographical overview of London's later stories set in Hawaii, presenting these pieces as some of London's best and most underrated writings.*]

"They don't know what they've got!" John Griffith London exclaimed about the American people when he landed in the Territory of Hawaii in 1907, on the first leg of a yachting trip through the Pacific.

His observations on the future fiftieth state, experienced during a five-month tour in that year, as well as during longer stays in 1915 and 1916, were passed on to his world-wide reading public in many articles and several books. His finest novel, the semiautobiographical *Martin Eden,* was written on the *Snark* cruise. A number of other great stories were likewise written in Hawaii. . . .

Two volumes of short stories that should be more widely known were written about the Hawaiian Islands and their people. London showed a great *aloha* for the Paradise of the Pacific over a period of thirteen years, and was proud to call himself a *kamaaina,* or old-timer, there in the islands where he had explored and had pioneered in surfboard-riding off Waikiki. And when on November 22, 1916, he was found dying in his home in the Valley of the Moon in California from uremic poisoning, he had been working on a novelette about race relations in Hawaii. (p. 3)

London first glimpsed the Big Island of Hawaii in the 1890's from the decks of the sealing ship *Sophie Sutherland.* . . .
But the voyage that was to take him around the Pacific on

his own specially built yacht had its origin during chats around a swimming pool at Glen Ellen, near Sonoma, California. Jack remarked that he would like to emulate Captain Joshua Slocum, who had girdled the globe on his tiny yacht *Spray.* The result of this idea was the "inconceivable and monstrous" adventures chronicled in London's volume *The Cruise of the "Snark"* (1911). This South Sea voyage ended after two years when its owner became seriously ill from an affliction that London believed came from exposure of a blond skin to tropical sunlight. . . .

Everything went wrong that could go wrong; even the San Francisco earthquake of 1906 conspired to delay the completion of the forty-three-foot ketch that was built at enormous expense to meet Jack's specifications. Thousands of people, yearning to escape to the alluring South Seas, applied to be unpaid members of the *Snark's* minuscule crew. (p. 4)

[During his first stay in Honolulu, Hawaii, London wrote] six short stories collected in *The House of Pride* (1912). Three of them mentioned the dread subject of leprosy, a word so fearful that as late as 1949 the Territorial Legislature passed a law that henceforth it should be known in Hawaii only under the name of "Hansen's disease."

London was fascinated by the isolation colony on Molokai for victims of the disease and their helpers, and spent five days there. He was amazed to find that the eight hundred inhabitants of the village were quite human and, on the whole, well adjusted. . . . Those who later accused Jack of misrepresenting conditions could have read in his chapter:

> All the foregoing is by way of preamble to the statement that the horrors of Molokai, as they have been painted in the past, do not exist. The Settlement has been written up repeatedly by sensationalists, and usually by sensationalists who have never laid eyes on it. Of course, leprosy is leprosy, and it is a terrible thing; but so much that is lurid has been written about Molokai that neither the lepers, nor those who devote their lives to them, have received a fair deal.

It is true, however, that of the six stories in *The House of Pride,* three concern the leper problem. Like Robert Louis Stevenson before him and James A. Michener after him, London was accused of exploiting a minor feature of the Hawaiian scene to terrify prospective visitors.

After his departure, the publication of the three stories aroused a tempest in the Honolulu newspapers. He was accused of making the world think that everybody in Hawaii was a gruesome leper. One letter signed "Bystander" termed London "a dirty little sneak, a sneak of the first water, a thoroughly untrustworthy man, an ungrateful and untruthful bounder."

In an exchange of lengthy letters between London and his friend Thurston, editor of the *Advertiser,* the two men aired their opinions concerning Hawaii's "peculiar institution" and its reception of criticism. "I think Hawaii is too touchy on matters of truth" London remarked;

> and while she complacently in her newspapers exploits the weaknesses and afflictions of other lands, gets unduly excited when her own are exploited. Furthermore, the several purely fictional stories on leprosy written by me have not shaken the world at all, Hawaii's fevered imagination to the contrary. . . . Stevenson's Father Damien letter

has more effect in a minute, and will go on having more effect in a minute, than all the stories I have written or ever shall write.

(pp. 9-10)

In *The House of Pride* appears one of the best known of the London stories, **"Koolau the Leper."** As with some of the other yarns, London drew upon local history and legend for its basis, but it is fiction, not fact, and the real events did not happen in just that way.

London probably first heard the tale of Koolau from his young crewman Bert Stolz on the rolling deck of the *Snark*, for Bert had been born on the island of Kauai, setting for the story, and his father had been the deputy sheriff who was killed during an attempt to capture the outlaw peaceably.

The true adventures of the real Koolau are in some ways more astounding even than the figure of London's creation. During the unsettled year of 1893, right after the overthrow of Queen Liliuokalani, the Provisional Government attempted to corral all known lepers and treat them at the Molokai center, since isolation was the only known palliative at the time. The thirty-one-year-old cowboy Koolau helped to round them up on Kauai, and then, discovering that he himself was stricken, agreed to go with the group by ship if his healthy wife, Piilani, could go along to attend him. But at the last minute she was held ashore on a baseless charge, and Koolau leaped overboard and swam back, to become the leader of a defiant leper band in the Kalalau Valley. He did murder Deputy Sheriff Louis H. Stolz, and did withstand a company of National Guardsmen armed with a Krupp gun. For three years Koolau, his wife Piilani, and their young son hid in the valley. Then the child, who had been infected with leprosy, died and was buried by the grieving couple. Two months later Koolau died, and was buried in a grave overlooking the valley of his exploits, in a grave hacked out beneath a cliff by Piilani with a small knife. The outlaw was dead, but his legend had just begun, and will be perpetuated for a long time by chatty tour guides.

The differences between the fiction and the true story are not important. London had created another tale on his favorite theme—the defiance of a strong man who feels that his cause is just and who will never give in unto death. The Koolau of his book is true in spirit to the desperate pariah of history who refused to yield even to a company of soldiers.

The story **"Good-by, Jack"** tells of a brilliant young millionaire who is also a brave man, but who at the end suffers a fear a thousand times more hideous than the fear he had endured by the narrator when he sees a writhing centipede. "I never knew!" Jack cries, when his friend says: "You, of all men, should have known." It is easy to be brave when one is sure there is no possible cause for infection by disease.

A third story, **"The Sheriff of Kona,"** also has a brave man for protagonist. He is also a lucky man, but he, whose duty requires him to send others into exile at Molokai, is ironically stricken with "the mark of the beast." The theme here, however, although there is an exciting midnight rescue from Molokai, is that Lyte Gregory feels a profound love for Kona, but can never return to his family and his paradise above the serene Kona sea; and nobody can do anything about it.

The setting for **"Aloha Oe"** is the Honolulu wharf in the days when visitors could come only by sea and the departure of a steamer was a gala event. At the railing, Dorothy Sam-brooke, fifteen-year-old daughter of a junketing United States senator, realizes that her friendship with Stephen Knight has blossomed into the love that comes once in a lifetime. But Steve is one-fourth Hawaiian, and "because there was tropic sunshine in his veins he could not marry her." This tale recalls a time that seems far distant. Nowadays Hawaiian ancestry is a marked social and political asset, and almost half the marriages in Hawaii are between people of different racial or national stocks. (pp. 10-12)

The finest story in *The House of Pride*, perhaps, is **"Chun Ah Chun."** Like the Koolau yarn, this also was clearly derived from London's recollection of a unique character in Hawaiian history, although again the needs of fiction unified the facts and eliminated many fascinating details. The real "Ah Chun" family was actually named Ah Fong.

The main character of this story was modeled on an Asian who came early to the Melting Pot of the Pacific. Chun Ah Fong was a young mandarin merchant who arrived in 1849—five years before the landing of the first shipload of imported Chinese field hands. He married Julia Hope Kamakia Paaikamokalani e Kinau Beckley Fayerweather, a girl who was descended from proud Hawaiian chiefs, whose grandfather was a British sea captain, and whose father was a Yankee sugar planter. Ah Fong made a fortune in business, and with his sixteen children—four boys and twelve girls—founded the most remarkable of Honolulu's cosmopolitan families. All but one of the children lived to be adult, and most of them married well—many of them to Caucasians.

Obviously, in London's short story he is not attempting a history of this fascinating family, but is once more showing a strong character solving his main problem by pursuing his main trait. James A. Michener, in his introduction to *A Hawaiian Reader* (1959), exercised his critical privilege to remark that when Jack London came to Hawaii

and saw at first hand a population—the Chinese—which had many of the characteristics he had espoused in mainland America, he was completely unable to understand what he saw. In **"Chun Ah Chun"** . . . he not only failed to comprehend what was happening in the Pacific; he actually denigrated an entire body of people, largely on racist grounds. . . . I have never understood how Jack London could be one man in California, and such a different man in Hawaii. . . . Yet the story **"Chun Ah Chun"** does have a sly warmth and much wit and remains one of the focal works in the London repertoire.

It is true that in many places elsewhere, Jack London glorified the battling, unyielding spirit of the Caucasian race. He went so far as to exclaim, during the Russo-Japanese War in 1904: "What the devil! I am first of all a white man and only then a Socialist!" Yet a careful reading of **"Chun Ah Chun"** should reveal that actually the fools and knaves of the story are the Caucasian men who by one means or another are persuaded to marry into the part-Chinese clan, and that the most admirable figure in the cast is the father, who does solve his problem intelligently and gracefully, and then retires to enjoy his success and contemplate philosophically the outcome of his actions. The story is great because it deals amusingly and with keen insight into an age-old human problem and offers a plausible solution.

When the Londons again sought refuge in Hawaii, during the two years before America entered World War I, Jack was at the height of his fame. Author of some fifty books, the best known, highest paid, and most popular writer in the world, he was nevertheless still filled with a boyish enthusiasm to see new sights. Visitors were more common in 1915 and 1916 than in 1907; Hawaii National Park . . . was established in 1916. Of the American people he said on this trip: "Because they have no other place to go, they are just beginning to realize what they've got." (pp. 12-14)

[Jack London and his wife Charmian] were back again at Honolulu on December 23 on the *Great Northern.* They found a comfortable cottage at 2201 Kalia Road, not far from the Halekulani Hotel. From this cottage Jack wrote a letter, on March 7, 1916, resigning from the Socialist Party. There, in a blue kimono, during the last year of his life, he wrote most of the stories reprinted in the posthumous volume *On the Makaloa Mat* (1919), as well as others not set in Hawaii. (p. 16)

The stories appearing in *On the Makaloa Mat* should be considered in the order in which they were written. It is notable that in this book London, although he had revisited the Molokai station, carefully omitted any mention of leprosy except that in **"Shin Bones"** the narrator does encounter on a spooky journey in a hidden valley "an old leper in hiding." In fact, London in that story goes so far as to avoid even mentioning the name of Molokai, and the setting is an imaginary island east of Oahu called "Lakanaii."

The title story of *On the Makaloa Mat* portrays two elderly sisters, sitting at Waikiki and revealing their secrets. Both are one-fourth Hawaiian, and both married to *haoles,* white men from New England who were destined to buy lands and make fortunes. The older one, Bella, confesses that, swept up in a royal progress around the Big Island, she had for two weeks shared with Prince Lilolilo the fine-woven *makaloa* mat, taboo to all but royalty. The tone is nostalgic, recalling the days when the nobility of the islands still exerted an imperious will.

In **"The Tears of Ah Kim"** the main character is a fifty-year-old Chinese who has risen from tow-rope coolie on the Yangtze River to shop owner in Honolulu. The various characterizations are amusing, but perhaps the main point of the story is: Why doesn't Ah Kim weep under the beatings of his mother's bamboo stick until a certain day?

In **"The Bones of Kahekili,"** Hardman Poole, haole ranch patriarch who has made himself a ruler of men, persuades an old Hawaiian cowboy to tell him the story of the death and burial of Chief Kahekili. (This name was that of a historic and powerful chief, ruler of all the islands except Hawaii, but he died in 1794, not in 1828, when London sets his tale.) The reminiscences of the old Hawaiian, who had been chosen as a human sacrifice, are exciting, but the theme of the story probably is found in the remarks of Hardman Poole on the nature of chiefs and chieftainship.

"Shin Bones" also reveals London's explorations into Hawaiian history and burial customs. Prince Akuli, descendant of the highest nobility, tells how he won his parents' consent to an Oxford education. At the age of fifteen he had accompanied an old retainer to a museum-like cave on the "Ironbound Coast" to collect the bones of his mother's mother. He had secretly brought back also the shin bones of Laulani, a Hawaiian Guinevere, and a spearhead made from the bones of her Lancelot. To possession at this early age of these reminders of humility, the prince owed more than to anything else.

"The Kanaka Surf" is a triangle story of three super-people—Lee and Ida Barton, who had early learned to be expert body-surfers in the biggest waves off Waikiki, and Sonny Grandison, social leader and rival far for Lee's wife. In the swells far beyond hope of rescue by the alert lifeguards on the Outrigger Club veranda, Lee feigns fatal cramps to test whether he can retain his wife. A possible flaw in this story is that the couple are both such super-beings that it is hard to excuse their all too human defects, and London does not make it easier by inveighing for several pages against weaklings and envious gossips. Beneath the fiction one can sense a good deal about Jack and Charmian and their relationships with Honolulu society.

In **"When Alice Told Her Soul,"** written when London had barely returned from his final visit to Hawaii, he tells of Abel Ah Yoh, a polyracial Billy Sunday who converts long-memoried but tight-tongued Alice Akana. When terror finally unloosens her tongue in the filled tabernacle, "Never was a more fearful and damning community narrative enunciated in the entire Pacific, north and south, than that enunciated by Alice Akana, the penitent Phryne of Honolulu."

Underlying the rollicking comedy of this Honolulu fable, which might have been concocted by one who had listened keenly to all the local gossip, was London's growing interest in C. G. Jung's *Psychology of the Unconscious,* in his copy of which he had underlined a passage pointing out that a neurotic derives special benefit when he can at last rid his libido of its various secrets.

Modern psychology is even more prominent in the last short story ever written by this master, **"The Water Baby,"** completed at Glen Ellen on October 2. Outwardly it is a simple reminiscence of fishing off Waihee with a seventy-year-old Hawaiian who thinks nothing of breaking off his conversation to dive down forty feet and kill a large octopus, and who otherwise passes the time by retelling the age-old story of Maui's deeds in the islands, or the tall tale of Keikiwai, the "water baby" who fools forty sharks. The narrator has been "born in the islands," but significantly his name is John Lakana—which is to say, Jack London. The two men discuss the riddles of religion and dreams, including the idea that life is all a dream. . . . (pp. 16-18)

Despite the air of lazy legend-telling, the story has modern profundity. Often dismissed as a primitivist, London in his last years was aware, long before the theories of Freud and Jung were topics of cocktail chat in the 1920's, of the role of dreams and the unconscious. His tales often dredge the deep-rooted myths of our species, and the ponderings even of a lowly old Polynesian may have meanings still to be discovered by the psychologists. This tale of **"The Water Baby"** was labeled by London's wife a Jungian parable, "clearly a symbolic representation of the Rebirth, the return of the Mother" (*The Book of Jack London,* 1921.) (pp. 18-19)

The following November 22, Jack was found in his bed at Glen Ellen, dying from uremic poisoning. Beneath the boulder on Sonoma Mountain that marks his grave was buried with him a withered ilima lei given to him in Hawaii by his ranch-owning friend Colonel Samuel Parker. Perhaps London's most touching epitaph was the expression of a Hawaiian lad who played the ukulele at a San Francisco theater:

> Better than any one, he *knew* us Hawaiians. . . .
> Jack London, the Story Maker. . . . The news
> came to Honolulu—and people, they seemed to

have lost a great friend—*auwe!* They could not understand. . . . They could not believe. I tell you this: Better than any one, he knew us Hawaiians.

(p. 19)

Much of Jack London's best writing, one must conclude, was done in Hawaii and the Pacific. Although the stories with a Pacific setting are often overlooked by readers of his other works, those describing the adventures to be found in this biggest of oceans, and particularly in the Hawaiian Islands he loved so well, should be remembered and read. (p. 20)

> *A. Grove Day, in an introduction to* Stories of Hawaii *by Jack London, edited by A. Grove Day, Appleton-Century, 1965, pp. 3-20.*

CLELL T. PETERSON (essay date 1966)

[*In the following excerpt, Peterson attempts to account for the popular and critical success of London's story "To Build a Fire" by comparing the piece to a more optimistic version that London published earlier under the same title.*]

Judged simply by the number of times it has been selected by the editors of anthologies, **"To Build a Fire"** is Jack London's most popular and presumably his best short story. What merit editors find in it, I can only speculate; but I imagine that it is admired as a fine example of a suspenseful story with a strong theme presented in vivid, realistic detail. All this, of course, it is; and it is interesting to recall in this connection that, aside from the death of the protagonist, the story treats of precisely the range of experience that London himself had had in the northland. He too, in his relations with cold, dogs, fires, and all the rest of the exotic *mise en scène,* had never become more than a *chechaquo* [or novice in the region], and writing within that narrow range of experience, he recreated a moment of truth about the Yukon more clearly and credibly than anywhere else in his fiction.

Valid as it is, however, an interpretation which halts at the careful contrivance of suspense, a strong theme—by which is meant, I suppose, the primitive struggle for survival—and precise, realistic details cannot explain the appeal of the story, which, like all serious fiction, hints at a depth and richness of meaning below the level of literal narration. In this paper I wish to discuss this "depth and richness of meaning," or theme, particularly in terms of the fable and the characters. To put the discussion into context, let me summarize the story even if its great popularity guarantees that most readers are familiar with it.

A man, whose name is not given, is traveling alone, except for an almost wild dog as companion, in the far north in the dead of winter. Although aware of the dangers of the journey, the man is confident. He is alert and careful; but even so he accidentally breaks through the surface of a frozen stream and gets his feet wet. When he fails in his attempts to build a fire to dry himself, he dies. His wolf-dog companion leaves the body to seek food and warmth with the dead man's companions waiting in camp.

The fable unfolds as a journey taken in the face of serious danger in which the conflicts between man and nature and between man and dog provide the drama. But I wish to consider here the journey itself, presented in the first sentence of the story in a passage that is both rhetorically impressive and charged with implication:

> Day had broken cold and gray, exceedingly cold and gray, when the man turned aside from the main Yukon trail and climbed the high earthbank, where a dim and little-traveled trail led eastward through the fat spruce timberland.

These details, admirably foreshadowing the events of the story, tell how a man leaves the well-trodden path of the familiar world of men to follow a faint and difficult trail into a world of mysterious ("dim and little-travelled") but significant ("fat spruce timberland") experience. The very rhythms of the passage reinforce the meaning. The shifts from the initial iambic rhythm to anapestic and back to iambic follow the movement of the passage from the scene itself. . . . The double stress upon "earth-bank" emphasizes the boundary between the realms of familiar and unfamiliar.

The journey thus brilliantly announced is, as I have implied, more than a literal journey, although the hard, realistic surface of the narrative may obscure what ought to be obvious. The nameless man (his anonymity is significant) is a modern Every man who, if not precisely summoned, nevertheless takes a pilgrimage the end of which "he in no wise may escape." At the realistic level, the direction of the journey is toward camp and safety, a return to the comfortable, sensual world of the known and familiar, but it becomes a journey into the unknown with the possibility of illumination as well as the risk of disaster. Hence another analogue, what Maud Bodkin, after Jung, has termed the archetypal theme of rebirth, suggests itself.

For Miss Bodkin, the rebirth theme consists of a double movement—downward toward disintegration and death and upward toward reintegration and life, but life greatly enriched. Jung terms this latter change "subjective transformation" and the result the "enlargement of personality." The pattern is similar to what Toynbee calls "withdrawal and return." . . . **"The Story of Jees Uck"** (1902), an obvious instance, tells of Neil Bonner, a spoiled young man who is forced by his father to leave the civilization that has corrupted him and to live in the northern wilderness. There he has experiences, including a liaison with Jees Uck, a native girl, which give him new insights and values. These he takes back to civilization where he becomes a prominent member of his society.

"To Build a Fire" is of this general type. The central character—like Neil Bonner . . .—has a misconception that must be changed, for living in such ignorance is a kind of death. . . . Extreme cold is a metaphor for a whole range of experiences beyond the man's awareness, and the point of the story is not that the man freezes to death but that he has been confronted with the inadequacy of his conception of the nature of things.

Neither the analogue of Everyman nor of the archetypal rebirth quite fits, however. The man, unlike Everyman, undergoes no redemption; nor, like Neil Bonner . . . does he return to civilization changed by the intensity and significance of his experience. He does not even have a moment of illumination as he dies. He comes nearest to insight when dying, he thinks, "When he got back to the States he could tell the folks what real cold was." The inadequacy of the vision is indicative; had he been capable of truly comprehending his experience, London implies, he might not have died. Inexact as the analogues are, however, they define the kind of story **"To Build a Fire"** is and show that its significance lies in something profound and universal in the fable.

Before turning to a discussion of the characters, I must call attention to several details of the setting that seem to me symbolic. The "dark hairline" of the main trail and the "pure snow" on the broad frozen Yukon suggest the narrow limits of the man's rational world compared with the universe beyond his knowledge and comprehension. The whiteness is not the whiteness of innocence but the blankness of the unknown, neither good nor evil but inexplicable, its meaning yet to be discovered. (pp. 15-17)

Although the man is the central character, it is valid to speak of both the dog and the man as characters. They are equally important to the story, and we know as much about one as the other. All we know of the man is that he is from the civilized land to the south and that he is both unimaginative and unreflective. He is not presented as young, strong, or heroic. The dog, his companion, is almost wild and retains its primitive instincts virtually intact.

London's point, that the man lacks imagination and does not think, would be obscure were it not for the careful contrast with the dog; for the man does think. Or, as London puts it, he is "quick and alert in the things of life." A common interpretation, I suspect, sees the man as a fool who dies for his folly, but a careful reading will disprove it. He is alert and attentive, and he handles himself well in a dangerous situation; but his thought is always practical and immediate, never looking beneath the surface of things. . . . The vastness of the scene London describes so vividly, the unbroken white extending for thousands of miles, means nothing to the man. And yet we realize that his self-confidence is, on the whole, justified, and we cannot dismiss him simply as a fool.

The distinction between the man's thought and the dog's instinct is explicitly made in three places. One passage will serve for example: "The dog did not know anything about thermometers. Possibly in its brain there was no sharp consciousness of a condition of very cold such as was in the man's brain. But the brute had its instinct." The reiteration of the contrast between man and dog points to the theme. London's Everyman, not civilized in any very significant way, is nevertheless modern, sensual, rational man; and what London is saying is that modern man, in accepting reason as a guide to short-sighted ends, has allowed his primal instincts to atrophy. (p. 17)

The theme, to say all this a little differently, springs from the contrast between our tidy, civilized world and the powerful forces beneath. Modern man reasons his way with false confidence, unaware that he may at any moment break through the shell of his comfortable, rational world into a universe of terrifying dimensions. The man in the story discovers these dimensions and forces, but the moment of illumination London seems to prepare us for never comes. The man dies with only a glimmering of insight.

In the story, breaking through the ice is both a realistic action with serious real consequences and a symbolic action which begins the destruction of the protagonist's confidence in a rationally ordered universe. In a different version of the fable (Crane's "Open Boat," for example), the protagonist would be plucked from disaster to emerge with an "enlargement of personality." London's grimmer story implies that man may have gone too far to save himself; and yet, if escape is possible, it may lie in surrendering upon occasion belief in reason and falling back upon the ancient, inarticulate guidance of instinct. The man does not comprehend this, but the reader does when he sees the dog's instincts save it.

A number of motifs occur repeatedly in London's fiction. Two of them, the struggle of man against nature and "love of life," appear in **"To Build a Fire."** Since it is always instructive to see a work of art in a larger context, I should like to comment briefly on two other stories in which these motifs appear and which, together with **"To Build a Fire,"** comprise an interesting triad.

The first is also called **"To Build a Fire,"** for London had already used the title for a story he sold to *Youth's Companion* in 1902. In the earlier story the man has a name, Tom Vincent, but no dog for companion; and he succeeds in building the fire that saves his life. Tom is typical of the triumphant Anglo-Saxons that figure frequently in London's fiction. (pp. 17-18)

He even imagines that he is stronger than the animals who crawl into hiding in the intense cold, but his confidence is soon shaken. The point London wants to make is simple and straightforward: "In the Klondike, as Tom Vincent found out . . . a companion is absolutely essential"; and Tom learned his lesson and "limped pitifully" back to camp with an "enlargement of personality," in Jung's phrase. But the fact that he did survive raises a question about London's thesis. In fact, Tom survived without a companion because "the love of life was strong in him" and would not let him sit down and die. "Love of life" in the story suggests both a tenacious clinging to mere existence and sheer joy in being young and strong; and although the ostensible theme is a practical warning about wilderness travel, a secondary theme celebrates human strength and endurance in opposition to nature.

The phrase "love of life" appealed to London and he used it again as theme and title for [**"Love of Life"**], a story published in *McClure's Magazine* in 1905. Two men, this time, are traveling through the perilous northern wilderness in late summer, on their way out with the gold that represents success in civilization. One man, unnamed, sprains his ankle— again the accident that brings ordinary man into direct contact with the dark forces of nature. His partner, Bill, callously deserts him, ironically as events prove, to save his own life. The deserted man, however, staggers and crawls for days. As he goes he sheds the emblems of man, first the useless gold and then the empty rifle and the knife. At the beginning of his journey he shoulders his pack and painfully straightens up "so that he could stand erect as a man should stand"; but the imagery shows his reversion to beast and then to mere living thing. . . . Eventually he reaches the shore of the Arctic Ocean where some members of a scientific expedition find [him]. . . .

Life itself had kept the man alive, "the life in him, unwilling to die," the fear of dying "that is to life germane and that lies twisted about life's deepest roots." Life force and body become disassociated: "He was very weary, but it refused to die." The man survived by jettisoning his human qualities. The point is lightly underscored, for his quondam companion died on the trail, still carrying the sack of gold he would not give up even to save his life.

Whereas in **"To Build a Fire"** (1902), "love of life" is characteristically human, and specifically characteristic of London's heroic Anglo-Saxon adventurers, **"Love of Life"** suggests that the naked will to live has little to do with humanity and nothing at all with civilization. **"To Build a Fire"** (1908) carries the shift of theme a step further. The protagonist does not wish to die, but he lacks the "love of life" that would force him to struggle to the end. We infer that the instinct to cling to life at any cost, like an instinctive awareness of cold or other danger, has decayed in civilization.

The story, however, takes a final twist and ends as tragedy. Denied any significant awareness of his inadequate vision of the universe, the man nevertheless faces up to his own human limitations. The realization that his efforts to stay alive are futile and absurd steels him in "meeting death with dignity," a response quite impossible to the survivor in **"Love of Life,"** and he succumbs to a death that is nothing but a "comfortable sleep."

The three stories are not, I think, random variations upon a theme. Rather they reflect the growth of London's thought and a movement from comic to tragic vision with an accompanying artistic development. [**"To Build a Fire"** (1902)] sees man and nature in opposition, with man, strong equally in youth and innocence, reaffirming the traditional myth of his dominion over nature. [**"Love of Life"**], disillusioned and reflecting London's melancholy pondering of Haeckel and Spencer, places man squarely within a materialistic nature. [**"To Build a Fire"** (1908)] ambiguously suggests that man has been corrupted from nature and therefore pays occasionally a fearful consequence. Ignorant of his apostasy and unable to see quite where he has gone wrong, man nevertheless is capable of new insights and the tragic vision that both ennobles and conceals his fall from nature. The third story is not better simply because it is better written, for the second story is its equal in style if not, perhaps, in structure, but because it is London's serious, mature treatment of a favorite theme. All of the by now familiar details of his mythic northland gain new vigor from the insight that fuses them into a taut, highly charged, meaningful whole that justly deserves its reputation. (p. 18)

Clell T. Peterson, "The Theme of Jack London's 'To Build a Fire'," in American Book Collector, *Vol. XVII, No. 3, November, 1966, pp. 15-18.*

EARLE LABOR AND KING HENDRICKS (essay date 1967)

[*Labor and Hendricks were among the foremost spokesmen for the appreciation of London's works during the 1960s. Labor is widely regarded as an authority on London and taught the first courses on the author's works offered at an American university and in Western Europe. In the following excerpt, Labor and Hendricks compare London's two versions of "To Build a Fire" and suggest that London's work will undergo substantial critical reassessment.*]

While Jack London's fiction awaits a proper critical assessment, **"To Build a Fire,"** that "brilliant little sketch whose prose rhythms . . . are still fresh" [see excerpt by Maxwell Geismar dated 1953], has firmly established itself as a perennial favorite among the world's readers. In it London managed to combine those qualities which distinguish his best work: vivid narrative, graphic description of physical action, tension (*e.g.,* human intelligence *vs.* animal intuition, man's intrepidity *vs.* cosmic force, vitality *vs.* death), a poetic modulation of imagery to enhance mood and theme, and—above all—a profound sense of irony. It is therefore hardly surprising that this masterpiece of short fiction is still available in a dozen contemporary anthologies.

What is surprising is that London sold the same title to two magazines. The first sale was made in December, 1901, to *The Youth's Companion.* . . . London received fifty dollars for the story. Six years later, after he had become world-famous, *Century Magazine* paid $400 for **"To Build a Fire."** Following publication of the story in August 1908, *Century* Editor R. W. Gilder discovered that he had paid for, and foisted upon his readers, apparently soiled goods. Understandably indignant, he lost little time in notifying the author of this discovery. London, who had been cruising the South Seas aboard *The Snark,* sent the following reply:

> Sydney, N.S.W., Australia
> Dec. 22, 1908
>
> Dear Mr. Gilder:— . . .
>
> A long, long time ago I wrote a story for boys which I sold to the *Youth's Companion.* It was purely juvenile in treatment; its motif was not only very strong, but very true. Man after man in the Klondike has died alone after getting his feet wet, through failure to build a fire. As years went by, I was worried about the inadequate treatment I had given that motif, and by the fact that I had treated it for boys merely. At last I came to the resolve to take the same motif and handle it for men. I had no access to the boys' version of it, and I wrote it just as though I had never used the motif before. I do not remember anything about the way I handled it for juveniles, but I do know, I am absolutely confident, that beyond the motif itself, there is no similarity of treatment whatever.
>
> I can only say that it never entered my head that there was anything ethically wrong in handling the same motif over again in the way I did, and I can only add that I am of the same opinion now, upon carefully considering the question. Please let me know how you feel about the matter.
>
> Sincerely yours,
>
> Jack London

The most cursory reading of the two versions . . . confirms London's defense: despite the similarity of motifs, the stories are radically different. Perhaps the most remarkable thing, in view of the circumstances of composition, is the recurrence of a few similar—and, at times, identical—phrases in both versions. In any case, London's reply would seem to have satisfied Gilder; for the matter was not pursued further.

But we wish to pursue it further here. . . .

[We] hope to demonstrate by comparing the two versions, that Jack London was not merely a prolific hack but, contrary to modern critical opinion, an astute craftsman who understood the difference between juvenile fiction and serious literary art. The first **"To Build a Fire,"** if we will grant the author his *donnée,* is a well-made boys' story; the second version is a classic for all ages. An appreciation of this distinction should not only enhance London's reputation but also sharpen our own insights into the ontological qualities of the short story as art form—a form whose aesthetic virtues have been too easily ignored by the critics.

There are a number of interesting features about the first **"To Build a Fire."** It was written early in London's career, during a period of financial depression when he was frequently in the depths of despair. Certain autobiographical implications are

London (far right) and his crew prior to the first voyage of his sailing vessel "The Snark." In the foreground is London's wife, Charmian.

fairly evident in the story: like its protagonist, London had been a robust "young fellow, big-boned and big-muscled, with faith in himself and in the strength of his head and hands"; also like Tom Vincent, the struggling young writer had found out, "not by precept, but through bitter experience," that—regardless of one's optimism, vigor, and self-confidence—man cannot travel alone; and London had furthermore, in his extremity, "set to work to save himself [by] heroic measures." . . . (pp. 334-36)

Though London may have written the first **"To Build a Fire"** "for boys merely," he nevertheless worked his form to perfection. This form, one of the oldest types of short fiction, is the *exemplum*. Because its primary function is moral edification, such structural elements as atmosphere and characterization are subordinated, in the *exemplum*, to theme; and what E. M. Forster has called the "mystery" of plot is sacrificed for the didactic explicitness of "story." London adheres closely to the conventions of his form by stating his moral at the outset ("a companion is absolutely essential") and reemphasizing it at the end ("*Never travel alone!*"). The narrative action is simple and direct; his "story" is an uncomplicated circle, moving from message through true-to-life illustration back to message. The tale's effectiveness depends upon two major factors: clarity of the statement and vividness of the illustration. An-

other important, if minor, factor is the attractiveness of his hero; Tom Vincent, notwithstanding his foolishness, is a sympathetic, clean-cut character—an admirable model for young men. The first **"To Build a Fire"** was, in short, one of the many fictional examples used by the editors of *The Youth's Companion* to vivify their weekly sermons to America's strenuous young manhood.

The second **"To Build a Fire"** is, as London himself indicated, an altogether different story. It is, for one thing, considerably longer than the earlier version (7,235 as compared to 2,700 words). Although expansion is of itself no criterion for artistic merit, in this case London obviously used his additional wordage for greater artistic effect, creating a narrative "mystery" and an "atmosphere" lacking in the first version. His awareness of the importance of such elements is revealed in one of his letters to a fellow writer: "Atmosphere stands always for the elimination of the artist, that is to say, the atmosphere is the artist; and when there is no atmosphere and the artist is yet there, it simply means that the machinery is creaking and the reader hears it." (p. 337)

Examination of the opening paragraph of the second **"To Build a Fire"** reveals the devices through which London allows atmosphere to function as commentary:

Day had broken cold and gray, exceedingly cold and gray, when the man turned aside from the main Yukon trail and climbed the high earth-bank, where a dim and little-travelled trail led eastward through the fat spruce timberland. It was a steep bank, and he paused for breath at the top, excusing the act to himself by looking at his watch. It was nine o'clock. There was no sun nor hint of sun, though there was not a cloud in the sky. It was a clear day, and yet there seemed an intangible pall over the face of things, a subtle gloom that made the day dark, and that was due to the absence of sun. This fact did not worry the man. He was used to the lack of sun. It had been days since he had seen the sun, and he knew that a few more days must pass before that cheerful orb, due south, would just peep above the sky line and dip immediately from view.

By varied repetition of a textural motif, London achieves the same kind of hypnotic impact that Hemingway is said to have learned from Gertrude Stein: certain images recur and cluster to produce a mood that is at once somber and sinister ("cold and gray, exceedingly cold and gray . . . a dim and little-travelled trail . . . no sun nor hint of sun . . . intangible pall . . . a subtle gloom . . . day dark . . . absence of sun . . . lack of the sun . . . days since he had seen the sun"). The story's dominant symbolism, the polarity of heat (sun-fire-life) and cold (darkness-depression-death), is carefully adumbrated at the outset so that the reader *senses* the protagonist's imminent doom. We are subtly oppressed by that "intense awareness of human loneliness" that Frank O'Connor has identified with the short story. . . . It is undoubtedly such scenes as this that prompted Maxwell Geismar to remark that "London's typical figure was a voiceless traveler journeying across the ghostly leagues of a dead world."

Unlike Tom Vincent, the protagonist of this **"To Build a Fire"** is nameless. He is the naturalistic version of Everyman: a puny, insignificant mortal confronting the cold mockery of Nature as Antagonist. Yet, though nameless, he is distinguished by certain traits of character: the man is practical, complacent, insensitive, and vain—he must, for example, excuse to himself the impractical human act of pausing for breath; he is unawed by the mysterious other-worldness of his surroundings; caught in this weird *Urwelt,* he is foolish enough to put his faith in mere clock-time.

What has been hinted in the beginning becomes explicit in the third paragraph, the only place in the story where the author's voice may be detected. The man lacks the one asset that might equalize the odds against him—imagination. . . . The scope of his imagination is signified in his one stock comment: "It certainly was cold," a fatally inept response that recurs with increasing irony as the man's situation deteriorates. It is also in this paragraph that the theme of the story is subtly implanted in the reader's mind: "It [the extreme cold] did not lead him to meditate upon his frailty as a creature of temperature, and upon man's frailty in general . . . and from there on it did not lead him to the conjectural field of immortality and man's place in the universe." London drops the comment so deftly that it hardly ripples in the reader's consciousness, yet it is this idea precisely that gives the story its final impact: "unaccommodated man" is indeed a frail and pitiable figure when pitted against the awful majesty of cosmic force. (pp. 338-39)

But the nameless protagonist of **"To Build a Fire"** is unaware of these deeper implications, as we learn not only from his

own behavior but also through the only other animated character in the story, the dog. The inclusion of this *ficelle* or "reflector" is the masterstroke of London's revised version. By employing the dog as foil, the author has obviated the necessity for further editorial comment. Instead of being *told* that one needs a companion in the Northland, we are made to *see* dramatically through his relationship with the animal that the man is a "loner." Because he lacks imagination, he fails to see, until too late, that a companion—even a dog—might possibly save him in a crisis; more important, he is revealed as a man lacking in essential warmth. There is no place in his cold practical philosophy for affection or for what London called elsewhere "true comradeship." To this man the dog is only another of "the things" of life, an object to be spoken to with "the sound of whip lashes." From his relationship to the animal, we may infer a broader relationship—that to mankind. The protagonist is, in other words, a hollow man whose inner coldness correlates with the enveloping outer cold. And there is a grim but poetic justice in his fate.

The dog serves as a foil in the following manner also: his natural wisdom of conduct is juxtaposed against the foolish rationality of his master's behavior. By shifting point of view from man to dog, London provides a subtle counterpointing that enhances both theme and structural tension. (p. 340)

And, finally, by using the animal as objective correlative, London has managed to give an extra twist of irony to the conclusion of his story. After the man's last desperate attempt to save himself and after his dying vision of rescue, we shift once more to the dog's point of view:

> The brief day drew to a close in a long, slow twilight. There were no signs of a fire to be made, and, besides, never in the dog's experience had it known a man to sit like that in the snow and make no fire. As the twilight drew on, its eager yearning for the fire mastered it, and with a great lifting and shifting of forefeet, it whined softly, then flattened its ears down in anticipation of being chidden by the man. But the man remained silent. Later the dog whined loudly. And still later it crept close to the man and caught the scent of death. This made the animal bristle and back away. A little longer it delayed, howling under the stars that leaped and danced and shone brightly in the cold sky. Then it turned and trotted up the trail in the direction of the camp it knew, where were the other food providers and fire providers.

Through its natural responses the dog conveys the finality of the man's death more forcibly—and more artistically—than any overt statement by the author might do. And in this concluding paragraph all the key elements of London's story—the ironic polarity of life and death, the intransigence of Nature's laws, the cosmic mockery of the White Silence—coalesce to produce a memorable effect. (pp. 340-41)

For more than a half-century now, men—as well as boys—have finished reading **"To Build a Fire"** with the same profound satisfaction—and a shiver of relief to be among the "food providers and fire providers." In view of the story's durability, it should be evident that Jack London was thoroughly sensitive to the meaning of the art of short fiction. He recognized moreover, as comparison of the two versions of **"To Build a Fire"** reveals, the intricate demands of the genre to which he committed most of his literary talent; and he knew the difference between juvenilia and adult fiction. Our critics would do well to exercise an equally fine discrimination in taking his measure as an artist. (p. 341)

Earle Labor and King Hendricks, "Jack London's Twice-Told Tale," in Studies in Short Fiction, *Vol. IV, No. 4, Summer, 1967, pp. 334-41.*

SUE FINDLEY (essay date 1969)

[*In the following excerpt, Findley compares London's use of Naturalist techniques in the short story "To Build a Fire" to that of Thomas Hardy and Joseph Conrad.*]

The year 1859, marking the publication of Darwin's *The Origin of Species,* is one of those years that occur rarely, a turning point, after which nothing is ever the same again. Darwin's central idea which he called "natural selection" but for which Huxley coined the more apt phrase "survival of the fittest" had ramifications not for biology alone but for many other branches of human knowledge. The influence of Darwin's thesis that the strong tend to survive has, to some extent at least, made twentieth century civilization what it is, and nowhere has this influence been more pronounced than in the realm of literature, specifically in literature as it embodies philosophical concepts. Freud extended the concept to include the cosmos itself as "the strong," by envisioning Nature as a personification, a force superior to man, the external enemy of man, a power sublime, pitiless, inexorable. With these attributes assigned to Nature, one has already made the leap to the idea designated by the literary term *pathetic fallacy*—the whole cosmos alive and morally conscious. In the imaginations of such literary artists as Thomas Hardy and Joseph Conrad this living cosmos is equated with evil, or to say the least, evil is a powerful constituent in the makeup of the universe, evil that "walks about . . . seeking whom it may devour" with the odds in its favor, and weak humanity as its natural prey. In the post-Darwinian era this literary philosophy came to be called naturalism. . . . (p. 45)

[Nowhere in his fiction has London treated naturalistic phenomena] more artistically than in his short story **"To Build a Fire."** Nature is the true protagonist in this story, man a puppet. It is no accident that in the opening sentence the reader meets the forces of Nature first, "Day had broken cold and gray" and man second, "when the man turned aside from the main Yukon trail and climbed the high earth bank." Significantly, this secondary character is never named; he is "the man" unworthy of such distinction and individuality as a name would impart. The second sentence reinforces the suggestion that Nature is a power to be reckoned with: "It was a steep bank, and he paused for breath at the top." In the third sentence London states that "there was no sun or hint of sun, though there was not a cloud in the sky." . . . With these economical deft strokes of the pen, the artist gave to his reader the protagonist, a cosmos instinct with evil.

In true Freudian fashion London next set about the task of indicating that the man was no match for the forces of Nature. The man was lacking in imagination. "He was quick and alert in the things of life, but only in the things, and not in the significances. Fifty degrees below zero meant eighty-odd degrees of frost . . . that was all. It did not lead him to meditate upon his frailty . . . and upon man's place in the universe." By now there remains no doubt; man's place is very minor indeed. However the man, lacking in perception as he was, pressed forward unaware, and London made this fact

vivid with the well-chosen synecdoche, "the eager nose that thrust itself aggressively into the frosty air."

At this point London introduced a third character, the dog, as a link between man and Nature but identified with Nature more closely than with man. Although it trotted at the man's heels, it was a "proper wolf dog" and the animal knew what the dull-witted human being did not know "that it was no time for traveling. Its instinct told it a truer tale than was told to the man by man's judgment." By the time the reader has reached this juncture, the man makes a pathetically gallant figure as he "held steadily on" down the faintly marked trail at the rate of four miles an hour. Overtones of catastrophe are clear in his numb cheekbones, and in the ice muzzle of tobacco juice surrounding his mouth. . . . Note the implications in London's choice of verb. Again London reminded the reader that the dog knew it should be lying "snug in a hole in the snow" waiting for a warming "curtain of cloud to be drawn across the face of outer space whence this cold came." London did not allow his reader to forget that this cold was immense and cosmic in scope, that if the planet is dwarfed and stricken by it, man is proportionately less significant. (pp. 46-7)

The man's struggle to build a fire in order that he might dry his footgear was unsuccessful, for Nature in a calculated move inverted the snow-laden branches to smother the last vestiges of the life-sustaining warmth. Not even that Titan Prometheus bearing his gift of fire can withstand the forces of cosmic evil. The denouement to such a mismatched contest as this between man and the universe was of course predictable from the beginning. London closed the account as it began with attention on the protagonist. Nature remained, standing exultant in its triumph. "The stars leaped and danced and shone brightly in the cold sky" when the man sat still and stiff, frozen in the cold snow. London barely managed to refrain from saying *"because* the man sat."

As suggested above there is a variation among the literary proponents of Darwin's and Freud's philosophy ranging from the conception of nature as lacking moral consciousness and as being indifferent to man's existence to the conception of nature as an active moral agent malevolent and malignant. Conrad and Hardy typify the latter group of literary philosophers while Crane seems more closely allied with the former. Interestingly enough, Jack London speaks for both camps, depending on whether or not he, himself, is opposing the powers of the universe. . . . [The] Nature of **"To Build a Fire"** is the Nature of Conrad and Hardy, actively aware and consciously evil. For "the man" with his lack of perception, intuition, or sensitivity clearly is not London's autobiographical hero. He is not a hero at all; nature is. (pp. 47-8)

Sue Findley, "Naturalism in 'To Build a Fire,' " in Jack London Newsletter, *Vol. 2, No. 2, May-August, 1969, pp. 45-8.*

EARLE LABOR (essay date 1974)

[*In his critical study* Jack London, *Labor discusses London's diverse and prolific career and argues for the author's inclusion among the world's most prominent writers. In the following excerpt from that work. Labor examines the origins of London's concerns, style, and temperament and offers an analysis of London's early stories set in Alaska.*]

> To understand the opening years of the new century one must study Jack Londonism.
>   —Fred Lewis Pattee, *The Development of the American Short Story* . . .

Because we have been conditioned by more than two generations of Realism, it is difficult to imagine the kind of fiction that dominated American magazines at the turn of the century. Perhaps the easiest way is to look at a few issues of the prestigious *Atlantic Monthly.* Volumes LXXXIV and LXXXV (1899 and 1900) disclose a genuine editorial concern for social and political relevance in the publication of such articles as Jacob A. Riis's series on the slums, Frank Norris's "Comida: An Experience in Famine" (an essay on the civilian war victims in Cuba), William James's *Talks to Teachers on Psychology,* and Prince Peter Kropotkin's *The Autobiography of a Revolutionist.* But the fiction in these volumes scarcely suggests such concern. For example, Mary Johnston's *To Have and To Hold*—a serialized historical romance which is reported to have doubled *Atlantic* circulation in 1900—is set in early seventeenth-century Virginia; and the action revolves about the love affair of Captain Ralph Percy and the lovely Jocelyn Leigh as they endure the tribulations of piracy, Indian savagery, and Lord Carnal's lecherous villainy. (p. 40)

[At this time, the] short story—virtually ignored in Realist theory—was worse yet. In the August, 1899, issue of the *Atlantic,* for instance, Elizabeth Stuart Phelps's "Loveliness: A Story" begins typically: "Loveliness sat on an eider-down cushion embroidered with cherry-colored puppies on a pearl satin cover. . . . For Loveliness was a little dog. . . . the essence of tenderness; set, soul and body, to one only tune. To love and be beloved—that was his life." . . .

[Such an example helps] to explain why the period has been called "the Mauve Decade" and "the decade of arrested development." We should remember, in all fairness to the *Atlantic* editors, that this period was the same one in which Leo Tolstoi's *The Awakening* was bowdlerized by the editors of *Cosmopolitan,* Thomas Hardy's *Jude the Obscure* was expurgated in *Harper's* under the fetching title of *Hearts Insurgent,* and Theodore Dreiser's *Sister Carrie* was suppressed on grounds of impropriety by Doubleday, Page & Company. Into this literary hothouse Jack London entered as a bracing draft of Arctic air. . . . (p. 41)

In *John Barleycorn* London contended, "Some are born to fortune, and some have fortune thrust upon them. But in my case I was clubbed into fortune, and bitter necessity wielded the club." The financial situation at home was acute when he returned from his Klondike trip in the summer of 1898. Jack had many talents, but no skill or trade. . . . He scored high on the civil service examinations for postman, but there were no vacancies. In desperation he turned once again to writing, not this time—or so he thought—as a career, but merely to put bread on the table at home. (p. 42)

In September, he sent the following letter to the editor of the San Francisco *Bulletin:*

> Dear Sir:
> I have returned from a year's residence in the Clondyke [*sic*], entering the country by way of Dyea and Chilcoot Pass. I left by way of St. Michaels, thus making altogether a journey of 2,500 miles on the Yukon in a small boat. I have sailed and traveled quite extensively in other parts of the world and have learned to seize upon that which is interesting, to grasp the true romance of things, and to understand the people I may be thrown amongst.
>
> I have just completed an article of 4,000 words, describing the trip from Dawson to St. Michaels in a rowboat. Kindly let me know if there would be any demand in your columns for it—of course, thoroughly understanding that the acceptance of the manuscript is to depend upon its literary and intrinsic value.
>
> Yours very respectfully,
>
> Jack London
>
> (*Letters from Jack London*)

In what would seem to have been one of the great blunders of publishing history, the editor returned the letter with a hasty reply scribbled on the bottom: "Interest in Alaska has subsided in an amazing degree. Then, again, so much has been written, that I do not think it would pay us to buy your story."

Most important, however, in London's early letter is the disclosure of three essential factors which account in large measure for his success as a writer: (1) "to seize upon that which is interesting," (2) "to grasp the true romance of things," (3) "to understand the people I may be thrown amongst." Human interest, romantic imagination, sympathetic understanding: these are the major ingredients in his work and—combined with the forces of luck, talent, and plain "dig"—made him one of the most popular writers of his generation. Another element, which he did not mention and which, indeed, he seemed hardly aware of—a genius for myth—made his achievement ultimately something more lasting than popular success. (pp. 42-3)

[Early 1899], the Oakland postmaster telephoned to say there was a vacancy for mail carrier and London could have the job if he was ready to go to work. The starting pay would be sixty-five dollars a month—twice what he had made as a common laborer—with opportunities for regular increases, as well as security and retirement benefits. One month of delivering mail would pay more than he had made from five years of writing—unless he counted the check just received from the *Black Cat:* the incredible sum of forty dollars for a mediocre science-fiction tale titled **"A Thousand Deaths,"** the kind of stuff he could now write with his eyes shut. Perhaps this sum was indicative of a real change in his luck; furthermore, his odds would be bettered by the deal offered him by *Overland* editor James Howard Bridge: if Jack would continue to produce stories as good as **"To the Man on Trail"** and **"The White Silence,"** which would be published in the January and February, 1899, numbers, he would be given not only $7.50 a sketch but also prime space in the magazine. Although the prestige of "the Gold Coast *Atlantic*" had become slightly tarnished (Ambrose Bierce now referred to it as "the warmed-*Overland Monthly*"), it was still a big-name magazine and, despite its picayune fees, might serve as a springboard for an unknown young writer.

The prospects for literary success had never been more tantalizing; on the other hand, the pressure to accept the certain income and the excellent security of the government job was urgent. . . . Had Chance decreed a vacancy ten days earlier, . . . America might have gained another servant of the public mails, inadvertently relegating the name "Jack London" to the deadletter office. (pp. 44-5)

Spring—the time of the open road—was approaching again; but this time the only road left open to Jack led him to success in the world of belles-lettres. That road is charted in two thumb-worn nickel composition books now secured under double lock in the Utah State University Library and simply labeled:

NO. 1	NO. 2
MAGAZINE SALES	MAGAZINE SALES
FROM 1898	FROM MAY 1900
TO MAY 1900	TO FEB. 1903

These two unpretentious notebooks not only confirm the legend of London's fabulous rise to success; they also tell, as King Hendricks has pointed out, "a graphic story of feverish work, disappointments and frustrations and of the tenacious determination to succeed."

Notebook No. 1, more noteworthy for its number of failures than its successes, reveals that London quite probably holds the record as America's most rejected author. Of the one hundred and three items listed, only fifty-seven were accepted for publication; and of these fifty-seven, only fifteen were accepted the first time they were submitted. Of the remainder, more than thirty items were permanently "retired" after multiple rejections; four were lost; and another four were rewritten and carried over to the second notebook. The one hundred and three items in the first book garnered more than four hundred rejections.

What is most impressive about these entries, in addition to the author's amazing persistence, is their variety: short stories, sonnets, triolets, humorous sketches, jokes, essays on subjects ranging from grammar to economics—anything, in short, that might sell for fifty cents upwards. (pp. 45-6)

[In the first third of Notebook No. 1], the retirement-acceptance ratio is two to one in favor of retirement; in the rest of the book, the ratio is almost exactly reversed—acceptances outnumber retirements better than two to one. The trend is confirmed in Notebook No. 2, thereby indicating that London had by May, 1900, found out his strengths and weaknesses. Gone are the crippled verses and lame jokes. More than half of the seventy-two entries are short stories; the rest are sketches and essays. Of these seventy-two, only two were retired, and one of these was later resurrected for publication in a book of London's essays.

One of the most significant entries in either notebook is the fifty-third item in Notebook No. 1: **"An Odyssey of the North,"** mailed to the *Atlantic Monthly* on June 10, 1899. Two days later Jack complained to his literary pen-pal Cloudesley Johns, "I am groping, groping, groping for my own particular style, for the style which should be mine but which I have not yet found" (*Letters from Jack London*). Six weeks later the *Atlantic* returned **"An Odyssey of the North"** with the note that, if he would shorten the manuscript by three thousand words, the story would be accepted. On August 1, he sent back the revised story; and on October 30 he received a check for one hundred and twenty dollars and also a complimentary one-year subscription.

Acceptance by America's premier literary monthly signified a major breakthrough. The *Overland Monthly* had provided literary respectability, and the *Black Cat* had given financial reassurance. The *Atlantic* gave Jack these things and something even more valuable: self-confidence. Henceforth there would be no further groping for his own particular style.

What was good enough for the *Atlantic* was surely good enough for the rest. By the winter of 1899, when he signed the contract with Houghton Mifflin for his first book [*The Son of the Wolf*]—a collection of the eight Klondike stories which had appeared in the *Overland,* along with **"An Odyssey of the North"**—London had abandoned the amateurish frenzy of his early writings and had settled into the steady professional pace he maintained for the rest of his life. . . . And by the time Houghton Mifflin released *The Son of the Wolf* in the spring of 1900, he had set not only the routine but also the style which would remain essentially unchanged throughout the rest of his career. "Let me tell you how I write," he explained in a letter to Elwyn Hoffman, . . . [an] early fan.

> In the first place I never begin a thing, but what I finish *before* I begin anything else. Further; I type as fast as I write, so that each day sees the work all upon the final MS. which goes for editorial submission. And *on* the day I finish the MS. I fold it up and send it off without once going back to see what all the previous pages were like. So, in fact, when a page is done, that is the last I see of it till it comes out in print.

This remarkable facility explains in part why it was that London had so little regard for much of his work and why there is so little change in his style. The changes had already taken place, for the most part, in the period of feverish apprenticeship before his first book appeared on the market.

Later, answering the critics who had raised their eyebrows over the incredible success of his hero in *Martin Eden,* London asserted,

> In three years, from a sailor with a common school education, I made a successful writer of him. The critics say this is impossible. Yet I was Martin Eden. At the end of three working years, two of which were spent in high school and the university and one spent at writing, and all three in studying immensely and intensely, I was publishing stories in magazines such as the *Atlantic Monthly*. . . .

London's success was an extraordinary literary phenomenon, and it occurred because his hard-earned mastery of narrative technique and his instinctive genius for myth meshed precisely with a change in cultural tastes and with the sudden national awareness that the frontier and all its dreams of glory were gone. (pp. 47-9)

Specific titles of London's works may be blurred among our other dim memories of youth, but few persons who have ever encountered his tales can totally forget [**"To Build a Fire,"** about] the lonely traveler who dies unmourned in the awesome cold of the Arctic winter because he has accidentally wet his feet and failed to build a fire; [or, **"Love of Life,"** which concerns] the lost miner who wanders across the Arctic waste land in a nightmarish odyssey of starvation and exposure, sustained solely by an incredible will to live. . . . There is something timeless about these stories. At the turn of the century, when they first appeared, there was also something very timely about them.

A reading public that had dieted on propriety and pap for more than a generation and whose appetite for strenuous action had been whetted by the colorful melodramas of Kipling and by the melodramatics of Theodore Roosevelt was hungry for the meaty fare of Jack London's Northland. . . . Others had already used the Klondike materials for profit, but their writings lacked the vividness and poetic cadence of London's style, a style which fused the vigorous and the picturesque. Furthermore, his was a fresh breed of fictional heroes. . . . Kipling had introduced a kindred type the decade before, and London was quick to acknowledge his debt to the master of the "plain tale."

But the Klondike argonauts were not merely copies of those leathery cockneys and Irishmen in the Queen's Army whose individualism was subverted to the uses of British Imperialism and whose sporting ethic was at times gratuitously cruel. London's Northland heroes were, by contrast, a ruggedly independent yet a remarkably compassionate breed who paid allegiance only to the inexorable laws of nature and to the authority of conscience, but who also possessed a capacity for selflessness and comradeship very much like the *agape* of primitive Christianity. Theirs was a situational ethic, predicated on integrity, charity, and pragmatism. (pp. 49-50)

This code of the Northland, with the mystique of comradeship at its heart, is dramatized in **"To the Man on Trail,"** the first of Jack's Klondike stories which had so excited the editors of the *Overland Monthly*. A Yuletide story, it is trimmed with the rich assortment of symbols, pagan as well as Christian, appropriate to the occasion. The setting is Christmas Eve in the cabin of the Malemute Kid, who dominates *The Son of the Wolf* collection as high priest of the code. Gathered together are representatives from a dozen different lands who are swapping yarns, reminiscing about home, and sharing the heady Christmas punch concocted by Kid. At midnight the convivialities are suddenly interrupted by the jingling of bells, "the familiar music of the dogwhip, the whining howl of the Malemutes, and the crunch of a sled"; then comes "the expected knock, sharp and confident" and the entrance of "the stranger." . . . (p. 51)

Jack Westondale, the stranger, explains that he is pursuing a gang of dog thieves. While the guest is eating the Christmas snack hospitably prepared for him, Kid studies his face and finds him worthy:

> Nor was he long in deciding that it was fair, honest, and open, and that he liked it. Still youthful, the lines had been firmly traced by toil and hardship. Though genial in conversation, and mild when at rest, the blue eyes gave promise of the hard steel-glitter which comes when called into action, especially against odds. The heavy jaw and square-cut chin demonstrated rugged pertinacity and indomitability. Nor, though the attributes of the lion were there, was there wanting the certain softness, the hint of womanliness, which bespoke the emotional nature.

Westondale apparently embodies all the vital traits of the code hero. . . . [The Kid] sends him on his way with fresh provisions and wise counsel. Fifteen minutes later the festivities are stopped a second time—by a nearly exhausted stranger who wears the red coat, not of St. Nick, but of the Royal Canadian Mounted Police. He demands fresh dogs and information about Westondale, who is running—he discloses—not for, but *from,* the law after having robbed a Dawson gambling casino of forty thousand dollars!

Though the revelers have kept silent according to Kid's example, they furiously demand an explanation after the Mountie has gone: why has Kid given sanctuary and aid to a man who has doubly violated the code by robbery and by deception?

> "It's a cold night, boys,—a bitter cold night," was the irrelevant commencement of his defense. "You've all traveled trail, and know what that stands for. Don't jump a dog when he's down. You've only heard one side. A whiter man than Jack Westondale never ate from the same pot nor stretched blanket with you or me. Last fall he gave his whole clean-up, forty thousand, to Joe Castrell, to buy in on Dominion. To-day he'd be a millionaire. But while he stayed behind at Circle City, taking care of his partner with the scurvy, what does Castrell do? Goes into McFarland's, jumps the limit, and drops the whole sack. Found him dead in the snow the next day. And poor Jack laying his plans to go out this winter to his wife and the boy he's never seen. You'll notice he took exactly what his partner lost,—forty thousand. Well, he's gone out; and what are you going to do about it?"

> The Kid glanced around the circle of his judges, noted the softening of their faces, then raised his mug aloft. "So a health to the man on trail this night; may his grub hold out; may his dogs keep their legs; may his matches never miss fire. God prosper him; good luck go with him; and"—

> "Confusion to the Mounted Police!" cried Bettles, to the crash of the empty cups.

Without belaboring his symbolism, London has provided a fitting epiphany to the conclusion of his Christmas carol; moreover, the situational ethic which informs the story was sure to appeal to a reading public less than one generation removed from frontier justice.

The mystique of comradeship is obversely dramatized in the fourth story in *The Son of the Wolf* collection, **"In a Far Country."** . . . In this tale about "two Incapables" named Carter Weatherbee and Percy Cuthfert, who elect to spend the long Arctic winter snugly marooned in a deserted cabin rather than suffer the hardships of breaking trail with their comrades for the thousand remaining miles to Dawson, London reiterates the idea that survival is not primarily a matter of physical fitness.

Both Incapables are healthy, husky men, whereas Merritt Sloper, the wiry little argonaut who functions as moral norm in this and in several other Klondike episodes, weighs less than a hundred pounds. . . . Sloper predicts the Incapables' fate as he and the remaining members of the party pull out from the cabin: . . . "[These] two men don't like work. They won't work. We know that. They'll be all alone in that cabin all winter,—a mighty long, dark winter."

At first, Sloper's prophecy appears to be wrong, for the Incapables seem determined to prove their compatibility; in addition, they are plentifully stocked with food and fuel. But, representatives of a degenerate society, they are fatally undersupplied in the moral staples needed for subsistence in the Northland. Weatherbee, formerly a clerk, is an unimaginative, materialistic fool who has joined the gold rush to make his fortune; Cuthfert, opposite as well as apposite, is the overripe cultural dilettante afflicted with "an abnormal development of sentimentality [which he mistakes] for the true spirit of romance and adventure." Moreover, the two men lack that "protean faculty of adaptability"—the capacity to slough off the callus of "self" along with the specious comforts of civilization—which is the most vital insurance against the dangers of the wilderness.

After an overeager show of industrious cooperation, they abandon the austere discipline of the code. Their spiritual degeneration, as they succumb to each of the Seven Deadly Sins, is initially dramatized in their social relationship. First, pride is manifest in a foolish arrogance which precludes the mutual trust requisite to survival in the wilderness. . . . (pp. 52-4)

Next appears lust, as they consume with sensual promiscuity their supply of sugar, mixing it with hot water and then dissipating "the rich, white syrup" over their flapjacks and breadcrusts. This is followed by sloth, as they sink into a lethargy which makes them "rebel at the performance of the smallest chore." . . . Accelerated by gluttony, their moral deterioration now begins to externalize itself in their physical appearance. . . . Covetousness and envy appear when they divide their sugar supply and hide their shares from each other, obsessed with the fear of losing the precious stuff.

The last of the cardinal sins, anger, is delayed awhile by another trouble: "the Fear of the North. . . . the joint child of the Great Cold and the Great Silence," which preoccupies each man according to his nature. For the dilettantish Cuthfert, the Fear manifests itself quietly and inwardly. . . . The coarser sensibilities of the clerk are more sensationally aroused in necrophilic nightmares. . . . (p. 55)

The symbolism grows richer as the drama moves toward its ghastly climax. Though London had not yet read the works of Sigmund Freud, his metaphors reveal an instinctive grasp of dream symbolism, particularly of the unconscious associations of sexual impotency and death. Cuthfert is obsessed with the absolute stillness of the phallic, arrow-shaped weathervane atop the cabin. . . . The metaphors of potency-life versus emasculation-death coalesce in the story's vivid climax, as anger completes the allegoric procession of the deadly sins. Thinking that his companion has pilfered his last tiny cache of the symbol-laden sugar, Weatherbee attacks Cuthfert in the cold fury of insanity and severs his spine with an axe . . . , and then falls heavily upon him as the bullet from his victim's Smith & Wesson explodes in his face.

The closing tableau—a grotesque inversion of the primal scene—dramatically reveals London's pre-Freudian intuitions: "The sharp bite of the axe had caused Cuthfert to drop the pistol, and as his lungs panted for release, he fumbled aimlessly for it among the blankets. Then he remembered. He slid a hand up the clerk's belt to the sheath-knife; and they drew very close to each other in that last clinch." Passages like this one apparently substantiate Maxwell Geismar's observation that London seemed to be more at home in the "world of dream and fantasy and desolate, abnormal emotion . . . than the world of people and society" and that "his best work was often a transcript of solitary nightmares." But such an assessment, notwithstanding the brilliance of Geismar's Freudian interpretation of London's life and work, is too limited. Though a considerable amount of his fiction does fit into this category, London's best is something more than "a transcript of solitary nightmares": it is the artistic modulation of universal dreams—*i.e.,* of myths and archetypes. (pp. 56-7)

"A great work of art is like a dream," explains Carl Jung in *Modern Man in Search of a Soul;* "for all its apparent obviousness it does not explain itself and is never unequivocal. A dream never says: 'You ought,' or 'This is the truth.' It presents an image in much the same way as nature allows a plant to grow, and we must draw our own conclusions." In his essay "Psychology and Literature" Jung draws a sharp line between the fundamental approaches of the artist: the "psychological mode" and the "visionary mode." The former, rational and objective, always takes its materials from the vast realm of conscious human experience. . . . (p. 57)

[The] visionary mode derives its materials from what Jung calls the "collective unconscious": the deep psychological reservoir of "racial memories" that transcend both personal consciousness and the individual unconsciousness—or, as he explains, "a certain psychic disposition shaped by the forces of heredity [from which] consciousness has developed."

Because the language of normal discourse is inadequate to express such visions, the artist must resort to the metaphorical language of symbol and myth. . . . The work of the visionary artist will therefore be informed by what Jung elsewhere calls "archetypes": symbols of such transcendent and universal force that they would seem to be instinctual predispositions toward certain forms of psychic response rather than simple conditioned or learned responses. (p. 58)

One of the many ironies of Jack London's career is that he thought of himself as a thoroughly professional craftsman working quite consciously in what Jung would have termed the "psychological mode"; but, while most of his works can be superficially thus categorized, those with the most enduring force derive their potency from his instinctive mythopoeic vision. Readily apparent in the great fiction like **"To Build a Fire"** and *The Call of the Wild,* evidence of the visionary and mythic may be traced throughout the Northland Saga. In an obscure tale like **"In the Forests of the North,"** for example, the hero is described as undergoing a "weary journey beyond the last scrub timber and straggling copses, into the heart of the Barrens. . . . the bad lands of the Arctic, the deserts of the Circle, the bleak and bitter home of the musk-ox and lean plains wolf." . . . Long journeys far beyond the last outposts of civilization that penetrate into the great blank places—mysterious quests deep into the *urwelt,* the elder world of racial memories beyond space and time—form the recurrent pattern of the Northland Saga; and even the unimaginative reader may sense that such journeys reach beyond the material world.

"In the saga," Mircea Eliade explains, "the hero is placed in a world governed by the gods and fate." In this same world London has placed his sourdoughs, Indians, and *chechaquos;* and the ruling gods are not flatly indifferent ones like the typical deities of Naturalistic literature; they are actively hostile and sometimes vengeful. In dramatizing these forces London's vision is essentially primordial rather than logical or "psychological," and the mode of his fiction is often symbolic rather than discursive. At his best, he reaches the level of other great American symbolists like Poe, Hawthorne, and Melville; and his primitive sensitivity to archetypes gives him a special affinity to Melville. (pp. 58-9)

In his brilliant study of the symbolic mode in primitivism, James Baird identifies the "authentic primitivist" as an extreme individualist, as "the egoist-romanticist, as Santayana has described him . . . who 'disowns all authority save that mysteriously exercised over him by his deep faith in himself,' " . . . a man who will "entertain the idea of God in every form" and who will demonstrate "the custom of making symbols for the meaning of his own existence before a God whose nature he sees as inscrutable." Sensing that the traditional symbols of his spiritually impoverished civilization have lost their potency, the primitivist will attempt to replace these with symbols derived from his own personal experience and from "the richest and least exhaustible alien cultures," particularly those of Polynesia and the Orient: "The symbolist's awareness of cultural failure becomes *atavism*, reversion, thoroughly dependent upon feeling, to the past in search for a prototypic culture. This atavism . . . permits the use of archetypal concepts in the making of new and 'personal' religious symbols."

This definition applies to Jack London as well as to Herman Melville. For all London's insistence on Realism, he was a blatant Romantic and an arrogant, inner-directed egoist with a profound faith in his own resources, who lived life as if it were "an absolute personal experiment." Born into an age when the larger religious structures of Western Civilization were tottering, and reared in a home without any formal religious orientation, London gravitated logically toward the secular doctrines of Karl Marx and Herbert Spencer; and he described himself as a revolutionary Socialist and as a materialistic monist. In theory, he generally managed to remain true to these faiths; in practice, however, he demonstrated time and again that he was an individualist and a dualist. And an instinctive mysticism, not a logical positivism, dominates his Northland fiction. An example is the following passage from **"The White Silence,"** the first story in *The Son of the Wolf*:

> The afternoon wore on, and with the awe, born of the White Silence, the voiceless travelers bent to their work. Nature has many tricks wherewith she convinces man of his finity,—the ceaseless flow of the tides, the fury of the storm, the shock of the earthquake, the long roll of heaven's artillery,—but the most tremendous, the most stupefying of all, is the passive phase of the White Silence. All movement ceases, the sky clears, the heavens are as brass; the slightest whisper seems sacrilege, and man becomes timid, affrighted at the sound of his own voice. . . . Strange thoughts arise unsummoned, and the mystery of all things strives for utterance. And the fear of death, of God, of the universe, comes over him,—the hope of the Resurrection and the Life, the yearning for immortality, the vain striving of the imprisoned essence,—it is then, if ever, man walks alone with God.

London's Northland Deity, like the "inscrutable tides of God" in Melville's *Moby-Dick,* is the polar opposite of the philanthropic God-in-Nature celebrated by such sentimental "exoticists" as Jean Jacques Rousseau and François René de Chateaubriand.

Furthermore, in conveying the awesome ruthlessness of this deity, London drew his metaphors from the same mythic stockpile that Melville had used a half-century before him. Melville had fashioned his own unique metaphor, or "autotype," by combining two archetypes: the *fish,* an ancient life-symbol of divine creative force and wisdom, and *whiteness,* the emblematic all-color of universal mystery and the metonymy for an impersonal, incomprehensible deity of infinite paradoxes and incommunicable truth. (pp. 60-1)

But where Melville had combined whiteness with the fish, an archetype of creation and the life-force, London fused it with images of space, silence, and cold—and he thereby created an autotype more subtly terrifying than the warm-blooded whale. . . . Cuthfert in **"In a Far Country"** is reduced to craven depression by "the ghastly silence [of] the solemn forest which seemed to guard an awful inexpressible something, which neither word nor thought could compass." . . . London's White Silence is not merely a convenient setting for adventurous plots; it emerges as a dramatic antagonist charged with the special potency of universal dream symbolism—that is, of myth.

This potency is displayed nowhere to better advantage than in **"To Build a Fire,"** a masterpiece of short fiction which has become one of the most widely anthologized works ever produced by an American author. The central motif is simple enough, as London himself suggested: "Man after man in the Klondike has died alone after getting his feet wet, through failure to build a fire." Plot and characterization are equally uncomplicated: a nameless *chechaquo* (newcomer to the Northland), accompanied by a large husky, is taking a day's hike across the frozen wilderness to join his partners at their mining claim. Although he has been warned by the old-timers against traveling alone in the White Silence, he, a strong, practical man, is confident of his ability to cope with the forces of nature. Yet we sense from the outset that he is doomed. . . . (pp. 62-3)

The key to the story's impact is not plot, but—as in much of London's best work—mood and atmosphere, which is conveyed through repetitive imagery of cold and gloom and whiteness. . . . (p. 63)

London's story manifests in its stark eloquence many of those same elements that Aristotle indicated in his *Poetics* as requisite to tragedy. It is a representation of an action that is serious, whole, complete, and of a certain magnitude. The action is rigorously unified, taking place between daybreak and nightfall. The protagonist, neither an especially good man nor an especially bad man, falls into misfortune because of a tragic flaw, notably hubris: an overweening confidence in the efficacy of his own rational faculties and a corresponding blindness to the dark, nonrational powers of nature, chance, and fate—

> But all of this—the mysterious, far-reaching hairline trail, the absence of sun from the sky, the tremendous cold, and the strangeness and weirdness of it all—made no impression on the man. . . . He was quick and alert in the things of life, but only in the things, and not in the significances. Fifty degrees below zero meant eighty-odd degrees of frost. Such fact impressed him as being cold and uncomfortable, and that was all. . . .

Here, as throughout the story, the narrator functions as the chorus, who mediates between the action and the reader and who provides moral commentary upon the action. The setting, a mask of the scornful gods, functions as antagonist. Aside from these, the only other character is the dog, who acts as foil or "reflector" by displaying the humility and natural wisdom which the man fatally lacks. . . . (pp. 63-4)

Also in keeping with the tragic mode is the sense of inevitability in the catastrophe which must befall the hero. Even when he builds his first fire for lunch, we know that the reprieve is temporary: "For the moment the cold of space was outwitted." There is no doubt in our suspense, only a dreadful waiting for the disaster. "And then it happened": the curt announcement is almost a relief. Still, knowing the cruel irony of the gods, we sense that although the man must surely die, he will first be mocked in his delusion of security. The man himself does not know this of course, but he does know the gravity of his situation. Having broken through the snow crust over a hidden spring and having wet his legs halfway to the knees, he realizes he must immediately build a fire. . . . (pp. 64-5)

[Later, the] man, working rationally and carefully, manages to build his fire and believes himself safe. . . . The irony is dramatic as well as tragic.

"Tragedy," according to Aristotle, "is a representation of an action that is not only complete but that consists of events inspiring fear and pity; and this effect is best produced when the events are at once unexpected and causally related." Moreover, the greatest tragedies are complex: the catastrophe is attended by a sudden reversal in the hero's situation to its opposite and by a discovery, or a change from ignorance to knowledge. . . . (p. 65)

Being human and therefore fallible, London's protagonist makes a simple, human mistake: he builds his fire under a large, snow-laden spruce tree; and the heat precipitates a small avalanche that blots out the fresh blaze. Reversal and discovery are virtually simultaneous: "The man was shocked. It was as though he had just heard his own sentence of death." . . . (pp. 65-6)

From this dramatic climax, the story moves through a brilliant dénouement toward its inescapable conclusion. Fighting off panic, the man tries vainly to build another fire; but his fingers are already dead from the cold. Next, he tries ineffectually to kill the dog, thinking he can warm his hands in its body. Then, panic-stricken, he tries running on his frozen feet until he falls exhausted into the snow. Finally, he grows calm and decides to meet death with dignity. . . . In thus resigning himself to his fate, the man achieves true heroic stature; and his tragic action inspires both pity and fear in leading his audience toward the cathartic relief prescribed by Aristotle. (p. 66)

"To Build a Fire" has established itself as a world classic, and while it is instructive to see how much of Aristotle's formula is dramatically reflected in this remarkable work of short fiction, we should realize that the story's greatness does not depend on this formal coincidence and that London himself was probably unaware of these nice parallels with Greek tragedy. The story is great because it derives its informing power from the common mystery that animates the plays of Sophocles and Aeschylus—and all great tragedians—and because it has articulated this mystery with such force that we become mutual participants in the celebration of what Joseph Conrad called "the unavoidable solidarity" of our human destiny. The ultimate source of tragedy is, as Herbert Muller points out, the simple fact that man must die; the great wonder is that, being the one animal who knows this fact, man is still capable of achieving dignity. So long as he possesses this heroic capability, "all is not vanity." (p. 67)

Earle Labor, in his Jack London, *Twayne Publishers, Inc., 1974, 179 p.*

JAMES I. McCLINTOCK (essay date 1975)

[*In his critical study* White Logic: Jack London's Short Stories, *McClintock examines the themes, motifs, and techniques of London's short fiction. In the following excerpt from that book, McClintock affirms death and violence as viable themes for London's tragic concerns and contends that the author's characters move from a belief in rationality or moral codes in the early works toward an awareness of the nonrational and fallible aspects of humanity in later stories, reflecting London's own changing world view.*]

[The] fundamental philosophical assumption behind the characterization of the Malemute Kid as he is presented in **"The Men of Forty-Mile," "The Priestly Prerogative,"** and **"The Wife of a King,"** the least artistic of the stories in *The Son of the Wolf,* is that man can master his fate by rationally comprehending the ways of men and the cosmos. He is at home in the "new land," a citizen of the Northland, and can "see it all around." He is a protector of the American Dream.

Most casual critics and some London scholars discuss the entire London canon of fiction as if, at its base, it merely reflects the American Dream that all inevitably leads to individual mastery and social perfection. For them the idealized Malemute Kid must represent the most important aspects of London's thought and fiction. (p. 79)

The condescension exhibited by such commentators is not wholly unjustified when discussing London's weaker fiction, but it has occupied too prominent a place in London criticism. For the triumphant Malemute Kid disappears early in 1899 from London's fiction, and birth is given to a new Kid, the one in **"The White Silence"** and **"An Odyssey of the North,"** who receives a terrifying glimpse of human finitude. After this revelation, the hero as completed and masterful man is no longer possible and the limited, code-practicing protagonist takes London's stage. Pessimism is the pervasive mood of *The Son of the Wolf;* pessimism, rather than optimism, sponsored the major themes of his stories from the beginning of his career. To **"The White Silence"** and **"An Odyssey of the North"** can be added two more excellent tales from *The Son of the Wolf*—**"The Wisdom of the Trail"** and **"In a Far Country"**—making in a collection of nine, four superior stories which deny the American Dream of drifting optimistically towards perfection. They present the nightmare of "things greater than our wisdom" which suggest tragedy, horror, irrationality and human impotence.

Rather than portraying characters who master themselves and their environments, London depicted them either reaching an uneasy accommodation with internal and external forces or being destroyed by them. In the best stories in *The Son of the Wolf* and the following collections, indifferent or even sadistically irrational forces inhibit man's puny efforts to control his fate; they are not man-oriented or man-controlled. Rather than nineteenth century preoccupations, London engaged twentieth century concerns: alienation, disenchantment, ironic ambivalence, and impotence. Early in his career he began to compose excellent stories within this pessimistic context and continued for ten years.

Although he wrote and published short stories from 1898 until his death in 1916, most of what are judged his superior stories were written in a ten year period between the fall of 1898 and the spring of 1909, when he stopped for a variety of personal reasons. During this decade he wrote stories which were eventually collected into the six volumes of Alaskan tales that established his fame then and continue it now: *The Son of the Wolf* (1898-99), *The God of His Fathers* (1900-01), *Children of the Frost* (1900-02), *The Faith of Men* (1901-03, but primarily 1903), *Love of Life* (1904-06) and

Lost Face (1905-08). The height of London's technical and thematic achievement is recorded in these six volumes of Alaskan stories. The "socialist" stories, the other group of tales upon which London's literary and popular fame rests, were also written during this decade, but they were written primarily during 1906 and 1907. The most important collection of these is **The Strength of the Strong.** In addition to the Northland and socialist stories, this ten year period also saw the composition of two volumes of tales set in a South Seas locale: **South Seas Tales** and **House of Pride** (written by 1908). The order of these three groups of short stories is not merely chronological; it also indicates a pattern of decline— the Northland stories are often excellent, the socialist and South Seas tales rarely as good.

The encounter of limited man with a mysterious cosmos, an encounter which defines the limits of rationality, is the major theme of London's best fiction. London continually readjusts the boundary between the rational and the suprarational: from the intuitive and rational Kid living in an imaginatively and rationally comprehensible universe, London begins to portray protagonists who live by various kinds of laws which they apply to the knowable parts of their existence while being aware of the ultimately unknowable and incomprehensible nature of life. At first these limited characters find some way to maintain identity; but eventually, the characters participate with, or are crushed by, the nonrational. London finally portrays protagonists who become victims of the irrational elements in the unknowable because there is no law which affords protection. This pattern of readjustments by limited characters to the "Unknown" is the dynamic thematic principle which gives life to London's finest short stories.

In the Malemute Kid stories that emphasize rationality, control and mastery, the poetic landscape of the "white silence" plays no integral part in the fates of the characters; in fact, it is almost unmentioned. In the best stories, the reverse is true and the landscape is constantly crushing in upon the characters' consciousness. That the stories which evoke the mythic wasteland are the same in which the protagonists fail to "see it all around" is no accident; for, as has been mentioned, the Alaskan landscape symbolizes the unchartered land of the spirit where man must confront but can not conquer the supra-rational if he is to experience life fully. . . . [London] was torn between the "greatness and the littleness of the human intellect . . . its power [and] its impotence." This is the lesson of [what he termed] the "white silence." . . . The Northland landscape is the "unknowable" which can not be comprehended through positivistic logic and must be evoked symbolically and poetically. . . . Again and again, London's best protagonists move into the unchartered, unknown land and experience awe, mystery and terror that arise spontaneously as the landscape speaks to them symbolically. The characters are compelled to confront the mysterious unknown and to learn either how to live amidst it or to perish. Like an aspect of mind, destructive forces cannot be escaped nor conquered. (pp. 80-3)

That the Unknowable is not completely accessible to logic is a sub-theme in both **"The White Silence"** and **"An Odyssey of the North."** While [in **"The White Silence"**], the Kid analyzes the alternatives he confronts when Mason is injured, he must consider the inevitability of his and Ruth's deaths as well as Mason's. He considers the logic of the crisis: "In the abstract, it was a plain mathematic proposition,—three possible lives against one doomed one" (the third is Mason's un-

born child). A sense of brotherhood makes him hesitate, but finally he acts in accord with the "mathematic proposition," with reason, and shoots Mason. The man of reason has killed rationally, but rather than mastery and conquest, the consequence is ambiguous. He has preserved his life, Ruth's and the unborn child's. But as important, he ironically has discovered the limits of his power, the limits of logic. The symbolic unknown has been brooding behind the events, and as he acts rationally, he experiences terror as the White silence "sneers." The non-rational unknown teaches the Kid the lesson that he is limited. Although he acts logically, he is aware that his action forces him to cross a boundary between rationality and a threatening non-rationality. Similarly in **"An Odyssey"** reason, legality in this case, tells Prince that Naass's slaying of Unga and Axel convicts Naass of murder. But the Kid intervenes with his observation that "there be things greater than our wisdom" that necessitate violence and killing. Why is beyond explanation. Even Naass, the killer, has discovered that premeditation has not led to mastery and that the personal implications of his actions are unclear. He senses that he can neither submit himself to the law for judgment (only the possibility that they will hang him and he "will sleep good" appeals to him) nor return to his native village and live on "the edge of the world." Neither the civilized nor the primitive, the rational nor the instinctual or nonrational, provide solace. Both are necessary components of the internal and external worlds, but even together they yield no completely satisfactory basis for action nor for understanding the consequences of action. At the end of the story, Naass remains undecided and confused. . . . (pp. 83-4)

The impotence of rationality when confronting the unknown in effect demands that London turn to violence and death. Only in death is there finality, and only in non-rational action can one identify himself with his environment. The "unknowable" symbolized by the Alaskan landscape is organically linked with violence and death. It is significant that in the stories that portray the Kid as master and conqueror not only is there no artistic evocation of the landscape, but no death either by murder or by accident. But in **"The White Silence"** and **"An Odyssey"** death is the basic experience which raises the crucial issue of the limits of man's powers in the unknown. Death is at the center of almost all of London's important stories. Placed in a crisis situation without comforting landmarks, the protagonist defines the border between the rational and the supra-rational, the known and the unknown, by acting violently. (pp. 84-5)

The predominance of death and violence in London's short stories disturbed some of the early critics who rejected him as a sensationalist, and very few later critics have realized that through violence London was probing experiences neglected by his contemporaries. Moreover, he probed with an integrity, sincerity and insight rarely associated with him. (p. 85)

The introduction of violence and death coupled with the unknown into London's fiction has important artistic consequences: it demands limited characters who can not predict all the implications of their actions nor understand all their consequences; the supra-rational is wedded to the rational and mystery to the known; tragedy rather than comedy becomes the mode; irony rather than a confident certainty becomes the mood.

"The Wisdom of the Trail" contains the elements that go into one kind of excellent London story: a limited protagonist ventures into the unknown; he lives by a code that permits, even demands, that he kill; and death tragically and ironically defines the fluid boundary between rationality and the threatening supra-rational.

[In **"The Wisdom of the Trail"**], Sitka Charlie, the Siwash Indian protagonist, who is the "sheer master of reality" in **"The Sun-Dog Trail,"** contracts with Captain and Mrs. Eppingwell to "go beyond the pale of the honor and the law" by undertaking "an unknown journey through the dismal vastness of the Northland." . . . The story opens on the trail, and Charlie has become the guide because he has the "wisdom of the trail" lacking in two other Indians, Kah-Chucte and Gowhee. . . . Charlie, uncertain of [the party's] exact location (he does not suffer a damning hubris about the unknown), knows that they have passed the "Hills of Silence" and are moving towards the Yukon River. His "wisdom" means more than a knowledge of geography however; it also means that he knows that "honor and law" are what precariously separate men from annihilation. He is a code hero. Tortured by the trail, Kah-Chucte and Gowhee break honor and law by stopping to rest and stealing a little, but life-sustaining, flour from the provisions. Charlie reminds them that they had contracted to live by the law, passes the judgment, and shoots them. Immediately afterwards he hears other shots that indicate that the travelers have reached the safety of the Yukon settlement.

The story invokes the mythic powers of the unknown that threaten tragically to destroy worthy individuals. Like the lesser characters on this ritualistic journey to confront the dangerous but fascinating unknown, Charlie has little notion of where he is and, at the end, is surprised to learn that he has reached safety. . . . Charlie survives for two reasons: The first, the will to live, he shares with the others since in all men "the ego seemed almost bursting forth with its old cry, 'I, I want to exist!' the dominant note of the whole living universe." The second, which he shares only with Captain and Mrs. Eppingwell, is that he is a code hero who lives by the "honor and the law" that "forbade a mighty longing to sit by the fire and tend his complaining flesh." This law demands that he be willing to kill coldly, lucidly, in order to maintain his dignity, control and life. What the code does is to give some certainty, some internal logic to human relationships. Without the law, chance rules and the human community dissolves into competing individuals who will not only destroy one another, but themselves as well. The code is an artificial, sometimes inhumane, order imposed upon the rationally unknowable cosmic condition and replaces, in London's fiction, individual, logical comprehension of an orderly universe.

The ending of **"The Wisdom of the Trail,"** like the endings of **"The White Silence"** and **"An Odyssey of the North,"** is an important turning point in London's fiction because it is ironic. A simple kind of dramatic irony is discernible in a story like **"The Men of Forty-Mile"** or **"The Wife of a King"** since the audience is privy to a joke upon one of the principals. Tragic irony is, however, impossible because the central consciousness in such stories has the power to restore order so that all is eventually resolved comically. But in **"The Wisdom of the Trail,"** even the best human is limited, permitting a more mature irony. The rigid, but orderly code, representing the zenith of man's control over himself and his environment, like the men who practice it, is not perfect. On the symbolic level, the code killing at the end and climax of the story

London in his study during the latter stages of his career.

brings salvation. The ritualistic murder purges the destructive element in man and "magically" Charlie and the Eppingwells discover that they have endured long enough to escape the white silence and find "the Men of the Yukon." Ironically and tragically, it is killing that brings life. But it is also the sign of tragic limitations in man and code. The code provides man with a way to exist, but not with a way to "see it all around." Charlie, practicing the code, discovers that the execution of the two Indians was unnecessary. Since the code is practiced not for sadistically punitive reasons, but, instead, to preserve life, it is tragically ironic that safety had been reached without the execution. Charlie's limited nature permits this irony and tragedy. But because he is aware of his limitations, represented by his miscalculation, and aware of the ironical and tragic quality of life, Charlie experiences no remorse. He accepts the situation because he has made a partially successful accommodation with the unknown and assumes that violence is unavoidable: He can "smile viciously at the wisdom of the trail" because he recognizes that violence and evil are inherent in nature. (pp. 85-8)

"In a Far Country," also in [*The Son of the Wolf*], concentrates on the grotesque misery in life; and in it, London attempts to reinforce his code premise by reversing the coin. London means to portray what happens when two men, Carter Weatherbee and Percy Cuthfert, face the unknown without the code. He intends these two to be deficients since they lack heroic qualities available to them. However, within the story there is an unintentional shift of emphasis that unveils a far deeper pessimism than revealed in any previous story. The malign, irrational powers of the cosmos are so predominant and so destructive that they make codes ludicrous attempts at self-deception. The basic irony of life found in . . .

"The Wisdom of the Trail" is resolved because life is no longer dear. In this story London explores the irrational demands made by the unknown and, implicitly, concludes that the deficient man in the beginning of the story is really the best he can be, a limited man. "Limited" and "deficient" become synonymous terms. The major part of the story becomes a parody of what London has claimed for the ritual journey into the unknown and for the practice of the code which demands love, imagination, and, sometimes, ritual killing in order to give a measure of dignity to limited human beings.

The story begins as if it were to be an exemplum for a text about Darwinian adaptability separating the fit from the unfit. Jacques Baptiste and Sloper are fit men who live by the code. They contract to guide the "Incapables" or deficients, Weatherbee and Cuthfert, into "the Unknown Lands" and begin the "arduous up-stream toil" of the long trail. But the two deficients refuse to meet the hardships of the trail and decide to remain during the heart of winter in a remote cabin. The rest and most important part of the story is an account of Weatherbee's and Cuthfert's physical and mental deterioration which climaxes in their killing one another.

Together, the two Incapables represent a perversion of the ideal man of reason and imagination: Weatherbee has the doggedly pedestrian and literal mind of an ex-clerk, and Cuthfert possesses a sentimental dilettante's imagination "which mistook . . . the true spirit of romance and adventure." They follow "civilized" codes of behavior and are unequipped, therefore, to confront the demands of the unknown as would Charlie or the Kid by exercising comradeship and discipline. So in the depths of winter, in *terra incognita,* without the protection of the rational-imaginative man's code as a buffer between life and death, they are vulnerable to the message and power of the "white logic." Defenseless as they are, the central power and interest in the story becomes the unknown and its death-dealing attributes. (pp. 89-90)

Fear inspired by the unknown causes the unimaginative Weatherbee to hallucinate men rising from two graves beside the cabin who tell him of their suffering. Death and suggestions of death continue to pervade the story. But it is through the imaginative man, Cuthfert, that the nature of the unknown is revealed. . . . Without the aid of the code to protect him, the message of the white logic captures his spirit. . . . (pp. 90-1)

Cuthfert's discovery that life is an illusion is captured in a passage that typifies some of London's most suggestive prose:

> Once, like another Crusoe, by the edge of the river he came upon a track,—the faint tracery of a snow-shoe rabbit on the delicate snow-crust. It was a revelation. There was life in the Northland. He could follow it, look upon it, gloat over it. He forgot his swollen muscles, plunging through the deep snow in an ecstasy of anticipation. The forest swallowed him up, and the brief midday twilight vanished; but he pursued his quest till exhausted nature asserted itself and laid him helpless in the snow. There he groaned and cursed his folly, and knew the track to be the fancy of his brain; and late that night he dragged himself into the cabin on hands and knees, his cheeks frozen and a strange numbness about his feet. A week later mortification set in.

This passage is a parody of the archetypal quest motif in London's other stories. Rather than to accommodation or mas-

tery, this quest leads to disillusionment. Archetypally, man wants to explore and discover (like Crusoe) and ecstatically follows a faint trail, despite the agonies of the flesh, so that he can affirm life. He enters the wilderness and passes the brief day of his life. At the end of the brief span, he loses his illusions and learns that life has been a cheat, and he is filled with an agonizing self-mockery. Exhausted, disillusioned, he senses his imminent death.

Cuthfert possesses London's third and final kind of imagination, the "thrice cursed gift of imagination." This kind of imaginative man does not "see it all around" so that he cannot act constructively, nor does he "understand the ways of the northland so sympathetically that he can anticipate its emergencies before they occur, always adapting himself to nature's laws." Instead, this imagination fills him with "soul-sickness, life sickness." . . . This is the imagination that allows London's limited and deficient characters to merge. The code, the law and the honor, are merely life-giving lies, frauds, tricks to avoid recognizing that life is a mockery and death and pain the reality. Cuthfert, despite the contempt with which London surrounds him in the opening of the story, perceives truths that make the basis of that contempt inoperative. Cuthfert is everyman; instead of being deficient, he turns out to be limited, the best that men can be. And the fundamental qualities of his life and eventual death are grotesquery, malevolency, degeneracy and insanity.

The end of the story is an ironic and grotesque parody of London's other stories that use the ritualistic killing to ennoble both killer and victim. Weatherbee, gone mad, approaches Cuthfert with an axe. . . . Cuthfert shoots him in the face, but Weatherbee swings the axe which "bit deeply at the base of the spine, and Percy Cuthfert felt all consciousness of his lower limbs leave him." They fall together in a final clinch, an image that ironically recalls to the reader the embrace of tender fellowship described two pages earlier and, more generally, London's emphasis upon comradeship as part of the code in other stories. This double killing, described in terms of lucid, rational action, does not ennoble. Instead, it is grotesque. . . . The disappearance of Baptiste and Sloper in the beginning of the story, despite London's intention, symbolizes the death of the code as anything more than a system of illusions.

In "In a Far Country," then, London explicitly attempts to reaffirm the necessity of the code, but implicitly he denies the efficacy of a code in the face of the message revealed to Cuthfert. London wanted desperately to announce the revitalizing nature of "true adventure" and intended to satirize the enervating effects of civilization upon Weatherbee and Cuthfert who were unequipped to live according to new laws demanded by the new land; but he found this impossible. Eagerness to believe succumbs to the impossibility of belief. Not only has mastery become impossible, but accommodation as well. . . . The stories which follow "In a Far Country" eventually make explicit its implicit concerns: *The God of His Fathers, Children of the Frost, The Faith of Men, Love of Life* and *Lost Face* pursue the nature of the code or the "law" as London makes a series of adjustments to the terrifying insights in "In a Far Country." No adjustment, however, could prevent him from coming to the edge of the abyss.

The Son of the Wolf collection of stories written in 1898 and 1899, in summary, has a range of talent and depth of insight unexpected in a first volume of short stories. Against a Northland landscape, poetically invoked because it is a symbol of the unknown which lies beyond factual, logical comprehension and control, characters actively explore the dimensions of their internal and external worlds. London dramatizes a mythic encounter with the tragedy that man's most highly prized attributes are merely self-sustaining illusions which cannot protect him from the terrifying suspicion that life is empty of significance and the irony that the best man's clearest thoughts and most purposeful actions have ambiguous consequences. Forced to live on the edge of annihilation and to participate in violence, code practicing protagonists act violently, even kill, so that they can revitalize the spirit of adventure and experience [and self-sufficiency]. . . . But finally, as in **"In a Far Country,"** the code is inoperable and characters kill because they are linked to a destructive cosmic evil which demands death and violence.

The importance of London's achievement in *The Son of the Wolf* and his independence from popular tastes can be appreciated, perhaps, when it is pointed out that W. M. Frohock in *The Novel of Violence in America* concludes that the treatment of violence by writers of the twenties, thirties and forties is the distinguishing mark of twentieth century American fiction. His generalizations about the elements of this fiction reveal London's originality as he labored in the first decade of this century. "At their best," Forhock writes, "these tragic novels . . . conceive of violence as the characteristic mark of the human, and acts of violence themselves are performed with great lucidity." . . . [London's best stories] join content and form artistically. Characters, in a crisis situation, kill or act violently but "lucidly" and, thereby, expand their conceptions of self and their connections with the cosmos. (pp. 91-5)

Although London's second collection of Alaskan stories, *The God of His Fathers* containing stories written during 1900 and 1901, continues the author's concern with violence, horror, the code and the unknown, it is generally inferior to *The Son of the Wolf*. **"Grit of Women,"** . . . despite its virtues, suffers slightly from a sentimental treatment of women that more seriously mars **"Siwash,"** another Sitka Charlie story, and **"The Great Interrogation."** This last story, like **"Which Makes Men Remember,"** **"Where the Trail Forks,"** **"A Daughter of the Aurora"** and **"At the Rainbow's End,"** all in the same volume, is flawed by thematic confusion. For example, in both **"The Great Interrogation"** and **"Where the Trail Forks"** the white protagonists' motives for kindness towards Indians are unclear—do they sacrifice themselves because they love and appreciate for themselves the good qualities of these women or do they merely act chivalrously as "white men"? Social comedy, like that found in the clumsy **"The Wife of a King,"** is resurrected in **"The Scorn of Women"** and given a perverse twist in **"A Daughter of the Aurora."** . . . **"Jan the Unrepentant"** is another **"The Men of Forty-Mile"** in its portrayal of comic violence erupting among isolated miners; but like most of these stories which have a parallel in *The Son of the Wolf*, it is more cynical about human nature. In [*The God of His Fathers*], too, there is less emphasis upon the demands of the mythic unknown and more upon the demands of the "law" of Anglo-Saxon race supremacy. Generally, then, this volume lacks the stature of its predecessor because of its recurrent appeals to sentimentality and adolescent humor, its thematic confusion and its use of race theory as an explanation for motive and action.

The title story of *The God of His Fathers* does, however, represent an important transition linking the best stories in *The Son of the Wolf* with the best stories in *Children of the Frost*,

London's third and, perhaps, finest collection. **"The God of His Fathers"** is an attempt to deny the implications of **"In a Far Country"** but without returning to the use of the personal code. London attempts a return to the theme of mastery by emphasizing a new law—race supremacy.

The story is set in the Northland's "forest primeval" at "the moment when the stone age was drawing to a close." Hay Stockard, his Indian wife and child, and Bill, his companion gold-seeker, are in an Indian camp attempting to get an assurance from Baptiste the Red, an independent, dignified but hostile half-breed chief, that his tribe will not molest them in the quest up the unchartered Koyukuk River. They are joined by another white man, Sturgis Owen, a self-righteous and fanatical priest. Baptiste the Red refuses to let them pass unless they renounce the Christian God whom he hates because priests had refused to legitimatize his birth, to solemnize his marriage to a white woman, and to punish the Factor who raped and killed Baptiste's daughter. Sturgis Owen refuses to blaspheme, and out of race pride the non-religious Stockard refuses to turn over the missionary to torture. A bloody battle results, at the end of which the missionary recants to save his life and Hay Stockard is killed, a martyr to the "God of his fathers,"—his race.

This is the first of London's stories in which race is the dominant theme. Race is the true God. . . . (pp. 95-6)

The story is sententiously phrased and loosely structured; nevertheless, it is significant in the development of London's major themes. Earlier, as has been shown, London had written poor stories attempting to show the mastery of the individual in an orderly cosmos; then, because of a deepening pessimism suggesting a more complex view of reality, he had written more probing stories using more artistic control in which limited protagonists like Sitka Charlie reached an accommodation with a hostile, chaotic cosmos by living by an imposed code; finally, he recorded the failure of individual accommodation in **"In a Far Country."** Having found individual identity impossible to integrate, London turns to race identification, a blood brotherhood, in **"The God of His Fathers"** and, thereby, returns to the theme of mastery. His pessimism is held in temporary abeyance. The individual human may be weak, but law and order are restored to the cosmos and link man (white men, at least) with nature. After the collapse of the powers of reason and imagination in **"In a Far Country,"** London now romantically asserts a unity beyond the appearance of flux. This time, however, his optimism depends upon mastery achieved by the aggregate rather than the individual. (p. 97)

Literarily, race theory had the advantage of allowing London to continue some of his best practices. He did not have to yield his concept of the limited individual. . . . Characters like Stockard, a blasphemous, adulterous, violent man, could serve the inevitable law which, ironically, demands that he support the fanatical Sturgis Owen and attack the more noble Indian, Baptiste the Red. Moreover, by means of race theory, London's impulse towards power and mastery could be joined with his sense of insignificance and powerlessness since all individuals are impotent participants in the working out of the inexorable natural law. . . .

However, the race theory has disadvantages as well. The protagonists, whom London means to be positively received, often degenerate into brutal fascists, especially when London's racism is less consciously used than in **"The God of His Fathers."** (p. 98)

Fortunately, the "unimaginative" white protagonist who carries out the dictates of his heredity by inflicting personal and social injustices is not often a positively portrayed hero in London's Northland short stories. There is injustice, but since London's more responsive emotional and philosophical milieu was a tragic and ironic sense of failure, his artistic efforts are more often sympathetic with the, albeit "inevitable," despair of the Indians who suffer at the hands of the white invaders. London might write that a white "unimaginative man" (in the sense that he is indifferent to and unaware of the human values of non-whites) is the ideal and that "we must come to understand that nature has no sentiment, no charity, no mercy" . . . but his Northland Indian stories in **Children of the Frost** show London, himself, "imaginative," "sentimental," "charitable," and "merciful."

The stories collected in **Children of the Frost** were composed from 1900 to 1902 at the same time London was writing those collected in **The God of His Fathers;** but they are more dramatic, mythic, tragic and ironic, a continuation of the best in **The Son of the Wolf.** Despite Earle Labor's claim that "most of the stories are mediocre in artistry," **"The League of Old Men"** and **"Keesh, the Son of Keesh,"** although sometimes too discursive, rise above some structural awkwardness by evoking the epic struggle of the individual rebelling against the demands of social and cosmic law and compare favorably with **"The White Silence"** and **"An Odyssey of the North." "The Death of Ligoun," "The Sickness of Lone Chief"** and **"The Law of Life"** are dramatically and economically written and capitalize upon the mellifluous style arising from the dignified language London associated with Indian speech. Technical flaws are not difficult to uncover; however, these stories were written at the height of London's apprenticeship in short story technique and theory. This means, for example, that this volume avoids the essay-exemplum form and concentrates on more dramatic forms. (pp. 99-100)

Although he would write other excellent stories, no single volume of short stories is as consistent in quality of artistry and control of theme as **Children of the Frost.** . . . Because of the Indian point of view, the special pleading and exhortations found in earlier stories are curtailed and the demand for ideal characters is diminished. . . . The Indians in all of these stories had possessed all that London's white conquerors came to the Northland to find: individual dignity, courage, contact with and adjustment to the elemental strength of nature, and a sense of community within the tribe. Such a theme was compatible with London's emotional gestalt and could be handled with a consistency unmatched in even the best stories in the first two volumes which threatened to break apart upon the ambivalent requirements of mastery and failure. The Indians are limited protagonists who are victims of both cosmic and social laws. London returns to his theme that human values are tragically inappropriate, but redeeming, in a hostile cosmos. But eventually, he suggests that they are not even redemptive.

Hay Stockard in **"The God of His Fathers"** is a martyr for his race: his death, and the deaths of other white men, will be redemptive for the Anglo-Saxon race. **"The League of Old Men"** in **Children of the Frost** is a companion story since it too employs race martyrdom as the dramatic situation; however, the latter story has the power of tragedy, while the former only pathos. Unlike Stockard who is a contributor to group mastery, Old Imber the Indian protagonist is a social and cosmic rebel and martyr. (pp. 100-01)

[In **"The League of Old Men"**], Old Imber, the last of his kind, a "bronze patriot," remembers his Edenic youth when "the land was warm with sunshine and gladness" and when "men were men." Therefore, he organizes a band of old men to assassinate the white men who had brought whiskey, gambling, smallpox and tuberculosis and had taken away women and young men and turned them against tribal customs and honor. Because of his pride, Imber refuses to accept white culture and rebels against it, consequently rebelling against the cosmic law. The "old men departed up river and down to the unknown lands," where they murdered. Eventually, only Imber was left, and exhausted, "it being vain fighting the law," he surrenders to the police. It is both tragic and ironic that men like Imber who are courageous, loyal and intelligent must suffer and die at the hands of contemptible whites acting out nature's "law." Imber's martyrdom is moving and even suggests to the judge something like the "things greater than our wisdom, beyond our justice" at the end of **"An Odyssey."** Moreover, the tragedy of this story goes beyond the pathetic death of Stockard since Imber's rebellion against and final submission to social and cosmic injustice will not be redemptive; his nobility ends with his death. So, although the situation and underlying beliefs might be the same as in **"The God of His Fathers,"** the emphasis shifts from the Hay Stockards of the North to the Red Baptistes and Imbers, from a somber optimism to inevitable tragedy. London has invested his racial theme with the rhetoric of defeat and submission rather than conquest and triumph.

"Keesh, the Son of Keesh," is similar in theme to **"The League of Old Men"** since it dramatizes the loss of racial identity as the non-whites fall before their Anglo-Saxon superiors. But, contrary to the critics' usual response to this story, it is more than social criticism that reveals London's ambivalency towards non-whites; for the theme of loss in **Children of the Frost** is more than the loss of racial identity. The tragic loss is the death of London's previously held illusions that some code, some system of belief, some systematic description of reality, would redeem men from fear, violence, death and despair, or at least that the archetypal journey would yield a self-sustaining myth as a buffer between man and the terrors of a meaningless universe.

Keesh, a young chief of the Thlunget Indians left his tribe to be educated in the "higher morality" by Mr. Brown, a Christian missionary, and had learned that killing is immoral. Since this emasculates him in the eyes of other Indians and allies him with the white oppressors, he is denied the hand of Su-Su, the daughter of the chief of the Tananaws. She agrees to disobey her father if Keesh will "bring me, not scalps, but heads . . . three at least." At first loyal to his catechism, Keesh finally decides to "go to hell" and returns to Su-Su's camp. . . . There he murders Su-Su's father and three other men who spoke against him, decapitates them and then allows Su-Su to guess what he has wrapped in the moose hide. After she plays her coy and sexually exciting guessing game, he rolls the heads before her. . . . A dog sniffs at the head of Su-Su's father and raises a "long wolf-howl" as the girl bares her throat to Keesh's knife, ending the story.

There is social criticism in this story. In eloquent speeches, the men whom Keesh eventually murders list the injustices: whites had married Indian women, breaking the unity of the tribe; had degraded the men by making them do "squaw work"; and are driving the Indians from their land. More-over, the whites are hypocritical since, although they speak of killing as both criminal and immoral, they kill at will. As in **"The League of Old Men"** it is tragic and ironic to London that the dignified Indian had to give way to cultural pressures.

But the power of the story [**"Keesh, the Son of Keesh"**] goes beyond social criticism. It arises from the tension between conflicting codes or value systems, each of which is unable to sustain positive human values. Neither the white man's way of life nor the Indian's code of honor leads to an integration of the spirit; instead, the one is hypocritical and, metaphorically, will not permit Keesh the basic privileges of a wife, children and honor, and the other is inhumanely grotesque. Life has become a mechanical ritual for Keesh: he contracts to undergo an ordeal, a ritualistic task, which leads to nihilism. Although he performs perfectly and exhibits the kind of control that saves the Kid and Sitka Charlie, the contract is demonic and the tortured ritual ultimately meaningless so that he is neither damned nor saved. Rather than a synthesis of the two systems, all that links the white and the Indian codes are ugly emotions and grotesque violence. . . . As London begins to doubt "Laws," codes and other abstract systems of belief, he turns to a greater emphasis upon ugly physical details as the most meaningful facts of existence. (pp. 102-04)

The only law of life is the law of death. In the most economically, and dramatically conceived and written story in [*Children of the Frost*], **"The Law of Life,"** Old Koskoosh perceives this as he sits by the fire waiting the inevitable conclusion of life and recalls the basic lessons taught him by experience:

> Nature was not kindly to the flesh. She had no concern for that concrete thing called the individual. Her interest lay in the species, the race . . . Nature did not care. To life she set one task, gave one law. To perpetuate was the task of life, its law was death.

What dignity the old man retains arises from his ability to perceive this law and his stoical resignation to it, although terror threatens to undermine his composure. He has performed well, having sired a chief and perpetuated the race, but the performance is mere "task." His stoicism, too, is not totally redemptive because the law is merely descriptive and is not humanly satisfying or meaningful. The fundamental quality of life remains its savagery and terror.

In this story, London gives his metaphor of the human situation which shows how far he has travelled from the optimism of his earliest stories. It is the poetry of this story that discloses the horror, the nightmare of existence. Left to die as the snow begins to fall, armed with a few sticks of wood to feed the small fire, the blind Koskoosh remembers that in his youth he had seen an old Moose cut from the herd by wolves, surrounded by them and, finally, felled and torn apart. . . . As in other stories, London uses savage animals as a reminder of the bestial quality of life that threatens to break loose and overwhelm man. The dogs in **"The White Silence"** overcome Ruth's discipline, significantly just after Mason has been crushed by the tree; a sick wolf stalks the man in **"Love of Life"**; and in **"Batard"** the half savage dog is always waiting for the opportunity to kill his master. The moose-wolf analogy to the old man's situation in **"The Law of Life"** is as powerful in its simplicity and implications as it is obvious. And

London continues the parallel and ends the story by applying it directly to Koskoosh's situation:

> . . . a ring of crouching, jaw-slobbered grey was stretched round about. The old man listened to the drawing in of the circle. He waved his brand wildly, and sniffs turned to snarls; but the panting brutes refused to scatter. . . . Why should he cling to life? he asked, and dropped the blazing stick into the snow. It sizzled and went out. The circle grunted uneasily, but held its own. Again he saw the last stand of the old bull moose, and Koskoosh dropped his head wearily upon his knees. What did it matter after all? Was it not the law of life?
>
> (pp. 107-08)

Life, in **"The Law of Life,"** is no longer of consequence. Koskoosh refuses to cling to life because it does not "matter after all" and drops the brand. The will to live that dominates all the men in **"The Wisdom of the Trail"** and is the fundamental irony in **"The Grit of Women"** is gone. The "white logic" has won despite London's earlier enthusiasm for racial law that promised order beyond the multiplicity of existence. (p. 109)

The theme of loss, then, in *Children of the Frost,* is more than an account of Indian cultures falling before the inevitable white supremacists. Romance had gone out of the Northland which had once promised a revitalization by immersion in the "stinging things of the spirit." . . . Truth terrifies; illusions are impossible to sustain. Death . . . has become a nightmare indistinguishable from life.

It would seem that London's pessimism had reached its nadir. However, the demonic asserts itself in the Alaskan stories which follow **"The Law of Life"**; nature is actively and motivelessly evil. The characters who live in this environment become one with its demonic, motiveless malignancy, as the grotesque pervades the stories in *The Faith of Men, Love of Life* and *Lost Face.*

"Simple horror," writes Austin Wright, "involves the emergence of grotesque evil in a character or world that initially appears to be morally neutral." The grotesque arises when we perceive "horror in the face of facts about life that we know to be universal, normal rather than abnormal." The world presented in **"Batard,"** first published in 1902 as **"Diable—a Dog"** and later included in *The Faith of Men,* is a place of horrors that is grotesque because the "abnormal" has become the universal norm. Evil has become the active force in man and the cosmos.

The two principals in **"Batard"** are Black Leclere, who struggles to master the malign forces in the "unknown," and his dog, Batard, who embodies those hostile powers. Eventually, the animal kills the man, and London has presented a perverse modification of his previously held cosmic view.

At first it would seem as if London's description of Leclere makes him as another ideal, imaginative character, perfectly suited to survive in the Northland. . . . But Leclere's imaginative power is London's third kind of imagination that allows one to perceive the horror, and he has become a "devil" in order to attempt matching the malign cosmic powers. Throughout the story, he tortures his dog, hoping to break his spirit and to master the unknown.

Batard, known as "Hell's Spawn" to the other men of the Northland, has inherited the savage and malignant spirit of the land. . . . Past, present and future demand doom for man and triumph for the diabolical "unconquerable essence" of savagery and iniquity. With a "fiendish levity" Batard finally knocks a cracker-box from under the defenseless Leclere and hangs him. The "unnatural," an illegitimate product of savagery and evil, has become the indomitable power of the unknown, of nature.

London's world view has altered perversely. Leclere, as do earlier protagonists, recognizes that he cannot escape the challenge of the unknown and refuses, therefore, advice to sell or kill Batard. But heroic confrontation does not save. Nor does comradeship, even when its principle is inverted: Leclere's and the dog's "hate bound them together as love could never bind." Violence in earlier stories had become a necessary evil that helped man to preserve his life and values; and violence pervades **"Batard"** as Leclere at first practices "crude brutalities" and, then, "refinements of cruelty." But he is unable to accommodate himself to the environment. Finally, the atavism that gave a measure of salvation to men like Hay Stockard, who responded to the call of blood ties, does not save Leclere. (pp. 109-11)

Love of Life and *Lost Face* were the last collections of Northland stories London produced, with the exception of his *Smoke Bellew* volume that London, himself, acknowledged as hack work. Many of the stories in *Love of Life* and *Lost Face* are obviously pot-boilers also or recreate the dehumanized world of **"Batard"** and **"Lost Face"** that threatens to become more bizarre than terrifying. "The central mood" in these two volumes, writes Maxwell Geismar, is "inhuman, but almost mechanical misery" [see excerpt dated 1953]; and the extreme of the grotesque brings the fiction close to the merely sensational. However, each volume included a story destined to become one by which London is remembered: **"The Love of Life"** in the first and **"To Build a Fire"** in the second. Published in 1905 and 1908, respectively, each had its genesis earlier when London was writing consistently good stories that had not yet become "mechanical" in their pessimism. . . . Neither story depicts the motiveless malignancy which brought the black imagery of oblivion to stories like **"Batard"**; but neither do they evoke the mystical whiteness of **"The White Silence."** Instead, a cold gray encloses the two protagonists as they move between, but never experience consciously, a redeeming illumination and a damning recognition of the powers of darkness.

"Love of Life" describes the ordeal of a nameless prospector who has been abandoned by his partner and must wander alone through the forbidding Alaskan landscape if he is to survive. Only his tenacious, instinctive will to live, despite the pain and apparent hopelessness of his situation, permit him to reach the safety of a ship anchored in an Arctic bay. Atavism saves him. This affirmation of the impulse towards life, modifies the theme of a perversity controlling the stories in these later volumes; nevertheless, the details used to dramatize his theme, threaten to contradict its import.

Although the theme of the story is the triumph of the will to endure, the patterns of the story convey disintegration. In the beginning there are two men, the nameless wanderer and Bill, his companion, and then just the one human; then, the man and diseased wolf, man and brute; finally, only the man is left, but now dehumanized, brute-like himself. . . . His awareness constricts, and he no longer looks slowly at the horizon but compulsively at his immediate surroundings: he counts his matches over and over; sees a moose he can not shoot, a

ptarmigan he can not catch, and finally he captures some fish the size of minnows as the physical world diminishes in its size and he becomes more impotent. . . . Increasingly, he becomes aware of his own physical state—his blurred vision, the rhythm of his breathing, the throbbing of his heart. Detailed, basic physical needs are foremost in the description as the man moves between sanity and delusions, between conscious and increasingly more frequent unconscious states. The real in his world has been reduced to his instinctual will to survive and the functioning of his involuntary physical processes within a context of pain and fear.

Before the man becomes totally unconscious, he does awaken to a new awareness of the world about him when he hears a cough. He discovers that he is being followed by a sick wolf that has been patiently stalking him. . . . The new awareness of the world is that it is diseased, destructive, death-dealing, tragic and grotesque. Finally, the man sinks his teeth into the wolf's throat, killing it, and drinks its blood. (pp. 113-15)

Up to this point in [**"Love of Life"**], London has depicted human physical and emotional disintegration. . . . He had done this artistically by exercising care with detail and control over his omniscient narration by limiting it, as in **"The Law of Life,"** to the prospector's awareness. His "love of life" theme, however, demanded that the character not die. Consequently, London added a two page, contrived epilogue from a totally omniscient point of view that describes the rescued man's return to the human community aboard ship. He portrays the man's compulsive eating and hoarding of food. In the last sentence, the narrator assures us that he would recover from the eccentric behavior. . . . The inartistically presented epilogue is unconvincing. Madness, pain, decay and disease are not easily dismissed. In effect, the arctic landscape has triumphed, and London's theme that life can be sustained through atavism unintentionally and ironically undercut. Life has been stripped of its dignity; not only has the code failed, but instinct as well.

"To Build a Fire" is London's most mature expression of his pessimism. The nameless "chechaquo" or tenderfoot who confronts the white silence in this short story possesses neither the imagination that gives man an intuitive grasp of the laws of nature and allows him to exercise his reason to accommodate himself to them, nor the "thrice cursed" imagination that convinces man of the absurdity of confronting the unknown with ridiculously finite human powers. . . . He does not recognize that man is so finite that the bitterly cold Alaskan landscape inevitably destroys the individual. The rest of the story suggests that man is totally unequipped to face the unknown and inherently too limited to explore life's mysteries and live. If the individual is to survive, he must avoid truth-seeking and "spirit-groping."

Only two other living beings are mentioned in **"To Build a Fire"**: the "old timer" and the dog who accompanies the tenderfoot along the "hair-line trail" into the "unbroken white" of the mysterious land. The old timer offers one way to survive, and as it turns out, the only way. In the autumn before the young man takes his fatal journey, "the old timer had been very serious in laying down the law that no man must travel alone in the Klondike after fifty below." . . . The lesson he attempts to teach the young wanderer is that if one hopes to survive, he must retreat from a solitary confrontation with cosmic power. . . . The kind of accommodation the Kid makes, practicing the code in order to adjust, is impossible. The dog, however, accompanies the reckless young man into the cold and does survive. Instinct protects him. Nevertheless, instinct gives no comfort to man, since it is unavailable to him. The dog has "inherited the knowledge" from his savage ancestors who, like he, had never been separated from the brutal landscape by civilization. . . . The old timer's imagination, then, warns that man cannot confront the depths of experience and live; the dog's instinct for survival is unavailable to man. Having been divorced from nature by civilization, no man is fit to undertake the most arduous journey.

In addition to imagination, the quality that permitted the Malemute Kid and other protagonists to survive in the Northland had been their knowledge of the concrete and their mastery of facts. Suspicious of abstractions, London had given his characters control over the factual. For example, Sitka Charlie may not understand the reasons for the bizarre occurrences in **"The Sun-Dog Trail,"** but he sees the details in the "picture" and knows how to respond to them effectively. The Kid, too, is able to master situations because he knows Northland lore, knows facts and can order them rationally. But by the time London had written **"To Build a Fire"** he had lost his faith in the potency of reason.

The chechaquo in this story has a command of facts and is "quick and alert in the things of life." Clell Peterson argues perceptively and convincingly that the young man is not, as many readers assume, merely "a fool who dies for his folly"; he is "not a fool" but the "modern, sensual, rational man" [see excerpt dated 1966]. Rather than a deficient character, he is another of London's limited protagonists; and his death denies the efficacy of reason. . . . London has even lost his faith in "facts": symbolically, the man falls through the snow into the water, the accident which begins his desperate struggle to live, because there are "no signs" indicating where the snow is soft. The man's tragic flaw has been his masculine pride in his rationality.

Neither the abstract nor the concrete, imagination nor reason, sustain life. The romantic and the realistic impulses both lead nowhere. Without their protection, the unknown becomes a destructive agent whose white logic is the "antithesis of life, cruel and bleak as interstellar space, pulseless and frozen as absolute zero." The landscape in **"To Build a Fire"** has become killer. What remains for London to do in this story, which everyone agrees he does masterfully, is to record the grotesque details which describe the nightmare of impaired physical activity that is the prelude to the modern man's death. In **"To Build a Fire"** London has employed a controlled artistry to present the theme that was struggling to life in **"In a Far Country."**

Now that London's everyman has become merely a helpless victim of the killing landscape, the mystical light goes out of the Alaskan sky. Rather than, as some would have it, portraying man's insignificance but unsystematically depicting affirmations of the American Dream, the reverse had happened: London tried to dramatize a new version of human dignity but unintentionally drifted towards the pessimism which undeniably informs these Northland stories. Throughout the best of his Alaskan stories, London had made a series of adjustments in order to stave off a darkening vision and to preserve some reason for "spirit-groping." Although his temperament and reading called upon him to affirm life, he exhausted the positive as he found himself forced to move from themes of mastery, to themes of accommodation, to themes

of failure. His honesty compelled him to deny affirmations. Even the archetypal quest motif and the evocative imagery of the wasteland, artistic elements which distinguish his stories from those of lesser writers, disappear from his fiction as he discovered that it is not undertaking the dangerous and desperate quest that determines the quality of life but, instead, inexorable, external forces of nature and man's irrationality, his link with that nature. The Alaskan nightmare had reached its conclusion, and London retreated from the "Unknown." (pp. 115-19)

> *James I. McClintock, in his* White Logic: Jack London's Short Stories, *Wolf House Books, 1975, 206 p.*

ROBERT BARLTROP (essay date 1976)

[*A member of the Socialist Party of Great Britain, Barltrop claims a strong identification with his working-class background. In the following excerpt, Barltrop defends London against critical charges of triviality and asserts that the author's popularity derives from his romantic treatment of personal experience rather than from the realism of his fiction, as many critics have asserted.*]

Jack London's books have not been taken seriously as literature. At best, he is seen as an enjoyable but unimportant writer, and his work is frequently treated with contempt. In *Intellectual America* Oscar Cargill refers to him, Upton Sinclair and Dreiser as 'witless, heavy-handed progeny' of earlier realist writers like Frank Norris. Later in the same book Cargill says there is little indication that Jack London and others of his school knew 'or cared to know' what 'the genuine primitive' was. Other critics acknowledge his popularity, but discount it on literary grounds.

Such judgements have not deterred readers of Jack London's books but often create a kind of guilt over reading them: the right to triviality is claimed, a little defiantly. However, it is not uncommon for literary criticism to forget what literature is. Most popular fiction is essentially ephemeral, having no virtue beyond meeting some need of the hour. . . . But if a writer continues to give satisfaction to large numbers of people for a long enough period, he becomes entitled to a place of respect in literature. The needs he meets have been shown to be not transient. It is sixty years since Jack London died, and seventy since his major books were written. Most of them are reprinted throughout the literate world. He cannot be dismissed. (p. 179)

Jack London's themes were taken directly from his own experiences, and his treatment of them took no account of being 'nice'. Many of his stories are autobiographical, narrating incidents in his life either openly in the first person, as in *The Road* and *John Barleycorn,* or with slight disguises of names and circumstances. Not infrequently he used the names of people he had known in a way which would be unthinkable to libel-haunted English writers. Ernest Everhard is one example, though he borrowed the name alone without otherwise involving the cousin he had once met. In several other cases he used a person whole, as it were, under the person's own name. From his Klondike days there were Elam Harnish, the hero of *Burning Daylight;* [and] Father Roubeau, the priest in **The Son of the Wolf**. . . . (p. 181)

His stories appear to be true. In matters of detail they undoubtedly were true. At times when he was challenged over authenticity he was always able to reply with the certainty of first-hand experience. (p. 182)

Yet the use of existing people and true events is not in itself realism. The fact is that Jack London's stories have their persistent appeal because, ultimately, they are not realistic at all: they are romantic fantasy. It is not just the case that they bring a world of distant excitement to town-dwellers; the world is adapted to be as the reader wants it, rather than as he would have found it. The drinking and gambling in Klondike saloons are without the misery which follows them in real life—it is all part of a swashbuckling, virile existence for strong men and beautiful women. The heroes combine superb physique with outstanding intellectual powers. Martin Eden and Ernest Everhard both have muscles which almost burst their clothes. Elam Harnish is 'a striking figure of a man . . . he had lived life naked and tensely, and something of all this smouldered in his eyes'. . . . But were Jack's associates in the Klondike really like this? It is unlikely, to say the least. Moreover, the obvious truth about the gold rush to the north is that it was inspired by the desire to get rich—whether or not one calls it greed is a matter of taste—more than anything else.

Nevertheless, Jack London's fantasies are not the same as the fantasies created by most popular writers. He had created them for himself. In practically everything he did in his life, romantic images obscured what things and people were really like. The failures in his personal relationships and his projects were certainly due to this; the idealisation of his experiences in his stories was not simply a selective view from a safe distance, but expectations he had taken into—and, apparently, preserved through—those experiences. One reason is that the experiences of oyster-pirating, the sea, tramping and the Klondike were all short-term, enabling him to feel a member of an exalted and glamorous brotherhood without the disenchanting effects of time. He entered and left them with mental pictures formed by his boyhood reading.

His vision was the same as his readers'. Just as they envisaged a northland full of manly adventures and populated by such characters as the Malemute Kid, so did he. He voiced their feeling that it was far above the life led by the majority of people, that it bred a higher type of man. . . . A number of the stories represent extremes of fantasy. The beautifully-told **"The Night Born"** is an example: the sort of sexual episode away from civilisation that most men daydream of at some time.

No doubt many thousands of people in Jack's own time half-believed they might have such adventures, given the opportunity. The legend of the frontiersmen was still potent. Jack's reputation for realism came partly from this belief, and also because his stories had a full measure of toughness. Death is frequent in them, usually by violence; disease, frostbite and scurvy appear regularly, and leprosy is used in several of the South Seas stories. In fact this is another aspect of romanticism. What is signified is the 'law of life' which Jack laid down. It replaces explanation and makes human efforts redundant: 'this is how it is', the author is saying.

Several of the stories are built round this principle. Perhaps the best is a boxing story, **"A Piece of Steak"**. Its chief character is a hard-up, ageing fighter who is matched with a rising younger man. His skill just fails to master the other's greater strength and speed. As he walks home, he thinks how narrow a thing it was and how he could have won if he had been able

to afford a piece of steak beforehand. The excellence of the story comes from leaving it there, without expressions of sentiment: in time the same thing will happen to the younger man. While we know it is true, there is the feeling that the writer likes the idea of it being true—'the law' is like God, disposing of man regardless of what he proposes.

This overlaying of romantic concepts on vivid, often harsh, experience produced inconsistency. Some of Jack London's stories fail because of his inability to break through the concepts and perceive what men and women would think and feel in such situations. **"An Odyssey of the North"**, for all its thrilling pursuit, fails in this way. Even **"Love of Life"**, one of the most powerful of his stories, comes close to bathos at the end when the man is rescued and among other human beings recovering from his ordeal.

Jack's worst work, the pot-boiler yarns, has been noted. His best is to be found in a number of short stories which establish him as one of the masters of that form. A collection of these outstanding stories would include **"The Apostate"**, **"The Mexican"**, **"Love of Life"**—the ending is an irrelevance rather than a weakness, **"A Piece of Steak"**, **"The Night Born"**, and **"To Build a Fire"**. There are six or seven others which are very good by any standard: **"The *Francis Spaight*"**, **"Under the Deck Awnings"**. **"Just Meat"**, **"The Benefit of the Doubt"**. In addition, *The Cruise of the Snark* and *The Road* are collections of episodes which can be read separately; **"Hoboes That Pass in the Night"** and **"Holding Her Down"** are little gems of writing which is both stimulating and informative.

The reason why these have, on the whole, been denied literary importance is their subject-matter. Whatever the quality of Jack London's stories, they are not taken seriously because their material does not reflect—indeed, it provides an escape from—life as the mass of people know it. This applies not only to the Klondike and the South Seas stories, but to those which are about boxers and tramps; equally, these represent attractive, disreputable sub-worlds of fantasy. Comparison can be made with American writers of the early part of this century—Sinclair Lewis, for example—who, with narrative ability inferior to Jack London's, won critical praise for their pictures of the known contemporary world. Since that world changes, there is no reason why London should not be recognised as a writer of high order. The place for him in literature is much on a level with Maupassant's. His view was too restricted for the place to be a topmost one, but in the field of imaginative story-telling his work cannot be bettered. (pp. 182-85)

Jack's early stories bear the marks of his study of Kipling. The narrative presents no problems, but there are self-conscious discourses in which he can be seen searching for aids to writing well. These quickly disappeared as confidence was gained, and after the first two or three books his style becomes distinctly his own. It is essentially a journalistic style, almost reporter-like when he is describing action. However, it contains another journalistic element which became the worst fault in his writing: repetition. The reiteration of phrases, from a useful device, was turned into a cheap way of obtaining emphasis. It is done a great deal in his letters when he is upbraiding, and can be seen in **"The Good Soldier"**. It is a continual irritation in the stories written in the last five years of his life. (p. 186)

However, the writing of Jack's best years is frequently superb. It contains not only movement without reiteration, but some beautiful descriptive passages. . . . These passages drew upon the notebooks he had kept and the imagery formed by his early reading. In later years he became preoccupied with finding plots and situations. He kept boxes of newspaper cuttings, and looked for themes in everything he read and saw. It has been suggested, on the basis of stories like **"Law of Life"**, **"Love of Life"**, **"To Build a Fire"** and **"The Apostate"**, that he functioned best as a writer when dealing with individuals isolated in a given background. A wider survey provides no support for this. Rather, it appears that he was dependent on turning up or being supplied with ideas for action against backgrounds with which he was familiar. The effectiveness of the results depended on his attitude to his work—more than anything, on what was happening in his personal life. (p. 187)

> Robert Barltrop, in his Jack London: The Man, the Writer, the Rebel, *Pluto Press, 1976, 206 p.*

CHARLES E. MAY (essay date 1978)

[*The editor of* Short Story Theories *(1976), a highly influential collection of studies on the history and status of short fiction, May seeks in his critical writings to reestablish the short story as a major narrative form in American literature. In the following excerpt, May uses London's story "To Build a Fire" to refute the attempts of various critics to exalt London by attributing unintended metaphysical or extraliterary intentions to his fiction.*]

Ten years ago Earle Labor and King Hendricks, perhaps the most avid partisans of Jack London, reproved critics for not giving London's fiction its "proper critical assessment" and urged that a "fine discrimination," equal to London's own, be exercised in taking his measure as an artist [see excerpt dated 1967]. . . . I have no major contribution to make toward this reassessment of London's fiction, but I do wish to express some reservations about the "discrimination" made in the last ten years in regard to [the story **"To Build a Fire"**], London's best-known piece of short fiction, which Labor calls "a masterpiece" and says is one of the most widely anthologized works ever written by an American author.

A common method of critics who wish to rescue a work that has not been highly valued is to subject it to a critical category that is highly valued. If the work "fits," even in the coarsest fashion, with physiognomy effaced and limbs lopped off, it is declared to have value because the category does. In especially difficult cases, not only must the work be reduced to an indistinguishable torso, but the Procrustean bed itself must be altered. Because the categorical bed of "naturalism" on which London has previously been laid seems to have laid him permanently to rest, more fashionable categories have been applied to disinter him. However, in applying universal terms to **"To Build a Fire,"** the critics have so ignored Wittgenstein's exhortation to "look and see" that they have not only failed to tell us anything helpful about the story, they have applied the terms so uncritically that the categories themselves are in danger of losing their heuristic value in telling us anything helpful about literature at all. Three such categories that have been applied to London's story to claim it is both thematically and structurally more significant than heretofore realized are: the short story as a generic form, the archetypal theme of rebirth, and the structure and theme of classical tragedy.

Labor and Hendricks' argument that **"To Build a Fire"** is a "masterpiece of short fiction" is based primarily on a comparison of the story with an earlier juvenile version by the same name. The superiority of the adult story over the juvenile one is a result of three basic artistic improvements. First of all, London adds "atmosphere" to adumbrate the story's dominant symbolism of "the polarity of heat (sun-fire-life) and cold (darkness-depression-death)." . . . Secondly, the protagonist in the juvenile story, a likeable and sympathetically identifiable young man named Tom Vincent has been changed to a nameless "naturalistic version of Everyman," representative of "unaccommodated man . . . pitted against the awful majesty of cosmic forces." Finally, the "masterstroke" of the adult version is the addition of the dog as a *ficelle,* an addition that not only makes us see dramatically by the man's harsh treatment of the animal that the protagonist is a "hollow man whose inner coldness correlates with the enveloping outer cold," but that also creates by "subtle counterpointing" the structural and thematic tension between the dog's "natural wisdom" and the man's "foolish rationality."

The logical fallacy of the argument is obvious. The fact that London's adult story is more carefully crafted than the juvenile version does not automatically mean that London understands the "intricate demands" of the short story genre, or that this particular story is a "masterpiece." Furthermore, an analysis of the craftsmanship of the work alone will do nothing either to enhance London's reputation or "sharpen our own insights into the ontological qualities of the short story as an art form." Anyone familiar with the history of short story criticism in America knows the kind of damage done to the reputation of the form by just this kind of craftsmanship criticism that proliferated in the handbooks and manuals during the very period when London was writing. (pp. 19-20)

The claim that **"To Build a Fire"** is a tragedy in the Aristotelian sense has been made both by James M. Mellard and by Earle Labor in his recent book-length study of London [see excerpt dated 1974]. . . . [Labor] uses Aristotle's *Poetics* to note the parallels between the story and Greek tragedy and suggests that the story is great because it articulates the mystery that animates the plays of Sophocles, Aeschylus, and all the great tragedians; that is, the common mystery of that "simple fact"—man must die.

I suspect that most, if not all, of these grandiose claims are based on this "simple fact" which is the central fact of the story—the protagonist dies. The basic critical fallacy of the various interpretations of the story is that the critics insist that the man's death has significance not because of any significance attributed to that death within the story, but rather because of the significance of death in the critical categories they have applied to the story. The man's death is significant because it symbolizes the frailty of unaccommodated man against cosmic forces, because it leads to psychic rebirth, because it is the tragic result of a tragic flaw and is confronted with "dignity." It should not have to be pointed out that the "significance" of a death in a piece of fiction depends not upon the imagination of the critics of that fiction, but rather upon the imagination of the author. And the "simple fact" of death is nothing but a simple fact if nothing is at stake but the "mere" loss of biological life, if the character who dies is nothing but a physical body killed to illustrate this "simple fact."

Labor and Hendricks inadvertently suggest the nature of the critical problem by calling the protagonist in the adult story a "naturalistic version of Everyman." The convention of the Everyman character in the sixteenth-century morality play from which the term comes, as well as in other allegories such as *The Faerie Queene* and *Pilgrim's Progress,* depends on the Everyman figure representing the soul, or, more narrowly, some specific moral or psychological aspect of man. The assumption of Naturalism, however, is that man is primarily a biological living body in a natural world of objects and forces. Thus, it follows that a naturalistic version of Everyman is simply Everyman as a body. And this is precisely what the protagonist is in London's story, and it is why the story has physical significance only, not the metaphysical significance the critics have attributed to it.

For Jack London, and consequently for the reader, the man in the story is simply a living body and the cold is simply a physical fact. To insist that the story is a symbolic dramatization adumbrated in a symbolic polarity between fire as life and cold as death is to run the risk of saying that the symbolic protagonist's symbolic failure to build the symbolic fire results in his symbolic death. Of course, such a statement is true in the sense that every art work can be said to "symbolize" or "mediate" a reality that is not identical with the verbal construct of the work itself. But such a statement tells us nothing about Jack London's story. Surely Labor and Hendricks realize that both Frank O'Connor and Pascal in their references to human loneliness and the terror of infinite spaces meant something more than the simple fear of being physically alone or losing physical life. Moreover, Labor and Hendricks' reaching for the inference that the man's treatment of the dog is an indication of his hollowness confuses the man's "inhumanity" as a naturalistic given of the story with a symbolic character flaw that leads to the "poetic justice" of his death.

London's central comment about the protagonist in the story itself clearly indicates the "naturalistic" nature of his Everyman: "The trouble with him was that he was without imagination. He was quick and alert in the things of life, but only in the things, and not in the significances." London says that the cold was a simple fact for the man. "It did not lead him to meditate upon his frailty as a creature of temperature, and upon man's frailty in general, able only to live within certain narrow limits of heat and cold; and from there it did not lead him to the conjectural field of immortality and man's place in the universe." If this comment "hardly ripples in the reader's consciousness," as Labor and Hendricks suggest, it is not because it is dropped so "deftly," but rather because London, like his protagonist, is without imagination in this story, because he too is concerned here only with the things of life and not with their significance. The reader may be led to meditate upon the physical limits of man's ability to live in extreme cold, but nothing in the story leads him to the metaphysical conjectural field of immortality and man's place in the universe. (pp. 21-3)

A close look at the story itself without the lenses of *a priori* categories reveals that the most significant repetitive motif London uses to chart the man's progressive movement toward death is the gradual loss of contact between the life force of the body and the parts of the body. . . . The separation is further emphasized when he burns the flesh of his hands without feeling the pain and when he stands and must look down to see if he is really standing. When he realizes that he is physically unable to kill the dog, he is surprised to find that he must use his eyes to find out where his hands are.

Finally, realizing that the frozen portions of his body are extending, he has a vision of himself that the story has been moving toward, a vision of the self as totally frozen body, not only without psychic life, but without physical life as well. Picturing the boys finding his body the next day, "he found himself with them, coming along the trail and looking for himself. And, still with them, he came around a turn in the trail and found himself lying in the snow. He did not belong with himself any more, for even then he was out of himself, standing with the boys and looking at himself in the snow." The discovery of self in London's story is not the significant psychic discovery of Oedipus or the Ancient Mariner, but rather the simple physical discovery that the self is body only.

Anyone who sees this purely physical fiction as a story with metaphysical significance does so not as a result of the imagination of Jack London, but as a result of the imagination of his critics. One can grant that the bare situation of the story has metaphysical potential without granting that London actualizes it, gives it validity. It is possible that the great white silence in the story could have had the significance it has in *Moby Dick,* that the cold of space could have had the significance it has in Crane's "The Blue Hotel," that the "nothingness" that kills the man could have had the significance it has in "Bartleby the Scrivener" or Hemingway's "A Clean, Well-Lighted Place." It is even possible that the obsessive concern with immediate detail could have had the significance it has in "Big Two-Hearted River." But without going into what makes such elements metaphysically significant in these true "masterpieces," it is sufficient to say that there is more in the context of these works to encourage such symbolic readings than in London's **"To Build a Fire."** (pp. 23-4)

> *Charles E. May, " 'To Build a Fire': Physical Fiction and Metaphysical Critics," in* Studies in Short Fiction, *Vol. 15, No. 1, Winter, 1978, pp. 19-24.*

CHARLES N. WATSON, JR.   (essay date 1983)

[*Watson is the author of the highly acclaimed biographical and critical study* The Novels of Jack London: A Reappraisal *(1983). In the following excerpt from his survey* The Haunted Dusk: American Supernatural Fiction, 1820-1920, *Watson discusses elements of spiritualism in London's short fiction.*]

Though all his life Jack London denied that he believed in the supernatural, he found himself compelled repeatedly to fend off the overtures of spiritualists who had mistaken him for a fellow believer. His reply to one such person, in early 1915, was polite but firmly discouraging. "When I tell you that I am hopelessly a realist and a materialist," he wrote,

> believing that when I die I am dead and shall be forever dead, you will understand how unable I am to join with you in the prosecution of your most interesting researches. . . . I was born amongst spiritualists and lived my childhood and boyhood life amongst spiritualists. The result of this close contact was to make an unbeliever out of me.

(p. 193)

Yet the inquiries of these spiritualists, if overeager, were not entirely groundless, for like so many of London's most insistent pronouncements, his declarations of skepticism conceal as much as they reveal. London was a man of complex, sometimes confused, emotional and intellectual stances—a man seldom able to embrace one position without also entertaining its opposite. Such ambivalence, rooted in his early childhood as well as in the intellectual uncertainties of the era, inevitably emerged in his fiction, especially in his stories of the occult. These stories are rarely among his best; indeed, he often dismissed them as potboilers. Yet behind the mask of his indifference or contempt lay a continuing fascination with nonrational experience. Though he had no patience with the cruder varieties of nineteenth-century spiritualism, he often hedged his rejection of occultism and actively explored such alternative psychic phenomena as mystical transcendence, creative inspiration, and subconscious motivation. (pp. 193-94)

London's mother, Flora Wellman, was eight years old and living in Massillon, Ohio, in 1851. . . . [Sometime afterward, Flora] became interested in the occult and eventually gravitated to San Francisco, where in 1874 she was living with a "professor" of astrology named William Henry Chaney, holding séances, and lecturing on spiritualism. The next year she became pregnant, creating a minor public scandal when she unsuccessfully attempted suicide and was then deserted by Chaney. Her child was born out of wedlock on 12 January 1876, but later in the same year she married a middle-aged widower, John London, who gave the future writer his name.

Although Jack London did not learn the full story of his birth until he was in his early twenties, he experienced its effects throughout his childhood. He always recalled with gratitude the kindness of his stepfather, but he felt his mother's emotional rejection. . . . [His] longing for emotional nurture, however, was counterbalanced by an opposite impulse: an early revulsion from his mother's hysterical fits and terrifying séances. Indian "controls" were apparently in vogue at this time, and Flora's favorite, a chieftain named Plume, made a habit of punctuating his messages with "unexpected yells and gibberish." It is not hard to see how London could have emerged from such a childhood with a deep ambivalence toward his mother and the forms of irrationality she represented. All his adult life he loathed feminine hysteria, scorned the supernatural, and embraced scientific rationalism with a confidence that at times bordered on complacency. (p. 194)

Yet even as he insisted on his immunity to the nonrational in all its forms, his deeply emotional nature asserted itself in his volatile personal life and intermittently in his fiction, from early apprentice work to later ideas for stories he never lived to write. Especially in his early years, he seems to have considered his stories of the occult mere finger-exercises and hack work, and in commenting on them he invariably insisted on his disbelief in their supernatural events. Yet what is remarkable is the consistency with which, in the clash between believer and skeptic, the last word goes to the believer. Characteristically, London portrayed the skeptic as something of a fool and the believer as a possessor of esoteric wisdom. Two of these stories date from London's earliest apprentice period, between his return from his tramp journey to the East in the fall of 1894 and his departure for the Klondike in the summer of 1897. Each deals with two young friends, sophomoric know-it-alls who pompously proclaim their disbelief in the supernatural to a man who proposes to put their disbelief to the test.

In **"A Ghostly Chess Game,"** the more skeptical of the two friends, Pythias, denounces séances as frauds: "Rapping, table-tipping, slate-writing and other physical manifestations," he adds, "are just as bad, being but little better bosh than clairvoyance, clairaudience, impersonation and trance-

mediumship." Pythias thus dismisses at a sweep the entire panoply of the spiritualist movement, while the more temperate Damon contents himself with rejecting the "very idea" of ghosts as "absurd." The language of these denunciations may at first seem to express London's own reaction against the spiritualism of his mother. Yet throughout the story the pomposities of the unbelievers are set against the seemingly plausible supernatural beliefs of their more knowing friend, George, whose wish that they may experience "a speedy conversion through the most horrible of proofs" is fulfilled in the ensuing action. Complacently proposing to test themselves by spending the night in a reputedly haunted mansion, the two find themselves uncannily reenacting a murder committed by the former resident. Though George comes to the rescue just in time to prevent Damon from strangling Pythias, the skeptics have presumably been cured of their disbelief.

In a later version of the same motif, **"The Mahatma's Little Joke,"** the skeptical friends are Jack and Charley, who begin by discussing whether apparently supernatural phenomena will ultimately be explained scientifically. The argument is resolved for them by the Mahatma of the title, a middle-aged savant whose face combines "the brooding wisdom of the sphinx and the mysterious solemnity of a Monte Cristo." After all, the Mahatma argues, a hundred years ago "telegraphy was beyond practical conception; and thus, to day the disintegration and reintegration of form by psychic impulses, is beyond both yours and the popular conception. . . . Do you take upon yourself the infinite knowledge necessary to declare that such is infinitely impossible?" . . . Once again London portrays dogmatic disbelief as arrant conceit. The Mahatma, moreover, like George in the earlier story, vanquishes the boys' doubts by performing a demonstration, translating the "astral form" of each into the body of the other, thereby allowing the two shy fellows to propose to each other's sisters "by proxy."

Both of these stories are amateurish and quite preposterous, and neither should be taken as clear evidence against London's often-repeated skepticism. To a degree, they merely exploit the popular taste for supernatural fantasy without committing the author to the slightest belief in the occult. Still, the Mahatma's advice to Jack and Charley is eminently reasonable. Surely, as he argues, it *is* "egotistical" to declare "infinitely impossible" those phenomena beyond the reach of present scientific knowledge. The Mahatma's definition of an enlightened agnosticism, in fact, differs little from the Spencerian attitude that London recommended to Cloudesley Johns in 1899. "Remember," he wrote, "the infidel that positively asserts that there is no God, no first cause, is just as imbecile a creature as the deist that asserts positively that there is a God, a first cause," and he goes on to remind Johns of the "adamantine line" that Spencer had drawn between "the knowable and the unknowable."

After he returned from the Klondike in 1898 and began his second period of apprenticeship, London continued to toy with ideas for occult fiction. Twice he made notes for further revisions of **"A Ghostly Chess Game,"** and in the same notebook the conflict between belief and disbelief was embodied in a plan for a story involving the "materializing" of a baby, who would then be "stolen by a skeptic." . . . [Three of London's] later stories suggest that even as he issued his periodic disclaimers of belief, he never rested easy in his skepticism.

The first such story, **"Planchette,"** was written in the spring of 1905, at a critical juncture in London's life. After nearly two years he was beginning to emerge from what he called his "long sickness," the period of depression following his separation from his first wife and the early months of his love affair with Charmian Kittredge. For the better part of 1904 and early 1905 his relationship with Charmian had deteriorated, but in the spring their love revived as they visited Charmian's aunt and uncle at Glen Ellen, rode over the wooded hills, and made excited plans to buy a nearby ranch, all the while looking forward to the time when London's divorce would become final and they could marry. On 28 May, however, Charmian experienced a momentary scare when her horse fell down a ditch with Jack in the saddle, and she recorded in her diary her relief that he was "unhurt, thank God." But though London broke no bones, the near miss tripped a wire in his imagination, uncovering a source of buried guilt—perhaps over his desertion of his first wife and their two daughters, perhaps over the secret of his birth, which he may not yet have revealed to Charmian. Whatever the cause, a day or two later he began a long story that re-created the circumstances of his accident, endowing them with a convincing aura of the occult.

The tale opens with a horseback ride during which Chris Dunbar tells the woman he loves, Lute Story, that he cannot marry her and cannot tell her why. Shortly afterward, Chris mounts Lute's horse, who suddenly bolts through the trees, stopping only after Chris has been badly gashed and bruised. For a moment the two wonder whimsically whether the horse was a victim of "obsession" or an "evil spirit." . . . [The] next afternoon Chris's own horse suddenly rears and falls backward into a rocky stream twelve feet below while Chris miraculously frees his feet from the stirrups and leaps clear. Back at the home of Lute's aunt and uncle, they try to forget these weird accidents amid the flurry of excitement over the planchette that has been produced for a session of spirit-writing. When Chris, jocular and skeptical, agrees to put the board to a test, he finds it scrawling: "BEWARE! BEWARE! BEWARE! Chris Dunbar, I intend to destroy you. I have already made two attempts upon your life, and failed. I shall yet succeed."

Chris continues to view the whole matter as a joke, but Lute is moved by the memory of the two horseback accidents and by the discovery that the handwriting of the message resembles that of her long-dead father. Though conscious of a "vague and nameless fear at this toying with the supernatural," she decides to try the planchette herself and promptly receives a message from her dead mother. "What if there be something in it?" she wonders aloud. "I am not so sure. Science may be too dogmatic in its denial of the unseen. The forces of the unseen, of the spirit, may well be too subtle, too sublimated, for science to lay hold of, and recognize, and formulate. Don't you see, Chris, that there is rationality in the very doubt?" Chris, however, will go no further than the agnosticism of a scientific rationalist: "We are playing with the subjective forces of our own being, with phenomena which science has not yet explained, that is all." . . . Chris thus states what the rational side of London's mind persistently believed.

Yet as the story moves quickly to a climax, its action refutes such rationalism in the most telling way: by making Chris pay for it with his life. As he and Lute tempt fate by taking a final ride, they ascend to the rim of a canyon, where they exult in their love and experience a moment of ecstatic communion with the rhythms of natural life. To their wonder-

struck vision, the stream below is like a Platonic idea, "a breath with movement, ever falling and ever remaining, changing its substance but never its form, an aërial waterway as immaterial as gauze and as permanent as the hills." . . . This moment of revelation, expressed in the language of religious mysticism, is entirely characteristic of the side of London's imagination that transcends his theoretical rationalism. In the next instant, moreover, it is validated by the fulfillment of the planchette's prophecy as Chris's horse plunges without warning into the canyon below. This time Chris does not leap clear.

"Planchette" may thus serve as a paradigm of London's double vision. It presents a character who is very much like London and who holds the skeptical views that London always professed. Yet the story as a whole constitutes a critique of those views, implying that a dogmatic materialism must give place, if not to open credulity, then at least to a suspension of disbelief consistent with the present state of scientific ignorance. In addition, the story offers two sources of nonrational experience. One of them is the sense of ineffable joy that Chris and Lute feel in their moment of mystical communion with nature. But another and darker source appears in Lute's "instinctive fear," expressive of "man's inheritance from the wild and howling ages when his hairy, apelike prototype was afraid of the dark." This is more than the familiar naturalistic insistence that, beneath the veneer of civilization, human beings harbor atavistic impulses. The key to its further dimension lies in Lute's remark that the whole experience, while it may be "delusion and unreal," is nevertheless "very real . . . as a nightmare is real." On the one hand, such an experience moves in the direction of Jung's theory of the collective unconscious, an inherited racial memory with its shadowy archetypes. Yet because it also involves Chris's unrevealed source of personal guilt, it touches those facets of the subconscious mind that had recently been explored by Freud.

A second story of occult experience, **"The Eternity of Forms,"** written in the fall of 1910, deals with the materialization of a ghost. Less successful artistically than **"Planchette,"** it reads like a second-rate Poe arabesque, with a fantastic plot involving a probable fratricide and all the complications of a mind disordered by guilt. Yet at the center of the tale, as at the center of **"Planchette,"** lies a conflict between belief and disbelief; and once again a skeptic is forced to pay dearly for his dogmatic rationalism. The story takes the form of extracts from a journal kept by an old man named Sedley Crayden in the last months of his life, while his sanity and health deteriorate following the mysterious death of his brother, James. Psychologically, the journal serves as a forum for Sedley's desperate effort to convince himself that he did not, in a fit of passion during a philosophical argument, murder his brother. Philosophically, it constitutes his final attempt to convince himself that his own rationalistic side of that argument was correct. But as the tale progresses and the evidence of the supernatural accumulates, his mind disintegrates along with his argument.

The focus of the brothers' conflict soon becomes clear. James, the idealist, believed in the "eternity of forms," while according to Sedley, "Form is mutable. This is the last word of positive science. The dead do not come back." Sedley is thus another of London's complacent dogmatists. . . . Even at this early stage, however, Sedley's desperate tone reveals that his "positive science" is beginning to weaken under attack. "It is not true that I have recanted," he cries. "I still believe that

I live in a mechanical universe." What prompts this outburst is the repeated materialization of the dead brother in the chair he occupied when alive. Like Chris Dunbar in **"Plan-chette,"** Sedley adopts every rational expedient to explain away this ghost, but under such continuous pressure his certitudes begin to crumble. At this point Sedley falls back on an explanation that, while not inconsistent with his rationalism, nevertheless ventures into little-understood areas of man's psychic and spiritual life. For a time he relishes his new sensations, which he can disarm by labeling them "hallucinations." He has wanted to "experience such phenomena" all his life. But having reached such a point, he takes a step beyond it and links the hallucinations to the less scientifically manageable phenomenon of "imagination." . . . From here it is but a short step to that characteristically romantic theory of creativity in which the human imagination assumes godlike powers. If a mere man can create a new entity, Sedley speculates, "then is not the hypothesis of a Creator made substantial?" And since he himself has exercised such powers, he is "unlike other men. I am a god. I have created."

The story then moves to its ironic ending, in which Sedley at last succeeds in banishing the ghost by displacing him—by occupying the chair and never moving from it until he dies. He has convinced himself that his rationalism, though "severely tried for a time," has passed the test, and that the ghost "never was." Yet he takes no chances: "I do not leave my chair. I am afraid to leave the chair." The ending thus leaves in suspension the protagonist's theoretical rationalism and practical credulity, although the story as a whole clearly dramatizes the inadequacy of his scientific dogmatism while affirming the facet of nonrational experience that London himself most fully embraced: the power of the creative imagination. (pp. 195-201)

It would be misleading to end with the implication that London rejected his scientific rationalism and became a convert to some sort of spiritual beliefs, as if he had come home to mother at last. One can go no further than to suggest that the conflict between belief and doubt continued throughout his life, providing him with an important source of imaginative power. . . . London never abandoned his lifelong rationalism. Yet he loved new experience, new knowledge, too well ever to fence himself off from any part of it. Though he continued to hope and believe that science held the key to all mysteries, he was never completely sure. (pp. 204-05)

Charles N. Watson, Jr., "Jack London: Up from Spiritualism," in The Haunted Dusk: American Supernatural Fiction, 1820-1920, *edited by Howard Kerr, John W. Crowley, and Charles L. Crow, The University of Georgia Press, 1983, pp. 191-207.*

FURTHER READING

Allen, Mary. "The Wisdom of the Dogs: Jack London." In her *Animals in American Literature*, pp. 77-96. Chicago: University of Illinois Press, 1983.
    Analysis of animals as figures of myth and allegory in London's fiction.

Bowen, James K. "London's 'To Build a Fire': Epistemology and the White Wilderness." *Western American Literature* V, No. 4 (Winter 1971): 287-89.
    Analysis of the story "To Build a Fire." In contrast to most critics, Bowen asserts that the protagonist's death results not from a lack of intuition but from limited mental faculties.

Calder-Marshall, Arthur. Introduction to *The Bodley Head Jack London, Vol. I*, pp. 7-16. Edited by Arthur Calder-Marshall. London: Bodley Head, 1963.
    Brief survey of representative stories from London's career.

Campbell, Jeanne. "Falling Stars: Myth in 'The Red One.'" *Jack London Newsletter* 11, Nos. 2 & 3 (May-December 1978): 86-96.
    Analysis of Jungian archetypes in the story "The Red One."

Collins, Billy G. "Jack London's 'The Red One': Journey to a Lost Heart." *Jack London Newsletter* 10, No. 1 (January-April 1977): 1-6.
    Interpretation of the story "The Red One" as indicative of London's pessimism toward the end of his life.

Chapman, Arnold. "Between Fire and Ice: A Theme in Jack London and Horacio Quiroga." *Symposium* XXIV, No. 2 (Spring 1970): 17-26.
    Critical comparison of London's story "To Build a Fire" and Uruguayan author Horacio Quiroga's "La insolación."

Courbin, Jacqueline M. "Jack London's Portrayal of the Natives in His First Four Collections of Arctic Tales." *Jack London Newsletter* 10, No. 3 (September-December 1978): 127-37.
    Favorable critical discussion of London's treatment of the North American Indian in his first four volumes of short fiction set in Alaska.

Dhondt, Steven T. "'There Is a Good Time Coming': Jack London's Spirit of Proletarian Revolt." *Jack London Newsletter* 3, No. 1 (January-April 1970): 25-34.
    Discussion of London's socialist beliefs as reflected in the stories "The Apostate" and "A Curious Fragment."

Gower, Ronald. "The Creative Conflict: Struggle and Escape in Jack London's fiction." *Jack London Newsletter* 4, No. 2 (May-August 1971): 77-114.
    Biographical and analytical reassessment of London's reputation in light of existing criticism of his works.

Graham, Don. "Jack London's Tale Told by a High-Grade Feeb." *Studies in Short Fiction* 15, No. 4 (Fall 1978): 429-33.
    Critical discussion of the short story "Told in the Drooling Ward." Graham regards this work as unique among contemporary English-language short fiction about the insane.

Labor, Earle. "From 'All Gold Canyon' to *The Acorn Planter*: Jack London's Agrarian Vision." *Western American Literature* XI, No. 2 (Summer 1976): 83-101.
    Rejection of London's reputation as a pessimist in which Labor examines works from the author's career to emphasize the evolution of a transcendental world view through which London believed the United States could achieve the harmonious integration of science and nature.

————. "'To the Man on Trail': Jack London's Christmas Carol." *Jack London Newsletter* 3, No. 3 (September-December 1970): 90-4.
    Examination of "To the Man on Trail," an early Christmas story London wrote for the *Overland Monthly.*

Lachtman, Howard. "Man and Superwoman in Jack London's 'The Kanaka Surf.'" *Western American Literature* VII, No. 2 (Summer 1972): 101-10.
    Critical discussion of the story "The Kanaka Surf." Lachtman interprets this work about marital rivalry and infidelity as London's attempt to relate a psychological drama within the framework of an adventure story.

Lundquist, James. *Jack London: Adventures, Ideas, and Fiction.* New York: Ungar, 1987, 212 p.

Biographical and critical analysis of London's life, politics, and career.

Mitchell, Lee Clark. " 'Keeping His Head': Repetition and Responsibility in London's 'To Build a Fire'." *Journal of Modern Literature* 13, No. 1 (March 1986): 76-96.
Analysis of London's use of such elements as alliteration and repetition in the story "To Build a Fire."

Ownbey, Ray Wilson, ed. *Jack London: Essays in Criticism.* Santa Barbara, Salt Lake City: Peregrine Smith, 1978, 126 p.
A collection of critical essays by Clarice Stasz, Sam S. Baskett, Earle Labor, and others.

Peterson, Clell T. "Jack London's Alaskan Stories." *American Book Collector* IX, No. 8 (April 1959): 15-22.
Brief biographical and critical survey of London's fiction.

Riber, Jørgen. "Archetypal Patterns in 'The Red One.' " *Jack London Newsletter* 8, No. 3 (September-December 1975): 104-06.
Identifies such literary archetypes as the quest motif, the wise old man, and the Great Mother in the story "The Red One."

Tavernier-Courbin, Jacqueline. *Critical Essays on Jack London.* Boston: G. K. Hall, 1983, 298 p.
Includes essays by Tavernier-Courbin, H. L. Mencken, Anatole France, Earle Labor, Susan Ward, and others. This volume is divided into sections on London's life, general commentary, specific works, and writing techniques.

Walcutt, Charles Child. "Jack London: Blond Beasts and Supermen." In his *American Literary Naturalism, a Divided Stream,* pp. 87-113. Minneapolis: University of Minnesota Press, 1956.
Discusses the influence of the theories of Charles Darwin and Herbert Spencer on London's adventure stories.

————. *Jack London.* American Writers Pamphlet no. 57. Minneapolis: University of Minnesota Press, 1966, 48 p.
Biographical and critical essay covering most of London's work.

Walker, Franklin, *Jack London and the Klondike.* San Marino, Cal.: Huntington Library, 1966, 288 p.
Relates London's Klondike adventures to their fictional counterparts in his Arctic tales.

Watson, Charles N., Jr. "Jack London's Yokohama Swim and His First Tall Tale." *Studies in American Humor* 3, No. 2 (October 1976): 84-95.
Examination of London's biographical experiences as reflected in the stories "A Night's Swim in Yeddo Bay" and "In Yeddo Bay."

Bobbie Ann Mason

1940-

American short story writer, novelist, and critic.

Mason has received considerable critical acclaim for her short story collections *Shiloh, and Other Stories* and *Love Life*. Set primarily in rural western Kentucky, Mason's fiction depicts a rapidly changing South in which individuals who once lived and worked on farms and shared deep-rooted family traditions are now employed by national retail stores, live in subdivisions, and experience the modern world largely through such commercial institutions as television, popular music, shopping malls, and fast-food restaurants. Unable to reconcile their present lives to their past, Mason's characters have been viewed as grotesques who are experiencing, in Anne Tyler's words, "the sense of bewilderment and anxious hopefulness that people feel when suddenly confronted with change." In her fiction, Mason employs a plain, laconic prose style replete with mentions of brand names to illustrate the banality of mass culture and its effects on the society she portrays.

Mason grew up on a farm in Paducah, Kentucky, where many of her stories are set. A withdrawn child, she spent much of her youth reading books and listening to popular music on the radio. After attending the University of Kentucky, Mason relocated to New York, where she worked as a writer for the fan magazines *Movie Life* and *TV Star Parade*. Later, while pursuing an advanced degree at the University of Connecticut, Mason met her future husband, whose support, coupled with her own growing assurance in her abilities, inspired her to write short stories, which she began submitting for publication to the *New Yorker* magazine. *New Yorker* fiction editor Roger Angell, while offering encouraging comments, rejected nineteen of Mason's submissions before finally accepting one of her stories in 1980.

The pieces in Mason's first book, *Shiloh, and Other Stories,* are set in and around Paducah, Kentucky, and document some of the social, economic, and moral changes that have accompanied the region's transition from farmland to commercial outpost. Most of these stories are marked by present-tense narration and inconclusive endings, and their protagonists are often torn between the security of their familiar lives and the desire to leave their surroundings and seek better circumstances. This conflict is illustrated in the story "Residents and Transients," in which a woman chooses to stay at her parents' farmhouse instead of accompanying her husband to the city after he receives a job transfer, stating simply, "I do not want to go anywhere." By the end of the story, however, the woman decides to join her husband after acknowledging the threat of stagnation and admitting that she truly misses him. Several of Mason's stories focus on troubled marriages caused by dissatisfaction with traditional gender roles, and her female characters often display more emotional strength and independence than their male counterparts. In "Shiloh," a homebound truck driver recovering from an accident tries to save his dissolving marriage by purchasing an organ for his wife Norma Jean. Ironically, however, she becomes obsessed with the accompanying "Sixties Songbook" and feels that she has missed something exciting in both her

marriage and her life. Later, the couple travel to Shiloh, the scene of a famous Civil War battlefield, in another attempt to revive their relationship, but the trip only reinforces Norma Jean's desire to leave her husband.

Mason's second volume of short stories, *Love Life,* also focuses upon characters confused by a society in transition and trapped between a desire for stability and a longing for change. In the story "Hunktown," for example, a man who secretly dreams of becoming a professional singer urges his wife to sell the family farm and move with him to Memphis, but she refuses, suspecting his motives and doubting his talent. Many of Mason's protagonists have become removed from their heritage and consequently seek refuge in television evangelism, call-in radio mysticism, or aerobic dancing. Michiko Kakutani observed: "[It is one of Mason's] strengths as a writer that she's able to look beyond the bluff facades of her characters and reveal the geography of their inner lives." Kakutani added: "[These] stories are not simply minimalist 'slice-of-life' exercises, but finely crafted tales that manage to invest inarticulate, small-town lives with dignity and intimations of meaning."

Mason has earned critical respect for her compelling and unsentimental depictions of rural, working-class people attempting to adjust to an increasingly modernized South. Her works describe not only commercial and material changes, but also more threatening alterations in societal mores. Most critics attribute Mason's success to her vivid evocation of Southern dialect and the physical and social geography of the region. Although some reviewers have faulted Mason's stories for displaying similarities in narrative tone and for lacking definite resolutions, most agree that they portray contemporary Southern life with accuracy, humor, and poignancy.

(For further information on Mason's life and career, see *Contemporary Literary Criticism*, Vols. 28, 43; *Contemporary Authors*, Vols. 53-56; *Contemporary Authors New Revision Series*, Vol. 11; and *Dictionary of Literary Biography Yearbook: 1987.*)

PRINCIPAL WORKS

SHORT FICTION

Shiloh, and Other Stories   1982
Love Life   1989

OTHER MAJOR WORKS

In Country   (novel)   1985
Spence + Lila   (novel)   1988

DAVID QUAMMEN   (essay date 1982)

[*Quammen is an American novelist, critic, and short story writer. In the following review of* Shiloh, and Other Stories, *he lauds Mason for her evocative portrayals of rural and working-class people coping with change in western Kentucky.*]

For several years short stories by Bobbie Ann Mason have been turning up—rather improbably, it seemed—in *The New Yorker* and *The Atlantic*. The improbability lay in the fact that Miss Mason writes almost exclusively about working-class and farm people coping with their muted frustrations in western Kentucky (south of Paducah, not far from Kentucky Lake, if that helps you), and the gap to be bridged *empathically* between her readership and her characters was therefore formidable. But formidable also is Miss Mason's talent, and her craftsmanship. *Shiloh and Other Stories,* her first collection, shows not only how good she can be but how consistently good she remains. The most improbable thing about this volume is that not a single page lags, hardly a paragraph fails, not one among 16 stories is less than impressive.

Loss and deprivation, the disappointment of pathetically modest hopes, are the themes Bobbie Ann Mason works and reworks. She portrays the disquieted lives of men and women not blessed with much money or education or luck, but cursed with enough sensitivity and imagination to allow them to suffer regrets. These are lives seen against an equally disquieted social landscape, where old grocery stores with front porches are being replaced by things called "the Convenient," where the grown daughters of ranch wives work as clerks at K Mart, where higher wisdom comes in via the Phil Donahue show. . . .

In this sad and scary moment of failing certainties it is time for the venerable tulip tree in the yard to be cut down, time for Granny to be moved to the nursing home, time for an arthritic old dog named Grover Cleveland to be put to sleep. Time too for a couple of Miss Mason's heroines to see the gynecologist about a lump in the breast. All the bad portents,

all the sickening changes seem somehow connected, uniting *Shiloh and Other Stories* as tightly as a good novel. One elderly woman says to her grown daughter: "Did you hear about the datsun dog that killed the baby?" She means dachshund. Ominous forces of disorientation are loose in Masonland. (p. 7)

Most compellingly, Miss Mason examines in her various truck drivers and salesclerks the dawning recognition—in some cases only a vague worry—of having missed something, something important, some alternate life more fruitful than the one that's been led. For instance, Norma Jean Moffitt of the story **"Shiloh"** sells cosmetics at a Rexall and has lately, for reasons unclear to her husband Leroy, begun developing her pectorals with barbells. Because he fears she is drifting away from him (and he is right), Leroy buys her an electric organ, upon which Norma Jean proceeds to master every tune in "The Sixties Songbook." "I didn't like these old songs back then," she says. "But I have this crazy feeling I missed something." And a long deferred car picnic with Leroy to the battlefield at Shiloh is not, it transpires, what she has in mind.

The message from Bobbie Ann Mason, which by her wit and skill she makes a fascinating matter, is that inexorable changes are coming upon the plain folk of western Kentucky. (p. 33)

> David Quammen, "Plain Folk and Puzzling Changes," in The New York Times Book Review, November 21, 1982, pp. 7, 33.

ROBERT TOWERS   (essay date 1982)

[*In the excerpt below, Towers praises Mason for her unbiased treatment of ordinary people in her fiction and for her ability to reveal the essence of domestic conflict.*]

Vision and technique come exhilaratingly together in Bobbie Ann Mason's collection of stories [*Shiloh and Other Stories*]. She is one of those rare writers who, by concentrating their attention on a few square miles of native turf, are able to open up new and surprisingly wide worlds for the delighted reader. Less tragically gloomy than Raymond Carver, Mason nonetheless resembles that fine writer in the way she lays bare the heart of a domestic drama; and like him she holds up for our inspection a whole class of unremarkable people who are seldom noticed in fiction. (p. 39)

Bobbie Ann Mason is wonderfully even-handed and nonjudgmental in the handling of her characters, male as well as female. They are what they are, she seems to say, as restless women strain against the confines of marriage, as restless men take off in pickup trucks for Texas or the Rockies, leaving their women stuck with more rent than they can afford to pay. Her interest in them is both friendly and detached—and it extends to cats and ancient, ailing dogs . . . and to mechanical objects as well: an injured truck-driver's rig "sits in the backyard, like a gigantic bird that has flown home to roost." She avoids extended descriptions, depending upon a few exactly observed details to establish her situations and scenes.

Individually effective as they are, there is a degree of sameness to the stories read as a collection. This is due partly to the rather narrow restrictions of class and circumstance and outlook within which the characters lead their untidy lives; it is due more, I think, to the fact that Mason seldom varies the form and rhythmic pattern of her pieces. She is a superb technician, but I wish she did not adhere quite so closely to the conventions that seem to apply chiefly to women writing for *The New Yorker*: i.e., the use of the present tense for narration and the avoidance of anything resembling a "closed" ending. Mason's stories are open-ended with a vengeance. Most often her conclusions swerve abruptly from the path that has been hitherto pursued and take off across the fields. A few resolutions might add some needed variety to an otherwise remarkable achievement. *Shiloh and Other Stories* is among the best of the recent good collections that have once again brought the short story to the forefront of literary interest. (p. 40)

> Robert Towers, "American Graffiti," in The New York Review of Books, *Vol. XXIX, No. 20, December 16, 1982, pp. 38-40.*

ROBERT NEWMAN   (essay date 1983)

[*In the following excerpt, Newman offers a favorable review of* Shiloh, and Other Stories.]

[Bobbie Ann Mason's *Shiloh, and Other Stories*] marks the debut of a writer with a gift for transmuting the regional flavor of small-town Kentucky into a full-bodied evocation of the difficulties of transition. Humor and warmth blend with confusion and pain in sixteen portraits of people contemplating or resisting change. . . .

Characters break down into residents and transients, the title of one of the stories. The residents seek to insulate themselves against the shifts of time by collecting paintings of watermelons, perpetually dialing the weather service, or projecting the illusion of the perfect family into a "miniature early American whatnot." For them, "perhaps the meaning of home grows out of the fear of open spaces."

The transients pursue meaning, take decisive actions, but find satisfaction elusive. (p. 92)

The conflict between residents and transients is revealed in the title story ["Shiloh"]. Leroy Moffitt, a truckdriver who is home recuperating from an accident, idly conjures a dream home from a popsicle stick model while his wife, Norma Jean, lifts weights, takes courses at the community college, and experiments with "unusual" foods like tacos and lasagna. Leroy tries to instill life into their disintegrating marriage by purchasing an electric organ for Norma Jean whose subsequent obsession with her *Sixties Songbook* dovetails with her insistence that "I have this crazy feeling that I missed something." Norma Jean's mother, Mabel, convinces herself that a vacation in Shiloh, the place of her own honeymoon, will shore up their marriage, but their view of the battlefield only strengthens Norma Jean's resolve to leave while Leroy realizes that "the inner workings of marriage, like most of history, have escaped him." As Norma Jean walks through the cemetery that mirrors the state of their relationship, Leroy still searches for hopeful signs despite a sky that is "unusually pale—the color of the dust ruffle Mabel made for their bed."

Departure and return are the behavioral and conceptual patterns that dominate Mason's characters. Cataclysmic breaks fade into ponderous attempts at self-discovery through familial and natural sources, and the revelations achieved are often communicated in the lovely and satisfying lines that close the stories. In **"Nancy Culpepper,"** the protagonist reconciles

past with present through the photograph of her great-aunt. In **"Offerings,"** acceptance of the rituals of nature yields vision and temporary contentment: "the night is peaceful, and Sandra thinks of the thousands of large golden garden spiders hidden in the field. In the early morning the dew shines on their trampolines, and she can imagine bouncing with an excited spring from web to web, all the way up the hill to the woods." (pp. 92-3)

Mason's resolutions are personal but not intrusive. The cultural reverberations wrought by transformations in the Southern landscape issue challenges to her characters, and they find both escape and wisdom in the sanctity of the familiar. Her adroit handling of dialogue, both in its precise intonations and in its ability to communicate silences, and her capacity to join metaphor with detail contribute texture to these portraits that begin to bear uncanny resemblances to relatives, friends, and self. (p. 93)

> Robert Newman, in a review of "Shiloh, and Other Stories," in Carolina Quarterly, *Vol. XXXV, No. 3, Spring, 1983, pp. 92-3.*

GREG JOHNSON   (essay date 1983)

[*In the following excerpt, Johnson provides an appreciative review of* Shiloh, and Other Stories.]

An intriguing narrative perspective, amounting to a kind of "double vision," distinguishes the stories in [*Shiloh, and Other Stories*]. On the one hand, this is regional fiction, rendering the lives of Kentucky people who still partake of long-established rural traditions. . . . Yet the stories are as contemporary as this morning's newspaper, crammed with details of video games and New Wave music, Colonel Sanders and "The Dukes of Hazzard." It is this meeting place of two vastly different cultures that Mason has taken as her special province. The stories . . . are unfailingly intelligent, detached, unsentimental; yet they do not condescend toward their characters, many of whom are uneducated and plainly bewildered by their loosening hold on the world around them.

In **"The Retreat,"** a young woman accompanies her preacher-husband on an annual church retreat, and slowly discovers that her marriage is unsatisfying, that her life has slipped mysteriously beyond her control. She deals with her frustration by playing a video game called Galaxians, which gives her a temporary sense of autonomy and power. Like most of the stories, **"The Retreat"** has no resolution, no easy answers: it simply evokes the character's moral confusion, her sense of entrapment. "I want to stay here by myself so I can think straight," she tells her bewildered husband, who has been reassigned to a church in another city. This need to "think straight," to orient the self within a confusing present and an unassimilated past, is an issue confronted again and again by Mason's characters.

Often the conflict is between generations, as in **"Drawing Names,"** a story about a young woman's doomed attempt to bring together her lover and her family (farm people who disapprove of drinking, much less premarital sex) for an old-fashioned Christmas dinner, or **"A New-Wave Format,"** about a fortyish bus driver involved with a girl half his age, Sabrina, who makes him feel out of date: "He used to think of himself as an adventurer, but now he believes he has gone through life rather blindly, without much pain or sense of loss." (pp. 196-97)

Mason's special strengths as a writer are her sense of place, her accuracy of detail, and her ability to mingle compassion with a good-humored vision of human absurdity. No one escapes her ironic eye: if she often smiles at her good country people and their narrow view of things, she also enjoys deflating the "sophistication" of her younger, urban characters. . . .

The collection as a whole, however, suffers from a uniformity of style that often borders on monotony. Nearly all the stories are written in the present tense, and although this is effective in some cases, in others it feels mannered and self-conscious; similarly, Mason's laconic narrative voice can become wearing when it continues unvaried through sixteen stories. Also, the dramatic situation of a young woman recently divorced, or abandoned by her husband, who is now forced to reassess her life and identity, appears once or twice too often. This is a most impressive collection, however, surely one of the best to be published by any writer, new or established, in the past decade. (p. 197)

> Greg Johnson, "Stories of the New South," in Southwest Review, Vol. 68, No. 2, Spring, 1983, pp. 196-97.

FRANCIS KING (essay date 1983)

[One of Britain's most respected contemporary writers, King is best known for his detailed, realistic works of fiction which exhibit a pessimistic view of modern humanity and a fascination with life's injustices. In the following excerpt, King offers a positive review of Shiloh, and Other Stories.]

Each story [in **Shiloh**] is a recreation of life, in all its quaint, baffling, funny, pathetic inconsequentiality, in one small, obscure corner of the world. Few of her English readers will ever have visited the towns that she describes, few are likely to do so. But it is probable that they will retain the impression that they have made a visit, in some other existence or in a dream, so intense is her evocation. . . .

One of Miss Mason's constant themes is the manner in which, with no decisive snap of the thread, human relationships become unravelled. In some instances, they remain that way; in others, the fabric knits up again, with no apparent effort by either of the parties. In the title story, **"Shiloh"**, for example, a truck-driver, out of work after an accident, observes, through a haze of marijuana smoke, how his tough, independent wife is slowly receding from him, in a new-found interest first in body-building and then in English composition. When he takes her to the Civil War battlefield of Shiloh, she, in effect, vanishes out of sight, leaving him with the desolating sense that, just as he has never understood the inner workings of history that erupted in so much carnage, so he has never understood the inner workings of the marriage that is now causing his own living death.

Again, in **"Still Life with Watermelon"**, a wife, whose husband has inexplicably taken off for Texas with a buddy—is the buddy perhaps, as her closest woman friend suggests, a homosexual?—obsessively paints one amateurish picture of watermelons after another, in the hope that a rich, eccentric collector of pictures of watermelons will buy one off her. Eventually, wife and husband are reunited. The journey to Texas has been a crazy adventure for him; and she, working away at her watermelons, has been on a journey no less crazy. Now they are together once more in all their usual ordinariness; but some faint recollection of their fugues into craziness will obstinately remain with them.

Another constant theme is the persistence with which the past works like a yeast in the present. In **"Nancy Culpepper"** for example, a young woman becomes obsessed with the ancestress whose name she bears. Her nonagenarian grandmother has a hoard of family photographs, which, now that she is about to go into an old people's home, the young woman hopes to claim for herself. Eventually, there, in her hands, is the faded photograph of another young woman, in an embroidered white dress, 'her eyes fixed on something so far away'—the future containing her namesake. Photographs, as the symbols, at once shadowy and powerful, of an ever-living past are used to eerie effect in stories other than this one.

As an incessant, intrusive counterpoint to the lives of these ill-educated characters, their television screens, in livingrooms, kitchens or bedrooms, project images of a world which they are doomed never to experience except at secondhand. Often, they pay more attention to the images of drama than to the actual dramas (love, bereavement, betrayal) in which they are engulfed.

> Francis King, "Fantasy Lives," in The Spectator, Vol. 251, No. 8093, August 20, 1983, p. 21.

WELCH D. EVERMAN (essay date 1983)

[Everman is an American critic and novelist. In the review excerpted below, he assesses the stories in Shiloh, and Other Stories as traditional in narrative form yet concerned with the nature of storytelling.]

The stories in **Shiloh** are well-written, straightforward narratives—stories in the traditional sense. For Mason, the story is not open to question. Rather, it is what it has always been—logical plot, detailed settings, recognizable characters. It is about life, and life is completely speakable. The dust jacket describes these stories as sharing "pinpoint accuracy of external detail and inner vision."

This is not true, of course. Mason's fictions are not accurate and detailed descriptions of the world beyond language where we live out our lives. . . . Mason is a very skilled writer, but if her fictive worlds are familiar, it is not because they resemble our world. It is because they resemble other fictions, other stories.

We know these stories. We have read them before, or at least we have read stories very much like them. We have told them ourselves—though perhaps not as well as Mason does. Again and again, we have used the familiar form of these stories to explain ourselves to ourselves. . . .

But even these stories that scrupulously avoid the question of storiness answer it by reminding us that stories are what we are. They teach us how to live. They give us means for interpreting our lives and ourselves.

Like us, Mason's characters are defined by stories, in this case by popular culture. They follow TV and the movies and interpret their lives accordingly.

> She hates the thought of a string of husbands, and the idea of a stepfather is like a substitute host on

a talk show. It makes her think of Johnny Carson's many substitute hosts.

We have learned that stories explain the truth of what we know, though in fact we don't always recall that these truths are only stories.

> Leroy has read that for most people losing a child destroys the marriage—or else he heard this on *Donahue*. He can't always remember where he learns things anymore.

Whether she intends it or not, Mason reminds us that it is important for us to question the nature of storiness, to question the stories we have received, to know what stories are. (p. 74)

> Welch D. Everman, "Breaking Silence," in The North American Review, *Vol. 268, No. 4, December, 1983, pp. 73-4.*

ROBIN BECKER (essay date 1984)

[*Becker is an American critic and poet. In the essay below, she examines Mason's treatment of male-female relationships, noting role reversals among many of the couples portrayed in* Shiloh, and Other Stories.]

The authors reviewed here—Ann Beattie, Bobbie Ann Mason and Alice Munro—all tell their stories in vastly different ways, but they share certain similarities which make critical comparisons possible. They observe, to a great extent, the traditional conventions of short fiction. Told from a particular point of view in the Jamesian sense, they preserve the unities of time and place, and, with the exception of dreams, they all take place in the real, phenomenal world. Although each writer depicts a range of situations, all three portray women in terms of their relations to men—marriage, separation and divorce. Heterosexual relations work as an amorphous moral, social and economic force, a backdrop for and occasionally the site of the story's plot. (p. 5)

Mason examines power and powerlessness by assigning to female characters behavior which ruptures the social fabric. The wives in *Shiloh and Other Stories* are in states of transition much like the Kentucky landscape which surrounds them, and which Mason depicts with relentless humor and sharp irony. In the title story **"Shiloh,"** Norma Jean studies body-building and takes courses at the local community college. Leroy, her husband, collects a disability pension since a tractor-trailer accident, does needlepoint (a *Star Trek* pillow cover), and struggles to articulate what is happening to him. "He has the feeling that they are waking up out of a dream together—that they must create a new marriage, start afresh." Leroy's impulses are admirable; his desire for a "new marriage" is wholly consistent with the theme of this and other stories, but Norma Jean sees things differently. "We *have* started all over again," says Norma Jean. "And this is how it turned out."

While satirizing the traditional roles in marriage, Mason portrays characters who feel the stirrings that lead to action. The comic role reversals surprise and startle. The husbands in these stories are white, working-class Southern men, neither rapists nor villains, and their marital difficulties are made to seem systemic, not individual. This is an important strategy, as it enables her to create characters for whom a more gender-free existence seems possible. The men are "feminized" by their distress, as the women are strengthened by work, a measure of sexual freedom (sometimes adulterous), and by their community with other women.

Georgeann, married to a preacher in **"The Retreat,"** experiences a "thrill of power" playing video games during a church retreat. "Your mind leaves your body," she tries to explain to her husband. Mason ably satirizes the values displayed at the church by leading Georgeann to a spiritual experience through electronic games. When her husband is transferred to another church sixty miles away, she refuses to go. This refusal, like others in the collection, jolts our notion of the traditional wife who willingly follows her husband as he pursues his career. The story is filled with metaphors of alienation. Her husband, dressed in a suit, looks "remote, like a meter reader." Georgeann wanders around the retreat "as if she is visiting someone else's dreams" (which she is). She imagines seagulls returning home "like hurled boomerangs." Her house looks "like something abandoned." A dying hen, weakening throughout the story, echoes Georgeann's waning faith in her role of wife and mother. Her husband, she notes early in the story, would "get the ax and chop its head off," because he "believes in the necessity of things." Now, having experienced a feeling of power and a quickening inside her, she knows what she must do. She kills the dying chicken by chopping off its head, her action symbolizing her need to take control over her life.

Marital disagreements are sometimes subsumed by other tensions, such as the urban/rural and traditional/high-tech dichotomies. In **"Residents and Transients,"** Mary prefers to remain in her parents' rural farmhouse when her husband Stephen is transferred to Louisville. Stephen is a travelling demonstrator of word-processing machines; in the canning kitchen where her mother processed green beans, Mary feeds her eight cats. Yankees are moving into the region; her parents are moving into a condo. Mason's lively word-plays accentuate the sense of dislocation and disorientation. When Mary expresses her sadness at the loss of the things she loves, Stephen tells her that provincial emotions lead to "nationalism, fascism—you name it." His misreading of history (and her feelings) illustrates a more insidious undercurrent here, the romantic myth that science and progress can solve social problems.

To Waldeen, contemplating a second marriage in **"Graveyard Day,"** a stepfather for her daughter is "something like a sugar substitute." Her first husband and her lover, both named Joe, keep getting confused in her mind. ("What she is really afraid of, she realizes, is that he will turn out to be just like Joe Murdock.") Her lover is unreal, like "some T.V. game-show host," like "an actor in a vaudeville show," and families with their shifting memberships are "like clubs." When her lover asks her why, if she loves him, she resists marrying him, she replies, "that's the easy part. Love is easy." Mason illustrates Waldeen's resistance to romantic love with images depicting her increasing sense of disorder. At the end, she takes a "flying leap" into the neat pile of leaves Joe has been raking all afternoon, scattering his tidy order, and, on another level, his narrow notions of her future as his wife.

The endings of Mason's stories frequently suggest the leaps necessary to produce change. Georgeann's gesture, Mary's refusal to leave the rural farmhouse, Waldeen's jump indicate the characters' needs for movement and replenishment. The longing for simplicity and a more "primitive" existence appears frequently in these fictions, while spiritual renewal seems in short supply. In **"Offerings,"** Mason creates a rural retreat for Sandra Lee, who lives alone in the country (her husband has left her) tending her garden, watching her cats kill birds and moles. The human world, too, is filled with images of sickness and death—her mother's post-operative body resembled "the Red Sea parting" and the tomato sauce looks like "bowls of blood." Sandra's grandmother observes that she has moved to the "wilderness," echoing the desire for an uninhabited, uncultivated place. Sandra is nourished by solitude and her intimacy with the creatures which seem, almost, to inhabit her house, and the story ends with her fantasy of escape into the woods. (pp. 5-6)

Beattie, Mason, and Munro present believable characters in believable situations. Like the early women writers, they concentrate on the struggle to achieve self-fulfillment, the nature of intimate relationships, the ways women compromise to remain within society's bounds. . . .

Beattie and Mason depict marriage as a way-station where women and men incubate their frustrations and articulate their desires. . . .

Mason delights us by laughing at our efforts while cheering us on. Her female characters work and tend to have more mobility (both social and personal) than the women depicted in fictions of an earlier age. The stories teem with characters on the brink of change, and she observes their struggles with respect and gentle humor. The articulation of pain remains, as Heilbrun says, the primary achievement of these women writers. . . .

Why do we read novels and short stories? For pleasure; for instruction; for the solace of seeing others in familiar dilemmas; for the opportunity to see what is unfamiliar, perhaps strange; for hope. These writers, in different ways, satisfy these requirements. They suggest that diversity is possible, that fiction will reflect varying lifestyles, political and sexual commitments, as well as new approaches to language. All three have nudged the genre forward. What remains is for women writers to continue to explore their experiences as successful, creative, autonomous people. There are risks still to be taken. (p. 6)

Robin Becker, "Fear-of-Success Stories?" in *The Women's Review of Books*, Vol. I, No. 7, April, 1984, pp. 5-6.

MAUREEN RYAN (essay date 1984)

[*In the following excerpt, Ryan discusses the ways in which Mason's characters in* Shiloh, and Other Stories *deal with personal, social, and cultural upheavals in the South.*]

Bobbie Ann Mason's short stories, published in 1982 in the award-winning collection *Shiloh and Other Stories,* are set in western Kentucky in a contemporary South marked by change. Small towns and farmhouses have made way for subdivisions with "new brick ranch houses of FHA-approved designs" and "mobile homes that have appeared like fungi." New shopping centers and industrial parks have displaced "the farmers who used to gather around the courthouse square on Saturday afternoons to play checkers and spit tobacco juice **("Shiloh")**. But the old farmers are barely missed; in the new TV-infested South they have been replaced by Johnny Carson and Phil Donahue as the oracles of humor and truth.

Mason's characters stumble through their lives in this protean world, puzzled by intimidating new mores. In **"The Climber,"** Dolores, apprehensively awaiting an appointment with a doctor who will diagnose the lump in her breast, hears "the Oak Ridge Boys . . . singing 'Elvira' on the radio. The Oak Ridge Boys used to be a gospel quartet when Dolores was a child. Now, inexplicably, they are a group of young men with blow-dried hair, singing country-rock songs about love." The New South is in many aspects a more liberal, expanded world; a middle-aged grandfather asks who bought the "toes," no longer referring to " 'nigger toes,' the old names for the chocolate-covered creams" **("Drawing Names").** Yet it is as well a plastic, superficial world of television, Sara Lee cheesecake, and Star Wars toys.

Against the backdrop of this modernized society, Mason's characters, most of them in early to late middle age, grapple with the vicissitudes of life and their own personal upheavals—marriage and divorce, illness and aging, family relationships. Their ambivalent attitudes—and Mason's—toward the events in their own lives parallel their uncertain reactions to the complexities of the world around them.

In Mason's South, middle-aged men recognize, hesitantly and belatedly, that they have missed out on much of life. In **"The Ocean,"** Bill Crittendon has sold his farm and invested in a deluxe camper, and he and his wife have set off to see the Atlantic Ocean because "he had once promised Imogene that they would see the world, but they never had. He always knew it was a failure of courage. After the war he had rushed back home. He hated himself for the way he had stayed at home all that time." (pp. 283-85)

Leroy Moffitt, the protagonist of the title story [**"Shiloh"**], is a disabled truck driver who has been unemployed for four months and whose suddenly sedentary life has inspired new perceptions. Having recently "grown to appreciate how things are put together," Leroy decides to build his wife Norma Jean a log cabin, because, as he recognizes, "the house they live in is small and nondescript." He begins to notice the rampant suburbanization of the once-rural community, but more threatening is his observation that Norma Jean has become stronger and more independent in his absence. When on a long-planned trip to the Civil War battleground in Shiloh, Tennessee, she announces that she is leaving him, Leroy reflects on the past. But he "knows he is leaving out a lot. He is leaving out the insides of history. History was always just names and dates to him. It occurs to him that building a house out of logs is similarly empty—too simple. And the real inner workings of a marriage, like most of history, have escaped him."

These confused men share an emotional impotence and ineffectuality that are manifested most obviously in their relationships with women. (p. 286)

Mickey Hargrove, in **"Private Lies,"** seems to resent the fact that "marriage to Tina was like riding a bus. She was the driver and he was a passenger. She made all the decisions—food, furniture, Kelly's braces, his socks. If he weren't married to Tina, he might be alone in a rented room, living on canned soup and Tang. Tina rescued him. With her, life had a regularity that was almost dogmatic." Yet he admires strong women and is attracted to his ex-wife because she has changed, has become "different, prettier and more assured." He is excited by the new Donna who has flown over Mount St. Helens ("He admired a woman who would charter a plane") and who has "learned all new techniques" of love-making.

In **"The Rookers,"** it is not Mary Lou Skaggs but her husband Mack who is suffering from the empty nest syndrome now that his youngest child has gone off to college. Mack does his carpentry work at home and becomes distressed if he must be away from the house for too long.

> Mary Lou has tried to be patient with Mack, thinking that he will grow out of his current phase. Sooner or later, she and Mack will have to face growing older together. Mack says that having a daughter in college makes him feel he has missed something, but Mary Lou has tried to make him see that they could still enjoy life. . . . She suggested bowling, camping, a trip to Opryland. But Mack said he'd rather improve his mind. He has been reading *Shōgun.* He made excuses about the traffic.

Mack is afraid of Mary Lou and her insistence upon living; "You're always wanting to run around . . . You might get ideas." He is content to stay at home with his television and his *Old Farmer's Almanac,* reading about the weather. Not until the story's end does Mary Lou recognize the motivation for her husband's fascination with the weather:

> Mary Lou suddenly realizes that Mack calls the temperature number because he is afraid to talk on the telephone, and by listening to a recording, he doesn't have to reply. It's his way of pretending that he's involved. He wants it to snow so he won't have to go outside. He is afraid of what might happen. But it occurs to her that what he must really be afraid of is women. Then Mary Lou feels so sick and heavy with her power over him that she wants to cry. She sees the way her husband is standing there, in a frozen pose. Mack looks as though he could stand there all night with the telephone receiver against his ear.

If many of Mason's female characters are stronger, more in control than their husbands and lovers, their assertiveness is as new and tentative as the men's awareness. Like Mason's men, her women are assessing their marriages and their lives.

Norma Jean Moffitt, pregnant and married at eighteen, has at thirty-four endured the death of a child, the incessant advice of a meddling mother, a husband on the road, and a job at the Rexall drugstore. No longer the child whom Leroy married, she is at his return taking a body-building class and later graduates to adult-ed composition at Paducah Community College. She gives up the electric organ and *The Sixties Songbook,* begins to cook "unusual foods—tacos, lasagna, Bombay chicken." And Leroy is not surprised when Norma Jean announces that she is leaving him, with the explanation that "in some ways a woman prefers a man who wanders."

Georgeann Pickett, in **"The Retreat,"** grows increasingly discontent with her marriage to a good but shallow minister who must supplement his modest salary with part time work as an electrician. Distressed because low attendance is about to force the closing of his small church, Shelby looks forward with eagerness to the annual church retreat and workshops like "The Changing Role of the Country Pastor." Georgeann, however, attends reluctantly. At a workshop on Christian marriage, she asks the participants—mostly other ministers' wives—"What do you do if the man you're married to—this is just a hypothetical question—say he's the cream of creation and all, and he's sweet as can be, but he

turns out to be the wrong one for you? What do you do if you're just simply mismatched?" But "everyone looks at her."

When she stumbles upon a video game in the lodge basement, Georgeann finds a refuge. Playing the game, Galaxian, she feels that "the situation is dangerous and thrilling, but Georgeann feels in control. She isn't running away; she is chasing the aliens." She cannot explain the attractions of the game to her bewildered husband, when he finds her much later. "You forget everything but who you are," she tries to tell him. "Your mind leaves your body. . . . I was happy when I was playing that game." When they return home to the children and Shelby's reassignment letter and the reality that they will have to move, Georgeann announces to her husband that she will not go with him.

Georgeann's inability to articulate to Shelby her feelings about the video game illustrates the failure to communicate that plagues Mason's marriages. Leroy, recognizing that his marriage is in jeopardy, wants to make a fresh start with his wife; he "has the sudden impulse to tell Norma Jean about himself, as if he had just met her. They have known each other so long they have forgotten a lot about each other. They could become reacquainted. But when the oven timer goes off and she runs to the kitchen he forgets why he wants to do this."

In her letters to her husband Tom, who has gone to Texas to play "born-again cowboy," Louise Milsap, in **"Still Life with Watermelon,"** is more "expressive" than she ever was during their four-year marriage. She recognizes that the incident that precipitated Tom's departure, in which she threw "a Corning Ware Petite Pan" at him, was merely an attempt to get his attention. Linda will not return to her husband, in **"Old Things,"** because, as she tells her mother, "I don't feel like hanging around the same house with somebody that can go for three hours without saying a word. He might as well not be there."

Most of Mason's stories are concerned with marriage and male-female relationships that reflect, in their instability and disquietude, the fluidity of this society. Mason recognizes, however, that in complicated times close and lasting relationships become—if more difficult—more imperative as well. In brief, often poignant scenes she offers glimpses of durable, satisfying marriages.

After Imogene, in **"The Ocean,"** expresses the hidden resentment she has long felt at having cared for her husband's invalid mother and, inadvertently, her own fears about growing old, Bill comforts her. Later, watching her sleep, he remembers when, just after their marriage and his induction into the service, he "watched her sleep for a full hour, wanting to remember her face while he was overseas. . . . Now Imogene's face was fat and lined, but he could still see her young face clearly." A recently separated Kay Stone returns home in **"Gooseberry Winter"** and, after a day's outing with her mother, in which the older woman tells her daughter about her unhappy childhood, watches as her parents plant flowers. "For a while she watches the relaxed way they work together, her father patiently digging holes, following her mother's directions. For all Mama's fears, she is comfortable with her husband, as though he were a refuge even now from her loveless past."

For Mason such scenes, however rare and transitory, demonstrate that marriage—indeed, any human relationship—can offer a permanence seldom found in a mutable world. As Kay notes, "she had thought that marriage was so much simpler than the intricacies of blood ties, so easy that it could be canceled, forgotten. But her parents make marriage seem as permanent as having children."

Having children may be more enduring than marriage in Mason's fictional world, but it is no less problematical. Many of her stories deal with aging parents and grandparents, and unhappy adult children returning home. The interaction among generations further illustrates the unrest that characterizes their society.

Although widowed Cleo Watkins cannot understand why her daughter would leave her faithful husband, Linda and her two children have moved in and overtaken Cleo's house. The grandmother is unable to adjust to the constant noise of the television, dishwasher, and telephone that the children create, and she "has forgotten to move effortlessly through the clutter children make." Neither can Cleo comprehend why her daughter buys new clothes and goes out without her children, nor can Linda accept her mother's refusal to create a new life for herself. When Cleo argues that "people can't just have everything they want all the time," Linda responds, ". . . people don't have to do what they don't want to as much now as they used to." "I should know that," Cleo says. "It's all over television. You make me feel awful."

The generation gap is dramatized too in **"Graveyard Day."** Waldeen Murdock, recently divorced, does not understand her ten-year-old daughter. "Her daughter insists that she is a vegetarian. If Holly had said Rosicrucian, it would have sounded just as strange to Waldeen." Holly is precocious and unhappy, and Waldeen wonders whether she misses her father, who has moved to Arizona. Joe McClain wants to marry Waldeen, but she knows that marriage is complicated. She loves Joe, she admits, but proclaims that "that's the easy part. Love is easy." She tries to explain to Joe that "you can't just do something by itself. Everything else drags along. It's all *involved*." Considering the effect of her remarriage on Holly, Waldeen sees that "Holly would have a stepfather—something like a sugar substitute." But "she hates the thought of a string of husbands, and the idea of a stepfather is like a substitute host on a talk show. It makes her think of Johnny Carson's many substitute hosts." Waldeen and Holly disagree about everything from the relative benefits of plastic vs. real flowers to whether the cat was neutered or nurtured, and after one of her spats with her very contemporary daughter, Waldeen "suddenly feels miserable about the way she treats Holly. Everything Waldeen does is so roundabout, so devious."

Devious is the word for Sandra's interaction with her grandmother in **"Offerings."** Sandra's husband has gone to Louisville to work at a K Mart, and Sandra, a country girl, has stayed behind. Her mother and grandmother come from Paducah to visit, and "they aren't going to tell Grandmother about the separation. Mama insisted about that. Mama has never told Grandmother about her own hysterectomy. She will not even smoke in front of Grandmother Stamper. For twenty-five years, Mama has sneaked smokes whenever her mother-in-law is around." Neither can Kay Stone tell her father about her separation from her husband, whom she has left because he will not accept the responsibility of dealing with his son from a former marriage. Only at the end of the story (again, after her mother's disclosure of a loveless child-

hood with an aunt and uncle) does Kay understand her reluctance to confide in her father.

> Kay realizes that although it is cowardly of her, she is not going to tell her father about the separation. She will let her mother tell him. She reasons that she wants to save him the embarrassment of letting her see his pain, but she knows she wants to avoid her own embarrassment at admitting to him her failure. . . . because he is her father and expects her to be happy, for her he has an authority that is . . . absolute . . . and so she cannot tell him what she feels. . . . Now, for the first time, Kay has an idea that her feeling of dread around her father is something like Gary's fear of dealing with his child, and she feels ashamed that she left Gary for having that kind of weakness.

Family ties are close in Mason's Kentucky, but the insecurities and anxieties of her characters are evident in their interactions with loved ones. If neither marriage nor familial relationships provide an answer for many of Mason's characters, some seek constancy in a return to the past.

Kay's epiphanic comprehension of her parents' marriage and her relationship with her husband and father is a result of her return home and a visit to her reluctant mother's birthplace. Picnicking in the pasture near the decaying house, Kay "tries to imagine being a girl in this place. . . . It could be fifty years ago. This landscape could be the whole world. In it, marriage, like death, could seem absolute and permanent. A storm would be like the breath of God." (pp. 286-91)

"Old Things" demonstrates most poignantly the authority of the past in Mason's world. Cleo Watkins is perplexed by the modern predilection for antiques, for she "has spent years trying to get rid of things she has collected. . . . She doesn't want to live in the past." Cleo does not perceive that her avoidance of life, her discontent with contemporary society, anchor her in a past that no longer exists. "Kids never seem to care about anything anymore," she reflects bitterly when her grandchildren act oblivious to their cluttered surroundings, and "she has put a chain on the door, because young people are going wild, breaking in on defenseless older women." Cleo envies a friend who has just taken a trip out West but maintains that she could not "take off like that" because "now there are too many maniacs on the road."

Although she declares that "there's no use trying to hang on to anything. You just lose it all in the end. You might as well not care," the story's denouement teaches Cleo that some of the past cannot—and should not—be forgotten. At a flea market, amidst the Depression glass and rusty farm tools, she spots a familiar object, a miniature what-not in which her husband used to keep his stamps and receipts. At the sight of the small box, with its drawers that form a scene of a train running through the meadow, Cleo's "blood is rushing to her head and her stomach is churning." As the story ends, she pays three dollars (too much) for the piece and, looking at the train, imagines that her happy family is aboard, crossing the valley, heading West: "Cleo is following unafraid in the caboose, as the train passes through the golden meadow and they all wave at the future and smile perfect smiles."

Although the past offers quiet solace from the hectic pace of modern life, Mason is aware of the dangers of ignoring the inexorable changes of society. Cleo, with her refusal to adapt to contemporary culture, personifies another Mason theme—the inordinate fear of life in this strange new world. At fifty-two Cleo feels and acts like an old woman; "everything seems to distress her, she notices." Mack Skaggs is also relatively young (in his late forties), but his agoraphobia and his ineffectual attempts to keep up with his college-student daughter (he struggles with *The Encyclopedia of Philosophy* only to discover that she is studying physics) are the pathetic actions and attitudes of a man completely overwhelmed by the world around him. In **"Still Life with Watermelon,"** Louise's husband goes off to Texas without her because, he claims, she is "afraid to try new things." She is initially angry at his accusations and his wanderlust, but at his return her feelings change. "Something about the conflicting impulses of men and women has gotten twisted around, she feels. She had preached the idea of staying home, but it occurs to her now that perhaps the meaning of home grows out of the fear of open spaces. In some people that fear is so intense that it is a disease, Louise has read."

Mary, in **"Residents and Transients,"** has, unlike most of these characters, experimented with various lifestyles, but she has returned to her roots in Kentucky. Now, although her husband has been transferred and has moved to the city to work and find them a home, she stays behind because, she says, "I do not want to go anywhere." Mary loves her parents' old farmhouse and worries about a world that sends her mother off to live in a mobile home in Florida. She knows that her mother, who loved her canning kitchen, would be appalled to find that her daughter has taken a lover and spends her afternoons with him drinking Bloody Marys made with the old woman's canned tomato juice. An obviously more educated and sophisticated woman than many of her neighbors in these stories, Mary too is torn between the serene seductions of an obsolete lifestyle and the intimidating uncertainties of a variable present and future. Eventually she recognizes the dangers of stasis: "I am nearly thirty years old," she proclaims. "I have two men, eight cats, no cavities. One day I was counting the cats and I absent-mindedly counted myself." Near the end of the story Mary relates to her lover the perception that will ultimately send her—however reluctantly—to Louisville and a new life with her husband:

> "In the wild, there are two kinds of cat populations . . . Residents and transients. Some stay put, in their fixed home ranges, and others are on the move. They don't have real homes. Everybody always thought that the ones who establish the territories are the most successful. . . . They are the strongest, while the transients are the bums, the losers . . . The thing is—this is what the scientists are wondering about now—it may be that the transients are the superior ones after all, with the greatest curiosity and most intelligence. They can't decide. . . . When certain Indians got tired of living in a place—when they used up the soil, or the garbage pile got too high—they moved on to the next place."

Bobbie Ann Mason's Kentucky is paradigmatic of the contemporary South, and to an extent of modern America. Overwhelmed by rapid and frightening changes in their lives, her characters and her readers must confront contradictory impulses, the temptation to withdraw into the security of home and the past, and the alternative prospect of taking to the road in search of something better. There are no easy answers, Mason tells us, a fact that makes her stories all the more satisfying. They are small stopping places, brief, refreshing respites from a complex world. (pp. 292-94)

Maureen Ryan, "Stopping Places: Bobbie Ann Mason's Short Stories," in *Women Writers of the Contemporary South*, edited by Peggy Whitman Prenshaw, University Press of Mississippi, 1984, pp. 283-94.

THULANI DAVIS (essay date 1986)

[In the essay on Southern women writers excerpted below, Davis admires Mason's ability to depict "personal emptiness" in her stories but expresses frustration over the narrow focus of her fiction and her creation of characters who cannot comprehend their unsatisfying conditions.]

Bobbie Ann Mason and Jayne Anne Phillips write about survival, a kind of survival so desperate it lacks connection to any lore—regional, familial, or personal. In their work the regional past is never taught, the family past never kept, and the language with which one makes personal bonds no longer exists. The personal past has become inexpressible, the persons inarticulate. Elizabeth Janeway has written that Flannery O'Connor's people "have moved further away from any settled structure of belief and behavior, to live like weeds in a stony desert. Innocence has been distorted by ignorance; but ignorance and malice are the result of a bad fit between the inner experience of life and the symbolic actions available to express it publicly." Mason's and Phillip's characters have much these same difficulties, with a vengeance. It's almost as if they've never seen a symbolic or meaningful (dare I say heroic?) action and wouldn't have anything to say about it if they had.

Touted as the bright talents of their generation, these two women have in common a tendency to describe the symptoms, the sensations of an unnamed malaise, without saying what is wrong. Their work is humorless, alienated. The books have a fitful quality, as if the characters are trying to express anxiety over things they've experienced but don't understand. It's an odd tension. Richard Wright was accused of creating a similar tension by devoting himself to a world in which he no longer belonged, failing to create even one character who, like Wright himself, might know this inarticulate world and yet have an intellectual grasp of it. In some of his work, and in the work of Mason and Phillips, readers can find themselves disintegrating as they read. The characters move through their days with no discernible internal life, until, luckily, in some passage of dream or madness, they stumble on a metaphor for their condition—a metaphor they will never understand. (p. 10)

In *Shiloh and Other Stories* and her novel, *In Country*, Bobbie Ann Mason creates victims of displacement, the demise of meaningful education, and the actual stripping of the land. The short story is Mason's forte, a form that shows off her ear for dialogue and brand-name detail. The people in *Shiloh* remember the subject of every Phil Donahue show, turn on the Christian station for the music, put snapshots of Charlie's Angels in their photo albums. Mason writes powerfully of personal emptiness. In a short piece called **"Big Bertha Stories,"** she compares strip mining to the U.S. role in Vietnam:

> We were stripping off the top. The topsoil is like the culture and the people, the best part of the land and the country. America was just stripping off the top, the best. We ruined it.

Mason feels connected to the Kentucky hills, but not to the southern literary tradition, having grown up completely unaware of it. Evidently she also grew up among people who did not do a lot of storytelling. . . .

Rootlessness itself is the subject of the contemporary southern women writers, and most of them narrow the focus of their work in such a way that there is no room for the rest of the world. They are whites who only see whites, unemployed folk who only know folks out of work, rich folks who never cross the tracks even if that's where they started out. They are young people who have no old people, simple speakers who have no family storytellers. The lost woman cannot place herself in the larger world and stake her claim there, except perhaps through anonymous, intangible identification with *all* the lost. The larger world is rarely acknowledged; the writer rarely grants her characters enough distance to perceive it. It's as if they're confined to the kitchen, despite narrative to the contrary. (p. 11)

> *Thulani Davis, "Rednecks, Belles, and K-Mart Women: Southern Women Stake Their Claim," in* VLS, *No. 42, February, 1986, pp. 10-13.*

ALBERT E. WILHELM (essay date 1986)

[*In the following essay, Wilhelm examines the struggle of Mason's characters in* Shiloh, and Other Stories *to establish a sense of identity in a rapidly changing southern society.*]

[Mason] grew up on a small dairy farm in rural Kentucky. A few years later she had migrated to New York City and was writing features on Fabian, Annette Funicello, and Ann-Margaret for *Movie Life* magazine. As a child her favorite reading materials were Nancy Drew and other girl sleuth mysteries. As a young woman she published a scholarly study of Nabokov's *Ada.*

Given these divergent circumstances of her own life, it is hardly surprising that Bobbie Ann Mason should be interested in culture shock and its jarring effects on an individual's sense of identity. This theme dominates the sixteen pieces in **Shiloh and Other Stories**. . . . Throughout this collection Mason dramatizes the bewildering effects of rapid social change on the residents of a typical "ruburb"—an area in Western Kentucky that is "no longer rural but not yet suburban." Again and again in these stories old verities are questioned as farm families watch talk-show discussions of drug use, abortion, and pre-marital sex. Old relationships are strained as wives begin to lift weights or play video games with strange men. In such contexts the sense of self is besieged from all sides and becomes highly vulnerable. As O. B. Hardison has observed, "Identity seems to be unshakable, but its apparent stability is an illusion. As the world changes, identity changes. . . . Because the mind and the world develop at different rates and in different ways, during times of rapid change they cease to be complementary. . . . The result is a widening gap between the world as it exists in the mind and the world as it is experienced—between identity formed by tradition and identity demanded by the present."

Mason's stories document many efforts to bridge such a gap. Although the behavior of her characters is diverse, two basic patterns are apparent. When faced with confusion about their proper roles, they tend to become either doers or seekers. They stay put and attempt to construct a new identity or they light out for the territories in the hope of discovering one. In short, they try to make over or they make off. Both patterns are, of course, deeply entrenched in American history. The former reflects the Puritan emphasis on building a new order through work. The latter repeats the typical response of the wanderer from Natty Bumppo to Jack Kerouac. (The occupations of Mason's characters frequently parallel these basic patterns. For example, many of her male characters are either construction workers or truck drivers.)

One good example of a character who attempts to construct a new identity is Norma Jean Moffitt in [**"Shiloh"**]. Even though her double given name may suggest a typical good-old Southern girl, Norma Jean is definitely striving to be a new woman. Like many of Mason's characters, her days are filled with the contemporary equivalents of what Arnold van Gennep has termed sympathetic rites—ceremonies "based on belief in the reciprocal action of like on like, of opposite on opposite, of the container and the contained . . . of image and real object or real being." For example, her efforts to build a new body by lifting weights reveal also her efforts to build a new self. She doesn't know exactly what to make of her husband and her marriage, so she frantically makes all sorts of other things. By making electric organ music she strives for new harmony. By cooking exotic new foods she hopes to become what she eats.

Her husband Leroy (no longer the king of his castle) has to dodge the barbells swung by Norma Jean, but he too is obsessed with making things. He occupies himself with craft kits (popsicle stick constructions, string art, a snap-together B-17 Flying Fortress) as if putting together these small parts can create a more comprehensive sense of order. No doubt he is also seeking *craft* in its root sense of *power* or *strength.* In an effort to create a real home, Leroy is even thinking of "building a full-scale log house from a kit." Having failed to make a family because of the accidental death of their baby, he and Norma Jean must now "create a new marriage." Although Leroy admits that a log cabin will be out of place in the new subdivisions, he apparently sees such a construction as a means of returning to a more stable past. He and Norma Jean could join together in a cabin-raising and revert to the time of those more resourceful Kentuckians like Abe Lincoln or Daniel Boone.

Another character whose work is ritualistic is Cleo Watkins in **"Old Things."** As a middle-aged widow she is on the shoulder of the fast lane, but she still feels the gusts of wind as change rushes by. For Cleo a typical day consists of a flurry of TV shows. Disturbing reports on *Today* fade into questionable jokes on *Tonight* which, in turn, give way to even more alarming developments on *Tomorrow.* Though insulated from much that is new in the larger world, she cannot escape the consequences of the breakup of her daughter's marriage. (In this story a "family circle" is little more than a magazine to be discarded when the recipes are clipped.) When Linda and her two children move in with Cleo, they turn her quiet home into pandemonium. Amidst the noise, the clutter, and the unpredictable comings and goings, Cleo asserts that she is "still in one piece." Perhaps this small measure of personal integrity is due, in part, to Cleo's craftsmanship. Like several other characters in Mason's fiction, Cleo is a seamstress, and she sews garments with such care that she seems to be trying to repair the rent fabric of society. The paper patterns she must use are "flimsy," but she produces outfits whose "double seams" will surely hold them together and whose "pockets with flaps" suggest a further effort to provide security.

Still another confused but meticulous craftsman is Mack Skaggs in **"The Rookers."** Frightened by people and the highways, he retreats to his basement workshop. As a twenty-fifth anniversary gift for his wife, he makes an elaborate card table whose top is a mosaic of wood scraps. With its twenty-one oddly shaped pieces, it suggests "that Mack was trying to put together the years of their marriage into a convincing whole and this was as far as he got." After making this giant jigsaw puzzle, he wants to build a home entertainment center—an intricately designed cabinet whose small compartments will hold everything in its proper place. In still another attempt to see his confused world as an orderly system, he reads *Cosmos* but, understandably, cannot bring himself to believe a word of it. Mircea Eliade has observed that "the cosmogonic myth serves as the paradigm . . . for every kind of making. Nothing better ensures the success of any creation . . . than the fact of copying it after the greatest of all creations, the cosmogony." In Mack's case, however, all attempts to create order remain truncated because he has no clear conception of his place in a larger order. When his wife's friends come to play Rook (a gregarious game named after a gregarious bird), he repeatedly calls the time-and-temperature number so that he can pretend to be involved with people without really having to talk to anyone. A passage from his daughter's physics text comments further on his dilemma. Photons, she explains, are tiny particles which disappear when one starts to look for them. In fact, they don't exist "except in a group." Mack's wife Mary Lou is much more interested in *Real People* than in quantum mechanics, but she understands the relevance of this lesson from physics to her own family's situation. "If you break up a group," she reflects, "the individuals could disappear out of existence." She has "tried to be patient with Mack, thinking that he will grow out of his current phase," but "sooner or later, she and Mack will have to face growing older *together* (emphasis added)."

As the reference to physics suggests, the basic problem for all of these characters is one of composition—integrating self with society and creating a convincing whole out of many disparate parts. (pp. 76-9)

Mason's stories usually portray contemporary characters whose sense of identity is threatened by mid-life crises or problems of aging. In **"Detroit Skyline, 1949"** she reverts to an earlier time and focuses on the passage from childhood to adolescence. In a pattern that is typical of many initiation stories, Peggy Jo leaves the protected environment of her farm home and journeys to the big city. Although she experiences much that is new, this journey of self-discovery is surely incomplete. In fact, she never actually sees Detroit—only a fuzzy picture of its tall buildings on the TV screen. The failure of Peggy Jo's pilgrimage is foreshadowed by the fates of several adults who have migrated north. Her Uncle Boone Cashon left the agrarian South for a job in the industrial North, and his two names (one the surname of a famous pioneer and the other an echo of the cliché "cash on the barrel head") probably suggest a conflict between his frontier heritage and the crass world where he now works. He has acquired a pleasant house complete with all-electric kitchen and television set. But instead of finding himself, he leads a fragmented life. He could never build a complete car because all he knows "is bumpers." Boone's daughter enjoys their relative affluence, but her reading material—Bromfield's *Pleasant Valley*—suggests perhaps a yearning for a more pastoral environment. For Lunetta Jones, another transplant from Kentucky, the problem of finding herself is even more severe. She always has elaborate descriptions of her fantastic clothes,

but her outfits are nothing more than "man bait" and she remains a faceless fashionplate. The climax of Peggy's experiences among these incomplete characters is her mother's miscarriage. Her mother loses the baby she didn't know she had, and Peggy's own search for a mature identity is abortive.

Other travellers in Mason's stories are too numerous to discuss in detail. In **"Graveyard Day"** Joe Murdock wants to go to California and "strike it rich" on a game show. Thus he serves as a parody of those more heroic but frequently disappointed pilgrims of gold-rush days. After much wandering Ed in **"The Rookers"** has made it to the west coast. He has gone to the edge of the continent and has acquired a new wife and a new house. The house, however, remains a hollow shell since he has nothing to put in it but a washer and dryer. Some of Mason's pilgrims manage to make extended journeys without taking a step. In **"The Retreat,"** for example, Georgeann explores both outer space and her own inner space merely by piloting a Galaxian rocket ship in an electronic game arcade. But when her quarters run out, her husband treats her like a mental case and takes her home to pray over her. No matter how far they may travel, many of Mason's searchers never really leave home. They are like the emblematic rabbit which has been hit by a car in **"Residents and Transients."** Plastered to the pavement, it can do nothing more than hop in place. "Its forelegs are frantically working, but its rear end has been smashed and it cannot get out of the road."

Like this rabbit the characters in Mason's stories are a cast of valiant strugglers. They attempt to create order through various sympathetic rites, but their magic is frequently powerless. They journey through wide expanses without ever finding a real sense of place. In spite of all their efforts they repeatedly find themselves caught in the dilemma described by Orrin Klapp: "In the accumulation of new things, it is possible for society to pass the optimum point in the ratio between the new and the old . . . between innovation and acculturation on the one hand and tradition on the other. Beyond this optimum point, where society is roused to creativity by introduction of new elements, is a danger point where consensus and integrity of the person break down." In her "few square miles of native turf," Mason graphically depicts such a society. (pp. 80-2)

Albert E. Wilhelm, "Making Over or Making Off: The Problem of Identity in Bobbie Ann Mason's Short Fiction," in The Southern Literary Journal, *Vol. XVIII, No. 2, Spring, 1986, pp. 76-82.*

MICHIKO KAKUTANI (essay date 1989)

[*In the review excerpted below, Kakutani praises Mason for revealing without condescension the inner lives of her small-town characters in* Love Life.]

For Ms. Mason, television is both the one constant in her characters' lives and a tawdry symbol of the rootless pop culture they inhabit. Like their predecessors in *Shiloh and Other Stories* (1982) and *In Country* (1985), the people in these stories [in *Love Life*] live in the New South of fast-food franchises and tanning boutiques, subdivisions and malls. . . .

Most of these folks have lost touch with their roots—family farms have been sold; family connections, severed or loosened—and as a result, many of them have turned to television evangelists and call-in psychics for support. Hobbies, too, help pass the time. "I think I'll take up aerobic dancing," one woman tells her niece. "Or maybe I'll learn to ride a motorcycle. I try to be modern."

In another story, a man who wants his wife to sell her father's farm so they can move to the city amuses himself by changing the lyrics of old songs: "Swing Low, Sweet Chariot" becomes "Sweet 'n Low, Mr. Coffee pot, perking for to hurry my heart"; and "The Old Rugged Cross" turns into "an old Chevrolet." As described by Ms. Mason, the altered lyrics not only make for a comic moment, but they also signify the characters' willingness to discard the past.

In fact, few of the people in *Love Life* are able to find any continuity in their lives. . . .

Whereas the couple in Ms. Mason's last book, *Spence and Lila,* have spent 40 years together on a farm that's become their entire world, the couples in this volume all seem to be reeling from the dislocations of modern life. In the case of a veteran named Donald, it's the aftereffects of Vietnam that prevent him from connecting with his wife and son: he tries regaling them with horrific stories from the war, but finds that the tales breed less sympathy than fear. In other instances, the causes of romantic or familial discord are less specific: too much liquor, too little affection, or maybe simply a realization that there's no longer anything (like television shows) in common.

In the title story ["Love Life,"] a waitress goes on a camping trip with a fellow waiter, their romance fades, she loses touch with him, and later hears he's been killed in an accident. In **"Airwaves,"** a couple get into a fight over who's going to pay the bills, and the woman abruptly departs, signing up at the local Army recruiting station for "Communications and Electronics Operations." And in **"Midnight Magic,"** a man watches his girlfriend recede from him as she becomes increasingly absorbed in a cult based on someone named Sardo, "a thousand-year-old American Indian inhabiting the body of teenage girl in Paducah."

It would be easy to patronize many of the people in *Love Life.* Their susceptibility to phony preachers, their fondness for enrolling in things like mail-order cosmetics clubs and eating at thematic restaurants decorated with stuffed wild animals—such foibles might render them the objects of satire in many writers eyes. But Ms. Mason instead displays an enduring affection for them and their circumscribed world.

Indeed, it is one of her strengths as a writer that she's able to look beyond the bluff facades of her characters and reveal the geography of their inner lives. Many, it turns out, are torn between breaking with the past and pursuing a high-flown, seemingly impossible dream or accepting their dreary daily routines—numbingly dull jobs or no jobs at all, imperfect relationships in which love and passion have given way to economic and emotional dependence.

Few of Ms. Mason's characters ever resolve their dilemmas— or if they do, their decisions take place off stage, beyond the knowledge of the reader. But if these stories catch their characters in medias res, they are not simply minimalist "slice-of-life" exercises, but finely crafted tales that manage to invest inarticulate, small-town lives with dignity and intimations of meaning.

Michiko Kakutani, "Watching TV and Being Rootless in the South," in The New York Times, *March 3, 1989, p. C35.*

LORRIE MOORE   (essay date 1989)

[*An American short story writer, novelist, and critic, Moore explores the themes of love and anguish from the perspectives of contemporary women in her short story collection* Self-Help *(1985) and her novel* Anagrams *(1986). In the following excerpt, Moore praises Mason's unpredictable and sympathetic portrayals of middle-class American life in* Love Life.]

Ms. Mason's strongest form may be neither the novel nor the story, but the story *collection*. It is there, picking up her pen every 20 pages to start anew, gathering layers through echo and overlap, that Ms. Mason depicts most richly a community of contemporary lives, which is her great skill. It could be argued that the quiet, cumulative beauty of Ms. Mason's **Shiloh and Other Stories** is rivaled in her oeuvre (which includes the novels *In Country* and *Spence + Lila*) only by her new collection, *Love Life.* There is depth here, in the way the word is used to describe armies and sports teams: an accumulation, a supply. When one story is finished, a similar one rushes in to fill its place. There is also profundity. Ms. Mason dips her pen in the same ink, over and over, because her knowledge of the landlocked Middle America she writes about—most of it centered in Kentucky and Tennessee—is endless and huge. Each small story adds to the reader's apprehension of that hugeness.

In Ms. Mason's new collection her themes of provincial entrapment and desire are present again, but here she has given them a new improvisatory sprawl. Though a few of the 15 stories in *Love Life* (such as the title one) repeat the figure-eight structure found in **"Shiloh"**—a narrative that loops gracefully through several combinations of characters, then arches back to the original one—many of the stories in *Love Life* splay out unexpectedly, skate off, or in, at odd angles, displaying a directional looseness. **"Midnight Magic"** introduces the dramatic thread of a town terrorized by an unknown rapist, but then ends off to one side of it, with the moral dilemma over the reporting of a hit-and-run accident. **"Piano Fingers"** begins with a husband's sexual boredom and ends with a father buying his daughter an electric keyboard from the piano store. Certainly the beginnings and endings do illuminate each other, but only indirectly, diffusely. Along the way elements are seldom developed in a linear fashion, and are often, once introduced, abandoned altogether.

But this unexpectedness keeps Ms. Mason's stories breathing and alive. Her writing is naked-voiced, without vanity. In **"State Champions,"** a memory of small-town adolescence, the middle-aged narrator is made to understand belatedly and obliquely the significance of her high school basketball team's state championship. Twenty years after the fact someone not from her community recollects for her. " 'Why, they were just a handful of country boys who could barely afford basketball shoes,' the man told me in upstate New York.

" 'They were?' This was news to me." Which leads, circuitously, to one of Ms. Mason's strongest stories about the illiteracy of the provincial heart. (p. 7)

For an edifying word on their troubles, Ms. Mason's characters watch the Phil Donahue show, where they find the various problems of their lives formulated for them. A woman in the story **"Hunktown"** says, "I can't stand watching stuff that's straight out of my own life." They seem to share a startling belief that their lives correspond to the television culture that has descended on them. But it is more hope than belief, a desire to refashion and locate themselves, to medicate their feelings of exile with cheap understanding.

For a good time they go to Paducah or Gatlinburg. "At a museum there, she saw a violin made from a ham can." They work in mattress factories, or plant tobacco, and when they brush up against glamour and wealth, it is in the form of people who own hot tubs or their "own bush-hog rental company." For spirituality there is the local Christianity—"He opens the Bible and reads from 'the Philippines' "—which may also include speaking in tongues. "He is speaking a singsong language made of hard, disturbing sounds. 'Shecky-beck-be-floyt-I-shecky-tibby-libby. Dabcree-la-crooo-la-crow.' He seems to be trying hard not to say 'abracadabra' or any other familiar words." Only one Mason character ventures off to a therapist, whom she calls " 'The Rapist,' because the word *therapist* can be divided into two words, *the rapist.*" When he tells her that perhaps she is trying to escape reality, she says, "Reality, hell! . . . Reality's my whole problem."

Ms. Mason's women tend to be practical, disillusioned, self-preserving. They belong to cosmetics clubs, wear too much makeup, have names like Beverly or Jolene. They are trapped mostly in their desire for Ms. Mason's men, who tend to be feckless, dreamy, drunk, between jobs. The sexes are a puzzle to each other here, and longing and distraction pervade their lives. Divorce seems the only remedy for a life where a couple "stayed married like two dogs locked together in passion, except it wasn't passion." Ms. Mason's use of the present tense in the majority of her stories serves as the expression of this trapped condition, but also as a kind of existential imperfect: the freeze in time suggests the flow; the moment stilled and isolated from the past and future is yet emblematic of them both, of the gray ongoingness of things.

Nevertheless, the characters in *Love Life* seem determined to amuse themselves. In **"Private Lies"**: "He liked to clown around, singing 'The Star-Spangled Banner' in a mock-operatic style; he would pretend to forget the words and then shift abruptly into 'Carry Me Back to Old Virginny.' He was a riot at parties." In **"The Secret of the Pyramids"**: "The last time he took her out to eat, they had to wait for their table, and Bob gave the name 'Beach' so the hostess would call out on the microphone, 'Beach Party.' " In **"Memphis"**: " 'I'm having a blast, too,' Beverly said, just as an enormous man with tattoos of outer-space monsters on his arms asked Jolene to dance." Their days are punctuated with attenuated joys and generosities. The large gestures of life are reduced by Ms. Mason to the smallest scale, inflaming them with meaning. "Steve's friend Pete squirts blue fluid on Steve's windshield—a personal service not usually provided at the self-serve island" (**"Midnight Magic"**).

If such living is morally hemmed in, strewn with the junk of our culture, it is all that Ms. Mason's characters can avail themselves of. Buried in the very gut of America, feeling deeply the lock and cage of the land, they send up antennae and receive what they are able to, what there is. If they are mocked and demeaned by what they consume, they do not know it; to mock and demean are coastal pastimes, of which they haven't the means to partake. "Liz wished she could go to the ocean, just once in her life," one narrator says. "That was what she truly wanted." Despite the immodest imperative of its title, this wonderful collection is less about the optimist's advice to love life than about the struggle and necessity

of some ordinary and valiant people to like it just a little. (pp. 7, 9)

Lorrie Moore, "What Li'l Abner Said," in The New York Times Book Review, *March 12, 1989, pp. 7, 9.*

RHODA KOENIG (essay date 1989)

[*In the review excerpted below, Koenig lauds Mason's skill in reproducing Southern dialect but detects uniformity in the stories in* Love Life.]

Their marriages sundering, their houses piling up with tacky and unsuitable furnishings, Mason's characters [in *Love Life*] lead the mournful and ramshackle lives of people in country songs. A woman asks herself whether she should quit her good job at the post office and move to Nashville just because her paunchy, middle-aged husband has decided to take a shot at the music business. She looks at the picture on his album cover and thinks, "He looked old. His expression seemed serious and unforgiving, as though he expected the world to be ready for him, as though this were his revenge, not his gift." A man decides to look for the daughter given away for adoption eighteen years ago but ends up having another affair with her mother. (One can see why he is drawn to an easy-going type. His wife is the kind who, when he goes out of town, makes him promise to stay in a hotel with a smoke alarm.)

When they bustle about and summon up some pluck or disgust, Mason's people have no trouble expressing their feelings. Getting out an old patchwork quilt, a spinster depressed by the history and eye-strain it represents says, "Shoot! It's ugly as homemade sin." Freshening her face in the rest room, a waitress decides, "I reckon I better put on some lipstick to keep the mortician away." When it comes to showing tenderness and sympathy, however, they are at a loss, their thorny lives giving them no clue to what is expected. Faced with a friend's grief over the death of her sister, a schoolgirl reflects on the background that keeps her out of the middle class as well as from full humanity.

> I didn't know what to say. I couldn't say anything, for we weren't raised to say things that were heart-felt and gracious. . . . Manners were too embarrassing. Learning not to run in the house was about the extent of what we knew about how to act. We didn't learn to congratulate people; we didn't wish people happy birthday. We didn't even address each other by name. And we didn't jump up and spontaneously hug someone for joy. Only cheerleaders claimed that talent. We didn't say we were sorry. We hid from view, in case we might be called on to make appropriate remarks.

Mason sometimes endows her characters with thoughts that are a little too sophisticated and well articulated for their circumstances. Her slices of life, as well, are often too many identical wedges from the same marked-down Sara Lee. But she has a good-hearted approach to her down-but-not-out folk, a good ear for their plaintive music. (p. 67)

Rhoda Koenig, "The Watchful I," in New York Magazine, *Vol. 22, No. 11, March 13, 1989, pp. 66-7.*

JUDITH FREEMAN (essay date 1989)

[*An American short story writer and critic, Freeman is the author of the short story collection* Family Attractions *(1987). In the excerpt below, Freeman offers a largely positive review of* Love Life.]

The stories in *Love Life* are all about love, it's true, but they are also about the ways in which ordinary people are caught up in the pernicious consumption of popular culture, which has packaged even love in riotously vulgar imagery proposing banal formulas for happiness. Phil Donahue is their guru; when he speaks, they listen up.

They are not fools, however; they are seekers with special poignancy because they rarely get the long view that might help them understand what's happening to them. What keeps them from buying the talk-show banalities whole hog are the rural-values common sense instilled over generations and not easily forgotten, but it's an unlikely combination of impulses, things constantly at odds, like a meal of collard greens and Big Macs.

In **"Hunktown,"** for instance, Joan is on her second marriage, to Cody, a good looking guy who's always wanted to cut a record album. He's laid off work and drinking too much, but he decides now's the good time to pursue his singing career, so he heads for Memphis, where he gets a few gigs. He wants Joan to sell the family farm and move to Memphis with him, but she says no. She's suspicious of his longing to be in the spotlight. She even thinks he might be cheating on her.

"You're not Elvis," she tells him. "And selling the place is too extreme. Things can't be all one way or the other. There has to be some of both. That's what life is, when it's any good." Cliché? Yes, there's a whole kettle of them here. But the story manages to find an emotional censor far removed from the banal, largely through the accumulation of beautiful detail, dead-on dialogue, and above all, the sense of a heartfelt quest for proper boundaries, which is at the center of all of Mason's writing.

Almost every story tells of divorce, confusion, longing, a sense of something missing from life. Characters often have the choice of remaining mired in unhappy relationships or trying to extricate themselves, but you don't get the sense that anyone succeeds in resolving anything.

If there is a shortcoming here it's that characters often seem too much alike. For instance, in the story **"Memphis,"** Beverly, who is being pressured by her ex-husband Joe to get back together, could almost be the same person as Liz, a woman who's cheating on her husband in **"Sorghum."** They even have the similar troubles: "You're so full of warmth you don't know what you want," Joe tells Beverly; "Danny was right about the way she always wanted something she didn't have," thinks Liz.

In **"Big Bertha Stories,"** a Vietnam vet suffering from postwar Trauma (who seems a little like Emmett from the novel *In Country*) is a strip-miner who only comes home sporadically, and entertains his wife and child with fantastic and rather frightening tales about a mythical machine called "Big Bertha." Although the story doesn't really take off until half

way through, it finally builds to a spooky conclusion as the wife leaves her shaking husband in a VA hospital: "Rest was what he needed." Later, she has a nightmare, and it seems she has now assimilated her husband's ghoulish obsessions. "In her dream, she is jumping on soft moss and then it turns into a springy pile of dead bodies."

"Private Lives" examines the guilt a divorced couple feel over giving up a baby for adoption 18 years earlier. They have an affair, as if this act might recapture some of what's been lost, but the story ends on a beach in Florida, with the couple walking along the sand, stepping on seashells, "crunching the fragments of skeletons."

Fragments of skeletons, a pile of dead bodies; these aren't reflections of a happy state of affairs. We are left wondering just what sort of world Mason has chosen to portray.

I think it's a world quite close to the one we actually live in, and I don't mean just the Paducahns. All around us, clichés rule and loneliness is epidemic. A memory of something lost bothers us. We seek extensions of ourselves, a *community,* and instead find only a conglomeration of private cells. The problems of the children (divorce, insecurity, unhappiness) are also the problems of the parents, as if a malaise has infected our guides and erased the generational line that once existed. Raymond Carver was the first in our time to echo the hollow state of affairs with perfectly reflective, flattened prose. Bobbie Ann Mason accomplishes a similar feat. These stories work like parables, small in scale and very wise, tales wistfully told by a masterful stylist whose voice rises purely from the heart of the country. (pp. 1, 11)

> *Judith Freeman, "Country Parables," in* Los Angeles Times Book Review, *March 19, 1989, pp. 1, 11.*

FURTHER READING

Arnold, Edwin T. "Falling Apart and Staying Together: Bobbie Ann Mason and Leon Driskell Explore the State of the Modern Family." *Appalachian Journal* 12, No. 2 (Winter 1985): 135-41.

> Compares Mason's treatment of family relations in *Shiloh, and Other Stories* to Driskell's in *Passing Through.*

Chambers, Andrea. "Bobbie Ann Mason's *In Country* Evokes the Soul of Kentucky and the Sadness of Vietnam." *People Weekly* 23, No. 18 (28 October 1985): 127-29.

> Feature story focusing upon Mason's novel *In Country,* her childhood, and her publishing career.

Havens, Lila. "Residents and Transients: An Interview with Bobbie Ann Mason." *Crazyhorse,* No. 29 (Fall 1985): 87-104.

> In-depth interview in which Mason discusses her themes and writing processes, her relation to the southern literary tradition, the influence of place and family on her work, and her relationship with the *New Yorker,* among other topics.

Yukio Mishima

1925-1970

(Pseudonym of Kimitake Hiroaka) Japanese short story writer, novelist, dramatist, film director, and actor.

Considered one of the most provocative and versatile modern Japanese writers, Mishima is known for his unorthodox views and eccentric personal life, as well as for his fiction. His works often reflect a dedication to the traditional values of imperialist Japan and are characterized by a preoccupation with aggression and violent eroticism. Critics often interpret Mishima's works from a biographical perspective, frequently placing him among the Japanese "I-novelists," who wrote autobiography in the guise of fiction. Known to the West primarily for his novels, Mishima also composed over twenty volumes of short stories. Only one of these, however—*Death in Midsummer, and Other Stories*—has been translated into English. Like his novels, this collection has garnered praise from both Eastern and Western literary critics, and its stories display Mishima's concern with a wide range of themes.

Mishima was born in Tokyo, where his father was a senior government official. His paternal grandmother, Natsu, was obsessively protective and would not allow Mishima to live on the upper level of their house with his parents, keeping him confined to her darkened sickroom until he reached the age of twelve. Perhaps because of this extreme isolation, Mishima had difficulty developing social relationships as a youth, and many biographers and critics have attributed his homosexual and nihilistic tendencies to these troubled early years. In his autobiographical novel *Confessions of a Mask,* Mishima gives an uninhibited account of his struggles to come to terms with these inclinations and recalls that since childhood his "heart's leaning was for Death and Night and Blood." Several critics have referred to this statement as an apt summary of Mishima's literary aesthetic, pointing to a tendency in both his personal life and his fiction to treat violence and death as sacred events. This passion and violence, which was characteristic of Mishima's personal life, is also conveyed throughout his fiction.

Mishima began writing stories in middle school, and in 1941, when he was sixteen, his short fiction piece "Hanazakari no mori" was published in the small, nationalist literary magazine *Bungei Bunka.* "Hanazakari no mori" focuses on the aristocracy of historical Japan and displays the early development of Mishima's acrid literary perspective. Many critics were impressed with the maturity of Mishima's style and voice in this work, and Zenmei Hasuda, a member of the *Bungei Bunka* coterie, encouraged Mishima to approach the prominent intellectuals of a group of Japanese Romanticists known as the *Nihon-Roman-ha.* Many tenets of this group's doctrine mirrored Mishima's personal convictions, and he was particularly fascinated by their emphasis on death and violence. Stressing the "value of destruction" and calling for the removal of party politicians in an attempt to preserve the cultural traditions of Japan, the *Nihon-Roman-ha* had a profound influence on Mishima.

After receiving a law degree from Tokyo University in 1947, Mishima accepted a position with the Finance Ministry. He

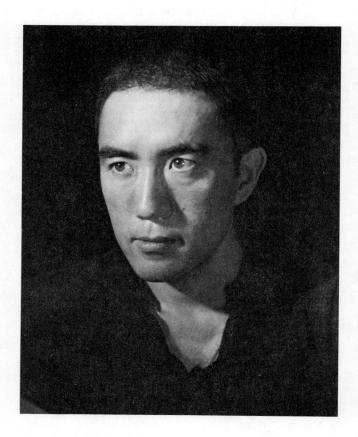

resigned within his first year, however, in order to devote himself entirely to writing. The extraordinary success of *Confessions of a Mask* solidified Mishima's reputation as an important voice in Japanese fiction, and his subsequent endeavors in literature and drama were greeted with high critical acclaim. He received numerous literary awards and a nomination for the Nobel Prize in 1965. Throughout his adult life, Mishima was disturbed by what he felt was Japan's "effeminate" image as "a nation of flower arrangers." He became increasingly consumed by a desire to revive the traditional values and morals of Japan's imperialistic past and was vehemently opposed to the Westernization of his country. His ensuing works further reflect both his political orientation and his personal philosophy of "active nihilism," which regards self-sacrifice as an essential gesture in achieving spiritual fulfillment. In affirmation of these personal convictions, Mishima committed *seppuku,* or *hari-kari,* a traditional Japanese form of suicide by disembowelment.

The themes of the ten pieces in *Death in Midsummer, and Other Stories* vary widely. The title story, in its focus on the tragic drowning deaths of two children, transcends cultural boundaries as it explores the ironic and emotional trauma of Tomoko and Masaru, the children's parents. In this story, Mishima uncovers the young couple's inability to confront their grief and exposes the contradictory feelings of guilt and happiness that accompany their gradual emotional recovery. Other works in the collection, including "The Priest of Shiga Temple and His Love," "Onnagata," and Mishima's modern *Noh* play *Dojoji*, deal more specifically with the traditional character of Japan. Critics note Mishima's delicate handling of the theme of homosexual love in "Onnagata," which focuses on the lives of female impersonators in the traditional Kabuki theater. In "Onnagata," as in his other stories, Mishima examines discomfitting emotional states with cool and uninhibited candor that is often startling to his readers.

Perhaps the most critically discussed work in *Death in Midsummer, and Other Stories* is "Patriotism." Exemplifying Mishima's tendency to present eroticism and death with shocking objectivity, this piece is considered crucial in understanding Mishima's nihilistic creed. According to Lance Morrow, "Patriotism" reveals Mishima's mastery of "what Russians call *poshlust*, a vulgarity so elevated—or debased—that it amounts to a form of art." Based on the dual suicide of a young married couple during the 1936 Ni Ni Roku incident in which a band of insurrectionists organized a rebellion against Japan's military forces on behalf of the emperor, the story centers on the union of the couple's physical and spiritual commitment to traditional ideals. Mishima himself described "Patriotism" as "neither a comedy nor a tragedy, but a tale of bliss." The couple's final sexual experience is treated as a prelude to their suicides, and the excruciating pain of the lieutenant's suicide is linked with erotic desire: "Was it death he was now waiting for? Or a wild ecstasy of the senses? The two seemed to overlap, almost as if the object of this bodily desire were death itself."

Often overshadowed by his dramatic personal life, Mishima's fiction eludes easy critical analysis. His sensational death by *seppuku* has prompted many critics to solicit biographical meanings from his works, while other commentators note a distinct contradiction between Mishima's modern personal lifestyle and his literary aesthetic. Although critics have accused Mishima of self-indulgent prose, he is widely respected for his distinctive style, and most observers agree that he has made a significant contribution to world literature.

(For further information on Mishima's life and career, see *Contemporary Literary Criticism*, Vols. 2, 4, 6, 9, 27; and *Contemporary Authors*, Vols. 97-100; Vols. 29-32, rev. ed. [obituary].)

PRINCIPAL WORKS

SHORT FICTION

Hanazakari no mori   1944
Manatsu no shi   1953
   [*Death in Midsummer, and Other Stories*, 1966]

OTHER MAJOR WORKS

Kamen no kokuhaku   (novel)   1949
   [*Confessions of a Mask*, 1959]
Kinkakuji   (novel)   1956
   [*The Temple of the Golden Pavillion*, 1959]
Taiyo to tetsu   (essay)   1968
   [*Sun and Steel*, 1970]
Haru no yuki   (novel)   1969
   [*Spring Snow*, 1972]
Homba   (novel)   1969

   [*Runaway Horses*, 1973]
Akatsuki no tera   (novel)   1970
   [*The Temple of Dawn*, 1973]
Tennin gosui   (novel)   1970
   [*The Decay of the Angel* 1974]
The Sea of Fertility: A Cycle of Four Novels   1972-1974

ROBERT J. SMITH   (essay date 1966)

[*Smith is an American anthropologist who has written and edited several studies of Japanese culture. In the following excerpt, Smith comments on Mishima's modern treatment of traditional themes and notes the underlying tone of anxiety and despair in* Death in Midsummer, and Other Stories.]

What a storyteller Mishima is! All those who people the tales offered here [in *Death in Midsummer*] are Japanese, but if the reader is hoping for a breath of the Fujiyama/cherry blossom/Madame Butterfly school of Japanese exoticism he would be well advised to look elsewhere. There are geisha, to be sure, one involved in an encounter with an old lover on Geary Street in San Francisco (**"Thermos Bottles"**), and a group of them on an odd pilgrimage through Tokyo on a night late in September (**"Seven Bridges"**). There is one story laid in old Japan, and it seems to me only mildly interesting (**"The Priest of Shiga Temple and His Love"**), for all its importance as the sole representative of a major stream of Mishima's work.

But for the rest, the men and women who people these pages are for the most part caught up in despair, situations of unbearable cruelty, or the deadly ennui of one of the world's most "modern" societies. The attractive levelheaded young couple of **"Three Million Yen,"** childless, very much in love, and prudently saving toward a family and a home, turn out to earn their money by giving public sexual performances for pay. The parents of **"Death in Midsummer,"** who lose two of their three children by drowning, will be recognized by all. **"Swaddling Clothes"** is a very slight piece, and **"The Pearl"** positively trivial, but the two remaining stories are in very different ways the two most powerful of the collection.

The first paragraph of **"Patriotism"** lulls the reader in any way familiar with the fictional treatments of harakiri in Japanese literature. The young army officer, paragon of loyalty, leaves a note that is testimony to his patriotic fervor and kills himself. His young wife follows him by cutting her throat, leaving her own apology to her parents for thus unfilially preceding them. In succeeding pages, they are revealed to have been an ideal young couple, "flowers of Japan" in her virulently nationalistic 1930's, deeply in love, and possessed of equal parts of idealism and control. Their story is a rapid slide into the horror of the mechanics of harakiri; Mishima's pace never falters as he drowns his reader in patriotic gore.

"Onnagata" is uncannily evocative of the world of the Kabuki theater and in particular of the peculiar quality of mystery of the female impersonators of that stage. The female impersonator of the title is one Mangiku, who is "like shoots of flame visible through the snow," and whose "stage presence was colorful, but with dark overtones. . . ." The relationship between this aloof beauty and the young man who holds a degree in classical Japanese literature and is attached to the theater is understandably complex. Mishima's handling of the appearance of a third party to the relationship is as devastatingly low-key as **"Patriotism"** is strident.

Dojoji is one of Mishima's "modern Noh plays." It seems to me to hold little interest for anyone unacquainted with the dramatic form or with the original *Dojoji* itself.

The collection offers an unusual opportunity to sample a wide range of the work of one of contemporary Japan's most popular authors. It is clear that he has paid a price for his popularity, but his is a formidable talent, as the best of these stories reveal. (pp. 380-81)

> *Robert J. Smith, in a review of "Death in Midsummer, and Other Stories," in* Arizona Quarterly, *Vol. 22, No. 4, Winter, 1966, pp. 380-81.*

ROBERT TRUMBULL　　(essay date 1966)

[*Trumbull served as a war correspondent in the Pacific Theater for the* New York Times *and has written extensively on the culture and literature of Southeast Asia. In the following excerpt, Trumbull notes the varied themes and styles in* Death in Midsummer, and Other Stories *and claims that this collection displays Mishima's artistic flexibility.*]

[In **Death in Midsummer**], Yukio Mishima unfolds to English-language readers a fuller range of his talents as he explores a variety of pathways into the complex Japanese personality.

Mishima, a 40-year-old giant in the contemporary Japanese literary world, is known internationally for *The Golden Pavilion* and other novels. Widely admired as a master of tragedy in the offbeat Japanese style, he reveals himself in this volume to be equally sure in comedy. Tragedy, however, is the quality of the title piece, **"Death in Midsummer."** This appealing account of a young family of the upper middle class contains elements of a sociological study, like many of the stories in this book, but plunges into dark psychic depths and ends in the inconclusive style of a *New Yorker* sketch.

Mishima's next tale, **"Three Million Yen,"** is again almost journalistic in conveying the motivations of a typical young couple in a lower stratum of present-day Japanese society. In a shattering twist, the story comes to a bizarre ending in which suggested depravity is of a strength to leave the reader gasping in surprise. **"Thermos Bottles"** relates an episode in the life of a travelling Japanese businessman, who, on a visit to San Francisco, encounters a former mistress from Japan and resumes the former relationship for one nostalgic night. Abruptly, the author shifts backward in time in the next story to describe the hopeless love of an ancient Buddhist priest for an Imperial concubine, thereby achieving a creation on a plane with classics of the Kabuki stage. The next is a slight piece that gets inside the minds of a trio of geishas and a simple country girl, on an enchanting evening when modern Tokyo seems to be pervaded with the atmosphere of old Edo, as this throbbing city was called in feudal times.

Just when the reader has become thoroughly accustomed to these atmospheric and psychological trinkets, Mishima suddenly unveils a violent aspect of Japanese character that is supposed to have died with the end of World War II. The author goes back to the context of 1936 to describe a *seppuku*, the ritual suicide more commonly (and erroneously) called *harikiri* in the West in vibrant and gory detail that becomes again a portrait of the Japanese mind.

The blood-drenched exposition of the old *bushido* spirit that may not be wholly dead in Japan is a tour de force in its grim genre. It is all the more astonishing to discover in the next piece, one of Mishima's "modern No plays," a Japanese type of humor that might have been modeled on an artless scene from an Elizabethan play. Even funnier, indeed hilarious, is his witty parable about the Japanese hostess who loses a pearl at a ladies' tea party, and the determination of each of her guests to replace the lost gem for reasons of her own.

Some of the most famous stories in Japanese literature deal with homosexual love. In the most delicate good taste, Mishima demonstrates his mastery of this taxing theme in his sensitive account of an episode in the mysterious world of Kabuki stars, called *onnagata,* who play women's roles better, it is said, than any actress could. The editors have saved a little masterpiece for the very end. It is perhaps best, for the reader's appreciation, to say only that it is a shocker in the finest tradition of the short story and of Hitchcock movies.

> *Robert Trumbull, "Encounters with Life," in* The New York Times Book Review, *May 1, 1966, p. 4.*

HOWARD HIBBETT　　(essay date 1966)

[*Hibbett is an American author, critic, translator, and editor of Japanese literature. In the following excerpt, he discusses Mishima's exploration of tragedy in* Death in Midsummer, and Other Stories, *noting and commenting on his integration of Eastern and Western perspectives in the collection.*]

Most Japanese "novelists" (*shosetsuka*) are in fact primarily writers of short stories, sketches, vaguely fictionalized essays, all of which are indiscriminately called *shosetsu.* Not surprisingly, in view of the age-old ascendancy of minute poetic forms in Japan, brevity has never been considered incompatible with the highest artistic value, and one often finds that "novels" which are acclaimed as masterpieces turn out, on inspection, to be stories or sketches of a few pages in length. Such works are particularly tempting to the translator but editors and publishers have seldom shown much interest in them. It is therefore more than ever gratifying to welcome [**Death in Midsummer,** a] fine collection of stories, with a play for good measure, by the internationally well-known novelist and dramatist Yukio Mishima.

Paradoxically, perhaps, the title story, **"Death in Midsummer,"** is at once the longest and the most moving. Two small children and their aunt, who suffers a heart attack, drown in the shallows off a lovely, unspoiled beach (discreetly identified as A) near the southern tip of the Izu Peninsula. Summer is at its blazing height, the setting is idyllic, and, though there is "anger in the rays of the sun," even the cruelty of the sea is masked by its scintillating beauty. Summed up in an epigraph from Baudelaire (*"La mort . . . nous affecte plus profondément sous le regne pompeux de l'été"*) and exquisitely illustrated in Japanese literature for more than a millennium, death in such a setting takes on a poignant irony.

But Mishima goes on to the aftermath: the customs that must be followed, the requirements of society, the private, irrational fluctuations of grief, and the old intrusive, unseemly emotions of irritation, resentment, jealousy. Tomoko and Masaru are a conventional young couple, with a conventional inability to face the reality of their true feelings. Masaru reacts by retreating into his work, by drinking late in the evenings, by allowing himself a trivial infidelity out of dissatisfaction with his failure to match his wife's sorrow. Yet even Tomoko finds forgetfulness stealing over her, distressingly improper as that seems, and life predictably asserts itself. "The outlines of the incident were slowly giving way, dimming, blurring, weathering, disintegrating." Still, her experience has been one that her husband could not share; she remains more vulnerable to the cruelty of the sea and the blinding midsummer sun.

In this simple but profound and beautifully finished story, more vividly than in even such ambitious novels as *After the Banquet* or *The Temple of the Golden Pavilion,* Mishima has succeeded in investing an "incident" with imaginative life. Psychological analysis in the classic French tradition is enhanced by awareness of the changing seasons, by a sensibility fusing passions, meditations, and landscapes in the great tradition of Japanese literature. Elsewhere in his work the incident sometimes remains stubbornly unrealized, richly detailed yet as remote from poetic truth as a bald newspaper account or a dry medieval chronicle.

The theater, however, has always stirred Mishima's imagination, and two of the finest pieces in the book are *Dojoji*—a Noh play as brilliant as any of his earlier *Five Modern Noh Plays*—and "Onnagata," a masterly study of emotional currents set up behind the scenes at the Kabuki by Mangiku, an aloof, seductive performer of feminine roles whose feelings offstage are as theatrical as his flamboyant entrances and exits. An admirer sits in his dressing room awaiting him— "The mirror suddenly burst into crimson flames as Mangiku returned to the room, filling the entrance with the rustle of his robes"—or sees him leave, under an umbrella with a surly young director, in a delicious parody of the exit of star-crossed lovers. Both as an evocation of the Kabuki magic and a study in involved emotions, the story shows Mishima at the height of his powers.

Notable among a number of other striking stories in this collection are "**The Priest of Shiga Temple and His Love,**" an elaborately embellished version of an old tale about the conflict between sacred and profane love, and "**Patriotism,**" a romantically exalted but gruesomely realistic account of the ceremonial suicide of a young army lieutenant and his wife. Sometimes the embellishments seem too elaborate, the incidents too obviously contrived into the semblance of a deeper significance. But there is no question of Mishima's versatility and lively talent; nor, thanks to the flawless translations . . . , is there any doubt of his virtuosity as a stylist.

> Howard Hibbett, "Man's Place in the Landscape," in Saturday Review, Vol. XLIX, No. 19, May 7, 1966, p. 93.

JOHN WAIN (essay date 1966)

[*A prolific English author of contemporary fiction and poetry, Wain is also recognized as a significant twentieth-century critic. Central to his literary criticism is a belief that, in order to assess the quality of a piece of literature, the critic must make both a moral and an imaginative judgment. In the following excerpt, Wain links the tenor of Mishima's fiction with the social identity of modern Japan and suggests that several of the pieces in* Death in Midsummer, and Other Stories *convey Mishima's desire to understand the changing social climate of his country.*]

Yukio Mishima is not only a very prolific and successful writer; he is also, by what seems to be common consent, the Japanese writer who exports most readily to the West. He has made numerous visits to America and at least one to England. His books are translated and issued by major publishers, and greeted with enthusiasm by important critics. The sensibility of modern Japan? If we set out to investigate Mishima in *that* spirit, we are certain to fall into half-baked theories, a foreigner's distorted generalizations. But how else can we approach it? Of all the arts, literature is most rooted in event, in society, in relationships. It does not blow over the face of the earth like the wind; it pushes up through the weather like a tree.

Thus, in the present collection of stories, **Death in Midsummer,** we find several which seem to be attempts on the part of a modern Japanese to comprehend the rigid traditional society that has crumbled away in his lifetime. The story "**Patriotism,**" for instance, is an unflinching effort to imagine what lies behind the bald announcement that a young officer and his bride of six months' standing, on a certain day and in a certain room of their modern city apartment, committed ceremonial suicide. There is no "plot"; or, rather, what holds one's attention is not the narrative; since the story begins by saying that the couple killed themselves, we do not read on in a state of suspense to find out what they will do. Mr. Mishima is here, as in several of his other stories, attempting the classic task of fiction: to establish and assess the reality that lies behind some concrete, take-it-or-leave-it happening. These young people killed themselves. For what reason? What was the view of life that imposed death on them as the only honorable way to face a certain situation? What was the upbringing that rooted them within this tradition? These questions, which may be no easier for a modern Japanese to answer than they are for us, are investigated patiently and convincingly. And the gory business of disemboweling oneself is described—as in this kind of story it must be, for there can be no drawing of veils—with a surgical directness that taxes the reader's endurance as it must have taxed the writer's.

Again, in "**The Seven Bridges,**" a traditional belief is explored in modern terms; but this time the exploration is combined with a "story" in the conventional sense, so that we read along to see what happens, and are not disappointed. This, to me, is the best piece in the book, and since I don't see how to discuss it without giving away the plot, I will say no more.

The amount of Japanese local color, as it were, varies from story to story and is not an important distinguishing feature. Yukio Mishima's identity as a writer, it seems to me, lies elsewhere. The mark of his work is an intense curiosity about the human spirit, and in particular about those moments of sudden illumination that come to us when, with our emotional responsiveness keyed up by an unfamiliar situation or an unusual stress, we have an abrupt vision of the world, and of our own situation, from some unexpected angle that makes everything look different. Mishima's stories very often pivot on these moments. The central character has a flash of intuition in which he or she understands some central truth: or, perhaps, is blinded by some central illusion. It hardly matters. These moments change people's characters. They are the inner sources of our energies, often unguessable by outside onlookers. (pp. 25-6)

In **Death in Midsummer,** the title story ends with a sudden psychological jump on the part of a woman who has been struggling, all through the story, with an impossible burden of guilt. The short play *Dojoji* culminates when a girl, who has hidden herself inside a (heavily symbolic) wardrobe in order to disfigure her face—a kind of ritual suicide in which she intends to kill her prettiness—suddenly realizes a truth about the relationship of experience to Nature, and comes out unscathed. In **"The Priest of Shiga Temple and His Love,"** the ascetic old priest catches sight of a beautiful courtesan and falls in love with her:

> He could only think that, in order to bring about that wonderous moment, something which had for a long time lurked deceptively within him had finally revealed itself. That thing was nothing other than the present world, which until then had been at repose, but which had now suddenly lifted itself out of the darkness and begun to stir.

"Suddenly," we note, the experience had "lifted itself out of the darkness." And everything was changed, as completely as when the boy heard the ship's siren.

Are we ready with our foreigner's generalizations? Shall we say that when a nation, long held in the plaster of Paris of a rigid code which regulated every detail of life from ethics to etiquette, suddenly finds itself wandering in the featureless desert of the 20th Century, its finer spirits can only turn inward? That the intense moment of illumination—even with false light—that comes from within, is all that is left to them to set against the triviality and emptiness of the world they now share with us?

Mr. Mishima has been compared by Western critics, with a startling range of European writers. Christopher Isherwood names Gide. Samuel E. Martin hesitates over Gide but plumps for Proust. Angus Wilson says that Mishima's char-

acterization has "Balzacian dimension and Flaubertian truth." *The Times Literary Supplement* speaks of his "almost Brechtian detachment." It seems that you get a lot for your money—Gide, Proust, Balzac, Flaubert and Brecht all in one. Under these circumstances I feel justified in adding one more. Yukio Mishima's intense descriptions of moments of inner revelation seem to me Wordsworthian. Wordsworth's poetry was written at a time when the rigid European society of the 18th Century—legalistic, Christian, hierarchical, incurious—had suddenly fallen into dust and that dust was being blown about by the wind of free speculation. The individual crisis took on a new scale. A man's own interior drama mattered more than the fate of a society, because the one included the other. Mishima? A minor Japanese Wordsworth? Take your pick: it's as good a guess as Balzac or Brecht anyway. (p. 28)

John Wain, "Japanese Modern," in The New Republic, *Vol. 155, No. 4-5, July 30, 1966, pp. 25-8.*

RONALD H. BAYES   (essay date 1967)

[*Bayes is an American poet, dramatist, and short story writer who regards Mishima as one of his main literary influences. In the following excerpt, Bayes points out similarities between the works of Mishima and German writer Thomas Mann and comments on Mishima's candid, unemotional style.*]

Death in Midsummer is painfully "of our time." More than this, the book affords the opportunity for sound display of Mishima's fantastic range and control. There is about Mishima's mystery of the prose form that which reminds one of Mann in "Death in Venice," "Mario and the Magician," and "Tonio Kröger." Certainly such tempered stuff is rare now— even among the most heralded of modern short stories.

It would appear that Mishima can deal with any subject matter in a direct way and that his strength and frankness never prove offensive. He is concerned with the sensational at times, but never for sensation's sake alone. His clear objectivity as a craftsman leaves one in awe, for in spite of its hardness and polish Mishima's prose does not abdicate compassion and respect for the figures moving within the created framework. **"Three Million Yen,"** is one of the finest stories in the new collection. It deals with innocent dreams made more tragic than usual when it is discovered that the frugal, idealistic young country couple who are saving for a "sound" future for themselves and the child they refuse to have until they have "enough" money, are earning toward that end by performing sexually before a set of jaded, wealthy, aging women who gather secretly in Tokyo. The story is made more telling in that the reader discovers the protagonists, Kenzo and Kiyoko, in a Disneyesque amusement area within a department store called "The New World."

"Thermos Bottles" has an infinite number of identification points for everyone aware of the changes within oneself and within, at the same time, this century. Here, as in other of his stories, comments that seem at first peripheral lock tight in Mishima: for instance the protagonist of **"Thermos Bottles,"** Kawase, in San Francisco on business, meets an old love (a former geisha) and as they are both an ocean away from home and years away from their old relationship, seriously ponders that

> It was as if the distance between past and present, usually so precise, had shrunk a few inches.

Mishima at age five with his grandmother Natsu in 1930.

He blamed the shrinkage on the foreign country. The Japanese system of measuring had gone askew. There were times when a sudden encounter abroad produced effusions that were cause for later regret, for the distance could not be forced back to normal afterward. The difficulty was not limited to relations between men and women. Kawase had had the experience with other men, and men who were not particularly close friends.

It is only later that the heart of Kawase's future is cut into by a grotesque business involving a child's thermos.

Mishima examines the many parts of love in as cool a manner as a surgeon might approach his duties. In his tale of the Old Priest of Shiga and his love for the Great Imperial Concubine we find classic power of description and economy together. In **"The Seven Bridges,"** the enigma of the selfish romantic silliness, to which no person is a stranger, is laid bare—and that its conclusion leaves the reader with one foot in the air is the very thing that refuses to let the reader off the hooking personal identification. The author is just as tough in **"Swaddling Clothes"** and in the book's title story.

"The Pearl," which is like many Oriental and many non-Oriental tales . . . does not sparkle. It is rather O. Henry-like and probably the weakest story in the collection. One of the strongest is **"Patriotism,"** which effectively copes with difficult sexual and personal-political detail. The eventual suicides in the story are handled in a manner that must provoke a type of objective aversion: but the acts are subjectively understandable to the point that one can completely set aside the aversion just as surely as one can in Greek tragedy. As for subject matter, Mishima may, in a few paragraphs, accomplish as much as Shaw does with his clever combat between Don Juan and The Devil in their discussion of war and patriotism. After her husband's suicide, the lovely bride, Reiko, makes her careful preparations to follow the lieutenant:

> Slowly, her socks slippery with blood, Reiko descended the stairway. The upstairs room was now completely still.

> Switching on the ground-floor lights, she checked the gas jet and the main gasplug and poured water over the smouldering, half-buried charcoal in the brazier. She stood before the upright mirror in the four-and-a-half-mat room and held up her skirts. The bloodstains made it seem as if a bold, vivid pattern was printed across the lower half of her white kimono. When she sat down before the mirror, she was conscious of the dampness and coldness of her husband's blood in the region of her thighs, and she shivered. Then, for a long while, she lingered over her toilet preparations. She applied the rouge generously to her cheeks, and her lips too she painted heavily. This was no longer make-up to please her husband. It was make-up for the world which she would leave behind, and there was a touch of the magnificent and the spectacular in her brushwork. When she rose, the mat before the mirror was wet with blood. Reiko was not concerned about this.

> Returning from the toilet, Reiko stood finally on the cement floor of the porchway. When her husband had bolted the door here last night it had been in preparation for death. For a while she stood immersed in the consideration of a simple problem. Should she now leave the bolt drawn?

The one dramatic work included in Mishima's book is called *Dojoji*. It is a deliberately contrived Noh-style play which takes place in a second-hand furniture store filled with both Oriental and Occidental antiques.

Dojoji, like the short stories, leaves one once again in awe of the scope of Yukio Mishima—feeling a little, perhaps, like the secondhand store's superintendent who warns the girl, Kiyoko, "Spring is a dangerous season." It is easy to feel toward Mishima as the dealer does toward Kiyoko when he warns her, "You'll be ruined. Your heart'll be torn to shreds. You'll end up no longer able to feel anything." But fortunately one will long recall Kiyoko's reply: "I'm not worried. Nothing can bother me, no matter what happens. Who do you suppose can wound me now?"

If his heart isn't torn to shreds, or even if it is and he can continue to write with such combined sensitivity, insight, and calm; with such lucidity—Mishima will indeed be the equal of Thomas Mann—if he isn't already. (pp. 41-2)

Ronald H. Bayes, in a review of "Death in Midsummer," in West Coast Review, *Vol. 2, No. 1, Spring, 1967, pp. 41-2.*

WILLARD KEENEY   (essay date 1967)

[In the following excerpt, Keeney claims that cultural differences impede Western readers' appreciation of Death in Midsummer, and Other Stories. *He suggests, however, that Mishima's treatment of modern themes is universal and enlightening.]*

Yukio Mishima's **Death in Midsummer** brings together a number of stories previously translated and published in American periodicals and several appearing in English for the first time. They elude total comprehension, perhaps because of the sensibility gap between occident and orient. Yet one of Mishima's constant themes is the universal psychology of guilt and desire, the form alone differing among cultures. In these stories the difference is frequently a function of Japanese tradition. In **"Patriotism,"** for example, a shining young military officer and his beautiful wife, passionately devoted to one another, trade the fulfillment of life for the fulfillment of death, committing ritual suicide because he feels disgraced by his comrades. Behind Mishima's careful understatement one feels an irony mocking the heroic delusion; yet elsewhere tradition becomes implicitly a positive value. **"Three Million Yen,"** for example, is set in a neon-lit pagoda replete with artificial flowers and artificial butterflies, located, naturally, on the site of what was the town pond. In **"Thermos Bottles,"** a Japanese businessman confronts his quondam mistress, now thoroughly Westernized, in a vain attempt to recapture the fragile union of youth. In **"The Priest of Shiga Temple and His Love"** a Buddhist priest and a palace concubine seek the "Pure Land," and in seeking the abstraction miss the tangible magic of their love for one another. Mishima's intensely personal, intensely emotional dilemmas are revealed through a prose of almost casual simplicity, studded with the disarming images of oriental poetry.

Willard Keeney, in a review of "Death in Midsummer," in The Southern Review, *Louisiana State University, n.s. Vol. 3, 1967, p. 1053*

MICHAEL STANDEN   (essay date 1967)

[*In the essay excerpted below, Standen comments on the objectivity of Mishima's fiction, suggesting that the traditional formality of Japanese culture facilitates Mishima's artistic detachment from his subjects.*]

Japan, by virtue of the political geography which has put Greece in the North Atlantic, is part of The West, but to some extent the reader of [*Death in Midsummer*] is bound to be on the look-out for local colour, the Old and New, like any tourist. Some stories partly satisfy such curiosity. In **"Onna-gata"** for example there is a conflict between a classical theatre troupe and the jumpy, becorduroyed director who is using them in a modern play. **"Thermos Flasks"** takes place largely in San Francisco where X, a business-man, runs into Y, a former mistress and geisha who is undergoing full westernization by her new protector. Occasionally Mishima makes direct comments but except in **"Three Million Yen"** such confliction is incidental to the main business of his stories.

Perhaps the oddest juxtaposition is found in **"Patriotism,"** the most striking of the ten pieces. We go into the house of Z, an army officer implicated in the unsuccessful mutiny of 1936. Aided by his wife, who then kills herself, he carries out a ritual suicide in a room heated by a gas-fire. Such an oriental proceeding in a westernized setting has all the incongruity we might expect, yet in the reading this is hardly noticeable. Yukio Mishima is not reporting on the customs of time and place but going through that to the human heart where there is neither East nor West.

It does matter that he is Japanese; for perhaps it helps him to find his artistic distance that there is greater formality in Japanese life. Certainly he exploits this ironically in the slight story **"The Pearl,"** but in **"Patriotism"** it has something to do with the heroism and tragedy which we experience in witnessing the couple's final sexual intercourse and the truly horrifying suicides. There are various other violent happenings in the book. In the title story [**"Death in Midsummer"**]for example (one of the best) two children are accidentally drowned whilst in the charge of the wife's sister-in-law. The parents' guilt and other reactions are traced through and the story ends—as do many of them—with the seemingly inconsequential which implies the essential carryover of the previous situation; in this case simply the wife on their return to Oki beach staring out to sea.

Neither violence nor sex is used for its own sake by Mishima and this distinguishes him from much Western fiction where the cultural climate so often encourages the writer to exploit his material for short-term gains. (pp. 55-6)

> *Michael Standen, in a review of "Death in Midsummer," in* Stand Magazine, *Vol. 9, No. 2, 1967, pp. 55-6.*

HENRY SCOTT-STOKES   (essay date 1974)

[*Scott-Stokes is a British journalist and author who has served as a Tokyo correspondent for such periodicals as the* New York Times, *the* London Times, *and the* Economist. *In the following excerpt from his biography of Mishima, Scott-Stokes discusses the autobiographical aspects of Mishima's story "Patriotism" in the context of the Ni Ni Roku incident.*]

Mishima was an excellent critic and a fair judge of his own writing. He remarked of [his short story] **"Patriotism"** that it contained "both the best and the worst features of my writing"; it may also be regarded as representative of his entire oeuvre. **"Patriotism,"** which Mishima wrote in the early autumn of 1960, is the story of a young Imperial Army lieutenant at the time of the Ni Ni Roku Incident of February 1936. The two principal factions in the Japanese Armed Forces at the time were both expansionist, wanting Japan to pursue a policy of foreign conquest. The Kodo-ha, the Imperial Way faction, favored a strike north against the Soviet Union; and the Tosei-ha, the Control faction, favored a strike south against Britain and other European colonial powers. The conflict came to a head with the Ni Ni Roku Incident, which was triggered by Kodo-ha officers seeking to forestall seizure of power by their Tosei-ha rivals. The action was spurred on by a plan for the dispatch of the First Division, many of whose officers were Kodo-ha members, to Manchuria—this would have greatly reduced the strength of the Kodo-ha in Tokyo. The Kodo-ha adherents, led by a few young officers—Takatsugu Muranaka, Asaichi Isobe, Teruzo Ando, Yasuhide Kurihara, and others—decided to strike against the authorities before that happened. Early on the morning of February 26, with the capital under a fresh fall of snow, the officers mobilized 1,400 men and seized control of the center of Tokyo after assassinating three leading members of the government. The action, they declared, was carried out on behalf of the Emperor and was aimed at his evil advisers. After a brief hesitation Hirohito himself ordered them to surrender. The revolt collapsed in four days.

The protagonist of Mishima's story, Lieutenant Takeyama, is an officer in a regiment stationed in Tokyo. He is a friend of the rebel officers and sympathizes with their aims, but he is left out of the plans because he is newly married. After the outbreak of the Ni Ni Roku, he is ordered to lead an attack on the rebels. His way out of the moral dilemma created for him by this order is to commit hara-kiri. His wife, Reiko, must also kill herself. In **"Patriotism,"** . . . Mishima described the hara-kiri of the young man in extraordinary detail. This is probably the most elaborate account of the samurai rite in the whole of Japanese literature, and it is all the more striking in that the author appears to endorse the ideology of Lieutenant Takeyama and his associates. The hara-kiri, subtly idealized by Mishima in the story, appears as a grisly act justified by a high ideal. . . . (pp. 231-33)

One other remarkable feature of the story is that Lieutenant Takeyama kills himself first, leaving Reiko to follow him in death afterward. She stabs herself in the throat with a knife, having firmly secured her skirts so that she shall not be found dead in an indecorous posture. The reason given for the husband taking precedence instead of the wife dying first, as would have been normal, is that "it was vital for the lieutenant, whatever else might happen, that there should be no irregularity in his death." The point is not easy to follow. What is clear is that the officer wants to be *watched* as he performs hara-kiri. **"Patriotism"** emerges, from this detail alone, as a work by an abnormal man.

Mishima wrote twice more about the Ni Ni Roku affair. In his play *Toka no Kiku,* and in his unclassifiable work *Eirei no Koe* ("The Voices of the Heroic Dead," 1966), an elegy for the war dead, and also an assault upon Emperor Hirohito for deserting the souls of the departed by intervening in the Ni Ni Roku Incident and by announcing his ningen sengen in 1946, Mishima endorsed the ideology of the rebel officers of

1936. He put the three works—**"Patriotism,"** *Toka no Kiku,* and *Eirei no Koe*—together in one volume, which he called his Ni Ni Roku trilogy. In a postscript to the trilogy he described his conclusion, which I condense a little here:

> I wrote **"Patriotism"** from the point of view of the young officer who could not help choosing suicide because he could not take part in the Ni Ni Roku Incident. This is neither a comedy nor a tragedy but simply a story of happiness . . . If they [husband and wife] had waited one more night, the attack on the Imperial Army [the rebels] would have been called off and the need for their deaths would have decreased, although the legal authorities would have caught up with him [Takeyama]. To choose the place where one dies is also the greatest joy in life. And such a night as the couple had was their happiest. Moreover, there was no shadow of a lost battle over them; the love of these two reaches to an extremity of purity, and the painful suicide of the soldier is equivalent to an honorable death on the field of battle. Somewhere I obtained the conviction that if one misses one's night one will never have another opportunity to achieve a peak of happiness in life. Instrumental in this conviction were my experiences during the war, my reading of Nietzsche during the war, and my fellow feeling for the philosopher Georges Bataille, the "Nietzsche of eroticism. . . ."

> Surely some great God died when the Ni Ni Roku Incident failed. I was only eleven at the time and felt little of it. But when the war ended, when I was twenty, a most sensitive age, I felt something of the terrible cruelty of the death of that God, and this was somehow linked with my intuition of what had happened when I was eleven. For a long time I was unable to understand the connection, but when I wrote *Toka no Kiku* and **"Patriotism"** there appeared a dark shadow in my consciousness as I wrote—and then it disappeared again without taking definite shape. This was a "negative" picture of the Ni Ni Roku Incident; the positive picture was my boyhood impression of the heroism of the rebel officers. Their purity, bravery, youth, and death qualified them as mythical heroes; and their failures and deaths made them true heroes in this world. . . .

(pp. 233-35)

> *Henry Scott-Stokes, in his* The Life and Death of Yukio Mishima, *Farrar, Straus and Giroux, 1974, 344 p.*

JOHN NATHAN (essay date 1974)

[*Nathan was a close friend of Mishima. In the following excerpt, he comments on Mishima's objective point of view in "Patriotism" and examines the relationship between events in this story and those surrounding Mishima's death.*]

The spring and early summer of 1960 were a time of violent political confrontation. The issue was the renewal of the Japan-U.S. Security Treaty of 1952 (*Anpo*). Not only the leftist opposition but also the press and public opinion were opposed to the treaty (which authorized the continuance of U.S. military bases in Japan in return for U.S. protection against Japan's hypothetical enemies) on the sensible grounds that it harnessed Japan to whatever military action in Asia the United States might see fit to take. The administration, however, anxious as always to comply with American desires, was de-

Mishima addressing the Japan Self-Defense Force moments before his suicide.

termined it should be renewed for a period of ten years. (pp. 173-74)

The security treaty was an issue which elicited violent feelings pro or con from nearly everyone. Mishima's response, however, suggests that in 1960 he was unburdened by any political consciousness whatsoever. (p. 174)

Yet by 1968 Mishima was promising his friends that he would "die with sword in hand" in the battle with the Left at the next renewal of the security treaty in 1970. By 1968, that is, he had become (or at least was sounding very much like) an ultranationalist. What enabled (or drove) the confessed nihilist in this short space of years to acquire faith?

The beginnings of an answer are to be found in a forty-page story called **"Patriotism"** which Mishima wrote late in the summer of 1960. The story was inspired by the Army Rebellion of 1936, which Mishima would invest with increasing symbolic importance as his own very special brand of patriotism evolved. (p. 175)

The hero of **"Patriotism"** is a handsome young lieutenant in the Imperial Guard whose comrades have kept him ignorant of the plot [to overthrow the government and restore supreme command of the armed forces to the emporer] out of compassion for his recent marriage. Early on the morning of the twenty-sixth the Lieutenant is summoned to the palace by an emergency bugle and is gone for two days. When he returns on the evening of the twenty-seventh he tells his young wife Reiko that he has resolved to kill himself rather than join an attack in the morning against his fellow officers, who have been branded rebels. Reiko expresses her desire to join her husband in death; the Lieutenant agrees. He purifies himself in a bath. The couple makes love a final time. Then, as Reiko looks on, the lieutenant disembowels himself. Reiko kisses her dead husband goodbye, sits in front of his body, and drives a dagger through her throat.

In an afterword, Mishima described **"Patriotism"** as "neither a comedy nor a tragedy, but a tale of bliss." A reader unfamiliar with Mishima, however, would have difficulty locating the bliss he asserts, particularly in the long and loving description of the lieutenant's *seppuku*, which is the climax of the tale:

> Despite the effort he had put into the blow himself, the lieutenant had the impression that someone else had struck his side agonizingly with a rod of iron. For a second or so his head reeled and he had no idea what had happened. The five or six inches of naked point vanished completely into his flesh. . . .

> He returned to consciousness. The blade had certainly pierced the wall of his stomach, he thought. It was difficult to breathe, his chest pounded, and in some deep distant region which he could hardly believe was a part of himself, a fearful excruciating pain came welling up as if the ground had opened to disgorge a boiling stream of molten lava. The pain came suddenly nearer, with terrifying speed. . . .

> So this was *seppuku!* he thought. It was as if the sky had fallen on his head and the world was reeling drunkenly. His will power and courage, which had seemed so robust before he made the incision, had now dwindled to something like a single hairlike thread of steel, and he was assailed by the uneasy feeling that he must advance along this thread, clinging to it with desperation. His clenched fist had grown moist. Looking down he saw that both his hand and the cloth about the blade were drenched in blood. His loincloth too was dyed a deep red. It struck him as incredible that, in this terrible agony, visible things could still be seen and existing things existed still. . . .

> The pain spread slowly outward from the inner depths until the whole stomach reverberated. It was like the wild clanging of a bell. Or like a thousand bells which jangled simultaneously at every breath and every throb of his pulse, rocking his whole being. The lieutenant could no longer stop himself from moaning. But by now the blade had cut its way through to below the navel, and when he noticed this he felt a sense of satisfaction, and a renewal of courage. . . .

> By the time the lieutenant had at last drawn the sword across to the right side of his stomach the blade was already cutting shallow and had revealed its naked tip, slippery with blood and fat. Suddenly stricken by a fit of vomiting, the lieutenant cried out hoarsely.

> The vomiting made the fierce pain fiercer still, and the stomach, which had thus far remained firm and compact, now abruptly heaved, opening wide its wound, and the entrails burst through, as if the wound too were vomiting. Seemingly ignorant of their master's suffering, the entrails gave an impres-

sion of health and almost disagreeable vitality as they slipped smoothly out and spilled over into the crotch. The lieutenant's head drooped, his shoulders heaved, his eyes opened to narrow slits, and a thin trickle of saliva dribbled from his mouth. . . .

And so on. To the end, when the lieutenant finally administers himself the *coup de grâce* by driving his blade through his throat, he is aware of terrible pain only. Nor does the solemn narrator ever hint that there is more to this than meets the reader's eye. If there is bliss in this death—and unquestionably for Mishima there is, though the lieutenant is not made privy to it—then it must be the bliss of excruciating pain.

But that was nothing new. Since the day Mishima had been aroused sexually for the first time by a painting of Saint Sebastian's martyrdom, youthful, martyred, and painful death had been a prospect of bliss. Neither was there anything new in the explicit connection established in **"Patriotism"** between erotic desire and death:

> Was it death he was now waiting for? Or a wild ecstasy of the senses? The two seemed to overlap, almost as if the object of this bodily desire were death itself. . . . As their tongues explored one another's mouths . . . they could feel their senses being fired to the red heat of steel by the agonies of death as yet nowhere prefigured. The pain they could not feel yet, the distant pain of death, had refined their awareness of pleasure.

But there is also a new element in **"Patriotism,"** something beginning to crystallize. "On a rare night such as this one," Mishima wrote in his afterword, "the love of man and wife reaches the zenith of purity and intoxication, and an agonizing death by one's own sword becomes a soldier's act of supreme sincerity, equal in every way to honorable death on the battlefield." The implication is that death must be more than merely agonizing if it is to be the means to erotic bliss: it must also be a soldier's death, "equal to honorable death on the battlefield." This in turn implies the necessity of some profound disturbance such as the February Rebellion in the absence of an actual state of war. It is here, in this search for a battlefield, that Mishima's interest in terrorism originates.

"Patriotism" suggests that Mishima's imagination is beginning to resolve a means of acquiring the death he desires and has always desired. Given that "rare night" on which all the requisites for bliss are within reach, what is it that enables the lieutenant actually "to seize the supreme moment in life"? His *patriotism*. And what is that? It is what Mishima soon would begin to equate with what he called "the essence of the Japanese spirit" and to define as *fanatic* (his choice of words) devotion to ideals which transcend rationality. This very special notion of patriotism is therefore very like if not identical to religious faith.

The lieutenant is a *devout* patriot. His actions both as a soldier and a husband have all the austerity, measure, and high solemnity of a Shinto prayer. And the basis for all his actions, the fundament of his moral world, is his devotion to the emperor, at once god and high priest of Shinto:

> On the shelf below the stairway, alongside the tablet from the Great Ise Shrine, were installed photographs of their Imperial Majesties, and every morning before leaving for duty the lieutenant would stand here with his wife and together they would deeply bow. The offering water was renewed each

morning, and the sacred sprig of *sakaki* was always green and fresh. Their lives were lived beneath the solemn protection of the gods and were imbued with an intense pleasure which set every fiber of their being atremble.

The solemnity which pervades the story and is the expression of the lieutenant's devoutness is unremitting, even in those delirious moments when he and his wife are making love: "Even in bed these two were frighteningly and awesomely serious. At the very height of frenzied passion their hearts were serious, serious to a point of solemnity." In another man this would seem an impossible contradiction. But the lieutenant's devoutness (patriotism) is so fundamentally a part of himself that it is indistinguishable from erotic desire; indeed, patriotism and erotic desire are identical:

> The lieutenant was confident there had been no impurity in that joy they had experienced when resolving upon death. They had both sensed at that moment—though not, of course, in any clear and conscious way—that the proper pleasure they shared in private was once again sanctified by the Supreme Imperative and the authority of the gods, and of a complete and unassailable morality. On looking into one another's eyes and discovering there proper death, they had felt themselves safe once more within impenetrable steel walls, armored in Beauty and Righteousness. Thus, so far from seeing any contradiction between his physical desire and the sincerity of his patriotism, the lieutenant was even able to consider the two as parts of the same thing.

If patriotism and erotic desire are identical, and if the object of erotic desire is death, then patriotism is also a desire for death. But it is more than simply desire; it is at the same time a means of obtaining death. For the obvious difference between a devout patriot and a mere romantic is that the patriot, provided he is also a warrior, has the physical wherewithal to fulfill his desire. All he requires are the proper circumstances, "that rare night when . . . agonizing death by *seppuku* becomes a soldier's act. . . ."

The seeds of **"Patriotism"** are contained in *Kyoko's House*. But there is a crucial difference between the boxer and the lieutenant. The boxer's evolution into a right-wing activist is presented ironically: he knows, if not in a fully conscious way, that the faith he professes is only a means to obtaining an "indescribable rapture" very like death. But the lieutenant's faith is airtight, proof against the slightest irony. The drama of **"Patriotism"** is played against a scroll which hangs in the decorational altar in the couple's room. The two Chinese characters on the scroll mean roughly "sincerity" but carry the additional connotation of the samurai's utter faith in his lord, in this case, the emperor. **"Patriotism"** is sincere: Mishima was careful to seal his story against whatever impulses to irony in himself might have prevented him from identifying completely with the lieutenant's devout world. When he wrote in the opening lines "The last moments of this heroic and dedicated couple were such as to make the gods themselves weep," he believed it. At least he desperately wanted to believe.

"Patriotism" is the earliest indication that Mishima's quest for death was leading him to Shinto mysticism and emperor worship. Before long his newly found faith in the emperor would become the basis of a nationalism, and a politicized Mishima would emerge. But just beneath the surface of the politics was the old desire for death. There is nothing unusual about a man who has never required faith abruptly embracing religion when he learns that he must die. But surely the reverse is extraordinary: the "patriotism" Mishima began to formulate in the summer of 1960 was in essence his attempt to acquire faith in order to die. (pp. 176-82)

> *John Nathan, in his* Mishima: A Biography, *Little, Brown and Company, 1974, 300 p.*

BARBARA WOLF   (essay date 1975-76)

[*In the essay excerpted below, Wolf discusses the thematic and stylistic scope of* Death in Midsummer, and Other Stories *and comments on the distinction between Mishima's personal life and his art.*]

Death in Midsummer is almost a microcosm of Mishima's whole work, representing most of his major styles except for the polemic and the directly confessional. Together, the stories suggest both where he was broad in his concerns and limited by his obsessions.

Death in Midsummer must be surprising to those familiar with Mishima only through headlines. [**"Death in Midsummer,"**] which opens the collection, is quite unrelated to nationalism, fascism, homosexuality, or seppuku. Rather, it is an elegy on the death of the innocent, and a study of the psychology of mourning. The main character, Tomoko, is the mother of two young children who are drowned in a commonplace incident at a resort. Mishima's method is one with many affinities but no equivalents. The narration is a controlled Tolstoyan analysis, phase by phase, of his character's evolving perceptions, proceeding to an epiphany that is left as ambiguous as a Zen koan or haiku, and that is therefore utterly *un*-Tolstoyan. There is also something rather like Poe or Dostoevsky in the extraordinary lucidity of the descriptions, coupled with the intense hysteria of the passions described. Yet although the passions are hysterical, the person who suffers them is fundamentally sound, and not at all like a character out of Dostoevsky or Poe. Tomoko's irrational state is simply normal for one in her circumstances.

In **"Death in Midsummer,"** the whole process of mourning is described as an unfolding of ironies and contradictions. Tomoko's grief is both hysterical and normal. Her recovery, which she feels is shameful, is perfectly natural. Her quest for meaning is both inevitable and futile. And to enrich the irony, the narrator places her ordeal in cosmic perspective: the children, who mean so much to their mother, mean nothing to Nature; they are swept away by a chance wave and not a sign is left on ocean, beach, or sky. The grief, the shame, the hunger for meaning, all define Tomoko as human; yet all are as irrational and futile as they are unavoidable. Tomoko's personal loss confronts her with something even more terrible: the void itself. Yet despite the void, as despite her grief, she goes on living, protected from destruction by the limitations of her intelligence, limitations not merely specific to her but essential to the species.

For all their outward diversity, the majority of Mishima's sympathetic characters come down to a type much like Tomoko: an individual entranced by inner conflicts, isolated from an exterior world as unconsciously cruel as it is beautiful. Yet it is the diversity that is more immediately obvious. At first sight, few works would seem less alike than **"Death in Midsummer,"** with its bourgeois setting, chaste tone, and unsophisticated protagonist, and so extravagant a period piece as **"The Priest of Shiga Temple and His Love."** Yet the latter piece too is ultimately reducible to a series of internal perceptions and riddling contradictions.

The story is told in prose of great elaborateness and beauty. An aged monk of famed sanctity falls in love at first sight with a Grand Concubine from the Heian court. Just as his whole life to that point has represented the renunciation of this world for the next, hers has represented the empty enjoyment of the present:

> The Great Priest was not young enough . . . to believe that this new feeling was simply a trick that his flesh had played on him. . . . [She] was nothing other than the present world, which until then had been in repose. . . . It was as if he had been standing by the highway . . . with his hands firmly covering his ears, and had watched two great ox-carts rumble past each other. All of a sudden he had removed his hands. . . .

But her response works at cross-purposes to his; as he seeks this world through her, she seeks the next through him. When they finally meet, it is in silence and tears. They feel some enormous event has occurred, but what it is is never made explicit, and no doubt it differs for each character, as it does for each reader. Religion and sensuality are both—and perhaps equally—triumphs of the spirit and follies of the flesh; but above all they are achievements and also deceptions of the imagination. Therefore, Mishima makes the Grand Priest's meeting with his love at once a consummation and an anticlimax, and as solitary an event as his return to his monastic cell.

For in **"The Priest and His Love,"** as in **"Death in Midsummer,"** the great struggles of the characters are not so much internalized as fundamentally internal. The characters live in worlds subjective to the point of isolation. Unable to share either values or feelings, they have nothing to go on but their own impulses and intuitions. Inner states may be set off by something outside the self, like the death of the children or the first glimpse of the Grand Concubine; but from that point on they assume an autonomous life and logic. The *moment* in Mishima tends to have such enormous consequences, because it so often represents a forced awakening from an innocence that is really a kind of unreflecting solipsism. In **"Death in Midsummer,"** Tomoko is literally napping at the moment her children drown; and the Great Priest has figuratively closed his senses to the present world.

Toshiko, heroine of the brief but powerful **"Swaddling Clothes,"** suffers a very similar awakening. When a low-ranking servant in her household unexpectedly gives birth to an illegitimate child, wealthy young Toshiko is shocked into pity and a kind of responsibility. She is aware for the first time of the injustice of the social order, and foresees a time when the despised infant must take revenge against her own pampered baby. This awakening, however, leads to nothing practical. Rather than offering material help, she is impelled toward a masochistic expiation. Deliberately going into the park at night, she invites assault by a young vagrant whom she identifies with the person the newborn outcast must become. Toshiko's sacrifice is both symbolically appropriate and fundamentally hysterical, a psychotic *acting out* rather than a purposeful *act*. Like that of Dostoevsky, and of Tolstoy in his last phase, Mishima's power seems largely a product of his own desperate sincerity, which is of a kind that can

find no outlet in the world of action. Such passion creates grand, symbolic gestures, and characters and situations that seem to demand them—in art if not in life. (pp. 848-50)

The incompatibility of emotion and aesthetic beauty is one of the several themes of **"Onnagata."** The drama critic, Masuyama, is fascinated by the art of the Kabuki female impersonator, Mangiku. Mangiku's femininity is greater than any woman's, just as his theatrical roles are more grandly passionate than life. But his only place is on stage, in that bastard world "born of the illicit union between dream and reality." When Mangiku takes his impersonation out of the theater and into the real world, he immediately disgraces himself and disillusions Masuyama.

With one exception, the rest of the stories in *Death in Midsummer* satirize the contemporary scene. **"The Pearl"** describes a club of housewives with nothing to do but manipulate each other. **"The Three Million Yen"** tells how a young married couple saves for middle-class possessions by giving sex shows for audiences like the housewives in **"The Pearl."** **"The Seven Bridges"** concerns a group of geishas, whose playful approach to a rite of their profession soon exposes their ugly selfishness. **"Thermos Bottles"** follows a smug businessman through his discovery that his perfect egoism has made him expendable to everyone. These modern types have neither beauty nor feeling to recommend them. They recognize nothing capable of transcending or ennobling the self, except possibly money.

How different from these, almost another species, are the Lieutenant and Reiko in **"Patriotism,"** as poetically idealized as their foils are satirically denigrated. **"Patriotism"** is an imaginative reconstruction of an actual double suicide performed by a young married couple trapped in a conflict of loyalties during the insurrection of 1936. The work is, in every sense, "highly wrought," a kind of heroic epic, or even opera, in prose. As charged with splendor and glory, with sensuality and death as *Tristan and Isolde,* it expresses the same striving after transcendence. The young couple's heedless sincerity endows them with the grandeur of figures in legend; or rather, it almost so endows them. But it is one thing to accept heroic gestures from personages at the dawn of history, acting upon archetypal situations, and another to accept them from twentieth-century persons committed to the wrong side of issues. Ironically, **"Patriotism"** succeeds for most readers only to the extent that Mishima's stylistic genius overbalances the theme he is apparently celebrating.

Every story in *Death in Midsummer* is rich in ironies, but perhaps the supreme irony is that the martyred lovers of **"Patriotism"** are the only truly happy characters in the whole volume. They alone are free from both triviality and alienation. They alone are in communion with each other and with the world. Their acceptance of a transcendent principle endows their emotions with beauty and meaning and permits them to live and die both serenely and intensely. Had they martyred themselves to almost any other ideal, it would be easier for liberal readers to sympathize and understand. For what is being celebrated in **"Patriotism"** is not thirties-style militarism per se, but the self-realizing force of idealism and the bliss of martyrdom. The specific principle is less the cause than the occasion.

Mishima's fiction is fiction, not polemics or propaganda. It is true that a good deal of what he wrote conveys an open or implicit criticism of modern society. True, he traced much of the inauthenticity of modern Japanese society to the rejection of tradition that followed defeat in the Pacific war. It is even true that in his last years he became a spokesman for a kind of right-wing reaction, and ultimately martyred himself for that cause. But it is also true that practically nothing in **Death in Midsummer,** except possibly **"Patriotism,"** reasonably lends itself to a right-wing, or even political, interpretation. And only one story in all ten, **"Onnagata,"** is even remotely concerned with homosexuality. Mishima, of course, did write polemics and confessions, but only on a few occasions did he disguise them as fiction.

That Mishima could conceive no better solution for Japan than to revive its past was less a misfortune for him as an artist than as a man. It so happened that the desperate sincerity, disciplined violence, and paradoxical gentleness of the samurai tradition had affinities with fundamental traits of his own nature: his discipline as artist and athlete, his sadomasochism as a sexual being, his despair as a Japanese, his emotionality as a person. These affinities were destructive to him as a man because they encouraged his tendency to hysteria. But the effect on his work was probably beneficial. Since Mishima universalized his private experience when he wrote, the passions and issues that concerned him personally were rarely allowed to intrude into his fictional universe. Within the limits of his sensibility, he could be an objective and dispassionate artist. Many of his characters do not resemble him at all, but are specimens of types held up for examination. Those in whom he did invest himself are far less likely to share his opinions and habits than his loneliness, his alienation, and his passionate integrity. In other words, the dovetailing of influences that produced hysteria in his life created intensity in his art, just as it did with Tolstoy, Dostoevsky, and Poe.

Mishima died attempting a double impossibility: to inspire Japan to reject the present and return to the past, and to make himself over into a man of the past, a samurai. When so futile a gesture is made in life, it can only appear as madness. But when it occurs in art, as in **"Swaddling Clothes"** or **"The Priest and His Love,"** then it takes on quite another meaning. We seek in art, after all, what we cannot have in a sane life: an unfettered expression of our feelings, wishes, fears, impulses, intentions; a direct confrontation with our human condition in all its madness and cruelty, its contradictions and tragic joys. Mishima declared that he wished to make a poem of his own life. That aspiration is the great romantic quest after the impossible, which in life must always lead to destruction but which is the source of the sublime in art. As an artist, Mishima may have been limited by his own obsessions, but he still gives a great deal of what we go to literature for. Because he kept his own opinions out, his characters and their situations transcend the time and place of their creation. Compared to that accomplishment, the success or failure of the rest of his life must fade into its relative insignificance. (pp. 851-52)

Barbara Wolf, "Mishima in Microcosm," in The American Scholar, *Vol. 45, Winter, 1975-76, pp. 848-52.*

FURTHER READING

Keene, Donald. "Mishima." *The New York Times Book Review* (3 January 1971): 4, 24-5.

>   Memorial tribute to Mishima. Keene reflects on his friendship with Mishima and comments on the artist's suicide.

———. "Mishima and the Modern Scene." *The Times Literary Supplement* (20 August 1971): 989-90.

>   Discusses Mishima's personal philosophy, reputation, and suicide. Keene notes contradictions between Mishima's lifestyle and his professed ideals.

Petersen, Gwenn Boardman. *The Moon in the Water: Understanding Tanizaki, Kawabata, and Mishima.* Honolulu: University Press of Hawaii, 1979, 366 p.

>   Introduces the major themes in Mishima's works and comments on the elements and style of Mishima's fiction within the context of Japanese literature.

Yourcenar, Marguerite. *Mishima: A Vision of the Void.* Translated by Alberto Manguel and Marguerite Yourcenar. New York: Farrar, Straus, and Giroux, 1986, 151 p.

>   Highly-acclaimed discussion of the biographical aspects of Mishima's fiction.

Katherine Anne Porter

1890-1980

American short story writer, novelist, essayist, critic, and translator.

Porter is widely acknowledged as one of the finest modern authors of short fiction in English. Writing in an unadorned prose style, Porter endowed her works with vivid, sensitive characterizations and garnered much critical admiration for her arresting blend of imagery, detail, and subtle irony. Her stories often revolve around the relationships and emotions of her characters and explore such concerns as the differences between appearance and reality and the consequences of self-deception. Porter's perceptive psychological studies typically draw from personal experience and depend on moments of illumination to express the essence of an incident. She is perhaps most highly regarded for her lengthier works of short fiction, particulary the novellas *Noon Wine* and *Pale Horse, Pale Rider,* which emphasize personal consequences within a social context. Porter wrote: "My whole attempt has been to discover and understand human motives, human feelings, to make a distillation of what human relations and experiences my mind has been able to absorb. I have never known an uninteresting human being, and I have never known two alike; . . . I am passionately involved with these individuals who populate all these enormous migrations, calamities; these beings without which, one by one, all the 'broad movements of history' could never take place."

Porter was born in Indian Creek, Texas. When she was two years old, her mother died, and the family moved to a farm in Hays County, near Austin, where Porter and her four siblings were reared by their paternal grandmother. This milieu, which Porter has called "this summer country of my childhood . . . , soft blackland farming country, full of fruits and flowers and birds," provided the setting and characters for many of Porter's short stories. Uncle Jimbilly and Nannie, for example, emancipated slaves who appear in several works, are based upon two of the farm's domestic servants, and Porter's grandmother, Catherine Anne, often surfaces as the authoritative, strong-willed matriarch. After her grandmother died in 1901, Porter was sent to several convent schools in Texas and Louisiana, until, at the age of sixteen, she ran away to get married. This marriage, her first of four, ended in divorce, and Porter subsequently moved to Chicago, where she worked as a journalist and as a movie extra for Essanay studios. Porter referred to herself as "a roving spirit," and her myriad travel experiences typically yielded the ideas for her stories. In 1918, while employed as the drama critic for the *Rocky Mountain News* in Denver, Colorado, Porter succumbed to influenza. The virus threatened her life and caused her hair to turn white, an ordeal that later formed the basis for *Pale Horse, Pale Rider.* After a brief, unhappy stint as a ghost writer while living in New York City's Greenwich Village, Porter traveled to Mexico, where she studied art and became involved in the Obregón Revolution of 1920, a movement to overthrow the regime of President Venustiano Carranza, who had failed to move Mexico toward social reform. The revolutionary program of educational, agrarian, and labor reorganization intrigued

Porter and influenced the nature of social commentary in her works. Porter's first published short story, "María Concepción," and several other early tales take place in Mexico—the country Porter deemed she knew best.

During the 1920s, Porter's stories appeared in such literary journals as *Century Magazine, Hound and Horn,* and the *Virginia Quarterly Review,* and were later collected in *Flowering Judas,* her first volume of short fiction. The stories won Porter critical acclaim and a Guggenheim fellowship that allowed her to travel extensively in Europe for many years. A cruise to Germany in 1932, where she met, among others, Adolf Hitler and Hermann Goering, inspired her only novel *Ship of Fools.* Written over a twenty-year period, the work describes an ill-assorted group of tourists traveling by ship from Vera Cruz, Mexico, to Bremerhaven, Germany, in 1931, and has been studied as an allegory of the moral malaise of Western civilization before World War II. Although she generally disliked Germany, Porter stayed there for a year following her cruise, and her experiences later rendered material for "The Leaning Tower," a short story concerning an American expatriate in Nazi Germany. After leaving Berlin in 1933, Porter lived in Paris, and the four years she spent there greatly influenced her life and career. In Paris Porter renewed many literary acquaintances and developed several lifelong friendships, most notably with such authors as Glenway Wescott and Ford Madox Ford. Porter also remarried and her writing flourished. Such nostalgic works as *Old Mortality,* "The Witness," and "The Grave" were composed or developed in Paris, and the distance and contrast of the city from Porter's native Texas gave her a fresh perspective on her childhood that allowed her to write of it with genuine warmth. Porter's perspective on her strict Southern upbringing was so changed that when she returned to the United States in 1936, she visited her family for the first time in eighteen years.

Porter continued to travel in America, and the books that evolved in Paris, *Pale Horse, Pale Rider* and *The Leaning Tower, and Other Stories,* were eventually published. Porter's critical renown brought her employment offers from many universities, and for years she earned income as both a lecturer and a writer-in-residence. With the publication and commercial success of *Ship of Fools,* Porter became financially independent, drastically reduced her speaking appearances, and moved to College Park, Maryland, a suburb of Washington, D.C. Her final work, *The Never-Ending Wrong,* was published when she was eighty-seven and concerns the Sacco and Vanzetti murder trial. Written from fifty-year-old notes that detail conversations Porter had with policemen, journalists, and protesters, *The Never-Ending Wrong* reflects Porter's concern with what she termed the "political injustice" involved in the case. Porter's lifelong pursuit to complete a biography of Cotton Mather remained unrealized when she died after a succession of strokes at the age of ninety.

George Hendrick observed that from the beginning of her career, Porter sought to "explore the human heart and mind and society itself, without lapsing into popular clichés." Porter often realized this ideal through treatment of grim, uncomfortable realities. The stories in *Flowering Judas,* for example, are united by the theme of betrayal. The title work explores the dilemma of an emotionally cocooned young American woman who joins forces with Mexican revolutionaries before learning of the group's cruelty. Although troubled by the heinous acts she tacitly supports, the woman remains with them, realizing her hypocrisy only after a political prisoner commits suicide with pills she has unknowingly provided. In "The Jilting of Granny Weatherall," a stream-of-consciousness work, Porter shifts from a political to a personal exploration of her theme. On her deathbed, Granny is haunted by the memory of the fiancée who deserted her at the alter sixty years ago. Although she married another man and raised many children, at her death she feels nothing but loss and passes away believing that God has also abandoned her.

Pale Horse, Pale Rider is comprised of three novellas—*Old Mortality, Pale Horse, Pale Rider,* and *Noon Wine*—that explore the uneasy correlations between life and death. *Old Mortality* is an ironic work that probes the authenticity of a family legend from the point of view of Miranda, a young girl commonly acknowledged as Porter's fictional counterpart. Raised in the South on her grandmother's farm and educated in convents, Miranda is a rebellious tomboy whose youthful perception of reality has been molded around the romantic myth of Aunt Amy. Remembered by the adults in the family as a beautiful young girl who lived a vibrant life, Amy died after only six weeks of marriage to the dashing Uncle Gabriel. When Miranda finally meets Gabriel, however, the legend begins to crumble, for he is in truth an overweight drunkard. Throughout the story, Miranda becomes increasingly aware

of her elders' misconceptions of the past, and *Old Mortality* ends as Miranda, determined not to repeat the mistakes of her family, naively makes a vow to live life free of illusion and deception. Porter continued her portrayal of Miranda in *Pale Horse, Pale Rider,* a treatment of wartime psychology set in Denver during World War I. While working as a drama critic for a local newspaper, Miranda falls in love with Adam, a young soldier. Seriously ill with influenza, Miranda lapses into a coma. When she awakens, the Armistice has been signed and Adam is dead, having caught the affliction from Miranda. Melancholy about facing a jubilant world that promises little happiness for her, Miranda greets post-war society with guilt and reluctance. In *Noon Wine,* which many contemporary critics consider her most outstanding work, Porter shifts the focus of her central theme of betrayal to a complex, cerebral study of murder. Royal Earle Thompson, a Texan farmer badly in need of a farmhand, hires Helton, a stranger from North Dakota who is an exemplary, amicable worker for nine years. One day, however, bounty hunters arrive on the ranch searching for Helton, who had escaped from an asylum for the criminally insane nine years earlier. Stunned by this turn of events and reluctant to lose his hired hand, Thompson kills the bounty hunters and later commits suicide after friends object to his transgression.

In her final short story collection, *The Leaning Tower,* Porter contemplates the constant change and growth of human relationships, often using a character's personal experience to represent the greater failures or triumphs of humanity. The first six stories revolve around Miranda and pivotal points of her childhood. Set on and around Grandmother Rhea's farm, these tales are largely autobiographical and provide readers with insight into Porter's structured Southern upbringing. "The Circus" centers on Miranda's first excursion to the circus. Almost immediately uncomfortable, Miranda is overwhelmed by the odor of the animals and the noises of the crowd, and is terrified by a clown's dangerous stunts on the high wire. When she returns home, her family is unsympathetic, and the young girl must cope with the trauma alone. In "The Grave," nine-year-old Miranda and her brother Paul are synchronously introduced to the enigmas of birth and death. While playing in their grandfather's empty gravesite, Paul shoots a rabbit, realizing too late that the animal was pregnant. Miranda is awed and saddened by the tiny dead babies in the mother's womb and subsequently represses the entire incident. Twenty years later, Miranda's memory is triggered by the sight of an Indian vendor's tray of candy rabbits. Now, instead of the fear she felt as a child, she only recalls with pleasure the memory of her brother as a twelve-year-old boy.

Throughout her life, Porter was a perfectionist in her art. She has written that she burned trunkfuls of inferior stories and, as a result, her *oeuvre* comprises less than thirty works of fiction. Although she received pervasive critical acclaim during her career, she never enjoyed wide readership or financial success until she wrote *Ship of Fools.* Ironically, critics concluded from the novel that Porter's excellence in short fiction could not be sustained in a longer work. Miranda remains Porter's most popular protagonist, and the Miranda stories have been viewed as attempts by Porter to come to terms with the repressed Southern world of her childhood. Her studies of the foibles of human nature, though often set in the Old South, transcend regionalism and explore such themes as the nature of evil, self-delusion, and the importance of individuality. In a posthumous tribute, Robert Penn Warren observed: "[Porter's fiction] bears the stamp of a personality distinctive, delicately perceptive, keenly aware of the depth and darkness of human experience . . . and thoroughly committed to a quest for meaning in the midst of the ironic complexities of man's lot. . . . What her work celebrates is the toughness and integrity of the individual."

(For further information on Porter's life and career, see *Contemporary Literary Criticism*, Vols. 1, 3, 7, 10, 13, 15, 27; *Contemporary Authors*, Vols. 1-4, rev. ed., Vol. 101 [obituary]; *Contemporary Authors New Revision Series*, Vol. 1; *Something about the Author*, Vols. 23, 39; *Dictionary of Literary Biography*, Vols. 4, 9; *Dictionary of Literary Biography Yearbook: 1980.*)

PRINCIPAL WORKS

SHORT FICTION

Flowering Judas   1930; expanded edition published as *Flowering Judas, and Other Stories,* 1935; second expanded edition, 1970
Hacienda: A Story of Mexico   1934
Noon Wine   1937
Pale Horse, Pale Rider: Three Short Novels   1939
The Leaning Tower, and Other Stories   1944; expanded edition, 1970
The Old Order: Stories of the South, from Flowering Judas, Pale Horse, Pale Rider, *and* The Leaning Tower   1955
The Collected Stories of Katherine Anne Porter   1964; expanded edition, 1965

OTHER MAJOR WORKS

The Days Before: Collected Essays and Occasional Writings (nonfiction)   1952; expanded edition published as *The Collected Essays and Occasional Writings of Katherine Anne Porter,* 1970
Ship of Fools   (novel)   1962
The Never-Ending Wrong   (nonfiction)   1977

ALLEN TATE   (essay date 1930)

[Tate's criticism is closely associated with the Agrarian movement. Concerned with political and social issues as well as literature, the Agrarians were dedicated to preserving the Southern way of life and traditional Southern values. Tate attacked the tradition of Western philosophy which he felt has alienated persons from themselves, one another, and from nature by divorcing intellectual from natural functions in human life. For Tate, literature is the principal form of knowledge and revelation which restores human beings to a proper relationship with nature and the spiritual realm. His most important critical essays are on modern poetry, and on Southern traditions and the legacy of the Civil War. A friend of Porter's since the mid-1920s, Tate admired the author professionally and personally, and later became involved romantically with her. In the following excerpt from an original review of Flowering Judas, *Tate praises Porter's autonomy from what he maintains is the most common vice of American authors: an overworked, sensationalistic style.]*

Miss Porter's mind is one of those highly civilized instruments of perception that seem to come out of old societies, where the "social trend" is fixed and assumed. The individual character as the product of such a background also has a certain constancy of behavior which permits the writer to ignore the now common practice of relating individual conduct to some abstract social or psychological law; the character is taken as a fixed and inviolable entity, predictable only in so far as familiarity may be said to make him so, and finally unique as the center of inexhaustible depths of feeling and action. In this manner Miss Porter approaches her characters, and it is this that probably underlies many of the very specific virtues of her writing.

For one thing, her style is beyond doubt the most economical and at the same time the richest in American fiction. Only in the first story [in *Flowering Judas*], **"Maria Concepcion,"** is there any uncertainty of purpose. In the five others there is not a word gone to waste—and there is no under-writing. There is none of that alternation of natural description and character exposition which is the hall-mark of formula-made fiction. There is much sensuous detail, but no decoration. For Miss Porter has a direct and powerful grasp of her material as a whole; this makes every sentence, whether of description, narration, or dialogue, create not only an inevitable and beautiful local effect, but contribute directly to the final tone and climax of the story.

For another thing, Miss Porter's stories are never told in the same way. Each character, or set of characters, in the given scene requires a different approach; their own inherent quality, their inviolable isolation as human beings, determines the form; and no two of these six stories have anything like the same form. While the quality of the style is the same in all of them—there is the same freshness of imagery, the same rich personal idiom—the method is always different. And—this is her great distinction—the method is always completely objective. It would be difficult to "place" an art like this, unless we may timidly call on the word classical. For here is a combination of those sensuous qualities usually accredited to a dissociative romanticism, with a clear, objective, full-bodied outside world.

Flowering Judas is not a promising book; it promises nothing. It is a fully matured art. We may only hope to have more of it. (pp. 352-53)

Allen Tate, "A New Star," in The Nation, New York, *Vol. CXXXI, No. 3404, October 1, 1930, pp. 352-53.*

EDITH H. WALTON   (essay date 1935)

[In the following excerpt, Walton presents a positive review of Flowering Judas, and Other Stories, *emphasizing Porter's character studies in "Theft" and "The Cracked Looking-Glass."]*

Like all people who are overtaken by legend, Katherine Anne Porter has a hard test to meet. *Flowering Judas* was originally published in 1930 in a small limited edition. It won immediately extravagant praise, but comparatively few readers had access to it and it has since become a collector's item. Although the book made Miss Porter's reputation and established her in the same company as Hemingway and Kay Boyle, her prestige, in many cases, has been largely based on hearsay. Now at last comes a new edition of *Flowering Judas,* including an extra four stories which Miss Porter, evidently a slow and fastidious craftsman, has written in the interval. The general public has been given a chance to verify the legend.

Descriptions by comparison are always unfair and misleading, but to say that she comes closer to Kay Boyle than to any of her contemporaries will perhaps give some notion of Miss Porter's quality. Both writers are stylists of a very high order, and both of them gravitate toward subtle and elusive material. To judge between them is impossible because Miss Porter has not yet produced a sufficient body of work, but it would seem at least as if she had certain advantages in her favor. Her style is not mannered, as Miss Boyle's has lately become, and her talent appears to be more robust and less rarefied.

Four of the stories have a Mexican setting, and two of them are new. Apparently Miss Porter is thoroughly familiar with the raggle-taggle of American radicals, artists and writers who haunt Mexico City. One of this crew, since become a prosperous journalist, tells his life history in **"That Tree,"** describing his marriage to the prim little school teacher from Minneapolis who was revolted by Mexican squalor and Mexico's casual ways. The other new story, which has appeared in a limited and expensive edition, is **"Hacienda,"** a long, curious, rambling tale. . . . Starting off with a superb and very funny description of the type of American who considers natives hardly human, it takes one to the ancient hacienda where a Russian movie of Mexico is being staged. It is a good story, full of sharp and lively observation, but it is a little too chaotic to be entirely successful.

By the excellence of the second pair of new stories one can measure the extent to which Miss Porter has developed and progressed. Some of the earlier, non-Mexican tales are not all that they might be. **"Magic,"** a grim episode laid in a brothel, definitely seems synthetic; **"The Jilting of Granny Weatherall,"** good as it is, is too reminiscent of other deathbed reveries; **"He,"** a tale of a cherished idiot son, does not entirely live up to its immensely effective ending. With the exception of **"Rope,"** so shrewd and amusing in its account of a senseless quarrel, none of the stories in this group is as good as **"Theft"** or **"The Cracked Looking-Glass."**

These two character studies—both of which, incidentally, have been reprinted in anthologies—do what the short story so seldom really achieves. They compress a whole life within their brief limits, hint at rich implications, permit one to bridge the gaps that are left unfilled. The more straightforward and the more vigorous of the two is **"The Cracked Looking-Glass,"** a portrait of a red-haired Irishwoman tied to a man too old to satisfy her exuberance. The story wanders, and Rosaleen's problems remain unsolved, but Miss Porter has packed into her casual narrative so much humor and teeming life that this tale alone would justify her reputation.

The critics who praised the original edition of *Flowering Judas* need have no uncomfortable second thoughts about the wisdom of their enthusiasm. Miss Porter has her faults—for her material is often thin and her underlying theme nebulous—but she appears to be a writer who is capable of depth and growth. She has humor, vitality and a wide range of subject matter. Above all, her style is so distinguished that even if it failed to progress further her work would still be a delight.

Edith H. Walton, "Katherine Anne Porter's Stories and Other Recent Works of Fiction," in The New York Times Book Review, *October 20, 1935, p. 6.*

CHRISTOPHER ISHERWOOD (essay date 1939)

[*Isherwood is an English-born writer known for his autobiographically-oriented accounts of pre-Nazi Berlin and for his detached, humorous observations of human nature and manners. As a young man during the 1930s, Isherwood was a member of the Marxist-oriented Oxford group of poets that included Stephen Spender and W. H. Auden. He was also one of the first non-American critics to review Porter's works. In the following excerpt, Isherwood discusses reactions to Porter's stories in England and comments on the psychological technique of* Noon Wine.]

It is a depressing proof of the inadequacy of the Anglo-American cultural exchange that Miss Porter's name isn't more widely known in England. I am ashamed to confess that, until I opened *Pale Horse, Pale Rider,* I had barely heard of her, and had never read any of her works. Here, therefore, are the first impressions of an ignorant foreigner.

It is, perhaps, natural for an Englishman to compare her stories with those of Katherine Mansfield—and not entirely to Miss Porter's disadvantage. Katherine Mansfield had genius, and the failings of genius. She lapses often into sentimentality; her writing is patchy and uneven; many of her effects are shamelessly faked. Miss Porter has no genius but much talent. Her average level is high, and she doesn't let you down. She is more fundamentally serious than Katherine Mansfield, less neurotic, closer to the earth. She is dry-eyed, even in tragedy: when she jokes, she does not smile. You feel you can trust her.

This volume contains three short novels: *Old Mortality, Noon Wine* and *Pale Horse, Pale Rider* itself. *Old Mortality* is about a portrait—the portrait of a certain Aunt Amy who "had been beautiful, much loved, unhappy, and . . . had died young." The legend of Aunt Amy is the whole fairy story of Grown-up Life, as it appears to two little girls, living at the end of the last century. "What is it going to be like?" they wonder, and ask their elders, who lie to them, of course. The years pass, and we meet one of the little girls, Miranda, again. She is now a young married woman. The legend of the portrait, and all it stood for for, has been exploded. But the question remains. (p. 312)

Pale Horse, Pale Rider is a study in war psychology. It takes place during the later months of 1918. Miranda, a young journalist, is falling in love with Adam, whose regiment is soon due to leave for the front. Miss Porter brilliantly evokes the horror of the time—the din of propaganda, the moral blackmail of the Liberty Bond salesmen, the almost suffocating claustrophobia of a life cramped down within its narrowest limits. As far as the eye can see, there is nothing but war: the two lovers can hardly remember any other kind of existence. Miranda scarcely dares to hope that Adam will survive—and she is right. He dies of influenza, caught while nursing Miranda. When she herself recovers, the Armistice has been signed. She opens her eyes to the new, free, empty life:

> No more war, no more plague, only the dazed silence that follows the ceasing of the heavy guns. . . . Now there would be time for everything.

I liked *Noon Wine* best of these three stories. It is an examination of "the nature of a crime," a subtle, psychological theme handled so directly, so concretely that one is reminded of Guy de Maupassant. Mr. Thompson, owner of a small farm in South Texas, hires a mysterious Swede named Helton, who says that he comes from North Dakota, and has no luggage but a collection of harmonicas. Mr. Helton is a model worker, and the Thompsons congratulate themselves upon their choice. Nine years go by, and one day another stranger arrives at the farm. He, too, is from Dakota, and he is looking for Mr. Helton—to win the reward offered for the recapture of an escaped homicidal maniac. Only an exceedingly skilled writer could have presented the ensuing tragedy so vividly and with such absolute conviction. The characterization is beautifully done, and the farm really comes to life, with all its sounds and smells.

Having praised so much, I pause, and wonder just what it is that prevents me from uttering the final, whole-hearted hurrah. The work of so important an artist as Miss Porter must be judged by the lowest, as well as the highest standards—and, curiously enough, it is by the lowest standards that she fails. She is grave, she is delicate, she is just—but she lacks altogether, for me personally, the vulgar appeal. I cannot imagine that she would ever make me cry, or laugh aloud. No doubt, she would reply that she doesn't want to. But she should want to. I wish she would give herself a little more freely to the reader. I wish she would paint with bolder, broader strokes. I wish she wouldn't be quite so cautious. (p. 313)

> Christopher Isherwood, "Miss Porter and Mr. Todd," in The New Republic, Vol. XCVIII, No. 1272, April 19, 1939, pp. 312-13.

LODWICK HARTLEY (essay date 1940)

[*Hartley was an American critic, short story writer, and poet. In the following excerpt, he discusses Porter's objective observations and detailed characterization.*]

Since the publication of *Flowering Judas and Other Stories* in 1930 few discriminating readers of the short story in America have spoken of Miss Porter without ecstasy. None has spoken of her without respect. As a stylist she has been mentioned in the same breath with Hawthorne, Flaubert, and Maupassant. Very recently Mr. Christopher Isherwood made proper apologies for her not being better known in England [see excerpt dated 1939]. Indeed, if her popularity has been confined to a relatively select group of American readers, the fault lies only with those who have not discovered her. Fortunately, the inclusion of her stories in anthologies is rapidly widening her audience.

To her friends the artist has already become a legend. Her life-thread stretches from Texas to Louisiana to Mexico to France and back again. From her experience and her travel she has collected material that is anything but irrelevant when it finds a place in her narrative art. She has observed with miraculous keenness. She has remembered with amazing accuracy. Not Marcel Proust himself could revivify a detail from the past with more telling effect.

Miss Porter produces slowly; hence her output for the past ten years has been very small. But in an age of overwriting and of pursy omnibus novels, her two slender volumes offer refreshing relief. She nowhere gives the impression of being

the too conscientious lapidary, polishing and repolishing until the original surface is entirely lost. One suspects that her small output has another explanation: namely, that she never writes unless she cannot escape writing. Thus, although she may take months to produce one story, her work always has a striking immediacy.

The task of classifying Miss Porter in the field of the narrative is not simple. *Flowering Judas* is ostensibly a collection of short stories; whereas the stories in *Pale Horse, Pale Rider*, her second volume, are presented as short novels. The vexing question of the difference between the short story and the short novel once more rears its ugly head. Perhaps the safest course for the critic is to ride on the horns of the dilemma. Through their concentration and limited range many of the stories in *Flowering Judas* clearly fall into the province of the short story. When the narrative turns on a specific psychological problem as does **"Rope"** or a highly particularized situation as does **"Magic"**, classification offers no real difficulty. But with all their compactness of expression, several of the stories in the first volume become remarkably expansive, and one quite frequently has the feeling that they are embryonic novels—or, what is more accurate, novels with all extraneous matter rigidly excised.

Although Miss Porter can produce short stories of superb quality, a survey of the whole of her work may convince one that she has never been wholly contented with the form. She senses acutely its limitations. She fears its unhappy tendency to turn on a trick ending or to develop into an anecdote. **"Magic"** is an excellent example of a successful attempt to keep an anecdote from seeming like one. The narrator tells a tale of cruelty and sympathetic magic, near the end of which the listener asks, with the normal desire for *dénouement*, "Yes, and then?" But there is no pointing of the conclusion. The climax comes with the perfect naturalness of being inherent in the tale. It is adroitly blunted. (What is less fortunate in this case is that it is made exegetic.) Again, in **"That Tree"** the author, finding herself faced with the possibility of a conventional ending, cleverly sidesteps and fixes the onus both of theme and technique on the egocentric journalist who is the central figure. "I've been working up to the climax all this time," he is made to remark when it is time for the story to make its turn. "You know, good old surprise technique. Now then, get ready." In both stories the author has triumphed over potential and technical difficulties by sheer cleverness. The double stroke in the second is extremely ingenious. (pp. 206-08)

In **"He"**, the story of a mother's love for a simple-minded son, Miss Porter has told a "straight story" with well-nigh perfect economy and concentration. For delicate emotional control it has rarely been excelled, and for stark simplicity of treatment it reminds one of Knut Hamsun. But Miss Porter's economy can produce more than magnificent bareness. In **"María Concepcíon"** it creates an effect of richness and color, admirably in keeping with a story of primitive passion and revenge. With all its impression of leisureliness, the story is a closely knit narrative. **"The Jilting of Granny Weatherall"** is a piece of stream-of-consciousness writing worthy of commanding envy from Mrs. Virginia Woolf or Miss Dorothy Richardson. Turning on a charming old lady's death-bed memory of a lost love, the story achieves a marvelously beautiful pattern in its patternlessness. (p. 208)

[Structurally, *Noon Wine* is] the finest achievement of Miss Porter's second volume. In Mr. Helton, the escaped Swedish lunatic, there is a portrait that in sureness of line surpasses another with which it bears comparison, that of Lennie in John Steinbeck's *Of Mice and Men*. Helton's methodical efficiency on the farm of Mr. Thompson—a Texan handicapped by a sickly wife and by his own genteel shiftlessness—makes the Swedish hired man so much a part of the life of his employer that Mr. Thompson is led to commit murder to protect him. The action moves so simply and unerringly as to command wonder. The last part of the story—Mr. Thompson's attempt to vindicate himself in the eyes of his neighbors—leans heavily on Guy de Maupassant's "A Piece of String", but the influence is perfectly assimilated.

The remaining two stories of the second volume are not so flawlessly planned. *Old Mortality,* constructed like a chronicle novel, presents the traditions of a Southern family as seen through the eye of two children, Miranda and Maria. The theme finds explicit statement:

> The loyalty of their father's in the face of evidence contrary to his ideal had its spring in family feeling, and a love of legend that he shared with the others. . . . Their hearts and imaginations were captivated by their past, a past in which worldly considerations had played a minor rôle.

The central figure is Aunt Amy, a perverse and strangely fascinating Southern belle who married without love and who died under mysterious circumstances. The first part of the story shows how this remarkable young lady is evoked from a family portrait and from family legend by the two little girls who bring the story into focus. The second part revolves about a visit made by the girls some years later to Aunt Amy's husband, Uncle Gabriel, who is continuing to pursue an old passion for race horses and who is married to a frustrated second wife. The third part deals with Miranda's revolt from the false and romantic notions of her family and of the life in which she was brought up. The story is told with great richness and beauty of detail, but its purpose is not entirely certain and its climax lacks the authority of complete inevitability. The development of Miranda throughout the story hardly justifies laying the "turn" of the story on her shoulders, especially since her revolt in the final analysis involves much more than the theme of the story demands for satisfactory completion.

Pale Horse, Pale Rider misses complete success for another reason. It, too, is expansive in its scope, containing material that a less skillful artist would have stretched into a full-length novel. It often approaches magnificence in its creation of the American scene during the World War: the hysteria, the jingoism, the frantic desire of youth to live before it was too late. Miranda, all but completely dissociated from the situation with which the preceding story concluded, is the central figure. Her love affair with the young soldier, Adam, is interrupted by her falling a victim of the influenza epidemic of 1918. She recovers only to find that Adam has succumbed and that she must face a life of emptiness. The defect here is not one of structure but of method. As I have already suggested, Miss Porter can use both the objective and the subjective methods with effectiveness; but when she combines the two, she does not move so surely as she might. In *Pale Horse, Pale Rider* the center of the picture is clear enough, but the edges seem blurred.

Miss Porter achieves her greatest success when she is most objective. At her best she challenges Maupassant. Complete detachment in **"Magic"** allows her to tell with ineffably cool

poise a story that might have been violently repulsive. In **"He"**, **"The Cracked Looking Glass"**, and *Noon Wine* the ability to hold her subjects at arm's length allows her to achieve fine structural symmetry and totality of effect. When Miss Porter identifies herself subjectively with her heroines, she at times loses strength and directness. Her art may also tend to lose the androgynous quality of great narrative genius and to become distinctively effeminate.

When Gustave Flaubert said that he *was* Madame Bovary, he was merely stating an artistic truism. Any good writer must *be* his characters if he is to make them live. However, this kind of identification is plainly dramatic or objective, and it is a vastly different matter from William Thackeray's projection of his own experience in Pendennis, Thomas Wolfe's in Eugene Gant, James Joyce's in Stephen Dedalus. Without knowing the biographical facts, we can hardly avoid identifying Miss Porter with the Miranda of her stories whether she appears under that name, or as Laura in **"Flowering Judas"**, or as the unnamed writer in **"Theft"** and **"Hacienda"**. Of Miranda we may reconstruct some sort of biography. In **"The Grave"** we see her as a charmingly tomboyish child in Texas. ("What I like about shooting," said Miranda with exasperating inconsequence, "is pulling the trigger and hearing the noise.") Her childhood, surrounded by the lavendered spuriousness of family legend, is continued in *Old Mortality.* In the same story we see her "immured" in a New Orleans convent and we learn of her elopement. *Pale Horse, Pale Rider* presents her as a journalist in the World War period. In **"Theft"** she is a writer in New York, and in **"Flowering Judas"** she is an American girl who divides her time between school teaching and socialistic activity in the "New" Mexico. In **"Hacienda"** she is again a writer who attaches herself to a group of Russians in the process of making a film on a pulque plantation.

These are external details in which the time-order is neither clear nor important. They are less illuminating than the psychological insights that go along with them. **"Flowering Judas"** and **"Theft"** offer the best indices to the soul-history of Miranda, the meaning of whose name is sufficiently symbolic. In both of these stories the heroine suffers from what Mr. John Crowe Ransom and Mr. Allen Tate have suggested as our *Zeitgeist*: "dissociation of sensibility" and the "locked-in ego." . . . The heroine of **"Flowering Judas"** has given herself to abstraction. Her rigidity of purpose is her sword, but ultimately it kills as well as protects. She is wooed by the obese Braggioni, a Revolutionist, and by a Troubadour with scarlet blossoms of the Judas tree in his hair, but her "notorious virginity" is to capitulate neither to the fleshly nor to the romantic symbol. . . . Her dilemma is stated perfectly in terms of the neglected wife of her most dogged pursuer: "To-night Laura envies Mrs. Braggioni, who is alone, and free to weep as much as she pleases about a concrete wrong." In sharp contrast to her inability to realize herself is Braggioni, an introvert of a vastly different type, who "loves himself with such tenderness and amplitude and eternal charity that his followers . . . warm themselves in the reflected glow, and say to each other: 'He has a real nobility, a love of humanity raised above mere personal affections.' "

Incorporated in a dream comes Laura's final self-accusation of murder and cannibalism, the ultimate sentimentality of which becomes fully apparent when one compares it with the conclusion of **"Theft"**, upon which I have already remarked. In **"Theft"** Miss Porter uses a simple incident, the theft of the heroine's purse by a janitress, to reveal a fundamental failure in the heroine's character and to explain her tragedy. Between the thief and the owner of the purse she develops a psychological situation of power. From it, however, we are led to a passage of wistful celebration. . . . [It] is by no means bad writing. It is even subtle writing. But it is the kind of thing that almost any number of competent people can do.

The conclusion of *Old Mortality* is another evidence of the kind of sentimentality that endangers the author's art—an indulgence of an emotional bias rather than the strict business of telling a "straight story" and giving "true testimony".

The greatest gift of Miss Porter is her consummate mastery of detail. Whatever may be her structural or emotional limitations, she has the uncanny power of evoking richness from minutiae. The gift is manifested everywhere in her work, but no more astonishing bit of observation can be found than in **"The Grave"**, a simple and tremendously powerful little story of two children's contact with the mysteries of life and death. Paul and Miranda have just killed a rabbit:

> . . . Miranda watched admiringly while her brother stripped the skin away as if he were taking off a glove. The flayed flesh emerged dark scarlet, sleek, firm; Miranda with thumb and finger felt the long fine muscles with the silvery flat strips binding them to the joints. Brother lifted the oddly bloated belly. "Look," he said, in a low, amazed voice. "It is going to have young ones."
>
> Very carefully he slit the thin flesh from the center ribs to the flanks, and a scarlet bag appeared. He slit again and pulled the bag open, and there lay a bundle of tiny rabbits, each wrapped in a thin scarlet veil. The brother pulled these off and there they were, dark grey, their sleek wet down lying in minute ripples, over pink skin, like a baby's head just washed; their unbelievably small delicate ears folded close, their little blind faces almost featureless.

Such an evocation of beauty from anatomical detail is not often excelled anywhere in the language. Miss Porter's power to take grossness out of the brutal and the violent is evidenced by her unflinchingly truthful handling of detail in **"Magic"**. Here one is convinced—as, indeed, one should be—that truth has an integrity preserving it eternally from obscenity.

"María Concepción" is warmly documented with Mexican life, and it glows with the primary colors of primitive art designs. . . . Details of a completely different sort make *Old Mortality* an excitingly beautiful tapestry. With a few accurate strokes Miss Porter can most successfully evoke the illusion of the past. Detail is used in **"Hacienda"** for yet another purpose. In fact, here it almost takes precedence over everything else in accomplishing the intent of the story. Miss Porter gives an absorbing panorama of life in contemporary Mexico. With a realistic and unsentimental eye she sees the peons, primitive creatures not many steps removed from animals. She presents with Chekhovian ruthlessness the decadent upper classes: Don Genaro, lover of speed and *chic;* Doña Julia, his wife, who affects the Hollywood Chinese note in costuming and an effete elegance in manner; Betancourt, "Mexican by birth, French-Spanish by blood, French by education . . . completely at the mercy of an ideal of elegance and detachment perpetually at war with a kind of Mexican nationalism which affected him like an inherited weakness of the nervous system."

Porter (far right) at eighteen months, with her sister Annie Gay and brother Harry Ray, photographed several months before the death of their mother.

Mastery of detail assures Miss Porter a high distinction in character delineation. She understands women better than men: the fiercely proud and fiercely tender Mrs. Whipple of **"He"** and the romantic Irish Rosaleen of **"The Cracked Looking Glass"** are her high watermarks. But her character studies of men also have authority. One thinks immediately of the journalist of **"That Tree"**, Mr. Thompson and Holton of *Noon Wine,* and the exasperatingly efficient Mr. Kennerly of **"Hacienda"**.

Among her Southern contemporaries in short prose fiction Miss Porter has few peers. She lacks the social emphasis of Mr. Erskine Caldwell, but she also lacks his sensationalism. She has nothing of Mr. William Faulkner's hypnotic quality, his violent power, or his flair for abnormal psychology; but neither has she any of his obliquity. At her best she is superior as a craftsman to both. At any point in her art she is one of the most talented of living American writers. (pp. 209-16)

Lodwick Hartley, "Katherine Anne Porter," in The Sewanee Review, *Vol. XLVIII, No. 2, April-June, 1940, pp. 206-16.*

EDMUND WILSON (essay date 1944)

[*Considered America's foremost man of letters in the twentieth century, Wilson wrote widely on cultural, historical, and literary matters, and is noted for several seminal critical studies. He is often credited with bringing an international perspective to American letters through his examinations of European literature. Although Wilson explored the historical and psychological implications of a work of literature, he rarely did so at the expense of a discussion of its literary qualities. Perhaps Wilson's greatest contributions to American literature were his tireless promotion of writers of the 1920s, 1930s, and 1940s, and his essays introducing the best of modern literature to the general reader. In the following excerpt, Wilson asserts that Porter's best stories explore human relationships through the use of female protagonists.*]

To the reviewer, Miss Porter is baffling because one cannot take hold of her work in any of the obvious ways. She makes none of the melodramatic or ironic points that are the stock in trade of ordinary short stories; she falls into none of the usual patterns and she does not show anyone's influence. She does not exploit her personality either inside or outside her work, and her writing itself makes a surface so smooth that the critic has little opportunity to point out peculiarities of color or weave. If he is tempted to say that the effect is pale, he is prevented by the realization that Miss Porter writes English of a purity and precision almost unique in contemporary American fiction. If he tries to demur that some given piece fails to mount with the accelerating pace or arrive at the final intensity that he is in the habit of expecting in short stories, he is deterred by a nibbling suspicion that he may not have grasped its meaning and have it hit him with a sudden impact some moments after he has finished reading.

Not that this meaning is simple to formulate even after one has felt its emotional force. The limpidity of the sentence, the exactitude of the phrase, are deceptive in that the thing they convey continues to seem elusive even after it has been communicated. These stories are not illustrations of anything that is reducible to a moral law, or a political or social analysis, or even a principle of human behavior. What they show us are human relations in their constantly shifting phases and in the moments of which their existence is made. There is no place for general reflections; you are to live through the experience as the characters do. And yet the writer has managed to say something about the values involved in the experience. But what is it? I shall try to suggest, though I am afraid I shall land in ineptitude.

Miss Porter's short stories lend themselves to being sorted into three fairly distinct groups. There are the stories of family life in working-class or middle-class households (there are two of these in *The Leaning Tower*), which, in spite of the fact that the author is technically sympathetic with her people, tend to be bitter and bleak, and, remarkable though they are, seem to me less satisfactory than the best of her other stories. The impression we get from these pieces is that the qualities that are most amiable in human life are being gradually done to death in the milieux she is presenting, but Miss Porter does not really much like these people or feel comfortable in their dismal homes, and so we, in turn, don't really much care. Another section of her work, however, contains what may be called pictures of foreign parts, and here Miss Porter is much more successful. **"The Leaning Tower,"** which gives its name to her new collection and which takes up two-fifths of the volume, belongs to this category. It is a study of Germany between the two wars in terms of a travelling American and his landlady and fellow-lodgers in a Berlin rooming house. By its material and its point of view, it rather recalls Christopher Isherwood's *Goodbye to Berlin,* but it is more poetic in treatment and more general in implication. The little plaster leaning tower of Pisa which has been cherished by the Viennese landlady but gets broken by her American tenant stands for something in the destruction of which not merely the Germans but also the Americans have somehow taken a criminal part (though the American is himself an artist, he finds that he can mean nothing to the Germans but the power of American money). (p. 72)

But perhaps the most interesting section of Katherine Anne

Porter's work is composed of her stories about women—particularly her heroine Miranda, who figures in two of the three novelettes that make up her previous volume, *Pale Horse, Pale Rider.* The first six stories of *The Leaning Tower* deal with Miranda's childhood and her family background of Louisianians living in southern Texas. This is the setting in which Miss Porter is most at home, and one finds in it the origins of that spirit of which the starvation and violation elsewhere make the subjects of her other stories. One recognizes it in the firm little sketches that show the relations between Miranda's grandmother and her lifelong colored companion, the relations between the members of the family, and the relations between the family and the Negro servants in general. Somewhere behind Miss Porter's stories there is a conception of a natural human spirit in terms of their bearing on which all the other forces of society are appraised. This spirit is never really idealized, it is not even sentimentalized; it can be generous and loving and charming, but it can also be indifferent and careless, inconsequent, irresponsible, and silly. If the meaning of these stories is elusive, it is because this essential spirit is so hard to isolate or pin down. It is peculiar to Louisianians in Texas, yet one misses it in a boarding house in Berlin. It is the special personality of a woman, yet it is involved with international issues. It evades all the most admirable moralities, it escapes through the social meshes, and it resists the tremendous oppressions of national bankruptcies and national wars. It is outlawed, driven underground, exiled; it becomes rather unsure of itself and may be able, as in *Pale Horse, Pale Rider,* to assert itself only in the delirium that lights up at the edge of death to save Miranda from extinction by war flu. It suffers often from a guilty conscience, knowing too well its moral weakness; but it can also rally bravely if vaguely in vindication of some instinct of its being which seems to point toward justice and truth.

But I told you this review would be clumsy. I am spoiling Miss Porter's stories by attempting to find a formula for them. . . . She is absolutely a first-rate artist, and what she wants other people to know she imparts to them by creating an object, the self-developing organism of a work of prose. (pp. 73-4)

Edmund Wilson, "Katherine Anne Porter," in The New Yorker, *Vol. XX, September 30, 1944, pp. 72-4.*

S. H. POSS   (essay date 1958)

[*In the following excerpt, Poss explains Porter's theme of self-definition through a chronological study of four Miranda stories: "The Circus,"* Old Mortality, Pale Horse, Pale Rider, *and "The Grave."*]

I should like to explore through the character of Miranda the What Is Worth Belonging To theme in four stories of Katherine Anne Porter, **"The Circus,"** *Old Mortality, Pale Horse, Pale Rider,* and pre-eminently, **"The Grave."** The stories collectively form a quasi-*bildungsroman* (or perhaps even *kunstlerroman*) pattern, for they manifest that typical structure of the genre which may be described as a secular version of the medieval notion of life as a pilgrimage from Babylon to Jerusalem: the young hero grows up, leaves home (to seek, in the fairy tale sources, his fortune), ventures into a world he has not made that is notoriously indifferent to his sensibilities, flounders about in this new, cold and alien milieu, wastes inordinate amounts of time and effort learning what it is he needs to know, and so on, finally (if he is lucky) to get straight on the road he has been destined to travel all along. During this dialectic of disorientation and re-integration, the hero seeks always to define himself, to grow up, to find out who he is and what he needs to become. At first he attempts to define himself within the present, within the society into which he is born; later, when he finds this definition inadequate to his own deep-lying though sometimes unarticulated idea of what he needs to be, when he cannot find in the present—and he almost never can—an image of himself that is as attractive as the one he carries in his heart, he asks that question which distinguishes the genre as much as its characteristic form: "Where are my own people and my own time?" (p. 21)

Since categories are convenient, I have elected to discuss the stories as a somewhat unbalanced trichotomy: **"The Circus"** and *Old Mortality* I consider dramatizations of a "failure," the responsibility for which is mutual, between an individual and various institutionalized myths; *Pale Horse, Pale Rider* presents a similar "failure" which is simultaneously heightened and mitigated by a momentary realization of an ideal state; and **"The Grave,"** the quintessence of the Miranda stories, provides a static suspension of irreconcilables. (To justify this arrangement of the stories, I ought to say that, quite apart from the symbolic order suggested above, the stories deal successively with Miranda growing up: she is a child in **"The Circus,"** a girl of eighteen in 1912 at the end of *Old Mortality,* and a young woman of twenty-four in *Pale Horse, Pale Rider.* In the first part of **"The Grave"** she is a girl of nine, but the second part takes place about twenty years later.)

"The Circus" illustrates the failure, for Miranda, of the American myth of Having Fun. The child is taken to see her first circus, but her response to it takes the form of a very nearly traumatic shock. She is terrified by the braying of the band and the antics of the performers, and is led in near-hysteria from the scene which her family had relished. Later, when she is kidded for her abnormal reaction, she feels resentful and ashamed without quite knowing why, though Miranda has just revealed to us that she lives in a different world from her contemporaries. Abnormal sensibility and acute and unwavering perceptions—the standard equipment of the artist—conspire to dramatize in her the conflict between the thing itself and the thing imagined that seems to exist less intensely in us all. She sees instantly the "truth" about clowns, their sad comedy, their cynical despair in playing the role of scapegoat. She sees the high-wire act as a kind of sacrificial rite which fills the crowd with "savage delight." And she is "completely subjugated by her fears," she is frightened because the knowledge of her difference has been impressed on her.

That the incident is more than an irrational childish caprice is underscored by Miranda's grandmother remarking later that she has never approved of circuses. The child's father surveys the children at dinner and says, "This basket of young doesn't seem to be much damaged," to which the grandmother replies, "The fruits of their present are in a future so far off, neither of us may live to know whether harm has been done or not. That is the trouble."

This "trouble" appears in *Old Mortality* as the question which Henry James had asked: "Where do my loyalties lie?" . . . Social estrangement is the theme of this story: its central concern is with the abortive attempt of one generation to define and understand its relationship to a previous one,

to determine what its attitude should be toward the past, toward tradition.

The antagonist of the story is a ghost. Amy, a recent ancestor of Miranda, was a beauty who had been "much loved, unhappy, and had died young." She epitomizes the values of the past ("mythic" in both the general and technical senses which Miranda and her sister cannot successfully integrate into their present lives. This inability of the sisters to reconcile the past impinging on the present results in an inability to be simply themselves: "They had lived not only their own years; but their memories, it seemed to them, began years before they were born . . ."

It is of course Amy, the ghost of the past, who provides vicarious life for the adults of Miranda's world, for around her are grouped a complex cluster of attitudes and ideals and associations which make up the myth of the Past: she is its synecdoche. Miranda, influenced all her life by this myth, attempted to suspend her disbelief in the deep-rooted and frequently absurd mores within which she had moved. But she cannot, finally, refuse to acknowledge the perceptions of her critical intelligence; when she returns home for an uncle's funeral, she knows it will be for the last time, and in the light of this knowledge, she observes the comfortable relationship between her father and his contemporaries, realizing with an insight whose force, we see later, is cumulative, "It is I who have no place. . . . Where are my own people and my own time?" (pp. 21-3)

We have seen that **"The Circus"** and *Old Mortality* dramatize the seeming impossibility of establishing a relationship between the public myths and the individual sensibility. *Pale Horse, Pale Rider* is a variation on this theme, for Miranda's momentary rapport between herself and the myth of Love makes more acute her "inability" (I include here extra-personal considerations) to sustain the relationship: her realization of an ideal state heightens and at the same time mitigates the ultimate failure between myth and individual.

Miranda, having been frustrated on successive planes of experience, is dubious of that "ecstatic reciprocal cannibalism," love, and *Pale Horse, Pale Rider* is concerned with the tension between her instincts and her cautioning knowledge. She has left one husband (barely mentioned in *Old Mortality*) and now, completely cut off, as she thinks, from her past, she is living a lonely life as an ill-paid "drama" critic on a small newspaper. The year is 1918; she is twenty-four and has met a young Army officer, Adam, who is expecting to be sent overseas.

Death and Love are the polarities on which the story is based; and Death, the Pale Rider, has two supremely powerful allies: the war, which exists as the ghost of an apprehension, a brooding omnipresent force; and a "plague," an influenza epidemic of epic proportions which seems "something out of the Middle Ages." There are in fact rather calculated allegorical efforts all through the story; for instance, "Adam," Miranda's figurative first man, is also the ideal male, fatalistically "committed without any knowledge or act of his own to death." His idealness and his role of sacrificial offering are summarized in Miranda's realization that he was "pure . . . all the way through, flawless, complete as the sacrificial lamb must be."

With characteristic perception, then, Miranda understands "that there was nothing at all ahead for Adam and her," and with this perception, her latent "schizophrenia" becomes acute. (This is not to make a case history of the story; I use the term in the most general sense.) She suffers an internal division: her instincts impel her toward love; her painfully gained knowledge causes her to recoil from it. And so, until the very moment when Miranda, infected with influenza, loses consciousness in Adam's arms, they are unable to acknowledge their love. Only when the "heavy soft darkness" of near-unconsciousness is upon her can she say, "I love you, and I was hoping you would say that to me, too"; and before she passes into a coma, she hears Adam say, "What do you think I have been trying to tell you all this time?"

The veil of separateness is lifted for an instant, and Miranda experiences a state of beatitude. Then, to emphasize the ephemerality of the union,

> almost with no warning at all, she floated into the darkness, holding his hand, in sleep that was not sleep but clear evening light in a small green wood full of inhuman concealed voices singing sharply like the whine of arrows and she saw Adam transfixed by a flight of these singing arrows that struck him in the heart and passed shrilly cutting their path through the leaves. Adam fell straight back before her eyes, and rose again unwounded and alive; another flight of arrows loosed from the invisible bow struck him and he fell, and yet he was there before her untouched in a perpetual death and resurrection.

This extraordinary dream, with Adam as a kind of composite Attis-Osiris-Adonis, seems to symbolize Miranda's final inability to share, even with the man she loves: she is the ultimate solipsist. It is not however her solipsistic sensibility so much as it is her acute awareness of it that makes her so fascinating and so meaningful in her despair, even as it is that same sensibility that confines her in her private hell, with a barely concealed wish for death. As the dream which opened the story shows, Miranda is familiar with death, while in her second dream she sets herself "angrily and selfishly" in the path of the arrows, crying "It's my turn now, why must you always be the one to die?" But "the arrows struck her cleanly through the heart and through his body and he lay dead, and she still lived, and the wood whistled and sang and shouted, every branch and leaf and blade of grass had its own terrible accusing voice." It is unnecessary to consult Freud here. (pp. 23-4)

We have traced Miranda's attempts to "belong," and we have seen that various myths have failed her: in **"The Circus,"** the myth of Having Fun, with all that implies; in *Old Mortality,* the myth of the Past; in *Pale Horse, Pale Rider,* the myth of Love. With **"The Grave,"** a rather enigmatic piece which seems universally to have instilled in its readers a definite reluctance to comment, at least in print, upon it, we come to that most consequential of archetypes, death and generation. Here, the contradictions of Miranda's life are not resolved but suspended, for **"The Grave"** presents an equilibrium that consists of a static suspension of the irreconcilables of the individual and the institution. Such at least is the theory; let us now see if it works.

The year of the story is 1903; Miranda is nine years old. The theme of the story is perfectly clear: the confrontation of a child with the mysteries of birth and death. Miranda has gone hunting "one burning day" with her brother Paul, and during their hiking about they have come upon an old graveyard from which the coffins have been removed, leaving the graves open and empty. Searching there, Miranda finds a screw head for a coffin in the shape of a silver dove and Paul finds a gold wedding ring. Each desires the other's treasure, so they trade gifts. Continuing the hunt, Paul shoots a rabbit, and discovers on skinning it that it was about to give birth. Strangely agitated at the sight of the embryo rabbits, Miranda tells her brother that she doesn't want the skin, and he swears her to secrecy regarding the incident: "Don't you ever tell a living soul that you saw this . . . Don't tell Dad because I'll get into trouble. He'll say I'm leading you into things you ought not to do." And "Miranda never told, she did not wish to tell anybody." She thought about the incident for a few days, then forgot it. Nearly twenty years later, in a strange land, she is "reasonlessly horrified" at being approached by a vendor who "held up before her a tray of dyed sugar sweets, in the shapes of all kinds of small creatures: birds, baby chicks, baby rabbits, lambs, baby pigs." She is reminded instantly of that day when she and her brother had found treasure in the graves, and with this recollection, she sees her brother, again twelve years old, standing in the sun as he had stood that day when he had found the gold ring in the cemetery of their family.

So much for the first level. We must now consider as accurately as possible just what is the nature of the symbolic rendering of experience which this story presents. (pp. 24-5)

[The] grave is death, the rabbit was life. But "when the coffin was gone a grave is just a hole in the ground." Further, these graves provide treasure—a silver dove for Miranda, and "a thin wide gold ring carved with intricate flowers and leaves" for Paul; though as we have seen they trade gifts, "with some little bickering." Let us consider again the literal level of the story—we now have a dead man's wedding ring on the thumb of a little girl who is being initiated into the anatomical mysteries of generation and death. After she put on the ring, Miranda began to feel dissatisfaction with her clothes, her appearance, which seem particularly grubby when contrasted with the "serene purity" of the fine gold ring) . . . . (We remember Miranda's secret belief in *Old Mortality* that she would "one day suddenly receive beauty, as by inheritance, riches laid suddenly in her hands through no deserts of her own.") Thus it appears that Miranda's dissatisfaction with her present state is a preparation of some sort for her coming initiation into the ambiguous miracle of life.

As the graves provided treasure for the children, so does the act of killing and skinning the [pregnant] rabbit. . . . Miranda, "excited but not frightened," exclaims, "Oh, I want to *see.*" . . . (p. 26)

Then, "quietly and terribly agitated," looking at the bloody skin, she exclaims "I don't want the skin . . ., I won't have it." "Paul buried the young rabbits again in their mother's body, wrapped the skin around her, carried her to a clump of sage bushes, and hid her away," then returned to swear Miranda to secrecy.

It is now evident that we have at least two graves in the story—the literal grave and the rabbit. Both graves produce treasure; both contribute in some obscure fashion to the last scene of the story. But it must always be remembered that the rabbit is simultaneously a symbol of generation and death; and part of the story's undeniable effect seems to result from the frightening ease with which "womb" and "tomb" elide.

There is, however, at least one more grave in the story, and this is the human mind.

Miranda never told, she did not even wish to tell. She thought about the whole worrisome affair with confused unhappiness for a few days, then it sank quietly into her mind *and was heaped over by accumulated thousands of impressions,* for nearly twenty years (my italics).

(p. 27)

What, now, can we identify as the master trope of this story? We observed at the outset that **"The Grave"** provides a "static suspension of irreconcilables": we now begin to see that there is a mythic element at work. The story is not so much concerned with a myth in the sense that **"The Circus,"** *Old Mortality* and *Pale Horse, Pale Rider* are: rather it is itself a mythic projection of the big death-birth archetype. It may be "interpreted" on at least four levels, and there may well be more. Applying the medieval four-fold "meaning-structure," we find that, in Dante's terms, **"The Grave"** exists simultaneously on the various levels of the literal, the allegorical, the moral, and the anagogical. On the literal level we have a little girl who finds treasure in a grave, witnesses the skinning of a pregnant rabbit, and who, twenty years later, is made so suddenly aware of that "burning day" that she is brought up short, tranced in her perception that the immensities and trivialities of her life have been rolled into "one overwhelming ball"; we see, allegorically, that she is made conscious of growth processes in herself as a result of having been confronted with the phenomenon of birth and death in nature ("She understood a little of the secret, formless intuitions in her own mind and body, which had been clearing up, taking form, so gradually and so steadily she had not realized that she was learning what she had to know"); on the moral level, we note Miranda's nearly simultaneous attraction toward and revulsion from the knowledge which she intuitively apprehends—she recoils from this knowledge at the same time that "she wanted most deeply to see and to know"—she perceives the dualism of experience, the fundamental affinity of pain and pleasure; and finally, on the anagogical level (which exists in and informs the literal level), we conclude that the end of the story, recapitulating the incident of that "one burning day" in all its unresolved paradoxicalness, seems to be saying something about two "facts," both of which possess the "felt universal relevance" of the myth: the "fact" of the essentially un-chronological nature of time, and the "fact" of non-personal immortality.

Thus we have traced Miranda's progress from cognition through ratiocination to myth. On successive planes of experience she finds the myths of Having Fun, of the Past, and of Love insufficient. As a result of this successive frustration on various levels, she moves steadily in the direction of an ever larger, more inclusive rationale—she experiences, she knows failure, she gathers herself for the test of experience on a new level. Then, with **"The Grave,"** the outward spiraling movement ceases, the past returns, transfigured, informed ("the dreadful vision faded"), and Miranda literally returns also. . . . But more than this, she is apparently reconciled, as the tone of the last words of the story suggests, with the strange necessity that her role of Artist-Outsider has forced on her of sustaining herself on what she had earlier repudiated. Therefore, the *bildungsroman* pattern we have been attempting to trace is completed by **"The Grave,"** which ends, appropriately, in a kind of acceptance, a homecoming, a discovery that the "kinsmen" for whom Miranda had searched so widely were, in a sense, within reach all along, if it had only been in her to see them. Thus the stories seem to demonstrate Kenneth Burke's idea that literature strives always to

move toward a homily, for at the last they "say" something almost Tolstoyan about the home and the family, about the kingdom being within one ("The mind is its own place"), about tradition and continuity and the individual heart and the immortality of the race. But they say this for the moment only, there is no suggestion of a permanent or absolute awakening to Truth, no semi-religious conversion. The illumination fades, the epiphany goes, the "dreadful vision" will come back. But provisionally the contradictions and irreconcilables are suspended, for the moment there is peace. (pp. 28-9)

S. H. Poss, "Variations on a Theme in Four Stories of Katherine Anne Porter," in Twentieth Century Literature, *Vol. 4, Nos. 1-2, April-July, 1958, pp. 21-9.*

SARAH YOUNGBLOOD (essay date 1959-60)

[*The following excerpt is from an essay regarded by many critics as the standard reading of* Pale Horse, Pale Rider. *Here Youngblood illustrates how this work's rich structure and imagery have earned Porter an important place among contemporary American authors.*]

Structurally, *Pale Horse, Pale Rider* can be viewed as three units or sections of action, each section presenting action of an increasingly psychological kind, in a setting generally different from the others. The first section introduces Miranda and extends to her collapse from illness; the second describes her night of delirium in the room of the boarding-house; the third presents her hospital experience. It will be noted that the first section opens with Miranda in the isolation of a dream, but this isolation is immediately intruded upon when she wakes to the reality of her room and the world she must enter for survival. Thereafter, the first section can be said to present Miranda-in-the-world, as, in the narrowing psychological focus of the story, the succeeding sections present Miranda-and-Adam, and Miranda alone. The last section would seem to be a reverse reflection of the first, since it concludes with Miranda's preparation to move back into the world.

In terms of spatial movement, the opening section is thus the largest and most inclusive. This spatial inclusiveness is appropriate to the initiation of themes in the novel, and all of the themes stated here in image or action figure in the later sections as motivation and explanation. The themes—political, social, psychological, and moral in their implications—require a certain largeness of stage for postulation, and this is available in the shifting scenes of the opening section: the room, the newspaper office, the theater, the dance-hall, the streets of the city. Also available is a necessarily large cast of characters, by which we follow Miranda's reaction to her world: the newspaper staff, the bond salesmen, the Junior League girls, the lovers in the dance hall, the soldiers in the hospital, the has-been vaudeville actor. . . . The presence of war is a conditioning factor in the action and themes of the novel. War is the "gong of warning" which wakes Miranda from sleep and beats the rhythm of the day for her. It focuses in the day-to-day world of Miranda the theme of death which haunts her dream, since war has unreined the "pale horse" of destruction. War posits, in the relationship of Adam and Miranda, the conflict of the individual's obligations to society, and to himself, since in a state of war, in the non-life that war creates (Miranda speaks of peacetime or pre-war time as "in life," making the distinction in time a distinction in being), Adam and Miranda are bound by obligations to society which prevent their unity, even though, ironically, the only dedications which could have value for them now in a war-world would be those based upon love for each other. They are compelled to fulfill obligations created by a society operating upon hatred, not love.

A corollary of this theme is the confusion of appearance and reality which so disturbs Miranda's equilibrium in the world. The war creates fear and suspicion, distrust and hypocrisy, which transforms daily reality into a disturbing set of distorting mirrors. "Towney" may, in the cloakroom, privately despair of the pressures placed upon her by flag-waving tyrants acting as patriots, but in the office later she can summon her "most complacent patriotic voice" to praise the idea of Hut Service. Miranda's wondering reaction to this is repeated in her later, rather terrified, reaction to the theater-crowd, which enthusiastically responds, in a kind of conditioned reflex, to the patriotic jargon of the bond salesman: "There must be a great many of them here who think as I do, and we dare not say a word to each other of our desperation, we are speechless animals letting ourselves be destroyed, and why? Does anybody here believe the things we say to each other?" These contradictions in apparent reality, "the disturbing oppositions in her day-to-day existence," find pervasive expression in the general pattern of hypocrisy which the cautious citizen in war must assume. It is noteworthy, therefore, that everything in Miranda's experience of the daily world that rightly should have been an act of love has degenerated to an act of duty done out of fear: the buying of bonds, the comforting of soldiers. This is a part of what she calls the "disturbing oppositions" in her existence, and one illustration of the appearance/reality theme. (pp. 344-46)

War conditions the action in other ways. It creates the necessity for a "code" or "system" among the younger generation, much like the code of Hemingway's characters, which makes possible for them a "proper view" of chaos, a proper existentialist formula of casualness and flippancy for maintaining cynical control: because the situation is absurd, behave as if it were amusing. When the bond-salesmen accuse Miranda of ignoring the war, she meets the absurdity of the accusation with her formal system:

> "Oh, the war," Miranda had echoed on a rising note and she almost smiled at him. It was habitual, automatic, to give that solemn, mystically uplifted grin when you spoke the words or heard them spoken. "C'est la guerre," whether you could pronounce it or not, was even better, and always, always, you shrugged.

Miranda's conversations with Adam in this section of the novel make use of "the kind of patter going the rounds" as a way of suppressing the sense of the chaotic which informs both characters. "Their smiles approved of each other, they felt they had got the right tone, they were taking the war properly." Above all, thought Miranda, "no tooth-gnashing, no hair-tearing, it's noisy and unbecoming and it doesn't get you anywhere." This is, finally, only another of the masks of reality war has forced them to assume. The system of attitudes is so rigidly adhered to that only delirium can finally compel Miranda to admit in speech to Adam the reality of her terror and her love.

The result of all these interacting implications of war is to assure the isolation of each individual. Since Miranda is the point-of-view character whose reactions are the strict concern of the reader, her isolation and her lucid awareness of

it require some examination. Enough has been said of the effect of war in her world to indicate her response to that external condition; the war-theme is, besides, the most obvious nucleus of implication in the story, and other elements demand more explication.

At the psychological level *Pale Horse, Pale Rider* is the dramatization of Miranda's death-wish, a dramatization presented in the ironic form of a reversal, and taking the metaphorical form of a journey. The title of the novel indicates the primacy of the death-theme (of which the war is only, for Miranda, a kind of specific vehicle; one feels that in a situation devoid of war conditions, another vehicle would have been present for her). The title also presents the major symbol of the story, which appears in Miranda's first dream in a kind of double vision. Miranda is pursued by the pale rider, "that lank greenish stranger," but she is also herself the pale rider on Graylie, the pale horse, since she carries the seeds of death within her. (pp. 346-47)

The pale rider allusion of the title is the most obvious, but others can be remarked in this first section of the novel. Adam's name is symbolic since he is "committed without any knowledge or act of his own to death," and since he is a vessel of innocence, golden "purity," as Miranda calls it: "Pure, she thought, all the way through, flawless, complete, as the sacrificial lamb must be." In this remark she views him simultaneously as Adam, Unfallen Man, and Isaac, the victim offered to propitiate the wrath of God. As the latter he shares with all the young soldiers the role of sacrificial victim. To increase the symbolic value of his character, his health is emphasized (in a symbolic pun he is compared to a "fine healthy apple"), and his golden, glowing appearance is repeatedly described, suggesting not only his health and handsomeness but also a certain "man of the Golden Age" quality which his physical perfection connotes and Miranda's idealism confirms. Adam himself, far from being a romantic, is a very stable and normal person, which Miranda senses, and she clings to a strength in him which she lacks. That she realizes the idealism of her view of him is made clear in the irony of the line immediately following her thought of him as a sacrificial lamb: "The sacrificial lamb strode along casually, accommodating his long pace to hers, keeping her on the inside of the walk in the good American style. . . ."

Related to this religious imagery associated with Adam is Miranda's remark about the epidemic of influenza: "It seems to be a plague . . . something out of the Middle Ages," since this calls into focus two sets of religious associations: the plague as a sign of God's wrath, and the danse macabre (in which the "lank stranger" symbol of death is also operative). The influenza epidemic is also, of course, the physical counterpart of the illness of society at war.

The second section of the novel opens, as does the first, with Miranda in sleep, waking to discover that a day has passed. In her illness her memory "turned and roved after another place she had known first and loved best," a place clearly Southern, which merges into a dream in which death is represented as a tropical jungle of vivid colors, sulphur-colored light, and the "hoarse bellow of voices." As in the first dream, Miranda commits herself to the journey but does not complete it: she boards the ship, but does not arrive at the jungle, the "secret place of death," before she wakes. Nevertheless, in her talk with Adam afterwards, she speaks as if she were already dead: "Let's tell each other what we meant to do," and her review of her life and attitudes is carefully kept in the past tense, except for her impulsive outburst about the sensuous delights of being alive: her love of weather, colors, sounds. In this conversation the religious theme again occurs, here introduced in an explicit discussion of religion between the characters. Miranda is revealed to be a Catholic, and her preoccupation with religion, anticipated by her earlier allusions, is emphasized here and will recur in later crises. The Negro spiritual which she and Adam try to sing (there are "about forty verses" and they can't remember the third line) gives another element of meaning to the title of the novel since it combines the religious and the love themes.

The scene is followed by another dream, in which Adam figures, and which repeats many of the images of the second dream: the jungle is here an "angry dangerous wood," the voices of the second dream recur, their sound compared to arrows which pierce Adam and Miranda. This curious simile, although its phallic symbolism is apparent, seems also to be a subconscious extension of Miranda's earlier remark, "I even know a prayer beginning O Apollo," since Apollo is associated with pestilence and plagues, which in Greek drama are often referred to as the darts or arrows of an angry Apollo. This is a pagan analogy of the medieval Christian view of plagues; and within the dream, the arrows which finally kill Adam but not Miranda symbolize the disease and its actual final results. In Miranda's mind the arrows are also associated with the everydayness of valentines and arrows, a symbolism she is later able to explain rationally. The attitude of Miranda reflected in the dream is also significantly changed from that of her first dream. The ambivalence of her desire for death is absent. "Like a child cheated in a game," she demands her right to die, and "selfishly" attempts to die and save Adam's life. He dies only because of her intervened presence, having before undergone "a perpetual death and resurrection," and this also foreshadows the actual outcome of the plot.

The time of the third section extends over a month; yet Miranda's experience in the hospital telescopes this time into a series of dreams. Her illness is enough advanced that even in the passages of time in which she is relatively conscious, her surroundings impinge upon her mind in the dimensions of dream-experience. For example, the incident of the two internes, hidden by a screen, removing a dead body from the bed next to hers, is to Miranda a "dance of tall deliberate shadows" (an image suggesting again the danse macabre theme, like churchwall paintings) whose significance she does not fully comprehend—the shroud of the corpse she describes as "a large stiff bow like merry rabbit ears dangled at the crown of his head." (pp. 347-49)

Miranda's dream of Dr. Hildesheim, who becomes, like the Hun torturer in her nightmare, a variant of the pale rider figure and almost a parody of it, indicates how deeply her mind has absorbed the jargon of the current propaganda which she hates. The dream, by verging on the ridiculous (he carries "a huge stone pot marked Poison in Gothic letters), is like a poetic-justice punishment vaguely threatened by the bond salesmen to those who don't buy bonds. Besides being a revealing comment on the insidious corruption wrought by propaganda, the brief nightmare contains two images which, in her later dream of paradise, reappear as transfigured symbols: the "pasture on her father's farm" and "a well once dry" with the "violated water" of the poison. The dream also reveals her present fear of death, a fear both conscious and subconscious. . . . (p. 350)

Porter at age fifteen, a year before her first "disasterous" marriage.

Her dreams in this period have the duality of her earlier daily experience: "Her mind, split in two, acknowledged and denied what she saw in the one instant," and this anticipates the final conflict between her rational will to die and her irrational instinct to live. It is ironic that the "angry point of light" symbolizing her will to live is the ultimate source of the radiance which spreads and curves into the rainbow of her paradise. This has a metaphorical logic also in that she has earlier desired death as escape but feared it as a dark jungle of evil things and of guilt. Here in her dream of paradise her mind postulates what death ideally should be (all that actual life is not), and its features are the opposite of those associated with death in the earlier nightmares. The jungle, the angry wood, becomes the meadow, the darkness becomes radiance, the incessant voices become silence and "no sound," the serpents and exotic evil animals become human beings transfigured in beauty who "cast no shadows"—that is, who no longer have any duality or ambivalence of being, but are "pure identities." In this paradise there is solitude for everyone (what Miranda desired in her dream-escape from her childhood home) but not loneliness or isolation: "each figure was alone but not solitary." The distinctive features of the paradise are silence, radiance, joy. (pp. 350-51)

She is drawn back from this paradise by the awareness that

"something, somebody was missing . . . she had left some-thing valuable in another country," and her remark that "there are no trees here" seems to be the form her memory of Adam, by association, takes (as in her earlier comparison of him to "a healthy apple"). The dead are absent, and she has consistently viewed Adam as committed to death, so that she is forced back through the wasteland of her march, "the strange stony place of bitter cold," to find him. There is also here the implication that all of the real world is the world of the "dead." The imagery of the world she returns to is domi-nantly that of violent noise, and gray colorless light, "where the sound of rejoicing was a clamor of pain" and "it is always twilight or just before morning, a promise of day that is never kept." To Miranda now "the body is a curious monster, no place to live in," as the flesh is alien to the returned mystic, and she is like "an alien who does not like the country in which he finds himself, does not understand the language." But the conspiracy must not be betrayed, the illusion that life is preferable must be maintained out of courtesy to the living. The irony of Miranda's situation is overwhelming: the "hu-mane conviction and custom of society" insist that life is best, and will force her to pay twice for the gift of death, making her endure again at some future date the painful journey to the blue sea and tranquil meadow of her paradise. It is a part of this irony that Adam, for whom she returned, is already dead. The casual understatement with which she and the reader are informed of his death is consistent with her situa-tion: since she has lost paradise, the other loss is inevitable and even unsurprising. It doesn't touch her because her heart is "hardened, indifferent. . . ."

She makes symbolic preparation for re-entrance into the world of "dead and withered beings that believed themselves alive," by requesting a number of significant things. They are her symbolic armor and mask, and they include cosmetics (". . . no one need pity this corpse if we look properly to the art of the thing" applies not only to her physical mask of cos-metics but to her mask of future behavior); a pair of gloves, which she calls *gauntlets;* and a walking stick. The last object is richly connotative. Its silvery wood and silver knob suggest Miranda's emphasis upon "the art of the thing," the appear-ance she must maintain. Its purpose is to help her, a kind of cripple, through her journey back again to death. When Towney warns against its expensiveness and comments that walking is hardly worth it, Miranda's "You're right" is an as-sured and cynical answer which arises out of her awareness of the symbolic act implied. Her mental image of herself as Lazarus come forth with "top hat and stick" is a dual vision of herself as he has been and as she will be in the world where appearances must be maintained; imagistically, we have come full circle again to the "disturbing oppositions" of that world of appearances. She is, with her walking stick, herself the pale rider, unhorsed and alone now, crippled by her first journey and preparing for her next: "Now there would be time for everything." (pp. 351-52)

> *Sarah Youngblood, "Structure and Imagery in Katherine Anne Porter's 'Pale Horse, Pale Rider,'" in* Modern Fiction Studies, *Vol. 5, No. 4, Winter, 1959-60, pp. 344-52.*

LEONARD PRAGER (essay date 1960)

[*In the following excerpt Prager addresses ironic elements of "Theft," asserting that the story's principal theme is "possession equals identity."*]

A woman discovers that her purse is missing, reconstructs the immediate past up to the moment of this discovery, un-covers a theft, recovers the stolen object from the thief—this is the simple action of Katherine Anne Porter's **"Theft,"** a story as rich in implication as it is effortless in its movement. In the concentrated language of the story, the title itself pro-vides the key metaphor and poses the basic equation: posses-sion equals identity. The protagonist is a woman and the purse which she has lost can readily be seen as sexual symbol; her problem of self-identity is concretely presented as the problem of an "emancipated" career woman who is starving emotionally in the Wasteland of urban anonymity and alien-ation. But on another level, and this the most far-reaching, *purse* means value, the lost purse uncertainty of values, the stolen purse betrayal of self. In the act of recalling the past, the protagonist takes an initial step in self-exploration.

The major portion of the story—almost two-thirds—consists of a flashback, a symbolic summary of the heroine's spiritual life. It begins: "She had intended to take the Elevated . . ." That she does not do so seems explicable in terms of chance. But such deflection of purpose, we come to see, is characteris-tic. Her ready surrender of will points to her uncertainty as a self. She is an anonymous "she" in the story precisely be-cause of her inability to claim herself for herself; to possess oneself is to assume an identity, a proper name. (p. 230)

In her recapitulation she introduces us to a series of male friends, the first being the shallow and theatrical Spaniard, Camilo, who "by a series of compromises had managed to make effective a fairly complete set of smaller courtesies, while ignoring the larger ones." Our attention is drawn to Camilo's new hat, which is as impractical as its wearer is suave. Camilo in a shabby hat would be merely shabby, but even an old weathered hat would seem right on Eddie—through this free association the protagonist's lover is intro-duced, a self-assured individual strongly contrasted with the vain Camilo. The latter wishes to see the heroine home: "It is written that we must be rained upon tonight, so let it be together." This inflated pronouncement does more than char-acterize its speaker. Here is the master of the smaller courte-sies proposing to play at a mutuality he cannot comprehend. (pp. 230-31)

The man-woman relationship in **"Theft"** represents the type of human relations in general, none of which is magically or-dered, all of which require outlay of effort. The device of the hats does not only realistically characterize the wearers. The hat is nothing less than maleness, as purse is femaleness. These sexual symbols must be understood in terms of the broadest meanings applicable to "sex." Camilo plays an exag-gerated male role; he is a kind of phallic exhibitionist. In the case histories of exhibitionists, the dead end of impotence is not infrequent. In the downpouring rain with a lady, Camilo wears his hat, but when he leaves her he hides his hat under his overcoat. He squanders and hoards his sexuality, which appears as a dissociated part of his personality. Eddie as-sumes the male role confidently, and is the only man in the story, we may infer from his letter, who can be decisive. The "rightness" with which Eddie can wear an old hat, can let time mellow it without undue concern, is a complex meta-phor for emotional maturity. The clinician would doubtless recognize Eddie as uniquely genital among a cast of oral and anal personalities. The amiable and "comfortable" Roger ap-pears to be realistic in protecting his hat from the rain. In this connection it is well to recall the protagonist's thoughts on

Eddie's hats, which seemed "as if they had been quite purposely left out in the rain . . ." The observation is revealing as regards the observer, who fails to understand that the basic function of a hat is to protect the head. The symbolic meaning is apparent: Eddie does not intellectualize, doesn't "use his head" to shield his feelings. He understands that it is the very vulnerability of the heart which makes genuine feeling possible. The quality of the protagonist's relationship with Roger suggests a mutual capacity for friendship where the demands of intimacy are not too great. She can tell Roger that it is time for him and Stella to do something definite, a prescription which fits her own case very well. Roger is a playwright trying to sell a play and he has decided on the strategy of "holding out." In the area of work he is apparently able to know what he is holding out for. There is implied in this juxtaposition of life and work the lack of realism involved in man-woman relationships which are damned from the outset by their goal of personal "happiness." Neither Roger, nor Stella, nor our protagonist, in their tortured love affairs, quite knows what he or she is "holding out" for. Undefined desire is projected in the form of impossible demands upon the other.

The culminating experience of insight is gradually foreshadowed, the reader increasingly aware of what the protagonist can only subconsciously perceive. She is, however, increasingly acute in her random thoughts about her friends and even about herself. Yet genuine insight erupts only when she dares to feel strongly. Seated with Roger in the taxi, she peers out the window "at the rain changing the shapes of everything, and the colors." This marks the first positive foreshadowing of insight, for the distortions she now views are those of the artist, distortions which twist things into their essentials. The new way of seeing thus hinted at is almost immediately consciously suppressed in the observation that the more the taxi skids, the calmer she feels. She is her old passive self again, surrendering to that which moves her, "make a move" for her, to her "general faith which ordered the movements of her life without regard to her will in the matter." On yet another level, the taxi ride to which she surrenders is a sexual wish fulfillment, a key to the dream life of an unfulfilled woman. (pp. 231-32)

Mounting the stairs to her apartment, the protagonist meets the viciously self-centered divorcé, Bill, who owes her fifty dollars; characteristically, she fails to insist upon payment, though she is critically in need of money. Arriving in her apartment she rereads Eddie's letter, obsessively rereading certain lines—"why were you so anxious to destroy . . . not worth all this abominable . . the end . . ."—and then she ritualistically destroys the letter. The following morning she discovers her purse has been stolen, and contrary to her typical passivity she rebels against this deprivation, one which is clearly linked to loss of Eddie's love. At first noting the theft, she thought "let it go," but at that moment "there rose coincidentally in her blood a deep almost murderous anger." This sudden breakthrough of feeling releases her for action—and for self-understanding: "She remembered how she had never locked a door in her life, on some principle of rejection in her that made her uncomfortable in the ownership of things . . ." The janitress denies stealing the purse and is bitterly told to keep it if she wants it so badly; by now its loss has stirred up awareness of a lifetime of losses, irreparable and painful defeats. Suddenly aware of her own vulnerability, her infantile certainty that her life will be ordered for her crumbles as she feels pity for herself: . . . . The janitress fi-

nally admits her guilt and returns the purse, cruelly taunting its owner as being too old to need pretty things any more. That the protagonist is no longer young is of the greatest importance. For the pathos of self-spoliation is compounded by "Time, the subtle thief of youth," the common enemy of mortals. The central character of **"Theft"** is a rootless sophisticate who experiences the terror of oblivion in fullest measure. She has not shored up her life with religious values through which to transcend time, nor rooted her being in the freedom of existential choice. The somber Edward Young writes that "Procrastination is the thief of time," and our protagonist has indeed been attempting to steal from the stealer, to ward off oblivion with obliviousness. Eddie's hats, we recall, grew old with him.

The story's final paragraph reveals a woman who has faced the pathos of her existence; following a flood of self-pity she sees with terrible clarity the self-defeating principle of her life: "She laid the purse on the table and sat down with the cup of chilled coffee, and thought: I was right not to be afraid of any thief but myself, who will end by leaving me nothing." The coffee would not stay hot by itself, the purse will not be magically filled with treasure. Yet she has regained her purse and gleaned a chilling truth which may help her warm her woman's soul. The power to deplete oneself need not be greater than the power to fill one's life with meaning. The story's central irony is that **"Theft"** comes principally through unwillingness to spend oneself. The protagonist's childishly-dimmed proprietary sense is a function of a more generalized flight from feeling. To own is to be responsible for, to be concerned with, to expend effort on. Her irrational certainty that the world will not take from her is but the negative of the infantile wish to be cared for regardless of what she does or does not do. The form of the wish betrays a fear of feeling and commitment. Illusion, however, powerful enough to imprison her soul, is no armor against reality, that force which both destroys and liberates. (pp. 233-34)

> Leonard Prager, "Getting and Spending: Porter's 'Theft,'" in Perspective, Vol. 11, No. 4, Winter, 1960, pp. 230-34.

JAMES WILLIAM JOHNSON   (essay date 1960)

[*Johnson is an American editor and educator who has written extensively on seventeenth- and eighteenth-century British literature. In the following excerpt, he arranges Porter's stories according to four basic themes: the controlling power of an individual's background, "cultural displacement," "the survival of individual integrity," and "man's slavery to his own nature."*]

As a serious writer, Miss Porter is concerned, of course, with certain general and pervasive themes: the workings of the human heart; appearance and reality; the epiphanic apperception of truth; the subterranean rills of individual emotion which produce the emotional torrents of an historical era; self-delusion and its consequences. But she tends to use these broader topics to re-enforce more limited themes, which dramatize themselves in a variety of characters and places. (pp. 601-02)

Initially, there is the theme of the individual within his heritage, the relationship of past to present in the mind. *Old Mortality* is the novella which embodies this topic most tellingly, with its three stages of development in the mind of its child-heroine and its alteration of the legendary past through a series of clashes which it has with the factual present. There are four short stories illustrating the same theme, all of them co-incidentally dealing with the same characters: **"The Old Order," "The Source," "The Witness," "The Last Leaf."** The two old ladies, one white and one black, in **"The Old Order"** talk always about the past, making it the very substance of the present and embalming the future with the dead. The Witness exists in the present but his mind dwells on what he believes happened long ago but actually did not. The Last Leaf, through her obdurant behavior in the present, gives the lie to sentimental memories of what the past was. And the Source is a farm which has become symbolic of a past stability and order which never existed except in golden retrospection.

These works treat what Miss Porter has recently called "the country of my heart." Autobiographical or not, they stand thematically with certain works of Faulkner, Mann, and Proust. Like Faulkner, Miss Porter is fascinated with the tragedy of the Old South and the effect of the legend on those who helped to create it. Like Mann, she sees the past as a wistfully perfect and stable order which is perfect only because it is completed, that is, dead. And like Proust, she emphasizes memories of human beings and the fragments of re-collected days and ways as the bits which make up the mosaic of present thought. She never exaggerates the past by using it mythopoeically or giving it a transcendence over the present because of its historicity. Instead, she sees the past simply as a former time peopled by human beings living unheroic lives, for the most part. To her as to Homer, the generations of men are as leaves which wax green and then fall; and there is always one last leaf to remind the living of the human reality of the past.

A second theme is cultural displacement. Whether one is exiled willingly or unwillingly from his own heritage, he finds himself in an alien culture which often permits him to discover the inherent nature of human evil. **"The Leaning Tower"** takes this as its thesis, with its depiction of a young American artist in Nazi Germany in the days when the beast is beginning to emerge once more from its subconscious jungle. This novella is profitably compared with the final chapters of Thomas Wolfe's *You Can't Go Home Again* and Christopher Isherwood's *Goodbye to Berlin,* which utilize the same fictional situation. Both Wolfe and Isherwood are content to evoke a general mood of brutality and totalitarianism; Miss Porter clothes it in flesh in the persons of Hans, Otto, and Lutte. Where Wolfe editorializes, using such words as "evil," "brutal," and "stupid," Miss Porter simply and severely records the reactions of a decent, essentially unvocal young man to the revealing but unspectacular behavior of three young Germans, an Austrian, and a Pole. Thus embodied, Nazism is a tangibly, recognizably ugly aspect of humanity rather than the vaguely terrifying, whispered accounts of "those people" to be found in Wolfe's version.

"Flowering Judas" is a shorter statement of the theme of cultural displacement and the discovery of evil. This much-anthologized and criticized story anticipates **"The Leaning Tower"** in many ways: the idealistic young American protagonist, the removal to a remotely exotic culture, the militaristic background, the underlying tradition of violence and force in the strange culture, the final realization of evil by the protagonist. Unlike Charles Upton, who discovers that selfishness and a feeling of inferiority explain the megalomania of an un-loved race, Laura of **"Flowering Judas"** finds herself guilty

of a cold idealism which has cut her off from human beings and has blighted the growth of compassion in her heart. Charles is capable of compassion but is ineffectual; Laura is efficient but frigid. With these differences in protagonist, **"Flowering Judas"** and **"The Leaning Tower"** are thematically closely akin. Braggioni is the prototype of the Nazi pigs of the novella, and his nameless victims are finally personified in the hapless Otto.

The third group of stories deals with unhappy marriages and the self-delusion attendant upon them. **"Rope,"** which serves as Miss Porter's version of the Battle of the Sexes, shows a violent squabble between a husband and wife over a trivial incident which reveals their deep-seated differences. **"That Tree"** explores a conflict of wills and temperaments between the male and female; and **"A Day's Work"** is a dreadfully sordid, if grotesquely funny, story about two mismatched and long-married people. **"The Cracked Looking Glass"** is the novella archetype of the theme, with its characterization of the fanciful Rosaleen, wed to the aging Dennis and trapped in rural New England. Similar in its external qualities to Eugene O'Neill's *Desire under the Elms,* the longer version of a mis-matched Irish immigrant couple (**"A Day's Work"** is the shorter) concerns itself with the wife's deficiencies in the marriage state. Rosaleen's unrealistic dreams of what her marriage should be have been so constantly eroded by the realities of her life that she has overworked her fancy almost to the point of dementedness.

Then there is the group of stories which have as their theme the death of love and the survival of individual integrity. *Pale Horse, Pale Rider,* the longest version, is a literal account of the death of love in the person of Adam, whose tragic death in the influenza epidemic of 1918 leaves Miranda, the "one singer," to mourn and to rebuild her life on the single principle of refusing to be comforted by a flight into religious illusion. **"The Downward Path to Wisdom"** is a study of the metaphoric death of love: at its conclusion the unwanted and rejected child discovers the core of his self in his little song of hatred. **"Theft"** shows a girl robbed of everything—things lost, borrowed books, unspoken words, "dying friendships and the dark inexplicable death of love"—until the theft of her purse reminds her that no loss but that of her hope in life and trust in others really matters. (pp. 602-05)

The fifth body of stories is those which deal with the theme of *Noon Wine:* man's slavery to his own nature and subjugation to a human fate which dooms him to suffering and disappointment. The destiny which decrees that Mr. Thompson, the self-indulgent child of pride, will benefit from the lucky hiring of the insane farm hand also assures that he will finally be crushed under its grinding wheel. Miss Porter firmly insists that man's suffering is inextricably related to what he is, though she also suggests that certain destructive forces—disease, death—are inevitable and inescapable in spite of one's character and she implies strongly that the struggle of mankind goes on before an aloof and indifferent cosmos. In **"Maria Concepcion,"** for instance, the footloose and irresponsible Juan is drawn back to the life-pattern incorporated in his wife, who dispassionately murders her rival to possess her husband's child. In **"Magic,"** the central figure, a young prostitute in a New Orleans bordello, struggles frantically to escape her enslaved existence, succeeding at last only to return voluntarily to the black tyranny of the madam. **"He"** shows the unavoidable tragedy of the abnormal child, the victim of a biological accident; but the suffering which His mother undergoes is compounded by her own foolish vanity and pride in refusing to accept the facts (her son's hopeless abnormality and her hatred of him). **"The Jilting of Granny Weatherall"** shows a dying old woman, stood up by the God she had supposed to exist, just as she had been jilted by an earthly fiancée and forced to live a life of disappointment and compensation. The violence and suffering, mental and physical, in these stories are denigrated by the ironic realization that man must face them with little choice, however senseless they may be. (pp. 605-06)

Such are the recurrent themes of Katherine Anne Porter's seventeen short stories and six novelle. If the above summary is oversimplified, its categories can be defended with more details than space permits here. The important point is that thematically Miss Porter is working with a limited group of ideas which she presents with a uniformly superb style and a multiformly ingenious handling of symbols. (p. 606)

During the 1940's, it was as symbolist that Miss Porter was most effusively praised by the totemist critics. In fact, criticism of her work became tantamount to an intellectual parlor game: "Let's see who can find the most abstruse symbols in **'Flowering Judas.'** " Her work survived this craze, which was largely unnecessary, since the truth is that her symbols operate on the most direct level and where she intends a multiplicity of meaning, Miss Porter almost always tells the reader so.

Her titles, for example, almost invariably summarize symbolically the state of affairs she deals with in her story: **"The Old Order," "The Circus," "Magic."** If the story is more than an expository dissertation on its topic, it is always about that topic fundamentally. When her titles are literary or allusive, as with **Noon Wine, Old Mortality,** or **Pale Horse, Pale Rider,** she works the substance of the quoted source into her own story: Mr. Helton, in **Noon Wine,** plays the symbolic tune on his harmonica and the missing words are eventually supplied by the odious Mr. Hatch, or Adam and Miranda, of **Pale Horse, Pale Rider,** chant the old slave tune while waiting for the ambulance to arrive. If Miss Porter uses an "objective correlative" as her title—**"The Leaning Tower," "The Cracked Looking Glass"**—it appears significantly in the story and someone comments on its connotations. Charles, of **"The Leaning Tower,"** breaks the plaster replica of the Pisan landmark; and when it is returned, repaired, to its place, he mulls over its meaning for its owner and tries to understand how it typifies the unsound culture of Nazi Germany. Rosaleen is constantly distressed about the cracked mirror, which blurs her face so unrecognizably; but her imperfect and unsatisfactory marriage as mirrored in her "cracked" imagination cannot be replaced, and so the cracked looking glass remains hanging in the kitchen, after Rosaleen has fully pondered the consequences of its doing so. (pp. 606-07)

The Porter symbolism also depends in obvious fashion on proper names. The masterful thing about the names of her characters is that they are appropriate for those people in those places. The names of real people are chosen from a cultural context which embodies certain values of the culture; thus when Miss Porter calls her heroine "Miranda," it is a suitable name for a little Southern girl of 1900, being Latinate and vaguely "literary." If as a fictional personage Miranda shares the innocence and optimism of Shakespeare's sheltered heroine, or if she literally becomes an "admirable" character because of her honesty and moral responsibility, Miss Porter's story is so much the richer. Miranda's last name, incidentally, is "Rhea," as we find from a close reading

of **Old Mortality.** "Rhea" is a fine old Southern name, thus appropriate; but Rhea was also the Greek Earth-Mother, and Miss Porter's Rheas live on the soil of a matriarchy run by a grandmother often described in divine terms. Such symbolism of nomenclature is not vital to the understanding of the stories, but it helps to reinforce characterization and theme. (pp. 607-08)

Many of Miss Porter's symbols are the very stuff of her narrative and operate without calling up allusions or forming patterns of meaning. Mrs. Thompson's dark glasses in **Noon Wine** are symbolic in this fashion, as are the animal gravestones of **"The Witness"** and the patchwork of **"The Old Order."** A few individual symbols appear several times in the stories without any incremental repetition or external frame of reference. Miss Porter is apparently fond of these and they fulfill a self-renewing purpose for her. Chief of these is her death-image of a swirling cloud or whirlpool of darkness narrowing down to a pin point of light. The meadow is often a symbol of freedom, and a horseback ride expresses independence. A spring of fresh water symbolizes innocence, truth, or faith. Tangling and weaving images appear in her stories of the individual in his heritage; and weak or vicious people are figuratively animalistic: they are "penguins" or they have "rabbit teeth" or "skunk heads." Merely to list such images, however, gives them a commonplace quality which within their contexts they do not have.

A few basic themes, an adroit use of symbols, a limpid prose style—these combine in Miss Porter's stories to the propagation of a fictional point of view which is amazingly consistent and complete. The logos of her fictional attitude toward life is something like this:

The child is born into a world seemingly ordered and reasonable but it is in fact chaotic, ridiculous, and doubt-ridden (**"The Old Order"**). He learns at an early age that he is an atomistic creature, often unloved (**"The Downward Path"**), and that the delightful spectacle of life masks fear, hatred, and bitterness (**"The Circus"**). He discovers that life and love must end in death (**"The Grave," "The Fig Tree"**). He must inevitably reject his heritage as lies and his family as hostile aliens **(Old Mortality);** but when he tries to substitute something else in their place, he is driven back by his own weaknesses to what he has been conditioned to (**"Maria Concepcion," "Magic"**). If he makes the break with the past and tries to replace the lost old love with a new, he is doomed to despair **(Pale Horse, Pale Rider).** If he tries to substitute another heritage for his own, he finds it full of evil (**"The Leaning Tower"**); or he discovers that he has lost his power to love through denying his own tradition (**"Flowering Judas"**). There is nothing for him to cling to but his desperate belief in his own courage and integrity (**"Theft"**) and what little of love and certainty he has in life (**"The Cracked Looking Glass"**). But life is senselessly cruel (**"He"**), full of frustration and contention (**"Rope," "That Tree," "A Day's Work"**); and it ends in annihilation and the extinction of all hope (**"The Jilting of Granny Weatherall"**). Such is Miss Porter's fictional philosophy. (pp. 610-11)

James William Johnson, "Another Look at Katherine Anne Porter," in The Virginia Quarterly Review, *Vol. 36, No. 4, Autumn, 1960, pp. 598-613.*

SHIRLEY E. JOHNSON (essay date 1961)

[*In the following excerpt, Johnson examines the theme of disillusionment as experienced by Porter's female chracters.*]

Katherine Anne Porter's women characters contribute to a statable thesis concerning women, their condition and role: loss of illusion and the consequent acceptance of, or resignation to, the new "reality." Porter clearly implies that only men and young girls are blind to the fallacy of romantic love. A woman's education is concerned primarily with discovering this fallacy to which she must reconcile herself. In Porter's world duty rather than love governs life. (p. 83)

Porter, with few exceptions, uses women as central characters. Some are young girls who must in time replace fictions concerning love and marriage with facts. Their story is, therefore, almost without exception, the story of disillusionment. The other women—spinsters or wives—having lost their illusions, carry on lives made tolerable only by resignation.

Miss Porter depicts the loss of illusion primarily through the stories of two young girls, Violeta of the story, **"Virgin Violeta,"** and Miranda, a character recurring in several stories, most notably *Old Mortality,* **"The Grave,"** and *Pale Horse, Pale Rider.* Violeta, fifteen, is secretly and painfully in love with her cousin Carlos who, oblivious of her, reads poetry to her sister Blanca. Violeta is tortured by the murmurs, smiles, and gestures which mark their private world. The convent school where she had been taught "modesty, chastity, silence, obedience with a little French and music and some arithmetic" has provided no instruction to fit the present moment. She wants passionately to cry, to say aloud, "I love Carlos," although the idea embarrasses her intensely. When Carlos and Blanca are ready for more poetry, Violeta desperately and defiantly intrudes upon their privacy by saying in a tone that excludes Blanca, "If you want your book, Carlos, I can find it. . . . I have had it for a whole week." After a moment's hesitation while the two awaken to the fact of her existence in the room, Carlos, aware for the first time of her challenge, goes to help find the book. Although Violeta has been yearning for something she cannot even name, she is totally unprepared for the disillusioning experience that follows:

> Carlos's hand came up in a curve, settled upon hers, and held fast. His roundish, smooth cheek and blond eyebrows hovered, swooped. His mouth touched hers and made a tiny smacking sound. She felt herself wrench and twist away as if a hand pushed her violently. And in that second his hand was over her mouth, soft and warm, and his eyes were staring at her fearfully close. Violeta opened her eyes wide also and peered up at him. She expected to sink into a look warm and gentle, like the touch of his palm. Instead, she felt suddenly, sharply hurt, as if she had collided with a chair in the dark. His eyes were bright and shallow, almost like the eyes of Pepe, the macaw. His pale, fluffy eyebrows were arched, his mouth smiled tightly. A sick thumping began in the pit of her stomach, as it always did when she was called up to explain things to mother superior. Something was terribly wrong. Her heart pounded until she seemed about to smother. She was angry with all her might, and turned her head aside in a hard jerk.

Miranda's disillusionment is treated more thoroughly. The reader can trace her history from the first bewilderment as a child to her resignation at twenty-four. Although she has been brought up to believe the romantic tales about love, her doubt is early stirred by the contradiction between the evidence of her eyes and her ears. By the time she and her sister are sent to the convent school, they already know that "It was no good at all trying to fit the stories to life, and they did not even try." (pp. 83-5)

An important step in Miranda's disillusionment comes when she and her sister first meet their almost legendary Uncle Gabriel. He had been pictured for them as the dashing, handsome, romantic man who had married their beautiful Aunt Amy. After her early and mysterious death, he had remarried. When they finally meet him, they are astonished and ask themselves, "Can that be our Uncle Gabriel? . . . Is that Aunt Amy's handsome romantic beau? Is that the man who wrote the poem about our Aunt Amy? Oh what did grown-up people mean when they talked, anyway?" What they saw was a "shabby fat man with bloodshot blue eyes, sad beaten eyes, and a big melancholy laugh, like a groan." After the race in which their uncle's horse wins, Miranda, her sister, and father go with Uncle Gabriel, who is by this time quite drunk, to meet his second wife. They stop finally before a "desolate-looking little hotel in Elysian Fields" and are led through a "long gas-lighted hall full of a terrible smell" and "up a long staircase with a ragged carpet." In a dismal room they are introduced to Aunt Amy's successor, Miss Honey, who, they are shocked to discover, is a bitter, hating, wholly unlovely woman. Experience is gradually teaching them that handsome gentlemen and beautiful ladies exist and love only in stories.

At seventeen, Miranda elopes and at eighteen feels only weariness when she thinks of her marriage, "as if it were an illness that she might one day hope to recover from." The end of the story records her loss of faith as she thinks, " 'I hate loving and being loved, I hate it.' And her disturbed and seething mind received a shock of comfort from this sudden collapse of an old painful structure of distorted images and misconceptions." (pp. 85-6)

In Porter's stories a man or woman, after marriage, may say, "I hate you," in a number of ways, but never, "I love you." In fact, most of the stories seem to say that love dies with marriage, to be replaced at best by an uneasy truce, at worst by a death struggle. In one description Porter presents a scene which might be taken as symbolizing the most malign possibilities of marriage. A woman repeatedly dreams of an incident she has once witnessed:

> As the bus rolled by, Jenny saw a man and a woman, some distance from the group, locked in a death battle. They swayed and staggered together in a strange embrace, as if they supported each other; but in the man's right hand was a knife, and the woman's breast and stomach were pierced. The blood ran down her body and over her thighs, her skirts were sticking to her legs with her own blood. With a jagged stone she was beating him on the head and his features were veiled in rivulets of blood. They were silent, and their faces had taken on a saintlike patience in suffering, abstract and purified of rage and hatred, in their one holy purpose to kill each other. Their flesh swayed about each other's bodies as if in love, their weapons were raised again, but their heads lowered little by little, until the woman's head rested upon his breast, and his head was on her shoulder, and holding thus they both struck again.

Most of Porter's stories, however, present a less violent picture. The typical marriage becomes essentially an alliance whose bonds are repeatedly strained to the limit, yet are strong enough to hold. In the story, **"Rope,"** the fact that the husband comes home with an unneeded piece of rope, but without the coffee upon which his wife's good temper depends, creates the situation which tests the bond.

> Had he brought the coffee? She had been waiting all day long for coffee. They had forgot it when they ordered at the store the first day.
>
> Gosh, no, he hadn't. Lord, now he'd have to go back. Yes, he would if it killed him. He thought, though, he had everything else. She reminded him it was only because he didn't drink coffee himself. If he did he would remember it quick enough. Suppose they ran out of cigarettes? Then she saw the rope. What was that for? Well, he thought it might do to hang clothes on, or something. Naturally she asked him if he thought they were going to run a laundry? They already had a fifty-foot line hanging right before his eyes? Why, hadn't he noticed it, really? It was a blot on the landscape to her.
>
> He thought there were a lot of things a rope might come in handy for. She wanted to know what, for instance. He thought a few seconds, but nothing occurred. They could wait and see, couldn't they? You need all sorts of strange odds and ends around a place in the country. She said, yes, that was so; but she thought just at that time when every penny counted, it seemed funny to buy more rope. That was all. She hadn't meant anything else. She hadn't just seen, not at first, why he felt it was necessary.
>
> Well, thunder, he had bought it because he wanted to, and that was all there was to it. She thought that was reason enough, and couldn't understand why he hadn't said so, at first.

Variations of this basic tension are treated in **"A Downward Path to Wisdom," "A Day's Work,"** and **"The Cracked Looking Glass."** In each, marriage is represented as being an unsatisfactory condition to which one is, nevertheless, committed. In **"A Day's Work"** the relationship at times becomes a version of the death struggle. The Irish-American Hallorans live together grimly, their antagonisms apparent in every word they speak. Here, as is frequently the case in Porter marriages, the woman is the dominating member. Mrs. Halloran has supported the family by taking in washing and ironing ever since Mr. Halloran lost his job during the depression. Before his marriage, Mr. Halloran had been warned by a friend, "There's a girl will spend her time holding you down. . . . You're putting your head in a noose will strangle the life out of you." But he did not then recognize what he has long since learned: that Lacey Mahaffy was a "woman born to make any man miserable." She is a rigid, hard, persevering woman whose grim philosophy is expressed in her advice to her unhappily married daughter, Maggie. "I told her to do right and leave wrong doing to the men. . . . I told her to bear with the trouble God sends as her mother did before her."

When Mr. Halloran comes home drunk but with a political job, the results reveal their basic antagonisms. In defiance of his wife's rejection of him, he hurls the flatiron at her, although he sees her only hazily. The "specter, whoever it was, whatever it was, sank and was gone." Out on the street he tells the cop, "I killed Lacey Mahaffy at last, you'll be pleased to hear. . . . It was high time and past." But he has not

killed her. He has only raised a great lumpy clout of flesh on her forehead. And he has only spurred on her desire for revenge. (pp. 86-8)

In Porter's spinsters one again finds women, their illusions lost, committed to a less than ideal life. But the resignation, colored by bitterness, is qualified by a still almost wistful longing for the love each has rejected. The three most fully developed spinsters, Eva of *Old Mortality,* Laura of **"Flowering Judas,"** and the unnamed women in **"Theft,"** are all intelligent, educated, sensitive women. But Eva, an unattractive, chinless old maid, who teaches Latin in a Female Seminary and fights for women's rights, belongs to an earlier era. She is depicted more as a caricature of the frustrated old maid, revealing her frustration in her jealous comments about her cousin Amy and her wistful references to a beautiful dress she had once had. Still she finds compensation and even a kind of fulfillment in her crusading.

However, the problems of the woman in **"Theft"** and Laura in **"Flowering Judas"** seem less capable of solution and thus more distressing. Each is plagued by an acute self-awareness coupled with a tendency to reject, specifically love and relationships. . . . In one sense, the condition of the Porter spinster, because negative, is even worse than that of the married woman.

Leslie A. Fiedler says in *Love and Death in the American Novel,* "It is maturity above all things that the American writer fears, and marriage seems to him its essential sign. For marriage stands traditionally not only for a reconciliation with the divided self, a truce between head and heart, but also for a compromise with society, an acceptance of responsibility and drudgery and dullness." If a writer's maturity is to be judged, at least in part, by his acceptance of marriage as the condition of life, Porter can clearly claim the label in so far as she presents the drudgery, dullness, and commitment required of marriage. However, one waits still for evidence of the maturity which allows characters to step beyond resignation to reconciliation and into the reciprocal relationship possible between two adult human beings. (p. 93)

> *Shirley E. Johnson, "Love Attitudes in the Fiction of Katherine Anne Porter," in* West Virginia University Philological Papers, *Vol. 13, 1961, pp. 82-93.*

DANIEL CURLEY (essay date 1963-64)

[*Curley is an American dramatist, poet, novelist, short story writer, and author of children's books. Here he explores the use of flashback and repetition in "The Grave."*]

Katherine Anne Porter's brief but powerful story **"The Grave"** provides some interesting clues as to the nature of her personal fable, because the fundamental concepts on which the story rests are that the mind of the writer is the grave of the past and that the art of the writer resurrects the past to a new life and a new meaning. (p. 377)

The story is set up in three parts. The body of the story is framed by a one paragraph prologue and a one paragraph epilogue. The prologue sketches family history and provides a background against which the body has amplified meaning. The history concentrates on the possessive grandmother who moved her husband's coffin with her from place to place in order to be sure of lying beside him for eternity. The body of

Porter with friend and admirer Monroe Wheeler (right) and her fourth husband, Albert Erskine (center). It was not until their wedding day that Erskine, then twenty-six, discovered Porter was nearly twice his age.

the story relates an incident in the life of nine-year-old Miranda and her brother Paul, twelve. The entire family burial plot has been dug up, and all the coffins have been moved to a public burial ground. The children are out hunting and visit the empty graves. Miranda finds a silver dove in her grandfather's grave, and her brother finds a delicately carved wedding ring in another grave. Miranda's brother wants the dove, because he knows that it is a screw head from a coffin—a priceless treasure to a boy—and Miranda wants the ring, because it is beautiful. They swap their treasures. This turn toward beauty is a crucial moment in Miranda's life, for until now she has been a tomboy. She seems at this point to be getting ready to accept the adult female role. Unfortunately, as the children continue their hunting, her brother kills a rabbit that turns out to be pregnant. This is another crucial moment, for Miranda now rejects the whole bloody female mess. She continues to reject it for twenty years until one day in Mexico circumstances conspire to recreate the event and cast a new light on it. This takes place in the epilogue, which is isolated from the body of the story by a time jump just as the prologue is isolated by a time summary. One hot day in a Mexican market full of the scent of fresh meat and corruption, Miranda, still a stranger in the world, is confronted with some dyed candy animals, rabbits among them. Her first re-

action is exactly the horror with which she looked at the mother rabbit and the babies, but as she relives the scene she adds something she had not noticed on her first visit to the grave; and the last sentence turns the entire story inside out: "Instantly upon this thought the dreadful vision faded, and she saw clearly her brother, whose childhood face she had forgotten, standing again in the blazing sunshine, again twelve years old, a pleased sober smile in his eyes, turning the silver dove over and over in his hands." (pp. 377-78)

One of the first things to be observed about the story is that it abandons the usual order of narration . . . for an order that reproduces the actual sequence of events with a twenty-year gap. What we would normally expect to see in a story of this sort is a beginning like this: Miranda is picking her path among the puddles and crushed refuse of a market street in a strange city of a strange country . . . and so on. She has a sudden emotional experience out of all proportion to the event, the presentation of a tray of candy animals. Suddenly she is a child again, and the bulk of the story takes place in flashback.

The usual theory is that the use of flashback will create an illusion of tighter time. In this case, the actual elapsed time of the story would be, probably, seconds, only long enough for Miranda to see and smell the candy animals and for her mind to reach back into the past, find her open grave, and come forward to the present. The writer might even present the entire experience as instantaneous. The use of flashback has a further advantage in that the reader is constantly aware that the body of the story is an illumination of the moment of truth or horror of the opening passage. He traces the material backward with the protagonist into the past and finds what he needs by way of explanation.

But let us look for a moment to see exactly what Katherine Anne Porter gains by following the direct order rather than the more usual inverse order. In the first place, we think we are reading a story of childhood. We think the moment of the child is the moment of the story. We are, in short, as bemused as the child herself. Instead of analyzing the situation from the vantage point of the mature writer (flashback approach) we are experiencing it from the point of view of the awakening child. The whole heartbreakingly beautiful world is opening before us.

Suddenly it vanishes, this strange and beautiful world of the child in which we find out things and they are True. The horror that Miranda experiences in the Mexican market is reproduced for us exactly as it came to her and exactly as similar experiences have come to us. In short, we have been sucked in again by our apparently boundless hope that some one of these days we are actually going to be blessed. By the time we reach the moment of horror, her childhood has become our childhood, and again we are ravished by the world. Instead, then, of being presented with a character experiencing a reaction entirely foreign to us, we are that character experiencing a truly terrible moment the background for which we know and the implications of which we are prepared to receive viscerally and completely long before we can even begin to work over the meanings with our mind.

In electing to tell the story this way, Miss Porter has clearly taken a risk, because it has meant stopping the story in its tracks to say, "Twenty years pass," but the risk pays off beautifully. When the world of childhood is so suddenly snatched away from us, our minds move in exactly the direction the story must move in: the doubts and insecurities of our own lives crowd in to remind us of the crushing sorrow of what does happen in twenty years. However, what makes the payoff truly magnificent is the way in which out of the very horror, out of the grave, treasure suddenly appears, blazing sunshine and the silver dove.

Not only does the story contain a jump of twenty years at the end, but the prologue introduces at the very beginning a much longer stretch of time and a different concept of time as external to and inclusive of the time of Miranda's own life. This immediately places the matter she has to experience, the lesson she has to learn, on quite a different level from the ordinary story of the passage into maturity. This opening statement of the themes, then, in spite of the fact that it seems at first to be simply a random setting down of isolated events in a purely naturalistic world, controls the entire development of the story by implying a kind of larger-than-life pattern against which the individual and apparently fragmentary pattern can deduce its own wholeness. The opening implies also that the individual learns through his individual experience, but what he learns is the collective experience. The totality of the story says this through its prologue, body, and epiphany. All parts are essential. The story cannot be seen in any one of them until all are there; then each of the parts is seen

to reflect the whole. The epiphany is that at which all things aim, but it cannot come to pass without the individual repetition of the collective experience.

The prologue of **"The Grave"** tells us of the grandmother who literally carries with her the body of her long-dead husband and at last is literally reunited with him as the result of her constancy and possessiveness. The repeatedly opened grave of the grandfather has its appropriate counterpart in the old woman's constant memory of him. We are sure of this at once, but the value of her constancy and possessiveness and the meaning of the reintegration of the severed flesh of husband and wife become clear only at the end of the story when Miranda's adult terror is vanquished by the memory of her childhood treasure and the final Christian image of the dove.

The open grave dominates as well the entire childhood episode—including the body of the mother rabbit: ". . . buried the young rabbits again in their mother's body. . . ." This grave imagery also prepares the way for the opening of the grave in Miranda's mind when the right combination of sight and smell and strangeness in the world touches the secret spring. Not only that, but the episode hints that an open grave is only a hole in the ground and may contain treasure. From the point of view of technique it is worth noticing that the sections of the story repeat themselves along these themes and anticipate the reconciliation of the end: the grave of memory opened and found to contain something more important than horror. (pp. 379-82)

> Daniel Curley, "Treasure in 'The Grave,'" in Modern Fiction Studies, Vol. IX, No. 4, Winter, 1963-64, pp. 377-84.

SAM BLUEFARB (essay date 1964)

[*In the following excerpt, Bluefarb analyzes "Flowering Judas," commenting on Porter's atypical treatment of the initiation motif.*]

The initiation motif in American fiction has frequently dealt with the loss of innocence. . . . Generally, an "end to innocence" in a fictional character has been followed by a brief period of inaction, even paralysis, which, while temporary, eventually leads to some sort of action. (p. 256)

In Katherine Anne Porter's **"Flowering Judas,"** there is a similar loss of innocence through an initiation. But the shock, and the paralysis that follows, do not necessarily lead to an "equal but opposite" reaction. On the contrary: what is produced in Laura, the main character, is a change in tempo of her work in the Mexican revolutionary movement. It does not bring that work to a stop; it merely brakes it to a slower pace. So that Laura, rather than withdraw her commitment to the revolution, continues in its service, except thereafter as a kind of somnambulant victim, a zombie, of the experience.

In Laura, innocence may be said to lie at the heart of her revolutionary idealism. Perhaps her awakening to the revolutionary cause is, in a sense, a socio-political extension of her Catholicism—like the mendicant priest who goes out into the world to "do good." Laura's presence in Mexico at the time of the revolution may be seen—as perhaps Laura herself sees it—as a providential act which would permit her (and not only permit, but inspire her) to do good.

But initiation not only involves the "clean side of the coin";

the dirty side must be discovered too. Her initiation, then, is one that includes both experiences—dedication to a noble revolutionary ideal, and the discovery that corruption, opportunism, and animal meanness exist within the "secure" secular morality of the revolutionary movement. And this discovery includes initiation at a second level: innocence ends when the sharp wound of reality is inflicted on an innocent. Not all revolutionary heroines are affected in the same way. Some, perhaps, are less sensitive than others. And some are better at rationalization. But Laura is—or was—sensitive, and she is the kind of person who is simply no good at rationalization, which might less euphemistically be called self-deception. Once the real world has broken through the diaphanous membrane of her revolutionary innocence—or virginity?—Laura has been reduced—or seduced—to the deflowered state of her spiritual zombiism. Loss of innocence, then, may take many forms. But Laura has remained intact at the sexual level: she is still a virgin.

Braggioni, the revolutionary leader, paradoxically does not symbolize the revolution's ideals. Rather, he represents the corrupt world, the world indeed against which revolutions are made! For he is neither an idealist—which Laura in her innocence had expected him to be—nor even the papier-mâché god of the revolutionary poster; he is a man like any other. If there is anything about him that reveals personality, it is a capacity for ruthlessness. . . . In a sense—and it is difficult not to sound melodramatic in setting up such a metaphor—Laura undergoes a rape of the soul at Braggioni's hands. But not entirely without "reasonable" cause. If Braggioni cannot "ruin" Laura as virgin, he will ruin her as idealist; he will either destroy her on his terms or, kept from that, on hers. If he can't touch her body, he will touch her where she is even more vulnerable. It is thus no accident that this story of revolutionary idealism gone sour, should be shot through with the violent imagery of depersonalized sexuality at one level, and with religious symbolism at another.

At first Braggioni—the name itself is suggestive of a multiplicity of associations—appears to Laura as a "gluttonous bulk." He has "become a symbol of her many disillusions, for a revolutionist should be lean, animated by heroic faith, a vessel of abstract virtues." But this is an accurate description of Laura herself! Yet she denies the thought, and tells herself: "This is nonsense . . . Revolution must have leaders, and leadership is a career for energetic men."

Energetic! One can almost see, in the use of this word, Laura's furtive admiration for Braggioni's primitive sexuality. Further, Braggioni's physical reality hardly coincides with Laura's preconceptions of a revolutionist: "lean, animated by heroic faith," the idealist, more thinker than activist, more the planner of revolutions than the maker of them, the impulsive rebel rather than the cool organizer of armed insurrection—in short, the complete antithesis of a Braggioni!

Not only is Braggioni the realistic antidote to the toxic agent of Laura's romanticism—her idealistic innocence; he is "real" with the kind of hard, brutal honesty that is not only designed to tell Laura the truth about herself, but will destroy all of her illusions. (pp. 256-58)

Cynics—or, if one prefers, realists—like Braggioni are usually capable of organizing revolutions, of *functioning* in situations untenable for idealists like Laura. (It is interesting to note that Laura begins to function as soon as she loses her

idealism, her innocence—becomes a zombie, that is.) Thus while it is possible for the idealist to remain something of a token revolutionary, it is far more probable that the cynic cannot only remain a genuine revolutionist, but can do so without breaking. (pp. 258-59)

Braggioni, then, seems to be a symbol of the professional revolutionist in all of his implications: an ideal to worship and a tyrant to despise. Ironically, he is clear-eyed enough to see himself neither as unmitigated good, nor as unadulterated evil; he is the impersonal force delegated by History to bring down the established social structure without even a thought for the social order that will replace it. And the added irony is that Braggioni's contempt is not merely limited to his political enemies; he has as much, or even more, for his friends and followers. His enemies see him as evil, while his followers, willfully blinding themselves to his excesses, see him as a shining symbol of revolutionary courage. Oversimplification is hard at work here, for he is neither. And this is brought home to Laura with brutal finality in the death of Eugenio, martyr not so much to the revolution as to the betrayal of its ideals by the Braggionis.

What has thus far amounted to one kind of appearance becomes for Laura quite another reality: revolutionaries are supposed to be thin and ascetic; Braggioni is fat and sensual. Revolutionaries are supposed to be vessels of dedication and self-sacrifice; Braggioni is shamelessly self-indulgent. For Laura, the people—spelled out in capital letters—are sacred; to Braggioni they are not sacred, but are pawns of the revolution. . . . (p. 259)

On the other hand, Laura denies herself; she is truly the soul of revolutionary womanhood. Self-sacrificing, she finds satisfaction in teaching the children to read and write. Once she perceives the truth about Braggioni, she plunges with even greater zeal into the struggle, but only as an unfeeling automaton now: she visits prisoners, smuggles letters out of jail, warns those outside, and exposes herself to all the hazards. She seems to be making up for Braggioni's failure. And while she denies herself, plunges ever further into revolutionary work, Braggioni strums Mexican love ballads on his guitar. While Laura feeds the voracious hunger of revolutionary duty, Braggioni makes the revolution itself the source for gratifying his own peculiar hungers.

There was a time when the girls had called him Delgadito, "thin one." But that was long ago—in the days of his own starved idealism. Miss Porter speaks of Laura's breasts as being full, "like a nursing mother's," as though lacking nurslings, Laura will give the milk of her existence to the revolution, to the Braggionis, who see in the revolution, as they do in the Lauras, the source of their own nourishment. What is it that Braggioni wants? Power over women sexually, and over men politically. And the two are not always mutually exclusive.

Yet, surprisingly, it is Braggioni, notwithstanding his hard outer shell, who unexpectedly reveals an inner frailty. And it is *Mrs.* Braggioni—she who represents the unlikely domestic side of the revolutionist—who triggers this frailty. Laura, herself frail and ethereal at first, becomes the zombie who can never weep; yet it is Braggioni, his hardness notwithstanding, who can still break under emotional strain. For if Braggioni suffers a guilt, it is the guilt induced by his cast-off wife, who will wash his feet on his return home, and whose tears will mingle with the remorse of Braggioni's own. Laura can only envy Mrs. Braggioni her tears, for they are shed over a concrete wrong. But Laura cannot shed tears either for a concrete wrong, or the abstract wrongs conceived in terms of revolutionary justice. Unlike Braggioni, who reveals a soft core within the hard shell, Laura's inner being has become hard; she cannot weep, and the children she teaches are not her own flesh. They are abstractions, dream children she might have had, like those other abstractions of the revolution. Indeed, their very concreteness is a constant reminder of this dilemma.

Perhaps Laura's "strength" as well as her weakness may be more clearly seen against her Catholic upbringing: dedication to a cause transcending a personal view of the world. But even as Laura feels she has severed her last tie with the church, she is still the prisoner of her own emotional necessity, of her past. She must still occasionally slip into a "crumbling little church" to whisper a clandestine Hail Mary!

Caught, then, between the rejected faith of her girlhood and a political faith that is its pale counterpart, Laura has gravitated towards the latter. Thus she has given herself to the revolution as another woman might give herself to a man—or a convent! Ironically, Laura, in rejecting her childhood orthodoxy, has ended up in the hell of another orthodoxy.

Having dedicated herself to what she believed to be the one true cause, Laura, when she sees that cause mired by cynicism, by men like Braggioni, can only push further into the wasteland of the world that has made that cynicism possible. She must thrust forth now into the real world which, in itself, has nothing to do with innocence or guilt, but is catalyst for both. In spite of her Judas nightmare which closes the story, Laura survives the loss of her innocence. And now, harder than Braggioni himself, she will take on the dedication of the zombie, which is finally much stronger than Braggioni's. For Braggioni the cynic is still, to some extent, alive: he can weep. Laura cannot even do that.

Yet no loss of innocence proceeds without some guilt. And guilt Laura certainly has—even if that guilt is in some curious way the force behind her "deadness." But that guilt does not proceed primarily from Eugenio's death by suicide, whose means Laura, Judas-like, had provided. If guilt there is, it is a guilt that Laura bears for her deepest—and repressed—yearnings, feelings which have little or nothing to do with revolution. Thus it is an almost appropriate piece of poetic justice that it should have been Braggioni the political "revolutionist" who became the means whereby Laura's non-political—and certainly non-religious—yearnings were awakened. (pp. 260-62)

> *Sam Bluefarb, "Loss of Innocence in 'Flowering Judas,' " in* CLA Journal, *Vol. VII, No. 3, March, 1964, pp. 256-62.*

JOSEPH FEATHERSTONE (essay date 1965)

[*Featherstone is a former contributing editor to the* New Republic *who has written extensively on theories of educational development. In this review of Porter's* Collected Stories, *Featherstone praises many aspects of Porter's tales, emphasizing their portrayal of struggles between morality and art.*]

Few writers in America or anywhere else have matched the purity of [Porter's] English, her powers of deep poetic concentration, her intelligence, her responsiveness to the inner life of her characters, her sharp sense of the pressing forces of history, nationality, and social atmosphere.

She is a contemporary of Faulkner, and although she has always stood completely alone as a literary figure, her art suggests some reflections on the First World War generation of American writers whose restless search for values and experiments with form introduced Americans to the modern age. She, too, questioned all that she inherited. She threw off the beliefs she was raised with, the quaint, hypocritical notions about the family, the human personality, love, art. This generation was through with all that. It was setting up a new order in the world. Politics and literature were going to be wholly transformed. . . .

[Porter] has lived much of her life outside this country, and few writers can equal her for sheer variety of characters and settings. She does city people, Texas blackland farmers, Mexicans, the American Irish, German-Americans and Germans in Germany; of all classes and generations. She never celebrates a region, although many of her stories might be called local color pieces. She gives the bitter essence of what a people's life is like, as if she were sketching an abstract stage set, and then concentrates on the dramatic revelation of character in the created setting. . . . The local color pieces lack the dense web of associations, the amount of felt living, memory and contemplation that go into the more autobiographical stories. But in their bleak, abstracted way, they are splendid. Mexican stories, like the flawless **"Maria Concepcion,"** have the beautiful and hollow ring of formal tragedy. **"Hacienda"** is a tale of some Russian film makers in Mexico to shoot a revolutionary epic—in real life the Russian director was Eisenstein—and through their tangled failures we begin to see what the camera captures, "the almost ecstatic death-expectancy which is in the air of Mexico," the peasant figures under a doom imposed by the landscape.

Some of her stories might be called political. Few apart from **"Flowering Judas"** bear directly on politics, but her historical and social sense is like a fine antenna, and certain pieces shimmer with the ominous presence of history. (p. 23)

Here and there are a few clean images and happy scenes, bright coins thrown into the threatening sea. They occur most often in the large number of stories dealing with Miss Porter's native Texas. Her Texas was the South, for it was peopled by Southerners from Virginia, Tennessee, the Carolinas, and Kentucky; and the values by which she judges the world derive from her family experiences in what she has called the Old Order. It must be understood, however, that the derivation is exceedingly subtle. (As well as selective: There are, for example, few traces in her art of her Catholic upbringing.) She has too much critical moral intelligence to become a genteel celebrant of the Southern heritage. There is even less of that in her than in Faulkner. She is, after all, a Southerner in exile. Still, the Texas stories—or rather the family experiences they are distilled from—seem to be the ultimate source of her sense of things in their right proportions.

Just how subtle the derivation is may be seen in an autobiographical short novel, ***Old Mortality,*** set in Texas in three spans of time between 1885 and 1912. There are many characters, each so vividly drawn that the story achieves the dense effect of a much longer work. The narrative is anecdotal, lingering over odd details and bits of family history in a deceptively casual way. The theme is every child's problem, making the stories grownups tell match reality as it begins to unfold. In this case the story is the rich tapestry of romance the family has woven around the figure of an Aunt Amy. As young Miranda's parents tell it, Amy's life touched their youth with poetry, "the nobility of human feeling, the divinity of man's vision of the unseen, the importance of life and death, the depths of the human heart, the romantic value of tragedy." Miranda and her sister examine the old, sepia-tinted photographs of Amy trying to reconstruct the legendary age of their parents' youth, the days of dark beauties pale as death, high-sounding words, eternal loves, and duels in the moonlight; for the children are held, as each new generation is, by the love of the living for what the faded relics and ribbons represent.

Growing up, alas, is a series of disillusionments. And in the final portion of the novel, Miranda returns home, a married woman now, to a funeral. On the train she meets old Cousin Eva, a spinster suffragette with a weak chin. Eva is the muckraking voice of the modern era, and she has a very different interpretation of the legends of magnolias and moonshine surrounding Amy and her circle. To Eva, the disenchanted modern, the legend is best debunked in terms of money and biology. . . . Miranda is appalled by this modern portrait of corruption under the lace and flowers of the Old Order, but she realizes that Eva's debunking is no more credible than the family romance. Still, the talk with Eva chills her, and she yearns to feel once again the solid and reassuring presence of her father. A curious thing happens when everyone arrives home: Miranda sees that her pious father and skeptical Cousin Eva belong together in some mysterious way. They view the past by radically different lights, but it is their past together, and Miranda is excluded from their fellowship. The older generation has a complicity of experience that Miranda will never share. (pp. 24-5)

Thus *Old Mortality* shows some of the complexity of Miss Porter's relation to the Southern past she rebels against. Much of that past is bogus and what is worth saving, ironically has to be re-created by each generation at a fearful cost. Some of the old truths are true; you find out which ones in the course of living a life.

I think her best stories are those of the Old South and Texas. In them, she creates, illumines, and places the tight family of the Old Order, with its accumulated weight of traditional living and its foolish conviction that the world would never change. The great theme of these stories is the initiation of young Miranda into a knowledge of the forces of cruelty, sexuality, and death. . . . From the spark of essential spirit that gleams through these stories from time to time, Katherine Anne Porter takes her stand. Morality and art are not the same for her—she is not *that* old-fashioned—but they meet in the question of order. The art that made these masterpieces is not primarily educative, though the stories are wise; it is not primarily enjoyable, though they give much pleasure. The special function of this art is to give shape to our existence: to achieve order and form and statement in a world "heaving with the sickness of millennial change." Even when her stories tremble on the edge of disintegration, even when they reveal the most unpleasant truths about ourselves and our age, they are replicas of life, complete and compelling. She has a triumphant ability to see a life and its surroundings as it is and as it might be: a knowledge of proper proportions. This is the sense of a great comic writer, of course, but the effect of most of these stories is relentlessly ironic, perhaps because proper proportions are so scarce in this world.

We feel, even of the weakest characters, that they are kin. She enables us to look on a figure with wonder and deep attention: When we see the mad Swede in *Noon Wine,* we get an inkling of what it must really be like to be crazy, to play the harmonica in a dazed unhappy way over and over again in the noon sun.

And the power of the telling remains. You remember, not just the grace and precision of the sentences, but the actual experience of having listened to the voice of a character's inner imagination. In *Pale Horse, Pale Rider,* the First World War and the influenza epidemic blend together in a delirious dance of death, and as you follow Miranda's nightmares, you forget the incomparable style in the comprehension of how it is to be young and alive and in love in a world full of death. (pp. 25-6)

> *Joseph Featherstone, "Katherine Anne Porter's Harvest," in* The New Republic, *Vol. 153, No. 10, September 4, 1965, pp. 23-6.*

ROBERT PENN WARREN (essay date 1965)

[*Warren is considered one of the most distinguished modern American writers. He received Pulitzer Prizes for both fiction and poetry, and in 1986, he was appointed by the Library of Congress as the first Poet Laureate of the United States. Warren began his career during the 1920s as a member of the Fugitive's, a group of Southern poets including John Crowe Ransom, Donald Davidson, and Allen Tate, who upheld traditional values of the agrarian South. Consequently, Warren's work is strongly regional in character, often drawing its inspiration from the land, the people, and the history of the South. Warren was one of Porter's closest friends and a zealous admirer of her works. In the following excerpt, he discusses Porter's treatment of inner tension and truth in her short stories.*]

In *The Collected Stories* of Katherine Anne Porter we have all of the short stories, including four (one, **"Holiday,"** a masterpiece) hitherto uncollected, along with five longer pieces—long stories and short novels. This is a large, solid book, and in its 500 packed pages we find the record of a life and the achievement of a rare, powerful, and subtle creative force. It is a beautiful and deeply satisfying book; and it promises to be a permanent and highly esteemed part of our literature.

Permanent: we may have some confidence in the permanence of this book because, from the beginning, forty-five years ago, the fiction of Katherine Anne Porter has been numinously present but never in fashion. It has had, very definitely, a public, and distinguished appreciation, but its appeal has always been intrinsic, and has never been derived from the accidents of context, social or literary, in which the work appeared. If we look back at the first collection, *Flowering Judas,* what do we find to remind us of the labels and textbook tags for the 'twenties? Or if we look back on the volume of long pieces, *Old Mortality, Noon Wine,* and *Pale Horse, Pale Rider,* published in a volume that goes by the name of the last, what do we find that reminds us of the polemics and posturing or, in any obvious way, of the social passion of the 'thirties? Only one story in this collection, the title story of the collection called *The Leaning Tower,* has an air of topicality, and that is the only one which, by the rigorous standard proposed by the rest of the book, can be called a failure. Against the background of shifting fashions, this fiction has always seemed fixed. It seems to have been there always, a part of our spiritual landscape to which one may turn now and then, as to a tree, rock, or hill, for a moment of reorientation. Despite the great richness of detail and the subtlety of tonal variations, the final effect is one of a classic severity: the memory, as it were, of our own old, half-forgotten inner experiences, suddenly seen in a vital form.

There is, however, a paradox here. Though outside the flux of fashion and beyond the journalism of the chic, this fiction is profoundly, radically, modern. And that, of course, is why it sometimes seems, at first glance, to be outside of what, at a particular moment, may merely appear to be modern. Because of its radical modernism—its root modernism—this fiction often undercuts what is only the accident of a moment.

The most obvious example of this is in the short novel *Old Mortality.* Here the legend of the Old South—appearing as a story of romantic family piety, with the beautiful and charming Aunt Amy, long dead, as the heroine—is subjected to a series of "unmaskings," is submitted to a series of tests by corrosives. The person who crucially confronts the legend of Amy, and for whom the unmaskings have a deep bearing on her own vision of life and on her own fate, is Miranda, a child when we first meet her, but at the end a grown girl.

As a child Miranda brings to the family stories merely the test of simple realism. If her romantic father can say, "Thank God, there never were any fat women in my family," the little girl remembers Aunt Keziah, up in Kentucky, "who, when seated, was one solid pyramidal monument from floor to neck." The corrosive of realism is succeeded by that of moral judgment, when Miranda discovers the disastrous effects of Aunt Amy's romantic story—this in the person of Cousin Gabriel, who, as a dashing young man, had married Amy but now is reduced to a whiskey-sodden, wheezing wreck of a man, a failing follower of the tracks, who tortures his present wife with the legend of Amy, a delusion from which he cannot disenthrall himself.

The next stages of the criticism of the legend occurs some years later when Miranda, on the train going back home to Gabriel's funeral, encounters Cousin Eva, who, like Gabriel, had been a victim of the romantic legend—poor, chinless Cousin Eva, who had failed as a belle and has spent her life teaching Latin in a female seminary or fighting gallantly for the cause of woman suffrage. Cousin Eva, out of the rancor of her old deprivation and defeat, offers Miranda two more kinds of unmasking for the legend. The gay parties of the legend had had a brutal economic undergirding; the parties and the love affairs were a "market." So here we have the very modern corrosive of Marx. But there is another very modern corrosive: "Cousin Eva wrung her hands. 'It was just sex,' she said in despair; 'their minds dwelt on nothing else. They didn't call it that, it was all smothered under pretty names, but that's all it was, sex. . . . None of them had, and they didn't need to have, anything else to think about, and they didn't really know anything about that, so they simply festered inside—they simply festered—' " So the corrosive of Freud is added to that of Marx.

Cousin Eva, with Marx and Freud, speaks for modernism against the romanticism of which Miranda's father is the chief exponent, and thus far, in the various unmaskings of the Southern myth—i. e. the "past" in general—we find a fiction appropriate to its period, the 'thirties. But even as Cousin Eva speaks her piece about sex, "Miranda found herself deliberately watching a long procession of living corpses, festering women stepping gaily towards the charnel house, their cor-

ruption concealed under laces and flowers, their dead faces lifted smiling, and thought quite coldly, 'Of course it was not like that. This is no more true than what I was told before, it's every bit as romantic.' "

So Miranda retorts that her own mother had been "a perfectly natural woman who liked to cook"—and with the phrase "natural woman," she gropes out for some truth beyond all the formulations that have been offered her. She is now eighteen, she had eloped only a year before, she has run through her own "romance," and now she is seeking solid footing for her own life. She suddenly thinks she may find the "natural" truth upon returning home, with her father. But this is not to be. When she arrives she finds that there is a secret, unhealable breach between her and her father, and that it is Eva to whom he turns—Eva, who, with her modern unmaskings, had seemed the enemy of his romanticism.

It now appears that Eva and the father are merely the "poles," as it were, of the past, the terms of the dialectic of the past, and Miranda is left isolated to find her own "truth" without reference to that past. So we come to the end. . . . (pp. 280-83)

Truth, the last words would imply, is not an absolute, but inheres in the dialectic of the life-process. Each age must create its own truth, out of its own polarities, its own tensions, and this truth, however provisional, is what must constitute its vital commitment. Each age, each person in fact, lives only in the quality—the passion and profundity, and at the same time the critical awareness—of this existential commitment.

This story is, as we have said, the most explicit treatment of this theme, at least in historical and social terms. But it is implicit in **"The Old Order."** Here the character of Miranda again confronts, as in *Old Mortality,* the past. Here is the struggle of the girl to find her own footing, but the struggle is not a simple objective one against the Old Order. She is involved in the values of that order, and the struggle is, finally, a subjective one, for she is fully aware of the virtues of the Old Order, and yearns for them. In **"The Jilting of Granny Weatherall"** we have a story which might well be in **"The Old Order,"** and a character very close to the grandmother there. We find the toughness and self-reliance of Granny Weatherall (the name is significant), her loyalties and kindnesses, her well-earned pride in her triumph of life. On her deathbed she can think of "sitting up nights with sick horses and sick negroes and sick children and hardly losing one." The fusion of a will to life and a moral attitude, a clear notion of the rules of the game of life and of the stakes for which it is played—that was what the Old Order offered. (pp. 283-84)

The virtues of the Old Order appear, however, as in *Old Mortality,* in the context of its limitations and defects. Since this fiction presents the Southern version of the Old Order, let us take, for example, the life of Nannie—the Black Mammy—as it winds in and out of the stories. There is the time when, as a pot-bellied child, scarcely more than a baby, she is sold at a slave-auction and the purchaser pokes her in the stomach, saying, "Regular crowbait." And the time when, a generation later, she is identified to the seller, now an old judge and respected citizen, who bawls out: "For God Almighty's sake! is that the strip of crowbait I sold to your father for twenty dollars?" Nannie finally airs the grievance to her mistress—whom, long after Emancipation, she had elected to stay with: " 'Looks lak a jedge might had better raisin',' she said gloomily, 'Looks lak he didn't keer how much he hurt a body's feelins.' " The episode, in its very muteness, is more telling than a catalogue of atrocities. And how complex are the ironies in the fact that Nannie impugns the "raisin' " of the judge—a point on which the Old Order, at any social level, would have had most pride.

If Miranda can look back and yearn for the toughness, the sense of obligation, and the moral certitude of the Old Order, she knows that she cannot have them on the same terms. She must find her own terms, in the New Order; but this means that she may find herself, in the end, as much in conflict with its prevailing values as with any of the past. This is implicit in, for example, *Pale Horse, Pale Rider;* and the theme appears in **"Flowering Judas"** and is hinted at in the opening of **"Holiday,"** and elsewhere. This is not to say that this theme is dominant, but it is often present, as a kind of under-theme, coloring and modifying whatever may be more dominant, providing another counterpoint or another irony.

The candor, the willingness to confront and explore inner tensions, the conviction that reality, the "truth," is never two-dimensional, is found in process not in stasis—all this gives the peculiar vibrance and the peculiar sense of a complex but severely balanced form to almost all of the other stories, even those not concerned with the generations or with an over-all society, but with more strictly personal issues. In a story like **"Theft"** the drama develops from the tension between "world-as-thief" and "self-as-thief," in a rigorous balance of argument subtly unfolding beneath the circumstantial surface of the narrative. In **"He,"** as in **"Holiday,"** the drama develops from the tension between love and compassion, on the one hand, and the gross force of need and the life-will, on the other. In **"Maria Concepcion"** the drama lies in a contrast between the code of civilization and the logic of natural impulse. In *Noon Wine* it revolves about the nature of motive and of guilt. Did Mr. Thompson really see a knife in the hand of Mr. Hatch? Did he brain the monstrous Hatch to save Mr. Helton's life or to defend the prosperity which Helton had brought him? Or had some other, more mysterious force guided his hand? Poor Mr. Thompson—he can never know and therefore must put the shotgun muzzle under his chin.

The dark pit where motives twine and twist is a place well known, of course, to our modernity; it is the milieu of much modern fiction. It is the milieu deeply pondered and scrupulously reported by Katherine Anne Porter. Not only are *Noon Wine* and *Old Mortality* studies of the ambiguity of motive; such studies are also found in **"Theft," "The Tree,"** and **"He,"** to take only three examples. But it is important to see the difference in effect between her treatment of such ideas and that found in writers whom we think of as specifically modern. For one thing, Katherine Anne Porter never confounds the shadowy and flickering shapes of the psychological situation with vagueness of structure in the story itself, or permits the difficulty of making an ethical analysis to justify a confusion in form. The fallacy of expressive form is not found here. In fact, it may be plausibly argued that the most powerful tension in her work is between the emotional involvements (how great they can, at times, be!) and the detachment, the will to shape and assess experience; and the effect of this is sometimes to make a story look and feel strangely different, unanalyzably different, from the ordinary practice. But there is a deeper and more significant difference. A great deal of the current handling of the psychology of motive is a kind of clinical reportage. In two respects the work of Katherine Anne Porter is to be distinguished from this. First,

she presumably believes that there is not merely pathology in the world, but evil—Evil with the capital *E,* if you will. Along with the pity and humor of her fiction there is the rigorous, almost puritanical, attempt to make an assessment of experience. Second, she presumably believes in the sanctity of what used to be called the individual soul. She may even go as far as Hawthorne does in "Ethan Brand," and elsewhere, in regarding the violation of this sanctity of the soul as the Unpardonable Sin. Not even those characters who are touched with evil or fatuity are deprived of a vital rendering; the ethical judgment is not a judgment abstractly passed on a robot, and the difficulty of judging any human being is not blinked.

If neither the ethical bias in the fiction of Katherine Anne Porter nor the notion of the sanctity of the individual soul seems, at first glance, modern, let us recall that both are related to an issue which undercuts the clinical and reportorial concerns often passing for modernity. The issue is this: given the modern world of technology and the great power state, on what terms, if any, can the individual survive? The abstractions that eat up the sense of the individual—they call forth her most mordant ironies. Of Braggioni, the "professional lover of humanity" who cannot love a person, she says: "He has the malice, the cleverness, the wickedness, the sharpness of wit, the hardness of heart, stipulated for loving the world profitably." And oh, the beauty of that word *stipulated!*

The chic phrase is the "crisis of identity," and a consideration of that crisis lies at the heart of this fiction. It lies so near the informing heart, so deep in fact, that it can be missed; for Katherine Anne Porter sees the question in radical terms: ethical responsibility and the sanctity of the individual soul. Without that much, she might argue, what would "identity" mean? It is chic to discuss the crisis of identity, but it is not chic to explore it in terms that count—that, in fact, undercut the chic. One might conceivably state the issue here in theological terms. But there is no need to do so, and it might be irrelevant to the author's view. The logical terms are enough.

To take another approach to the whole question, there is a more personal aspect to the tensions underlying these stories. The story of Miranda is that of a child, then of a young woman, trying, in the face of the Old Order, and then of the New, to find her own values, to create her own identity. The exact ratio of fact and fiction in Miranda's story, and of autobiography and fiction in the portrait, is something which we cannot—and in one sense, the author herself cannot—know. It is not even important for us, or for the author, to know. Clearly there is a degree of overlap and projection, but, clearly again, there is one important difference between Miranda and her creator. The creator is an artist, and her own rebellions, rejections, and seekings, as shadowed forth however imperfectly and with whatever distortions, inevitably have some deep relation to this role in real life. No doubt the artist, in all periods, is stuck with some sense of difference, of even alienation, no matter how stoutly, or cynically, he may insist on identifying himself with his world; and in our period this alienation of the artist—even the "pathology of the artist"—is not only an element in his experience but often a theme of his work. It is, in one perspective, a theme of this book, in much the same sense that it is a theme of the work of Hawthorne, James, Kafka, or Mann. (pp. 284-87)

The artist must find the right distance from life, put the right shape or frame on life, and at the same time must render, to a greater or lesser degree, its quality, its urgency. These paradoxical demands simply repeat the personal tensions of apartness and involvement. Such tension in this fiction has been peculiarly fruitful, because there is a willed candor in the author's assessment of her role. She knows the deep ambivalences in that role: the world—life—is a beloved enemy. If on one hand, life must be mastered in the dialectic of her form, on the other hand, life must be plunged into—or realized as though one had plunged into it and were totally immersed. The dialectic of her form is peculiarly severe, as I have tried to indicate in discussing **Old Mortality,** and even in stories like **"Flowering Judas"** and **"He,"** which seem at first glance more casually devised in their progression, will be found a deeply set logic. But in all the stories, even when the ordering is most rigorous, there is the same vividness of circumstantiality. The vividness of the details of the physical world is unwavering. The mouth of Braggioni, the fat revolutionist in **"Flowering Judas,"** opens "round and yearns sideways, his balloon cheeks grow oily with the labor of song. . . . He sighs and his leather belt creaks like a saddle girth." When Granny Weatherall lighted the lamps, the "children huddled up to her and breathed like little calves waiting at the bars in the twilight." In **"Virgin Violetta,"** in reference to Carlos: "His furry, golden eyebrows were knitted sternly, resembling a tangle of crochet wool." In **"The Old Order,"** we have the annual arrival of the grandmother back at the farm: the "horses jogged in, their bellies jolting and churning, and Grandmother calling out greetings in her feast-day voice."

Here is a poetry of the rich texture of the world. It is a poetry that shows a deep emotional attachment to the world's body. But this is not a self-indulgent poetry, and its richness is derived from precision—precision of observation and precision of phrase. From, shall we say, the hard intellectuality that veins and hardens that love, that manifests itself elsewhere, and more fundamentally, in the dialectic of form.

As the love of the texture of the world is set against this intellectuality, so the world of feeling is set against the dialectic. It is a rich world of feeling. Gaiety, good humor, and humor abound here. The whole first section of **Old Mortality** spills over with it. In the second section we have the delicious humor of the little girls "immured" in the convent, and even in the last section, there are flashes of humor in the encounter with the formidable Cousin Eva.

Gaiety, good humor, and humor represent, however, only one segment of the spectrum of feeling found in this book. There is the heart-wrenching moment, for instance, at the end of **"He,"** when all the tortured complexities of Mrs. Whipple's attitude toward her idiot son are absorbed into a sudden purity of focus. Or the moment in **"The Old Order"** when Nannie, after the words of the judge who had sold her years ago as "crowbait," bursts out to her mistress. Or in **"Holiday,"** when the mute cripple, who works as a servant in the house of her own parents, shows the narrator the blurred photograph of a fat, smiling baby, and then turns it over to point to the name—her own name—written carefully on the back. Or in **Noon Wine,** when after her husband has given her "a good pinch on her thin little rump," Mrs. Thompson says, "Why, Mr. Thompson, sometimes I think you're the evilest-minded man that ever lived," and then takes "a handful of hair on the crown of his head" and gives it "a good slow pull." Then: " 'That's to show you how it feels, pinching so hard when you're supposed to be playing,' she said, gently." Whether it is the bleak purity of emotion in **"He,"** or this flash of unexpected warmth and tenderness

in the life of the Thompsons, Katherine Anne Porter has the gift for touching the key of feeling. She never exploits this gift, never indulges in random emotionality; she knows that the gift must not be abused or it will vanish like fairy gold.

She knows, too, that shifts in feeling are essential if we are to sense the movement of life. A feeling suddenly explodes against the counterpoint of other feelings, other tones, as the pathos of the scene at the hotel in the second part of **Old Mortality** bursts against the humor associated with the little girls in the convent. And always, the feeling appears against the backdrop of the rigorously unfolding form of the story. Katherine Anne Porter has some austerity of imagination that gives her a secret access to the spot whence feeling springs. She can deny herself, and her own feelings, and patiently repudiate the temptation to exploit the feelings of the reader, and therefore can, when the moment comes, truly enter into the heart of a character; and in that self-denial may find, and affirm, herself. One hesitates to think what price may have been paid for this priceless gift.

I have been speaking of some of the tensions and themes in this book. They spring from the author's will to see "all" of a thing. She must explore, as it were, the inner resonances and paradoxes of her own sensibility. She is willing to undergo the painful discipline of trying to keep uncorrupted her own consciousness. One feels that for her the act of composition is an act of knowing, and that for her, knowledge is the end of life—and that for her, knowledge, imaginatively achieved, is, in the end, life. Without it, all the bright texture of the world and experience would be only illusion.

She knows, we are forced to believe, that if one is to try to see "all," one must be willing to see the dark side of the moon. She has a will, a ferocious will, to face, but face in its full context, what Herman Melville called the great "NO" of life. If stoicism is the underlying attitude in this fiction, it is a stoicism without grimness or arrogance, capable of gaiety, tenderness, and sympathy, and its ethical point of reference is found in those characters who, like Granny Weatherall, have the toughness to survive but who survive by a loving sense of obligation to others, this sense being, in the end, only a full affirmation of the life-sense, a joy in strength. On her deathbed, as we recall, Granny Weatherall, thinking of all the sick animals and people she had sat up with, night after night, can cry out in triumph to her long-dead husband: "John, I hardly ever lost one of them!"

Like all strong art, this book is, paradoxically, both a question asked of life and a celebration of life; and the author of it knows in her bones that the more corrosive the question asked, the more powerful may be the celebration. (pp. 288-90)

Robert Penn Warren, "Uncorrupted Consciousness: The Stories of Katherine Anne Porter," in The Yale Review, *Vol. LV, No. 2, December, 1965, pp. 280-90.*

WINFRED S. EMMONS (essay date 1967)

[*In the following excerpt, Emmons discusses Porter's stories set in the South and Southwest, maintaining that they are not limited by their regionalism because the truths realized by her characters are universal.*]

Miss Porter is often classified as a "Southern" writer, and it is true that a strong flavor of the old South runs through many of her stories. To call her a Southern writer is to invite comparison with other Southern writers of high caliber, particularly Eudora Welty and William Faulkner; in the comparison their paths diverge. Everybody has noted the flavor of the South in Miss Porter's writings, but nobody has complained about it, as some critics have done about the works of Faulkner and Miss Welty. Both of the latter incorporate details and attitudes into their work which can be understood only by somebody who knows the South intimately; the Southern quality in Miss Porter's works is less intense. None of her characters, except her Negroes, are so Southern as to be incapable of living almost anywhere.

Miss Porter says that having written the stories collected in *Flowering Judas,* she felt herself turning toward her own past and her own family, or in her own phrase, "the native land of my heart." Her native land was the South, transplanted to central Texas and populated mainly by people from Virginia, Tennessee, the Carolinas, and Kentucky. . . . After her mother died, when Katherine was three years old, she made her home with her Grandmother Porter, who lived in Kyle, a small town between San Marcos and Austin. She is rumored to have attended "convent schools" at times, but the most lasting influences on her, judging from her fiction, were those of her grandmother's household and her grandmother's farm. (pp. 1-2)

The society in which she was reared was civilized for the most part, but there was always the threat of potential violence breaking through. Quiescent feuds existed among the "good families," and her own father was supposed to have taken a shot at another man once, though not according to the rules of the *code duello.* Frontier types sometimes attended church armed; even in her grandmother's home, guns were everywhere and the children were taught how to use them. Her father's lapse into violence, which considerably antedated her own birth, had been colored by time into romance; but more immediate and much less romantic was the shotgun blast followed by a scream that Miss Porter remembers from her childhood.

The source from which local violence was expected was the Plain People; presumably, the plainer the people, the greater the violence. *Noon Wine,* the only one of her regional stories in which violence is a major element, deals with the Plain People, who are in this story ordinary country folks. When Miss Porter deals with such people in her stories, she endows them with a certain dignity; but in the society of her childhood they were viewed with condescension by the "good families," just as they would be today. A man who sprang from humble origins could never get away from them; he might marry above his station, and if the children turned out well, they might be allowed their mother's status, but their father's origin would never be forgotten. Miss Porter is a snob, in a very pleasant way; it is the way she was raised.

But even in *Noon Wine* Miss Porter had not taken her readers to the true native land of her heart; that small country was her grandmother's household and farm, and it is found in *Old Mortality* and in the seven pieces grouped under the heading, **"The Old Order,"** in *The Collected Stories.* In her native land as it appears in her stories, the knowledge of violence that the child Katherine Anne Porter possessed was not passed on to the child Miranda, who is Miss Porter's fictional self. There the children were bossed, corraled, overseen, and tyrannized over, as well as being kissed, prayed over, and loved. They had their very own Uncle Remus, who rejoiced

in the name of Uncle Jimbilly; when terror entered Miranda's world, it came by way of circuses and incongruities, not through shotgun blasts and flashing knives. The general capacity for violence must have been there, but perhaps some grace about her grandmother denied it expression. Or Miss Porter may have merely decided, for artistic reasons of her own, to ignore whatever domestic violence there may have been. (pp. 2-3)

If the word "regional" is to be used in any pejorative sense, Miss Porter is not a regional writer; the regionalism of her work is in no sense a limiting factor on her writing, as it is occasionally in the works of other regional writers. In all of her writings, her main concern is people, and her people are universal. The truths that some of her people arrive at are universal, too. (p. 4)

Old Mortality is the least regional of Miss Porter's regional stories and also the most autobiographical in the sense that Miranda's life is indicated, in a sketchy way, from early childhood to the age of about seventeen. As such, it has value as providing an indication of what Miss Porter grew out of and what she grew into, aside from its virtues as a story. (p. 5)

In "Reflections on Willa Cather," Katherine Anne Porter describes the world in which things were going to happen to her as disintegrating, chaotic, and unstable; nothing remained firm, not even the distinction between the sexes; the world after World War I as described by Miss Porter sounds remarkably like the world after World War II in many ways. She ironically observes that not only in governments and organized crime but also in the arts, there was a frantic concern with the New.

The capitalization of "New" is Miss Porter's and it underscores the irony with which she viewed the world into which she escaped from the family legend, at least after a few years. The "art of rejection" attributed to Miss Porter was certainly applied with discrimination to her childhood experiences; the fact that she came to be heartily sick of hearing family annals hashed and rehashed and substituted for more immediate matters does not mean that she rejected her family, a fact that even the hasty reader must observe. Nor does it mean that she rejected the values the family stood for; as a matter of fact, Miss Porter's amused irony when confronted with the New seems to parallel a considerable reverence for the Old, which is probably not really old but timeless.

Miss Porter's first published stories were set in Mexico, which at the time she called her "familiar country," and she was familiar with it from having resided there at various times in the early twenties. The New, in **"Flowering Judas,"** probably seems newer to Laura, the central character, because it is also foreign and exotic; it is also unsatisfactory, and she cannot actually get involved in it. The Obregon revolution is supposed to change the face of Mexico and lift up the downtrodden, but in its visible symbols it is not coming off. Braggioni, the revolutionary leader who is Laura's superior, is a cynical mass of suet who nevertheless manages to be sinister. A true revolutionist ought to be lean, faithful, virtuous, and dedicated to the cause; Braggioni, however, is more interested in high eating and low women than in revolutionary virtues. (pp. 7-8)

But if the New is unsatisfactory in **"Flowering Judas,"** in **"Hacienda"** it is repulsive; the revolution has been betrayed, the old tyrants have been displaced, and the successful revolutionists have only set up a new tyranny. The film company, which has a hard core of Russian communists, is more concerned with getting a moving picture made than it is with the peons on the hacienda where the movie is being shot. The peons manage to live with a kind of happiness that has been handed down to them out of time and that has nothing to do with revolutions. Early in the story the point is made that the *pulque* hacienda has not changed, and it is the unchanged life that is most attractive there, not the fruits of the revolution. In her regional stories, the life of her childhood is also preserved unchanged and provides an ironic though tacit comment on the New world. (p. 9)

In *Old Mortality* Miss Porter had woven fiction out of the romantic and realistic elements of her childhood; in *Noon Wine* she achieved one of her finest purely fictional effects in that the material she used was entirely outside the bounds of her own immediate experience, though it was part of the atmosphere of the native land of her heart. But in the group of stories and sketches grouped under the large title **"The Old Order"** in *The Leaning Tower and Other Stories* (1944), she returns to her own home and the personal experiences and impressions she received there. The line between fiction and fact is not always easy to draw among them, but **"The Fig Tree"** and **"The Grave"** seem most story-like of the seven pieces. The only thing that gives the seven pieces unity is that they all deal with the family of Miranda, which is Miss Porter's family in her stories, and the central setting is the grandmother's farm in central Texas. The grandmother is dominant in four of the pieces and important in two others; and the first of the pieces, **"The Source,"** deals only with her and the influence she exerted.

Miss Porter's sense of humor is seldom quiescent; had she been the typical twentieth century rebel, she could have made of the grandmother a figure of fun and condemned her tolerantly as an old tyrant. But like Clarence Day the elder, though she had her foibles, she was still a person to be respected; in **"The Source"** the respect accorded the grandmother approaches reverence.

Such respect is possible only in a society disposed to respect authority, and the grandmother's authority is practically feudal, though she herself would be the last to admit it. Unlike her granddaughter (either Miranda or Katherine Anne) she embodies a strong streak of sentimentality and romanticism. When planning the annual trip to her farm, she imagines herself as walking at leisure among the orchard trees, wearing a straw shepherdess hat, watching the peaches ripen, and tying up vagrant tendrils of honeysuckle. But what she actually wears is a sunbonnet, and what she actually does is to put the sagging society that inhabits her farm back on a sound basis. In her absence things have gone to pot; it is her office to restore cosmos out of the many tendencies toward chaos.

Given this view of her activities, one might make a mythic figure out of the grandmother, but fortunately Miss Porter does not do so; the old lady is merely an old lady with a sense of order and an iron will. On arriving at the farm she immediately sweeps through the house, the yards, the gardens, and past the barns making mental notes of what needs doing. But it is with her human responsibilities, the Negroes on the place, that the most immediate action is called for.

The hidebound segregationist would love Miss Porter's Negroes; they are in their place and presumably satisfied in it. They seem cheerful, they are reasonably improvident, and without their white folks they would revert to savagery. With

names like Littie and Hinry, Dicey, Bumper, and Keg, the Negroes are old-fashioned stereotypes who would not be out of place at Swallow Barn or on the farm of Mark Twain's Uncle John Quarles. Similarly, the activist civil rights worker would despise them as a set of Uncle Toms, dismissing them exactly as he dismissed Huck Finn's good friend Nigger Jim. Both would be wrong; Miss Porter is not making any point with the Negroes she portrays, and one of them, old Nannie, is endowed with more character than most of the white people in the stories. (pp. 10-12)

The second of the **"Old Order"** pieces, **"The Journey,"** begins with a flashback into the grandmother's past, to her early childhood, and ends with her death. (In *The Leaning Tower* its title is **"The Old Order."**) In between is developed her relation with her ex-slave and present companion, old Nannie, with just enough chronological development to sketch a basis for the kind of woman the grandmother came to be. As the piece opens, the reader is informed that the grandmother and Nannie share a passion for cutting out quilt scraps and piecing them together; and while they cut and piece, they reminisce over their long life together. The story has the sort of easy flow and an artistic touch of the disjointed quality that such a conversation would have; Miss Porter doubtless listened to much of this kind of talk when she was a child. (pp. 12-13)

Nannie came into the life of Miss Sophia Jane (described as five years old, spoiled and prissy, and the very caricature of a pre-Civil War child, complete with ringlets and pantalettes) as a nubbly-headed, pot-bellied child of about the same age, with arms and legs like sticks. The little Negro is so interesting as to distract Miss Sophia Jane's attention from the pony her father has brought her, which is to be the first in a long line of her saddle horses named Fiddler. But there was to be only one Nannie, and she, we are told, outwore Miss Sophia Jane.

Beginning as plaything and playmate, after a worming that cures her pot belly, and thriving on good food, Nannie passes through stages of personal maid and black mammy to the children Miss Sophia Jane bears after her marriage, to emancipated slave and voluntary companion. Nannie is also married, at about the time of her mistress's wedding, to another slave; and thenceforth the two women seem in constant competition with their pregnancies. It is in the rearing of children that one episode contributes to the making of the grandmother that is to be.

It was, at least in fiction, standard practice for black mammies to nurse their mistresses' children, but considerably less common for the favor to be reciprocated. Miss Sophia Jane, however, did so, when Nannie was near death from puerperal fever. Her husband pleaded with her that such conduct was improper, and her mother did the same, but Sophia Jane was adamant; she had already begun to develop her basic character, which blended justice, pride, humanity, and simplicity. If she had a weakness, it was a tendency to resent criticism, but her resentment was logically based on her knowledge of her own superiority to those around her. She derived a sensual pleasure from nursing Nannie's child and her own, and thenceforth nursed her own children. (pp. 13-14)

"The Last Leaf" is Uncle Jimbilly's piece; it is the shortest and weakest of the **"Old Order"** pieces, and is weak only because Uncle Jimbilly comes close to being the standard old Negro. His former slavery has left few if any scars on his soul, though his hands are gnarled from years of labor; he works when he feels like it and must be approached politely if he is to work at all. Mostly, in this sketch, he is an appurtenance to an idealized farm-life for children, for Uncle Remus-like, he tells them stories and amuses them. He also probably helps educate them, because the horrendous stories he tells of the tortures inflicted on slaves are faintly embarrassing to the children who hear them, though Uncle Jimbilly freely admits that he never received any such torture himself.

Slight though the sketch is, however, his character is given dimension through contrast; outwardly merely senile and pathetic, with his purplish skull showing through the wisps of greenish-gray hair, he betrays a harmless truculence in talking to the children who listen to his yarns. He is full of vague threats; he annoys easily and is always going to do something terrible to somebody, such as pull out his teeth and make a set of false teeth for Old Man Ronk, the tramp who is suffered to live in an unoccupied Negro cabin. . . . To the children, however, he is no merely comic figure; there is a deliciously vague sense of menace about him and his threats.

Uncle Jimbilly is comic with just a touch of pathos; Nannie, in **"The Last Leaf,"** is dignified and even majestic as she awaits death. The grandmother had said to her when they last parted that this might be their last farewell on earth, and they had embraced and kissed each other's cheeks and promised to meet each other in heaven. After all, they had grown up together, slept together, fought together when very young, and young Miss Sophia Jane had relieved Nannie of all discipline but her own. After the death of the grandmother, the last of her discipline and sense of propriety is lodged in old Nannie.

Nannie is no fat, jolly Aunt Jemima; she is described as thin, tall, a thick, sooty black in color, and with a nobly modeled face that has been worn to the bone. Her white folks have taken her service and devotion for granted over the years; but with the grandmother dead, it becomes apparent that her devotion was to the grandmother personally for the most part, not to her family. She had been glad to be emancipated from slavery but had told her mistress that she would stay with her as long as her mistress wished, and the two could not have got along without each other. But with her mistress dead, her work is done, and she makes preparation to await her own death in comfort.

Moving into a vacant cabin, she furnished it with odds and ends from the big house which her amused white folks are glad to give her. (pp. 15-17)

Now it turns out that Uncle Jimbilly is actually Nannie's husband, though they have ignored each other for years. But with Nannie ensconced in a house of her own, the dim embers of domesticity flare up briefly in Uncle Jimbilly, whose dwelling is a small attic over the smokehouse. When he first sees her, sitting on her steps and smoking her pipe, he ambles over casually and joins her, observing by way of making conversation that she must have a lot of room in her house. But Nannie will have none of him; she has done her work, and she does not intend to pass her last days waiting on any man. And Uncle Jimbilly creeps back to his attic and goes near her no more. (p. 17)

These four pieces provide an incomplete, home-centered mosaic of the childhood of Miranda, and it is through her eyes and memory, presumably, that the picture takes shape, though Miranda herself appears nowhere in the four sketch-

es. The world is dominated by wise old women, and the men who appear, however briefly, are woman-dominated. The children lead a life of freedom and are without much law, except when the grandmother is there to administer it; and they love her, though they are glad to see her go back to town and leave them to themselves. If any deep meaning, other than the goodness of living in a world that is regulated but not too well-regulated, is present, it is well-concealed. The children's penchant for having funerals for deceased small animals indicates no particular preoccupation with death; children in the country who live around animals are early acquainted with death, as they are with mating and with birth. There must have been crises that arose among the children and even among the adults, just as there was an outside world that Miss Porter tells us she was conscious of as a child, but none of these enters into the background world presented in the four sketches. What unpleasantness was there was present only in the reminiscences of the grandmother and of Nannie.

The other three **"Old Order"** pieces are stories, and all deal with some kind of developmental crisis in Miranda. With a minimum of straining, it may be said that Miranda learns something in each of the stories, though in the first it is difficult to say exactly what it is that she learns. At any rate Miranda has an experience in each story, and the three experiences demonstrate the profound truth that experience may be either pleasant or unpleasant. And Miss Porter's wry perception of truth colors them all. (p. 18)

In **"The Fig Tree"** Miranda moves a step or two closer to adult knowledge than she does in **"The Circus,"** and what she learns can be labeled; the facts of death are more firmly established for her at the end of the story.

One central theme of the story revolves around character-contrast. Miranda's grandmother, like the other grownups around her, is incapable of giving a direct answer to a question unless that answer is "No" to a request. Grownups talk around things, not about them. But Great-Aunt Eliza, the grandmother's sister of whom she disapproves in sisterly fashion, is different; she can and will give direct answers when direct answers are possible. Miranda knows that all grownups are not alike, and Great-Aunt Eliza is nice, even if she does dip snuff and smell like snuff and give snuffy gumdrops as bribes to great-nieces to get them out from under foot.

But all this remains to be discovered; as preparations are completed for a trip to Cedar Grove, the farm, Miranda walks in the fig grove near the house, and there she discovers a dead chicken. She is familiar with dead things and identifies them as such by their being motionless. All sorts of things die, including mothers, and Miranda is quite calm about it all; but she does provide funerals for all the dead things she finds, complete with coffin, flowers, and a stone at the head of the grave. Miss Porter arrives at the death theme by means of a process of random association in Miranda's mind: the speech-ways of adults are strange (they won't give direct answers, etc.); they don't always use the right names (her father calls Grandmother "Mama," but Mama is dead); being dead involves dying, and dying happens to everything.

Dead things are motionless and presumably noiseless, so after Miranda has hastily buried the dead chicken, she is horrified to hear a sad little sound like "Weep, weep" that seems to come out of the ground. . . . On hearing the sound, Miranda's immediate conclusion is that she has buried the chicken alive; before she is able to resurrect it, the hurrying family

Porter with Allen Tate in Washington, D.C., 1944. Porter's brief liaison with the married Tate several years earlier had by this time evolved into a deep friendship.

hustles her into the carryall for the trip to Cedar Grove, and her guilt and horror at what she thinks she has done makes her miserable.

But on arriving at Cedar Grove the worry is pushed out of her mind by the conflict between her grandmother and her great-aunt Eliza. Her grandmother is on the fragile side, and is finicky in her ways, insisting that there is only one way to do a thing and no other. Great-Aunt Eliza is mountainous in build and more relaxed in her attitude toward life. One habit she has that is distasteful to the grandmother is dipping snuff in the time-honored country fashion of scooping it out of the brown bottle with the frazzled end of a chewed twig and then rubbing her gums with it. The grandmother also finds distasteful Eliza's hobby of science, which involves among other things clambering up and down a ladder to the chickenhouse roof, where she has had a telescope mounted on a tripod. (pp. 20-2)

To lose security is to lose innocence, and Miranda loses hers when she sees the moon through Great-Aunt Eliza's telescope. It is like another world. Like this one? Miranda asks. And Great-Aunt Eliza replies that nobody knows. The phrase "nobody knows" runs like a tune through Miranda's head; there is an intoxicating joy in this new agnosticism, in the release from her grandmother's certainties.

But there is joy in certainty, too. Returning to the house from Great-Aunt Eliza's observatory, walking through the fig grove, once again Miranda hears the "weep, weep" sound and her forgotten horror returns. But Eliza does know about this phenomenon: it is the sound made by tree frogs, and it means that it is going to rain. And Miranda has not buried a chicken alive; the burden of guilt and horror is taken away. There is joy in learning things; some of the things she will learn eventually will not bring joy, but that is a more complex lesson and will come later. (p. 23)

All of the **"Old Order"** pieces came, in one way or another, out of Miss Porter's memory of her personal life, and the people they deal with are all Porters or the Porters' Negroes. Except for the bare hints given in **"The Grave,"** the surrounding countryside might as well not have existed. But one of the hints in the story is the picture of the old country women who

criticize Miranda's overalls and shirt. . . . The old women are the kind that smoke corncob pipes, and they had treated her grandmother with the utmost respect; at least they knew their place. But now they view the granddaughter askance, peering at her out of their gummy old eyes and conferring their wisdom on her in their uncultured speech, which Miranda hears with a certain *noblesse oblige* that is appropriate to a member of a good family when dealing with the Plain People; she is, as they say she ought to be, ashamed of herself, but not because of her clothes. It is because she knows that it is rude and ill-bred to shock people, even repulsive old crones. All the Plain People are not old crones, of course, but they are the social class that old crones come out of. Given the social sense that Miss Porter had, it is noteworthy that she was able to transcend it and write two stories of the plain people in which the *noblesse oblige* is transmuted into sympathy and understanding.

The first of these, **"He,"** appeared in her first volume, ***Flowering Judas and Other Stories.*** He is the otherwise nameless son of Mr. and Mrs. Whipple, who apparently have no first names; Miss Porter's relentless use of the honorific Mr. and Mrs. when dealing with the poorer whites in her stories serves the same purpose that their use in life did to her grandmother; it helps to maintain a distance, both social and esthetic, but at the same time the small dignity conferred is not grudged, nor is any irony implied. The Whipples do have a certain dignity, though small.

He is an idiot. Mrs. Whipple very possibly hates Him, and it is certain that she wishes He had never been born; but she practices the eleventh commandment, which is to put up the appearance of virtue if one cannot manage the real thing. So she is forever saying that she loves Him more than her two other children put together; she says it frequently around the neighbors, though she says it plenty for the benefit of Mr. Whipple.

Mrs. Whipple maintains the appearance of optimism about all of life, not only her afflicted child. The Whipples are not fortunate people, and Mr. Whipple is always saying that it looks as if their bad luck will not ever let up, but Mrs. Whipple believes in taking what the Lord sends and calling it good. And she maintains that there is a lot more to Him than anybody but her realizes, and she resents any slur cast upon His capacities, whether by Mr. Whipple or a neighbor.

One incident might indicate that part of the bad Whipple luck stems from Mrs. Whipple's desire to keep up appearances, for she insists that a suckling pig be slaughtered for a company dinner when her brother and his family come over one Sunday, while Mr. Whipple complains that that pig would mean three hundred pounds of pork later. But aside from this incident, the fate of the Whipples seems dependent entirely on fortune.

He is blessed with a strong body, however, and for that reason He is sometimes taken advantage of, though there is no pattern of deliberate persecution. He seems not to mind the cold, so when His sister, Emly, has a cold in the head, she gets the extra blanket off His cot. But when He almost has pneumonia during the winter, He gets a blanket from the bed of Mr. and Mrs. Whipple, and His cot is placed by the fire. When He gets His clean clothes dirty, His mother boxes His ears, and then the look on His face hurts her feelings. He helps His father with the farm work, and the family seems to treat Him as much like a normal person as possible. But when He slips on the ice and begins to have fits and His legs swell, the doctor, after doing all he can do for Him, suggests that they have Him put in the County Home for treatment and care. And He will also, incidentally, be off their hands.

Mrs. Whipple objects, saying that they do not begrudge Him anything they give Him, and besides she does not want to take charity. Mr. Whipple says that since he is a taxpayer, it is not exactly charity; and finally Mrs. Whipple is persuaded, though saying that as soon as He is well, they will bring Him home. But they know He will never get better.

And they do not think He knows what goes on anyway, but on the way to the County Home, Mrs. Whipple can see tears in His eyes; He scrubs at the tears, snuffles, and gulps. Mrs. Whipple puts her arms around Him and cries out of a broken heart; she had loved Him all she could, but there were the others of the family who had to be considered, too. There is no way she can make up to Him for His life; it is a pity He was ever born. On this note the story ends. Everybody has done his best, but He was a problem that nobody could solve. The reader may hope that Mrs. Whipple's bright outlook will somehow return; it has seemed to be her natural state and would doubtless be more pleasant to her than the defeated pragmatism of her husband. And it is possible that their luck might change for the better some day. Sometimes luck works that way, and Mrs. Whipple's desire for order and a better life might find a way to help luck along.

People like the Whipples are deserving of sympathy, but no purpose is served in sentimentalizing them. Inherently they are neither virtuous nor vicious, nor are they any more contemptible than any people are when bereft of civilizing influences. If they are deserving of punishment for their failure to produce order and beauty out of their chaotic lives, the lives they lead are punishment enough. (pp. 25-8)

[In] **"Holiday"** the narrator, who has arranged to spend a month as a paying guest of the Müller family, enters into their lives and achieves a kind of intimacy with the family that is duplicated elsewhere only in Miranda's childhood world. The Müllers are represented as living in a German community in Texas near the Louisiana line, complete with *Turnverein* and dominant German folkways. Exactly why Miss Porter placed the community near the Louisiana line, where in fact German settlement was sparse, is not clear; perhaps she felt that the lower half of extreme east Texas was more hurricane-prone than the regions of thicker German settlement, and she does work a storm into the story, though at the wrong season for hurricanes.

The Müller family is patriarchal, in the fine old German fashion, being dominated by Father Müller and his second self, Mother Müller. Married sons have brought their brides to live in their father's house; the daughters who marry bring their husbands there, too. Wives stand behind their husbands at mealtime to wait on them; it is a wife's place to serve her husband. When Hatsy's new husband wishes to help her with some heavy milk pails, he is fiercely rebuked by Mother Müller; handling milk is not a man's business—an attitude she shares completely with Mr. Thompson of *Noon Wine.*

"Holiday" is almost too heavily loaded with the basic elements of life: during the narrator's presumably short stay, there are a wedding, a birth, and a funeral. During that time the season changes from the winter to full-blown spring, and near the end of the story, a hurricane-like storm occurs. All these elements of the story are used as foundations on which to erect a description of the Müller family, who react in their own way to the forces that drive their world.

The sense of family is even stronger among the Müllers than among Miranda's family; the Müllers react as an organism, and the narrator sees it mainly as an organism, of which the center is Father Müller. Father Müller himself is a type of the *Herr*-tyrant, and Mother Müller is a type, too, but each has individual touches. Hatsy is more individual than most of the others, though this may be only because the narrator is thrown with her to a greater extent and has a better chance to see her as a person.

But the only real individual is the crippled Ottilie, whom the narrator does not even recognize as a member of the family until late in the story. Ottilie does most of the cooking, in spite of a kind of palsy that makes her shake continually; she cannot speak; and except for making use of her labor, the family behaves as if she were not there. When it develops that Ottilie is the oldest Müller daughter and that she was a normal child till the crippling disease struck her at the age of five, the reader is apt to wax indignant at the Müllers for using her labor instead of cherishing her as a perpetual invalid; he may already have become indignant at the servile condition accepted and even enjoyed by the Müller women before their husbands. But Miss Porter takes some pains to emphasize that in the society they lived in, the Müllers rightly considered that anyone able to work must work; there were no provisions for coddling invalids.

As always, Miss Porter's pathos is not developed in terms of sentimentality; the reader who feels sorry for Ottilie does so without Miss Porter's aid. Life is to be accepted, and when it is hard, the person living the life must have strength if he is not to be crushed. Meanwhile, throughout, Miss Porter's sense of humor, which though often ironic is never cruel, flashes continually.

Many readers will find the passages of nature-description the most enjoyable parts of the story, and only in this story does Miss Porter include such passages. Noteworthy among them are descriptions of the blooming orchard trees englobed in light from the fireflies and of the eruption of spring following the storm.

Another rare quality in the story is the respectful and affectionate relationship between husbands and wives. The warmth between Annetje and her husband is part of the Müller household; harsh and crabbed as they may seem otherwise, the first thought of Father Müller and Mother Müller is for each other, and when Mother Müller dies, the old man weeps like a child. In the Müller family there is the same sense of discipline and of order that pervades Miranda's family, without any hint that anyone would like to escape from tyranny. None of the Müllers seems to feel that there is anything to escape from.

This probably includes even Ottilie, whom the narrator, on her long holiday, takes for a short holiday while the family attends Mother Müller's funeral. They go for a drive in the new spring, riding in a rickety spring wagon; it is probably the first time anyone has done anything for Ottilie's pleasure since her crippling illness, and she responds to it. She claps her hands for joy and makes yelping sounds that are unmistakably laughter; Ottilie's holiday is a success. But this new joy marks no beginning of a new life for her. For both the narrator and Ottilie are equally the puppets of fate; they have escaped for that one day and will savor the joy while they have it during the lovely, festive afternoon. Ottilie's festive afternoon is the time when her mother is being buried. And there will be plenty of time for her to be taken back, to prepare supper for the returning family. (pp. 34-6)

The world as seen by Miss Porter is essentially normal, in the sense that it can be accepted by a majority of the literate public and even by much of the non-literate public. Some critics have found strong evidence of Christian values in Miss Porter's stories; it is certainly not too much to say that the values they embody are nowhere opposed to Christian values. Such values are perverted in some of her characters, but there is nowhere in her stories the cult of *nada* as developed by Hemingway and others, not even as a straw man to be set up and beaten. In the regional stories, no characters have, as primary interests, the gratification of appetites. When such a character does appear, such as Braggioni in **"Flowering Judas,"** there is nothing admirable about him, though he is not used as a whipping boy either. Such people are phenomena, when they do appear, and are not to be moralized over in any direct way. Only by implied contrast with such characters as the grandmother and Old Nannie, or even with Mr. Helton and the Müller family, do they rate condemnation.

In the contrast of the young with the old, there must be an element of rebellion; otherwise the young would not seem to be young. But both operate within an unspoken code that emphasizes decorum. The children may long for the grandmother's departure so that they may pass their days out from under her thumb, but there is nothing Byronic or ultra-romantic about their longing; and when the escape does come, no passionate production is made of it. The lessons of decorum and order have been learned too well; and even if the center of things is confusing and things are not always what they seem, the problem lies in a person's not being able to order a *plenum,* not in a preconceived despair based on a *nada.* Given reasonable cooperation by Fate, Miss Porter's young people seem to have a good chance of turning out reasonably well, in spite of the reservations of the grandmother and Old Nannie.

Style is the hardest aspect of writing to discuss coherently, unless one wants to indulge in rhetorical studies which would throw up a cloud of pedantic dust to replace the magical haze a good style helps to produce. This is not to say that Miss Porter's style is hazy, but there is magic in the universality of the memories she uses and in the phrases in which she embodies them. Having grown into a tall, cream-colored brunette, Miranda had decided that she would always wear a trailing white satin gown. "Maria, born sensible, had no such illusions. 'We are going to take after Mamma's family,' she said. 'It's no use, we are. We'll never be beautiful, we'll always have freckles. And you,' she told Miranda, 'haven't even a good disposition.' "

One feature of Miss Porter's style is the humor that so often plays just under the surface, leavening whatever other qualities may be present. And one source of humor, in a world that cultivates the mealy mouth and the disposition to call a spade an agricultural implement, is clear vision and forthright language. Plentifully endowed with these qualities herself, Miss Porter builds them into her characters. In **Noon Wine,** as Mr. Thompson goes about his pathetic task of trying to explain to the neighbors how he really is not a murderer, he arrives at the McClellan house. The McClellans are white trash and know it; as Mr. Thompson hesitates in telling his tale, "the two listening faces took on a mean look, a greedy, despising

look, a look that said plain as day, 'My, you must be a purty sorry feller to come round worrying about what we think, we know you wouldn't be here if you had anybody else to turn to—my, I wouldn't lower myself that much, myself.' " For Miss Porter to have told this from the omniscient point of view of the narrator would have deprived it of humor by making it didactic; as it is, the clear vision is assimilated to the character of the McClellans and gives them a brief roundness of character with a sense of humor, mean though their sense of humor is.

But her sense of humor is not always employed in some "significant" way; it is often present for its own sake, and then, perhaps, it is to be most enjoyed. (pp. 37-9)

In her essay on Willa Cather, consciously or unconsciously, she draws two more or less valid parallels with herself. Miss Cather got most of her education at home by reading good literature; so did Miss Porter. And she says, referring to the look of genius which Miss Cather lacked, "Well, Miss Cather looks awfully like somebody's big sister or maiden aunt, both of which she was." By some strange coincidence, the first reaction I ever had to reading Katherine Anne Porter was something like this: "She sounds just like somebody's very intelligent, highly sophisticated maiden aunt who used to live in the country."

Her sense of truth has seldom been challenged, based as it is on what one may hope to be timeless verities; her style is both firm and supple, like a good sword blade, and can stand comparison with that of any other person who has ever written fiction in English. (p. 40)

> *Winfred S. Emmons, in his* Katherine Anne Porter:
> The Regional Stories, *Steck-Vaughn Company,*
> *1967, 43 p.*

JOSEPH WIESENFARTH (essay date 1969)

> [*Wiesenfarth is an American author who has written works on Jane Austen, George Eliot, and Henry James. In the following excerpt, he explores irony in "The Jilting of Granny Weatherall."*]

[In **"The Jilting of Granny Weatherall"**], surface order keeps from awareness the demands of a more radical personal need. . . . (p. 48)

On her deathbed Granny Weatherall's emotional and spiritual well-being is threatened by the revival of her memory of the fiancé who jilted her. George left her at the altar when she was twenty years old, and in her eightieth year Granny is threatened by his appearance. . . . The smoky cloud from hell, the thought of George, threatens to obscure "the bright field where everything was planted so orderly in rows." This image is a minature of the conflict in **"The Jilting of Granny Weatherall."** Which will prevail, the cloud or the orderly bright field—the memory of George or the order that has made life's day bright enough to render one cloud unimportant?

Granny gave order to her life after her jilting. Now in retrospect she praises: it is good to "spread out a plan of life and tuck in the edges orderly." "She had fenced in a hundred acres once, digging the post holes herself and clamping the wires with just a negro boy to help." Even now Granny feels like jumping out of bed, "rolling up her sleeves and putting the whole place to rights again." Granny sees her life as orderly and complete: "Everything came in good time. Nothing left out, left over." She even feels that she has death under control: "She had spent so much time preparing for death there was no need for bringing it up again." Ellen Weatherall is convinced, therefore, even though the "whole bottom dropped out of the world" when she was jilted, that she has "found another [life] a whole world better." (pp. 48-9)

Granny made her new life out of things that compose the worlds of most women: "I had my husband . . . and my children and my house like any other woman." Besides this Granny had her religion: "She had her secret comfortable understanding with a few favorite saints who cleared a straight road to God for her." It is only fitting that Father Connolly should come to her deathbed to minister to her: "the table by the bed had a linen cover and a candle and a crucifix." This reminds Granny of an altar and of the day that she was left at it by George: "What if he did run away and leave me to face the priest by myself?"

Her daughter Cornelia reminds Granny of Hapsy, a daughter whom she seems to love most but who also seems to have caused her most pain. Hapsy also recalls George. Hapsy seems to have been Granny's last child, the "one she had truly wanted." Hapsy becomes confused with Granny's very self: "She had to go a long way back through a great many rooms to find Hapsy standing with a baby on her arm. She seemed to herself to be Hapsy also, and the baby on Hapsy's arm was Hapsy and himself and herself, all at once, and there was no surprise in the meeting." Granny keeps asking for Hapsy. At one time she thinks that Lydia is Hapsy, at another she mistakes Cornelia for Hapsy; altogether she asks for Hapsy on five occasions. But Hapsy never comes. As Granny is dying, presumably in pain, watching the light within her, aware of the priest nearby, Hapsy does not come, just as George did not come under similar circumstances sixty years ago. Disorder breaks through the order of Granny's life; no sign comes to give meaning to the delay of the heavenly bridegroom, who merges with Hapsy (who does not come) and with George (who did not come), and Granny is overwhelmed: "She could not remember any other sorrow because this grief wiped them all away. Oh, no, there's nothing more cruel than this—I'll never forgive it. She stretched herself with a deep breath and blew out the light."

The disorder of Granny's past—inevitably associated with the order of her having been wife, mother, and Catholic—forces itself through the surface order that has been covering it, and Granny's fear of George's return to memory materializes. With the memory of him comes a darkness that prevents her from seeing the order of her life just as previously in her memory the "whirl of dark smoke" covered "the bright field where everything was planted so carefully in orderly rows." Granny, who had so carefully controlled life, cannot control death: "Oh, my dear Lord, do wait a minute. I meant to do something about the Forty Acres, Jimmy doesn't need it and Lydia will later on. . . ." But death will not wait for Granny to put the last shreds of her life in order. She is once again left to face the priest alone. Granny is forced to a final decision: she blows out the light of her life.

One must avoid being simplistically moral and declaring that Granny tried to love God without forgiving the man who jilted her, that she did not heed the command to leave her gift at the altar and make peace with her fellow man before trying to offer it, and that therefore Granny came to the end of her days like one of the foolish virgins without sufficient oil in her lamp to attend the bridegroom's coming. Each of these statements may be partly true, and the imagery of the story may even support such a reading. But one must not read the story so simply, for Granny tried to do what she thought right. Her success was limited because she thought that in being orderly she could be human. She forgot that the order of her life was compelled into being the day she was jilted; she forgot that the jilting was as much a part of her personal existence as the married life and the religion that made up for it; she forgot that the jilting was the source of disorder as well as order; and that the elements of that order—as the structure of the story shows—lead ineluctably to their disorderly source.

In this connection the most telling sentence in **"Granny Weatherall"** is "Beads wouldn't do, it must be something alive." As Granny dies she drops her rosary and grasps the hand of her son. The central fact of Granny's life has been her jilting at age twenty; the remaining sixty years of her life constituted her attempt to reorder life through marriage, rearing a family, and devotion to her religion. But each of these implies for Granny something other than "alive." Like the beads she drops, they constitute a conventional order; but they are really meaningless since they are without a vitalizing human principle. Thus, as her life ends, the fact of her jilting shows itself as her life-source and challenges the conventional order of her existence. Granny finds that all the order she has put into her life has not enabled her to cope with the tragedy of her jilting sixty years before. Here, at the moment of death, she learns that neither marriage, nor children, nor religion suffices to bring her a peace of soul and human wholeness that can reconcile her to the once unfaithful George. At this moment of death a question earlier posed is answered for Granny: "Oh, no, oh, God, there was something else besides the house and the man and the children. Oh surely they were not all? What was it?"

Love was denied Granny the day she was jilted and she herself never again dared to love. But without love Granny's radically human hurt was never healed: "To a woman all reformation, all salvation from any sort or ruin," writes Dostoyevski [in his *Notes from the Underground*], "and all moral renewal is included in love and can only show itself in that form." Granny required a love more human than any order she had created to heal the rankling wound left in her soul by George's infidelity. This need to love could have no approximation in her life. In spite of all that she did and all that she overcame to give her life some meaning, Granny was unsuccessful because she never again dared seek a love as vital as the one she was once cruelly denied. Rather she settled for the safer and seemingly less dangerous way of order. But Granny's life of order, as we have seen, "is rent in sunder by internal oppositions."

"The Jilting of Granny Weatherall," then, is not a moral tale about forgiveness, a gospel parable in modern dress. We are not asked in this story to face with a shudder the damnation of an octogenarian. The next world enters the story to give meaning to this world. The boundary situation is here for the sake of the land of the living, not of the dead. We are directed to look at Granny Weatherall and to realize what she—trapped by the inability to understand the paradox of order—cannot: that in spite of showing great courage, that in spite of pushing against the stone of her jilting, that in spite of doing more than many another person might have done in similar circumstances, she has lived a less than truly satisfying life. We are asked to see that the problem of existence has been vexing and difficult for Granny and that she has not satisfactorily solved it. In short, we are asked to see in **"The Jilting of Granny Weatherall"** that to weather all is not necessarily to live—to see that beads alone will never do, that there "must [always] be something alive." (pp. 51-4)

Joseph Wiesenfarth, "Internal Opposition in Porter's 'Granny Weatherall,'" in Critique: Studies in Modern Fiction, *Vol. XI, No. 2, 1969, pp. 47-55.*

JAN PINKERTON (essay date 1970)

[*In the following excerpt, Pinkerton discusses Porter's treatment of black and white relationships in Southern families, finding an awareness of the era's injustices in such stories as "The Last Leaf" and "The Journey."*]

The stories which Katherine Anne Porter grouped under the title **"The Old Order"** [in her *Collected Stories*] are usually considered attempts on her part to understand the interrelationship of her past and present worlds—and this, to be sure, is their principal theme. Critical discussion has not focused, however, on another aspect of these stories: the author's portrayal of the relationship between blacks and whites in her Southern family. Clearly presented is the bitterness she saw even in the most "favored" and "faithful" of black servants; under the surface of a genteel and seemingly harmonious turn-of-the-century Southern family, she gives glimpses of the apparently docile black's recognition of his long-standing injustices and of his desire for compensation. The compensation he desires disturbs no social order, but at least it affords mental satisfaction to the man who is fully aware, beyond most white understanding at that time, that he has been and remains the victim of injustice.

The brief story **"The Witness"** deals most obviously with this theme. Uncle Jimbilly, once a slave and now a servant, is conscious of the unjust treatment dealt his race and has found a number of personal compensations that offer no threat to "the old order" but yet clearly serve to balance a mental scoresheet. He is, for one thing, a teller of tales to the children of the family—horror tales of the whippings and brutalities of slavery times.

Uncle Jimbilly's descriptions, even to the youngest of ears, are unsparing:

Dey used to take 'em out and tie 'em down and whup 'em . . . wid gret big leather strops inch thick long as yo' ahm, wid round holes bored in 'em so's evey time dey hit 'em de hide and de meat done come off dey bones in little round chunks . . . Dey spread dry cawn-shucks on dey backs and set 'em afire and pahched 'em, and den dey poured vinega all ovah 'em.

Of course they died, he responds to the children's question: "dey died . . . by de thousands and tens upon thousands." Uncle Jimbilly, obviously, obtains satisfaction from the reaction of his young audience; they "listened with faint tinglings of embarrassment" and "wriggled a little and felt guilty." Yet his stories, complete with their numerical exaggerations, must be told only to children, not to adults; Uncle Jimbilly knows who his audience must be. He understands, in other words, the boundaries within which he can express his bitterness and soothe his sense of injustice.

Moreover, the old man asserts his independence within acknowledged boundaries in a number of other ways. He has

worked hard all his life, but it is understood that he does his work "just as he pleased and when he pleased"; the ex-slave must be treated gingerly. He is, to the children, irritable and easily annoyed, and they have to be careful when they ask favors of him.

Uncle Jimbilly has a habit of making threats—exorbitant threats, and therefore not to be taken seriously—yet again revealing his attempts at mentally balancing old scores:

He was always going to do something quite horrible to somebody and then he was going to dispose of the remains in a revolting manner. He was going to skin somebody alive and nail the hide on the barn door, or he was just getting ready to cut off somebody's ears with a hatchet and put them on Bongo, the crop-eared brindle dog.

These descriptions, too, are unsparing. But to what other whites, except to this group of responsive children, can he reveal his bitterness and yet stay within the limits of the socially acceptable? It is in the form, then, of guilt-producing stories, of a general irascibility and of fearful if meaningless threats, that the turn-of-the-century black servant compensates for his sufferings and for those of his people. (pp. 315-16)

Uncle Jimbilly . . . is bitter—and to a degree undoubtedly beyond what the whites, to whom he is a favored servant, could ever understand. Also bitter—although also favored by whites—is Nannie, Jimbilly's wife and the lifelong companion to the children's grandmother. Nannie, too, despite the harmony of her relationship with the grandmother, has a strong sense of the injustice under which she has lived. In the story **"The Journey"** we are told of her reaction to the freeing of the slaves: "Emancipation was a sweet word to her. It had not changed her way of living in a single particular . . . Still, Emancipation had seemed to set right a wrong that stuck in her heart like a thorn." (p. 316)

[Like Uncle Jimbilly, Nannie] finds her own personal device for compensation—again within the framework of the socially acceptable, yet entailing on her part a more dramatic act of defiance. The grandmother dies, and yet Nannie, now herself quite old, continues her life of hard work; as is related in another story, **"The Last Leaf,"** the children did not realize till much later the extent to which they were taking her for granted: "Years afterward, Maria, the elder girl, thought with a pang they had not really been so very nice to Aunt Nannie. They went on depending upon her as they always had, letting her assume more burdens and more, allowing her to work harder than she should have."

When a cabin on the property becomes vacant, Nannie announces that she wishes to move in: "She wanted a house of her own, she said; in her whole life she never had a place of her very own." The children are astonished; they had never realized that she, the favored companion, had wishes of her own, had desires independent of the desires of the family. It is, they realize, a rebuke to them. . . . (pp. 316-17)

This chastening, in other words, is another form of the compensation Uncle Jimbilly found in making them feel guilty about slavery. Nannie, like Uncle Jimbilly in his story-telling, was disturbing no social order; as an elderly, faithful servant she had a socially recognized right to this "reward" of retirement.

What the author makes clear, however, is her independent, seemingly defiant attitude. . . .

She, like Uncle Jimbilly, is fully aware that the score has never been even, and she is now going to get what satisfaction she can out of the system that had long perpetrated injustice upon her.

Here, then, is another facet of Katherine Anne Porter's sensitivity to issues that, while intensely personal, are yet ultimately "social" in import. Even in these stories in which her main theme is a wish to understand her own past—"the old order" into which she was born—she shows at the same time an understanding of the bitterness behind seemingly "harmonious" black-white relationships. Long before the current spotlight of sociology was focused on the South, she had in her most personal way shown nuances in social inequality that many Americans are still far from comprehending. (p. 317)

Jan Pinkerton, "Katherine Anne Porter's Portrayal of Black Resentment," in University Review, *Vol. XXXVI, No. 4, June, 1970, pp. 315-17.*

JOSEPH WIESENFARTH (essay date 1973)

[*In the following excerpt, Wiesenfarth analyzes the incipient disorder of Porter's fictional world, noting her practice of depicting individual dilemmas that evoke universal problems.*]

Taken collectively, as a record of her attempt to understand, Katherine Anne Porter's stories project a disordered world in which conflict is generated in lives where self-knowledge and love have failed to find their place. If individual men and women fail, how can those collocations of men and women we call nations succeed? With a classically hard-headed sense of human frailty, Porter insists that many cannot succeed where two or three have failed. To diagnose the "cause of human ills," then, she goes straight to the individual to test his self-knowledge and his love.

"I have not much interest in anyone's personal history after the tenth year," Porter writes, "not even my own. Whatever one was going to be was all prepared for before that." Her story **"The Downward Path to Wisdom"** is a gloss on this remark. It tells how a child of kindergarten age, Stephen, becomes "badly mixed up in his mind." It opens one morning with Stephen eating peanuts in his parents' bedroom.

> "Bright-looking specimen, isn't he?" asked Papa, stretching his long legs and reaching for his bathrobe. "I suppose you'll say it's my fault he's dumb as an ox."
>
> "He's my little baby, my only baby," said Mama richly, hugging him, "and he's a dear lamb." His neck and shoulders were quite boneless in her firm embrace. He stopped chewing long enough to receive a kiss on his crumby chin. "He's sweet as clover," said Mama. The baby went on chewing.
>
> "Look at him staring like an owl," said Papa.
>
> Mama said, "He's an angel and I'll never get used to having him."
>
> "We'd be better off if we never *had* had him," said Papa.

To the father the retarded child is a bird or a beast, an owl or an ox; to the mother he is more politely inhuman: he is a lamb, he is clover, he is an angel. In the narrator's words, Stephen with his parents is "like a bear cub in a warm litter."

Porter in College Park, Maryland, on her eighty-fifth birthday.

To his parents the child is never a person and consequently to the observer his parents are less than human. (pp. 85-6)

This story, told from a child's point of view, is anything but childish. It is an account of civilized disorder in a respectable middle-class family. The child, like everyone else in the story, can gain no self-understanding within the context of the family. Moreover, Stephen's world of needs is as foreign to his elders as theirs of codes is to him, and they use the child's unwitting mistakes to fight maliciously with each other. . . . The child who is presumed retarded is the natural symbol of the truly retarded grownups. Given enough people like those who surround Stephen and martyr him, hating themselves without knowing it, the world would be entitled to its measure of terrible confusion and awful failure. Certainly this is Porter's logic in **"The Downward Path to Wisdom."** (p. 87)

If Stephen's story is that of a child in search of himself—of his attempt to find his "I" as Stephen rather than as "Baby" or "Fellow" or "Bad Boy"—the short novel **Noon Wine** is the story of a man without any personal identity or desire for self-knowledge. It is the story of a man making every attempt to live an orderly life without ever learning that order must emanate from within.

When the strange and quiet Olaf Helton appears one day on his run-down farm, Mr. Royal Earle Thompson takes him on as a hired man. Through the industry of Helton over a period of nine years the farm is put on a paying basis and the lives of Thompson, his wife and two sons are set in a semblance of order. With Helton on the farm, Thompson is able to achieve that measure of social prestige that alone has attracted him. One day, however, his idyll comes to an end with the arrival of Homer T. Hatch, a bounty hunter, who reports that Helton is an escaped lunatic. In a foray, during which Helton's life seems endangered by Hatch, Thompson's lawyer has the weak-eyed Mrs. Thompson lie for her husband by saying that she witnessed the whole incident. This causes Ellie to suspect her husband of murder, and Thompson himself, with qualms about his courtroom conduct, attempts to convince each of his neighbors of his innocence by having his wife repeat her lie to each of them singly. But all is to no avail. Neither Thompson's wife nor his sons nor any of his neighbors sees him as anything but a murderer. Thus this man who lived on the good opinion of others really died the moment he killed Hatch. His suicide merely certifies the death of the *persona* which he had substituted for the self he never knew.

In this story Mr. Thompson only knows the importance of appearance. "All his carefully limited fields of activity were related somehow to Mr. Thompson's feeling for the appearance of things, his own appearance in the sight of God and man. 'It don't *look* right,' was his final reason for not doing anything he did not wish to do." The collapse of the appearance of 'looking right' is his death. The complete inadequacy of Thompson is pictured in the run-down condition of the farm at the beginning of the novel and the disintegration of his family life at the end. Into this disordered existence comes Mr. Helton, whom the Thompsons think queer because he is not like them; that is, he is a person in his own right. But it is Helton, the benign lunatic, who sets the farm in order and even effects a temporary familial harmony by way of his own orderly life. And at the end of each day he reaffirms the new order by his ritual playing of the same song on one of his harmonicas. The story confronts one, then, with the extraordinary irony of an insane man creating order among sane people and reminding the sane people of this order through the symbolic order of his music. The irony is compounded when Hatch, a servant of society, arrives and announces: "Fact is, I'm for law and order, I don't like to see lawbreakers and loonatics at large." Here a servant of the society from which Mr. Thompson exacts life-giving respect comes in the name of law and order to destroy order and to return the Thompsons' life to worse than pre-Heltonian chaos.

Noon Wine, then, is the dramatization of the life of a man without any form of self-reliance based on self-knowledge and, consequently, without any ability to set up a meaningful mode of existence to sustain himself and his family. The source of his failure within the limits of the story is in the lie he lives—in the *persona* which cannot cope with the reality of evil in the person of Hatch, who contests Thompson's mediocrity for the possession of a good in the person of Helton.

Other stories of Katherine Anne Porter explore both of the dimensions that *Noon Wine* dramatizes: first, law and order as a substitute for personal and real order; second, life as impoverished by a failure of truth and love. "Magic" and "Theft," respectively, capture these themes in their essence. "Magic" is a story in which a human being is valuable only as a commodity. It tells simply of a madam who through magic secures the return of a dismissed prostitute when her clientele becomes disorderly because of the absence of the popular Ninette. The girl's return reestablishes social tranquility. Even the police are pleased. Here in a story Kafkalike in its savagery the profoundest human disorders are masked by the order of a brothel. Love becomes lust and freedom becomes servitude in a situation where disorder wears the costume of order. The point that Porter makes is that a society which proceeds without a recognition of the dignity of the human person and of his responsibility to a meaningful love has as its analogue the whirligig order of a brothel.

The savagery of "Magic" is balanced by the pathos of "Theft." Here a woman of perhaps early middle-age has her gold purse stolen by her janitress. All the woman has allowed herself to miss—especially the love of the man who gave her the purse—comes vividly to mind. The woman finds that anyone who steals her purse steals trash, because, basing her life on a vague general faith, she has been the thief of her own happiness. The purse calls from her memory the unpleasant ghosts of missed opportunities and innumerable losses, and her life converges in a pathetic epiphany that leaves her, in the last sentence, staring into a cup of cold coffee that she has substituted for the wine of life.

The failure of Ninette in "Magic" and the woman in "Theft" is the disordering failure of human love. The one is forced to accept the imposed order of love as lust, the other must see in her gold purse the poverty of her existence. Life without love in these two stories is revealed mainly as endurance, and endurance itself is an inadequate answer for human life.

This inadequacy of endurance divorced from love is realized in stories like "He" and "A Day's Work," in which the demands for social recognition and religious devotion are used by Mrs. Whipple and Mrs. Halloran as substitutes for self-knowledge and love of another. The one seeks to fulfill herself by having her neighbors recognize the extent to which she has sacrificed herself to care for her idiot son, and the other attempts to enforce Christian virtue on her husband by way of Catholic observance without liking him at all. "He" ends with Mrs. Whipple learning that her child, though simple, has feelings which are deep and that her loudly professed love for him has hidden a secret death-wish which her neighbors clearly understand: "His head rolled on her shoulder: she had loved Him as much as she possibly could, there were Adna and Emly who had to be thought of too, there was nothing she could do to make up to Him for His life. Oh, what a mortal pity He was ever born. They came in sight of the hospital, with the neighbor driving very fast, not daring to look behind him." "A Day's Work" ends with Lacey Halloran beating her helpless husband with a knotted wet towel because, among other things, he drinks and filches change from her hoard and habitually walks through their flat in sock feet. One thinks of Porter's remark on Thomas Hardy's Angel Clare in Lucy Halloran's case: "His failure to understand the real nature of Christianity makes a monster of him at the great crisis of his life." (pp. 87-90)

Given the fragility of human existence as Porter has written of it, how does one learn the nature of love and seek spiritual rebirth? One has to reverse the processes seen in the stories discussed. Passion, sexual or otherwise, must be admitted and consciously dealt with. Order must be created realistically from within rather than imposed from without. Self-righteousness must be avoided. And things must take a place secondary to human relationships. In "The Cracked Looking-Glass." Rosaleen tries to order her life by dreams because her marriage to Dennis, twenty-five years her senior, is painful to her. Yet all her dreams prove lies. There are she and Dennis and no one else. The cracked-looking glass is a mirror of their marriage, not a distortion of her beauty. Dennis, not "The Lover King," must be the object of her love. She must admit these things and accept them and she finally does when their truth is forced upon her mind. She then breaks the pattern of her life, refuses to believe in dreams and in romantic love, and takes Dennis to herself: "She sat up and felt his sleeves carefully. 'I want you to wrap up warm this bitter weather, Dennis,' she told him. 'With two pairs of socks and the chest protector, for if anything happened to you, whatever would become of me in this world?' " Rosaleen has done what Porter in "St. Augustine and the Bullfight" describes as converting an adventure into an experience. "Adventure is something you seek for pleasure, or even for profit, like a gold rush or invading a country; for the illusion of being more alive than ordinarily, the thing you will to occur; but experience is what really happens to you in the long run; the truth that finally overtakes you." Rosaleen seeks adventure in New York at the movies and in Boston with Hugh Sullivan and even near home with Guy Richards, but Rosaleen discovers her real life must be with Dennis. She draws on her adventures to find her experience, and faithful to him she breaks the pattern of illusion that has put the crack in the looking-glass that symbolized their marriage. (pp. 92-3)

[The] astringent and subtle art of truth which Porter practices so relentlessly is a certain sign of hope in human life. One who does not want another to see does not for half a century hold up a mirror to his nature. Katherine Anne Porter's stories show man how and why he is spiritually blind and how and why he hates and they show with as much intensity, if more rarely, how and why he can be reborn and love again. Her stories are the shape of existence, fiction that is truth, art that is life. They are stories that live by faith in the man whose illness they diagnose. As such, they will endure. (p. 94)

Joseph Wiesenfarth, "Negatives of Hope: A Reading of Katherine Anne Porter," in Renascence, *Vol. XXV, No. 2, Winter, 1973, pp. 85-94.*

BARBARA HARRELL CARSON (essay date 1977)

[*In the following excerpt, Carson examines feminist stances assumed by many of Porter's fictional women and evidenced in their unwillingness to adopt assigned social roles.*]

In Katherine Anne Porter's *Old Mortality,* Miranda Rhea watches her uncle's horse, Miss Lucy, win a race in a hundred-to-one long shot. Seeing the animal's bleeding nose, her wild eyes and trembling knees, Miranda thinks in anguish, "That was winning, too." In many ways, the painful victory of the old mare (including the odds against it) epitomizes the victories of the human females in Porter's Miranda stories. For them, too, triumph and defeat are virtually indistinguishable. As if to underline the significance of the metaphorical race, Porter often presents her women on horseback, galloping for all they are worth toward Mexico or away from death or just around the farm, to convince themselves of their undiminished vigor. But whether they are involved only in symbolic contests or in literal races as well, her women—Miranda, Miranda's Grandmother (Sophia Jane Rhea), her Aunt Amy, her cousin Eva, and even, in her own way, the Grandmother's old servant, Nannie—all, with varying degrees of awareness, seek the same prize. We would call it, in the worn phraseology of our day, a valid selfhood. Porter herself speaks of it as entry "into . . . an honest life." If the words are vague, the concept is not. At its center are the recognition and use of one's own powers and abilities even in the face of custom, the discovery of truth for oneself (including the truth of one's own desires), and the strength to face that

truth and act from that basis. It is, in short, the creation of an essence for oneself through self-initiated actions, rather than the passive acceptance of a role assigned by others.

Porter deals with the struggle for literal self-possession by the women of the Rhea family in nine stories: the seven sketches gathered under the title **"The Old Order"** in *The Collected Stories* and the two longer works, *Old Mortality* and *Pale Horse, Pale Rider.* Although the stories (except for *Pale Horse, Pale Rider*) are set in the South, the problems faced by these women apply beyond these geographical limits. The region that had, with such a hyperbole of lofty sentiments, elevated woman to a pedestal, convinced her of her own sacredness, and walled her in a crinoline prison, offered to the writer a perfect crucible for the study of what happens in general when the lady decides to abdicate her throne—or at least gets the feeling that it is not, after all, a very comfortable seat.

The black servant Nannie did not, of course, occupy the feminine pedestal (although as "Mammy" she did share in the "matriarchal tyranny" exercised by the Grandmother). Nevertheless, she is important to Porter's treatment of women for several reasons. For one, Nannie suggests Porter's view of woman's true condition. Although different in complexion and status, the other women in the Miranda stories are, at least at some time in their lives, as surely bound as Nannie to their society, to tradition, and to family. Porter makes Nannie's symbolic role explicit when she emphasizes that the slave Nannie and Miss Sophia Jane had been "married off" within days of each other—the passivity implied is chilling—and had started simultaneously "their grim and terrible race of procreation." (pp. 239-40)

However, Nannie does not serve Porter merely as a symbol. A realistic character in her own right, she is also a woman who manages to break her bonds and assert her honest self. In **"The Last Leaf,"** the Grandmother dead, Nannie leaves the family she has served all her life, retreats to a cabin in the woods, takes off her neat servant's cap [and] dons the kerchief of her ancestral tribe. . . . Her final rejection of servitude and sacrifice takes place when Uncle Jimbilly, the husband whom she had long ago stopped living with, hints that he would like to share her cabin with her. She tells him pointedly, " 'I don' aim to pass my las' days waitin on no man. . . . I've served my time, I've done my do, and dat's all.' "

But Nannie's spirited self-emancipation is not unequivocal. Her coming to her "honest self" is late; it is limited; and even in her total emotional self-sufficiency there is great irony. Others had always meant burdens for Nannie; now in rejecting those externally imposed burdens she rejects, too, their sources. She does not care, we are told, whether her children loved her or not; she wants only to be alone; she "wasn't afraid of anything." She is left finally only with herself. This reduction to the core of self—this recognition of one's ability to survive alone and of the validity of one's own desires—is a good starting point (it is the one Miranda discovers in *Pale Horse, Pale Rider*). But as a conclusion it is nihilistic, grim in its lack of connection with others, barren of emotions and of productivity. All Nannie has left to look forward to is restful night, both the immediate and the final one.

Death as liberator—perhaps the only one for those who can fight things as they are on no other terms—is also a theme in *Old Mortality* in the story of Amy Rhea Breaux. Owner of the original mare Miss Lucy (of which Miranda's bleeding winner is, significantly, only one in a long line of avatars),

Amy has been dead over a decade at the beginning of *Old Mortality.* In life she had been the victim of the weakness of her strengths. Had she been less perceptive she would, no doubt, have been happy as the belle of her day; had she been more perceptive she would have known what to do about her unhappiness. As it was, she sensed the emptiness of her life, but she had neither the understanding to define clearly what troubled her, the vision to see how she could successfully oppose it, nor the will or ability to effect that opposition, except fitfully. She cried out, " 'Mammy, I'm so sick of this world. I don't like anything in it. It's so *dull* . . .' " But she possessed only the tools of the coquette to fight that dullness with. . . . Only once did her rejection of her empty life reach a serious level. After her brother Harry shot a man to save her "honor," she galloped off with him to the Mexican border in the one great self-willed horse ride of her life. But Amy had not had the strength to sustain her defiance. Passivity soon replaced action, literally and psychologically. She returned home in a state of collapse, nearly immobilized, unable even to dismount by herself.

Although Amy was unaware of it, a good part of what she struggled against so vainly and inarticulately was represented in the brotherly defense that occasioned her ride. Her great enemy was the monolithic family, the family as viceroy of society and tradition, which determines how the individual will act and which, indeed, squeezes individuality out and makes the person (and particularly the woman—Harry could, after all, ride to Mexico with impunity) just a unit expressing the larger whole. (pp. 240-42)

Years later, her cousin Eva reminisced bitterly of Amy: " 'She rode too hard, and she danced too freely, and she talked too much. . . . I don't mean she was loud or vulgar, she wasn't, but she was *too free.*' " The truth, of course, is just the opposite: Amy had not been free at all, except in things that mattered little. Finally, unwilling to live on other people's terms and unequipped to alter the emptiness of her existence, she chose simply to make that emptiness final. There is little question that her death from an overdose of drugs was suicide. Only in taking her life could she condemn the life she had been meted. (p. 243)

Forgetting Amy's rebellion, her cries of boredom, the hints of a suicide motivated by a deep dissatisfaction with their kind of life, the family transformed her in their memories into the ideal belle. But there is more here. The family was involved in an ancient protective ritual. Like primitive people who worship what they fear and so regulate its powers, Amy's family reasserted its control over the woman who challenged it, by declaring her an "angel." They negated what her life and death really meant by worshiping what they said she stood for. By mythologizing her, they restored the woman to her "proper" place. (pp. 243-44)

In Nannie, Amy, and Eva, Porter presents the terms of woman's fight for an independent and honest life. The opponents she faces are delineated: family, tradition, her own vacillation between desire for independence and need for others, her lack of preparation—philosophical, psychological, and practical—for establishing any relationship with others except the traditional ones requiring sacrifice of her own selfhood. The usual outcome of the fight has also been adumbrated: the emotional negativism, the defeat, the pain, and the delusion that are involved in even the smallest victories. These themes are repeated and elaborated in the stories about the Grandmother and Miranda.

In their youths both of these women suffered from what Simone de Beauvoir in *The Second Sex* has called being made other than self. Family, society, romantic mythology (including, for the Grandmother, the idealistic literature she was brought up on, and, for Miranda, the idealization of Amy)—all conspire to shape their attitudes, goals, and actions. But both Sophia Jane and Miranda manage somehow to preserve a secret self, an area of honesty within. For both women the process of moving toward an authentic life is one of unmasking that secret self and acting on the basis of inner rather than external motivations.

The double life from which the Grandmother emerged is described, largely in flashbacks, in the first two stories of **"The Old Order."** As a young girl, she appeared to be the belle of Southern stereotypes, "gay and sweet and decorous, full of vanity and incredibly exalted daydreams . . ." But in the rest of this sentence, in the rhetorical irony so typical of her, Porter reveals the hidden side of Sophia Jane. Those "incredibly exalted daydreams . . . threatened now and again to cast her over the edge of some mysterious frenzy." Dreams of loss of her virginity, envy of "the delicious, the free, the wonderful, the mysterious and terrible life of men," visions of the "manly indulgences" of her "wild" cousin—and future husband—Stephen: all these had filled her thoughts, giving evidence of her sense of the inadequacies of her life and offering compensations for its dullness. (p. 245)

Her marriage to the dashing cousin had been, no doubt, motivated at least in part by the hope that it would grant access to the mysterious, exciting world that seemed to be his. Instead, marriage had revealed that the "wild" Stephen was spineless and self-indulgent, having neither ambition nor adhesiveness. Sophia Jane's true character began to develop as she tried to change his, her strength growing, for the most part secretly, in proportion to his weakness. To compensate for the sensual pleasure denied her in her marriage bed, she had begun, with her fourth child, to nurse her own children (and when Nannie was sick, her black foster child, too) in defiance of custom and her shocked husband and mother.

Yet except for this one overtly defiant act, Sophia Jane seems, on the whole, to have accepted the passive role in marriage. Even while despising her husband, she had been ruled by him. In fact, this must have been at least a partial cause for her hatred: her being forced by the conventions of marriage to submit to his decisions, while recognizing her own superiority. Many critics have pointed out the failure of love in Porter's women, overlooking the very good reasons for that failure. How can real love exist between people who know each other only by their false, public masks? How can a woman love when she is on all sides being forced to sacrifice that honest self from which, alone, love can come? How can she love when according to her training, love, for a woman, means exactly that sacrifice? (p. 246)

However, just as the Grandmother's symbolic counterpart, the literally enslaved Nannie, won one type of emancipation during the war, so, after her fashion, did Sophia Jane. She found herself in one of those "epochs of social disintegration" during which, according to de Beauvoir, "woman is set free." It was in the war that Sophia Jane's husband received the wound from which he would afterwards die, allowing her "finally [to] emerge into something like an honest life. . . ." Then "with all the responsibilities of a man but with none of the privileges," she had made her secret self (assertive, willful, self-conscious in the basic sense of the term) her public self. She took charge not only of her own existence, but of all her family, both black and white. Her sense of responsibility extended finally to the fate of Nannie's soul and the color of the children born in the black quarters. And it is precisely this assumption of responsibility that indicates the true measure of the Grandmother's triumph. To take, by an act of will, the burden of one's world on one's own shoulders, to create obligations for oneself—that is the mark of the traditional hero. It is also the mark of the authentic self, which can be defined only in process, never in stasis.

Porter continually emphasizes the importance of action in the Grandmother's new life. Before her husband's death, her contact with the world of decision-making, planning, working—outside of her genteel wifely labors at home—had come only in her daydreams and in her usually unspoken criticism of her husband's failures in these areas. As a widow, however, she had set out for Louisiana with her nine children, repaired a house, planted an orchard, sold the house, moved on to Texas, built a house, had the fields fenced and crops planted, all the while driving herself as she drove her children and servants and horses.

But if she had achieved much, she had also suffered and lost a great deal. Independence had come to her only in what seemed an utter life-or-death dilemma. In such extremities, the one involved can scarcely appreciate the victory that results. For the hero the triumph is often only grim and ugly toil. For the Grandmother it meant realizing that she had driven her children too hard and fed them too little. It meant that her very strength had hardened her to enable her to endure: "griefs never again lasted with her so long as they had before." And it had meant weakening her children, probably because, feeling guilty about her own strength, she had begun to vacillate between firmness and indulgence, spoiling particularly her sons and making them unfit for effective living.

Nevertheless, the action to which she had been freed continued to characterize her life. Even in old age, when the reader first sees her, she cannot rest from her habit of doing. **"The Source,"** a description of her yearly visit to the family farm, is dominated by the whirlwind of her activity: the flurry surrounding her arrival, her brisk supervisory walk through the house and yards, the uproar created by the soapmaking and washing and painting and dusting and sewing under her direction. (pp. 246-48)

"The Journey" (originally called **"The Old Order"**) . . . deals with the Grandmother's retreat, in her last years, from significant action into a romantic evasion of reality. Even though the story makes clear that the Grandmother keeps busy literally until the day of her death (when she is working on moving a fifty-foot adobe wall), its imagistic emphasis is on lack of action. This apparent contradiction is resolved if one sees the imagery of stasis as underscoring the philosophical and psychological change that has taken place in the Grandmother in her old age. Her real passivity now lies in accepting the values and beliefs of the order she once chafed under. She and Nannie sit fingering the "material" of the past; making patchwork quilts of it; "gilding" each piece (with edgings of lemon-colored thread and linings of yellow silk); covering heirlooms with velvet and removing them—as she has, in effect, removed herself—from useful life. In reordering the past (or "carefully disordering" it, as she does the pieces in the quilts), the Grandmother idealizes it in spite of its bitterness, dreaming of a cessation of change and a return to the old ways. She overlooks her own life of hard work

and censures her new daughter-in-law for "unsexing herself." (Porter suggests the daughter-in-law's participation in the race for integrity—the Grandmother describes her as "self-possessed"—by noting that her idea of a perfect honeymoon would have been riding on a cattle roundup.) She was, the Grandmother decides, "altogether too Western, too modern, something like the 'new' woman who was beginning to run wild, asking for the vote, leaving her home and going out in the world to earn her own living . . ."

How can we account for the Grandmother's forgetting the price of her own liberation and reverting to the prison of custom? The guilt the Grandmother felt toward her sons, with its suggestion of her early ambivalence concerning her strength, could itself have forced her back into the solace of traditional life patterns. Here at least there would be authority to blame if things went wrong; the other way, there was only self. Or maybe the Grandmother's reversion is more simply explained. Perhaps it is merely that freedom for women, in her time, could come only in moments of cultural chaos. When the talents that enabled her to survive and flourish were no longer so much in demand, after the reestablishment of the *status quo ante bellum,* society itself could have reclaimed her simply by no longer offering arenas for the exercise of her selfhood.

Whatever the reasons, by the time of **"The Journey"** she has fallen back upon a belief in "authority," and in "the utter rightness and justice of the basic laws of human existence, founded as they were on God's plans . . ." So the cycle has come round full. The Grandmother, who, with Nannie, had wished that "a series of changes might bring them, blessedly, back full-circle to the old ways they had known" has, as in fairy tales, been granted the wish unwittingly asked for. She has returned to her original dichotomized psychological state; she is once again playing a role; her secret self is once more hidden by the mask of her public face. It is as if Porter is suggesting that liberation is a non-transferable commodity and must be won anew by each individual.

But Porter's point is not so simple as that, for in sacrificing her real self—with its doubts, hesitancies, and social heresies—the Grandmother does give something of value to the next generation. We are told that the children "loved their Grandmother; she was the only reality to them in a world that seemed otherwise without fixed authority or refuge . . ." Porter's irony in all this is multi-layered, quite properly posing more questions than it answers. Must the freed woman of one generation inevitably become the oppressor of the next? Can order be established only at the expense of freedom? Is one—order or freedom—more valuable than the other? Or do they always exist in a dynamic relationship, one rising cyclically from the other? It is surely the Grandmother's very role as defender of order that, at least in part, makes possible Miranda's fight for freedom, by giving her a strong adversary to exercise her selfhood against. (pp. 248-50)

A major part of what Miranda has to fight against in her attempts to save her "individual soul" is the romantic vision of reality represented by the Grandmother's mythology and perpetuated by all of her family. This is the problem she faces in *Old Mortality.* Here Miranda finds previous generations' versions of reality contradicted on all sides by the evidence offered by her own senses. . . . But even as Miranda frets about the family's habit of making their own past into "love stories against a bright blank heavenly blue sky," she is beginning to gild her life in the same way. She speaks with her sister Maria of being "immured" in their convent school, because "it gave a romantic glint to what was otherwise a very dull life for them . . ." Already her chances of discovering reality, exterior and interior, are threatened.

The problem reaches its climax in the final section of *Old Mortality,* where Miranda, now eighteen and a year married, is confronted with two versions of the Amy story. As devil's advocate, she voices the family's romantic legend, while Cousin Eva Parrington gives the sordid, "Freudian," and ostensibly more realistic side. It is to Miranda's credit that she sees that Eva's tale is as romantic in its own way as the family's version. This awareness leaves her, however, with little certainty about what the truth really is. . . . Miranda will never be able to escape the past completely. But there is strength in it as surely as there is weakness. From it had come the essentially Existentialist precept behind her question about life, the idea that life is a process defined by actions directed toward a goal. If she works from this premise given her by the past, while still acting, as she resolves here, from the basis of her own will and her own vision of reality, Miranda will be able to establish an authentic selfhood and avoid passively accepting a role or a view of reality created by others. She will, in Existentialist terms, become subject rather than object, and if she can sustain this identity derived from willed action, she will find all the freedom possible to her in this world.

At the end of *Old Mortality,* Miranda's plans are vague, but she has at least decided to stop being like her Shakespearean namesake, watching in awe the phantom shows created by her forebears. Her name implies not only "the wonderer," but also "the seeing one." True to the second implication, she has determined to discover reality for herself. Her mind, we are told, "closed stubbornly against remembering, not the past but the legend of the past, other people's memory of the past, at which she had spent her life peering in wonder like a child at a magic-lantern show." Since this is her determination, we are not surprised to learn in *Pale Horse, Pale Rider* that she has left her home and family and started a career. It may seem ironical, however, that she is still watching shows created by others, now as theater critic for a western newspaper (a "female job" to which she was relegated after compassion allowed her to suppress a news item about a scandalous elopement). By the end of the story, however, Miranda has become a critic of the *theatrum mundi,* a reviewer of reality, who will be, not just a passive "wonderer," but a creator. (pp. 251-52)

Perhaps the best internal evidence that the way Miranda will claim her "honest self" is through art lies in the title *Pale Horse, Pale Rider.* It comes from the song that Miranda, sick with influenza, sings with Adam, the man she has known for ten days and is falling in love with. In the old spiritual, Miranda says, the pale horse of death takes away lover, mother, father, brother, sister, the whole family, but is always implored to "leave one singer to mourn." Miranda is left, after multiple remembered deaths of family members and after the death of Adam, as the one who will sing of the others. As she once wrote about the theater of the stage, she will now write of the theater of life. This interpretation is supported by the frequent comparisons of life to plays or to movies, occurring throughout the story. Bill, the city editor of the Blue Mountain *News,* behaves "exactly like city editors in the moving pictures, even to the chewed cigar"; Chuck, the tubercular sportswriter, dresses his part from turtlenecked sweater to

tan hobnailed boots; the restaurant next door to the newspaper, like all its cinematic counterparts, it seems, is nicknamed "The Greasy Spoon"; Miranda finds Liberty Bond salesmen in her office and on the stage of the theater; she and Adam talk to each other in the prescribed flippancies of the day as if they are role-playing; even the vision that comes to her when she is near death is couched in imagery of the theater: she sees that "words like oblivion and eternity are curtains hung before nothing at all."

Just as it took a war to release the Grandmother's true, subjective self in action, so it takes a war to free Miranda's to art. In her case, however, the war is clearly internal as well as external. As surely as Miranda fights against death from influenza at the end of World War I, she also fights—as a woman struggling for psychological and creative independence— against the death that comes from intellectual passivity, from the failure to act or to create, from the surrender of one's honest self. The story opens, significantly, with a description of an almost totally motionless Miranda, just beginning to feel the symptoms of her disease. She is half in a coma. . . . Only through a stubborn act of will, conscious refusal to die, will Miranda make it to the other side. In *Old Mortality* the child Miranda dreamed of being a jockey when she grew up, envisioning the day "she would ride out . . . and win a great race, and surprise everybody, her family most of all." Her victory will, like Miss Lucy's, be filled with suffering, but this is her day to ride. Although her pulse lags and her heart is almost lifeless, in her mind there is still action: she dreams of mounting her horse and riding to escape death—physical death and that other death, that sacrifice of self, associated with the spider web, or tangled fishing lines, of family.

But if the family was, in her past, the major source of temptations to passivity, other lures have presented themselves in her new life, calling on her to deny her integrity. Even though she believes the war "filthy," it takes all the strength she can muster to resist the intimidations of the men selling Liberty Bonds (the pun is perfect), who assert that she is the lone holdout in all the businesses in the entire city. She surrenders at least momentarily to social pressure when she puts in her time visiting hospitalized soldiers. . . . Even Adam and the love she feels for him seem a threat to her free will—Adam who keeps her "on the inside of the walk in good American style," who helps her "across street corners as if she were a cripple," who would have carried her over mud puddles had they come across any, and whom she does not want to love, not now, but whom she feels forced to love *now,* because their time seems so short. (pp. 252-55)

With Adam's death and her own delirious vision of oblivion, Miranda gives up all illusions, all hopes, all love. She is left with what Nannie had found only at the end of her life: that reduction to the very core of selfhood, that "hard unwinking angry point of light" that Miranda saw in her death sleep and heard say, " 'Trust me. I stay.' " She is left with the awareness of the power of her own will (strong enough to conquer death); of her ability to survive alone; and of an identity, a reality that is hers without dependence on any one else. But unlike Nannie, Miranda has the time and the emotional and practical equipment to make this center a starting point instead of a final station. As she returns from her race with death, she is not only a Lazarus come forth, but a "seer" in another sense now, a *vates,* who has looked into the depths and will, no doubt, be compelled to tell about it in certain seasons to come, when Pegasus replaces that other pale horse.

"The Grave" in **"The Old Order"** had revealed to Miranda that treasure can come from a tomb; her art will be another proof of the truth of this promise.

The likelihood that Miranda will express her selfhood in art may also suggest her superiority to her Grandmother in Porter's view. Porter once indicated her agreement with E. M. Forster's belief that "there are only two possibilities for any real order: art and religion." The essential difference is significant: religion, the Grandmother's source of order in old age, has its anchor outside the self, in institutions, rules, dogmas. Art, on the other hand, has an interior source; the self becomes creator. Religion, as the Grandmother practiced it, means limitation of the self; art, expression of the self. For Porter it is the center that will hold. As she wrote in her introduction to **Flowering Judas and Other Stories**: "[The arts] cannot be destroyed altogether because they represent the substance of faith and the only reality. They are what we find again when the ruins are cleared away. And even the smallest and most incomplete offering at this time can be a proud act in defense of that faith."

And that is winning, too. (pp. 255-56)

> *Barbara Harrell Carson, "Winning: Katherine Anne Porter's Women," in* The Authority of Experience: Essays in Feminist Criticism, *edited by Arlyn Diamond and Lee R. Edwards, The University of Massachusetts Press, 1977, pp. 239-56.*

ROBERT PENN WARREN   (essay date 1980)

[*In this posthumous tribute, Warren honors Porter's distinctive style and the "historical awareness" of her fiction.*]

In my view, the final importance of Katherine Anne Porter is not merely that she has written a number of fictions remarkable for both grace and strength, a number of fictions which have enlarged and deepened the nature of the story, both short and long, in our time, but that she has created an *oeuvre*—a body of work including fiction, essays, letters, and journals—that bears the stamp of a personality distinctive, delicately perceptive, keenly aware of the depth and darkness of human experience, delighted by the beauty of the world and the triumphs of human kindness and warmth, and thoroughly committed to a quest for meaning in the midst of the ironic complexities of man's lot. . . . A review of her *oeuvre* reveals that, in spite of its sharp impression of immediacy, it is drenched in historical awareness.

Most obviously, we have the story of Miranda—a sharply defined person, but also a sort of alter ego of the author. In **Old Mortality,** Miranda, first as a child, then as a young woman with a broken marriage returning to a family funeral, grows into an awareness of the meaning of myth and time. In the beginning of the story Miranda inspects the myth of the beautiful Aunt Amy, doomed to an early and perhaps disgraceful death. The romantic story is first subjected to a child's realistic scrutiny, then to an old-fashioned moral judgment, and finally to the modern judgment of Marx and Freud (although these names never appear). Miranda, at the end, swears that she will be done with all old tales, old romance, that she will live her own life, will know the truth "about what happens to me." This is a promise she makes to herself, and this would be the end of a certain kind of story. But this story ends with three simple phrases: ". . . making a promise to herself, in her hopefulness, her ignorance." And indeed, these three phrases *are* the story. What kind of truth can we know about our own being, our own fate?

Later, in **Pale Horse, Pale Rider,** we see Miranda again, she and her lover set against the hysteria of war, the lover dying, she herself dying into a new order of life—the life of the great ruthless machine of the modern world. (pp. 10-11)

This question is always present in the work of Katherine Anne Porter: What does our history—of the individual or in the mass—mean? World War II is only one episode in that long question, with the horror of Nazism only an anguishing footnote to a great process in which we are all involved. In the face of the great, pitiless, and dehumanizing mechanism of the modern world, what her work celebrates is the toughness and integrity of the individual. And the great virtue is to recognize complicity with evil in the self. We may be foolishly hopeful, or ignorant, as young Miranda making her promise to herself. But even in the face of the savage irony of history, could she otherwise affirm her integrity? (p. 11)

> *Robert Penn Warren, "The Genius of Katherine Anne Porter," in* Saturday Review, *Vol. 7, No. 16, December, 1980, pp. 10-11.*

FURTHER READING

Allen, Charles A. "The Nouvelles of Katherine Anne Porter." *The University of Kansas City Review* XXIX, No. 2 (December 1962): 87-93.

> A balanced examination of *Noon Wine, Old Mortality,* and *Pale Horse, Pale Rider.* Allen asserts that the stories' protagonists are "victim[s] of a hostile society" and evaluates Porter as an "artist, psychologist, and moralist."

Baldeshwiler, Eileen. "Structured Patterns in Katherine Anne Porter's Fiction." *South Dakota Review* II, No. 2 (Summer 1973): 45-53.

> Categorizes Porter's works into three groups: (1) those with a traditional syllogistic pattern; (2) those using memory as a fictional device; and (3) expository, dramatic stories in which knowledge is gained through emotional revelations.

Brinkmeyer, Robert H., Jr. " 'Endless Remembering': The Artistic Vision of Katherine Anne Porter." *The Mississippi Quarterly* XL, No. 1 (Winter 1986-1987): 5-19.

> Discusses Porter's use of the South as the dominant setting in her stories of the 1920s. Brinkmeyer maintains that, having previously rejected her personal background as fictional material, Porter's works of this decade begin to explore the problems of denying "one's memory." Includes a detailed discussion of "The Jilting of Granny Weatherall."

Hartley, Lodwick, and Core, George, eds. *Katherine Anne Porter: A Critical Symposium.* Athens, Ga.: University of Georgia Press, 1969, 242 p.

> Contains seventeen essays by such writers as Cleanth Brooks, Eudora Welty, and Robert Penn Warren.

Hendrick, George. *Katherine Anne Porter.* Chicago: University of Illinois, 1965, 176 p.

> Includes biographical information, a critical discussion of Porter's complete works, and an extensive bibliography.

Joselyn, Sister M., O.S.B. " 'The Grave' as Lyrical Short Story." *Studies in Short Fiction* 1, No. 3 (Spring 1964): 216-21.

Highly regarded essay commenting on the use of poetic elements in "The Grave."

Kaplan, Charles. "True Witness: Katherine Anne Porter." *Colorado Quarterly* VII, No. 3 (Winter 1959): 319-27.

A chronological study of the Miranda stories, emphasizing "The Circus."

Mooney, Harry John, Jr. *The Fiction and Criticism of Katherine Anne Porter.* Pittsburgh: University of Pittsburgh Press, 1957, 58 p.

Examines various aspects of Porter's writing, stressing their political implications.

Pierce, Marvin. "Point of View: Katherine Anne Porter's *Noon Wine.*" *The Ohio University Review* III (1961): 95-113.

Detailed analysis of point of view in the eight sections of *Noon Wine.*

Porter, Katherine Anne. "*Noon Wine:* The Sources." *The Yale Review* XLVI, No. 1 (September 1956): 22-39.

Insightful essay in which Porter reflects on her childhood memories and the social patterns of the Old South, revealing the origins of the characters, scenes, and plot of *Noon Wine.*

Redden, Dorothy S. " 'Flowering Judas': Two Voices." *Studies in Short Fiction* VI, No. 2 (Winter 1969): 194-204.

Contends that "Flowering Judas" is Porter's "most remarkable story of tension sustained, threatened and reestablished." Redden examines how the work's paradoxes are illuminated through Porter's dual perspective.

Schwartz, Edward Greenfield. "The Fictions of Memory." *Southwest Review* XLV, No. 3 (Summer 1960): 204-15.

Critically acclaimed article exploring the moral dilemmas of Porter's protagonists and focusing on the Miranda stories.

Smith, J. Oates. "Porter's *Noon Wine:* A Stifled Tragedy." *Renascence* XVII, No. 3 (Spring 1965): 157-62.

Praises Porter's unsentimental, understated treatment of tragedy in *Noon Wine.*

Stout, Janis P. "Miranda's Guarded Speech: Porter and the Problem of Truth-Telling." *Philological Quarterly* 66, No. 2 (Spring 1987): 259-78.

Agrees with the widely held critical theory that Miranda is Porter's fictional counterpart. Stout suggests that Miranda is also "the ethical measure and center of Porter's fiction" and her role is "not only as center of consciousness but as touchstone of value."

Thompson, Barbara. "Katherine Anne Porter: An Interview." *The Paris Review* 8, No. 29 (Winter-Spring 1963): 87-114.

Lengthy interview in which Porter remarks on her childhood and adolescence, sources of her stories, influences on her work, and her philosophy of life and writing.

Van Zyl, John. "Surface Elegance, Grotesque Content: A Note on the Short Stories of Katherine Anne Porter." *English Studies in Africa* 9, No. 2 (September 1966): 168-75.

Considers Porter's main theme the confrontation of illusion and reality and discusses the self-knowledge attained by protagonists who ultimately question their pasts.

Voss, Arthur. "Symbolism and Sensibility: Katherine Anne Porter." In his *The American Short Story: A Critical Survey,* pp. 288-301. Norman: University of Oklahoma Press, 1973.

Explores the psychological insights and characterizations of *Flowering Judas, Pale Horse, Pale Rider,* and other works.

Warren, Robert Penn. "Irony with a Center: Katherine Anne Porter." *The Kenyon Review* IV (Winter 1942): 29-42.

Considered one of the most influential essays on Porter. Warren views Porter as a distinctive author whose work is founded on an irony that implies "a refusal to accept ready-made formulas, hand-me-down morality."

Wescott, Glenway. "Katherine Anne Porter Personally." In his *Images of Truth: Remembrances and Criticism,* pp. 25-58. London: Hamish Hamilton, 1962.

Combines personal reminisces with literary criticism.

Wiesenfarth, Brother Joseph. "Illusion and Allusion: Reflections in 'The Cracked Looking-Glass.' " *Four Quarters* XII (November 1962): 30-7.

Examines an often-neglected story and traces the influence of Henry James and James Joyce on Porter's technique.

Winsten, Archer. "Presenting the Portrait of an Artist." *New York Post* (6 May 1937): 17.

A significant early interview in which Porter offers information on her family history and explains her writing methods.

Young, Marguerite. "Fictions Mystical and Epical." *The Kenyon Review* VII (Winter 1945): 152-54.

Addresses the theme of continuity in Porter's works. Young maintains that Porter's "great service to the short story has been that in her hands it acquires a new stature and significance."

J(ames) F(arl) Powers

1917-

American short story writer, novelist, and critic.

Powers is a highly regarded contemporary satirist whose works typically focus on the foibles of institutional Catholicism. Displaying both humor and compassion, Powers lampoons frailties among members of the Catholic clergy and illuminates conflicts between the religious and secular worlds. An acknowledged literary craftsman, Powers has frequently been commended for his authentic renderings of Midwestern speech patterns, his use of detail to reveal character, and his economical prose style that often features elements of wordplay. Mary Gordon observed: "It is in the close, packed atmosphere of parishes and monasteries that the comedy of Powers grows and flourishes: an odd, rare bloom: satiric, harsh, and yet not condemning, falling with an undisguisable relish upon the clergy's faults yet based upon a tough and weary faith in what these clergymen so ineptly represent."

Powers was born into a middle-class Catholic family in the small, predominantly Protestant city of Jacksonville, Illinois, a situation dramatized in his early story, "Jamesie." As a young man during the Depression, Powers moved to Chicago and worked a series of jobs while attending Northwestern University. During the early years of World War II, he experienced a spiritual epiphany that led him to embrace pacifism, and the works that arose from this formative period reflect Powers's burgeoning social conscience. His first collection of short fiction, for example, *Prince of Darkness, and Other Stories,* includes the pieces "The Eye," "The Trouble," and "He Don't Plant Cotton," which express, in Powers's words, "anger at the plight of the Negro." In another story, "Renner," Powers condemns anti-Semitism, comparing the title character's experiences in Nazi Germany with the more subtle but equally destructive forms of bigotry he encounters as an immigrant in Chicago.

A recurring theme in Powers's fiction is the attainment of spiritual rebirth through a crisis of faith. In "Lions, Harts, Leaping Does," a much-anthologized piece which, unlike most of Powers's fiction, is meditative rather than satirical, Father Didymus, recently retired from teaching geometry, struggles with his conflicting beliefs in God and reason. Just before his death, however, the priest loses sense of his material being and fully experiences the presence of grace. Similarly, in his novels, Powers portrays his characters' spiritual resurrections as resulting from the passing of their material concerns.

Throughout his career, Powers has reshaped chapters from his novels-in-progress for publication as short stories. "The Green Banana," "Twenty-Four Hours in a Strange Diocese," and "Wrens and Starlings," for example, were initially published as stories during the 1950s. They later appeared in revised form in Powers's first novel, *Morte d'Urban.* Powers also published two seminal chapters from his second novel, *Wheat That Springeth Green,* as the stories "Bill" and "Priestly Fellowship," first in the *New Yorker,* and subsequently in his collection *Look How the Fish Live.* Eleanor B. Wymard noted that a comparison of Powers's novels and the short stories that have evolved from them illustrates sensitivity to the demands of each genre, "for in the short stories Powers depends upon economical exposition to clarify conflict and resolution, whereas the chapters . . . relish ambiguity and paradox."

In much of his fiction, Powers explores ironies in the clergy's dual commitment to the spiritual and material worlds. "The Forks," for example, portrays a confrontation between the spiritual realm, represented by the Church and the sanctimonious young Father Eudex, and the material domain, symbolized by the local monsignor and the Rival Tractor Company, an unscrupulous organization that underpays its employees and distributes its excess profits as charity to members of the clergy. The monsignor, however, understands the social duties required of the clergy more clearly than pietistic Father Eudex, and by the story's end, Father Eudex realizes that his fellow curates have used their portions of the tractor firm's money for charitable works, while he has accomplished nothing worthwhile by destroying his own check. In this and other stories, including "Priestly Fellowship" and "The Keystone," Powers censures those members of the clergy whose overweening spirituality interferes with their service to humanity.

In other stories, Powers humorously emphasizes the similarities between religious and secular life. "Prince of Darkness" is a sympathetic portrayal of Father Ernest "Boomer" Burner, whose dream of becoming a famous golfer is as unrealistic as his desire to administer a parish of his own so that his mother may be his housekeeper. "Bill" and "The Keystone" depict power struggles in the businesslike atmosphere of a church rectory. "Blue Island," "The Poor Thing," and the title piece in *The Presence of Grace* explore spiritual bankruptcy within the bourgeois Catholic laity. Wymard remarked: "Although Powers has been attacked and defended for his attitudes toward the Roman Catholic priest, the spiritual orientation of his fiction neither rises nor falls on his portrayal of the inner sanctum of the rectory. It provides simply an external structure for his pursuing the deeper problem that our generation is condemning itself to unfulfillment by ceasing to search for Mystery and Truth."

(For further information on Powers's life and career, see *Contemporary Literary Criticism,* Vols. 1, 4, 8; *Contemporary Authors,* Vols. 1-4, rev. ed.; and *Contemporary Authors New Revision Series,* Vol. 2.)

PRINCIPAL WORKS

SHORT FICTION

Prince of Darkness, and Other Stories   1947
The Presence of Grace   1956
Look How the Fish Live   1975

OTHER MAJOR WORKS

Morte d'Urban   (novel)   1962

Wheat That Springeth Green   (novel)   1988

JOHN V. HAGOPIAN   (essay date 1968)

[*In the following excerpt from his book-length study,* American
critic and fiction writer Hagopian analyzes Powers's early secular stories as technical and thematic precursors of his more celebrated works concerning the Catholic clergy.*]

The popularity of Powers' narratives of rectory life—a subject only he has successfully embodied in American fiction—
has unfortunately burdened him with an invidious reputation
as a narrow specialist on the priesthood. But, from the very
beginning to the publication of *Morte d'Urban,* he has produced magnificent stories on a wide variety of secular themes:
a compassionate portrayal of the mind of a European refugee
from Fascism (**"Renner"**); the pathos of old age (**"The Old
Bird, A Love Story"**); the simpleminded saintliness of an exploited domestic (**"The Poor Thing"**); the innocent victim of
ruthless salesmanship in the new suburbs (**"Blue Island"**);
the painful discovery of the inexorable cruelty of nature
(**"Look How the Fish Live"**); a little boy's betrayed adulation
of a baseball player (**"Jamesie"**); and the troubled human values involved in racial hatred and violence (**"He Don't Plant
Cotton," "The Eye,"** and **"The Trouble"**). Had Powers never
written a story about a priest, some of these pieces would
alone ensure his status as a distinguished writer. (p. 37)

Powers' five stories on Negro themes—**"He Don't Plant Cotton," "The Trouble," "The Eye," "Interlude in a Book
Shop,"** and **"The Blessing"**—were all written in the early
1940's; and he has confessed that they were written out of
"anger at the plight of the Negro." **"He Don't Plant Cotton,"**
written in 1942, has as its central character a Negro jazz
drummer named "Baby," based on the famous Baby Dodds.
This Negro refuses to degrade himself in his own eyes by submitting to the demands of the society around him, but he does
not quite have the capacity for pure hatred of the whites as
do the piano player, Dodo, and the singer, Libby. Baby resents waiting for streetcars in the cold Chicago winter, playing popular ballads and slick swing tunes instead of honest
jazz; but he does it without self-corrosive rancor. A Southern
Negro from New Orleans, he paradoxically enjoys lapsing
into the Negro stereotype expected of him during the singing
of "Ole Man River." When drunken Mississippians at the
night club demand that the musicians "tote that bar, lift that
bale" all night long, Libby leads the revolt. . . . (pp. 37-8)

The rebellion gives them a sense of joy and dignity:

> Baby was even a little glad it had happened. A feel-
> ing was growing within him that he had wanted to
> do this for a long time—for years and years, in a
> hundred different places he had played. . . .
> Waves of warm exhilaration washed into him, en-
> dearing him to himself. No, he smiled, I'm sorry,
> no favors today."

In **"He Don't Plant Cotton,"** Powers poignantly shapes an
image of the Negro's long experience of *humiliation* in the
North and shows that endurance has its limits. In **"The Eye"**
he takes up the theme of the *violence* which the Negro has endured in the South. The victim is again a Negro musician,
Sleep Bailey, a deaf piano player who has heroically rescued

a white girl from drowning. To reward him, the girl's boy
friend, Clyde Bullen, wants to take up a collection among his
friends in the pool hall; but one of them balks, insinuating
that the scratches and bruises sustained by the Negro during
the rescue is evidence that he had attempted to rape the girl.
When a hospital report reveals that the girl is seven months
pregnant, a lynch cry is raised; and the mob seeks out Sleep
Bailey, who awaits them while calmly playing the piano: "If
I'm here I guess I got no call to be scared. . . . Don't it prove
nothing if I'm here, if I didn't run away? Don't that prove
nothing?" Having been pressured into leading the mob,
Clyde Bullen then makes an inchoate, desperate struggle with
his conscience and tries in vain to stop the lynching.

Despite the stereotype and stock situations, the story is not
without interest. Powers does not focus attention on the innocent victim, but with a certain brute force he employs the device of an internal narrator, Roy, who is a brainless oaf like
the barber in Ring Lardner's "Haircut." Like the barber, Roy
has no idea of what really happened. It is obvious to the reader, but not to the moronic narrator, that Clyde's refusal to
join the chorus of condemnation of the Negro is manifest evidence of his own guilt. Clyde himself is the father of the girl's
child, and she was rescued while attempting to drown herself
to escape the shame of being an unmarried mother.

Apart from the intricate technique of narrative irony, what
is significant is that Clyde does not readily and willingly take
up the lynch cry to cover his own responsibility. To be sure,
he does not confess his guilt, but neither can he bury it; and
he finally turns his fury on the mob in a futile attempt to stop
the murder of the Negro. Thus, in an unusual twist away
from another stereotype—the Northern liberal's view of the
Southern white bigot—Powers presents a conscience-stricken
protagonist who cannot escape his own deep-seated morality.

The third of the Negro stories, **"The Trouble,"** also is a first-
person narrative dealing with racial violence. . . . Powers'
anger is controlled by a symbolically significant structure and
by a rather subtle imagery. Although **"The Trouble"** may not
be entirely successful, it reveals a considerable advance over
the earlier Negro stories and distinctly shows Powers moving
toward artistic maturity.

The point of view is that of a little Negro boy, a member of
a family from New Orleans that has migrated to Chicago in
search of employment in the war plants. But Powers ignores
the sociological aspects of the wartime race riots to focus on
the spiritual crisis of the little boy. (pp. 38-40)

[The] race riot remains for the boy a spectacle, a macabre entertainment, until the battered body of his mother is carried
into the house. The Negro doctor, the boy's father, and then
the new parish priest are summoned; but there is some speculation about whether the priest will bother to come—for, as
the father says, "his predecessor couldn't stand to save black
souls."

From the window the boy watches his grandmother go out
at the height of the riot to buy candles; and, to his astonishment, he observes her covertly providing sanctuary to a white
man fleeing from a Negro mob. But the father confronts the
man with a threat to kill him if the mother dies. Finally the
priest arrives, and at that point in the narrative the conflict
between the races modulates into a spiritual conflict with the
father. The priest's administering the final sacrament influences the boy's father to abandon his threat to kill the loathsome white man: " 'I wouldn't touch you.' That was all. He

moved slowly back to Mama's bed and his big shoulders were sagged down like I never saw them before."

Both the father and the priest despise the white man, but both manifest the divine injunction, "Be ye angry and sin not: let not the sun go down upon your wrath" (Ephesians 4:26). The presence of grace is in these Negroes; even the little boy's sister Carrie, who had refused to submit to a "white" God, kneels to pray. The change in the father, the final crisis of the story, is foreshadowed by the earlier one in the boy, who at the beginning "wanted to see some whites get killed for a change." He experiences a momentary ambivalence when it appears that his wish may come true and then falls into grace:

> I did not see what difference it could make to Mama if the white man lived or died. It only had something to do with us and him. . . . *The trouble is somebody gets cheated or insulted or killed and somebody else tries to make it come out even by cheating and insulting and killing the cheaters and insulters and killers. Only they never do. I did not think they ever would* (italics mine).

When the father too is infused with this spirit, the story, which opened with violence, closes with charity, which "suffereth long, and is kind" (I Corinthian, 13:4): Thus **"The Trouble"** supports Evelyn Waugh's observation that Powers' "whole art is everywhere infused and directed by his Faith." Even if this story also supports Robert Daniels' complaint that "the Negro stories in particular are badly didactic," it employs a pattern of animal imagery that indicates a firm artistic control behind the child-narrator's simple idiom. Early in the story, the boy compares the white man to rats, "the biggest live game you can find in ordinary times." Later one of the militant Negroes, quoting Claude McKay, declares: "If we must die, let it not be like hogs hunted and penned in an inglorious spot." When the fleeing white man appears in the alley, he blows a bugle "like the white folks do when they go fox hunting."

But these manifestations of man's animal nature modulate into Christian charity when the priest, Father Crowe (a white man with the name of a black bird), comes to administer Extreme Unction to the dying mother. Such an image pattern in a story written in anger and in one sitting at the typewriter is evidence of Powers' growing skill. Powers himself says of **"The Trouble,"** that "It's not a terribly good story, but it's not a bad story. I don't work like that anymore. Now it takes me a month or two to write a story."

Apart from the three Negro stories which Powers collected in **Prince of Darkness,** there are two which he quite properly omitted. They deserve attention, however, because they anticipate certain themes in his more mature fiction: the morality of everyday life, and the conflict between idealism and practicality within the Catholic Church. The first of these themes is embodied in an early sketch, **"Interlude in a Bookshop,"** which was published in the liberal Negro journal, *Opportunity.* The story shows the moral superiority and the moral victory of the Negro with a levity that foreshadows the wit of Powers' later work. Two moral pigmies, Mr. Flynn, a short man, and Mr. Mosby, a shorter man, find their usual competitive zeal in serving booklovers dampened by the entrance of a Negro woman into the shop. After she buys an inexpensive paperback from the truculent Mr. Flynn, he hands her the unwrapped purchase with a lie:

"We never wrap small purchases on account of paper shortage."

"That's all right. . . . I can put it right in my bag. Is it severe?"

"What?"

"The paper shortage?"

"Oh, yes, yes indeed."

Mr. Flynn is no match for the perceptiveness and the poise of the woman. When she continues to browse and begins to show signs of becoming a heavy purchaser, Mr. Mosby tries to take over the sale. Eventually, each clerk tries to get in ahead of the other. Flynn wins the sale, but a crisis arises when the woman offers to pay by check. His apprehensions disappear, however, when he notes that the signature on the check is that of a famous Negro opera singer.

Then, Mr. Mosby, seeing an opportunity for revenge, suggests that the opera singer personally autograph a copy of her recently published book for Mr. Flynn. Mosby knows that "poor Flynn would have to buy the book now" and would thus lose whatever commission he made on the sale. This sly trick skews the story away from a final Negro-white confrontation to show how greed and vindictiveness among whites can be even stronger forces than racial prejudice. In the last paragraph, another clerk, the crotchety Mr. Channing, looks into Bartlett's to find a quotation about Fame and Gold o'ercoming all. Although there is nothing especially distinguished about **"Interlude in a Bookshop,"** Powers undoubtedly gained perspective by looking at serious issues from a comic point of view.

Another early story, **"Blessing,"** published in the Catholic monthly *The Sign,* was also omitted from **Prince of Darkness.** Like **"The Trouble,"** it deals with a test of faith in a Catholic Negro family that becomes the victim of racial violence. A Negro boy, converted to Catholicism by a young curate, in turn converts his brothers, sisters, and widowed mother. Though many in the parish clearly resent the presence of Negroes at Mass, the pastor himself determines to give the mother instruction. The children transfer to the parochial school, and the family moves into a run-down house near the church. Frightened by anonymous threats of arson, the mother summons the curate to bless her house; but, just as the blessing is concluded, the dwelling goes up in flames. The curate, undaunted, determines to take the family into the rectory—"if they would come now."

The story is in three parts; the gravest flaw is the shift from scene to summary in part two, which consists of a long, moralistic letter from the curate to his brother, describing his hopes and fears. Of course, the device of the letter is not necessarily in itself a poor technique, but this one introduces its message with the rhetoric one might expect from a callow priest: "I am about to embark upon a subject I've tried, but failed miserably, to be calm about. It is one that concerns all of us Catholics, as such, in this country: mortally." Now this sort of utterance from a character in [Powers' 1962 novel] *Morte D'Urban* would certainly be ironic. When Father Urban says such a thing, he doesn't mean it; and when he becomes the kind of priest who can genuinely mean it, he is no longer able to say it. But Powers' moral fervor in the **"Blessing"** drives him to use fiction as propaganda for a liberal, humane, and socially-oriented Catholicism, and he loses control as an artist. There is, of course, nothing wrong about the values expressed, but they are *expressed* rather than embodied in art.

Nevertheless, it is instructive to note what values dominate Powers' thought, for he has never repudiated them—he has simply learned to dramatize them more subtly and effectively. (pp. 40-4)

But the **"Blessing"** does manifest artistic power in other ways: vivid descriptive details ("his sockless toes budding brownly from the ends of his shoes"); dramatic foreshadowings (the flames of the candles in the house during the blessing anticipate and contrast with the cruel, crackling fire that destroys the house); images that communicate more than the central intelligence of the story comprehends ("he saw the streetlight turn yellow, flare up too brightly, and finally go out, leaving the street in darkness"—the arsonists at work have put out the light of faith and reason); and significant realistic details ("As the priest pulled the widow and son out of the burning house, he saw his hat hung within easy reach, but he would not take it and was a little sickened to think he had thought of it at all.")

In this story is the germ of an idea that grew to become one of the most salient features of Powers' most characteristic fiction—the comedy of a pastor's relations with his curate:

> Many people, including priests, do not understand the Pastor (call him strict, anti-social, etc.), but I believe I am beginning to know the man. You may remember my misgivings when I learned I was to be his curate at St. Gregory's. He is an implacable enemy to all easy piety, and—should I say, as a consequence?—the most saintly priest I know. I recall the first brush we had. He woke up one morning with a beautiful boil on his neck. I remarked (not in all seriousness) that he was fortunate to have such a boil. Why fortunate? he growled. Suffering is a means to perfection, Father, I replied. Huh! he snorted, I suppose that's why the Bishop sent me you!

In this situation is the beginning of such relationships as those of Father Burner and Father Malt in **"Prince of Darkness,"** Father Fabre and his pastor in **"The Presence of Grace"** and **"A Losing Game,"** Father Udovic and the Bishop in **"Dawn,"** Father Early and the Bishop in **"Zeal,"** and of Bill and Joe in the novel [*Wheat that Springeth Green*].

As an intense young liberal in the early 1940's, Powers was, of course, concerned with social issues other than the Negro problem. His one story dealing with the problem of the Jews, **"Renner,"** is so atmospheric and suggestive that the reviewer for the London *Times Literary Supplement* found it the only story in **Prince of Darkness** in which "the author's subtlety of approach obscures his intention." The story is subtle, but not obscure; and it is an immensely superior work of art in comparison to any of the Negro stories. It requires more concentrated attention and more astuteness from the reader before it yields its force and meaning.

"Renner" is several stories merged into one, a brilliant, unified complexity showing Fascism in the drama of everyday life—in the present and the past, in Europe and America. As the narrator says of the anti-Semites, "such men are everywhere, never without a country." For the first time in Powers' fiction, an internal narrator approaches intelligence, maturity, and perceptiveness, but ultimately even he cannot fully understand the experience thrust before his consciousness from worlds he has never known. (pp. 44-5)

The narrator is confronted with two lines of force that move through the story: (1) the ongoing drama of the present—Emil, the proprietor of the restaurant with his card-playing friends reacting to a Jewish businessman who comes in for dinner; and (2) the autobiography of Renner, an Austrian exile from Fascism who encounters virulent forms of it in the United States. The climax of the story occurs when these two narrative lines collide; but the meaning of that impact is left implicit: men of good will are confused and powerless in a world without Christian values.

As the story opens, the narrator reveals that he had never known the "good old days" evoked by their setting, but he observes that among the "swillish brown paintings" of fat tippling friars in cellars and other subjects there are "no fishes on platters." Thus the opening paragraph suggests the paradox of appearance and reality, for the surface display of geniality obscures the absence of Christianity. The narrator is only partially aware of—indeed, morally indifferent to—the significance of what he sees and hears. For example, he notes that there was "something dimly sinister about Emil," the proprietor, but he fails to probe for it. . . . In ordinary social situations such indifference might be to the narrator's credit; here it suggests a desire to avoid difficulties. (p. 46)

Behind the narrator, of course, is Powers, who causes the story to move in alternate rhythmic pulses of time toward its climax when Renner's sudden gesture of indignation at the card players freezes in paralysis and defeat. The narrative movement toward that closure is intricately structured: (1) five episodes of the present alternate with five episodes of Renner's past; (2) then a brief abstract discussion of Christianity, followed by (3) Renner's account of the immediate past event that triggers the climax in the present . . . .

This alternation of the American present with the European past emphasizes the similarity in the moral corruption of the two areas as if to say that chauvinism, the rejection of foreigners, and the mockery of Jews lead everywhere to the same spiritual rottenness. (p. 47)

The first religious reference in the story is casual enough, but it alerts us to the fact that the narrator must be a Catholic, and a naïve one at that. Upon learning that Renner's uncle had been president of the Vienna Academy of Art, he muses: "Achievement through violence or succession or cunning or even merit is common enough. But president of an academy of art—now there was an inscrutable honor, beyond accounting for, like being an archbishop (except in Italy), only more so." Among other relations, this passage reaffirms our awareness of the narrator's relative naïveté; for, as Powers' other stories show, "cunning or even merit" is often the factor that determines status in religious hierarchies. The narrator says of Renner, "his species, spiritually speaking, tends to make itself at home in exile;" but it is obvious that Renner will never be at home anywhere since he cannot limit his Christianity to "the community fund, doing good, and brisk mottoes on the wall." All these, Renner says, are ways of "copulating with circumstance." (p. 49)

There is an immense poignancy to Renner's experience, a poignancy contained by the narrator's self-control, his avoidance of excess emotion, his evasion of embarrassing confrontations, and his willingness to compromise: "I told Emil the beer was good, very—when he waited for more—very good beer." The poignancy is also paradoxically both tempered and heightened by the ironic wit: "It's too bad der Fuehrer couldn't paint a little. Another bad painter, we could have stood that. . . . The Austrian army was not the most formidable in the world, except of course at regimental balls," the geometry teacher would "get furious and throw the squares and triangles at the pupils." This is the same ironic technique that is handled with sustained power in the later stories and in *Morte D'Urban.*

"The Old Bird, A Love Story" is, among the ten pieces that Powers published in the years 1943-45, remarkable for its quiet restraint and dignity, its controlled evocation of pathos, its gentle insight into the marital love of the aged. It has no black wit, no scorching irony, no inflamed, reformist zeal, no didactic rhetoric. It is strange to find this work among the early stories—strange but satisfying—because it confirms the observation that Powers began as a pure artist as well as a social reformer. Fortunately, the artist in him eventually triumphed. More than any other story in *Prince of Darkness,* **"The Old Bird"** exemplifies one reviewer's observation that "the expert technique of these stories is as unemotional and photographic as the later Hemingway, consisting mainly of placing the model in a clear light and shooting."

"The Old Bird" depicts a day in the life of an old man, Mr. Newman, who, although he has a horror of intruding where he isn't wanted, is driven by the approach of Christmas to seek a job. After running the gauntlet of the information girl, the employment interviewer, and the boss of the shipping department, he puts in an exhausting day's work and returns home to his sympathetic wife. As this summation indicates, the story is not a powerfully dramatic narrative but a poignant character study built up with sensitively observed details. (pp. 50-1)

Quite agitated, [Mr. Newman] is ushered into the office of Mr. Shanahan, the interviewer:

> Mr. Shanahan, his eyes . . . reading the letter, noiselessly extended a hand toward Mr. Newman. A moment later he moved his head and it was then that Mr. Newman saw the hand. Mr. Newman paled. Caught napping! A bad beginning. He hastened to shake Mr. Shanahan's hand, recoiled in time. Mr. Shanahan had only been reaching for the application. Mr. Newman handed it to Mr. Shanahan and said, "Thank you," for some reason."

Such skill in looking simultaneously at and through Mr. Newman is impressive. The humor mocks with compassion.

Because of the wartime labor shortage, Mr. Newman is hired—not for office work, as he had hoped, but in the shipping room. However, as the elevator descends, his spirit sinks as he learns that the job doesn't pay much at the beginning but that the name of the firm would make it easier for him to find another position should he leave this one; and, "out of the elevator and in the lower depths, Mr. Shanahan said he would like to make sure Mr. Newman understood the job was only temporary." Then, Mr. Newman suffers one humiliation after another at the hands of Mr. Hurley; he manages to get through the day to head for home in a mood "unfamiliar to him, one of achievement and crazy gaiety."

This mood is dissipated, however, by the heavy snows, the crowded streetcars, and his confusion in trying to find a way of telling his wife of his success—and failure. He confronts "the truest condition of their married life. . . . She was the

audience . . . and he was always on stage, the actor who was never taken quite seriously by his audience, no matter how heroic the role." He shamelessly exaggerates the fine qualities of the old-line firm that had hired him, only to have his fantasies collapse with her enthusiastic response: "Then maybe they'll keep you after Christmas, Charley!" Because she loves him and understands him, she does not challenge his inept lie: "Yes. You know, I think they will. I'm sure of it." And, as in the poignant conclusion of Joyce's "The Dead" and Powers' own **"Lions, Harts, Leaping Does,"** "Snowflakes tumbled in feathery confusion past the yellow light burning in the court, wonderfully white against the night, smothering the whole dirty, roaring, guilty city in innocence and silence and beauty." As Marcus Klein says of Nabokov's short stories, "There is the rare accuracy, just so much of sorrowing and just so much of scrutiny, which is what we mean by compassion."

But such a delicate balance of sorrowing and scrutiny is lacking in **"Jamesie,"** Powers' autobiographical narrative about a nine-year-old boy who discovers that his idol is corrupt. The story has invited comparison with Hemingway's "My Old Man" and with Sherwood Anderson's "I Want to Know Why." Its motif is one which has attracted almost every significant American writer since Hawthorne's "My Kinsman, Major Molineux." But **"Jamesie"** is not a distinguished piece of work, probably because a young writer looking back on his own boyhood cannot achieve sufficient psychic distance and control to shape his materials into genuine art. Powers himself has confessed to a certain embarrassment at the obvious autobiographical elements, most prominent of which are his own name and the town in which he was born (Jayville is Jacksonville).

It is difficult to shape a richly textured emotional experience in the perspective and idiom of a boy. In Faulkner's "That Evening Sun," Lionel Trilling's "The Other Margaret," and Robert Penn Warren's "Blackberry Winter," that difficulty is avoided by making the initiation into evil a reminiscence or an observation of a sophisticated adult. Another difficulty when the central intelligence of the story is much less perceptive than the reader is an anti-climactic conclusion. Faulkner and Warren succeed by employing a rich symbolism and by introducing elements of complex atmosphere and threatened violence; Trilling, by making the child's discovery parallel that of a concomitant discovery by the adult. Hemingway and Anderson are superior in that they create a tension between a stronger drama of corruption and a taut, slangy prose style. But Powers, by keeping everything simple and ordinary, both in event and narrative technique, must finally rely on sentimentality. (pp. 52-3)

John P. Sisk has, in effect, linked **"Jamesie"** with Powers' earlier stories by his observation that "implicitly or explicitly the literature of innocence is social criticism." Such a flat pronouncement is contradicted by such stories as Hawthorne's "Roger Malvin's Burial" and "My Kinsman, Major Molineux" and Graham Greene's "The Basement Room," where the evil that shatters innocence is either personal or cosmic, but not—strictly speaking—social. Nevertheless, Sisk's observation is appropriate to **"Jamesie,"** a narrative in which perhaps the only subtle element is the implicit suggestion that in an American milieu, corrupted by the commercial ethic, it is not surprising that [Jamesie's hero] Lefty should prove vulnerable. (p. 54)

However deftly the evil of Lefty is shown to be consonant

with the evils of the larger society in which it occurs, and however felicitously the attractions of that evil may be expressed in an occasional image, the language and the dramatic structure of **"Jamesie"** are at best mediocre. Neither can be compared, for example, with these qualities in **"The Trouble,"** which remains artistically and morally Powers' only worthy contribution to the literature of young innocence encountering evil. . . .

[Only] two of the nine stories in his second collection, *The Presence of Grace* (1956) are secular—**"The Poor Thing"** and **"Blue Island."** Both of them are superior to all the earlier secular stories, with the exception of **"Renner,"** and they are equal to the best of the religious stories in that collection. (p. 55).

Blue Island is . . . a suburb of Minneapolis where Ralph Davicci, a liquor dealer and proprietor of cheap bars, has installed his pregnant bride Ethel. Lonely and eager for the approval of their upper middle-class neighbors, they easily fall victim to Mrs. Hancock, a sordid female who, under the guise of arranging a get-together coffee hour, uses their home to stage a party for selling kitchen utensils.

As a sociological study of class disorientation and alienation, **"Blue Island"** is easily the equal of anything by, say, John O'Hara; but as a work of art it is far superior. Written with a Joycean scrupulous meanness, **"Blue Island"** is actually the sustained interior monologue of Ethel Davicci who, despite her life among the riffraff, remains a well-meaning, good-hearted, dumb blonde. Ethel is alert to the possibility of danger, oblivious of the real tactics of Mrs. Hancock, and gradually caught in her clutches. Here Powers' subtle technique of implications requires the closest possible attention of the reader. . . . [Throughout] the story, one finds not merely a realistic description of a milieu and dialogue, as in O'Hara, but a presentation closer to Joyce's techniques of implication in *Dubliners.*

The story has four parts: (1) Ethel's encounter with Mrs. Hancock and the invitations to the coffee hour, (2) Ralph's anxiety over the success of the affair—and exposition accounting for that anxiety, (3) preparations, (4) the debacle of the coffee hour and its aftermath. The aftermath concludes with the arrival of Ralph, who had apparently been hovering nervously and solicitously in the background: "He was carrying a big club of roses." This last image embodies a powerful epiphany, serving the same function as "I'll say a *Hail Mary*" at the end of Joyce's "Counterparts" or "Now there would be time for everything" at the end of Katherine Anne Porter's "Pale Horse, Pale Rider."

Had the story been simply another sophisticated *New Yorker* hatchet job on life in the new suburbs, it could have ended with Ethel's discovery of the nausea of her neighbors who clearly resented being tricked into serving as a captive audience for a Shipshape utensils saleswoman:

> In a minute, she'd have to get up and go down to them and do something—but then she heard the coat hangers banging back empty in the closet downstairs, and the front door opening, and finally, closing. There was a moment of perfect silence in the house before her sudden sob. . . .

That is clearly a satisfactory point of closure. But Powers follows it with Ethel's final dialogue with Mrs. Hancock and Ralph's arrival. Thus the ending of part four nearly parallels

the ending of part one. Yet the gain of narrative power does not derive merely from the structural parallel; more important is that last line about his "carrying a big club of roses." It reveals in a flash that Ralph, not Mrs. Hancock, is ultimately responsible for these events. In his excess zeal for status and acceptance in a milieu utterly foreign to his own heritage or to his wife's personality, he has created the situation that has made misery inevitable. He has clubbed her with inept kindness.

That denouement explains and justifies the large role that Ralph plays in the middle two acts of this pathetic little domestic drama. The exposition in part two is smoothly introduced as Ethel considers how Ralph has changed since they moved to Blue Island. Formerly a happy extrovert, he is now tense and inhibited. . . . (pp. 55-7)

Ralph Davicci had renounced his own Italian family and his nickname of "Rocky," and he had ceased being a practicing Catholic; he dressed too ostentatiously well; he attempted to play golf and read the *Reader's Digest;* and he pressed his wife into a life for which she was not suited. The whole episode of the coffee hour and of Ethel's failure is therefore merely an oblique way of understanding the inevitable wrong of a man's not being true to himself. Ethel and Mrs. Hancock are antagonists, and Ethel is the ironically conceived central intelligence; but Ralph Davicci is the protagonist and the ultimate cause of the events.

Sister M. Bernetta Quinn is mistaken in her notion that **"Blue Island"** is the only story in *The Presence of Grace* that "has no explicit religious references." To be sure, the fact that Ralph does not attend church is cited only once, but this important detail reveals that Ralph is alienated from himself. John P. Sisk has observed that both **"Blue Island"** and **"The Poor Thing,"** two stories in which naïveté and indecision make one an easy victim of the machinations of others, "end in a kind of darkness that is unusual in Powers." The explanation may lie in Powers' firm conviction that "you can't win in this world. In my secular stories this world is the only one there can be, but in the clerical stories there is always the shadow of another world." Considered in this larger perspective, the apostasy of Ralph Davicci is no longer a minor matter; in terms of the grand design of the whole of Powers' fiction, it explains everything.

In **"The Poor Thing"** Catholicism plays a more prominent role than in **"Blue Island,"** which means that the astringency of the irony is increased. The Daviccis' failure to upgrade their social status is pathetic, but at least Ralph's commitment to social success was not hypocritical. However, when a character like Dolly in **"The Poor Thing"** professes to be a pious Catholic while actually sucking the lives out of all who come within reach of her wheelchair, the quality of the rendered experience isn't so much pathos as it is a kind of dumb amazement at the enormity of petty moral corruption. Apart from the Catholic element, the interpersonal actions of the two stories are quite similar: for selfish reasons, a petty power figure (Ralph Davicci, Mrs. Shepherd) manipulates a well-meaning, weak, decent human being (Ethel, Teresa) into the clutches of a moral monster (Mrs. Hancock, Dolly).

Teresa, an elderly retired spinster with an inadequate pension, is cajoled by Mrs. Shepherd—a bad shepherd leading her sheep to a fleecing—into "temporarily" accepting a position as companion to Dolly, a lifelong invalid, penny-pincher, and emotional leech. Even Teresa's unusual patience cannot endure the bizarre demands and indignities heaped upon her by the invalid, and she quits the job—only to be tricked, in a whiplash conclusion, into returning. The final irony is that the poor thing is Teresa and not the invalid Dolly. Once again, Powers reverses the stereotypes: priests are not always priestly; athletes, not always good sportsmen; Southerners, not always racial bigots eager for a lynching; and the invalid, not always a pitiful creature.

But the impact of this story does not depend solely upon the reversal of stock responses, which is simply an old O. Henry trick. Here Powers plumbs the depths of Catholic moronia and pulls up nauseating images from the sediment, and he does so with a precision and economy of effort that keeps the artistic gesture clean. (pp. 58-9)

Furthermore, the central character is not the invalid; it is Teresa, who resembles the humbler, more recent St. Therese de Lisieux, the simple nun canonized in 1925, rather than the great mystic of Avila. St. Therese was considered remarkable for her childlike simplicity, exemplifying the "little way," achieving goodness by performing the humblest deeds and by carrying out the most trivial actions. When, at the end of the story, Dolly greets Teresa with the ironic epithet, "You poor thing!," it is not merely her hypocrisy that must be observed, for the epithet would be applied even to St. Therese by many even more perceptive than Dolly. By the highest Catholic standards, implicitly evoked in the story, Teresa is not merely a soft touch; in many respects, she approaches saintliness.

However, Teresa does not quite achieve saintliness because she is, to a certain extent, trapped and corrupted by her own pride and her material needs. . . . Unlike the saint whom she resembles, she does adjust to circumstances which she is powerless to change; but her heart and most of her deeds are kind and charitable. Her moral character is left for the reader to determine for himself because, even on the level of the ordinary realism, Powers eschews direct comment.

In fact, he never so much as labels the significance of speech or gesture, with a revealing adjective. The inescapable consequence is often an ambiguity for which there is no authorial resolution. (pp. 59-60)

The "Dolly" to whom Teresa becomes companion is a plastic, inhuman contrivance—a thing of wires and flexes who is not genuinely aware that she possesses a soul: "The poor thing who met Teresa at the door in a wheelchair wore an artificial flower in her artificial hair." She has a bad habit of giggling slightly and pushing up her wig, inch by inch, showing more and more scalp. This grotesque creature with the baby face spends hours listening to soap operas on the radio and keeping books on the indulgences she gains through her special devotions. That this is a form of living death is reinforced by Dolly's inordinate interest in death—in cancer and the "leopard colonies" where "one by one, their members fall off." . . . (pp. 60-1)

Dolly, however, is not so much evil as simply moronic. She *means* to be a pious, sentimental Catholic, but her way of expressing it is unbelievably stupid. In fact, it is a real challenge to Powers' daring and ingenuity to present one of Dolly's poems:

> A sight more lovely and sweet
> Nowhere on earth have I seen
> Than the little bundles of meat
> In Mother's arms I mean.

The fact that Teresa kept this poem—the only one she did keep—confirms that even grotesquerie will not repel her from sentimental values. Horrible as she is, Dolly is nevertheless a pathetically dependent human being whom no saintly person can utterly reject. The enormity of the lie that provokes Teresa into returning to her is in itself a measure of Dolly's desperate need. But her return to Dolly, too, is ambiguous because Teresa is coerced into it by the fact that she has been accused of theft, cannot get a reference from Dolly, and is thus at the mercy of the employment agency. Hence, the pious conclusion is leavened by the iron demands of realism.

Powers seems frequently drawn to poignant or sentimental situations, but he is utterly unable to present them in sentimental terms. There is, for example, none of the pathos of Steinbeck's *paisanos,* or the cuteness of O'Hara's Pal Joey. At the very least, there is a certain restraint, detachment, and matter-of-factness, as in **"The Old Bird"**; more often there is a frame of dead-pan, mock-ironic humor, as in **"The Poor Thing."** But Powers' astringent wit does not negate sentiment; rather, it controls the qualities of character and situation which in lesser hands would degenerate into sentimentality. One of the most effective means by which Powers avoids mushiness is by removing himself from the story and letting it be simply the record of what transpires in the mind of a character. And one of the means by which he gains astringency and irony is by compressing and abruptly juxtaposing in a jarring rhythmic progression the observations and experiences of his central intelligence.

In that way, he can unemotionally display the dignity of Negro musicians who reach their limit of compromise, the compassion of a wife for her aging husband, the anguish of a boy discovering evil, the indignation of a refugee at a demonstration of racial prejudice, or the saintliness of a simple woman who serves the needs of an invalid moron. The character from whose point of view Powers projects these experiences is, in the collected stories, never one who fully understands and articulates the meaning of that experience. If not a child, an adolescent, or a moron, the narrative medium is usually, like the priest in **"The Blessing"** or the refugee's friend in **"Renner,"** a person somehow incapable of imagining or perceiving the full significance of evil about him.

However, in . . . **"Look How the Fish Live,"** which appeared in 1957 after the publication of *The Presence of Grace,* the narrative mind is more probing, more meditative than usual. Like Elwin in Trilling's "The Other Margaret" or the schoolteacher in Katherine Anne Porter's "Holiday," the central intelligence of this story actively pursues the meaning of the experience he is undergoing—and achieves insight after considerable struggle to ward it off. Without a trace of the high hilarity or the hard ironic humor of his other stories, **"Look How the Fish Live"** is sustainedly sad. George Scouffas says that it "comes perhaps closest of all his stories to overt despair over the human condition"; and Scouffas is right because, for the first and only time, the protagonist is not only caught in the grip of unalterable cosmic circumstances but is fully aware of it.

Appropriately for a meditative story, the pace is very slow. Each sequence of action and dialogue is followed by the narrator's pondering the significance of it. But again Powers characteristically probes a tremendous issue in homely, modest terms. Powers is outside the grand tradition in American literature, which presents man's confrontation with nature in terms of the huge, wild creatures of the wilderness or the sea.

The heroes of *Moby Dick, The Bear,* and *The Old Man and the Sea* are all displaced from the normal, day-to-day milieu; but Powers in **"Look How the Fish Live"** is working in a smaller and more recent movement, which includes such stories as Sherwood Anderson's "The Egg," Katherine Anne Porter's "The Grave," and William Goyen's "The White Rooster"—stories which dramatize man's conflict with nature in civilized environments. And the familiar environment paradoxically heightens rather than diminishes the horror and the anguish (just as man's inhumanity to man is no less destructive in a rectory or in a suburban living room than in a courtroom or in a prison). (pp. 61-3)

John V. Hagopian, in his J. F. Powers, *Twayne Publishers, Inc., 1968, 174 p.*

RICHARD KELLY (essay date 1969)

[*In the following excerpt, American critic Kelly discusses Powers's use of dramatic irony in his story "The Forks."*]

In his short story **"The Forks"** J. F. Powers depicts two very different kinds of priests. On the one hand is Monsignor, a man very much at home with the things of this world. He wears a Panama hat, uses "Steeple" cologne, and drives a long black car, "new like a politician's." (p. 316)

His curate, Father Eudex, on the other hand, reads the radical *Catholic Worker,* neglects to shave under his armpits (not to mention his failure to use "Steeple"), contemplates buying a Model A in opposition to Monsignor's contention that a shabby car is unbefitting to a priest, works in his undershirt with Monsignor's gardener, and sympathizes with labor unions.

In short, Powers has placed in one rectory an old, worldly traditionalist and a young, idealistic radical—and the drama that unfolds from their interaction is what the story is about. On the surface, Powers seems to be satirizing the worldly Monsignor and lauding the saintly curate, but such a reading, I hope to show, is inaccurate and ignores the dramatic structure of the entire story.

Judging the two characters by the standards of their own church, one's initial reaction is to censure Monsignor's materialism and to admire Father Eudex's Christ-like values. Father Eudex is humble (he works like a common laborer in Monsignor's garden), is on the side of social justice (the labor unions), is simple (ignores the claims of respectability and ephemeral social graces), and is possessed of an unassailable integrity (destroys his check from the Rival Tractor Company). All of his actions are Christian exemplars, but his motivation is ambiguous.

It is not entirely coincidence that Father Eudex is the exact opposite of Monsignor in almost every respect. Father Eudex's character develops in deliberate opposition to his pastor's. Instead of modelling his life directly on Christ's, he fashions it after what he views as the antithesis of Christ—Monsignor. Indeed, one may know the tree by the fruit it bears until one encounters a curious hybrid like Father Eudex. (pp. 316-17)

The very title of the story suggests the opposition between the two priests. After dinner, Monsignor notices that his curate has failed to use all the silverware provided at his plate and declares that "Father Eudex did not know the forks." The implication is that the young man's idealism is naive and a

little foolhardy, that it has blinded him to religious, social, and political exigencies.

The title also suggests a fork in the road, as if to say that the way of truth diverges in the lives of both men, that each of them has gone astray from the true spirit of Catholicism. The name Eudex itself is significant in this regard. Powers typically selects suggestive names for his characters, like Father Urban, Father Firman, and Mrs. Stoner. Hardly a common family name, Eudex is slightly disguised Latin for *iudex,* judge. Father Eudex's actions evolve from a series of negative judgments he makes of his pastor's behavior. Furthermore, Father Eudex, not Monsignor, is the person whom the reader must carefully judge and whom Powers does judge throughout the story, as will be shown.

Powers unites and recapitulates the opposing forces in his two characters in the ironic exchange between Mrs. Klein and Father Eudex. Believing Father Eudex to be cut from the same cloth as Monsignor, Mrs. Klein seeks his advice as to how she may best invest the money which her husband left her upon his death. Father Eudex, assuming that she wants to contribute to some noble cause, naively advises her that "the worthiest is the cause of the poor" and that she should "give what you have to someone who needs it." Her response is—

> "You're a nice young man," Mrs. Klein said, rather bitter now and bent to get away from him. "But I got to say this—you ain't much of a priest. And Klein said if I got a problem, see the priest—huh! You ain't much of a priest! What time's your boss come in?"

In one sense Mrs. Klein is accurate in her assessment of Father Eudex: he does fail to understand the parishioners who live in a world strangely like that of Monsignor, a world with obvious imperfections but still one that must be understood if it is to be significantly changed; and Father Eudex is perhaps too deliberate in his zeal, too high-minded, and too naive to come to terms with its representative, Mrs. Klein. It is in his encounter with the complex world that Father Eudex's failure as a priest is most crucial. . . . (p. 317)

Powers judges Father Eudex not only through the curate's perverse opposition to Monsignor and through the character of Mrs. Klein, but through an allusion to the parable of the talents. The Rival Tractor Company, in order to solve the excess-profits problem, annually mailed checks to local clergymen. Father Eudex is the only character in the story reluctant to accept the money, which he views as the company's dishonest attempt to win away sympathy from its union workers who have frequently struck against Rival. On the surface, Father Eudex again does the "right" thing:

> Father Eudex walked into the bathroom. He took the Rival check from his pocket. He tore it into little squares. He let them flutter into the toilet. He pulled the chain—hard.
>
> He went to his room and stood looking out the window at nothing. He could hear the others already giving an account of their stewardship, but could not judge them. I bought baseball uniforms for the school. I bought the nuns a new washing machine. I purchased a Mass kit for a Chicago missionary. I bought a set of matched irons. Mine helped pay for keeping my mother in a rest home upstate. I gave mine to the poor. And you, Father?

Father Eudex, like his biblical counterpart who foolishly buried his one talent, is found wanting in his stewardship. Like Eliot's tragic Thomas à Becket, Father Eudex has committed the greatest treason: he did the right thing for the wrong reason.

The total character of Father Eudex, however, is complicated. Perverse, idealistic, naive, he is nevertheless not a "bad" priest, only a human one, even as Monsignor is human. Although the parable of the talents clearly implies a judgment upon Father Eudex, the Rival Tractor Company is not analogous to the just Master in the Bible. Consequently, one's final judgment of Father Eudex is tempered with mercy and disallows the sentence of God: "But as for the unprofitable servant, cast him forth into the darkness outside, where there will be weeping and gnashing of teeth." One may assume that Father Eudex has a good number of years ahead of him in which to make peace with the complex, ironic world in order to prepare his answer to the final, ultimate, and overwhelming question, "And you, Father?" (p. 318)

> *Richard Kelly, "Father Eudex, the Judge and the Judged: An Analysis of J. F. Powers' 'The Forks,'" in* University Review, *Vol. XXXV, No. 4, June, 1969, pp. 316-18.*

ANATOLE BROYARD (essay date 1975)

[*In the excerpt below from his review of* Look How the Fish Live, *Broyard, an American essayist on literature and popular culture, focuses on weaknesses in Powers's understated style.*]

[The stories in J. F. Powers' *Look How the Fish Live*] are the sort that are generally praised as being marvelously understated. It would usually follow that the author's style, in his understatement, is delightfully lucid. Now, it seems to me that the majority of writers are understaters: there is almost always more to their characters and situations than they manage to convey. And often as not, writers do have a lucid style, which merely means that they are easily understood, rational, or clear.

But one can grow tired of understatement and lucid styles. It might be more satisfying to read stories overstuffed with significance, written in a prose, not necessarily lucid—perhaps even cloudy—which strains to express the irrational fullness of life. Understatement and lucidity may not be the natural instruments for capturing the peculiar quality of contemporary experience.

An understated story suggests that there are still areas in which things can be expressed in a "civilized" manner. So there are, and one is tempted to say that, for this very reason, they are not urgently in need of expression. A lucid style implies that there is nothing to get excited about—but if there isn't, why write? . . .

The better stories in *Look How the Fish Live* . . . concern themselves with the small, rather secular malaises that nag at the lives of priests. A bishop who is fond of using the word keystone as a metaphor is dismayed to find that his newly built cathedral has no keystones in its arches. Modern architecture has rendered them unnecessary; they would give the cathedral a heavy, horizontal feeling. Where the bishop had expected to find a keystone, there is only a crack, which is supposed to emphasize the vertical.

Now this has the makings of a splendid metaphor, but Mr.

Powers so discreetly understates it, dresses it so nakedly in his lucid style, that its possibilities are limited. The way the story is written, the bishop's character too seems to lack a keystone. One thinks of Gaudi, who designed what was intended to be the largest cathedral in the world, then deliberately put the pews so close together that the worshippers would be prevented from crossing their legs.

Another story in *Look How the Fish Live* pursues a silly man for 18 pages in order to arrive at the observation, based on a dead baby bird, that "a man couldn't commiserate with life to the full extent of his instincts and opportunities." Again, the author has something interesting in mind, but he starves it to death. His stories flirt with passions only to reject them as unseemly. When Henry James wanted to dramatize an idea like this one, he conveyed the feeling implicit in the situation by understating it lucidly 20 or 30 times, by turning understatement and lucidity into an obsession and a symbolic syntactical torment.

"One of Them," as far as I can make out, is a story about a monosyllabic priest—silent almost to the point of imbecility—whose sense of the divine order of things can only find expression in insisting that his curate eat peaches with a spoon, not a fork, and that he must leave the guest towels in the bathroom for the exclusive use of guests. Somewhere here, there is the possibility of a story, but Mr. Powers has seized it at its furthest remove, as if he had gone through its every declension of appeal to arrive at the very least.

"Bill" goes even further, if possible, in this direction. It is, quite simply, a description of a pastor who cannot discover, and will not ask, his new curate what his name is. The story is furnished, literally, with nothing but furniture, the greater part of it dealing with the bed, desk, lamps, table and so on, that the pastor buys in preparation for the arrival of his anonymous assistant. There is so little tangible evidence of the author's intention that one can only surmise that the story is mourning some lost sense of ceremony or respect in the modern church.

The bishop who was deprived of his keystone is revived in another story about a woman who saw a "vision" of the Virgin Mary. The Virgin spoke to the woman and gave her a message. The fact that the message was "keep Minnesota green" suggests all sorts of ironical things about what is happening to the church. But once more Mr. Powers, in his resolute understatement, disdains to develop his theme and kills the bishop off instead in a car accident. Unless we are willing to assume that the author has no idea what he is doing, we can only conclude that he intends for us to accept the bishop's death in the context of "keep Minnesota green." I'm damned, in both the ecclesiastical and the colloquial sense, if I know what it means.

In its treatment of the church and the clergy, *Look How the Fish Live* reminds me of the impulse that led to the translation of the mass from Latin into English. This decision attempted to bring the church to the people rather than the people to the church. It was probably the sensible thing to do, and some people would say that this was a powerful argument against it.

> *Anatole Broyard, "Look How the Fish Die," in* The New York Times, *September 25, 1975, p. 41.*

ELEANOR B. WYMARD (essay date 1976)

[In the following excerpt, Wymard explores the theme of waning spiritual values in the stories in Powers's Look How the Fish Live.]

[As] an angry young man, Powers oversimplifies the complex relationship between belief and literature with the blatant statement, "the upholstery of Christianity has held up better than the idea and practice."

Although never again so obviously stated, this germinal concept goads Powers' mature writing with compelling purpose, revealing the central unity and vital spirit of his creativity. In *Look How the Fish Live* (1975), Powers continues to expose the "upholstery of Christianity" to real light, as he tries, with edgy patience, to make some sense out of a condition that is, indeed, very human.

To gain some sense of Powers' vision in [*Look How the Fish Live*], it is important to consider the original dates of publication of some of the pivotal short stories, especially in relationship to Vatican II. The structural arrangement of these ten pieces—seven short stories, a three-act practical joke, and "two cautionary tales"—also reveals Powers' judgment that religious values in America need to be deepened and revitalized.

"The Keystone" (1963), coinciding with Vatican II, directly protests that the time has waned for good-humored tolerance of an inflexible ecclesiastical organization, for Powers is clearly critical of the institutional Church. Certainly the building of a cathedral—minus the keystone of the arches—is the central symbol of the story, but the real issue is the very nature of the monstrosity. The horror of Bishop Dullinger's dream to build a cathedral in the twentieth century city of man lies in the ignorance shared by the hierarchy, architects, contractors, and laborers who do not recognize that they are compromising the uniqueness of their own worship by camouflaging the fresh forms of today under the manufactured guises of another age. The artificiality of the Cathedral of Ostergothenburg is a metaphor for a Church that mimics a medieval culture but fails to respond to the challenge that new stones be carved for today. (pp. 182-83)

The essential issue of ["The Keystone"] involves the price the Church has paid for existing within a tight system of structured promotions which brew internal dissension and power struggles. At one time, for example, Bishop Dullinger had "given some thought to building the cathedral out of fieldstones . . . just as they came from the hand of God and were collected by farmers from their fields. . . . Monsignor Gau . . . had more or less discouraged the idea. . . ."

The missing keystone in the arches of the new cathedral is, then, the central symbol of the story: "In the middle of every arch there were *two stones; Where the keystone should have been there was just a crack.*" The archetypal symbol from 1 Peter, 2:4-8, refers to Christ as the keystone among the "living stones," that is, all life, the good and evil of reality. But the keystone is missing in the new cathedral because it is a hybrid form, proposed, designed, and executed by those ignorant of Christ's message to make all things new in him.

In **"The Keystone"** Powers is concerned that a Church which neglects the cultivation of aesthetic and intellectual excellence, neglects, too, the pursuit and expression of truth. Bishop Dullinger's scrapping of the diocesan hierarchial chart is not the act of a man with insight, but the gesture of one who

feels useless and lonely because he no longer has need to examine his conscience daily according to "Good Rules for Businessmen."

In May, 1963, the publication date of **"The Keystone,"** Vatican II was already underway. Twenty years before that, however, J. F. Powers was a prophet of that Council, for his concern has always been with the eccentricities of a Church turned inward. The tonal theme of **"The Keystone"** expresses the fear that the Church faces the curious danger of becoming an empty Gothic shell unless it tries to relate Revelation more meaningfully to the problems of contemporary life.

What does Vatican II mean then to the art and theme of Powers? The clerical stories in *Look How the Fish Live* are a scathing indictment that the Church has simply changed its upholstery. Simpson, the newly ordained curate in **"One of Them"** (1975), "stopped looking for the action, and sometimes settled down [to read] *Enthusiasm: A Chapter in the History of Religion: With Special Reference to the XVII and XVIII Centuries,* by Monsignor Knox (a convert), and shook his head at the hysteria in the Church then, as he did at the hysteria in the Church now, thinking, *Plus ça change the more it's the same. . . .*" But Simpson is no visionary: his idea of action is to canvass the office and boiler room in search, not of mystery, but of answer—in this case, the literal key to the door of the parish house. (p. 183)

According to Powers, the clergy, despite hopes and promises, are not yet confronting the awesome mystery of salvation, for they still reduce the pain of living to the superficial grievances of the rectory. In the case of the newly ordained, Incarnation, Redemption, and Resurrection are communicated by vestibule posters screaming LOVE, PEACE, and JOY. Although the vocabulary has changed, Powers' clergy are still absorbed in trivia. The Bishop of Ostergothenburg, only in his retirement, lives to bring "good news."

The inhumanity of the rectory is painful: pastors live for days without knowing a curate's name, and stay forever in their bedrooms at the head of the stairs, sealed off from the problems of the microcosmic parish. Powers hits directly at their celibacy as the reason for their alienation and loneliness. In search of **"Priestly Fellowship"** (1969), Father Joe encouraged Bill, his new assistant, to invite some seminary friends for a Sunday night buffet, but one of them is Conklin, a seminary drop-out. When conversation turns to celibacy, Joe, with unwitting smugness, says, "And when you consider we work at it [celibacy] full time, unlike the laity—well, it makes you wonder, doesn't it?"

The irony of Conklin's response, "It did me," is lost on Bill. Implied in Powers' title, **"Priestly Fellowship,"** is an exposé of the Church as human organization in juxtaposition to the Church as Mystical Body, the ideal brotherhood of all men united in the fatherhood of God. Such understatement, Powers would claim, makes for "stronger beer." To say that Powers sees no hope in the institutional Catholic Church is not to assert that he sacrifices faith in the Word. By exposing the frailty of the Church's human ways, Powers urges a necessary return to the essential Christian mysteries, blinded by mores, rubrics, and now, by strobe lights.

Placed first in the collection, the title story, **"Look How the Fish Live"** (1957), is a religious fable expressing the basic tenet of Powers' theme. Although the narrative action is slight, the plot is complex because it brings new awareness to the protagonist, an unnamed father of a family brood living in a rambling frame house surrounded by a yard which is "four city lots and full of trees, a small forest and game preserve in the old part of town." The father has never been "soft" toward the small animals who live in the yard, but on this particular day he ruminates about the "balance of nature" when he returns home to find his children trying to nurse a forgotten baby dove, while the mother dove sits "unconcerned" in a tree and soon flies away. After the bird is killed by a cat and the father buries it, Mr. and Mrs. Hahn, neighbors, stroll by and comment on the effectiveness of an insecticide for mosquitoes. The protagonist interrupts:

> "I'm sick of it all. . . . Insects, birds, and animals of all kinds. . . . Nature."
>
> Mr. Hahn smiled. "There'd be too many of those doves if things like that didn't happen. . . . Look how the fish live."
>
> He looked at the man with interest. This was the most remarkable thing Mr. Hahn had ever said in his presence. But of course Mr. Hahn didn't appreciate the implications.

Violence is potentially unchained when Mr. Hahn wants to kill the cat that killed the bird. When the father persists, "I'm sick of it all . . . children . . . women . . . and men," Mr. Hahn exclaims, "That doesn't leave much, does it?" The father ponders quietly, however:

> Who was left? God. It wasn't surprising, for all problems were at bottom theological. He'd like to put a few questions to God. God, though, knowing his thoughts, knew his questions, and the world was already in possession of all the answers that would be forthcoming from God. . . . A man had to accept his God-given limitations.

Powers seeks to reveal truth as it exists in the created order of things: his task is not to impose new order, but to explore pattern and design as they are subject to a higher perspective. When the father of **"Look How the Fish Live"** realizes his own imposition of an order upon existence, he concludes that neither can he be passive. So he plants a headstone on the grave of the dove and hopes that the cat may someday trip; after all, it *is* the nature of the cat to pursue the bird. As an artist, then, Powers is not in the Joycean tradition, a priest of the imagination creating his own independent order; instead, he traces the order of life to God. The role of Powers, as man and artist, is to discover and interpret that order, occasionally stubbing his toe and shouting angrily at enigmas he cannot understand, simply because it is the nature of human beings to behave so. (pp. 183-84)

Although Powers has been attacked and defended for his attitudes toward the Roman Catholic priest, the spiritual orientation of his fiction neither rises nor falls on his portrayal of the inner sanctum of the rectory. It provides simply an external structure for his pursuing the deeper problem that our generation is condemning itself to unfulfillment by ceasing to search for Mystery and Truth. The unnamed father [in the story, **"Tinkers"**] is the spokesman for Powers' repeated them that, although the order of life is inscrutable, man, by using his uniquely human powers, can question his existence and thereby come to a realization of, not only his finitude, but also his freedom. For Powers, the ironies, perplexities, and paradoxes of the human situation ultimately seem to make some sense and achieve some order only if viewed from a van-

tage point that embraces eternity. "Who was left? God." (pp. 184-85)

Eleanor B. Wymard, "The Church of J. F. Powers," in Commonweal, *Vol. CIII, No. 6, March 12, 1976, pp. 182-84.*

ARLENE SCHLER (essay date 1977)

[*In the excerpt below, Schler asserts that Powers's story "Lions, Harts, Leaping Does" is informed by the theology of St. John of the Cross, a sixteenth-century Spanish mystic.*]

The fiction of J. F. Powers moves dialectically; the characters achieve no final conclusion to their movements but rather struggle through expectancies, compromises and contradictions, only to reach ambiguity. When Didymus, one of Powers' complex contemporary clerics, closes his eyes at the conclusion of Powers' masterful short story **"Lions, Harts, Leaping Does"** and imagines the snow darkly falling, he finds himself drowning in ambiguity: he has struggled throughout the story to find some assurance of his spiritual salvation but dies, it seems, without any. The lack of assurance has led to the general academic interpretation that Didymus is not saved. (p. 159)

J. F. Powers, through Didymus, examines the difficulty a rational man, even a cleric, has in discerning the road to salvation. What are the signs? What are the feelings? What assurances are there? Although Didymus, a Franciscan friar, knows that the spirit of his vows of poverty, chastity and obedience "opened the way and revealed to the soul . . . the means of salvation," perhaps Didymus, himself, is not the best judge of his spiritual status. After all, he is identified with doubting Thomas. "Didymus" is the twin name for Thomas. And Didymus deliberately doubts his own demonstration of sanctity; for every humble Christian act he performs he purposely finds some profane, prideful action to cancel it. Like doubting Thomas, Didymus acts more the man of reason than of faith. After all the years Didymus has taught geometry he considers himself more rational than spiritual: he puts himself, uneasily though, "foremost among the wise in their own generation, the perennials seeking after God when doctor, lawyer and bank fails."

Didymus, rather than content himself with an optimistic but perhaps erroneous conclusion, preoccupies himself with fear of hell and with self-reproval for being lukewarm towards God. Yet does Didymus encounter any road signs to heaven which he ignores or misses that would give an objective indication of his spiritual status? The story does contain an objective measure of the condition of his soul—the sixteenth-century theological system of the Spanish mystic St. John of the Cross.

The most obvious reference to St. John's system is the title of the story—**"Lions, Harts, Leaping Does"**—a translation of a line from St. John's poem "Cántico Espiritual." Didymus while dying, hears the passage containing this line from "Cántico Espiritual" read aloud by Titus, a fellow friar. St. John devotes his theological system to explaining and identifying the spiritual steps to salvation; he poetically and prosaically describes the psychological dilemmas suffered by the soul in its ascent towards God. (pp. 159-60)

Key metaphors and symbols from St. John's works appear in Powers' short story; the presence and sequence of appearance of these metaphors and symbols are the road signs on Didymus' ascent to heaven. The metaphor of the night and the symbols of the house and ladder are significant in St. John's poetry; the night, the house and ladder signify certain theological arguments offered by St. John in his poem "la Noche Oscara del Alma" ("Dark Night of the Soul") and explained in his book *Subida del Monte Carmelo* (*Ascent of Mount Carmel*). The metaphor of the night and the symbols of the house and ladder operate within the short story and explain the struggles in Didymus' spiritual ascent.

Superimposing St. John's theological system on **"Lions, Harts, Leaping Does"** reveals that when Didymus closes his eyes at the end of the story, he has ended his earthly existence at some point in the illuminative life—the second stage of the soul in its path to salvation. Right before he dies, he tries to surrender himself completely to God but fails. The life of union with God cannot be achieved on earth; only the purgative and illuminative stages can be realized in the mundane. Because St. John, through his own vivid experiences, knew the divine signs of salvation to be difficult for rational man to recognize, he invented his theological system. Applying his system to the story determines that Didymus' soul, despite Didymus' own conclusion, is not in peril but somewhere on the road to glory.

According to the Saint's prose commentaries in *Subida del Monte Carmelo,* the metaphor of the night in his poem "la Noche Oscura del Alma" designates the "darkness" that envelops the soul while searching for faith to guide it to God. Faith involves the extinction of reason, and "compared with the insight of natural reason the knowledge of faith is dark. . . ." In the story while Didymus seeks faith he moves in a physical darkness. The story begins with Titus, a brother, reading the biographies of the Popes to Didymus in a cell forsaken by the "winter daylight." When Didymus attempts to pray in the chapel at four in the afternoon that winter day, he observes that no light passes through the stained glass windows. Finally, he questions the salvation of his soul as he lies dying during the night.

In "la Noche Oscura del Alma" the house represents the carnal appetites which cage in man, obstructing him in his pursuit of God. Didymus is identified with his pet canary held captive in a cage: "They were captives he and the canary and the only thing they craved was escape." Didymus decides to free the canary: although confined to a wheelchair from a recent fall, he determinedly lifts his deteriorating body from the wheelchair to reach the bird cage hanging by the window. Straining, he opens the cage and then "fell over on his face and lay prone on the floor." That night "unsuffering and barely alive," he acknowledges that his mind and eye improve in sensitivity "because his body, now faint, no longer blurred his vision." Didymus' bodily functions and needs no longer distract him. The bird's cage (house) permits him to be released from his own "house"—his body which houses his soul—and thereby attain the first step of spiritual salvation which is pacification of carnal desires.

In the transition from the purgative to illuminative life, according to St. John, the soul gradually and reluctantly relinquishes its reliance upon the rational and sensible faculties to a dependence upon faith. Before his incapacitating fall Didymus admits himself to be a man of reason who is distracted by a cacophony of outside stimulation. When Didymus first becomes ill, he passes time by musing at the dead winter landscape outside his window. Since he has not yet passed

through the purgative life, his sensibilities are at war and the "ground . . . appeared to be involved in a struggle of some kind, possibly to overlap each other, constantly shifting." (pp. 160-62)

Didymus observes nature through the "faith" he professes "in his faculties" and savors "the cosmic truth in the falling drops and the mildly trembling branches. There was order. . . ." Didymus shows no leap of faith; he demonstrates himself to be, before his incapacitating fall, a man of science—dependent upon his sensible faculties to understand God's universe. He does, however, make the transition from a man of reason to a man of faith. Since after his debilitating fall his body no longer blurs his vision, the landscape, whose alternating harmony and cacophony once distracted him, is now perceived with equanimity: " . . . he could count the snowflakes, all of them separately, before they drifted, winding, below the sill." And Didymus, now purged of bodily desires, finds that he " . . . suddenly could pray." When he attempted to pray earlier in the story, he disgracefully fell asleep.

With his evidence of faith and his passing through the purgative life, Didymus enters the illuminative life—that period during which his will must be purified of all thoughts and desires contrary to the Divine. While waiting for death to take his wearied body, he feels that "he wanted nothing in the world for himself at last. This may have been the first time he found his will amenable to the Divine." But even so close to sublimity, Didymus debates the evidence of his sanctity with himself, demonstrating the struggle a rational man goes through while trying to rely on faith. Didymus, even while reciting his Hail Marys, trying "to turn his thoughts from himself, to join them to God," ponders "how at last he did—didn't he NOW?—prefer God above all else." Didymus fears that his humility before God is a disguise for inverted pride; rather than counter his question of despair with hope for his salvation, he deliberately sins after reciting his Hail Marys "by flooding his mind with maledictions." (p. 162)

St. John explains that this confused and agonized state of the soul in its ascent to heaven is to be expected: "There is no desire for anything else but God and one suffers, by reason of not loving and serving God enough." Didymus is experiencing the active and frustrating mental purgation of his will of all thoughts and acts contrary to the Divine. He is passing through the active night of the soul as opposed to the passive night of the soul in which the soul can peacefully embrace the Divine because it has already been purged. The soul must encounter the active night of the soul before the passive night of the soul which is closer to the life of union with God. Didymus, then, is ascending the road to salvation in the sequence set forth by St. John in "la Noche Oscura del Alma": only a soul purged of carnal desires can participate in the illuminative life where the soul is first actively purged of all thoughts contrary to the Divine and eventually is tranquilly submerged in the Divine.

The illuminative life in St. John's poetry is symbolized by the ladder and the metaphor of the night, a night darker than experienced in the purgative life. In the poem "la Noche Oscura del Alma," the soul, purged of carnal desires, ascends through the illuminative life towards union with God by a secret staircase or literally a concealed ladder ("escala disfrazada"). . . . After he passes through the purgative life, Didymus acts out the final stages of his earthly life in a darker night and observes a celestial ladder.

While night descends Didymus, dying in bed, listens to Titus, appropriately enough, read to him from St. John of the Cross. Titus reads the "lions, harts, leaping does" passage, as well as the commentary on the passage; the passage reflects the distractions and obstructions the soul encounters in its ascent towards God. In the midst of Titus' recitation, Didymus asks him to shut off the light; only the glow of moonlight illuminates the room. Automatically the night has grown darker for Didymus—another road sign to heaven.

And like the ascending soul in St. John's poem, Didymus, after the lights are out, beholds that "a full moon let down a ladder of light." St. John explains in *Subida del Monte Carmelo* that the ladder connotes the steps that the soul travels while climbing towards God after the appeasement of the senses. While the soul ascends the ladder it must extinguish all thoughts opposed to the Divine and gradually depend totally on faith for guidance. Didymus beholds the ladder at exactly the right moment: after he has purged his carnal desires through his incapacitating fall, after the night has grown darker and before he has demonstrated his faith through prayer—evidence of purging of his will.

Didymus at the final moments of earthly life and the final words of the story enters, then, the illuminated life of the soul. According to St. John only the purgative and illuminative lives can be achieved in earthly life; the life of union with God can be achieved only in heaven. Didymus right before his expiration "with his whole will . . . tried to lose himself in the sight of God, and failed." Has Didymus begun his ascent on the ladder to heaven only to find that it goes nowhere? Perhaps Didymus tried to begin his sainthood too early. As explained in "la Noche Oscura del Alma," the soul's complete surrender to God can be effectively achieved only in heaven, but also when the soul reaches closer to union with God, the night becomes lighter, as if dawn were approaching. The night of Didymus' demise does not gradually become lighter. In fact, Didymus' final earthly vision is the snowflakes "darkly falling" in the interior of his mind. Perhaps his attempt to ascend higher in the illuminative life is premature; his will is still being purged in the active night of the soul.

Since the last words on Didymus' spiritual ascent end on a dark note, Powers, it seems, has again led his character into ambiguity. Didymus is confused about his spiritual status because he cannot find the final divine sign that will allow him to conclude that his salvation, like a geometric proof, is *quod erat demonstrandum*. He fails to recognize, though, any of the positive signs, as revealed through St. John of the Cross, that he is on the right path to heaven. This ambiguity could be a hopeful indication, at least in St. John's system, that his soul is in the midst of active pursuit of God within the illuminative life. Also, Didymus' ambiguity could be an unavoidable condition of his mundane life, for only God can ultimately judge his soul. . . . Didymus' confusion should not persuade the reader, therefore, that Didymus will be denied ultimate deliverance. (pp. 163-64)

The ultimate question—the salvation of Didymus—cannot be answered during the course of the short story, for the final judgment of Didymus' soul will be rendered only in his afterlife. (p. 164)

Arlene Schler, "How to Recognize Heaven When You See It: The Theology of St. John of the Cross in J. F. Powers' 'Lions, Harts, Leaping Does,'" in Studies in Short Fiction, *Vol. 14, No. 2, Spring, 1977, pp. 159-64.*

ELEANOR B. WYMARD (essay date 1977)

[*In the essay excerpted below, Wymard compares chapters of Powers's first novel,* Morte d'Urban, *with the short stories that evolved from them and demonstrates Powers's understanding of the differences between the short story and novel forms.*]

When J. F. Powers published *Morte D'Urban* (1962), he sprung no surprises. Many chapters were already known by readers of *The New Yorker, The Kenyon Review, The Critic,* and *Esquire.* Although J. V. Hagopian has pointed out that many critics err in "seeing *Morte D'Urban* as an episodic satire rather than a unified novel," no one has examined the kind of rewriting Powers did to adapt chapters to the short story form. The revisions reveal, however, his awareness of the distinct demands of the two *genres,* for in the short stories Powers depends upon economical exposition to clarify conflict and resolution, whereas the chapters of *Morte D'Urban* relish ambiguity and paradox. Even though stylistic changes often appear to be slight, the stories do not copy the words of the novel, nor does the novel copy the words of the stories.

Having published his first . . . novel after proving himself for twenty years as a writer of short stories, Powers was aware that *Morte D'Urban* could raise a thorny structural problem. He reveals such concerns in a 1960 interview with Donald McDonald: "I'm writing a novel but due to my circumstances I write chapters and turn them into short stories and sell them as stories, which they are actually—I'm afraid they're more stories than chapters—to *The New Yorker* and that's how I get by." Powers stresses, moreover, that his novel is not a "longer short story." His stylistic problem was the danger of "too many words" in the novel; yet he recognized that he could not simply "cut" the words so significant to the differentiation of the structure of the chapters of the novel and that of the short stories. The former and the latter were to him as different as an "Old Fashioned with a cherry" and a "Martini."

Chapter one of *Morte D'Urban,* **"The Green Banana,"** was the first to be published as a short story [in 1956]. . . . It is easy to understand why Powers worried about "too many words" because the indirection of the novel often had to be sacrificed for exposition in the short story. Father Urban's first meetings with Billy Cosgrove, for example, are captured with immediate detail in the "Overture," but in **"The Green Banana,"** the short story, Powers pins them down through retrogression: "It had been a lucky day for the Order when, about a year before, Billy turned up, after Mass, in the sacristy of a suburban church where Father Urban was appealing for funds." Through flashback, Powers marshals the past that is necessary to realize the shock of the transfer of Father Urban to Duesterhaus. In the novel, however, Powers stresses the moment-by-moment living of Father Urban because the process of his growth is dependent upon a sequential ordering of events.

A well-placed word in **"The Green Banana,"** for example, modifies the ambiguity of Urban's behavior, whereas the paradox of his motivation and his quiet metamorphosis are the thematic kernel of the novel. This difference demands a change in technique, apparent at the end of **"The Green Banana"** when Urban and Jack finish a sumptuous dinner in the Pump Room:

> "Shouldn't drink so much," Father Urban said.
> "You can't handle it."

"No," Father Jack said, "I can't. As a matter of fact, I've never cared for it in any form. One of the hardest things about the priesthood for me—the wine."

"Why didn't you say so?" said Father Urban crossly, but he knew why Jack hadn't said so. Jack, out of place in these surroundings but determined not to show it, was dead game.

Powers is not so explicit in the novel: " 'Why didn't you say so?' Father Urban knew why, though. Jack had been trying to keep his end up." **"The Green Banana"** is the first chapter of *Morte D'Urban,* and, as such, Urban faces an open future that Powers cannot cheaply direct with a charged word like *crossly.* In the *New Yorker* version, Powers rounds off the story with defined certainties about the abrasive difference between Urban and Jack. . . . The texture of the novel implies rather than states the contrast between the personalities of Urban and Jack. The entire novel, through its structure, develops their differences on a gradual continuum. (pp. 84-5)

A consideration of Powers' "feel" for form reveals that **"Twenty-Four Hours in a Strange Diocese"** [1962] is not re-worked simply to change the name of Father Urban to Father Nightengale. The *Esquire* story begins and ends, for example, in Ostergothenburg. This structural maneuver eliminates the initial incident of the chapter about the blossoming of the golf course, an event important to the novel because it implies exactly the opposite of Urban's unheralded entry into Ostergothenburg. Unrecognized and unappreciated there, Urban feels secure to return to his successes at the Hill. Ironically foreshadowed in the golf game at the beginning of this chapter, however, is the impinging defeat of Father Urban, for his arrogant superiority at golf challenges the Bishop to a return duel. The novel involves, then, a careful plotting of past, present, and future to reveal the death in life, life in death of Urban, whose lifetime experiences are more complex than those of Father Nightengale, who spends **"Twenty-Four Hours in a Strange Diocese."**

In the short story, **"Wrens and Starlings"** [1960], Powers is again concerned with the tensions of a day. He recollects first, however, the trials of Urban at Duesterhaus, leading into the major incident, the crucial match fought to capture and defend the golf course, the Clementines' land of plenty. Whereas the short story ends with Monsignor Renton, Wilf, and the Bishop lionizing Father Urban in his hospital bed, a scene effectively conveying unity and the victory of Urban as the champion of the Clementines, the chapter in *Morte D'Urban* ends precisely with the accident, leaving the hospital scene to "God Writes. . . ."

Such a change is not arbitrary. In *Morte D'Urban* the beaning is the crisis of Urban's life, not simply an accident that rallies the clergy together for the preservation of St. Clement's Hill. Powers reconciles the tension of the day by ending his short story in Urban's hospital room, but in the novel Powers is concerned with the tensions of a life-time. The larger theme of *Morte D'Urban* stretches the pattern of recovery and reconciliation outside the limits of a short story that seems to cover the same material. In the short stories, Father Urban is seen in one-to-one relationships: battling the Clementines or the Bishop, catering to Billy, swallowing his pride with Father John. But the lens of the novel widens the spatial world of Father Urban, indicating opaque dimensions shaped by a merger of the Arthurian legacy with American myth and Christian mystery. The very essence of *Morte D'Urban* is ex-

pressed, then, through its structure, a structure that is deeper and more complex than the premiere short stories, even if considered together, reveal. (pp. 85-6)

Eleanor B. Wymard, "On the Revisions of 'Morte D'Urban,' " in Studies in Short Fiction, *Vol. 14, No. 1, Winter, 1977, pp. 84-6.*

MICHAEL TRUE (essay date 1978)

[*In the following excerpt, True analyzes Powers's fiction from an anthropological perspective, asserting that his novels and stories document the evolution of the Catholic Church in the United States since the 1940s.*]

The fiction of J. F. Powers is, among other things, one of the important artifacts of American Catholicism, and the significance of his stories, including **"The Hair Shirt"** (1978)—probably a section from a novel announced some years ago—can hardly be overestimated, in their revelations about what has happened to that institution over the past 35 years.

I do not mean to impose limitations on the significance of Powers's stories by concentrating on their cultural or anthropological implications, but merely to describe one way of reading them. I agree, in general, with Peter de Vries's statement, in 1963, that Powers's stories are not necessarily about the church at all, but about "that much older community, the human race." The church just happens to be his world, as Hemingway's world was war and violent death, or Flannery O'Connor's was the South and backwoods prophets. As a subject, the church appears to have chosen him, rather than he the church. What happens with that subject, how people relate to one another or how they refuse to relate to one another, is what amuses and delights us and what keeps us hoping for more stories and novels from this modern master of prose fiction.

Having said that, one turns, nonetheless, to the subject at hand, looking at Powers's work from a decidedly Catholic viewpoint. There we find, of all things, ourselves: cradle Catholics in disarray, our religious ground cut out from under us, clergy wandering about the rectory, nervous about their lives, their earthly fortunes and their tarnished honor. Amid the irony and humor, the reader is conscious, too, of the serious nature of this comedy. Living in Powers's world is like living, at times, in one of those monastic orders, with a skull (memento mori) constantly in view. Death haunts several of the characters, clerical and lay, in the recent collection, *Look How the Fish Live* (1975), as it did in earlier ones, especially in **"Lions, Harts and Leaping Does"** (1943) and in the novel *Morte d'Urban,* which received the National Book Award in 1963.

Since the very beginning, Powers has captured the Catholic scene with almost painful accuracy. . . .

"The Lord's Day" and **"The Valiant Woman,"** both published in the mid-1940's and frequently anthologized, were some of the first delineations of what actually happened in the Catholic ghetto. These and later stories describe the schools, rectories and convents with something of the stark realism of James T. Farrell's *Studs Lonigan,* savoring the parochial scene for its comic, rather than its tragic, implications. They tell about power struggles between priests and nuns, younger and older clergy, about who shall control whom and for what purposes.

Rereading them, in light of the Second Vatican Council and of Powers's later work, one is struck by the fact that however remote the precise conditions of that earlier Catholic scene, the characters and incidents continue to live vividly in the stories. The conflicts so perfectly described seem eternal and the sense of the world as strong as that in the novels of Jane Austen, however distant the reader may be from the physical world that the characters inhabit. The fiction seems to gather strength from the fact that some aspects of the American Catholic scene described there, in pure, naturalistic detail, may have disappeared forever.

In **"The Lord's Day,"** for example, the main character is a mother superior of a small group of nuns "forced" into counting the Sunday collection for the local pastor. Throughout the story, she tries, unsuccessfully, to maneuver the pastor of the nearby church into repairing the convent's kitchen stove. Through dialogue and a minimum of commentary, the reader witnesses the nun's defeat, the sort of minor humiliation that symbolizes the powerlessness of women at the mercy of the dominating male clergy. (p. 202)

Though often regarded as a traditionalist in matters ecclesiastical, Powers, in this story, "exposed" the oppressive nature of sexism among the clergy, in a story written 20 years before Mary Daly's *The Church and the Second Sex,* and long before similar issues came to occupy a central place in church forums.

In **"The Valiant Woman,"** one gets a picture of the opposite situation, the power that a woman, a housekeeper at a parish rectory, has over the clergy she "serves." Mrs. Stoner, an Irishwoman widowed early in life, has devoted her best years to the care and subtle torture of Father John Firman. In the most famous card game in literature since Belinda met the Baron at Hampton Court in Pope's "The Rape of the Lock," Powers describes two modern antagonists on the field of battle, that is, at a game of honeymoon bridge. The priest, who—like the nun in **"The Lord's Day"**—suffers defeat, is the central consciousness.

Mrs. Stoner, the housekeeper, having banished Father Firman's old seminary friend, following an early birthday dinner, prepares the table and cards and openly plans her attack.

> She played for blood, no bones about it, but for her there was no other way; it was her nature, as it was the lion's, and for this reason [Father Firman] found her ferocity pardonable, more a defect of the flesh, venial, while his own trouble was all in the will, mortal. He did not sweat and pray over each card as she must, but he did keep an eye out for reneging and . . . he was always secretly hoping for aces.

(pp. 202-03)

Even though women are still excluded from major administrative and liturgical posts, it is hard to imagine things ever again being quite as oppressive for women religious as they were for the nun in **"The Lord's Day"**; and the Catholic scene is just not as clubby now, even for housekeepers, as it was when **"The Valiant Woman"** was written. In spite of the change, however, Powers shows that the subjects for satire are still as numerous among American Catholics as they ever were.

In **"Fellowship,"** for example, or **"Bill,"** both from *Look How the Fish Live,* the church is still the frame, if not the central picture, for Powers's fiction. Generally, it is tilted fur-

ther to emphasize the peculiarities of the postconciliar church, but not so far as to completely distort the view. As a fiction writer, he is, if anything, surer in his satiric vision. The characters, as in Sinclair Lewis's classic short story, "The Man Who Knew Coolidge," often reveal themselves in conversation. Yet Powers's stories have a sophistication, a highly polished style and a consistency in point of view that Lewis seldom maintained. He is tolerant of his characters' small-town mendacities, as Lewis was, ultimately, of Carol Kendicott's or even George Babbitt's, but there is no sudden conversion or shift in attitude. All is presented from a Horatian rather than a Juvenalian perspective, Powers's satire belonging to the tradition of Alexander Pope's milder ridicule rather than that of Samuel Johnson's moral indignation.

They are stories about what happens to people who no longer believe strongly in the principles that are supposed to govern their lives. They are about priests whose arid lives suggest that although their faith has departed, they are stuck with the same old job and a kind of hell that other people inflict upon them. In the midst of such emptiness and loneliness, they hope for **"Priestly Fellowship,"** as they hoped, in an earlier story, for **"The Presence of Grace."** Likely as not, they end up with a rectory in chaos and a new assignment that brings not peace, but a sword.

Although *Look How the Fish Live* includes several stories that have nothing to do with parish life, Powers is more often than not at his best on the old ground. The old ground, the church, has shifted slightly, but his seismograph measures the changes more accurately than any sociological study. Although a young curate with long hair and a bishop with a flair for public relations look and act somewhat differently from those that appeared in his stories a generation ago, they belong to the same old gang. The fact that their world is more complex may suggest that the changes in the church deprived Powers momentarily of the caricatures that a satirist manipulates to his own advantage. But the nature of the changes, superficial in their implications, appears to have strengthened, rather than weakened, his hold on that world. Everything, he suggests, including even the most ancient institutions, teeters on the brink of commercialism, and the earlier version is thus confirmed by subsequent developments.

"Farewell," a recent story, represents the best in the later style. There, the central figure, John Dullinger, Bishop of Ostergothenburg, Minn.—a diocese and clergy owned and operated solely by J. F. Powers—reflects upon his change of status, as the former auxiliary, Bishop Gau, assumes command. (p. 203)

In this story and in a companion piece, **"Keystone,"** the structure of the church, physically and intellectually, has clearly weakened. The new bishop, a public-relations expert with a talent for administration (he recently set up a "successful" diocesan procurement office) replaces a traditionalist, whose administration is remembered, according to the Ostergothenburg Times, "not least for its churches." Dullinger watches as his plan for a cathedral with keystones in the arches gives way to the auxiliary bishop's plan for a cathedral without keystones and, later, as hairline cracks begin to appear "here and there in the fabric of the structure." For all his limitations, the retiring bishop has a certain dignity, reserve and generosity that others lack. He responds immediately to calls for help from parish priests in the boondocks who are ill and to one seeking guidance about a local parishioner who "thought she'd seen an apparition of our Lady in a tree on several likely occasions." The reader is left to wonder if the younger, flashier Bishop Gau will age as well.

Two other stories from the same collection, **"Bill"** and **"Priestly Fellowship,"** dramatize the effect of change in another context, the conflict between a middle-aged pastor, hungry for companionship, and a young curate just out of the seminary. The first story contrasts the rather formal, impersonal manner of the pastor and the casual, impersonal manner of the curate who, to the consternation of his new boss, manages to withhold any knowledge about his background, including his last name. For Father Joe, "Bill" exemplifies the younger generation's lack of professional skills, having been ordained "without even a hunt and peck command of typing." And the parishioners these days are even more unpredictable. . . . (pp. 203-04)

Perhaps in presenting the old bishop and Father Joe sympathetically, Powers is simply casting his lot with those, like the late Evelyn Waugh—whose work he admired—who ridicule all change in the church, as if it were their private club. As a moralist and satirist, he would thus follow the traditional pattern. But his picture of American Catholicism, in its Midwestern guise, is subtler than that, and must be viewed in a wider context. He reflects, first of all, a constituency that has been in the midst of change for some time, where liturgical and social reforms antedated Vatican II. Some of them centered, in fact, at St. John's University, Collegeville, Minn., where Powers presently teaches. He is no desperate Boston or New York Jansenist anxious for apocalypse of the New Jerusalem—a fact that may account for the impatience reflected in a recent comment about Powers's later message and style.

In a surprisingly negative review of *Look How the Fish Live,* for example, Tom McHale, author of several "Catholic" novels, including *Principato* and *Farragan's Retreat,* wrote that Powers had not grown as a writer, over the years; worse, McHale argued, Powers measured "the beat of his world in tiny pats, when a good hard slam is what it needs." It is as if someone were criticizing Henry James for not behaving like Micky Spillane. But McHale's review points toward a significant difference in sensibility between a Jesuit-educated Eastern Catholic who behaves as if there were no escape from the church and a relaxed Midwesterner, mildly puzzled and intrigued by all the fuss. "The church is a frigging cancer," according to one of McHale's characters in *Principato,* the vehemence of the character's remark, like the hostility of the review, suggesting the distance between McHale's absurdist humor and Powers's more tolerant satire. It is a difference not only in material, but also in tone, and like many matters of literary judgment, it reflects principally a difference in taste. As a reader, one has the luxury of enjoying and admiring both styles, but for anyone interested in the church as an institution, Powers's work is, I think, eminently more revealing, whether one speaks of the early work or the very latest published story. . . .

Powers's view that the changing church has not changed at all may turn out to be the most accurate—and disturbing—view we have. (p. 204)

> Michael True, "The Changing Church and J. F.
> Powers," in America, Vol. 139, No. 9, September 30,
> 1978, pp. 202-04.

MARY GORDON (essay date 1982)

[*Gordon is an American novelist whose works have been well received for their subtle evocations of the effects of a Catholic upbringing and education. In the excerpt below, Gordon examines the components of Powers's comedy.*]

Powers is a comic writer of genius, and there is no one like him. In vain one looks for precedents—English scenes of comical clerical life in Sterne or Trollope or Goldsmith do not do; the English tone is sweeter, for those clergymen never have to worry if the community wants someone like them around. In those novels, if the clerics themselves do not represent personal power, they represent an institution whose power is unquestioned. The furtive, hot desire for assimilation is impossible to imagine in the rural towns where those parsons christen, marry, bury. And the high drama circling around the priests of Bernanos or Graham Greene flies nowhere near the carefully barbered, untonsured heads of the Powers clergy. It is America that Powers writes about, and the peculiar situations of its Catholic priests illumines the larger world that they inhabit as the lives of outsiders who remain outside by the fixed nature of their identities must always do.

The isolated world—the pilgrimage, the madhouse, the country house, the colonial outpost—is a natural setting for the kind of comedy whose implications are at once moral and social. Life is denser in such places; personalities conform to types and types to personality; objects tell as they do not where the press of things and people is less close. It is in the close, packed atmosphere of parishes and monasteries that the comedy of Powers grows and flourishes: an odd, rare bloom: satiric, harsh, and yet not condemning, falling with an undisguisable relish upon the clergy's faults yet based upon a tough and weary faith in what these clergymen so ineptly represent. Powers's voice is dry, supremely ironic; it is a difficult one for Americans, who like their comedy, it seems, with fewer modulations, and do not read him. (p. 29)

[Powers] has one subject: priests; his stories on other topics are far less memorable. His great and unique talent lies in his ability to record the daily lives of priests; he does this with sympathy, yet with close, hilarious attention to the errors of their lives spelled out by their possessions and their diction.

He writes without romance and without rancor, perhaps because he sees the priests he likes as largely powerless. He never expects heroics from them; the irony of their lives that he so clearly sees is that the expectation of heroics is implicit in their vocation. Yet they inhabit the actual world, west of Chicago, and they are unexceptional, average Americans, who must live out the history of apostolic succession in a mode particularly American. Truly American, they cannot really comprehend the European ideal of the Roman Church. Like the millionaire who builds himself a villa in Michigan—installing copies of the Venus de Milo in each of his ten bathrooms—they both misunderstand the ideal and rudely try to force domestication on it. In addition, being priests, they are necessarily alone—unsure tenants, poor relations, dependent upon the charity of strangers whom they must, if they are true to their vows, serve, impress, and keep as strangers.

The story **"The Forks"** concerns a pastor and a curate; it is a story about power and authority, youth and age, idealism and *Realpolitik* as well as about the uneasy cohabitation of God and Mammon. The pastor, known only as Monsignor, has taken Christ's counsel to the unjust steward: he has made friends for himself with the Mammon of wickedness, so well that he is far more at ease with local businessmen than he is with the Roman Church. (pp. 29-32)

Monsignor imagines himself a man of culture and his curate a boor. But his notion of European culture is entirely Midwestern; in an outburst of outraged sensibility, he complains that his housekeeper has included green olives in the "tutti-frutti" salad he has asked for; he plans a lady garden in the back of the rectory, calling for a fleur-de-lis, a sundial, a cloister walk "running from the rectory to the garage." Father Eudex, the curate, who tries to help the janitor with the job of digging, sees the project as expensive, and, in this country, "Presbyterian."

Yet the center of the story is not truly social comedy, but a serious moral-religious issue. The local tractor company, a successful concern with an execrable record toward its employees, solves its excess profits problem by sending out regular checks as "donations" to the local clergy. Father Eudex, whose sympathies are strongly pro-labor, understands the checks to be the most blatant whitening of the sepulchers, but he doesn't know what he should do with his—send it to the missions, hand it over to the company's workers' strike fund? The pastor advises him to put it toward the new car he has been wanting, a car that will make the right kind of point about his station.

Father Eudex makes his decision after a parishioner comes to him seeking not spiritual but financial advice, and accuses him of not being "much of a priest" when he suggests she give some money to the poor. He flushes the tractor company's check down the toilet in a rapture of righteous divestment. But Powers ends the story with Father Eudex's priggish reflection on the superiority of his position to that of his fellow clerics who might have used their checks for good works. The final disembodied line, "And you, Father?" refuses to settle the question whether virtue lies in the pure act, with its wage of pride, or in the muddled gift, which serves the poor by abetting the wicked.

In **"Prince of Darkness,"** Powers introduces us to the inner life of Father Ernest Burner, an entirely mediocre timeserver, a glutton, a cynic, adolescent in his desire to be on the opposite side of whatever position is taken by the younger curate. Powers's attitude and tone are complicated, and are the source of the story's comedy. Burner lives in front of a mythic backdrop; even Powers's most secular readers know the image of the devoted pastor burning himself out for his flock. Burner knows he fails but does not change. He is a romantic whose sin is sloth, the least romantic of the lot. He fantasizes a heroic life, a martyr's death. Even if we have our doubts, even if we suspect that the *Dies Irae* might find Father Burner hiding under his bed—Powers shows us Burner putting golf balls into his roman collar, claiming that he is off to visit the sick when he is taking flying lessons, leaving a used match in the holy water font—we cannot help seeing the pathos of his adolescent dreams, even his most down-to-earth one: being named a pastor. We don't want him to have to write his mother again, telling her that he has been appointed assistant yet another time and that she will have to wait even longer to fulfill their joint dream of her becoming his housekeeper. . . . (p. 32)

We never see Powers's priests doing any harm to the laity. There are no scenes of tormeted penitents being denied con-

solation. It is impossible, for example, to be genuinely worried about the penitent in this confessional scene:

"Were you married by a priest?"

"Yes."

"How long ago was that?"

"Four years."

"Any children?"

"No."

"Practice birth control?"

"Yes, sometimes."

"Don't you know it's a crime against nature and the Church forbids it?"

"Yes."

"Don't you know that France fell because of birth control?"

"No."

"Well, it did. Was it your husband's fault?"

"You mean—the birth control?"

"Yes."

"Not wholly."

"And you've been away from the Church ever since your marriage?"

"Yes."

"Now you see why the Church is against mixed marriages. All right, go on. What else?"

"I don't know . . ."

"Is that what you came to confess?"

"No. Yes. I'm sorry, I'm afraid that's all."

"Do you have a problem?"

"I think that's all, Father."

"Remember it is your obligation, and not mine, to examine your conscience. The task of instructing persons with regard to these matters—I refer to the connubial relationship—is not an easy one. Nevertheless, since there is a grave obligation imposed by God, it cannot be shirked. If you have a problem—"

"I don't have a *problem*."

The language is perfect: "pure" Powers, the "problem," the "connubial relationship," the logical leap from birth control to the fall of France and the penitent's understandable confusion. But, after all, she doesn't have a "problem," she'll be all right. In Powers's stories, no one suffers nearly so much as the priests themselves.

In **"The Valiant Woman,"** the priestly suffering occurs at the hands of a truly monstrous housekeeper, the worst possible type of shrewish wife. Father Firman, the pastor, is as trapped as any tormented husband; he can't bear the guilt of getting rid of Mrs. Stoner, and besides, he can't afford to pension her off. Yet she has ruined his life:

> She hid his books, kept him from smoking, picked his friends . . ., bawled out people for calling after dark, had no humor, except at cards and then it was grim, very grim, and she sat hatchet-faced every morning at Mass. But she went to Mass, which was all that kept the church from being empty some mornings. She did annoying things all day long. She said annoying things into the night. She said she had given him the best years of her life.

Powers flawlessly brings home the real horror of the woman, hostile, omnipresent, self-satisfied, encyclopedically misinformed.

> She smiled pleasantly at Father Nulty. "And what do you think of the atom bomb, Father?"
>
> "Not much," Father Nutly said. . . .
>
> "Did you read about this communist convert, Father?"
>
> "He's been in the Church before, . . . and so it's not a conversion, Mrs. Stoner."
>
> "No? Well, I already got him down on my list of Monsignor's converts. . . . And that congresswoman, Father? . . ."
>
> "And Henry Ford's grandson. . . . I got him down. . . ."
>
> "But he's only one by marriage, Father, . . . I always say you got to watch those kind."

In **"Lions, Harts, Leaping Does,"** Powers explores once again the nature of the priesthood, but here his approach is not comic. The story is anomalous in Powers's canon; its tone is meditative, somber; there are dream passages, visionary sections. We meet Father Didymus, a Franciscan friar, in the last days of his life. Didymus is a perfectionist, a *perfectionalist* one might say, tormented by his failure to live up to the Franciscan ideal, an ideal of poverty, simplicity, sanctity. He is a teacher of geometry and suffers, though he comes late to an awareness of it, from pride in his ability to make nice moral distinctions; the spiritual life becomes for him a geometric problem: which solution is the most elegant, the most seemingly, the most formally satisfying? In having lived this way, he has entirely lost charity, the necessary center of the ideal to which he strives to conform.

In the character of Brother Titus, a single-minded lay brother, the ideal of charity is embodied. Every day he sits and reads to Didymus, from Bishop Bale's book of martyrs, "a denunciation of every pope from Peter to Paul IV." Titus is truly interested in only two books, *The Imitation of Christ* and *The Little Flowers of St. Francis;* he knows them by heart and would prefer to read only from them. But in the spirit of genuine brotherhood, he reads what Didymus wants. "Father Didymus, his aged appetite for biography jaded by the orthodox lives, found this work fascinating. . . . It was in sober fact a lie."

One cannot come to a genuine understanding of Powers's work without a careful reading of this story, for it is a story informed by faith. Judiciously spread through the text, coming always from the mouth of Titus, are quotes from spiritual writers that provide the unassailable standard against which all Powers's priests live their flawed lives. "O how joyous and how delectable is it to see religious men devout and fervent in the love of God, well mannered and well taught in ghostly learning." Titus, deficient in intelligence, cannot be ordained to the priesthood, yet he, of all Powers's characters, comes closest to the priestly ideal. Didymus's incisive yet ungenerous intellect keeps him from sanctity. When his brother, also a priest, asks Didymus to visit him on his deathbed, Didymus refuses, on the grounds that to go would indicate excessive earthly attachments. At the news of his brother's death, he realizes that the decision not to go to his brother has been a sinful one, a sin of pride and of lack of charity. "Harshly, Didymus told himself he had used his brother for a hair shirt."

When he comes to this realization, he opens himself up to true sanctity, giving up all delusion. He is also struck with an affliction of the eye which renders the visible world a chaotic jumble to him: "The background of darkness became a field of varicolored factions, warring, and, worse than the landscape, things like worms and comets wriggled and exploded before his closed eyes." It is the final loss to the geometrician, this believer in natural order as a prefiguration of the supernatural.

Powers has not written again in this vein, but **"Lions, Harts, Leaping Does"** shares some of the concerns of his one novel, *Morte D'Urban.* In *Morte D'Urban,* we can see the extended use Powers makes of the priesthood as a kind of metonymic device to explore the themes of community, America, the spiritual/moral life. (pp. 32, 34)

Perhaps [novelist and priest Andrew] Greeley should read J. F. Powers; it might remind him of the comic possibilities inherent in American religion, which Americans nearly always forget. Because we tend to see religion as unsusceptible to humor we have outlandish expectations of it, expectations which only a demagogue can pretend to fulfill. In the face of the most recent events in American religion, and its stars—[Cardinal] Cody, Greeley, Jerry Falwell, even—Powers's vision, clear, ironic, and secure, continues to refresh and nourish. (p. 36)

Mary Gordon, "The Priestly Comedy of J. F. Powers," in The New York Review of Books, *Vol. XXIX, No. 9, May 27, 1982, pp. 29, 32, 34-6.*

FURTHER READING

Barr, Donald. "Doors That Open on a World in Little." *The New York Times Book Review* (18 March 1956): 5.
> Applauds the development of directness and authentic dialogue in Powers's style.

Goyen, William. "A Too-Measured Prose." *The Nation* 182, No. 19 (12 May 1956): 413.
> Enumerates the limitations of Powers's prose style.

Lebowitz, Naomi. "The Stories of J.F. Powers: The Sign of the Contradiction." *The Kenyon Review* XX, No. 3 (Summer 1958): 494-99.
> Examines Powers's use of humor in resolving tensions between the actual and the ideal in several of his stories.

Peden, William. "The Tightrope Writers." *The Virginia Quarterly Review* 32, No. 3 (Summer 1956): 470-74.

Delineates elements of Powers's prose.

Quinn, M. Bernetta, O. S. F. "View from a Rock: The Fiction of Flannery O'Connor and J. F. Powers." *Critique* II, No. 2 (Fall 1958): 19-27.
  Explores the role of Catholicism in the works of O'Connor and Powers.

Rago, Henry. Review of *Prince of Darkness and Other Stories,* by J. F. Powers. *The Commonweal* XLVI, No. 19 (22 August 1947): 457-58.
  Praises Powers's technical skill and attention to detail.

True, Michael. "J. F. Powers, Flannery O'Connor and Their Satiric Muse." *America* 143, No. 9 (4 October 1980): 183-85.
  Compares Powers's and O'Connor's satiric visions of the Catholic Church in the United States.

Waugh, Evelyn. "Scenes of Clerical Life." *The Commonweal* LXIII, No. 26 (30 March 1956): 667-68.
  Assesses Powers's progress as a writer and predicts great success for his career.

Wymard, Eleanor B. "J. F. Powers: Comic Caricature and Christianity." *Cross Currents* XXXII, No. 3 (Fall 1982): 316-22.
  Examines Powers's use of caricature and other devices to convey the humor of spiritual issues.

Robert Penn Warren

1905-1989

American poet, novelist, short story writer, editor, essayist, critic, and dramatist.

Warren is widely acclaimed as one of the most distinguished figures in contemporary American literature. He received Pulitzer Prizes for both fiction and poetry, and in 1986, he was appointed by the Library of Congress as the first Poet Laureate of the United States. The tenor of Warren's writing conveys a passionate allegiance to his Southern heritage, and he often relies on dialect to render authentic characterizations and impart the local color of the rural South. While many of his works are based on actual regional incidents and legends, Warren focuses on the universal moral issues that engulf those events. Particularly in his short fiction, Warren dramatizes situations that pit his characters' ideals against their pragmatic concerns, and in such stories as "Prime Leaf," "Blackberry Winter," and "When the Light Gets Green," Warren contrasts the perspectives of youths and adults to illustrate these conflicts. Though Warren's work in the short story genre consists of a single volume, *The Circus in the Attic, and Other Stories,* and several uncollected pieces, it is nonetheless regarded as a significant component of his literary achievement.

Warren was born and raised in Guthrie, Kentucky. From an early age, he was instilled with an appreciation of his Southern agricultural heritage, and he attributed much of his knowledge and interest in history, poetry, and the oral tradition to his maternal grandfather, with whom he spent his childhood summers. In 1921, Warren enrolled at Vanderbilt University in Nashville, Tennessee, and studied under poet and critic John Crowe Ransom. At the invitation of Ransom, Warren became the youngest member of the Fugitives, a group of writers that also included Donald Davidson and Allen Tate. Between 1922 and 1925, these writers published the *Fugitive,* a literary journal containing poetry and criticism that upheld the values of southern agrarian regionalism against the cultural influences of the North's industrial economy. Viewing the poet as an outcast and prophet, the Fugitives honored classical literature and metaphysical verse and espoused formal diction and meter in modern poetry. After receiving further education at several noted institutions, including Oxford University in England, Warren began teaching English at Louisiana State University. There in 1935, with fellow faculty members Cleanth Brooks and Charles W. Pipkin, he co-founded the literary journal the *Southern Review,* an important literary magazine that served as an organ for the New Criticism. This approach to literature, which favored close textual analysis of a work, originated in part from discussions held by the Fugitives and the group that evolved from them, the Agrarians. Warren also collaborated with Brooks in writing the textbooks *Understanding Poetry* (1938) and *Understanding Fiction* (1943), influential works that introduced the New Criticism to several generations of teachers and students.

During his years as a student, Warren published many of his poems and essays in literary magazines. In 1935, his first collection of verse, *Thirty-Six Poems,* appeared and was well re-

ceived. The poems in this and his other early volume, *Eleven Poems on the Same Theme,* were deeply influenced by the theories of the Fugitives. In his later verse, however, Warren adopted a more personal tone and a looser metrical style. In addition to his outstanding reputation as a poet, Warren is well known for his Pulitzer Prize-winning novel, *All the King's Men,* a tale of political corruption loosely based on the character and career of Louisiana populist politician Huey Long. Among his other most important works are *Promises: Poems, 1954-1956* and *Now and Then: Poems, 1976-1978,* both of which won Pulitzer Prizes, and *Selected Poems, 1923-1975.*

Warren published his first short story, "Prime Leaf," in 1930, his final year at Oxford. This piece initially appeared in Paul Rosenfeld's literary annual, the *American Caravan* and was later included in *The Circus in the Attic, and Other Stories.* Set in Kentucky during the Black Patch Tobacco War of 1907, "Prime Leaf" examines the relationship between a father and son, focusing on events that test the two men's allegiances to their ideals and to each other. The action of the piece centers on the father's association with a group of tobacco farmers who have resorted to violence in their attempts to drive up tobacco prices. Angered by the group's brutality, the farmer severs his ties with them, an action which leads, following a series of confrontations with the group, to the murder of his son. As in many of his works, Warren employs an historical setting in "Prime Leaf," but he couches the story's episodes within the context of the emotional struggles and moral decisions faced by the father and his son. These types of filial confrontations are prominent throughout Warren's writings, and several critics consider "Prime Leaf" to be a preliminary treatment of the themes more extensively examined in his novel *Night Rider.*

In "Blackberry Winter," also collected in *The Circus in the Attic,* and Warren's most frequently anthologized story, he traces the fading of a boy's naiveté. The tale is related through the middle-aged narrator's recollections of an unseasonably cold June morning when he was nine years old after a violent storm had flooded the creek, damaging crops and leaving marks of destruction across the countryside. Throughout this story, Warren establishes a causal relationship between nature's sudden, devastating burst and a rash of unusual events in the community, as he recounts the startling images that the boy, Seth, sees. "Stringy and limp" bodies of drowned chicks, a crowd of people watching a dead cow float downstream, garbage strewn across the usually tidy lawn of Seth's friend Little Jeb, and a clash with a knife-wielding city tramp introduce Seth to a harsh reality that he had previously not known.

Critical reaction to *Circus in the Attic, and Other Stories* has varied. While some commentators suggest that Warren's narrative art is better served by the more expansive format of the novel, others praise Warren for his precise and sensitive descriptions of both setting and character and consider several of his stories to be among the finest in the short story genre. Though Warren's reputation has been fixed by his successes in poetry, criticism, and novels, his short stories are generally regarded as valuable and have augmented his high standing among literary critics.

(For further information on Warren's life and career, see *Contemporary Literary Criticism,* Vols. 1, 4, 6, 8, 10, 13, 18, 39, 53; *Contemporary Authors,* Vols. 13-16; *Contemporary Authors New Revision Series,* Vol. 20; *Something about the Author,* Vol. 46; *Dictionary of Literary Biography,* Vols. 2, 48; and *Dictionary of Literary Biography Yearbook: 1980.*)

PRINCIPAL WORKS

SHORT FICTION

Blackberry Winter   1946
The Circus in the Attic, and Other Stories   1947; reprinted, 1968

OTHER MAJOR WORKS

John Brown: The Making of a Martyr   (nonfiction)   1929
Thirty-Six Poems   (poetry)   1935
Night Rider   (novel)   1939
Eleven Poems on the Same Theme   (poetry)   1942
At Heaven's Gate   (novel)   1943
Selected Poems, 1923-1943   (poetry)   1944
All the King's Men   (novel)   1946
Brother to Dragons: A Tale in Verse and Voices   (novel) 1953
Promises: Poems, 1954-1956   (poetry)   1957
Selected Essays   (essays)   1958
Selected Poems, 1923-1975   (poetry)   1976

Now and Then: Poems, 1976-1978   (poetry)   1978

GRANVILLE HICKS   (essay date 1948)

[*Hicks was an American literary critic whose famous study* The Great Tradition: An Interpretation of American Literature since the Civil War *(1933) established him as the foremost advocate of Marxist critical thought in Depression-era America. During this period, Hicks believed it was the task of literature to confront sociopolitical issues. After 1939, Hicks denounced communist doctrine and adopted a less stringently ideological posture in his literary criticism. In the following review, Hicks comments on the vivid images, poignant narratives, and poetic quality of Warren's short stories while suggesting that the short story format stifles the thematic development of several pieces in* The Circus in the Attic, and Other Stories.]

According to the author's note, "The earliest story in [**The Circus in the Attic**] was written in 1930, the latest in 1946, but the order here is not chronological." As a matter of fact, the first appears to be last and the other way round, for "**Prime Leaf,**" the final story in the volume, appeared in *American Caravan IV* in 1931, whereas the first—and title—story was published in *Cosmopolitan* last autumn.

Between the two dates, Warren has written not only the other stories in this book but also poetry, criticism and three novels—an impressive record for a man who has been teaching almost continuously during the entire period. Slowly, much more slowly than many of his contemporaries, he has won a substantial reputation and finally, with *All the King's Men,* some sort of general recognition. (p. 5)

This collection of short stories consolidates rather than advances its author's position in contemporary literature. Since he has dedicated **The Circus in the Attic** to Katherine Anne Porter, it is not irrelevant to observe that his talent is for the novel just as markedly as hers is for the short story. One must immediately point out, however, that the best of his stories are very good. It is a satisfaction to reread "**Prime Leaf,**" for example, and to find in it once more the precision of detail and the directness in narration that were so impressive when it appeared in *American Caravan* sixteen years ago. Such a story as "**Blackberry Winter**" reminds us, as do so many passages in the novels, that Warren is a poet; but its delicacy is perhaps a commoner gift than the hard, unflinching awareness of "**The Patented Gate and the Mean Hamburger**"—a George Ade kind of title that is apt but misleading. As for "**The Circus in the Attic,**" it is a fine story, but the long, tangential introduction about the heroes of Bardsville is more memorable than the story of Bolton Lovehart.

The question Warren seems to be asking himself, both in the short stories and in the novels, is: How can you get at the significance of a human being? It is a natural enough question for a novelist, but it creates difficulties for a short-story writer. Warren tries again and again to get a whole life into a few thousand words. He is notably successful when he relies on condensed narrative, as in the title story, the pair of stories about Elsie Barton, and in the tale of a big-league pitcher, "**Goodwood Comes Back.**" He does less well when he makes a single incident carry the weight of a full biography, as in his two stories of academic life, "**The Life and Work of Professor Roy Millen**" and "**The Unvexed Isles.**"

The fact seems to be that what Warren wants to say takes

more room than the short story affords, not because he is concerned with a mass of incidental detail but because he is interested in the whole complex interrelation of causes and consequences. Once in a while he can make an incident stand by itself—he does it beautifully in **"Christmas Gift"**—but usually he seems cramped and unhappy. He has incorporated an independent tale in each of his novels and these three stories are better than any in this book, presumably because Warren knew that each would have its proper framework and was therefore under less of a strain in writing them.

At any rate, one feels, especially in some of the later stories, that Warren is trying too hard. When he wrote **"Prime Leaf,"** he was content to tell a straightforward story, and he told it extraordinarily well. Now, under his compulsion to bring out larger implications, he winds into his tales. His convolutions are invariably interesting, but one misses the clarity and drive of **"Prime Leaf."**

On the other hand, he has become adroit in handling the devices that he seems to find necessary and he has developed a colloquial style that is just about as good as anything one can find in contemporary literature. He has also acquired greater and greater subtlety in his explorations of personality. Says the narrator in **"The Circus in the Attic,"** speaking of an iconoclastic veteran, "They would not have believed him or his truth, for people always believe what truth they have to believe to go on being the way they are." The way people are is, of course, the concern of every writer of serious fiction. As the quotation shows, Warren knows just how elusive the goal is that he is pursuing, but he pursues it with rigorous honesty and a sharper vision than most. (pp. 5, 28)

Granville Hicks, "Warren's Short Stories," in The New York Times Book Review, *January 25, 1948, pp. 5, 28.*

HENRY NASH SMITH (essay date 1948)

[*Smith is an American critic who has edited several volumes of critical studies on Mark Twain. In the following excerpt, Smith comments on the vivid characterizations and nostalgic themes in* The Circus in the Attic, and Other Stories. *Although Smith finds that the quality of these pieces varies, he suggests that the collection shows the development of Warren's talent.*]

The novelties and short stories collected in Mr. Warren's [*The Circus in the Attic*], displaying his development over a period of seventeen years, show how his imagination has nourished itself upon Proustian exploration of a remembered world of childhood in Northwestern Tennessee. The chronological line is not neat and simple, but it is nevertheless clear that he has moved from isolated moments of recapturing the past toward a fuller and fuller imaginative grasp of the society within which he grew up. This tendency culminates in the vivid political awareness of *All the King's Men.*

The most prominent theme of the earlier stories is the integral relation between a rural folk and the land, and the normal source of conflict or disaster is the violation of this organic pattern by some outside force. The stranger in **"Blackberry Winter"** is potentially such a force, although the menace he embodies is kept at the edge of a child's consciousness. Luke Goodwood, the hunter and baseball player, is fatally shattered when he is drawn away from the land to attempt a career in professional baseball. Jeff York kills himself when his

wife forces him to sell his farm so she may buy a hamburger stand in town. The divisive and tragic impulses at work in the novelette **"Prime Leaf"** originate in the meaningless fluctuations of tobacco prices in distant markets.

But the outside forces could not affect the society if they did not encounter some answering evil within it. This is often a kind of irrational compulsion, as in the two companion stories about Elsie Barton and her daughter. Benjamin Beaumont the tobacco buyer and Frank Barber the railroad detective and bootlegger, both felt as alien and sinister, are the immediate sources of evil, but here the attention is fixed rather on the dark currents of motivation in the two women. If Mr. Warren finds in his characters compulsions that recall Faulkner, his treatment of them is quite different, for he analyzes them with clinical thoroughness and brings to the surface matters that Faulkner ordinarily keeps buried and mysterious.

Despite the occasional triumphs of these earlier pieces, none of them, is an entirely satisfactory thing-in-itself. They suggest, in fact, that Mr. Warren is a novelist rather than a short-story writer. The awareness of society as a complex structure of individuals and classes can hardly be rendered in a brief flash. This is even more certainly true of the concern with the relation between past and present which is so central in Mr. Warren's work. The psychological basis of this interest is perhaps the very process of childhood reminiscence, which revives the past within a present from which it is irretrievably separated by time. The Tennessee folk whom Mr. Warren depicts so well and whose vernacular speech he puts to such remarkable use are themselves, a product of time, of long residence in a given environment. Indeed, the whole character of Southern society as it appears derives from its traditional quality, which confers upon every aspect of life a ceremonial order. These matters are not adapted to the quick intensity of the short story.

But Mr. Warren needs only a slightly greater space to manage them perfectly. The newly published novelette which is the title piece of *The Circus in the Attic* manages to pack into sixty pages an historical perspective stretching back a century and a half, an accurate diagram of social relationships in a Tennessee town, an analytical biography of the central character, and adequate portraits of half a dozen others. Bolton Lovehart, the hero, is imprisoned by his mother's cannibalistic fixation on him. After several desperate and pathetic efforts to escape, which he himself only dimly understands, he finds in the secret hobby of carving a toy circus from wood compensation for the actual life she has forbidden him to lead. By the time his mother dies at eighty-seven he is past fifty and no longer able to take advantage of his freedom. These themes and various subordinate ones, such as the impact of the Second World War on the community, are managed with an autocratic precision that could hardly have been predicted on the basis of the work preceding *All the King's Men. The Circus in the Attic* confirms the impression left by that novel, that within the past couple of years Mr. Warren has raised himself to a new command over his materials and by that fact has entered the first rank of American writers. (pp. 14-15)

Henry Nash Smith, "Proustian Exploration," in The Saturday Review of Literature, *Vol. XXXI, No. 5, January 31, 1948, pp. 14-15.*

WILLIAM VAN O'CONNOR (essay date 1948)

[*An associate of Warren's and a proponent of the New Criticism, O'Connor evaluated literature through close textual analysis of symbol, image, and metaphor. Here O'Connor focuses on the thematic tensions in* The Circus in the Attic, and Other Stories.]

Most of the fourteen stories in Robert Penn Warren's *The Circus in the Attic* are studies of frustration in the various strata of a society. It may not be far fetched to say that *The Circus in the Attic* and *Dubliners,* despite differences in style and setting, have more in common than either has with any other collection of stories by a single author.

The only story with a non-Southern setting, **"The Unvexed Isles,"** is that of a man who knows the meaning of belonging to persons and to a place, that through them he achieves his definition and satisfactions. In the hands of another author, the story might be turned into a sophisticated notation of middle-aged frustration; in Warren's hands it becomes a study in self knowledge. Variations upon this theme are developed in **"When the Light Gets Green,"** a child's first awareness that one is not really alive unless he knows that others love, want or need him, and **"Her Own People,"** a story suggesting, partly through its ironic title, that the state of *belonging* may evolve from human relationships that transcend the boundaries of race.

In **"Goodwood Comes Back"** and **"The Love of Elsie Barton: A Chronicle"** we watch the violences visited upon individuals who are incapable of love or unwilling to commit themselves to anything except the pretense of it, and to that only for the conveniences it makes possible. Luke Goodwood, who attempts to live in isolation, (wanting to belong to a patch of ground near good places to hunt and fish but not wanting to belong to people) marries a girl "to get the little piece of ground he spoke of." Bad blood developed between Luke and his brother-in-law "because Luke and his wife didn't get along so well together. . . . Whatever it was, her brother shot Luke with Luke's own shotgun in the kitchen one morning. He shot him three times. The gun was a .12 gauge pump gun, and you know what even one charge of a .12 gauge will do at close range, like a kitchen." Elsie Barton, whom we see first (before the flashback) as an eccentric, was incapable of loving anyone, school mates, husband, or daughter. Her isolation, lack of feeling and passivity cause her unpremeditated rape by a man as alive as she is dead. Marriage and a child do not affect her. Only after her husband is dead and her daughter has left her does she find herself at ease, feeling "it was right to be alone, that this was best." Warren points up the significance of her story when, describing her getting into a carriage for a long trip, he says she "drove off into the enormous world she would never understand."

Perhaps the most pervasive theme in the volume is that our expectations of innocence as a permanent factor in human existence are gradually and ineluctably contradicted by experience. **"The Life and Work of Professor Roy Millen"** illustrates a psychological phenomenon which Poe called the "imp of the perverse" (a subject Warren has discussed in his essay on *The Ancient Mariner*). Sometimes the awareness comes early, as it does to the young boys in **"Blackberry Winter," "Testament of Flood,"** and **"Christmas Gift."** In the first of these, a tramp, vicious and physically ugly, becomes a symbol for the young boy. When the tramp saw the boy following him he turned and said: "You don't stop following me and I cut your throat you little son-of-a-bitch.' That was what

he said, for me not to follow him. But I did follow him, all the years." In the second of them, a high school boy is scorched by the knowledge that the world of adult sins has invaded his province. In the third of them, there is a ten year old who seems fully capable of standing up to and accepting the evil he finds around him but who already is marked by it and who seems to have had it bred into his own bones and blood. Warren manages a scene with great pathos when, after evoking for us the granite-like hardness of the child and, as it were, assuring us that he is lost forever from innocence, he reminds us dramatically of the irony involved:

> The boy, almost surreptitiously, took a stick of candy from his pocket, broke off half, and stuck it between his lips. He looked at the man's sharp expressionless profile. Then he held out a piece to him. Without a word the man took it and stuck it between his lips, sucking it.
>
> They moved forward between the empty fields.

In the title story we have a theme that Blake might have employed—evil has its uses and can serve good ends. Each of the chief characters in **"The Circus in the Attic"** knows his own weakness, his former failures and the unhappiness his betrayals or deficiencies have caused or might still cause. Each nurtures, as it were, the memory of his secret guilt because in the light of it the joy in love he has is greater than what is deserved.

These, generally speaking, then are the themes in Warren's short stories. None of them will surprise those readers who are acquainted with his novels or his poetry. We should ask whether these stories rank, within the genre of short fiction, with the work Warren has done in the novel and in poetry. They do. By and large, they exhibit the same insight, the same capacity for dramatizing a theme down to its last subtle implication, the same ability to render native speech, the texture of the physical world and to suggest character and motive through gesture or phrase. (Probably no other contemporary writer has the same ability to capture the *feel* of a pre-1914 rural America.) Karl Shapiro says that the poet childlike "remembers all his life. And cannily constructs it fact by fact." If Warren were not also a poet the pages of his fiction undoubtedly would not have the luminous detail that makes a fact or situation or person fill the reader's mind in the way each does when caught through the wide-open eyes and in the awe-struck mind of a child. (pp. 251-53)

> William Van O'Connor, "Robert Penn Warren's Short Fiction," in The Western Review, Vol. 12, No. 4, Summer, 1948, pp. 251-53.

JOHN M. BRADBURY (essay date 1958)

[*An American critic, Bradbury is the author of several studies on Southern literary movements and editor of a critical volume on Warren. In the following excerpt from his book on the Fugitive movement, Bradbury examines the relationship between Warren's short stories and his novels.*]

"Prime Leaf" is not only Warren's first considerable short story, but the first of several re-creations of the historic background of his region. Furthermore, it is interesting as a preliminary handling of the subject which his first novel, *Night Rider,* will treat more complexly and more "philosophically." In this case, Warren goes directly at his subject, without tactical maneuvers and without the addition of any special stylistic increment such as will distinguish the novels. The theme is already, in simplified form, one of Warren's particular themes, the conflict between the ideal and the practical, the problem of ends and means. The point-of-view character, old Mr. Hardin, who is the prototype of Captain Todd of *Night Rider* and represents the unyielding integrity of the gentleman-farmer traditions, is pitted against his stubbornly practical son and finally against the whole organization of night-riding tobacco growers, whose zeal in their clearly just cause has led them into violent tactics. Since the point of view, and therefore most of the sympathy, is carried by a character who remains solidly fixed in his position, the conflict lacks the complexity lent it in *Night Rider,* where protagonist Percy Munn must face the outer struggle and the reflection of it in his inner conflicts at every step.

This story, further, lacks the symbolic richness of Warren's later work. For the most part, he is content with his "documentation of the world." **"Prime Leaf"** develops a final tragic irony as the son, now following to the letter the uncompromising code of old Mr. Hardin, is shot down by those whom he had previously defended. Though the meaning pattern is thus completed, it is not reinforced by a contained pattern of imagery. Warren's documentation of his characters and the setting is careful and convincing, as his action is firm and compelling, but the images do not "rise to symbol," so that the story does not reach to the status of, let us say, poem-myth, to which his later work constantly strives.

In the other early stories [in *Circus in the Attic*], it is largely the realistic texture that absorbs the author. They are a series of explorations into the life of his region, the inflections of its voices, the rounds of its habits, its secret guilts and satisfactions, the moods of its rocks and fields and streams. Sometimes these stories recall the vignettes of [Sherwood Anderson's] *Winesburg, Ohio,* without the pointed preoccupation with psychic frustration and with a more inclusive, more evenly modulated, if often ironic, sympathy. Often, too, they bring to mind Chekhov's simple pathetic chronicles and his significant glimpses of small experience. Only occasionally does a story, like **"The Patented Gate and the Mean Hamburger,"** extrude its point—in this case Agrarian—or not quite convincingly enforce its irony, like the stories about college professors, **"The Life and Work of Professor Roy Millen"** and **"The Unvexed Isles."**

The life in these stories is varied and often richly textured in the telling. The embittered animalish life of a shiftless sharecropper family is pictured in **"Christmas Gift"** against a finely etched foreground of winter snow, rocks, and mud, and presented in the light of a prematurely tough young boy's responses. In **"Her Own People,"** the pathetic story of an uprooted and stubborn Negro servant is exposed through the comico-serious give-and-take of the master-mistress intimacies. The desperation that forces itself into the placid life of an average town girl (**"The Love of Elsie Barton"**) is chronicled in a level Chekhovian style that suggests the level of town comment. And the hidden sin which occasions **"The Confession of Brother Grimes"** is revealed by means of a salted ironic commentary which forecasts the style of *All the King's Men.*

There are several boy stories, compounds of pathos and irony, and a fine old-man-boy story, **"When the Light Gets Green,"** a delicately handled boy's view of a grandfather's ultimate capitulation to the basic indifferences of nature and man. In most cases, the life chronicle or the notation of an incident is offered without commentary, but with a sidelong glance down the direction of the pattern's significance. When the point of view is limited by a first-person presentation, it is a boy's view or a removed view, so that a comprehensive understanding is automatically ruled out. In the removed view of **"Goodwood Comes Back,"** for example, the important crises are simply reported to the narrator, and only in Goodwood's own inadequate reminiscence and in the severely limited speculation of the reason for Goodwood's murder are there hints at the total ironic configuration.

In the third-person stories, Warren's practice is to limit the comprehension either by the point-of-view character's inherent limitations, as in the professor stories, or by the implication of point of view carried in the style. In the latter case, the style is flavored generally to a sort of man-about-country-town level, an amalgam of amused gossip and mildly ironic comment, but limited by an implied narrow range of understanding and by similarly implied observational restrictions. **"The Patented Gate"** illustrates the type. Though an "I" is casually inserted early, the narrator soon becomes completely absorbed in the communal view. Here, there are a number of independent comments on various stages of the family transfer from country to city life, but a complete absence of total evaluation, save as the bold symbols of farm gate and hamburger stand supply it. **"The Love of Elsie Barton"** projects its major incidents in a dramatically presented sequence, and the style level is keyed down to the "average" level which Elsie represents. No comment is offered until the final, "they drove off into the enormous world which she would never understand." The statement comes out not as an author conclusion but as a kind of communal head-shaking over the noticeable lack in Elsie, which is unexplainable by the common lights.

All of these stories illustrate Warren's acute ear for the various vernaculars of the region, as well as his eye for the illuminating detail and his command of the striking phrase. Furthermore, almost all of them exhibit a wide range of human sympathy and understanding. The rather pervasive ironic view has much of [John Crowe] Ransom's aloof observer incorporated in it, but it seems always more immediately concerned than Ransom ever allows himself to appear. There are stories in which the harsh irony of many early Ransom poems obtains: **"A Christian Education," "The Confession of Brother Grimes,"** and **"The Life and Work of Professor Roy Millen"**; and it is noteworthy that these concern the professional preacher and the professional educator, both abstracted in the event from large contact with "the world's body." But Elsie Barton, the town girl; "Milt's little bastard," the sharecropper son; the uprooted servant Viola; Jeff York and his city-yearning wife; ballplayer Goodwood; and the dying grandfather are all treated with notable, if often gently ironic, sympathy.

Few of these stories carry a symbolic extension to any considerable degree of complexity or depth. It is different, however, with the other two stories included in *Circus in the Attic*, both of them written after the first novels had appeared. **"Blackberry Winter,"** which was originally published in a limited special edition in 1945, is, I think, one of the finest short stories that American writers have produced. It had its origin, Warren has told us, in a group of recollections of farm boyhood: a boy's outrage at incongruously cold unbarefoot weather in June, an outseason flood, the equally incongruous appearance of a city-bred tramp coming from the wrong direction and wanting farm work. All these "blackberry winter" elements were originally set down in their compelling naturalistic detail before the congruity of the incongruous images began to find its ultimate extension. Warren nowhere in the story sacrifices the original sharply registered surface: the drowned chicks with their feebly curled feet and "the fluff plastered" to the limp bodies, the necks "long and loose like a little string of rag," the eyes "with that bluish membrane over them which makes you think of a very old man who is sick and about to die"; the sharecropper boy who, in his patched overalls and "mud-stiff brogans," surprises himself by saying out loud, " 'Reckin anybody ever et drownt cow?' " as he watches the flooded stream and its cargo; the train play with the little colored boy playmate set against the colored mother's "woman-mizry"; the indecent fastidiousness of the tramp and his flick knife.

But all of the details are finally relevant, and poignantly so, as the tramp's parting words, cursing the boy who cannot help trail after him as he leaves, echo back: " 'You don't stop following me and I cut your throat, you little son-of-a-bitch.' " And the boy-narrator adds, "But I did follow him, all the years." All the incongruities and the contrasting stabilities, both with their own meaningful ambiguities, come suddenly into focus: the deadness of the chickens and their finicky handling, the train playing and the "mizry," the cow and the hungry boy, the firmness and gentleness of the father, the tricks of the boy to stay illegally barefooted, the oak-bodied everlasting Negro hand who finds that "the yearth is tahrd," plain "tahrd of sinful folks."

"The Circus in the Attic," which dates from 1946, has less immediate surface interest and develops at a slower pace. A late example of the life chronicle which Warren first had tested in stories like **"Elsie Barton,"** and which he had developed in the "bump" stories included in the novels, **"The Circus"** reverts to the communal viewpoint, supplemented here by direct native comments through the course of the narrative. In addition, analyses of motive and states of mind are introduced, but these are always partial and held within the limits of the character's own insight. Direct scenic presentation is necessarily confined to brief climactic moments, but the vigorous and often poetic narrative style is constantly enlivened by the colorful voices of the town.

"Circus in the Attic" is the chronicle of a man, Bolton Lovehart; of a town, the Bardsville of *Night Rider;* and of Southern town aristocracy in general. A mature example of Warren's typical, several-leveled complexity, it exhibits amply his "philosophical" transformation of image into symbol and of human experience into patterns of meaning. The first section of the narrative gives us the town, sharply described in its modern dress of factory, Negro slum, business center, and residential heights; and its early ambiguous history, which is symbolized in the now neglected heroes' monument to the Civil War town "saviors," one a "likker killer" only, the other a stubborn defender of his rights. The second section introduces the protagonist, descendant of pioneer long-rifle stock, exhibited first as a child in the image of an effete aristocracy, a velveted Lord Fauntleroy. Soon the image becomes that of a puppet, manipulated carefully and sheltered against the touch of the "common" by his mother, who embodies both the emasculating social snobbery and its supporting unrealistic religious heritage. (The ironic development has the church supply Bolton with an eminently realistic Snopesish wife, who actually descends from Bolton's own stock.)

From the beginning of the story, metaphors of the "circus performer" and "celluloid film" have been introduced; in the second section there are further images of this artificial life: the puppet, "spangles," a skirt flaring "like a dancer," "a photograph in an album," prepare the major symbol. When the circus actually appears, it is "barbarous" to Bolton, and his love-smothered need for animalism, for sin, drives him to it. Later, it is this same need, "like a blind fish from a cave, hurled into light," which drives Sara Darter to seduce Bolton under the portraits of her grandfathers. Trapped again by his mother, his first refuge is the new movie theatre, where, as ticket-taker, he acts the part of an "impressario." Finally, the secretly carved circus succeeds as the substitute for the real life that has been continually thwarted. An artificial life, an art for life's sake life, has replaced the attempt to live. Bolton learns now that "you can only love perfectly in terms of a great betrayal." His mother has pointedly identified herself with Christ and become absolutely necessary to the Judas role which enables him to live in a semblance of the good-evil world of reality.

When his mother's heart proves in its turn a Judas to her, Bolton's circus loses its *raison d'être* and becomes a sacrifice on the altar of his new commitment to life, in marriage and in vicarious war participation. Only when he is betrayed, first by his stepson's death in the Italian campaign, then by his wife, who is killed in the process of an adulterous affair, does Bolton revert permanently to the circus, which has now become coterminal with death, with the now artificial tradition of "aristocratic" Southern town life, with the "heroes," early and late, and with Bardsville itself. And it is the final pattern of Bolton's life.

"The Circus" is less poignant, less immediate in its appeal than **"Blackberry Winter."** Its drama and its color thin out during the war era sequences where too much must be presented in summary, but it has brilliant moments: the opening section of description; and the old-timer's version of the historic raid, particularly the scene of her heart's final betrayal of "pretty little, nice little Louise Bolton" Lovehart (the ironic significance of the name is apparent). Chiefly, however, **"The Circus"** provides a useful introduction into Warren's novelistic methods. (pp. 196-202)

John M. Bradbury, "Warren's Fiction," in his The Fugitives: A Critical Account, *The University of North Carolina Press, 1958, pp. 195-230.*

ROBERT PENN WARREN   (essay date 1959)

[In the following essay, Warren discusses the development of his short story "Blackberry Winter."]

I once wrote a story called **"Blackberry Winter."** It has the form of a recollection, many years after the events narrated, by a fictional first person. On a June morning, a young boy on a farm in Tennessee is being prevented by his mother from going barefoot because a gully-washer the night before makes the morning unseasonably cold. As they argue, they see a tramp, a citified tramp, coming up the lane, and wonder how he ever got back there in the river woods. The mother gives the tramp some work. The boy goes off to explore the damage and excitement of the storm, and then to play with the son of Dellie, the cook, who is sick in one of the tenant cabins. In a moment of annoyance Dellie, ordinarily a loving mother, savagely cuffs her son. The boy, disturbed, goes to hunt Old

Jebb (Dellie's common-law husband) who says this isn't merely blackberry winter—that the earth maybe is tired the way Dellie is, and won't produce any more. The boy goes back to the house and sees his father firing the tramp. The tramp is about to resent the firing, but the father overawes him, and the tramp goes off, the boy following until the tramp turns and snarls at him. Then there is a little summary of what had happened to the boy's family and Dellie's family in later years. Then:

> That is what has happened since the morning when the tramp leaned his face down at me and showed his teeth and said: 'Stop following me. You don't stop following me and I cut yore throat, you little son-of-a-bitch.' That was what he said, for me not to follow him. But I did follow him, all the years.

I remember with peculiar distinctness the writing of the story, especially the tension between a sense of being trapped in a compulsive process, and the flashes of self-consciousness and self-criticism. I suppose that most attempts at writing have some such tension, but here the distinction between the two poles of the process was peculiarly marked, between the ease and the difficulty, the elation and, I am tempted to say, the pain.

The vividness with which I remember this may come from the time and situation in which the story was written. It was the winter of 1945-46, just after the war, and even if one had had no hand in the blood-letting, there was the sense that one's personal world would never be the same. I was then reading Melville's poetry, and remember being profoundly impressed by "The Conflict of Convictions," a poem about the American Civil War. Whatever the rights and wrongs, the war, Melville said, would show the "slimed foundations" of the world. There was the sense in 1945 that we had seen the slimed foundations, and now as I write this, the image that comes to mind is the homely one from my story—the trash washed out from under Dellie's cabin to foul her pridefully clean yard. So Melville, it seems, belongs in the package.

For less remote background, I had just finished two long pieces of work, a novel called *All the King's Men* and a study of Coleridge's "The Ancient Mariner." Both of these things were impersonal, that is, about as impersonal as the work of a man's hand may be. At the same time I was living in a cramped apartment over a garage in a big, modern, blizzard-bit Northern city. So the circumstances of my life and the work that had held me for so long were far from the rural world of my childhood. As for my state of mind, I suppose I was living in some anxiety about my forthcoming pieces of work, and in the unspoken, even denied conviction that, with my fortieth birthday lately passed, I was approaching some watershed of experience.

Out of this situation the story began, but by a kind of accident. Some years earlier I had written a story about a Tennessee sharecropper, a bad story that had never been published; now I thought I saw a way to improve it. So with that story I began to turn my feelings back into an earlier time. I can't say whether I began writing **"Blackberry Winter"** before I rewrote the other story. It doesn't really matter much. What mattered was that I was going back. I was fleeing, if you wish. Hunting old bearings and bench-marks, if you wish. Trying to make a fresh start, if you wish. Whatever people do in their doubleness of living in a present and a past.

I recollect the particular thread that led me back into the past: the feeling you have when, after vacation begins, you are allowed to go barefoot. Not that I ever particularly liked to go barefoot. But the privilege was important, an escape from the tyranny of winter, school, and, even, family. It was like what the anthropologists call rite of passage. But it had another significance; it carried you over into a dream of nature, the woods, not the house, was now your natural habitat, the stream not the street. Looking out into the snow-banked alley of that iron latitude, I had a vague nostalgic feeling and wondered if spring would ever come. It finally came—and then on May 5 there was again snow, and the heavy-handed blooms of lilac were beautiful with their hoods of snow and beards of ice.

With the recollection of going barefoot came another, which had been recurrent over the years: the childhood feeling of betrayal when early summer gets turned upside down and all its promises are revoked by the cold spell, the gully-washer. So by putting those two recollections together, I got the story started. I had no idea where it was going, if anywhere. Sitting at the typewriter was merely a way of indulging nostalgia. But something has to happen in a story, if there is to be more than a dreary lyric poem posing as a story to promote the cause of universal boredom and deliquescent prose. Something had to happen, and the simplest thing ever to have happen is to say: *"Enter, mysterious stranger."* And so he did.

The tramp who thus walked into the story to cut short the argument between mother and son had been waiting a long time in the wings of my imagination—an image based, no doubt, on a dozen unremembered episodes from childhood, the city bum turned country tramp, suspicious, resentful, contemptuous of hick dumbness, bringing his own brand of violence into a world where he half-expected to find another kind, enough unlike his own to make him look over his shoulder down the empty lane as dusk came on, a creature altogether lost and pitiful, a dim image of what, in one perspective, our human condition is. But then, at that moment, I was thinking merely of the impingement of his loose-footedness and lostness on a stable and love-defined world of childhood.

Before the tramp actually appeared, however, I had known he was coming, and without planning I began to write the fourth paragraph of the story, about the difference between what time is when we grow up and what it was when we stood on what, in my fancy phrase in the story, I called the glistening auroral beach of the world—a phrase which belonged to a boy who had never seen a beach but whose dreams were of the sea. Now the tramp came up, not merely out of the woods, but out of the darkening grown-up world of time.

The boy, seeing the tramp, tries to think of him coming up through the woods. He sees the image of the tramp blundering along, not like a boy who might stand in absolute quiet, almost taking root and growing moss on himself, trying to feel himself into that deep vegetative life. This passage, too, was written on impulse, but as soon as it began I knew its import; I was following my nose, trusting, for better or worse, my powers of association in relation to an emerging pattern of contrasts. It was natural, therefore, after a little about the tramp's out-of-water-ness, to set over against him the brisk self-sufficiency of the mother at the time of the incident, and then over against that portrait a thought of the time later when she would be dead and only a memory—though back then in the changeless world of childhood, as the narrator says, it had never crossed the boy's mind that "she would ever be dead."

In the instant I wrote that clause I knew, not how the story would end, for I was still writing by guess and by God, but on what perspective of feeling it would end. I knew that it would end with a kind of detached summary of the work of time, some hint of the adult's grim orientation toward that fact. From now on, the items that came on the natural wash of recollection came not only with their, to me, nostalgic quality, but also with the freighting of the grimmer possibilities of change—the flood, which to the boy is only an exciting spectacle but which will mean hunger to some, the boy's unconscious contempt for poor white trash like Milt Alley (the squatter who lived up the hill), the recollection of hunger by the old man who had ridden with Nathan Bedford Forrest, Dellie suffering her "woman mizry." But before I had got to Dellie, I already had Old Jebb firmly in mind with some faint sense of the irony of having his name remind one—or at least, me—of the dashing Confederate cavalryman killed at Yellow Tavern.

Perhaps what I did with Dellie had, in fact, stemmed from the name I gave Old Jebb. Even if the boy would see no irony in that echo of J. E. B. Stuart's fame, he would get a shock when Dellie slapped her beloved son, and would sense that that blow was, in some deep way, a blow at him. I knew this, for I knew the inside of that prideful cabin, and the shock of early realization that beneath mutual kindliness and regard a dark, tragic, unresolved thing lurked. And with that scene with Dellie I felt I was forecasting the role of the tramp in the story. The story, to put it another way, was now shifting emphasis from the lyricism of nostalgia to a concern with the jags and injustices of human relationships. What had earlier come in unconsciously, reportorially, in regard to Milt Alley, now got a conscious formulation.

I have said the end was by now envisaged as a kind of summary of the work of time on the human relationships. But it could not be a mere summary; I wanted some feeling for the boy's family and Jebb's family to shine through the flat surface. Now it struck me that I might build the summary with Jebb as a kind of pilot for the feeling I wanted to get; that is, by accepting, in implication at least something of Jebb's feeling about his own life, we might become aware of our human communion. I wanted the story to give some notion that out of change and loss a human recognition may be redeemed, more precious for being no longer innocent. So I wrote the summary.

When I had finished the next to the last paragraph I still did not know what to do with my tramp. He had already snarled at the boy, and gone, but I sensed in the pattern of things that his meaning would have to coalesce now with the meaning I hoped to convey in the summary about the characters. Then, for better or worse, there it was. In his last anger and frustration, the tramp had said to the boy: "You don't stop following me, and I cut yore throat, you little son-of-a-bitch."

Had the boy stopped or not? Yes, of course, literally, in the muddy lane. But at another level—no. In so far as later he had grown up, had really learned something of the meaning of life, he had followed the tramp all his years, in the imaginative recognition, with all the responsibility which such a recognition entails, of this lost, mean, defeated, cowardly, worthless, bitter being as somehow a man.

So what had started out as an escape into the simplicities of childhood from the complications of the present, had turned, as it always must if we accept the logic of our lives, into an attempt, however bumbling, to bring something meaningfully out of that simple past into the complication of the present. And now, much later, I see that this story, and the novel then lately finished, and my reading of Coleridge's poem all bore on the same end.

I should give a false impression if I imply that this story is autobiographical. It is not. I never knew these particular people. And no tramp ever leaned down at me and said for me to stop following him or he would cut my throat. But if one had, I hope that I would have been able to follow him anyway, in the way the boy in the story does. (pp. 4-5, 36)

Robert Penn Warren, "Writer at Work: How a Story Was Born and How, Bit by Bit, It Grew," in The New York Times Book Review, *March 1, 1959, pp. 4-5, 36.*

LEONARD CASPER　(essay date 1960)

[*Casper is an American poet, short story writer, editor, and critic who has written extensively on Philippine literature. In the following excerpt from his full-length study on Warren, Casper discusses the retrospective quality of* The Circus in the Attic, and Other Stories.]

During his undergraduate days at Vanderbilt, Robert Penn Warren had written several short stories that he disliked so thoroughly that he decided to abandon fiction permanently. But the friendship that developed with Katherine Anne Porter during the late 1920's, while Warren was at Yale, helped to change his mind. At the same time he had been impressed by the fact that Caroline Gordon was publishing stories about his own region. While he was away at Oxford his thoughts of home grew more lustrous, so that when the editors of *The American Caravan,* which had already printed his poetry, requested fiction, he remembered the tobacco country of his childhood, the turbulence of its economic wars that sundered son and parent, and wrote **"Prime Leaf."**

The Circus in the Attic and Other Stories, collected in 1948, corroborates that early turning homeward. Most of Warren's short fiction is an ingathering of Southern rural life. His best stories have been adult reminiscences of durable childhood events, combined retrospection and introspection, the older scrupulous mind infecting with its guilt the reopened flesh of the past that has never quite been lost, or wholly lived in.

Of this group, **"Blackberry Winter,"** held in such esteem by its author that it was published as a book in 1946, justifiably has already entered the histories of its genre. The story is narrated by a man in his early forties, recalling how his immaculate boyhood mind, at nine, had watched only with curiosity the city-clothed stranger who, snapping the silence of green twilight suspended under forest trees, approached his father's farm. While the man earned his feed by burying chicks and poults drowned in the latest storm, the boy watched with neighboring farmers their possessions stream irrecoverably, in a swollen current, past the fields of flooded tobacco plants. Still, his father sat straight in his saddle.

Yet the world had changed. The boy found a yardful of trash washed out from under the cabin of his father's "prideful" help, and old Jebb predicted that the cold snap in June would go on. The Lord had tired of sinful folks and was blessing the earth with earned rest. Later when his father, explaining that he was unable to hire anyone now, still offered a dollar, the stranger cursed the farm and left, dogged by the curious boy whom he also cursed. "That was what he said, for me not to follow him. But I did follow him, all the years." The boy has been initiated into irrevocable manhood in a world of time.

"Blackberry Winter" makes no attempt to romanticize rural hardships. Its concern is with intuition more than with sentiment. Flood, the drowned poults, the dead cow, the ruined tobacco crop—these are expected. They are countered with calmness, by women replanting flowers in their wake and by men who stoically compare their calamities with those of General Forrest's cavalry. But just as the displaced stranger fails to comprehend such composure, so does the boy consider it too commonplace to notice. The flood, the hillmen's hunger, the "woman mizry," all are no more than personal inconveniences, preventing his going barefoot. Only the mean, defeated stranger can engage his curiosity about the meaning of a man. Leaving, not literally but imaginatively, he moves into time, the unforeseen world of change, beyond the charmed circle of childhood's "submarine" forests. His action is the natural motion of birth, of parturition. Yet, remembering it, he feels a sadness beyond nostalgia: guilt at having come so late to an appreciation of his family and its undramatic daily weathering. While reaching out to make the strange familiar, he has let the customary become mysterious. The farm is quickly lost, his parents die, his playmate is imprisoned. Now any act of attention or of contrition seems ineffectual. Even old Jebb who endures like Tiresias or ancestral memories is immortally aware of mortal suffering and human loss, the expense of knowledge.

To this same moral landscape belongs Grandfather Barden of "When the Light Gets Green," whose portrait, taken alone, would seem cropped. Nothing remains of his ex-cavalryman's physique except a thin posture of dignity and a sure hand on the horse. During a heavy hail in the summer of 1914, threatening his son-in-law's tobacco, he collapses, and later waits to die upstairs, unloved. His grandson lies, pretending to love him; although Barden dies not then but four years later, the boy feels ashamed of his inability to love and his rejection of the old man who had no son of his own. The now adult narrator is puzzled by his own sadness and shame. Everything remembered about the old man is pleasant, except for what the boy feels about his grandfather's shrunkenness. Is this pity, or involuntary self-pity, the twist in the loins at the realization of imminent disability? (It is an ominous green that shines before the calamity of storms; after his lie, the boy cannot face himself in the dresser mirror, which is "green and wavy like water.") Is it an incapacity to associate himself with age and change, the required disaster that makes him reject the old man? In both this story and "Blackberry Winter" there is a curious nostalgia for a past, painful because its obligations are beyond comprehension. The sense of kinship works in secret.

In "Christmas Gift" one of Milt Alley's sons is shown the same respect given the father, "white trash" hillsman, in "Blackberry Winter." The boy is shy and burdened. En route to deliver his sister of an illegitimate child, a doctor lets the boy roll a cigarette and in return receives a stick of candy—mutual tokens for those who survive adversity.

Measured by the authentic simplicity of such stories, "Goodwood Comes Back" and "The Patented Gate and the Mean Hamburger" seem contrived. Goodwood, after drinking his way out of professional baseball, finally marries a girl who has what he really wanted all the time, half interest in some out-country land. One day her brother kills him because "bad blood" had developed between them. The cause of violence is never explained except for the hint that Goodwood loved solitude too much. He should have farmed his land instead of spending his time off in the woods shooting or fishing. But the narrator seems unsure of the significance of his story. The characters of "The Patented Gate and the Mean Hamburger" are again hard-living would-be, yeoman farmers. After thirty years of labor Jeff York finally owns a small farm with a gate that can be opened without getting down from a buggy. But, because his wife's one pleasure is hamburgers, he sells his farm, buys her a stand, and hangs himself on his patented gate. She happily learns in time to fling "a mean hamburger." The conclusion, by paring down her character to grotesque dwarfdom, destroys the credibility that the story maintains as long as Jeff is its center. For sacrificing so much for such a woman, he himself is whittled down until his suicide becomes more bewildering than pathetic.

The same indeterminate interest unsettles "The Confession of Brother Grimes" and "A Christian Education." In the first of these stories Warren's cosmic web philosophy appears to be parodied. When preacher Grimes's relatives suffer sometimes without apparent cause, he admits that God is punishing him, through them, for dyeing his hair black over twenty years. More provocative but equally elusive is the confession of the narrator in "A Christian Education." Silas Nabb, raised to ignore all provocation, nevertheless one day on a picnic cruise attacks a boy who has harassed him with dirty jokes and in the commotion falls overboard. The boy-narrator makes no attempt to save Silas until forced to do so. Swimming down, he wants to lie in that remote silence, looking up, "trying to see where the light made the water green." But the drowned body's touch forces him up to the surface, shrunken with guilt. The fact that much later Nabb's brother, not brought up a Christian, is imprisoned for shooting a man forestalls any attempt to interpret the story as a text on child education. As a result the Nabbs seem nearly superfluous in this story whose one convincing scene is that in which the narrator acknowledges the enormity of his crime. Yet his own attitude toward the story he tells is ambivalent. In the death and rescue scenes his manner is candid; reporting on the Nabbs he is distant, sarcastic. His own confession comes accidentally, the reader's attention having been directed meanwhile toward people whom the narrator neither knows nor cares to know. As a result the characters are made to appear eccentric, although it is the narrative line itself that is off center.

What happens when the "central register" of a story is only a semiconscious character is clear in the contrast between "The Love of Elsie Barton: A Chronicle" and its sequel. Elsie is a woman of mystery even to herself. Her life seems bent on fulfilling some ineluctable pattern to which she must patiently acquiesce. When she is violated by Ben Beaumont (who understands neither himself nor his interest in her), she refuses to struggle. Their subsequent marriage makes her feel even more "trapped in that alien body." Ben's passion is as much an involuntary reflex as is his wife's passivity. Confronted by the unrelieved incomprehension of these characters, the reader has to invent his own cause for pity. "Testament of Flood," however, gains by being told through the mixed feelings of a young boy who loves and hates Elsie's daughter. Filled with a sense of his own ugliness, yet wanting this beautiful girl who dates older men, he is suddenly saturated with gossip about her and realizes that already she is dead and tragically inaccessible, and he in his knowledge and impotence older than anyone alive.

An equal irony certifies the characterizations in **"Her Own People."** Fired for her temper, Viola, a Negro cook, lies in her rented bed waiting to die unwanted. She has no other home but death. Her employers are angry with her because she has made them examine themselves and their own niggardly relationship with life. The home for which *they* are sick is the one they were never married enough to build.

The two stories about academic life included in this volume develop the theme of the rejected past introduced in other stories. **"The Life and Work of Professor Roy Millen"** studies a man whose childhood has been difficult, his young manhood painful. When a student maneuvers him into saying that he once visited Paris, he becomes so enraged with his own lie, the denial of his early life, that he repudiates the student rather than recommend him for the requested Paris scholarship. In **"The Unvexed Isles"** a professor's temptation to reject the truth of his origin is complicated by the discovery that his wife finds attractive the sophistication of one of his students. To keep his wife, the professor is at first prompted to behave with equal sophistication. Instead he reminds them all of the modest midwestern farm that was his home, and his wife is trapped by his honesty. For a moment after the student has left in dismay, the professor, fearing the silence that frosts the interval between his wife and himself, feels profoundly homesick for the first time. But he senses, too, that the home to which one returns is never the home he left. Home is a spirit that each two people must construct on some past image. Whatever his wife is, insufficient or merely tired, he is also. Yet even these resources for building a life together are better than pretenses. Such a conclusion is more compelling than that of its companion story largely because the introductory action, by refusing to stay withheld in one man's mind, allows what it symbolizes to affect and alter the contents of the three minds involved.

Short fiction has never satisfied Warren's love of and respect for circumstantial detail and development. His best short stories have been incomplete; divided halves in search of each other. Both early and late, he has trained for his longer works with novelettes: 1931, **"Prime Leaf"**; 1947, **"The Circus in the Attic."** In the later, sprawling story, having successively isolated himself from his heroic ancestry (he is the only survivor of Bardsville's first settler) and his possessive mother, Bolton confines himself to the secret carving of a soft-pine circus. It has become his personal monument to honor what he most desires: something undemanding, to which he can belong (as the town has its own monument to glorify itself in two Civil War "heroes," one actually too drunk to run from the Yankees, the other a temporary turncoat). He has always been afraid to explore the motives for his own "civil wars," knowing that under the rational answers will be "the blank-faced need swaying in the dark, coiled like the spring of his being." He contents himself with his circus and with keeping an inadequate history of the county (he has never known even his pioneer ancestor's name). Then for a while he identifies himself with his stepson when the boy is drafted. But after the boy's death, as victory in war approaches, fewer people listen to Bolton's enthusiasms, and, when his wife and a certain captain are killed in a highway accident together, he retires to carve another circus in his lonely attic. His daughter-in-law, remarrying, discovers guiltily that she loves her new husband even more than she did the old, but her joy is too

real to be denied. Nor does it matter. In some future all those who lived will be equally blessed by the blurring of memory.

Perhaps the novelette is intended to mean that history is a circus, an entertainment, a projection of each man's mind carved to suit its own half-seen needs. History deserves to be satirized when it pretends to be exact and omniscient, instead of admitting to the erection of self-satisfying monuments. No man knows with complete intimacy and accuracy his own motives. No man can enter and survey the mind of another. Consequently history is elaborate myth or the feeble interpretation of external action only.

Such a reading of **"The Circus in the Attic"** could find parallels in the attitude of the historian-narrator in *World Enough and Time,* or the philosophy of history in the foreword of *Brother to Dragons.* Nevertheless, even if these resemblances establish the intention of **"Circus in the Attic,"** the novelette is still hobbled by having to adopt the method that it satirizes. The characterizations are so disproportionate in interest assigned them that Bolton survives as the central figure only by force of accident. The storytelling method is so hopelessly remote from extraordinary human insight that it seems to assent to, rather than censure, the notion that all men are equally unimportant—that each simply has his own source of intoxication, his own dark compulsion and destiny, his own mystification.

Warren's earliest novelette is equally extravagant. Its whole first section of dialogue is ballast better overboard. Once under way, **"Prime Leaf"** is essentially a straightforward tale of action about a family's near division during the tobacco wars. Old Man Hardin steps out of the farmers' association rather than use force against objectors to price fixing. However, his son, whom he had originally convinced to join the association, refuses to quit immediately. Their reconciliation occurs when young Hardin kills a man raiding the Hardins' property. The old man rides with him part way to town, honorably bringing him to justice and bringing justice to him, but on the way the father is ambushed and killed. After its awkward beginning, **"Prime Leaf"** explores with powerful intimacy the divisions and alliances of its inhabitants.

What makes **"Prime Leaf"** an exceptional story in the Warren canon is that none of its characters wonders who he is or what the nature is of man, God, or society. Although most of the short stories have the same locale as the novelettes—Kentucky and Tennessee—the impression repeatedly given is that of an alien world. The narrator, after having rejected this background early in life, discovers now, as he tries to recall it, that in turn it has rejected him. Although he left in order to "define" himself, he feels that his present life is either false or inconsequential. He suffers genuine nostalgia in recalling his youth, though its circumstances were hard or even perilous. He remembers the dignity won by the poorest of hillsmen. His motives for rejecting home now seem obscured. Yet he blames only himself, believing that there can be no identity for him without obligations. In order to prove that he has an existence at least partially independent of ancestral forces fused in him, he necessarily must couple a sense of guilt with his sense of loss. The presence of evil in his life is dim but undeniable, and he is one of its sources.

Even where motivation is darkest, it is this concept of the individual struggling to emerge from determining forces and yet somehow merely multiplying their efficiency which provides a near-tragic tone to the more successful stories of Robert Penn Warren. The others fail when the characters are so unaware of their own situation that no feeling in them, or consequently for them, can result. It is not unnatural for a writer to try to express the irrational acts of subterranean man, for who needs a spokesman more than the mute? Yet Warren has seldom found short fiction adequate to the aura of associations that subsumed incitements require. Perhaps also, in some part, he claims for the author areas of the unverifiable, those psychic portions unexplained by science and often never dreamed of by Freud. In this area myth, however finite, is privileged to move, but often no myth is forthcoming. Such stories become mere chronicles, parodies of Warren's concepts. There is puzzlement without sadness, an alien world with no competing vision, dark compulsion without resistance. As a result such stories seem bad copies of Sherwood Anderson's "grotesques," which Warren once criticized for presenting motivation in terms of oversimplified but still unexplained impulses. (pp. 92-100)

> Leonard Casper, in his Robert Penn Warren: The Dark and Bloody Ground, *University of Washington Press, 1960, 212 p.*

CHESTER E. EISINGER   (essay date 1963)

[*Eisinger, an American critic and editor, is the author of the critical study* Fiction of the Forties. *In the following excerpt from that work, he assesses the gradual maturation of Warren's characters and points out structural deficiencies in several short stories.*]

The conservative southern imagination may be best summed up, for the 1940's, in the work of Robert Penn Warren. He belongs to this period, as Faulkner does not. But, like Faulkner, he is a writer of such considerable achievement that he cannot be totally contained within a formula. Or perhaps it would be better to say that Warren reveals, better than any other writer except Faulkner, the potentials for a universal interpretation of experience that lie in southern conservatism.

The particularities of Warren's revisionist and conservative position may be framed in a dialectic of affirmations and repudiations. Such a formulation may ignore the spontaneity of Warren's mind, but it will have the advantage of setting before us the naked girders in the structure of his thought. To begin, then, he rejects the heritage of eighteenth-century Enlightenment. He finds its optimistic view of human nature shallow and its faith in reason and abstract principle misplaced; most of all he fears its untrammeled individualism, which leads to the autonomy and thus to the heresy of the self, by which he means a destructive overconfidence in the capacities of the self-isolating individual, cut off from society and God. He accepts a more complicated and darker view of man, whose good is always susceptible to corruption. He is suspicious of reason and impatient with abstractions, since he brings to bear on life an ironic and sceptical vision which abhors dogmatic decisions and makes a virtue of provisional resolutions. While he regards the realization of the self or of human identity as the highest, final goal of man, he believes this realization can be achieved only by reference to authority beyond the self. He rejects the heritage of nineteenth-century science, which is responsible for our God-abandoned world of today and which has bred the variety and multiplicity that contribute so heavily to the disintegration of society and of individual consciousness. He accepts an unorthodox orthodoxy which rests on the validity of religious myth and religious metaphor; out of the Christian conception of the communion of men will come unity to replace the present fragmentation. He rejects the industrialism and the metropolitanism of the twentieth century because they too stifle the human personality. And they cut man off from the fructifying past. He affirms the enduring value of the past, of its tradition and its myth, in establishing the continuity of human identity in the present and for the future. He rejects the romantic, "democratic" conception of the West as the land of golden opportunity, settled by Frederick Jackson Turner's individualistic and independent frontiersmen. This myth of America he inverts, and he sees the West as a region of license and as an escape from responsibility. The West is the world of nature. While man is in and of nature, as Warren recognizes, man must nevertheless separate himself from nature if he is to achieve the discipline commensurate with his humanity. For Warren, in short, Jeffersonian liberalism, Darwinian science, and American industry comprise an unholy trinity that has spread its infection throughout the modern world, fragmenting our universe, inducing a chaos of beliefs, destroying the possibility for stable society, and threatening the existence of the human personality itself. He is at war with all these forces. (pp. 198-99)

In 1947 Warren collected his short stories in a volume called *The Circus in the Attic and Other Stories.* My feeling is that the stories do not, on the whole, succeed. When they are not discursive and loose in structure, like the title story, they are too neatly packaged, like **"The Patented Gate and the Mean Hamburger."** The humor and the irony are sometimes so obvious that it is difficult to understand why Warren should have wanted to preserve such work; I have in mind especially **"A Christian Education"** and **"Confession of Brother Grimes."**

The most authentic note Warren strikes in this volume is that of reminiscence, because looking backwards gives scope to his piety and opportunity to assess the growing-up process. These characteristics make meaningful such stories as **"When the Light Gets Green"** and **"Blackberry Winter."** The second story treats the maturation theme as a series of disorientations from the lovely green world of nature and the secure, isolated world of the farm. "When you are a boy . . . you want to stand there in the green twilight until you feel your very feet sinking into and clutching the earth like roots and your body breathing slow through its pores like the leaves. . . ." But one cannot retain the innocence of boyhood. The stranger, who does not grow into the ground, brings the meaningless viciousness of the urban world to the boy. The dead cow in the river and the old veteran of Forrest's cavalry bring home the horror of nature and life to the boy. Even the familiar and gentle Dellie, now irascible and mean in her illness, shows the unhappy reality that lies under the surface of human life; and her usually spotless yard, now littered with filth brought out by the flooding creek, signalizes the destructiveness of nature. Not everyone can survive the knowledge of good and evil and the wrenching away from nature. The boy in this story does. But the men in stories like **"Goodwood Comes Back"** and **"The Patented Gate"** cannot do it; they thus reveal themselves as only half-men.

"The Circus in the Attic," the title story, is another approach to the dualism of life, an examination of the relation between the world of illusion and the world of reality as it bears on the discovery of truth. Warren seems to be showing that what is important is what men choose to live by. In so doing they make an enduring truth, and it makes no difference whether or not it is a verifiable truth. The counsels of imperfection and tentativeness contained in this story, like the use of time as a continuity which helps to create a truth that never was, are typical of the Warren syndrome, even as the indecisive conduct of the story is an aberration from the disciplined form he so often provides. (pp. 223-24)

> Chester E. Eisinger, "The Conservative Imagination," in his Fiction of the Forties, *The University of Chicago Press, 1963, pp. 146-230.*

JAMES B. SCOTT (essay date 1964)

[*Scott is an American critic noted for writing the first full-length study of Djuna Barnes. In the following excerpt from his volume on Warren, Scott traces symbols and patterns that emphasize the theme of betrayal in* The Circus in the Attic, and Other Stories.]

Robert Penn Warren has constructed his series of tales, **The Circus in the Attic and Other Stories,** around the common theme of betrayal. Some of the betrayals described are effected by people, and some by time. In other instances, the characters betray themselves. The consequences of these betrayals range from the declaration of independence from his farm parents which sets a young boy on the road to becoming an artist to more violent eventualities such as murder. The final trio of stories, however, demonstrates man's potential for self-realization when he resists the impulse to betray himself.

Little critical attention has been paid to this dimension of Warren's fiction. John M. Bradbury [see essay dated 1958] has correctly identified the importance of betrayal as theme in **"The Circus in the Attic,"** but fails to extend its application to the other stories, and thus to recognize a unifying principle in the entire collection.

"Blackberry Winter," the second story, seems to be a symbolic statement of both Warren's literary technique and his direction. The story is written in the first person singular and invites comparison between the narrator, a boy of nine, and Warren himself. The boy remembers that the ninth June of his life was a cold one. The boy wishes to go outdoors without shoes, but his mother insists that it is too cold. He says that it is June, and she rejoins that it is "blackberry winter." The expression signifies a very late, unexpected cold spell, hence "blackberry winter" is a regional denotation for a time which is out of the normal sequence. The boy may be ready enough in the conscious part of his mind to agree with his mother that a cold spell has come in June, but his whole person, the non-reasoning part, rebels, and so he behaves as though it were not blackberry winter. He disobeys his mother by going barefoot. Later, when he is thoroughly chilled, he will incline, when talking with Jebb, to agree with his mother's position. This is the crux of the boy's makeup: it is both blackberry winter and June for him. He comes to accept two kinds of time: one is chronological, is measured by calendars and clocks, and the other is circumstantial; it is measured psychologically.

Big Jebb accepts the cyclical nature of time and change, but seems convinced that the cycle may not repeat itself. Perhaps it will never get warm again, for the earth is tired. Jebb's thinking is influenced by his wife's sickness: she is in menopause, when the life process refuses to come full circle in the old way and renew itself. In this sense, she is an artistic corre-

spondence (in Jebb's mind) for the earth itself. About the one, Jebb was wrong, but what matters is not that he was wrong about the earth, but that the boy, without certain foreknowledge, discredited the notion and chose to defend his mother's point of view. He would prefer to have it be June, but at the least he prefers to call it blackberry winter rather than the terminus of all life and enterprise. This is, of course, very natural for a nine-year-old boy, but the story can also be considered as symbolic of the artist's direction. In this latter sense, Warren seems to say that his will be a positive view of life, even in the chill of a bad cold-snap, when the whole world seems to be going wrong, rather than a negative view which reads the signs in terms of a more limited, personal kind of experience, such as either Jebb's or that of a boy who at first isn't willing to admit that it is both June and blackberry winter. If it is both, Warren seems to say, then it must be recognised that it is both.

This much, at least, must be said about time in these stories; but the message of the story suggests still another kind of dichotomy, and one that is not easily divorced from time. No sooner does the boy's mother tell him it is blackberry winter than he sees a tramp approaching across the field. The tramp's dress indicates that he is out of place in the southern, rural scene. Worn and dirty as they are, he wears city clothes. Just as a sense of time's running counter to itself has been suggested, so the man suggests in everything about his person and appearance a reality which is out of place. He reacts to handling dead chicks with obvious disgust. His surly behavior, and his willingness to draw a knife suggest that he has probably gotten into some kind of trouble for which he is not willing to pay. He has chosen instead to avoid the places of law and order. He has placed himself outside of society, a move in which the boy will follow him.

The point of the story comes clearest in the symbolism of shoes. The " . . . strong, scuffed brown shoes . . ." the boy was supposed to wear are a more modest version of his father's " . . . strong cowhide boots . . . splashed with good red mud and set solid upon the bricks. . . ." These are the boots, which, if he follows in his father's footsteps, the boy will someday wear. Juxtaposed against his father's are the shoes of the tramp who regards the farm as a disgusting place. He wears " . . . the pointed-toe, broken, black shoes, on which the mud looked so sad and out of place." The latter, the shoes of the tramp, are those the boy elects to follow.

It should not be supposed, however, that the boy has any intention of fitting into the tramp's shoes; he follows them, but keeps a few paces off to the right. For the whole story has been a description of a boy's attempt to do without any shoes at all. The significance of shoes, as a comfort styled to the demands of the environment, is suggested by the boy's rejected strong shoes, his rejected father's good boots, the strong brogans of the "pore white" boy whom he sees at the flood, and by those of the tramp from an urban area. Broken as the tramp's shoes are, they are still shoes that would not look so out of place in more civilized areas as his father's boots, which would look pretty farmerish. This choice runs consistently through Warren's stories. As a barefoot writer of fiction, Warren has chosen to place himself outside of any form of social system. This is the independence a writer must insist upon.

The image of the barefoot boy combines both Robinson Crusoe and his man Friday:

You do not understand that voice from back in the kitchen which says that you cannot go barefoot outdoors and run to see what has happened and rub your feet over the wet shivery grass and make the perfect mark of your foot in the smooth, creamy, red mud and then muse upon it as though you had suddenly come upon that single mark on the glistening auroral beach of the world. You have never seen a beach, but you have read the book, and how the footprint was there.

Here the boy is his own discoverer, Robinson Crusoe, and, simultaneously, his own discovery, Friday. The image is an apt one for Warren's purposes, for it combines the step-by-step chronological time represented by Friday, with the circumstantial time which brings a civilized man, represented by Robinson Crusoe, strangely clad in the skins of beasts, to the beach of a desert island. This "auroral beach" marks the beginning of an experience of discovery. Part of the boy's discovery will have to be stated in terms of chronological time, for over the years the footprint will change. Another part of the discovery will depend, as it did for Crusoe, upon a certain isolation of the individual, away from the ordinary perceptions of life, and one that is symbolized by the boy's insistence upon going barefoot, even though he stands a good chance, like the barefoot chicks, of perishing before he has lived long enough to make the discoveries.

While the boy felt the right kind of, almost stereotyped, emotions toward his parents, he chose a different life. His father died from injuries he received from a mowing machine. This was harmonious, poetically just; his mother died, presumably, of a broken heart. This too was fitting. Old Jebb, who prayed for strength to endure, endured. Jebb's son, who was badly treated by jealous neighbors, ended in the penitentiary. All of the pieces fall in place but one: the boy elected to follow the tramp. He is seen, years later, writing a story called **"Blackberry Winter."**

If the narrator of the story is to be equated with Warren, **"Blackberry Winter"** is revealing as to the choice, the mental processes, and the early age at which these must have been taking place in the writer. The story suggests that it will be the person who is not stereotyped, who is somehow out of place, together with the author's determination to treat time simultaneously in and out of sequence—it is June but it is also blackberry winter—that will form the chief characteristics of Warren's literary "pursuit." It should also be noticed that the regional term used for the title suggests, in addition, that Warren will be concerned with the South. In the symbolic sense I have suggested, the choice the boy makes at the age of nine constitutes the first, and necessary, betrayal—it is the author's betrayal of his heritage.

The title story of the collection, **"The Circus in the Attic,"** illustrates well the counter-currents of time, place, and betrayal. Bolton Lovehart, an elderly resident of Bardsville, bridges time from the first settling of that southern region by a white man, Bolton's great-great-grandfather, to the present. The town's unofficial historian, he spends a good part of his life in a gradually diminishing attempt to write the history of Carruthers County. It is repeatedly made clear that Bolton is a failure in this endeavor. He doesn't know the truth about Cassius Perkins and Seth Sykes, the town heroes. He doesn't know the truth about how his own great-great-grandfather led a party of settlers to what is now Carruthers County and settled it. He doesn't even know the truth about the town's most recent hero, Jasper Parton, his own stepson. He is the

town authority on the progress of World War II, but no evidence is presented that he is any more than a popular, if attentive, observer of this event.

Nevertheless, Bolton Lovehart is the one person in Bardsville about whom Warren must write his story, for Bolton precipitates the story, much in the fashion that a catalyst precipitates a chemical change without itself being thereby changed. Bolton has been made what he is by a number of complicated circumstances: his own naturally inquisitive bent—as a boy he collected arrowheads and interested himself in a number of matters—his fairly intelligent mind—he read widely for some years—and his mother, who dominated him with effusive "love." Actually, she tried to project her will by investing it in her son. This attempt was so successful that from his earliest years Bolton became a kind of puppet, controlled by invisible wires. He naturally struggled against this control and made various attempts to compensate, as best he could, by seeking some form of escape. He was drawn to a baptismal ceremony where he became a Baptist (his mother was Episcopalian) in hopes both of eluding his mother and of hurting her. Then he ran away to join a circus: a place which collects oddities. The circus represented the only kind of ready-made society in which Bolton could feel free. Years later, he tried to escape by becoming a ticket taker at the town's first motion-picture house. Here again, the world of make-believe offered a nightly refuge from hateful reality. In all these attempts he was frustrated by his mother.

The only safe place, as it developed, was in the attic of his own house. Here he had hoarded all his treasures from the past; here he worked on his book and started his circus. It should be recognised at once that the attic of a house corresponds to some part of a man's mind. We all have an attic of memory to which we can go, if we don't mind the dust, the detritus of time, and the closeness of the air. Most of us only go there when we have something at hand that we don't know what to do with. We put it in this attic and only glance at it again when we make the rare journey up to put still another object out of sight. But Bolton Lovehart lived in daily communion with this part of his mind. Thus even at the age of 67 he kept the boy in himself very much alive. The figures he carved out of blocks of soft pine were dream figures: they represented a world reshaped closer to his heart's desire.

The most interesting specimens of his skill are his ringmaster and his masterpiece, the girl acrobat. The acrobat, with her blue eyes and skirt of silk, is so light on her feet she scarcely seems to touch the ground, and in truth, she spends a good part of her time in the air. Intense, but easy, effortless grace characterizes her, and is suggested even in repose. Compare her with Bolton's motionless mother who, for more than fourteen years now, has not stood upon her feet. Notice the little doll's painted smirk, and compare it with the tint of rouge on the mother's cheeks, and the painted smirk she wears, the one that serves for a smile. Bolton has succeeded in creating a figure of woman that will not dominate him; far from it, she is dominated, in a gently tyrannical way, by the ringmaster with his "ferocious black mustache." He is another form of Bolton Lovehart, but now the tables are turned. Everything, even the ages, are turned. The ringmaster was created before the girl acrobat, hence is older, and in fact, he looks older.

Thus the circus Bolton Lovehart carved in his attic became, for some years, the reality, against which the external world seemed pale. His greatest satisfaction, however, was not the creation of those figures; it was the certain knowledge, all the hours he worked on them, that his mother did not know what he was doing. She thought he was working on his book, and of course one can work for years on a book without making any visible signs of progress. Like a boy, he enjoyed what he did because it was secret, and because he knew his mother would put an instant stop to his efforts if she ever found out what he was up to. He was getting away with being naughty.

When at the age of 87 his mother's fictitious heart trouble turned real and she died in the night, Bolton, left without motive to continue his carving, discontinued.

He was 59 when he married. His only previous experience with a woman had been a generation before, when he had courted Sara Darter. She had seen through his mother's illness—had recognised it as a device to keep her son with her. Out of spite Sara seduced Bolton and then left town the following day, never to return. Bolton no doubt felt that he had been betrayed. Marriage provided him with a new reality, so he left the world of the attic for the world of the streets. He used the war as a pretense for talking about himself and his family, and his wife soon learned to hate him for this. She did not interfere in his entertainment of the soldiers, even after the war, and Bolton was free to believe that her motives were generous and pure. But they were not. They were no purer than Bolton's motives for entertaining men in uniform, or, really, uniform men; for Bolton all his life had been in the entertainment business. This was satisfying to him, for now he was the ringmaster, with the pretty, blue-eyed girl acrobat wife. Had he been more true to himself, Bolton might have seen more deeply into the sources of his own actions, and so his wife's. Finally, when she and an officer crashed into the tailgate of a truck, Bolton understood. He realized that he had been betrayed a third time by a woman. First it had been Sara Darter who got tired of waiting, seduced him, and left as though nothing had happened. Next it had been his mother. For years she had secretly betrayed him with her phony cardiac condition. Finally, his wife had died with another man—she too had betrayed him.

At the end of the story, Bolton Lovehart is back with his circus in the attic. The attic of his mind contains not only the imperfect wooden figures, but also the imperfect human figures. He never really understood what was happening around him. He didn't understand his mother, Sara Darter, his wife, Jasper Parton, the soldiers who drank his beer and ate his sandwiches, the other heroes, Cassius Perkins and Seth Sykes, or, and this is the worst failure of all, he never understood himself. Bolton was a misfit in his environment, out of place and out of time, betrayed by everyone, and betrayed by himself.

"When the Light Gets Green" also combines the three elements of time, in and out of sequence, place and betrayal. The story seems to deal with the bald statement that old men have disagreeable habits, together with most weak hams, and that once they have outlived their usefulness, are no longer really wanted. The title image of green light is premonitory of death. The light gets green just before lightning strikes. In this story green light presages hail, destructive to tobacco, and tobacco was the grandfather's whole life. The green light is also the reflection from the wavy green mirror in the grandfather's room. It reveals the old man's image in a way strikingly like that of a dead man when seen at the bottom of a frozen stream in winter. The old man himself recognises the meaning of these signs. He realizes that no one loves him, and

that it is time to die. Coming from an old man, the feeling he expresses seems awkward, even embarrassing. But this is a human truth: even old men want to be loved. The grandson who tells the story realizes that in sober truth he doesn't love his grandfather. He tells his grandfather he loves him, he even tells himself he does, and listens to his voice saying it, but that does not make it real. Thus the betrayal in the story is one wrought chiefly by time. It is simply in the nature of things for men to be part of the great cycle. When the cycle is completed, it is time to die. The old man was unfortunate enough to last another four years after this realization.

"The Patented Gate and the Mean Hamburger" is similar to **"Blackberry Winter."** Jeff York, of "pore white" stock, has broken the traditional caste of squatterdom by getting to own his own farm. Thus he is exceptional for men of his background, for he has more persistence, and more power of rejection. The way he sets his " . . . cast-iron brogans down deliberately on the cement . . ."; reminds one of the father in **"Blackberry Winter,"** whose strong cowhide boots stood so firmly on the bricks. York's wife, when she is at home, wears the same kind of shoes her husband wears. But every Saturday, when he takes her to town, she appears on the street in polished, black leather high heels. These shoes are somewhat reminiscent of the tramp's shoes in **"Blackberry Winter."** Her secret ambition and her secret vanity are revealed by the high heels. Mrs. York longs to be sophisticated; she does not want to be a farmer's wife. When she breaks a chain of centuries of tradition by trading her husband's farm for a hamburger stand, he hangs himself.

But Mrs. York learns to walk erect in her high heels without lurching at every step. That is the onward march of progress; that is life in modern times. The invisible print of Mrs. York's high heels on concrete led, step by inexorable step, to betrayal of her husband's entire sense of identity. Even though it took years, it had to happen. Perhaps Jeff York should not have taken his wife into the dogwagon in the first place, but how could he have foreseen its significance? Consider the father in **"Blackberry Winter."** How could he have known he was betraying himself when he told the tramp to get off his property?

"Her Own People" involves the betrayal of a near-white servant girl by Negro and white alike. She is a "white folks nigger" who has little colored blood, and dislikes what little she has. She wants to be a lady and live elegantly, but her blood prevents her. So she works for a white family and behaves with all the affected mannerisms of gentility that she imagines are a part of white folks' ways. Her own people are the only ones, except for her employers, who understand her. They are probably the only ones who are her own color. She is in the transitional state represented by Mrs. York before she got the dogwagon, and she too is rather awkward in her high heels. Mrs. York, it will be recalled, learned, after a while, how to wear them with some grace. There doesn't seem to be much hope that Viola will. Society just can't find a place for her yet. Probably she will have to stay with her own people a few generations more.

Warren shows that Viola is not welcome in a Negro home. The black people treat her like a Negro, and Viola expects to be treated white, or at least something approaching white. The final scene brings out the paradoxical nature of the problem. The white couple has just left Viola lying in her bed in the Negro home where she isn't welcome and knows it, and they have refused to take her back. The white couple knows that she is their responsibility, just as every white American knows that every American Negro is his responsibility. But they choose to turn their backs on the problem. "Go back where you came from," is what, in effect, they say. And they try to overlook the fact that they have changed her so that she can't go back.

Then there is an abrupt change in the remaining three stories in this collection. Warren says in a note to the book: "The earliest story in this book was written in 1930, the latest in 1946, but the order here is not chronological." It seems fitting that Warren chose not to arrange his stories in chronological time. The alternative is, of course, to arrange them according to what I have been calling, for lack of a better term, circumstantial time. The last three stories are Warren's statements of affirmation: these are stories in which men do not betray themselves.

"The Life and Work of Professor Roy Millen" sketches in the past of a man who did not realize there could be so good a life as he came to know after his marriage to the daughter of the English Department chairman at a state university. His life has been a satisfying one, although his wife's declining health in later years made it impossible for him to go abroad to do certain studies for a book he has been writing. Now, his wife dead, he is about to go abroad, for the first time in his life, to complete those studies. Into the picture comes his best student requesting a recommendation so that he may be granted a scholarship to pursue his postgraduate study in Paris. The boy has received "A's" for his work in the English Department. But during their conversation he reveals a side of his personality that Millen had not been able to see in the normal functions of class recitation and written work. The boy is too glib; he isn't sufficiently humble; above all, because he has a natural ability with language, and because his parents are well off, he has never come to grips with life. Millen senses the fact that this boy's best interests will be served if he is made to earn what he receives. Millen checks the enthusiastic recommendation he was dictating. Not for nothing were all those years lived. In privacy, he writes another letter of recommendation carefully observing that the student has a natural facility with language, but that his character seems superficial; he lacks " . . . the spirit of patient inquiry, and what might be termed the philosophical bent."

What seems to be studied meanness, and what, without question, has something to do with the professor's own sufferings to achieve place, causes him to deny the easy way to the student. But looked at further, Millen's life, with all its hard work at the start, turned out to be better than he could have dreamed. Perhaps this is a favor he is doing for the student. No one can say what would have happened had the student been granted the easy way; such a letter as Millen wrote effectually closes that door. Perhaps Millen was wrong in his estimation, perhaps he was right. It does not really matter. What matters is that Millen checked the natural impulse to betray himself, and to betray what all his years of effort represented, and in the end did not. He remained true to himself.

"The Unvexed Isles" is a companion story. The English professor again has come up from penury to recognition. He has married a woman whose parents are wealthy, but whose wealth does not improve his. The professor and his wife have enough for a gracious, stay-at-home way of life, but not enough for a train ticket to Baltimore for his wife. Their life is a full and satisfying one.

There to take his farewell for the Christmas holidays is, again, the exceptional student. Again he is well to do, much more so, in fact, than in the first story. This student is a New Yorker, wears tailored clothes, drives an expensive car, and (no doubt) escorts an expensive young girl, richly clad in silk and fur, to various expensive places. He (no doubt) necks with the richly clad girl. His fleet, empty conversation about his going to Bermuda for Christmas upsets Professor Dalrymple, who now feels that he is an outsider to both the student and his own wife's parents. His wife, he realizes, is caught in the meshes of his poverty. She can't go home for Christmas because she married a poor man. She would know better now, he tells himself, than to marry an English professor. He takes savage pleasure in torturing himself with the thought that the lipstick on the student's cigarette is from kissing Mrs. Dalrymple while he was in the pantry. Later, he will admit that this was an over-dramatization of his feelings in a bad moment. Later, he will realize that his wife would marry him again. He is not really a poor man. The silver-mounted siphon, the silver ice-bucket, the best whiskey in Russell Hill (and Professor Dalrymple does not care for whiskey), the comfortable home, all give the lie to the cost of a train ticket to Baltimore.

Mrs. Dalrymple, who once wrote poetry of some account, simply escaped from her parents into a world more compatible with her spirit. If she cannot afford to leave her husband over Christmas, it is because they can't afford to jeopardize their way of life. All of this the professor realizes by the end of the story.

Deliberately, at the moment of the student's farewell, Professor Dalrymple rapidly sketches in the poverty-stricken, tortured background he turned into something more satisfying, and more worthy of a man's best efforts. He makes his guest see something the boy does not wish to believe. Later, the student may see the contrast, and may perhaps realize that it is not his own efforts that bought the ticket to Bermuda. If he ever does, which is unlikely, he may choose, like Mrs. Dalrymple, not to buy such tickets at all. Dalrymple upset his wife somewhat by his actions, but he knows that she will see that he has saved their self-respect, and has cherished the effort that gives meaning to self-sacrifice and to life.

Momentarily betrayed by emotions of self-pity, Dalrymple and Millen both reveal in the crisis a toughened resiliency of spirit that long training has given them. Both men are caught in what for them were the most mortifying of circumstances. Both were temporarily swayed, but returned to self-command, and to ascendance over their worlds. Both were able to avoid self-betrayal.

Warren's first two affirmations are relatively painless. Victory is achieved without any shattering defeats. In the final story of the collection, **"Prime Leaf,"** actually Warren's first published story, Warren reminds us that the man who is true to himself can still be betrayed, under certain circumstances, and that integrity is sometimes preserved at a fearful cost. Mr. Hardin, the old man, has been persuaded to join the tobacco association by his close friend, Bill Hopkins. His son, Big Thomas, was strongly against joining but in the end followed his father's example. The association represents a kind of democracy based on the principle of doing the greatest amount of good for the greatest number of people. When the association abandons ethical means to achieve its ends and uses the nightriders to coerce farmers into joining the association, Hardin resigns as board member on the principle that there isn't anything in the world that is worth doing irrespective of the means used to do it. Then he spends his time sitting on the gate: he is still a member, but an inactive one. As soon as it is clear that the nightriders are actually destroying private property, he resigns outright. His son protests that he doesn't want to be ruined by his father's "notions," but in the end he too quits. He quits because his father shows him that in order to be true to the association he must be false to himself. He knows he will have to join the nightriders if he means to affirm his faith in the association, and this means that he must be ready to help destroy the labors of his own friends and neighbors. This is a more serious matter to him than doing what is best for the greatest number of men, no matter how. So the nightriders come and they burn down the Hardins' barnful of tobacco. The old man takes this development calmly, this is the price he knew had to be paid, but his son, who is not very reflective, and hasn't foreseen the inevitable consequences of quitting, is outraged. He shoots and seriously injures one of the nightriders, Bill Hopkins. He returns home to await the sheriff and to defend his home from the nightriders. His father persuades him that the honorable course would be to give himself up to the sheriff. So father and son start for town together, but at a fork in the road the old man turns off the leaves his son to go into town alone. His motives for this action are not made clear, proabably because there is no single motive. Big Thomas suspects that his father may be turning off because it would look as though he were bringing his son in to justice. This is a valid surmise. It also seems possible that the old man suspects foul play along the road and does not wish to pay the price for his son's crime. This is also a legitimate possibility, and the old man himself is aware of this. He has already said to his grandson: " 'No, I wouldn't call Bill Hopkins a coward, I guess I can't tell who's a coward.' " The old man knows that a lot of nightriders are cowards who probably delight in destroying the property of other men. Hardin is faced with the alternatives of calling his own decisions acts of heroism or of cowardice. When he persuades Big Thomas to give himself up he seems to affirm his principles once more, and thus to give them meaning. In this sense, his going to visit the man his son has wounded, while at that very minute he knows his own son may be sacrificed to the brutality of his own act by others even more brutal, represents an act of affirmation of the highest order.

The old man and his son had joined the association in good faith. The men of the association betrayed themselves when they introduced the use of violence. In such a situation, in such a society, the only way Big Thomas could have protected his wife and son would have been to negate his own principles.

Warren chooses not to show the face of the grieving father. It is enough to see the grandson, who, after all, is next. The old man's grief could tell us nothing. What may look like cowardice was the old man's greatest sacrifice, and his greatest act of affirmation. Crucified by time and circumstance, he can still see to the welfare of the man who brought all his grief upon him, but who, after all, acted according to his ideas of rightness.

These stories are an examination into the complexities of time and change. Circumstantial time, so subjective in nature, can betray men into impatience, as in **"Prime Leaf,"** but then chronological time must betray men by its inexorable march, as in **"When the Light Gets Green."** Warren reveals a finely

attuned sensitivity to the determinism of events, which must happen in order, for causes and effects usually are not simultaneous. The suffering attendant upon various betrayals Warren has described is unavoidable, just as many of the betrayals are themselves inescapable. Bolton Lovehart, for example, did not choose his mother. But not all. For men can resist the impulse to self-betrayal, as the final three stories suggest. As in **"Blackberry Winter,"** Warren's position denies the validity of Jebb's belief that the end is near. A bad cold-snap, such as the nightriders Bill Hopkins set in motion, though it may do its damage, is only part of the Great Cycle, abnormal as, in the shorter view, this may seem. And, Warren seems to say, a man owes it to himself to stand firm to his principles, no matter how the wind changes. (pp. 74-84)

James B. Scott, "The Theme of Betrayal in Robert Penn Warren's Stories," in Thoth, *Vol. V, No. 2, Spring, 1964, pp. 74-84.*

RICHARD ALLAN DAVISON (essay date 1968)

[*In the following excerpt, Davison examines the "rite-of-passage" theme in Warren's story "Blackberry Winter."*]

The ability to use physical imagery and human actions as vehicles for psychological and philosophical observations on man is the commanding distinction of Robert Penn Warren's art. His most carefully constructed images dramatically realize a "dialectal configuration" which embodies a struggle to explore fully the significance of human experience. This artistic struggle is found in Warren's best fiction in a way that generates a rare brand of sympathetic excitement in the classroom.

In none of his short stories is the quest for understanding better realized than in the oft-anthologized, frequently taught **"Blackberry Winter"**; in no story has he better integrated his imagistic patterns. **"Blackberry Winter"** is one of Warren's best and, deservedly, most popular stories. Through this dramatization of a child's rite of passage Warren explores the complications of a nine-year-old farm boy's initiation into the complexities of the adult world largely by centering the most telling imagery on the young protagonist's feet. Warren virtually charts the sensitive reactions of the boy's feet to external stimuli. The responses of Seth's bare feet serve as indications of his changing awareness of the mystery, uncertainty and evil in the world from which his parents have so long sheltered him. The forty-four year old narrator (Warren's actual age at the time of composition) couches his youthful recollections and mature observations largely in this physical imagery. And when the narrator tells his story in the first person he adds breadth of meaning to the imagery by creating the sense of a double vision. Through this double point of view the reader is both caught up in the action of the story from the perspective of a boy's callow awareness (as one is in *Huck Finn*) and able to maintain the artistic distance of the mature narrator.

The persona's "double vision" extends the range of suggestiveness of the imagery by balancing naive reportage with mature observations. For instance, he conceptualizes about Time as "not a movement, a flowing . . . but . . . a kind of climate in which things are, and . . . a thing . . . stands solid in Time like the tree that you can walk around." Then he translates his adult comments on time into the terms of his childhood: "When you are nine, you know that there are things that you don't know, but you know that when you know something you know it. You know how a thing has been and you know that you can go barefoot in June." The statement is similar to Dylan Thomas' remark in "Child's Christmas in Wales" that "One Christmas was so much like another . . . that I can never remember whether it snowed for six days and six nights when I was twelve or whether it snowed for twelve days and twelve nights when I was six." Warren's handling of the persona's relation to his boyhood is reminiscent also of Whitman's creation of a sense of telescoped time in "Out of the Cradle Endlessly Rocking" in which the mature narrator states that he is "a man, yet by these tears a little boy again." The man's awareness merges with the boy's.

Through the physical imagery that is filtered through the persona in **"Blackberry Winter"** then, the reader is engaged in a dramatic immediacy reinforced by a technique analogous to the imagistic techniques of writers as diverse as Whitman and Salinger. Warren's employment of such central tactile imagery is more dramatically successful than either Whitman's use of an uninitiate child's bare feet in "Out of the Cradle Endlessly Rocking" or Salinger's organic use of the feet to depict Seymour's abnormal mental state in "A Perfect Day for Banana Fish." With Warren, furthermore, we are fortunate to have direct evidence of the author's partial (at least) awareness of the importance of such an imagistic use of feet. In a critical article on the genesis of **"Blackberry Winter"** [see excerpt dated 1959] Warren writes:

> I recollect the particular thread that led me back into the past: the feeling you have when after vacation begins, you are allowed to go barefoot. Not that I particularly liked to go barefoot. But privilege was important, an escape from the tyranny of winter, school, and even family. It was like what anthropologists call rite of passage. But it had another significance; it carried you over into a dream of nature; the woods, not the house, was now your natural habitat, the stream, not the street. . . .

> With the recollection of going barefoot came another, which had been recurrent over the years: the childhood feeling of betrayal when early summer gets turned upside down and all its promises are revoked by the cold spell, the gully-washer.

Warren's comments enlighten the theme but they also suggest that in the actual imagistic embodiment of all that Seth's bare feet represent the author (à la Robert Frost) may have written better than he knew.

Purely on the sensory level Seth's bare feet, in their reactions to the temperature and texture of their surroundings, motivate his actions which place him in "learning" situations. His shoes represent ambivalent values: shoes protect and inhibit. The need for protection from the elements and the freedom from the restrictions of civilization are represented by shoes and shoelessness respectively. His shoes are also associated with parental guidance and security. Seth's responses to his feet motivate virtually all of his physical actions as he moves towards the adult emotional maturity that comes only in exchange for an equal portion of innocence.

At first the warmth of the house makes unreal his mother's worry over his getting a chill by going barefoot. He stands "working [his] bare toes slowly on the warm stone." He wants to go outside without shoes and does not want to "let her see that [he] was barefoot." His thoughts are dominated by the physical pleasure of rubbing his "feet over the wet shivery grass and [making] the perfect mark of [his] foot in the smooth, creamy red mud. . . ." The boy's main concern seems to be for physical comfort and sense gratification. But he also desires literally and figuratively to make his mark in the world, to make choices untrammeled by parental restrictions. The narrator describes the boy's feet as parts of nature "sinking into and clutching the earth like roots. . . ." It is only the unexpected visit of the tramp from the outside world, however, that prevents Seth's mother from exercising her authority by forcing Seth to put on shoes. The tramp's inappropriately foreign (to Seth's world) city shoes are diametrically opposed to the naturalness of Seth's own bare feet. The boy decides to watch the tramp work in the yard because of his wish to remain barefoot and out of the sight of his mother and a growing curiosity about the outside world. Warren repeatedly contrasts Seth's bare feet with the tramp's shoes. The tramp's ignorance of rural matters parallels Seth's inexperience outside of the country. There is also an analogue to Seth's innocence in the helplessness of the chickens drowned in the early spring storm as the tramp picks them up by their limp feet and disdainfully disposes of them. The drowned chicken's "feet curl in that feeble, empty way. . . . He . . . began to pick up the other chicks, picking each one up slowly by a foot and then flinging it into the basket with a nasty, snapping motion."

Warren frequently uses animals in the story as a way of revealing character. The farm dogs, the horse, mule, and the dead cow all serve to reinforce his explorations of character. The cow, for example, has jumped a fence as Seth will figuratively have to do and its drifting down the creek toward the river foreshadows Seth's drift through experience.

Seth sees the dead cow after the tramp's uncivil response to his presence has prompted him to join his father and other rural observers of the devastation wrought by the gully washer. Seth's father does not comment on his son's bare feet but, like Seth's mother, serves as a buffer to the boy's growing awareness of pain in the world. "He whisked [him], light as a feather, up to the pommel of his McClennan saddle." His presence lessens the horror of the dead bloated cow and mutes the awareness of the blatant poverty of the Alleys. A gangly neighbor boy "on a scraggly little old mule" wonders if "anybody ever et drownt cow." Nobody seems to listen to the old man who answers, "You live long enough and you'll find a man will eat anything when the time comes." But the grownup Seth has remembered this further witness to various standards in the world. Seth's parents' strength and dignity have allowed him more gradually to absorb the harsh effects of an interplay of innocence and experience. Seth watches the spectacle from the back of his father's mare, where he has been lifted. In contrast, the sullen neighbor boy's "mud-stiff brogans, hanging off his skinny, bare ankles," are scanty protection from the agony of experience as he digs his heel into his mule's "lank and scrofulous hide" and rides away alone.

Seth rides back toward home firmly pressed against his father's strong body with a physical and emotional contentment unknown in the vulnerable life of the poor neighbor boy. But when his father sets him down to the ground at the farm, experience begins to become as penetrating to his innocence as palpably as does the cold penetrate his feet. It is Seth's cold feet (chilled from the mud) and knowledge of his mother's authority that send him running for physical warmth and the companionship of a life-long friend, Dellie, their Negro servant. He had always warmed himself emotionally in Dellie's presence. She had reinforced his childhood innocence, but as he runs with chilled feet toward the symbol of past security he has to pick his way "past the filth [of the present], being careful not to get [his] bare feet on it." Just as Dellie has proved anything but irascible in the past so the trash has always been hidden from view under the well-kept servants' cottage. The storm has destroyed Dellie's flowers and the "little grass there was in the yard . . . reminded [him] of the way the fluff was plastered on the skin of the drowned chicks that the strange man had been picking up in [his] mother's chicken yard." It took the traumatic gully washer to turn things upside down in Seth's young life—to spew forth trash, float dead cows, drown chickens and flowers and summon surly tramps. Seth is being prepared for further probing into his mental and emotional awareness.

At Dellie's cabin he endures more deeply "traumatic" experience: Dellie's new menopausal hostility to him and her seemingly unmotivated cruelty to little Jeb. Little Jeb will be scarred by such traumas and sent to the penitentiary for killing another Negro. Seth does not yet comprehend this dark side of human experience figured in Dellie's "change of life"; for this is, in fact, a figuring forth of all that he will learn from his metaphorical following of the tramp "all the years."

Seth runs from the painful hostility of Dellie's cabin "not caring whether or not [he] stepped in the filth which had washed out from under the cabin." From there he runs to the stables, again from fear of his mother's catching him with bare feet. When he sees Big Jeb shelling corn in the nearby crib, he stops for security and comfort, and because of his childish fear of parental punishment he has gradually given in to a curiosity of what is beyond a world where blackberry winters and gully-washers are synonymous and human response is unpredictable. One sees a carefully drawn parallel between Dellie's menopause and Seth's change of life.

Significantly, Seth's feet get increasingly cold as Jeb hints at even more mystery and uncertainty in life. As Seth gets colder, for a time his security weakens in proportion to the chill. The blackberry winter is also associated with Seth's boyhood innocence that is gradually diminished. Seth's confidence in past beliefs is further shaken when Jeb questions whether they are really experiencing blackberry winter and, in effect, contradicts the boy's mother. All this uncertainty is somehow linked to the unknown world of the city tramp— the tramp Seth's mother and father do not fear and that he himself must learn to comprehend. The tramp knows of the river that is two miles from the creek which borders the farm. From the swollen creek Seth must walk to the river; but that is the next stage of his encounter with experience.

Seth's physical journey of the single morning described in the story comes full circle after he leaves Big Jeb and returns home. He is just in time to witness his father drive off the tramp because the tramp has abused his father for refusing him a permanent job. Warren describes this crucial scene again by focusing on the action below the knees. The tramp's muddy, "broken, black" city shoes slowly retreat before the "strong cowhide" boots of Seth's father. Seth's world which has been shaken so severely is given a renewed but different kind of security and he is given the courage to figuratively follow the tramp. He has not merely retreated to past innocence. His father's action helps him to withstand and come to grips with the upsets of this day. Seth is eventually to embrace a fuller courage that is a blend of a renewed parental trust and

deepening personal experience. These incidents of a single morning microcosmically embody the agonies and joys—the sufferings—that span a boy's whole adolescence. But such suffering has led to a wisdom that allows the mature narrator to come to terms with the shocks of his childhood and to cope with the potentially tragic human situation. These are the kinds of experiences that prepare Seth for the death of his parents a few years hence and allow him to direct his bare feet along the path to the road beyond the creek and to the fast flowing river that parallels the broader perspectives of adult life. And through the artistic synthesis of imagery, action and statement the reader has vicariously shared this particular individual's encounter with universal experience. A highly personal experience has been integrated in a way that renders it transcendent.

In **"Blackberry Winter"** the teacher and poet in Robert Penn Warren are marvelously blended. The feet that propel Seth through his journey Warren has used to probe and assess the adult implications of childhood experiences. It is through a mixture of mystery and incisiveness that he has so successfully transmuted the actions and objects surrounding a small boy into a dialectical configuration which has the universal implications of all honest quests for understanding. (pp. 482-88)

> *Richard Allan Davison, "Physical Imagery in Robert Penn Warren's 'Blackberry Winter',"* in The Georgia Review, *Vol. XXII, No. 4, Winter, 1968, pp. 482-88.*

ROBERT PENN WARREN [INTERVIEW WITH RUTH FISHER]   (interview date 1972)

[*In the following excerpted interview, Warren discusses criticism of his work and his personal perceptions of his fiction. He also comments on the significance of his short stories in relation to his novels and poems.*]

Fisher: Has being a teacher of literature had much influence on the way you write? Does it, for example, encourage an analytical approach to structure?

Warren: This is a question that in one sense is unanswerable. Because I can't say what I would be if I weren't me. I don't want to dodge it on that basis, though. I won't dodge it at all. I'll try to answer. I would have to answer by saying how I would like to go at it, and how I trust that I do sometimes.

To take a preliminary notion, whatever we do—teaching or reading criticism or practicing it a little—has an effect on us. It gets inside us. We can't throw it away, except by a feat of total amnesia. Even then it's lurking in your brain somewhere, and you are different because of its presence. But to turn to the general question of how ideas may affect the process of writing—we have to recognize that they can appear at different levels of consciousness. Some writers, and some very good ones indeed, are intensely self-conscious in the practice of their art. They bring a great deal to bear at the level of "knowing." For better or for worse, I try to forget, not remember, what little I know. I try to "feel" into the structure of my story. Literally, I want to get the kinetic sense of the plot movement, of the swell and fall of action, of the intense moment and the relaxed moment. But—and this is a big *but*—when things begin to feel wrong, that is when I try to analyze the reason why things are wrong. Finding out the reason for the wrongness will not give you rightness, but it clears the way, perhaps, for rightness to come. In general, however, I try to immerse myself in the immediate concerns of the thing I'm doing. You have to pray that what you have learned and thought in the past will, by instinct as it were, bear fruit now. But, of course, once you have a draft, you must become "critic"—must try to estimate, analyze, explain to yourself. That is in so far as things have gone wrong.

It's the same—learning to write, if you can every say you have "learned"—as learning to drive a tennis ball. A coach can look at the action and analyze it into various stages, say body position, placement of feet at the moment of contact, grip on racket, shoulder position, etc. All these things can be separated out as problems. Now the coach may say, "Do it again, your racket is wrong, you turned your arm too far down." In other words, he is trying to analytically break up the action. The coach wants the player to know intellectually each phase of action, because the player, left to himself and acting *naturally,* has failed to strike the ball correctly. The player failed naturally. Therefore he analyzes the failure by taking the parts of action and locating the source of error. The player may drill himself on these actions and, bang, the ball comes and he has a beautiful return. But when he hit the ball, he was not thinking; he had gone beyond thinking; it was in the bloodstream. There is total unawareness in the moment of action.

Fisher: Is that how you write?

Warren: That's how you want to write. Writing is not caught in a single motion like a tennis ball. You can stop and look back and assess as you go along. But the principle is the same, I think. Certainly if you study four or five years in college and then take two years to write a certain book, you are not trying to remember everything that you learned in college. You are trying to write a good book. You think about the actual process as it exists in the moment of action. Now the moment of action in writing a book is longer than that of striking a tennis ball, but the parallels are real in the significant moment of action. You want to be able to have the right flash of "inspiration." Where does it come from? It comes from all of you, all of the things you have learned, the kind of man you have made yourself by the time you are 25 or 50. You have lived into this moment of inspiration. Let's take the case where people get total inspiration, like a revelation from on high.

Take the case of Coleridge and "Kubla Khan" and the laudanum. Coleridge takes the laudanum and goes to sleep and has a dream. The dream is both visual and verbal. He sees the things and the words are there, too. He is awakened by a man at the door, and he writes it all down. That's a lovely way to write poetry. But this doesn't happen often. How did it happen?

Let's take the case of a famous chemist. Kekulé had been working for two or three years trying to arrive at a formula for the benzene ring. He couldn't work it out. He tried intellectually for several years. One night, after working on his chemistry textbooks in a stuffy room, he fell asleep over his work. He had a nightmare about snakes biting each other. He woke up with the snake images in his head, and said, "My God! that's the formula." He spent the rest of the night working out the mathematics for the snake formula.

Fisher: (Interruption) And you do this, in your writing?

Warren: Now, wait, now, don't rush me.

What happens to Coleridge and what happens to Kekulé: Coleridge can dream a poem, the chemist can dream a formula; but Coleridge could never dream a chemical formula and Kekulé could never dream "Kubla Khan." The dream can only come out of the person who owns the dream already. The dream work is done on the material that is already available in the man. There can be no revelation to a man to whom the revelation would not be a summing up of his own experience. His conscious, intellectual efforts may have failed to solve his problem (or write his poem), but the solution thanks to all his past history and presumably recent efforts too, is "in" him and emerges fulfilled. There's nothing irrational about such a process, for the end product—that of Kekulé's formula or Coleridge's poem—embodies the law of the medium appropriate to it. This can happen because we, at the conscious and the unconscious levels, are all one piece.

Now what I am trying to get at is this, in so far as writing is concerned. You try by all your strength to be rational, to study, and to think (as well as to be open, receptive) to prepare yourself for the moment when all your work will—apparently—become superfluous. When the idea will take over, effortlessly. But as Pasteur put it, Fortune favors only the prepared spirit. The idea "comes" to him. These ideas come mysteriously. You can't say I'm going to have an idea now. You have to be in the condition to have an idea. The trick in writing is to get in a certain condition to have an idea. In other words, it won't come by logical manipulation. You have to find what for you may lead you to these happy moments. You have to learn the art of blankness. And learn to "live right." Whatever that is for you. (pp. 5-7)

Fisher: You were quoted at Haverford College in September as saying that in order to write poetry, you had to stop writing short stories. What are some of the obstacles that one encounters when writing both short stories and poetry?

Warren: I wouldn't draw any principle from this. It just happened. I don't fully understand it myself. There was a period in my life for ten years when I couldn't finish a short poem. I had fifty or sixty of them. They would die on me. Something went wrong with them. It was a period when I was writing a lot of fiction. I wrote a couple of novels, and a long poem in that period, *Brother to Dragons.* I wrote the best short story I ever wrote in my life in that period, but it was the last short story I ever wrote. I wrote a novelette in that period, too, that I like very much, relatively speaking. But I was through with stories and I knew I would never write another. And as soon as I swore off short fiction, I had a new way in for writing short poems—a new relation to "subject"—to experience.

Fisher: (Interruption) What was that short story, the best one you ever wrote?

Warren: Well, it was as good as any I have written, and I don't like many of my stories at all. It was a story called **"Blackberry Winter."** The novelette I refer to is called **"Circus in the Attic."** I believe that was in the winter of '46.

Fisher: But you don't find this problem with the novel and poetry? There is no conflict there? (back to original question).

Warren: I suppose that the situation has something to do with scale. The original idea—the intuition, shall we say—for a short story might very well lead to a poem, but as long as I was dabbling with stories the story would usually preempt it—not let it grow into a poem or at least would somehow inhibit it. When I stopped writing stories, lost my pleasure in writing them, I somehow felt free to regard the little things that had seemed made for stories as now appropriate for poems. To find poetry in a more circumstantial, realistic base, with a more immediate relation to the material. And this led, I guess, to a change in style. What I am saying would not be true of the idea for a novel. Mere scale would make the difference.

Fisher: Is there a difference, then, in the writer's mind in the relationship among the three—short stories, poetry and novels? What is the relationship? What is the difference in the level?

Warren: Well, I can only tell you what's in this writer's mind. Me.

Fisher: Because you have written all three and quite brilliantly.

Warren: Well, thank you.

The short stories were always a kind of accident for me. All young people write stories first, so I wrote a few stories. But I wrote poems for years before I wrote short stories. I published a lot of poems before I wrote any fiction seriously. But short stories always seemed to have a way of limiting your risk in fiction. I was trying to write the best story I could, of course. I started writing novels before I wrote short stories. I wrote a novelette first, and then I wrote a novel before I wrote any short stories at all. I came to them almost . . . well, I don't know how I really came to short stories. Except maybe, I was very hard up and hoped for the quick buck. Which didn't come.

I wrote quite a few short stories, but I never had the same feeling for them as I had for poems or novels. This is me. I am not theorizing about anybody else. (pp. 8-9)

> *Robert Penn Warren and Ruth Fisher, "A Conversation with Robert Penn Warren," in* Four Quarters, *Vol. XXI, No. 4, May, 1972, pp. 3-17.*

FURTHER READING

Bohner, Charles. *Robert Penn Warren.* Boston: Twayne Publishers, 1981, 176 p.

> A survey of Warren's literary career that discusses and analyzes dominant themes in Warren's fiction and offers brief commentary on *The Circus in the Attic, and Other Stories.*

Breit, Harvey. "Talk with Mr. Warren." *The New York Times Book Review* (25 June 1950): 20.

> Brief interview in which Warren comments on his teaching career and discusses the theme of his book *Brother to Dragons: A Tale in Verse and Voices* (1953).

Ellison, Ralph, and Walter, Eugene. "Robert Penn Warren." *Paris Review* IV, Nos. 16-17 (Spring-Summer 1957): 112-40.

> Extensive interview in which Warren discusses his early interests in literature, his association with the Fugitives, and his personal and critical approaches to literature.

Frank, Joseph. *Hudson Review* 1 (Spring 1948): 285-86.

> Brief, largely unfavorable review of *The Circus in the Attic, and Other Stories.*

Freemantle, Anne. *The Commonweal* XLVII, No. 22 (12 March 1948): 547.

> Comments on Warren's shifting narrative voices in *The Circus in the Attic, and Other Stories,* concluding that the variance of perspective is distracting and results in disjointedness and unconvincing characterizations.

Shaw, Patrick W. "A Key to Robert Penn Warren's 'When the Light Gets Green.'" *College English Association: Critic* 38, No. 2 (January 1978): 16-18.

> Examination of the symbolic use of the word "green" in Warren's short story.

Weathers, Winston. "'Blackberry Winter' and the Use of Archetypes." *Studies in Short Fiction* 1, No. 1 (Fall 1963): 45-51.

> Detailed discussion of Warren's use of traditional thematic structures that convey archetypal images in "Blackberry Winter."

Short Story Criticism

Indexes

Literary Criticism Series
Cumulative Author Index

SSC Cumulative Nationality Index

SSC Cumulative Title Index

This Index Includes References to Entries in These Gale Series

Contemporary Literary Criticism

Presents excerpts of criticism on the works of novelists, poets, dramatists, short story writers, scriptwriters, and other creative writers who are now living or who have died since 1960. Cumulative indexes to authors and nationalities are included, as well as an index to titles discussed in the individual volume. Volumes 1-56 are in print.

Twentieth-Century Literary Criticism

Contains critical excerpts by the most significant commentators on poets, novelists, short story writers, dramatists, and philosophers who died between 1900 and 1960. Cumulative indexes to authors, nationalities, and titles discussed are included in each new volume. Volumes 1-34 are in print.

Nineteenth-Century Literature Criticism

Offers significant passages from criticism on authors who died between 1800 and 1899. Cumulative indexes to authors, nationalities, and titles discussed are included in each new volume. Volumes 1-24 are in print.

Literature Criticism from 1400 to 1800

Compiles significant passages from the most noteworthy criticism on authors of the fifteenth through eighteenth centuries. Cumulative indexes to authors, nationalities, and titles discussed are included in each new volume. Volumes 1-11 are in print.

Classical and Medieval Literature Criticism

Offers excerpts of criticism on the works of world authors from classical antiquity through the fourteenth century. Cumulative indexes to authors, titles, and critics are included in each volume. Volumes 1-3 are in print.

Short Story Criticism

Compiles excerpts of criticism on short fiction by writers of all eras and nationalities. Cumulative indexes to authors, nationalities, and titles discussed are included in each new volume. Volumes 1-4 are in print.

Children's Literature Review

Includes excerpts from reviews, criticism, and commentary on works of authors and illustrators who create books for children. Cumulative indexes to authors, nationalities, and titles discussed are included in each new volume. Volumes 1-19 are in print.

Contemporary Authors Series

Encompasses five related series. *Contemporary Authors* provides biographical and bibliographical information on more than 92,000 writers of fiction, nonfiction, poetry, journalism, drama, motion pictures, and other fields. Each new volume contains sketches on authors not previously covered in the series. Volumes 1-127 are in print. *Contemporary Authors New Revision Series* provides completely updated information on active authors covered in previously published volumes of *CA*. Only entries requiring significant change are revised for *CA New Revision Series*. Volumes 1-28 are in print. *Contemporary Authors Permanent Series* consists of updated listings for deceased and inactive authors removed from the original volumes 9-36 when these volumes were revised. Volumes 1-2 are in print. *Contemporary Authors Autobiography Series* presents specially commissioned autobiographies by leading contemporary writers. Volumes 1-10 are in print. *Contemporary Authors Bibliographical Series* contains primary and secondary bibliographies as well as analytical bibliographical essays by authorities on major modern authors. Volumes 1-2 are in print.

Dictionary of Literary Biography

Encompasses three related series. *Dictionary of Literary Biography* furnishes illustrated overviews of authors' lives and works and places them in the larger perspective of literary history. Volumes 1-87 are in print. *Dictionary of Literary Biography Documentary Series* illuminates the careers of major figures through a selection of literary documents, including letters, notebook and diary entries, interviews, book reviews, and photographs. Volumes 1-6 are in print. *Dictionary of Literary Biography Yearbook* summarizes the past year's literary activity with articles on genres, major prizes, conferences, and other timely subjects and includes updated and new entries on individual authors. Yearbooks for 1980-1988 are in print. A cumulative index to authors and articles is included in each new volume.

Concise Dictionary of American Literary Biography

A six-volume series that collects revised and updated sketches on major American authors that were originally presented in *Dictionary of Literary Biography*. Volumes 1-4 are in print.

Something about the Author Series

Encompasses three related series. *Something about the Author* contains heavily illustrated biographical sketches on juvenile and young adult authors and illustrators from all eras. Volumes 1-57 are in print. *Something about the Author Autobiography Series* presents specially commissioned autobiographies by prominent authors and illustrators of books for children and young adults. Volumes 1-8 are in print.

Yesterday's Authors of Books for Children

Contains heavily illustrated entries on children's writers who died before 1961. Complete in two volumes.

Literary Criticism Series
Cumulative Author Index

This index lists all author entries in the Gale Literary Criticism Series and includes cross-references to other Gale sources. References in the index are identified as follows:

AAYA: *Authors & Artists for Young Adults,* Volumes 1-2
CAAS: *Contemporary Authors Autobiography Series,* Volumes 1-10
CA: *Contemporary Authors* (original series), Volumes 1-127
CABS: *Contemporary Authors Bibliographical Series,* Volumes 1-2
CANR: *Contemporary Authors New Revision Series,* Volumes 1-28
CAP: *Contemporary Authors Permanent Series,* Volumes 1-2
CA-R: *Contemporary Authors* (revised editions), Volumes 1-44
CDALB: *Concise Dictionary of American Literary Biography,* Volumes 1-4
CLC: *Contemporary Literary Criticism,* Volumes 1-56
CLR: *Children's Literature Review,* Volumes 1-19
CMLC: *Classical and Medieval Literature Criticism,* Volumes 1-3
DLB: *Dictionary of Literary Biography,* Volumes 1-84
DLB-DS: *Dictionary of Literary Biography Documentary Series,* Volumes 1-6
DLB-Y: *Dictionary of Literary Biography Yearbook,* Volumes 1980-1988
LC: *Literature Criticism from 1400 to 1800,* Volumes 1-11
NCLC: *Nineteenth-Century Literature Criticism,* Volumes 1-24
SAAS: *Something about the Author Autobiography Series,* Volumes 1-8
SATA: *Something about the Author,* Volumes 1-56
SSC: *Short Story Criticism,* Volumes 1-4
TCLC: *Twentieth-Century Literary Criticism,* Volumes 1-34
YABC: *Yesterday's Authors of Books for Children,* Volumes 1-2

Author Index

Aquin, Hubert 1929-1977. . . . . **CLC 15**
See also CA 105; DLB 53

Aragon, Louis 1897-1982. . . . . . . **CLC 3, 22**
See also CA 69-72; obituary CA 108;
DLB 72

Arbuthnot, John 1667-1735 . . . . **LC 1**

Archer, Jeffrey (Howard) 1940- . . . . **CLC 28**
See also CANR 22; CA 77-80

Archer, Jules 1915- . . . . **CLC 12**
See also CANR 6; CA 9-12R; SATA 4

Arden, John 1930- . . . . **CLC 6, 13, 15**
See also CAAS 4; CA 13-16R; DLB 13

Arenas, Reinaldo 1943- . . . . **CLC 41**

Arguedas, Jose Maria
1911-1969 . . . . **CLC 10, 18**
See also CA 89-92

Argueta, Manlio 1936- . . . . **CLC 31**

Ariosto, Ludovico 1474-1533. . . . . **LC 6**

Arlt, Roberto 1900-1942 . . . . **TCLC 29**
See also CA 123

Armah, Ayi Kwei 1939- . . . . **CLC 5, 33**
See also CANR 21; CA 61-64

Armatrading, Joan 1950- . . . . **CLC 17**
See also CA 114

Arnim, Achim von (Ludwig Joachim von
Arnim) 1781-1831 . . . . **NCLC 5**

Arnold, Matthew 1822-1888 . . . . . . **NCLC 6**
See also DLB 32, 57

Arnold, Thomas 1795-1842 . . . . . . **NCLC 18**
See also DLB 55

Arnow, Harriette (Louisa Simpson)
1908-1986 . . . . **CLC 2, 7, 18**
See also CANR 14; CA 9-12R;
obituary CA 118; SATA 42, 47; DLB 6

Arp, Jean 1887-1966. . . . . **CLC 5**
See also CA 81-84; obituary CA 25-28R

Arquette, Lois S(teinmetz) 1934-
See Duncan (Steinmetz Arquette), Lois
See also SATA 1

Arrabal, Fernando 1932- . . . . . . **CLC 2, 9, 18**
See also CANR 15; CA 9-12R

Arrick, Fran 19??- . . . . **CLC 30**

Artaud, Antonin 1896-1948 . . . . **TCLC 3**
See also CA 104

Arthur, Ruth M(abel) 1905-1979. . . . **CLC 12**
See also CANR 4; CA 9-12R;
obituary CA 85-88; SATA 7;
obituary SATA 26

Artsybashev, Mikhail Petrarch
1878-1927 . . . . **TCLC 31**

Arundel, Honor (Morfydd)
1919-1973 . . . . **CLC 17**
See also CAP 2; CA 21-22;
obituary CA 41-44R; SATA 4;
obituary SATA 24

Asch, Sholem 1880-1957 . . . . **TCLC 3**
See also CA 105

Ashbery, John (Lawrence)
1927- . . . **CLC 2, 3, 4, 6, 9, 13, 15, 25, 41**
See also CANR 9; CA 5-8R; DLB 5;
DLB-Y 81

Ashton-Warner, Sylvia (Constance)
1908-1984 . . . . **CLC 19**
See also CA 69-72; obituary CA 112

Asimov, Isaac 1920- . . . . **CLC 1, 3, 9, 19, 26**
See also CLR 12; CANR 2, 19; CA 1-4R;
SATA 1, 26; DLB 8

Astley, Thea (Beatrice May)
1925- . . . . **CLC 41**
See also CANR 11; CA 65-68

Aston, James 1906-1964
See White, T(erence) H(anbury)

Asturias, Miguel Angel
1899-1974 . . . . **CLC 3, 8, 13**
See also CAP 2; CA 25-28;
obituary CA 49-52

Atheling, William, Jr. 1921-1975
See Blish, James (Benjamin)

Atherton, Gertrude (Franklin Horn)
1857-1948 . . . . **TCLC 2**
See also CA 104; DLB 9

Atwood, Margaret (Eleanor)
1939- . . . . **CLC 2, 3, 4, 8, 13, 15, 25, 44;**
SSC 2
See also CANR 3; CA 49-52; DLB 53

Aubin, Penelope 1685-1731? . . . . **LC 9**
See also DLB 39

Auchincloss, Louis (Stanton)
1917- . . . . **CLC 4, 6, 9, 18, 45**
See also CANR 6; CA 1-4R; DLB 2;
DLB-Y 80

Auden, W(ystan) H(ugh)
1907-1973 . . . . . **CLC 1, 2, 3, 4, 6, 9, 11,**
14, 43
See also CANR 5; CA 9-12R;
obituary CA 45-48; DLB 10, 20

Audiberti, Jacques 1899-1965 . . . . . . **CLC 38**
See also obituary CA 25-28R

Auel, Jean M(arie) 1936- . . . . **CLC 31**
See also CANR 21; CA 103

Austen, Jane 1775-1817. . . . **NCLC 1, 13, 19**

Auster, Paul 1947- . . . . **CLC 47**
See also CA 69-72

Austin, Mary (Hunter)
1868-1934 . . . . **TCLC 25**
See also CA 109; DLB 9

Avison, Margaret 1918- . . . . **CLC 2, 4**
See also CA 17-20R; DLB 53

Ayckbourn, Alan 1939- . . . . **CLC 5, 8, 18, 33**
See also CA 21-24R; DLB 13

Aydy, Catherine 1937-
See Tennant, Emma

Ayme, Marcel (Andre) 1902-1967. . . **CLC 11**
See also CA 89-92; DLB 72

Ayrton, Michael 1921-1975. . . . . **CLC 7**
See also CANR 9, 21; CA 5-8R;
obituary CA 61-64

Azorin 1874-1967 . . . . **CLC 11**
See also Martinez Ruiz, Jose

Azuela, Mariano 1873-1952. . . . . . . **TCLC 3**
See also CA 104

"Bab" 1836-1911
See Gilbert, (Sir) W(illiam) S(chwenck)

Babel, Isaak (Emmanuilovich)
1894-1941 . . . . **TCLC 2, 13**
See also CA 104

Babits, Mihaly 1883-1941 . . . . **TCLC 14**
See also CA 114

Bacchelli, Riccardo 1891-1985 . . . . . **CLC 19**
See also CA 29-32R; obituary CA 117

Bach, Richard (David) 1936- . . . . **CLC 14**
See also CANR 18; CA 9-12R; SATA 13

Bachman, Richard 1947-
See King, Stephen (Edwin)

Bacovia, George 1881-1957 . . . . **TCLC 24**

Bagehot, Walter 1826-1877 . . . . . . **NCLC 10**
See also DLB 55

Bagnold, Enid 1889-1981. . . . . **CLC 25**
See also CANR 5; CA 5-8R;
obituary CA 103; SATA 1, 25; DLB 13

Bagryana, Elisaveta 1893- . . . . **CLC 10**

Bailey, Paul 1937- . . . . **CLC 45**
See also CANR 16; CA 21-24R; DLB 14

Baillie, Joanna 1762-1851 . . . . **NCLC 2**

Bainbridge, Beryl
1933- . . . . **CLC 4, 5, 8, 10, 14, 18, 22**
See also CA 21-24R; DLB 14

Baker, Elliott 1922- . . . . **CLC 8**
See also CANR 2; CA 45-48

Baker, Russell (Wayne) 1925- . . . . . . **CLC 31**
See also CANR 11; CA 57-60

Bakshi, Ralph 1938- . . . . **CLC 26**
See also CA 112

Baldwin, James (Arthur)
1924-1987 . . . . . **CLC 1, 2, 3, 4, 5, 8, 13,**
15, 17, 42, 50
See also CANR 3; CA 1-4R; CABS 1;
SATA 9; DLB 2, 7, 33;
CDALB 1941-1968

Ballard, J(ames) G(raham)
1930- . . . . **CLC 3, 6, 14, 36; SSC 1**
See also CANR 15; CA 5-8R; DLB 14

Balmont, Konstantin Dmitriyevich
1867-1943 . . . . **TCLC 11**
See also CA 109

Balzac, Honore de 1799-1850 . . . . . **NCLC 5**

Bambara, Toni Cade 1939- . . . . **CLC 19**
See also CA 29-32R; DLB 38

Banim, John 1798-1842 . . . . **NCLC 13**

Banim, Michael 1796-1874 . . . . . . **NCLC 13**

Banks, Iain 1954- . . . . **CLC 34**

Banks, Lynne Reid 1929- . . . . **CLC 23**
See also Reid Banks, Lynne

Banks, Russell 1940- . . . . **CLC 37**
See also CANR 19; CA 65-68

Banville, John 1945- . . . . **CLC 46**
See also CA 117; DLB 14

Banville, Theodore (Faullain) de
1832-1891 . . . . **NCLC 9**

Baraka, Amiri
1934- . . . . **CLC 1, 2, 3, 5, 10, 14, 33**
See also Baraka, Imamu Amiri; Jones,
(Everett) LeRoi
See also DLB 5, 7, 16, 38

Benchley, Robert 1889-1945 .... TCLC 1
See also CA 105; DLB 11

Benedikt, Michael 1935- .... CLC 4, 14
See also CANR 7; CA 13-16R; DLB 5

Benet, Juan 1927-................ CLC 28

Benet, Stephen Vincent
1898-1943 .... TCLC 7
See also YABC 1; CA 104; DLB 4, 48

Benet, William Rose 1886-1950 ... TCLC 28
See also CA 118; DLB 45

Benford, Gregory (Albert) 1941-.... CLC 52
See also CANR 12, 24; CA 69-72;
DLB-Y 82

Benn, Gottfried 1886-1956........ TCLC 3
See also CA 106; DLB 56

Bennett, Alan 1934- .... CLC 45
See also CA 103

Bennett, (Enoch) Arnold
1867-1931 .... TCLC 5, 20
See also CA 106; DLB 10, 34

Bennett, George Harold 1930-
See Bennett, Hal
See also CA 97-100

Bennett, Hal 1930-................ CLC 5
See also Bennett, George Harold
See also DLB 33

Bennett, Jay 1912-................ CLC 35
See also CANR 11; CA 69-72; SAAS 4;
SATA 27, 41

Bennett, Louise (Simone) 1919-..... CLC 28
See also Bennett-Coverly, Louise Simone

Bennett-Coverly, Louise Simone 1919-
See Bennett, Louise (Simone)
See also CA 97-100

Benson, E(dward) F(rederic)
1867-1940 .... TCLC 27
See also CA 114

Benson, Jackson J. 1930-......... CLC 34
See also CA 25-28R

Benson, Sally 1900-1972 .... CLC 17
See also CAP 1; CA 19-20;
obituary CA 37-40R; SATA 1, 35;
obituary SATA 27

Benson, Stella 1892-1933........ TCLC 17
See also CA 117; DLB 36

Bentley, E(dmund) C(lerihew)
1875-1956 .... TCLC 12
See also CA 108; DLB 70

Bentley, Eric (Russell) 1916-....... CLC 24
See also CANR 6; CA 5-8R

Berger, John (Peter) 1926- ..... CLC 2, 19
See also CA 81-84; DLB 14

Berger, Melvin (H.) 1927-........ CLC 12
See also CANR 4; CA 5-8R; SAAS 2;
SATA 5

Berger, Thomas (Louis)
1924- .... CLC 3, 5, 8, 11, 18, 38
See also CANR 5; CA 1-4R; DLB 2;
DLB-Y 80

Bergman, (Ernst) Ingmar 1918-..... CLC 16
See also CA 81-84

Bergson, Henri 1859-1941 .... TCLC 32

Bergstein, Eleanor 1938- .... CLC 4
See also CANR 5; CA 53-56

Berkoff, Steven 1937-............ CLC 56
See also CA 104

Bermant, Chaim 1929-............ CLC 40
See also CANR 6; CA 57-60

Bernanos, (Paul Louis) Georges
1888-1948 .... TCLC 3
See also CA 104; DLB 72

Bernhard, Thomas 1931- .... CLC 3, 32
See also CA 85-88

Berriault, Gina 1926-............. CLC 54
See also CA 116

Berrigan, Daniel J. 1921-.......... CLC 4
See also CAAS 1; CANR 11; CA 33-36R;
DLB 5

Berrigan, Edmund Joseph Michael, Jr.
1934-1983
See Berrigan, Ted
See also CANR 14; CA 61-64;
obituary CA 110

Berrigan, Ted 1934-1983 .... CLC 37
See also Berrigan, Edmund Joseph Michael,
Jr.
See also DLB 5

Berry, Chuck 1926- .... CLC 17

Berry, Wendell (Erdman)
1934- .... CLC 4, 6, 8, 27, 46
See also CA 73-76; DLB 5, 6

Berryman, Jerry 1914-1972
See also CDALB 1941-1968

Berryman, John
1914-1972 ..... CLC 1, 2, 3, 4, 6, 8, 10,
13, 25
See also CAP 1; CA 15-16;
obituary CA 33-36R; CABS 2; DLB 48;
CDALB 1941-1968

Bertolucci, Bernardo 1940- .... CLC 16
See also CA 106

Besant, Annie (Wood) 1847-1933 ... TCLC 9
See also CA 105

Bessie, Alvah 1904-1985.......... CLC 23
See also CANR 2; CA 5-8R;
obituary CA 116; DLB 26

Beti, Mongo 1932- .... CLC 27
See also Beyidi, Alexandre

Betjeman, (Sir) John
1906-1984 .... CLC 2, 6, 10, 34, 43
See also CA 9-12R; obituary CA 112;
DLB 20; DLB-Y 84

Betti, Ugo 1892-1953 .... TCLC 5
See also CA 104

Betts, Doris (Waugh) 1932-.... CLC 3, 6, 28
See also CANR 9; CA 13-16R; DLB-Y 82

Bialik, Chaim Nachman
1873-1934 .... TCLC 25

Bidart, Frank 19??-................ CLC 33

Bienek, Horst 1930-............. CLC 7, 11
See also CA 73-76

Bierce, Ambrose (Gwinett)
1842-1914? .... TCLC 1, 7
See also CA 104; DLB 11, 12, 23, 71;
CDALB 1865-1917

Billington, Rachel 1942-.......... CLC 43
See also CA 33-36R

Binyon, T(imothy) J(ohn) 1936- .... CLC 34
See also CA 111

Bioy Casares, Adolfo 1914-.... CLC 4, 8, 13
See also CANR 19; CA 29-32R

Bird, Robert Montgomery
1806-1854 .... NCLC 1

Birdwell, Cleo 1936-
See DeLillo, Don

Birney (Alfred) Earle
1904- .... CLC 1, 4, 6, 11
See also CANR 5, 20; CA 1-4R

Bishop, Elizabeth
1911-1979 ...... CLC 1, 4, 9, 13, 15, 32
See also CA 5-8R; obituary CA 89-92;
CABS 2; obituary SATA 24; DLB 5

Bishop, John 1935-............... CLC 10
See also CA 105

Bissett, Bill 1939-............... CLC 18
See also CANR 15; CA 69-72; DLB 53

Biyidi, Alexandre 1932-
See Beti, Mongo
See also CA 114

Bjornson, Bjornstjerne (Martinius)
1832-1910 .... TCLC 7
See also CA 104

Blackburn, Paul 1926-1971 ...... CLC 9, 43
See also CA 81-84; obituary CA 33-36R;
DLB 16; DLB-Y 81

Black Elk 1863-1950 .... TCLC 33

Blackmore, R(ichard) D(oddridge)
1825-1900 .... TCLC 27
See also CA 120; DLB 18

Blackmur, R(ichard) P(almer)
1904-1965 .... CLC 2, 24
See also CAP 1; CA 11-12;
obituary CA 25-28R; DLB 63

Blackwood, Algernon (Henry)
1869-1951 .... TCLC 5
See also CA 105

Blackwood, Caroline 1931- .... CLC 6, 9
See also CA 85-88; DLB 14

Blair, Eric Arthur 1903-1950
See Orwell, George
See also CA 104; SATA 29

Blais, Marie-Claire
1939- .... CLC 2, 4, 6, 13, 22
See also CAAS 4; CA 21-24R; DLB 53

Blaise, Clark 1940-............... CLC 29
See also CAAS 3; CANR 5; CA 53-56R;
DLB 53

Blake, Nicholas 1904-1972
See Day Lewis, C(ecil)

Blake, William 1757-1827 .... NCLC 13
See also SATA 30

Blasco Ibanez, Vicente
1867-1928 .... TCLC 12
See also CA 110

Blatty, William Peter 1928-........ CLC 2
See also CANR 9; CA 5-8R

Blessing, Lee 1949-.............. CLC 54

Blish, James (Benjamin)
1921-1975 .... CLC 14
See also CANR 3; CA 1-4R;
obituary CA 57-60; DLB 8

Blixen, Karen (Christentze Dinesen)
    1885-1962
    See Dinesen, Isak
    See also CAP 2; CA 25-28; SATA 44

Bloch, Robert (Albert) 1917-....... CLC 33
    See also CANR 5; CA 5-8R; SATA 12;
    DLB 44

Blok, Aleksandr (Aleksandrovich)
    1880-1921 .... TCLC 5
    See also CA 104

Bloom, Harold 1930- .... CLC 24
    See also CA 13-16R

Blount, Roy (Alton), Jr. 1941- ..... CLC 38
    See also CANR 10; CA 53-56

Bloy, Leon 1846-1917............ TCLC 22
    See also CA 121

Blume, Judy (Sussman Kitchens)
    1938-.................... CLC 12, 30
    See also CLR 2, 15; CANR 13; CA 29-32R;
    SATA 2, 31; DLB 52

Blunden, Edmund (Charles)
    1896-1974 .... CLC 2, 56
    See also CAP 2; CA 17-18;
    obituary CA 45-48; DLB 20

Bly, Robert (Elwood)
    1926- .... CLC 1, 2, 5, 10, 15, 38
    See also CA 5-8R; DLB 5

Bochco, Steven 1944?- .... CLC 35

Bodker, Cecil 1927- .... CLC 21
    See also CANR 13; CA 73-76; SATA 14

Boell, Heinrich (Theodor) 1917-1985
    See Boll, Heinrich
    See also CA 21-24R; obituary CA 116

Bogan, Louise 1897-1970..... CLC 4, 39, 46
    See also CA 73-76; obituary CA 25-28R;
    DLB 45

Bogarde, Dirk 1921-.............. CLC 19
    See also Van Den Bogarde, Derek (Jules
        Gaspard Ulric) Niven
    See also DLB 14

Bogosian, Eric 1953- .... CLC 45

Bograd, Larry 1953-.............. CLC 35
    See also CA 93-96; SATA 33

Bohl de Faber, Cecilia 1796-1877
    See Caballero, Fernan

Boiardo, Matteo Maria 1441-1494 .... LC 6

Boileau-Despreaux, Nicolas
    1636-1711 .... LC 3

Boland, Eavan (Aisling) 1944-...... CLC 40
    See also DLB 40

Boll, Heinrich (Theodor)
    1917-1985 ... CLC 2, 3, 6, 9, 11, 15, 27,
                                         39
    See also Boell, Heinrich (Theodor)
    See also DLB 69; DLB-Y 85

Bolt, Robert (Oxton) 1924-........ CLC 14
    See also CA 17-20R; DLB 13

Bond, Edward 1934-....... CLC 4, 6, 13, 23
    See also CA 25-28R; DLB 13

Bonham, Frank 1914-............. CLC 12
    See also CANR 4; CA 9-12R; SAAS 3;
    SATA 1, 49

Bonnefoy, Yves 1923-.......... CLC 9, 15
    See also CA 85-88

Bontemps, Arna (Wendell)
    1902-1973 .... CLC 1, 18
    See also CLR 6; CANR 4; CA 1-4R;
    obituary CA 41-44R; SATA 2, 44;
    obituary SATA 24; DLB 48, 51

Booth, Martin 1944-.............. CLC 13
    See also CAAS 2; CA 93-96

Booth, Philip 1925-............... CLC 23
    See also CANR 5; CA 5-8R; DLB-Y 82

Booth, Wayne C(layson) 1921- ..... CLC 24
    See also CAAS 5; CANR 3; CA 1-4R

Borchert, Wolfgang 1921-1947 ..... TCLC 5
    See also CA 104; DLB 69

Borges, Jorge Luis
    1899-1986 ... CLC 1, 2, 3, 4, 6, 8, 9, 10,
                    13, 19, 44, 48; SSC 4
    See also CANR 19; CA 21-24R; DLB-Y 86

Borowski, Tadeusz 1922-1951...... TCLC 9
    See also CA 106

Borrow, George (Henry)
    1803-1881 .... NCLC 9
    See also DLB 21, 55

Bosschere, Jean de 1878-1953..... TCLC 19
    See also CA 115

Boswell, James 1740-1795.......... LC 4

Bottoms, David 1949-............. CLC 53
    See also CANR 22; CA 105; DLB-Y 83

Boucolon, Maryse 1937-
    See Conde, Maryse
    See also CA 110

Bourget, Paul (Charles Joseph)
    1852-1935 .... TCLC 12
    See also CA 107

Bourjaily, Vance (Nye) 1922- .... CLC 8
    See also CAAS 1; CANR 2; CA 1-4R;
    DLB 2

Bourne, Randolph S(illiman)
    1886-1918 .... TCLC 16
    See also CA 117; DLB 63

Bova, Ben(jamin William) 1932-.... CLC 45
    See also CLR 3; CANR 11; CA 5-8R;
    SATA 6; DLB-Y 81

Bowen, Elizabeth (Dorothea Cole)
    1899-1973 ..... CLC 1, 3, 6, 11, 15, 22;
                                     SSC 3
    See also CAP 2; CA 17-18;
    obituary CA 41-44R; DLB 15

Bowering, George 1935-........ CLC 15, 47
    See also CANR 10; CA 21-24R; DLB 53

Bowering, Marilyn R(uthe) 1949-... CLC 32
    See also CA 101

Bowers, Edgar 1924- .... CLC 9
    See also CA 5-8R; DLB 5

Bowie, David 1947- .... CLC 17
    See also Jones, David Robert

Bowles, Jane (Sydney) 1917-1973.... CLC 3
    See also CAP 2; CA 19-20;
    obituary CA 41-44R

Bowles, Paul (Frederick)
    1910- .... CLC 1, 2, 19, 53; SSC 3
    See also CAAS 1; CANR 1, 19; CA 1-4R;
    DLB 5, 6

Box, Edgar 1925-
    See Vidal, Gore

Boyd, William 1952-............ CLC 28, 53
    See also CA 114, 120

Boyle, Kay 1903- .... CLC 1, 5, 19
    See also CAAS 1; CA 13-16R; DLB 4, 9, 48

Boyle, Patrick 19??-............... CLC 19

Boyle, Thomas Coraghessan
    1948-.................... CLC 36, 55
    See also CA 120; DLB-Y 86

Brackenridge, Hugh Henry
    1748-1816 .... NCLC 7
    See also DLB 11, 37

Bradbury, Edward P. 1939-
    See Moorcock, Michael

Bradbury, Malcolm (Stanley)
    1932-...................... CLC 32
    See also CANR 1; CA 1-4R; DLB 14

Bradbury, Ray(mond Douglas)
    1920-........ CLC 1, 3, 10, 15, 42
    See also CANR 2; CA 1-4R; SATA 11;
    DLB 2, 8

Bradley, David (Henry), Jr. 1950-.. CLC 23
    See also CA 104; DLB 33

Bradley, John Ed 1959-........... CLC 55

Bradley, Marion Zimmer 1930-..... CLC 30
    See also CANR 7; CA 57-60; DLB 8

Bradstreet, Anne 1612-1672......... LC 4
    See also DLB 24; CDALB 1640-1865

Bragg, Melvyn 1939- .... CLC 10
    See also CANR 10; CA 57-60; DLB 14

Braine, John (Gerard)
    1922-1986 .... CLC 1, 3, 41
    See also CANR 1; CA 1-4R;
    obituary CA 120; DLB 15; DLB-Y 86

Brammer, Billy Lee 1930?-1978
    See Brammer, William

Brammer, William 1930?-1978 ..... CLC 31
    See also obituary CA 77-80

Brancati, Vitaliano 1907-1954..... TCLC 12
    See also CA 109

Brancato, Robin F(idler) 1936-..... CLC 35
    See also CANR 11; CA 69-72; SATA 23

Brand, Millen 1906-1980.......... CLC 7
    See also CA 21-24R; obituary CA 97-100

Branden, Barbara 19??-........... CLC 44

Brandes, Georg (Morris Cohen)
    1842-1927 .... TCLC 10
    See also CA 105

Branley, Franklyn M(ansfield)
    1915-...................... CLC 21
    See also CANR 14; CA 33-36R; SATA 4

Brathwaite, Edward 1930-........ CLC 11
    See also CANR 11; CA 25-28R; DLB 53

Brautigan, Richard (Gary)
    1935-1984 .... CLC 1, 3, 5, 9, 12, 34, 42
    See also CA 53-56; obituary CA 113;
    DLB 2, 5; DLB-Y 80, 84

Brecht, (Eugen) Bertolt (Friedrich)
    1898-1956 .... TCLC 1, 6, 13
    See also CA 104; DLB 56

Bremer, Fredrika 1801-1865..... NCLC 11

Brennan, Christopher John
    1870-1932 .... TCLC 17
    See also CA 117

Casey, Warren 1935-
See Jacobs, Jim and Casey, Warren
See also CA 101

Casona, Alejandro 1903-1965 ...... **CLC 49**
See also Alvarez, Alejandro Rodriguez

Cassavetes, John 1929- .... **CLC 20**
See also CA 85-88

Cassill, R(onald) V(erlin) 1919-... **CLC 4, 23**
See also CAAS 1; CANR 7; CA 9-12R;
DLB 6

Cassity, (Allen) Turner 1929- .... **CLC 6, 42**
See also CANR 11; CA 17-20R

Castaneda, Carlos 1935?- .... **CLC 12**
See also CA 25-28R

Castro, Rosalia de 1837-1885 ..... **NCLC 3**

Cather, Willa (Sibert)
1873-1947 ...... **TCLC 1, 11, 31; SSC 2**
See also CA 104; SATA 30; DLB 9, 54;
DLB-DS 1; CDALB 1865-1917

Catton, (Charles) Bruce
1899-1978 .... **CLC 35**
See also CANR 7; CA 5-8R;
obituary CA 81-84; SATA 2;
obituary SATA 24; DLB 17

Cauldwell, Frank 1923-
See King, Francis (Henry)

Caunitz, William 1935- .... **CLC 34**

Causley, Charles (Stanley) 1917-..... **CLC 7**
See also CANR 5; CA 9-12R; SATA 3;
DLB 27

Caute, (John) David 1936-........ **CLC 29**
See also CAAS 4; CANR 1; CA 1-4R;
DLB 14

Cavafy, C(onstantine) P(eter)
1863-1933 .... **TCLC 2, 7**
See also CA 104

Cavanna, Betty 1909-............ **CLC 12**
See also CANR 6; CA 9-12R; SATA 1, 30

Cayrol, Jean 1911-............... **CLC 11**
See also CA 89-92

Cela, Camilo Jose 1916-........ **CLC 4, 13**
See also CANR 21; CA 21-24R

Celan, Paul 1920-1970 ...... **CLC 10, 19, 53**
See also Antschel, Paul
See also DLB 69

Celine, Louis-Ferdinand
1894-1961 ..... **CLC 1, 3, 4, 7, 9, 15, 47**
See also Destouches,
Louis-Ferdinand-Auguste
See also DLB 72

Cellini, Benvenuto 1500-1571 .... **LC 7**

Cendrars, Blaise 1887-1961 .... **CLC 18**
See also Sauser-Hall, Frederic

Cernuda, Luis (y Bidon)
1902-1963 .... **CLC 54**
See also CA 89-92

Cervantes (Saavedra), Miguel de
1547-1616 .... **LC 6**

Cesaire, Aime (Fernand) 1913-.. **CLC 19, 32**
See also CA 65-68

Chabon, Michael 1965?-.......... **CLC 55**

Chabrol, Claude 1930-........... **CLC 16**
See also CA 110

Challans, Mary 1905-1983
See Renault, Mary
See also CA 81-84; obituary CA 111;
SATA 23; obituary SATA 36

Chambers, Aidan 1934- .... **CLC 35**
See also CANR 12; CA 25-28R; SATA 1

Chambers, James 1948-
See Cliff, Jimmy

Chandler, Raymond 1888-1959 ... **TCLC 1, 7**
See also CA 104

Channing, William Ellery
1780-1842 .... **NCLC 17**
See also DLB 1, 59

Chaplin, Charles (Spencer)
1889-1977 .... **CLC 16**
See also CA 81-84; obituary CA 73-76;
DLB 44

Chapman, Graham 1941?-
See Monty Python
See also CA 116

Chapman, John Jay 1862-1933 ..... **TCLC 7**
See also CA 104

Chappell, Fred 1936- .... **CLC 40**
See also CAAS 4; CANR 8; CA 5-8R;
DLB 6

Char, Rene (Emile)
1907-1988 .... **CLC 9, 11, 14, 55**
See also CA 13-16R; obituary CA 124

Charyn, Jerome 1937- .... **CLC 5, 8, 18**
See also CAAS 1; CANR 7; CA 5-8R;
DLB-Y 83

Chase, Mary Ellen 1887-1973 ...... **CLC 2**
See also CAP 1; CA 15-16;
obituary CA 41-44R; SATA 10

Chateaubriand, Francois Rene de
1768-1848 .... **NCLC 3**

Chatterji, Bankim Chandra
1838-1894 .... **NCLC 19**

Chatterji, Saratchandra
1876-1938 .... **TCLC 13**
See also CA 109

Chatterton, Thomas 1752-1770 .... **LC 3**

Chatwin, (Charles) Bruce 1940-..... **CLC 28**
See also CA 85-88

Chayefsky, Paddy 1923-1981....... **CLC 23**
See also CA 9-12R; obituary CA 104;
DLB 7, 44; DLB-Y 81

Chayefsky, Sidney 1923-1981
See Chayefsky, Paddy
See also CANR 18

Chedid, Andree 1920-............ **CLC 47**

Cheever, John
1912-1982 ..... **CLC 3, 7, 8, 11, 15, 25;
SSC 1**
See also CANR 5; CA 5-8R;
obituary CA 106; CABS 1; DLB 2;
DLB-Y 80, 82; CDALB 1941-1968

Cheever, Susan 1943-.......... **CLC 18, 48**
See also CA 103; DLB-Y 82

Chekhov, Anton (Pavlovich)
1860-1904 ...... **TCLC 3, 10, 31; SSC 2**
See also CA 104, 124

Chernyshevsky, Nikolay Gavrilovich
1828-1889 .... **NCLC 1**

Cherry, Caroline Janice 1942-
See Cherryh, C. J.

Cherryh, C. J. 1942-.............. **CLC 35**
See also DLB-Y 80

Chesnutt, Charles Waddell
1858-1932 .... **TCLC 5**
See also CA 106; DLB 12, 50

Chester, Alfred 1929?-1971 .... **CLC 49**
See also obituary CA 33-36R

Chesterton, G(ilbert) K(eith)
1874-1936 .... **TCLC 1, 6; SSC 1**
See also CA 104; SATA 27; DLB 10, 19,
34, 70

Ch'ien Chung-shu 1910-.......... **CLC 22**

Child, Lydia Maria 1802-1880 .... **NCLC 6**
See also DLB 1

Child, Philip 1898-1978 .... **CLC 19**
See also CAP 1; CA 13-14; SATA 47

Childress, Alice 1920-.......... **CLC 12, 15**
See also CLR 14; CANR 3; CA 45-48;
SATA 7, 48; DLB 7, 38

Chislett, (Margaret) Anne 1943?- ... **CLC 34**

Chitty, (Sir) Thomas Willes 1926-
See Hinde, Thomas
See also CA 5-8R

Chomette, Rene 1898-1981
See Clair, Rene
See also obituary CA 103

Chopin, Kate (O'Flaherty)
1851-1904 .... **TCLC 5, 14**
See also CA 104, 122; DLB 12;
CDALB 1865-1917

Christie, (Dame) Agatha (Mary Clarissa)
1890-1976 ...... **CLC 1, 6, 8, 12, 39, 48**
See also CANR 10; CA 17-20R;
obituary CA 61-64; SATA 36; DLB 13

Christie, (Ann) Philippa 1920-
See Pearce, (Ann) Philippa
See also CANR 4

Christine de Pizan 1365?-1431?....... **LC 9**

Chulkov, Mikhail Dmitrievich
1743-1792 .... **LC 2**

Churchill, Caryl 1938-......... **CLC 31, 55**
See also CANR 22; CA 102; DLB 13

Churchill, Charles 1731?-1764....... **LC 3**

Chute, Carolyn 1947-............ **CLC 39**

Ciardi, John (Anthony)
1916-1986 .... **CLC 10, 40, 44**
See also CAAS 2; CANR 5; CA 5-8R;
obituary CA 118; SATA 1, 46; DLB 5;
DLB-Y 86

Cicero, Marcus Tullius
106 B.C.-43 B.C. .... **CMLC 3**

Cimino, Michael 1943?-........... **CLC 16**
See also CA 105

Clair, Rene 1898-1981 .... **CLC 20**
See also Chomette, Rene

Clampitt, Amy 19??-.............. **CLC 32**
See also CA 110

Clancy, Tom 1947-............... **CLC 45**

Clare, John 1793-1864 .... **NCLC 9**
See also DLB 55

Farrell, James T(homas)
1904-1979 . . . . CLC 1, 4, 8, 11
See also CANR 9; CA 5-8R;
obituary CA 89-92; DLB 4, 9; DLB-DS 2

Farrell, J(ames) G(ordon)
1935-1979 . . . . CLC 6
See also CA 73-76; obituary CA 89-92;
DLB 14

Farrell, M. J. 1904-
See Keane, Molly

Fassbinder, Rainer Werner
1946-1982 . . . . CLC 20
See also CA 93-96; obituary CA 106

Fast, Howard (Melvin) 1914- . . . . . . CLC 23
See also CANR 1; CA 1-4R; SATA 7;
DLB 9

Faulkner, William (Cuthbert)
1897-1962 . . . . CLC 1, 3, 6, 8, 9, 11, 14,
　　　　　　　　　　　18, 28, 52; SSC 1
See also CA 81-84; DLB 9, 11, 44;
DLB-Y 86; DLB-DS 2

Fauset, Jessie Redmon
1884?-1961 . . . . CLC 19, 54
See also CA 109; DLB 51

Faust, Irvin 1924- . . . . CLC 8
See also CA 33-36R; DLB 2, 28; DLB-Y 80

Fearing, Kenneth (Flexner)
1902-1961 . . . . CLC 51
See also CA 93-96; DLB 9

Federman, Raymond 1928- . . . . . . CLC 6, 47
See also CANR 10; CA 17-20R; DLB-Y 80

Federspiel, J(urg) F. 1931- . . . . CLC 42

Feiffer, Jules 1929- . . . . CLC 2, 8
See also CA 17-20R; SATA 8; DLB 7, 44

Feinstein, Elaine 1930- . . . . CLC 36
See also CAAS 1; CA 69-72; DLB 14, 40

Feldman, Irving (Mordecai) 1928- . . . . CLC 7
See also CANR 1; CA 1-4R

Fellini, Federico 1920- . . . . CLC 16
See also CA 65-68

Felsen, Gregor 1916-
See Felsen, Henry Gregor

Felsen, Henry Gregor 1916- . . . . CLC 17
See also CANR 1; CA 1-4R; SAAS 2;
SATA 1

Fenton, James (Martin) 1949- . . . . . . CLC 32
See also CA 102; DLB 40

Ferber, Edna 1887-1968 . . . . CLC 18
See also CA 5-8R; obituary CA 25-28R;
SATA 7; DLB 9, 28

Ferlinghetti, Lawrence (Monsanto)
1919?- . . . . CLC 2, 6, 10, 27
See also CANR 3; CA 5-8R; DLB 5, 16;
CDALB 1941-1968

Ferrier, Susan (Edmonstone)
1782-1854 . . . . NCLC 8

Feuchtwanger, Lion 1884-1958 . . . . . TCLC 3
See also CA 104

Feydeau, Georges 1862-1921 . . . . . . TCLC 22
See also CA 113

Fiedler, Leslie A(aron)
1917- . . . . CLC 4, 13, 24
See also CANR 7; CA 9-12R; DLB 28

Field, Andrew 1938- . . . . CLC 44
See also CA 97-100

Field, Eugene 1850-1895 . . . . NCLC 3
See also SATA 16; DLB 21, 23, 42

Fielding, Henry 1707-1754 . . . . LC 1
See also DLB 39

Fielding, Sarah 1710-1768 . . . . LC 1
See also DLB 39

Fierstein, Harvey 1954- . . . . CLC 33

Figes, Eva 1932- . . . . CLC 31
See also CANR 4; CA 53-56; DLB 14

Finch, Robert (Duer Claydon)
1900- . . . . CLC 18
See also CANR 9; CA 57-60

Findley, Timothy 1930- . . . . CLC 27
See also CANR 12; CA 25-28R; DLB 53

Fink, Janis 1951-
See Ian, Janis

Firbank, Louis 1944-
See Reed, Lou

Firbank, (Arthur Annesley) Ronald
1886-1926 . . . . TCLC 1
See also CA 104; DLB 36

Fisher, Roy 1930- . . . . CLC 25
See also CANR 16; CA 81-84; DLB 40

Fisher, Rudolph 1897-1934 . . . . TCLC 11
See also CA 107; DLB 51

Fisher, Vardis (Alvero) 1895-1968 . . . . CLC 7
See also CA 5-8R; obituary CA 25-28R;
DLB 9

FitzGerald, Edward 1809-1883 . . . . NCLC 9
See also DLB 32

Fitzgerald, F(rancis) Scott (Key)
1896-1940 . . . . TCLC 1, 6, 14, 28
See also CA 110; DLB 4, 9; DLB-Y 81;
DLB-DS 1

Fitzgerald, Penelope 1916- . . . . . . CLC 19, 51
See also CA 85-88; DLB 14

Fitzgerald, Robert (Stuart)
1910-1985 . . . . CLC 39
See also CANR 1; CA 2R;
obituary CA 114; DLB-Y 80

FitzGerald, Robert D(avid) 1902- . . . CLC 19
See also CA 17-20R

Flanagan, Thomas (James Bonner)
1923- . . . . CLC 25, 52
See also CA 108; DLB-Y 80

Flaubert, Gustave
1821-1880 . . . . NCLC 2, 10, 19

Fleming, Ian (Lancaster)
1908-1964 . . . . CLC 3, 30
See also CA 5-8R; SATA 9

Fleming, Thomas J(ames) 1927- . . . . CLC 37
See also CANR 10; CA 5-8R; SATA 8

Flieg, Hellmuth
See Heym, Stefan

Flying Officer X 1905-1974
See Bates, H(erbert) E(rnest)

Fo, Dario 1929- . . . . CLC 32
See also CA 116

Follett, Ken(neth Martin) 1949- . . . . CLC 18
See also CANR 13; CA 81-84; DLB-Y 81

Foote, Horton 1916- . . . . CLC 51
See also CA 73-76; DLB 26

Forbes, Esther 1891-1967 . . . . CLC 12
See also CAP 1; CA 13-14;
obituary CA 25-28R; SATA 2; DLB 22

Forche, Carolyn 1950- . . . : . . . . CLC 25
See also CA 109, 117; DLB 5

Ford, Ford Madox 1873-1939 . . . TCLC 1, 15
See also CA 104; DLB 34

Ford, John 1895-1973 . . . . CLC 16
See also obituary CA 45-48

Ford, Richard 1944- . . . . CLC 46
See also CANR 11; CA 69-72

Foreman, Richard 1937- . . . . CLC 50
See also CA 65-68

Forester, C(ecil) S(cott)
1899-1966 . . . . CLC 35
See also CA 73-76; obituary CA 25-28R;
SATA 13

Forman, James D(ouglas) 1932- . . . . CLC 21
See also CANR 4, 19; CA 9-12R; SATA 8,
21

Fornes, Maria Irene 1930- . . . . CLC 39
See also CA 25-28R; DLB 7

Forrest, Leon 1937- . . . . CLC 4
See also CAAS 7; CA 89-92; DLB 33

Forster, E(dward) M(organ)
1879-1970 . . . . CLC 1, 2, 3, 4, 9, 10, 13,
　　　　　　　　　　　15, 22, 45
See also CAP 1; CA 13-14;
obituary CA 25-28R; DLB 34

Forster, John 1812-1876 . . . . NCLC 11

Forsyth, Frederick 1938- . . . . . . CLC 2, 5, 36
See also CA 85-88

Forten (Grimke), Charlotte L(ottie)
1837-1914 . . . . TCLC 16
See also Grimke, Charlotte L(ottie) Forten
See also DLB 50

Foscolo, Ugo 1778-1827 . . . . NCLC 8

Fosse, Bob 1925- . . . . CLC 20
See also Fosse, Robert Louis

Fosse, Robert Louis 1925-
See Bob Fosse
See also CA 110

Foucault, Michel 1926-1984 . . . . CLC 31, 34
See also CA 105; obituary CA 113

Fouque, Friedrich (Heinrich Karl) de La
Motte 1777-1843 . . . . NCLC 2

Fournier, Henri Alban 1886-1914
See Alain-Fournier
See also CA 104

Fournier, Pierre 1916-
See Gascar, Pierre
See also CANR 16; CA 89-92

Fowles, John (Robert)
1926- . . . . CLC 1, 2, 3, 4, 6, 9, 10, 15, 33
See also CA 5-8R; SATA 22; DLB 14

Fox, Paula 1923- . . . . CLC 2, 8
See also CLR 1; CANR 20; CA 73-76;
SATA 17; DLB 52

Fox, William Price (Jr.) 1926- . . . . . CLC 22
See also CANR 11; CA 17-20R; DLB 2;
DLB-Y 81

Frame (Clutha), Janet (Paterson)
    1924- .... CLC 2, 3, 6, 22
    See also Clutha, Janet Paterson Frame

France, Anatole   1844-1924 .... TCLC 9
    See also Thibault, Jacques Anatole Francois

Francis, Claude   19??- .... CLC 50

Francis, Dick   1920- .... CLC 2, 22, 42
    See also CANR 9; CA 5-8R

Francis, Robert (Churchill)   1901-... CLC 15
    See also CANR 1; CA 1-4R

Frank, Anne   1929-1945 .... TCLC 17
    See also CA 113; SATA 42

Frank, Elizabeth   1945- .... CLC 39
    See also CA 121

Franklin, (Stella Maria Sarah) Miles
    1879-1954 .... TCLC 7
    See also CA 104

Fraser, Antonia (Pakenham)
    1932- .... CLC 32
    See also CA 85-88; SATA 32

Fraser, George MacDonald   1925-.... CLC 7
    See also CANR 2; CA 45-48

Frayn, Michael   1933-...... CLC 3, 7, 31, 47
    See also CA 5-8R; DLB 13, 14

Fraze, Candida   19??- .... CLC 50

Frazer, Sir James George
    1854-1941 .... TCLC 32
    See also CA 118

Frazier, Ian   1951- .... CLC 46

Frederic, Harold   1856-1898 ...... NCLC 10
    See also DLB 12, 23

Fredro, Aleksander   1793-1876..... NCLC 8

Freeling, Nicolas   1927- .... CLC 38
    See also CANR 1, 17; CA 49-52

Freeman, Douglas Southall
    1886-1953 .... TCLC 11
    See also CA 109; DLB 17

Freeman, Judith   1946- .... CLC 55

Freeman, Mary (Eleanor) Wilkins
    1852-1930 .... TCLC 9; SSC 1
    See also CA 106; DLB 12

Freeman, R(ichard) Austin
    1862-1943 .... TCLC 21
    See also CA 113; DLB 70

French, Marilyn   1929-......... CLC 10, 18
    See also CANR 3; CA 69-72

Freneau, Philip Morin   1752-1832.. NCLC 1
    See also DLB 37, 43

Friedman, B(ernard) H(arper)
    1926- .... CLC 7
    See also CANR 3; CA 1-4R

Friedman, Bruce Jay   1930-.... CLC 3, 5, 56
    See also CANR 25; CA 9-12R; DLB 2, 28

Friel, Brian   1929-............. CLC 5, 42
    See also CA 21-24R; DLB 13

Friis-Baastad, Babbis (Ellinor)
    1921-1970 .... CLC 12
    See also CA 17-20R; SATA 7

Frisch, Max (Rudolf)
    1911- .... CLC 3, 9, 14, 18, 32, 44
    See also CA 85-88; DLB 69

Fromentin, Eugene (Samuel Auguste)
    1820-1876 .... NCLC 10

Frost, Robert (Lee)
    1874-1963 ... CLC 1, 3, 4, 9, 10, 13, 15,
                                26, 34, 44
    See also CA 89-92; SATA 14; DLB 54

Fry, Christopher   1907-....... CLC 2, 10, 14
    See also CANR 9; CA 17-20R; DLB 13

Frye, (Herman) Northrop   1912- .... CLC 24
    See also CA 8; CA 5-8R

Fuchs, Daniel   1909-.......... CLC 8, 22
    See also CAAS 5; CA 81-84; DLB 9, 26, 28

Fuchs, Daniel   1934-.............. CLC 34
    See also CANR 14; CA 37-40R

Fuentes, Carlos
    1928- .... CLC 3, 8, 10, 13, 22, 41
    See also CANR 10; CA 69-72

Fugard, Athol   1932-... CLC 5, 9, 14, 25, 40
    See also CA 85-88

Fugard, Sheila   1932- .... CLC 48

Fuller, Charles (H., Jr.)   1939-..... CLC 25
    See also CA 108, 112; DLB 38

Fuller, (Sarah) Margaret
    1810-1850 .... NCLC 5
    See also Ossoli, Sarah Margaret (Fuller
    marchesa d')
    See also DLB 1; CDALB 1640-1865

Fuller, Roy (Broadbent)   1912-.... CLC 4, 28
    See also CA 5-8R; DLB 15, 20

Fulton, Alice   1952-............... CLC 52
    See also CA 116

Furphy, Joseph   1843-1912....... TCLC 25

Futrelle, Jacques   1875-1912 ...... TCLC 19
    See also CA 113

Gaboriau, Emile   1835-1873 ...... NCLC 14

Gadda, Carlo Emilio   1893-1973 .... CLC 11
    See also CA 89-92

Gaddis, William
    1922- .... CLC 1, 3, 6, 8, 10, 19, 43
    See also CAAS 4; CANR 21; CA 17-20R;
    DLB 2

Gaines, Ernest J.   1933-...... CLC 3, 11, 18
    See also CANR 6; CA 9-12R; DLB 2, 33;
    DLB-Y 80

Gale, Zona   1874-1938 .... TCLC 7
    See also CA 105; DLB 9

Gallagher, Tess   1943-............. CLC 18
    See also CA 106

Gallant, Mavis   1922- .... CLC 7, 18, 38
    See also CA 69-72; DLB 53

Gallant, Roy A(rthur)   1924- .... CLC 17
    See also CANR 4; CA 5-8R; SATA 4

Gallico, Paul (William)   1897-1976 ... CLC 2
    See also CA 5-8R; obituary CA 69-72;
    SATA 13; DLB 9

Galsworthy, John   1867-1933....... TCLC 1
    See also CA 104; DLB 10, 34

Galt, John   1779-1839 .... NCLC 1

Galvin, James   1951-.............. CLC 38
    See also CA 108

Gann, Ernest K(ellogg)   1910- ...... CLC 23
    See also CANR 1; CA 1-4R

Garcia Lorca, Federico
    1899-1936 .... TCLC 1, 7
    See also CA 104

Garcia Marquez, Gabriel (Jose)
    1928- .... CLC 2, 3, 8, 10, 15, 27, 47, 55
    See also CANR 10; CA 33-36R

Gardam, Jane   1928-.............. CLC 43
    See also CLR 12; CANR 2, 18; CA 49-52;
    SATA 28, 39; DLB 14

Gardner, Herb   1934- .... CLC 44

Gardner, John (Champlin, Jr.)
    1933-1982 .... CLC 2, 3, 5, 7, 8, 10, 18,
                                28, 34
    See also CA 65-68; obituary CA 107;
    obituary SATA 31, 40; DLB 2; DLB-Y 82

Gardner, John (Edmund)   1926-..... CLC 30
    See also CANR 15; CA 103

Garfield, Leon   1921-............. CLC 12
    See also CA 17-20R; SATA 1, 32

Garland, (Hannibal) Hamlin
    1860-1940 .... TCLC 3
    See also CA 104; DLB 12, 71

Garneau, Hector (de) Saint Denys
    1912-1943 .... TCLC 13
    See also CA 111

Garner, Alan   1935-............... CLC 17
    See also CANR 15; CA 73-76; SATA 18

Garner, Hugh   1913-1979 .... CLC 13
    See also CA 69-72

Garnett, David   1892-1981 .... CLC 3
    See also CANR 17; CA 5-8R;
    obituary CA 103; DLB 34

Garrett, George (Palmer, Jr.)
    1929-.................... CLC 3, 11, 51
    See also CAAS 5; CANR 1; CA 1-4R;
    DLB 2, 5; DLB-Y 83

Garrigue, Jean   1914-1972 .... CLC 2, 8
    See also CA 5-8R; obituary CA 37-40R

Gary, Romain   1914-1980.......... CLC 25
    See also Kacew, Romain

Gascar, Pierre   1916-.............. CLC 11
    See also Fournier, Pierre

Gascoyne, David (Emery)   1916- .... CLC 45
    See also CANR 10; CA 65-68; DLB 20

Gaskell, Elizabeth Cleghorn
    1810-1865 .... NCLC 5
    See also DLB 21

Gass, William H(oward)
    1924- .... CLC 1, 2, 8, 11, 15, 39
    See also CA 17-20R; DLB 2

Gautier, Theophile   1811-1872 ..... NCLC 1

Gaye, Marvin (Pentz)   1939-1984 ... CLC 26
    See also obituary CA 112

Gebler, Carlo (Ernest)   1954-....... CLC 39
    See also CA 119

Gee, Maurice (Gough)   1931-....... CLC 29
    See also CA 97-100; SATA 46

Gelbart, Larry (Simon)   1923- ...... CLC 21
    See also CA 73-76

Gelber, Jack   1932-........... CLC 1, 6, 14
    See also CANR 2; CA 1-4R; DLB 7

Gellhorn, Martha (Ellis)   1908- ..... CLC 14
    See also CA 77-80; DLB-Y 82

Genet, Jean
    1910-1986 ... CLC 1, 2, 5, 10, 14, 44, 46
    See also CANR 18; CA 13-16R; DLB 72;
    DLB-Y 86

Gent, Peter 1942-................ **CLC 29**
See also CA 89-92; DLB 72; DLB-Y 82

George, Jean Craighead 1919-...... **CLC 35**
See also CLR 1; CA 5-8R; SATA 2;
DLB 52

George, Stefan (Anton)
1868-1933 .... **TCLC 2, 14**
See also CA 104

Gerhardi, William (Alexander) 1895-1977
See Gerhardie, William (Alexander)

Gerhardie, William (Alexander)
1895-1977 .... **CLC 5**
See also CANR 18; CA 25-28R;
obituary CA 73-76; DLB 36

Gertler, T(rudy) 1946?- .... **CLC 34**
See also CA 116

Gessner, Friedrike Victoria 1910-1980
See Adamson, Joy(-Friederike Victoria)

Ghelderode, Michel de
1898-1962 .... **CLC 6, 11**
See also CA 85-88

Ghiselin, Brewster 1903-.......... **CLC 23**
See also CANR 13; CA 13-16R

Ghose, Zulfikar 1935-............. **CLC 42**
See also CA 65-68

Ghosh, Amitav 1943- .... **CLC 44**

Giacosa, Giuseppe 1847-1906 ...... **TCLC 7**
See also CA 104

Gibbon, Lewis Grassic 1901-1935... **TCLC 4**
See also Mitchell, James Leslie

Gibbons, Kaye 1960- .... **CLC 50**

Gibran, (Gibran) Kahlil
1883-1931 .... **TCLC 1, 9**
See also CA 104

Gibson, William 1914-............. **CLC 23**
See also CANR 9; CA 9-12R; DLB 7

Gibson, William 1948-............. **CLC 39**

Gide, Andre (Paul Guillaume)
1869-1951 .... **TCLC 5, 12**
See also CA 104

Gifford, Barry (Colby) 1946-....... **CLC 34**
See also CANR 9; CA 65-68

Gilbert, (Sir) W(illiam) S(chwenck)
1836-1911 .... **TCLC 3**
See also CA 104; SATA 36

Gilbreth, Ernestine 1908-
See Carey, Ernestine Gilbreth

Gilbreth, Frank B(unker), Jr.
1911- .... **CLC 17**
See also CA 9-12R; SATA 2

Gilchrist, Ellen 1935-.......... **CLC 34, 48**
See also CA 113, 116

Giles, Molly 1942- .... **CLC 39**

Gilliam, Terry (Vance) 1940-
See Monty Python
See also CA 108, 113

Gilliatt, Penelope (Ann Douglass)
1932- .... **CLC 2, 10, 13, 53**
See also CA 13-16R; DLB 14

Gilman, Charlotte (Anna) Perkins (Stetson)
1860-1935 .... **TCLC 9**
See also CA 106

Gilmour, David 1944-
See Pink Floyd

Gilroy, Frank D(aniel) 1925-........ **CLC 2**
See also CA 81-84; DLB 7

Ginsberg, Allen
1926- .... **CLC 1, 2, 3, 4, 6, 13, 36**
See also CANR 2; CA 1-4R; DLB 5, 16;
CDALB 1941-1968

Ginzburg, Natalia 1916-...... **CLC 5, 11, 54**
See also CA 85-88

Giono, Jean 1895-1970.......... **CLC 4, 11**
See also CANR 2; CA 45-48;
obituary CA 29-32R; DLB 72

Giovanni, Nikki 1943- .... **CLC 2, 4, 19**
See also CLR 6; CAAS 6; CANR 18;
CA 29-32R; SATA 24; DLB 5, 41

Giovene, Andrea 1904-............. **CLC 7**
See also CA 85-88

Gippius, Zinaida (Nikolayevna) 1869-1945
See Hippius, Zinaida
See also CA 106

Giraudoux, (Hippolyte) Jean
1882-1944 .... **TCLC 2, 7**
See also CA 104

Gironella, Jose Maria 1917-....... **CLC 11**
See also CA 101

Gissing, George (Robert)
1857-1903 .... **TCLC 3, 24**
See also CA 105; DLB 18

Gladkov, Fyodor (Vasilyevich)
1883-1958 .... **TCLC 27**

Glanville, Brian (Lester) 1931-...... **CLC 6**
See also CANR 3; CA 5-8R; SATA 42;
DLB 15

Glasgow, Ellen (Anderson Gholson)
1873?-1945................. **TCLC 2, 7**
See also CA 104; DLB 9, 12

Glassco, John 1909-1981 .... **CLC 9**
See also CANR 15; CA 13-16R;
obituary CA 102

Glasser, Ronald J. 1940?- .... **CLC 37**

Glendinning, Victoria 1937-...... **CLC 50**
See also CA 120

Glissant, Edouard 1928-.......... **CLC 10**

Gloag, Julian 1930- .... **CLC 40**
See also CANR 10; CA 65-68

Gluck, Louise (Elisabeth)
1943- .... **CLC 7, 22, 44**
See also CA 33-36R; DLB 5

Gobineau, Joseph Arthur (Comte) de
1816-1882 .... **NCLC 17**

Godard, Jean-Luc 1930-.......... **CLC 20**
See also CA 93-96

Godden, (Margaret) Rumer 1907-... **CLC 53**
See also CANR 4, 27; CA 7-8R; SATA 3,
36

Godwin, Gail 1937-........ **CLC 5, 8, 22, 31**
See also CANR 15; CA 29-32R; DLB 6

Godwin, William 1756-1836...... **NCLC 14**
See also DLB 39

Goethe, Johann Wolfgang von
1749-1832 .... **NCLC 4, 22**

Gogarty, Oliver St. John
1878-1957 .... **TCLC 15**
See also CA 109; DLB 15, 19

Gogol, Nikolai (Vasilyevich)
1809-1852 .... **NCLC 5, 15; SSC 4**
See also CAAS 1, 4

Gokceli, Yasar Kemal 1923-
See Kemal, Yashar

Gold, Herbert 1924-........ **CLC 4, 7, 14, 42**
See also CANR 17; CA 9-12R; DLB 2;
DLB-Y 81

Goldbarth, Albert 1948-......... **CLC 5, 38**
See also CANR 6; CA 53-56

Goldberg, Anatol 1910-1982 .... **CLC 34**
See also obituary CA 117

Goldemberg, Isaac 1945-.......... **CLC 52**
See also CANR 11; CA 69-72

Golding, William (Gerald)
1911- .... **CLC 1, 2, 3, 8, 10, 17, 27**
See also CANR 13; CA 5-8R; DLB 15

Goldman, Emma 1869-1940....... **TCLC 13**
See also CA 110

Goldman, William (W.) 1931-.... **CLC 1, 48**
See also CA 9-12R; DLB 44

Goldmann, Lucien 1913-1970 ...... **CLC 24**
See also CAP 2; CA 25-28

Goldoni, Carlo 1707-1793 .... **LC 4**

Goldsberry, Steven 1949-......... **CLC 34**

Goldsmith, Oliver 1728?-1774....... **LC 2**
See also SATA 26; DLB 39

Gombrowicz, Witold
1904-1969 .... **CLC 4, 7, 11, 49**
See also CAP 2; CA 19-20;
obituary CA 25-28R

Gomez de la Serna, Ramon
1888-1963 .... **CLC 9**
See also obituary CA 116

Goncharov, Ivan Alexandrovich
1812-1891 .... **NCLC 1**

Goncourt, Edmond (Louis Antoine Huot) de
1822-1896 .... **NCLC 7**

Goncourt, Jules (Alfred Huot) de
1830-1870 .... **NCLC 7**

Gontier, Fernande 19??-........... **CLC 50**

Goodman, Paul 1911-1972.... **CLC 1, 2, 4, 7**
See also CAP 2; CA 19-20;
obituary CA 37-40R

Gorden, Charles William 1860-1937
See Conner, Ralph

Gordimer, Nadine
1923- .... **CLC 3, 5, 7, 10, 18, 33, 51**
See also CANR 3; CA 5-8R

Gordon, Adam Lindsay
1833-1870 .... **NCLC 21**

Gordon, Caroline
1895-1981 .... **CLC 6, 13, 29**
See also CAP 1; CA 11-12;
obituary CA 103; DLB 4, 9; DLB-Y 81

Gordon, Mary (Catherine)
1949- .... **CLC 13, 22**
See also CA 102; DLB 6; DLB-Y 81

Gordon, Sol 1923-................ **CLC 26**
See also CANR 4; CA 53-56; SATA 11

Guthrie, A(lfred) B(ertram), Jr.
1901- . . . . **CLC 23**
See also CA 57-60; DLB 6

Guthrie, Woodrow Wilson 1912-1967
See Guthrie, Woody
See also CA 113; obituary CA 93-96

Guthrie, Woody 1912-1967 . . . . **CLC 35**
See also Guthrie, Woodrow Wilson

Guy, Rosa (Cuthbert) 1928- . . . . **CLC 26**
See also CANR 14; CA 17-20R; SATA 14;
DLB 33

Haavikko, Paavo (Juhani)
1931- . . . . **CLC 18, 34**
See also CA 106

Hacker, Marilyn 1942- . . . . **CLC 5, 9, 23**
See also CA 77-80

Haggard, (Sir) H(enry) Rider
1856-1925 . . . . **TCLC 11**
See also CA 108; SATA 16; DLB 70

Haig-Brown, Roderick L(angmere)
1908-1976 . . . . **CLC 21**
See also CANR 4; CA 5-8R;
obituary CA 69-72; SATA 12

Hailey, Arthur 1920- . . . . **CLC 5**
See also CANR 2; CA 1-4R; DLB-Y 82

Hailey, Elizabeth Forsythe 1938- . . . **CLC 40**
See also CAAS 1; CANR 15; CA 93-96

Haley, Alex (Palmer) 1921- . . . . . . **CLC 8, 12**
See also CA 77-80; DLB 38

Haliburton, Thomas Chandler
1796-1865 . . . . **NCLC 15**
See also DLB 11

Hall, Donald (Andrew, Jr.)
1928- . . . . **CLC 1, 13, 37**
See also CAAS 7; CANR 2; CA 5-8R;
SATA 23; DLB 5

Hall, James Norman 1887-1951 . . . **TCLC 23**
See also SATA 21

Hall, (Marguerite) Radclyffe
1886-1943 . . . . **TCLC 12**
See also CA 110

Hall, Rodney 1935- . . . . **CLC 51**
See also CA 109

Halpern, Daniel 1945- . . . . **CLC 14**
See also CA 33-36R

Hamburger, Michael (Peter Leopold)
1924- . . . . **CLC 5, 14**
See also CAAS 4; CANR 2; CA 5-8R;
DLB 27

Hamill, Pete 1935- . . . . **CLC 10**
See also CANR 18; CA 25-28R

Hamilton, Edmond 1904-1977 . . . . **CLC 1**
See also CANR 3; CA 1-4R; DLB 8

Hamilton, Gail 1911-
See Corcoran, Barbara

Hamilton, Ian 1938- . . . . **CLC 55**
See also CA 106; DLB 40

Hamilton, Mollie 1909?-
See Kaye, M(ary) M(argaret)

Hamilton, (Anthony Walter) Patrick
1904-1962 . . . . **CLC 51**
See also obituary CA 113; DLB 10

Hamilton, Virginia (Esther) 1936- . . . **CLC 26**
See also CLR 1, 11; CANR 20; CA 25-28R;
SATA 4; DLB 33, 52

Hammett, (Samuel) Dashiell
1894-1961 . . . . **CLC 3, 5, 10, 19, 47**
See also CA 81-84

Hammon, Jupiter 1711?-1800? . . . . **NCLC 5**
See also DLB 31, 50

Hamner, Earl (Henry), Jr. 1923- . . . **CLC 12**
See also CA 73-76; DLB 6

Hampton, Christopher (James)
1946- . . . . **CLC 4**
See also CA 25-28R; DLB 13

Hamsun, Knut 1859-1952 . . . . . . **TCLC 2, 14**
See also Pedersen, Knut

Handke, Peter 1942- . . **CLC 5, 8, 10, 15, 38**
See also CA 77-80

Hanley, James 1901-1985 . . . **CLC 3, 5, 8, 13**
See also CA 73-76; obituary CA 117

Hannah, Barry 1942- . . . . **CLC 23, 38**
See also CA 108, 110; DLB 6

Hansberry, Lorraine (Vivian)
1930-1965 . . . . **CLC 17**
See also CA 109; obituary CA 25-28R;
DLB 7, 38; CDALB 1941-1968

Hansen, Joseph 1923- . . . . **CLC 38**
See also CANR 16; CA 29-32R

Hansen, Martin 1909-1955 . . . . **TCLC 32**

Hanson, Kenneth O(stlin) 1922- . . . . **CLC 13**
See also CANR 7; CA 53-56

Hardenberg, Friedrich (Leopold Freiherr) von
1772-1801
See Novalis

Hardwick, Elizabeth 1916- . . . . **CLC 13**
See also CANR 3; CA 5-8R; DLB 6

Hardy, Thomas
1840-1928 . . . **TCLC 4, 10, 18, 32; SSC 2**
See also CA 104, 123; SATA 25; DLB 18,
19

Hare, David 1947- . . . . **CLC 29**
See also CA 97-100; DLB 13

Harlan, Louis R(udolph) 1922- . . . . . **CLC 34**
See also CA 21-24R

Harling, Robert 1951?- . . . . **CLC 53**

Harmon, William (Ruth) 1938- . . . . . **CLC 38**
See also CANR 14; CA 33-36R

Harper, Frances Ellen Watkins
1825-1911 . . . . **TCLC 14**
See also CA 111; DLB 50

Harper, Michael S(teven) 1938- . . **CLC 7, 22**
See also CA 33-36R; DLB 41

Harris, Christie (Lucy Irwin)
1907- . . . . **CLC 12**
See also CANR 6; CA 5-8R; SATA 6

Harris, Frank 1856-1931 . . . . **TCLC 24**
See also CAAS 1; CA 109

Harris, George Washington
1814-1869 . . . . **NCLC 23**
See also DLB 3

Harris, Joel Chandler 1848-1908 . . . **TCLC 2**
See also YABC 1; CA 104; DLB 11, 23, 42

Harris, John (Wyndham Parkes Lucas)
Beynon 1903-1969
See Wyndham, John
See also CA 102; obituary CA 89-92

Harris, MacDonald 1921- . . . . **CLC 9**
See also Heiney, Donald (William)

Harris, Mark 1922- . . . . **CLC 19**
See also CAAS 3; CANR 2; CA 5-8R;
DLB 2; DLB-Y 80

Harris, (Theodore) Wilson 1921- . . . . **CLC 25**
See also CANR 11; CA 65-68

Harrison, Harry (Max) 1925- . . . . . . **CLC 42**
See also CANR 5, 21; CA 1-4R; SATA 4;
DLB 8

Harrison, James (Thomas) 1937-
See Harrison, Jim
See also CANR 8; CA 13-16R

Harrison, Jim 1937- . . . . **CLC 6, 14, 33**
See also Harrison, James (Thomas)
See also DLB-Y 82

Harrison, Tony 1937- . . . . **CLC 43**
See also CA 65-68; DLB 40

Harriss, Will(ard Irvin) 1922- . . . . . . **CLC 34**
See also CA 111

Harte, (Francis) Bret(t)
1836?-1902 . . . . **TCLC 1, 25**
See also CA 104; SATA 26; DLB 12, 64;
CDALB 1865-1917

Hartley, L(eslie) P(oles)
1895-1972 . . . . **CLC 2, 22**
See also CA 45-48; obituary CA 37-40R;
DLB 15

Hartman, Geoffrey H. 1929- . . . . **CLC 27**
See also CA 117

Haruf, Kent 19??- . . . . **CLC 34**

Harwood, Ronald 1934- . . . . **CLC 32**
See also CANR 4; CA 1-4R; DLB 13

Hasek, Jaroslav (Matej Frantisek)
1883-1923 . . . . **TCLC 4**
See also CA 104

Hass, Robert 1941- . . . . **CLC 18, 39**
See also CA 111

Hastings, Selina 19??- . . . . **CLC 44**

Hauptmann, Gerhart (Johann Robert)
1862-1946 . . . . **TCLC 4**
See also CA 104

Havel, Vaclav 1936- . . . . **CLC 25**
See also CA 104

Haviaras, Stratis 1935- . . . . **CLC 33**
See also CA 105

Hawkes, John (Clendennin Burne, Jr.)
1925- . . . . . . **CLC 1, 2, 3, 4, 7, 9, 14, 15,
27, 49**
See also CANR 2; CA 1-4R; DLB 2, 7;
DLB-Y 80

Hawthorne, Julian 1846-1934 . . . . . **TCLC 25**

Hawthorne, Nathaniel
1804-1864 . . . **NCLC 2, 10, 17, 23; SSC 3**
See also YABC 2; DLB 1, 74;
CDALB 1640-1865

Hayashi Fumiko 1904-1951 . . . . **TCLC 27**

Haycraft, Anna 19??-
See Ellis, Alice Thomas

Hitchcock, (Sir) Alfred (Joseph)
    1899-1980 .... **CLC 16**
    See also obituary CA 97-100; SATA 27;
    obituary SATA 24

Hoagland, Edward 1932- .... **CLC 28**
    See also CANR 2; CA 1-4R; SATA 51;
    DLB 6

Hoban, Russell C(onwell) 1925- .. **CLC 7, 25**
    See also CLR 3; CA 5-8R; SATA 1, 40;
    DLB 52

Hobson, Laura Z(ametkin)
    1900-1986 .... **CLC 7, 25**
    See also CA 17-20R; obituary CA 118;
    SATA 52; DLB 28

Hochhuth, Rolf 1931- .... **CLC 4, 11, 18**
    See also CA 5-8R

Hochman, Sandra 1936- .... **CLC 3, 8**
    See also CA 5-8R; DLB 5

Hochwalder, Fritz 1911-1986 ...... **CLC 36**
    See also CA 29-32R; obituary CA 120

Hocking, Mary (Eunice) 1921- ..... **CLC 13**
    See also CANR 18; CA 101

Hodgins, Jack 1938- .... **CLC 23**
    See also CA 93-96; DLB 60

Hodgson, William Hope
    1877-1918 .... **TCLC 13**
    See also CA 111; DLB 70

Hoffman, Alice 1952- .... **CLC 51**
    See also CA 77-80

Hoffman, Daniel (Gerard)
    1923- .... **CLC 6, 13, 23**
    See also CANR 4; CA 1-4R; DLB 5

Hoffman, Stanley 1944- .... **CLC 5**
    See also CA 77-80

Hoffman, William M(oses) 1939- ... **CLC 40**
    See also CANR 11; CA 57-60

Hoffmann, Ernst Theodor Amadeus
    1776-1822 .... **NCLC 2**
    See also SATA 27

Hoffmann, Gert 1932- .... **CLC 54**

Hofmannsthal, Hugo (Laurenz August
    Hofmann Edler) von
    1874-1929 .... **TCLC 11**
    See also CA 106

Hogg, James 1770-1835 .... **NCLC 4**

Holberg, Ludvig 1684-1754 .... **LC 6**

Holden, Ursula 1921- .... **CLC 18**
    See also CANR 22; CA 101

Holderlin, (Johann Christian) Friedrich
    1770-1843 .... **NCLC 16**

Holdstock, Robert (P.) 1948- .... **CLC 39**

Holland, Isabelle 1920- .... **CLC 21**
    See also CANR 10; CA 21-24R; SATA 8

Holland, Marcus 1900-1985
    See Caldwell, (Janet Miriam) Taylor
    (Holland)

Hollander, John 1929- ...... **CLC 2, 5, 8, 14**
    See also CANR 1; CA 1-4R; SATA 13;
    DLB 5

Holleran, Andrew 1943?- .... **CLC 38**

Hollinghurst, Alan 1954- .... **CLC 55**
    See also CA 114

Hollis, Jim 1916-
    See Summers, Hollis (Spurgeon, Jr.)

Holmes, John Clellon 1926-1988.... **CLC 56**
    See also CANR 4; CA 9-10R;
    obituary CA 125; DLB 16

Holmes, Oliver Wendell
    1809-1894 .... **NCLC 14**
    See also SATA 34; DLB 1;
    CDALB 1640-1865

Holt, Victoria 1906-
    See Hibbert, Eleanor (Burford)

Holub, Miroslav 1923- .... **CLC 4**
    See also CANR 10; CA 21-24R

Homer c. 8th century B.C.- .... **CMLC 1**

Honig, Edwin 1919- .... **CLC 33**
    See also CANR 4; CA 5-8R; DLB 5

Hood, Hugh (John Blagdon)
    1928- .... **CLC 15, 28**
    See also CANR 1; CA 49-52; DLB 53

Hood, Thomas 1799-1845. .... **NCLC 16**

Hooker, (Peter) Jeremy 1941- ..... **CLC 43**
    See also CANR 22; CA 77-80; DLB 40

Hope, A(lec) D(erwent) 1907- .... **CLC 3, 51**
    See also CA 21-24R

Hope, Christopher (David Tully)
    1944- .... **CLC 52**
    See also CA 106

Hopkins, Gerard Manley
    1844-1889 .... **NCLC 17**
    See also DLB 35, 57

Hopkins, John (Richard) 1931- ...... **CLC 4**
    See also CA 85-88

Hopkins, Pauline Elizabeth
    1859-1930 .... **TCLC 28**
    See also DLB 50

Horgan, Paul 1903- .... **CLC 9, 53**
    See also CANR 9; CA 13-16R; SATA 13;
    DLB-Y 85

Horovitz, Israel 1939- .... **CLC 56**

Horwitz, Julius 1920-1986. .... **CLC 14**
    See also CANR 12; CA 9-12R;
    obituary CA 119

Hospital, Janette Turner 1942- ..... **CLC 42**
    See also CA 108

Hostos (y Bonilla), Eugenio Maria de
    1893-1903 .... **TCLC 24**

Hougan, Carolyn 19??- .... **CLC 34**

Household, Geoffrey (Edward West)
    1900- .... **CLC 11**
    See also CA 77-80; SATA 14

Housman, A(lfred) E(dward)
    1859-1936 .... **TCLC 1, 10**
    See also CA 104; DLB 19

Housman, Laurence 1865-1959 ..... **TCLC 7**
    See also CA 106; SATA 25; DLB 10

Howard, Elizabeth Jane 1923- ... **CLC 7, 29**
    See also CANR 8; CA 5-8R

Howard, Maureen 1930- ..... **CLC 5, 14, 46**
    See also CA 53-56; DLB-Y 83

Howard, Richard 1929- ...... **CLC 7, 10, 47**
    See also CA 85-88; DLB 5

Howard, Robert E(rvin)
    1906-1936 .... **TCLC 8**
    See also CA 105

Howe, Fanny 1940- .... **CLC 47**
    See also CA 117; SATA 52

Howe, Julia Ward 1819-1910 ..... **TCLC 21**
    See also CA 117; DLB 1

Howe, Tina 1937- .... **CLC 48**
    See also CA 109

Howells, William Dean
    1837-1920 .... **TCLC 7, 17**
    See also CA 104; DLB 12, 64;
    CDALB 1865-1917

Howes, Barbara 1914- .... **CLC 15**
    See also CAAS 3; CA 9-12R; SATA 5

Hrabal, Bohumil 1914- .... **CLC 13**
    See also CA 106

Hubbard, L(afayette) Ron(ald)
    1911-1986 .... **CLC 43**
    See also CANR 22; CA 77-80;
    obituary CA 118

Huch, Ricarda (Octavia)
    1864-1947 .... **TCLC 13**
    See also CA 111

Huddle, David 1942- .... **CLC 49**
    See also CA 57-60

Hudson, W(illiam) H(enry)
    1841-1922 .... **TCLC 29**
    See also CA 115; SATA 35

Hueffer, Ford Madox 1873-1939
    See Ford, Ford Madox

Hughart, Barry 1934- .... **CLC 39**

Hughes, David (John) 1930- .... **CLC 48**
    See also CA 116; DLB 14

Hughes, Edward James 1930-
    See Hughes, Ted

Hughes, (James) Langston
    1902-1967 ..... **CLC 1, 5, 10, 15, 35, 44**
    See also CANR 1; CA 1-4R;
    obituary CA 25-28R; SATA 4, 33;
    DLB 4, 7, 48, 51

Hughes, Richard (Arthur Warren)
    1900-1976 .... **CLC 1, 11**
    See also CANR 4; CA 5-8R;
    obituary CA 65-68; SATA 8;
    obituary SATA 25; DLB 15

Hughes, Ted 1930- ..... **CLC 2, 4, 9, 14, 37**
    See also CLR 3; CANR 1; CA 1-4R;
    SATA 27, 49; DLB 40

Hugo, Richard F(ranklin)
    1923-1982 .... **CLC 6, 18, 32**
    See also CANR 3; CA 49-52;
    obituary CA 108; DLB 5

Hugo, Victor Marie
    1802-1885 .... **NCLC 3, 10, 21**
    See also SATA 47

Huidobro, Vicente 1893-1948 ..... **TCLC 31**

Hulme, Keri 1947- .... **CLC 39**

Hulme, T(homas) E(rnest)
    1883-1917 .... **TCLC 21**
    See also CA 117; DLB 19

Hume, David 1711-1776. .... **LC 7**

Humphrey, William 1924- .... **CLC 45**
    See also CA 77-80; DLB 6

Jiles, Paulette   1943-.............. CLC 13
See also CA 101

Jimenez (Mantecon), Juan Ramon
1881-1958 .... TCLC 4
See also CA 104

Joel, Billy   1949-................. CLC 26
See also Joel, William Martin

Joel, William Martin   1949-
See Joel, Billy
See also CA 108

Johnson, B(ryan) S(tanley William)
1933-1973 .... CLC 6, 9
See also CANR 9; CA 9-12R;
obituary CA 53-56; DLB 14, 40

Johnson, Charles (Richard)
1948- .... CLC 7, 51
See also CA 116; DLB 33

Johnson, Denis   1949-............. CLC 52
See also CA 117, 121

Johnson, Diane   1934-....... CLC 5, 13, 48
See also CANR 17; CA 41-44R; DLB-Y 80

Johnson, Eyvind (Olof Verner)
1900-1976 .... CLC 14
See also CA 73-76; obituary CA 69-72

Johnson, James Weldon
1871-1938 .... TCLC 3, 19
See also Johnson, James William
See also CA 104; DLB 51

Johnson, James William   1871-1938
See Johnson, James Weldon
See also SATA 31

Johnson, Lionel (Pigot)
1867-1902 .... TCLC 19
See also CA 117; DLB 19

Johnson, Marguerita   1928-
See Angelou, Maya

Johnson, Pamela Hansford
1912-1981 .... CLC 1, 7, 27
See also CANR 2; CA 1-4R;
obituary CA 104; DLB 15

Johnson, Uwe
1934-1984 .... CLC 5, 10, 15, 40
See also CANR 1; CA 1-4R;
obituary CA 112

Johnston, George (Benson)   1913-... CLC 51
See also CANR 5, 20; CA 1-4R

Johnston, Jennifer   1930-.......... CLC 7
See also CA 85-88; DLB 14

Jolley, Elizabeth   1923-............ CLC 46

Jones, David
1895-1974 .... CLC 2, 4, 7, 13, 42
See also CA 9-12R; obituary CA 53-56;
DLB 20

Jones, David Robert   1947-
See Bowie, David
See also CA 103

Jones, D(ouglas) G(ordon)   1929-.... CLC 10
See also CANR 13; CA 113; DLB 53

Jones, Diana Wynne   1934- .... CLC 26
See also CANR 4; CA 49-52; SATA 9

Jones, Gayl   1949-............... CLC 6, 9
See also CA 77-80; DLB 33

Jones, James   1921-1977.... CLC 1, 3, 10, 39
See also CANR 6; CA 1-4R;
obituary CA 69-72; DLB 2

Jones, (Everett) LeRoi
1934- .... CLC 1, 2, 3, 5, 10, 14, 33
See also Baraka, Amiri; Baraka, Imamu
Amiri
See also CA 21-24R

Jones, Madison (Percy, Jr.)   1925-... CLC 4
See also CANR 7; CA 13-16R

Jones, Mervyn   1922-.......... CLC 10, 52
See also CAAS 5; CANR 1; CA 45-48

Jones, Mick   1956?-
See The Clash

Jones, Nettie   19??-.............. CLC 34

Jones, Preston   1936-1979 .... CLC 10
See also CA 73-76; obituary CA 89-92;
DLB 7

Jones, Robert F(rancis)   1934-....... CLC 7
See also CANR 2; CA 49-52

Jones, Rod   1953- .... CLC 50

Jones, Terry   1942?-
See Monty Python
See also CA 112, 116; SATA 51

Jong, Erica   1942-.......... CLC 4, 6, 8, 18
See also CA 73-76; DLB 2, 5, 28

Jonson, Ben(jamin)   1572-1637....... LC 6
See also DLB 62

Jordan, June   1936-.......... CLC 5, 11, 23
See also CLR 10; CA 33-36R; SATA 4;
DLB 38

Jordan, Pat(rick M.)   1941- .... CLC 37
See also CA 33-36R

Josipovici, Gabriel (David)
1940- .... CLC 6, 43
See also CA 37-40R; DLB 14

Joubert, Joseph   1754-1824 .... NCLC 9

Jouve, Pierre Jean   1887-1976...... CLC 47
See also obituary CA 65-68

Joyce, James (Augustine Aloysius)
1882-1941 .... TCLC 3, 8, 16, 26; SSC 3
See also CA 104, 126; DLB 10, 19, 36

Jozsef, Attila   1905-1937......... TCLC 22
See also CA 116

Juana Ines de la Cruz   1651?-1695 .... LC 5

Julian of Norwich   1342?-1416?....... LC 6

Just, Ward S(wift)   1935-........ CLC 4, 27
See also CA 25-28R

Justice, Donald (Rodney)   1925-... CLC 6, 19
See also CA 5-8R; DLB-Y 83

Kacew, Romain   1914-1980
See Gary, Romain
See also CA 108; obituary CA 102

Kacewgary, Romain   1914-1980
See Gary, Romain

Kadare, Ismail   1936- .... CLC 52

Kafka, Franz
1883-1924 .... TCLC 2, 6, 13, 29
See also CA 105

Kahn, Roger   1927-.............. CLC 30
See also CA 25-28R; SATA 37

Kaiser, (Friedrich Karl) Georg
1878-1945 .... TCLC 9
See also CA 106

Kaletski, Alexander   1946-........ CLC 39
See also CA 118

Kallman, Chester (Simon)
1921-1975 .... CLC 2
See also CANR 3; CA 45-48;
obituary CA 53-56

Kaminsky, Melvin   1926-
See Brooks, Mel
See also CANR 16

Kane, Paul   1941-
See Simon, Paul

Kanin, Garson   1912-.............. CLC 22
See also CANR 7; CA 5-8R; DLB 7

Kaniuk, Yoram   1930-............ CLC 19

Kantor, MacKinlay   1904-1977 .... CLC 7
See also CA 61-64; obituary CA 73-76;
DLB 9

Kaplan, David Michael   1946- ...... CLC 50

Karamzin, Nikolai Mikhailovich
1766-1826 .... NCLC 3

Karapanou, Margarita   1946-....... CLC 13
See also CA 101

Karl, Frederick R(obert)   1927-..... CLC 34
See also CANR 3; CA 5-8R

Kassef, Romain   1914-1980
See Gary, Romain

Katz, Steve   1935-................. CLC 47
See also CANR 12; CA 25-28R; DLB-Y 83

Kauffman, Janet   1945-............ CLC 42
See also CA 117; DLB-Y 86

Kaufman, Bob (Garnell)
1925-1986 .... CLC 49
See also CANR 22; CA 41-44R;
obituary CA 118; DLB 16, 41

Kaufman, George S(imon)
1889-1961 .... CLC 38
See also CA 108; obituary CA 93-96; DLB 7

Kaufman, Sue   1926-1977 .... CLC 3, 8
See also Barondess, Sue K(aufman)

Kavan, Anna   1904-1968........ CLC 5, 13
See also Edmonds, Helen (Woods)
See also CANR 6; CA 5-8R

Kavanagh, Patrick (Joseph Gregory)
1905-1967 .... CLC 22
See also obituary CA 25-28R; DLB 15, 20

Kawabata, Yasunari
1899-1972 .... CLC 2, 5, 9, 18
See also CA 93-96; obituary CA 33-36R

Kaye, M(ary) M(argaret)   1909?-.... CLC 28
See also CA 89-92

Kaye, Mollie   1909?-
See Kaye, M(ary) M(argaret)

Kaye-Smith, Sheila   1887-1956..... TCLC 20
See also CA 118; DLB 36

Kazan, Elia   1909-.............. CLC 6, 16
See also CA 21-24R

Kazantzakis, Nikos
1885?-1957............. TCLC 2, 5, 33
See also CA 105

Kazin, Alfred   1915- .... CLC 34, 38
See also CAAS 7; CANR 1; CA 1-4R

Keane, Mary Nesta (Skrine)   1904-
See Keane, Molly
See also CA 108, 114

Keane, Molly   1904-............... CLC 31
See also Keane, Mary Nesta (Skrine)

Author Index

Porter, Katherine Anne
1890-1980 . . . . . **CLC 1, 3, 7, 10, 13, 15,
27; SSC 4**
See also CANR 1; CA 1-4R;
obituary CA 101; obituary SATA 23, 39;
DLB 4, 9; DLB-Y 80

Porter, Peter (Neville Frederick)
1929- . . . . **CLC 5, 13, 33**
See also CA 85-88; DLB 40

Porter, William Sydney   1862-1910
See Henry, O.
See also YABC 2; CA 104; DLB 12;
CDALB 1865-1917

Potok, Chaim   1929- . . . . **CLC 2, 7, 14, 26**
See also CANR 19; CA 17-20R; SATA 33;
DLB 28

Pound, Ezra (Loomis)
1885-1972 . . . . . **CLC 1, 2, 3, 4, 5, 7, 10,
13, 18, 34, 48, 50**
See also CA 5-8R; obituary CA 37-40R;
DLB 4, 45, 63

Povod, Reinaldo   1959- . . . . **CLC 44**

Powell, Anthony (Dymoke)
1905- . . . . **CLC 1, 3, 7, 9, 10, 31**
See also CANR 1; CA 1-4R; DLB 15

Powell, Padgett   1952- . . . . **CLC 34**

Powers, J(ames) F(arl)
1917- . . . . **CLC 1, 4, 8; SSC 4**
See also CANR 2; CA 1-4R

Pownall, David   1938- . . . . **CLC 10**
See also CA 89-92; DLB 14

Powys, John Cowper
1872-1963 . . . . **CLC 7, 9, 15, 46**
See also CA 85-88; DLB 15

Powys, T(heodore) F(rancis)
1875-1953 . . . . **TCLC 9**
See also CA 106; DLB 36

Prager, Emily   1952- . . . . **CLC 56**

Pratt, E(dwin) J(ohn)   1883-1964 . . . . **CLC 19**
See also obituary CA 93-96

Premchand   1880-1936 . . . . **TCLC 21**

Preussler, Otfried   1923- . . . . **CLC 17**
See also CA 77-80; SATA 24

Prevert, Jacques (Henri Marie)
1900-1977 . . . . **CLC 15**
See also CA 77-80; obituary CA 69-72;
obituary SATA 30

Prevost, Abbe (Antoine Francois)
1697-1763 . . . . **LC 1**

Price, (Edward) Reynolds
1933- . . . . **CLC 3, 6, 13, 43, 50**
See also CANR 1; CA 1-4R; DLB 2

Price, Richard   1949- . . . . **CLC 6, 12**
See also CANR 3; CA 49-52; DLB-Y 81

Prichard, Katharine Susannah
1883-1969 . . . . **CLC 46**
See also CAP 1; CA 11-12

Priestley, J(ohn) B(oynton)
1894-1984 . . . . **CLC 2, 5, 9, 34**
See also CA 9-12R; obituary CA 113;
DLB 10, 34; DLB-Y 84

Prince (Rogers Nelson)   1958?- . . . . . **CLC 35**

Prince, F(rank) T(empleton)   1912- . . **CLC 22**
See also CA 101; DLB 20

Prior, Matthew   1664-1721 . . . . **LC 4**

Pritchard, William H(arrison)
1932- . . . . **CLC 34**
See also CA 65-68

Pritchett, V(ictor) S(awdon)
1900- . . . . **CLC 5, 13, 15, 41**
See also CA 61-64; DLB 15

Procaccino, Michael   1946-
See Cristofer, Michael

Prokosch, Frederic   1908- . . . . **CLC 4, 48**
See also CA 73-76; DLB 48

Prose, Francine   1947- . . . . **CLC 45**
See also CA 109, 112

Proust, Marcel   1871-1922 . . **TCLC 7, 13, 33**
See also CA 104, 120; DLB 65

Pryor, Richard   1940- . . . . **CLC 26**

Puig, Manuel   1932- . . . . **CLC 3, 5, 10, 28**
See also CANR 2; CA 45-48

Purdy, A(lfred) W(ellington)
1918- . . . . **CLC 3, 6, 14, 50**
See also CA 81-84

Purdy, James (Amos)
1923- . . . . **CLC 2, 4, 10, 28, 52**
See also CAAS 1; CANR 19; CA 33-36R;
DLB 2

Pushkin, Alexander (Sergeyevich)
1799-1837 . . . . **NCLC 3**

P'u Sung-ling   1640-1715 . . . . **LC 3**

Puzo, Mario   1920- . . . . **CLC 1, 2, 6, 36**
See also CANR 4; CA 65-68; DLB 6

Pym, Barbara (Mary Crampton)
1913-1980 . . . . **CLC 13, 19, 37**
See also CANR 13; CAP 1; CA 13-14;
obituary CA 97-100; DLB 14

Pynchon, Thomas (Ruggles, Jr.)
1937- . . . . **CLC 2, 3, 6, 9, 11, 18, 33**
See also CANR 22; CA 17-20R; DLB 2

Quasimodo, Salvatore   1901-1968 . . . **CLC 10**
See also CAP 1; CA 15-16;
obituary CA 25-28R

Queen, Ellery   1905-1982 . . . . **CLC 3, 11**
See also Dannay, Frederic; Lee, Manfred
B(ennington)

Queneau, Raymond
1903-1976 . . . . **CLC 2, 5, 10, 42**
See also CA 77-80; obituary CA 69-72;
DLB 72

Quin, Ann (Marie)   1936-1973 . . . . . . **CLC 6**
See also CA 9-12R; obituary CA 45-48;
DLB 14

Quinn, Simon   1942-
See Smith, Martin Cruz

Quiroga, Horacio (Sylvestre)
1878-1937 . . . . **TCLC 20**
See also CA 117

Quoirez, Francoise   1935-
See Sagan, Francoise
See also CANR 6; CA 49-52

Rabe, David (William)   1940- . . . **CLC 4, 8, 33**
See also CA 85-88; DLB 7

Rabelais, Francois   1494?-1553 . . . . **LC 5**

Rabinovitch, Sholem   1859-1916
See Aleichem, Sholom
See also CA 104

Rachen, Kurt von   1911-1986
See Hubbard, L(afayette) Ron(ald)

Radcliffe, Ann (Ward)   1764-1823 . . **NCLC 6**
See also DLB 39

Radiguet, Raymond   1903-1923 . . . . **TCLC 29**

Radnoti, Miklos   1909-1944 . . . . . . **TCLC 16**
See also CA 118

Rado, James   1939- . . . . **CLC 17**
See also CA 105

Radomski, James   1932-
See Rado, James

Radvanyi, Netty Reiling   1900-1983
See Seghers, Anna
See also CA 85-88; obituary CA 110

Rae, Ben   1935-
See Griffiths, Trevor

Raeburn, John   1941- . . . . **CLC 34**
See also CA 57-60

Ragni, Gerome   1942- . . . . **CLC 17**
See also CA 105

Rahv, Philip   1908-1973 . . . . **CLC 24**
See also Greenberg, Ivan

Raine, Craig   1944- . . . . **CLC 32**
See also CA 108; DLB 40

Raine, Kathleen (Jessie)   1908- . . . **CLC 7, 45**
See also CA 85-88; DLB 20

Rainis, Janis   1865-1929 . . . . **TCLC 29**

Rakosi, Carl   1903- . . . . **CLC 47**
See also Rawley, Callman
See also CAAS 5

Ramos, Graciliano   1892-1953 . . . . . **TCLC 32**

Rampersad, Arnold   19??- . . . . **CLC 44**

Ramuz, Charles-Ferdinand
1878-1947 . . . . **TCLC 33**

Rand, Ayn   1905-1982 . . . . **CLC 3, 30, 44**
See also CA 13-16R; obituary CA 105

Randall, Dudley (Felker)   1914- . . . . . . **CLC 1**
See also CA 25-28R; DLB 41

Ransom, John Crowe
1888-1974 . . . . **CLC 2, 4, 5, 11, 24**
See also CANR 6; CA 5-8R;
obituary CA 49-52; DLB 45, 63

Rao, Raja   1909- . . . . **CLC 25, 56**
See also CA 73-76

Raphael, Frederic (Michael)
1931- . . . . **CLC 2, 14**
See also CANR 1; CA 1-4R; DLB 14

Rathbone, Julian   1935- . . . . **CLC 41**
See also CA 101

Rattigan, Terence (Mervyn)
1911-1977 . . . . **CLC 7**
See also CA 85-88; obituary CA 73-76;
DLB 13

Ratushinskaya, Irina   1954- . . . . **CLC 54**

Raven, Simon (Arthur Noel)
1927- . . . . **CLC 14**
See also CA 81-84

Rawley, Callman   1903-
See Rakosi, Carl
See also CANR 12; CA 21-24R

Rawlings, Marjorie Kinnan
1896-1953 . . . . **TCLC 4**
See also YABC 1; CA 104; DLB 9, 22

Robinson, Kim Stanley 19??- . . . . **CLC 34**

Robinson, Marilynne 1944- . . . . **CLC 25**
See also CA 116

Robinson, Smokey 1940- . . . . **CLC 21**

Robinson, William 1940-
See Robinson, Smokey
See also CA 116

Robison, Mary 1949- . . . . **CLC 42**
See also CA 113, 116

Roddenberry, Gene 1921- . . . . **CLC 17**

Rodgers, Mary 1931- . . . . **CLC 12**
See also CANR 8; CA 49-52; SATA 8

Rodgers, W(illiam) R(obert)
1909-1969 . . . . **CLC 7**
See also CA 85-88; DLB 20

Rodriguez, Claudio 1934- . . . . **CLC 10**

Roethke, Theodore (Huebner)
1908-1963 . . . . . . **CLC 1, 3, 8, 11, 19, 46**
See also CA 81-84; CABS 2; SAAS 1;
DLB 5; CDALB 1941-1968

Rogers, Sam 1943-
See Shepard, Sam

Rogers, Will(iam Penn Adair)
1879-1935 . . . . **TCLC 8**
See also CA 105; DLB 11

Rogin, Gilbert 1929- . . . . **CLC 18**
See also CANR 15; CA 65-68

Rohan, Koda 1867-1947 . . . . **TCLC 22**

Rohmer, Eric 1920- . . . . **CLC 16**
See also Scherer, Jean-Marie Maurice

Rohmer, Sax 1883-1959 . . . . **TCLC 28**
See also Ward, Arthur Henry Sarsfield
See also DLB 70

Roiphe, Anne (Richardson)
1935- . . . . **CLC 3, 9**
See also CA 89-92; DLB-Y 80

**Rolfe, Frederick (William Serafino Austin
Lewis Mary)** 1860-1913 . . . . . . **TCLC 12**
See also CA 107; DLB 34

Rolland, Romain 1866-1944 . . . . **TCLC 23**
See also CA 118

Rolvaag, O(le) E(dvart)
1876-1931 . . . . **TCLC 17**
See also CA 117; DLB 9

Romains, Jules 1885-1972 . . . . **CLC 7**
See also CA 85-88

Romero, Jose Ruben 1890-1952 . . . **TCLC 14**
See also CA 114

Ronsard, Pierre de 1524-1585 . . . . **LC 6**

Rooke, Leon 1934- . . . . **CLC 25, 34**
See also CA 25-28R

Roper, William 1498-1578 . . . . **LC 10**

Rosa, Joao Guimaraes 1908-1967 . . . **CLC 23**
See also obituary CA 89-92

Rosen, Richard (Dean) 1949- . . . . **CLC 39**
See also CA 77-80

Rosenberg, Isaac 1890-1918 . . . . **TCLC 12**
See also CA 107; DLB 20

Rosenblatt, Joe 1933- . . . . **CLC 15**
See also Rosenblatt, Joseph

Rosenblatt, Joseph 1933-
See Rosenblatt, Joe
See also CA 89-92

Rosenfeld, Samuel 1896-1963
See Tzara, Tristan
See also obituary CA 89-92

Rosenthal, M(acha) L(ouis) 1917- . . . **CLC 28**
See also CAAS 6; CANR 4; CA 1-4R;
DLB 5

Ross, (James) Sinclair 1908- . . . . **CLC 13**
See also CA 73-76

Rossetti, Christina Georgina
1830-1894 . . . . **NCLC 2**
See also SATA 20; DLB 35

Rossetti, Dante Gabriel
1828-1882 . . . . **NCLC 4**
See also DLB 35

Rossetti, Gabriel Charles Dante 1828-1882
See Rossetti, Dante Gabriel

Rossner, Judith (Perelman)
1935- . . . . **CLC 6, 9, 29**
See also CANR 18; CA 17-20R; DLB 6

Rostand, Edmond (Eugene Alexis)
1868-1918 . . . . **TCLC 6**
See also CA 104

Roth, Henry 1906- . . . . **CLC 2, 6, 11**
See also CAP 1; CA 11-12; DLB 28

Roth, Joseph 1894-1939 . . . . **TCLC 33**

Roth, Philip (Milton)
1933- . . . . . . **CLC 1, 2, 3, 4, 6, 9, 15, 22,
31, 47**
See also CANR 1, 22; CA 1-4R; DLB 2, 28;
DLB-Y 82

Rothenberg, Jerome 1931- . . . . **CLC 6**
See also CANR 1; CA 45-48; DLB 5

Roumain, Jacques 1907-1944 . . . . . . **TCLC 19**
See also CA 117

Rourke, Constance (Mayfield)
1885-1941 . . . . **TCLC 12**
See also YABC 1; CA 107

Rousseau, Jean-Baptiste 1671-1741 . . . **LC 9**

Roussel, Raymond 1877-1933 . . . . . **TCLC 20**
See also CA 117

Rovit, Earl (Herbert) 1927- . . . . **CLC 7**
See also CANR 12; CA 5-8R

Rowe, Nicholas 1674-1718 . . . . **LC 8**

Rowson, Susanna Haswell
1762-1824 . . . . **NCLC 5**
See also DLB 37

Roy, Gabrielle 1909-1983 . . . . **CLC 10, 14**
See also CANR 5; CA 53-56;
obituary CA 110

Rozewicz, Tadeusz 1921- . . . . **CLC 9, 23**
See also CA 108

Ruark, Gibbons 1941- . . . . **CLC 3**
See also CANR 14; CA 33-36R

Rubens, Bernice 192?- . . . . **CLC 19, 31**
See also CA 25-28R; DLB 14

Rudkin, (James) David 1936- . . . . . . **CLC 14**
See also CA 89-92; DLB 13

Rudnik, Raphael 1933- . . . . **CLC 7**
See also CA 29-32R

Ruiz, Jose Martinez 1874-1967
See Azorin

Rukeyser, Muriel
1913-1980 . . . . **CLC 6, 10, 15, 27**
See also CA 5-8R; obituary CA 93-96;
obituary SATA 22; DLB 48

Rule, Jane (Vance) 1931- . . . . **CLC 27**
See also CANR 12; CA 25-28R; DLB 60

Rulfo, Juan 1918-1986 . . . . **CLC 8**
See also CA 85-88; obituary CA 118

Runyon, (Alfred) Damon
1880-1946 . . . . **TCLC 10**
See also CA 107; DLB 11

Rush, Norman 1933- . . . . **CLC 44**
See also CA 121

Rushdie, (Ahmed) Salman
1947- . . . . **CLC 23, 31, 55**
See also CA 108, 111

Rushforth, Peter (Scott) 1945- . . . . . **CLC 19**
See also CA 101

Ruskin, John 1819-1900 . . . . **TCLC 20**
See also CA 114; SATA 24; DLB 55

Russ, Joanna 1937- . . . . **CLC 15**
See also CANR 11; CA 25-28R; DLB 8

Russell, George William 1867-1935
See A. E.
See also CA 104

Russell, (Henry) Ken(neth Alfred)
1927- . . . . **CLC 16**
See also CA 105

Rutherford, Mark 1831-1913 . . . . . . **TCLC 25**
See also DLB 18

Ruyslinck, Ward 1929- . . . . **CLC 14**

Ryan, Cornelius (John) 1920-1974 . . . **CLC 7**
See also CA 69-72; obituary CA 53-56

Rybakov, Anatoli 1911?- . . . . **CLC 23, 53**
See also CA 126

Ryder, Jonathan 1927-
See Ludlum, Robert

Ryga, George 1932- . . . . **CLC 14**
See also CA 101; DLB 60

**Sévine, Marquise de Marie de
Rabutin-Chantal** 1626-1696 . . . . . **LC 11**

Saba, Umberto 1883-1957 . . . . **TCLC 33**

Sabato, Ernesto 1911- . . . . **CLC 10, 23**
See also CA 97-100

Sachs, Marilyn (Stickle) 1927- . . . . . **CLC 35**
See also CLR 2; CANR 13; CA 17-20R;
SAAS 2; SATA 3, 52

Sachs, Nelly 1891-1970 . . . . **CLC 14**
See also CAP 2; CA 17-18;
obituary CA 25-28R

Sackler, Howard (Oliver)
1929-1982 . . . . **CLC 14**
See also CA 61-64; obituary CA 108; DLB 7

Sade, Donatien Alphonse Francois, Comte de
1740-1814 . . . . **NCLC 3**

Sadoff, Ira 1945- . . . . **CLC 9**
See also CANR 5, 21; CA 53-56

Safire, William 1929- . . . . **CLC 10**
See also CA 17-20R

Sagan, Carl (Edward) 1934- . . . . **CLC 30**
See also CANR 11; CA 25-28R

Vliet, R(ussell) G(ordon)
1929-1984 .... **CLC 22**
See also CANR 18; CA 37-40R;
obituary CA 112

Voight, Ellen Bryant 1943- .... **CLC 54**
See also CANR 11; CA 69-72

Voigt, Cynthia 1942- .... **CLC 30**
See also CANR 18; CA 106; SATA 33, 48

Voinovich, Vladimir (Nikolaevich)
1932- .... **CLC 10, 49**
See also CA 81-84

Von Daeniken, Erich 1935-
See Von Daniken, Erich
See also CANR 17; CA 37-40R

Von Daniken, Erich 1935- .... **CLC 30**
See also Von Daeniken, Erich

Vonnegut, Kurt, Jr.
1922- .... **CLC 1, 2, 3, 4, 5, 8, 12, 22, 40**
See also CANR 1; CA 1-4R; DLB 2, 8;
DLB-Y 80; DLB-DS 3

Vorster, Gordon 1924- .... **CLC 34**

Voznesensky, Andrei 1933- ...... **CLC 1, 15**
See also CA 89-92

Waddington, Miriam 1917- .... **CLC 28**
See also CANR 12; CA 21-24R

Wagman, Fredrica 1937- .... **CLC 7**
See also CA 97-100

Wagner, Richard 1813-1883 .... **NCLC 9**

Wagner-Martin, Linda 1936- ...... **CLC 50**

Wagoner, David (Russell)
1926- .... **CLC 3, 5, 15**
See also CAAS 3; CANR 2; CA 1-4R;
SATA 14; DLB 5

Wah, Fred(erick James) 1939- ...... **CLC 44**
See also CA 107; DLB 60

Wahloo, Per 1926-1975 .... **CLC 7**
See also CA 61-64

Wahloo, Peter 1926-1975
See Wahloo, Per

Wain, John (Barrington)
1925- .... **CLC 2, 11, 15, 46**
See also CAAS 4; CA 5-8R; DLB 15, 27

Wajda, Andrzej 1926- .... **CLC 16**
See also CA 102

Wakefield, Dan 1932- .... **CLC 7**
See also CAAS 7; CA 21-24R

Wakoski, Diane
1937- .... **CLC 2, 4, 7, 9, 11, 40**
See also CAAS 1; CANR 9; CA 13-16R;
DLB 5

Walcott, Derek (Alton)
1930- .... **CLC 2, 4, 9, 14, 25, 42**
See also CA 89-92; DLB-Y 81

Waldman, Anne 1945- .... **CLC 7**
See also CA 37-40R; DLB 16

Waldo, Edward Hamilton 1918-
See Sturgeon, Theodore (Hamilton)

Walker, Alice
1944- .... **CLC 5, 6, 9, 19, 27, 46**
See also CANR 9; CA 37-40R; SATA 31;
DLB 6, 33

Walker, David Harry 1911- .... **CLC 14**
See also CANR 1; CA 1-4R; SATA 8

Walker, Edward Joseph 1934-
See Walker, Ted
See also CANR 12; CA 21-24R

Walker, George F. 1947- .... **CLC 44**
See also CANR 21; CA 103; DLB 60

Walker, Joseph A. 1935- .... **CLC 19**
See also CA 89-92; DLB 38

Walker, Margaret (Abigail)
1915- .... **CLC 1, 6**
See also CA 73-76

Walker, Ted 1934- .... **CLC 13**
See also Walker, Edward Joseph
See also DLB 40

Wallace, David Foster 1962- .... **CLC 50**

Wallace, Irving 1916- .... **CLC 7, 13**
See also CAAS 1; CANR 1; CA 1-4R

Wallant, Edward Lewis
1926-1962 .... **CLC 5, 10**
See also CANR 22; CA 1-4R; DLB 2, 28

Walpole, Horace 1717-1797 .... **LC 2**
See also DLB 39

Walpole, (Sir) Hugh (Seymour)
1884-1941 .... **TCLC 5**
See also CA 104; DLB 34

Walser, Martin 1927- .... **CLC 27**
See also CANR 8; CA 57-60

Walser, Robert 1878-1956 .... **TCLC 18**
See also CA 118

Walsh, Gillian Paton 1939-
See Walsh, Jill Paton
See also CA 37-40R; SATA 4

Walsh, Jill Paton 1939- .... **CLC 35**
See also CLR 2; SAAS 3

Wambaugh, Joseph (Aloysius, Jr.)
1937- .... **CLC 3, 18**
See also CA 33-36R; DLB 6; DLB-Y 83

Ward, Arthur Henry Sarsfield 1883-1959
See Rohmer, Sax
See also CA 108

Ward, Douglas Turner 1930- .... **CLC 19**
See also CA 81-84; DLB 7, 38

Warhol, Andy 1928-1987 .... **CLC 20**
See also CA 89-92; obituary CA 121

Warner, Francis (Robert le Plastrier)
1937- .... **CLC 14**
See also CANR 11; CA 53-56

Warner, Rex (Ernest) 1905-1986 .... **CLC 45**
See also CA 89-92; obituary CA 119;
DLB 15

Warner, Sylvia Townsend
1893-1978 .... **CLC 7, 19**
See also CANR 16; CA 61-64;
obituary CA 77-80; DLB 34

Warren, Mercy Otis 1728-1814 ... **NCLC 13**
See also DLB 31

Warren, Robert Penn
1905- .... **CLC 1, 4, 6, 8, 10, 13, 18, 39,
53; SSC 4**
See also CANR 10; CA 13-16R; SATA 46;
DLB 2, 48; DLB-Y 80

Washington, Booker T(aliaferro)
1856-1915 .... **CLC 34**
See also CA 114; SATA 28

Wassermann, Jakob 1873-1934 ..... **TCLC 6**
See also CA 104

Wasserstein, Wendy 1950- .... **CLC 32**
See also CA 121

Waterhouse, Keith (Spencer)
1929- .... **CLC 47**
See also CA 5-8R; DLB 13, 15

Waters, Roger 1944-
See Pink Floyd

Wa Thiong'o, Ngugi
1938- .... **CLC 3, 7, 13, 36**
See also Ngugi, James (Thiong'o); Ngugi wa
Thiong'o

Watkins, Paul 1964- .... **CLC 55**

Watkins, Vernon (Phillips)
1906-1967 .... **CLC 43**
See also CAP 1; CA 9-10;
obituary CA 25-28R; DLB 20

Waugh, Auberon (Alexander) 1939- ... **CLC 7**
See also CANR 6, 22; CA 45-48; DLB 14

Waugh, Evelyn (Arthur St. John)
1903-1966 ... **CLC 1, 3, 8, 13, 19, 27, 44**
See also CANR 22; CA 85-88;
obituary CA 25-28R; DLB 15

Waugh, Harriet 1944- .... **CLC 6**
See also CANR 22; CA 85-88

Webb, Beatrice (Potter)
1858-1943 .... **TCLC 22**
See also CA 117

Webb, Charles (Richard) 1939- ...... **CLC 7**
See also CA 25-28R

Webb, James H(enry), Jr. 1946- .... **CLC 22**
See also CA 81-84

Webb, Mary (Gladys Meredith)
1881-1927 .... **TCLC 24**
See also DLB 34

Webb, Phyllis 1927- .... **CLC 18**
See also CA 104; DLB 53

Webb, Sidney (James)
1859-1947 .... **TCLC 22**
See also CA 117

Webber, Andrew Lloyd 1948- ...... **CLC 21**

Weber, Lenora Mattingly
1895-1971 .... **CLC 12**
See also CAP 1; CA 19-20;
obituary CA 29-32R; SATA 2;
obituary SATA 26

Wedekind, (Benjamin) Frank(lin)
1864-1918 .... **TCLC 7**
See also CA 104

Weidman, Jerome 1913- .... **CLC 7**
See also CANR 1; CA 1-4R; DLB 28

Weil, Simone 1909-1943 .... **TCLC 23**
See also CA 117

Weinstein, Nathan Wallenstein 1903?-1940
See West, Nathanael
See also CA 104

Weir, Peter 1944- .... **CLC 20**
See also CA 113

Weiss, Peter (Ulrich)
1916-1982 .... **CLC 3, 15, 51**
See also CANR 3; CA 45-48;
obituary CA 106; DLB 69

Author Index

SSC Cumulative Nationality Index

SSC Cumulative Title Index

459

Title Index